CRIMINOLOGY

CRIMINOLOGY

Tenth Edition

by the late
Edwin H. Sutherland
and
Donald R. Cressey
University of California
Santa Barbara

J. B. LIPPINCOTT COMPANY
Philadelphia   New York   San Jose   Toronto

This is a revised edition of Edwin H. Sutherland and
Donald R. Cressey's *Criminology*, copyright 1974, by
J. B. Lippincott Company. Original copyright, 1924, by
J. B. Lippincott Company, under the title *Criminology*, of
which Edwin H. Sutherland was sole author. Rewritten and
reset under the title *Principles of Criminology*, with Sutherland
as sole author, in 1934, 1939, and 1947. Rewritten and reset,
with Edwin H. Sutherland and Donald R. Cressey as co-authors,
in 1955, 1960, 1970, and 1974.

Library of Congress Cataloging in Publication Data

Sutherland, Edwin Hardin, 1883-1950.
   Criminology.

   Bibliography: p.
   Includes indexes.
   1. Crime and criminals.   2. Criminal justice,
Administration of.   I. Cressey, Donald Ray, 1919-
joint author.   II. Title.
HV6025.S83 1978   364   78-5652
ISBN-0-397-47384-2

Title

Printed in the United States of America

10 9 8 7 6 5 4 3 2 1

Book produced by Ken Burke & Associates

Copyeditors: Frank Meltzer and Judith Fillmore
Text designers: Judith Fillmore and Ken Burke
Cover designer: Christy Butterfield
Compositor: Computer Typesetting Services, Inc.
Printer: The Murray Printing Company

Preface

The revision of this edition of *Criminology* is the most extensive since the book first appeared more than fifty years ago. Those familiar with earlier editions will find essentially the same order of presentation, with modifications of some chapter titles, but substantial portions of all chapters have been rewritten.

The field of criminology has been changing at an accelerating rate in the past decade. More and more research reports and essays have been oriented to policy issues rather than to behavioral-science issues. A few years ago, most of the critical debates focused on theoretical questions about why some people commit crimes while others do not, and on why crime rates are high in some groups but not in others. These debates were allied with broader theoretical issues in psychology, psychiatry, social psychology, and sociology. Today, criminology is much more oriented to law and public policy.

It is an exaggeration to say that criminology formerly tried to *understand* crime and the methods of dealing with it, but criminology today attempts to *do something about* crime and the practices of agencies ranging from police departments to parole boards. This is an exaggeration because many criminologists continue to show deep concern for understanding the crime-generating processes in society, including those processes inadvertently set in motion by state agencies charged with reducing the incidence of crime. Research and discussion stimulated by labeling theory, structural-frustration ("opportunity") theory, differential-association theory, control theory, and conflict theory continue. Research and discussion allied with other theories about why persons and groups behave the way they do also continue: modern psychological-learning theory ("operant theory"), psychiatric theory, psychoanalytic theory, and even biological theory.

But it is not an exaggeration to say that criminology's theoretical concerns recently have been supplemented by more practical objectives—how to reduce the incidence of delinquency and crime, how to make criminal-justice procedures more rational or fair, how to influence legislation, and so on. Some of the criminological debates have thus become lively discussions of policy issues that are, or should be, of concern to all citizens—disparities in sentences, the deterrent effect of punishment, the proper role of police officers, the effectiveness of rehabilitation programs, the plea-bargaining practices of prosecutors, the closing of prisons, the abolition of the indeterminate sentence, and so on.

I have tried to capture the essence of most of these debates, especially in Part Two. Yet the tenth edition of *Criminology*, like earlier editions, has a sociological and social-psychological orientation. Part One and Chapters 13 through 15 of Part Two, especially, provide a theoretical background for understanding what the new debates (some of which are really not so new) are all about. Moreover, theoretical issues continue to be of critical importance. Obviously, every policy and program for doing something about crime is based, implicitly or explicitly, on a theory about individual or group behavior. In this edition more attention is given to radical or critical theories of crime and punishment, but I have also discussed new research papers and essays that are relevant to other theoretical and practical issues.

In its nine previous editions, the first four written by the late Edwin H. Sutherland (1883–1950), *Criminology* emphasized the organization and system-atization of knowledge. This edition adheres to that tradition. The differential-association principle and other sociological and social-psychological perspectives are used in an attempt to make sense of the wide variations in criminal and delinquent behavior, and in crime and delinquency rates. These and similar principles are also used to explain the wide variations in criminal-justice policies and programs, and the differences in the behavior of the numerous state officials who are directly concerned with delinquency and crime.

Because *Criminology* organizes knowledge about criminological questions, the careful reader will have a sense of participation, of being involved. My objective is to provide students with a theoretical foundation so they can participate in criminological debates, not just observe them. Thus this textbook has a thesis. It takes a position on most issues, especially those that I have personally researched.

Many textbooks resemble encyclopedias or other reference books in that they annotate research reports and essays on a long list of topics, give definitions of technical terms, and describe technical processes without analyzing them. This promotes a tendency to "talk down" to readers or to burden them with masses of detail. *Criminology* is oriented differently. Although it has its share of purely descriptive and historical paragraphs and pages, it is a book about *ideas* rather than cops and robbers or the mechanics of criminal-law administration. Instead of confining itself to reporting what various people have written about crime and punishment, the book attempts to make a statement about crime and punishment. Important points are reinforced by repetition, sometimes immediately, sometimes in later chapters.

It is not possible to say everything at once, nor is it possible to discuss every topic first. Obvious as these truths may seem, they severely handicap most modern criminological writers. "Criminal behavior" and "high crime rates" can hardly be appreciated by those whose knowledge of criminal-law, law-enforcement, and criminal-justice practices is deficient. Likewise, an understanding of the actions of criminal-justice institutions, agencies, and personnel requires knowledge of law violators and their backgrounds. Criminal behavior and criminal-justice processes are not divisible. We know, for example, that any law violation is likely to be termed "criminal behavior" because someone has been arrested and processed, and not solely because the person involved was observed engaging in precisely defined criminal conduct and then arrested. We also know that the personnel of criminal-justice agencies have as much to do with manufacturing high crime rates as do criminals. But because it is not possible to discuss all of this at the same time, I have chosen to focus on criminals (Part One) before examining criminal-justice administration (Part Two). Readers are advised, however, to treat Chapters 1, 13, 14, and 15 as a unit, to study these chapters first, and to refer to them when reading other chapters. (Readers who are familiar with earlier editions of *Criminology* will note that these four chapters have been extensively revised.)

Once again I have decided that Professor Sutherland's formal statement of the theory of differential association should not be modified. The theory has been found defective, and suggestions for its modification have been made. These suggestions have been incorporated in this edition. However, if considered as a "principle" rather than as a "theory," differential association continues to make good sense of most of the phenomena in the delinquency and crime area. It was a harbinger of the "conflict orientation" that is now becoming popular in sociological circles once again. The formal statement, as written by Superland, continues to be tested, analyzed, discussed, and extended. It would be inappropriate to modify the theory in such a way that research work now in progress would be undermined. Moreover, the "great debates" about the present statement of the theory probably are of more value to students than would be a revised formal statement that would take some of the criticisms into account. Finally, the theory in its present form has become rather basic to the thinking of American researchers, who refer to "the theory of differential association," or just "differential association," without citing Sutherland or anyone else, apparently on the assumption that readers are familiar with the theory and its origins. I continue to believe that it would not be wise to revise the statement in such a way that these references become meaningless.

One last but by no means minor point: I have neutered *Criminology*.

Criminals, prisoners, and probationers are commonly described as "he." This is not a serious error, for most criminals, prisoners, and probationers are indeed males. But it is incorrect to accept the common practice of referring to all police officers as police*men*, and all judges, parole-board members, prosecutors, and criminologists as "he." I made this error in previous editions because I am a product of my cultural environment. In this edition of *Criminology*, the sex of most anonymous actors, especially high-status ones, is not indentifiable.

Santa Barbara, California   Donald R. Cressey
March, 1978

Contents

PART ONE

THE STUDY OF
DELINQUENCY AND CRIME

1

Criminology and Criminal Law

Criminology is the body of knowledge regarding juvenile delinquency and crime as social phenomena. It includes within its scope the processes of making laws, of breaking laws, and of reacting toward the breaking of laws. These processes are three aspects of a somewhat unified sequence of interactions. Certain acts which are regarded as undesirable are defined by the political society as crimes. In spite of this definition some people persist in the behavior and thus commit delinquencies or crimes; the political society reacts by punishment, intervention, and prevention. This sequence of interactions is the subject matter of criminology.

Criminology has three interrelated divisions, as follows: (1) the sociology of criminal law, which is an attempt at systematic analysis of the conditions under which penal laws develop and also at explanation of variations in policies and procedures used in police departments and courts; (2) the sociology of crime and social psychology of criminal behavior, which is an attempt at systematic analysis of the economic, political, and social conditions in which crime and criminality are either generated or prevented; and (3) the sociology of punishment and correction, which is an attempt at systematic analysis of policies and procedures for reducing the incidence of crime.

The scholarly objective of criminology is the development of a body of knowledge regarding this process of law, crime, and reaction to crime.[1] Much of this body of knowledge will continue to come from observations of the success or failure of practical efforts to reduce the incidence of crime and delinquency. Such knowledge will contribute to the development of other social sciences, and in this

---

[1]As suggested in the first paragraph above, this objective pertains to juvenile delinquency as well as to crime. For purposes of editorial convenience, however, the phrase *and juvenile delinquency* will not be added every time the word *crime* is used, nor will the phrase *and delinquent behavior* be added whenever *criminality* or *criminal behavior* is mentioned.

way will contribute to an understanding of social behavior. But if practical programs wait until theoretical knowledge is complete, they will wait for eternity, because theoretical knowledge is increased most significantly by determining why some practical programs work while others do not, and by observing that some practical programs have undesirable and unanticipated consequences. Years ago, John Dewey described the relationship between knowledge and practice as follows:

> . . . It is a complete error to suppose that efforts at social control depend upon the prior existence of a social science. The reverse is the case. The building up of social science, that is, of a body of knowledge in which facts are ascertained in their significant relations, is dependent upon putting social planning into effect. . . . Physical science did not develop because inquirers piled up a mass of facts about observed phenomena. It came into being when men intentionally experimented, on the basis of ideas and hypotheses, with observed phenomena to modify them and disclose new observations. This process is self-corrective and self-developing. Imperfect and even wrong hypotheses, when *acted upon*, brought to light significant phenomena which made improved ideas and improved experimentations possible. The change from a passive and accumulative attitude into an active and productive one is the secret revealed by the progress of physical inquiry.[2]

While experimentation may increase theoretical knowledge and thereby contribute to ultimate improvements in policies, it is unnecessarily wasteful unless it is directed by the best-organized and critical thought available. Moreover, experimentation with humans, unlike natural science experiments, poses grave ethical problems, even when directed by the best-organized critical thought. The average citizen is confronted by a confusing and conflicting complex of popular beliefs and programs in regard to crime. Some of these are traditions from eighteenth-century philosophy; some are promulgations of special-interest groups; and some are emotional reactions. Organized and critical thinking in this field is therefore peculiarly difficult and also peculiarly necessary.

CONVENTIONAL DEFINITION OF CRIME AND THE CRIMINAL LAW

Criminal behavior is behavior in violation of a criminal law. No matter what the degree of immorality, reprehensibility, or indecency of an act, it it not a criminal act unless it is outlawed by the state. The criminal law, in turn, is a list of specific forms of human conduct which has been outlawed by political authority, which applies uniformly to all persons living under that political authority, and which is enforced by punishment administered by the state. The characteristics which distinguish this body of rules regarding human conduct from other rules are, therefore, *politicality*, *specificity*, *uniformity*, and *penal sanction*. However, these are characteristics of an ideal, completely rational system of criminal law; in practice the differences between the criminal law and other bodies of rules for

[2]John Dewey, "Social Science and Social Control," *New Republic*, 67:276–77, 1931.

human conduct are not clear-cut. Also, the ideal characteristics of the criminal law are only rarely features of the criminal law in action.

CHARACTERISTICS OF THE CRIMINAL LAW

The vast majority of the rules which define certain behavior as criminal are found in constitutions, treaties, common law, enactments by the legislatures of the state and its subdivisions, and in judicial and administrative regulations. However, the criminal law is not merely a collection of written proscriptions. The agencies of enforcement are the police and the courts, and these agencies, with the legislature, determine what the law is. According to one school of thought, police and courts merely "apply" the law in an evenhanded manner to all persons who come before them. However, both the techniques used by justice administrators in interpreting and applying the statutes and the body of ideals held by them are a part of the law in action, as truly as are the written statutes.

The court decision in one controversy becomes a part of the body of rules used in making decisions in later controversies. Consequently, law students must read court decisions in order to learn law. Further evidence supporting this view that the courts as well as the legislatures make law is found whenever the nation is confronted with the problem of selecting a justice of the Supreme Court. At such times it is explicitly recognized that the nature of the law itself, not merely its administration, is determined to a considerable extent by the proportion of liberals and conservatives on the supreme bench. Also, between the courts and the legislature are intermediate agencies such as police departments. Many statutes are never enforced; some are enforced only on rare occasions; others are enforced with a striking disregard for uniformity. Enforcement and administrative agencies are affected by shifts in public opinion, in budget allocations, and in power. As a consequence, the law often changes while the statutes remain constant.

Politicality is regarded almost universally as a necessary element in criminal law. The rules of the trade union, the church, or the family are not regarded as criminal law, nor are violations of these rules regarded as crimes. Only violations of rules made by the state are crimes. But this distinction between the state and other groups is quite arbitrary. It is difficult to maintain when attention is turned to societies where patriarchal power, private self-help, popular justice, and other forerunners of legislative justice are found. This may be illustrated by the gypsies, who have no territorial organization and no written law, but who do have customs, taboos, and a semijudicial council which makes definite decisions regarding the propriety of behavior of members of the group and often imposes penalties. These councils have no political authority in the territory in which they happen to be operating, but they perform the same function within the gypsy group that courts perform in the political order.[3] Similarly, early Chinese immigrants in Chicago

---

[3]See Jean-Paul Clebert, *The Gypsies*, trans. Charles Duff (London: Vista Books, 1963), pp. 123–33; and Anne Sutherland, "Gypsies, the Hidden Americans," *Transaction: Social Science and Modern Society*, 12:27–33, 1975.

established an unofficial court which had no political authority, but which, in practice, exercised the functions of an authorized court in controversies among the Chinese people. The American Cosa Nostra, labor unions, and university student associations all have legislative and judicial systems for administering the functional equivalent of the criminal law among their members.[4] Thus, the element of politicality is arbitrary, not sharply defined.

Specificity is included as an element in the definition of criminal law because of the contrast in this respect between criminal law and civil law. The civil law may be general. An old German civil code, for instance, provided that whoever intentionally injured another in a manner contrary to the common standards of right conduct was bound to indemnify him. The criminal law, on the other hand, generally gives a strict definition of a specific act, and when there is doubt as to whether a definition describes the behavior of a defendant, the judge is obligated to decide in favor of the defendant. In one famous case, for example, the behavior of a person who had taken an airplane was held to be exempt from the punitive consequences of violating a statute regarding the taking of "self-propelled vehicles," on the ground that at the time the law was enacted "vehicles" did not include airplanes.[5] Some laws, to be sure, are quite general, as the laws in regard to nuisances, conspiracy, vagrancy, disorderly conduct, use of the mails to defraud, and official misfeasance. The criminal law, however, contains no general provision that any act which, when done with culpable intent, injures the public can be prosecuted as a punishable offense. Consequently it frequently happens that one act is prohibited by law while another act, which is very similar in nature and effects, is not prohibited and is not illegal.[6]

Uniformity or regularity is included in the conventional definition of criminal law because law attempts to provide evenhanded justice without respect to persons. This means that no exceptions are made to criminal liability because of a person's social status; an act described as a crime is crime, no matter who perpetrates it. Also, uniformity means that the law-enforcement process shall be administered without regard for the status of the persons who have committed crimes or are accused of committing crimes. This ideal is rarely followed in practice, in part because it results in injustices. Rigid rule is softened by police and judicial discretion. The principle of uniformity demands, for example, that all armed robbers be treated exactly alike, but police officers, judges, and others take into account the circumstances of each robbery and the characteristics of each offender, a process which has come to be called *individualization*.[7] Such use of discretion is not unlike equity, a body of rules which supplements law and which developed as a method of doing justice in particular situations where iron

[4]See Donald R. Cressey, *Theft of the Nation: The Structure and Operations of Organized Crime in America* (New York: Harper and Row, 1969), pp. 162–220.
[5]McBoyle v. United States, 283 U.S. 25 (1931).
[6]See Jack P. Gibbs, "Crime and the Sociology of Law," *Sociology and Social Research*, 51:23–38, 1966.
[7]See Chapter 15.

regularity would not do justice. In criminal law matters, legislators have conferred upon judges and administrative bodies the authority to set the length of a prison term after taking individual characteristics into account. Accordingly, much of what happens to persons accused of delinquency or crime is determined in a process of negotiation about just what the law is and how or whether it should be applied.[8]

Penal sanction, as one of the elements of the conventional definition of criminal law, refers to the notion that violators will be punished or at least threatened with punishment by the state. Punishment under the law differs from punishment imposed by a mob because it is supposed to be applied dispassionately by representatives of the state in such manner that it will win the approval of the cool judgment of impartial observers. A law which does not provide a penalty that will cause suffering is quite impotent and, in fact, no criminal law at all. However, the punishment provided may be very slight; in the courts of honor a verdict was reached, a party was declared guilty, and the disgrace of the declaration of guilt was the only punishment. In view of the difficulty of identifying the criminal law of nonliterate societies, where the institution of "the state" is not obvious, the suggestion has been made that the penal sanction is the only essential element in the definition of criminal law, and that wherever a society's rulers enforce proscriptions by a penal sanction, there criminal law exists. This is in contrast to the tort law, where the court orders defendants to reimburse plaintiffs, but does not punish them for damaging the plaintiffs.

The punitive aspects of criminal law have been supplemented by attempts to discover and use methods which are effective in reducing crime and forestalling criminality, whether they are punitive or not. Juvenile courts, for example, do not in theory determine the guilt or innocence of defendants and punish those who are guilty; they merely act in behalf of a child who is in need of help. In practice, however, except for youngsters who are called delinquent because they have been neglected, or who are "predelinquent," juvenile delinquencies are acts which would be crimes if committed by an adult. Juvenile court procedures represent an attempt to avoid labeling children criminals, but they nevertheless do not exempt youths from responsibility for acts which are crimes if committed by adults. Consequently, juvenile delinquencies continue to be punishable by law, even if the punishment is kept in the background.[9] Similarly, the states and the federal government for a generation or two have been enacting laws for the regulation of manufacturing, commerce, agriculture, and other occupations. The persons affected by such laws are ordinarily respectable and powerful, and the legislatures have adapted criminal law procedures to the status of these persons. Violations of these laws are crimes, but they are not always tried in the criminal courts. Instead,

---

[8]See Arthur Rosett and Donald R. Cressey, *Justice By Consent: Plea Bargains in the American Courthouse* (Philadelphia: Lippincott, 1976).
[9]See Chapter 19.

they are handled in civil and equity courts or in administrative commissions; the conventional penalties of fine and imprisonment are kept in the background to be used only as a last resort, and coercion in the first instance consists of injunctions and cease-and-desist orders. Thus persons of social importance avoid the "stigma of crime," just as, to a lesser degree, juvenile delinquents do. The acts remain as crimes, however, for they are punishable by law.[10]

The conventional view is that a crime is an offense against the state, while, in contrast, a tort in violation of civil law is an offense against an individual. A particular act may be considered as an offense against an individual and also against the state, and is either a tort or a crime or both, according to the way it is handled. A person who has committed an act of assault, for example, may be ordered by the civil court to pay the victim a sum of $500 for the damages to his interests, and may also be ordered by the criminal court to pay a fine of $500 to the state. The payment of the first $500 is not punishment, but payment of the second $500 is punishment.

This distinction between individual damage and social harm is extremely difficult to make in the legal systems of nonliterate societies, where court procedures are relatively informal. Even in modern society, the distinction is dubious, for it rests upon the assumption that "individual" and "group" or "state" are mutually exclusive. For practical purposes, the individual is treated as though he or she were autonomous, but in fact an act which harms an individual also harms the group in which the victim has membership. Also, in modern society the indefiniteness of the distinction between torts and crimes is apparent when the victim of an act which is both a tort and a crime uses the criminal law as a method of forcing restitution which could not be secured with equal facility in the civil courts. Prosecutors frequently complain about the use of the criminal law as a collecting agency, especially because the victim who is reimbursed by the offender prior to trial then refuses to act as a witness.

THE SOCIOLOGY OF CRIMINAL LAW

For many centuries, philosophers of jurisprudence have attempted by deductive reasoning to determine the principles underlying the development and use of criminal law. Divine will, the will of the sovereign, nature, reason, history, public opinion, and other principles have been presented.[11] Sociologists have, since about 1960, taken up the search for principles, but in the name of the sociology of law. Generally speaking, sociologists have recently revived an interest in the sociology of law that flourished in the 1920s, although it was not called by that name. Many of the recent specialists in the sociology of law have taken a clue from Roscoe

[10]Edwin H. Sutherland, "Is 'White Collar Crime' Crime?" *American Sociological Review*, 10:132–39, 1945; idem, *White Collar Crime* (New York: Dryden Press, 1949), pp. 29–55.
[11]See M. P. Golding, ed., *The Nature of Law: Readings in Legal Philosophy* (New York: Random House, 1966); and W. Friedman, *Legal Theory*, 5th ed. (New York: Columbia University Press, 1967).

Pound, the principal figure of "sociological jurisprudence," a school of legal philosophy.[12] This is reasonable, because fifty years ago Pound took many of his clues from sociologists like E. A. Ross, Albion W. Small, and especially from Lester F. Ward. Pound stated that a final answer to the question, "What is law?" is impossible because law is a living, changing thing, which may at one time be based on sovereign will and at another time on juristic science, which may at one time be uniform and at another time give much room for judicial discretion, which may at one time be very specific in its proscriptions and at another time much more general.[13]

Pound's statement is a call for the study of "law in action," and sociologists are beginning to respond. Pound maintained that the law regulates social interests and arbitrates conflicting interests, claims, and demands. Sociologists are beginning to see that the emergence of criminal laws, like the administration of justice, reflects the wishes of interest groups.[14] In pluralistic societies, the criminal law does not merely balance various social interests; it *is* a balance of social interests. As Quinney has said,

First . . . society is characterized by diversity, conflict, coercion, and change, rather than by consensus and stability. Second, law is a *result* of the operation of interests, rather than an instrument which functions outside of particular interests. Though law may operate to control interests, it is in the first place *created* by interests. Third, law incorporates the interests of specific persons and groups in society. Seldom is law the product of the whole society.[15]

Four principal theories regarding the origin of the criminal law as an agency of social control, and of specific criminal laws, can be discerned. Three of the theories invoke a *consensus model*, whereby a group or society expresses its will or spirit in the form of criminal law, while the fourth uses a *conflict model* consistent with the observation that politically organized society is based on an interest structure. It should be understood that our presentations of these theories are gross oversimplifications. The problem of trying to account for the origins of criminal law is but part of the very difficult task of trying to account for the origin of social order itself.[16]

One of the oldest theories regards the criminal law as originating in torts, or wrongs to individuals. According to this theory, harms at first produced efforts at self-redress by the injured parties and were therefore treated as injuries to particular individuals. Later, by a series of transitions, the group took charge of the

[12]Roscoe Pound, *Interpretations of Legal History* (New York: Macmillan, 1923), Chap. 3.

[13]See Edwin M. Schur, *Law and Society: A Sociological View* (New York: Random House, 1968).

[14]See Austin T. Turk, "Law as a Weapon in Social Control," *Social Problems*, 23:276–91, 1976.

[15]Richard Quinney, "Introduction: Toward A Sociology of Criminal Law," in *Crime and Justice in Society*, ed. Richard Quinney (Boston: Little, Brown, 1969), p. 25. See also idem., *The Social Reality of Crime* (Boston: Little, Brown, 1970), pp. 15–25; and *Criminology* (Boston: Little, Brown, 1975), pp. 37–41.

[16]See Desmond P. Ellis, "The Normative Solution," *American Sociological Review*, 36: 692–703, 1971.

transaction, and the wrongs came to be regarded as injuries to the group or to the state. These transitions included a requirement that the avenger announce an intention of seeking revenge; a requirement that the avenger secure the consent of the group before taking vengeance; regulation of the amount of injury that could be done to the wrongdoer by the injured party; limitation of time and place in which vengeance could be secured; public investigation of the merits of the case in connection with the requirements previously mentioned or independently of these; and participation of some members of the group in the efforts of the injured party to secure self-redress.[17]

There can be no doubt that some crimes did originate in torts and became crimes through one or more of the steps described. The theory is inadequate, however. It assumes the priority of the individual to the group, and this assumption is not justified, for it is certain that in early societies some wrongs were regarded as wrongs against the group. Such wrongs were regarded as dangerous to the group directly, as in treason and in violations of the hunting rules, or indirectly, as in sacrilege and witchcraft, which might bring down the wrath of the gods upon the group.[18] Furthermore, for those crimes which originated from torts, the process is not adequately described. It is at this point, in part, that some of the other theories are concentrated.

A second theory holds that the criminal law originated in rational processes of a unified society. When harms occurred, the society, acting in its corporate capacity as a state, took action and made a regulation to prevent a repetition of them. The criminal law, like specific criminal laws, is a rational codification of the "will of the people" or of "public opinion."[19] It is obvious that some criminal laws are made in a rational manner, but the theory is inadequate as a general description of how the criminal law has developed. It assumes a unity of opinion and purpose that in fact exists only as an ideal type. Further, it assumes that all the people have equal access to the political processes by which wrongs and harms are identified as such and then outlawed. Finally, it minimizes the irrational components in these processes. In modern times, at least, enactment of statutes, is frequently more an expression of emotion than anything else.[20] Something occurs which upsets an interest group and there is a rush to the legislature to secure a prohibition of such acts. One of the founders of American sociology, Professor Robert Park, said in one of his lectures, "We are always passing laws in America.

[17]See Rafael Karsten, "Blood Revenge and War Among the Jibaro Indians of Eastern Ecuador," in *Law and Warfare*, ed. Paul Bohannan (Garden City, N. Y.: Natural History Press, 1967), pp. 312–13.

[18]S. R. Steinmetz, *Ethnologische Studien zur ersten Entwicklung der Strafe* (Leiden: Harrassowitz, 1894), vol. II, pp. 327–48; H. Oppenheimer, *The Rationale of Punishment* (London: University of London Press, 1913), pp. 66–91; and E. Adamson Hoebel, *Law of Primitive Man: A Study in Comparative Legal Dynamics* (Cambridge: Harvard University Press, 1954).

[19]See N. Friedman, *Law in a Changing Society* (Berkeley: University of California Press, 1959); and Michael Barkun, *Law Without Sanctions* (New Haven, Conn.: Yale University Press, 1968).

[20]See Edwin H. Sutherland, "The Diffusion of Sexual Psychopath Laws," *American Journal of Sociology*, 56:142–48, 1950.

We might as well get up and dance. The laws are largely to relieve emotion, and the legislatures are quite aware of that fact."

A third theory is that the criminal law originated in and is a crystallization of the *mores*. Customs developed with little or no rational analysis, but after persisting for a time, they achieved an ethical foundation. Infractions of such customs produced antagonistic reactions from the group, and these reactions were expressed in the form of criminal law with penal sanctions. While primitive law and the common law of England might reflect some consensus of this kind, there clearly is little general "public opinion" at the base of modern statutes which deal with airplanes, labor unions, factories, automobiles, television, and taxes.[21]

A fourth theory is that criminal law originated in conflict between interest groups. When an interest group secures the enactment of a law, it secures the assistance of the state in a conflict with a rival interest group. Indeed, an interest group or coalition of interest groups may become the state. Behavior in opposition to it, whether by members of rival interest groups or by others, thus becomes criminal. According to this theory, wrongful and harmful acts are characteristic of all classes in present-day society; the upper classes are subtle in their wrongdoing, the underprivileged classes are direct. The upper classes are politically important, and for that reason have power to outlaw the wrongful acts of the underprivileged classes. At the same time, the upper classes are politically powerful enough to define crimes and implement the criminal law in such a manner that many of the wrongful acts of the upper classes do not come within the scope of the criminal law. In this theory, the criminal law originates in the conflict of groups and in the inconsistency of the mores.[22]

Chambliss has used this theory in an analysis of the emergence of vagrancy laws in England and the United States.[23] His thesis is that these laws emerged in order to provide an abundance of cheap labor to landowners during a period in which serfdom was breaking down. When landowners were no longer dependent upon cheap labor, and when industrialists and businessmen supplanted landowners as a powerful interest group, the vagrancy laws remained dormant. But after the turn of the sixteenth century, emphasis was placed on "rogues" and others suspected of being engaged in criminal activities, rather than on the "idle" and "those refusing

[21]See Richard C. Fuller, "Morals and the Criminal Law," *Journal of Criminal Law and Criminology*, 32:624–30, 1942; and Clarence Ray Jeffery, "Crime, Law, and Social Structure," *Journal of Criminal Law, Criminology, and Police Science*, 47:423–35, 1956.

[22]See Lynn McDonald, *The Sociology of Law and Order: Conflict and Consensus Theories of Crime, Law, and Sanctions* (London: Faber and Faber, 1976); Austin T. Turk, "Law, Conflict, and Order: From Theorizing Toward Theories," *Canadian Review of Sociology and Anthropology*, 13:282–94, 1976; and Harold E. Pepinsky, *Crime and Conflict: A Study of Law and Society* (New York: Academic Press, 1976).

[23]William J. Chambliss, "A Sociological Analysis of the Law of Vagrancy," *Social Problems*, 12:67–77, 1964. See also Barbara A. Hanawalt, "Economic Influences on the Pattern of Crime in England, 1300–1348," *American Journal of Legal History*, 18:281–97, 1974; and Douglas Hay, Peter Linebaugh, John G. Rule, E. P. Thompson, and Carl Winslow, *Albion's Fatal Tree: Crime and Society in Eighteenth-Century England* (New York: Pantheon Books, 1975.)

to work." This shift reflected the increased importance of commerce in England. A new interest group of great importance to the society emerged, and the vagrancy laws were altered so as to afford protection to this group.

From this perspective, and in light of the discussion in the preceding section, crime can be seen to involve four elements: (1) a value which is appreciated by a group or a part of a group which is politically powerful; (2) isolation of or normative conflict in another part of this group so that its members do not appreciate the value or appreciate it less highly and consequently tend to endanger it; (3) political declaration that behavior endangering the value is henceforth to be a crime; and (4) pugnacious resort to coercion decently applied by those who appreciate the value to those who are perceived to disregard the value. When a crime is committed, all these relationships are involved. Crime *is* this set of relationships when viewed from the point of view of a social system rather than of the individual. The theory of differential association, to be discussed in Chapter 4 and later sections, can logically be derived from the notion that crime consists of this set of relationships.

No positive conclusion can be reached about the comparative efficiency of the various theories concerning the origin of criminal law. Certainly some criminal laws—such as those prohibiting sacrilege, witchcraft, and, possibly, murder—are expressions of consensus. But, just as certainly, criminal laws prohibiting vagrancy, cattle rustling, automobile theft, and discrimination against blacks and women are expressions of special interests. Research on social aspects of criminal law is greatly needed. While the medical profession is constantly engaged in research work as to the origin of diseases and the effects of treatment, the legal profession has until recently engaged in practically no research work of an analogous kind. Even now, professors of law concentrate their research work on study of what the law *is*. Four of the small number of exceptions to this approach are the analysis by Jerome Hall of the development of the law of theft in modern society, the analysis by a group of Norwegian scholars of the changes in the laws relevant to domestic servants, the analysis by William Chambliss of vagrancy laws, and the more general analysis by Leon Radzinowicz of the development of criminal law in England.[24]

THE DIFFERENTIAE OF CRIME

The rules of criminal law contain only definitions of specific crimes, such as burglary, robbery, and rape, but legal scholars have been able to abstract certain general principles from such definitions. These general principles are said to apply

[24]Jerome Hall, *Theft, Law, and Society*, 2d ed. (Indianapolis: Bobbs-Merrill, 1952); Vilhelm Aubert, Torstein Eckhoff, and Knut Sveri, *En Lov i Sökelyset: Sosialpsykologisk undersökelse ave den Norske Hushjelplov* [A law in the searchlight: social psychological research on the Norwegian law pertaining to domestic servants] (Oslo: Akademisk Forlag, 1952); Leon Radzinowicz, *A History of English Criminal Law and Its Administration from 1750*, vols. 1–4 (New York: Macmillan, 1948–1968).

to all crimes and are the criteria ideally used in determination of whether any particular behavior is or is not criminal. They are consistent with the ideal characteristics of the whole body of the criminal law—politicality, specificity, uniformity, and penal sanction—and, in fact, they may be viewed as translations of the ideal characteristics of the criminal law into statements of the ideal characteristics of all crimes. The concern is shifted from determination of the characteristics of a body of rules to determination of the general characteristics of the many specific acts described in those rules. Thus, for example, penal sanction is a general characteristic of the criminal law, and liability to legally prescribed punishment is a characteristic of all acts or omissions properly called crimes. Obviously, a set of criteria used for deciding whether or not any specific act is a crime must be more precise than statements of the general characteristics of a body of rules.

One extensive and thorough analysis of crimes has resulted in a description of seven interrelated and overlapping differentiae of crime.[25] Ideally, behavior would not be called crime unless all seven differentiae were present. The following brief description of the differentiae is greatly simplified.

1. Before behavior can be called crime there must be certain external consequences called a *harm*. Behavior called a crime, such as burglary or robbery, for example, has a harmful impact on social interests; a mental or emotional state is not enough. If a man decides to commit a crime but changes his mind before he does anything about it, he has committed no crime. The intention is not taken for the deed.

2. The harm must be one that has been outlawed. Engaging in antisocial, immoral, or reprehensible behavior is not crime unless the behavior has been specifically outlawed in advance. Penal law does not have a retroactive effect; there is a long-standing tradition against the enactment of ex post facto legislation.

3. There must be *conduct*. That is, there must be an intentional or reckless action or inaction which brings the harmful consequences about. One who is physically forced to pull the trigger of a gun does not commit murder, even if someone dies from the bullet.

4. *Criminal intent*, or *mens rea*, must be present. Hall suggests that legal scholars have often confused intentionality (deliberate functioning to reach a goal) and motivation (the reasons or grounds for the end-seeking).[26] *Mens rea* is identified with the former, not with the latter. The "motives" for a crime might be "good," but the intention itself might be an intention to effect an outlawed harm, a criminal intent. Thus, if a man decides to kill his starving children because he feels that they will pass on to a better world, his motive is good, but his intent is

[25]Jerome Hall, *General Principles of Criminal Law*, 2d ed. (Indianapolis: Bobbs-Merrill, 1960). See especially pp. 14–26.

[26]Ibid., pp. 84–93.

wrong. Persons who are insane at the time they perpetrate legally forbidden harms do not commit crimes, because the necessary *mens rea* is not present.[27]

5. There must be a fusion or concurrence of *mens rea* and conduct. This means, for example, that a police officer who goes into a house to make an arrest and who then commits a crime while still in the house after making the arrest cannot be considered a trespasser from the beginning. The criminal intent and the conduct do not fuse or concur.

6. There must be a *causal* relation between the outlawed harm and the voluntary misconduct. The conduct of one who fails to file an income tax form is failure to take pen and ink, fill out the form, and so on; the harm is the absence of a form in the collector's office. In this case, the causal relation between the two obviously is present. But if, for example, one person shot another (conduct) and the victim suffocated while in a hospital recovering from the wound, the relationship between conduct and harm (death) is not so clear-cut.

7. There must be legally prescribed punishment. Not only must the harm be identified and announced in advance but, as indicated above, the announcement must carry a threat of punishment to violators. The voluntary conduct must be punishable by law.

These differentiae of crime are all concerned with the nature of the behavior which can properly be called crime, but in making decisions about most cases each criterion need not be considered separately and individually. If the *mens rea*, conduct, and legally proscribed harm are obviously present, for example, the causal relation between harm and misconduct almost certainly will be present. In sum, the differentiae represent the kinds of subject matter with which both criminal lawyers and criminal-law theorists must deal.

There are, of course, many exceptions to the generalization that these are the elements of all crimes. Criminal-law theory is not a body of precise principles, and consequently there are deviations from that which is logical and ideal. Similarly, the criminal law in action differs from the criminal law in principle. For purposes of illustration, we may cite three major exceptions to the above differentiae.

First, criminal intent, in the ordinary meaning of the concept, need not be present for some crimes. In some cases—the so-called strict-liability cases—the offender's intent is not considered. Instead, the person is held responsible for the results of his or her conduct, regardless of his or her intention. The handling of statutory rape is a case in point—no matter how elaborate the calculations, inquiries, or research which a male utilizes in reaching the conclusion that his female companion is above the age of consent, if he has sexual relations with her and it is subsequently shown that she was below the age of consent, he has committed statutory rape. Certain public-welfare offenses, such as traffic offenses and the selling of adulterated food, are handled under the same rule. Similarly,

[27]See Herbert Fingarette, *The Meaning of Criminal Insanity* (Berkeley: University of California Press, 1972); see also the discussion in Chapter 8 below.

under the "felony-murder–misdemeanor-manslaughter doctrine" defendants are held criminally liable for much more serious offenses than they intended to commit. If a person sets fire to a building and a fireman dies trying to extinguish the flames, the offender is liable for murder; if the offense had been a misdemeanor rather than arson, the offender would have been liable for manslaughter.

Hall has severely criticized this doctrine and the general conception of strict liability in the criminal law. He contends that it is "bad law," stating that "there is no avoiding the conclusion that strict liability cannot be brought within the scope of penal law."[28] A behavioristic school in jurisprudence, however, insists that the intent can be determined only by the circumstances of the act, and that a translation of these circumstances into mental terms confuses rather than clarifies the procedure. It contends that the doctrine of *mens rea* should be greatly modified or even abandoned. In criminology, the inclusion in the concept "crime" of behavior which was not intended by the actor makes general theoretical explanation of all crime extremely difficult. No current theoretical explanation of criminal behavior can account for strict-liability offenses.

Second, *motive* and *intention* are confused in many court decisions. In the crime of libel, for instance, motive is explicitly considered. In many states, one cannot publish truthful, albeit damaging statements about another unless the motive is good. Criminal conspiracy also frequently involves consideration and evaluation of a defendant's motives as well as intention. In most instances, however, motivation is ideally taken into account only in the *administration* of the criminal law, that is, in making a decision as to the severity of the punishment which should be accorded a criminal.

Third, the criminal law in action is quite different from the criminal law discussed and analyzed by legal scholars. One reason is this: In reality, every criminal law is quite vague, despite the fact that each appears to be precise and rigorous in its definition of what is outlawed. Criminal laws and the "elements" of each crime are necessarily stated in quite general terms. No law-making body, far removed from occurrences of behavior "on the street," can say precisely what it is that it wants outlawed and made punishable by law. One form of burglary, for example, is a breaking into and entering the house of another at night with intent to commit a felony. Each of the essentials is a legal element of the crime of burglary—breaking, entering, house, night, intent, and felony. Also, each of the essentials seems to be a precise and specific version of one or more of the seven differentia listed above. But not one of the essentials of burglary refers to something real, in the way the word *cat* refers to something real. Consequently, police officers, prosecutors, magistrates, defense attorneys, judges, and others

---

[28]Hall, *General Principles of Criminal Law*, p. 336. See also Jerome Hall, "Analytic Philosophy and Jurisprudence," *Ethics*, 77:14–28, 1966; and Colin Howard, *Strict Responsibility* (London: Sweet and Maxwell, 1963).

must necessarily decide that a specific incident is or is not *close enough* to what the burglary statute seems to outlaw.

When an incident looks something like a burglary, criminal justice personnel must ask, "With what intent did John Doe enter the house on the night of the entry?" In most cases, the correct answer is, "No one knows." Even defendants cannot always say what their intentions were. Nevertheless, criminal justice personnel must answer the question in black-or-white terms—either the defendant had criminal intent or did not.

Similarly, criminal justice personnel must decide other issues in the either-or terms of criminal law, even if the so-called elements and differentia are quite vague. For example, *night* differs from *day* only in degree, but the law in the books does not provide for the decision as to whether conduct and a harm and a *mens rea* occurring together but at daybreak or in the evening is or is not burglary. More generally, the legal institution requires that each suspect and defendant be found either guilty or not guilty; it does not acknowledge the common-sense notion that some criminals are a little bit guilty while others are very guilty indeed. Under the "living law" or "law in action" (consisting of legal decisions made in concrete cases), however, suspects and defendants are in effect held to be "guilty enough" or "not guilty enough."

Criminal justice personnel give concrete reality to law on the books by inserting folk knowledge and common sense into it. Thus they make law by giving meaning to statutes through "playing it by ear"—deciding that a specific incident does or does not resemble what the stated law seems to outlaw. For example, even a specific case involving all of the elements of burglary is not necessarily a burglary in a literal sense. Instead, it might be considered a burglary *for all practical purposes;* or it might be considered no crime at all because it does not seem to resemble closely enough, *for all practical purposes,* what the law on the books says burglary is.

It was observation along these lines that led Justice Oliver Wendell Holmes (1841–1935) to assert that judges make law rather than use it. Thus, he said, judges select appropriate law to cite as justification for the decisions they have reached.[29] As police officers, prosecutors, and defense lawyers "play it by ear" they also decide, first, that a case is or is not burglary, and then they find written law which supports that decision. There is, thus, a fusion of criminal law ("Is the suspect guilty of burglary?") and administration of criminal law ("What, if anything, should the state do with, to, and for this person?"). Whether a man is guilty of burglary or not depends in part on whether someone thinks he should be sent to jail or prison or sent home; if the decision is to send him home, then the elements of burglary will not be found in his case. The outcome of this decision-making process is a living law or law in action that is more just than literal enforcement of criminal statutes would be. But the same living law also makes the conduct of a

[29]Oliver Wendell Holmes, *The Common Law* (Boston: Little, Brown, 1881), pp. 1, 27, 36. See also Holmes, "The Path of the Law," *Harvard Law Review*, 10:457–78, 1897.

"bad guy" (for example, a young, tough, black male with a prior criminal record) a burglary, and the conduct of a "good guy" (such as a middle-aged, middle-class, well-mannered, respectable, white male) a mere case of trespassing or no crime at all.[30]

THE RELATIVITY OF CRIME

The criminal law has had a constantly changing content. Many early crimes were primarily religious offenses, and these remained important until recent times; now few religious offenses are included in penal codes.[31] During Iceland's Viking era, it was a crime for a person to write verses about another, even if the sentiment was complimentary, if the verses exceeded four stanzas in length. A Prussian law of 1784 prohibited mothers and nurses from taking children under two years of age into their beds. The English villein (free common villager) in the fourteenth century was not allowed to send his son to school, and no one lower than a freeholder was permitted by law to keep a dog. The following have at different times and in different places been crimes: printing a book, professing the medical doctrine of circulation of the blood, driving with reins, selling coin to foreigners, having gold in the house, buying goods on the way to market or in the market for the purpose of selling them at a higher price, writing a check for less than one dollar. On the other hand, many of our present laws were not known to earlier generations—quarantine laws, traffic laws, sanitation laws, factory laws.

Laws differ, also, from one jurisdiction to another at a particular time. The laws of some states require automobile owners to paste certificates of ownership or inspection certificates on the windshield, while adjoining states prohibit the pasting of anything on the windshield. Georgia once had a $1000 fine or six months' in jail as the maximum penalty for adultery, while in Louisiana adultery was not a crime at all.

In a particular jurisdiction at a particular time there are wide variations in the interpretation and implementation of the written law. As we suggested earlier, these variations are related to the specific characteristics of the crimes, to the status of the offenders, and to the status of the enforcers.[32] Sudnow has shown that what is "burglary" or "robbery" or almost any other crime is highly negotiable.[33] Further, gross forms of fraud, such as those committed by confidence men, are

---

[30]See Howard Daudistel and William B. Sanders, "Detective Work: Patterns of Criminal Investigations," chap. 8 in *The Sociologist as Detective: An Introduction to Research Methods*, ed. William B. Sanders (New York: Praeger, 1974), pp. 166–84; see also Howard Daudistel, "Deciding What the Law Means: An Examination of Police-Prosecutor Discretion" (Ph.D. diss., University of California, Santa Barbara, 1976); and Harold E. Pepinsky, "Police Patrolmen's Offense-Reporting Behavior," *Journal of Research in Crime and Delinquency*, 13:33–46, 1976.

[31]Kai T. Erikson, *Wayward Puritans: A Study in the Sociology of Deviance* (New York: Wiley, 1966).

[32]See Donald J. Black and Albert J. Reiss, Jr., "Police Control of Juveniles," *American Sociological Review*, 35:63–77, 1970.

[33]David Sudnow, "Normal Crimes: Sociological Features of the Penal Code in a Public Defender Office," *Social Problems*, 12:255–76, 1965.

easily detected by the regular police, but expert investigators must deal with the subtler forms of fraud which flourish in many areas of business and of the professions. When such experts are provided by politicians interested in making subtle fraud "real crime," what has been mere chicanery is interpreted and dealt with as crime. In this sense, also, crime is relative to the status of the criminals and the situations in which they violate law.

CLASSIFICATION OF CRIMES

Because crime is not a homogeneous type of behavior, efforts have been made to classify crimes. They are frequently classified in respect to atrocity as felonies and misdemeanors. The more serious are called felonies and are usually punishable by death or by confinement in a state prison; the less serious are called misdemeanors and are usually punishable by confinement in a local prison or by fines. As a classification of crimes this is not very useful, and it is difficult to make a clear-cut distinction between the classes. Though one may agree that assaults, as a class, are more serious offenses than permitting weeds to grow on a vacant lot in violation of a municipal ordinance, the effects of permitting the weeds to grow, in a particular case, may be more serious because of the hay fever produced by the pollen and the resulting incapacitation of many people. The fact that many things which are classed as felonies in one state are classed as misdemeanors in nearby states shows how difficult it is to make a real distinction between them. Even within a single state the distinction is often vague. Moreover, a crime labeled a felony in a state's criminal code might not be viewed by the public as a more serious offense than some misdemeanors. For example, one sample of the public rated selling marijuana (often a misdemeanor) more serious than "killing spouse's lover after catching them together," and using heroin was more strongly condemned than killing someone in a barroom brawl.[34]

The greatest objection to the classification of crimes as felonies and misdemeanors is that it is used also as a classification of criminals. The individual who commits a felony is a felon; the individual who commits a misdemeanor is a misdemeanant. It is assumed that misdemeanants are less dangerous and more susceptible to the reformative effects of mild punishment than felons. But it is quite fallacious to judge either dangerousness or the probability of reformation from one act, for an individual may commit a misdemeanor one week, a felony the second week, and a misdemeanor the third. The acts do not represent changes in the individual's character or dangerousness.

Moreover, the definition of a crime as misdemeanor or felony is influenced by various considerations other than atrocity or dangerousness. Since 1852, when a felony was first defined in Massachusetts as a crime punishable by confinement in the state prison, at least four major changes have been made in the laws of that state determining the conditions under which a sentence is served in state prison

---

[34]Peter H. Rossi, Emily Waite, Christine E. Bose, and Richard E. Berk, "The Seriousness of Crimes: Normative Structure and Individual Differences," *American Sociological Review*, 39:224–37, 1974.

rather than in a jail or house of correction. These changes, which also changed crimes from felonies to misdemeanors or the reverse, were not made because of alterations in views regarding the atrocity of crimes but for purely administrative reasons, generally to relieve the congestion of the state prison. In the administration of justice, thousands of persons charged with committing felonies successfully arrange to have the charge reduced to a misdemeanor, and the distinction between the two classes of offense is lost. Consequently there seems to be good reason to abandon this classification.

Wilhelm Bonger, the Dutch criminologist, classified crimes by the motives of the offenders as economic crimes, sexual crimes, political crimes, and miscellaneous crimes (with vengeance as the principal motive).[35] But no crime can be reduced to one motive. A desire for excitement or vengeance may be very important in such crimes as burglary, which Bonger classified as economic crime. The classification is clearly inadequate.

Crimes are frequently classified for statistical purposes as crimes against the person, crimes against property, and crimes against public decency, public order, and public justice. Most recorded crimes are crimes against public order or public morality, such as disorderly conduct and drunkenness; next in frequency come the crimes of dishonesty without violence. Of the persons arrested by the police in 1975, 31 percent were arrested for drunkenness or disorderly conduct or driving under the influence of alcohol. The crimes which are regarded as most serious are relatively few, according to this criterion. Homicide constituted 0.5 percent, rape 0.3 percent, burglary 6 percent, and robbery 1.7 percent, a total for these serious offenses of 8.5 percent of all arrests.[36] It is probable that if all cases of fraud could be recorded, fraud would rank close to drunkenness and disorderly conduct in frequency.

In a classification of crimes for theoretical purposes, each class should be a sociological entity, differentiated from the other classes by variations in causal processes. Professional crime, for instance, would be a class, or more likely a combination of classes, differentiated from other crimes by the regularity of this behavior, the development of techniques, and the association among offenders and consequent development of a group culture. Within this class might be included some cases of murder, arson, burglary, robbery, and theft, but not all of the cases in any of those legal categories.[37] Similarly, specific criteria for describing cases as "criminal violation of financial trust" have been developed, with the

[35]W. A. Bonger, *Criminality and Economic Conditions* (Boston: Little, Brown, 1916), pp. 536–37. This book was first published, in French, in 1905.

[36]Federal Bureau of Investigation, U.S. Department of Justice, *Uniform Crime Reports for the United States, 1975* (Washington, D. C.: Government Printing Office, 1975), p. 179.

[37]See Chapter 12. See also Don C. Gibbons and Donald L. Garrity, "Some Suggestions for the Development of Etiological and Treatment Theory in Criminology," *Social Forces*, 38:51–58, 1959; Jack F. Gibbs, "Needed: Analytical Typologies in Criminology," *Southwestern Social Science Quarterly*, 12:321–29, 1960; and Marshall B. Clinard and Richard Quinney, *Criminal Behavior Systems*, 2d ed. (New York: Holt, Rinehart and Winston, 1973).

result that some, but not all, cases of embezzlement, confidence game, forgery, larceny by bailee, and other crimes are included.[38] The new classification avoided the error of extending a legal concept beyond its legal meaning (for example, calling all the behavior "embezzlement") and at the same time it provided a rigorous definition of the behavior being studied. Jerome Hall has made an excellent analysis of theft from this point of view.[39] It is not worthwhile at present to attempt a complete classification of crimes from this viewpoint. Such a classification should be based on research work rather than on *a priori* speculation.

THE CRIMINAL

Who is a criminal? An answer consistent with the previous discussion is: a person who commits a crime. However, in the democratic legal tradition even a person who admits to having committed a crime is not designated a criminal until criminality has been *proven* by means of the accepted court procedures.

But attention is directed away from serious criminological problems by the assertion that a person who commits a crime is a criminal. This is so because, as we suggested earlier, the criteria used to define and designate behavior such as burglary, robbery, larceny, and fraud are actually quite imprecise. Is a boy a delinquent if no one labels him a delinquent? How can a person be said to have violated the law and, thus, to have engaged in criminal behavior if the law is not what is in the statute books but, instead, is what is in the heads of police officers, prosecutors, judges, and others? Such questions have become of great theoretical importance in recent years, and sociological criminologists, especially, are divided on the answers. There are three different positions.

A legally oriented group is confident that statutes adequately describe criminal behavior and, therefore, that anyone who violates a statute is a criminal, whether apprehended or not. This position is at the very foundation of all modern systems of criminal justice. Criminal law and procedure require specificity in definitions, as we indicated above, and this requirement necessarily is based on the assumption that a person is a criminal or not in the same way that a person is blue-eyed or not. While adequate and of critical importance for legal purposes, this position ignores the fundamental problem of determining just how specific a law must be before it can be said to be specific.

A second group goes to the opposite extreme, arguing essentially that the law on the books is irrelevant—persons of little power are criminals according to the law in action, but more powerful people are not. Although this argument is based on the known fact that the criminal justice processes do not treat all persons equally,

[38]Donald R. Cressey, *Other People's Money: A Study in the Social Psychology of Embezzlement* (Glencoe, Ill.: Free Press, 1953), pp. 19–22; idem, "Criminological Research and the Definition of Crimes," *American Journal of Sociology*, 56:546–51, 1951.
[39]Hall, *Theft, Law, and Society.*

it fails to account for another known fact, namely that most poor and powerless people do not get into trouble with the police.

A third group takes an in-between position, holding that statutory definitions, despite their vagueness, are used as reference points by ordinary citizens and criminal justice personnel alike. Thus, most persons know it is against the law to rob, even if they cannot define robbery and, indeed, tend to confuse it with burglary. Similarly, as police officers and others categorize crimes as robberies, and label as robbers the people perpetrating them, their orientation is to the legal norms. Even though there is always some latitude in the decision as to whether a specific piece of behavior is or is not a robbery, it is not hard to tell a robbery from fraud, nor hard to differentiate robbers from confidence men or from innocent bystanders.

The third approach is used throughout the remainder of this book. The criminologist may call behavior criminal if it reasonably falls within a certain class of acts defined as a crime (for example, robbery), and the criminologist may call a person a criminal (for example, a robber) if it is reasonable to believe the person committed an act of this class. Just as there is justification for writing of "crimes known to the police" and "unsolved crimes," there is justification for writing of "criminal behavior," "unapprehended criminals," and "criminals at large," even if no one has been arrested or even detected. One who takes this position finds it possible to study the conditions in which crime arises, flourishes, and diminishes, and the conditions in which persons behave criminally and thus become criminals. Study of interaction between persons who exhibit criminal behavior on the one hand and persons who do or do not label the behavior as crime and do or do not stigmatize its perpetrators as criminals, on the other hand, is the essence of the sociology of law, the sociology of crime, and the social psychology of criminals, as well as of the sociology of punishment and corrections.[40]

This answer—that a criminal is one who can be reasonably assumed to have committed a crime—raises other questions, however, for even the criminal law does not specify the length of time a person remains a criminal after he or she has been shown to have committed a crime. Is a man a criminal only during the time he is committing the crime, until he has "paid the penalty," or during the remainder of his life? These questions are difficult to answer because we use the words *criminal* and *delinquent* to stigmatize persons. Thus, criminality is a status ascribed to persons in a process of interaction between law violators and law enforcers, so that persons are considered "criminal" for varying lengths of time.[41] In public thought, the word *criminal* sometimes is used to refer only to those who have been ostracized by state officials, and the term thus is a synonym for

[40]See Austin T. Turk, *Criminality and the Legal Order* (Chicago: Rand McNally, 1969); idem, *Legal Sanctioning and Social Control* (Washington, D. C.: Government Printing Office, 1972).
[41]See Turk, "Law as a Weapon in Social Conflict."

"outlaw." It is in this sense that Tarde, a pioneering French criminologist, stated that criminals are "social excrement."[42]

Some criminologists restrict the term *criminal* to those persons who conform to a social type. The term then refers to the violator of law who has a body of skills, attitudes, and social relationships which signify maturity in criminal culture. This usage is analogous to the practice of reserving the terms *plumber*, *electrician*, or *preacher* for those who engage regularly and expertly in those occupations. If the term is restricted in this manner, the many occasional violators of law, even those who commit murder, are not criminals. Most of the inmates of state prisons are not *criminals* by this criterion. The use of the word *criminal* in this manner does not direct attention to most of the pertinent problems of criminology.

POSSIBILITY OF A SCIENCE OF CRIMINOLOGY

Criminology is not a science. However, those criminologists concerned with all its divisions, at least, hope it will become one as valid propositions are developed about the processes of making laws, breaking laws, and reacting to the breaking of laws, and about the interrelations among these processes. All such generalizations may be considered an outcome of the study of crime causation. Although the concept of *cause* is being abandoned in criminology, as in science generally, it continues to direct attention to the need for study of conditions under which crime and criminality originate, flourish, and decline. Indeed, unless certain changes in economic, political, and social conditions can be said to result in (that is, cause) changes in the criminal law, a sociology of criminal law is not possible. And unless researchers can say that similar conditions produce (cause) changes in crime rates and in reactions to them, neither a sociology of crime nor of punishment and corrections is possible either.[43]

It is frequently said, however, that criminology cannot possibly become a science. According to this argument, general propositions of universal validity are the essence of science, and these can be made only about stable and homogeneous units; social processes such as lawmaking, lawbreaking, and reaction to lawbreaking are far from being stable and homogeneous, varying from time to time and place to place; therefore, generalizations about these processes cannot be made, and scientific studies of them are impossible.

The emphasis on propositions that fit all cases of lawmaking, lawbreaking, and reactions to lawbreaking is not found among all criminologists. Indeed, most of them stress statistical correlations between, say, repressive legislation, or crime rates, or imprisonment, on the one hand, and social conditions such as unemployment on the other, or else stress various factors in the personalities or backgrounds of individual lawmakers, criminals, or police officers. Most criminologists agree, however, that generalizations are of great value in the long run, and also agree on

[42]Gabriel Tarde, *Penal Philosophy*, trans. Rapelje Howell, Modern Criminal Science Series (Boston: Little, Brown, 1912), p. 222. This book was first published, in French, in 1890.
[43]See Chapter 15.

the desirability of organizing research studies so that specific propositions may be tested. As indicated above, it is possible for the criminologist, by selection of criminal cases, to define the subject matter of a specific study in creative ways. Similarly, it is possible for the criminologist to select specific kinds of lawmaking or law-enforcement cases for study and then to generalize about them.

Sellin implicitly acknowledged the criticism described above and suggested that criminologists study all violations of conduct norms, whether crime or not. He argued that a solid basis for a science of criminology cannot be found unless the arbitrary definitions of the legislatures are replaced by definitions drawn up by scientists and for scientific purposes.[44] Even if this be done, it is not possible to escape the evaluations of behavior which are made by groups and the labeling decisions that are made as a result. Courage, for instance, cannot be defined as a fixed aspect of behavior, for behavior which is called courageous in one situation is called cowardly in another, and the difference in the names applied to the behavior makes the behavior different. Juvenile delinquency and some forms of crime have the same attribute. Physiologically, acts can be defined apart from group evaluations; sociologically they cannot be. In this respect crime is like all other social phenomena, and the possibility of a science of criminal behavior is similar to the possibility of a science of any other behavior. Social science has no stable unit, as it deals with phenomena involving group evaluations.

A sound explanation of crime must necessarily be extremely broad and may not be especially enlightening or valuable for purposes of reducing crime rates. In medicine, a great leap forward was made principally by defining and explaining particular diseases. Similarly, in criminology the significant explanations probably will relate not to crime as a whole, but to particular types or classes of crimes, each class being precisely defined. Obviously, legal definitions should not confine the work of criminologists; they should be free to push across the barriers of legal definitions whenever they see noncriminal behavior which resembles criminal behavior, as the Schwendingers have done.[45] It is an error, however, to call such noncriminal behavior *crime*, no matter how repulsive it may be.[46]

Some criminologists, generally lawyers and others not trained in social or behavioral science, do not participate in the effort to make criminology a science. Instead, they emphasize studies of the effects of penal legislation on crime. Their studies of lawmaking, lawbreaking, and the reactions to lawbreaking are attempts to determine the efficiency of criminal law and its administration.[47]

[44]Thorsten Sellin, *Culture Conflict and Crime* (New York: Social Science Research Council, 1938). See also Denis Szabo, *Déviance et Criminalité* (Paris: Armand Colin, 1970), p. 17.

[45]Herman and Julia Schwendinger, "Defenders of Order or Guardians of Human Rights?" *Issues in Criminology*, 5:123–57, 1970. See also Thomas Ford Hoult, *Social Justice and Its Enemies: A Normative Approach* (New York: Halsted Press, 1975).

[46]See Donald R. Cressey, "Foreword" to Edwin H. Sutherland, *White Collar Crime*, new ed. (New York: Holt, Rinehart and Winston, 1961), pp. 4–8.

[47]See Marc Ancel, *Social Defence: A Modern Approach to Criminal Problems* (London: Routledge and Kegan Paul, 1965).

THE PROBLEM OF CRIME

The practical objective of criminology, supplementing the scientific or theoretical objective, is to reduce the amount of pain and suffering in the world. This objective is consistent with humanitarian concerns for good medical care, good nutrition, and decent housing for all. Some crimes cause obvious pain and suffering to individual victims. Other crimes harm citizens more indirectly—for instance, treason, political corruption, and business fraud. Even more generally, every citizen can in one sense be said to suffer from the huge drain on the economy caused by crime, estimated to be about $125 billion for the United States alone in 1976.[48] This comes to about $343 million per day, and the annual total sum involved in such property transfers and other transactions far exceeds the annual defense budget. More realistically, every citizen suffers from crime if only because huge proportions of the world's tax budgets go to maintaining police departments, courts, probation and parole departments, jails, and prisons. In the United States, this cost is officially estimated to be about $40 million per day ($15 billion annually), but it might be closer to $62 million per day, or $22.7 billion annually.[49] Much more significant is suffering in the form of uneasiness and even terror that crime sometimes produces. Sadly enough, this suffering is experienced predominantly by categories of persons who are most subject to prejudice and discrimination—those who are poor, black, Spanish speaking, female, or aged.[50]

Criminals suffer too. Control of behavior by criminal law is control by deliberately inflicting pain and suffering on those who do not conform. A law without provision for such punishment, we have seen, is no criminal law at all. It follows that the amount of pain and suffering in the world will be reduced if criminologists can find some way to divert, in the name of crime prevention or something else, some of the young people who seem to be marching headlong toward the painful experience of imprisonment. It also follows that only the bare minimum of pain will be inflicted on convicted criminals if criminologists can determine what the bare minimum is and, consistently find nonpunitive ways of dealing with offenders. For that matter, the pain and suffering experienced by criminals will be reduced as criminologists produce more good evidence in support of the notion that many existing penal laws can be repealed without increasing the pain and suffering experienced by citizens at large; decriminalization of drunkenness, gambling, certain sexual conduct, and marijuana smoking are steps in this direction.

The financial losses from fraudulent business transactions are probably many times as great as the financial losses from burglary, robbery, and ordinary larceny.

---

[48]U. S. Congress, Joint Economic Committee, *Report*, 1976. Summarized in *The New York Times*, January 2, 1977.

[49]U. S. Department of Justice, Law Enforcement Assistance Administration, *Expenditures and Employment Data for the Criminal Justice System, 1974* (Washington, D. C.: Government Printing Office, 1976), p. 2.

[50]See Cora A. Martin and Ann S. Reban, *Criminal Victimization of the Aged in Texas* (Denton, Texas: North Texas State University, Center for Community Services, 1976), pp. 38–44.

Each working day trusted employees make off with over $8 million of their employers' cash or merchandise, a total annual loss of over $2 billion. In comparison, it was estimated that in 1965 crimes against the person resulted in a loss of approximately $815 million. This figure takes into account the value of property taken, loss of earnings, medical and hospital expenses, and related costs. Losses from property crimes amount to about $4 billion annually, but the cost of illegal goods and services, such as prostitution and gambling, is estimated to be about $8 billion.[51] One chain of stores has about five hundred burglaries and robberies a year, with a total loss of about $100,000 a year. The same chain had one embezzlement which caused a loss of more than $600,000. A management consulting firm found dishonesty in 50 percent of the assignments it undertook in one year, when there was no prior hint of dishonesty. The firm makes surveys of employee morale, performance in connection with plant layout, efficiency, and other matters which are essentially engineering in nature. In more than 50 percent of these cases they found dishonesty. The same firm unearthed more than $60 million worth of dishonesty in one year with more than 60 percent attributable to supervisory and executive personnel.[52] Such business losses are ordinarily passed on to the consumer in the form of higher prices.

Loss of status in the community is frequently a result of crime. The victim of rape, especially, suffers this loss, and the loss is immensely magnified by the continued publicity given to it in the newspapers. Loss of status may also be suffered by persons not ordinarily considered to be victims, such as the mother of a prostitute or the wife and children of a murderer or embezzler. The victim is sometimes immediately aware of the loss suffered, but the realization is frequently delayed. Children employed in violation of child-labor laws, for instance, may not have an immediate realization of the loss they suffer by this crime and, in fact, may never realize the relation of childhood labor to subsequent career.

In crimes of personal violence, the victims and offenders are generally of the same social group and have residences not far apart. Blacks murder blacks, Italians murder Italians, and Chinese murder Chinese. These crimes of personal violence are generally committed against persons with whom the offenders have personal dealings.[53] Crimes against property, however, are generally committed against strangers. They may be direct and personal, as in robbery or burglary, or may be much more general and public, as in consumer frauds, price fixing, or fraudulent advertisements. In modern society these general and impersonal crimes produce

[51]President's Commission on Law Enforcement and Administration of Justice, *Task Force Report: Crime and Its Impact—An Assessment* (Washington, D. C.: Government Printing Office, 1967), pp. 45–53.

[52]Norman Jaspan with Hillel Black, *The Thief in the White Collar* (Philadelphia: Lippincott, 1960), p. 10.

[53]Harold Garfinkel, "Research Note on Inter- and Intra-Racial Homicides," *Social Forces,* 27:369–81, 1949; President's Commission, *Task Force Report: Crime and Its Impact,* p. 82; Marvin E. Wolfgang and Franco Ferracuti, *The Subculture of Violence: Towards an Integrated Theory in Criminology* (London: Tavistock, 1967); and Richard Block, "Homicide in Chicago: A Nine-Year Study (1965–1973)," *Journal of Criminal Law and Criminology,* 66:496–510, 1976.

more suffering than do direct and personal property crimes, but there is widespread agreement that they are less serious than the direct ones. For example, one sample of citizens gave a score of 6.4, on a nine-point scale of seriousness, to "Burglary of a home and stealing a TV set," but a score of only 4.6 was given to "Fixing prices of machines sold to business."[54] Although the impersonal crimes generally represent no antagonism toward victims, they do represent a ruthless pursuit of interests at variance with the interests of the victims.

It is urged by some persons that crime makes certain contributions to society which offset these losses to some extent. For example, crime is said to promote the solidarity of the group, just as does war.[55] While it is true that a group or community is sometimes welded together by a spectacular crime of murder or rape, many other crimes both reflect and promote dissension, suspicion, and division in society. Moreover, the solidarity which is aroused by a spectacular crime or series of crimes is generally rather futile, for it is an emotional expression which soon passes. In this respect crime, like war, may have some effect in producing group solidarity, but the values can be produced more effectively in other ways.[56]

Again, it is urged that we must have crime in order to prevent morality from going to an extreme. If, under an existing regime, all criminals were eliminated, the standards would be set a little higher. If those at the bottom who violated the new standards were eliminated, the standards would be set still higher. Thus the society would become more and more strict in its morality until the situation became impossible. This argument, also, is not entirely convincing. At least, many primitive groups retained essentially the same standards with practically no violations for long periods of time.[57]

SUGGESTED READINGS

Aubert, Vilhelm. "Researches in the Sociology of Law." *American Behavioral Scientist*, 7:16–20, December, 1963.
Becker, Howard S. *Outsiders: Studies in the Sociology of Deviance.* New York: Free Press, 1963.
Black, Donald. *The Behavior of Law.* New York: Academic Press, 1976.

[54]Rossi et al., "The Seriousness of Crimes." See also Charles W. Thomas, Robin J. Cage, and Samuel C. Foster, "Public Opinion on Criminal Law and Legal Sanctions: An Empirical Examination of Two Conceptual Models," *Journal of Criminal Law and Criminology*, 67:110–16, 1976.
[55]George Herbert Mead, "The Psychology of Punitive Justice," *American Journal of Sociology*, 23:577–602, 1918; A. C. Hall, *Crime in its Relation to Social Progress* (New York: Columbia University Press, 1902), pp. 1–10. See also Robert A. Dentler and Kai T. Erikson, "The Functions of Deviance in Groups," *Social Problems*, 7:98–107, 1959; Lewis A. Coser, "Some Functions of Deviant Behavior and Normative Flexibility," *American Journal of Sociology*, 68:172–81, 1962; and Pat Lauderdale, "Deviance and Moral Boundaries," *American Sociological Review*, 41:660–76, 1976.
[56]See Chapter 14.
[57]William J. Chambliss and Robert B. Seidman, *Law, Order, and Power* (Reading, Mass.: Addison-Wesley, 1971), pp. 19–25.

Black, Donald, & Maureen Milesky, eds. *The Social Organization of Law*. New York: Academic Press, 1973.

Chambliss, William J., & Robert B. Seidman. *Law, Order, and Power*. Reading, Mass.: Addison-Wesley, 1971.

Cicourel, Aaron V. *The Social Organization of Juvenile Justice*. New York: Wiley, 1968.

Clinard, Marshall B., & Richard Quinney. *Criminal Behavior Systems: A Typology*. 2d ed. New York: Holt, Rinehart and Winston, 1973.

Denfield, Duane. *Streetwise Criminology*. Morristown, N. J.: General Learning Press, 1974.

Ellis, Desmond P. "The Hobbesian Problem of Order: A Critical Appraisal of the Normative Solution." *American Sociological Review*, 36:692–703, 1971.

Evan, William M., ed. *Law and Society*. New York: Free Press, 1962.

Fallers, Lloyd E. *Law Without Precedent: Legal Ideas in Action in the Courts of Colonial Busoga*. Chicago: University of Chicago Press, 1969.

Friedman, Lawrence M. *Law and Society: An Introduction*. Englewood Cliffs, N. J.: Prentice-Hall, 1977.

Glaser, Daniel, ed. *The Handbook of Criminology*. Chicago: Rand McNally, 1974.

Hall, Jerome. *General Principles of Criminal Law*. 2d ed. Indianapolis: Bobbs-Merrill, 1960.

Hall, Jerome. *Theft, Law, and Society*. 2d ed. Indianapolis: Bobbs-Merrill, 1952.

Hann, Robert G. "Crime and the Cost of Crime: An Economic Approach." *Journal of Research in Crime and Delinquency*, 9:12–30, 1972.

Hess, Henner. "Repressive Crime and Criminal Typologies: Some Selected Types," *Contemporary Crises*, 1:91–108, 1977.

Hills, Stuart L. *Crime, Power, and Morality*. Scranton, Pa.: Chandler, 1971.

Hindelang, Michael J. "Public Opinion Regarding Crime, Criminal Justice, and Related Topics." *Journal of Research in Crime and Delinquency*, 11:110–16, 1974.

Hobsbawm, E. J. *Primitive Rebels*. New York: W. W. Norton, 1959.

Lauderdale, Pat. "Deviance and Moral Boundaries." *American Sociological Review*, 41:660–76, 1976.

Newman, Graeme. *Comparative Deviance: Perception and Law in Six Cultures*. New York: Elsevier, 1976.

Pepinsky, Harold E. *Crime and Conflict: A Study of Law and Society*. New York: Academic Press, 1976.

Quinney, Richard. *Class, State and Crime: On the Theory and Practice of Criminal Justice*. New York: David A. McKay, 1977.

Radzinowicz, Leon. *A History of English Criminal Law and Its Administration from 1750*, vols. 1–4. New York: Macmillan, 1948–1968.

Rossi, Peter H., Emily Waite, Christine E. Bose, & Richard E. Berk. "The Seriousness of Crimes: Normative Structure and Individual Differences." *American Sociological Review*, 39:224–37, 1974.

Schafer, Stephen. *Theories in Criminology*. New York: Random House, 1969.

Schur, Edwin M. *Law and Society*. New York: Random House, 1969.

Schwartz, Richard D., & Jerome H. Skolnick. *Society and the Legal Order: Cases and Materials in the Sociology of Law*. New York: Basic Books, 1970.

Straus, Murry A. "Leveling, Civility, and Violence in the Family." *Journal of Marriage and the Family*, 36:13–29, 1974.

Sutherland, Edwin H. *White Collar Crime*. New York: Dryden Press, 1949.

Thomas, Charles W., Robin J. Cage, & Samuel C. Foster. "Public Opinion on Criminal Law and Legal Sanctions: An Empirical Examination of Two Conceptual Models." *Journal of Criminal Law and Criminology*, 67:110–16, 1976.

Treves, Renato, & J. F. Glastra van Loon. *Norms and Actions: National Reports on Sociology of Law*. The Hague: Martinus Nijhoff, 1968.

Turk, Austin T. *Criminality and Legal Order*. Chicago: Rand McNally, 1969.

Turk, Austin T. "Law as a Weapon in Social Conflict." *Social Problems*, 23:276–91, 1976.

Turk, Austin T. "Law, Conflict and Order: From Theorizing Towards Theories." *Canadian Review of Sociology and Anthropology*, 13:282–94, 1976.

Unger, Roberto Mangabeira. *Law and Modern Society: Towards a Criticism of Social Theory*. New York: Free Press, 1974.

Wolfgang, Marvin E., ed. *Crime and Culture*. New York: Wiley, 1968.

2

Measures of Delinquency
and Crime

The statistics about crime and delinquency are probably the most unreliable and most difficult of all social statistics. It is impossible to determine with accuracy the amount of crime in any given jurisdiction at any particular time. Some behavior is labeled "delinquency" or "crime" by one observer but not by another. Obviously a large proportion of all law violations goes undetected. Other crimes are detected but not reported, and still others are reported but not officially recorded. Consequently any record of crimes, such as crimes known to the police, arrests, convictions, or commitments to prison, can at most be considered an index of the crimes actually committed. But these "indexes" of crime do not maintain a constant ratio with the true rate, whatever it may be. We measure the extent of crime with elastic rulers whose units of measurement are not defined.

Ordinarily, a statistical index, such as the "cost of living index," is a compilation of fluctuations in a sample of items taken from the whole; the relationship to the whole is known, and the index serves as a convenient shortcut to a sufficient approximation of variation in the whole. But in crime statistics the rate as indicated by any set of figures cannot be a sample, for the whole cannot be specified. Both the true rate and the relationship between the true rate and any index of this rate are capricious "dark figures" which vary with changes in police policies, court policies, and public opinion.[1] The variations in this "dark figure" in

[1]Donald R. Cressey, "The State of Criminal Statistics," *National Probation and Parole Association Journal*, 3:230–41, 1957; Albert D. Biderman and Albert J. Reiss, Jr., "On Exploring the Dark Figure of Crime," *Annals of the American Academy of Political and Social Science*, 374:1–15, 1967; Donald J. Black, "Production of Crime Rates," *American Sociological Review*, 35:733–47, 1970; Howard S. Becker, "Practitioners of Vice and Crime," in *Pathways to Data*, ed. Robert A. Habenstein (Chicago: Aldine, 1973), pp. 30–49; and Lois B. DeFleur, "Biasing Influences on Drug Arrest Records: Implications for Deviance Research," *American Sociological Review*, 40:88–103, 1975.

crime statistics make it almost foolhardy to attempt a comparison of crime rates of various cities, and it is hazardous even to compare national rates or the rates of a given city or state in a given year with the rates of the same jurisdiction in a different year. International comparisons are even more difficult.

CRIMES KNOWN TO THE POLICE

The crimes which are reported to the police and recorded by the police are designated "crimes known to the police." These statistics have not been established as an index of the true crime rate. Yet the decision to use this rate is probably the best way out of a bad situation, for as Professor Sellin has repeatedly pointed out, "The value of criminal statistics as a basis for measurement of criminality in geographic areas decreases as the procedures take us farther away from the offense itself."[2] That is, these police records are a more reliable index than arrest statistics; arrest statistics are more reliable than court statistics; and court statistics are more reliable than prison statistics.

Arrests are made in only a small proportion of all the crimes which become known to the police. For example, in 1975 arrests were made in only 11 percent of the cases of motor vehicle theft known to the police in 1496 American cities. The ratio of arrests to 100 known offenses was 99 for murder, 42 for rape, 28 for robbery, 34 for aggravated assault, 15 for burglary, and 21 for larceny-theft.[3] Even within a single police department, many crimes are "lost" between recording and arrest, the exact number varying with the honesty and efficiency of the police department and with individual police officers' practices regarding handling cases informally, without actual arrest. In 1975, the police of 6449 cities who reported crimes to the Federal Bureau of Investigation "cleared by arrest" 78 percent of the murders, 51 percent of the rapes, 64 percent of the aggravated assaults, 27 percent of the robberies, 18 percent of the burglaries, 20 percent of the larcenies, and 14 percent of the automobile thefts known to them.[4]

Similar rates are reported for European countries, but statistical comparisons are hazardous because "clearance" is defined in so many different ways.[5] No matter how defined, high clearance rates do not necessarily reflect diligent detective work on the part of the police. But because they often are viewed as indexes of police efficiency, they tend to be highly inflated. Police commonly use a technique called "slate cleaning" to improve their clearance rate. For example, a man might confess to a hundred burglaries, thus "clearing" them, in return for a promise that he will be granted a light sentence upon conviction of the

[2]Thorsten Sellin, "The Significance of Records of Crime," *Law Quarterly Review*, 67:489–504, 1951.

[3]Federal Bureau of Investigation, U.S. Department of Justice, *Uniform Crime Reports for the United States, 1975* (Washington, D. C.: Government Printing Office, 1976), p. 176.

[4]Federal Bureau of Investigation, *Uniform Crime Reports*, p. 166.

[5]See Manuel Lopez-Rey, *Crime: An Analytical Appraisal* (London: Routledge and Kegan Paul, 1970), pp. 60–62; Karl O. Christiansen and Gram Jensen, "Crime in Denmark—A Statistical History," *Journal of Criminal Law, Criminology, and Police Science*, 63:82–92, 1972; and Black, "Production of Crime Rates."

burglary for which he was arrested. Probably not more than 5 percent of all crimes committed in the United States are cleared by means of field detective methods.

Similarly, many crimes are "lost" between arrest and prosecution. Just as some types of crime are cleared by arrest more frequently than others, some types of crime are more frequently prosecuted than others. In 1496 cities in the United States in 1975, persons were held for prosecution in 99 percent of the murder cases, 42 percent of the rape cases, 34 percent of the aggravated assault cases, 28 percent of the robbery cases, 15 percent of the burglary cases, 20 percent of the larceny cases, and 11 percent of the automobile theft cases known to the police.

In addition, many crimes are "lost" between prosecution and conviction; this process, too, is selective—some types of crime are "lost" more frequently than others. In 2925 cities in 1975, 48 percent of the persons charged with murder were found guilty, as compared to 33 percent of those charged with rape, 44 percent of those charged with aggravated assault, 36 percent of those charged with robbery, 27 percent of those charged with burglary, 44 percent of those charged with larceny, and 20 percent of those charged with automobile theft.

Similarly, it is obvious that prison statistics are not in constant ratio to the crimes committed, for there are wide variations in the use of fines, probation, and other alternatives to imprisonment. These variations indicate that if crimes known to the police are a good index of crimes committed, then arrests, prosecutions, convictions, and commitments to prison are not—at least for purposes of comparing types of crime.

However, even the number of crimes known to the police is not an adequate index of crime. There are six examples of evidence for this assertion.

1. The number of crimes known to the police is certainly much smaller than the number actually committed. National surveys done for President Johnson's Crime Commission revealed that the incidence of crime in the United States is several times the incidence of crime reported in *Uniform Crime Reports.*[6] More recent surveys carried out by the Census Bureau on behalf of the Law Enforcement Assistance Administration have shown the same thing, as have "victimization surveys" in Canada, Australia, and several European nations.[7] In one such survey, a sample of 10,000 households (about 22,000 persons) and 2000 businesses was drawn in each of twenty-six American cities, and respondents were asked whether they had recently been the victims of specific crimes. The results suggest that, at least for eight cities studied intensively, "crimes known to the police" as recorded

---

[6]President's Commission on Law Enforcement and Administration of Justice, *The Challenge of Crime in a Free Society* (Washington, D. C.: Government Printing Office, 1967), p. 20.

[7]For discussion of this work, see Michael J. Hindelang, *Criminal Victimization in Eight American Cities: A Descriptive Analysis of Common Theft and Assault* (Cambridge, Mass.: Ballinger, 1976); Richard W. Dodge, Harold R. Lentzner, and Frederick Shenk, "Crime in the United States: A Report on the National Crime Survey," chap. 1 in *Sample Surveys of the Victims of Crime*, ed. Wesley G. Skogan (Cambridge, Mass.: Ballinger, 1976), pp. 1–26; and Richard F. Sparks, "Crimes and Victims in London," chap. 3 in *Sample Surveys*, ed. Skogan, pp. 43–71.

in *Uniform Crime Reports* include only about half of the rapes, aggravated assaults and robberies, and about a third of the burglaries and larcenies experienced by citizens. Automobile theft, however, was not underrepresented in the *Uniform Crime Reports*, probably because this crime must be reported in order for the victim to collect insurance.[8] The respondents said they had reported only about half of all personal robberies and about 45 percent of all household burglaries to the police; for crimes in which the victim was a business rather than an individual or a household, about 90 percent of the robberies and about 75 percent of the burglaries were reported.[9] Studies indicate that in one year the detectives of a Chicago department store arrested two-thirds as many adult women for shoplifting as were formally charged with petty larceny of all forms (including shoplifting) by the police in the entire city of Chicago, and that store detectives turn only about 25 percent of apprehended victims over to the police.[10]

Victims may consider the crime insignificant and not worth reporting; they may hope to avoid embarrassing the offender, who may be a relative, school friend, or fellow employee; they may wish to avoid publicity which might result if the crime were reported; they might have agreed to the crime, as in gambling and some sexual offenses; they may wish to avoid the inconvenience of calling the police, appearing as a witness, and so on; they may be intimidated by the offender; they may be antagonistic to the police or opposed to the punitive policies of the legal system; or they may feel that the police are so inefficient that they will be unable to catch the offender even if the offense is reported.[11] The police themselves overlook many offenses, often because "enforcing the law" would be unfair to the suspect, because the law is vague, because booking the offender would be too much work, or because arresting the offender is too dangerous.[12]

2. The number of crimes known to the police is a reasonably accurate index of crime only if the police are honest, efficient, and consistent in making their reports. Police have an obligation to protect the reputation of their cities, and when this cannot be done efficiently under existing administrative machinery, it is sometimes accomplished statistically. Politicians up for reelection are likely to be accused of neglect of duty if the crime rate has gone up during their administration, and they are likely to be praised if the crime rate has declined. Consequently, political administrations often try to show statistically that during their term in office the crime rate declined. Individual police officers select out for recording and further processing only a proportion of the crimes, delinquencies,

---

[8]Hindelang, *Criminal Victimization*, pp. 396–401.

[9]Ibid, pp. 360–363.

[10]Loren E. Edwards, *Shoplifting and Shrinkage Protection for Stores* (Springfield, Ill.: Charles C. Thomas, 1958), p. 130; and Roger K. Griffin, "Shoplifting: A Statistical Study," *Security World*, November, 1970, pp. 21–25. For additional information on shoplifting, see Mary Owen Cameron, *The Booster and the Snitch* (New York: Free Press, 1970).

[11]F. H. McClintock, "The Dark Figure," *Collected Studies in Criminological Research*, vol. V, 1970, pp. 9–34.

[12]See DeFleur, "Biasing Influences on Drug Arrests."

and suspected crimes and delinquencies they observe. No one knows what the proportion is in each case. It is known, however, that officers with professional training process more delinquents than those without professional training.[13] Variations in crime rates among cities or among other jurisdictions must be interpreted with extreme caution, for the differences may be due merely to differential recording practices in the various police departments and by individual police officers.

3. The value of crimes known to the police as an index of crime is sharply limited by the fact that the ratio of crimes committed to crimes reported and recorded varies according to offense. In the first place, some offenses, such as murder, are more likely to be discovered than others. More generally, the *meaning* which people attach to criminal behaviors—how serious, harmful, or immoral they are perceived to be—also dramatically influences whether acts become known and recorded:

. . . We cannot use the *total* recorded criminality. We must extract from that total the data for only those offenses in which the recorded sample is large enough to permit the assumption that a reasonably constant relationship exists between the recorded and the total criminality of these types. We may make that assumption *when the offense seriously injures a strongly embraced social value, is of a public nature in the sense that it is likely to come to the attention of someone beside the victim, and induces the victim or those who are close to him to cooperate with the authorities in bringing the offender to justice.*[14]

4. The organization of control agencies affects the volume of crime known to the police. The sheer number of police officers obviously affects how much crime is processed, especially if these officers work during the night, when the true crime rate is likely to be high. Further, a police department with a "drug division," for example, is likely to know of more drug offenders than a department without such a division, thus creating variations in perception of "the drug problem." Moreover, police departments often organize "drives" against one kind of crime or another, thus manipulating the numbers and rates of crimes known to them.[15]

5. Variations in the criminal law may affect the volume of crimes known to the police, reducing the value of the measure for comparative purposes. Behavior which is a crime in one place or time may not be a crime in another place or time; the difference reduces the value of crimes known to the police for long-range comparative purposes. Further, categorization of an offense in one of the classifications used for recording may be unsystematized and irregular, so that variation in a particular offense is created when none exists in fact. Whether a suspect is charged with petty theft, burglary, or grand larceny sometimes depends

[13]James Q. Wilson, "The Police and the Delinquent in Two Cities," in *Controlling Delinquents*, ed. Stanton Wheeler (New York: Wiley, 1967).

[14]Sellin, "The Significance of Records of Crime," pp. 496–97.

[15]See DeFleur, "Biasing Influences on Drug Arrest Records."

on the whim of the police officer recording the offense. Most contemporary "kidnapping," for example, is just taking control of a victim in the course of a robbery. Magistrates pay little attention to the charges against the vagrants who come before them; as a consequence, there may be more commitments of vagrants to houses of correction in a given period of time than there are arrests for vagrancy. Similarly, comparisons of the crime rates of various countries are seriously limited by wide variations in the national legal systems. For example, *robo* in the Argentine penal code includes what the United States codes call robbery, but it also includes some kinds of behavior which the typical United States code would call burglary or breaking and entering.[16] International comparisons would be of decided value in securing an understanding of criminality because these statistics show the wider variations which may not be apparent within a particular country. In Scandinavia, considerable interest has developed in a program for the international codification of criminal laws and for the development of international statistics of crime and criminals. The essential problem is to develop units that can be used for international comparisons.

6. The number of crimes known to the police must, for purposes of comparison, be stated in proportion to the population or to some other base, and the determination of this base is often difficult. United States census figures on the general population collected in the first year of a decade often must be used throughout the decade as the base for computing crime rates. Because the increasing United States population is not taken into account, the number of crimes per 100,000 population appears to increase each year throughout the decade. For example, if 1970 population figures are used to compute the crime rates for both 1970 and 1979, the latter year shows a higher rate, not because of an increase in crime, but because the population increase between 1970 and 1979 is not included in the base for the 1979 rate. Also, the population figures must be corrected for variations in age, sex, racial composition, and urban-rural composition, and much of this information is available only in the years in which the census is taken.[17] Moreover, in many cases it is necessary to have other information. For instance, the number of automobile thefts in a community must be stated in proportion to the number of automobiles in the community. More generally, crimes of theft should be stated in proportion to the amount of property available to be stolen, not merely in proportion to population. Moreover, Engelmann and Throckmorton have argued convincingly that a more accurate view of all crime rates is obtained if the number of crimes is stated in proportion to the frequency of interaction among people, rather than merely in proportion to

[16]Lois B. DeFleur, "A Cross-Cultural Comparison of Offenders and Offenses: Cordoba, Argentina, and the United States," *Social Problems*, 14:483–92, 1967.

[17]See Ronald Chilton and Adele Spielberger, "Is Delinquency Increasing? Age Structure and the Crime Rate," *Social Forces*, 49:487–93, 1971.

the number of people.[18] The difficulty of securing an adequate base for computing a rate is evident.

SOURCES OF STATISTICS ON CRIME IN THE UNITED STATES

Police, court, and prison statistics may be published by the agency which manufactures them, or they may be reported to a central state or federal agency which organizes, combines, and publishes the statistics from many agencies. Only rarely do the local or central agencies do more than catalog the incidence of various crimes. Computation of rates, analyses of interrelationships between various statistical facts, and the making of inferences about the statistics are left to outside research workers. The various agencies, in other words, merely take censuses of various dimensions of the criminal population, just as the Department of Commerce takes censuses of the total United States population. Some of the agencies try to identify the limitations of the statistics which they publish, but most of them do not.

Federal Reports

Since 1930, the United States Department of Justice has published a periodical bulletin on crime statistics, *Uniform Crime Reports*. The number of known crimes reported to the FBI by the police of about 3000 cities and towns is used as an index of "major" crimes (murder, rape, aggravated assault, burglary, robbery, larceny, and automobile theft), and "arrests" (fingerprint records sent to the FBI) are used as an index of other crimes. The bulletin was first published monthly, became a quarterly in 1932, was converted into a semiannual publication during World War II, and became an annual publication in 1959. Local police departments are supplied with a manual on reporting, but participation by police departments is voluntary. Consequently, not all communities are covered, and the large metropolitan centers are overrepresented. For example, the 1975 statistics are based on reports from law enforcement agencies representing 97 percent of the population living in the standard metropolitan statistical areas, but only 83 percent of the rural population; the total population represented in one set of statistics numbered 187 million, while the total population of the United States was more than 213 million.[19]

The *Uniform Crime Reports* have many limitations, and the FBI will not vouch for their accuracy. Nevertheless, they are persistently used as evidence about the amount and nature of crime in the United States. Table 1 shows the estimated

[18]Hugo O. Engelmann and Kirby Throckmorton, "Interaction Frequency and Crime Rates," *Wisconsin Sociologist*, 5:33–36, 1967. See also Sarah L. Boggs, "Urban Crime Patterns," *American Sociological Review*, 30:899–908, 1965.

[19]Federal Bureau of Investigation, *Uniform Crime Reports*, 1975, pp. 3, 153. For a history of this bulletin and a critique of the statistics reported in it, see Marvin E. Wolfgang, "Uniform Crime Reports: A Critical Appraisal," *University of Pennsylvania Law Review*, 111:708–38, 1963.

number of serious crimes reported as known to the police in 1975, and Table 2 shows the number of police department arrests recorded by the FBI in 1975 on the basis of the fingerprint cards sent to it. In the latter table it should be noted that only 23.7 percent of the arrests were for the seven "major" crimes and that there is a great discrepancy between the estimated number of major crimes committed (Table 1) and the number of arrests for those crimes (Table 2).

The Department of Justice also publishes statistics on commitments to state and federal penal institutions in the United States. This series, *National Prisoner Statistics*, was originally published by the Bureau of the Census, with the title *Prisoners in State and Federal Prisons and Reformatories*. In 1950 the series was transferred to the Federal Bureau of Prisons, and in 1971 to the Law Enforcement Assistance Administration. Included are data on the number of commitments to the various institutions, the number of prisoners present at the end of each year, and the number of prisoners discharged under each of the various systems of release. The annual report of the Federal Bureau of Prisons, *Federal Prisons* (formerly named *Federal Offender*), gives statistical data on persons convicted of violations of federal laws. Table 3 presents *National Prisoner Statistics* data on the recent trends in rates of commitments to both state and federal institutions.

Local coroners keep records of known homicides. Since 1900, the National Office of Vital Statistics (or a similar agency) has published in *Vital Statistics of the United States* an annual homicide rate based on these records. Until about

Table 1   Estimated Number of Major Crimes in the United States, 1975

Crime Index Classification	Estimated Crime, 1975		Percent Change over 1974	
	Number	Rate per 100,000 Inhabitants	Number	Rate
Total	11,256,600	5281.7	+ 9.8	+ 8.9
Murder	20,510	9.6	− 1.0	− 2.0
Forcible rape	56,000	26.3	+ 1.3	+ 0.4
Robbery	464,970	218.2	+ 5.1	+ 4.3
Aggravated assault	484,710	227.4	+ 6.2	+ 5.4
Burglary	3,252,100	1525.9	+ 7.0	+ 6.1
Larceny, $50 and over	5,977,700	2804.8	+13.6	+12.7
Auto theft	1,000,500	469.4	+ 2.4	+ 1.6

SOURCE: Federal Bureau of Investigation, *Uniform Crime Reports*, 1975, p. 11.

NOTE: The estimated crime totals for the United States appearing in this table are not comparable to such totals published in *Uniform Crime Reports* in the years prior to 1959. "Negligent manslaughter" has been omitted. "Larceny" no longer includes petty offenses, and "rape" no longer includes "statutory rape."

Table 2   Total Arrests, Distribution by Sex, 1975

Offense Charged	Number Total	Male	Female	Percent Total	Male	Female
Total	**8,013,645**	**6,751,545**	**1,262,100**	**100.0**	**100.0**	**100.0**
Criminal homicide	19,526	16,611	2,915	.2	.2	.2
Forcible rape	21,963	21,748	215	.3	.3	
Robbery	129,788	120,650	9,138	1.6	1.8	.7
Aggravated assault	202,217	175,823	26,394	2.5	2.6	2.1
Burglary—breaking or entering	449,155	421,729	24,426	5.6	6.3	1.9
Larceny—theft	958,938	659,671	299,267	12.0	9.8	23.7
Auto theft	120,224	111,868	8,356	1.5	1.7	.7
Other assaults	352,648	303,903	48,745	4.4	4.5	3.9
Arson	14,589	12,942	1,647	.2	.2	.1
Forgery and counterfeiting	57,803	41,091	16,712	.7	.6	1.3
Fraud	146,253	96,249	50,004	1.8	1.4	4.0
Embezzlement	9,302	6,406	2,896	.1	.1	.2
Stolen property—buying, receiving, possessing	100,903	90,141	10,762	1.3	1.3	.9
Vandalism	175,865	161,809	14,056	2.2	2.4	1.1
Weapons—carrying, possessing, etc.	130,933	120,493	10,440	1.6	1.8	.8
Prostitution and commercialized vice	50,229	12,928	37,301	.6	.2	3.0
Sex offenses [except forcible rape and prostitution]	50,837	46,932	3,905	.6	.7	.3
Narcotic drug laws	508,189	438,129	70,060	6.3	6.5	5.6
Gambling	49,469	45,136	4,333	.6	.7	.3
Offenses against family and children	53,332	47,109	6,223	.7	.7	.5
Driving under the influence	908,680	835,073	73,607	11.3	12.4	5.8
Liquor laws	267,057	228,933	38,124	3.3	3.4	3.0
Drunkenness	1,176,121	1,093,103	83,018	14.7	16.2	6.6
Disorderly conduct	632,561	520,999	111,562	7.9	7.7	8.8
Vagrancy	59,277	53,080	6,197	.7	.8	.5
All other offenses [except traffic]	1,037,754	870,289	167,465	12.9	12.9	13.3
Suspicion	29,038	25,037	4,061	.4	.4	.3
Curfew and loitering law violations	112,117	89,316	22,801	1.4	1.3	1.8
Runaways	118,817	81,347	107,470	2.4	1.2	8.5

SOURCE: Federal Bureau of Investigation, *Uniform Crime Reports*, 1975, p. 191.

Table 3 Prisoners in Institutions and Received from Court, 1939–1973, Rates per 100,000 of the Estimated Civilian Population

	Present at End of Year			Received from Court		
Year	All Institutions	Federal Institutions	State Institutions	All Institutions	Federal Institutions	State Institutions
1940	132.0	14.6	117.3	55.5	11.5	44.1
1945	100.5	14.0	86.5	40.0	10.7	29.4
1950	110.3	11.4	98.9	46.1	9.5	36.7
1955	113.4	12.3	101.1	47.9	9.3	38.5
1960	118.6	12.9	105.7	49.3	7.6	41.7
1965	109.5	10.9	98.6	45.4	6.6	38.8
1970	96.7	9.8	86.8	39.1	5.9	33.1
1973	97.8	10.9	86.9	59.6	7.0	52.5

SOURCE: Federal Bureau of Prisons, "Prisoners in State and Federal Institutions for Adult Felons, 1968–1970," *National Prisoner Statistics*, no. 47, April, 1972, table 1, p. 2, and table 2, p. 3; and U.S. Department of Justice, Law Enforcement Assistance Administration, *Prisoners in State and Federal Institutions, 1971–1973*, NTS Bulletin—National Prisoner Statistics, no. SD-NTS-SFP-1, 1974.

1930, only the coroners' statistics from the New England states were summarized, but now the entire population of the United States is covered. These statistics were issued by the Bureau of the Census until 1946; now that bureau merely reprints—in *Statistical Abstracts of the United States*—the data published by the U.S. Public Health Service. Table 4 shows that the number of deaths by homicide per 100,000 adults increased in the middle 1960s and has remained rather constant since that time. However, these statistics on homicide do not necessarily show that murders and manslaughter, as ordinarily understood, have increased. Homicide includes justifiable and noncriminal violence, such as killing in self-defense, killing a prisoner who is trying to escape, and similar acts. It also includes deaths caused by negligence, now common in automobile accident cases. Because *Vital Statistics* does not report the portion of all homicides which are justifiable or due to negligence, the publication tells us little about trends in murder, as popularly understood. It should be noted further that coroners' reports pertain to medical causes of death, and not to arrests or prosecutions of persons accused of murder.

The homicide rate per 100,000 population fluctuates markedly from country to country. The United States consistently shows a rate higher than most European countries and lower than most South American countries, as illustrated in Table 5.

Statistics on juvenile delinquency are also published by the federal government, through the Children's Bureau of the Social Security Administration. Until 1955, only about 400 courts, out of approximately 3000 courts that deal with children's cases, made reports to the bureau. In 1955, the bureau revised its statistical reporting plan to include a national sample representative of all juvenile

Table 4 Number and Rate of Homicides, United States: 1930 to 1970

Years[a]	Number	Rate[b]
1930	10,331	12.4
1935	10,396	11.2
1940	8,329	8.6
1945	7,547	7.7
1950	7,942	7.2
1955	7,418	6.4
1960	8,464	6.5
1965	10,712	8.0
1970	16,848	11.6
1971	18,787	12.6
1972	19,638	13.0
1973	20,465	13.3

SOURCE: U.S. Bureau of the Census, Statistical Abstract of the United States, 1975, 96th ed. (Washington, D.C.: Government Printing Office, 1975), table 256, p. 154.

[a]Prior to 1960, excludes Alaska and Hawaii. Excludes armed forces abroad.

[b]Per 100,000 resident population 16 years old and over; enumerated as of April 1 for 1930, 1940, 1950, 1960, and 1970; estimated as of July 1 for all other years.

courts. The earlier Children's Bureau statistics have been criticized on the ground that a very small proportion of the population was represented, that the standards for reporting were not uniform, that definitions of delinquency vary from jurisdiction to jurisdiction, that the ages of children over whom the courts have

Table 5 Homicide Rates for Selected Countries (per 100,000 Population), 1972

Country	Rate	Country	Rate
El Salvador	29.5	Israel	1.5
Guatemala	20.4[a]	Germany (FRG)	1.4
Mexico	14.3	Japan	1.3
Thailand	12.7	Italy	1.1
United States	9.1[a]	France	0.9
Venezuela	7.8	Poland	0.9
Cuba	3.7	England/Wales	0.8
Canada	2.3	Norway	0.7
Hungary	2.1	Netherlands	0.5
Hong Kong	1.8	Spain	0.3

SOURCE: World Health Organization (WHO), World Health Statistics Annual, 1972, vol. 1 (Geneva, 1975), p. 234.

[a]Data for 1971.

Table 6 Trend in Delinquency Cases Disposed of by Juvenile Courts, United States, 1960–1973

Year	Delinquency Cases[a,b]	Child Population (10–17 Years of Age)	Rate[c]
1960	510,000	25,368,000	20.1
1965	697,000	29,536,000	23.6
1970	1,052,000	32,614,000	32.3
1971	1,125,000	32,969,000	34.1
1972	1,112,000	33,120,000	33.6
1973	1,143,000	33,377,000	34.2

SOURCE: U.S. Department of Health, Education, and Welfare, *Juvenile Court Statistics, 1970* (Washington, D.C.: National Center for Social Statistics, 1975), p. 11.

[a]Excluded are the ordinary traffic cases handled by juvenile courts, except where traffic cases, usually the more serious ones, are adjudicated as "juvenile delinquency" cases and are reported as such.

[b]Data for 1960 and 1965 estimated from the national sample of juvenile courts. Data for 1970–1973 estimated from all courts reporting, whose jurisdictions included almost three-fourths of the population of the U.S.

[c]Based on the number of delinquency cases per 1000 U.S. child population.

jurisdiction vary, and that there are variations in the proportions of juvenile delinquents who are referred to the courts.[20] Table 6 shows the recent trends in juvenile delinquency, as measured by a representative national sample.

State Reports

Generally, the states are less efficient than the federal government in making crime statistics available. In most states, one or more departments or bureaus obtain reports from a particular type of county or municipal official, but no attempt is made to use a uniform system of reporting in order to make the resulting summaries comparable. The attorney general may receive information from district attorneys; the department of correction may receive information from sheriffs; the department of public welfare from juvenile courts and welfare agencies dealing with delinquency, and so on. In a few states, the only criminal statistics are those published by individual institutions or agencies. Only thirteen states—including California, Hawaii, Louisiana, Massachusetts, Michigan, Minnesota, New York, Pennsylvania, Rhode Island, South Dakota, and Texas—have central statistical bureaus which collect and publish statistical information drawn from reports made by a variety of local, county, or state agencies. For some states, crimes known to the police, arrests, and convictions are summarized, but in most states the statistics are restricted to the number of persons admitted to probation,

[20]See James F. Short, Jr., and F. Ivan Nye, "Extent of Unrecorded Juvenile Delinquency: Tentative Conclusions," *Journal of Criminal Law, Criminology, and Police Science*, 49:296–302, 1958.

prison, or parole. The data in Table 7 are from the Bureau of Statistics, California Department of Justice; this bureau acts as a statistical agency for the Department of Corrections.

Other Reports

Statistics on specific crimes are published regularly by some federal and state agencies, and certain private organizations maintain running accounts of the offenses committed against them. The Federal Deposit Insurance Corporation, the Treasury Department, and the Department of Justice, for example, all publish annual indexes of the number of violations of certain federal laws. Similarly, the American Bankers Association keeps records of offenses against banks; fidelity bonding companies keep records of crimes against bonded business firms, and large corporations record their annual losses to various kinds of crime. Ordinarily, the statistics reported by a single agency or private organization are not comparable with the statistics compiled and published for the entire nation or for an entire state.

Government agencies and private foundations also have promoted and con-

Table 7 *Male Prisoners Newly Received from Court, California, 1970 and 1971*

	1970		1971		
Offense	Number	Rate per 100,000 Population[a]	Number	Rate per 100,000 Population[a]	Percent Change in Rate— 1971 over 1970
Total	**4,472**	**22.02**	**4,272**	**20.82**	**– 5.7**
Homicide	421	2.08	443	2.16	+ 3.8
Robbery	995	4.91	962	4.69	– 4.5
Assault	329	1.62	354	1.73	+ 6.8
Burglary	646	3.19	637	3.10	– 2.8
Theft, except auto	326	1.61	295	1.44	– 10.6
Auto theft	139	0.69	123	0.60	– 13.0
Forgery and checks	198	0.98	208	1.01	+ 3.1
Sex offenses	247	1.22	243	1.18	– 3.3
Narcotics	921	4.54	781	3.81	+ 16.1
Other offenses	250	1.23	226	1.10	– 10.6

SOURCE: *California Prisoners*, 1972 (Sacramento: Department of Corrections, 1973), p. 10.

[a]Estimates of population from State Department of Finance, Financial and Population Research Section.

ducted a number of crime surveys, one general aim of which has been the discovery of the proportions of crimes not reported in the usual statistics of crime. Among the more famous surveys are the Cleveland survey, the Missouri survey, the Illinois survey, the study by the Wickersham commission, the Oregon survey, the Attorney General's survey, and the recent survey made by the President's Commission.[21]

Occasionally, a comprehensive firsthand investigation by an independent research worker produces new statistical indexes. Short and Nye long ago demonstrated that statistics compiled from reports of delinquencies by offenders are acceptable and desirable in scientific analyses, and studies of self-reported crimes and delinquencies are now quite common.[22]

THE PERVASIVENESS OF CRIME IN THE UNITED STATES

Crime is much more general and pervasive than the ordinary statistics indicate, and an entirely incorrect impression regarding criminality is formed if conclusions are based only on these statistics. Opposition to law has been a tradition in the United States. Popular rebellions against laws constitute an almost continuous series from the early colonial period to the present. Violations of many of the early laws were quite as general as were violations of the Prohibition act in the 1920s and violations of current laws prohibiting gambling, homosexual conduct, and possession of marijuana. The manufacture of nails and of other commodities in violation of English law, the sale of firearms and of liquor to Indians, smuggling and other violations of laws regulating commerce, Shays's Rebellion in 1787, the Whisky Rebellion in 1794, trading with the enemy during the War of 1812, riots against the Catholics, the Irish, and the Mormons, Dorr's Rebellion in 1841–1842, trading in slaves, harboring fugitive slaves, Negro disfranchisement, violation of antitrust laws, violation of banking laws, violation of prohibition laws, and violation of draft laws during the Vietnam War are some of these popular rebellions.[23] The earlier violations of this type cannot be measured statistically,

[21]Roscoe Pound and Felix Frankfurter, eds., *Criminal Justice in Cleveland* (Cleveland: The Cleveland Foundation, 1922); Missouri Association for Criminal Justice, Survey Committee, *The Missouri Crime Survey* (New York: Macmillan, 1926); Illinois Association for Criminal Justice, *The Illinois Crime Survey* (Chicago: Illinois Association for Criminal Justice, 1929); National Commission on Law Observance and Enforcement, *Reports* (Washington: Government Printing Office, 1931); Wayne L. Morse and Ronald H. Beattie, *Survey of the Administration of Justice in Oregon* (Eugene: University of Oregon Press, 1932); *Attorney General's Survey of Release Procedures*, 5 vols. (Washington: Government Printing Office, 1939–40); President's Commission on Law Enforcement and Administration of Justice, *The Challenge of Crime in a Free Society* (Washington, D. C.: Government Printing Office, 1967), pp. 21–22.

[22]James F. Short, Jr., and F. Ivan Nye, "Reported Behavior as a Criterion of Deviant Behavior," *Social Problems*, 5:207–13, 1957–58. For analyses of some of the early studies using this procedure, see Roger Hood and Richard Sparks, *Key Issues in Criminology* (London: World Universities Library, 1970); and Travis Hirschi, *Causes of Delinquency* (Berkeley: University of California Press, 1969).

[23]See Kai T. Erikson, *Wayward Puritans: A Study in the Sociology of Deviance* (New York: Wiley, 1966).

and it is not possible to determine from the descriptions whether the number of persons involved in popular rebellions has increased or decreased.

The criminal tradition is also reflected in the fact that certain occasions are defined as holidays from morality. Halloween, New Year's Eve, election nights, spring celebrations, campus demonstrations, and important football victories are occasions of this nature. On these occasions, crimes are committed by persons who ordinarily would not commit them. These crimes may take the form of destruction of property and of assaults. Individual crimes are committed primarily in a spirit of exuberance, and they coincide with institutionalized collective behavior involving many persons. There is much evidence that the delinquency of juveniles in deteriorated urban areas is an extension of this attitude through the entire year.

Labor strikes were once very much like these moral holidays. More recently, student strikes have resembled them. There is a gathering of persons with a common interest, an attitude during the early period of the strike which is much like that of a picnic, and an exuberance which is like that of the spring celebration. Assaults and destruction of property occur on these occasions, just as on other holidays from morality.[24] The violation of law, however, is much more purposive in the strike than in these other outbursts. Factory workers, skilled tradesmen, farmers, and students, without much differentiation, violate the laws on such occasions. These holidays from morality are so generally recognized that penalties for lawlessness seldom result.

The fact that almost all persons have at some time deliberately committed crimes, often of a serious nature, is further evidence of our criminal tradition. In interviews, a sample ($N = 2510$) of American men who were 20 to 30 years old in 1974 were asked if they had ever committed each of ten illegal acts.[25] Seventy percent of the men reported public intoxication and 60 percent admitted that they had driven an automobile while intoxicated (8 percent had been arrested for driving while intoxicated). The next most common of the other eight offenses was shoplifting—44 percent of the men reported this form of theft. Thirteen percent admitted breaking and entering, 6 percent admitted automobile theft, 3 percent admitted face-to-face stealing, 3 percent illegal gambling, and another 3 percent bad checks. Also, 1 percent admitted to having forged a prescription and another 1 percent confessed to armed robbery.[26] Overall, 31 percent of the respondents indicated that they had been arrested for an offense involving something other than a traffic violation; 8 percent had appeared in juvenile court, and 12 percent of

---

24See the discussion by David F. Luckenbill and William B. Sanders, "Criminal Violence," chap. 3 in *Deviants: Voluntary Actors in a Hostile World,* ed. Edward Sagarin and Fred Montanino (Morristown, N. J.: General Learning Press, 1977), pp. 88–156.

25John A. O'Donnell, Harwin L. Voss, Richard R. Clayton, Gerald T. Slatin, and Robin G. W. Room, *Young Men and Drugs—a Nationwide Survey* (Washington, D. C.: National Institute on Drug Abuse, Research Monograph No. 5, 1976), pp. 81–82, 90–92.

26For definitions of these and the other illegal acts used in this study, see Table 12 in chap. 6.

the men indicated that they had been convicted of a crime. Four percent of the whites and 14 percent of the blacks had served prison sentences.

Significantly, this study also indicated that there is a high correlation between reported criminal conduct and the probability of being arrested, convicted, or imprisoned. Thus, the men who were arrested or who appeared in juvenile court, or who were committed to a juvenile correctional institution, were convicted of a crime, or sentenced to prison were more likely to report one or more criminal acts than those without such experiences. Table 8 shows, for example, that 78 percent of the men sent to a juvenile institution reported one or more of the listed acts, in comparison with 19 percent of those with no commitment as juveniles. The comparable figures for those who did and did not serve prison sentences are 67 and 17 percent, respectively. The data in the table suggest, in short, that a distinction should be made between the incidence of criminal *behavior* on the one hand, and the *labeling* of the person perpetrating that behavior on the other. The conclusion seems to be that labeling is by no means only "in the eye of the beholder," but flows from participating in behavior which has been outlawed.

Studies in several European countries and other American studies similarly suggest that the number of crimes committed is far greater than the number reported in crime statistics. A Finnish study showed that only 5 percent of self-reported larcenies and 1 percent of self-reported violations of alcohol laws were detected by police.[27] In a study of juvenile delinquencies, Short found that a group of sixty-five male college students reported that they had committed an average of 9.9 offenses against property, 12.3 behavior-problem offenses, 9.6 offenses against persons, 16.5 sex offenses, 20.8 "casual offenses," and 12.6 miscellaneous offenses. A group of ninety-four training-school boys reported that they had committed an average of 13.4 offenses against property and 19.1 behavior-problem offenses; their average number of other offenses was about the same as that of the college students. In comparison with the training-school boys, the students had only very rarely been arrested for their offenses.[28] One explanation for this differential lies in the fact that police and other officials use discretion in making arrests, often to the advantage of middle-class suspects who do not fit the stereotype of the "bad actor."[29]

White-collar crimes—crimes committed by persons of respectability and high social status in the course of their occupations—also are extremely widespread,

[27]Inkeri Anttila and R. Jaakkola, "Unrecorded Criminality in Finland," *Kriminologinen Tutkimuslaitos,* 2:5–22, 1966.

[28]James F. Short, Jr., "A Report on the Incidence of Criminal Behavior, Arrests, and Convictions in Selected Groups," *Research Studies of the State College of Washington,* 22:110–18, June, 1954. See also Short and Nye, "Reported Behavior as a Criterion of Deviant Behavior," and Maynard L. Erickson and Lamar T. Empey, "Court Records, Undetected Delinquency and Decision-making," *Journal of Criminal Law, Criminology, and Police Science,* 54:456–69, 1963.

[29]Aaron V. Cicourel, *The Social Organization of Juvenile Justice* (New York: John Wiley, 1968); Irving Piliavin and Scott Briar, "Police Encounters with Juveniles," *American Journal of Sociology,* 70:206–14, 1964.

Table 8   Self-Reported Criminal Acts, by Contacts with the Criminal Justice System

Self-Reports	Arrested (786) Yes	(1724) No	Juvenile Court Appearance (205) Yes	(2305) No	Juvenile Commitment (59) Yes	(2541) No	Crime Conviction (303) Yes	(2207) No	Prison Sentence (135) Yes	(2375) No
Public intoxication or driving while intoxicated	87%	69%	87%	69%	87%	74%	89%	73%	84%	74%
Shoplifting before age 18	53	33	65	37	73	38	55	37	54	38
Other self-reported criminal acts admitted:										
None	60	89	38	84	22	81	47	85	33	83
One	23	9	29	12	24	14	26	12	26	13
Two or more	17	2	33	4	54	5	27	3	41	4
(One or more)	(40)	(11)	(62)	(16)	(78)	(19)	(53)	(15)	(67)	(17)

SOURCE: O'Donnell et al., *Young Men and Drugs*, p. 96.

but an index of their frequency is not found in police reports. Prosecution for this kind of crime is frequently avoided because of the political or financial importance of the parties concerned, because of the apparent triviality of the crimes, or because of the difficulty of securing evidence sufficient for prosecution, particularly in the cases of crimes by corporations.[30] Even more important, methods other than prosecution in the criminal courts are frequently used to deal with white-collar criminals—action may be taken in the civil courts or in hearings before boards and commissions. Consequently, a precise statement regarding the extent of white-collar crime is impossible. Differences in administrative procedures, however, do not justify the designation of this behavior as something other than crime.[31] In general, underlying these failures to prosecute white-collar criminals is the lack of a developed feeling of moral indignation in the persons of power who are involved and, to some extent, in the general public.[32] The reaction to robbery and assault is severe, for they involve direct sensory processes and are based on social relations which have existed for many centuries. But theft by fraudulent

[30]For a summary statement, see Carl B. Klockars, "White Collar Crime," chap. 5 in *Deviants: Voluntary Actors in a Hostile World*, ed. Sagarin and Montanino, pp. 220–58.

[31]See Edwin H. Sutherland, "White Collar Criminality," *American Sociological Review*, 5:1–12, 1940.

[32]See Vilhelm Aubert, "White-Collar Crime and Social Structure," *American Journal of Sociology* 58:263–71, 1952; John C. Spencer, "White-Collar Crime," in *Criminology in Transition*, ed. Tadeusz Grygier, Howard Jones, and John C. Spencer (London: Tavistock, 1965), pp. 233–66; André Normandeau, "Les Deviations en

advertisements and by violations of antitrust laws are recent developments which affect persons who may live thousands of miles away from the thief. Moral codes have not been developed in regard to this behavior. White-collar criminals, however, are by far the most dangerous to society of any type of criminal from the point of view of effects on human rights and democratic institutions. Ethical codes deploring such offenses have not developed, and the victims of white-collar crimes have not been able to persuade criminal justice personnel to be as indignant about white-collar crime as they are about robbery, automobile theft, and vandalism.[33]

An analysis has been made of the number of instances in which seventy of the largest United States mining, manufacturing, and mercantile corporations violated, over a period of about 40 years, the laws regulating the following practices: restraint of trade; misrepresentation in advertising; infringements of patents, trademarks, and copyrights; "unfair labor practices" as defined by the National Labor Relations Act and other laws; rebates; financial fraud and violation of trust; violations of war regulations; and some miscellaneous activities.[34] The records reveal that every one of the seventy corporations violated one or more of the laws, with an average of about thirteen adverse decisions per corporation and a range of from one to fifty adverse decisions per corporation. The corporations had a total of 307 adverse decisions on charges of restraint of trade, 222 adverse decisions on charges of infringements, 158 adverse decisions under the National Labor Relations Act, 97 adverse decisions under the laws regulating advertising, and 196 adverse decisions on charges of violating other laws.

Thus, the official records revealed that these corporations violated the law with great frequency. The habitual-criminal laws of some states impose severe penalties on criminals convicted the third or fourth time. If this criterion were extended to corporations, about 90 percent of the large corporations studied would be considered habitual white-collar criminals. Moreover, this enumeration of official decisions is far from complete, and it is concerned with violations of only a few laws. Even a complete enumeration of all adverse decisions against all corporations would represent only a crude index of the total amount of crime perpetrated by these corporations.

Financial corporations and institutions also have a high incidence of hidden

Affaire et de Crime en Col Blanc," *Revue International de Criminologie et de Police Technique*, 4:247–48, 1965; Hans Joachim Schneider, "Wirtschaftkriminalität in Kriminologischer und Strafrechtlicher Sicht," *Juristenzeitung*, 15:461–67, 1972; Klaus Tiedemann and Jean Cosson, *Straftaten und Strafrecht im Deutschen und Französischen Bank- lund Kreditwesen* (Cologne: Carl Heymanns Verlag, 1973); Klaus Tiedemann and Christoph Sasse, *Delinquenzprophylaxe, Kreditsicherung und Datenschutz in der Wirstschaft* (Cologne: Carl Heymanns Verlag, 1973); and Klaus Tiedemann, *Kartellrechtsverstösse und Strafrecht* (Cologne: Carl Heymanns Verlag, 1976).

[33]George C. S. Benson and Thomas S. Engeman, *Amoral America* (Stanford, Cal.: Hoover Institution Press, 1975); and Donald R. Cressey, "Restraint of Trade, Recidivism, and Delinquent Neighborhoods," chap. 8 in *Delinquency, Crime, and Society*, ed. James F. Short, Jr. (Chicago: University of Chicago Press, 1976), pp. 209–38.

[34]Edwin H. Sutherland, *White Collar Crime* (New York: Dryden Press, 1949).

criminality. The comptroller of the currency reported that about three-fourths of the national banks examined in a particular quarter were found to be violating the national banking laws. Dishonesty was found in 50.4 percent of the national bank failures during the period 1865–1899, and in 61.4 percent during the period 1900–1919.[35] Some years ago, lie detector tests of the employees of certain Chicago banks showed that 20 percent of them had taken money or property from the bank, and in almost all cases these tests were supported by subsequent confessions.[36] A recent study of bank losses estimated that robbers took about $27 million in 1973, while in the same year about $150 million was stolen by bank employees.[37]

Fraud, also, is frequently a white-collar crime. The statistics on crime in European countries show a general trend toward a decrease in crimes of violence and an increase in crimes involving fraud. It is probable that the trend is even more pronounced in America, but neither the trend nor the present extent of fraud can be determined by available statistics. It is probable, also, that fraud is the most prevalent crime in America. Misleading balance sheets, which public accountants have been able to invent and develop; wash sales, by which the value of a security is fraudulently determined; concessions in rent by real estate dealers for the purpose of fraudulently increasing the sales price of property; excessive and misleading claims made by the manufacturers, vendors, and advertisers of patent medicines, toothpaste, cosmetics, and many other articles; transfer of deteriorated securities from the banker's own possession to the trust funds under her direction; and a considerable part of present-day salesmanship and of advertising—all these examples illustrate this kind of criminality. These things represent either active fraud with the intent to deceive the prospective purchaser or else misrepresentation by silence.

Expert techniques of concealment have developed in many occupations for the purpose of preventing the purchaser from learning the defects of the commodity. Not many farmers would sell hogs with the knowledge that the hogs were infected with cholera and would die within a few days, and those farmers who did this would be regarded as dishonest, even if the misrepresentation consisted merely in silence regarding the danger. On the other hand, not many brokers or bankers would hesitate to sell securities which, by advance information, they had learned would soon be worthless, and the few who did refrain from immediate sale would be regarded as foolish. The physical disease of the hogs is more readily appreciated than the financial disease of the securities, and the effects are likely to be more definitely recognized. Defects in commodities are frequently concealed, and labels often misrepresent. Shirting of inferior quality may be filled with clay in order that the defects may be hidden until the sale is consummated. This is essentially the same principle that was used by the old horsetrader in concealing

[35]These statistics were included in the annual reports of the Comptroller of the Currency and of the Department of the Treasury until 1923, when they were discontinued.

[36]Fred E. Inbau, "Scientific Evidence in Criminal Cases," *Journal of Criminal Law and Criminology*, 24:1140–58, 1934.

[37]Erich Goode, "On Behalf of Labeling Theory," *Social Problems*, 22:570–83, 1975.

the blemishes in his horses. Manufacturers offer merchants a wide variety of "list prices" for the same item, so that the merchants can advertise that they sell at a very small percentage of "list price." These cases of misrepresentation and fraud have not been subject to prosecution in most cases, for the courts have operated on the principle *caveat emptor*, which has meant that purchasers must protect themselves against ordinary dishonesty and could appeal to the courts for protection only against *extraordinary* dishonesty. President Roosevelt in 1933 insisted that the principle be reversed and *caveat vendor* be substituted, especially with regard to securities.

An immense amount of fraud is involved in insurance, both on the part of the insured and the insurers. Murders are committed, houses burned, automobiles destroyed, and sickness or injury feigned in order that insurance may be collected. Fraud in personal injury cases is unusually extensive, and was once an important source of income for unscrupulous lawyers known as "ambulance chasers," who generally worked on contingent fees. Fraud in these cases seldom results in prosecution, although murder and arson may be occasion for prosecution of those crimes as such. The insurance company is seldom free to prosecute for fraud, for it seldom has clean hands. The insurance company adopts the usual policy that "business is business" and that sentiment must be eliminated; it makes a settlement at the lowest possible figure rather than at the figure which the nature of the loss justifies. For this purpose, claim agents, lawyers, and physicians for the insurance company frequently practice misrepresentation. Physicians for the company, for instance, frequently minimize the extent of injuries, in the expectation that the physician on the other side will magnify them. Also, in many cases the claim agent collects an additional sum for settlement and divides this with the attorney for the injured party.

Fraud is also present in the legal profession. Popular feeling inclines to the belief that a lawyer cannot be successful if completely honest and that almost any law firm will take any case within its field of specialization no matter how extreme the dishonesty required for representing the interests of the client. Though absence of official statistics makes it impossible to determine the truth or falsity of this popular opinion, it probably exaggerates the extent of dishonesty in the profession. While fraud is still common, flagrant practices seem to have decreased in the past generation, due to increased "professionalization" of legal occupations. Bar associations have been organized to promote codes of ethics and to prosecute unethical and openly criminal practices. Nevertheless, the "spirit of combat" in legal trials continues to make it necessary for some lawyers to practice fraud and misrepresentation by misstatement and concealment of whole truth if they are to win cases.[38] Such practices generally are not grounds for disbarment proceedings by bar associations but, again, they illustrate our criminalistic traditions.

[38]See Monroe H. Freedman, *Lawyers' Ethics in an Adversary System* (Indianapolis: Bobbs-Merrill, 1975).

Fraudulent reports of property and income for tax purposes are general. The person who reported personal property honestly would generally be regarded as a freak, for the only method by which individuals can avoid paying more than their share of taxes is by accepting the common level of dishonesty. Most citizens would probably prefer to make honest reports, if they were assured that others would do the same. Dishonesty in reporting incomes has become more dangerous, but the general methods of concealing a part of the income or making fraudulent claims for exemptions are extremely widespread.

Many churches and denominational colleges have misapplied funds, under the direction of boards of trustees composed of clergy, lawyers, and businessmen. Gifts for endowments have been used for current expenses; gifts for missions have been used for pastors' salaries; and funds have been misapplied in many other ways.

The extraordinary development of fraud in modern life has been an aspect of the drive for profits, which in itself has been regarded as one of the primary virtues, and which, for that reason, has appeared to remove somewhat the taint from illegal practices. Persons practicing fraud have ordinarily felt no pangs of conscience, for the effects of fraudulent behavior have not become apparent in individual victims known to the defrauders, but have been impersonal and diffuse. If the effects were discernible in particular persons known to the defrauders, and if the practices were not purified by attachment to the virtuous search for profits, many business and commercial practices would be clearly recognized as crimes.

Although bribery is not always white-collar crime, it is another extremely prevalent crime for which arrests are seldom made. Bribery of public officials is a crime both for the bribe-taker and the bribe-giver. Influencing private persons by giving them gifts, money, or services is not crime, but it is closely akin to bribery in effects and attitudes. Both public and private "influence peddling" may be in the form of a direct exchange of money, but it is much more frequently a concealed and indirect method of putting a person under obligation to return a service.

In many cities and states an immense amount of white-collar bribery of public officials occurs in connection with the purchase of supplies, the making of contracts, the enforcement of regulations, and the enactment of legislation. Bribery can be involved when fuel oil is purchased; when school books are selected; when roads or buildings are constructed; when land is bought for public purposes; when franchises are granted to railroads, bus companies, and other public utility companies; and on hundreds of other occasions. Agents of book-publishing companies have testified regarding their methods of bribing school boards, and many public investigations have shown the wide prevalence of bribery of public officials. In some cities, any strictly honest purchase of commodities is an oversight. Much of the wealth of some public officials was secured from these bribes, and it came from the most important of the financial and commercial concerns as well as from agents of the so-called underworld.[39]

Enforcement of regulations regarding insurance, banking, factories, housing, building construction, streets, garbage, public utilities, weights and measures, and most other important functions is often a matter of bargaining between the agents of the state and the agencies subject to the law. The process, once started, grows and involves firms which were previously honest. The honest firm is forced to bribe the inspector in order to protect itself against arbitrary and persecutory enforcement of laws, but the inspector's expectation of securing bribes has grown out of bribes given previously by other concerns. Campaign contributions may protect a firm against demands for petty graft and may be effective in protecting agencies and interests against laws which may decrease profits.

Corruption is extremely prevalent, also, in private business. Buyers for department stores, hotels, factories, railways, and almost all other concerns which make purchases on a large scale accept and sometimes demand gifts or money payments. In doing so, they violate the trust their employer has placed in them, although not necessarily in a criminal way. The cost of the gifts is added to the price of the merchandise being sold, so that the employer and, eventually, the consumer actually is forced to subsidize the employee. Agents of general credit bureaus and of credit bureaus of special trade associations have reported that they are frequently approached by businessmen who offer bribes if information which tends to lower their credit rating is concealed, or if their credit rating is raised. Persons who have had experience in both business and politics claim that the honesty standards among politicians are higher than they are among businessmen.

Aiding and abetting criminals is itself a crime. Although, for obvious reasons, this crime is seldom reported to the police, the number of persons who, in the course of their business, aid and abet criminals is very great. Restaurants and bars are sometimes the sanctuaries of gunmen, though the proprietors may not themselves engage in crimes of violence. Some lawyers are regularly retained to advise professional and organized criminals and to protect them in case of arrest. Such a lawyer is an essential part of any criminal organization. Certainly some part of the perjury by witnesses in trials grows out of the suggestions and instructions of lawyers. Reputable business concerns frequently purchase the proceeds of thefts with a clear realization of the source of the commodities. The manufacturers and distributors of weapons, especially of machine guns, of silencers, and of material for bombs are important assistants of criminals. All large

[39]See John A. Gardiner, *The Politics of Corruption: Organized Crime in an American City* (New York: Russell Sage Foundation, 1970); John A. Gardiner and David J. Olson, eds., *Theft of the City: Readings on Corruption in Urban America* (Bloomington, Ind.: Indiana University Press, 1974); Alexander B. Callow, Jr., ed., *The City Boss in America: An Interpretive Reader* (New York: Oxford University Press, 1976); and Jack D. Douglas and John M. Johnson, eds., *Official Deviance: Readings in Malfeasance, and Other Forms of Corruption* (Philadelphia: Lippincott, 1977).

cities and most smaller ones have persons who make a business of "fixing" cases for professional thieves. Certain police officers, bailiffs, clerks, prosecutors, and judges cooperate with these "fixers," either for direct money payments or under orders from political leaders who control appointments and elections.

The police constantly break the laws. The laws of arrest are rigidly limited, but some police officers exercise their authority with little reference to these limitations and in violation of law. If illegal arrests are regarded as kidnappings, then the number of kidnappings by the police is thousands of times as great as the number of kidnappings by burglars and robbers. The courts, similarly, are not immune from criminal contagion, and this is true especially of the lower courts.

CONCLUSIONS

The statistics on crimes known to the police, like those on arrests, prosecutions, and imprisonments, give a distorted picture of crime in the United States or in the world. In the first place, the true incidence of even ordinary "street crime" such as burglary and larceny seems to be much higher than the incidence reported in *Uniform Crime Reports* and similar compilations. In the second place, the crime and delinquency statistics that are officially assembled seem to exaggerate the difference between the crime rate of poor people and the crime rate of people who are well-off financially. Indeed, the people of the business world are probably more criminalistic than are the people of the slums. The crimes of the slums are direct physical actions—a blow, a physical grasping and carrying away of the property of others. The victim thinks of the criminal as a particular individual, and citizens generally think of criminals as individual predators who prey on individual victims. The crimes of the business world, on the other hand, are indirect, devious, anonymous, and impersonal. A vague resentment against the political and economic system which both permits and fosters such exploitation may be experienced by direct and indirect victims alike, but when particular individuals cannot be thought of as the culprits, the antagonism is not institutionalized.[40] The perpetrators thus do not feel the resentment of their victims, and the criminal practices continue, spread, and go unreported.

Sociologists in recent years have devised methods of data collection which make it unnecessary to rely upon arrest statistics and other compilations in order to study delinquency and crime. Studies using techniques such as participant observation, interviews, questionnaires, surveys of unreported crimes and victimization, and plain logical argument have given a broader perspective on the "crime problem." Sutherland and others showed, further, that statistics on white-collar crimes are not routinely assembled and that, therefore, it is a mistake to view "the crime problem" as though it were a problem dealing with "the criminal classes" in slums.

Nevertheless, the very conception of some behavior as "criminal" or "delin-

---

[40]See Fred T. Allen, "Corporate Morality: Is the Price Too High?" *Wall Street Journal*, October 17, 1975, p. 14.

quent" depends upon conditions outside the behavior itself, making it all but impossible to count accurately, by any technique, the incidence of crime or delinquency. Put another way, whether a specific act is called a crime or something else is often a matter of interpretation and negotiation.[41] At one time, sociologists analyzed what were then considered the statistical "facts" about crime, among other things. Now they are beginning to realize that the facts are not, like sticks and stones, independent of the persons who assemble them.[42] Accordingly, criminologists no longer just study "crime" or "criminal behavior" in an objective sense; it is also necessary to study the process by which the statistical information and other facts are manufactured, assembled, and published. Some observers of this change have called it a shift toward a "sociology of criminal law" because the concern is for the process by which criminal justice personnel and others decide what is to be called crime "really" and "after all." Quinney has more accurately called the change a shift to the study of "the politics of crime."[43] Thus the concept of crime and delinquency statistics must be broadened to include the fact that the "measures" of crime and delinquency involve *labeling* of behavior as criminal or delinquent. As Quinney has noted:

Instead of assuming that criminal statistics indicate only the *incidence of criminal behavior* in a population, we now assume as well that criminal statistics reflect differentials in the *administration of criminal law*. These two conceptions of criminal statistics may not necessarily be regarded as mutually exclusive. A third meaning of the statistics is that they reflect a combination of the first two conceptions, a mixture of the *incidence of criminality* and the *administration of criminal law*.[44]

SUGGESTED READINGS

Akman, Dogan D., & André Normandeau. "Towards the Measurement of Criminality in Canada." *Acta Criminologica* 1:135–254, 1968.

Black, Donald R. "Production of Crime Rates." *American Sociological Review*, 35:737–47, 1970.

Brooks, John. *The Go-Go Years*. New York: Weybright and Talley, 1973.

Bryant, Clifton D., ed. *Deviant Behavior: Occupational and Organizational Bases*. Chicago: Rand McNally, 1974.

---

[41]See Arthur Rosett and Donald R. Cressey, *Justice by Consent: Plea Bargains in the American Courthouse* (Philadelphia: Lippincott, 1976).

[42]See Donald R. Cressey, "The State of Criminal Statistics," *National Probation and Parole Association Journal*, 3:230–241, 1957; John I. Kitsuse, "Societal Reactions to Deviant Behavior: Problems of Theory and Method," *Social Problems*, 9:247–56, 1962; John I. Kitsuse and Aaron V. Cicourel, "A Note on the Uses of Official Statistics," *Social Problems*, 11:131–39, 1963; Donald J. Newman, "The Effect of Accommodations in Justice Administration on Criminal Statistics," *Sociology and Social Research*, 46:144–55, 1962; Stanton Wheeler, "Criminal Statistics: A Reformulation of the Problem," *Journal of Criminal Law, Criminology, and Police Science*, 58: 317–24, 1967; and Albert D. Biderman and Albert J. Reiss, Jr., "On Exploring the 'Dark Figure' of Crime," *Annals of the American Academy of Political and Social Science*, 374:1–15, 1967.

[43]Richard Quinney, "Crime in Political Perspective," *American Behavioral Scientist*, 8:19–22, 1964.

[44]Richard Quinney, *Criminology: Analysis and Critique of Crime in America* (Boston: Little, Brown, 1975), p. 21.

Doleschal, Eugene. *Criminal Statistics.* Washington, D. C.: Government Printing Office, 1972.

Edelhertz, Herbert. *The Nature, Impact, and Prosecution of White-Collar Crime.* Washington, D. C.: Government Printing Office, 1970.

Erickson, Maynard L., & Lamar T. Empey. "Court Records, Undetected Delinquency, and Decision-Making." *Journal of Criminal Law, Criminology, and Police Science,* 54:456–69, 1963.

Gehlke, C. E. "Development of Criminal Statistics in the Past Century." *Proceedings of the American Prison Association,* 1931, pp. 176–90.

Geis, Gilbert, & Robert F. Meir, eds. *White Collar Crime: Offenses in Business, Politics, and the Professions.* New York: Free Press, 1977.

Hindelang, Michael J. *Criminal Victimization in Eight American Cities: A Descriptive Analysis of Common Theft and Assault.* Cambridge, Mass.: Ballinger, 1976.

Kamisar, Yale. "How to Use, Abuse—and Fight Back with—Crime Statistics." *Oklahoma Law Review.* 25:239–58, 1972.

Lejins, Peter P. "Uniform Crime Reports." *Michigan Law Review,* 64:1011–30, 1966.

Price, J. E. "A Test of the Accuracy of the Crime Statistics." *Social Problems,* 14:214–22, 1966.

Quinney, Richard. "The Study of White Collar Crime: Toward a Reorientation in Theory and Research." *Journal of Criminal Law, Criminology, and Police Science,* 55:208–14, 1964.

Robinson, Louis N. "History of Criminal Statistics (1908–1933)." *Journal of Criminal Law and Criminology,* 24:125–39, 1933.

Sellin, Thorsten, & Marvin E. Wolfgang. *The Measurement of Delinquency.* New York: Wiley, 1964.

Skogan, Wesley G., ed. *Sample Surveys of the Victims of Crime.* Cambridge, Mass.: Ballinger, 1976.

Smigel, Erwin O., & H. Laurence Ross, eds. *Crimes Against Bureaucracy.* New York: Van Nostrand, 1970.

Sutherland, Edwin H. *White Collar Crime.* New York: Dryden Press, 1949.

Walker, Nigel. *Crimes, Courts and Figures: An Introduction to Criminal Statistics.* London: Penguin, 1971.

Wheeler, Stanton. "Criminal Statistics: A Reformulation of the Problem." *Journal of Criminal Law, Criminology, and Police Science,* 58:317–24, 1967.

Wolfgang, Marvin E. "Uniform Crime Reports: A Critical Appraisal." *University of Pennsylvania Law Review,* 111:708–38, 1963.

3

Perspectives and Methods

Systematic study of crime rates and criminal behavior is of rather recent origin. During the medieval and early modern periods many unorganized and ephemeral explanations of crimes were stated and accepted. Probably the principal explanation during this time was that crime was due to innate depravity and the instigation of the devil. The English indictment used as late as the nineteenth century not only accused the defendant of violating the law, but also of "being prompted and instigated by the devil and not having the fear of God before his eyes." And the Supreme Court of North Carolina, as late as 1862, declared: "To know the right and still the wrong pursue proceeds from a perverse will brought about by the seductions of the evil one."

During the period when this explanation was used most frequently the conception of natural causation was not developed even with reference to such things as disease, and, of course, was not developed with reference to criminality. The idea that crime is a natural outcome of the way a society is organized, not of something outside the society, was not imaginable. Neither was it possible even to imagine that offenders and others could have the status of persons—little or no interest was manifested in motives, intentions, circumstances, or other immediate conditions of the offender or the offense. Consistently, the notion that crime and criminality can be modified by changing the economic, political, and social conditions that produce them was entirely foreign. The general principle in crime control was that of heaping tortures on the damned in accordance with divine example.

OUTLINE OF SCHOOLS OF CRIMINOLOGY

Schools of criminology have developed during the last two centuries. A "school of criminology" is a system of thought, together with supporters of that system of

54

Table 9 Schools of Criminology

School	Date of Origin	Content of Explanation	Methods
Classical-Neoclassical	1765	Hedonism	Armchair
Cartographic	1830	Ecology, culture, composition of population	Maps, statistics
Socialist	1850	Economic determinism	Statistics
Typological 1. Lombrosian	1875	Morphological type, born criminal	Clinical, statistics
2. Intelligence testers	1905	"Feeblemindedness"	Clinical, statistics tests
3. Psychiatric	1905	Psychopathy	Clinical, statistics
Sociological and social psychological	1915	Groups and social processes	Clinical, statistics, fieldwork

thought. The system of thought consists of a theory of crime causation integrated with policies of change implied in the theory. Obviously, many popular "explanations" of crime are not included in this definition. But every interventionist policy is based, implicitly or explicitly, on a theory or set of assumptions about why people commit crime. The relationship between theories and policies will be elaborated in Part 2.

The principal schools of criminology are listed in Table 9. These schools can be distinguished from each other only in the writings of the more extreme adherents, who were customarily the early writers in each school. Furthermore, the outline below cannot do justice to the many variations in each school of thought or to the interrelations among the schools. The dates of origin are approximate. Each of these schools will be described briefly, and in later chapters the more pertinent research pertaining to each school will be discussed.

The Classical School

The classical school of criminology and of criminal law developed in Italy and England during the last half of the eighteenth century and spread to other European countries and to America. It was based on hedonistic psychology. According to this psychology, man governs his behavior by considerations of pleasures and pains; the pleasures anticipated from a particular act may be balanced against the pains anticipated from the same act, or the algebraic sum of pleasures and pains from one act may be balanced against the algebraic sum of pleasures and pains from another act. The actor was assumed to have a free will and to make his choice with reference to the hedonistic calculation alone. This was regarded as a complete explanation of crime, and no need for research on economic, personal, political, or social conditions associated with crime and criminality could be imagined.

In 1764, Beccaria made the principal application of the hedonistic doctrine to penology.[1] His objective was to make punishment less arbitrary and severe than it had been. He contended that all persons who violated a specific law should receive identical punishment, regardless of age, sanity, position, or circumstance. This policy was justified on the ground that the punishment must be precisely specified in advance so that all persons could take it into account in the calculation of pains and pleasures that would result from violation of the law. According to this school, the penalty should be just severe enough so that the pains would exceed the pleasures derived from violation of the law. But persons were not prohibited from committing crimes. Even today, criminal laws, unlike the Ten Commandments, do not prohibit citizens from engaging in fraud, robbery, murder, and other offenses. Based on the hedonistic doctrine, they simply tell state officials to punish misbehaving citizens in prescribed ways. The basic idea was, and is, that crime rates will be minimal if fear of state agents is maximal. This principle is usually called deterrence, but a more realistic name for it is terror.

The emphasis on uniform punishments for all people committing the same crime was soon modified at two points: first, children and "lunatics" were exempted from punishment on the ground that they were unable to calculate pleasures and pains intelligently; and, second, the penalties were fixed within narrow limits rather than absolutely, so that a small amount of judicial discretion was possible.

The modified classical doctrine is the essence of the neoclassical school of criminology. With these modifications, the classical doctrine became the backbone of the body of the criminal law which has persisted in popular thought and judicial decisions to the present day.[2]

The psychology underlying the work and policies of the classical-neoclassical school, and of much contemporary criminal law, is now generally questioned. It is individualistic, intellectualistic, and voluntaristic. It assumes freedom of the will in a manner which gives little or no possibility of investigating the politics of crime or of developing a sociology or psychology of crime and criminals. All the

---

[1]Cesare Beccaria, *An Essay on Crimes and Punishments* (London: Almon, 1767); see also Marcello T. Maestro, *Voltaire and Beccaria as Reformers of the Criminal Law* (New York: Columbia University Press, 1942). Bentham applied the hedonistic psychology to legislation: Jeremy Bentham, *An Introduction to the Principles of Morals and Legislation* (London: Pickering, 1823).

[2]The doctrines of the classical and neoclassical schools are discussed in more detail in Chapters 13, 14, and 15, and Chapters 16–27 are devoted primarily to analysis of attempts to put these doctrines into practice.

schools which developed in the nineteenth and twentieth centuries accepted the hypothesis of natural causation, and for that reason they are sometimes called positivistic.

The Cartographic School

The cartographic or geographic school used methods similar to those used in more recent years by ecologists and epidemiologists. Its originators were concerned primarily with the distribution of crimes in certain areas, both geographical and social. They saw crime as a necessary expression of social conditions. Quetelet and A. M. Guerry were the leaders of this approach in France, and they had a large number of followers in that country, in England, and Germany. The school flourished from about 1830 to 1880. In addition to analyzing distributions of general crime rates and correlating them with distributions of other social conditions, adherents of the school made special studies of juvenile delinquency and of professional crime which are comparable with those of the present century.[3] The basic notion was, and is, that crime is caused by the conflicts of values arising when legal norms fail to take into consideration the behavioral norms that are specific to the lower socioeconomic classes, various age groups, religious groups, and interest groups living in certain geographic areas. Early proponents of the school also saw crime rooted in "poverty, misery and de-pravity,"[4] but they tended to hold each individual criminal responsible for falling to his or her lowly state. Later proponents merged with the socialist school.

The Socialist School

The socialist school of criminology, based on the ideas of Marx and Engels, began about 1850 and emphasized economic determinism. Marx himself had little to say about crime and criminals. His ideas about the origin and maintenance of social inequality were "applied" to the study of crime by others. The resulting theory of crime causation was so simplistic that it can hardly be called Marxist.

Marx's basic idea was that inequality and poverty result from private ownership of the means of production, a system which exploits the working classes. To the criminologists, this came to mean that inequality and poverty cause people to turn to crime. Although the mechanisms by which poverty might "work" to produce crime were not spelled out, the research studies done by even the early members of this school were scientific. They started by hypothesizing that crime rates are affected by economic conditions such as fluctuations in the business

---

[3]Alfred Lindesmith and Yale Levin, "The Lombrosian Myth in Criminology," *American Journal of Sociology*, 42:653–71, 1937; Yale Levin and Alfred Lindesmith, "English Ecology and Criminology of the Past Century," *Journal of Criminal Law and Criminology*, 27:801–16, 1937.

[4]Henry Mayhew, *London Labour and the London Poor: Cyclopedia of the Conditions and Earnings of Those That Will Not Work* (London: Charles Griffin, 1861), 1:6.

cycle, and then tested the hypothesis with statistical data in a manner which enabled others to repeat the work and test the conclusions.[5]

The earlier studies used statistical methods, measures of crime, and measures of economic conditions that are quite naive by present-day standards. Nevertheless, many empirical studies—most of them done by non-Marxists—show that variations in crime rates are associated with variations in economic conditions. Modern Marxian criminologists are more theoretical than empirical. They tend to reject the idea that criminology can or should be scientific. They explore our consciousness, examine how we understand the world, seek a critical understanding of official reality, and question the state and its legal system. The emphasis is thus on the sociology of criminal law, rather than on the sociology of lawbreaking or of reactions to it.

Typological Schools

Three schools of criminology which have been called "typological" or "biotypological" have developed. They are similar in their general logic and methodology; all are based on a postulate that criminals differ from noncriminals in certain traits of personality, which promote unusual tendencies to commit crimes in situations in which others do not commit crimes. The three typological schools differ from each other as to the specific traits which differentiate criminals from noncriminals.

The Lombrosians Lombroso was the leader of a school which came to be called the "Italian school," or the "positive school." The first statement of his theory was in a pamphlet published in 1876; it grew to a three-volume book in subsequent editions.[6] In its earlier and more clear-cut form this theory consisted of the following propositions: (1) Criminals are, by birth, a distinct type. (2) This type can be recognized by stigmata or anomalies, such as asymmetrical cranium, long lower jaw, flattened nose, scanty beard, and low sensitivity to pain.[7] The criminal type is clearly represented in a person with more than five such stigmata, incompletely represented by three to five, and not necessarily indicated by less than three. (3) These physical anomalies do not in themselves cause crime; rather they identify the personality which is predisposed to criminal behavior, and this personality is either a reversion to the savage type—an atavism—or else a product of degeneration. (4) Because of their personal natures, such persons cannot refrain from crime unless the circumstances of life are unusually favorable. (5) Some of

[5]For a report on some of the early studies using a Marxist approach (Friedrich Engels, 1892; Filippo Turatio, 1883; Bruno Battaglia, 1886; Joseph Van Kan, 1903; Willem Bonger, 1905), see Stephen Schafer, *Introduction to Criminology* (Reston, Va.: Reston Publishing Company, 1976), pp. 75–78.

[6]Cesare Lombroso, *L'uomo delinquente* (Torino, Italy: Bocca, 1896–97). See also Marvin E. Wolfgang, "Pioneers in Criminology: Cesare Lombroso (1835–1909)," *Journal of Criminal Law, Criminology, and Police Science,* 52:361–391, 1961.

[7]The belief that criminals have unique physical characteristics appeared long before Lombroso. See C. Bernaldo de Quiros, *Modern Theories of Criminality,* trans. Alfonso de Salvio (Boston: Little, Brown, 1911), pp. 4–5.

Lombroso's followers concluded that the several classes of criminals, such as thieves, murderers, and sex offenders, are differentiated from each other by physical stigmata.

The Lombrosian school was at first directed against the classical school. It provoked considerable controversy by asserting, like the cartographic and socialist schools before it, that engaging in criminal conduct is determined by conditions beyond the control of the actor and is not therefore to be understood as an exercise in free will. Later it was directed against Tarde's attempt to reconcile moral responsibility with determinism and against his theory of imitation.[8] The controversy then focussed on the question of biological versus social determinism. As a result of these controversies, Lombroso gradually modified his conclusions, especially as to the "born criminal," and reduced the proportion of criminals who were "born criminals" from approximately 100 percent to about 40 percent. Garofalo, Ferri, and other followers of Lombroso made other modifications, so that the school lost its clear-cut characteristics.

The conception that criminals constitute a distinct physical type was disproved to the satisfaction of most scholars when Goring, an English physician, made a comparison of several thousand criminals and several thousand noncriminals and found no significant difference between them.[9] Lombroso and his followers had never made a careful comparison of criminals and noncriminals and had little knowledge of the "savage" whom the criminals were supposed to resemble. The morphological emphasis has continued in modified form in South America. It was in vogue in the United States until about 1915, and it continues, currently, in attempts to locate the cause of some criminality in chromosomal imbalances.[10]

The Intelligence Testers   When the Lombrosian school fell into disrepute, its logic and methodology were retained, but "feeblemindedness" was substituted for physical type as the characteristic which differentiated criminals from noncriminals. This school was represented most clearly by Goddard's theory that "feeblemindedness," inherited as a Mendelian unit, causes crime for the reason that the mentally retarded person is unable to appreciate the consequences of his or her behavior or appreciate the meaning of law.[11] Goddard's tests showed that almost all criminals were "feebleminded," and he asserted, also, that almost all "feebleminded" persons were criminals. As intelligence tests became standardized and were applied to a larger number of criminal and noncriminal persons, the importance attributed to mental retardation in the causation of crime decreased greatly, and this school of thought dissolved.

[8]Gabriel Tarde, *Penal Philosophy* trans. Rapelje Howell and Edward Lindsey (Boston: Little, Brown, 1912). This book was first published in 1890.
[9]Charles Goring, *The English Convict* (London: His Majesty's Stationery Office, 1913).
[10]M. F. Ashley Montagu, "Chromosomes and Crime," *Psychology Today*, 2:42–49, October, 1968; and Donald J. West, ed., *Criminological Implications of Chromosome Abnormalities* (Cambridge: Institute of Criminology, 1969).
[11]H. H. Goddard, *Feeblemindedness* (New York: Macmillan, 1914).

The Psychiatric School   The psychiatric school is a continuation of the Lombrosian school without the latter's emphasis on morphological traits. In the earlier years it emphasized, as did Lombroso, psychoses, epilepsy, and "moral insanity," but it has attributed increasing importance to emotional disturbances and other minor psychopathies as the school of intelligence testers fell into disrepute. Also, in the later history of this school, it has held that these emotional disturbances are acquired in social interaction rather than by biological inheritance. Many variations are found within this school, but the major influence has been the Freudian theory, especially in its earlier form, which placed great emphasis on frustration and "the unconscious." The central thesis is that a certain organization of the personality, developed entirely apart from criminal culture, will result in criminal behavior regardless of social situations. For example, Aichhorn claimed that a delinquent personality is formed in the first few years of a child's life. If a boy is not socialized in a manner such that he learns to control his instincts for pleasure, he will come into conflict with society. His ego will be faulty because he was unable to adjust to the problem of leaving the pleasures of childhood for the reality of adult life.[12] The most extreme writers hold that all or almost all criminals develop by processes similar to this; the less extreme writers attempt to isolate a smaller fraction of the criminals for explanation in this manner. The notion that criminals must as a matter of policy be "treated" rather than punished is part of this school of thought.

The Sociological and Social Psychological School
Of all the schools of criminology, this one is the most varied and diverse. Analysis of crime in a sociological manner actually began with the cartographic and socialist schools. Also, many nineteenth-century European scholars belonging to neither of these schools interpreted crime as a function of social environment. Among these were Von Liszt (Germany), Prins (Belgium), Van Hamel (Holland), and Fointsky (Russia). Tarde, a French social psychologist and a contemporary of Lombroso, refuted the prevailing biological notions and developed a theory emphasizing the importance of "imitation" in crime causation. His basic notion was that one behaves according to the customs of his society; if a man steals or murders, he is merely imitating someone else.

The greatest development of the sociological school has taken place in the United States. Late in the nineteenth century, criminology was accepted as a field of study by the growing university departments of sociology, and in the United States since that time systematic studies of crime and criminals have been made primarily by sociologists. A survey made in 1901 indicated that criminology and penology were among the first courses offered under the general title "sociology"

---

[12]August Aichhorn, *Wayward Youth* (New York: Viking Press, 1936). See the more general discussion in David Feldman, "Psychoanalysis and Crime," chap. in Bernard Rosenberg, Israel Gerver, and F. William Howton, eds., *Mass Society in Crisis* (New York: Macmillan, 1964), pp. 50–58.

in United States colleges and universities,[13] and the *American Journal of Sociology* included articles and book reviews on criminology when it was first published in 1895. However, American sociologists, like most European scholars, were deeply impressed by many of the Lombrosian arguments,[14] and it was not until about 1915, after the publication of Goring's work, that a strong environmentalist position was cultivated. It was probably this trend which prompted a sociologist to write in 1914:

> The longer the study of crime has continued in this country, the greater has grown the number of causes of crime which may be described as social. This is the aspect in the development of American criminology which has given to that study in this country the title of "The American School."[15]

The central thesis of the sociological school is that criminal behavior results from the same processes as other social behavior. Analyses of these processes as they pertain to criminality have taken two principal forms. First, sociologists have attempted to relate variations in crime rates to variations in social organization, including the variations in larger institutional systems. The following are some of the social conditions which have been discussed in relation to variations in the crime rates of societies and subsocieties: the processes of mobility, culture conflict, normative conflict, competition, and stratification; political, religious, and economic ideologies; population density and composition; and the distribution of wealth, income, and employment. This kind of analysis fell into disfavor in the years between about 1940 and 1955, principally because criminologists have become extremely cautious about basing generalizations on the available crime statistics. Because variations in crime rates may represent mere differences in statistical procedures, rather than real variations in the frequency of crime, sociological analysis of the variations is extremely hazardous. Sociologists are now concentrating much time and attention on the processes by which various agencies manufacture sets of crime and delinquency statistics. Nevertheless, the trend in criminology since about 1955 has been toward analysis of the relationships between aspects of the social structure and variations in crime rates, especially variations by social class.

Second, sociologists have attempted to identify the processes by which persons become criminals. These analyses are related to general theories of social learning and have utilized such concepts as imitation, attitude-value, compensation, frustration-aggression, differential association, and reinforcement. The principal

---

[13]Frank L. Tolman, "The Study of Sociology in Institutions of Learning in the United States," *American Journal of Sociology* 7:797–838, 1902; 8:85–121, 1902; 8:251–72, 1902; 8:531–58, 1903.

[14]See, for example, Carroll D. Wright, *Outline of Practical Sociology* (New York: Longmans Green, 1899); Maurice F. Parmelee, *The Principles of Anthropology and Sociology in Their Relations to Criminal Procedure* (New York: Macmillan, 1908); Phillip Parsons, *Responsibility for Crime* (New York: Columbia University Press, 1909).

[15]John L. Gillin, "Social Factors Affecting the Volume of Crime," in *Physical Basis of Crime: A Symposium* (Easton, Pa.: American Academy of Medicine, 1914), pp. 53–67.

orientation at present is generally taken from the social psychological theories of John Dewey, George Mead, Charles Cooley, and W. I. Thomas, and the development of criminal behavior is considered as involving the same learning processes as does the development of the behavior of a banker, teacher, or student. The content of learning, not the process itself, is considered the significant element which determines whether one becomes a criminal or a noncriminal.

EPIDEMIOLOGY AND INDIVIDUAL CONDUCT

The basic controversy in criminology in the United States at present is that between the psychiatric school and the sociological school. Members of the sociological school recognize that psychogenic traits must be taken into account in the explanation of criminal behavior, and members of the psychiatric school have recognized the importance of social and cultural conditions. But there is disagreement over the extent to which "personality" and "culture" should be emphasized in criminological theories, largely because there is no consensus as to the specific manner in which personality and culture interact to produce specific forms of noncriminal behavior.

Some writers in both schools have made classifications of criminals, with the conception that one class is due to personality and another to culture.[16] It is sometimes said that sociologists study crime rates while psychiatrists study individual conduct, and that the two kinds of resulting theory need not be consistent. These practices seem to form a basis for merging the psychiatric and sociological approaches to an explanation of criminal behavior, but they really just avoid the difficult problem of determining the relationship between culture and personality. The problem of how, or whether, basic personality traits and culture combine remains a point of controversy.

Perhaps a new school of criminology will soon develop. Ideally, the theory forming the basis of this school will have three distinct but consistent aspects. First, there will be a statement that explains the statistical distribution of criminal behavior in time and space (epidemiology), from which predictive statements about unknown statistical distributions can be derived. Second, there will be a statement that identifies the process or processes by which persons come to exhibit criminal behavior, from which can be derived predictive statements about the behavior of individuals. Third, there will be demonstration of how both lawmaking and reactions to lawbreaking can be made consistent with the explanations of crime rates and criminality.

Concentration on only one segment of this theoretical problem is sometimes necessary, but it is erroneous and inefficient to ignore the other segments or to

---

[16]A. R. Lindesmith and H. W. Dunham, "Some Principles of Criminal Typology," *Social Forces*, 19:307–14, 1941; Guy Houchon, "Contribution à la Methode Differentielle en Criminologie," *Revue Internationale de Criminologie et de Police Technique*, 18:19–32, 1964; and Richard O. Nahrendorf, "Typologies of Crime and Delinquency: Classification or Methodology?" *Sociologia Internationalis*, 5:15–33, 1967.

turn them over to another academic discipline. This means that as time goes on, the psychiatric school, which now concentrates on individual criminality, will attempt to explain crime rates with a consistent set of theory, that those sociologists who concentrate only on explaining the distribution of crime will develop a consistent set of theory to explain individual criminal conduct, and that the resulting merger of psychiatric and sociological theory will be utilized by lawyers and others who write new criminal codes and devise procedures for their administration. Modern behavioral psychology, which is neither sociological nor psychiatric nor punitive in orientation, probably will be at the base of this "new" criminology.[17]

THE MULTIPLE-FACTOR APPROACH

In contrast with the preceding schools of criminology, which are oriented to integrated theory, many scholars have insisted that crime is a product of a large number and great variety of factors, and that these factors cannot now, and perhaps cannot ever, be integrated theoretically. That is, they insist that no scientific theory of criminal behavior is possible. The multiple-factor approach, which is not a theory, is used primarily in discussions of individual cases of crime, but one form of this approach is also used in analyses of variations in crime rates.

Persons who study individual cases by means of this approach are convinced that one crime is caused by one combination of circumstances or "factors," while another crime is caused by another combination of circumstances or factors. This eclecticism is often considered more rigorously empirical than explanations stated in terms of an integrated theory. William Healy's emphasis upon multiple causation in the cases of individual delinquents, at a time when many persons were seeking arguments for discounting the biological and physical explanations of crime, played an important role in the rise of this assumption.[18] Healy was determined that no theoretical orientation or preconception would influence his findings and that he would simply observe any "causal factor" present. The inevitable consequence of such crass empiricism was the discovery, in a now-famous study, of no less than 170 distinct conditions, every one of which was considered as conducive to delinquency.[19] The following is an example of multiple-factor thinking about individual cases:

Elaborate investigations of delinquents give us conclusive evidence that there is no single predisposing factor leading inevitably to delinquent behavior. On the other hand, the delinquent child is generally a child handicapped not by one or two, but usually by seven or eight counts. We are safe in concluding that almost any child can overcome one or two handicaps, such as the death of one parent or poverty and poor health. However, if the child

[17]See Harvey Wheeler, ed., *Beyond the Punitive Society: Operant Conditioning—Social and Political Aspects* (San Francisco, W. H. Freeman, 1973).

[18]William Healy, *The Individual Delinquent* (Boston: Little, Brown, 1915).

[19]Cyril Burt, *The Young Delinquent*, 4th ed. (London: University of London Press, 1944), p. 600.

has a drunken unemployed father and an immoral mother, is mentally deficient, is taken out of school at an early age and put to work in a factory, and lives in a crowded home in a bad neighborhood, nearly every factor in his environment may seem to militate against him.[20]

Although this statement seems to be based on an assumption that each factor is of equal importance, adherents of the multiple-factor notion ordinarily argue that either the presence of one or two "important" factors or seven or eight "minor" factors will cause delinquency.

When variations in crime rates are the object of consideration, conditions found to be statistically associated with high crime rates are taken as the units of study. Thus, in the United States, males have a higher crime rate than females, blacks than whites, young adults than middle-aged, and city residents than rural residents. The advocates of the multiple-factor approach to the study of crime rates make little or no attempt to discover processes common to males, blacks, young adults, and city residents. However, they do not impute causal power to the factors either; this is in contrast to the persons who use the multiple-factor approach in studying individual cases. Ogburn used this procedure in one of the early comparisons of crime rates of American cities.[21] Reckless pioneered its use, under the name "actuarial approach," in the study of differential reactions to the lawbreaking of various categories of citizens, its most common usage at present:

> The actuarial approach assumes that individuals have a greater or lesser liability to be caught and reported as violators [of the criminal law] by virtue of the position they occupy in society as determined by their age, sex, race, nativity, occupational level, and type of residence. The behavior which is studied is only that which is reported in contrast to that which is not recorded. The liability is strictly that of becoming the sort of violator who is reported.[22]

Some adherents of multiple-factor "theory" take pride in their eclectic position, pointing to the narrow, particularistic explanations of other schools and to their own broadmindedness in including all types of factors.[23] Others agree on the desirability of a generalized and integrated theory and on the possibility of developing such a theory in the long run, but they point to the breakdown of all such explanations and insist that the most economical procedure for the present generation is to accumulate factual knowledge rather than add to the futile attempts at new generalizations. Often the contribution of multiple-factor studies to criminal-law administration, rather than to the development of a body of scientific principles, is emphasized.

[20]Mabel A. Elliott and Francis E. Merrill, *Social Disorganization* (New York: Harper, 1941), p. 111.

[21]William F. Ogburn, "Factors in the Variation of Crimes Among Cities," *Journal of the American Statistical Association*, 30:12–34, 1935.

[22]Walter C. Reckless, *The Etiology of Delinquent and Criminal Behavior* (New York: Social Science Research Council, 1943), p. 74.

[23]See Sheldon Glueck, "Theory and Fact in Criminology," *British Journal of Delinquency*, 7:92–109, 1956.

Albert Cohen has made one of the best critiques of the multiple-factor approach in criminology, and some of the comments above are from his work.[24] There are three major points in the critique, which is directed at the approach as it is used in the study of individual cases. He points out, first, that there has been a confusion of explanations by means of a *single factor* and explanation by a *single theory* or system of theory applicable to all cases. A single theory does not explain crime in terms of a single factor, and it is often concerned with a number of variables. A *variable* is a characteristic or aspect—such as velocity or income— with respect to which something may vary. We make statements of fact in terms of the *values* of these variables, for example, "The crime rate is high among persons with incomes of less than $3000 per year." The pertinent variable here is income, and its value is $3000. But neither a statement of one fact ("single factor") nor a series of such statements ("multiple factors") about crime is a theoretical explanation of crime. A theoretical explanation, a single *theory*, organizes and relates the variables. It is an abstract statement of how the known variations in the values of one variable are related to known variations in the values of other variables. A test of the theory is how well it accounts for all of the variations in the values of the variables.

Cohen's second point is that factors are not only confused with causes, but each factor also is assumed to contain *within itself* a capacity to produce crime, a fixed amount of crime-producing power. Thus, one factor is not always considered powerful enough to produce crime in individual cases—several factors must conspire to do so. As Cyril Burt said, "It takes many coats of pitch to paint a thing thoroughly black." Sometimes the basis for imputing causal power to a factor in an individual case is statistical association between high crime rates and that factor. Thus, if a study of various areas of a city has revealed that high crime rates and "poor housing" are usually found together, an investigator studying a juvenile delinquent who lives in a poor house may assign causal power to the condition of the house. Or if the delinquency rate among "only children" is high, causal power may be assigned to the fact that a particular child is an only child. Statisticians have pointed out that this practice is fallacious, and it is not an intrinsic part of the "actuarial approach."[25] Another consideration is that sometimes the basis for imputing causal power to a factor cannot be determined at all, for it is based upon rather subjective, intuitive judgments of the investigators. Furthermore, each factor is assumed to be independent of all other factors and to operate independently of the actor's definition of the situation. However, the factor "only child," for example, obviously has no intrinsic qualities which produce delinquency or nondelinquency; instead, the *meaning* of being an only child varies with

[24]Albert K. Cohen, "Juvenile Delinquency and the Social Structure" (Ph.D. dissertation, Harvard University, 1951), pp. 5–13. See also his *Delinquent Boys: The Culture of the Gang* (Glencoe, Ill.: Free Press, 1955).

[25]William S. Robinson, "Ecological Correlations and the Behavior of Individuals," *American Sociological Review*, 15:351–57, 1950; Leo A. Goodman, "Some Alternatives to Ecological Correlation," *American Journal of Sociology*, 64:610–25, 1959.

differences in local customs, national and ethnic mores and various other social conditions.

Third, Cohen points out, the "evil-causes-evil fallacy" usually characterizes multiple-factor studies, although it is neither a necessary part of the approach nor peculiar to it. This fallacy is that "evil" results (crime) must have "evil" precedents (broken home, psychopathic personality, and so on). Thus, when we "explain" crime or almost any other social problem, we tend merely to catalog a series of sordid and ugly circumstances which any decent citizen would deplore, and attribute causal power to those circumstances. In criminology, this fallacious procedure might stem from a desire to eradicate crime without changing other existing conditions which we cherish and esteem; that is, criminologists tend to identify with the existing social order and seek causes of crime in factors which might be eliminated without changing social conditions that they hold dear, or that may be safely deplored without hurting anyone's feelings.

METHODS OF STUDYING CRIME

Explanations of crime have been derived from two general types of methodology. The first is the commonsense approach by which people become acquainted with a community, a business, politics, or any social issue. This methodology is used by the historian and by all social scientists. It consists of collecting and arranging data that are believed to be significant. It is not the methodology of science outlined in textbooks on logic. It is impressionistic and deals with general tendencies rather than with specific interpretations. Consequently, the person using it is able to take into account a great variety of conditions which could not be considered if the methodology were more precise. One of the most important of these omissions in contemporary criminology is concern for the immense amount of white-collar fraud. These crimes seem to have permeated modern life and to have social effects which are far more serious than the effects of "street crime." However, these impressions cannot be documented statistically or by any precise methodology.

The second general methodology is systematic study of persons who are arrested or convicted of crimes or of the statistics of such arrests and convictions. This methodology is more precise and "scientific" than the first; it deals with specific variables and, usually, specific types of criminal behavior.[26] The more popular techniques or "methods" included within the scope of this methodology are discussed below. In later chapters, many examples of research studies utilizing the various methods will be given.

Statistics of Crimes

One common criminological method is the determination of the correlation between arrests or convictions and certain specific physical or social variables.

---

[26]See Guy Houchon, "Modèles de Recherche et Equipment en Criminologie," *Annales de la Faculté de Droit de Liège*, 1965, pp. 241–304.

Bonger used this method and presented a mass of materials purporting to show a close correlation between crime rates and economic conditions.[27] Others have used the same method in an effort to determine the statistical significance of seasons, of unemployment, of congestion of population. Thus, the correlations may be between crime rates and certain conditions over a period of time, or they may be between crime rates and certain conditions in space. One of the difficulties of this method has been the lack of reliable crime statistics, and lack of concern for the processes by which statistics are produced. Another difficulty is that, at most, it merely identifies general relationships. It may determine, for instance, that more crimes are committed against the person in hot weather than in cold weather, but it does not tell whether this is due to the direct effect of temperature upon temper, or to a greater frequency of contacts between people in hot weather than in cold weather, or to a greater frequency of intoxication in hot weather, or to some other variable. Consequently this method is of value in collecting data but does not necessarily lead to theoretical statements about the data.

Statistics of Traits and Conditions of Criminals

A second statistical method is comparison of the frequency with which one or more traits or conditions appears among criminals with the frequency with which it occurs among noncriminals. Thus, personality tests have been used to determine the relative frequency of emotional disturbances among criminals and noncriminals. Also, enumerations have been made of the criminals who come from homes broken by death, divorce, and desertion of one or both parents in comparison with the number of law-abiding persons who come from such homes. Similarly, race, sex, age, nativity, alcoholism of self or of parents, education, and other conditions are studied. In the course of such studies many traits and conditions are compared, but in general each one is abstracted from the others. Often, as indicated above, each trait showing a relatively high incidence among criminals is considered one of many "factors" in crime. No pretense is made of studying any criminal as a unit, and no effort is made to determine the conditions producing the criminality of particular persons by this method.

Valuable information preliminary to the formulation of a theory, may be secured in this way. The ideal study of this kind would reveal that certain traits or conditions were present among all criminals, or all criminals of a certain type, and that these traits or conditions were absent among all noncriminals. But there are several difficulties and inadequacies in this method:

1. There is practically no information accessible in regard to criminals, as such. The only information generally available concerns prisoners. Prisoners are a selected group of criminals, and an enumeration of their traits or conditions would, presumably, yield results different from an enumeration of the same traits

---

[27] W. A. Bonger, *Criminality and Economic Conditions* (Boston: Little, Brown, 1916).

or conditions of all criminals. This is a difficulty that confronts any method of studying criminals, but it is more distinctly a limitation of this method than of some of the others because this method depends on mass information. Apparently, the best that can be done at present is to recognize the apparent biases in the statistics and to try to make allowances for them, or to attempt to secure other statistics regarding criminals not adequately represented in prisons.

2. The data regarding arrestees and prisoners are doubtful in many respects. Such evident conditions as race, sex, and age can be determined with a fair degree of accuracy, but it is impossible to secure other data, such as income, home conditions, or employment history, without intensive investigations in the communities in which the prisoners lived prior to arrest. Beyond these rather formal items, reliable information can be secured only with great difficulty. Even when prisoners are cooperative, unreliability enters because of errors of memory, perception, and interpretation.

3. When this method is used, it is necessary to make comparisons with the general population and also with specialized occupational, racial, sex, age, and other groups from which criminals come. It is often necessary to assume, therefore, that the sample of the general population does not include persons who have violated the criminal law without detection or apprehension. This assumption is unwarranted. Standards for the entire population and especially for particular groups are lacking. It has been customary for those who use this method to enumerate their cases and then, without knowing how prevalent the same traits are in the general population, assert that the enumerated traits are important "causes of" or "factors in" crime. For instance, it is frequently reported that a specified part of the criminal population is found, on examination, to be psychopathic, and that this trait is therefore extremely important in the causation of crime. But no one knows how large a percentage of the general population would also be found, by the same standards, to be psychopathic. It was once frequently asserted that "feeblemindedness" was much more common among criminals than among noncriminals, but the general administration of army tests during World War I revealed that the proportion of the population estimated to be "feebleminded" had been far too small.

4. No matter how many traits or conditions are enumerated, this method cannot by itself provide a framework for understanding the mechanisms by which crime and criminality are produced. We may find, for instance, that the male is ten times as criminalistic, judged by commitments to prison, as the female. But males are also ten times as likely to be killed by lightning. Is this a sex difference, or a result of differences in occupations, or the general mode of life, or something else? If we find that there is a close correlation between the criminality of juveniles and the alcoholism of their parents, we want to know whether the child is delinquent because the parent spends money for alcohol that ought to be used to obtain necessities for the child, or because the discipline of the home is irregular or brutal, or because the child becomes emotionally disturbed, or because

alcoholism of parents creates a condition whereby the child comes into contact with an excess of delinquent behavior patterns. As a leading social psychologist stated more than fifty years ago, "Taken in themselves, statistics are nothing more than symptoms of unknown causal processes."[28]

5. Sometimes the traits and conditions which are compared are so loosely defined that their frequency distribution in the two populations can only be asserted, not demonstrated. The incidence of "constitutional inferiority," "bad home environment," and "psychological tensions," for example, cannot be determined with accuracy simply because the concepts are so vague that investigators cannot agree on their presence or absence in individual cases.

6. The statistical enumeration of an excess of certain traits and conditions among delinquents or criminals gives no clues as to why some offenders who do not possess the traits or conditions are criminals, or why some persons who do possess them are not delinquents or criminals. Thus, for example, a good statistical study will tell us how much more frequently delinquency occurs in children from homes broken by divorce, desertion, or death than in children from homes not so broken. But we need to know more than that—why some persons from intact homes are nevertheless delinquent, and why some children from broken homes do not become delinquent.[29] Ideally, we should have information that will enable us to state that persons with such-and-such attitudes or who live under such-and-such social conditions will all become delinquent. Perhaps it will never be possible to construct precise rules of this kind, but it is certain that the statistics of traits of criminals will not be sufficient in themselves.[30] The differential association theory presented in Chapter 4 is an attempt to organize, integrate, and give meaning to statistical information about crimes and criminals, among other things.

Individual Case Study

In the individual case-study method, the criminal, rather than the trait or condition, is regarded as the unit. The traits and conditions of one criminal are all studied together. It is not necessary to abstain from statistics in this method, and it differs from the method just described largely in that the individual, rather than any abstracted trait or condition, is the unit of study. The same traits may be studied by each method. If the importance of the home environment to crime is determined by a comparison of the grades or indices of the homes of delinquents and of nondelinquents, it is not the individual case method. If the importance of the home environment is determined by a consideration of the home in relation to the rest of the life situation of a criminal, it is the individual case method. The differences in the methods are further emphasized by recalling that the purpose of

---

[28]W. I. Thomas, *The Unadjusted Girl* (Boston: Little, Brown, 1923), p. 244.

[29]See the discussion in Chapter 10.

[30]See Marvin E. Wolfgang and Harvey A. Smith, "Mathematical Models in Criminology," *International Social Science Journal*, 18:200–233, 1966.

the comparison of the home indices of criminals and noncriminals is to determine the relative frequency of home conditions of specified kinds among the two groups. The purpose of the individual case study is to determine how and why certain types of homes produce delinquency—how they produce delinquency, rather than how frequently delinquency is found in them.

The study of individual cases can be made on a multiple-factor level, or it can be used to discover meaningful hypotheses to be tested by other methods or by analyses of other cases. The first use of the method, the enumeration of multiple factors, has already been discussed. The assertion that a certain combination of factors caused the delinquency in an individual case often rests on an implicit, "hidden" theory which the person making the study has in mind. It is important, in scientific work, that these implicit theories be made explicit. In his pioneer study of delinquents, Healy listed factors located by means of reviewing the child's family and developmental histories, by examining the child's environment (including home and neighborhood), by taking physical and psychological measurements, and by making medical and psychiatric examinations.[31] The list of specific items under these heads covers nine pages in his book. But Healy emphasized the importance of studying psychological factors such as mental dissatisfaction, irritative mental reactions to environmental conditions, obsessional imagery, adolescent mental instabilities and impulsions, emotional disturbances, worries and repressions, antisocial grudges, mental peculiarities or aberrations, and mental defects.[32] This would indicate that the causal factors considered as significant to the delinquency of each case actually were those which supported a hidden psychiatric hypothesis about delinquency. In later books, Healy explicitly stated this hypothesis and reported on specific efforts to test it by the method of examining the traits of delinquents and nondelinquents.[33] An alternative interpretation is that the earlier case studies were conducted on an exploratory basis, and that the psychiatric theory was suggested by them. While this hypothesis is doubtful in this particular instance, exploratory examination of case histories, including life histories and autobiographies of criminals and delinquents, can provide significant hypotheses about the etiology of criminal behavior.

The individual case-study method is subject to two general criticisms: (1) Explanations of the specific delinquencies are too much subject to the individual whim or prejudice of the investigator. Consequently, there is danger of making much of conditions which are really insignificant and neglecting conditions that are very significant. This means that the investigator sees in the materials of an

---

[31]Healy, *The Individual Delinquent*, pp. 53–63.

[32]Ibid., pp. 28, 32.

[33]William Healy and Augusta F. Bronner, *New Light on Delinquency and Its Treatment* (New Haven: Yale University Press, 1936).

individual case those things which fit into his or her own preexisting scheme for explaining delinquency. even if that scheme is not stated. The check on this explanation is the judgment of other investigators who examine the same case and carefully state their hypotheses. (2) Most of the persons making case studies are employed by agencies dealing with delinquents, and their studies must result in advice regarding procedure. Consequently, there is a probability that the studies will be directly oriented toward temporary modification of delinquency rather than toward understanding delinquency. The items which can be readily modified may be selected as causes, or considerations of practicability in dealing with the offender may determine both the kind of statistics produced and the explanation which is given. There is a tendency to be concerned with any physical or other defect that may need to be corrected, even if it is not considered relevant to the individual's criminality.

Limited Case Study

In an attempt to explain drug addiction, Lindesmith used a method aimed at the production of generalizations rather than a multiple-factor "theory." This system also has been used in a study of embezzlers.[34] The method involves case studies, directed by explicit hypotheses, of rigorously defined categories of behavior. The procedure has essentially the following seven steps: (1) A rough definition of the behavior to be explained is formulated. (2) A hypothetical explanation of the behavior is formulated. (3) One case is studied in the light of the hypothesis with the object of determining whether the hypothesis fits the facts in that case. (4) If the hypothesis does not fit the facts, either the hypothesis is reformulated or the behavior to be explained is redefined so that the case is excluded. This definition must be more precise than the first one, and it may not be formulated *solely* to exclude a negative case. The negative case is viewed as a sign that something is wrong with the hypothesis, and redefinition takes place so that the cases of behavior being explained will be homogeneous. (5) Practical certainty may be attained after a small number of cases has been examined in this way, but the location by the investigator, or anyone else, of a negative case disproves the explanation and requires a reformulation. (6) This procedure of examining cases, redefining the behavior, and reformulating the hypothesis is continued until a universal relationship is established, each negative case calling for a redefinition or a reformulation. The negative case—that is, the one which does not fit the hypothesis—is the important point in the procedure, for it calls for redefinition or reformulation. (7) For purposes of proof, cases outside the area circumscribed by the definition are examined to make certain that the final hypothesis does not

[34]Alfred R. Lindesmith, *Opiate Addiction* (Bloomington, Ind.: Principia Press, 1947), and *Addiction and Opiates* (Chicago: Aldine, 1968); Donald R. Cressey, *Other People's Money: A Study in the Social Psychology of Embezzlement* (Glencoe, Ill.: Free Press, 1953). See also Howard S. Becker, *Outsiders: Studies in the Sociology of Deviance* (New York: Free Press, 1963).

apply to them. This step is in keeping with the observation that scientific generalizations consist of descriptions of conditions which are always present when the phenomenon being explained is present but which are never present when the phenomenon is absent.

This method is not statistical in the ordinary sense, nor is it the case-study method in the ordinary sense. It combines the individual case-study method and the method of statistical examination of traits of criminals, for it examines individual cases of criminality in the light of a hypothesis and then, for purposes of proof, attempts to determine whether or not that hypothesis also pertains to cases of noncriminality. At the same time, however, it differs from either of these methods: it does not attempt to secure a general picture of the person, but only such facts as bear upon the hypothesis, and it attempts to go beyond statistical tendencies to a theoretical explanation. The method has been criticized on the ground that it merely produces precise definitions of various types of behavior, rather than explanations of that behavior.[35]

Study of the Criminal "In the Open"

Another method of studying crime is by association with criminals "in the open." Those who have had intimate contacts with criminals know that criminals are not "natural" in police stations, courts, and prisons, and that they must be studied in their everyday life outside of institutions if they are to be understood. By this is meant that the investigator must associate with them as one of them, seeing their lives and conditions as the criminals themselves see them. In this way, observations can be made on attitudes, traits, and processes which can hardly be made in any other way. Also, observations are of unapprehended criminals, not the criminals selected by the process of arrest and imprisonment.

An excellent study of persons receiving stolen goods was recently made by this method.[36] Unlike its author, however, few individuals have the ability to secure the trust of criminals. After all, criminals have little to gain and much to lose by allowing observers to hang around with them. Further, one observer cannot build upon the work of another to a very great extent, for precise, controlled techniques of observation can scarcely be employed. Moreover, it cannot be assumed that criminals know much about crime and criminal behavior, even if they volunteer information regarding the processes by which they became criminals. Nevertheless, study of criminals in natural settings can generate useful and fruitful hypotheses, especially if the study is guided by the principles of the limited case method.[37]

---

[35]Ralph H. Turner, "The Quest for Universals in Sociological Research," *American Sociological Review,* 18:604–11, 1953.
[36]Carl B. Klockars, *The Professional Fence* (New York: Free Press, 1974).
[37]Cf. Ned Polsky, *Hustlers, Beats, and Others* (Chicago: Aldine, 1967).

Experimental Method

It is possible to test hypotheses regarding causes of delinquency or crime by changing the behavior of groups or individuals, under controlled conditions. This is somewhat like the experimental method of the physical and biological sciences, although the control is much less complete in social situations. In criminology, experiments in social reform attempt to change the crime rate by altering the conditions believed to create and maintain it, or to change the behavior of individual criminals by changing them or the conditions in which they live. If, for example, it is believed that certain aspects of social structure produce high crime rates, then it is likely to be predicted that if those structural conditions are changed experimentally, the crime rate will go down. The Chicago Area Projects were undertaken primarily to test the hypothesis that community disorganization causes high crime rates, and the Mobilization for Youth Project in New York was an experiment designed to test whether increasing the economic opportunities available to young people would result in less delinquency.[38] Similarly, hypotheses regarding the processes by which persons become criminals can be tested by trying to change criminals by methods based on the hypotheses. The Cambridge-Somerville Youth Study was an experiment of this kind,[39] as are most attempts to change criminals by clinical methods.

However, the results of such experiments must be interpreted with extreme caution. Evidence that a crime rate goes down or that a person's behavior changes in the expected direction when a program of change based on a theory is instituted cannot by itself be taken as evidence that the theory correctly describes the social conditions which made the crime rate high or the process by which the behavior was originally acquired. The change might have been produced by things rather extraneous to the program of change, or the program might have been based on several theories, rather than on a single theory. The careful observation and elimination of such extraneous elements is the essence of a *controlled* experiment.

CONCLUSION

All the methods which have been described have a proper place in the attempt to understand crime and criminal behavior. Much futile argument has been devoted to controversies between methods and especially to the controversy between the statistical and the nonstatistical methods. The value of any method is determined by its relation to the problem which is stated, and the statement of a problem is justified by the position of that problem in the total body of knowledge. At a particular stage in the development of knowledge some problems are more important than others, and consequently some methods are more useful than others.

---

[38]See the discussion in Chapter 16.
[39]See the discussion in Chapter 26.

The "exploratory method" is needed continuously. This is a congeries of methods, including statistical descriptions and comparisons in the form of averages, percentages, and correlations; field observations, and armchair speculations. This exploratory method is justified in new areas of study because it may pave the way for later definitive studies based on general theory. Both in the total field of criminology and in smaller areas within this field, the exploratory method is the only method available for developing hypotheses and theories. Several generalizations have been made by different schools of thought regarding crime and criminal behavior as a whole. None of these generalizations is completely satisfactory, and revision of them calls for new hypotheses to be tested. Similarly, if a particular area of criminal behavior, such as kleptomania or automobile theft, is selected for study, the researcher must become acquainted with the available statistical data and use other exploratory methods before he or she is prepared to formulate definite hypotheses regarding it.

The principal argument presented in this chapter is that the multiple-factor approach, defined as mere enumeration of a series of conditions related in some manner or other to criminal behavior, is not adequate. The pride which some criminologists take in this multiple-factor approach is entirely misplaced. This "theory" should be recognized as an admission of defeat, for it means that criminological studies must always be exploratory. The criminologist can carry conclusions beyond multiple factors and reduce the series of factors to simplicity by the method of logical abstraction.

For purposes of understanding crime and criminal behavior, definitive generalizations are needed regarding crime rates and criminal behavior generally, with specifications of the general theory applied to particular criminal behaviors. The relation between the general theory and the particular crimes and criminal behaviors is analogous to the relation between a germ theory of disease and the particular germs which cause particular diseases.

Work along both of these lines is desirable. Continued efforts should be made to state valid generalizations regarding criminal behavior as a whole, and continued efforts should be made to explain particular criminal behaviors. Research work of the former type should guide the efforts of those who are attempting to explain particular criminal behaviors, and conclusions from the studies of particular areas of criminal behaviors should lead to revisions of the generalizations regarding criminal behavior as a whole. Just as the germ theory of disease does not explain all diseases, so it is possible that no one theory of criminal behavior will explain all criminal behavior. In that case, it will be desirable to define the areas to which any theory applies, so that the several theories are coordinate and, when taken together, explain all criminal behavior.[40]

[40]Cf. Marshall B. Clinard and Andrew L. Wade, "Toward the Delineation of Vandalism as a Sub-Type in Juvenile Delinquency," *Journal of Criminal Law, Criminology, and Police Science*, 48:493–99, 1958; Don C. Gibbons and Donald L. Garrity, "Some Suggestions for the Development of Etiological and Treatment Theory in

SUGGESTED READINGS

Burgess, E. W. "The Study of the Delinquent as a Person." *American Journal of Sociology*, 28:657–80, 1923.

Cantor, Nathaniel. "The Search for Causes of Crime." *Journal of Criminal Law and Criminology*, 22:854–63, 1932.

Cicourel, Aaron V. *Method and Measurement in Sociology.* New York: Free Press, 1965.

Chiricos, Theodore G., & Gordon P. Waldo, "Socioeconomic Status and Criminal Sentencing: An Empirical Assessment of a Conflict Proposition." *American Sociological Review*, 40:753–72, 1975.

Clinard, Marshall B. "Contributions of Sociology to Understanding Deviant Behaviour." *British Journal of Delinquency*, 13:110–29, 1962.

Cressey, Donald R. *Other People's Money: A Study in the Social Psychology of Embezzlement.* Glencoe, Ill.: Free Press, 1953.

Davis, John A. "Justification for No Obligation: Views of Black Males Toward Crime and the Criminal Law." *Issues in Criminology*, 9:69–87, 1974.

Doleschal, Eugene. *Crime and Delinquency Research in Selected European Countries.* Washington, D.C.: Government Printing Office, 1971.

Gibbons, Don C. "Observations on the Study of Crime Causation." *American Journal of Sociology*, 77:262–78, 1971.

Hartung, Frank E. "A Critique of the Sociological Approach to Crime and Correction," *Law and Contemporary Problems*, 23:703–34, 1958.

Hirschi, Travis, & Hanan C. Selvin. *Delinquency Research: An Appraisal of Analytic Methods.* New York: Free Press, 1967.

Kitsuse, John I. & Malcolm Spector, "Social Problems and Deviance: Some Parallel Issues." *Social Problems*, 22:584–594, 1975.

Klockars, Carl B. *The Professional Fence.* New York: Free Press, 1974.

Lindesmith, Alfred R. *Addiction and Opiates.* Chicago: Aldine, 1968.

Mannheim, Hermann, ed. *Pioneers in Criminology.* Chicago: Quadrangle Books, 1960.

Martin, John M., Joseph P. Fitzpatrick, & Robert E. Gould. *The Analysis of Delinquent Behavior: A Structural Approach.* New York: Random House, 1970.

Meier, Robert F. "The New Criminology: Continuity in Criminological Theory." *Journal of Criminal Law and Criminology*, 67:461–69, 1977.

Miller, Walter B. "Ideology and Criminal Justice Policy: Some Current Issues." *Journal of Criminal Law and Criminology*, 64:141–62, 1973.

Newman, Graeme R. "Clinical and Legal Perceptions of Deviance." *Australian and New Zealand Journal of Criminology*, 9:37–47, 1976.

Quinney, Richard. *The Social Reality of Crime.* Boston: Little, Brown, 1970.

Radzinowicz, Leon. *Ideology and Crime.* London: Heinemann, 1966.

Reckless, Walter C. "American Criminology." *Criminology: An Interdisciplinary Journal*, 8:4–20, 1970.

Criminology," *Social Forces*, 38:51–58, 1959; Nahrendorf, "Typologies of Crime and Delinquency,"; Theodore N. Ferdinand, *Typologies of Delinquency* (New York: Random House, 1966); Edwin D. Driver, "A Critique of Typologies in Criminology," *Sociological Quarterly*, Summer, 1968, pp. 356–73; Marshall B. Clinard and Richard Quinney, *Criminal Behavior Systems: A Typology*, 2nd ed. (New York: Holt, Rinehart and Winston, 1973); and Don C. Gibbons, "Offender Typologies—Two Decades Later," *British Journal of Criminology*, 15:97–108, 1975.

Reiss, Albert J., Jr. "Putting Sociology into Policy." *Social Problems*, 17:289–94, 1970.

Slawski, Carl J. "Crime Causation: Toward a Field Synthesis." *Criminology: An Interdisciplinary Journal*, 3:375–96, 1971.

Sykes, Gresham M. "The Rise of Critical Criminology." *Journal of Criminal Law and Criminology*, 65:206–13, 1974.

Taylor, Ian, Paul Walton, & Jock Young. *The New Criminology: For A Social Theory of Deviance.* London: Routledge & Kegan Paul, 1973.

Taylor, Ian, Paul Walton, & Jock Young, eds. *Critical Criminology.* London: Routledge & Kegan Paul, 1975.

Wheeler, Stanton. "The Social Sources of Criminology." *Sociological Inquiry*, 32:139–59, 1962.

Wilkins, Leslie T. *Social Deviance: Social Policy, Action, and Research.* Englewood Cliffs, N. J.: Prentice-Hall, 1965.

Wilson, Thomas P. "Conceptions of Interaction and Forms of Sociological Explanation." *American Sociological Review*, 35:697–710, 1970.

Wolfgang, Marvin E. "Criminology and the Criminologist." *Journal of Criminal Law, Criminology, and Police Science*, 54:155–62, 1963.

4

A Sociological Theory
of Criminal Behavior

The preceding discussion has suggested that a scientific explanation consists of a description of the conditions which are always present when a phenomenon occurs and which are never present when the phenomenon does not occur. Although a multitude of conditions may be associated in greater or lesser degree with the phenomenon in question, this information is relatively useless for understanding or for control if the data are left as a hodgepodge of unorganized factors. Scientists strive to organize their knowledge in interrelated general propositions, to which no exceptions can be found.

THE PROBLEM FOR CRIMINOLOGICAL THEORY

If criminology is to be scientific, the heterogeneous collection of multiple factors known to be associated with crime and criminality must be organized and integrated by means of explanatory theory which has the same characteristics as the scientific theory in other fields of study. That is, the conditions which are said to cause crime should be present when crime is present, and they should be absent when crime is absent. Such a theory or body of theory would stimulate, simplify, and give direction to criminological research, and it would provide a framework for understanding the significance of much of the knowledge acquired about crime and criminality in the past. Furthermore, it would be useful in minimizing crime rates, provided it could be "applied" in much the same way that the engineer "applies" the scientific theories of the physicist.

There are two complementary procedures which may be used to put order into criminological knowledge. The first is logical abstraction. Blacks, males, urban-dwellers, and young adults all have comparatively high crime rates. What do they have in common that results in these high crime rates? Research studies have shown that criminal behavior is associated, in greater or lesser degree, with such social and personal pathologies as poverty, bad housing, slum-residence, lack of recreational facilities, inadequate and demoralized families, mental retardation, emotional instability, and other traits and conditions. What do these conditions have in common which apparently produces excessive criminality? Research studies have also demonstrated that many persons with those pathological traits and conditions do not commit crimes and that persons in the upper socio-economic class frequently violate the law, although they are not in poverty, do not lack recreational facilities, and are not mentally retarded or emotionally unstable. Obviously, it is not the conditions or traits themselves which cause crime, for the conditions are sometimes present when criminality does not occur, and they also are sometimes absent when criminality does occur. A generalization about crime and criminal behavior can be reached by logically abstracting the conditions and processes which are common to the rich and the poor, the males and the females, the blacks and the whites, the urban- and the rural-dwellers, the young adults and the old adults, and the emotionally stable and the emotionally unstable who commit crimes.

In developing such generalizations, criminal behavior must be precisely defined and carefully distinguished from noncriminal behavior. Criminal behavior is human behavior, and has much in common with noncriminal behavior. An explanation of criminal behavior should be consistent with a general theory of other human behavior, but the conditions and processes said to produce crime and criminality should be specific. Many things which are necessary for behavior are not important to criminality. Respiration, for instance, is necessary for any behavior, but the respiratory process cannot be used in an explanation of criminal behavior, for it does not differentiate criminal behavior from noncriminal behavior.

The second procedure for putting order into criminological knowledge is differentiation of levels of analysis. The explanation or generalization must be limited, largely in terms of chronology, and in this way held at a particular level. For example, when Renaissance physicists stated the law of falling bodies, they were not concerned with the reasons why a body began to fall except as this might affect the initial momentum. Galileo did not study the 'traits" of falling objects themselves, as Aristotle might have done. Instead, he noted the relationship of the body to its environment while it was falling freely or rolling down an inclined plane, and it made no difference to his generalization whether a body began to fall because it was dropped from the hand of an experimenter or because it rolled off the ledge of a bridge due to vibration caused by a passing vehicle. Also, a round object would roll off the bridge more readily than a square object, but this fact was not significant for the law of falling bodies. Such facts were considered as existing on a different level of explanation and were irrelevant to the problem of explaining the behavior of falling bodies.

Much of the confusion regarding crime and criminal behavior stems from a failure to define and hold constant the level at which they are explained. By analogy, many criminologists and others concerned with understanding and defining crime would attribute some degree of causal power to the "roundness" of the object in the above illustration. However, consideration of time sequences among the conditions associated with crime and criminality may lead to simplicity of statement. In the heterogeneous collection of factors associated with crime and criminal behavior, one factor often occurs prior to another (in much the way that "roundness" occurs prior to "vibration," and "vibration" occurs prior to "rolling off a bridge"), but a theoretical statement can be made without referring to those early factors. By holding the analysis at one level, the early factors are combined with or differentiated from later factors or conditions, thus reducing the number of variables which must be considered in a theory.

A motion picture made several years ago showed two boys engaged in a minor theft; they ran when they were discovered; one boy had longer legs, escaped, and became a priest; the other had shorter legs, was caught, committed to a reformatory, and became a gangster. In this comparison, the boy who became a criminal was differentiated from the one who did not become a criminal by the length of his legs. But "length of legs" need not be considered in a criminological theory because it is obvious that this condition does not determine criminality and has no necessary relation to criminality. In the illustration, the differential in the length of the boys' legs apparently was significant to subsequent criminality or noncriminality only to the degree that it determined the subsequent experiences and associations of the two boys. It is in these experiences and associations, then, that the mechanisms and processes which are important to criminality or noncriminality are to be found.

TWO TYPES OF EXPLANATIONS OF CRIMINAL BEHAVIOR

Scientific explanations of criminal behavior may be stated either in terms of the processes which are operating at the moment of the occurrence of crime or in terms of the processes operating in the earlier history of the criminal. In the first case, the explanation may be called "mechanistic," "situational," or "dynamic"; in the second, "historical" or "developmental." Both types of explanation are desirable. The mechanistic type of explanation has been favored by physical and biological scientists, and it probably could be the more efficient type of explanation of criminal behavior. As Gibbons said:

In many cases, criminality may be a response to nothing more temporal than the provocations and attractions bound up in the immediate circumstances. It may be that, in some kinds of lawbreaking, understanding of the behavior may require detailed attention to the concatination of events immediately preceding it. Little or nothing may be added to this understanding from a close scrutiny of the early development of the person.[1]

However, criminological explanations of the mechanistic type have thus far been notably unsuccessful, perhaps largely because they have been formulated in

[1]Don C. Gibbons, "Observations on the Study of Crime Causation," *American Journal of Sociology,* 77:262–78, 1971.

connection with an attempt to isolate personal and social pathologies among criminals. Work from this point of view has, at least, resulted in the conclusion that the immediate determinants of criminal behavior lie in the person-situation complex.

The objective situation is important to criminality largely to the extent that it provides an opportunity for a criminal act. A thief may steal from a fruit stand when the owner is not in sight but refrain when the owner is in sight; a bank burglar may attack a bank which is poorly protected but refrain from attacking a well-protected bank. A corporation which manufactures automobiles seldom violates the pure food and drug laws, but a meat-packing corporation might violate these laws with great frequency. But in another sense, a psychological or sociological sense, the situation is not exclusive of the person, for the situation which is important is the situation as defined by the person who is involved. That is, some persons define a situation in which a fruit-stand owner is out of sight as a "crime-committing" situation, while others do not so define it. Furthermore, the events in the person-situation complex at the time a crime occurs cannot be separated from the prior life experiences of the criminal. This means that the situation is defined by the person in terms of the inclinations and abilities which he or she has acquired. For example, while a person could define a situation in such a manner that criminal behavior would be the inevitable result, past experiences would, for the most part, determine the way in which he or she defined the situation. An explanation of criminal behavior made in terms of these past experiences is a historical or developmental explanation.

The following paragraphs state such a developmental theory of criminal behavior on the assumption that a criminal act occurs when a situation appropriate for it, as defined by the person, is present. The theory should be regarded as tentative, and it should be tested by the factual information presented in the later chapters and by all other factual information and theories which are applicable.

DEVELOPMENTAL EXPLANATION OF CRIMINAL BEHAVIOR

The following statements refer to the process by which a particular person comes to engage in criminal behavior:

1. *Criminal behavior is learned.* Negatively, this means that criminal behavior is not inherited, as such; also, the person who is not already trained in crime does not invent criminal behavior, just as a person does not make mechanical inventions unless he has had training in mechanics.

2. *Criminal behavior is learned in interaction with other persons in a process of communication.* This communication is verbal in many respects but includes also "the communication of gestures."

3. *The principal part of the learning of criminal behavior occurs within intimate personal groups.* Negatively, this means that the impersonal agencies of

communication, such as movies and newspapers, play a relatively unimportant part in the genesis of criminal behavior.

4. *When criminal behavior is learned, the learning includes (a) techniques of committing the crime, which are sometimes very complicated, sometimes very simple; (b) the specific direction of motives, drives, rationalizations, and attitudes.*

5. *The specific direction of motives and drives is learned from definitions of the legal codes as favorable or unfavorable.* In some societies an individual is surrounded by persons who invariably define the legal codes as rules to be observed, while in others he is surrounded by persons whose definitions are favorable to the violation of the legal codes. In our American society these definitions are almost always mixed, with the consequence that we have culture conflict in relation to the legal codes.

6. *A person becomes delinquent because of an excess of definitions favorable to violation of law over definitions unfavorable to violation of law.* This is the principle of differential association. It refers to both criminal and anticriminal associations and has to do with counteracting forces. When persons become criminal, they do so because of contacts with criminal patterns and also because of isolation from anticriminal patterns. Any person inevitably assimilates the surrounding culture unless other patterns are in conflict; a southerner does not pronounce r because other southerners do not pronounce r. Negatively, this proposition of differential association means that associations which are neutral so far as crime is concerned have little or no effect on the genesis of criminal behavior. Much of the experience of a person is neutral in this sense, for instance, learning to brush one's teeth. This behavior has no negative or positive effect on criminal behavior except as it may be related to associations which are concerned with the legal codes. This neutral behavior is important especially as an occupier of the time of a child so that he or she is not in contact with criminal behavior during the time the child is so engaged in the neutral behavior.

7. *Differential associations may vary in frequency, duration, priority, and intensity.* This means that associations with criminal behavior and also associations with anticriminal behavior vary in those respects. Frequency and duration as modalities of associations are obvious and need no explanation. Priority is assumed to be important in the sense that lawful behavior developed in early childhood may persist throughout life, and also that delinquent behavior developed in early childhood may persist throughout life. This tendency, however, has not been adequately demonstrated, and priority seems to be important principally through its selective influence. Intensity is not precisely defined, but it has to do with such things as the prestige of the source of a criminal or anticriminal pattern and with emotional reactions related to the associations. In a precise description of the criminal behavior of a person, these modalities would be rated in quantitative form and a mathematical ratio would be reached. A formula

in this sense has not been developed, and the development of such a formula would be extremely difficult.

8. *The process of learning criminal behavior by association with criminal and anticriminal patterns involves all of the mechanisms that are involved in any other learning.* Negatively, this means that the learning of criminal behavior is not restricted to the process of imitation. A person who is seduced, for instance, learns criminal behavior by association, but this process would not ordinarily be described as imitation.

9. *While criminal behavior is an expression of general needs and values, it is not explained by those general needs and values, since noncriminal behavior is an expression of the same needs and values.* Thieves generally steal in order to secure money, but likewise honest laborers work in order to secure money. The attempts by many scholars to explain criminal behavior by general drives and values, such as the happiness principle, striving for social status, the money motive, or frustration, have been, and must continue to be, futile, since they explain lawful behavior as completely as they explain criminal behavior. They are similar to respiration, which is necessary for any behavior, but which does not differentiate criminal from noncriminal behavior.

It is not necessary, at this level of explanation, to explain why persons have the associations they have; this certainly involves a complex of many things. In an area where the delinquency rate is high, a boy who is sociable, gregarious, active, and athletic is very likely to come in contact with the other boys in the neighborhood, learn delinquent behavior patterns from them, and become a criminal; in the same neighborhood the psychopathic boy who is isolated, introverted, and inert may remain at home, not become acquainted with the other boys in the neighborhood, and not become delinquent. In another situation, the sociable, athletic, aggressive boy may become a member of a scout troop and not become involved in delinquent behavior. The person's associations are determined in a general context of social organization. A child is ordinarily reared in a family; the place of residence of the family is determined largely by family income; and the delinquency rate is in many respects related to the rental value of the houses. Many other aspects of social organization affect the associations of a person.

The preceding explanation of criminal behavior purports to explain the criminal and noncriminal behavior of individual persons. As indicated earlier, it is possible to state sociological theories of criminal behavior which explain the criminality of a community, nation, or other group. The problem, when thus stated, is to account for variations in crime rates, which involves a comparison of the crime rates of various groups or the crime rates of a particular group at different times. The explanation of a crime rate must be consistent with the explanation of the criminal behavior of the person, since the crime rate is a summary statement of the number of persons in the group who commit crimes and the frequency with which they commit crimes. One of the best explanations of crime rates from this point of view is that a high crime rate is due to social disorganization. The term *social disorganization* is not entirely satisfactory, and it seems preferable to substitute for it the term *differential social organization*. The postulate on which this theory is based, regardless of the name, is that crime is rooted in the social organization and is an expression of that social organization. A group may be organized for criminal behavior or organized against criminal behavior. Most communities are organized for both criminal and anticriminal behavior, and, in that sense the crime rate is an expression of the differential group organization. Differential group organization as an explanation of variations in crime rates is consistent with the differential association theory of the processes by which persons become criminals.

DIFFERENTIAL ASSOCIATION AND INDIVIDUAL CRIMINALITY

Professor Sutherland introduced the theory of differential association in the 1939 edition of *Criminology*. He modified the theory in the 1947 edition, but this version was not changed in subsequent editions. Neither has it been changed in the current edition. The theory is still being tested, analyzed, criticized, and extended. It would be inappropriate to modify the statement in such a way that the research work of a number of persons would be undermined. Accordingly we shall merely elaborate on the basic statement by describing some of the principal interpretive errors apparently made by readers and some of the principal criticisms advanced by criminologists and others.[2]

Some Literary Errors

The basic statement of the theory of differential association is not clear. In two pages, nine propositions are presented, with little elaboration, purporting to explain both the epidemiology of crime and delinquency and the presence of criminality or delinquency in individual cases. It therefore is not surprising that Sutherland's words do not always convey the meaning he seemed to intend. Most significantly, as we shall see later, the statement gives the impression that there is little concern for explaining variations in crime and delinquency rates. This is a serious error in communication. In reference to the delinquent and criminal behavior of individuals, however, the difficulty in communication seems to arise as much from failure to study the words presented as from the words themselves. Five principal errors, and a number of minor ones, have arisen because readers do not always understand what Sutherland seemed to be trying to say.

First, it is common to believe, or perhaps to assume momentarily, if only for purposes of research and discussion, that the theory is concerned only with contacts or associations with criminal and delinquent behavior patterns. Vold, for

---

[2]The remainder of this chapter is a modification of Donald R. Cressey, "Epidemiology and Individual Conduct: A Case from Criminology," *Pacific Sociological Review*, 3:47–58, 1960. Students interested in documentation of the points made here should refer to this article, which is reprinted in Donald R. Cressey and David A. Ward, eds., *Crime, Delinquency, and Social Process* (New York: Harper and Row, 1969), pp. 557–77.

example, says, "One of the persistent problems that always has bedeviled the theory of differential association is the obvious fact that not everyone in contact with criminality adopts or follows the criminal pattern.'[3] At first glance, at least, such statements seem to overlook or ignore the words "differential" and "excess" in the theory, which states that a person becomes delinquent because of an *excess* of definitions favorable to violation of law over definitions unfavorable to violation of law. "This is the principle of differential association. It refers to both criminal and anticriminal associations and has to do with counteracting forces." DeFleur and Quinney rearranged and analyzed the nine assertions of the differential association theory in the logical language of set theory.[4] This work both discovered and demonstrated that "the principle" or "the theory" is in all nine assertions, not in the sixth assertion (about the excess of definitions) alone. But it also showed clearly that the sixth assertion does not say that persons become criminals because of associations with criminal behavior patterns; it says that they become criminals because of exposure to an *overabundance* of such associations, in comparison with associations with anticriminal behavior patterns. After restating the theory of differential association in the language of set theory, DeFleur and Quinney translated their finished product back into English as follows:

Overt criminal behavior has as its necessary and sufficient conditions a set of criminal motivations, attitudes, and techniques, the learning of which takes place when there is exposure to criminal norms in excess of exposure to corresponding anticriminal norms during symbolic interaction in primary groups.[5]

Clearly, then, it is erroneous to state or imply that the theory is invalid because a category of persons—such as police officers, prison workers, or criminologists—have had extensive association with criminal behavior patterns but yet are not criminals.

Second, it is commonly believed that the theory says persons become criminals because of an excess of associations with criminals. Because of the manner in which the theory is stated, and because of the popularity of the "bad companions" theory of criminality in our society, this error is easy to make. The theory of differential association is concerned with ratios of associations with *patterns of behavior*, no matter what the character of the person presenting them. Phrases such as "definitions of legal codes as favorable or unfavorable," "definitions favorable to violation of law over definitions unfavorable to violation of law," and "association with criminal and anticriminal patterns" are used throughout the formal statement. Thus, if a mother teaches her son that "Honesty is the best policy," but also teaches him, perhaps inadvertently, that "It is all right to steal a

[3]George B. Vold, *Theoretical Criminology* (New York: Oxford University Press, 1958), p. 194.
[4]Melvin L. DeFleur and Richard Quinney, "A Reformulation of Sutherland's Differential Association Theory and a Strategy for Empirical Verification," *Journal of Research in Crime and Delinquency*, 3:1–22, 1966.
[5]Ibid., p. 7.

loaf of bread when you are starving," she is presenting him with an anticriminal behavior pattern and a criminal behavior pattern, even if she herself is honest, noncriminal, and even anticriminal. One can learn criminal behavior patterns from persons who are not criminals, and one can learn anticriminal behavior patterns from hoods, professional crooks, habitual offenders, and gangsters.

Third, in periods of time ranging from five to twelve years after the first publication of the above statement (1947), at least five authors have erroneously believed that the theory consists of the version published in 1939.[6] This error is not important to the substance of the current statement of the theory, but discussing it does tell something about the nature of the theory. The 1939 statement was qualified so that it pertained only to "systematic" criminal behavior rather than to the more general category "criminal behavior."[7] The word "systematic" was then deleted, and Sutherland explained that it was his belief that all but "the very trivial criminal acts" were "systematic," but he deleted the word because some research workers were unable to identify "systematic criminals," and other workers considered only an insignificant proportion of prisoners to be "systematic criminals."[8] The theory now refers to all criminal behavior. Limitation to "systematic" criminality was made for what seemed to be practical rather than logical reasons, and it was abandoned when it did not seem to have practical utility.

Fourth, it is commonplace to say that the theory is defective because it does not explain why persons have the associations they have, or identify the *sources* of definitions favorable or unfavorable to delinquency and crime.[9] Although such expressions are valuable statements of what is needed in criminological research, they are erroneous when applied to differential association. Determining why persons have the associations they have is a highly relevant research problem, and we shall later see that when the differential association theory is viewed as a principle that attempts to account for variations in crime rates it does deal in a

[6]Robert G. Caldwell, *Criminology* (New York: Ronald Press, 1956), pp. 182–84; Ruth S. Cavan, *Criminology*, 2d ed. (New York: Crowell, 1955), p. 701; Mabel A. Elliott, *Crime in Modern Society* (New York: Harper and Bros., 1952), p. 274; Richard R. Korn and Lloyd W. McCorkle, *Criminology and Penology* (New York: Holt, 1959), pp. 297–98; Vold, *Theoretical Criminology*, pp. 197–98.

[7]See Edwin H. Sutherland, *Principles of Criminology*, 3d ed. (Philadelphia: Lippincott, 1939), pp. 5–9. This statement proposed generally that systematic criminality is learned in a process of differential association but then went on to use "consistency" as one of the modes of affecting the impact of the various patterns presented in the process of association. Thus, "consistency" of the behavior patterns presented was used as a general explanation of criminality, but "consistency" also was used to describe the process by which differential association takes place. Like the word "systematic," "consistency" was deleted from the next version of the theory.

[8]Edwin H. Sutherland, "Development of the Theory," in *Edwin H. Sutherland on Analyzing Crime*, ed. Karl Schuessler (Chicago: University of Chicago Press, 1973), p. 21.

[9]Gwynn Nettler, *Explaining Crime* (New York: McGraw-Hill, 1974), p. 199; and Gene Grabiner, "The Limits of Three Perspectives on Crime: 'Value-Free Science,' 'Objective Law,' and 'State Morality,' " *Issues in Criminology*, 8:35–48, 1973.

general way with differential opportunities for association with an excess of criminal behavior patterns. Nevertheless, the fact that the "individual conduct" part of the theory does not pretend to account for a person's associations or for the origins of definitions favorable to crime cannot be considered a defect in it.

Fifth, other authors have erroneously taken "theory" to be synonymous with "bias" or "prejudice," and have condemned the statement on this ground. For example, in connection with criticizing Sutherland for deleting "systematic" from the earlier version of his theory, Caldwell wrote that at the time the revision was made "we had not acquired enough additional facts to enable [Sutherland] to explain all criminal behavior.[10] This statement does not clearly recognize that facts themselves do not explain anything, and that theory tries to account for the relationships between known facts, among other things. Confusion about the role of theory also is apparent in Clinard's statement that the theory is "arbitrary," Glueck's statement that "social processes are dogmatically shaped to fit into the prejudices of the preexisting theory of 'differential association,' " and Jeffery's statement that "the theory does not differentiate between criminal and noncriminal behavior, since both types of behavior can be learned."[11]

Additional errors stemming from the form of the formal statement, from lack of careful reading of the statement, or from assumptions necessary to conducting research, have been made, but not with the frequency of the five listed above. Among these less frequently made errors are (1) confusion of the concept "definition of the situation" with the word "situation"; (2) confusion of the notion that persons associate with criminal and anticriminal behavior patterns with the notion that it is *groups* that associate on a differential basis; (3) belief that the theory is concerned principally with learning the *techniques* for committing crimes; (4) belief that the theory refers to learning of behavior patterns that are neither criminal nor anticriminal in nature, (5) belief that "differential association," when used in reference to professional thieves, means maintaining "a certain necessary aloofness from ordinary people";[12] (6) failure to recognize that the shorthand phrase "differential association" is equivalent to "differential association with criminal and anticriminal behavior patterns," with the consequent assumption that the theory attempts to explain all behavior, not just criminal behavior; and (7) belief that the theory is concerned only with a raw ratio of associations between the two kinds of behavior patterns and does not

[10]Caldwell, *Criminology*, p. 182.

[11]Marshall B. Clinard, *Sociology of Deviant Behavior* (New York: Rinehart, 1957), p. 204; Sheldon Glueck, "Theory and Fact in Criminology," *British Journal of Delinquency*, 7:92–109, 1956; Clarence Ray Jeffery, "An Integrated Theory of Crime and Criminal Behavior," *Journal of Criminal Law, Criminology, and Police Science*, 49:533–52, 1959.

[12]Walter C. Reckless, *The Crime Problem*, 2d ed. (New York: Appleton-Century-Crofts, 1955), p. 169. This kind of error may stem from Sutherland himself, for in his work on the professional thief he used the term "differential association" to characterize the members of the behavior system, rather than to describe the process presented in the first statement of his theory, two years later. See Edwin H. Sutherland, *The Professional Thief* (Chicago: University of Chicago Press, 1937), pp. 206–7.

contain the statement, explicitly made, that "differential association may vary in frequency, duration, priority, and intensity.[13]

Some Popular Criticisms

Identification of some of the defects that various critics have found in the theory also should make the theory clearer. Five principal types of criticism have been advanced in the literature. It would be incorrect to assume that a criticism advanced by many readers is more valid or important than one advanced by a single reader, but commenting on every criticism would take us too far afield. We can only mention, without elaboration, some of the criticisms advanced by only one or two authors.

It has been stated or implied that the theory of differential association (1) is defective because it omits consideration of free will, (2) is based on a psychology assuming rational deliberation, (3) ignores the role of the victim, (4) does not explain the origin of crime, (5) does not define terms such as "systematic" and "excess," (6) does not take "biological factors" into account, (7) is of little or no value to "practical men," (8) is not comprehensive enough because it is not interdisciplinary, (9) is not allied closely enough with more general sociological theory and research, (10) is too comprehensive because it applies to noncriminals, (11) assumes that all persons have equal access to criminal and anticriminal behavior patterns, and (12) assumes that some behavior patterns are objectively "criminal." Some of these comments represent pairs of opposites, one criticism contradicting another, and others seem to be based on one or more of the errors described above. Still others are closely allied with the five principal types of criticism, and we shall return to them.

One popular form of criticism of differential association is not, strictly speaking, criticism at all. A number of scholars have speculated that some kinds of criminal behavior are exceptions to the theory. Thus, it has been said that the theory does not apply to rural offenders, to landlords who violate rent control regulations, to criminal violators of financial trust, to "naïve check forgers," to white-collar criminals, to certain delinquents,[14] to perpetrators of "individual" and "personal" crimes, to irrational and impulsive criminals, to "adventitious"

[13]If these "modalities," as Sutherland called them, are ignored, then the theory would equate the impact of a behavior pattern presented once in a television drama with the impact of a pattern presented numerous times to a child who deeply loved and respected the donor. It does not so equate the patterns. See Eric Linden and James C. Hackler, "Affective Ties and Delinquency," *Pacific Sociological Review*, 16:27–46, 1973.

[14]Marshall B. Clinard, "The Process of Urbanization and Criminal Behavior," *American Journal of Sociology*, 48:202–13, 1942; idem, "Rural Criminal Offenders," *American Journal of Sociology*, 50 38–45, 1944; idem, "Criminological Theories of Violations of Wartime Regulations," *American Sociological Review*, 11:258–70, 1946; Donald R. Cressey, "Application and Verification of the Differential Association Theory," *Journal of Criminal Law, Criminology, and Police Science*, 43:43–52, 1952; Edwin M. Lemert, "Isolation and Closure Theory of Naïve Check Forgery," *Journal of Criminal Law, Criminology, and Police Science*, 44:293–307, 1953; Daniel Glaser, "Criminality Theories and Behavioral Images," *American Journal of Sociology*, 61:441, 1956; and Travis Hirschi, *Causes of Delinquency* (Berkeley: University of California Press, 1969), pp. 14–15, 229–30.

and/or "accidental" criminals, to "occasional," "incidental," and "situational" offenders, to murderers, nonprofessional shoplifters and noncareer type of criminals, to persons who commit crimes of passion and to persons whose crimes were perpetrated under emotional stress.[15] It is important to note that only the first six comments—those referring to rural offenders, landlords, trust violators, check forgers, some white-collar criminals, and some delinquents—are based on research. At least two authors have simply stated that the theory is subject to criticism because there are exceptions to it; the kind of behavior thought to be exceptional is not specified.[16] Quinney has argued, more generally, that behavior patterns are not objectively criminal so that *any* attempt to explain *any* criminal behavior is necessarily fallacious on its face; nevertheless, he has devised a strategy for refining the differential association theory so it can be put to test.[17]

The fact that most of the comments are not based on research means that the criticisms are actually proposals for research. Should a person conduct research on a particular type of offender and find that the theory does not hold, then a revision of the theory is called for, provided the research actually tested the theory, or part of it. As indicated, this procedure has been used in six instances, and these instances need to be given careful attention. Hirschi, for example, has concluded on the basis of empirical research that *absence* of control, not the presence of behavior patterns favorable to delinquency, is what increases the likelihood that delinquent acts will be committed.[18] But in most cases, there is no evidence that the kind of behavior said to be exceptional is exceptional. For example, we do not know that "accidental" or "incidental" or "occasional" criminals have not gone through the process specified in the theory. Perhaps it is sometimes assumed that some types of criminal behavior are "obviously exceptional." However, one theoretical analysis indicated that a type of behavior that appears to be obviously exceptional—"compulsive criminality"—is not necessarily exceptional at all.[19]

A second principal kind of criticism attacks the theory because it does not adequately take into account the "personality traits," "personality factors," or "psychological variables" in criminal behavior. This is real criticism, for it suggests that the statement neglects an important determinant of criminality. Occasion-

[15]See Nettler, *Explaining Crime*, p. 197; and Steven Giannell, "Criminosynthesis," *International Journal of Social Psychiatry*, 16:83–95, 1970.

[16]Harry Elmer Barnes and Negley K. Teeters, *New Horizons in Criminology*, 3d ed. (Englewood Cliffs, N. J.: Prentice-Hall, 1959), p. 159; Donald R. Taft, *Criminology* (New York: Macmillan, 1956), p. 340.

[17]Richard Quinney, *Criminology: An Analysis and Critique of Crime in America* (Boston: Little, Brown, 1975), pp. 96–99, 100–111.

[18]Hirschi, *Causes of Delinquency*, p. 229. See also Gary F. Jensen, "Parents, Peers and Delinquent Action: A Test of the Differential Association Perspective," *American Journal of Sociology*, 78:562–75, 1972; John R. Hepburn, "Testing Alternative Models of Delinquency Causation," *Journal of Criminal Law and Criminology*, 67:450–60, 1977; and Joseph H. Rankin, "Investigating the Interrelations Among Social Control Variables and Conformity," *Journal of Criminal Law and Criminology*, 67:470–80, 1977.

[19]Donald R. Cressey, "The Differential Association Theory and Compulsive Crimes," *Journal of Criminal Law, Criminology, and Police Science*, 45:49–64., 1954.

ally, the criticism is linked with the apparent assumption that some kinds of criminality are "obviously" exceptional. However, at least a dozen authors have proposed that the statement is defective because it omits or overlooks the general role of personality traits in determining criminality.

In an early period Sutherland stated that his theory probably would have to be revised to take account of personality traits.[20] Later he pointed out what he believed to be the fundamental weakness in his critics' argument: *Personality traits* and *personality* are words that merely specify a condition, like mental retardation, without showing the relationship between that condition and criminality. He posed three questions for advocates of personality traits as supplements to differential association: (1) What are the personality traits that should be regarded as significant? (2) Are there personal traits to be used as supplements to differential association, which are not already included in the concept of differential association? (3) Can differential association, which is essentially a *process* of learning, be combined with personal traits, which are essentially the *product* of learning?[21]

Sutherland did not attempt to answer these questions, but the context of his discussion indicates his belief that differential association does explain why some persons with a trait like "aggressiveness" commit crimes, while other persons possessing the same trait do not. It also reveals his conviction that terms like *personality traits*, *personality*, and *psychogenic trait components* are, when used with no further elaboration to explain why a person becomes a criminal, synonyms for *unknown conditions*.[22]

Closely allied with the "personality trait" criticism is the assertion that the theory does not adequately take into account the "response" patterns, "acceptance" patterns, and "receptivity" patterns of various individuals. The essential notion here is that differential association emphasizes the social process of transmission but minimizes the individual process of reception. Stated in another way, the idea is that the theory deals only with external variables and does not take into account the meaning to the recipient of the various patterns of behavior presented in situations which are objectively quite similar but nevertheless variable, according to the recipient's perception of them. One variety of this type of criticism takes the form of asserting that criminals and noncriminals are sometimes reared in the "same environment"—criminal behavior patterns are presented to two persons, but only one of them becomes a criminal.

Sutherland was acutely aware of the social psychological problem posed by such concepts as "differential response patterns." Significantly, his proposed solution to

---

[20]Sutherland, "Development of the Theory," pp. 25–27.

[21]Edwin H. Sutherland, *White Collar Crime* (New York: Dryden Press, 1949), p. 272. See also Harwin L. Voss, "Differential Association and Containment Theory—a Theoretical Convergence," *Social Forces*, 47:381–91, 1969.

[22]See the discussion in Chapter 7.

the problem was his statement of the theory of differential association.[23] One of the principal objectives of the theory is to account for differences in individual responses to opportunities for crime and in individual responses to criminal behavior patterns presented. To illustrate, one person who walks by an unguarded and open cash register, or who is informed of the presence of such a condition in a nearby store, may perceive the situation as a "crime-committing" one, while another person in the identical circumstances may perceive the situation as one in which the owner should be warned against carelessness. The difference in these two perceptions, the theory holds, is due to differences in the prior associations with the two types of definition of situation, so that the alternatives in behavior are accounted for in terms of differential association. The differential in "response pattern," or the difference in "receptivity" to the criminal behavior pattern presented, then, is accounted for by differential association itself.[24] Cressey has argued that one of the greatest defects in the theory is its implication that receptivity to any behavior pattern presented is determined by the patterns presented earlier, that receptivity to those early presentations was determined by even earlier presentations, and so on back to birth.[25] But this is an assertion that the theory is difficult to test, not an assertion that it does not take into account the differential response patterns of individuals.

If receptivity is viewed in a different way, however, the critics appear to be on firm ground.[26] The theory does not identify what constitutes a definition favorable to or unfavorable to the violation of law. The same objective definition might be favorable or unfavorable, depending on the relationship between the donor and the recipient. Consequently, the theory indicates that differential associations may vary in "intensity," which is not precisely defined but "has to do with such things as the prestige of the source of a criminal or anticriminal pattern and with emotional reactions related to the associations." This statement tells us that some associations are to be given added *weight*, but it does not tell us how, or whether, early associations affect the *meaning* of later associations. If earlier associations determine whether a person will later identify specific behavior patterns as favorable or unfavorable to law violation, then these earlier associations determine the very meaning of the later ones, and do not merely give added weight to them. In other words, whether a person is prestigeful or not prestigeful to another may be determined by experiences that have nothing to do with criminality and anticriminality. Nevertheless, these experiences affect the meaning (whether favorable or unfavorable) of patterns later presented to the person

[23]See Edwin H. Sutherland, "Susceptibility and Differential Association," in *Edwin H. Sutherland on Analyzing Crime*, ed. Schuessler, pp. 42–43. See also Solomon Kobrin, "The Conflict of Values in Delinquency Areas," *American Sociological Review*, 16:653–61, 1951.

[24]Cf. Elihu Katz, Martin L. Levin, and Herbert Hamilton, "Traditions of Research on the Diffusion of Innovation," *American Sociological Review*, 28:237–52, 1963.

[25]Cressey, "Application and Verification of the Differential Association Theory."

[26]I am indebted to Albert K. Cohen for assistance with this paragraph and with other points.

and, thus, they affect receptivity to the behavior patterns.[27] For example, in one experiment a rich-looking person and a poor-looking person were employed as models. The models crossed a street against a traffic light, and the experimenters noted how many pedestrians followed them in their lawbreaking. More people imitated the rich-looking model, possibly because to many persons, observing another person crossing the street against the light is not objectively favorable or unfavorable. If a poor person does it, it might be a behavior pattern unfavorable to law violation, but if a rich person does it, the pattern might have a quite different meaning.[28]

A fourth kind of criticism is more damaging than the first three, for it insists that the ratio of learned behavior patterns used to explain criminality cannot be determined with accuracy in specific cases. Short, for example, has pointed out the extreme difficulty of operationalizing terms such as "favorable to" and "unfavorable to"; nevertheless, he has devised various measures of differential association and has used the term in a series of significant studies.[29] Glaser has noted that the "phrase 'excess of definitions' itself lacks clear denotation in human experience." Glueck has asked, "Has anybody actually counted the number of definitions favorable to violation of law and definitions unfavorable to violation of law, and demonstrated that in the predelinquency experience of the vast majority of delinquents and criminals, the former exceeds the latter?" And Hirschi has concluded both that the theory is "virtually nonfalsifiable" and that predictions from it "tend to be trivial."[30] In a study of trust violators, Cressey found that embezzlers could not identify specific persons or agencies from whom they learned their behavior patterns favorable to trust violation. The general conclusion was, "It is doubtful that it can be shown empirically that the differential association theory applies or does not apply to crimes of financial trust violation or even to other kinds of criminal behavior."[31] Similarly, Stanfield has noted the extreme difficulty of measuring the variation and content of "frequency, duration, priority, and intensity."[32]

It should be noted that these damaging criticisms of the theory of differential association as a precise statement of the mechanism by which persons become

[27]This actually is the important point Vold was making in the quotation cited at footnote 3, above. See also Don C. Gibbons, *Society, Crime, and Criminal Careers: An Introduction to Criminology* (Englewood Cliffs, N. J.: Prentice-Hall, 1968), pp 204–6.

[28]M. M. Lefkowitz et al., "Status Factors in Pedestrian Violation of Traffic Signals," *Journal of Abnormal and Social Psychology*, 51:704–6, 1955.

[29]James F. Short, Jr., "Differential Association and Delinquency," *Social Problems*, 4:233–39, 1957; and James F. Short, Jr. and Fred L. Strodtbeck, *Group Process and Gang Delinquency* (Chicago: University of Chicago Press, 1965).

[30]Glaser, "Criminality Theories and Behavioral Images"; Glueck, "Theory and Fact in Criminology," p. 96; and Hirschi, *Causes of Delinquency*, pp. 14–15.

[31]Cressey, "Application and Verification of the Differential Association Theory," p. 52.

[32]Robert E. Stanfield, "The Interaction of Family Variables and Gang Variables in the Aetiology of Delinquency," *Social Problems*, 13:411–17, 1966.

criminals do not affect the value of the theory as a general principle which organizes and makes good sense of the data on crime rates. As we shall see below, a theory accounting for the distribution of crime, delinquency, or any other phenomenon can be valid even if a presumably coordinate theory specifying the process by which deviancy occurs in individual cases is *incorrect*, let alone untestable.

The fifth kind of criticism states in more general terms than the first four that the theory of differential association oversimplifies the process by which criminal behavior is learned. At the extreme are assertions that the theory is inadequate because it does not allow for a process in which criminality is said to be "chosen" by the individual actor. Some such assertions maintain that a social psychology and sociology of criminals and crime is impossible, and their authors ask for a return to something like the "free will" tenets of the classical school of criminology. Interestingly enough, such assertions have in recent years been announced by social psychologists and sociologists.[33] More realistic criticism ranges from simple assertions that the learning process is more complex than the theory states or implies, to the idea that the theory does not adequately take into account some specific type of learning process, such as differential identification or operant conditioning.

But it is one thing to criticize the theory for failure to specify the learning process accurately and another to specify which aspects of the learning process should be included and in what way.[34] Clinard, Glaser, and Matthews, among others, have introduced the process of identification.[35] Weinberg, Sykes and Matza, Cressey and Frazier, among others, have stressed other aspects of more general social psychological theory.[36] Adams has, on the basis of a laboratory

[33]David Matza, *Becoming Deviant*, (Englewood Cliffs, N. J.: Prentice-Hall, 1969), p. 107; Steven Box, *Deviance, Reality, and Society* (London: Holt, Rinehart and Winston, 1971), p. 21; Ian Taylor, Paul Walton, and Jock Young, *The New Criminology: For a Social Theory of Deviance* (London: Routledge and Kegan Paul, 1973), p. 128.

[34]Despite the fact that Sutherland described a learning process, it should be noted that he also said, "The process of learning criminal and anticriminal behavior patterns involves all the mechanisms that are involved in any other learning."

[35]Clinard, "The Process of Urbanization and Criminal Behavior"; idem, "Rural Criminal Offenders"; idem, "Criminological Theories of Violations of Wartime Regulations"; Glaser, "Criminality Theories and Behavioral Images"; idem, "Differential Association and Criminological Prediction," *Social Problems*, 8:6–14, 1960; idem, "The Differential Association Theory of Crime," in *Human Behavior and Social Process*, ed. Arnold Rose (Boston: Houghton Mifflin, 1962), pp. 425–43; Victor Matthews, "Differential Identification: An Empirical Note," *Social Problems*, 15:376–83, 1968.

[36]S. Kirson Weinberg, "Theories of Criminality and Problems of Prediction," *Journal of Criminal Law, Criminology, and Police Science*, 45:412–29, 1954; idem, "Personality and Method in the Differential Association Theory," *Journal of Research in Crime and Delinquency*, 3:165–72, 1966; Gresham Sykes and David Matza, "Techniques of Neutralization: A Theory of Delinquency," *American Sociological Review*, 22:664–70, 1957; Cressey, "Application and Verification of the Differential Association Theory"; idem, "The Differential Association Theory and Compulsive Crimes"; idem, "Social Psychological Foundations for Using Criminals in the Rehabilitation of Criminals," *Journal of Research in Crime and Delinquency*, 2:49–59, 1965;

experiment, noted the importance of such "nonsocial" variables as money, drugs, and sex in the reinforcement and maintenance of delinquent behavior.[37] Jensen consistently found that boys who associate with delinquents are more likely to be delinquent than boys who do not, but this occurs independently of the effect of these associations on their attitudes and beliefs.[38] Even these attempts are, like the differential association statement itself, more in the nature of general indications of the kind of framework or orientation one should use in formulating a theory of criminality than they are statements of theory. Burgess and Akers have given a most promising lead in this area by specifying that the conditions and mechanisms through which delinquent and criminal behavior are learned are those indicated in the theory of human learning variously referred to as reinforcement theory, operant behavior theory, and operant conditioning theory.[39]

The theory of differential association does not concentrate exclusively on individual criminality. It is also concerned with making sense of the gross facts about delinquency and crime.[40] Examination of Sutherland's writings clearly indicates that when he formulated the theory he was greatly, if not primarily, concerned with organizing and integrating the factual information about crime rates. In his account of how the theory of differential association developed, he made the following three relevant points:

> More significant for the development of the theory were certain questions which I raised in class discussions. One of these questions was, Negroes, young-adult males, and city dwellers all have relatively high crime rates: What do these three groups have in common that places them in this position? Another question was, even if feeble-minded persons have a high crime rate, why do they commit crimes? It is not feeble-mindedness as such, for some feeble-minded persons do not commit crimes. Later I raised another question which

idem, "The Language of Set Theory and Differential Association," *Journal of Research in Crime and Delinquency*, 3:22–26 1966; Charles E. Frazier, *Theoretical Approaches to Deviance* (Columbus, Ohio: Bobbs-Merrill, 1976), pp. 113–114.

[37]Reed Adams, "The Adequacy of Differential Association Theory," *Journal of Research in Crime and Delinquency*, 11:1–8, 1974. See also Clarence Ray Jeffery, "Criminal Behavior and Learning Theory," *Journal of Criminal Law, Criminology, and Police Science*, 56:294–300, 1965.

[38]Jensen, "Parents, Peers and Delinquent Action."

[39]Robert L. Burgess and Ronald L. Akers, "A Differential Association—Reinforcement Theory of Criminal Behavior," *Social Problems*, 14:128–47, 1968. See also Ronald L. Akers, Robert L. Burgess, and Weldon T. Johnson, "Opiate Use, Addiction, and Relapse," *Social Problems*, 15:459–69, 1968.

[40]One of Sutherland's own students, colleagues, and editors has said, "Much that travels under the name of sociology of deviant behavior or of social disorganization is psychology—some of it very good psychology, but psychology. For example, Sutherland's theory of differential associations, which is widely regarded as preeminently sociological, is not the less psychological because it makes much of the cultural milieu. It is psychological because it addresses itself to the question: How do people become the kind of individuals who commit criminal acts? A sociological question would be: What is it about the structure of social systems that determines the kinds of criminal acts that occur in these systems and the way in which such acts are distributed within these systems?" (Albert K. Cohen, "The Study of Social Disorganization and Deviant Behavior," chap. 21 in *Sociology Today*, ed. Robert K. Merton, Leonard Broom, and Leonard S. Cottrell, Jr. [New York: Basic Books, 1959], p. 452).

became even more important in my search for generalizations. Crime rates have a high correlation with poverty if considered by areas of a city but a low correlation if considered chronologically in relation to the business cycle; this obviously means that poverty as such is not an important cause of crime. How are the varying associations between crime and poverty explained?[41]

It was my conception that a general theory should take account of all the factual information regarding crime causation. It does this either by organizing the multiple factors in relation to each other or by abstracting them from certain common elements. It does not, or should not, neglect or eliminate any factors that are included in the multiple-factor theory.[42]

The hypothesis of differential association seemed to me to be consistent with the principal gross findings in criminology. It explained why the Mollaccan children became progressively delinquent with length of residence in the deteriorated area of Los Angeles, why the city crime rate is higher than the rural crime rate, why males are more delinquent than females, why the crime rate remains consistently higher in deteriorated areas of cities, why the juvenile delinquency rate in a foreign nativity group is high while the group lives in a deteriorated area and drops when the group moves out of the area, why second-generation Italians do not have the high murder rate their fathers had, why Japanese children in a deteriorated area of Seattle had a low delinquency rate even though in poverty, why crimes do not increase greatly in a period of depression. All of the general statistical facts seem to fit this hypothesis.[43]

The formal statement of the theory indicates, for example, that a high crime rate in urban areas can be considered the end product of criminalistic traditions in those areas. Similarly, the fact that the rate for all crimes is not higher in some urban areas than it is in some rural areas can be attributed to differences in conditions which affect the probabilities of exposure to criminal behavior patterns.[44] The important general point is that in a multigroup type of social organization, alternative and inconsistent standards of conduct are possessed by various groups, so that an individual who is a member of one group has a high probability of learning to use legal means for achieving success, or learning to deny the importance of success, while an individual in another group learns to accept the importance of success and to achieve it by illegal means. Stated in another way, there are alternative educational processes in operation, varying with groups, so that a person may be educated in either conventional or criminal means of achieving success. As indicated above, this situation may be called "differential social organization" or "differential group organization." "Differential group

---

[41]Sutherland, "Development of the Theory," p. 15.

[42]Ibid., p. 18.

[43]Ibid., pp. 19–20.

[44]Cf. Henry D. McKay, "Differential Association and Crime Prevention: Problems of Utilization," *Social Problems*, 8:25–37, 1960.

organization" should explain the crime rate, while differential association should explain the criminal behavior of a person. The two explanations must be consistent with each other.

It should be noted that, in the three quotations above, Sutherland referred to the differential association statement as both a "theory" and a "hypothesis," and did not indicate any special concern for distinguishing between differential association as it applies to the epidemiology of crime and differential association as it applies to individual conduct. In order to avoid controversy about the essential characteristics of theories and hypotheses, it seems preferable to call differential association, as it is used in reference to crime rates, a principle. Many "theories" in sociology are in fact principles that order facts about rates—now called epidemiology—in some way. Durkheim, for example, invented what may be termed a "principle of group integration" to account for, organize logically, and integrate systematically the data on variations in suicide rates. He did not invent a theory of suicide, derive hypotheses from it, and then collect data to determine whether the hypotheses were correct or incorrect. He tried to make sense of known facts about rates, and the principle he suggested remains the most valuable idea available to understand the differences in the rates of suicide between Protestants and Jews, urban-dwellers and rural-dwellers, and so on.

The differential association statement, similarly, is a "principle of normative conflict" which proposes that high crime rates occur in societies and groups characterized by conditions that lead to the development of extensive criminalistic subcultures. The principle makes sense of variations in crime rates by observing that modern societies are organized for crime as well as against it, and then observing further that crime rates are unequally distributed because of differences in the degree to which various categories of persons participate in this normative conflict.[45] Sutherland invented the principle of normative conflict to account for the distribution of high and low crime rates; he then tried to specify the mechanism by which this principle works to produce individual cases of criminality. The mechanism proposed is differential association:

> The second concept, differential association, is a statement of [normative] conflict from the point of view of the person who commits the crime. The two kinds of culture impinge on him or he has association with the two kinds of cultures and this is differential association.[46]

THE VALUE OF DIFFERENTIAL ASSOCIATION

As an organizing principle, normative conflict makes understandable most of the variations in crime rates discovered by various researchers and observers, and it

---

[45]See Raymond D. Gastil, "Homicide and a Regional Culture of Violence," *American Sociological Review*, 36:412–27, 1971.
[46]Sutherland, "Development of the Theory," pp. 20–21.

also focuses attention on crucial research areas.[47] The principle of normative conflict does not make good sense out of all the statistical variations, but it seems to make better sense out of more of them than do any of the alternative theories.

On the other hand, it also seems safe to conclude that differential association is not a precise statement of the process by which one becomes a criminal. The idea that criminality is a consequence of an excess of intimate associations with criminal behavior patterns is valuable because, for example, it negates assertions that deviation from norms is simply a product of being emotionally insecure or living in a broken home, and then indicates in a general way why only some emotionally insecure persons and only some persons from broken homes commit crimes. Also, it directs attention to the idea that an efficient explanation of individual conduct is consistent with explanations of epidemiology. Yet the statement of the differential association process is not precise enough to stimulate rigorous empirical test, and it therefore has not been proved or disproved. This defect is shared with broader social psychological theory. Although critics agree, as we have indicated, that the differential association statement oversimplifies the process by which normative conflict "gets into" persons and produces criminality, an acceptable substitute that is consistent with the principle of normative conflict has not appeared.

It is important to observe, however, that the "individual conduct" part of the theoretical statement does order data on individual criminality in a general way and, consequently, might be considered a principle itself. Thus, "differential association" may be viewed as a restatement of the principle of normative conflict, so that this one principle is used to account for the distribution of criminal and noncriminal behavior in both the life of the individual *and* in the statistics on collectivities. In this case, both individual behavior data and epidemiological rate data may be employed as indices of the variables in the principle, thus providing two types of hypotheses for testing it.[48] Glaser has shown that differential association makes sense of both the predictive efficiency of some parole prediction items and the lack of predictive efficiency of other items.[49] In effect, he tested the principle by determining whether parole prediction procedures which could have proven it false actually failed to prove it false. First, he shows that a majority of the most accurate predictors in criminology prediction

[47]Cf. Llewellyn Gross, "Theory Construction in Sociology: A Methodological Inquiry," chap. 17 in *Symposium on Sociological Theory*, ed. Llewellyn Gross (Evanston, Ill.: Row, Peterson, 1959), pp. 548–55. See also Donald R. Cressey, "The State of Criminal Statistics," *National Probation and Parole Association Journal*, 3:230–41, 1957; and DeFleur and Quinney, "Reformulation of Sutherland's Differential Association Theory."

[48]I am indebted to Daniel Glaser for calling this point to my attention.

[49]Glaser, "Differential Association and Criminological Prediction." See also idem, "A Reconsideration of Some Parole Prediction Factors," *American Sociological Review*, 19:335–41, 1954; and idem, "The Efficiency of Alternative Approaches to Parole Prediction," *American Sociological Review*, 20:283–87, June, 1955; and Daniel Glaser and Richard R. Hangren, "Predicting the Adjustment of Federal Probationers," *National Probation and Parole Association Journal*, 4:258–67, 1958; and David M. Downes, *The Delinquent Solution: A Study in Subcultural Theory* (London: Routledge and Kegan Paul, 1966), pp. 97–98.

research are deducible from differential association theory, while the least accurate predictors are not deducible at all. Second, he shows that this degree of accuracy does not characterize alternative theories. Finally, he notes that two successful predictors of parole violation—type of offense and noncriminal employment opportunities—are not necessarily deducible from the theory, and he suggests a modification that would take this fact into account.

SUGGESTED READINGS

Adams, Reed. "Differential Association and Learning Principles Revisited." *Social Problems*, 20:458–70, 1973.

Adams, Reed. "The Adequacy of Differential Association Theory." *Journal of Research in Crime and Delinquency*, 11:1–8, 1974.

Akers, Ronald L. *Deviant Behavior: A Social Learning Approach.* Belmont, Calif.: Wadsworth, 1973.

Athens, Lonnie H. "The Self and the Violent Criminal Act." *Urban Life and Culture*, 3:98–112, 1974.

Bensman, Joseph, & Israel Gerver. "Crime and Punishment in the Factory: The Function of Deviancy in Maintaining the Social System." *American Sociological Review*, 28:588–98, 1963.

Clark, Robert E. *Reference Group Theory and Delinquency.* New York: Behavioral Publications, 1972.

Clinard, Marshall B., & Daniel J. Abbott. *Crime in Developing Countries: A Comparative Perspective.* New York: Wiley, 1973.

Cressey, Donald R. "Epidemiology and Individual Conduct: A Case From Criminology." *Pacific Sociological Review*, 3:47–58, 1960.

DeFleur, Melvin L., & Richard Quinney. "A Reformulation of Sutherland's Differential Association Theory and a Strategy for Empirical Verification." *Journal of Research in Crime and Delinquency*, 3:1–22, 1966.

DeLamater, John. "On the Nature of Deviance." *Social Forces*, 46:445–55, 1968.

Gibbons, Don C. "Observations on the Study of Crime Causation." *American Journal of Sociology*, 77:262–78, 1971.

Glaser, Daniel. "Differential Association and Criminological Prediction." *Social Problems*, 8:6–14, 1960.

Gorecki, Jan. "Crime and Causation Theories: Failures and Perspectives." *British Journal of Sociology*, 25:461–77, 1974.

Hall, Peter M. "Identification with the Delinquent Subculture and Level of Self-Evaluation." *Sociometry*, 29:146–58, 1966.

Harris, Anthony R. "Sex and Theories of Deviance: Toward a Functional Theory of Deviant Type-Scripts." *American Sociological Review*, 42:3–16, 1977.

Hirschi, Travis. *Causes of Delinquency.* Berkeley: University of California Press, 1969.

Jeffery, Clarence Ray. "Criminal Behavior and Learning Theory." *Journal of Criminal Law, Criminology, and Police Science*, 56:294–300, 1965.

Lemert, Edwin M. *Human Deviance, Social Problems, and Social Control.* Englewood Cliffs, N. J.: Prentice-Hall, 1967.

Linden, Eric, & James C. Hackler. "Affective Ties and Delinquency." *Pacific Sociological Review*, 16:27–46, 1973.

Liska, Allen E. "Interpreting the Causal Structure of Differential Association Theory." *Social Problems,* 16:485–92, 1969.

Lofland, John. *Deviance and Identity.* Englewood Cliffs, N. J.: Prentice-Hall, 1969.

Matthews, Victor M. "Differential Identification: An Empirical Note " *Social Problems,* 15:376–83, 1968.

Matza, David. *Becoming Deviant.* Englewood Cliffs, N. J.: Prentice-Hall, 1969.

Naess, Siri. "Comparing Theories of Criminogenesis." *Journal of Research in Crime and Delinquency,* 1:171–80, 1964.

Paschke, Walter R. "The Addiction Cycle: A Learning Theory–Peer Group Model." *Correctional Psychiatry and Journal of Social Therapy,* 16:74–81, 1970.

Reiss, Albert J., Jr. & Lewis Rhodes. "An Empirical Test of Differential Association Theory." *Journal of Research in Crime and Delinquency,* 1:5–18, 1964.

Schuessler, Karl F. *Edwin H. Sutherland on Analyzing Crime.* Chicago: University of Chicago Press, 1973.

Severy, Lawrence J. "Exposure to Deviance Committed by Valued Peer Group and Family Members." *Journal of Research in Crime and Delinquency,* 10:35–46, 1973.

Short, James F., Jr. "Differential Association as a Hypothesis: Problems of Empirical Testing." *Social Problems,* 8:14–25, 1960.

Slawski, Carl J. "Crime Causation: Toward a Field Synthesis." *Criminology,* 3:375–96, 1971.

Stratton, John R. "Differential Identification and Attitudes Toward the Law." *Social Forces,* 46:256–62, 1967.

Tec, Nechama. "The Peer Group and Marijuana Use." *Crime and Delinquency,* 18:298–309, 1972.

Trassler, Gordon. *The Explanation of Criminality.* London: Routledge and Kegan Paul, 1962.

Vold, George B. *Theoretical Criminology.* New York: Oxford University Press, 1958.

Voss, Harwin L. "Differential Association and Containment Theory: A Theoretical Convergence." *Social Forces,* 47:381–91, 1969.

Weinberg, S. Kirson. "Personality and Method in the Differential Association Theory." *Journal of Research in Crime and Delinquency,* 3:165–72, 1966.

5

Crime, Delinquency, and Social Structure

In nonliterate and peasant societies the influences surrounding a person are relatively steady, uniform, and consistent. Until the early part of this century, China exemplified this situation perfectly except in a few coastal cities. Individuals were surrounded by all of their relatives, and this larger family determined each person's career and ambitions. The principal satisfactions were found in cooperation with that group, which was considered as extending beyond one's own life into the distant future. Within this group each person had almost perfect security, for the group cared for its members in case of sickness, accident, old age, insanity, or any other emergency. Such charity involved no stigma or disgrace. The large family, moreover, was supported by the surrounding community, which also was harmonious in its traditional culture.

Despite industrialization, contemporary China is experiencing a return to this form of organization. Local communities are in many respects self-supporting and self-contained societies. There is consistency in the behavior patterns presented to persons in the socialization process. Accordingly, there are few opportunities for individualism in behavior, and the behavior of individuals is almost predictable. Therefore, few crimes are committed.[1]

Such group cohesion is illustrated by certain Labrador Indians, who have been characterized as follows:

They are primary in pattern since, through the intimate association of individuals forming them, the social fusion of kin results in producing a community whole within which there is a tendency toward harmony and the most thoroughgoing cooperation. Strife is scarcely present, violence strenuously avoided; competition even courteously disdained. These, they think, lead to ridicule. In their place are met subjection of self, generosity in respect to

[1]See Harold E. Pepinsky, *Crime and Conflict: A Study of Law and Society* (New York: Academic Press, 1976).

property, service, and opinion, the qualities which we often speak of as being found in "good sports" and which seem to develop as social habits. And these are the qualities that to them represent honor and a welcome place in the thoughts of their associates.[2]

Similarly, the Zuni Indians of western New Mexico disapprove of conflict, controversy, and strife:

Among the Zuni a man is not supposed to stand up for his rights; he is looked down upon if he gets into any sort of conflict or achieves notoriety. The best that one Zuni may say of another is that he "is a nice polite man. No one ever hears anything from him. He never gets into trouble."[3]

DIFFERENTIAL SOCIAL ORGANIZATION

At present no such consistency and uniformity is evident in Western civilization, although certain isolated rural settlements approach it. In contemporary urban society, a child is confronted with various ways of behaving even within the home, for no parent can act consistently in modern life; parents themselves are the recipients of many alternative roles and behavior patterns.[4] Similarly, groups outside the home have standards of conduct which often are extremely different from those within the home. A great deal of behavior is in the nature of role-playing; when roles are conflicting or ambiguous, the behavior is inconsistent. In a pioneering study, Sellin described the normative conflicts within contemporary communities thus:

Every person is identified with a number of social groups, each meeting some biologically conditioned or socially created need. Each of these groups is normative in the sense that within it there grow up norms of conduct applicable to situations created by that group's specific activities. As a member of a given group, a person is not only supposed to conform to the rules which it shares with other groups, but also to those which are peculiarly its own. A person who as a member of a family group—in turn the transmitting agency for the norms which governed the groups from which the parents come—possesses all its norms pertaining to conduct in routine life situations, may also as a member of a play group, a work group, a political group, a religious group, etc., acquire norms which regulate specialized life situations and which sustain, weaken, or even contradict the norms earlier incorporated in his personality. The more complex a culture becomes, the more likely it is that the number of normative groups which affect a person will be large, and the greater is the chance that the norms of these groups will fail to agree, no matter how much they may overlap as a result of common acceptance of certain norms. A conflict of norms is said to exist when more or less divergent rules of conduct govern the specific life situation in

[2]Frank G. Speck, "Ethical Attributes of Labrador Indians," *American Anthropologist*, 35:559–94, 1933.

[3]Robert Redfield, "Primitive Law," *University of Cincinnati Law Review*, 33:1–22, 1964. See also R. K. Denton, *The Semai: A Non-Violent People of Malaya* (New York: Holt, Rinehart and Winston, 1968); Michael Banton, "Authority in the Simpler Societies," *Police Journal*, 43:261–67, 1970; and B. K. Bantawa, "Juvenile Delinquency in Nepal," *United Nations Asia and Far East Institute for the Prevention of Crime and the Treatment of Offenders, Resource Materials*, No. 10, 1975, pp. 116–18.

[4]See Aubrey Wendling and Delbert S. Elliott, "Class and Race Differentials in Parental Aspirations and Expectations," *Pacific Sociological Review*, 11:123–33, 1968.

which a person may find himself. The conduct norm of one group of which he is a part may permit one response to this situation, the norm of another group may permit perhaps the very opposite response.[5]

This condition of normative conflict is ordinarily considered social "disorganization" or "unorganization" because the directives for conformity on the part of the person are not uniform and harmonious. In this condition, the society does not possess consensus with respect to societal goals or else does not possess consensus regarding means of achieving agreed-upon societal goals. Consequently, the individual is confronted with alternative goals or means, or exists under conditions in which the norms of many members of the society are unknown to other members.[6] Each male is "transformed from being defined as his father's son into a citizen."[7] Then he finds that behavior which is "right" or "correct" in one group is "wrong" or "improper" from the point of view of other groups in which he has membership; or, in the condition of *anomie*, he literally does not know how to behave, for he does not know what is expected of him.

The presence of this heterogeneous set of conflicting norms is considered social disorganization largely on the ground that an earlier form of social organization has disappeared or is disappearing. Actually, the social conditions in which the influences on the person are relatively inharmonious and inconsistent are themselves a kind of social organization. Such social organization is characteristic of all except the most isolated contemporary Western societies, although there are wide variations in the degree of heterogeneity and in the pervasiveness of the normative inconsistencies.[8]

So far as delinquency and crime are concerned, a heterogeneity of norms in a society means that both a delinquent or criminal subculture and an antidelinquent or anticriminal subculture have developed. The society has become organized in such a way that a premium has been placed both on refraining from crime and on perpetrating crime. A person may now be a member of a group organized against crime and at the same time be a member of a group organized for criminal behavior. The individual participates in delinquent subcultures as well as in nondelinquent and antidelinquent subcultures. Under such conditions of differential group organization, one would expect the crime rates to be relatively high, for there are "rules for crime" as well as "rules against crime." A sociological problem of first-rate importance is discovery of the conditions under which these rules for crime and rules for delinquency have developed. The task here is not to

[5]Thorsten Sellin, *Culture Conflict and Crime* (New York: Social Science Research Council, 1938), pp. 29–30. See also John Dewey, *Human Nature and Conduct* (New York: Henry Holt, 1930), p. 130.

[6]See Judith Blake and Kingsley Davis, "Norms, Values, and Sanctions," chap. 13 in *Handbook of Modern Sociology*, ed. Robert E. L. Faris (Chicago: Rand McNally, 1964) pp. 456–84.

[7]Daniel Lerner, "Comparative Analysis of Processes of Modernization," in *The Modern City in Africa*, ed. Horace Miner (New York: Praeger, 1967).

[8]C. W. Kiefer, "The Psychological Interdependence of Family, School, and Bureaucracy in Japan," *American Anthropologist*, 72:66–75, 1970.

identify the processes by which criminal behavior patterns are adopted by an individual or a group; it is to identify the processes which brought the behavior patterns into existence in the first place.

DEVELOPMENT OF NORMATIVE CONFLICT

One recent impetus to development of delinquent and criminal subcultures was the colonization of America, which threw the Old World out of economic balance. This was followed by the final breakup of the feudal system, in which the ownership of the land had been limited, and in which the fixed social classes had mutual duties to each other. Experimental science developed, resulting in the rise of modern technology. With the development of machinery, the production of wealth passed from the control of the consumer to the control of the capitalist; the laborers followed their work from the home to the factory; and thus the city developed around the factory and the marketplace. As world commerce began to develop, the traditional restrictions on economic activity were irksome, and rebellion against these restrictions resulted in a system of relatively free competition, with an accompanying individualistic ideology according to which social welfare is best attained if every person works only for his or her own selfish interests. Thus, the new system placed great emphasis upon individual enterprise, and it became shameful for an individual to withdraw from economic competition. Each person was expected to pursue private ends in the most efficient manner possible, and the expected result was increased economic wealth for all.

The democratic revolutions, with their accompanying ideologies of natural and inalienable rights, cannot be clearly separated from this economic revolution. Participants in the relatively new economic system resisted any measures which would inhibit free competition, and the slogan "the least government the best" was given homage. Each participant rebelled against restrictions on his or her own behavior and therefore attempted to keep government weak. However, as competition developed, it became apparent that competitive advantages could be secured through governmental manipulation. Individuals and industries secured tariffs, franchises, patents, and other special privileges. Both by emphasis on a "hands-off" policy and by emphasis on special privileges, government was made less effective as a controller of behavior.

The attitudes and ideology which developed with the industrial and democratic revolutions were opposed to the authoritarian principle in government and in other institutions. Economic and political individualism was useful at the time of revolt against the fixed statuses and restrictions of the feudal system and against the absolutism of the political system. But individualism is not a positive principle of social organization, and when the revolutions ended, the usefulness of the negative principle also ended. Since that time, the ideology of individualism has encouraged each citizen to disregard social welfare in the interest of selfish satisfactions.[9] Under such conditions of normative conflict, the significance of

---

[9]See Kenneth L. Karst, "Individual, Community, and Law," in *Law and the American Future*, ed. Murray L. Schwartz (Englewood Cliffs, N. J.: Prentice-Hall, 1976), pp. 68–73.

laws becomes relative—some are obeyed and others are not, depending on whether one "believes in" them.[10] Businessmen, like gangsters, believe that public welfare need not be considered, for it will be best realized if persons work for their own selfish interests.[11] The gangster is a man who acquires by individual merit and a gun that which is denied him by the complex orderings of a stratified society. As Veblen said:

> The ideal pecuniary man is like the ideal delinquent in his unscrupulous conversion of goods and persons to his own ends, and in a callous disregard of the feelings and wishes of others and of the remoter effects of his actions, but he is unlike him in possessing a keener sense of status and in working more farsightedly to a remoter end.[12]

Similarly, with the industrial and democratic revolutions the ambition for luxurious standards of life became effective for all social classes, since the values which previously restricted these standards to the nobility had been altered. Emile Durkheim, the noted French sociologist, made the following observation about stable societies:

> The economic ideal assigned each class of citizens is itself confined to certain limits, within which the desires have free range. But it is not infinite. This relative limitation and the moderation it involves make men contented with their lot while stimulating them moderately to improve it; and this average contentment causes the feeling of calm, active happiness, the pleasure in existing and living which characterizes health for societies as well as for individuals. Each person is then at least, generally speaking, in harmony with his condition, and desires only what he may legitimately hope for as the normal reward of his activity. Besides, this does not condemn man to a sort of immobility. He may seek to give beauty to his life; but his attempts in this direction may fail without causing him to despair.[13]

But rapid technological advancements and discovery of vast unexploited markets raised the level of aspirations by presenting what appeared to be unlimited possibilities for accumulation of wealth.[14] After the disappearance of the nobility, businessmen constituted the elite, and wealth became respected above all other attainments; necessarily, poverty became a disgrace. Wealth was therefore identi-

---

[10]See Marshall B. Clinard, *The Black Market: A Study of White Collar Crime* (New York: Rinehart, 1952), pp. 331, 334.

[11]See Edward A. Duddy, "The Moral Implications of Business as a Profession," *Journal of Business*, 15:70–71, 1945; and Harry V. Ball and Lawrence M. Friedman, "The Use of Criminal Sanctions in the Enforcement of Economic Legislation," *Stanford Law Review*, 17:197–223, 1965.

[12]Thorstein Veblen, *Theory of the Leisure Class* (New York: Macmillan, 1912), p. 237. See also David Matza and Gresham M. Sykes, "Juvenile Delinquency and Subterranean Values," *American Sociological Review*, 26:712–19, 1961.

[13]Emile Durkheim, *Suicide: A Study in Sociology*, trans. John A. Spaulding and George Simpson (Glencoe, Ill.: Free Press, 1951), p. 250. This book was first published in Paris in 1897.

[14]For contemporary examples, see Irving L. Horowitz, *Three Worlds of Development: The Theory and Practice of International Stratification* (New York: Oxford University Press, 1966); S. Kirson Weinberg, "Urbanization and Male Delinquency in Ghana," *Journal of Research in Crime and Delinquency*," 2:85–94, 1965; and Marshall B. Clinard and Daniel J. Abbott, *Crime in Developing Countries: A Comparative Perspective* (New York: Wiley, 1973).

fied with worth, and worth was made known to the public by conspicuous consumption. The desire for symbols of luxury, ease, and success, developed by competitive consumption and by competitive salesmanship, spread to all classes, and the simple life was no longer satisfying. Now, "it is everlastingly repeated that it is man's nature to be eternally dissatisfied, constantly to advance, without relief or rest, toward an indefinite goal. The longing for infinity is daily represented as a mark of moral distinction. . . . The doctrine of the most ruthless and swift progress has become an article of faith.[15]

Planned acquisition through hard work and careful saving became a virtue, and failure to acquire became evidence of poor character. The doctrine of equality meant that each man was to compete against all comers, even if his social and economic status put him at great disadvantage in doing so. As Durkheim said:

> Overweening ambition always exceeds the results obtained, great as they may be, since there is no warning to pause here. Nothing gives satisfaction and all this agitation is uninterruptedly maintained without appeasement. Above all, since this race of an unattainable goal can give no other pleasure but that of the race itself, if it is one, once it is interrupted the participants are left empty-handed. At the same time the struggle grows more violent and painful, both from being less controlled and because competition is greater. All classes contend among themselves because no established classification any longer exists. Effort grows, just when it becomes less productive.[16]

In sum, this analysis maintains that in the attempt to locate and train the most talented persons to occupy technical roles, industrial societies maintain that goals of personal, material success are available to all, regardless of social origins. By maintaining that great economic rewards are available to all, and by maintaining that achievement of the rewards is a sign of moral worth,[17] an optimum number of persons can be motivated to compete for the rewards. But the social structure of industrialized societies is not necessarily consistent with this set of values, this culture. The social structure is the patterned sets of relationships among people and, as Merton has pointed out, in industrial societies this structure effectively blocks access to success goals for some parts of the population.[18]

One result is invention of a set of values which makes it "all right," even if illegal, to achieve success by routes other than the standard ones provided in the social structure. A set of values of this kind is "deviant," or "delinquent," or "criminal," in the sense that it inspires persons to achieve success by means which are not sanctioned by the legal institutions of society. Normative conflict is present, and both individuals and groups now have the opportunity to learn

[15]Durkheim, *Suicide*, p. 257.

[16]Ibid., p. 253.

[17]See Max Weber, *The Protestant Ethic and the Spirit of Capitalism*, trans. Talcott Parsons (London: Allen and Unwin, 1930).

[18]Robert K. Merton, *Social Theory and Social Structure*, rev. and enl. ed. (Glencoe, Ill.: Free Press, 1957), chaps. 4 and 5.

illegitimate as well as legitimate means for achieving personal success. In this kind of social arrangement, multiple moralities develop. The "rules of the game" embodied in criminal laws may be known to those who evade them, but the emotional supports which accompany conformity to these rules are offset by the stress on the success goal and by the "rules for violating rules" which develop in these circumstances. As Merton has said: "It is only when a system of cultural values extols, virtually above all else, certain *common* success-goals for the population at large while the social structure rigorously restricts or completely closes access to approved modes of reaching these goals *for a considerable part of the same population,* that deviant behavior ensues on a large scale.[19]

Cloward and Ohlin have summarized the general observations on the origins of delinquent and criminal subcultures and, thus, the observations on the origins of normative conflict, in the following terms:

> Interaction among those sharing the same problem [discrepancies between aspiration and opportunity] may provide encouragement for the withdrawal of sentiments in support of the established system of norms. Once freed of allegiance to the existing set of rules, such persons may devise . . . delinquent means of achieving success. A collective delinquent solution to an adjustment problem is more likely to evolve by this process in a society in which the legitimacy of social rules can be questioned apart from their moral validity. . . . What seems expedient, rational, and efficient often becomes separable from what is traditional, sacred, and moral as a basis for the imputation of legitimacy. Under such conditions it is difficult for persons at different social positions to agree about the forms of conduct that are both expedient and morally right. Once this separation takes place, the supporting structure of the existing system of norms becomes highly vulnerable.[20]

Many types of delinquent, criminal, and deviant subcultures exist in contemporary society, with the result that normative conflict is present on a large scale. Accordingly, no juvenile gang, neighborhood group, ethnic group, or social class needs to invent a criminal subculture in order to take on a high rate of criminality. Although new sets of values which make delinquency and criminality "all right" even if illegal are invented from time to time, most apparent inventions are merely variations on themes invented long ago. As Bordua has observed, "Each generation does not meet and solve anew the problems of class structure barriers to opportunity but begins with the solution of its forbears. This is why reform efforts can be so slow to succeed.[21]

[19]Ibid., p. 146. It should be noted that in this statement Professor Merton slips into a theory of deviant behavior, rather than limiting himself to a theory of the origin of deviant subcultures. Deviant behavior on a large scale can arise only *after* invention of deviant subcultures. This point will be discussed in Chapter 9.

[20]Richard A. Cloward and Lloyd E. Ohlin, *Delinquency and Opportunity: A Theory of Delinquent Gangs* (Glencoe, Ill.: Free Press, 1960), pp. 108–9.

[21]David J. Bordua, "Delinquent Subcultures: Sociological Interpretations of Gang Delinquency," *Annals of the American Academy of Political and Social Science,* 338:119–36, 1961.

However, it appears that various types of delinquent subcultures have arisen, and thrive, at different locations in the social structure. The evidence is fragmentary, impressionistic, and uncoordinated, but it seems to indicate that some types of delinquent and criminal subcultures have arisen in large metropolitan centers and particularly in those areas of cities that are characterized by poverty, while other types have arisen in middle-class areas or, as indicated by values conducive to the commission of white-collar crimes, in upper-class areas.

Because the sets of delinquent and criminal values are located in different parts of the social structure, they are not equally available for adoption by all segments of the society. Working-class persons living in areas inhabited by certain racial and ethnic groups in large American cities have available for adoption a different kind of criminal subculture than do upper-class persons.[22] High delinquency and crime rates of various kinds become, from this perspective, "location data" which direct the attention of researchers to the study of the origin and continuation of various kinds of delinquent and criminal subcultures in various parts of the society.

In one of the best studies using such location data as a stimulus to exploration of the origin of a type of delinquent subculture, Cohen examined "non-utilitarian" delinquency.[23] Statistical data indicated that a destructive kind of "hell-raising" vandalism was more prevalent among working-class boys than among middle-class boys. Traditionally, criminologists have assumed that such data indicate the existence of a delinquent subculture and, thus, a high incidence of normative conflict among working-class boys, and then they have gone on to try to explain how the delinquent subculture is taken over by individual boys. Cohen, on the other hand, followed the leads provided by Durkheim and Merton and asked why such a subculture is there to be taken over. The theory he developed in response to this question maintains that the nonutilitarian delinquent subculture has arisen in response to a conflict between the aspirations inspired by middle-class values and the ability and opportunity that working-class boys have for fulfilling these aspirations. Middle-class values have been incorporated into the law and into other general codes of legitimate and moral conduct, codes which prescribe proper conduct for everyone.

At the same time, however, society is organized in such a way that all working-class persons cannot achieve the goals implied in these values—goals such as personal "success" and achievement of the kind requiring rational, honest labor, careful long-range planning, and deferral of gratifications. For example, while all youths might be inspired with the notion that anyone who works honestly and soberly can graduate from college, and with the idea that it is advantageous to graduate from college, the fact is that some youths entering this competition will be defeated, for they are not adequately equipped for the competition. In response to this conflict between values and social structure, rules have been developed for

[22]See Irving Spergel, *Racketville, Slumtown, Haulburg: An Exploratory Study of Delinquent Subcultures* (Chicago: University of Chicago Press, 1964).

[23]Albert K. Cohen, *Delinquent Boys: The Culture of the Gang* (Glencoe, Ill.: Free Press, 1955), esp. pp. 121–37.

achieving personal success by turning the middle-class rules "upside down." Once this subculture had been invented, youths could achieve a symbol of status, for example, either by doing well in school or by vandalizing the school at night. Or, more generally, they could achieve a symbol of status either by getting a good education, working hard, and saving their money until they were able to join the country club, or by doing none of these things and, instead, ripping up the country club's golf greens late at night.

It should be noted that Cohen's theory does not attempt to account for the delinquency or nondelinquency of any particular juvenile. It is a theory that explains why certain values are more readily available for learning by some youths than by others. Since the rules for nonutilitarian delinquency are carried, by and large, by working-class persons, they are more readily available for learning by working-class persons than by middle-class persons. Further, since the rules for delinquency arise in connection with differences between culturally defined aspirations regarding success, on the one hand, and opportunities for achieving this success, on the other. they are more readily available for learning by boys than by girls.

Walter B. Miller's study of working-class delinquency showed more concern for diffusion of delinquency values within the working class than for the origin of these rules for delinquency among working-class people. Unlike Cohen, he has not developed a specific theory which attempts to account for the development of certain of the rules for delinquency. Instead, Miller develops the notion that working-class values include a delinquent subculture.[24] Accordingly, he finds the origin of the delinquent subculture in the values of the working class, but he does not report in detail on the structural conditions leading to the invention of these values. Essentially, Miller sees working-class values emerging from the shaking-down process of immigration, internal migration, and vertical mobility.[25] Normative conflict has developed on a class basis, and, accordingly, rules for delinquency are present for learning by lower-class boys.

For example, Miller observes an intense concern for "toughness" and "masculinity" in lower-class culture, a concern which is expressed in a set of rules demanding that boys "act tough" in certain circumstances. Since "acting tough" and "being tough" often are defined as delinquency by the agencies of law enforcement, the stress on toughness amounts to a delinquent subculture. Miller emphasizes the importance of the structure of the family relationships in the working class to development of this delinquent subculture in that class:

A significant proportion of lower-class males are reared in a predominantly female household and lack a consistently present male figure with whom to identify and from

[24]Walter B. Miller, "Lower Class Culture as a Generating Milieu of Gang Delinquency," *Journal of Social Issues*, 14:5–19, 1958.

[25]See Bordua, "Delinquent Subcultures"; and Walter B. Miller, "Implications of Urban Lower Class Culture for Social Work," *Social Service Review*, 33:219–36, 1959.

whom to learn essential components of a "male" role. Since women serve as a primary object of identification during the pre-adolescent years, the almost obsessive lower-class concern with "masculinity" probably resembles a type of compulsive reaction-formation.[26]

Miller's thesis has been reduced by Cloward and Ohlin to three main propositions: (1) The lower class is characterized by distinctive values. (2) These values vary markedly from the middle-class values which undergird the legal code. (3) The result is that conformity with certain lower-class values may automatically result in violation of the law.[27] As Miller says, "Engaging in certain cultural practices which comprise essential elements of the total life pattern of lower-class culture automatically violates certain legal norms.[28] This observation is consistent with one made earlier by two astute observers of American social life:

> Activities [such as] gregarious theft and gang warfare by the boys and gregarious sex by the girls appear to be channels for the playful, sociable and conformist impulses of the lower-class youth. If, in many urban areas, we find a lower-class boy or girl who is not delinquent in this sense, we can be fairly sure that he or she is either headed up the class ladder or is psychologically deviant or both, being unwilling or unable to join in the group activities sanctioned by peers.[29]

Cloward and Ohlin have attempted to account for the invention of delinquent subcultures in terms which closely resemble those used by Cohen. Their concern, like that of Miller, is more for the question of why delinquent subcultures persist and diffuse once they are invented, than for the question of how they get invented in the first place. Nevertheless, they follow the writings of Durkheim and Merton to the conclusion that at least three different types of delinquent subcultures have been invented as a response to a clash between values which promote unlimited economic aspirations and a social structure which restricts accomplishment of the aspirations. They then go on to observe that among some segments of the population even the possibilities of legitimately achieving *limited* success goals are also restricted, and they find three delinquent subcultures being invented in these areas of poor opportunity.

Two of these subcultures provide illegal avenues to success goals; these are the "criminal subculture," which contains rules for the pursuit of material gain by means such as theft, extortion, and fraud, and the "conflict subculture," which contains rules for the achievement of status through manipulation of force or the threat of force. The other subculture, the "retreatist subculture," contains rules favoring the consumption of drugs. The basic notion here is that the subcultures are invented when aspirations are frustrated and when the frustration is diagnosed

[26]Miller, "Lower Class Culture as a Generating Milieu of Gang Delinquency," p. 9.

[27]Cloward and Ohlin, *Delinquency and Opportunity*, p. 65.

[28]W. C. Kvaraceus and W. B. Miller, *Delinquent Behavior: Culture and the Individual* (Washington: National Education Association, 1959), pp. 68–69.

[29]Reuel Denney and David Riesman, "Leisure in Urbanized America," in *Reader in Urban Sociology*, ed. Paul K. Hatt (Glencoe, Ill.: Free Press, 1951), p. 471. See also David M. Downes, *The Delinquent Solution: A Study in Subcultural Theory* (London: Routledge and Kegan Paul, 1966).

as due to the conditions of the social order rather than to personal attributes of the interacting but frustrated population.[30]

If, once invented, a delinquent subculture is to persist, there must be devices for passing the norms, values, and rules for delinquency on to newcomers, whether these newcomers are children of the participants or immigrants from another area where the subculture does not exist. For example, the "criminal subculture" described by Cloward and Ohlin is rather stable, and one source of this stability is the network of bonds that exists between age levels.[31] Children are linked with adolescent delinquents and share their normative conflict; adolescent delinquents, in turn, are linked with young adult offenders, who, in turn, are linked with adult criminals.[32] The delinquent subculture is carried by a broad, age-linked population. On the other hand, the "conflict subculture" is less stable, probably because devices for socializing newcomers into it have not developed to the same degree. While any newcomer must learn the values of the conflict subculture, the subculture is carried by adolescents, not by children and adults. Accordingly, those persons who have been socialized do not move onward through a set of age-graded patterns; they tend to be guided by other values when they reach young adulthood, rather than moving on to an "adult" form of violence. The population carrying the values of the conflict subculture is small and diffuse.

Discovery of the processes leading to the invention of delinquent and criminal subcultures whose existence establishes normative conflict in a society does not explain either the behavior of individual delinquents and criminals or the distribution of crime and delinquency rates. Even in societies disproportionately stressing success goals to the degree that delinquent subcultures are invented, most persons do not use illegitimate means for achieving the approved ends. Rather, in a multigroup type of social organization, conflicting standards of conduct are possessed by various groups. Normative conflict is not distributed evenly throughout the society. An individual who is a member of one group will use one means for achieving the success goal, while an individual having membership in another group will use another means.

McKay has pointed out that alternative educational processes are in operation

[30]Cloward and Ohlin, *Delinquency and Opportunity*, pp. 111–24. See also Wendling and Elliott, "Class and Race Differentials"; and Wan Sang Han, "Discrepancy in Socioeconomic Level of Aspiration and Perception of Illegitimate Expediency," *American Journal of Sociology*, 74:240–47, 1968.

[31]Cloward and Ohlin do not make a careful distinction between gang activities and the delinquent subcultures on which gang activities are based, with the result that it is difficult to determine when they are concerned with the invention of a delinquent subculture and when they are concerned with the distribution of the values of this subculture to individuals. See the discussion of gangs in Chapter 9. For an excellent study of the way the behavioral rules making up a deviant subculture get invented, see John K. Irwin, "Surfers: A Study of the Growth of a Deviant Subculture" (Master's thesis, Department of Sociology, University of California, Berkeley, 1965).; and idem, "Deviant Behavior as a Subcultural Phenomenon," in *The Sociology of Subcultures*, ed. David O. Arnold (Berkeley: Glendessary Press, 1970), pp. 109–11.

[32]See Gerald Robin, "Gang Member Delinquency," *Journal of Criminal Law, Criminology, and Police Science*, 55:59–65, 1964.

and that a child may be educated in either "conventioral" or criminal means of achieving success.[33] Cloward has shown that even unsanctioned means of attaining success are not available to everyone; some persons may be "double failures," in the sense that neither legitimate nor illegitimate means for achieving success are available to them:

> Note, for example, variations in the degree to which members of various classes are fully exposed to and thus acquire the values, education, and skills which facilitate upward mobility. It should not be startling, therefore, to find similar variations in the availability of illegitimate means.[34]

MOBILITY

The industrial and democratic revolutions were accompanied by increased mobility as well as by a conflict between increased aspirations and conditions of the social structure. The new condition of mobility was compatible with the individualistic ideology, and it was at the same time incompatible with political absolutism. In the first place, the large family and the homogeneous neighborhood, which had been the principal agencies of social control, disintegrated, primarily as a result of mobility. They were replaced by the small family, consisting of parents and children, detached from other relatives, and by a neighborhood in which the *mores* were not homogeneous. Many family functions were transferred to other social institutions, resulting in a weak family unit in which the members had relatively few activities or interests in common. Similarly, the neighborhood ceased to function as an effective socializing agency in which the pressures for conformity were intimate, personal, and consistent.

Second, with increased mobility the problem of control was greatly intensified, for the boundaries of frequent and effective interaction were extended from the local community to nations and then to most of the earth in the form of commerce, travel, newspapers, and other means of communication. When interaction was confined to the local community, spontaneous and sentimental influences controlled behavior, for the effect of the behavior of a person was immediately apparent to self and to others. When interaction extended beyond the area of intimate association, the effects of the behavior were not immediately discernible either to the members of any local community or to the participants in the broader area of interaction.

Because of increased mobility, a condition of anonymity was created, and the agencies by which control had been secured in almost all earlier societies were

---

[33]Henry D. McKay, "The Neighborhood and Child Conduct," *Annals of the American Academy of Political and Social Science*, 261:32–42, 1949. See also South Side Community Committee, *Bright Shadows in Bronzetown* (Chicago: South Side Community Committee, 1949), pp. 26–28.

[34]Richard A. Cloward, "Illegitimate Means, Anomie, and Deviant Behavior," *American Sociological Review*, 24:164–76, 1959. See also Albert K. Cohen and James F. Short, Jr., "Research in Delinquent Subcultures," *Journal of Social Issues*, 14:20–37, 1958.

greatly weakened.[35] It is probable that the family and neighborhood would have been relatively impotent to control their members in activities with outsiders, even if they had been retained in their original strength, for these agencies cannot be effective in the control of behavior occurring far away from their location. A certain national loyalty, somewhat comparable to the loyalties in the earlier primary groups, flourished in connection with the doctrine of the divinity of royalty. But apparently the common people did not take this doctrine as seriously as did royalty, and when the belief in the doctrine disintegrated, no effective substitute was found.

We may conclude that mobility of persons and of commodities widens the area within which control becomes necessary and at the same time weakens the local agencies of control in the communities into which the migrants move. On the one hand, "over-attention to movement and under-attention to settlement are the villains that destroy local defensible community space."[36] On the other hand, "people who occupy a marginal status are continually confronted with the necessity of forming moral judgments. Situations that would be routine for other people call for choice."[37] However, this conclusion is not based on sufficient evidence to justify a definitive statement regarding the significance of mobility to criminality. It is possible that rapid changes in technology may create a situation in which the criminal laws, written for social conditions as they existed before the technological changes, must almost necessarily be violated if the new technologies are to be retained.[38] However, certain students of law have insisted that the prevalence of crime is due to the fact that the law has been extended much more rapidly than the general *mores*, and that when the law is not thus supported by general *mores* it is relatively unimportant and is violated frequently. In either case, the most relevant variable is the normative conflict which has arisen to provide alternative patterns of conduct, some of which are clearly violations of the criminal law.[39] The author of *Future Shock* has put the matter this way:

In each year since 1948 one out of five Americans changed his address, picking up his children, some household effects, and starting life anew at a fresh place. Even the greatest migrations of history, the Mongol hordes, the westward movement of Europeans in the nineteenth century, seem puny by comparison. . . . Any relocation, of necessity destroys a complex web-work of old relationships and establishes a set of new ones. It is this

[35]See Joel Samaha, *Law and Order in Historical Perspective: The Case of Elizabethan Essex* (New York: Academic Press, 1974); and Douglas Hay, Peter Linebaugh, John G. Rule, E. P. Thompson, and Cal Winslow, *Albion's Fatal Tree: Crime and Society in Eighteenth-Century England* (New York: Pantheon, 1975).

[36]H. L. Niebert, "Crime Prevention by Urban Design," *Transaction: Social Science and Modern Society*, 12:41–47, 1974.

[37]Tomatsu Shibutani, *Society and Personality* (Englewood Cliffs, N. J.: Prentice-Hall, 1961), p. 578.

[38]W. F. Ogburn, *Social Change*, 2d ed. (New York: Viking Press, 1952), pt. 4.

[39]See Weinberg, "Urbanization and Male Delinquency in Ghana"; and Denis Szabo, "Societe de masse et inadaptations psycho-culturelles," *Revue Francaise de Sociology*, 6:472–86, 1965.

disruption that, especially if repeated more than once, breeds the "loss of commitment" that many writers have noted among the highly mobiles.[40]

A few studies of the relationship between horizontal mobility and the crime rate have been made, most of them in the 1930s, but they have been directed toward analysis of the direct effects of mobility in a contemporary situation. They fail to measure the full significance of mobility, for the effects of this process on criminality are principally indirect and are diffused over a period of time and over a wide area.[41] A few data are presented, however, as illustrations of the first efforts to study this process. McKenzie found a correlation of 0.39 between juvenile delinquency and mobility by wards in Columbus, and Sullenger found a correlation of 0.34 in a similar study in Omaha.[42] Carpenter concluded that a criminal group studied in Buffalo was much more migratory than a control group in the same city.[43] A more recent study, of a sample of 787 Dutch children, showed that children who had never moved had the lowest delinquency rates, that those who had moved 1–3 times had intermediate rates, and that children who had moved four or more times had the highest delinquency rates.[44] A national survey of the United States has shown that blacks, who have higher crime rates than whites, also move more often than whites, though their mobility is more local.[45] Reiss showed that 39 percent of a group of delinquent probationers in Chicago had resided at their present address for less than three years, and the Gluecks found that 33.6 percent of their delinquents, as compared with only 14.8 percent of the nondelinquents, were at their present address for less than one year.[46]

These statistics give some understanding of the reason why the word *traveler* in medieval England was used in popular discourse to designate the thief. Such statistics, however, are entirely inadequate as demonstrations of the significance of horizontal mobility, for the important point is that mobility has affected all persons in modern society and not merely those who are nonresidents at the time of a crime:

Urbanization and industrialization have affected the development of community relationships by increasing the rate of family mobility. Mobility has eroded the sense of

[40]Alvin Toffler, *Future Shock* (New York: Bantam Books, 1970), pp. 78–79.

[41]O. Kinberg, "On So-Called Vagrancy," *Journal of Criminal Law and Criminology*, 24:552–583, 1933; and Clinard and Abbot, *Crime in Developing Countries*, pp. 108–127.

[42]R. D. McKenzie, "The Neighborhood," *American Journal of Sociology*, 28:156, 1921; T. E. Sullenger, *Social Determinants in Juvenile Delinquency* (New York: John Wiley, 1936), p. 179 See also Sullenger, "The Social Significance of Mobility: An Omaha Study," *American Journal of Sociology*, 55:559–564, 1950.

[43]Niles Carpenter and William M. Haenszel, "Migratoriness and Criminality in Buffalo," *Social Forces*, 9:254–55, 1930.

[44]W. Buikhuisen and H. Timmerman, "Verhuizing en Criminaliteit" [Moving and Crime], *Nederlands Tijdschrift voor Criminologie*, 12:34–39, 1970.

[45]Ronald J. McAllister, Edward J. Kaiser, and Edgar W. Butler, "Residential Mobility of Blacks and Whites: A National Longitudinal Survey," *American Journal of Sociology*, 77:445–56, 1971.

[46]Albert J. Reiss, Jr., "The Accuracy, Efficiency, and Validity of a Prediction Instrument," *American Journal of Sociology*, 56:552–61, 1951. Sheldon and Eleanor T. Glueck, *Unraveling Juvenile Delinquency* (New York: Commonwealth Fund, 1950), p. 80.

community, diminishing opportunity for the development of role relationships based on roots in a neighborhood. It is important to have a variety of role contacts, particularly across age groups; yet increasingly in urban areas adults interact with friends who are scattered throughout the metropolitan area and not with individuals who live in the same building or block. There is a reduction of long-term interest in youth on the part of conforming adults outside the family. Young people are mobile, meeting friends away from home and away from the neighborhood where informal social controls are more likely to be exercised. Once a certain proportion of the population has developed this postindustrial pattern, one can no longer speak of it as a community.[47]

CULTURE CONFLICT

Like "social disorganization," the concept of *culture conflict* has been used to refer to social conditions characterized by a lack of consistency in the influences which direct the individual. The concept has not been clearly formulated, however, for it sometimes is used as a synonym for normative conflict and sometimes is restricted to only the normative conflict arising from migration of conduct norms from one area to another.[48] As we have seen, normative conflict can develop *within* a culture, without the introduction of norms from other cultural areas. It also can arise when the norms of one cultural area come into conflict with those of another. Most of the American research on the relationships between culture conflict and crime has been concerned with normative conflict arising in the latter process, the interpenetration of cultural codes. This emphasis no doubt reflects an interest in America's "immigrant problem."[49]

Conflicts between the norms of behavior in divergent cultural codes may arise in at least three ways. First, the codes may clash on the border of contiguous culture areas. Speck observed, for example, that:

> Where the bands popularly known as the Montagnais have come more and more into contact with Whites, their reputation has fallen lower among the traders who have known them through commercial relationships within that period. The accusation is made that they have become less honest in connection with their debts, less trustworthy with property, less truthful, and more inclined to alcoholism and sexual freedom as contacts with the frontier towns have become easier for them.[50]

With increased mobility and the development of communication processes, the border between such divergent cultures has become extremely broad, for knowledge concerning divergent conduct norms no longer arises solely out of direct personal contacts. The old social relations and standards of behavior which had been adequate for control while Palestine was relatively isolated from the rest

---

[47]Paul C. Friday and Jerald Hage, "Youth Crime in Postindustrial Societies: An Integrated Perspective," *Criminology*, 14:347–68, 1976. See also H. MacCoby, "The Differential Political Activity of Participants in a Voluntary Association," *American Sociological Review*, 23:524–32, 1958.

[48]See Donald R. Cressey, "Culture Conflict, Differential Association, and Normative Conflict," chap. 4 in *Crime and Culture: Essays in Honor of Thorsten Sellin*, ed. Marvin E. Wolfgang (New York: Wiley, 1968), pp. 43–54.

[49]See Chapter 7.

[50]Speck, "Ethical Attributes of Labrador Indians," p. 561.

of the world have proved inadequate in more recent years, when the cultures of other groups have been introduced into Israel through impersonal means. Remarkable changes in criminality have occurred.[51] Similar effects have also been observed in South Africa:

> An important factor in producing criminal behavior is culture conflict. This discontinuity is seen in the movement of hundreds of thousands of Bantus from the "Veld," the native reserves, and even other parts of Africa to the cities where a new set of physical and personal associations surrounds the individual. There is a breakdown in primary controls that follows detribalization with the introduction of cash economy, accelerated mobility, personal anonymity, and new leisure time pursuits. . . . One aspect of nonconforming behavior has been gang life among the [African] juvenile offenders.[52]

Second, in colonization the laws and norms of one cultural group may be extended to cover the territory of another, with the result that traditional ways of behaving suddenly become illegal. For example, when Soviet law was extended to Siberian tribes, women who obeyed the Soviet law and laid aside their veils were killed by their relatives for violating the norms of the tribes. Wearing a veil was illegal from the point of view of Soviet law, and not wearing a veil was illegal from the point of view of tribal law. Similarly, before French law was introduced in Algeria, the killing of an adulterous woman was the right and duty of the woman's father or brother; but under the French law such killing became a crime punishable by death.

Third, when participants in one culture migrate to another culture, they may take with them ways of behaving which clash with the norms of the receiving culture. This process is the reverse of the one just discussed, and it occurs when the migrant group is politically weaker than the group whose territory is invaded. If the Algerians in the above illustration had moved to France, they would have introduced divergent norms in that nation.

After a period of dominance by English customs and laws, many conflicting norms were introduced in the United States by this process. Generally, the immigrant population, having reached maturity in the Old World environment, remains relatively isolated and has a relatively low crime rate when the immigrants settle in America, but some studies show that the sons of immigrants have a much higher crime rate than their parents or the native-born of native parentage, apparently because the second generation, like the Siberian women, finds it difficult to identify the proper ways of behaving.

TENDENCIES TOWARD INTEGRATION

During the last century, especially, the individualistic system in business and politics has been modified in its material aspects. Free competition was ruining

[51]See Shlomo Shoham, "Culture Conflict as a Frame of Reference for Research in Criminology and Social Deviation," chap. 5 in *Crime and Culture*, ed. Wolfgang, pp. 55–82.

[52]R. Williamson, "Crime in South Africa: Some Aspects of Causes and Treatment," *Journal of Criminal Law, Criminology, and Police Science*, 48:185–92, 1957. See also Clinard and Abbott, *Crime in Developing Countries*.

individuals, and they abandoned it in favor of collective activities. Huge multinational corporations, huge banks, chain stores, chain theaters, chain newspapers, and broadcasting networks developed. Trade associations, labor unions, chambers of commerce, and many other associations also were formed. To an increasing extent, the behavior and opportunities of individuals are determined and defined by these collectivities and associations.[53] The ideology of individualism still remains in a world of corporate activity. This may be seen in the frequency with which the directors and officers of corporations are traitors to their stockholders, in the competition between associations for financial advantages, and in many other ways. But the general development has been from feudalism and absolutism to individualism, and from individualism to private collectivism.

In the United States, the national wealth has been increasingly controlled by fewer and fewer corporations, primarily because the corporations gaining government privileges have been able to use them to gain still more privileges. Favorable legislation has been piled on favorable legislation, monopolies have monopolized monopolies, and merged corporations have merged with merged corporations until government and big business have become at the highest levels one enterprise rather than two.[54] As the late Senator Philip Hart of Michigan put it, "When a corporation wants to discuss something with its political representative, you can be sure it will be heard. When a company operates in thirty states, it will be heard by thirty times as many representatives."[55] One result of such legislative listening has been a fusion of corporation and government or, perhaps more accurately, transformation of the nation into a huge corporation with its own board of directors at the top.

There seems to be no real inclination to unscramble corporate mergers and thus to abandon the system of private collectivism in favor of a return to the competitive system of earlier generations. It is just possible, on the contrary, that individualism and normative conflict will diminish as more and more people, especially poor ones, are given full membership in the socialistic system which the corporate complex demanded and created. Such integration is, after all, what is implied by the term "welfare state."

Four tendencies toward social integration, aside from the corporate activities described above, seem to have appeared in the modern world First, a wider uniformity of behavior and a greater degree of identification of self with others are secured by newspapers, radio, theaters, television, and public education. This interest, however, tends to be restricted in scope or is concerned with ephemeral incidents. Its importance may be indicated in relation to bribery of athletes. In

[53]See Manfred Rehbinder, "Status, Contract, and the Welfare State," *Stanford Law Review*, 23:941–55, 1971; and Robert Childres and Stephen J. Spitz, "Status in the Law of Contract," *New York University Law Review*, 47:1–31, 1972.

[54]See Donald R. Cressey, "Restraint of Trade, Recidivism, and Delinquent Neighborhoods," in *Delinquency, Crime and Society*, ed. James F. Short, Jr. (Chicago: University of Chicago Press, 1976), pp. 209–38.

[55]Quoted by Milton Viorst, "Gentlemen Prefer Monopoly: The Impotence of Antitrust Law," *Harper's Magazine*, 245:32–38, November, 1972.

1919, when a notorious gambler and gangster bribed some of the baseball players in the world series to throw the game, a tremendous pressure for punishment of the players and the briber was exerted. Bribery of a member of the president's cabinet provoked less popular antagonism than the bribery of these baseball players. An almost identical reaction to bribery of college basketball players occurred thirty years later. The players were dismissed and in some states laws were enacted which made the penalty for giving bribes in athletic contests more severe than the penalty for robbery with a gun. On this point, the public, or that part of it which counted in athletics, presented a united front. It is possible that baseball or some other sport could become the nucleus around which public morality may be unified, as has been claimed of cricket in England; but in general the public interests, like the communication media which largely create them, are fluctuating, unstable, and concerned with unimportant things.

A second tendency toward uniformity of thought and attitudes was seen in the artificial efforts to develop nationalsim in Europe, as in the Nazi regime in Germany, Fascism in Italy, Sovietism in Russia, and dictatorships in other countries. These movements, like the New Deal in the United States and more recent manifestations of a "welfare state" both in the United States and abroad, were gropings toward social organization to replace the individualism which had broken down or was breaking down economically, legally, and politically.

Third, the rise of suburban living in the United States, a leveling-off of the birth rate, and the near-elimination of immigration should permit the development of a cultural homogeneity that has not been possible since the early nineteenth century. The passing of the population-expansion phase of our history, together with industrial decentralization, may lead to a cessation of city growth, may permit the development of neighborhoods and residential suburbs of a primary-group type, and may reduce the speculative aspect of economic life.

A fourth tendency toward homogeneity may be found in the development of scientific activities and intellectual honesty. The proportion of scientific people in modern society is not large, but the results of science have permeated all society to a greater or lesser extent. The attitude of scientific inquiry is an important variable to be considered in analysis of changes in some of the old institutions. A characteristic of the changes in social organization described earlier was their incompatibility with intellectual honesty.[56]

SUGGESTED READINGS

Arnold, David O., ed. *The Sociology of Subcultures.* Berkeley: Glendessary Press, 1970.
Arnold, Thurman. *The Folklore of Capitalism.* New Haven: Yale University Press, 1937.
Bell, Daniel. "Crime as an American Way of Life." *Antioch Review,* 13:131–54, 1953.
Blake, Judith, & Kingsley Davis. "Norms, Values, and Sanctions." Chapter 13 in *Handbook of Modern Sociology,* edited by Robert E. L. Faris, pp. 456–484. Chicago: Rand McNally, 1964.

[56]Noam Chomsky, "The Responsibility of Intellectuals," *The New York Review of Books,* February 23, 1967; and Kai T. Erikson, "Sociology: That Awkward Age," *Social Problems* 19:431–36, 1972.

Bordua, David J. "Delinquent Subcultures: Sociological Interpretations of Gang Delinquency." *Annals of the American Academy of Political and Social Science,* 338:119–136, 1961.

Clinard, Marshall B., & Daniel J. Abbott. *Crime in Developing Countries: A Comparative Perspective.* New York: Wiley, 1973.

Cloward, Richard A., & Lloyd E. Ohlin. *Delinquency and Opportunity: A Theory of Delinquent Gangs,* Glencoe, Ill.: Free Press, 1960.

Cohen, Albert K. *Delinquent Boys: The Culture of the Gang.* Glencoe, Ill.: Free Press, 1955.

De Fleur, Lois B. *Delinquency in Argentina: A Study of Cordoba's Youth.* Pullman, Wash.: Washington State University Press, 1970.

Dewey, John. "Individualism, Old and New." *New Republic,* 61:239–241, 294–296; 62:13–16, 184–188, 1930.

Durkheim, Emile. *Suicide: A Study in Sociology.* Translated by John A. Spaulding and George Simpson. Glencoe, Ill.: Free Press, 1951.

Gurr, Ted Robert. *Rogues, Rebels, and Reformers: A Political History of Urban Crime and Conflict.* Beverly Hills, Calif.: Sage, 1976.

Hall, A. C. *Crime in Its Relation to Social Progress.* New York: Columbia University Press, 1902.

Hay, Douglas, Peter Linebaugh, John G. Rule, E. P. Thompson, & Cal Winslow. *Albion's Fatal Tree: Crime and Society in Eighteenth-Century England.* New York: Pantheon, 1975.

Hobsbawm, E. J. *Primitive Rebels.* New York: W. W. Norton, 1959.

Kaplow, Jeffry. *The Names of Kings: The Parisian Laboring Poor in the Eighteenth Century.* New York: Basic Books, 1972.

Matza, David, & Gresham M. Sykes. "Juvenile Delinquency and Subterranean Values." *American Sociological Review,* 26:712–719, 1961.

Miller, Walter B. "Subculture, Social Reform and the 'Culture of Poverty'." *Human Organization,* 30:111–125, 1971.

Quinney, Richard. *Class, State and Crime: On the Theory and Practice of Criminal Justice.* New York: David McKay, 1977.

Samaha, Joel. *Law and Order in Historical Perspective: The Case of Elizabethan Essex.* New York: Academic Press, 1974.

Sellin, Thorsten. *Culture Conflict and Crime.* New York: Social Science Research Council, 1938.

Short, James F., Jr., & Fred L. Strodtbeck. *Group Process and Gang Delinquency.* Chicago: University of Chicago Press, 1965.

Spergel, Irving. *Racketville, Slumtown, Haulburg: An Exploratory Study of Delinquent Subcultures.* Chicago: University of Chicago Press, 1964.

Veblen, Thorstein. *Theory of the Leisure Class.* New York: Macmillan, 1912.

Weber, Max. *The Protestant Ethic and the Spirit of Capitalism.* Translated by Talcott Parsons. London: Allen and Unwin, 1930.

Wirth, Louis. "Culture Conflicts and Delinquency." *Social Forces,* 9:484–492, 1931.

Wirth, Louis. "Urbanism as a Way of Life." *American Journal of Sociology,* 44:1–24, 1938.

Wolfgang, Marvin E., ed. *Crime and Culture: Essays in Honor of Thorsten Sellin.* New York: Wiley, 1968.

6

Age and Sex Ratios

Although crime and criminality are by definition social phenomena, people have for centuries entertained the notion that they are the products of nonsocial causes. This notion has been expressed in many essays and research studies on the relationship between crime rates and certain physical conditions of the earth, and on the relationship between criminality and certain aspects of the biological makeup of the criminal. The data have been largely confined to arrest and incarceration rates and to criminals who are arrested and prosecuted; the white-collar criminal and the unapprehended criminal are not represented. This chapter treats age and gender as social statuses rather than as biological characteristics. Thus, age and gender affect associations with criminal behavior patterns and anticriminal behavior patterns. Physical and biological conditions which do not affect social interaction are not statistically associated with crime and criminality.

PHYSICAL ENVIRONMENT

For many generations, scholars attempted to find relationships between crime and physical conditions which would enable them to demonstrate physical determinants of criminal behavior. There are no recent studies. Older studies reported that crimes against property are more frequent in winter months and that crimes against the person are more frequent in summer months; and, analogous to this, that crimes against property increase, and crimes against the person decrease, with the distance from the equator. Other scholars have said that crimes are frequent in mountainous areas and infrequent in plains areas, or are frequent near the coast and infrequent in the interior.[1] It has been claimed also that crime rates vary with changes in barometric pressure and with wind direction.[2]

[1] The research studies on this point are reviewed in G. Aschaffenburg, *Crime and Its Repression* (Boston: Little, Brown, 1913), pp. 16–30; Gerhard J. Falk, "The Influence of the Seasons on the Crime Rate," *Journal of*

These reports and claims may be appraised in two propositions. First, the association between crime rates and these physical conditions at best is slight; in some cases not even a slight association has been demonstrated. Second, these physical conditions provide the habitat for human life and consequently may facilitate or impede contacts among human beings; perhaps in that sense these conditions are related to opportunities for criminal behavior. For example, the greater frequency of crimes against the person in summer months is probably due to the greater frequency of contacts among human beings in those months rather than to the effects of temperature on propensity to criminality. It has not been demonstrated that changes in physical conditions change either the attitudes and values which are conducive to criminal behavior or the attitudes and values conducive to noncriminal behavior.

HEREDITY

In the early part of the present century the discussion of causes of crime was concentrated on the controversy between heredity and environment, and this controversy continues, with decreasing attention, in the present generation. Five methods have been used in the effort to reach conclusions on the question of whether criminality is hereditary: comparison of criminals with the "savage," family trees, Mendelian ratios in family trees, statistical associations between crimes of parents and of offspring, and comparison of identical and fraternal twins.

Lombroso and his followers used comparisons of criminals and "savages" as their method of studying inheritance of criminality.[3] They held that the typical criminal was a born criminal and attributed this to atavism, or throwback to lower animal and savage life. Their principal evidence that criminality was atavistic was the resemblance of the criminal subjects to the savage, but the characteristics of the savage were assumed, not determined by reliable methods. The result was that Lombroso had no significant proof or explanation of the inheritance of criminality.

Family trees have been used extensively by certain scholars in the effort to prove that criminality is inherited. Perhaps the most famous example is the study of the Jukes family by Dugdale and Estabrook, who reported that of about 1200 members of this family, 140 were criminals, 7 were convicted of murder, 60 of theft, and 50

Criminal Law, Criminology, and Police Science, 43:199–213, 1952; and Sidney J. Kaplan, "The Geography of Crime," in *Sociology of Crime*, ed. Joseph S. Roucek (New York: Philosophical Library, 1961), pp. 160–92.

[2] G. A. Mills, "Suicide and Homicide in Their Relation to Weather Changes," *American Journal of Psychiatry*, 91:669–77, 1934; Manfred Curry, "The Relationship of Weather Conditions, Facial Characteristics, and Crime," *Journal of Criminal Law and Criminology*, 39:253–61, 1948; Ernest LaRoche and Louis Tillery, "Weather and Crime in Tallahassee during 1954," *Journal of Criminal Law, Criminology, and Police Science*, 47:218–19, 1956; and Alex D. Pokorny and Fred Davis, "Homicide and Weather," *American Journal of Psychiatry*, 120:806–8, 1964.

[3] See Chapter 3 above.

of prostitution.[4] Dugdale's methods were so questionable that his conclusions have been roundly denounced.[5] Moreover, even if a study of family trees accurately shows that a trait appears in successive generations, this finding does not prove that the trait is inherited. The use of the fork in eating has been a trait of many families for several generations, but this does not prove that a tendency to use a fork is inherited.

Over sixty years ago, Goring tried to prove by elaborate correlations that the criminalistic tendency is inherited, and that environmental conditions are of slight importance to criminality. He found that, measured by imprisonment, criminality of fathers and sons was correlated by a coefficient of $+.60$, which is very nearly the same as the coefficient for stature, eye color, and other physical traits; brothers had a coefficient of correlation for criminality of $+.45$, which also is approximately the same as for physical traits.[6] Goring reasoned that if the influence of environmental factors on his two correlations were very low, heredity would, by elimination, be the explanation. He divided environmental factors into "contagion" and "force of circumstances," such as poverty and ignorance, and his argument regarding them is as follows: (1) The resemblance of fathers and sons regarding criminality is not due to "contagion." The coefficient of correlation is no higher in crimes of stealing, in which fathers are examples for their sons, than in sex crimes, which fathers ordinarily attempt to conceal from their sons, and in which therefore they are not examples. (2) The resemblance is not due to the "force of circumstances" because, after the influence of defective intelligence is eliminated by the use of partial correlations, the correlation between criminality and "force of circumstances" is negligible.

The defects in Goring's arguments undermined his conclusion that criminality is inherited. There are three principal defects: (1) He did not measure the influence of "environment." He considered only eight environmental conditions, which represent a relatively small part of the total environment. (2) His comparison of stealing and sex offenses is based on an assumption that parental contagion is restricted entirely to techniques of crimes and he did not consider the possibility that transmission of values is more important. (3) He restricted his study to male criminals, although he mentions the fact that the ratio of brothers to sisters in respect to imprisonment is 102 to 6. If criminality is inherited to the same extent that color of the eyes is inherited, it must affect females to the same extent as males unless it is sex-linked. However according to Goring, since the biological predisposition to crime is made up entirely of physical and mental inferiority, sex linkage is not plausible.

The fifth method of measuring the relation of heredity to criminality is the

[4]Richard Dugdale, *The Jukes: A Study in Crime, Pauperism, and Heredity* (New York: Putnam, 1877); A. H. Estabrook, *The Jukes in 1915* (Washington, D.C.: Carnegie Institution, 1916).

[5]Samuel H. Adams, "The Juke Myth," *Saturday Review*, 38:48–49, April 2, 1955.

[6]Charles Goring, *The English Convict* (London: His Majesty's Stationery Office, 1913), p. 369.

comparison of identical twins (the product of a single egg) with fraternal twins (the product of two eggs fertilized by two sperm). Heredity is identical in the former and different in the latter. Lange made a study of thirty pairs of adult male twins; thirteen of the pairs were identical twins, and seventeen pairs were fraternal twins. One member of each pair was a criminal, and whenever the twin was also criminal, the pair was termed "concordant." The problem was to determine whether concordance would be more frequent among the group of identical twins than among the group of fraternal twins. He found that 77 percent of the pairs of identical twins and only 12 percent of the pairs of fraternal twins were concordant, that is, both criminal. The similarity of identical twins with reference to criminality was thus 6.4 times as great as the similarity of fraternal twins.[7] This great similarity was assumed to be a measure of the inheritance of criminality, but it is subject to skepticism on two points. First, the number of cases of each type is very small, and a shift of one or two cases from one category to the other would produce a significant difference in the conclusions. Second, the classification of a particular pair of twins as identical or fraternal is doubtful in many cases, since evidence as to the birth process is seldom available.

Lange's work was hailed as proof of the inheritance of criminality. However, three later studies of twins in European countries by methods similar to those of Lange show for all the cases in the three studies that the frequency of similarity in criminal behavior among identical twins was only 1.4 times as great as the frequency among fraternal twins.[8] One of the most extensive studies of the criminality of twins was later made by Rosanoff and others on adult criminality, juvenile delinquency, and child behavior problems. This study showed, for all types of cases combined, approximately three times as much concordance among identical twins as fraternal twins.[9] The procedures in this study, however, are so inaccurate that the conclusions are worthless. This may be illustrated with reference to the juvenile delinquents in the study. A juvenile delinquent was rigorously defined as a child under eighteen years of age brought before the juvenile court on a delinquency petition and either placed on probation or committed to a correctional institution. According to the brief descriptions given in the Rosanoff report, all delinquents of the fraternal type conform to this definition, while nine of the twenty-nine male juvenile delinquents of the identical-twin type fail to conform to the definition, and consequently should not be included as concordant cases. If correction be made for those cases which do

[7] Johannes Lange, *Verbrechen als Schicksal* (Leipzig: Thieme, 1919); trans. by Charlotte Haldane, with the title *Crime and Destiny* (New York: Boni, 1930).

[8] A. M. Legras, *Psychose en Criminaliteit bei Tweelingen* (Utrecht: Kemink, 1932); F. Stumpfl, *Die Ursprünge des Verbrechens* (Leipzig: Thieme, 1936); Heinrich Kranz, *Lebensschicksale Krimineller Zwillinge* (Berlin: Springer, 1936).

[9] A. J. Rosanoff, Leva M. Handy, and Isabel A. Rosanoff, "Etiology of Child Behavior Difficulties, Juvenile Delinquency, and Adult Criminality," *Psychiatric Monographs*, no. 1 (Sacramento: California Department of Institutions, 1941).

not conform to the definition, concordance appears among identical twins only 1.1 times as frequently as it appears among fraternal twins. This difference is not sufficiently great to create a presumption of inheritance.

The most extensive study of twins is now being completed in Denmark. All six thousand pairs of twins born in Denmark between 1880 and 1910 are being studied. A preliminary report indicates that the name of at least one member of nine hundred pairs of these twins had by 1968 been entered in Denmark's Central Police Register.[10] Concordance was found in 36 percent of 67 pairs of one-egg male twins and in 12 percent of 114 pairs of two-egg male twins, in 21 percent of 14 pairs of one-egg female twins and in 4 percent of 23 pairs of two-egg female twins, and in 4 percent of 226 pairs of two-egg male-female twins. Concordance, whether of one-egg or two-egg twins, was higher for serious crimes than for minor offenses, for females than for males, and for twins reared in rural districts as compared with twins reared in urban areas.

Even if a difference between the two types of twins in reference to concordance in criminality is accepted, the conclusion that criminality is inherited does not necessarily follow. The difference between the two types of twins may be explained in whole or in part by the fact that the environments of identical twins are more nearly alike psychologically than the environments of fraternal twins. Because of the difficulty of distinguishing one identical twin from the other, the reactions of other persons toward identical twins will be more nearly alike than the reactions of others toward fraternal twins. These reactions of others are the most important part of the environment. In general, therefore, the study of twins has failed as completely as other procedures to demonstrate the inheritance of criminality.

Some recent research has indicated that sex chromosome imbalances are disproportionately represented among patients in mental hospitals, and this finding has led to a flurry of studies of criminals. The general hypothesis is that an extra Y chromosome, or more, in males causes the individual to be uncontrollably aggressive. However, it has not been shown that chromatin abnormality produces criminality, or even aggressiveness. A recent review of research concluded: "XYY males in an institutional setting are *less* violent or aggressive when compared to matched chromosomally normal fellow inmates; and their criminal histories involve crimes against property rather than person."[11]

Two positive propositions and one negative proposition can be stated as conclusions regarding the relation of heredity to crime. First, criminals, like all

---

[10] Karl O. Christiansen, "Threshold of Tolerance in Various Population Groups Illustrated by Results from Danish Criminological Twin Study," in *Ciba Foundation Symposium on the Mentally Abnormal Offender,* ed. A. V. S. Reuck and Ruth Porter (London: J. and A. Churchill, 1968), pp. 107–16.

[11] Richard S. Fox, "The XYY Offender: A Modern Myth?", *Journal of Criminal Law, Criminology, and Police Science,* 62:59–73, 1971. See also Theodore R. Sarbin and Jeffrey E. Miller, "Demonism Revisited: The XYY Chromosomal Anomaly," *Issues in Criminology,* 5:195–207, 1970; and Barbara J. Culliton, "Patients' Rights: Harvard is Site of Battle over X and Y Chromosomes," *Science,* 186:715–17, 1974.

human beings, have some inherited traits which make it possible for them to behave like human beings. This proposition, however, does not aid in explaining why some human beings commit crimes and others do not. Second, some inherited characteristics may be significantly related to criminal behavior by virtue of the fact that members of a society have learned to react to them in a certain way. For example, color of the skin is reacted to in a certain way in the United States, and the crime rate is high among dark-skinned people. But this proposition is not relevant to explaining criminality on the basis of heredity, for traits which are not inherited may be reacted to in a significant way and may likewise be associated with criminal behavior. The third proposition is that, except in the two senses previously stated, heredity has no connection whatever with criminal behavior. It is obviously impossible for criminality to be inherited as such, for crime is defined by acts of legislatures, and these vary independently of the biological inheritance of the violators of the laws.

ANATOMY

Lombroso insisted that criminals differ from noncriminals with reference to certain anatomical traits which he called "stigmata of degeneracy." He found these deviations in all parts of the anatomy, but placed particular emphasis on deviations in the shape of the cranium. Goring made careful measurements of several thousand prisoners in comparison with the general population and reached the conclusion that prisoners differed anatomically from the general population only in being slightly shorter in stature and slightly lighter in weight. Goring's work is generally accepted as having demolished the early Lombrosian view that criminals are characterized by certain stigmata and constitute an inferior biological type However, in the late 1930s Hooton, an American anthropologist, attempted to revive the Lombrosian theory. He made elaborate measurements of thousands of prisoners and of a few nonprisoners. He found some differences between the two classes and concluded that "the primary cause of crime is biological inferiority."[12] Other studies, however, have generally reached the conclusion that criminals are not significantly different in physical traits from noncriminals.[13]

The general body build, or somatotype, also has received considerable attention as a possible explanation of criminal behavior.[14] Kretschmer developed a classifica-

[12] E. A. Hooton, *Crime and the Man* (Cambridge, Mass.: Harvard University Press, 1939), p. 130. See also idem, *The American Criminal: An Anthropological Study* (Cambridge, Mass.: Harvard University Press, 1939).
[13] These studies have been reviewed and summarized in W. Norwood East, "Physical Factors in Criminal Behavior," *Journal of Clinical Psychopathy*, 8:7–36, 1946. See also Robert K. Merton and M. F. Ashley Montagu, "Crime and the Anthropologist," *American Anthropologist*, 42:384–408, 1940.
[14] An excellent summary and appraisal of the general morphological theories of criminal behavior has been made by William A. Lessa, "An Appraisal of Constitutional Types," *Memoirs of the American Anthropological Society*, no. 62. (*American Anthropologist*, vol. 45, no. 4, pt. 2, 1943); and "Somatomancy—Precursor of the Science of Human Constitution," *Scientific Monthly*, 75:355–65, 1952.

tion of somatotypes in relation to psychoses and general personality. Attempts have been made to use Kretschmer's classification in the study of criminals, but thus far no relationship has been found between his body types and criminal behavior. Sheldon also attempted to differentiate criminals from noncriminals on the basis of body type.[15] He found three somatotypes—the endomorphic, which is round and soft; the mesomorphic, which is round and hard; and the ectomorphic, which is thin and fragile—and claimed that three temperamental types and three psychiatric types are closely related with these somatotypes. After making a study of two hundred young adults in a Boston welfare agency, whom he described as "more or less delinquent," he concluded that delinquents are different from nondelinquents in their somatotypes and in their related temperamental and psychiatric types. Also he assumed that these differences are in the direction of inferiority and that the inferiority is inherited. His data, in fact, do not justify the conclusion that the delinquents are different from the nondelinquents in general, the conclusion that the difference, if it exists, indicates inferiority, or the conclusion that the inferiority, if it exists, is inherited.[16]

The Gluecks used the logic of Kretschmer and Sheldon in a study of juvenile delinquents.[17] Like Sheldon, they adopted a system characterized by a noted physical anthropologist as a "new Phrenology in which the bumps of the buttocks take the place of the bumps on the skull."[18]

AGE RATIOS IN CRIME

Despite all their limitations, statistics on crime give information important to our understanding of crime and to hypotheses and theories about it. Similarities and differences in crime rates for certain categories of persons are so consistent that a gross relationship between the category and crime can reasonably be concluded to exist. In these cases, it is practical to assume that if the part of an observed relationship which is due merely to the methods of collecting and recording statistics were eliminated, a real relationship would still remain. After specifying this assumption, we can go ahead and use the statistics.

Even if they are gross, relationships which consistently appear and which cannot be readily "explained away" by citing the differential reactions of the

[15] William H. Sheldon, *Varieties of Delinquent Youth: An Introduction to Constitutional Psychiatry* (New York: Harpers, 1949). For a more recent and much more sophisticated study along these lines, see Juan B. Cortes with Florence M. Gatti, *Delinquency and Crime: A Biophychological Approach* (New York: Seminar Press, 1972).

[16] See Edwin H. Sutherland, "Critique of Sheldon's *Varieties of Delinquent Youth*," *American Sociological Review*, 16:10–14, 1951.

[17] Sheldon and Eleanor T. Glueck, *Physique and Delinquency* (New York: Harper, 1956). See also Sanford J. Fox, "Delinquency and Biology," *University of Miami Law Review*, 16:65–91, 1961.

[18] S. L. Washburn, "Review of W. H. Sheldon, *Varieties of Delinquent Youth*," *American Anthropologist*, 53:561–63, 1951.

persons and agencies manufacturing delinquency and crime statistics must be taken into account in any theory of crime and criminality. There are at least six types of such consistent relationships that are of great theoretical significance to students of crime and criminality. Age and sex are discussed here, race and nativity in Chapter 7, size of community in Chapter 9, and social class in Chapter 11.

Many varieties of statistics, in many jurisdictions, in many different years, collected by many types of agencies, uniformly report such a high incidence of crime among young persons, that it may reasonably be assumed that there is a statistically significant difference between the rate of crime among young adults and the rate among other age groups. Statistics are likely to exaggerate the crime rate of young adults: old people may have prestige enough to avoid fingerprinting and arrest, and young children might not be arrested as readily as either young adults or old adults, leaving young adults to bear the responsibility for more than their share of all the crimes committed. But there does seem to be a difference, even if it is not as great as the statistics indicate when taken at face value. In this sense, there are two general relationships between age and criminality.

First, the age of maximum general criminality is during or shortly before adolescence. Recent English statistics show that the age category of maximum convictions for indictable crimes is 14–17. While American statistics place this age slightly higher, these statistics are based on fingerprints submitted by local police departments to the Federal Bureau of Investigation, and American police departments seldom take fingerprints of young people. Similarly, in Scandinavian countries, 13–15 is the age of maximum criminality, and in Australia it is about 15–18.[19] Table 10 shows the American arrest rates for various age groups in 1975.

Second, the age of maximum criminality is not the same under all conditions. The extent to which the crime rate among young persons exceeds the crime rate among other age groups varies by offense, sex, place, and time. There are eight specific variables that must be considered here.

1. The age of maximum criminality varies with the type of crime. For example, males aged 15–19 have higher arrest rates for auto theft and burglary than any other group of males. Table 11 presents some recent data on the percentages of all arrests which were arrests of young persons. The table shows, for instance, that homicides and assaults are committed by persons who are much older, on the average, than are the persons who commit automobile theft and burglary. Persons under the age of 25 constituted 45 percent of all homicide arrests, 77 percent of the arrests for robbery, 85 percent of the arrests for burglary, 75 percent of the arrests for larceny, and 85 percent of the arrests for motor vehicle theft.

---

[19] F. H. McClintock and N. Howard Avison, *Crime in England and Wales* (London: Heinemann, 1968), p. 165; Knut Sveri, *Kriminalitet og Alder* (Criminality and Age) (Stockholm: Almquist and Wiksell, 1960), pp. 80, 161; and Paul Ward and Greg Woods, *Law and Order in Australia* (Sydney: Angus and Robertson, 1972), p. 77.

Table 10   Arrest Rates for Different Age Groups, 1975 (Rates per 100,000 Inhabitants)

Age Group	Arrest Rates for All Offenses (Excluding Traffic)	Arrest Rates for Willful Homicide, Forcible Rape, Robbery, Aggravated Assault	Arrest Rates for Burglary, Breaking or Entering, Larceny-Theft, Motor Vehicle Theft
10 and under	44.17	1.00	19.12
11–14	355.51	12.48	148.27
15–19	1238.70	60.06	282.44
20–24	882.71	49.42	147.02
25–29	521.36	30.66	70.35
30–34	341.24	17.93	35.79
35–39	260.74	11.84	21.35
40–44	224.78	8.26	15.25
45–49	199.48	5.85	11.91
50–59	259.60	6.22	14.59
60 and over	115.16	2.83	9.05

SOURCE: Federal Bureau of Investigation, U.S. Department of Justice, *Uniform Crime Reports for the United States, 1975* (Washington, D.C.: Government Printing Office, 1976), pp. 188–89.

Table 11   Percent of Arrests Accounted for by Different Age Groups, 1975

Offense Charged	Persons Under 18	Persons 18–24	Persons 25 and Over
Willful homicide	9.54	35.32	55.13
Forcible rape	17.58	40.43	41.97
Robbery	34.26	42.74	22.98
Aggravated assault	17.56	32.02	50.40
Burglary, breaking and entering	52.58	32.62	14.79
Larceny-theft	45.05	30.39	24.55
Motor vehicle theft	54.53	30.06	15.40
Violent crime (willful homicide, forcible rape, robbery, aggravated assault)	23.05	36.42	40.51
Property crime (burglary, breaking or entering, larceny-theft, motor vehicle theft)	48.01	31.02	20.96

SOURCE: Federal Bureau of Investigation, *Uniform Crime Reports 1975*, p. 130.

Studies of self-reported crimes show similar distributions. In interviews, a sample (N = 2510) of all American men who were 20 to 30 years old in 1974 were asked if they had ever committed any of ten listed illegal acts.[20] The results, showing age distributions, are summarized in Table 12. The table shows, for example, that shoplifting is much more likely to be a youthful activity than armed robbery, illegal gambling, or writing bad checks.

In a study of homicides committed in Philadelphia, Wolfgang found that the age group 20–24 predominated, with a homicide rate of 12.6 per 100,000; the

Table 12   Self-Reported Criminal Acts, by Age

Criminal Act	Number Admitting	Percent of Total	Percent		
			Before 18	After 18	Before and After 18
Been drunk or intoxicated in a public place?	1754	70	4	66	30
Driven a car while drunk?	1512	60	2	73	25
Shoplifted something from a store?	1103	44	71	10	19
Broken into a house, school, or place of business?	314	13	60	28	13
Stolen a car?	145	6	67	25	8
Stolen anything from a person, face-to-face?	83	3	42	36	22
Run numbers, or had a job which involved illegal gambling?	74	3	15	74	11
Forged, or passed bad checks?	70	3	22	75	3
Forged prescriptions or passed scrip?	37	1	3	92	5
Been armed with or used a weapon of any kind while committing a theft or robbery?	36	1	11	66	23

SOURCE: O'Donnell, et al., *Young Men and Drugs*, p. 84.

[20] John A. O'Donnell, Harwin L. Voss, Richard R. Clayton, Gerald T. Slatin, and Robin G. W. Room, *Young Men and Drugs—A Nationwide Survey* (Washington, D.C.: National Institute on Drug Abuse, Research Monograph No. 5, 1976), p. 84.

median age of the offenders was 31.9. Similar studies of homicide in Chicago and Canada showed the modal age of the offenders to be 20–24.[21]

The type of crimes committed by adult felons in California prisons shows a marked variation by age. Among the male felons received in 1972, the highest median age at admission was for the offense group "lewd act with child," 36.5 years. Other high median ages were 32.2 years for forgery and checks and 29.8 for "opiate derivatives." The lowest median ages were for robbery (24.1 years) and auto theft (26.6 years). Among female felons, the highest median age was for the women convicted of narcotics offenses, 28.9 years. Women admitted for forgery and bad checks were the second oldest group (28.5 years), and those admitted for homicide were the youngest (27.4 years).[22]

2. The age of maximum criminality varies by sex. Generally speaking, females commit crimes at later ages than do males. In 1975, for example, 47.7 percent of the American males arrested for larceny were under 18 years of age, but 41.5 percent of the females arrested for the same offense were under 18. Yet sex offenses (excluding rape and prostitution), narcotic drug offenses, crimes against family and children, driving while intoxicated, homicide, and forgery appear earlier in the lives of women than in the lives of men. In 1975, 29.5 percent of the females and 20.5 percent of the males arrested for sex offenses were under age 18.[23]

3. The age of first delinquency varies from place to place. In areas with high rates of delinquency, the children who become delinquent do so at an earlier age than do the children living in areas with low rates of delinquency.

. 4. The type of crime most frequently committed by persons of various ages varies from place to place. In some areas of Chicago, delinquent boys between 12 and 13 years old commit burglaries, while in other areas delinquent boys of those ages commit petty larcenies or engage in gang violence. In rural areas, offenders of any specified age are likely to be convicted of crimes different from those committed by offenders of the same age who live in urban areas.

5. For all crimes, and for most specific crimes, the rate decreases steadily from the age of maximum criminality to the end of life. This conclusion is derived from the general statistics of many nations. In the United States, burglary and automobile theft decrease rather regularly after ages 15–19, as does the crime rate generally; homicide decreases after ages 20–24, where it is concentrated, but not regularly.[24] Some crimes decrease more dramatically with increasing age than do

---

[21] Marvin E. Wolfgang, "A Sociological Analysis of Criminal Homicide," *Federal Probation*, 25:48–55, 1961; Harwin L. Voss and John R. Hepburn, "Patterns in Criminal Homicide in Chicago," *Journal of Criminal Law, Criminology, and Police Science*, 59:499–508, 1968; and Paul Reed, Teresa Bleszynski, and Paul Gaucher, *Homicide in Canada: A Statistical Synopsis* (Ottawa: Statistics Canada, 1976), p. 90.

[22] *California Prisoners, 1972* (Sacramento: Department of Corrections, 1973), pp. 32–33.

[23] Federal Bureau of Investigation, *Uniform Crime Reports 1975*, p. 187.

[24] See Kyriakos S. Markides and George S. Tracy, "The Effect of the Age Structure of a Stationary Population on Crime Rates," *Journal of Criminal Law and Criminology*, 67:351–55, 1976.

others; for example, the evidence is fairly conclusive that larceny decreases in old age more than do sex offenses.[25]

6. The crime rates among different age groups vary from time to time. Juvenile delinquency rates seem to have increased enormously during the last twenty years in proportion to the crime rates at older ages.

7. Both the probability that a crime will be repeated and the length of time between first and second offenses vary with the age at which the first offense is committed. Generally speaking, the younger a person is when the first offense is committed, the higher the probability that the person will commit a second offense and the shorter the interval between first offense and second offense.[26] A Danish study found that, in a group of 569 adult male offenders, 70 percent of those whose first offense was committed at age 20 or below had committed at least one additional offense.[27]

8. Juvenile delinquency is probably related in some manner to adult criminal behavior, but it is not correct to say that the juvenile delinquent of today is the adult criminal of tomorrow, as has frequently been stated. The error is due to the fact that practically all juveniles commit delinquencies, but not all of them develop into adult criminals. There is evidence that, after about age 25, the percentage of criminals who are first offenders increases with increasing age. Moreover, young persons tend to be arrested for offenses that are rare in other age groups. This specialization as to offenses is called *criminal differentiation*, and it is high among persons aged 14–19, decreases until about age 35, and then increases. The increase in criminal differentiation after age 35 does not reach the high level of the late teens, and the increase probably reflects an increasing "specialization" in drunkenness among older persons. Gibbs and Short have shown that age differentiation in crime is highly correlated with occupational differentiation in the United States. Thus, high criminal differentiation among the young probably means that young Americans are restricted in occupational experiences and, thus, in opportunities to commit some offenses.[28]

In sum, the available statistics on crime tell us that young persons have higher crime rates than older persons, but that there are variations in the ratio of young persons to other persons in the criminal population. Thus, crime rates vary with

[25] David O. Moberg, "Old Age and Crime," *Journal of Criminal Law, Criminology, and Police Science*, 43:764–76, 1953; Martin Roth, "Cerebral Disease and Mental Disorders of Old Age as Causes of Antisocial Behavior," in *The Mentally Abnormal Offender*, ed. Reuck and Porter, pp. 36–37.

[26] Thorsten Sellin, "Recidivism and Maturation," *National Probation and Parole Association Journal*, 4:241–50, 1958; Hermann Mannheim and Leslie T. Wilkins, *Prediction Methods in Relation to Borstal Training* (London: Her Majesty's Stationery Office, 1955), p. 64.

[27] Preben Wolf, "A Contribution to the Topology of Crime in Denmark," *Scandinavian Studies in Criminology*, 1:201–26, 1965.

[28] Jack P. Gibbs and James F. Short, Jr., "Criminal Differentiation and Occupational Differentiation," *Journal of Research in Crime and Delinquency*, 11:89–100, 1974.

age, but in any age group the rates vary with specific social conditions. Age appears to have an important effect, directly or indirectly, on the frequency and type of crime committed.

One of the theories presented as an explanation of the age ratios in crime is that they are due directly to biological traits such as physical strength and vigor: crimes are committed frequently by persons who are strong and active and infrequently by persons who are weak and passive. Another biological theory is that inheritance is the direct cause—persons strongly predisposed by heredity to commit crime do so at a very young age, while those with a weaker tendency delay longer.

These biological theories obviously provide no explanation of many of the variations in the age ratios in crime; indeed it may be said that they do not explain even one of the facts outlined above when that fact is considered in its ramifications. On the other hand, all of these facts are consistent with the differential association theory and the general principle that crime and criminality are products of social experiences and social interaction.

SEX RATIOS IN CRIME

Sex status is of greater statistical significance in differentiating criminals from noncriminals than any other trait. If you were asked to use a single trait to predict which children in a town of 10,000 people would become criminals, you would make fewer mistakes if you chose sex status as the trait and predicted criminality for the males and noncriminality for the females. The prediction would be wrong in many cases, for most of the males would not become criminals, and a few of the women would. But you would be wrong in more cases if you used any other single trait, such as age, race, family background, or a personality characteristic. As is the case with age, there are two general relationships to be observed between crime and sex status.

First, the crime rate for men is greatly in excess of the rate for women—in all nations, all communities within a nation, all age groups, all periods of history for which organized statistics are available, and for all types of crime except those peculiar to women, such as infanticide and abortion.[29]

In the United States, the rate of arrest of males is presently about five times the rate of arrest for females; about ten times as many males as females are convicted; about fifteen times as many males as females are committed to correctional institutions of all kinds; and about twenty times as many males as females are committed to prisons and reformatories housing serious offenders. A sample survey of all inmates housed in state correctional institutions in 1974 showed that 97 percent were males.[30] Approximately 80 percent of the delinquency cases in juvenile courts are boys. These statistics are supported by studies of self-reported

[29]See Hans Göppinger, *Kriminologie* (Munich: C. H. Beck, 1971), pp. 336–38.
[30]James J. Stephan, *Survey of Inmates of State Correctional Faculties, 1974* (National Prisoner Statistics Special Report, Washington, D.C.: Government Printing Office, 1976), p. 24.

delinquency, but the ratio of males to females in such studies is lower than that indicated by official sources.[31]

A similar general pattern prevails in other nations. In 1967, the sex ratio of Canadians convicted of indictable offenses was 1519; but for offenses against property with violence the ratio was 3820. (The sex ratio is always expressed as the number of males per 100 females. A ratio over 100 thus means that males exceed females, while a ratio of less than 100 means that females exceed males.) In an Australian community, 24 percent of the total offenders referred to the children's court in 1972–73 were girls. This sex differential was even more noticeable with respect to the number of offenses, girls being responsible for only 15 percent of the total.[32] In India, on the other hand, only 4 percent of the juveniles apprehended in 1970 were girls.[33] In random samples (3032 men and 606 women) of Danish citizens who were between the ages of 20 and 70 in 1953, 19 percent of the men and 2 percent of the women were listed in the official registers of criminals in Denmark, a sex ratio of 4800.[34] Even if correction could be made for the statistical bias in favor of females, the male crime rate probably would still greatly exceed that of females.[35]

Second, the extent to which the crime rate among males exceeds the crime rate among females is not the same under all conditions. There are variations in the sex ratio in crime, just as there are variations in the age ratio in crime.

1. The extent to which the rate for males exceeds the rate for females varies from one nation to another. Male criminals are about 350 times more numerous as females in Belgium and 2750 times as numerous in Algiers and Tunis in proportion to the populations of the several groups. In Ceylon 97 percent of the persons admitted to training schools and prisons in 1969–70 were male, and of the persons admitted to the prisons of Greece in 1968, 90 percent were male.[36] The sex ratio among 807,000 Japanese criminals investigated by the police in 1967 was 1600; of 3143 criminals investigated for robbery, only 36 were females.[37] Nine

31 Michael J. Hindelang, "Age, Sex, and the Versatility of Delinquent Involvements," *Social Problems*, 18:522–35, 1971.

32 June Fielding, "The Social Control of Female Delinquency: Occupational Ideologies of Policewomen, Welfare Workers, and Magistrates," (M.A. thesis, Australian National University, Canberra, 1975), pp. 3.7–3.12.

33 S. D. Gokhale and N. K. Sohoni, "The Juvenile Justice System in India," in United Nations Social Defence Research Unit, *Juvenile Justice: An International Survey* (Rome: U.N. Social Defence Research Unit, 1976), pp. 15–54.

34 Wolf, "Contribution to the Topology of Crime in Denmark."

35 Cf. Otto Pollak, *The Criminality of Women* (Philadelphia: University of Pennsylvania Press, 1950), pp. 44–56, 154; Bertha J. Payak, "Understanding the Female Offender," *Federal Probation*, 27:7–12, December, 1963; and M. Chesney-Lind, "Judicial Enforcement of the Female Sex Role: The Family Court and the Female Delinquent," *Issues in Criminology*, 8:51–69, 1973.

36 Ceylon Commissioner of Prisons, *Administrative Report for 1969–1970* (Colombo: Government Press, 1972), p. 132; C. D. Spinellis, *Crime in Contemporary Greece* (Athens: Athenian Institute of Anthropos, 1971), p. 27.

37 Japanese Ministry of Justice, *Statistical Data on Criminality in Japan* (Tokyo, 1970), p. 8.

studies in various nations and districts of Africa since 1955 show sex ratios ranging from 20,400 to 900.[38] The sex ratio in crime tends to be lowest in countries in which females have the greatest freedom and equality with males, such as western Europe, Australia, Canada, and the United States, and to be highest in countries in which females are closely supervised, such as Algiers. If countries existed in which females were politically and socially dominant, the female rate, according to this trend, would exceed the male rate.

2. The extent to which the rate for males exceeds the rate for females varies with the social positions of the sexes in different groups within a nation. An analysis of statistics in prewar Poland indicated sex ratios that ranged from 176 to 1163 in forty-two groups in categories according to age, province of residence, rural-urban residence, religion, and civil status.[39] In the United States, the sex ratio is less extreme among blacks than it is among whites, and it is probable that black males and females more closely resemble each other in social standing than do white males and females. In 1974, the sex ratio among nonwhites committed to Michigan prisons was 2035, but the ratio among whites was over 3700; and the sex ratio among blacks in Florida prisons in 1973 was 2044 as compared to 2585 for whites.[40] In a study conducted in Stamford, Connecticut, Forslund found the arrest rate for Negro males to be 6.42 times the rate for Negro females, and the arrest rate for white males to be 10.5 times that of white females; the sex ratio of conviction rates for blacks was 882, and for whites it was 1531.[41]

3. The extent to which the rate for males exceeds the rate for females varies with the size of community of residence. In American cities the crime rate of females is closer to the crime rate of males than is the case in rural areas and small towns. The ratio of male arrests to female arrests for crimes against the person in Massachusetts in 1970 was 17 to 1 in "towns," most of which have less than twelve thousand population, and 11 to 1 in cities above twelve thousand; for offenses against property the ratio was 8 to 1 in towns and 6 to 1 in cities.[42]

4. The extent to which the crime rate among males exceeds the crime rate among females varies with age. In the United States, the sex ratio among persons committed to penal institutions tends to increase with increasing age. At ages 15–

---

38 G. Houchon, "Les Mécanismes Criminogènes dans une Société Urbaine Africaine," *Revue Internationale Criminologie et de Police Technique*, 21:271–92, 1967. See also S. Kirson Weinberg, "Female Delinquency in Ghana West Africa: A Comparative Analysis," *International Review of Modern Sociology*, 3:65–73, 1973.

39 L. Radzinowicz, "Variability in the Sex Ratio of Criminality," *Sociological Review*, 29:76–102, 1937.

40 Michigan Department of Corrections, *Annual Report, 1974* (East Lansing: Michigan Department of Corrections, 1975), p. 24; Florida Division of Corrections, *Annual Report, 1972–1973* (Tallahassee: Author, 1973), p. 54.

41 Morris A. Forslund, "A Comparison of Negro and White Crime Rates," *Journal of Criminal Law, Criminology, and Police Science*, 61:214–17, 1970.

42 *Statistical Reports of the Commissioner of Correction, 1963* (Boston: Massachusetts Public Document No. 115, 1971) p. 65. Communities of less than twelve thousand are "towns," but a community with more than twelve thousand residents becomes a city only if it chooses to give up the "town" designation.

17 the sex ratio is about 1200, while at 60–64 it is about 5000. The statistics of convictions for indictable crimes in England and Wales in 1973 show a sex ratio of 648 for all ages; however, for the ages under 17 the ratio is 999; for the years 17–21 it is 904; and for the ages 21 and over it is 482.[43] In earlier years, these data were compiled for all age groups, and they indicated that after age 10 the two sexes became progressively more alike with advancing age until the age of 40, with little change thereafter. For Norway in 1959, the male rate per thousand population of the same age was only three times the female rate at age 60 and over, eight times the female rate at ages 40–59, and twelve times the female rate at ages 25–39. The greatest differences were at ages 9, 12, and 24, where the male rate exceeded the female rate by 30 times, 36 times, and 30 times, respectively.[44]

5. The extent to which the crime rate among males exceeds the crime rate among females varies with area of residence within a city. Generally, the higher the crime rate of an area, the lower the sex ratio in crime.

6. The extent to which the crime rate among males exceeds the crime rate among females varies with time. There is evidence that the sex ratio is decreasing. The trend for the United States in recent years is shown in Table 13, which was compiled by Rita James Simon.[45] In 1938, 5 percent of the persons under age 18 whose arrests were reported to the FBI, were females; in 1947 females were 10 percent; in 1957 they were 13 percent; in 1964 they were 16 percent; in 1967 they were 18 percent, and in 1975 they were 21 percent. Between 1960 and 1975 the male arrest rate for serious crimes increased 119 percent, but the female rate increased 374 percent.[46] In England and Wales, the sex ratio of persons convicted of indictable crimes in 1965 was 667; in 1972 it was 629. In war years, when women take over the occupations of men and in other ways approach social equality with men, the female crime rate increases.

7. Among young criminals, the extent to which the crime rate for males exceeds the crime rate for females varies with the degree of integration in the family. Among delinquents from broken homes, the sex ratio is lower than it is among delinquents from unbroken, "integrated" homes.[47] Further, there is some evidence from specialized studies that the sex ratio in delinquency is lower in families in which male children outnumber the females than in families in which the number of each sex is more nearly equal.[48]

[43] Great Britain Central Statistical Office, *Annual Abstract of Statistics, 1974* (London: Her Majesty's Stationery Office, 1974), p. 86.

[44] Sveri, *Kriminalitet og Adler* p. 64.

[45] Rita James Simon, *The Contemporary Woman and Crime* (Washington, D.C., Government Printing Office, 1975), p. 37. See also Joseph G. Weis, "Liberation and Crime: The Invention of the New Female Criminal." *Crime and Social Justice*, 6:17–27, 1976.

[46] Federal Bureau of Investigation, *Uniform Crime Reports, 1975*, p. 183.

[47] Jackson Toby, "The Differential Impact of Family Disorganization," *American Sociological Review*, 22:505–12, 1957; and Weinberg, "Female Delinquency in Ghana West Africa: A Comparative Analysis."

[48] Raymond F. Sletto, "Sibling Position and Juvenile Delinquency," *American Journal of Sociology*, 39:657–69.

Table 13 Percentage of Females Among Arrests, 1953–72

Year	All Crimes	Serious Crimes[a]
1953	10.84	9.40
1954	10.97	8.89
1955	11.00	9.12
1956	10.91	9.06
1957	10.63	9.29
1958	10.61	9.73
1959	10.68	10.54
1960	11.04	10.95
1961	11.26	11.47
1962	11.47	12.38
1963	11.68	12.65
1964	11.93	13.54
1965	12.12	14.37
1966	12.33	14.80
1967	12.67	15.03
1968	13.08	15.04
1969	13.82	16.58
1970	14.58	18.04
1971	15.07	18.34
1972	15.27	19.25

	Percent	Percent
Average rate of change, 1953–72	+0.23 per year	+0.52 per year
Average rate of change, 1958–72	+0.33	+0.68
Average rate of change, 1967–72	+0.52	+0.84

SOURCE: Federal Bureau of Investigation, *Uniform Crime Reports.*
NOTE: Arrest data for cities with populations 2500 and above.

[a]Serious crimes are all those included in the crime index, except rape.

CONCLUSION

As indicated, no other trait has a great statistical importance as does sex in differentiating criminals from noncriminals. But simply knowing that most criminals are male is not an explanation of crime and criminality. Some scholars have claimed that the higher rate of delinquency of the male sex is due to the biological characteristics of the male. This conclusion has no more justification than the conclusion that the death rate of males being struck by lightning six times more often than females is due to the biological differences between the sexes.

The variations in the sex ratio in crime are so great that it can be concluded that maleness is not significant in the causation of crime in itself but only as it indicates social position, supervision, social interaction, and other social relations. Moreover, since boys and girls live in the same homes, in equal poverty, with equally ignorant parents and live in the same neighborhoods, which are equally lacking in facilities for organized recreation, these conditions of the social environment cannot be considered as causes of delinquency either. The significant difference is in the social positions of the girls and women as compared with the boys and men, and the difference in social positions either determines the frequency and intensity of the delinquency and antidelinquency patterns which impinge upon them or determines the frequency of opportunities for crimes which are available to them.

Probably the most important difference is that the girls are supervised more carefully and behave in accordance with anticriminal behavior patterns taught to them with greater care and consistency than do boys. From infancy, most girls are taught that they must be nice, while boys are taught that they must be rough and tough.[49] This difference in care and supervision presumably arose simply because females can become pregnant. The importance of avoiding the personal and familial consequences of illicit pregnancy led to special protection of the girl, not only in respect to sex behavior but also in respect to social codes in general.[50] Grosser has shown that stealing has a different functional significance for boys and girls; it can be integrated with and can express features of the masculine adolescent role, but it cannot do so for the basic features of the feminine role.[51] A study of the epidemiology of marijuana use demonstrated quite conclusively that males and not females are the "carriers" of this behavior pattern. It is reasonable to conclude that, in this epidemiological sense, males are the "carriers" of most delinquent and criminal behavior patterns.[52]

[49] Jocelynne A. Scutt, "Role Conditioning Theory: An Explanation for Disparity in Male and Female Criminality," *Australian and New Zealand Journal of Criminology,* 9:25–35, 1976.

[50] Talcott Parsons has presented the thesis that girls are less delinquent than boys partially because the girls receive an apprenticeship training from their mothers for the careers into which they are to enter, while boys remain, during the same age, isolated from the occupational activities of their fathers, which leads to frustration of the boys and consequent delinquency. If this thesis were valid, the delinquency rate of the two sexes should be more nearly alike in rural districts where both boys and girls receive this apprenticeship training, than in urban districts, where the girls alone receive this training. But Toby has shown that the delinquency rates are more nearly the same for the two sexes in the urban districts, where the training in this respect differs more widely. See Talcott Parsons, *Essays in Sociological Theory* (Glencoe, Ill.: Free Press, 1949), pp. 219, 257–259; Toby, "Differential Impact of Family Disorganization."

[51] George H. Grosser, *Juvenile Delinquency and Contemporary American Sex Roles* (Ph.D. diss., Harvard University, 1952). See, however, Paul C. Friday, "Research on Youth Crime in Sweden: Some Problems in Methodology," *Scandinavian Studies,* 46:20–30, 1974. This study found that Swedish male adolescents stole items which seemed to reflect concern for status, wealth and prestige in the male youth group—gasoline, cigarettes, condoms, and stylish clothing.

[52] Jeffery B. Freeland and Richard S. Campbell, "The Social Context of First Marijuana Use," *International Journal of the Addictions,* 8:317–24 1973. See also Janet Lever, "Sex Differences in the Games Children Play," *Social Problems,* 23:479–87, 1976.

The general conclusion from this survey of data regarding physical and physiological conditions is that these conditions have not, in any case, been demonstrated to be a direct force in the production of crime or delinquency. On the contrary, it is apparent that these conditions are significant only to the extent that they affect social interaction.

SUGGESTED READINGS

Adler, Freda. *Sisters in Crime: The Rise of the New Female Criminal.* New York: McGraw-Hill, 1975.

Albert, Ethel M. "The Roles of Women: A Question of Values." Chapter in *Man and Civilization: The Potential of Women,* edited by Seymour M. Farber and Roger H. L. Wilson, pp. 105–115. New York: McGraw-Hill, 1963.

Bertrand, Marie-Andree. "Self-Image and Delinquency: A Contribution to the Study of Female Criminality and Woman's Image." *Acta Criminologica,* 2:71–138, 1969.

Fink, Arthur E. *Causes of Crime: Biological Theories in the United States, 1800–1915.* Philadelphia: University of Pennsylvania Press, 1938.

Friedenberg, Edgar Z. *The Vanishing Adolescent.* New York: Dell, 1962.

Gibbs, Jack P., & James F. Short, Jr. "Criminal Differentiation and Occupational Differentiation." *Journal of Research in Crime and Delinquency,* 11:89–100, 1974.

Harries, Keith D. "Cities and Crime: A Geographic Model." *Criminology,* 14:369–86, 1976.

Harris, Anthony R. "Sex and Theories of Deviance: Toward a Functional Theory of Deviant Type-Scripts." *American Sociological Review,* 42:3–16, 1977.

Hindelang, Michael J. "Age, Sex, and the Versatility of Delinquent Involvements." *Social Problems,* 18:522–35, 1971.

Klein, Dorie. "The Etiology of Female Crime: A Review of the Literature." *Issues in Criminology,* 8:3–30, 1973.

Lopez-Rey, Manuel. *Crime: An Analytic Appraisal.* New York: Praeger, 1970.

Morris, Ruth. "Female Delinquency and Relational Problems." *Social Forces,* 43:82–99, 1964.

Simon, Rita James. *The Contemporary Woman and Crime.* Washington, D.C.: Government Printing Office, 1975.

Toby, Jackson. "The Differential Impact of Family Disorganization." *American Sociological Review,* 22:505–12, 1957.

Wolfgang, Marvin E. "Pioneers in Criminology: Cesare Lombroso (1835–1909)." *Journal of Criminal Law, Criminology, and Police Science,* 52:361–69, 1961.

Wolfgang, Marvin E., Robert Figlio, & Thorsten Sellin. *Delinquency in a Birth Cohort,* Chicago: University of Chicago Press, 1972.

7

Race and Nativity Ratios

Any general theory of crime and criminal behavior should make sense of age and sex ratios in crime, and of the variations in these ratios. The same theory also should account for race and nativity ratios in crime and their variations.

STATISTICAL PROBLEMS

Crimes are sometimes regarded as a direct product of racial traits, and racial traits are regarded as biologically determined. For example, some persons believe that blacks are a primitive race and are innately inclined toward crime. This belief is composed of two constituent notions: that blacks cannot control their emotions and consequently have a high rate of crime against the person, and that they have no moral sense regarding property rights and consequently have a high rate of crime against property.[1] A survey of the facts regarding the crimes of various races in the United States would indicate whether such biological notions are valid, but it is difficult to obtain the facts. The statistics on the crimes of various racial groups are by no means facts.

In the first place, the classification of persons as "white," "black," or something else is arbitrary. Fifty years ago Herskovits drew a sample of 5000 "Negroes" from all parts of the United States, but his anthropological study of them suggested that at most 22 percent were of unmixed ancestry.[2] It is reasonable to assume that this proportion has decreased in the last half-century. There is no avoiding the fact that

[1] See the discussion by Gunnar Myrdal, *An American Dilemma*, rev. ed. (New York: Harpers, 1962), p. 655.
[2] Melville J. Herskovits, *The Anthropometry of the American Negro* (New York: Columbia University Press, 1930), p. 177. See also Marvin E. Wolfgang and Bernard Cohen, *Crime and Race: Conceptions and Misconceptions* (New York: Institute of Human Relations Press, American Jewish Committee, 1970); and Henry P. Lunsgaarde, "Racial and Ethnic Classifications: An Appraisal of the Role of Anthropology in the Law Making Process," *Houston Law Review*, 10:641–54, 1973.

at least 80 percent of the offenders contributing to the "black" crime rate are part "white."

In the second place, arrest rates and other official statistics are reported for selected areas and cities, but the population of the several races in those areas cannot be determined. Even racial classifications based on social definitions or regional legislation do not indicate how persons are classified for census purposes. In many estimates of crime by blacks, the arrest rate of blacks in a city, state, or area is determined by comparing the number of arrests with the total population of blacks in the United States.

A third error in the statistics arises because the procedures used in the administration of criminal justice are biased against minority groups, especially blacks. Later chapters—especially those dealing with the police and courts—will identify some of these biases. The transgressions of blacks are much more visible than the transgressions of white middle-class persons.[3] Numerous studies have shown that blacks are more likely to be arrested, indicted, convicted, and committed to an institution than are whites who commit the same offenses; and many other studies have shown that blacks have a poorer chance than whites of receiving probation, suspended sentence, parole, commutation of a death sentence, or pardon.[4] Thus, almost any "index" of the crime rate is likely to exaggerate the rate for blacks as compared with the rate for whites.

However, it is also true that many crimes committed by blacks—especially those committed against other blacks—receive no official attention from the police or courts, and this practice of overlooking some crimes offsets to some unknown degree the bias in other arresting, reporting, and recording practices. An extensive study of the administration of justice indicated that many guilty persons are acquitted because the conduct complained about is considered normal to the subculture of the defendant.[5] For example, in commenting on

[3] See William J. Chambliss, ed., *Crime and the Legal Process* (New York: McGraw-Hill, 1969), pp. 85–89; and Leroy C. Gould, "Who Defines Delinquency: A Comparison of Self-Reported and Officially Reported Indices of Delinquency for Three Racial Groups," *Social Problems*, 16:325–36, 1969.

[4] See the discussion of differential imposition of punishments in Chapter 14 below. See also, for example, Nathan Goldman, *The Differential Selection of Juvenile Offenders for Court Appearance* (New York: National Council on Crime and Delinquency, 1963); Irving Piliavin and Scott Briar, "Police Encounters with Juveniles," *American Journal of Sociology*, 60:206–14, 1964; Robert M. Terry, "The Screening of Juvenile Offenders," *Journal of Criminal Law, Criminology, and Police Science*, 58:173–81, 1967; Michael J. Hindelang, "Equality Under the Law," *Journal of Criminal Law, Criminology, and Police Science*, 60:306–13, 1969; Morris A. Forslund, "A Comparison of Negro and White Crime Rates," *Journal of Criminal Law, Criminology, and Police Science*, 61:214–17, 1970; Edward Green, "Race, Social Status, and Criminal Arrest," *American Sociological Review*, 35:476–90, 1970; William R. Arnold, "Race and Ethnicity Relative to Other Factors in Juvenile Court Dispositions," *American Journal of Sociology*, 77:211–27, 1971; Charles E. Reasons, "Racism and Prisoner's Rights," *Issues in Criminology*, 9:3–20, 1974; David M. Peterson and Paul C. Friday, "Early Release from Incarceration: Race as a Factor in the Use of 'Shock Probation,' " *Journal of Criminal Law and Criminology*, 66:79–87, 1975; and Leo Carroll and Margaret E. Mondrick, "Racial Bias in the Decision to Grant Parole," *Law and Society Review*, 11:93–107, 1976.

[5] Donald J. Newman, *Conviction: The Determination of Guilt or Innocence Without Trial* (Boston: Little, Brown, 1966) pp. 155–59.

differential treatment of certain sex cases, a judge remarked: "In statutory rape or carnal knowledge cases the man might be just above the legal age and the girl just below. Usually in such cases, particularly among the Negroes, there is mutual consent and in the Negro group this type of behavior is not particularly frowned upon and is felt to be normal. You have to take this factor into consideration." In urban black communities the problems of divergent *mores*, real or assumed, are most apparent at the police level. While discrimination against blacks is manifested in arresting them more readily than whites for many types of crime, it also is manifested in police activity resulting in underarresting blacks for conduct which would likely result in arrest in other precincts. Underarrest, in turn, affects conviction rates. Newman concluded:

Assaults involving Negro perpetrators and Negro victims commonly do not result in arrest, unless extremely serious, on the general philosophy that such conduct is normal in this subculture. The police have an informal policy of discouraging Negro assault victims from filing complaints, and it was reported that officers newly assigned to primarily Negro districts quickly adopt this practice regardless of the attitudes and policies they brought with them from white districts. . . . The policy of underarresting Negroes for such crimes as assault has a deceptive influence on conviction and sentencing statistics. For example, if only assault conviction records were used as the basis for comparing court treatment of the two races, it might appear as if there were a court bias against Negro defendants. Most Negroes charged with assault are convicted while a higher percentage of whites similarly charged are dismissed or acquitted; furthermore, the Negro defendant is more likely to receive a longer or more severe sentence. The difference, of course, is primarily due to differential arrest practices.[6]

The practice of underarresting blacks is sometimes based on the notion that strict enforcement against the more visible crimes of lower-class persons is a form of discrimination. But it sometimes is based on the prejudiced assumption that poor persons, especially blacks, are degenerates who cannot be expected to live up to the standards of morality codified in the law. One judge interviewed by Newman dismissed an assault charge against the male partner in a white "hillbilly" common-law relationship, then explained: "These people couldn't care less about marriage, divorce or other relationships. They are ignorant and their moral standards are not like ours. They come from the backwoods in the South where even incest is the accepted thing." Another judge, obviously subscribing to the notion that blacks are an inferior people with natural proclivities to crime, discouraged rigorous enforcement against gambling among Negroes on the ground that this "would merely drive them onto the streets, with a consequent rise in rapes, burglaries, and other serious crimes."

Some crimes of other minority groups also are overlooked, often for different reasons, and with entirely different consequences to the crime statistics. For example, Chambliss and Nagasawa reported that in the Seattle area delinquencies of Japanese-Americans were underreported principally because teachers, coun-

[6]Ibid., p. 157.

selors, police, and other officials *believe* that Japanese-Americans are well behaved. Moreover, part of the Japanese culture is to show respect for one's elders, and for others in positions of authority, so when a policeman encounters a Japanese-American it is hard for him to believe that a youth so polite, neat, and middle-class in demeanor could be involved in any very serious delinquency. By way of contrast, "Coolness, indifference, and a tough exterior are prized possessions of Negro youth. When youths who operate in this world are confronted with an accuser, their response is likely to do more to convince him of their guilt and their problem than to allay his qualms about the seriousness of their suspected or known delinquent behavior."[7]

That these suggested differences are by no means universal was revealed by a study in which Japanese-American delinquents and their parents were compared with Japanese-American nondelinquents and their parents. The delinquents and their families were much less "Japanese" than the nondelinquents, especially in terms of more use of lower-class argot, sloppy dress, hair style, and general physical appearance. The social participation patterns of the delinquents were typically with non-Japanese lower-class persons.[8]

A number of localized studies have shown that racial membership of *both the offender and the victim* is of great importance in determining the official reaction to crimes committed by blacks. For example, Bullock found that juries tend to give blacks convicted of murder shorter sentences than whites, while blacks convicted of burglary receive longer sentences than whites. Murder by blacks tends to be an intraracial crime, while burglary by blacks is mainly interracial.[9]

Table 14 shows the distribution of arrests reported by police agencies to the FBI in 1975.[10] While differential reporting and arresting practices probably affect in a significant way the proportions of arrests for crimes such as assault, burglary, possession of weapons, prostitution, and disorderly conduct, they probably are less closely related to crimes such as murder and robbery. Indeed, several studies have shown that blacks are more often arrested, convicted, and imprisoned than whites because blacks are more often involved in serious and repeated offenses, not because of biases against blacks by individual criminal justice officials.[11]

---

[7] William J. Chambliss and Richard H. Nagasawa, "On the Validity of Official Statistics—A Comparative Study of White, Black, and Japanese High-School Boys," *Journal of Research in Crime and Delinquency*, 6:71–77, 1969.

[8] Harry H. L. Kitano, "Japanese-American Crime and Delinquency," *Journal of Psychology*, 66:253–63, 1967.

[9] Henry Allen Bullock, "Significance of the Racial Factor in the Length of Prison Sentences," *Journal of Criminal Law, Criminology, and Police Science*, 52:411–17, 1961. Many similar studies are discussed in Charles E. Reasons and Jack Kuykendal, eds., *Race, Crime, and Justice* (Pacific Palisades, Calif.: Goodyear Publishing Company, 1972); and in Elton Long, James Long, Wilmer Leon, and Paul B. Weston, *American Minorities: The Justice Issue* (Englewood Cliffs, N.J.: Prentice-Hall, 1975).

[10] Federal Bureau of Investigation, U.S. Department of Justice, *Uniform Crime Reports for the United States*, 1975 (Washington, D.C.: Government Printing Office, 1975), p. 192.

[11] See, for example, Lyle W. Shannon, "Types and Patterns of Delinquency Referral in a Middle-Sized City," *British Journal of Sociology*, 3:24–36, 1963; Edward Green, *Judicial Attitudes in Sentencing* (New York: St.

RACE RATIOS

Despite the limitations of the official statistics on the crimes committed by members of various races, it seems reasonable to assume that in the United States the general crime rate among blacks is considerably higher than the rate among whites. If we make this assumption, then we can observe that there are two general relationships between crime and race, just as there are two general relationships between crime and age, and between crime and sex. We shall focus on a comparison of the rates of blacks and of whites.

First, the general crime rate of blacks exceeds the rate among whites. The official statistics of arrest per 100,000 population of the same race 15 years of age and over for the entire United States suggests that the black population has arrest rates about three to four times those of the white population. One study traced 9945 boys born in 1945 and living in Philadelphia at least from 1955 through 1962.[12] Over all, 35 percent of the boys had at least one contact with the police for something other than a traffic violation, but this percentage was 50 for the nonwhites as compared with 29 for the whites. Moreover, of all the offenses committed by the boys, 56 percent were committed by nonwhites who made up 29 percent of the birth cohort. When weighted for seriousness, the nonwhite rate was 4.6 times the white rate.[13] In a nationwide study, interviews with a sample (N = 2510) of American men who were 20 to 30 years old in 1974 revealed that 39 percent of the blacks and 30 percent of the whites had been arrested for a nontraffic offense. Also, 9 percent of the blacks and 8 percent of the whites had appeared in juvenile court; 17 percent of the blacks and 11 percent of the whites had been convicted of a crime; 14 percent of the blacks and 4 percent of the whites had been imprisoned.[14] The rate of commitment of blacks to state and federal prisons is about six times the white rate. The arrest of Indians and Chinese are about three times the rate of whites, but the Japanese have a rate lower than that of whites. The commitment rates of Indians and Chinese are also similar to the rate of blacks, but the commitment rate for Japanese is only about half that of whites.

Second, the extent to which the crime rate among blacks exceeds the crime rate of whites varies with social conditions. In some conditions the crime rate for blacks is not as far in excess of the rate for whites as it is in other conditions, and in

Martins Press, 1962); Donald J. Black, "Production of Crime Rates," *American Sociological Review*, 35:733–48, 1970; Norman L. Weiner and Charles V. Willie, "Decisions by Juvenile Officers," *American Journal of Sociology*, 77:199–210, 1971; William R. Arnold, "Race and Ethnicity in Juvenile Court Dispositions," and Robert G. Culbertson, "Commitment Practices in Indiana's Juvenile Courts," *Juvenile Justice*, 24:25–30, 1973.

12 Marvin E. Wolfgang, Robert Figlio, and Thorsten Sellin, *Delinquency in a Birth Cohort* (Chicago: University of Chicago Press, 1972).

13 Marvin E. Wolfgang, "Crime in a Birth Cohort," *Proceedings of the American Philosophical Society*, 17:404–11, 1973.

14 John A. O'Donnell, Harwin L. Voss, Richard R. Clayton, Gerald T. Slatin, and Robin G. W. Room, *Young Men and Drugs—A Nationwide Survey* (Washington, D.C.: National Institute on Drug Abuse, Research Monograph No. 5, 1976), pp. 90–93.

Table 14 Total Arrests by Race, 1975 (7,993 agencies; 1975 estimated population 169,455,000)

Offense charged	White	Negro	Indian	Chinese	Japanese	All Others (Includes Race Unknown)
				Percent Distribution		
Total	**72.2**	**25.2**	**1.5**	**0.1**	**0.1**	**0.9**
Criminal homicide:						
(a) Murder and nonnegligent manslaughter	43.4	54.4	0.9	0.1	0.1	1.1
(b) Manslaughter by negligence	78.0	18.7	0.7	0.1	0.1	2.5
Forcible rape	52.3	45.4	0.9	—	0.1	1.3
Robbery	39.5	58.8	0.7	0.1	0.1	0.9
Aggravated assault	58.2	39.5	1.2	0.1	—	1.0
Burglary—breaking and entering	69.8	28.4	0.7	—	0.1	0.9
Larceny—theft	67.2	30.6	0.7	0.1	0.1	1.2
Auto theft	70.7	26.4	1.3	0.1	0.1	1.4
Subtotal for above offenses	**65.1**	**32.8**	**0.8**	**0.1**	**0.1**	**1.1**
Other assaults	64.3	33.6	1.1	0.1	0.1	1.0
Arson	79.3	19.2	0.6	—	—	0.8
Forgery and counterfeiting	66.3	32.5	0.6	0.1	—	0.5
Fraud	70.5	28.5	0.6	—	—	0.3
Embezzlement	68.5	30.5	0.5	—	—	0.4
Stolen property: buying, receiving, possessing	64.9	33.8	0.5	0.1	—	0.7
Vandalism	83.3	15.2	0.8	—	—	0.7
Weapons: carrying, possessing, etc.	56.7	41.4	0.7	0.1	0.1	1.0
Prostitution and commercialized vice	45.0	53.6	0.4	0.1	0.1	0.8
Sex offenses (except forcible rape and prostitution)	78.6	19.3	1.0	0.1	0.1	0.9
Narcotic drug laws	78.7	19.8	0.5	0.1	0.1	0.8
Gambling	25.0	72.0	0.1	0.2	0.6	2.1
Offenses against family and children	70.4	28.0	1.1	—	—	0.5
Driving under the influence	84.0	13.1	1.3	0.1	0.1	1.4

Table 14   (cont'd.)

Offense charged	Percent Distribution					
	White	Negro	Indian	Chinese	Japanese	All Others (Includes Race Unknown)
Liquor laws	88.6	8.1	2.6	—	—	0.7
Drunkenness	76.1	19.3	3.9	—	—	0.6
Disorderly conduct	67.4	30.2	1.8	—	—	0.6
Vagrancy	58.4	39.3	1.6	0.1	—	0.6
All other offenses (except traffic)	70.6	27.1	1.1	0.1	0.1	1.1
Suspicion	59.4	39.3	0.8	—	—	0.5
Curfew and loitering law violations	72.4	25.6	1.1	—	0.1	0.7
Runaways	87.8	10.1	1.2	—	0.1	0.9

SOURCE: Federal Bureau of Investigation, *Uniform Crime Reports for the United States, 1975*, p. 192.

still other conditions the rate for blacks is lower than the rate for whites. At least five variations in the race ratio must be noted.

1. In the United States, the extent to which the rate for blacks exceeds the rate for whites varies by region. The excess is highest in the western states and lowest in the southern states, with northern states occupying an intermediate position.[15] In Philadelphia in 1954, blacks made up 20 percent of the population but accounted for 50 percent of the arrests; in Michigan and Ohio at about the same time blacks were 7 percent of the population but about 40 percent of the prison population.[16] The differences in rates are not distributed in the same way for all offenses; for homicide, for example, the difference is greatest in the South and least in New England. Similarly, Hayner long ago showed that there were variations in the crime rates of Indians in different tribes, and that the variations were related to the tribes' contacts with white culture and to their economic resources.[17]

[15] The high ratio in the West may be due in part to the fact that blacks in that area tend to be unduly concentrated in the young adult group and in cities, both of which have high crime rates.

[16] William H. Kephart, "The Negro Offender," *American Journal of Sociology*, 60:46–50, 1954; Vernon Fox and Joann Volakakis, "The Negro Offender in a Northern Industrial Area," *Journal of Criminal Law, Criminology, and Police Science*, 46:641–47, 1956; and Ohio Legislative Service Commission, *Capital Punishment*, Staff Research Report No. 46 (Columbus: Ohio Legislative Service Commission, 1961), p. 62.

[17] Norman S. Hayner, "Variability in the Criminal Behavior of American Indians," *American Journal of Sociology*, 47:602–13, 1942. See also Hans von Hentig, "Delinquency of the American Indian," *Journal of Criminal Law and Criminology*, 36:75–84, 1945; Sidney M. Willhelm, "Black Man, Red Man, and White

2. The extent to which the crime rate of blacks exceeds the crime rate of whites varies with sex status. Forslund found the following variations in the arrest and conviction rates per 100,000 of the same status in Stamford, Connecticut:[18]

	White Males	White Females	Negro Males	Negro Females
Arrest Rate	1829	175	10,696	1666
Conviction Rate	1746	114	14,177	1607

Thus the conviction rate for black males was about eight times that for white males, but the rate for black females was about 14 times the rate for white females. Similarly, in Wolfgang's study of all criminal homicides occurring in Philadelphia during a five-year period, the rate per 100,000 by race and sex of offenders showed the following rank order: black males—41.7, black females—9.3, white males—3.4, and white females—0.4.[19] A study of criminal homicide in Chicago showed higher rates, but in the same rank order: nonwhite males—54.8. nonwhite females—11.6, white males—6.6, and white females—0.7.[20]

3. The extent to which the crime rate of blacks exceeds the crime rate of whites varies with the offense. When based on imprisonment rates, the excess is greatest for assault and homicide and lowest for rape. Table 14 shows the proportions of blacks, whites, and others arrested for various crimes in 1975. The proportions of blacks among the persons arrested for murder and nonnegligent manslaughter, for robbery, and for gambling were high. While blacks were 54 percent of those arrested for murder and nonnegligent manslaughter in 1975, they were only 28 percent of those arrested for burglary and 20 percent of those arrested for violation of narcotic drug laws. It also is known that the excess of crime among blacks is higher for second offenses than it is for first offenses.

McKeown correlated arrest rates for specified crimes in fifty-five cities of 100,000–250,000 population and thirty-six cities over 250,000 with the percentage of black population in those cities. For murder and nonnegligent manslaughter the coefficients of correlation ranged from $+.67$ to $+.87$, justifying the conclusion that cities with a high percentage of blacks in their population have high rates

American: The Constitutional Approach to Genocide," *Catalyst*, Spring, 1969, pp. 1–62; Charles E. Reasons, "Crime and the American Indian," in *Native Americans Today: Sociological Perspectives*, ed. Howard Bahr, Bruce Chadwick, and Robert Day (New York: Harper and Row, 1972); and John Hagan, "Criminal Justice and Native People: A Study of Incarceration in a Canadian Province," *Canadian Review of Sociology and Anthropology*, 11:220–36, 1974.

[18] Forslund, "A Comparison of Negro and White Crime Rates."

[19] Marvin E. Wolfgang, "A Sociological Analysis of Criminal Homicide," *Federal Probation*, 25:48–55, 1961.

[20] Harwin L. Voss and John R. Hepburn, "Patterns in Criminal Homicide in Chicago," *Journal of Criminal Law, Criminology, and Police Science*, 59:499–508, 1968.

of murder and nonnegligent manslaughter. The coefficients for other types of crimes vary widely from one year to another or from one class of cities to the other, and justify no conclusion regarding the relation between black population and crime rates of cities.[21] Moreover, it has been shown that in southern cities, which have large percentages of blacks, the white populations have very high rates of murder and manslaughter. In Houston, Lundsgaarde consistently found that the census tracts having the heaviest concentration of blacks also had the greatest number of homicides, but one census tract comprised of 247 whites and 3525 blacks (93 percent) *had no homicides at all.*[22] Clearly, the relatively high murder and manslaughter rates in cities and areas which have large proportions of blacks cannot be attributed to a racial factor.

4. The extent to which the crime rate of blacks exceeds the crime rate of whites varies with time. There is no long-range evidence on this point, but it seems probable that the amount of excess has been increasing during the last fifty years. Recent statistics suggest that the amount of excess is increasing for some offenses but decreasing for others. During the period 1960–1965, the black arrest rate for robbery increased 24 percent while the white rate increased 3 percent. But for crimes of violence (murder, rape, aggravated assault) the black rate increased only 5 percent, while the white rate increased 27 percent. The rates per 100,000 of the same race for burglary, larceny, and automobile theft arrests increased along parallel lines—33 percent for blacks and 24 percent for whites.[23]

An earlier study indicated that in three decades the black juvenile delinquency rate in Chicago increased seven times, while the black population increased only three times.[24] The comparable data on the rate and population increases for whites are not available. Black children have a relatively low delinquency rate when they first settle in a deteriorated area, but their delinquency rate increases with length of residence until a peak is reached; this generally has taken about five years.[25]

5. The extent to which the crime rate of blacks exceeds that of whites varies with educational status. Older studies indicated little crime among graduates of black colleges, but it is likely that educated blacks have been increasingly convicted of crime in recent years, while small semirural black communities with high degrees of illiteracy have remained relatively free of crime. In cities, however,

[21] James Edward McKeown, "Poverty, Race, and Crime," *Journal of Criminal Law and Criminology*, 39:480–84, 1948.

[22] Henry P. Lundsgaarde, *Murder in Space City: A Cultural Analysis of Houston Homicide Patterns* (New York: Oxford University Press, 1977), p. 50.

[23] President's Commission on Law Enforcement and Administration of Justice, *Task Force Report: Crime and Its Impact: An Assessment* (Washington, D.C.: Government Printing Office, 1967), p. 78.

[24] Earl R. Moses, "Community Factors in Negro Delinquency," *Journal of Negro Education*, 5:220–27, April, 1936.

[25] Ibid. See also *idem*, "Differentials in Crime Rates Between Negroes and Whites," *American Sociological Review*, 12:411–20, 1947.

the crime rate of highly educated blacks is much lower than the rate of poorly educated whites.

In short, such statistics as are available indicate that blacks have higher crime rates than whites, but that the ratio of crime rates among blacks to crime rates among whites varies with specific social situations. These variations cannot be explained by biological differences among the races. They can be explained only by social interaction.

One notion that seeks to explain these racial ratios is that the minority group status, as such, somehow produces a high crime rate. In fact, however, the crime rate of Japanese-Americans is a sufficient refutation of this notion, for Japanese-Americans have a lower crime rate than the majority group.

A second notion is that the high crime rate of minority groups is due to frustrations produced by discrimination.[26] Again, Japanese-Americans meet discrimination and are presumably frustrated, but they do not have a high crime rate. Furthermore, while frustration is a vague term which cannot be measured or even defined, the feeling of frustration is probably more pronounced in the upper socioeconomic class of urban blacks, whose crime rate is low, than in the lower class of urban blacks, whose crime rate is high. A variation of the frustration theory is limited to the high rate of assaults and homicides by blacks. This theory is that blacks build up a great feeling of anger because of the discriminations against them, that they do not dare express their anger against the powerful white population, and that they release this anger in attacks on their fellow blacks. This theory, which is a theory of displacement of emotion, was formulated some years ago by Dollard.[27]

A third theory is that it is the economic status of the minority group, which is a product of discrimination, that explains the high crime rate of the group. This theory will be discussed in some detail in Chapter 11. The basic idea is that the differential between the blacks' economic status and their recently aroused hope that they will at last be permitted to participate in "the American dream" has produced a potential for direct action in the form of crime. In a significant study along these lines, Davis found that blacks in Los Angeles have developed a rich vocabulary of motives which "de-legitimize" the legal system, making criminal conduct seem both reasonable and justified.[28] In a statistical study of delinquency of black and white children by census tracts in Detroit, Blue showed that when economic status is held constant, the partial correlation between race and juvenile delinquency is $+.52$, while when race is held constant, the correlation between

---

[26] See Gerhard J. Falk, "Status Differences and the Frustration Aggression Hypothesis," *International Journal of Social Psychiatry*, 5:214–22, 1959.

[27] John Dollard, *Caste and Class in a Southern Town* (New Haven, Conn.: Yale University Press, 1937).

[28] John A. Davis, "Justification for No Obligation: Views of Black Males Toward Crime and the Criminal Law," *Issues in Criminology*, 9:69–87, 1974.

economic status and juvenile delinquency is –.59.[29] This indicates that economic status is slightly more closely related to juvenile delinquency than is race. Similarly, in a study of census tracts in Lexington, Kentucky, Quinney determined that the crime rate correlation with economic status was –.52; with family status it was –.16; and with ethnicity it was +.47. The area correlations with delinquency rates were –.38 for economic status, –.35 for family status, and +.48 for ethnic status.[30]

Statistically speaking, blacks are poor—in 1974, about 11 percent of the families in the United States were black, but 25 percent of the poverty families (those with incomes of $5038 or less) were black. Furthermore, 30 percent of all black families were classified as "poor," as compared with 7.5 percent of the white families.[31] However, Japanese-Americans resemble other minority groups in their low economic position but differ from them in crime rates. Finally, the popular notion that poverty causes crime ignores the fact that most blacks who are in poverty, like most whites who are in poverty, do not get into trouble with the law. Moreover, this notion is not a satisfactory explanation of criminal behavior because it does not specify how poverty might possibly "work" to produce the delinquency and crime it is said to produce.[32]

According to the differential association theory, race ratios and the variations in them result from variations in associations with criminal and anticriminal patterns. In the United States, race may be related to associations in either or both of two ways. First, the inheritance of certain characteristics to a large extent determines the social and economic level at which many members of a race live. This status casts persons into situations where either anticriminal behavior patterns or certain criminal patterns impinge upon them with great frequency and intensity. Blacks do not commit white-collar crimes as frequently as do whites, because they are not as frequently in association with the criminalistic values of white-collar criminals and, consistently, are not as frequently in white-collar jobs. They commit crimes which are typical of that part of the society with which they come in contact. Second, confinement of a race to a given locale may mean that many members of the race, especially juveniles, can hardly escape the traditions which are characteristic of the locale.[33] The traditions may be essentially

[29] John T. Blue, "The Relationship of Juvenile Delinquency, Race, and Economic Status," *Journal of Negro Education*, 17:469–77, 1948. See also Kenneth Polk, "Juvenile Delinquency and Social Areas," *Social Problems*, 5:215–17, 1957–58; H. Miller, "Changes in the Number and Composition of the Poor," in *Poverty in America*, ed. M. Gordon (San Francisco: Chandler, 1965), pp. 86–87; and St. Clair Drake, "The Social and Economic Status of the Negro in the United States," *Daedalus*, 94:771–810, 1965.

[30] Richard Quinney, "Crime, Delinquency, and Social Areas," *Journal of Research in Crime and Delinquency*, 1:149–54, 1964.

[31] *Statistical Abstracts of the United States*, 1975, p. 395.

[32] See Chapter 11.

[33] See Marvin E. Wolfgang, *Patterns in Criminal Homicide* (Philadelphia: University of Pennsylvania Press, 1958), pp. 65–70, 180–81; Mozell Hill, "The Metropolis and Juvenile Delinquency Among Negroes," *Journal*

anticriminal, but in contemporary inner-city ghettos some of the traditions are in direct conflict with the morality reflected in the criminal law.

NATIVITY RATIOS

While assimilation of vast numbers of immigrants is no longer considered a serious social problem in the United States, analysis of data on the nativity of criminals remains a problem of great theoretical significance. During the years when immigration was at its height, many persons argued that immigration was the chief cause of crime. The mechanisms by which immigration produces crime were not specified, but the following were suggested: (1) Immigrants come from inferior racial stock, or there is a larger proportion of inferior individuals in the racial stock of immigrants than among native whites, and this degeneracy leads to criminality. (2) Immigrants are not trained in the codes and ideals of America and, therefore, commit crimes out of ignorance. (3) Immigrants are frequently poverty-stricken, and this condition of poverty and the resulting frustration create personal maladjustments of various kinds, including delinquency and criminality. (4) Immigrants are highly mobile and thus are isolated from the inhibiting and restraining influences of primary groups. Each of these notions is based upon the assumption that there is an excessive rate of criminality among the immigrants. This assumption is not warranted. Many research studies have consistently shown that the general crime rate of immigrants is lower than the general crime rate of the native-born. These studies have also yielded a set of statistical data about the nativity ratio in crime and about the variations in this ratio. Consideration of these data casts doubt on the validity of all four notions. As is the case with age, sex, and race, there are two general relationships between crime and nativity.

First, computed on the basis of population numbers only, the native-white rates of arrest and imprisonment in the United States are about twice as high as the rates for foreign-born whites. Similarly, the crime rate for native Australians is about twice the rate for immigrants arriving after World War II, and in 1966 the crime rate of the native population of Düsseldorf, Germany, was about twice the rate of foreign-born workers.[34] Further, the conviction rate of native-born Canadian males aged 15–49 was 87/10,000 in 1951–54, but the rate for foreign-born males was 43. The rates for specific foreign-born groups ranged from 63 for the United States to 42 for Germany, 37 for Asia, and 17 for Italy.[35]

of Negro Education, 28:277–85, 1959; Claude Brown, *Manchild in the Promised Land* (New York: Macmillan, 1965); and Victor Eisner, *The Delinquency Label: The Epidemiology of Juvenile Delinquency* (New York: Random House, 1969), pp. 87–107.

[34] Commonwealth Immigration Advisory Council, *Third Report of the Committee Established to Investigate Conduct of Migrants* (Canberra, Australia: Commonwealth Government Printer, 1957), p. 4; Franco Ferracuti, "European Migration and Crime," Chapter 12 in *Crime and Culture: Essays in Honor of Thorsten Sellin,* ed. Marvin E. Wolfgang (New York: Wiley, 1968), pp. 189–219.

[35] P. J. Griffen, "Rates of Crime and Delinquency," Chapter 4 in *Crime and Its Treatment in Canada,* ed. W. T. McGrath (Toronto: Macmillan, 1965), p. 83.

When correction is made for the fact that the age and sex distributions of the populations are not the same, the difference between the two groups becomes even greater. For example, 52.5 percent of the immigrants in Australia and only 29 percent of the native Australians are in the "crime-committing ages" (15 to 35), so the correction for age gives the immigrants an even lower comparative crime rate. A study of the crime rates of Italian immigrants in Zurich, Switzerland, also showed that the crime rate of an immigrant group—in this case, Italians—was lower than that of the native-born despite an unfavorable age ratio.[36] In the earlier studies it was often concluded that immigrants contributed more than their quota of crime, but the present findings rebut this conclusion.

Second, the extent to which the crime rate of native whites exceeds the rate among immigrants is not the same under differing social conditions:

1. The extent to which the crime rate among native whites exceeds the crime rate of the foreign-born varies with offenses. Certain types of crime are characteristic of one immigrant group, while other types of crime are characteristic of a different immigrant group. Some groups have high rates for drunkenness and other misdemeanors, and low rates for felonies, while other groups have high rates for felonies and low rates for misdemeanors.

A high rate of commitment to jails and workhouses, as in the case of the Irish and Finnish immigrants, is an expression of the drinking habits of those groups. Of German immigrants committed to federal and state prisons in 1932–1936, 4.5 percent were committed for homicide, 3.6 percent for assault, and 14.3 percent for burglary, while of Italian immigrants the percentages were 10.7, 9.4, and 7.1. Thus, the Italians had twice the proportion of homicides and assaults, and half the proportion of burglaries. In Stockholm in 1965, 65 percent of the Yugoslavs convicted of crimes had committed crimes against persons, and only 12 percent were drunk at the time of the crime; Greeks, on the other hand, had only 24 percent convictions of crimes against the person, and almost all of them were committed while the offender was intoxicated.[37]

Thus certain crimes or groups of crimes are characteristic of certain national groups. These same types of crimes are, usually, characteristic of the home countries, also. The Italian and Turkish immigrants residing in Germany in 1965 had high rates of conviction for murder and assault; Italy and Turkey also have high murder and assault rates.[38] Italians in America have a low rate of arrest for drunkenness, and drunkenness is comparatively rare in Italy. The traditions of the home country are transplanted to the host country and determine the relative positions of the immigrant groups with reference to the types of crimes.[39]

[36] Ferracuti, "European Migration and Crime," p. 205.
[37] Ibid., pp. 210–11.
[38] Ibid., pp. 211–212.
[39] Lyle W. Shannon, "The Economic Absorption and Cultural Integration of Immigrant Workers," *American Behavioral Scientist*, 13:36–56, 1969.

2. The extent to which the crime rate of native whites exceeds the rate among foreign-born persons varies from one immigrant group to another. Eastern European immigrants in Australia have crime rates about three times as high as southern European immigrants and almost twice as high as northern European immigrants.[40] Of the foreign-born groups in Switzerland, the Austrians have the highest crime rate, followed by Germans, Italians, Arabs, Turks, and French.[41] Similarly, in the United States in the years when immigration was at its height, persons of Irish nativity had crime rates three to five times as high as German immigrants. The crime rate among Japanese immigrants was exceptionally low.[42] The rate among the children of these immigrants was also exceptionally low, but the grandchildren began to take on the crime rates of the areas where they resided.[43] A study of our adult Puerto Rican citizens residing in Brooklyn showed, similarly, that the crime rates were disproportionately low.[44] Another study showed that Puerto Rican children were not overrepresented in New York City's juvenile courts.[45]

3. The extent to which the crime rate of native whites exceeds the rate among the foreign-born varies from one native white group to another. The native white sons of immigrants tend to have crime rates higher than those of their fathers but lower than other native whites. Even this variation changes with specific circumstances. Sometimes the rates for the children of immigrants are higher than those for native whites of native parentage. The rate of referral of Mexican-American children to the Los Angeles County Probation Department for juvenile delinquency twenty years ago was three times the rate for "Anglos" (whites not of Mexican or Oriental descent) and slightly higher than the rate for blacks.[46] Forty years ago, Ogburn found that crimes known to the police had a negative correlation with the number of children of immigrants in three groups of cities, and that the negative association persisted when other factors were held constant;

---

[40] Commonwealth Immigration Advisory Council, *Third Report*, p. 18. This publication does not specify the nations involved. For a summary of early research on the crime rates of various immigrant groups in America, see Arthur Lewis Wood, "Minority Group Criminality and Cultural Integration," *Journal of Criminal Law and Criminology*, 37:498–510, 1947.

[41] Ferracuti, "European Migration and Crime," p. 208.

[42] Norman S. Hayner, "Delinquency Areas in the Puget Sound Region," *American Journal of Sociology*, 39:314–28, 1933.

[43] Gerald H. Ikeda, "Japanese Americans Fight Delinquency," *California Youth Authority Quarterly*, 12:3–6, 1959; Harry H. L. Kitano, "Japanese-American Crime and Delinquency."

[44] Julius Alter, "Crimes of Puerto Ricans in Brooklyn" (Master's thesis, Department of Sociology, Brooklyn College, 1958).

[45] Clarence O. Senior, *Strangers—Then Neighbors* (New York: Anti-Defamation League of B'nai B'rith, 1961), p. 31. See also New York City Board of Education, *The Puerto Rican Study, 1953–1957* (New York: New York City Board of Education, 1958), p. 120.

[46] Joseph W. Eaton and Kenneth Polk, *Measuring Juvenile Delinquency* (Pittsburgh: University of Pittsburgh Press, 1961), pp. 20, 28.

the coefficients of correlation in the three groups of cities ranged between –0.34 and –0.54.[47]

The Bureau of the Census, in its *Report on Federal and State Prisons* for 1933, presented a table regarding nativity of prisoners in twenty-six states in which reports regarding nativity were complete enough for comparison. In seventeen of these states the children of immigrants had a rate of commitment lower than that for native whites of native parentage, while in the other nine states their rate of commitment was higher. In one of the last studies of the crimes of the foreign-born in the United States, Taft made an analysis of this table, with corrections for variations in age distribution, and concluded that the states in which the second generation had lower rates were those in which the older immigration (northern and western Europe) was predominant, and the states in which they had higher rates were those in which the newer immigration (southern and eastern Europe) was predominant.[48] Taft's study also showed that the children of immigrants had higher rates of commitment than their parents in all except one of the twenty-six states, and that offspring of mixed parentage had lower rates of commitment than offspring of foreign parentage in seventeen states and higher rates in nine states.

4. The amount of the excess of crime among the native-born varies with age. Among immigrants who arrive in the United States when they are in early childhood, the crime rate is higher than among immigrants arriving in middle age.[49] Young immigrants take on the relatively high crime rate of native whites to a greater extent than do middle-aged immigrants. Further, the sons of immigrants tend to change from the types of crime characteristic of their parents to those characteristic of the native-born. This is illustrated in Table 15, a comparison of Irish immigrants, the children of Irish immigrants, and the native whites of native parentage with reference to a few crimes of which they were convicted in the New York Court of General Sessions at the turn of the century.[50] The same tendency appears, also, in a comparison of the first and second generations of Italian immigrants with reference to crimes of personal violence in Massachusetts, as shown in Table 16.[51] This seems to show that the tendency to commit crimes of

[47] William F. Ogburn, "Factors in the Variation of Crime among Cities," *Journal of the American Statistical Association*, 30:21–24, 1935. See also McKeown, "Poverty, Race and Crime," and Hans von Hentig, "The First Generation and a Half: Notes on the Delinquency of Native Whites of Mixed Parentage," *American Sociological Review*, 10:792–98, 1945.

[48] D. R. Taft, "Nationality and Crime," *American Sociological Review*, 1:724–36, 1936.

[49] Van Vechten, "Criminality of the Foreign-Born."

[50] U.S. Immigration Commission, "Immigration and Crime," *Report*, vol. 36 (Washington, D.C.: Government Printing Office, 1910), p. 14; see also pp. 15–16 and 67–68.

[51] Computed from reports of the Massachusetts Department of Correction, 1914–1922; population was secured from the Massachusetts State Census of 1915; the census of 1920 does not give the necessary information; Italians of all ages were included, and native-born, both white and nonwhite, of all ages, were used in computation of the native white rate. A similar analysis for the state of New Jersey was made long ago by Stofflet. E. H. Stofflet, "A Study of National and Cultural Differences in Criminal Tendency," *Archives of Psychology*, no. 185, 1935.

Table 15 Conviction Rates of Specified Groups

Offense	Irish Immigrants	Children of Immigrants	Native Whites of Native Parentage
Homicide	2.3	1.0	0.5
Rape	0.0	0.3	0.7
Gambling	1.2	2.7	3.6

personal violence, which is seen so clearly in the Italian immigrants, is a matter of tradition—a tradition which is not passed on to the second generation.

5. The extent to which the crime rate of native whites exceeds that of immigrants varies with the length of time the immigrants have been in the host country. Both immigrants and their sons tend to take on the crime rate of the specific part of the community in which they locate. The delinquency rates of the second generation are comparatively low when the immigrant group first settles in a community, and they increase as contacts with the surrounding culture multiply. The rate remains low in those foreign colonies which are comparatively isolated from the surrounding culture. However, the rate is lowest in the heart of the colony and increases on the borderlines where the group comes into contact with other groups. Moreover, the rates are comparatively low in the immigrant groups which have moved away from the areas of deterioration into better residential areas.[52]

Even the immigrant group itself tends to approach the crime rate of the host country. A study of crime rates in France in the nineteenth century indicated that migrants moving from one province to another changed their crime rates in the direction of the rate of the host province, whether the rate in the host province was higher or lower than the rate in the province from which they migrated.[53] Similarly, in the first five years of residence in an area of high delinquency in Los Angeles, 5 percent of the children in an immigrant group appeared before the juvenile court; after five more years, 46 percent appeared; and after another ten years, 83 percent of the children came before the court.[54] The delinquency rate increased with length of stay in the area, presumably because the immigrant group was assimilating that part of American culture which it experienced, including

[52]Evelyn Buchan Crook, "Cultural Marginality in Sexual Delinquency," *American Journal of Sociology*, 39:493–500, 1934; Hayner, "Delinquency Areas"; Andrew W. Lind, "The Ghetto and the Slum," *Social Forces*, 9:206–15, 1930; idem, "Some Ecological Patterns of Community Disorganization in Honolulu," *American Journal of Sociology*, 36:206–20, 1930; Helen G. McGill, "The Oriental Delinquent in the Vancouver Juvenile Court," *Sociology and Social Research*, 22:428–38, 1938.

[53]Henri Joly, *La France Criminelle* (Paris: Cerf, 1889), pp. 45–46.

[54]Pauline V. Young, "Urbanization as a Factor in Juvenile Delinquency," *Publications of the American Sociological Society*, 24: 162–66, 1930.

Table 16 Frequency of Commitments to State Prison and State Reformatory of Massachusetts for Murder, Manslaughter, and Assault, in Specified Groups, 1914–1922, per 100,000 in Each Group in 1915

Nativity and Parentage	Commitment Rate
Born in Italy	192
Native-born, one or both parents born in Italy	24
Native-born, of native parentage	24
Native-born, one or both parents born in any foreign country	22

the delinquency rates. In a personal communication, Dr. Young recently pointed out that in the 1940s the group dispersed to the suburbs, and that by 1970 the image of them as delinquents had completely vanished among law enforcement agencies.

Taken together, the above variations in the nativity ratio force a rejection of each of the four theories described above; each theory is contradicted by at least one of the variations. Also, the fact that there is generally no undue amount of crime among the foreign-born undermines the assumption on which each of the theories is based.

The variations can be explained in terms of differential associations with criminal and anticriminal behavior patterns. Since immigrants often live in poverty, are mobile, and are affected by many other conditions which are described as "criminogenic," it has been argued that their apparently low general crime rate must be due to statistical errors.[55] There is no necessary conflict here, however. Most immigrants have developed respect for law in their home countries, and these habits, ideals, and codes persist after they reach America, so that they are not as criminalistic as native Americans. They are, nevertheless, affected by the behavior patterns of the people living in the areas where they settle, and these patterns are likely to involve norms conducive to delinquency and crime.[56] The comparatively low crime rate of recent southern European migrants in Australia has been attributed to the fact that most such migrants enter Australia under the sponsorship of a member of their own family already in that country; the migrants who had spent many years in displaced-persons camps in Europe made up the group responsible for the greatest number of crimes committed by aliens.[57]

Thus, the important variables in the differential crime rates of the several

[55] Donald R. Taft, "Does Immigration Increase Crime?" *Social Forces*, 12:69–77, 1933.

[56] See Elena Padilla, *Up From Puerto Rico* (New York: Columbia University Press, 1958), p. 229; Richard A. Cloward and Lloyd E. Ohlin, *Delinquency and Opportunity* (Glencoe, Ill.: Free Press, 1960), pp. 194–211; and Daniel Bell, "Crime as an American Way of Life," *Antioch Review*, 13:131–54, 1953.

[57] Commonwealth Immigration Advisory Council, *Third Report*, pp. 5, 18.

nationality groups are the strength and consistency of the traditions which they assimilated in their home countries and the strength and consistency of the traditions with which they come in contact in the new country. These traditions also explain the differences in the types of crime characteristic of the various immigrant groups and the variations in the types of crime and crime rates of the children of immigrants as compared with their parents. An expert on demography and migration has formulated the principle as follows: "The characteristics of migrants tend to be intermediate between the characteristics of the population at origin and the population at destination."[58]

SUMMARY AND CONCLUSIONS

In this chapter and in Chapter 6 we have considered some of the data about the relationship of crime and delinquency to age, sex, race, and nativity. Although these are only some of the social conditions with which crime rates vary, the list is sufficiently long to enable us to draw the important conclusion that crime is social behavior that is closely associated with other kinds of social behavior. In Chapters 9 and 11 we will consider additional sets of data, those pertaining to relationships between crime and size of community and between crime and social class. Here we need only observe that one set of facts indicates that the crime rate is higher for young adults than for persons in later life, higher for males than for females; higher for blacks than for whites; and higher for native-born than for foreign-born. Such differences may be described as ratios—the age ratio in crime, the sex ratio in crime, and so on. A second set of facts shows that these ratios are not constant. They vary in definite ways, depending on social conditions.

These ratios and variations in ratios make up some of the facts that a general explanation of crime must fit. They may be called definitive facts, for they define or limit the explanations of crime that can be considered valid. For example, an explanation that attributes crime to poverty helps make good sense out of the overrepresentation of blacks in the criminal population, but the theory falls flat when we recall that females, who are equal in poverty with males, have very low crime rates; when we recall that immigrants, who are probably at least as poor as their sons, usually have crime rates lower than their sons; when we recall that even poor blacks do not have high crime rates in their old age, and so on. Similarly, an explanation of crime in terms of a hereditary characteristic or of a psychological trait such as aggression must show that the characteristic is much more frequent among males than among females, among black women than white women, among young persons as compared to old persons, among native whites as compared to immigrants; and it must show that the trait occurs very infrequently among some immigrant groups—among southern European immigrants in Australia, for example.

None of the general explanations of crime makes good sense of all the ratios and

---

[58] A. S. Lee, "A Theory of Migration," *Demography*, 3:47–57, 1966.

variations in ratios. Some of them explain one set of facts, and others explain another set of facts, but none of them explains all the facts. However, the theory of differential association and concordant sociological theories that have as their general point the observation that crime and criminality are products of social experience and social interaction make better sense out of more of the facts than do other general theories.

SUGGESTED READINGS

Black, Donald J. "Production of Crime Rates." *American Sociological Review*, 35:733–48, 1970.

Bonger, W. A. *Race and Crime*. Translated by Margaret M. Horduk. New York: Columbia University Press, 1943.

Bullock, Henry Allen. "Significance of the Racial Factor in the Length of Prison Sentences." *Journal of Criminal Law, Criminology, and Police Science*, 52:411–17, 1961.

Carroll, Leo, & Margaret E. Mondrick. "Racial Bias in the Decision to Grant Parole." *Law and Society Review*, 11:93–107, 1976.

Eaton, Joseph W., & Kenneth Polk. *Measuring Juvenile Delinquency*. Pittsburgh: University of Pittsburgh Press, 1961.

Falk, Gerhard J. "Status Differences and the Frustration Aggression Hypothesis." *International Journal of Social Psychiatry*, 5:214–22, 1959.

Forslund, Morris A. "A Comparison of Negro and White Crime Rates." *Journal of Criminal Law, Criminology, and Police Science*, 61:214–17, 1970.

Geis, Gilbert. "Statistics Concerning Race and Crime." *Crime and Delinquency*, April, 1965, pp. 142–50.

Goldberg, N. "Jews in the Police Records of Los Angeles, 1933–1937." *Yivo Annual of Jewish Social Science*, 5:266–91, 1950.

Gould, Leroy C. "Who Defines Delinquency: A Comparison of Self-Reported and Officially Reported Indices of Delinquency for Three Racial Groups," *Social Problems*, 16:325–36, 1969.

Green, Edward. "Race, Social Status, and Criminal Arrest." *American Sociological Review*, 35:476–90, 1970.

Kitano, Harry H. L. "Japanese-American Crime and Delinquency." *Journal of Psychology*, 66:253–63, 1967.

Reasons, Charles, & Jack L. Kuykendal. *Race, Crime, and Justice*. Pacific Palisades, Calif.: Goodyear, 1972.

Rudwick, Elliott M. "Race Labeling and the Press," *Journal of Negro Education*, 31:177–81, 1962.

Silverman, Robert A. "Criminality Among Jews: An Overview." *Issues in Criminology*, 6:1–39, 1971.

Swigert, Victoria Lynn, & Ronald A. Farrell. "Normal Homicides and the Law." *American Sociological Review*, 42:16–32, 1977.

Terry, Robert M. "The Screening of Juvenile Offenders." *Journal of Criminal Law, Criminology, and Police Science*, 58:173–81, 1967.

Wolfgang, Marvin E., & Bernard Cohen. *Crime and Race: Conceptions and Misconceptions*. New York: Institute of Human Relations Press, American Jewish Committee, 1970.

Wolfgang, Marvin E., Arlene Kelly, & Hans C. Nolde. "Comparison of the Executed and the Commuted Among Admissions to Death Row." *Journal of Criminal Law, Criminology, and Police Science*, 53:301–11, 1962.

Personality

A widely held belief is that criminal behavior is due to some pathological characteristic or trait of the personality which exists prior to the criminal behavior and is the cause of it. The Lombrosian notion that criminals constitute a distinct physical type has continued as a neo-Lombrosian notion that maintains the same logic but substitutes psychopathological type for physical type. Some scholars have found the explanation of crime in mental defectiveness, others in schizophrenia, others in psychopathic personality, and others in a composite group of emotional disturbances. However, psychiatrists differ as to the importance of these pathological traits; some assert that practically all criminals are psychopathic; others assert that 10 percent or even less are psychopathic.

Mental disorders have been classified in many ways. One of the simpler classifications includes three groups, namely, mental defect or mental retardation; psychosis; and neuropathic conditions, which include psychopathic personality, and the psychoneuroses.

MENTAL DEFECT

Mental retardation was once used almost as a specific explanation of crime. The explanation was explicitly stated in propositions that all or almost all criminals are "feebleminded." It also was stated implicitly in the proposition that "feebleminded" persons commit crimes, in the absence of special inhibiting conditions, because they do not have sufficient intelligence to appreciate the reasons for laws and the consequences of violations of law; in the proposition that "feeblemindedness" and, thus, the tendency to commit crimes is inherited as a unit character in accordance with Mendel's law of heredity; and in the proposition that a policy of sterilization or segregation of the "feebleminded" is the only effective method of preventing crime and of dealing with criminals.

This statement of propositions does not include the many exceptions made by various authors, and perhaps is unfair even to Harry H. Goddard, who was in the early period the most extreme adherent of the idea that mental defect causes crime. More than fifty years ago Goddard stated:

Every investigation of the mentality of criminals, misdemeanants, delinquents, and other antisocial groups has proven beyond the possibility of contradiction that nearly all persons in these classes, and in some cases all, are of low mentality. . . . It is no longer to be denied that the greatest single cause of delinquency and crime is lowgrade mentality, much of it within the limits of feeble-mindedness.[1]

Goddard's conclusion, and the other propositions as well, dominated psychological research in criminology as well as social policy about crime for two decades. More than 350 studies of the intelligence of delinquents and criminals were conducted in the 1920s and 1930s. This research ultimately led to the conclusion that the relationship between crime and mental retardation is slight, and the practice of sterilizing retarded persons as a crime-prevention measure stopped.[2] As intelligence tests and the methods of testing improved, the proportion of low IQ persons found in the general population increased, reducing the differences noted between criminals and noncriminals. Further, when allowance was made for the selection process involved in arrest, conviction, and imprisonment, the distribution of the intelligence test scores of delinquents and criminals became even more similar to the distribution in the general population. Studies of mentally retarded persons in the community showed no excess of criminality among them, and studies of mentally retarded offenders showed that they had prison disciplinary records, parole violation rates, and recidivism rates about the same as other offenders. Most significantly, also, intelligence (as measured by tests) proved to be modifiable, as was shown both by retesting of individuals and by comparisons of foster children reared in different environments.[3] Recent psychological thought regarding the relationship between mental deficiency and crime tends to parallel that of Coleman, who makes the following statement:

Popular opinion, based on outdated psychological findings, has it that the great majority of inmates of penal institutions are mentally defective and that mentally defective

[1] H. H. Goddard, *Human Efficiency and Levels of Intelligence* (Princeton: Princeton University Press, 1920), pp. 73–74. See also idem, *Juvenile Delinquency* (New York: Dodd, Mead, 1921), p. 22.

[2] The results of the studies are analyzed in Edwin H. Sutherland, "Mental Deficiency and Crime," chap. 15 in *Social Attitudes*, ed. Kimball Young (New York: Holt, 1931), pp. 357–75; L. D. Zeleny, "Feeble-mindedness and Criminal Conduct," *American Journal of Sociology*, 38:564–78, 1933; Clara F. Chasswell, *The Relation Between Morality and Intellect* (New York: Columbia University Press, 1935); Simon H. Tulchin, *Intelligence and Crime* (Chicago: University of Chicago Press, 1939); Mary Woodward, *Low Intelligence and Delinquency* (London: Institute for the Study and Treatment of Delinquency, 1963); and W. A. M. Black and A. R. Hornblow, "Intelligence and Criminality," *Australian and New Zealand Journal of Criminology*, 6:83–92, 1973.

[3] See Kenneth Eells, *Intelligence and Cultural Differences: A Study of Cultural Learning and Problem Solving* (Chicago: University of Chicago Press, 1951).

individuals are especially prone to criminal behavior. Indeed, one of the major reasons why institutionalization was first recommended for the mental defective was to protect society from his supposed "criminal propensities." More recent psychological evidence has conclusively demonstrated, however, that inferior mentality is neither the specific cause nor the outstanding factor in crime and delinquency. Although a higher percentage of delinquent children come from the ranks of the mentally defective, particularly from those of borderline intelligence, it is not the mental deficiency per se but the inability of the child to make adequate school or social adjustments that usually results in his delinquency.[4]

PSYCHOSES

Although mental disorders have been studied for many generations, much disagreement still prevails regarding definitions, classifications, causes, methods of diagnosis, therapy, extent in the general population, and frequency in the criminal population. It is improper to speak of adjustment problems as "disease" or even "illness."[5] However, if the disease analogy is used, then the phenomenon is not one disease but a large number of diseases, differing from each other as much as bronchitis differs from tuberculosis. Paresis is a fairly well-established disease with clear symptoms and demonstrable organic origin, but schizophrenia is extremely indefinite in regard to both symptoms and origin.

Increasing emphasis is being placed on the role of social relations in the etiology of many of the psychoses. In a pioneering work along this line, Faris and Dunham studied the residences of psychotic patients received in the public and private hospitals of Illinois and showed a definite relationship between social organization and the incidence of psychoses. Generally, they found that the previous places of residence clustered around the center of the city and decreased in frequency toward the city limits. Moreover, they found that all psychoses did not follow the same pattern of distribution, that one type of social organization tended to produce schizophrenia, another type to produce manic-depressive disorders.[6] More recent studies show both a close relationship between social class position and various kinds of mental disturbance,[7] as well as a close relationship between posthospital performance and social class—the higher the class, the better the performance.[8] One investigator has emphasized that delusional ideas and abnor-

[4] James C. Coleman, *Abnormal Psychology and Modern Life* (Glenview, Ill.: Scott, Foresman, 1950), pp. 476–77. See also Franco Ferracuti, "Il Contributo Die Tests Psicologici Alle Teorie Criminologiche Ed Alla Diagnosi Dei Criminali Mentalmente Anormali," *Quaderni Di Criminologia Clinica*, 2:495–506, 1960.

[5] Thomas S. Szasz, *The Myth of Mental Illness: Foundations of a Theory of Personal Conduct* (New York: Hoeber-Harper, 1961). See also idem, *The Manufacture of Madness* (New York: Harper and Row, 1970); and Herbert Fingarette, *The Meaning of Criminal Insanity* (Berkeley: University of California Press, 1972).

[6] R. E. L. Faris and H. W. Dunham, *Mental Disorders in Urban Areas: An Ecological Study of Schizophrenia and Other Psychoses* (Chicago: University of Chicago Press, 1939).

[7] August B. Hollingshead and Frederick C. Redlich, *Social Class and Mental Illness* (New York: Wiley, 1958).

[8] Simon Dinitz, Mark Lefton, Shirley Angrist, and Benjamin Pasamanick, "Psychiatric and Social Attributes as Predictors of Case Outcome in Mental Hospitalization," *Social Problems*, 8:322–28, 1961.

mal reaction patterns are transferred from one person to another, and that this phenomenon is found among persons in close and prolonged personal contact, even when there is no blood relationship.[9]

The major characteristic which psychotics have in common is complete breakdown or severe impairment of the means of communication; they lose contact with "reality." They sometimes are completely isolated from the values of their social groups and, in fact, do not maintain membership in social groups. In other cases the isolation is less extreme. Accordingly, many psychotics do not manage their lives in a way considered satisfactory by most persons, and they sometimes get into trouble with the law. Psychoses may produce social harms in various ways. A hallucinatory voice may repeat a command to kill, and the voice may finally be obeyed. An innocent person may be attacked as a means of revenge for or defense against an imagined misdeed. However, only some of the persons classed as psychotic are dangerous, and certainly not all psychotic persons are hospitalized.

Psychiatric examinations of criminals on admission to state prisons generally show not more than 5 percent to be psychotic, and in many institutions less than 1 percent are so classified. This variation is affected both by the preconceptions of the examiners and by variations in the manner of handling defendants who plead that they are "insane," not "criminal." In one clinic, no delinquent was diagnosed as "normal," on the curious ground that "normality is a vague concept because everybody simply projects his own ideal of perfection into it."[10] Offenders admitted to houses of correction and to jails have a slightly higher rate of psychoses than those admitted to prisons. Even so, the rate is seldom higher than 5 percent of the admissions and in many studies is reported to be about 2 percent. The offenders in these institutions often have alcoholic psychoses, from which they may quickly recover. Moreover, when the harms committed are not serious, the courts are not as likely to declare defendants insane and commit them to hospitals rather than to penal institutions.

The fact that a criminal is psychotic does not mean that the crime was due to the psychosis. In a highly significant early study, Silverman reported that the social backgrounds of 500 psychotic inmates of the Federal Medical Center were remarkably similar to those of nonpsychotic federal prisoners.[11] However, he did find that psychotic prisoners were considerably different from psychotic persons outside prisons. This suggests that the social backgrounds which produced

---

[9] Alexander Gralnick, "Folie a Deux—The Psychosis of Association: A Review of 103 Cases and the Entire English Literature, with Case Presentations," *Psychiatric Quarterly,* 16:230–63, 1942.

[10] Pierre Rube, "Psychiatric Clinic for Adolescent Delinquents," *Quarterly Journal of Child Behavior,* 4:24–56, 1952.

[11] Daniel Silverman, "The Psychotic Criminals: A Study of 500 Cases," *Journal of Clinical Psychopathology,* 8:301–27, 1946. See also idem, "Psychoses in Criminals: A Study of 500 Psychotic Prisoners," *Journal of Criminal Psychopathology,* 4:703–30, 1943.

criminal behavior in the nonpsychotic prisoners also produced criminal behavior in the psychotic prisoners.

Many psychotic persons do not commit crimes or legal harms of any kind. This was demonstrated long ago by Dunham, who studied 870 male schizophrenic patients aged 15–29 in Illinois hospitals. He found that only 24 percent had records of juvenile delinquency or adult crime, and a large proportion of these records were for minor offenses; approximately 20 percent of these records were in connection with the current commitment to the hospitals; the paranoid had a significantly higher rate of crime than the catatonic.[12] A similar study of 1262 patients in a state hospital in Michigan showed that 21.1 percent had records of definite crimes, and an additional 4.4 percent had records of threatened or attempted crimes; of these, 39 percent had the recorded behavior before the recognized onset of psychosis, 61 percent after the onset.[13] The law-abiding behavior of most psychotics is explained partly by the types of psychoses and partly by the fact that their attitudes and other behavior patterns were law-abiding prior to the onset of the psychosis and persisted after the mental disturbance occurred.

Research on the exact role of psychoses in crime is complicated by the fact that a person who is "insane" at the time he commits a legally-forbidden harm does not commit a crime. A man charged with a crime may defend himself in court by showing that he was insane at the time the act occurred, just as another man may plead that his act occurred in self-defense. This means, for example, that a man who is insane at the time he kills another has committed no crime; he is committed to a hospital for treatment, rather than to a prison for punishment. Hence, if the legal concept *insanity* were synonymous with the psychiatric term *psychosis*, there would be no problem regarding the role of the psychoses in criminality, for persons would be *either* psychotic *or* criminal. In the current medico-legal situation, however, insanity differs from what many psychiatrists have in mind when they speak of psychoses. Consequently, a court may find a defendant to be criminal (that is, not insane and guilty), while a psychiatrist may diagnose the same defendant as schizophrenic or, generally, psychotic.

Generally, the term *insanity* is used to describe legally harmful behavior perpetrated under circumstances in which the actor did not know the nature or quality of the act or did not know right from wrong. These rules for determining insanity were formulated in England in 1843 and are known as the *M'Naghten rules*. Most psychiatrists hold that they do not incorporate the many advances in their profession since that time. The most frequent argument against them is that

[12] H. Warren Dunham. "The Schizophrene and Criminal Behavior," *American Sociological Review*, 4:352–61, 1939. See also J. Kloek, "Schizophrenia and Delinquency," in *The Mentally Abnormal Offender*, ed. A. V. S. Reuck and Ruth Porter (Boston: Little, Brown, 1968), pp. 19–28.

[13] Milton H. Erickson, "Criminality in a Group of Male Psychiatric Patients," *Mental Hygiene*, 22:459–76, 1938.

in some kinds of behavior the actor does know right from wrong but *nevertheless* exhibits the harmful behavior because it is prompted "from within" by a force that the person is powerless to resist.[14] This argument has had some effect on criminal law theory, for at present the courts of several states hold that punishment for perpetration of a legal harm can be avoided by showing that, while the defendant knew right from wrong, his or her behavior was prompted by an "irresistible impulse."

About twenty years ago the Court of Appeals in the District of Columbia rejected the M'Naghten rules for determining insanity, holding simply that a defendant is not criminally responsible if his or her act was the product of "mental disease or mental defect."[15] The M'Naghten rules have also been modified in about six other states. In most states the vagueness of both the criminal law concepts and psychiatric concepts allows some criminals to be declared insane and thereby to escape punishment while also allowing some psychotics to be punished for crime rather than treated for mental disease.

During the last generation, development of the electroencephalograph technique, a recording of a so-called brain wave, has enabled researchers to compare delinquents and criminals and psychotics without actually declaring the delinquents to be psychotic or insane. A recent study of Israeli juvenile delinquents found them to have a high incidence of EEG abnormalities, and this finding was supported by results of Rorschach tests.[16] However, a comprehensive review of thirty years of research on this subject concluded: "Despite numerous electroencephalographic (EEG) studies indicating varying but high rates of abnormality in adult criminals, there is no proof that brain damage or abnormality as reflected in the EEG is a necessary precondition for the development of antisocial reactions."[17]

PSYCHOPATHIC PERSONALITY

The terms *psychopath, psychopathic personality,* and *constitutional psychopathic inferior* are used with little or no differentiation to refer to persons who are regarded as emotionally abnormal but who do not manifest the break with reality that characterizes psychotics. Some psychiatrists have classified psychopathic personalities in three groups—the egocentric, the inadequate, and the vagabond—and many descriptive terms have been applied to each category. Other scholars classify them into schizoid types, paranoid types, cyclothymic types, sexual deviants, alcoholics, and drug addicts. According to Goldstein, a criminal lawyer,

[14] See Manfred S. Guttmacher and Henry Weihofen, *Psychiatry and the Law* (New York: W. W. Norton, 1952), pp. 401–23; and Donald R. Cressey, "The Differential Association Theory and Compulsive Crimes," *Journal of Criminal Law, Criminology, and Police Science,* 45:29–40, 1954.

[15] Durham v. United States, 214 F.2d 862–76 (1954).

[16] Marcel Assael, Reuven Kohen-Raz, and Suzy Alpern, "Developmental Analysis of EEG Abnormalities in Juvenile Delinquents," *Diseases of the Nervous System,* 28:49–54, January, 1967.

[17] E. Robins, "Antisocial and Dyssocial Personality Disorders," in *Comprehensive Textbook of Psychiatry,* ed. A. M. Freedman and H. I. Kaplan (Baltimore: Williams and Wilkins, 1967), pp. 955–55.

psychopaths are unable to form close social relationships and, for that reason, are abnormally amoral or immoral:

[The psychopath] is commonly regarded as having either an antisocial character or no character at all. Though his cognitive faculties are likely to be intact, he is unable to defer his gratifications; he does as he pleases, often in a way which seems unmotivated by conventional standards, and feels neither anxiety nor guilt if he hurts others in the process. This is because he forms no lasting or close relationships. Far more than the psychotic, he is likely to find himself in violation of the criminal law. But because he will seem very much like the "normal" man in most respects, he will be less able to persuade a jury that he should be "acquitted."[18]

The method of diagnosing psychopathic personality is not at all standardized or objective; consequently, a person may be psychopathic or not, depending upon the preconceptions of the person making the examination. Because it is difficult to define or identify a psychopath, the label *psychopathic personality* can be applied to almost anyone. Investigators who are convinced that all, or almost all, criminals must have "bad" personalities can attribute the criminality of persons showing no ordinary psychoses or neuroses to psychopathic personality. Indeed, some years ago delinquency of one kind or another constituted the most frequently utilized symptomatic basis for diagnosis of psychopathic personality. The concept is often designated a "wastebasket category" into which not-otherwise-explicable criminal behavior is tossed. Preu made the following statement regarding the concept:

The term "psychopathic personality," as commonly understood, is useless in psychiatric research. It is a diagnosis of convenience arrived at by a process of exclusion. It does not refer to a specific behavioral entity. It serves as a scrapbasket to which is relegated a group of otherwise unclassified personality disorders and problems.[19]

The vagueness of the term as used in criminology is indicated by the fact that under the administration of one psychiatrist 98 percent of the inmates admitted to the state prison of Illinois were diagnosed as psychopathic personalities, while in similar institutions with different psychiatrists not more than 5 percent were so diagnosed. In some social agencies it is not uncommon to find that as many as a dozen different psychiatric diagnoses and interpretations—some of them flatly contradictory—have been made on a single delinquent boy.

Numerous persons have attempted to define the concept *psychopathic personality* with some degree of rigor and to account for the formation of psychopathic personalities.[20] The most careful investigations of psychopathic personalities

---

[18] Abraham S. Goldstein, *The Insanity Defense* (New Haven, Conn.: Yale University Press, 1967), pp. 33–34. See also Leonard P. Ullman and Leonard Krasner, *A Psychological Approach to Abnormal Behavior* (Englewood Cliffs, N. J.: Prentice-Hall, 1969), p. 31.

[19] P. W. Preu, "The Concept of Psychopathic Personality," in *Personality and the Behavior Disorders* ed. J. McV. Hunt (New York: Ronald Press, 1944), vol. 2, pp. 922–37. See also Ullman and Krasner, *A Psychological Approach to Abnormal Behavior*, pp. 445–65.

among criminals were made by Cason many years ago. In reviewing the literature, he found 202 terms which have been used more or less synonymously with the term *psychopath*.[21] He then counted fifty-five "traits or characteristics" which are generally held to be present among psychopaths, and thirty behaviors which are frequently characterized as "forms of psychopathic behavior." A study of the inmates held at the Psychopathic Unit of the Federal Medical Center revealed that some inmates exhibited many of the thirty different forms of psychopathic behavior, and some had few of the behaviors. He selected two groups—the twenty-three inmates having the largest number of the psychopathic behaviors and the twenty-nine inmates having the smallest number—and determined the frequency with which each of the fifty-five traits or characteristics appeared in each group. He found that forty-seven of the fifty-five traits had no statistical significance in differentiating the most psychopathic from the least psychopathic, and, of the eight remaining traits, six were just barely significant. With the exception of the two traits—intolerance and making threats—the traits which are generally regarded as characterizing the psychopaths were not as useful in differentiating the most psychopathic from the least psychopathic as were the facts that a person was born in the eastern states, had engaged in farming, or had violated the Dyer Act against automobile thefts.[22] These studies seem to justify a conclusion that the concept *psychopathic personality* is as useless in the interpretation of criminal behavior as was the older concept *moral imbecile* which has been completely discarded by scholars in this field.

During the years immediately following World War II, several states became panic-stricken because of a small number of serious sexual attacks, and their legislatures hurriedly enacted "sexual psychopath" laws, which spread through certain sections of the United States. Because no one has been able to identify a sexual psychopath any more than any other psychopath, the laws have been absurd in principle and futile in operation.[23]

OTHER PERSONALITY DEVIATIONS

Emotional instability and other traits of personality have been studied independently of the concept of psychopathic personality, and criminal behavior is frequently attributed to one or more of these traits. One of the principal research procedures consists of administering a personality test to a group of delinquents

[20]See, for example, Karl A. Menninger, "Recognizing and Renaming 'Psychopathic Personalities,' " *Bulletin of the Menninger Clinic*, 5:150–56, 1941; and M. D. Gynther, "Crime and Psychopathology," *Journal of Abnormal and Social Psychology*, 64:378–80, 1962.

[21]Hulsey Cason, "The Psychopath and the Psychopathic," *Journal of Criminal Psychopathology*, 4:522–27, 1943.

[22]Hulsey Cason, "The Symptoms of the Psychopath," *Public Health Reports*, 61:1833–68, 1946.

[23]See Edwin H. Sutherland, "The Sexual Psychopath Laws," *Journal of Criminal Law and Criminology*, 40:534–54, 1950; idem, "The Diffusion of Sexual Psychopath Laws," *American Journal of Sociology*, 56:142–48, 1950.

and then comparing their scores with the scores of a control group composed of nondelinquents. Dozens of tests, rating scales, and other devices for measuring personality traits have been used. Studies have been made of instincts, emotions, moods, temperaments, moral judgments, ethical discriminations, as well as of such specific tendencies as aggressiveness, caution, conformity, conscientiousness, deception, self-assurance, social resistance, suggestibility, and many others. Years ago it was pointed out that if these tests had really measured the things they were intended to measure, our knowledge of human behavior would be nearly complete, but that, as a matter of fact, the units are not adequately defined, the tests do not measure the things they purport to measure, and the results have not been validated by reference to other data.[24]

Some psychiatrists who have attempted to avoid the vagueness of the psychopathic personality concept have merely substituted personality deviations of various kinds. For example, of the 2537 individuals coming before the Psychiatric Clinic of the New York City Court of General Sessions in one year, 19.4 percent were diagnosed as psychopathic, but 76.1 percent were found to have personality deviations such as agressiveness, emotional instability, and shiftlessness.[25] However, no personality tests were utilized, and the technique for locating such deviations is not precisely described. Moreover, there is no assurance that the deviations found among the criminals would not also be found among the general population.

Twenty-five years ago, Schuessler and Cressey summarized the results of all studies in which the personality-test scores of delinquents and criminals were compared with the scores of control groups. In the 113 studies of this kind, the whole range of traits was included, as was the whole range of tests, including the Rorschach and other projective tests. One conclusion of their analysis was that not a single trait was shown in this series of studies to be more characteristic of delinquents than of nondelinquents. The general observation was that "the doubtful validity of many of the obtained differences, as well as the lack of consistency in the combined results, makes it impossible to conclude from these data that criminality and personality elements are associated.[26]

A follow-up survey which examined later studies of this kind suggests that the results obtained by personality testing are more positive than in the years surveyed by Schuessler and Cressey. Of the ninety-four studies, twenty-nine of which used the Minnesota Multiphasic Personality Inventory, seventy-six (81 percent) found a difference between criminals and noncriminals. Of the studies using tests other

[24] W. I. Thomas and Dorothy S. Thomas, *The Child in America* (New York: Knopf, 1936), p. 263.

[25] Walter Bromberg, "American Achievements in Criminology," *Journal of Criminal Law, Criminology, and Police Science*, 44:166–76, 1953.

[26] Karl F. Schuessler and Donald R. Cressey, "Personality Characteristics of Criminals," *American Journal of Sociology*, 55:476–84, 1950. Essentially the same conclusion was reached after a review of some of the same studies by Lawson G. Lowrey, "Delinquent and Criminal Personalities," in *Personality and the Behavior Disorders*, ed. Hunt, pp. 794–821.

than the MMPI, differences were found in 75 percent of the applications. However, after examining the studies closely, the investigators concluded: "Although the results are an improvement over those reported in the Schuessler-Cressey study, the same types of problems and criticisms generally prevailed. . . . The findings are far from conclusive.[27]

The frustration-aggression hypothesis is frequently combined with the deviant-personality-trait conception of delinquency and crime, whether the personality traits are labeled psychopathy or not. It is assumed that unusual frustration results in emotional disturbance which produces aggression, and that delinquency is the consequence. The belief that aggression is a necessary consequence of frustration is certainly incorrect. Most persons are frustrated, but only a few of them are aggressive. The belief that aggression has some necessary connection with delinquency and crime is equally incorrect. Most persons who seem to be aggressive are not criminals, and most criminals do not seem to be aggressive. If one were to select the tenth of the population which is most aggressive, assuming that aggression could be measured, it is not at all certain that this aggressive population would contain an unusual proportion of criminals.

The best general study of personal traits in relation to delinquency is still the one made by Healy and Bronner about forty years ago.[28] This was an analysis of 105 delinquents treated over a three-year period in three clinics, in comparison with 105 nondelinquent siblings who lived in the same homes and neighborhoods and were matched with the delinquents, as far as possible, by age and sex. The study resulted in a finding that 91 percent of the delinquents and only 13 percent of their nondelinquent siblings had emotional disturbances. This difference is striking and for a time it was regarded as final proof that delinquency is due largely to emotional disturbance. However, this interpretation is open to question for the following three reasons:

1. The difference between the delinquents and their nondelinquent siblings was probably exaggerated. The staff of the clinics was composed almost entirely of psychiatrists and psychiatric social workers, and members of these professions were trained to interpret delinquency in terms of emotional disturbance. Also, the staff became much better acquainted with the delinquents than with the nondelinquents, since they carried on three-year treatment programs for delinquents, and on that account would have been more likely to discover emotional disturbances among the delinquents. The inadequacy of the investigations of the nondelinquents was revealed by the report that only 21 percent of them were "even mildly delinquent."[29] Among university students in classes in criminology,

---

[27] Gordon P. Waldo and Simon Dinitz, "Personality Attributes of the Criminal: An Analysis of Research Studies, 1950–65," *Journal of Research in Crime and Delinquency*, 4:185–201, 1967.

[28] William Healy and Augusta F. Bronner, *New Light on Delinquency and Its Treatment* (New Haven, Conn.: Yale University Press, 1936).

[29] Ibid., p. 54.

about 98 percent report that they were at least "mildly delinquent" in childhood.

2. Emotional disturbances among delinquents, even if not exaggerated, were not demonstrated to be the cause of the delinquency; delinquent behavior may cause emotional disturbance. No organized effort was made in this study to determine whether the emotional disturbance preceded the delinquent behavior.

3. The process by which emotional disturbance produces delinquent behavior was not adequately investigated. The basic argument was a deceptively simple one: a boy is emotionally disturbed, so he commits a delinquent act. Emotional disturbance, however, does not in itself explain delinquent behavior, as is shown by the 13 percent of the nondelinquents who were said to be emotionally disturbed. The alternative hypothesis is that emotional disturbance produces delinquency when it isolates a person from law-abiding behavior patterns or decreases the prestige of persons presenting such patterns, or when it throws an individual into association with delinquent behavior patterns.[30] Under the same conditions of association, delinquent behavior results in those who are not emotionally disturbed.

ALCOHOLISM

Estimates of the number of alcoholics in the United States range from 4.5 million to 6.8 million.[31] Alcoholism is significant in criminology in two respects. First, it may be a crime in itself or may be directly related to violations of certain laws, such as those prohibiting public intoxication and drunken driving. Police arrest statistics submitted to the FBI in 1975 indicated that out of a total of about 8 million arrests, approximately 1.2 million were for drunkenness; 908,000 were for drunken driving; and another 692,000 arrests were for disorderly conduct and vagrancy, offenses which often involve drunkenness.

Second, alcoholism may indirectly contribute to the violation of other laws, such as those prohibiting murder, rape, assault and battery, vagrancy, and nonsupport of families. Interviews with a sample (N = 2510) of all American men who were 20 to 30 years old in 1974 indicated that 97 percent had used alcohol sometime in their lives. The men were asked if they had ever committed any of ten listed crimes, including shoplifting, breaking and entering, automobile theft, face-to-face stealing, and armed robbery. Those who reported heavy use of alcohol were more likely to report each of the acts than were nondrinkers or light or moderate drinkers. Among the 76 nonusers, 5 percent admitted to breaking and entering and 16 percent reported shoplifting; they did not report any other criminal acts. Among the 933 heaviest users, 18 percent admitted to breaking and

30Cf. John Janeway Conger and Wilbur C. Miller, *Personality, Social Class, and Delinquency* (New York: Wiley, 1966), pp. 110–29.

31Richard H. Blum, "Mind-Altering Drugs and Dangerous Behavior: Alcohol" appendix B. in President's Commission on Law Enforcement and Administration of Justice, *Task Force Report: Drunkenness* (Washington, D.C.: Government Printing Office, 1967), pp. 29–49.

entering, 56 percent admitted shoplifting, 9 percent reported automobile theft, 5 percent admitted stealing, and 2 percent admitted armed robbery.[32] In another nationwide study, interviews with a sample (N = 10,000) of the 191,400 persons held in custody under the jurisdiction of state correctional officers in early 1974 found that 43 percent of the inmates reported that they had been drinking at the time of the offense resulting in imprisonment. Approximately half of these persons said their drinking had been "heavy."[33]

Two major problems for a theory of criminal behavior are posed by the alcoholic or drunken criminal. The first of these is whether a man who is under the influence of alcohol will violate laws which he would not violate if he were not under that influence; if he does violate the law under such circumstances, he may not be acting under the influence of differential association. No clear-cut research work has been done on this problem, and no definite answer can be given. However, considerable information which points in the direction of a negative answer is available. It is known that when people in certain areas become intoxicated, they are almost certain to start fights and violate criminal laws; this is particularly true of the lower socioeconomic class. On the other hand, intoxication in other parts of American society may result only in singing, exchange of dirty stories, or crying. These differences appear to operate in larger groups and do not merely differentiate one person from another.[34] Furthermore, it may be said that even if a man, without change in his associations, acts differently when under the influence of alcohol than at other times, this may conceivably be because he has learned from associations with others certain ways of acting when intoxicated. He may have learned that when he is becoming intoxicated he should act joyful, and consequently he begins to sing, or he may have learned that he should act tough, and consequently he picks a fight. And he may have learned that intoxication is a good excuse for behavior which would be regarded as inexcusable otherwise. The best review and analysis of studies linking alcohol and crime noted that the problem of causal inference is an extraordinarily difficult one:

> On the basis of available information it is plausible to assume that alcohol does play an important and damaging role in the lives of offenders, particularly chronic inebriates, and in the production of crime. Yet one cannot be sure on the basis of the work done to date that the alcohol use of offenders exceeds that of nonoffenders with similar social and personal characteristics (if any such match is possible). One cannot be sure that the alcohol use of offenders is any greater at the moments of their offense than during their ordinary noncriminal moments. One cannot be sure that the alcohol-using offenders

[32] John A. O'Donnell, Harwin L. Voss, Richard R. Clayton, Gerald T. Slatin, and Robin G. W. Room, *Young Men and Drugs—a Nationwide Survey* (Washington, D.C.: National Institute on Drug Abuse, Research Monograph No. 5, 1976), pp. 13, 83.

[33] James J. Stephan, *Survey of Inmates of State Correctional Facilities, 1974*, National Prisoner Statistics Special Report No. SD-NPS-SR-R, March, 1976 (Washington, D.C.: Government Printing Office, 1976), pp. 6, 26.

[34] Craig MacAndrew and Robert B. Edgerton, *Drunken Comportment: A Social Explanation* (Chicago: Aldine, 1969); see also Sherri Cavan, *Liquor License: An Ethnography of Bar Behavior* (Chicago: Aldine, 1966).

would not have committed some offense had they not been drinking. One is not sure that the alcohol use of offenders differs from that of the other persons possibly present in the same or like situations which inspired or provoked the criminality of one and not the other. Finally, and this is an important point in view of the fact that all studies have been done on apprehended offenders, one does not know that the relationship now shown between alcohol use and crime is not in fact a relationship between being caught and being a drinker rather than in being a criminal and being a drinker.[35]

The second problem is whether alcoholism is a form of psychopathy. Many psychiatrists in making classifications of psychopathies interpret alcoholism as a form of vagabondage, or an abnormal method of escaping from reality. Scores of papers have been written from the point of view of this interpretation, and it may be regarded as a generally accepted belief. As a matter of fact, however, this has never been demonstrated, and the concept of escape is so vague that it cannot readily be tested.

Moreover, it is commonly asserted that persons who become alcoholic do so because of certain personality traits. An analysis was made, however, of all the available studies in which alcoholics had been given personality tests in comparison with nonalcoholics or with the general population, and one conclusion was that alcoholics had not been demonstrated to have any trait or traits which differentiate them from nonalcoholics. Another conclusion which may be drawn from the studies is that there is no such thing as a prealcoholic personality, that is, a type of person who is more likely than others to become an alcoholic.[36]

Alcoholism has been defined as a disease by many health organizations, including the American Medical Association and the World Health Organization. But further evidence that alcoholism is not primarily an expression of personal pathology is found in the fact that the Alcoholics Anonymous organization, which has approximately half a million members, has had some success in treating alcoholics. Although it can be argued that only the alcoholics without personal pathologies join the organization, those who do interact with ex-alcoholics gain assistance in overcoming their craving for alcohol. Alcoholics Anonymous has demonstrated that it is not necessary to attempt to find and treat some underlying defect in the alcoholic's personality.

NARCOTIC DRUGS

Interviews with a sample (N = 2510) of all American men who were 20 to 30 years old in 1974 indicated that, at some time in their lives, 31 percent had used opiates, 14 percent had used cocaine, and 6 percent had used heroin, a special kind of opiate.[37] Drug use, like alcoholic intoxication, is often regarded as a symptom of psychopathy. However, Lindesmith long ago showed conclusively that no distinc-

---

[35] Blum, "Mind-Altering Drugs," p. 43.

[36] Edwin H. Sutherland, H. G. Schroeder, and C. L. Tordella, "Personality Traits and the Alcoholic: A Critique of Existing Studies," *Quarterly Journal of Studies on Alcohol*, 11:547–61, 1950.

[37] O'Donnell, et al., *Young Men and Drugs*, p. 13.

tion can be made between psychopathic and normal persons in the genesis of drug addiction. Any person may begin to use narcotic drugs casually, either from motives of curiosity and observance of folkways in variant cultures or even in complete ignorance of the fact that he or she is using narcotic drugs, which happened especially in earlier generations in connection with medical prescriptions and patent medicines for digestive ailments. Any person, regardless of the traits of his or her personality, who thus uses narcotic drugs casually until distress is suffered when the drugs are withdrawn, and who becomes aware of the relation between this distress and the withdrawal of the drugs is a drug addict. Psychopathic and normal persons behave uniformly in this respect.[38]

Unlike drunkenness, drug addiction itself is not a crime. It never has been a crime under federal law, and a California law making it one was declared unconstitutional by the United States Supreme Court. What is illegal is purchase, possession, or sale of narcotics and, in some states, nonmedical use of narcotics and narcotics paraphernalia. Like the skid-row drunk, the addict thus lives in an almost perpetual state of law violation.

A large percentage of state and federal prisoners have committed drug-related crimes. In 1972, about 60 percent of the men and women committed to Connecticut correctional institutions were drug dependent.[39] In some county jails, as many as 80 percent of the inmates are confined for drug-related offenses. Interviews with a sample (N = 10,000) of all inmates in state correctional institutions in 1974 indicated that about 15 percent of them had used methadone, 45 percent had used cocaine, and 50 percent had used heroin at some time in their lives. Thirty-one percent of the methadone users, 27 percent of the cocaine users, and 69 percent of the heroin users said they used the drug daily. Approximately 3 percent of the 191,400 inmates (43 percent of the drug users) were under the influence of these or other drugs (including amphetamines, barbituates, and marijuana) at the time of the offense resulting in imprisonment.[40]

Narcotic drugs are often said to be factors in the genesis of other criminal behavior. Eleven percent of the persons arrested in 1965 by the New York City police for felonies against property were admitted drug (mostly heroin) users. The proportion of drug users among those arrested for petty larceny was about the same, but the figure for involvement of admitted drug users in arrests for felonies against the person was only 2 percent.[41]

Studies of criminality among addicts, rather than of drug use among criminals, show a much greater association between criminality and addiction. For example,

[38] Alfred R. Lindesmith, *Addiction and Opiates* (Chicago: Aldine, 1968).

[39] Connecticut Department of Correction, *Annual Report* (Hartford, Conn.: Connecticut Department of Correction, 1973), p. 27.

[40] Stephan, *Survey of Inmates of State Correctional Facilities*, pp. 6–7, 27.

[41] President's Commission on Law Enforcement and Administration of Justice, *Task Force Report: Narcotics and Drug Abuse* (Washington, D.C.: Government Printing Office, 1967), p. 10.

all of the male addicts certified to the New York Narcotic Addiction Control Commission for treatment in summer and fall, 1970, reported commission of criminal offenses, and 79 percent had arrest records.[42] Those arrests that did not involve drug-law violations were principally for petty theft and vagrancy. Of 1096 drug users admitted to a federal clinic in Lexington, Kentucky during a three-year period, 990 (90 percent) admitted having been arrested or having been engaged in illegal activities.[43] With alcohol excluded from the definition of drugs, 44 percent of the sample had been arrested before any drug use; when alcohol and marijuana were both excluded, 53 percent reported an arrest before they used any drug, but half of these admitted arrests were for illegal gambling. When the respondents were questioned about illegal activities, rather than arrests, 23 percent admitted that they had committed robbery, burglary, or larceny before drug use, and 74 percent admitted to committing at least one of these crimes during their lifetimes, suggesting a dramatic increase in criminal activity after the onset of drug use. Not surprisingly, the greatest increase occurs in the sale of drugs—before drug use only one percent admitted this offense, but prior to hospitalization 62 percent reported selling drugs.

Such increases do not occur in nations that handle drug addicts in such a way that they are not cast into association with criminal behavior patterns.[44] A recent British study found that male opiate addicts were neither more nor less likely than other groups of male offenders of similar age and number of previous convictions to be convicted of offenses during a two-year follow-up period.[45]

A precise description of the process by which narcotic drugs are related to criminal behavior has not been made. An interview study of American men who were 20 to 30 years old in 1974 found a strong statistical association between the extent of drug use and self-reported criminal acts, but the study did not provide clear support either for the idea that drug use leads to criminality or for the idea that criminal activity leads to drug use: "While only preliminary analyses have been conducted, the fact that drug use sometimes occurs first and at other times criminal behavior precedes use indicates that if there is a causal connection between drug use and criminal behavior, it is not a simple one."[46]

[42] James A. Inciardi and Carl D. Chambers, "Unreported Criminal Involvement of Narcotic Addicts," *Journal of Drug Issues*, 2:57–64, 1972.

[43] Harwin L. Voss and Richard C. Stephens, "Criminal History of Narcotic Addicts," *Drug Forum*, 2:191–202, 1973. See also Robert S. Weppner, "Drug Abuse Patterns of Vietnamese War Veterans Hospitalized as Narcotic Addicts," *Drug Forum*, 2:43–53, 1972.

[44] Alfred R. Lindesmith, *The Addict and the Law* (Bloomington, Ind.: Indiana University Press, 1965), pp. 124–28.

[45] Joy Mott and Marilyn Taylor, *Delinquency Amongst Opiate Users*, Home Office Research Report No. 23 (London: Her Majesty's Stationery Office, 1974). See also Andrzej Marek and Stawomir Redo, "Stan Naromanii W Polsce—Próba Oceny," [Drug addiction in Poland—an attempt at evaluation], *Studia Kryminologiczne, Kryminalstyczne i Penitencjarne*, 4:253–82, 1976.

[46] O'Donnell, et al., *Young Men and Drugs*, p. 97.

The popular belief that these drugs make their users reckless and violent is only one of several myths common in our culture and utilized in public policy regarding drug use.[47] The opiates, in fact, have the opposite effect. It is not true, either, that drug addicts and drug peddlers are moral degenerates who want to convert nonusers into addicts. The earliest explanations of addict criminality, however, held that use of narcotics impaired "many of the higher moral or ethical feelings."[48] Indeed, the Treasury Department, which polices drug addiction on the federal level under a tax law, once held that "drug addiction causes a relentless destruction of character and releases criminal tendencies."[49] Consistent with this myth is the idea that addicts take drugs and then commit crimes because they have more than their share of traits which may be taken as evidence of weakness, psychopathy, and abnormality. Harry Anslinger (chief of the Federal Bureau of Narcotics for thirty-two years) and William Tompkins found this myth and theory incompatible with the perceived need to criminalize the behavior of drug addicts, so they created a new myth and theory, the idea that it is criminals who become addicts, not the other way around:

This parasitic drug addict is a tremendous burden on the community. He represents a continuing problem to the police through his depredations against society. He is a thief, a burglar, a robber; if a woman, a prostitute or shoplifter. The person is generally a criminal before he becomes addicted. Once addicted he has the greatest reason in the world for continuing his life of crime.[50]

As theories, both of these myths have been refuted by numerous studies showing that criminality sometimes precedes drug addiction and that addiction sometimes precedes criminality.[51]

Perhaps the greatest myth of all is the idea that after persons have become addicted they are "forced" to steal or pimp or prostitute themselves in order to maintain their habits. Because the need is great, the idea goes, and because satisfaction of the need is expensive, drug-related crime naturally follows drug addiction. One of the earliest transformations of this popular and wide-spread myth into theory was made by Kolb in 1939:

They [addicts] suffer more character deterioration because of the physical enslavement that makes them feel inferior, because they must neglect work in order to search for

---

[47] Charles E. Reasons, "Images of Crime and the Criminal: The Dope Fiend Mythology," *Journal of Research in Crime and Delinquency*, 13:133–44, 1976.

[48] Alexander Lambert, "Report of the Committee on Drug Addiction," *American Journal of Psychiatry*, 87:433–538, 1930.

[49] Quoted by William Eldridge, *Narcotics and the Law* (Chicago: University of Chicago Press, 1962), p. 26.

[50] Harry R. Anslinger and William Tompkins, *Narcotics* (New York: Funk and Wagnalls, 1953), p. 197.

[51] See Dan Waldorf, *Careers in Dope* (Englewood Cliffs, N. J.: Prentice-Hall, 1973); and Leroy C. Gould, "Crime and the Addict: Beyond Common Sense," in *Drugs and the Criminal Justice System* ed. James A. Inciari and Carl D. Chambers (Beverly Hills, Calif.: Sage Publications, 1974).

narcotics; *because they are impelled to become parasites and thieves in order to keep up their supply,* because for the same reasons they must associate with questionable characters.[52]

In discussing juvenile drug users, Finestone later presented a less emotional version of the myth but nevertheless transformed it into a theory of economic compulsion:

Once addicted, however, these adolescents, who previously had been only marginally involved in delinquency, were forced into regular criminal activity in order to raise money to maintain their supply of narcotics.[53]

Coleman is among the few social scientists who have systematically studied the effects which the forced-to-steal myth has on addicts.[54] He notes, first, that the crime rate among heroin users is high and that the nondrug offenses in which addicts become involved are generally of the fund-raising variety. In 1965 the average daily cost to the admitted heroin user in New York City was about fourteen dollars.[55] Three to five dollars in merchandise or other goods must be stolen to realize one dollar in cash, so to support a drug habit by stealing cost between forty and seventy dollars worth of stolen goods every day. This was an average—some addicts' habits cost much more in 1965, and the average is higher now than it was then.

Coleman observes, secondly, that "street addicts" in the United States are quick to voice the opinion that once they became addicted they were "forced" to steal, often from their parents, wives, and best friends. One addict gave Coleman the following description of the junkie's normative system:

The only values were heroin and money. There were no moral values. There was nothing unethical or immoral because there was nothing you wouldn't do to get heroin. With everything geared toward heroin, there were no human values All people were concerned with was staving off insanity and feeling good.[56]

The third and most important point of Coleman's analysis is this: So far as drug mythology is concerned, American street addicts are no different from physicians, social scientists, psychiatrists, and social workers who have accepted the

[52] Lawrence Kolb, *Drug Addiction: A Medical Problem* (Springfield, Ill.: Charles C. Thomas, 1962), pp. 69–70. Emphasis added.

[53] Harold Finestone, "Narcotics and Criminality," *Law and Contemporary Problems*, 22:60–85, 1957.

[54] James William Coleman, *Addiction, Crime, and Abstinence: An Investigation of Addict Behavior* (Ph.D. diss., University of California, Santa Barbara, 1975); and idem, "The Myth of Addiction," *Journal of Drug Issues*, 6:135–41, 1976. See also Herbert Fingarette, "Addiction and Criminal Responsibility," *Yale Law Journal*, 84:413–44, 1975; the discussion by Fingarette, Coleman, and others in idem, "What is This Affliction?" *The Center Magazine*, 9:46–58, 1976; and Ann Fingarette Hasse, "Drug Intoxication and Criminal Responsibility: Old Dilemmas and a New Proposal," *Santa Clara Law Review*, 16:249–65, 1976.

[55] President's Commission, *Task Force Report: Narcotics and Drug Abuse*, p. 10. Coleman, *Addiction, Crime, and Abstinence*, pp. 18–19. See also Waldorf, *Careers in Dope*, pp. 16–20.

[56] Coleman, *Addiction, Crime, and Abstinence*, pp. 18–19.

forced-to-steal myth without critical evaluation. Because street addicts share the myth, they act as though it were true, just as nonaddicts do. They become liars, thieves, and hustlers because they have *learned* that once a person is an addict "there is nothing the person won't do to get a fix." Most Americans are reared to know the adage, "It is all right to steal a loaf of bread when you are starving," and they then steal when they define themselves as being in a situation of economic necessity. Consistently, it is part of the process of becoming a street addict to learn the adage, "Addicts are forced to use narcotics and forced to steal to support the addiction."

Fourth, Coleman's research indicates that although street addicts exhibit the kind of behavior the forced-to-steal myth would lead us to expect, other types of addicts do not. Marginal addicts, for example, live on the edges of the street addicts' subculture, associate with them in order to secure their sources of supply, but reject the junkie's criminal behavior and manipulative attitude toward others. One marginal addict offered the following reasons for giving up narcotics:

I wanted to be independent of it. I knew then that if I continued I would have to resort to stealing to maintain my habit and this I couldn't tolerate because it was contrary to my character. The others were robbing and stealing but I couldn't be a part of that.[57]

Most such addicts work at legitimate jobs and are not heavily involved in crime aside from the violations of law inherent in the use of narcotics. One marginal addict expressed his low opinion of the criminally oriented street addict in this way:

I wasn't really around a lot of people who were using. I knew one or two. Many of my friends now are not heroin users. And I can't really personally stand junkies. You know, they come over to the house and talk jive talk and jail talk. I try to get them out of the house. I don't consider them my friends and I don't trust any of them. I think you have to watch them every minute. They'll put anything they can pick up in their pockets.[58]

Similarly, most of the American servicemen who became addicted in Vietnam did not become readdicted upon their return to the United States and did not get involved in crime.[59] The difference between these addicts and street addicts is obvious: They did not participate in a myth stating that addicts become persons who are forced to use drugs and who are then forced to steal and commit other crimes:

"Heads" [military drug users in Southeast Asia], even those habituated to heroin, did not consider themselves "addicts" or "junkies" in the usual sense of the word. In fact, they abhorred behavior patterns associated with the civilian stereotype (e.g. crime, chronic drug

[57] March Ray, "The Cycle of Abstinence and Relapse Among Heroin Addicts," *Social Problems*, 4:160–67, 1961.
[58] Coleman, *Addiction, Crime, and Abstinence*, p. 20.
[59] Lee Robins, *The Vietnam Drug User Returns* (Washington, D.C.: Government Printing Office, 1974).

use, dereliction), and "heads" who exhibited these characteristics were excluded from the social system. Thus there may have been good reason for veterans to discontinue opiate use after returning home: The game must be played by different rules and the new rules require behavior which is incompatible with the "head" self-concept.[60]

Coleman concludes that the American mythology of the drug user as a dope fiend who prowls the streets committing crimes in order to buy drugs has become a self-fulfilling prophecy. Spurred by their common problems—particularly the need to defend themselves against a hostile society and to maintain their supply of drugs—narcotics users in the United States developed a distinctive subculture which came to encourage their ruthless style of amoral opportunism.

The myth of addiction encourages criminal behavior . . . because of the rationalizations the myth provides. The addict can excuse any deviance because he is not really responsible for it. He feels he is forced to lie or steal in order to support his habit. But such beliefs are more than rationalizations in the traditional sense—that is, *ex post facto* explanations of one's behavior designed to reduce negative self-evaluation. These beliefs actually become part of the addict's basic motivational structure by creating a set of symbolic definitions favorable to continuing addiction and its accompanying deviance. Addicts commit crimes *because* they believe their need for drugs forces them to do so.[61]

This theory is entirely consistent with differential association theory and is, in fact, based on the idea of "rationalization" as used in that theory and discussed in Chapter 12 below.

PSYCHOANALYSIS AND CRIME

A large proportion of the persons working with delinquents and criminals implicitly or explicitly use some form of psychoanalytic theory in their explanations of criminality. There really are many psychoanalytic theories; not one, but all emphasize unconscious emotional difficulties of some kind in the causation of crime.[62] The conventional Freudian theory contends that the mind is composed of three portions or parts: id, ego, and superego. The id consists of "original tendencies," or "impulses" which are possessed at birth. The id impulses are not adapted to social life and must be repressed or expressed in socially acceptable ways if persons are to maintain themselves in social life. Basically, this is a frustration of drives common to all. The superego is the embodiment of the moral

---

[60] M. Rohrbaugh, G. Eads, and S. Press, "Effects of Vietnam Experience on Subsequent Drug Use Among Servicemen," *International Journal of the Addictions*, 24:25–40, 1974.

[61] Coleman, "The Myth of Addiction," p. 139.

[62] For an excellent introduction to psychoanalytic theory, see Charles Brenner, *An Elementary Textbook of Psychoanalysis* (New York: Doubleday, 1974). For an excellent summary of psychoanalytic explanations of delinquent acts and of delinquent types of personality, see Nigel Walker, *Crime and Punishment in Britain* (Edinburgh: University of Edinburgh Press, 1965), pp. 69–72. For an excellent critique of such explanations, see David Feldman, "Psychoanalysis and Crime," in Bernard Rosenberg, Israel Gerver, and F. William Howton, eds., *Mass Society in Crisis* (New York: Macmillan, 1964), pp. 50–58.

codes of society, and the id impulses are directed in view of the superego by the ego. The id usually is tamed, but often the impulses remain in the unconscious; the ego represses or forces them into the unconscious because they are painfully in conflict with social conventions. They get into consciousness only in symbolic form, as in dreams or in overt behavior which does not mean what, on its face, it seems to mean. The criminal is a person who has failed to tame the impulses sufficiently, or who has failed to transform them into socially acceptable ways of behaving. Criminal behavior, therefore, may be the direct expression of original urges; it may be symbolic expression of repressed desires; or it may be the result of an ego which has become maladjusted because of the conflicting forces exerted on it by the id and the superego.[63]

The Oedipus complex concept, for example, is based on the premise that incest is a basic desire of human beings—every male loves his mother and is jealous of his father because of the father's sex relations with the mother. In this situation, the id could take over, and the father would be murdered and the mother raped. Or the id urges may be repressed or inhibited because of the strong social taboos against their expression. Or they may be partially repressed, in which case the person may murder his father in some symbolic way, or he may commit an act which is symbolic of the act of sexual intercourse with his mother. Either kind of symbolic act may be a crime—he may "murder" his father by forging checks on his bank account, or he may "rape" his mother by burglarizing a dwelling house. But crime may arise in another way also. Whenever the id dominates the superego, as in instances where it asserts itself through unconscious wishes and desires for intercourse with the mother, the ego feels guilty, for the superego is always operating. To get rid of the guilt feelings, the ego may seek punishment, and, since punishment follows crime, a crime may be committed. The existence of clues to detection and apprehension, such as a fingerprint left at the scene of a crime, is interpreted as evidence of this phenomenon.[64]

The major difficulty with such theory is the fact that the variables cannot be studied scientifically. There is no way to prove or disprove the theory, for the elements of it cannot be observed or measured. From the point of view of a nonbeliever the symbolism often is fantastic, and psychoanalysts have no way of demonstrating the relation between the symbols and the things they are supposed to represent. Moreover, one who argues that psychoanalytic theory is scientifically invalid in many respects is sometimes psychoanalyzed by the defenders of the

---

[63]For examples of the use of such theory in criminology, see David Abrahamsen, *The Psychology of Crime* (New York: Columbia University Press, 1960); Kate Friedlander, *The Psychoanalytic Approach to Juvenile Delinquency* (New York: International Universities Press, 1947); Franz Alexander and Hugo Staub, *The Criminal, the Judge, and the Public: A Psychological Analysis*, rev. ed. (Glencoe, Ill.: Free Press, 1956); and Hyman Grossbard, "Ego Deficiency in Delinquents," *Social Casework* 43:71–78, 1962.

[64]See S. Glover, *The Roots of Crime* (London: Imago, 1960), p. 302.

theory, on the assumption that he himself must necessarily be expressing some deeply hidden, secret, emotional conflict rather than a worthwhile criticism.[65]

CONCLUSIONS

The neo-Lombrosian notion that crime is an expression of psychopathy is no more justified than was the Lombrosian notion that criminals constitute a distinct physical type. Some studies have found a large proportion of criminals to be abnormal, but it is possible that these findings arise from poor standardization in methods of diagnosis of abnormality. The preconception of this school of thought was shown in extreme form in a psychiatric report which held that a diagnosis of mental disease "is permissible even when the criminal has shown no evidence of mental disease other than his criminal behavior."[66] According to this recommendation, the abnormality which is to be used as the explanation of criminal behavior may be inferred from the criminal behavior which it explains. Perhaps this is why one psychiatrist has been able to say, "In all my experience I have not been able to find one single offender who did not show some mental pathology. . . . The 'normal' offender is a myth."[67]

Research studies conducted by scholars representing different schools of thought have found no trait of personality to be associated with criminal or delinquent behavior. No consistent, statistically significant differences between personality traits of delinquents and personality traits of nondelinquents have been found. The explanation of criminal behavior, apparently, must be found in social interaction, in which both the behavior of a person and the overt or prospective behavior of other persons play their parts.

SUGGESTED READINGS

Alexander, Franz, & Hugo Staub. *The Criminal, the Judge, and the Public: A Psychological Analysis*. Rev. ed. Glencoe, Ill.: Free Press, 1956.

Becker, Jerome, & Doris S. Heyman. "A Critical Approach to the California Differential Treatment Typology of Adolescent Offenders." *Criminology*, 10:3–59, 1972.

Christie, Nils. "Law and Medicine: The Case Against Role Blurring." *Law and Society Review*, 5:357–66, 1971.

Coleman, James William. "The Myth of Addiction." *Journal of Drug Issues*, 6:135–41, 1976.

Conger, John Janeway, & Wilbur C. Miller. *Personality, Social Class, and Delinquency*. New York: Wiley, 1966.

DeFleur, Lois B. "Biasing Influences on Drug Arrest Records: Implications for Deviance Research." *American Sociological Review*, 40:88–103, 1975.

---

[65] Cf. Ernest Jones, *The Life and Work of Sigmund Freud*, vol. 2, *The Years of Maturity, 1901–1919* (New York: Basic Books, 1955), p. 127.

[66] Quoted in M. Ploscowe, "Some Causative Factors in Criminality," National Commission on Law Observance and Enforcement, *Report No. 13, Report on Causes of Crime*, vol. 1 (Washington, D.C.: Government Printing Office, 1931), p. 57.

[67] David Abrahamsen, *Who Are the Guilty? A Study of Education and Crime* (New York: Rinehart, 1952), p. 125.

Fingarette, Herbert. *The Meaning of Criminal Insanity.* Berkeley: University of California Press, 1972.

Fingarette, Herbert. "Addiction and Criminal Responsibility." *Yale Law Journal*, 84:413–44, 1975.

Gendin, Sidney. "Insanity and Criminal Responsibility." *American Philosophical Quarterly*, 10:99–110, 1973.

Glaser, Frederick B., & John C. Ball. "The British Narcotic Register in 1970." *Journal of the American Medical Association*, 216:1177–82, 1971.

Goode, Erich. *The Drug Phenomenon: Social Aspects of Drug Taking.* Indianapolis: Bobbs-Merrill, 1973.

Guze, Samuel B. *Criminality and Psychiatric Disorders.* New York: Oxford University Press, 1976.

Halleck, Seymour L. *Psychiatry and the Dilemma of Crime.* New York: Harper and Row, 1967.

Hare, R. D. *Psychopathy: Theory and Research.* New York: Wiley, 1970.

Inciardi, James A., & Carl D. Chambers. "Unreported Criminal Involvement of Narcotic Addicts." *Journal of Drug Issues*, 2:57–64, 1972.

Lindesmith, Alfred R. *Addiction and Opiates.* Chicago: Aldine, 1968.

Lindesmith, Alfred R. *The Addict and the Law.* Bloomington, Ind.: Indiana University Press, 1965.

O'Donnell, John A., & John C. Ball, eds. *Narcotic Addiction.* New York: Harper and Row, 1966.

Pittman, David J., ed. *Alcoholism.* New York: Harper and Row, 1967.

Reasons, Charles E. "Images of Crime and the Criminal: The Dope Fiend Mythology," *Journal of Research in Crime and Delinquency*, 13:133–44, 1976.

Rettig, Richard P., Manuel J. Torres, & Gerald R. Garrett. *Manny: A Criminal-Addict's Own Story* (Boston: Houghton Mifflin. 1977.)

Scheff, Thomas J. *Being Mentally Ill.* Chicago: Aldine, 1966.

Smart, Frances. *Neurosis and Crime.* London: Duckworth, 1970.

Ullman, Leonard P., & Leonard Krasner. *A Psychological Approach to Abnormal Behavior.* Englewood Cliffs, N. J.: Prentice-Hall, 1969.

Volkman, Rita, & Donald R. Cressey. "Differential Association and the Rehabilitation of Drug Addicts," *American Journal of Sociology*, 69:129–42, 1963.

Voss, Harwin L., & Richard C. Stephens, "Criminal History of Narcotic Addicts," *Drug Forum*, 2:191–202, 1973.

Walker, Nigel, & Sarah McCabe. *Crime and Insanity in England: New Solutions and New Problems.* Edinburgh: University Press, 1973.

Yablonsky, Lewis. *Synanon: The Tunnel Back.* Baltimore: Penguin Books, 1967.

Yockelson, Samuel, & Stanton E. Samenow. *The Criminal Personality.* New York: Jason Aronson, 1976.

9

Cultural Patterns

In the different culture areas of the earth, crime rates have ranged between zero and one hundred percent. Most cultural areas, of course, have crime rates between these two extremes, but the rates—whether high or low—seem to be transmitted as traditions over many generations. Like variations in the age, sex, race, and nativity ratios in crime, variations in crime patterns from area to area pose challenging problems for a theory of crime and criminal behavior.

REGIONAL PATTERNS

Crime rates vary from one nation to another and also among the sections of each nation. Ferri, the noted Italian criminologist, reported near the end of the nineteenth century that the rate of convictions for homicides per million population varied widely in different provinces in each of the principal European countries. In Italy, twenty-seven provinces had rates of less than fifty, while thirteen provinces had rates of more than two hundred. Convictions for homicide in Sardinia were more than fourteen times as frequent in proportion to population as in Lombardy.[1] At about the same time, Aschaffenburg, a respected German criminologist, found that offenses against the person were much higher in East Prussia, Bavaria, and the Palatinate than in other German provinces. He also observed that convictions for larceny were much higher in the provinces adjoining the Russian frontier than elsewhere in Germany, while resistance to and attack on officers were most frequent in seaports and in manufacturing districts.[2]

The rate of serious crimes known to the police in England is highest in the counties containing and adjacent to London, second highest in the counties

[1] Enrico Ferri, *L'omicido nell' antropologia criminale* (Torino, Italy: Bocca, 1895), pp. 241–325.
[2] Gustav Aschaffenburg, *Crime and Its Repression* (Boston: Little, Brown, 1913).

containing the principal seaports, third highest in the manufacturing counties in the central part of England, and lowest in the agricultural and mining counties. This same distribution was found in 1893, except that the southwestern agricultural counties, which had a low crime rate generally, had the highest rate of any section of the country for offenses against morals. At an earlier period, according to Pike, the counties in England in which crime was most prevalent were those adjoining Scotland, because of the lack of organized government in those counties, and these high rates continued until the final amalgamation of the counties.[3]

Joly, a French criminologist, found similar variations among the eighty-six departments (counties) of France.[4] However, he made his study much more significant than the other early studies by going on to analyze the changes which occurred in the crime rates of persons migrating from one department to another. He showed that as people moved from one district to another they abandoned the crime rate of the first district and took on the crime rate of the second one. He found, for example, that Corsica's crime rate was the second highest of the eighty-six districts when it was computed by counting the number of crimes committed by Corsicans living in Corsica. But Corsica's crime rate dropped to sixty-fifth in the eighty-six districts when the crime rate was computed by counting the number of crimes committed by Corsicans living anywhere in France. At home the Corsicans had high crime rates, but those who moved from Corsica abandoned the criminal tradition. Joly also showed that persons who migrated from areas with low crime rates took on the higher crime rate of the district to which they moved. Thus, the district that ranked eighty-fifth in crime at home rose to thirty-sixth rank when prosecutions away from home were included, indicating that persons who emigrated became acculturated to a culture containing high crime rates. Persons moving to Corsica would commit more crimes than they did at home; persons moving from Corsica would commit fewer crimes than they did at home. Some departments retained the same rank in the two methods of computing the rates, but others showed these very significant changes, suggesting that people take on the crime rate of the area in which they reside.

The *Uniform Crime Reports* data presented in Table 17 show the variation in the frequency of specific types of crime in different regions of the United States. Subject to the qualifications mentioned in Chapter 2 and elsewhere, the statistics indicate that New England had the lowest rates for homicide, rape, and aggravated assault. The East South Central region (Alabama, Kentucky, Mississippi, and Tennessee) had the lowest burglary, larceny, and motor vehicle theft rates. The highest rates for forcible rape, burglary, and larceny were found in the Pacific states (Alaska, California, Hawaii, Oregon, and Washington); the highest aggravated assault and homicide rates appeared in the South Atlantic region (all East Coast

---

[3]Luke O. Pike, *A History of Crime in England* (London: Smith, Elder, 1873–76).
[4]Henri Joly, *La France Criminelle* (Paris: Cerf, 1889), pp. 45–46.

Table 17   U.S. Crime Rates, 1975, by Geographical Division

Division	Homi-cide	Forcible Rape	Robbery	Aggra-vated Assault	Burglary	Larceny-Theft	Motor Vehicle Theft
All areas	9.6	26.3	218.2	227.4	1525.9	2804.8	469.4
New England	3.7	15.2	154.8	158.2	1529.5	2416.0	1015.5
Middle Atlantic	8.9	22.9	348.1	222.1	1421.2	2256.3	534.1
East North Central	9.1	26.5	240.4	194.1	1389.3	3024.2	473.5
West North Central	5.5	18.4	126.2	135.8	1157.4	2663.0	328.0
South Atlantic	12.9	27.3	202.9	306.0	1610.1	2879.7	339.3
East South Central	12.7	20.2	119.7	195.8	1114.3	1747.0	273.3
West South Central	12.4	26.9	144.7	206.9	1491.0	2643.7	351.0
Mountain	7.9	32.6	137.1	244.5	1805.2	3717.6	404.6
Pacific	9.4	39.3	243.6	297.5	2106.0	3705.0	585.0

SOURCE: Federal Bureau of Investigation, U.S. Department of Justice, *Uniform Crime Reports for the United States, 1975* (Washington, D.C.: Government Printing Office, 1975), pp. 50–55.
NOTE: Figures represent offenses per 100,000 inhabitants.

states south of Pennsylvania); the highest robbery rate occurred in the Middle Atlantic states (New Jersey, New York, Pennsylvania); the highest motor vehicle theft rate was in New England.

By individual states, North Dakota had the lowest homicide, forcible rape, robbery, aggravated assault, and burglary rates; Mississippi the lowest rate for larceny-theft; and West Virginia the lowest motor vehicle theft rate. Alabama had the highest homicide rate; Arizona the highest larceny-theft and burglary rates; New York the highest robbery rate; South Carolina the highest aggravated assault rate; Nevada the highest forcible rape rate; and Massachusetts the highest motor vehicle theft rate.

Forty years ago, Lottier analyzed sectional crime rates in the United States and reported a center of concentration for murder in the southeastern states, with somewhat regular gradients to the north and west; robbery was concentrated in the middle central states, with an axis running from Tennessee and Kentucky to Colorado, and with decreasing rates on either side of this axis. Shannon repeated this study fifteen years later and found essentially the same pattern. The rate for crimes against the person showed definite regional concentration, but crimes against property did not show such marked concentration, probably because they were not based on the total property values in the states in question.[5]

[5]Stuart Lottier, "Distribution of Criminal Offenses in Sectional Regions," *Journal of Criminal Law and Criminology,* 29:329–44, 1938. Lyle W. Shannon, "The Spatial Distribution of Criminal Offenses by States," *Journal of Criminal Law, Criminology, and Police Science,* 45:264–73, 1954.

Certain types of towns also have high crime rates. Lombroso reported that in every province in Italy certain villages had acquired reputations for special crimes; one was noted for murder, another for robbery, and another for swindling. Artena, for instance, had thirty times as many highway robberies as the average community in Italy, and had been noted as a home of robbers since the twelfth century.[6] Similarly, certain types of towns in America have been noted for high crime rates for short periods. Frontier towns, river towns, and resort towns are somewhat outstanding in this respect. Mining towns generally have higher rates than agricultural towns of the same size.

Such broad comparisons of crime rates have been made in many countries over a long period of time. In general, the various geographical divisions hold nearly the same ranks year after year. For regions, the ranks remain nearly the same whether the crime rates are computed for the larger cities or for the smaller cities in the regions. Various attempts have been made to explain the differences. Aschaffenburg believed that the differences in rates of crimes against the person in different provinces in Germany were related to the consumption of alcohol, while larceny was related to poverty, and crimes against public officials to the heterogeneity of population. In the United States, the high crime rates in the southern states are generally interpreted as due to the large number of blacks, but it is evident that homicides, at least, cannot be explained so simply, for the death rate by homicide for white persons in the South is about five times as high as in New England, and the black homicide rate in New England is slightly lower than the white homicide rate in the same area.

Pettigrew and Spier, like Hackney and Gastil, have attributed these variations to differences in community organization and traditions of orderliness.[7] Such explanation is consistent with Joly's early findings regarding crime rates in France and with the differential association theory, which predicts that if the ratio of criminal behavior patterns to anticriminal behavior patterns in a region remains approximately the same, the crime rate will remain approximately the same. Once started, customs of crime or noncrime are passed on to generation after generation, just as other customs are. For example, in Upper Egypt, as in Sicily, a tradition which requires that revenge be taken for insults and other harms has given this region extraordinarily high homicide rates for centuries. On the other hand, the same region has extraordinarily low rates of conviction for drunkenness, owing to a strong antialcohol tradition stemming from the Islamic religion. An illustration

---

[6] Cesare Lombroso, *Crime, Its Cause and Remedies* (Boston: Little, Brown, 1911).

[7] T. F. Pettigrew and R. Spier, "The Ecological Structure of Negro Homicide," *American Journal of Sociology*, 47:621–29, 1962; Raymond D. Gastil, "Homicide and a Regional Culture of Violence," *American Sociological Review*, 36:412–27, 1971; and Sheldon Hackney, "Southern Violence," in *The History of Violence in America*, ed. Hugh Davis Graham and Ted Robert Gurr (New York: Bantam Books, 1969), pp. 505–27. But also see Colin Loftin and Robert H. Hill, "Regional Subculture and Homicide: An Examination of the Gastil-Hackney Thesis," *American Sociological Review*, 39:714–24, 1974; and Howard S. Erlanger, "Is There a 'Subculture of Violence' in the South?" *Journal of Criminal Law and Criminology*, 66:483–90, 1976.

of such traditions in exaggerated form was found in the thievery patterns of the criminal tribes of India:

> The Bhamptas are a tribe who give an infinity of trouble. . . . The Bhampta is a marvellously skillful pickpocket and railway thief. He frequents fairs, landing-places, bazaars, temples—any place, in fact, where there is a crowd. He is always on the lookout for his prey. . . . The Bhamptas are trained to crime from their earliest childhood, so it is not wonderful that they should become very expert. The children are initiated into the profession of their life by lessons in the pilfering of shoes, cocoanuts, and any odds and ends that they may come across. If they are slow or stupid they are encouraged to improve by the application of a stick. The boys soon become adept. . . . Adults generally work in small gangs of three or four. One of them stealthily removes an ornament from someone in the crowd, or adroitly picks a pocket, or, jostling the victim, boldly snatches his bag or satchel, and instantly passes his booty to one of his accomplices, who in turn passes it on to another; and in an incredibly short space of time the stolen property is far away. . . . Again a Bhampta sees a well-to-do person in the street. He makes a great show of brutally beating a small boy. The boy screams and yells and rushes for protection to the prosperous-looking stranger, who shields the child and expostulates with the Bhampta. The latter in apparent anger snatches away the boy from his protector, while the young rascal, who has been well trained, kicks and struggles for all that he is worth. The sympathizer has had enough of it, and is glad to let the youngster go. Later on he realizes that his purse has disappeared.[8]

RURAL-URBAN PATTERNS

Statistics from many countries, and in many periods of time, indicate that urban areas have higher crime rates than rural areas. Two general types of relationship between crime and size of community can be observed, just as two types of relationship were observed between crime and age, sex, race, and nativity.

First, official statistics indicate that the number of serious crimes per 100,000 population tends to increase with the size of the community. In 1975, the rate of robberies known to the American police varied from 43.4 in towns of less than 10,000 population to 682.6 in cities of over 250,000. This trend is roughly the same for other types of crime and in other years, except that in cities over one million, the rates for some crimes are lower than the rates for cities of 500,000–1,000,000, and these latter cities sometimes have rates lower than cities of 250,000–500,000, and so on.

Similar tendencies have been reported for African, Latin American, and European countries and for Canada. For instance, of all males born in Norway in 1933, 5.08 percent had become registered offenders by January 1, 1958. Among the boys living in Oslo, however, 9 percent had become offenders, as compared to 8 percent of the residents of other cities and 4 percent of the country residents.[9]

[8] Edmund C. Fox, *Police and Crime in India* (London: S. Paul, 1911), pp. 234–37. See also Paul F. Cressey, "The Criminal Tribes of India," *Sociology and Social Research*, 20:503–11; 21:18–25, 1936; and Clarence H. Patrick, "The Criminal Tribes of India, with Special Emphasis on the Mang Garudi: A Preliminary Report," *Man in India*, 48:244–57, 1968.

[9] Nils Christie, *Unge Norske Lovovertredere* [Young Norwegian Lawbreakers] (Oslo: Universitetsforlaget, 1960), pp. 76, 304.

Among a sample of 3032 Danish men who in 1953–1954 were 21 years of age or more, 9.6 percent were violators of the criminal code. Thirteen percent of the men living in Copenhagen were violators as compared to 8.8 percent of those living in towns with populations of 2000–19,000, and to 6.2 percent of those living in rural districts and small towns with less than 2000 inhabitants.[10]

Self-reports on involvement with criminal justice agencies also show a concentration of crime and delinquency in cities. Interviews with a sample (N = 2510) of all American men who were 20 to 30 years old in 1974 showed positive correlations between city size and arrest, juvenile court appearance, convictions of a crime, and imprisonment. For example, 13 percent of the men who lived in cities of 500,000 or more had gone to juvenile court, as compared to 6 percent of the residents of rural areas. Similarly, 15 percent of the men who grew up in cities of one million or more had been convicted of a crime, in comparison with 10 percent among rural residents. There was also a linear relationship between serving a prison sentence and city size—4 percent of the rural residents and 11 percent of those who as juveniles resided in cities of one million or more served prison sentences.[11]

Offenses committed by rural criminals might not be reported or recorded as readily as offenses committed in urban areas, but the urban rate generally so far exceeds the rural rate that it is reasonable to conclude that there is in fact a great excess of crime in urban places.[12] Moreover, a large proportion of urban crime also is overlooked, and it is not at all certain that this proportion is any less than the proportion of rural crime that is overlooked.

Second, the extent to which the crime rate in urban areas exceeds the crime rate in rural areas is not the same under all conditions. In some rural areas the crime rate is higher than the rate in urban areas. The pattern varies in at least three significant ways.

1. The amount of the excess of crime in urban areas varies by offenses. In American cities of over 250,000, murder and rape rates are about five times as high as the rates in towns of 10,000; burglary, larceny, and aggravated assault are about

---

[10] Preben Wolf, "Crime and Social Class in Denmark," *British Journal of Criminology*, 13:5–17, 1962.

[11] John A. O'Donnell, Harwin L. Voss, Richard R. Clayton, Gerald T. Slatin, and Robin G. W. Room, *Young Men and Drugs—A Nationwide Survey* (Washington, D.C.: National Institute on Drug Abuse, Research Monograph No. 5, 1976), pp. 91–93.

[12] See Denis Szabo, *Crimes et Villes* (Louvain: Catholic University of Louvain, 1960); Abdellatif El Bacha, "Quelques Aspects Particuliers de la Délinquance Juvénile dans Certains Villes du Royaume du Maroc," *International Review of Criminal Policy*, 20:21–23, 1962; William Clifford, "The Evaluation of Methods Used for the Prevention and Treatment of Juvenile Delinquency in Africa South of the Sahara," *International Review of Criminal Policy*, 21:17–32, 1963; Abdelwahab Bouhdiba, *Criminalité et Changements Sociaux en Tunisie* (Tunis: University of Tunis, 1965); Leonore R. Kupperstein and Jaime Toro-Calder, *Juvenile Delinquency in Puerto Rico* (San Juan: University of Puerto Rico, 1969); Carl D. Chambers and Gordon H. Barker, "Juvenile Delinquency in Iraq," *British Journal of Criminology*, 11:176–82, 1971; C. D. Spinellis, *Crime in Contemporary Greece* (Athens: Athenian Institute of Anthropos, 1971), pp. 20–23; and Peter N. Grabosky, "Patterns of Criminality in New South Wales, 1788–1973," *Australian and New Zealand Journal of Criminology*, 7:215–29, 1974.

three times as high; automobile theft is more than six times as high, and robbery about twenty-five times as high. In certain respects, the number of crimes decreases as the distance from the large city increases. Burglaries or robberies were committed against 60 percent of the stores belonging to a chain in the city of Chicago in a two-year period, while only 30 percent were burglarized or robbed in the suburban area within 25 miles from the center of Chicago in the same period. Moreover, the proportion of stores burglarized or robbed decreased by 25–mile zones steadily until it reached 6.2 percent in the zone 100–125 miles away from the city.

Lottier, in a more extensive analysis of the distribution of crimes, found that murders, assaults, rapes, and robberies known to the police decreased consistently in the commutation area of Detroit to a distance of 20 miles from the city hall, but that burglaries, auto thefts, and larcenies did not show a consistent decrease. He also found the same crimes against the person decreasing in the entire metropolitan area of Detroit within a radius of 200 miles, but again the crimes against property showed no such consistent decrease. He suggested that the difference in the two types of crimes may be due to the fact that crimes against the person were calculated in proportion to the number of persons, but crimes against property were not calculated in proportion to the amount of property.[13] Boggs, similarly, recently proposed that even crimes against the person are not accurate because they are not calculated in proportion to the number of "exposures" of offenders and victims to each other.[14]

For the United States as a whole, the rural rates are slightly higher than the urban rates for homicide, about equal for rape, about one-half as high for assault, and from about one-fourth to about one-third as high for robbery, burglary, larceny, and motor vehicle theft.

2. The amount of the excess of crime in urban areas varies by region. In an earlier period, frontier towns, river towns, and resort towns were noted for high crime rates, despite the fact that they were not large in size. Further, Radzinowicz demonstrated that in the southern districts of Poland the crime rates decreased as communities increased in size, that even in other sections of Poland many small communities had higher crime rates than many large communities, and that communities of the same size varied immensely in crime rates.[15] Also, in some other European countries the rates for larger cities have been shown to be lower than the rural rates. Christie's study of Norwegian males showed a clear overrepresentation of offenders in the most densely populated areas, which also had the highest number of policemen per 1000 inhabitants. However, the most sparsely populated area—Finnmark, the northernmost county in Norway—had an offender rate which was approximately the same as that of the densely populated industrial areas. Finnmark, which is populated by Lapps as well as by Norwegians,

[13]Stuart Lottier, "Distribution of Criminal Offenses in Metropolitan Regions," *Journal of Criminal Law and Criminology*, 29:37–50, 1938.

[14]Sarah L. Boggs, "Urban Crime Patterns," *American Sociological Review*, 30:899–908, 1965.

[15]Leon Radzinowicz, "Criminality by Size-Groups of Communities," manuscript, 1946.

also has one policeman for each 500 inhabitants, as compared to a ratio of 1 to 12,000 in other sparsely populated counties and to a ratio of 1 to 400 in Bergen and Oslo.[16]

Older studies of Iowa and Kansas found regular increases in delinquency rates from the most rural to the most urban counties. However, a study of the distribution of delinquency in Wisconsin indicated that the counties containing cities had high delinquency rates, but that certain isolated rural logging counties also had high rates. Wiers found in Michigan that the most urban county had the highest delinquency rate, but that the sparsely settled logging counties had higher rates than the southern agricultural counties.[17] It must be concluded that certain contemporary rural sections have special criminalistic traditions, just as in an earlier period certain frontier areas had such traditions.

3. The amount of excess of crime in urban areas varies in time. There is evidence that as improved communication and transportation have reduced the differences between urban and rural districts, the differences in the crime rates of the two areas have decreased. The *Uniform Crime Reports* data indicate that, since about 1945, the rural rate in the United States has increased more rapidly than the urban rate. The suburban rate also is increasing faster than the urban rate. This general trend is found in some but not all areas of the United States and in some but not all nations of the world. In Sweden, the conviction rate in rural districts has in the past seventy-five years steadily approached the conviction rate in city districts. The same trend is found in France, but the opposite trend is found in Finland.

The excessive criminality of the city has been explained as due to the impersonality and greater criminal opportunities of city life in comparison with rural life.[18] This explanation is consistent with hundreds of sociological studies of cities and of urbanization, all of which have noted that "the urban way of life is characterized by extensive conflicts of norms and values, rapid social change, increased mobility of the population, emphasis on material goods and individualism and an increase in the use of formal rather than informal social controls."[19]

[16] Christie, *Unge Norske Lovovertredere*, pp, 78–80, 305.

[17] Charles N. Burrows, "Criminal Statistics in Iowa," *University of Iowa Studies in the Social Sciences*, vol. 9, no. 2, 1930; Mapheus Smith, "Tier Counties and Delinquency in Kansas," *Rural Sociology*, 2:310–22, 1937; Morris G. Caldwell, "The Extent of Juvenile Delinquency in Wisconsin," *Journal of Criminal Law and Criminology*, 32:148–57, 1941; and Paul Wiers, "Juvenile Delinquency in Rural Michigan," *Journal of Criminal Law and Criminology*, 30:211–22, 1939; see also idem, *Economic Factors in Michigan Delinquency* (New York: Columbia University Press, 1944).

[18] See Marshall B. Clinard, "The Process of Urbanization and Criminal Behavior: A Study of Culture Conflicts," *American Journal of Sociology*, 48:202–13, 1942; idem, "The Relation of Urbanization and Urbanism to Criminal Behavior," in *Contributions to Urban Sociology*, ed. Ernest W. Burgess and Donald J. Bogue (Chicago: University of Chicago Press, 1964), pp. 541–59; Richard Quinney, "Structural Characteristics, Population Areas, and Crime Rates in the United States," *Journal of Criminal Law, Criminology, and Police Science*, 57:45–62, 1966; and Marshall B. Clinard and Daniel J. Abbott, *Crime in Developing Countries: A Comparative Perspective* (New York: Wiley, 1973), pp. 85–91.

[19] Clinard and Abbott, *Crime in Developing Countries*, p. 85.

Recently, a survey of crime in Latin America concluded that city persons are much more likely than rural dwellers to encounter norms that contradict those enforced by the government.[20] In Iraq, another recent study noted that the city, in addition to presenting a heterogeneity of norms, substitutes individualism for family or community cohesiveness, is impersonal and anonymous, and therefore presents greater opportunities for crime.[21] So far as social controls are concerned, what has been said about persons experiencing the "modernization" of African communities pertains as well to any young man who moves from a small town to a metropolis: He is "transformed from being defined as his father's son into a citizen."[22]

Further, patterns of criminal behavior have become established in some rural districts, and persons migrating to those districts tend to become criminals, just as do persons migrating to urban areas in which criminal behavior patterns are prevalent. A study of the delinquents living in Daka found that the delinquents born in rural areas began their delinquent careers rather late, and their delinquency rate increased with age; the urban-born delinquents started their delinquent careers earlier than did those from rural areas, but their delinquency rate decreased with age.[23] Thus, the significant conditions are the area's ratio of anticriminal behavior patterns to procriminal behavior patterns, and the nature and extent of participation in these behavior patterns.[24] It should be noted, however, that relatively little organized research work has been done on rural criminality. Clinard has made the best studies, concluding that rural criminality is explained by the person's identification with delinquents and a conception of himself as reckless and mobile, an explanation which is consistent with differential association theory.[25]

[20]Robert Bergalli, *Criminologia en America Latina: Cambio Social Normative y Comportamientos Desviadas* (Buenos Aires: Ediciones Pannedille, 1972).

[21]M. N. Kadhim, "Some Aspects of the Participation of the Public in the Prevention and Control of Crime and Delinquency in Iraq," paper presented at the Fourth United Nations Congress on the Prevention and Treatment of Offenders, Kyoto, Japan, 1970, pp. 4–5. Quoted by Clinard and Abbott, *Crime in Developing Countries*, p. 90.

[22]Daniel Lerner, "Comparative Analysis of Processes of Modernization," in *The Modern City in Africa*, ed. Horace Miner (New York: Praeger, 1967).

[23]Study cited in G. Houchon, "Les Mécanismes Criminogènes dans une Société Urbanien Africaine," *Revue Internationale de Criminologie et de Police Technique*, 21:271–92, 1967. See also T. C. N. Gibbens and R. H. Ahrenfeldt, *Cultural Factors in Delinquency* (London: Tavistock, 1966), pp. 40–41.

[24]See Teruo Matsushita, "Crime in Japan: A Search for the Causes of Low and Decreasing Criminality," *Resource Materials of the United Nations Asia and Far East Institute for the Prevention of Crime and Treatment of Offenders*, No. 12, 1976, pp. 36–48.

[25]Clinard, "Process of Urbanization." See also idem, "Rural Criminal Offenders," *American Journal of Sociology*, 50:38–45, 1944; "A Cross-cultural Replication of the Relation of Urbanism to Criminal Behavior," *American Sociological Review*, 25:253–57, 1960; William P. Lentz, "Rural Urban Differentials and Juvenile Delinquency," *Journal of Criminal Law, Criminology, and Police Science*, 47:331–39, 1956.

INTRACITY PATTERNS

It has been evident for many decades that criminals and delinquents are much more numerous in some city areas than in others. Shaw and McKay have amplified this information and organized it in relation to the general pattern of the large American city.[25] By an analysis of the rates of delinquency in various areas of Chicago and other cities, they reached six conclusions.

First, the rates of delinquency vary widely in different neighborhoods. None of the boys residing in some areas are arrested, while in other neighborhoods more than one-fifth of the boys are arrested in one year. This variation has been found in many cities, and the neighborhoods with the highest rates have been designated as *delinquency areas.*

Second, the rates are generally highest in the low-rent areas near the center of the city and decrease with the distance from the center of the city. Also, the rates are high near large industrial or commercial subcenters of the city and decrease with distance from those subcenters.

Third, the areas which have high rates of truancy also have high rates for all juvenile court cases, as well as for arrests and adult commitments to the county jail. The areas which have high rates for boy delinquencies also have high rates for girl delinquencies.

Fourth, some areas have had high rates for more than fifty years, although the ethnic composition of the population of the areas has changed almost completely. When Germans and Swedes occupied an area near the center of the city, their children had high rates of delinquency; when they were replaced by Polish, Italian, or other national groups, and then by blacks, the juvenile delinquency rates in the area were essentially the same.

Fifth, the delinquency rate of a particular national group such as German or Polish shows the same general tendency as the delinquency rate for the entire population, namely, to be high in the areas near the center of the city and low toward the outskirts of the city.

Sixth, delinquents living in areas of high delinquency rates are the most likely to become recidivists, and among all recidivists they are likely to appear in court several times more often than those from areas with low delinquency rates.

The above conclusions have been criticized on the ground that the statistics from which they were drawn were not valid measures, but the conclusions have

[26]Clifford R. Shaw and Henry D. McKay, *Juvenile Delinquency and Urban Areas,* rev. ed. (Chicago: University of Chicago Press, 1969). See also V. V. Stanciu, *Criminalité a Paris* (Paris: Presses Universitaires de France, 1967). For excellent summaries of research on delinquency areas, see Terrence Morris, *The Criminal Area* (London: Kegan Paul, 1958); Judith A. Wilks, "Ecological Correlates of Crime and Delinquency," appendix A in President's Commission on Law Enforcement and Administration of Justice, *Task Force Report: Crime and Its Impact—An Assessment* (Washington, D.C.: Government Printing Office, 1967), pp. 138–56; and Harwin L. Voss and David M. Peterson, eds., *Ecology of Crime and Delinquency* (New York: Appleton-Century-Crofts, 1971).

been substantiated by studies in other localities by other authors.[27] The question which has been raised most persistently, perhaps, is whether the statistics of arrests or of juvenile court appearances do not give a biased measure of delinquencies because of the poverty of the families in the areas which are reported as having the highest delinquency rates.[28] Wealth and social position certainly provide a degree of immunity against arrest and incarceration, even for children. Also, some national or religious groups maintain informal and even formal welfare organizations which take problem cases that would otherwise be referred to the police or to the juvenile court, while other national and religious groups have no such organizations. Even when allowance is made for these probable statistical biases, some concentration of ordinary crime and delinquency seems to remain. In the District of Columbia some years ago, the juvenile court statistics showed *less* concentration of cases in the high-delinquency areas than did the unofficial statistics of other agencies.[29] Of course, white-collar crime is not concentrated in the areas which have the highest official delinquency rates.

The "concentration," it should be noted, is a concentration of the residences of criminals and delinquents, rather than of the crimes and delinquencies themselves. Generally, the places at which crimes are committed are close to the residences of the criminals. This is especially characteristic of crimes against the person, for the offender and the victim are usually of the same race, the same economic class, and also of the same neighborhood.[30] A study in Seattle indicated that serious property crimes, such as larceny and robbery, tend to occur in the central segment of the city, and are perpetrated by persons residing in that

[27] Bernard Lander, *Towards an Understanding of Juvenile Delinquency* (New York: Columbia University Press, 1954); Kenneth Polk, "Juvenile Delinquency and Social Areas," *Social Problems*, 5:214–17, 1957; David J. Bordua, "Juvenile Delinquency and Anomie," *Social Problems*, 6:230–38, 1958; William Bates, "Caste, Class, and Vandalism," *Social Problems*, 9:349–58, 1962; Charles V. Willie and Anita Gershenovitz, "Juvenile Delinquency in Racially Mixed Areas," *American Sociological Review*, 29:740–44, 1964; Ronald J. Chilton, "Continuity in Delinquency Area Research: A Comparison of Studies for Baltimore, Detroit, and Indianapolis," *American Sociological Review*, 29:71–83, 1964; Richard Quinney, "Crime, Delinquency, and Social Areas," *Journal of Research in Crime and Delinquency*, 1:149–54, 1964; and Charles V. Willie, "The Relative Contribution of Family Status and Economic Status to Juvenile Delinquency," *Social Problems*, 14:326–35, 1967. Some of this research is summarized and analyzed in Lawrence Rosen and Stanley H. Turner, "An Evaluation of the Lander Approach to Ecology of Delinquency," *Social Problems*, 15:189–200, 1967; Robert A. Gordon, "Issues in the Ecological Study of Delinquency," *American Sociological Review*, 32:927–44, 1967; Gerald T. Slatin, "Ecological Analysis of Delinquency: Aggregation Effects," *American Sociological Review*, 34:894–907, 1969; and Don C. Gibbons, *Delinquent Behavior*, 2d ed. (Englewood Cliffs, N. J.: Prentice-Hall, 1976), pp. 105–14.

[28] Christen T. Jonassen, "A Re-evaluation and Critique of the Logic and Some Methods of Shaw and McKay," *American Sociological Review*, 14:608–17, 1949; and Jackson Toby, "The Differential Impact of Family Disorganization," *American Sociological Review*, 22:505–12, 1957.

[29] Edward E. Schwartz, "A Community Experiment in the Measurement of Juvenile Delinquency," *National Probation Association Yearbook*, 1945, pp. 157–81.

[30] Thomas A. Reppetto, *Residential Crime* (Cambridge, Mass.: Ballinger, 1974), p. 48.

segment of the city. For example, 63 percent of the robberies and 40 percent of the burglaries were committed in the central segment, and 41 percent of those arrested for robbery and 34 percent of those arrested for burglary resided in the central segment.[31]

Although the concentration of the residences of delinquents and ordinary criminals near the industrial and commercial centers is demonstrated in an adequate sample of large American cities, the centers of concentration are not the same in European, Asiatic, or Latin American cities. In fact, a study of residences of criminals in Peking indicated a concentration in the slum areas at the gates of the city rather than in the center of the city, and much the same distribution is reported in the older European cities, although special studies of residences of delinquents have not been made. DeFleur found that in Cordoba, Argentina, the residences of delinquents are in pockets of poverty scattered throughout the city, with some concentration in the central zone and in the peripheral zones.[32] In some smaller cities in the United States, the residences of delinquents are in the low-rent areas adjacent to the railway tracks or to the refuse dumps on the outskirts of town. Because of the rapid expansion of American cities, especially those east of the Rocky Mountains, the areas of poverty in these cities tend to be located near the center. Thus, the high delinquency areas tend to be concentrated in the areas of greatest poverty, whether those areas are near the center of the city or on the outskirts.[33] It is not correct, however, to conclude from this that poverty is the cause of crime.

Two principal interpretations of the concentration of delinquents have been presented. The first is in terms of social organization in the neighborhood. The areas of concentration in large American cities, and especially Chicago, where the problem has been studied most intensively, are areas of physical deterioration, congested population, decreasing population, economic dependency, rented homes, foreign and black population, and few institutions supported by the local residents. Lawlessness has become traditional; adult criminals are frequently seen and have much prestige. Gangs have continued to exist, with changing personnel, for fifty years in some of these areas. In such areas, delinquencies begin at an early age, and maturity in crime is also reached at an early age. Boys 14 or 15 years of age steal automobiles and commit robberies, while in other areas delinquents of the same age are committing petty thefts. They not only acquire skill in the execution of crimes, but also prepare for avoidance or mitigation of penalties. They know the

---

[31] Calvin F. Schmid, "Urban Crime Areas: Part II," *American Sociological Review*, 25:655–78, 1960.

[32] Lois B. DeFleur, "Ecological Variables in the Cross-Cultural Study of Delinquency," *Social Forces*, 45:556–70, 1967. See also N. S. Hayner, "Criminogenic Zones in Mexico City," *American Sociological Review*, 11:428–38, 1946; and Theodore Caplow, "The Social Ecology of Guatemala City," *Social Forces*, 28:113–33, 1949.

[33] See John Mack, "Full-time Miscreants, Delinquent Neighbourhoods, and Criminal Networks," *British Journal of Sociology*, 15:38–53, 1964.

techniques of "fixing," of intimidating witnesses, of telling plausible stories in court, of appeals to sympathy. Consequently the influences toward delinquency and crime are strong and almost constant.

At the same time, the antidelinquent influences are few, and organized opposition to delinquency is weak. Parent-teacher associations do not exist, nor do other community organizations which are supported principally by the people of the neighborhood. Because the population is mobile and heterogeneous, it is unable to act cohesively in dealing with its own problems. Schools, social work agencies, police patrols, businesses, and even churches are staffed by people who reside elsewhere, and these agencies are for the most part formal and external to the life of the area.[34]

The residents of these areas probably know much better than do the members of the middle classes the details of any graft and dishonesty in their city's politics. The American culture which they see is a culture of competition, corruption, deceit, graft, crime, delinquency, and immorality. They see practically nothing of the culture of cooperation, decency, and law-abidingness in which some Americans are immersed from infancy. Thus they come in contact with a rather lawless neighborhood, and the rather dishonest public culture of America, but are isolated from the predominantly law-abiding culture of the primary groups in the middle-class American population.

That they would behave differently if they came into contact with a different culture pattern has been shown in a comparison of a delinquency area of Boston with a delinquency area of Cairo. In the Boulac area of Cairo, a high-delinquency area, 35 percent of the delinquents arrested in one year had committed crimes against the person, while in the Roxbury section of Boston, only 8 percent of delinquent arrests were for such crimes. Similarly, 65 percent of the Roxbury delinquents, but only 25 percent of the Boulac delinquents, committed crimes against property. These variations are the result of cultural differences in what American and Egyptian slum-dwellers learn about an individualistic orientation to life—that is, in what they know is true about the role of "fate" in their personal affairs, as compared to the role of other persons. Boulac residents have learned that their misfortunes are caused by other people. They behave accordingly:

In Boulac society, the individualism of Roxbury society is lacking. . . . Persons, in themselves, are more important to an individual than his belongings. When an individual's success, or his status, or his recognition is hindered or threatened, he usually thinks in terms of some person or persons hindering his success, or threatening his status, or discouraging his recognition. Thus he may try to revenge himself by removing the cause—in this case, the person concerned.[35]

[34] See Peter H. Rossi and Richard A. Berk, "Local Political Leadership and Popular Discontent in the Ghetto," *Annals of the American Academy of Political and Social Science*, 391:111–27, 1970.

[35] Saied Euwies, "A Comparative Study of Two Delinquency Areas," *National Review of Criminal Science* (U.A.R.), 2:1–15, 1959.

The second interpretation is that competitive processes select out inferior persons who would have high delinquency and crime rates wherever they lived. As a matter of fact, those who reside in areas of high delinquency at a particular time are of three types: recent immigrants, remnants of the earlier residential groups, and failures who have moved into the cheaper rent areas from the better residential districts. In studies of delinquency in nonmetropolitan areas, Polk and Halferty found that small towns contain a "trouble-making subculture," and that school failures drift into it after having been "locked out" of the system supporting accomplishments by legitimate means. Participants in the subculture become delinquent, and they also become socially handicapped. Even when they migrate to urban areas, they are not able to participate fully in legitimate opportunity structures because they are economically, educationally, socially, and culturally disadvantaged.[36]

The most important evidence on this point, however, is Shaw and McKay's finding that the delinquency rate remained practically constant over a fifty-year period despite an almost complete change in the ethnic composition of the population. This indicates that the delinquency rate is more likely to be a function of social conditions in an area than of the individual traits and conditions of the people who reside there. When some national groups, such as Swedes or Mexicans, first settled in an area of deterioration in an American city, the children did not play with the children of the residents and did not become delinquent. But, as contacts developed, the delinquency rates increased. Consistently, a detailed study showed that when an immigrant group first settled in Los Angeles, only 5 percent of the children of juvenile court age appeared in juvenile courts; five years later this percentage had increased to 46, and after another decade 83 percent of their children appeared in juvenile court.[37] The ethnic characteristics in this case remained constant, but the opportunities for assimilation of the culture of the American city increased, and in their neighborhood this meant assimilation of delinquency and crime.

The location of delinquency areas near the commercial or industrial centers is related to the rents in those centers. But low rents do not cause delinquency. Rents are low because accommodations are poor, and the accommodations are not improved because of the expectation that the commercial and industrial activities will expand, causing the nearby areas to be annexed to the business sections. When poor migrants arrive, they settle in these areas of deterioration where the

[36] Kenneth Polk and David S. Halferty, "Adolescence, Commitment, and Delinquency," *Journal of Research in Crime and Delinquency*, 3:82–96, 1966; Kenneth Polk, "Delinquency and Community Action in Non-metropolitan Areas," appendix R in President's Commission on Law Enforcement and Administration of Justice, *Task Force Report: Juvenile Delinquency* (Washington, D.C.: Government Printing Office, 1967), pp. 343–47.

[37] Pauline V. Young, "Urbanization as a Factor in Juvenile Delinquency," *Publications of the American Sociological Society*, 24:162–66, 1930; idem, *The Pilgrims of Russia-Town* (Chicago: University of Chicago Press, 1932).

rents are low, but some of them move out to better residential districts as soon as they accumulate sufficient capital. In this case, their delinquency rates go down. Blacks, Puerto Ricans, and Mexicans have dispersed less than other ethnic groups, and for that reason are likely to continue to have problems of delinquency.

Although areas of high delinquency contain an abundance of prodelinquent behavior patterns, most residents of such areas are not criminal or delinquent, and these persons live under the same conditions of poverty as do the criminals and delinquents. For example, within any given area, the female delinquency rate is customarily much lower than the male delinquency rate, although the wealth of parents, housing conditions, and many other conditions are the same for girls and boys. Furthermore, even in areas with relatively high delinquency rates, less than half of the boys can be identified as past or present delinquents. Mack found that, in a Scottish city, the precinct with the highest crime rate produced an annual average of eleven offenders per one hundred households during a ten-year period; the highest-density street in this precinct produced twenty offenders per one hundred houses per year. For this street, 32 percent of the households produced two or more offenders over a period of ten years, and another 7 percent of the households had a record of only one offender in the period. Thus, three out of five households in the most criminal area of the city had no criminal record at all, and only one out of three was "criminally active" in the sense that two or more offenders were produced in ten years.[38]

One explanation of the presence of nondelinquents in areas of high delinquency is the limitation on contact with delinquency patterns, even in the most delinquent areas. A delinquency area is seldom solidly delinquent; rather, there are certain streets or parts of streets on which at a particular time most delinquents reside, and on other streets the children may associate with each other in relative isolation from the behavior patterns of delinquents. Sometimes one or more ethnic groups within a general residential area are isolated from the rest of the population, or a few members of one such group may be isolated within a larger area of another nationality. For example, in the 1930s the delinquency rate in Seattle's Japanese colony, which was in a very deteriorated, high-delinquency area, was lower than in the best residential areas.[39] Further, some children are kept from frequent or intimate contact with delinquency patterns because of their retiring, quiet, and unaggressive dispositions, and others, especially girls, are kept from such associations by careful and capable parents or siblings. Some children may refrain from delinquency because they have formed attachments at school with teachers, or at other agencies with other leaders, or with their own parents; and their interests have been developed and their lives organized around lawful activities.[40]

[38]Mack, "Full-time Miscreants," p. 44.

[39]Norman S. Hayner, "Delinquency Areas in the Puget Sound Region," *American Journal of Sociology*, 39:314–28, 1933.

[40]See William F. Whyte, *Street Corner Society* (Chicago: University of Chicago Press, 1943), pp. 104–8; and Travis Hirschi, *Causes of Delinquency* (Berkeley: University of California Press, 1969).

A second, but consistent, explanation is that punishment of delinquents makes the career of a delinquent unattractive to some of the children in the areas of high delinquency. Of the young adults in the so-called Forty-Two Gang in Chicago some years ago, about one-third were killed by the police or by private parties, and another third were committed to prisons or reformatories. Killing young criminals or committing them to prison is a dramatic, but generally ineffective, way of presenting anticriminal behavior patterns to those who remain behind. Nevertheless, some of the boys in the vicinity must have avoided delinquency because of the outcomes of the older boys in the gang.

Yet punishment sometimes inadvertently operates as a prodelinquent influence, despite the attempt to use it as a device for presenting anticriminal behavior patterns. All children are somewhat delinquent, but only some are caught, punished, and thus publicly defined and labeled as delinquents. This first public appearance as a delinquent or criminal is highly critical, for thereafter the child's associations with law-abiding persons are restricted, and he or she is thrown into association with the behavior patterns of other delinquents. A boy who is consistently criminal is not defined as law-abiding if he commits a single lawful act, but a boy who is consistently law-abiding is likely to be publicly defined as a criminal if he is caught committing a single criminal act.

It is clear that even in the areas of highest delinquency many nondelinquent and antidelinquent behavior patterns are available.[41] Whether a particular youth becomes delinquent or not depends upon the ratio of his or her participation in this kind of behavior pattern, as compared with prodelinquency behavior patterns, just as is the case with a youth that lives in a more affluent area. The difference is in the availability of the two kinds of behavior pattern, not in the process by which they are learned.[42]

THE GANG

Among the influences in a neighborhood, the mutual stimulation of children in association is one of the most important. Many studies have shown that delinquencies are generally committed by two or more children acting together. Of 500 delinquents studied by the Gluecks, 492, or 98.4 percent, chummed largely with other delinquents. The 500 nondelinquents used as a control group lived in similar neighborhoods, yet only 37, or 7.4 percent, of them had intimates among delinquents.[43] In a study of the first delinquencies of boys admitted to the Ohio Boys Industrial School, it was found that the median age of the first contact with the police or courts for delinquency was 13.1 years; of boys whose first official delinquency occurred before this age, 77 percent were with companions when the

---

[41] Cf. Solomon Kobrin, "The Conflict of Values in Delinquency Areas," *American Sociological Review*, 16:653–61, 1951.

[42] See Jon E. Simpson, Simon Dinitz, Barbara Kay, and Walter C. Reckless, "Delinquency Potential of Pre-Adolescents in High-Delinquency Areas," *British Journal of Delinquency*, 10:211–15, 1960.

[43] Sheldon and Eleanor Glueck, *Unraveling Juvenile Delinquency* (New York: Commonwealth Fund, 1950), p. 164.

act occurred; of those whose first delinquency occurred after the age of 13.1, 73 percent were with companions.[44] Reiss and Rhodes found that the probability of an individual boy committing a specific kind of delinquent act depends upon the commission of that act by his two best friends. However, the relationship varies considerably with the type of delinquency. Vandalism and petty larceny were commonly committed by two or three members of the "best friends" triad. But in most of the triads in which at least one member committed automobile theft or assault, in fact only one member committed the offense.[45]

In most areas of high delinquency a few youths are organized for crime in definite working groups in which the labor is precisely divided. These groups are likely to be called "gangs" by the youths and others. In a robbery gang, for example, one young man drives the car, a second acts as lookout, while a third carries the gun and has the principal responsibility of entering the store. The assignment of tasks, of course, varies with the type of offense. This kind of organization is comparable to the division of labor in troupes of professional pickpockets, who do not call their working units "gangs."

The term *delinquent gang* usually refers to a larger and much more amorphous organization. However, the definition of *gang* is not clear. Inquiries among university students indicate that more than two-thirds of the men had, during childhood, been members of groups which were called gangs, and that about a third of the women had such memberships. Most of these groups were described as harmless in their activities, though inclined to mild rowdyism, and the name *gang* was applied largely in a spirit of bravado. Bloch and Niederhoffer attribute gang behavior of this kind to the problems which arise during the transition from child to adult; they find gang behavior in many cultures.[46]

These childhood gangs are different from neighborhood delinquent gangs. In some areas of high delinquency, all the boys who live on one street, or the boys of one ethnic group, belong together for the purposes of fights and are known by a common name. Frequently a portion of the neighborhood boys of about the same age and somewhat similar attitudes toward delinquency or toward "play" (which often involves delinquency) have a common meeting place on a corner and engage in many common activities without any other formal organization. A stranger would not be permitted to associate with these groups, which are sometimes called "clubs," and certain boys in the neighborhood might be ostracized, but the organization is not that of a working group of criminals.[47]

[44] Thomas G. Eynon and Walter C. Reckless, "Companionship at Delinquency Onset," *British Journal of Criminology*, 12:162–70, 1961.

[45] Albert J. Reiss, Jr., and Lewis Rhodes, "An Empirical Test of Differential Association Theory," *Journal of Research in Crime and Delinquency*, 1:5–18, 1964.

[46] Herbert A. Bloch and Arthur Niederhoffer, *The Gang: A Study in Adolescent Behavior* (New York: Philosophical Library, 1958).

[47] See Ruth Horowitz and Gary Schwartz, "Honor, Normative Ambiguity, and Gang Violence," *American Sociological Review*, 39:238–51, 1974.

Other delinquent gangs are more formally organized, with names, leaders, passwords, and slogans, and these gangs may persist, with changing personnel, for several decades.[48] Delinquent gangs of this kind disseminate techniques of delinquency and behavior patterns favorable to delinquency, protect members engaged in delinquency, and maintain continuity in delinquency. It is not necessary that there be bad boys inducing good boys to commit offenses. It is generally a mutual stimulation as a result of which each boy commits delinquencies which he would not commit alone. Nevertheless, these gangs are not primarily instruments for committing crime, and they might be called "groups" rather than gangs if they do not get into too much trouble.[49]

So far as structure is concerned, then, a neighborhood delinquent gang may be a loose federation of small cliques, a street club with rather informal and rapidly changing leadership, or an organization with an age hierarchy and specific leadership. Among 225 gangs studied in Warsaw, only 24 percent had an age hierarchy and specific leadership; another 24 percent were said to have "rudimentary organization," and the remaining 52 percent were "non-organized."[50]

One analysis has characterized both the loose federations of cliques and the street clubs as "near groups," rather than as groups.[51] The argument underlying this characterization is that these gangs are merely associations of individual boys who are trying to work out their own emotional problems in gang activities. There is little consensus, little identification with the group, and rapidly changing leadership. Thrasher observed the unstable quality of Chicago delinquent gangs in the 1920s and many other researchers have observed it in more recent times.[52] It is not at all certain, however, that emotionally disturbed boys are attracted to delinquent gangs in a disproportionate degree. One study of street clubs in Chicago found only about 10 percent of the members emotionally disturbed enough to be referred to a casework agency.[53] It appears, however, that even the gangs which are territorially organized and which have senior, junior, and midget sections, are so poorly integrated that the gang may disintegrate if a leader is

---

[48] See R. Lincoln Keiser, *The Vice Lords* (New York: Holt, Rinehart and Winston, 1969); and David Dawley, *A Nation of Lords* (Garden City, N. Y.: Doubleday, 1973).

[49] Walter B. Miller, "American Youth Gangs: Past and Present," chap. 10 in *Current Perspectives on Criminal Behavior*, ed. Abraham S. Blumberg (New York: Knopf, 1974), pp. 210–39.

[50] A. Pawelczynska, "Grupy nieletnich przestepców," *Archives Kryminologi*, 1:113–63, 1960.

[51] Lewis Yablonsky, "The Delinquent Gang as a Near-Group," *Social Problems*, 7:108–17, 1959.

[52] Frederic M. Thrasher, *The Gang* (Chicago: University of Chicago Press, 1927), pp. 35–37; Peter Scott, "Gangs and Delinquent Groups in London," *British Journal of Criminology*, 7:8–21, 1956; James F. Short, Jr., and Fred L. Strodtbeck, *Group Process and Gang Delinquency* (Chicago: University of Chicago Press, 1965), p. 200; David M. Downes, *The Delinquent Solution: A Study in Subcultural Theory* (London: Routledge and Kegan Paul, 1966), pp. 198–99; and Malcolm W. Klein and Lois Y. Crawford, "Groups, Gangs, and Cohesiveness," *Journal of Research in Crime and Delinquency*, 4:63–75, 1967.

[53] Charles H. Shireman, *The Hyde Park Youth Project, May 1955—May 1958* (Chicago: Welfare Council of Metropolitan Chicago, n.d.), p. 147

arrested or moves out of the neighborhood.[54] The staff of a research project studying two areas of high delinquency in Chicago had contact with thirty-five groups, all of which had names such as Aristocrats, Dukes, Top Boys. Fifteen months later, the staff had contact with forty-four groups, but only fifteen were continued from the previous year; twenty of the old groups had disappeared from the list, and twenty-nine new names had appeared.[55]

Delinquent gangs may be classified according to activities as well as according to the type of organization involved. One such classification developed from observations of the kinds of delinquent subcultures arising in the slum areas of large American cities: gangs oriented to criminal activities, gangs oriented to conflict and violence, and gangs oriented to the use of drugs.[56] This classification refers to gangs in different locations and in different periods of history, and it does not differentiate groups organized to complete certain criminal projects, such as committing robbery or using heroin, from groups of boys who hang out together and commit occasional crimes together. In 1963, Short and his co-workers could find no criminally oriented gangs in Chicago, and it took more than a year of extensive inquiries to locate a drug-oriented group.[57] It should be emphasized, moreover, that no classificatory system is airtight—gangs that fight also steal occasionally, and some of their members use drugs.[58]

In all three types of gangs listed by Cloward and Ohlin, members of the gangs follow norms which are in opposition to those held by law-abiding groups of the larger society. They have "withdrawn their attribution of legitimacy to certain of the norms maintained by law-abiding groups of the larger society and have given it, instead, to new patterns of conduct which are defined as illegitimate by representatives of official agencies."[59] This does not mean that gang members are oriented only to the norms of the gang; it means instead that they are characterized by what Horowitz and Schwartz call "normative ambiguity"—they

---

[54] See George W. Kelling, "Leadership in the Gang," chap. 7 in *Gang Delinquency*, ed. Desmond S. Cartwright, Barbara Thomson, and Hershey Schwartz (Monterey, Calif.: Brooks/Cole, 1975), pp. 111–26.

[55] Hans W. Mattick and Nathan S. Caplan, *The Chicago Youth Development Project* (Ann Arbor, Mich.: University of Michigan Institute for Social Research, 1964), pp. 96, 104.

[56] Richard A. Cloward and Lloyd E. Ohlin, *Delinquency and Opportunity: A Theory of Delinquent Gangs* (Glencoe, Ill.: Free Press, 1960). See also Yablonsky's classification: delinquent gangs, violent gangs, and social gangs. The latter are not delinquent. Lewis Yablonsky, *The Violent Gang* (New York: Macmillan, 1962), pp. 149–50. Cohen and Short stimulated classifications of these kinds by identifying three kinds of male delinquent subcultures: the "parent" subculture, the conflict-oriented subculture, and the drug addict subculture. Albert K. Cohen and James F. Short, Jr., "Research in Delinquent Subcultures," *Journal of Social Issues*, 14:20–37, 1958.

[57] James F. Short, Jr., Ray A. Tennyson, and Kenneth I. Howard, "Behavior Dimensions of Gang Delinquency," *American Sociological Review*, 28:411–28, 1963.

[58] James F. Short, Jr., "Street Corner Groups and Patterns of Delinquency: A Progress Report," *American Catholic Sociological Review*, 24:13–32, 1963.

[59] Cloward and Ohlin, *Delinquency and Opportunity*, p. 19.

move between two antithetical codes for conduct, one of which is "conventional" and one of which is "delinquent."[60]

The activities of gangs are consistent with rules which are specifically provided and supported by the delinquent subcultures described in Chapter 5, but the activities of the members, and of the gangs themselves, should not be confused with the delinquent subcultures. Because of inconsistencies in social structure, certain forms of delinquent activity have become substitutes for legitimate means of gaining status. This kind of delinquent activity is subcultural delinquency, and the "rules for delinquency" which underlie it constitute a delinquent subculture. However, explanation of the process by which such "rules" come into existence, develop, and change, is different from explanation of the behavior of delinquents, whether these delinquents perform their delinquencies alone or in gangs.[61]

The delinquent gang is, above all, an important agency for diffusion of the values that make up delinquent subcultures. Acts of delinquency which have the support of a gang are likely to recur with great frequency, for delinquent behavior can be used to achieve acceptance and status in the gang. This means that a boy's social position in the gang can be maintained only if he can "score" now and then, or if he can exhibit the behavior patterns of a "real man" or a "thief,"[62] or if he can on occasion exhibit "heart," and skill in the use of violence. Gangs are almost constantly engaged in negotiations with each other, and, as demonstrations of strength, many agreements, alliances, and contracts are made. "These are generally pseudobargains, which serve as means for gang members to flex muscles they are unsure they have."[63] In one city, the bulk of the assaultive incidents among members of street gangs involved contests in which the preservation and defense of gang honor was the central issue and where "little of the deliberately-inflicted property damage represented a diffuse outpouring of accumulated hostility

---

[60] Horowitz and Schwartz, "Honor, Normative Ambiguity, and Gang Violence." See also James F. Short, Jr., "Gang Delinquency and Anomie," in *Anomie and Deviant Behavior*, ed. Marshall B. Clinard, (New York: Free Press, 1964), pp. 98–127; and Edward Rothstein, "Attributes Related to High School Status: A Comparison of Perceptions of Delinquent and Non-delinquent Boys," *Social Problems*, 10:75–83, 1962.

[61] The following material is patterned after the presentation by Cloward and Ohlin, *Delinquency and Opportunity*, pp. 10–11, but it stresses the difference between gang activities and the delinquent subcultures on which gang activities are based. Cloward and Ohlin are vague about whether theirs is a theory about the behavior of delinquents, a theory about delinquent gangs, or a theory about the origin of delinquent subcultures. Their use of the terms *gang* and *subculture* synonymously contributes to this vagueness. We consider as primary the problem of explaining how delinquent values come into existence, and we view the problem of how these values are diffused as secondary. Cloward and Ohlin state that they are concerned with the first problem: "Why do delinquent norms, or rules of conduct, develop?" (p. ix). However, their book is devoted principally to discussion of how delinquent rules of conduct, once they are in existence, get distributed to individuals.

[62] See John Irwin and Donald R. Cressey, "Thieves, Convicts and the Inmate Culture," *Social Problems*, 10:142–55, 1962; and John Irwin, *The Felon* (Englewood Cliffs, N. J.: Prentice-Hall, 1970).

[63] Yablonsky, *The Violent Gang*, p. 157.

against arbitrary objects."[64] In short, it was found that nonutilitarian violence in the form of assaults on innocent victims is very rare. Consistently, a study of Chicano gangs in Chicago found a high incidence of assaults and killings, all done in defense of honor:

> Gang violence occurs when honor becomes a pressing issue in interpersonal relations and when the participants feel they cannot gracefully talk their way out of a situation that impugns their dignity and self-respect.[65]

Gang activities furnish continuity between criminal activities as a juvenile and criminal activities as an adult. Not all gang members become adult criminals, by any means, but gang activities sometimes afford the young an opportunity to acquire the values and skills that are necessary to the competent adult criminal. Even if gang members are more likely to exhibit a lack of commitment to conformity than a positive commitment to lawbreaking, as several studies have shown to be the case, their low stake in conformity gets them into trouble.[66] A study of 711 active black gang members in Philadelphia indicated that the rate for each type of delinquency rose gradually each year from the average age of first contact with the police (13.4 years) to a peak at 15–16 years, and then decreased in the last year of juvenile status.[67] The average time between the first and second contacts with the police was 14 months, while the average interval between the ninth and tenth contacts was 3.6 months. Of 580 gang members who moved out of juvenile status in a 9-month period, 41 percent acquired criminal records in this period. These data indicate that once gang delinquencies begin, there is a chain reaction in which each delinquent act becomes a stimulus for commission of another act within a briefer period of time, indicating gang members' increasing acceptance of the norms and values of the gang.

Further, participation in gang activities makes a delinquent difficult to change, for his behavior belongs to an explicit network of expectations and obligations. Most delinquent and criminal behavior is the property of groups rather than of individuals, in the way the French language or the English language is the property of collectivities rather than of individuals, but in the case of gang behavior, the ownership of the delinquency is more explicit and obvious. Accordingly, efforts to induce a member to feel shame or guilt are blocked by the rationalizations and reassurances which the group provides. "He can freely admit that killing is

[64] Walter B. Miller, "Violent Crime in City Gangs," *Annals of the American Academy of Political and Social Science*, 343:97–112, 1966.

[65] Horowitz and Schwartz, "Honor, Normative Ambiguity, and Gang Violence." p. 242.

[66] Scott Briar and Irving Piliavin, "Delinquency, Situational Inducements, and Commitment to Conformity," *Social Problems*, 13:25–45, 1965; Robert A. Gordon, "Social Level, Disability, and Gang Interaction," *American Journal of Sociology*, 73:42–62, 1967; and Hirschi, *Causes of Delinquency*, pp. 155–56.

[67] Gerald D. Robin, "Gang Member Delinquency: Its Extent, Sequence, and Typology," *Journal of Criminal Law, Criminology, and Police Science*, 55:59–69, 1964.

morally wrong and that fighting is foolhardy, and, at the same time, contend that one must defend one's honor even if this leads to homicide."[68]

The members of groups or cliques organized primarily for pursuit of material gain by such illegal means as theft, burglary, and extortion take on some of the attributes of professional thieves or participants in organized crime. Such cliques are likely to exist within a gang context, but they are not, in the usual sense of the term, delinquent gangs themselves.

Data from a large, white street-corner group without discernible delinquency specialization . . . suggest that "criminal cliques" may develop within such groups. In the observed case a clique of eight boys formed exclusively around rationally directed theft activities— auto stripping, burglary, shoplifting, etc. This clique did not hang together in the corner, but met in one another's homes. When on the corner they hung with other members of the larger group. They participated in the general hanging and drinking patterns, and in occasional altercations with various adults as part of the larger group, but not as a distinguishable clique. Only in their pattern of theft activities were they a clique. For at least two years they were reasonably successful in these activities, in terms of money and goods acquired, in fencing or selling directly to customers, and in avoiding arrest or "fixing" arrests when they were apprehended.[69]

Such groups adopt values which regard members of the conventional world as suckers, which see the world of business as a world of rackets, and the world of politics as a world of graft.

But, the solutions to problems of lower-class boys provided by delinquent gangs are primarily *status* rewarding, so the gang's organizational goal, if there is one, need not be economic gain.[70] In conflict gangs, for example, the role-model is the youth who displays the courage and bravery of the hero, the successful warrior. A youth can obtain "rep" in such a gang if he is tough and violent; he must not be weak. Short and Strodtbeck have shown that leaders of conflict gangs often respond to status threats by instigating aggression against persons outside the gang.[71]

In street groups whose members use drugs, the participant learns that to be important he must be detached from the life-style and everyday activities of "squares,"[72] but he must not "retreat." He must "hustle," meaning that he lives by his wits rather than by routine labor. What Cloward and Ohlin call the retreatest gang (the addict subculture) thus is not retreatest at all. In this subculture, persons

---

[68] Horowitz and Schwartz, "Honor, Normative Ambiguity, and Gang Violence," p. 247.

[69] Short and Strodtbeck, *Group Process and Gang Delinquency*, p. 98. See also Downes, *The Delinquent Solution*, pp. 116–25.

[70] Short, "Street Corner Groups and Patterns of Delinquency," p. 22.

[71] Short and Strodtbeck, *Group Process in Gang Delinquency*, pp. 185–98. See also Desmond S. Cartwright, Hershey Schwartz, and Barbara Tomson, "Status and Gang Delinquency," chap. 3 in *Gang Delinquency*, ed. Cartwright, Tomson and Schwartz, pp. 57–76.

[72] Harold Finestone, "Cats, Kicks, and Color," *Social Problems*, 5:3–13, 1957.

are accorded prestige for working regularly and hard in the nonconventional occupations summarized by the term "hustle."[73]

Cloward and Ohlin's thesis is that gang behavior is motivated by failure, or the anticipation of failure, in achieving successful goals by socially approved means. This thesis is similar to that of Albert K. Cohen, who stresses the function of the gang in resolving the status frustrations of working-class boys.[74] Lower-class male adolescents find themselves at a competitive disadvantage in gaining access to legitimate routes to success. If they attribute their failure to injustice in the social system, rather than to their own inadequacies, they may (1) bend their efforts to reforming the social order, (2) dissociate themselves from it, or (3) rebel against it. "Democratizing the criteria of evaluation without at the same time increasing the opportunities available to lower-class youngsters will accentuate the conditions that produce feelings of unjust deprivation."[75] A sense of injustice, then, springs from a sense of being discriminated against.

It should not be concluded, however, that persons with limited opportunities, or persons who are discriminated against, perceive these restrictions as status deprivation. For example, boys (but not girls) from rural areas and small towns have lower occupational aspirations than those from urban places—independent of intelligence and socioeconomic differences. Low-status rural youth, therefore, are less likely than low-status city youth to perceive their status as a consequence of deprivation.[76] Consistently, a study of delinquency in the most affluent nations of the world concluded: "Resentment of poverty is more likely to develop among the relatively deprived of a rich society than among the objectively deprived in a poor society."[77] Using a crude measure of perceived status deprivation, Reiss and Rhodes found that only 28 percent of a sample of delinquents and 16 percent of a sample of nondelinquents perceived that their clothing and housing were not as good as that of their fellow students.[78] Similarly, an Ohio State study found only a slight association between delinquency and perception of limited opportunity, and a Chicago study indicated that many of the values of

[73] Alan G. Sutter, "Worlds of Drug Use on the Street Scene," ch. in *Delinquency, Crime, and Social Process*, ed. Donald R. Cressey and David A. Ward (New York: Harper and Row, 1969) pp. 802–29.

[74] Albert K. Cohen, *Delinquent Boys: The Culture of the Gang*, (Glencoe, Ill : Free Press, 1955).

[75] Cloward and Ohlin, *Delinquency and Opportunity*, p. 121.

[76] William H. Sewell and Alan M. Orenstein, "Community of Residence and Occupational Choice," *American Journal of Sociology*, 60:551–63, 1965.

[77] Jackson Toby, "Affluence and Adolescent Crime," appendix H in President's Commission on Law Enforcement and Administration of Justice, *Task Force Report: Juvenile Delinquency and Youth Crime* (Washington, D.C.: Government Printing Office, 1967), pp. 132–44. See also Erdman P. Palmore and Phillip E. Hammond, "Interacting Factors in Juvenile Delinquency," *American Sociological Review* 29:848–54, 1969; and Larry Karacki and Jackson Toby, "The Uncommitted Adolescent: Candidate for Gang Socialization," *Sociological Inquiry*, 32:203–15, 1962.

[78] Albert J. Reiss, Jr., and A. Lewis Rhodes, "Status Deprivation and Delinquent Behavior," *Sociological Quarterly*, 4:136–49, 1963.

members of delinquent gangs closely resemble the values of the middle class.[79] DeFleur has pointed out that Latin cultures have been characterized by rigid class structures in which "remaining in one's station" is more heavily emphasized than striving for status. Accordingly, short-run hedonism, rather than status deprivation, is a major motive for delinquency.[80]

The gang-formation process is initiated when the individual delinquent finds encouragement and reassurance for acts of deviance by "searching out others who have faced similar experiences and who will support one another in common attitudes of alienation from the official system."[81] The gang of peers forms a new social world in which the legitimacy of the individual's delinquent conduct is strongly reinforced. Occasionally the "social world" extends far beyond any gang, becoming a social movement. This was somewhat the character of the "hippie" and "student protest" cults of the 1960s.[82]

Once individuals start seeking support from others who feel alienated from the prevailing social norms, a gang has begun to form. But before gang activities can begin, there must be effective interaction between the actors in a collective problem-solving process.[83] Cohen describes this problem-solving process as a "conservation of gestures," which serves at least four important functions.[84] First, it permits the gang members to explore the extent to which each is willing to go in accepting alternative rules for action. Second, it enables them to explore the extent to which they can rely on each other for support if they take a daring, rebellious, or delinquent path. Third, it gives each member an opportunity to test the degree to which his or her techniques for neutralizing the influences of law-abiding society are accepted by others.[85] Fourth, it enables the gang collectively to try out various courses of delinquent action and to judge the commitment that each member of the gang is willing to make to each type of action.

This process of alienation is abetted by the very processes by which law-abiding society attempts to deal with delinquent activities. As deviance has developed as

[79]Judson R. Landis, Simon Dinitz, and Walter C. Reckless, "Implementing Two Theories of Delinquency: Value Orientation and Awareness of Limited Opportunity," *Sociology and Social Research*, 47:408–16, 1963; Robert A. Gordon, James F. Short, Jr., Desmond S. Cartwright, and Fred L. Strodtbeck, "Values and Gang Delinquency: A Study of Street-Corner Groups," *American Journal of Sociology*, 69:109–28, 1963. See also Delbert S. Elliott, "Delinquency and Perceived Opportunity," *Sociological Inquiry*, 32:216–26, 1962; and Delbert S. Elliott and Harwin L. Voss, *Delinquency and Dropout* (Lexington, Mass.: D. C. Heath, 1974), pp. 133–36.

[80]Lois B. DeFleur, *Delinquency in Argentina: A Study of Cordoba's Youth* (Pullman, Wash.: Washington State University Press, 1970), p. 148.

[81]Cloward and Ohlin, *Delinquency and Opportunity*, p. 126.

[82]John C. Ball and Frida G. Surawicz, "A Trip to San Francisco's 'Hippieland': Glorification of Delinquency and Irresponsibility," *International Journal of Offender Therapy*, 12:63–69, 1968.

[83]Cohen, *Delinquent Boys*, p. 59.

[84]Ibid., pp. 60–61. Cf. Cloward and Ohlin, *Delinquency and Opportunity*, pp. 140–42.

[85]Gresham M. Sykes and David Matza, "Techniques of Neutralization: A Theory of Delinquency," *American Sociological Review*, 22:664–70, 1957.

an area of concern in sociology, an increasing number of sociologists have begun to write about the importance of "labeling" in the amplification of deviance.[86] Behavior which might be rather routine to the actor becomes a problem only because someone else, usually a state official, labels it "deviant."[87] In the case of delinquency, this labeling process might ignore one actor who has violated the law but stigmatize another as a delinquent. Tannenbaum referred to this process as a "dramatization of evil":

The first dramatization of "evil" which separates the child out of his group for specialized treatment plays a greater role in making the criminal than perhaps any other experience. It cannot be too often emphasized that for the child the whole situation has become different. He now lives in a different world. He has been tagged. A new and hitherto nonexistent environment has been precipitated out for him.

The process of making the criminal, therefore, is a process of tagging, defining, identifying, segregating, describing, emphasizing, making conscious and self-conscious; it becomes a way of stimulating, suggesting, emphasizing, and evolving the very traits that are complained of.[88]

Consistently, one of the earliest studies of delinquent gangs pointed out that the societal reactions to gang behavior make gang members more acutely aware of the gang's isolation from the values of the law-abiding community:

It does not become a gang, however, until it begins to excite disapproval and opposition, and thus acquires a more definite group-consciousness. It discovers a rival or an enemy in the gang in the next block; its baseball or football team is pitted against some other team; parents or neighbors look upon it with suspicion or hostility; "the old man around the corner," the storekeepers, or the "cops" begin to give it "shags" (chase it); or some representative of the community steps in and tries to break it up. This is the real beginning of the gang, for now it starts to draw itself more closely together. It becomes a conflict group.[89]

---

[86] See the following early examples: Edwin M. Lemert, *Social Pathology* (New York: McGraw-Hill, 1951); John I. Kitsuse, "Societal Reaction to Deviant Behavior: Problems of Theory and Method," *Social Problems*, 9:247–56, 1962; Kai T. Erikson, "Notes on the Sociology of Deviance," *Social Problems*, 9:307–14, 1962; and Howard S. Becker, *Outsiders: Studies in the Sociology of Deviance* (New York: Free Press, 1963).

[87] For samples and summaries of the extensive literature on this subject, see Jack D. Foster, Simon Dinitz, and Walter C. Reckless, "Perceptions of Stigma Following Public Intervention for Delinquent Behavior," *Social Problems*, 20:202–9, 1972; Jack P. Gibbs, "Issues in Defining Deviant Behavior," ch. in *Theoretical Perspectives on Deviance* ed. Robert A. Scott and Jack D. Douglas (New York: Basic Books, 1972), pp. 39–68; William D. Payne, "Negative Labels: Passageways and Prisons," *Crime and Delinquency*, 19:33–40, 1973; Anne Rankin Mahoney, "The Effect of Labeling Youths in the Juvenile Justice System: A Review of the Evidence," *Law and Society Review*, 8:583–614, 1974; Prudence Robins, "Imputations of Deviance: A Retrospective Essay on the Labeling Perspective," *Social Problems*, 1:1–11, 1975; and Jay R. Williams, *Effects of Labeling the "Drug-Abuser,"* Monograph No. 6 (Washington, D.C.: National Institute on Drug Abuse Research 1976).

[88] Frank Tannenbaum, *Crime and the Community* (New York: Ginn, 1938), pp. 19–20.

[89] Thrasher, *The Gang*, p. 30.

The specific direction taken in a gang's activities depends upon access to various directives for illegal actions, as well as upon the accessibility to directives for legal actions. Thus, a gang, like a person, takes a delinquent course rather than a nondelinquent course because a delinquent subculture in the form of rules, norms, values, and beliefs is more readily available than an antidelinquent subculture with its rules, norms, values, and beliefs. In this connection, Miller maintains that the dominant motivation underlying gang behavior is the attempt by gang members to achieve standards of value as they are defined in lower-class urban areas.[90] By the same token, a gang participates in one kind of delinquency rather than another because of the norms, values, and beliefs available to it.

A young man frustrated by his condition of poverty may relieve his tension by accepting a nondelinquent solution, such as renouncing all worldly things and becoming a hermit, or moving into the political arena to effect economic reforms. Alternatively, he may simply work harder, holding down two jobs at the same time.[91] Or he may solve the problem by adopting any of a number of delinquent solutions, one of which might be a burglary pattern, or a shoplifting pattern, or even an embezzlement pattern. Which of the delinquent solutions is adopted by the individual depends upon their availability to him.[92] Similarly, whether a delinquent moves in the direction of a particular kind of delinquency depends upon the availability of directives for action, and of training for action. In this connection, Cloward and Ohlin say that "the individual must have access to appropriate environments for the acquisition of values and skills associated with the performance of a particular role, and he must be supported in the performance of the role once he has learned it."[93]

Consistently, delinquent gangs arise in areas where access to legitimate channels to success-goals are denied, and where values supporting alternative actions are available. Thus, the gang seems to be composed of young men who are unable to "make it" legitimately, and who are able to seize upon patterns for manipulation of violence as a route to high status. Some support for this point is found in Short's observation that of sixteen Chicago gangs containing a total of 598 members, the six gangs *most* oriented to conflict, and three of the four gangs *least* oriented to conflict, were black.[94] This suggests that the status deprivation of blacks produces conflict-oriented gangs only when the conflict values available to be learned outweigh the nonconflict values. As Short et al. have said: "Given

[90] Walter B. Miller, "Lower Class Culture as a Generating Milieu of Gang Delinquency," *Journal of Social Issues*, 14:5–19, 1958.

[91] Harold L. Wilensky, "The Moonlighter: A Product of Relative Deprivation," *Industrial Relations*, 3:105–24, 1963.

[92] Richard A. Cloward, "Illegitimate Means, Anomie, and Deviant Behavior," *American Sociological Review*, 24:164–76, 1959. See also Howard S. Becker, "Marihuana Use and Social Control," *Social Problems*, 3:25–44, 1955; and "Becoming a Marihuana User," *American Journal of Sociology*, 59:235–42, 1953.

[93] Cloward and Ohlin, *Delinquency and Opportunity*, p. 148.

[94] Short, Tennyson, and Howard, "Behavior Dimensions of Gang Delinquency," p. 425.

culturally supported requirements for aggressive responses, such characteristics of lower-class life as public drinking, milling behavior, and a high incidence of guns may precondition the occurrence of acts of violence which involve individuals who could not have been differentiated from their peers by any personality assessment, even an hour before the occurrence of violence."[95]

In sum, delinquent gangs provide alternative channels for gaining status or symbols of status. Gang members are likely to be persons lacking in the role-playing ability necessary to meet the demands of the school, and unsatisfactory school experience, in turn, further narrows the range of opportunities to them—they do not have the social skills to "get along" with employers, fellow workers, and in new and strange situations generally.[96] Indeed, gang members do not even get along with each other.[97] Short has recently noted that these disabilities make it extremely difficult, even in a process of "politicalization," to transform gang members into law-abiding citizens.[98] Gangs provide opportunities, some of them illegitimate, for overcoming these handicaps. The specific forms of the illegitimate channels of opportunity provided by a gang depend upon the traditions of the people in the area—traditions of beliefs, values, and rules of conduct that are integrated closely enough so that they can be called a "subculture."[99]

Yablonsky, like Cloward and Ohlin, has argued that gang members are boys who have been satiated with delinquency behavior patterns and, at the same time, alienated from antidelinquency behavior patterns.[100] Hirschi has seemingly argued that delinquent behavior patterns are not important and that delinquent acts occur when the youth's bonds to his family and school are weak or broken, but Elliot and Voss have shown that for male students two of the most powerful predictors of delinquency are association with delinquent classmates and commitment to peers.[101] Nettler, like Sykes and Matza, has argued that the behavior of gang members, like that of other delinquents, is based on values extending from those held by most members of the society, and that delinquency, therefore, is

[95] James F. Short, Jr., Fred L. Strodtbeck, and Desmond S. Cartwright, "A Strategy for Utilizing Research Dilemmas: A Case from the Study of Parenthood in a Street Corner Gang," *Sociological Inquiry*, 32:185–202, 1962.

[96] Short and Strodtbeck, *Group Process and Gang Delinquency*, pp. 214–47; Gordon, "Social Level, Disability, and Gang Interaction"; and Jack L. Roach and Orville R. Gursslin, "The Lower Class, Status Frustration, and Social Disorganization," *Social Forces*, 43:506–17, 1974.

[97] Hirschi, *Causes of Delinquency*, pp. 145–48.

[98] James F. Short, Jr., "Gangs, Politics, and the Social Order," chap. 5 in *Delinquency, Crime, and Society*, ed. James F. Short, Jr. (Chicago: University of Chicago Press, 1976), pp. 129–63; and idem, "Youth Gangs and Society: Micro- and Macrosociological Processes," *Sociological Quarterly*, 15:3–19, 1974.

[99] See Irving Spergel, "Deviant Patterns and Opportunities of Pre-Adolescent Negro Boys in Three Chicago Neighborhoods," in *Juvenile Gangs in Context: Theory, Research and Action*, ed. Malcolm W. Klein (Englewood Cliffs, N. J.: Prentice-Hall, 1967), pp. 38–54.

[100] Yablonsky, *The Violent Gang*, pp. 170–94. See also Martin R. Haskell, "Toward a Reference Group Theory of Juvenile Delinquency," *Social Problems*, 8:220–30, 1961.

[101] Hirschi, *Causes of Delinquency*, pp. 157–58; Elliot and Voss, *Delinquency and Dropout*, p. 204.

better understood as a form of conformity than as a form of deviance.[102] Miller has made the following summary statement about why juvenile gangs arise, and why they persist in the face of changing circumstances:

> The youth gang remains as a persisting form because it is a product of a set of conditions that lie close to the basic building blocks of our social order. These include the necessary division of labor between the family and the peer group in the socialization of adolescents, the masculinity and collective-action emphases of the male subculture, the stress on excitement, congregation, and mating in the adolescent subculture, the importance of toughness, smartness, and trouble in the subcultures of lower-status populations, the density and territoriality patterns which figure in the subcultures of urban and urbanized locales. It is these social conditions and their related subcultures which, taken in conjunction, generate the American youth gang, and, insofar as these conditions and subcultural concerns retain continuity through time, so does their product—the gang—retain continuity.[103]

NEIGHBORHOOD AGENCIES

Individuals and institutions in a neighborhood may intentionally or inadvertently disseminate delinquent and criminal behavior patterns. The "fence," the junk dealer, and the ordinary citizen who is willing to purchase stolen goods stimulates delinquencies both by failing to present antidelinquency patterns to children who offer stolen goods for sale and by presenting the procriminal behavior patterns implicit in the purchase of the goods.

Many illegal agencies are located in specific areas because residents want the services they provide, while other illegal agencies are located in the same areas because residents do not have the power to keep them out. Bookmaking establishments, illegal lotteries, and loansharking enterprises, for example, depend on local residents for patronage and are thus meeting a neighborhood demand for services. Houses of prostitution are another matter, for their patrons ordinarily do not come from the local area. The residents oppose them, but are unable to produce the legal and political pressures necessary to close them down or force them out. Blacks and other minority groups suffer most from such vice districts, now commonly called "combat zones." A situation existing in Chicago over a half-century ago continues today in many American cities:

> The chief of police [of Chicago] in 1912 warned prostitutes that so long as they confined their residence to districts west of Wabash Avenue and east of Wentworth Avenue, they

[102] Gwynn Nettler, "Good Men, Bad Men, and the Perception of Reality," *Sociometry*, 24:279–94, 1961.

[103] Walter B. Miller, "Youth Gangs in the Urban Crisis Era," ch. 4 in *Delinquency, Crime, and Society*, ed. Short, pp. 91–128 (at pp. 118–119). See also idem, *Violence By Youth Gangs and Youth Groups as a Crime Problem in Major American Cities* (Washington, D.C.: Government Printing Office, 1975); Solomon Kobrin, "The Impact of Cultural Factors on Selected Social Problems of Adolescent Development in the Middle and Lower Class," *American Journal of Orthopsychiatry*, 32:387–89, 1962; and Barbara Tomson and Edna R. Fiedler, "Gangs: A Response to the Urban World," chaps. 8 and 9 in *Gang Delinquency*, ed. Cartwright et al., pp. 127–54.

would not be disturbed. This area contained at that time the largest group of Negroes in the city, with most of their churches, Sunday Schools and societies. . . . That many Negroes live near vice districts is not due to their choice, nor to low moral standards, but to three causes: (1) Negroes are unwelcome in desirable white residence localities; (2) small incomes compel them to live in the least expensive places regardless of surroundings; while premises rented for immoral purposes bring notoriously high rentals, they make the neighborhood undesirable and the rent of other living quarters there abnormally low; and (3) Negroes lack sufficient influence and power to protest effectively against the encroachments of vice.[104]

The presence of prostitution in an area is not likely to produce sex delinquencies because of the sex standards involved. But prostitutes and pimps do by their presence serve as occupational role models for neighborhood girls and boys. If one makes the reasonable assumption that most mothers do not want their daughters to be prostitutes, then it is correct to say that ghetto mothers are victims of prostitution in a way that middle-class suburban mothers are not. By their very presence in an area, prostitutes provide girls with an occupational alternative available to few middle-class girls. The same thing is done for boys by the presence of pimps, bookmakers, loansharks (who sometimes double as fences), drug sellers, the operators of illegal lotteries, and other organized criminals in an area. Organized criminals rarely try to recruit neighborhood youths into their occupations; instead, some youths work hard to convince organized criminals to give them jobs.[105] Thus, organized criminals in a neighborhood contribute to more general crime and delinquency rates in three interrelated ways.[106] First, by their opulence the persons engaged in organized crime demonstrate to the people of the neighborhood, and especially to the young, that crime does pay. Second, by their very presence they demonstrate the existence of a rich vein of corruption in political and law enforcement organizations, making it difficult for parents to convince their children that people get ahead in the world by good, hard, honest labor in the service of family, country, man, and God. Third, the presence of organized crime in a neighborhood lowers the status of the people in the district, just as do conditions of squalor, with the result that anticriminal admonitions become less effective—the people have less to lose if convicted of crime.[107] The late Reverend Martin Luther King, Jr., summed up the contemporary situation as follows:

The most grievous charge against municipal police is not brutality, although it exists. Permissive crime in ghettos is the nightmare of the slum family. Permissive crime is the

---

[104] Chicago Commission on Race Relations, *A Study of Race Relations and a Race Riot* (Chicago: Chicago Commission on Race Relations, 1922), pp. 343–44.

[105] See Irving Spergel, *Racketville, Slumtown, Haulburg: An Exploratory Study of Delinquent Subcultures* (Chicago: University of Chicago Press, 1968); and Gerald D. Suttles, *The Social Order of the Slum: Ethnicity and Territory in the Inner City* (Chicago: University of Chicago Press, 1968).

[106] See Donald R. Cressey, "Organized Crime and Inner-City Youth," *Crime and Delinquency*, 16:129–38, 1970.

[107] Jackson Toby, "Social Disorganization and Stake in Conformity: Complimentary Factors in the Predatory Behavior of Hoodlums," *Journal of Criminal Law, Criminology, and Police Science*, 48:12–17, 1957.

name for organized crime that flourishes in the ghetto—designed, directed, and cultivated by the white national crime syndicates operating numbers, narcotics, and prostitution rackets freely in the protected sanctuaries of the ghettos. Because no one, including the police, cares particularly about ghetto crime, it pervades every area of life.[108]

Recreational agencies also contribute to the delinquency of the children in a neighborhood. It has become commonplace to state that most of the delinquencies of children occur in the search for recreation. One general notion in this regard is that the only recreations generally available in deteriorated neighborhoods are those furnished by commercial concerns. Since these concerns are interested primarily in securing a profit, they offer whatever recreation produces the largest revenue, regardless of the welfare of the patrons. On this ground, neighborhood dance halls, pool rooms, school stores, pin-ball parlors, roller-skating rinks and other recreational enterprises are said to be "injurious" to juveniles. A more realistic interpretation is that such institutions merely serve as gathering places for neighborhood youths, thus providing opportunities for dissemination of delinquent attitudes and standards. The same process of dissemination occurs when youths gather on street corners, in public playgrounds, or in schools.

Another notion is that the *absence* of places of organized public recreation, particularly playgrounds, somehow contributes to the delinquency rate of a neighborhood. This idea, that delinquency rates are low when the incidence of "wholesome" recreation is high, is a conclusion about delinquency causation, and it has been reached by dubious methods and logic. It is obvious that delinquency, like baseball or swimming, is a "spare-time" activity, but this does not mean that delinquency results from an absence of baseball fields or swimming pools. An elaborate and detailed study of high school students found that level of participation in the school's extracurricular activities is not predictive of delinquency; in fact, youth who are highly involved in these activities report rates of delinquency higher than those with limited involvement.[109]

From the point of view of the differential association theory, there are three possible ways in which playground participation may be related to delinquent behavior. First, the activities may have little effect on the participants' attitudes regarding delinquency but may keep them from committing delinquencies during some of their waking hours; they cannot play baseball and participate in burglaries at the same time. Second, the playground may become the gathering place of the delinquents in the neighborhood and may, in fact, serve to promote a strong in-group feeling among them. Some delinquent gangs are baseball teams or basketball teams as well. Participants thus come into contact with delinquent behavior patterns. Third, the playground director or recreational leader may be

---

[108] Martin Luther King, Jr., "Beyond the Los Angeles Riots: Next Stop, The North," *Saturday Review*, November 13, 1965, p. 34.
[109] Elliott and Voss, *Delinquency and Dropout*, p. 206.

able to present antidelinquent behavior patterns to the participants, or the participants may in other ways come into contact with antidelinquent behavior patterns.

Thus, participation in the playground activities may be neutral, or it may be conducive to either delinquency or nondelinquency, depending upon the nature of the associations experienced. If the neighborhood baseball team is made up of delinquents, then a girl who is an excellent and enthusiastic baseball player is more likely to become delinquent than is a boy who abhors baseball, other things being equal. On the other hand, if the members of the neighborhood baseball team are antidelinquent in their attitudes and behavior patterns, then the probability that a good and enthusiastic baseball player will become delinquent is lower than the probability that a girl or boy who abhors baseball will become delinquent, other things being equal.

"Other things" never are equal, however. The boy who hates baseball may be an excellent and enthusiastic pool player in a neighborhood where pool players view stealing as a form of play, thus increasing the probability of his delinquency if he engages in his favorite form of recreation. But if the values of the pool players are antidelinquent, then the probability of his delinquency is diminished. By the same token, a girl who loves YWCA basketball and hates tennis may become delinquent if the basketball team goes shoplifting on occasion and the neighborhood tennis players do not. The process of selecting delinquent or antidelinquent companions depends in part, then, on the person's recreational interests and abilities. Yet it would be absurd to explain youngsters' delinquency or nondelinquency by assessing their ability to play baseball, pool, tennis, or basketball.

Further, selection or rejection of delinquent or antidelinquent companions is itself a function of previous associations with antidelinquent and delinquent behavior patterns. An excellent baseball player with strong antidelinquent identification and intimate association with antidelinquent behavior patterns might give up baseball rather than play with delinquents. A boy or girl without such strong counteracting values may join the team and become delinquent. Thus, an individual's selection of a delinquent, nondelinquent, or antidelinquent play group depends on prior associations with delinquent and antidelinquent behavior patterns, just as does the individual's delinquency itself. Moreover, a person with reference groups which are antidelinquent in their behavior patterns may join a baseball team made up of delinquents and not become a delinquent at all. This reference-group principle has long been noted by social psychologists:

As he [man] passes from one group situation to another from time to time, he reacts to the demands, pressures, and appeals of new group situations in terms of the person he has come to consider himself and aspires to be. In other words, he reacts in terms of more or less consistent ties of belongingness in relation to his past and present identifications and his future goals for security of his identity, and also status and prestige concerns. . . . The groups to which an individual relates himself need not always be the groups in which he is actually moving. His identifications need not always be with groups in which he is registered, is seen to be, or announced to be a member. . . . In many cases, of course, the individual's reference groups are at the same time his membership groups. However, in cases where the individual's membership groups are not his reference groups, it does not follow that the groups in which he actually interacts will not have an effect on him.[110]

SUGGESTED READINGS

Arnold, David O., ed. *The Sociology of Subcultures.* Berkeley, Calif.: The Glendessary Press, 1970.

Blake, Judith, & Kingsley Davis. "Norms, Values, and Sanctions," Chapter 13 in *Handbook of Modern Sociology,* edited by Robert E. L. Faris, pp. 456–84. Chicago: Rand McNally, 1964.

Cartwright, Desmond S., Barbara Tomson & Hershey Schwartz. *Gang Delinquency.* Monterey, Calif.: Brooks/Cole, 1975.

Clinard, Marshall B., & Daniel J. Abbott. *Crime in Developing Countries: A Comparative Perspective.* New York, Wiley, 1973.

Cloward, Richard A., & Lloyd E. Ohlin. *Delinquency and Opportunity: A Theory of Delinquent Gangs.* Glencoe, Ill.: Free Press, 1960.

Cohen, Albert K. *Delinquent Boys: The Culture of the Gang.* Glencoe, Ill.: Free Press, 1955.

Cohen, Albert K. *Deviance and Control.* Englewood Cliffs, N. J.: Prentice-Hall, 1966.

Cohen, Albert K. "The Sociology of the Deviant Act: Anomie Theory and Beyond." *American Sociological Review,* 30:5–14, February, 1965.

Cohen, Albert K., & James F. Short, Jr. "Research in Delinquent Subcultures." *Journal of Social Issues,* 14:20–37, 1958.

DeFleur, Lois B. *Delinquency in Argentina: A Study of Cordoba's Youth.* Pullman, Wash.: Washington State University Press, 1970.

Downes, David M. *The Delinquent Solution: A Study in Subcultural Theory.* London: Routledge and Kegan Paul, 1966.

Gibbs, Jack P., & Maynard L. Erickson. "Crime Rates of American Cities in an Ecological Context." *American Journal of Sociology,* 82:605–20, 1976.

Glaser, Daniel, ed., *Crime in the City.* New York: Harper and Row, 1970.

Gordon, Robert A. "Issues in the Ecological Study of Delinquency." *American Sociological Review,* 32:927–44, 1967.

Helfgot, Joseph. "Professional Reform Organizations and the Symbolic Representation of the Poor." *American Sociological Review,* 39:475–91, 1974.

Hirschi, Travis. *Causes of Delinquency.* Berkeley: University of California Press, 1969.

Horowitz, Ruth, & Gary Schwartz, "Honor, Normative Ambiguity, and Gang Violence," *American Sociological Review,* 39:238–51, 1974.

Klein, Malcolm W. *Street Gangs and Street Workers.* Englewood Cliffs, N. J.: Prentice-Hall, 1971.

Krisberg, Barry. *The Gang and the Community.* San Francisco: R and E Research Associates, 1975.

Longmoor, E. S., & Erle F. Young. "Ecological Interrelationships of Juvenile Delinquency, Dependency, and Population Mobility." *American Journal of Sociology,* 41:598–610, 1936.

Mahoney, Anne Rankin. "The Effect of Labeling Youths in the Juvenile Justice System." *Law and Society Review,* 8:583–614, 1974.

---

[110] Muzafer and Carolyn W. Sherif, *Groups in Harmony and Tension* (New York: Harper, 1953), pp. 160–61. See also idem, *Reference Groups: Explorations into Conformity and Deviation of Adolescents* (New York: Harper and Row, 1964); and Tamotsu Shibutani, *Society and Personality: An Interactionist Approach to Social Psychology,* (Englewood Cliffs, N. J.: Prentice-Hall, 1961), pp. 247–80, 571–73.

Morris, Terrence. *The Criminal Area*. London: Kegan Paul, 1958.

Nieberg, H. L. "Crime Prevention By Urban Design." *Transaction: Social Science and Modern Society*, 12:41–47, 1974.

Polk, Kenneth. "Juvenile Delinquency and Social Areas." *Social Problems*, 5:214–17, 1957–58.

Quinney, Richard. "Structural Characteristics, Population Areas, and Crime Rates in the United States." *Journal of Criminal Law, Criminology, and Police Science*, 57:45–62, 1966.

Reppetto, Thomas A. *Residential Crime*. Cambridge, Mass.: Ballinger, 1974.

Robin, Gerald D. "Gang Member Delinquency: Its Extent, Sequence, and Typology." *Journal of Criminal Law, Criminology, and Police Science*, 55:59–69, 1964.

Robinson, W. S. "Ecological Correlations and the Behavior of Individuals." *American Sociological Review*, 15:351–57, 1950.

Short, James F., Jr. *Delinquency, Crime, and Society*. Chicago: University of Chicago Press, 1976.

Short, James F., Jr., & Fred L. Strodtbeck. *Group Practices and Gang Delinquency*. Chicago: University of Chicago Press, 1965.

Spergel, Irving. *Racketville, Slumtown, Haulburg: An Exploratory Study of Delinquent Subcultures*. Chicago: University of Chicago Press, 1964.

Suttles, Gerald D. *The Social Order of the Slum: Ethnicity and Territory in the Inner City*. Chicago: University of Chicago Press, 1968.

Voss, Harwin L., & David M. Peterson, eds. *Ecology of Crime and Delinquency*. New York: Appleton-Century-Crofts, 1971.

Whyte, William F. *Street Corner Society*. Chicago: University of Chicago Press, 1943.

10

Family Patterns and Processes

Because the family has almost exclusive contact with children during the period of greatest dependency and greatest plasticity, as well as continued intimate contact over a subsequent period of several years, it plays an exceptionally important role in determining the behavior patterns which any individual follows. No child is so constituted at birth that it must inevitably become a delinquent or that it must inevitably be law-abiding, and the family is the first agency to affect the direction which a particular child will take. Probably it is for this reason that a large proportion of the criminological research and thinking during this century has been directly or indirectly concerned with the relationship between crime and delinquency on the one hand and various kinds of home conditions and child-rearing practices on the other hand.

Although each family unit is expected to train its children in some efficient way so that they will not become criminals, there is no real science of child-rearing, and such knowledge as is developed is not available to or utilized by many families. The task of child-training was comparatively simple in early societies but has become extremely difficult in modern life. In preliterate life both parents were reared in a rather simple, harmonious culture, as were also the grandparents, other relatives, and neighbors The result was rather steady and consistent directives that formed the character of children and adults with a minimum of conflicts. This is impossible in modern society, where the persons in charge of socializing the child cannot be consistent. Parents are in conflict with each other, with grandparents, with schoolteachers, and with movie and television actors. Moreover, parents are in conflict, probably more than previously, for the affection of the child. In this situation harmonious directives by consistent authorities is impossible.

It is not even possible for individual parents themselves to be consistent, for they do not have the support of a consistent culture to keep their policies stable. These inconsistencies affect the degree of conformity which parents can exact from children and, generally, the degree to which children can be controlled. Further, conformity to parental standards depends largely upon the prestige of the parents, and this is affected by both the consistency of the demands they make upon a child and by their status in the community. The poverty, physical features, competitive ability and comparative attainments, language, and social status of the parents in comparison with other persons with whom the child is acquainted may destroy the prestige of the parents so that the behavior patterns presented are relatively ineffective. Verbal description and structuring of proscribed behavior is particularly important; parents vary in this ability to communicate effectively with their children, and there is a correlation between children's verbal inadequacies and delinquency.[1]

FAMILY PATTERNS

Homes from which delinquent children come are often characterized by one or more of the following conditions: (1) other members of the family are criminalistic, immoral, or alcoholic; (2) one or both parents are absent by reason of death, divorce, or desertion; (3) there is a lack of parental control because of ignorance, indifference, or illness; (4) home uncongeniality exists as evidenced by domination by one member, favoritism, oversolicitude, overseverity, neglect, jealousy, crowded housing conditions, or interfering relatives; (5) religious or other cultural differences, or differences in conventions and standards are present; (6) there are economic difficulties, such as unemployment, poverty, both parents working, or poor arrangement of financial affairs.[2]

Three general methods have been used in the effort to determine the importance of such conditions as "factors" in delinquency. An older method tried to evaluate the home as a whole, by means of some rating device or scale. A "normal" standard for homes was set, and then it was concluded that individual home conditions were the cause of delinquency if most delinquents came from homes below this norm. The fallacy, of course, was in the setting of the arbitrary and artificial norm. Further, the rating of an individual home as "bad" or "good" was to a large extent determined by the values and the social-class position of the investigator. The use of such rating scales showed that, while children who get into the juvenile courts came, in more than fair proportion, from homes ranked as "poor" or "bad," none of the children in some homes of this kind, and only some

[1]Gordon B. Trasler, *The Explanation of Criminality* (London: Routledge & Kegan Paul, 1962); idem, "Socialization," in Gordon B. Trasler et al., *The Formative Years* (London: British Broadcasting Corporation, 1968); and idem, "Criminal Behavior," *Handbook of Abnormal Psychology*, 2d. ed, ed. H. J. Eysenck (London: Pitman Medical Publications, 1970). See also Walter Brandis and Dorothy Henderson, *Social Class, Language, and Communication* (London: Routledge & Kegan Paul, 1970).

[2]See Lynn Davies and E. C. Dax, "The Criminal and Social Aspects of Families with a Multiplicity of Problems," *Australian and New Zealand Journal of Criminology*, 7:197–213, 1974.

of the children in other such homes got into the juvenile court, while on the other hand some delinquent children came from homes ranked as "good."

A second method tried to evaluate the influence of the home in individual cases. By using this method in two pioneering studies, Healy first estimated that the home was a "major factor" in delinquency in 19 percent of a series of a thousand cases studied in Chicago and a "minor factor" in 23 percent; 230 of a thousand delinquents came from homes having "extreme lack of parental control." In a second study of a series of a thousand cases in Chicago, Healy and Bronner estimated that 46 percent came from homes said to have "extreme lack of parental control."[3] This method permits the investigator to evaluate the meaning which a particular set of home conditions has for the specific child, and thereby to make allowances for the fact that "bad" homes do not always produce delinquent children. However, the method is subjective, and the findings are likely to reflect the preconceptions of the investigator. During a period when rather strict discipline is the fad in child-rearing, homes without such discipline are likely to be designated as delinquency-producing; but when permissiveness is the fad in child-rearing, then the homes using strict discipline are likely to be so designated. Furthermore, whether the home is designated as a factor in the delinquency of a child may depend on the likelihood that the home can be modified by welfare agencies—a home which can be modified may more readily be designated as a factor than one which apparently cannot be modified. Social class differences in language and linguistic abilities, for example, are likely to be ignored, while specific child-rearing practices are noted.

A third method is statistical. The technique varies from simple calculation of the comparative incidence of certain home conditions among delinquent and nondelinquents to more sophisticated techniques of holding certain variables constant while determining the degree of association between delinquency and another variable. Thus the method aims at the identification of certain specific home conditions which are associated with delinquency, rather than at measuring the influence of the home as a whole. This is the most popular method currently in use, and it will be illustrated in the following sections.[4]

Criminality in the Home
One of the most obvious elements in the delinquency of some children is the criminalistic behavior of other members of the child's family. The Gluecks found

[3]William Healy, *The Individual Delinquent* (Boston: Little, Brown, 1915), pp. 130–31, 134; William Healy and Augusta F. Bronner, "Youthful Offenders," *American Journal of Sociology*, 22:50, 1916. See also Healy and Bronner, *New Light on Delinquency and Its Treatment* (New Haven, Conn.: Yale University Press, 1936).

[4]For an excellent review and critique of the work with this method, prepared for the President's Commission, see Hyman Rodman and Paul Grams, "Juvenile Delinquency and the Family: A Review and Discussion," appendix L of President's Commission on Law Enforcement and Administration of Justice, *Task Force Report: Juvenile Delinquency and Youth Crime* (Washington, D.C.: Government Printing Office, 1967), pp. 188–221. See also Travis Hirschi, *Causes of Delinquency* (Berkeley: University of California Press, 1969); and Delbert S. Elliott and Harwin L. Voss, *Delinquency and Dropout* (Lexington, Mass.: D. C. Heath, 1974).

drunkenness, crime, or immorality in the homes of 90.4 percent of 500 delinquent boys and in the homes of 54 percent of the 500 nondelinquents comprising the control group.[5] The McCords found that the sons of criminals had a higher rate of criminality than did the sons of noncriminals.[6] Interestingly enough, however, the sons of criminals who were rejected by their fathers had higher crime rates than those who were not. Johnson hypothesizes that this difference comes about because "rejection by the father creates aggressive tendencies which are channeled into crime because the father serves as a role model,"[7] an interpretation which is consistent with the theory of differential association.

Thus the homes in which some delinquents are reared are to a significant degree situations in which patterns of delinquency are present.[8] These patterns do not generally result in exact copies by the children; rather it is the attitudes toward certain kinds of delinquency and criminality which are likely to be most significant. It has been shown that farm boys who prefer farming as an occupation, as compared with farm boys who prefer nonfarm occupations, more frequently have participated in a family value system functionally related to farming.[9] There is no reason to believe that boys participating in a value system favorable to crime should not, similarly, enter criminality more frequently than those not participating in such direct, primary-type influences. Two psychiatrists have concluded that parents' unwitting sanction or indirect encouragement is a major cause of, and the specific stimulus for, truancy and various kinds of delinquency.[10] Wolfgang and Ferracuti have shown that a "subculture of violence" exists in the American urban lower class, and this subculture is carried by families as well as by other groups.[11] Severy studied 296 delinquent and nondelinquent high school students—selected so that half were males and half were Mexican-Americans—over a four-year period. Among these youths, if there was low original exposure to deviance of family members (crudely measured by offense rates, "seriousness of offenses," and "depth of involvement in the formal legal structure"), increasing exposure led

[5]Sheldon and Eleanor Glueck, *Unraveling Juvenile Delinquency* (New York: Commonwealth Fund, 1950), pp. 110–11. See also idem, *Five Hundred Criminal Careers* (New York: Knopf, 1930), pp. 111–12; *One Thousand Juvenile Delinquents* (Cambridge, Mass.: Harvard University Press, 1934), p. 79; and *Five Hundred Delinquent Women* (New York: Knopf, 1934), p. 72.

[6]Joan McCord and William McCord, "The Effects of Parental Role Model on Criminality," *Journal of Social Issues,* 14:66–75, 1958.

[7]Elmer H. Johnson, *Crime, Correction, and Society,* rev. ed. (Homewood, Ill.: Dorsey Press, 1968), p. 88.

[8]See Harriett Wilson, "Juvenile Delinquency, Parental Criminality, and Social Handicap," *British Journal of Criminology,* 26:7–18, 1975.

[9]Murray A. Straus, "Personal Characteristics and Functional Needs in the Choice of Farming as an Occupation," *Rural Sociology,* 21:257–66, 1956; see also A. O. Haller and William H. Sewell, "Occupational Choices of Wisconsin Farm Boys," *Rural Sociology,* 32:37–55, 1967.

[10]Adelaide M. Johnson and S. A. Szurek, "Etiology of Antisocial Behavior in Delinquents and Psychopaths," *Journal of the American Medical Association,* 154:814–17, 1954.

[11]Marvin E. Wolfgang and Franco Ferracuti, *The Subculture of Violence: Towards an Integrated Theory in Criminology* (London: Social Science Paperbacks, 1967), pp. 153–63.

to deviance, but when family exposure was originally high, increasing exposure led to rejection of delinquency.[12]

The Broken Home

The modification of home conditions by death, divorce, or desertion has generally been believed to be an important reason for delinquency of the children. This belief is found even in nonliterate tribes, for the Ama-Xosa, a Bantu tribe in southern Africa, have a proverb, "If the old bird dies, the eggs are addled." Research reports indicate that from 30 to 60 percent of delinquents come from broken homes, and the percentages tend to cluster around 40 percent.

Polk has shown that the judicial process tends to select children from broken homes; among the cases of male juveniles which the Los Angeles Probation Department closed at intake in one year, 43 percent were from broken homes, while 50 percent of those placed on probation and 58 percent of those institutionalized came from broken homes.[13] Similarly, Nye found that 24 percent of the most delinquent boys in a high school came from broken homes, as did 48 percent of the boys in a training school, indicating that a selective principle was operating.[14]

In a recent one-year period, 71 percent of all felony cases admitted to Florida prisons came from broken homes—64 percent of the white prisoners and 80 percent of the black prisoners. Half the prisoners' homes had been broken before they were 13 years old.[15] Similarly, of the young people committed to the California Youth Authority in 1973, 65 percent of the males and 68 percent of the females had parents who were not living together due to divorce, separation, or death.[16] Weinberg studied 67 institutionalized female delinquents, 107 institutionalized male delinquents, and 74 nondelinquent female school children (all between 11 and 16 years of age) in Accra, Ghana.[17] Half of the parents of the female delinquents were divorced or separated, compared with 29 percent of the female nondelinquents and 34 percent of the male delinquents. Further, 16

[12] Lawrence J. Severy, "Exposure to Deviance Committed by Valued Peer Group and Family Members," *Journal of Research in Crime and Delinquency*, 10:35–46, 1973.

[13] Kenneth Polk, "A Note on the Relationship Between Broken Homes, Disposition, and Juvenile Delinquency," manuscript, 1958.

[14] F. Ivan Nye, *Family Relationships and Delinquent Behavior* (New York: Wiley, 1958), pp. 43–44, 47–48; see also Philip M. Smith, "Broken Homes and Juvenile Delinquency," *Sociology and Social Research*, 39:307–11, 1955.

[15] Florida Division of Corrections, *Seventh Biennial Report* (Tallahassee: Florida Division of Corrections, 1971). pp. 100–1.

[16] California Department of the Youth Authority, *Annual Report, 1973*, (Sacramento: California Department of the Youth Authority, 1973) p. 11. See also T. C. N. Gibbens, *Psychiatric Studies of Borstal Lads* (Oxford: Oxford University Press, 1963); and Charlotte Banks, "Violence," *The Howard Journal*, 9:1–13, 1965.

[17] S. Kirson Weinberg, "Female Delinquency in Ghana West Africa: A Comparative Analysis," *International Review of Modern Sociology*, 3:65–73, 1973.

percent of the female delinquents and 16 percent of the male delinquents lived "on their own resources," but none of the school girls were self-supporting.

So far as delinquency itself is concerned, statistics on broken homes are meaningless except in comparison with similar percentages for nondelinquent children or for the total population. Burt found about twice as many broken homes in a delinquent group as he did in a control group in England, and the Gluecks found about the same ratio among a group of delinquent boys and a control group in the United States.[18] In a recent Florida study, Chilton and Markle found that 40 percent of 5326 children aged 10–17 referred to juvenile court came from broken homes, as compared with 17 percent of the children aged 10–17 in the general population.[19] Years ago, Barker found that the coefficient of correlation between the juvenile delinquency rate of an area and the percentage of parents divorced was +.79, which could mean that both the delinquency rate and the divorce rate are determined largely by other conditions such as local community culture.[20]

Christie studied all boys born in Norway in 1933; by the time these males were 25 years old, 5 percent of them were registered offenders. The homes of 17.4 percent of the offenders and 12.7 percent of the nonoffenders were broken by death, divorce, or separation.[21] This suggests that the broken home is not closely linked with the delinquency of adolescent males. But Monahan found that the proportion of delinquent girls coming from broken homes is greater than the proportion of delinquent boys coming from such homes, and the proportion of delinquent blacks coming from such homes is greater than the proportion of whites.[22] This suggests that a break in the home has a greater influence on girls than on boys and on blacks than on whites.

Toby suggested that such weak control is exercised over adolescent males in American families that there is little difference between supervision in a well-integrated family and a disorganized one. Hence, no appreciable relationship between broken homes and delinquency is to be expected among adolescent males. But for girls and preadolescents the well-integrated family gives firm supervision, whereas the disorganized family is unable to do so. Therefore, girls and preadolescents from disorganized households are more likely to be exposed to criminogenic influences than girls and preadolescents from well-integrated households.[23]

[18] Glueck and Glueck, *Unraveling Juvenile Delinquency*, p. 122.

[19] Roland J. Chilton and Gerald E. Markle, "Family Disruption, Delinquent Conduct, and the Effect of Subclassification," *American Sociological Review*, 37:93–99, 1972.

[20] Gordon H. Barker, "Family Factors in the Ecology of Juvenile Delinquency," *Journal of Criminal Law and Criminology*, 30:881–91, 1940. See also Walter Slocum and Carol L. Stone, "Family Culture Patterns and Delinquent-Type Behavior," *Marriage and Family Living*, 25:202–8, 1963.

[21] Nils Christie, *Unge Norske Lovovertredere* [Young Norwegian lawbreakers] (Oslo: Universitetsforlaget, 1960), pp. 105, 111.

[22] Thomas P. Monahan, "Family Status and the Delinquent Child: A Reappraisal and some New Findings," *Social Forces*, 35:250–58, 1957.

[23] Jackson Toby, "The Differential Impact of Family Disorganization," *American Sociological Review*, 22:505–12, 1957.

However, the findings of the recent Florida study by Chilton and Markle are not consistent with the data on which Toby's conclusions are based. In this study, the differences between the broken home rates among boys and girls are greater for persons referred for "status offenses" such as ungovernability, running away, and truancy, than for persons referred for behavior which would be crime if it were committed by an adult.[24] These differences are shown in Table 18, which also shows that broken homes (1) are more frequently present in the lives of preadolescents (ages 10–13) than in the lives of adolescents, and (2) are more frequently present in the lives of black children than in the lives of white children.

The Chilton and Markle study also found a modest positive association between seriousness of offense and family situation for children charged with offenses which would be crimes if committed by adults—50 percent of the white children referred to juvenile court for offenses such as robbery, rape, and homicide came from broken homes, as compared to 36 percent of those referred for offenses such as drunkenness, vandalism, and drug-law violations. For black children, the percentage of children not living with both parents was very similar for those charged with the most serious offenses (69 percent) and those charged

Table 18 Percentages of Children 10–17 Not Living in Husband-Wife Families for Those in the General Population, Those Charged with Offenses Applicable to Juveniles Only, and Those Charged with Other Offenses

Classification	General Population (age 10–17)	Children Charged with Offenses	
		Applicable to Juveniles Only	Which Would Be Crimes for Adults
All classes	17.0	39.7	40.0
Male	17.0	37.2	40.2
Female	17.0	43.6	39.0
Black	42.8	58.1	58.5
White	13.1	33.7	28.5
Black male	42.8	56.8	59.3
White male	13.1	50.7	28.3
Black female	42.8	60.4	54.7
White female	13.1	38.5	29.6
Age 10–13	15.2	45.8	41.6
Age 14–17	18.9	37.9	39.6

SOURCE: Roland J. Chilton and Gerald E. Markle, "Family Disruption, Delinquent Conduct, and the Effect of Subclassification," *American Sociological Review*, 37:93–99, 1972.

---

[24] See also H. Ashley Weeks, "Male and Female Broken Home Rates by Types of Delinquency," *American Sociological Review*, 5:601–9, 1940; Nye, *Family Relationships and Delinquent Behavior*; Theodore N. Ferdinand, "The Offense Patterns and Family Structures of Urban, Village, and Rural Delinquents," *Journal of Criminal Law, Criminology, and Police Science*, 55:86–93, 1964; and Richard S. Sterne, *Delinquent Conduct and Broken Homes* (New Haven, Conn.: College and University Press, 1964).

with the least serious offenses (67 percent), suggesting that family situation may be less important in generating serious misconduct among black children, particularly boys, than it is among whites. But the study also found that, for low-income families, seriousness is unaffected by family situation, suggesting that the family's economic situation is more important than its composition in understanding a child's apprehension for delinquency. Among the children of Florida, at least, differential exposure to criminal behavior patterns on the part of all poor, adolescent, and black boys and girls—as compared to exposure on the part of rich, preadolescent, and white boys and girls—seems to be more important to delinquency than the presence or absence of broken homes in each of these categories. Differential reporting and recording practices may, of course, invalidate this conclusion.

Discipline and Training

Almost everyone agrees that the most important difference between the situations of delinquent and nondelinquent children is in "home discipline." As Peterson and Becker note, "If one endorses the common assumption that capacities for internal control are complexly but closely related to previously imposed external restraints, then parental discipline assumes focal significance as a factor in delinquency."[25] The Gluecks found "unsuitable" supervision by the mother in the homes of 64 percent of the delinquent children and in the homes of only 13 percent of the nondelinquents; also, discipline by the mother was "lax" in 57 percent of the delinquents' homes and in 12 percent of the nondelinquents' homes.[26] Bandura and Walters found that parents of aggressive-destructive boys relied to a greater extent than did the parents of a control group on disciplinary methods involving ridicule, physical punishment, and deprivation of privileges.[27] Trasler has noted that the punishment-oriented type of child-rearing—used primarily in working-class families—results in less successful socialization to law-abiding norms than do the love-oriented and "character building" practices of middle-class families.[28]

Home discipline, which often means "training" or "socialization," fails most frequently because of inability, indifference, and neglect. While it cannot be concluded that children of working mothers are necessarily neglected, the fact that a mother works often affects the training of the child.[29] In the homes of some

[25] Donald R. Peterson and Wesley C. Becker, "Family Interaction and Delinquency," chap. in *Juvenile Delinquency: Research and Theory*, ed. Herbert C. Quay (New York: Van Nostrand, 1965), pp. 36–99.

[26] Glueck and Glueck, *Unraveling Juvenile Delinquency*, pp. 113, 131.

[27] Albert Bandura and Richard H. Walters, "Dependency Conflicts in Aggressive Delinquents," *Journal of Social Issues*, 14:52–65, 1958.

[28] Trasler, "Criminal Behavior," in *Handbook of Abnormal Psychology*, 2nd ed., ed. Eysenck (London: Pitman Medical Publications, 1970). See also Robert Everett Stanfield, "The Interaction of Family Variables and Gang Variables in the Aetiology of Delinquency," *Social Problems*, 13:411–17, 1966.

[29] Elizabeth Herzog, *Children of Working Mothers* (Washington, D. C.: Department of Health, Education, and Welfare, 1960), pp. 18–20; Eleanor E. MacCoby, "Children and Working Mothers," *The Child*, 5:83–89, 1958.

lower-class working mothers, like the homes of some nonworking mothers, the children are thrown on their own resources as soon as they are physically able. As a result, they are thrust into contact with the behavior patterns of persons outside the home. A study of 312 boys in Los Angeles probation camps found that they were characterized by premature autonomy, attitudinal distance from the family, and lack of factual knowledge about family members.[30] Such lack of stake in conformity has a double impact in inner-city areas: neglect of training by parents and lack of respect for parents are more extensive in slum areas than in middle-class residential areas, and at the same time delinquent subcultures thrive in the slums of American cities. Consequently, the probability that a neglected child will come into contact with an excess of delinquent behavior patterns is higher in ghetto areas than in others.

Many of the complaints in juvenile courts originate with parents who charge their own children, especially girls, with ungovernability. Such public accusation against a child by its own parents weakens the subsequent influence over the child. This behavior of parents is sometimes due to lack of affection and concern for the child, sometimes to exasperation which is often expressed inconsistently and sometimes violently. Moreover, this behavior of parents seems to be concentrated largely in the lower socioeconomic classes, where there is a relative lack of nonjudicial resources for dealing with the problem behavior of children. The boy or girl who appears in the juvenile court is labeled a criminal, despite legal theory to the contrary, and as a result the child is impeded in adjusting to the larger society, while at the same time, the society is impeded in adjusting to the child.

A special problem of training and discipline appears in the migrant family. Parents who were effective in training their children in the communities of Europe or in the rural areas of the southern United States often find themselves incompetent in the slum areas of the large American city. The rules for living are different, and the community-control agencies are different. Children usually acquire the new ways of behaving before their parents do, and then look on their parents with contempt. It is therefore difficult for the parents to make the homes attractive to the children, or to control the children, with the result that the children are often thrown upon their own resources, which means the resources of the delinquent subcultures which surround them.[31]

GENERAL PROCESSES

From the preceding analysis of home conditions in relation to delinquency, five principal processes appear. First, children may assimilate within the home by observation of parents or other relatives the attitudes, codes, and behavior

[30] Peter S. Venizia, "Delinquency as a Function of Intrafamily Relationships," *Journal of Research in Crime and Delinquency*, 5:148–73, 1968.

[31] See S. N. Eisenstadt, "Delinquency Group-Formation Among Immigrant Youth," *British Journal of Delinquency*, 2:34–45, 1951; and Richard A. Cloward and Lloyd E. Ohlin, *Delinquency and Opportunity* (Glencoe, Ill.: Free Press, 1961), pp. 194–211.

patterns of delinquency. They then become delinquent because they have learned delinquency at home.

Second, parents determine both the geographic and the social class locus of the home in the community, and the locus of the home, in turn, largely determines the kind of behavior patterns the child will encounter. If the home is in a high-delinquency area, the probability that the child will encounter many delinquent patterns is greater than it is if the home is located in a low-delinquency area. Similarly, being a member of a lower socioeconomic class may affect the child's denial or acceptance of the dominant values of the society. Hirschi found that 51 percent of about one thousand youths who reported on their own delinquencies had friends who had been picked up by the police; of those who reported that they had committed none of a number of listed delinquent acts, this percentage was 37, but of those who reported one or more of the acts the percentage was 63. Put another way, of the 533 respondents who said that at least one friend had been picked up by the police, 62 percent admitted committing at least one of the delinquent acts; but of 520 who said that none of their friends had been picked up by the police, only 27 percent admitted to a listed delinquent act.[32] Consistently, a recent study of girls appearing before a juvenile court in Great Britain found that at least 80 percent of the girls had a close associate who had been before a court; about half of the girls had a member of their immediate family who had also been in court. The investigator concluded:

If a girl comes from a family, or a housing area, where delinquent behavior is prevalent she will see herself as part of that social environment; her friends will tend to come from the same environment, and her easiest course of behavior will be to fall in line with the expectations of those around her. The likelihood of her becoming involved in group offenses, or of frequenting certain clubs or having a delinquent friend is thereby greatly increased.[33]

Third, the home may determine the prestige values of various persons and also the type of persons with whom intimacy later develops. Children learn to respect or reject members of certain minority groups, police officers, teachers, and others. They learn to appraise persons by their bearing, clothing, language, or occupation as important or unimportant, and this appraisal later affects acceptance or rejection of the behavior patterns which are presented. Children learn, in other words, to pay little attention to the behavior patterns, whether criminal or anticriminal, presented by some persons, and to pay close attention to those presented by other persons.

Fourth, a child may be driven from the home by unpleasant experiences and situations or withdraw from it because of the absence of pleasant experiences, and

[32]Hirschi, *Causes of Delinquency*, p. 99.

[33]Jean Davies, "Girls Appearing Before a Juvenile Court," in Jean Davies et al., *Further Studies of Female Offenders*, Home Office Research Study No. 33 (London: Her Majesty's Stationery Office, 1976), p. 63.

thus cease to be a functioning member of an integrated group. Nye found that delinquency is higher in unbroken but unhappy homes than it is in broken homes.[34] Hirschi found that children unattached to their parents are much more likely to have delinquent friends than those who do feel parental attachment, and that delinquency of companions is strongly related to delinquency regardless of the level of attachment to the father.[35] The child may become prematurely autonomous, overtly displaying indifference both to the expectations of parents and to their disapproval.[36] In the best study that has been made of this process, Werthman showed how lower-class juvenile gang boys lose membership in groups conducive to nondelinquency, including family groups, and at the same time become members of groups owning values and norms which support stealing and fighting. He suggests that by the time a delinquent boy is ready to assume adult responsibility, his choices have been so limited by his premature autonomy that he is incapable of making the transition to a nondelinquent role.[37]

A recent study of Swedish adolescents found that the greater the frequency of interaction with the family the less the frequency of serious theft, and the greater the interaction with friends the higher the frequency of theft. Consistently, a comparative study of Canadian and Swiss boys suggested that the Swiss boys are more family oriented and also less delinquent, while Canadian boys favor peer orientations and engage in more criminal acts. And an American longitudinal study of high school students found that alienation from home and school, association with delinquent friends, and delinquent behavior are bound together in a mutually reinforcing process.[38] Another study with consistent findings searched for differences in the psychological characteristics of successful and unsuccessful parolees in a community treatment project.[39] The successes, as compared to the failures, were not in conflict or dissatisfied with their parents. The failures, on the other hand, had a strong need for emancipation from adult structure and for early attainment of the symbols of young adult status; they also

[34]Nye, *Family Relationships and Delinquent Behavior*, p. 47.

[35]Hirschi, *Causes of Delinquency*, p. 103. See also Elliott and Voss, *Delinquency and Dropout*, pp. 150–51.

[36]Venizia, "Delinquency as a Function of Intrafamily Relationships."

[37]Carl Werthman, "The Function of Social Definitions in the Development of Delinquent Careers," appendix J of *Task Force Report: Juvenile Delinquency and Youth Crime*, pp. 155–70. See also idem, "Juvenile Delinquency and Moral Character," chap. in *Delinquency, Crime, and Social Process*, ed. Donald R. Cressey and David A. Ward (New York: Harper and Row, 1969), pp. 611–32; and S. Weinberg, "Female Delinquency in Ghana West Africa: A Comparative Analysis."

[38]Paul C. Friday, "Research on Youth Crime in Sweden: Some Problems in Methodology," *Scandinavian Studies*, 46:20–30, 1974; and Paul C. Friday and Jerald Hague, "Youth Crime in Postindustrial Societies," *Criminology*, 14:347–68, 1976. Edmund W. Vaz and J. Casparis, "A Comparative Study of Youth Culture and Delinquency: Upper Class Canadian and Swiss Boys," *International Journal of Comparative Sociology*, 12:1–23, 1971; and Elliott and Voss, *Delinquency and Dropout*, p. 203.

[39]Eric Werner and Ted Palmer, "Psychological Characteristics of Successful and Unsuccessful Parolees: Implications of Heteroscedastic and Nonlinear Relationships," *Journal of Research in Crime and Delinquency*, 13:165–78, 1976.

were committed to defending and remaining loyal to delinquent associates who were in trouble.

The important point of these studies is that isolation from the family is likely to increase the child's associations with delinquent behavior patterns and decrease his or her associations with antidelinquent behavior patterns. Other recent studies, however, have challenged this basic point, principally by questioning the meaning of phrases such as "delinquency behavior patterns" and "definitions favorable and unfavorable to violation of law." Stated in exaggerated form, the position taken by some investigators is that individual youngsters are naturally bad and invent their own criminality, so "associations with delinquency behavior patterns" are not necessary to delinquency; what is relevant is whether youngsters, assumed to be self-propelled toward delinquency, are controlled or not controlled by a family.[40] More reasonable is the observation that "the view that the child must somehow be taught crime in intimate, personal groups greatly overstates the case."[41] Adams observed in a laboratory experiment that "nonsocial variables" such as money and sex reinforce delinquent behavior, and he noted that these reinforcements cannot be considered "definitions" or behavior patterns with which one "associates" in the usual sense of the term.[42] Gibbons, as well as Briar and Piliavin, noted, too, that situational variables have an effect on whether a child becomes a delinquent, regardless of the actor's ratio of associations with criminal behavior patterns and anticriminal behavior patterns.[43] But Jensen has more directly challenged the point that a child who loses membership in a family will become delinquent or not depending on whether he or she comes into contact with behavior patterns supporting delinquency. In this study, which used the same data base used by Hirschi, parental supervision and delinquent peers were both found to influence delinquency involvement "regardless of definitions favorable and unfavorable to the violation of the law."[44] The point, thus, is not that delinquent peers are unimportant determinants of the behavior of a youth who becomes prematurely autonomous and comes into association with the peers. Instead, the disagreement is with the idea that companions who are delinquent

[40]Hirschi, *Causes of Delinquency*, p. 229.

[41]John R. Hepburn, "Testing Alternative Models of Delinquency Causation," *Journal of Criminal Law and Criminology*, 67:450–60, 1976.

[42]Reed Adams, "The Adequacy of Differential Association Theory," *Journal of Research in Crime and Delinquency*, 11:1–8, 1974. See also idem, "Differential Association and Learning Principles Revisited," *Social Problems*, 20:458–70, 1973; and Clarence Ray Jeffery, "Criminal Behavior and Learning Theory," *Journal of Criminal Law, Criminology, and Police Science*, 56:294–300, 1965.

[43]Don C. Gibbons, "Observations on the Study of Crime Causation," *American Journal of Sociology*, 77:262–78, 1971; Scott Briar and Irving Piliavin, "Delinquency, Situational Inducements, and Commitment to Conformity," *Social Problems*, 13:35–45, 1965. See also Eric Linden and James C. Hackler, "Affective Ties and Delinquency," *Pacific Sociological Review*, 16:27–46, 1973; and Michael J. Hindelang, "Causes of Delinquency: A Partial Replication and Extension," *Social Problems*, 20:471–87, 1973.

[44]Gary F. Jensen, "Parents, Peers, and Delinquent Actions: A Test of the Differential Association Perspective," *American Journal of Sociology*, 78:562–75, 1972.

either deliberately or inadvertently convert a youngster away from a commitment to conventional values and toward a dedicated commitment to a specific set of countervalues. This image of delinquent companions as persons who try to sell their friends on the idea that delinquency is a good thing is not the one intended by differential association theory. Not inconsistent with this theory is the finding that a boy who is closely attached to his parents, like a boy who is not attached to his parents at all, may drift into delinquency because, though not committed to delinquent norms, he "goes along" with friends who commit delinquencies now and then.[45] A social relationship which reinforces or otherwise encourages delinquency is a behavior pattern favorable to delinquency, whether the recipient develops a set of beliefs which positively require delinquent behavior or not.

The fifth general process relating to delinquency is that the home may fail to train the child to deal with community situations in a law-abiding manner. That is, delinquency patterns may not be present in the home, but the home may be neutral with respect to delinquency of the child. This failure to present antidelinquency patterns may be due to neglect of training because of the absence of the parents or because of the unconcern of parents, or it may be due to overprotection in the form of failure to acquaint the child with the kinds of delinquencies he or she will be expected to resist or with the taboos of the outside world. Moreover, as Trasler has pointed out, some parents may be unable to verbalize the norms their children will later be expected to follow.[46] Again, whether such a "neutral" child becomes delinquent or not will depend upon the child's associations with delinquent and antidelinquent patterns outside the home.

Most of the conditions which have been found to be associated with delinquency can be interpreted in relation to the fourth and fifth of the processes which have been outlined. The fact that the parents are divorced or that the father is dead, that the family income is low, that the housing facilities are very inadequate, that the parents are incapable of coping with the behavior of the child, are unconcerned, or are extremely harsh in their discipline—all of these may fall within the framework of the fourth and fifth processes. In both of those processes, the active condition is assimilation of delinquent behavior patterns from associates, whether the associates are adults or children. These two processes are important because they increase the probability that a child will come into contact with delinquents and will be attracted by delinquent behavior.

A sixth process has also been suggested. This is the persistence in the community of habits of disobedience formed in the home. This notion is frequently discussed in commonsense terms as the failure of the child to develop habits of obedience. It also is discussed in psychiatric terms as resentment of authority. Both views assume that there is a generalized attitude toward authority.

[45]David Matza, *Delinquency and Drift* (New York: Wiley, 1964), p. 63.
[46]Trasler, *The Explanation of Criminality.*

That is questionable. Disobedience of one kind or another develops in a large proportion of the children reared in modern homes due to the impossible demands made on them and to the inconsistency in the enforcement of home regulations. But children who are very disobedient at home are frequently well-behaved in the home of a neighbor or in school, and vice versa. Psychoanalysts have emphasized the Oedipus complex as an important source of delinquency. This complex consists of hatred of the father because of rivalry for the affections of the mother; because the father is the authority in the home, the boy transfers hatred of authority when he becomes active in the outside community. It is difficult to determine the extent to which such transference occurs. A study of seventy-four adult male prisoners found no correlation between the subjects' attitudes toward law and morality and their attitudes toward their parents.[47]

A seventh process is also frequently suggested: psychological tensions and emotional disturbances in the home. There is no doubt that tensions accompanying or resulting from favoritism, rejection, insecurity, harshness, rigidity, irritation, and other conditions characterize many homes and affect many children. Observation of such home conditions among delinquent groups has resulted in the proposition: "The problem child is a child with problems." The delinquent is considered as emotionally disturbed, and the emotional disturbance is considered a product of emotional disturbances in the home. Psychiatrists and psychoanalysts have brought this notion into prominence, and it probably is the most popular interpretation of juvenile delinquency at present. However, it is not at all certain that there is an undue incidence of emotional disturbances among delinquents or in the homes of delinquents.

Furthermore, a most significant theoretical question regarding this interpretation of delinquency has not been adequately answered. Granted that juvenile delinquents sometimes come from homes characterized by family tensions and emotional disturbances, how do these tensions produce delinquency? Obviously, they may produce delinquency through the fourth and fifth processes described above; that is, through increasing the probability of contacts with delinquent behavior patterns or through failure of the family to acquaint the child with the taboos of the community. Children do not become delinquent just because they are unhappy. Children living in unhappy homes may take on delinquency patterns if there are delinquency patterns around for them to acquire. Certainly they will not start giving away their personal possessions according to the custom of some Indian tribes, for this pattern is not present in urban America.[48]

DELINQUENT AND NONDELINQUENT SIBLINGS

It might be expected that all children in "bad" homes would become delinquent. As a matter of fact, many of the children in any given type of home are not

---

[47] Norman Watt and Brendan A. Maher, "Prisoners' Attitudes Toward Home and the Judicial System," *Journal of Criminal Law, Criminology, and Police Science*, 49:321–30, 1958.

[48] Cf. Warren Dunham and Mary E. Knauer, "The Juvenile Court in Its Relationship to Adult Criminality," *Social Forces*, 32:290–96, 1954.

delinquent, probably because home conditions are rarely the same for all the children in a family. The home changes greatly in some cases by reason of the death of a parent, a change in economic status, formation or discontinuance of habits and attitudes by parents, or other conditions. Also, parental affection and supervision vary considerably in a home at a particular time for the different children, so that a boy might not, on that account, have the same home as his brother. Finally, many of the associations which an individual has with delinquent and antidelinquent behavior patterns outside the home are adventitious. It is not necessary to believe that every turning point in the life of an individual is a choice directed by a deep-seated and fundamental trait of personality, by desperation or frustration, or by a deliberate teaching of new values by someone holding them.

Many studies have been made of the relation between birth order and achievement, intellectual ability, psychopathy, aggressiveness, and other traits of personality and of behavior. The earlier studies generally showed inferiority in the firstborn child, but the later studies have reduced this difference, due principally to an improvement in the statistical procedures. The result is that it is now doubtful whether order of birth has any association with traits of personality or behavior. Two explanations have been offered for the difference which has been found or assumed. One of these is biological and is to the effect that the firstborn child is inferior because of the greater difficulty of his birth process. The other explanation is in terms of social relations and includes undeveloped skill of parents in training the child, solicitude of parents because of the newness of the experience, and conflict for the child in passing from a favored position as an only child to a subordinate position when a second child is born.

American studies of birth order and delinquency or crime were made mostly in the 1920s and 1930s, and they were often limited to a small number of cases. A study of two groups of juvenile probationers in England showed an overrepresentation of intermediate-aged children, as compared with oldest and youngest in the family.[49] The investigators suggested that this relationship occurs because parents give most of their attention to the oldest and the youngest children, thus "squeezing" the intermediate children out of the family and into gangs. A recent New York study of 246 adult and juvenile probationers found that only 10 percent of the sixty-seven firstborn individuals violated probation, while 32 percent of the later-born probationers violated. The difference was attributed to differential child-rearing practices that had made firstborn individuals more willing clients of probation treatment programs.[50]

The "only child" is generally supposed to be extraordinarily prone to delinquency, but the studies which have been made do not consistently bear this out.

---

[49]J. P. Lees and L. J. Newson, "Family or Sibship Position and Some Aspects of Juvenile Delinquency," *British Journal of Delinquency*, 5:46–65, 1954.

[50]James B. Mullin, "Birth Order as a Variable of Probation Performance," *Journal of Research in Crime and Delinquency*, 10:29–34, 1973.

The Gluecks found that their group of delinquent boys contained lower proportions of oldest children, youngest children, and only children than did the control group.[51] Nye found that oldest and only children show less delinquency behavior than intermediate and youngest children.[52] Wattenberg reviewed the studies of delinquency and only children and concluded that the *meaning* of being an only child varies among different national, racial, religious, and economic groups, and that, consequently, the status of only child has no consistent relationship to delinquency or other behavior problems.[53]

MARITAL STATUS

The marital status of adult persons appears to have considerable significance in relation to crime. In the United States, the rate of commitment to prisons and reformatories per 100,000 population of the same marital status is lowest for the married, next to the lowest for widowed, next for the single, and highest for the divorced. These ranks, however, are affected in part by age. Divorced persons have the highest commitment rate at each age, and this is true for each of the sexes. Divorced males 20 to 24 years of age have a rate of commitment about six times as high as either single males of the same age or married males of the same age, while divorced females of that age have a rate about ten times as high as either single females or married females of the same age. Married males have a lower commitment rate than single males in all age groups except 15 to 19; the rate is only slightly lower in the age group 20 to 24, but is significantly lower in later ages. For females, however, the married women have a higher commitment rate at each age except 25 to 34, but the difference is not very great except in the age group 15 to 19. It has been found, also, that married persons succeed on parole more frequently than persons of any other marital class, and that those who are compatibly married succeed more often than those incompatibly married.

These statistics, which are based on commitments to prisons in the United States, are in substantial agreement with the statistics from most European countries. One exception is in Greece, where in 1960 married persons had a conviction rate much higher than did either single widowed, or divorced persons—65 percent of the convicted criminals were married, as compared with 42 percent of the Greek population; 33 percent were single, as compared with 49 percent of the general population; and 2 percent were widowed or divorced, as compared with 7 percent of the Greek population.[54] It is not correct, however, to conclude from these statistics that marital status is a direct causal factor in crime. Instead, it can be concluded that marital status is important to criminality

---

[51] Glueck and Glueck, *Unraveling Juvenile Delinquency*, p. 120.

[52] Nye, *Family Relationships and Delinquent Behavior*, p. 37. See also Raymond A. Mulligan, "Family Relationships and Juvenile Delinquency," *Pacific Sociological Review*, 1:40, 1958.

[53] William W. Wattenberg, "Delinquency and Only Children: A Study of a 'Category,' " *Journal of Abnormal and Social Psychology*, 44:356–366, July, 1949.

[54] C. D. Spinellis, *Crime in Contemporary Greece* (Athens: The Athenian Institute of Anthropos, 1971), p. 35.

and noncriminality because it determines the kinds of behavior patterns with which persons come in contact.

SUGGESTED READINGS

Adams, Reed. "The Adequacy of Differential Association Theory." *Journal of Research in Crime and Delinquency*, 11:1–8, 1974.

Barker, Gordon H. "Parental Organization Affiliation and Juvenile Delinquency." *Journal of Criminal Law, Criminology, and Police Science*, 44:204–7, 1953.

Brandis, Walter, & Dorothy Henderson. *Social Class, Language, and Communication*. London: Routledge and Kegan Paul, 1970.

Chilton, Roland, J., & Gerald E. Markle. "Family Disruption, Delinquent Conduct, and the Effect of Subclassification." *American Sociological Review*, 37:93–99, 1972.

Elliott, Delbert S., & Harwin L. Voss, *Delinquency and Dropout*. Lexington, Mass.: D. C. Heath, 1974.

Friday, Paul C., & Jerald Hague. "Youth Crime in Postindustrial Societies." *Criminology*, 14:347–68, 1976.

Hartnagel, Timothy F. "Father Absence and Self Conception Among Lower Class White and Negro Boys." *Social Problems*, 18:152–63, 1970.

Hepburn, John R. "Testing Alternative Models of Delinquency Causation." *Journal of Criminal Law and Criminology*, 67:450–60, 1976.

Hirschi, Travis. *Causes of Delinquency*. Berkeley: University of California Press, 1969.

Jensen, Gary F. "Parents, Peers, and Delinquent Actions: A Test of the Differential Association Perspective." *American Journal of Sociology*, 78:562–75, 1972.

Linden, Eric, & James C. Hackler. "Affective Ties and Delinquency." *Pacific Sociological Review*, 16:27–46, 1973.

Nye, F. Ivan. *Family Relationships and Delinquent Behavior*. New York: Wiley, 1958.

Quinney, Richard. "Crime, Delinquency, and Social Areas." *Journal of Research in Crime and Delinquency*, 1:149–54, 1964.

Severy, Lawrence J. "Exposure to Deviance Committed by Valued Peer Group and Family Members. *Journal of Research in Crime and Delinquency*, 10:35–46, 1964.

Sottong, David C. "The Dilemma of the Parent as a Culture Bearer." *Social Casework*, 36:302–6, 1955.

Sterne, Richard S. *Delinquent Conduct and Broken Homes*. New Haven, Conn.: College and University Press, 1964.

Straus, Murray A. "Power and Support Structure of the Family in Relation to Socialization." *Journal of Marriage and the Family*, 26:318–26, 1964.

Straus, Murray A. "Leveling, Civility, and Violence in the Family." *Journal of Marriage and the Family*, 36:13–29, 1974.

Toby, Jackson. "The Differential Impact of Family Disorganization." *American Sociological Review*, 22:505–12, 1957.

Toby, Jackson. "Violence and the Masculine Ideal: Some Qualitative Data." *Annals of the American Academy of Political and Social Science*, 364:19–27, 1966.

Trasler, Gordon, B. *The Explanation of Criminality*. London: Routledge and Kegan Paul, 1962.

Vincent, Clark E. "Mental Health and the Family." *Journal of Marriage and the Family*, 29:18–39, 1967.

11

Institutional Patterns

The basic social institutions—familial, economic, governmental, educational, and religious—are organized systems for meeting social needs. Each is a subdivision in the structure of every society, and each organizes some aspects of the behavior of individuals. But the specific form and content of the institutions have varied historically, and we showed in Chapter 5 that changes in crime rates, and in the very conceptions of crime, have accompanied these changes. The specific form and content of the institutions also vary from one contemporary society to another, and anthropologists, economists, political scientists, sociologists, and many others have for centuries been trying to determine how, or whether, variations in institutional patterns are linked with variations in patterns of delinquency and crime.

However, intersocietal comparisons of institutional structures and operations are, like intersocietal comparisons of crime rates, very difficult and very hazardous. Perhaps it is for this reason that most recent research on the subject has been directed at analysis of the role of the various institutions in determining patterns of crime and delinquency in single societies. In the United States, for example, hundreds of studies have looked at variations in individual families and then tried to link these variations with patterns of delinquency, as we showed in Chapter 10. Similarly, hundreds of other studies have examined variations in economic variables, political variables, and the like, and then tried to link them with variations in the crime rates of various groups and categories of persons. The family institution and the economic institution, especially as the latter affects the distribution of wealth, have received more attention than the other institutions.

THE ECONOMIC INSTITUTION

Many studies have been made of the relation between poverty and crime rates. Studies of the economic status of criminals have indicated that the lower economic class has a much higher official crime rate than the upper economic class. This conclusion has been derived from two types of data: those on the social class membership of criminals and delinquents, and those on delinquency and crime rates of persons living in areas of poverty as compared to the rates of persons living in other areas of cities. On the other hand, numerous studies have suggested that crime rates do not increase significantly in periods of economic depression. A survey will be made of the principal findings of these three kinds of studies, and then suggestions for reconciling the apparently contradictory conclusions will be made.

Social Class Ratios

The reliability of the official statistics on the socioeconomic backgrounds of criminals has been questioned even more severely than have statistics on such variables as age, race, and area of residence. Many persons maintain that the law-enforcement processes tend to select working-class persons, just as they tend to select blacks. Thus it is believed that if a member of the working class and a member of the upper class are equally guilty of some offense, the person from the working class is more likely to be arrested, convicted, and committed to an institution. Chambliss, for example, has put the matter this way:

The lower-class person is (1) more likely to be scrutinized and therefore to be observed in any violation of the law, (2) more likely to be arrested if discovered under suspicious circumstances, (3) more likely to spend time between arrest and trial in jail, (4) more likely to come to trial, (5) more likely to be found guilty, and (6) if found guilty, more likely to receive harsh punishment than his middle- or upper-class counterpart.[1]

Further, most white-collar crimes are not included in sets of official crime statistics. It is not possible at present to compile quantitative data regarding the white-collar crime rate, and therefore it is not possible to make accurate comparisons of the total criminal behavior of the several classes. When white-collar crimes are taken into account, however, they throw doubt on the conclusion that crime is concentrated in the lower economic classes.

For ordinary "street crimes," most careful research studies suggest that there is administrative bias toward persons of lower socioeconomic status at various points in the criminal justice process, but some studies do not. After reviewing the research studies and essays written on the relationship between delinquency and economic conditions, two sociologists concluded that the best evidence indicated that delinquency is basically a working-class phenomenon.[2] However, more recent studies have challenged this conclusion. For example, one of the early studies of "self-reported" delinquency found that lower-class boys were significantly over-represented in the population of training schools; however, when high school students were asked to report on their minor delinquencies, no significant

---

[1] William J. Chambliss, *Crime and the Legal Process* (New York: McGraw-Hill, 1969), p. 86.
[2] H. L. Wilensky and C. N. Lebeaux, *Industrial Society and Social Welfare* (New York: Free Press, 1965), p. 189.

differences in the different socioeconomic classes were found.[3] A study of juvenile court practices showed that delinquent boys living in low-income areas of Philadelphia were more likely (40 percent) to be sentenced to an institution than were boys living in higher-income areas (29 percent), but in a heavily indus-trialized Midwestern city socioeconomic status (as determined by father's occupation) was found to be unrelated to police referrals to juvenile courts or to the dispositions of cases made by the courts.[4] A recent statistical study of more than 10,000 felons sentenced to the prisons of North Carolina, South Carolina, and Florida found no relationship between length of sentence and socioeconomic status, but most of the persons receiving sentences were of socioeconomic status much lower than the average for the general population.[5]

It seems reasonable to assume that if statistical and administrative biases could be removed, there would be a residual but nevertheless real difference between the behavior of lower-class persons and members of other social classes, so far as serious juvenile delinquency and adult criminality are concerned. If this assump-tion, which says nothing about white-collar crime, is accepted, then the following two observations are warranted.

First, in the United States, official statistics indicate that the largest proportion

---

[3]F. Ivan Nye, James F. Short, Jr., and Virgil J. Olson, "Socioeconomic Status and Delinquent Behavior," *American Journal of Sociology,* 63:381–89, 1958. See also Robert A. Dentler and Laurence J. Monroe, "Social Correlates of Early Adolescent Theft," *American Sociological Review,* 26:733–43, 1961; Maynard L. Erickson and Lamar T. Empey, "Court Records, Undetected Delinquency, and Decision-Making," *Journal of Criminal Law, Criminology, and Police Science,* 54:456–69, 1963; Ronald L. Akers, "Socioeconomic Status and Delinquent Behavior: A Retest," *Journal of Research in Crime and Delinquency,* 1:38–46, 1964; Maynard L. Erickson and Lamar T. Empey, "Class Position, Peers, and Delinquency," *Sociology and Social Research,* 49:268–82, 1965; William R. Arnold, "Continuities in Research: Scaling Delinquent Behavior," *Social Problems,* 13:59–66, 1965; Harwin L. Voss, "Socioeconomic Status and Reported Delinquent Behavior," *Social Problems,* 13:314–24, 1966; William J. Chambliss and Richard H. Nagasawa, "On the Validity of Official Statistics—A Comparative Study of White, Black, and Japanese High-School Boys," *Journal of Research in Crime and Delinquency,* 6:74–77, 1969; Travis Hirschi, *Causes of Delinquency* (Berkeley, Calif.: University of California Press, 1969); Jay R. Williams and Martin Gold, "From Delinquent Behavior to Official Delinquency," *Social Problems,* 20:209–29, 1972; and Delbert S. Elliott and Harwin L. Voss, *Delinquency and Dropout* (Lexington, Mass.: Lexington Books, 1974). Most of these studies asked boys and girls about their own petty misbehavior (for example, skipping school or defying parents) rather than about theft, burglary, robbery, and similar offenses. The earliest of these studies, and others, are summarized in Roger Hood and Richard Sparks, *Key Issues in Criminology* (London: World University Library, 1970).

[4]Terence P. Thornberry, "Race, Socioeconomic Status, and Sentencing in the Juvenile Justice System," *Journal of Criminal Law and Criminology,* 64:90–98, 1973; Robert M. Terry, "Discrimination in the Handling of Juvenile Offenders by Social Control Agencies," *Journal of Research in Crime and Delinquency,* 4:218–30, 1967. See also William R. Arnold, "Race and Ethnicity Relative to Other Factors in Juvenile Court Dispositions," *American Journal of Sociology,* 77:211–27, 1971; and Norman C. Weiner and Charles V. Willie, "Decisions by Juvenile Officers," *American Journal of Sociology,* 77:199–210, 1971. Several similar studies, showing contradictory results on the question of whether police and other agencies are directly influenced in their discretionary decisions by the socioeconomic status of suspects, are summarized in Don C. Gibbons, *Delinquent Behavior,* 2d ed. (Englewood Cliffs, N. J.: Prentice-Hall, 1976), pp. 38–43.

[5]Theodore G. Chiricos and Gordon P. Waldo, "Socioeconomic Status and Criminal Sentencing: An Empirical Assessment of a Conflict Proposition," *American Sociological Review* 40:753–72, 1975.

of delinquent and criminal populations come from the working class, and there is some evidence that the "street-crime" rates of working-class juveniles and adults exceed the rates of other persons. In institutionalized populations, about two-thirds to three-fourths of the men, and about nine-tenths of the women, are members of the working class.

In an analysis of income and delinquency, Chilton found that the forty-two census tracts in Marion County (Indianapolis), Indiana, that had the highest average incomes contained 40 percent of the juvenile-court-age children but produced only 17 percent of the juvenile court cases. The forty-two census tracts with the lowest income contained 37 percent of the juvenile-court-age children but accounted for 65 percent of the juvenile court cases. The law violations by the children in the low-income tracts were heavily weighted with burglary, robbery, assault, and carrying dangerous weapons, while in the high-income-tract children, violations were overrepresented in trespassing, vandalism, automobile theft, receiving stolen goods, and violations of curfew, traffic, and liquor laws.[6] Consistently, Quinney found in Lexington, Kentucky, that the crime rates in census tracts correlated −.52 with the economic status of the persons living in those tracts, +.47 with ethnic status, and −.16 with family status. The area correlations with deliquency rates were −.38 for economic status, +.48 for ethnic status, and −.35 for family status.[7]

In their pioneering study of social class differences, Warner and Lunt found that while the two lower classes constituted only 57 percent of Yankee City's population, 90 percent of the arrests during a seven-year period were arrests of members of these two classes.[8] Ninety percent of the 932 felons convicted in Washington, D.C., in 1964–1965 had incomes less than $5000; 56 percent of the adult population of Washington at the time earned less than $5000.[9] A study in Denmark indicated that 10 percent of a group of offenders came from the upper or middle class, while 27 percent of the general population was in these classes.[10]

Many other studies have shown the same tendency for adult and juvenile

[6]Ronald J. Chilton, "Middle-Class Delinquency and Specific Offense Analysis," chap. in *Middle-Class Juvenile Delinquency*, ed. Edmund W. Vaz (New York: Harper and Row, 1967), pp. 91–101. See also Ronald J. Chilton, "Continuity in Delinquency Area Research: A Comparison of Studies for Baltimore, Detroit, and Indianapolis," *American Sociological Review*, 29:71–83, 1964.

[7]Richard Quinney, "Crime, Delinquency, and Social Areas," *Journal of Research in Crime and Delinquency*, 1:149–54, 1964. See also Laurence Rosen and Stanley H. Turner, "An Evaluation of the Lander Approach to Ecology of Delinquency," *Social Problems* 15:189–200, 1967; Robert A. Gordon, "Issues in the Ecological Study of Delinquency," *American Sociological Review*, 32:927–44, 1967; Kenneth Polk, "Urban Social Areas and Delinquency, *Social Problems*, 14:320–25, 1967; and Charles V. Willie, "The Relative Contribution of Family Status and Economic Status to Juvenile Delinquency," *Social Problems*, 14:326–35, 1967.

[8]William Lloyd Warner and Paul S. Lunt, *The Social Life of a Modern Community* (New Haven: Yale University Press, 1941), pp. 373–77.

[9]President's Commission on Crime in the District of Columbia, *Report* (Washington, D.C.: Government Printing Office, 1966), p. 130.

[10]Preben Wolf, "Crime and Social Class in Denmark," *British Journal of Criminology*, 13:5–17, 1962.

delinquents to be concentrated in the lower economic class.[11] One study indicated that prisoners rank themselves lower than they rank their fathers on socioeconomic status, perhaps indicating that the prisoners were unable to maintain the family level of status, let alone improve it through upward mobility.[12]

Second, the extent of overrepresentation of working-class persons in the criminal population is not the same under all conditions. In some situations, working-class people have crime rates lower than those of other classes.

1. The ratio of working-class persons to other persons in the criminal population varies by social group. A follow-up study of youngsters in an aid-to-dependent-children welfare program showed that by age 19, 34 percent had become known to the police or juvenile court.[13] However, in the Japanese colony in Seattle prior to World War II the children had a very low delinquency rate, despite the fact that the residents were of the working class and were in as great poverty as residents of the area surrounding the colony, who had high delinquency rates. Moreover, residents of certain rural areas may be in extreme poverty with little incidence of crime. Shaw found that for the eighty-seven counties of Minnesota the correlation between crime rates and the percentage of the populations on welfare combined with the percentage of the populations seeking work was only +.213. By way of contrast, he found a correlation of +.717 between the degree of urbanization of the counties and their crime rates.[14] During the Great Depression, Sheldon discovered no close relationship between the indexes of economic status and juvenile delinquency when other factors were held constant, but found a significant relationship between indexes of social disorganization and juvenile delinquency when economic factors were held constant.[15] More recently, Clark and Wenninger studied the self-reported crimes of public high school students, sixth through twelfth grades, in four communities chosen to represent four class levels—a rural farm area, a lower-class neighborhood within a city, an industrial city, and upper-class (mostly executive and professional) area within a city. They found that the incidence of self-reported crimes became greater as one moved from rural farm to upper urban to industrial city to lower urban.[16] This study

[11] For summaries, analyses, and bibliographies, see Ivar Berg, "Economic Factors in Delinquency," appendix O in President's Commission on Law Enforcement and Administration of Justice, *Task Force Report: Juvenile Delinquency and Youth Crime* (Washington, D.C.: Government Printing Office, 1967), pp. 305–16; and Lynn McDonald, *Social Class and Delinquency* (London: Faber and Faber, 1969).

[12] Harold Bradley and Jack D. Williams, *Intensive Treatment Program: Second Annual Report* (Sacramento, Calif.: Department of Corrections, 1958), p. 16.

[13] Erdman B. Palmore and Phillip E. Hammond, "Interacting Factors in Juvenile Delinquency," *American Sociological Review*, 29:848–54, 1964. See also T. Vinson and R. Homel, "Crime and Disadvantage: The Coincidence of Medical and Social Problems in an Australian City," *British Journal of Criminology*, 15:21–31, 1975.

[14] Van B. Shaw, "The Relationship Between Crime Rates and Certain Population Characteristics in Minnesota Counties," *Journal of Criminal Law and Criminology*, 40:43–49, 1949.

[15] Henry D. Sheldon, "Problems in the Statistical Study of Juvenile Delinquency," *Metron*, 12:201–23, 1934.

[16] John P. Clark and Eugene P. Wenninger, "Socio-Economic Class and Area as Correlates of Illegal Behavior Among Juveniles," *American Sociological Review*, 27:826–34, 1962.

shows, basically, that *location* is more important to delinquency than is *social class* in its pure form. Differences among the socioeconomic classes *within* the areas studied were generally insignificant. The study makes clear that the "working class," so overrepresented in the crime statistics, consists of the lower-class persons living in the lower-class areas of large urban communities. The middle-class children living in the same areas reported delinquencies in about the same measure as did the lower-class children.[17]

Similarly, girls who live in areas of poverty in the typical American city are in as great poverty as boys, but their delinquency rate is much lower than the delinquency rate of boys. Moreover, members of some poverty-stricken groups have literally starved to death rather than violate laws. In the years immediately following World War II economic conditions in Japan were so bad that "the people had to decide whether to commit a crime or die from hunger," and a judge who refused to violate the law by participating in the black market died of starvation.[18] The following is a report on a period of famine in India:

Through all these months the white Brahmin cattle wandered by the hundreds through the streets of Calcutta, as they always have, stepping placidly over the bodies of the dead and near-dead, scratching their plump haunches on taxi fenders, sunning themselves on the steps of the great Clive Street banks. No one ever ate a cow; no one ever dreamed of it. I never heard of a Bengali Hindu who would not perish with all his family rather than taste meat. Nor was there any violence. No grocery stall, no rice warehouse, none of the wealthy clubs or restaurants ever was threatened by a hungry mob. The Bengalis just died with that bottomless docility which, to most Americans, is the most shocking thing about India.[19]

2. The ratio of working-class persons to other persons varies by offense. The kind of crime, as contrasted with the fact of crime, is very significantly related to economic status. One's position in the economic structure determines opportunities, facilities, and the requisite skills for specialized crimes.[20] Most studies showing high ratios of working-class persons have concentrated on crimes against property, such as larceny and burglary. Homicide, also, has been shown to be highly concentrated in lower income groups. Lalli and Turner, for example, found that the homicide rate of the lowest occupational groups (laborers, but not farm laborers) is much higher than the rate of other groups.[21] Similarly, Wolfgang found that 90 to 95 percent of the offenders in his homicide study were at the lower end

---

[17] Cf. Wilensky and Lebeaux, *Industrial Society and Social Welfare*, p. 186; and Howard L. and Barbara G. Myerhoff, "Field Observations of Middle Class 'Gangs' " *Social Forces*, 42:328–36, 1964.

[18] Jinyo Kaneko, "Changing Roles of the Police in Japan," *United Nations Asia and Far East Institute for the Prevention of Crime and the Treatment of Offenders, Resource Materials*, No. 10, October, 1975, pp. 28–37.

[19] John Fischer, "India's Insoluble Hunger," *Harper's Magazine*, 190:438–45, 1945 (at p. 439).

[20] Jack P. Gibbs and James F. Short, Jr., "Criminal Differentiation and Occupational Differentiation," *Journal of Research in Crime and Delinquency*, 11:89–100, 1974.

[21] Michael Lalli and Stanley H. Turner, "Suicide and Homicide: A Comparative Analysis by Race and Occupational Levels," *Journal of Criminal Law, Criminology, and Police Science*, 59:191–200, 1968.

of the occupational scale.[22] There is some evidence, however, that the ratio is somewhat lower for sex offenses, and in fact the crime rate of the working class may be lower than the rates of other classes for some sex offenses.[23] Similarly, a Detroit study indicated that working-class persons are not as overrepresented in the population of automobile thieves as they are in other delinquent and criminal populations.[24] And, of course, working-class persons have lower crime rates than other persons for such offenses as embezzlement, misrepresentation in advertising, violation of antitrust laws, and issuing worthless stocks.

Variations by Area[25]

Ogburn found a significant association between poverty and crime in a comparison of sixty-two cities.[26] Shaw and McKay compared residential areas within each of twenty-one cities and found a large and consistent relationship between crime and poverty; they also found very high positive correlations by residential areas between boy and girl delinquency rates, and also between boy delinquency rates and adult crime rates.[27] In an English city, Morris found a correlation of $+.74$ between delinquency rates and percentage of overcrowded homes, and a correlation of $-.76$ between delinquency rates and the percentage of middle-class households.[28] A study of the relationship between homicide rates and the median incomes in twenty-one areas of Cleveland shows that the homicide rate falls rapidly as the median income rises and, indeed, is almost zero in the highest income areas.[29]

Correlations between crime rates and other indexes of poverty also indicate that crime is associated with areas of poverty. For instance, the economic values of houses in a delinquency area are low; the delinquency rate is higher among renters than among property owners; and the physical condition and equipment of houses in delinquency areas are poor. Reiss and Rhodes studied 9238 white

[22] Marvin E. Wolfgang, *Patterns in Criminal Homicide* (Philadelphia: University of Pennsylvania Press, 1958), p. 37.

[23] A. C. Kinsey, W. B. Pomeroy, and C. E. Martin, *Sexual Behavior in the Human Male* (Philadelphia: Saunders, 1948), pp. 327–93. See also John H. Gagnon and William Simon, *Sexual Conduct* (Chicago: Aldine, 1973).

[24] William W. Wattenberg and James Balistrieri, "Automobile Theft: A 'Favored-Group' Delinquency," *American Journal of Sociology*, 57:575–79, 1952.

[25] See the discussion of intracity distributions in Chapter 9.

[26] W. F. Ogburn, "Factors in the Variation of Crime Among Cities," *Journal of the American Statistical Association*, 30:12–34, 1935. See also Karl F. Schuessler, "Components of Variations in City Crime Rates," *Social Problems*, 9:314–23, 1962; Richard Quinney, "Structural Characteristics, Population Areas, and Crime Rates in the United States," *Journal of Criminal Law, Criminology, and Police Science*, 57:45–52, 1966; Karl F. Schuessler and Gerald Slatin, "Sources of Variation in U.S. City Crime, 1950 and 1960," *Journal of Research in Crime and Delinquency*, 1:127–48, 1964; and Victor Eugene Flango and Edgar L. Sherbenou, "Poverty, Urbanization, and Crime," *Criminology*, 14:331–46, 1976.

[27] Clifford R. Shaw and Henry D. McKay, *Juvenile Delinquency and Urban Areas* (Chicago: University of Chicago Press, 1942), pp. 141 ff. See also the studies cited in notes 6 and 7 above.

[28] Morris, *Criminal Areas*, p. 169.

[29] Robert B. Bensing and Oliver Schroeder, *Homicide in an Urban Community* (Springfield, Ill.: Charles C. Thomas, 1960).

male Tennessee delinquents of all social classes and found, among other things, that (1) both in areas of high delinquency and in areas of low delinquency, the low-status boy has the greater chance of becoming delinquent; (2) no matter whether he is of high, middle, or low status, the chances that a boy will be a delinquent are greater if he resides in a high-delinquency-rate area than if he resides in a low-delinquency-rate area; (3) the more the lower-class boy is in a minority in the school and residential community, the less likely he is to become a delinquent.[30] All these findings are consistent with the implication in the theory of differential association that socioeconomic status is important to delinquency and crime primarily as it affects the probability of association with delinquent and criminal behavior patterns.

Variations in Time
The relation between crime rates and poverty also has been studied by examination of data on the relationship between fluctuations in business conditions and fluctuations in crime rates. Here, poverty is measured by the poor business conditions constituting an economic depression, rather than by socioeconomic class or by area of residence. Studies of this kind of have been under way for more than a century and the early ones have been summarized and appraised by Sellin.[31] The methods used have not always been carefully devised, and the measures of both crime and business conditons have varied widely, with the result that no positive, definite, and valid generalizations can be made. The following are the closest approximations to conclusions from the studies.

1. The general crime rate does not increase significantly in periods of economic depression.[32]

2. Serious crimes have a slight and inconsistent tendency to rise in periods of economic depression and fall in periods of prosperity. Thomas found a correlation of $-.25$ between all indictable crimes and economic prosperity in England and Wales for the period 1857–1913, Ogburn a similar coefficient ($-.35$) in New York State for the period 1870–1920, and Phelps a coefficient of $-.33$ in Rhode Island for the period 1898–1926.[33]

---

[30] Albert J. Reiss, Jr., and Albert Lewis Rhodes, "The Distribution of Juvenile Delinquency in the Social Class Structure," *American Sociological Review*, 26:720–32, 1961.

[31] Thorsten Sellin, *Research Memorandum on Crime in the Depression* (New York: Social Science Research Council, 1937). See also W. A. Bonger, *Criminality and Economic Conditions*, trans. H. P. Horton (Boston: Little, Brown, 1916).

[32] Albert H. Hobbs, "Relationship Between Criminality and Economic Conditions," *Journal of Criminal Law and Criminology*, 34:5–10, 1943; James F. Short, Jr., "A Note on Relief Programs and Crimes During the Depression," *American Sociological Review*, 17:226–29, 1952; and Llad Philips, Harold Votey, and Darold Maxwell, "Crime, Youth, and the Labor Market," *Journal of Political Economy*, 80:491–505, 1972.

[33] Dorothy S. Thomas, *Social Aspects of the Business Cycle* (London: Routledge, 1925), pp. 143–44. W. F. Ogburn, "Business Fluctuations as Social Forces," *Social Forces*, 1:73–78, 1923; H. A. Phelps, "Cycles of Crime," *Journal of Criminal Law and Criminology*, 20:107–21, 1929. See also George B. Vold, *Theoretical Criminology* (New York: Oxford University Press, 1958), pp. 177–81.

3. Property crimes involving violence show a tendency to increase in periods of depression, but property crimes involving no violence, such as larceny, show only a very slight and inconsistent tendency to increase in depression periods.[34] Radzinowicz found a clear-cut increase in crimes against property in Poland in the depression years of the early thirties.[35] None of the studies which cover longer periods of time has shown such significant relationship, perhaps because extraneous factors, such as variations in laws and in administration of the laws, play less part in the longer period.

4. Drunkenness tends to increase in periods of prosperity according to some studies, but shows no significant change according to others. Dorothy Thomas found a correlation of + .34 between prosperity and prosecutions for drunkenness in England in 1857–1913,[36] but Winslow found no significant relation in Massachusetts between prosecutions for drunkenness and unemployment.[37]

5. Crimes against the person show no consistent relationship to the business cycle. Some studies have reported increases in crimes against the person in periods of prosperity and find, also, that increase in consumption of alcohol accompanies the increase in crimes against the person.

6. Juvenile delinquency tends to increase in periods of prosperity and to decrease during periods of depression.[38] Glasser and Rice have suggested that combining statistics on juvenile crime with statistics on adult crime may give the erroneous impression that the general crime rate (all ages) does not change in periods of depression.[39]

Conclusions

Before a general positive conclusion about the relationship between poverty and crime is derived from these three kinds of studies, two negative conclusions should be drawn. First, the official criminal statistics, being biased as to class by the exclusion of white-collar crimes and by differences in arresting practices, exaggerate the extent to which crimes are concentrated in the lower class; excessive

---

[34] See James F. Short, Jr., "A Social Aspect of the Business Cycle Re-examined: Crimes," *Research Studies of the State College of Washington*, 20:36–41, 1952.

[35] L. Radzinowicz, "The Influence of Economic Conditions on Crime," *Sociological Review*, 33:1–36, 139–53, 1941.

[36] Thomas, *Social Aspects of the Business Cycle*, pp. 143–44.

[37] Emma A. Winslow, "Relationships between Employment and Crime Fluctuations as Shown by Massachusetts Statistics," *Report on the Causes of Crime*, National Commission on Law Observance and Enforcement, no. 13, vol. I (Washington, D.C.: Government Printing Office, 1937), pp. 257–333.

[38] J. O. Reinemann, "Juvenile Delinquency in Philadelphia and Economic Trends," *Temple University Law Quarterly*, 20:576–83, 1947; Lowell J. Carr, *Delinquency Control* (New York: Harper, 1950), pp. 83–89; Paul Wiers, "Wartime Increases in Michigan Delinquency," *American Sociological Review*, 10:515–23, 1945; idem, *Economic Factors in Michigan Delinquency* (New York: Columbia University Press, 1944); David Bogen, "Juvenile Delinquency and Economic Trend," *American Soicological Review*, 9:178–84, 1944.

[39] Daniel Glaser and Kent Rice, "Crime, Age, and Employment," *American Sociological Review*, 24:679–86, 1959.

criminality of the lower class, except in the official crime records, is still questionable. Second, even if the official statistics are accepted, they give conflicting evidence. Criminal behavior is related consistently to poverty and low economic status according to studies which compare residential areas of criminals and noncriminals, but is related inconsistently or not at all to poverty and low economic status when chronological periods are compared.

The conflicting kinds of evidence suggest that poverty has certain social accompaniments when considered geographically which are lacking when considered chronologically, and that it is these accompaniments of poverty, rather than the economic need, which result in criminal behavior. Persons in poverty do not merely suffer from a *lack* of resources and power; they are weighed down with an overabundance of unwanted things.[40] Poverty in the modern city customarily means segregation in low-rent areas, where people are isolated to a considerable degree from anticriminal patterns and thrust into contact with many criminal behavior patterns. It generally means unemployment and no future potential for work, accompanied by low social status, little to lose, little to respect, and a sense of powerlessness.[41] It typically means bad housing conditions, poor health, and invidious comparisons in other physical and physiological conditions. It may mean that both parents are away from home during most of the hours the children are awake, and are fatigued and irritable when at home. It often means that the child is withdrawn from school at the earliest permissible age to enter an unskilled occupation which is not interesting or remunerative and which offers few opportunities for economic advancement. Low socioeconomic status in a small town may have few of these attributes of a culture of poverty.[42] On the other hand, a depression does not modify significantly the associations of many persons, for rents decrease and families generally occupy the same houses and have the same neighbors as formerly.[43] Poverty, therefore, is related to crime through its social accompaniments. The general conclusion is that poverty affects crime and criminality as it determines associations with criminal behavior patterns or isolation from anticriminal behavior patterns.

THE GOVERNMENTAL INSTITUTION

There has been much speculation but relatively little research on the institution of government and the political processes in relation to criminal behavior. Two

[40]See Vigdis Christie, "Poverty, Social Contact, and Social Class," *Acta Sociologica*, 19:375–86, 1976.

[41]G. Marwell, "Adolescent Powerlessness and Delinquency," *Social Problems*, 14:35–47, 1966. See also A. Mosciskier, "Delinquency in Regions Under Intensified Industrialization and the Relation Between Dynamics of Delinquency and the Dynamics of Socioeconomic Processes," *Archives of Criminology*, 4:223–28, 1969; and Franco Ferracuti, Simon Dinitz, and Esperanza Acosta de Brenes, *Delinquents and Nondelinquents in Puerto Rico* (Columbus, Ohio: University of Ohio Press, 1975).

[42]See Michael Harrington, *The Other America* (New York: Macmillan, 1963); Oscar Lewis, *La Vida* (New York: Random House, 1966; and Flango and Sherbenou, "Poverty, Urbanization, and Crime."

[43]Ruth Shonle Cavan and Katherine H. Ranck, *The Family and the Depression* (Chicago: University of Chicago Press, 1938).

possibilities for research may be suggested. First, various forms of government might be compared, such as a capitalist democracy and a communist dictatorship of the proletariat. Other comparisons, with less economic involvement, might be made between a democratic system and an absolute monarchy, a dictatorship, or a system of government by tribal council, with the objective of determining the extent to which criminal behavior is related to the general form of the political institution. The reason no organized research work has been done on this problem and the reason such research is not feasible need hardly be mentioned—the lack of comparable data for different nations and systems.

Second, comparison might be made of specific political variables within a nation, such as a Democratic administration with a Republican administration, or the particular policies of one administration with those of another. Discussion of this subject has resulted in many conflicting claims, but the problem seems peculiarly insusceptible to scientific research. In fact, crime statistics are probably related only vaguely to the true incidence of crime in the United States partly because various political administrations juggle the figures so as to "prove" that their policies have reduced crime while the policies of the opposition have increased or would increase crime. Quinney has made an eloquent plea for study of what he calls "the politics of crime."[44] Because of the absence of organized research on the influence of government on crime rates, analogous to that in the area of economic conditions, this problem can be discussed only in general terms.

A few centuries ago government had prestige because it was based on the divine right of the sovereign. General opposition to strong government developed because of the necessity of breaking away from the regulations which persisted from the feudal period, because of the democratic fear of absolutism, and because of the new problems of the frontiers. Despite this distrust, the widening area of social interaction and the deadly effects of competition drove many groups to appeal to government for assistance. New criminal laws and administrative regulations were enacted in an attempt to control personal behavior in a world of competing strangers, but the laws and regulations tended to receive support only from special interest groups. The result was, and is, the anomalous condition of a great amount of legislation and little respect for legislation. Each group rebels against the legislation forced upon it by other groups, and in a competitive process each group attempts to secure legislation to regulate other groups. It is easy to break laws derived from a source that one does not greatly respect, and it is easy to manipulate policies in the interest of one's group when few people have much interest in the welfare of all.

Clinard long ago noted that in America the prevailing public attitude toward law obedience is that all laws except those dealing with very serious offenses should be violated if one can get away with it, or that laws should be selectively

---

[44]Richard Quinney, "Crime in Political Perspective," *American Behavioral Scientist*, 8:19–22, 1964.

obeyed according to one's interests.[45] The first can be seen in attitudes toward tax evasion, business frauds, political corruption, shoplifting, speeding, drunken driving, and marijuana smoking. The second can be seen in the selective obedience of laws governing business, labor, agriculture, and military service.[46]

The general disrespect for law and disrespect for law-making and law-enforcement agencies is reflected in widespread law breaking, but it also is seen in the attitudes of persons who do not break laws. Legislative bodies, considered as corporate bodies rather than as individuals, are often viewed with contempt, suspicion, and distrust. Novels dealing with legislatures and city councils in the United States over the last five or six generations have presented these bodies as corrupt, boss-ridden, and inefficient, which they sometimes are. Similarly, police officers are regarded as brutal, corrupt, and inefficient. The public attitude toward the courts is perhaps a little more favorable but inclines toward ridicule and contempt for the lower courts for defects of dishonesty, individual inefficiency, and squalid surroundings. In many groups, individuals would generally prefer to be caught breaking almost any nonfelony law rather than be detected eating potatoes with a knife, and in certain groups even some felonies are less serious than breaches of etiquette.

Officials charged with the enforcement of laws may avoid their responsibility altogether or may enforce the laws only sporadically. The cyclical pattern of "reform" so common to American municipalities is partly a function of sporadic enforcement. But in the United States we have arranged our program for the combat of crime so that we may in fact maintain crime, putting an impossible burden on police and other local officials. They must ignore some crimes—especially organized crime—because they serve on the front line of diplomacy between those citizens who want laws enforced and those who do not. On the one hand, there are community interests in morality, governmental efficiency, and law enforcement. But on the other hand there are also community interests in immorality, soft political jobs, favors, domestic tranquility, and law violation. When both sets of interests are powerful, police "on the beat" and their superiors must decide what constitutes an "appropriate level" of law enforcement. As the President's Commission concluded, with reference to organized crime, "Politicians will not act unless the public so demands; but much of the urban public wants the services provided by organized crime and does not wish to disrupt the system that provides these services."[47] Gardiner's study of "Wincanton," a

---

[45] Marshall B. Clinard, "Secondary Community Influences and Juvenile Delinquency," *Annals of the American Academy of Political and Social Science,* 261:42–54, 1949.

[46] For examples of selective obedience see Marshall B. Clinard, *The Black Market* (New York: Rinehart, 1952); Robert E. Lane, "Why Businessmen Violate the Law," *Journal of Criminal Law, Criminology, and Police Science,* 44:151–65, 1953; and Erwin O. Smigel, "Public Attitudes Toward Stealing as Related to the Size of the Victim Organization," *American Sociological Review,* 21:320–27, 1956.

[47] President's Commission on Law Enforcement and Administration of Justice, *Task Force Report: Organized Crime* (Washington, D.C.: Government Printing Office, 1967), pp. 15–16.

middle-sized industrial city where municipal officials had long been paid to overlook illegal gambling, suggested that the citizens approved the gambling or were tolerant of it, but were hostile toward corruption.[48] The citizens, in other words, "display both a desire for or toleration of illicit services and a demand for honesty on the part of local officials." Gardiner concluded that the residents of Wincanton fail to see that a community cannot have illegal gambling without corruption. One outcome of conflicting community demands, with consequent assignment of diplomatic rather than law-enforcement functions to the police, is a negotiated social order. A balance is struck; an "understanding" is operationalized; crime is tolerated.

When a person is caught, the problem is to "fix" things. This occurs very commonly in so-called law-abiding groups in relation to traffic violations, drunken driving, gambling, smuggling, and business crimes. In other circles, fixing occurs in relation to shoplifting, picking pockets, burglary, robbery, and murder. There is a prevalent belief among prisoners that their own cases could have been "fixed" if they had had sufficient money. According to that belief, the only reason for being arrested or convicted is poverty. It is probable that no part of the population is better acquainted with corruption and graft in the legislative, judicial, and executive branches of government than are the professional criminals.

Some cities are under the control of political machines, which are sometimes bipartisan and which continue their control regardless of the party in power. However, whether a city is ruled by a political machine or not, its politicians must render services to those who have elected them, even though the benefactions come from the public treasury and even though their dispensation may be in violation of law. Among the services from which the politicians are most likely to derive the greatest political gains, and even direct financial gains, are those which are rendered to persons who violate the law or who wish to prevent the enactment of laws injurious to them. It is these services which are generally regarded as corruption.[49]

The first of these services is protection of law violators. In response to a questionnaire worded in such a way as to avoid implying any misconduct, 62 percent of the party leaders from eight New Jersey counties said they often helped citizens get things straightened out when they are in difficulty with the law; 72 percent said they often helped deserving people get public jobs.[50] Some politicians go further; they sell illegal licenses to engage in prostitution, gambling, violation of liquor laws, loan-sharking, and other organized crime activities.[51] This form of

[48] John A. Gardiner, *The Politics of Corruption: Organized Crime in an American City* (New York: Russell Sage Foundation, 1970).

[49] For numerous examples, see Jack D. Douglas and John M. Johnson, eds., *Official Deviance: Readings in Malfeasance, Misfeasance, and Other Forms of Corruption* (Philadelphia: Lippincott, 1977).

[50] Richard T. Frost, "Stability and Change in Local Politics," *Public Opinion Quarterly*, 25:230–39, 1961.

[51] See Donald R. Cressey, *Theft of the Nation: The Structure and Operations of Organized Crime in America* (New York: Harper and Row, 1969).

corruption is in fact so important that organized criminals sometimes themselves seek and obtain positions of importance in local politics. More often, they engage in direct bribery, or contribute heavily to political campaigns, or both, in return for their immunity. When these conditions prevail, individual police officers must tolerate violations of law. The chief of police is equally impotent, for he himself is under the control, either directly or indirectly, of the same politicians. The immunity, moreover, is extended to organized criminals even when it becomes evident that this means protection of groups engaged in robbery, burglary, murder, and other serious crimes, as was the case in many of the organized bootlegging groups during the period of national prohibition. Equally important is the immunity granted to many huge and "respectable" business concerns which violate laws dealing with fire hazards, safety devices, sanitation, water and air pollution, and other manufacturing and commercial considerations that are ostensibly regulated by government. Certainly a large part of all campaign contributions comes from those who expect immunity in the violation of the law, and only a few of the persons who expect immunity are organized criminals. The Chamber of Commerce of the United States estimates that three billion dollars are spent annually on bribery, kickbacks, and payoffs in transactions between business and government, between companies, and between management and labor.[52]

Second, many city councilmen, mayors, and other legislators receive support because of the protection they can furnish against injurious legislation. This protection is sometimes sought by organized criminals, but generally, it is more useful to business and labor interests. Public utilities, oil companies, agricultural groups, real estate developers, and liquor groups have been particularly active in this sphere. Many industries make huge contributions to political campaigns in order that they may have the goodwill of those who control the legislatures, thus preventing enactment of legislation that these industries regard as injurious. This is a form of bribery only slightly concealed.

But corrupt officials are not always merely minor or supporting actors in the crimes in which they are involved. A third form of corruption involves the selling of legitimate licenses, contracts for public works, and franchises. Here, corrupt officials are the star actors playing major roles in the criminal dramas. They get rich by charging under-the-table fees for building permits and liquor licenses, and for awarding contracts for buildings, parks, pavements, and services such as garbage collection and street sweeping.[53] The contractors, of course, pass the extra costs along to the consumer The extent to which persons in important political positions become wealthy after securing office is often evidence of the extent of this collusion with private contractors to plunder the public treasury.

[52]Chamber of Commerce of the United States, *White Collar Crime* (Washington, D.C.: U. S. Chamber of Commerce, 1974), pp. 6, 15.
[53]For examples, see Gardiner, *The Politics of Corruption*, pp. 82–92.

A fourth form of political corruption is inherent in the patronage system. In some political organizations each candidate for an elective office is required to agree in advance that the appointive offices will be filled by the organization. A patronage secretary or a patronage committee may be publicly recognized as in charge of this function. The principal opposition to state patronage systems comes from township and county politicians, who insist that patronage is the function of local organizations rather than of state organizations. And the principal opposition to federal patronage comes from state organizations.

It is important to the political organization, whether national, state, or local, that it control patronage, for it is through patronage that many of its services are rendered to individuals and groups. First, it may thus reward its members who have worked hard in election campaigns; the result is appointment of inferior persons whose principal loyalty is to a politician, whose salaries frequently are an incidental part of their incomes, and who sometimes do not even show up for work. Second, through control of patronage the political organization can regulate the granting of immunity, in return for campaign contributions, to those who violate the law. One of the members of the patronage committee in Illinois some years ago was the president of one of the principal banks of the state. He had membership on the patronage committee because the officials of the banks, utility companies, insurance companies, and similar concerns wanted him to be a member—they were interested in the selection of bank examiners, public utility commissioners, and other similar officers, who would be friendly and could be controlled. Nowadays, merit appointments are replacing appointments by patronage committees, primarily because patronage does not meet the needs of present-day political operations, but even highly qualified persons must generally have the right political connections if they are to be appointed to office.[54]

In a fifth form of corruption, a government official conspires with a business-man or labor leader to cheat the citizens represented by the official. For example, companies with a franchise to tow away illegally parked cars might charge citizens an extra dollar for the service, then pay the dollar to a city official for the privilege of holding the franchise. The persons granting the franchises and the persons holding them are costars in this crime.

A sixth form of corruption is fraud in voting. There is no way of knowing how many votes in any given contemporary election are fictitious, but it is certain that, in some elections, some of them are. However, multiple voting, deliberate miscounting of ballots, and theft of ballots cast for opponents all seem to have diminished since the days when all-powerful political machines governed American cities, counties and states.[55]

---

[54]See Frank J. Sorauf, "The Silent Revolution in Patronage," in *The City Boss in America*, ed. Alexander B. Callow, Jr. (New York: Oxford University Press, 1976), pp. 280–88.

[55]See Alexander B. Callow, Jr., "Vote Early and Often," *New York Times Magazine*, September 27, 1964, pp. 60–66; and idem, *The Tweed Ring* (New York: Oxford University Press, 1966).

The seventh form of corruption is similar to the first. But in this form, the relationship is between a corruptee and a corrupter who is also a victim. The small shopkeeper and the automobile driver are sometimes the victim of simple extortion on the part of officials. When a police officer, for a fee, grants a merchant the privilege of violating the law (the first kind of corruption), he or she supports the more important criminal role of the merchant, who is the principal actor. But when a police officer threatens a citizen with harassment until a bribe is paid, the citizen becomes a supporting actor rather than a star. The citizen's role is that of both criminal (briber) and victim.

As a result of these influences which corrupt politics, honest operation of the police and of the courts is limited. Corrupt politics has a more significant relationship to organized crime and to white-collar crime than to juvenile delinquency and the felonies for which persons are committed to prison. Nevertheless, juvenile delinquency and adult violations of the criminal code are intimately related to the politics of the local community. The fact that organized crime and white-collar crime activities float on a swamp of corruption teaches an insidious lesson to American youth, and especially to innercity youth, who, in order to survive, must be astute observers of the facts of life: The government is for sale; lawlessness is the road to wealth; honesty is a pitfall; morality is a trap for suckers. How can a youth be expected to respect authority when the model authority figure, the police officer, is known to be on the payroll of criminals? How can we reasonably expect young people of the inner city to have standards of honesty, decency, and morality higher than the standards they observe in their own public officials?

THE RELIGIOUS INSTITUTION

Because organized religion has been instrumental in developing and maintaining a sacred morality among mankind, and since crime often involves violation of this standard of morality, it may rightfully be concluded that a close relationship exists between crime and the religious institution. After making this observation, some persons go on to make religion the fundamental variable in a theory of crime causation. For example, one Christian criminologist has written, "The Christian believes the underlying cause of criminality is man's alienation from God."[56] From this point of view, the very existence of criminality demonstrates a failure on the part of the institution of religion to train members of society to behave morally, so it is easy to conclude that lack of religious training is the basic cause of crime. However, this conclusion merely emphasizes the fact that some persons commit crimes, and it does not really explain why they do so.

To the extent that criminality and immorality are synonymous, the problem in criminology is to explain or account for the fact that some persons behave immorally and some do not, and it is not sufficient to state merely that the

[56]Richard D. Knudten, *The Christian Encounters Crime in American Society* (St. Louis: Concordia, 1969), p. 7.

absence of morality is the cause of immorality. There is no specific evidence regarding the effect of religion, considered as something different from anticriminal values, on crime. Father Fitzpatrick, who analyzed the relationship of religion to delinquency and crime for President Johnson's Crime Commission, drew the following three conclusions:

(1) The relationship of religion to deviant behavior, in this case crime or delinquency, is very obscure. Religion itself is a very varied experience, and its relationship to social behavior is equally varied. It may be irrelevant to deviant behavior; as an instrument of social control it may seek to prevent deviancy; it may positively provoke deviancy. (2) When religion functions as an element in social control, its role may be very ambiguous. It may become the instrument of interest groups in the struggle for power, either protecting vested interests or becoming the motivating force for revolt. (3) In a number of situations in the United States, religiously related programs involving minority groups or the underprivileged may enjoy a bond of identification with the underprivileged which may enable them to be particularly effective.[57]

An older study indicated that delinquents had more favorable attitudes toward religious issues than did nondelinquents, but a study of 915 girls attending classes in religious instruction revealed that this training "did not contribute to the subjects' ability to apply the principles of moral law to life situations."[58] Similarly, whether or not children attend Sunday school seems to bear only a slight relationship to delinquency. Kvaraceus found that 91 percent of 761 delinquent children were affiliated with some church, and that 54 percent attended church regularly, that 20 percent attended occasionally, and that only 26 percent rarely visited a church. Other studies have reported similar percentages.[59] These studies, of course, do not indicate the percentage of regular church attendants who commit delinquencies, and this percentage is a prerequisite for a detailed analysis of the relationship between church attendance and delinquency.

A questionnaire study of 21,270 Tennessee high school students showed that boys with no religious preference had almost twice as high a delinquency rate as boys with a preference, after the rates had been adjusted for occupational status,

[57] Joseph P. Fitzpatrick, S.J., "The Role of Religion in Programs for the Prevention and Correction of Crime and Delinquency," President's Commission on Law Enforcement and Administration of Justice, *Task Force Report: Juvenile Delinquency and Youth Crime* (Washington, D.C.: Government Printing Office, 1967), pp. 315–30.

[58] Warren C. Middleton and Paul J. Fay, "Attitudes of Delinquent and Non-Delinquent Girls Toward Sunday Observance, the Bible, and War," *Journal of Educational Psychology,* 32:555–58, 1941; Carmen V. Diaz, "A Study of the Ability of Eleventh Grade Girls to Apply the Principles of Moral Law to Actual and Hypothetical Life Situations" (Ph.D. diss., Fordham University, 1952).

[59] William C. Kvaraceus, "Delinquent Behavior and Church Attendance," *Sociology and Social Research,* 28:284–89, 1944; William W. Wattenberg, "Church Attendance and Juvenile Misconduct," *Sociology and Social Research,* 34:195–202, 1950; Sheldon and Eleanor Glueck, *Unraveling Juvenile Delinquency* (New York: Commonwealth Fund, 1950), p. 166; M. Dominic, "Religion and the Juvenile Delinquent," *American Catholic Sociological Review,* 15:256–64, 1954; John Travers and Russel Davis, "A Study of Religious Motivation and Delinquency," *Journal of Educational Sociology,* 34:205–20, 1961.

subject and parent religious participation, age, and family structure. The rates were highest for youths whose parents did not go to church, lowest for those whose parents attended the same church, and intermediate for those whose parents attended different churches. Jews had the lowest rates. Catholics had the highest rates, but black male Catholics had rates much higher than white male Catholics, while white female Catholics had higher rates than black female Catholics. Baptists and fundamentalists had higher rates than nonfundamentalists except in the case of white females, where the rates were about the same.[60]

Among adults in America, Baptists and Catholics have the highest rate of commitment to those prisons which report religious affiliations. However, about two-thirds of the membership in the Roman Catholic and Baptist churches comes from the working class, so it is probable that something other than religious affiliation produces this overrepresentation. A Canadian study showed considerable differences in conviction rates for members of different religious denominations. The highest rate of convictions for indictable offenses per 100,000 population 16 years and older, was 398, for members of Salvation Army. Rates for other denominations were 373 for Roman Catholics, 267 for Anglicans, 244 for Baptists, 237 for Greek Orthodox, 228 for Presbyterians, 212 for United Church, 194 for Lutherans, and 164 for members of the Pentecostal church. The lowest rate, 112, was for Jews.[61] A census taken in the penal institutions of the Netherlands showed that Protestants and Catholics were slightly overrepresented, as compared with the general population of the Netherlands, while "other denominations" were slightly underrepresented.[62]

A study of 13,836 Los Angeles delinquents classified 58 percent of them as Protestant, 35 percent as Catholic, 3 percent as Jewish, and 3 percent as "other." The population of Los Angeles at the time was estimated to include 22 percent Catholics and 7 percent Jews.[63] Jews in all parts of the United States and in Europe also have low crime and delinquency rates, and this condition has been attributed to close family and community ties.[64] An older but rigorous analysis of the differences in crime rates of the several denominations in Hungary also resulted in the conclusion that these differences were due not to the variations in the creeds but to variations in the economic, educational, and family status of the members, to the differences in places of residence, and to variations in age and sex.[65]

[60] Albert Lewis Rhodes and Albert J. Reiss, Jr., "The 'Religious Factor' and Delinquent Behavior," *Journal of Research in Crime and Delinquency*, 7:83–98, 1970.

[61] P. J. Griffen, "Rates of Crime and Delinquency," chap. 4 in *Crime and Its Treatment in Canada*, ed. W. T. McGrath (Toronto: Macmillan, 1965).

[62] W. H. Nagel, "Criminality and Religion," *Tidschrift voor Strafrecht*, 69:263–91, 1960.

[63] Calvin Goldscheider and Jon E. Simpson, "Religious Affiliation and Juvenile Delinquency," *Sociological Inquiry*, 37:397–310, 1967.

[64] Robert A. Silverman, "Criminality Among Jews: An Overview," *Issues in Criminology*, 6:1–38, 1971.

[65] Ervin Hacker, *Der Einfluss der Konfession auf die Kriminalität in Ungarn* (Miskolc, Hungary: Jun, Ludvig, Janovits, 1930).

THE EDUCATIONAL INSTITUTION

Crime and delinquency often are attributed to poor education, just as they are attributed to poor family training and poor religious training. This attribution is more a mere notation of the schools' failure to supply youth with moral and democratic ideals than a theory of delinquency or criminality. It is an expression of indignation by persons who think the difference in delinquency and criminality between the educated and uneducated should be greater than it is. But it is only in recent years that schools have been expected to take over many of the socializing functions of the family and other primary groups, rather than merely specializing on diffusion of knowledge. Even now, schools do not have the specific function of preventing delinquency, although they, like the family, are expected to inculcate juveniles with certain anticriminal values and to provide interesting activities which keep juveniles off the labor market and out of trouble. An eleven-year longitudinal study concluded that school relationships are the third most pervasive relationship in delinquency, following only family and peer group.[66] Another follow-up study, so technically sound that it may be noted as the best study to date of these three relationships, does not even rank the school behind the family and peer group; it found that the school, not the family or "the streets," is the critical social context for the generation of delinquent behavior.[67] Both of these studies, and others, suggest that delinquency and crime are related to the school in much the same way they are related to family conditions, namely, through the effects which school activities have on the students' associations with delinquent and antidelinquent behavior patterns.

On the basis of inadequate statistics, which do not include white-collar crimes, it appears that crime decreases with the amount of formal education. Of the Canadians convicted of indictable crimes in 1961, the rate per 100,000 population 16 years of age and over was 242 for those with no schooling, 369 for those with elementary school only, 252 for those with a high school education, and 66 for those with an educational level above high school.[68] A 1974 nationwide survey of Americans in the custody of state correctional authorities indicated that 99 percent had not completed college, 61 percent had not completed high school, and 26 percent had not gone beyond the eighth grade.[69] Statistics compiled by states show the same low levels of education. Tests given to males received by California prisons each year place about 40 percent below the eighth grade and about 10 percent below the fifth grade; 4 percent are illiterate.[70] It is probable that these levels of educational achievement are lower than the levels among nonoffenders in

[66]J. Feldhusen, J. Thurston, and J. Benning, "A Longitudinal Study of Delinquency and Other Aspects of Children's Behavior," *International Journal of Criminology and Penology*, 1:341–51, 1973.

[67]Elliott and Voss, *Delinquency and Dropout*, p. 204.

[68]Griffen, "Rates of Crime and Delinquency," p. 79.

[69]James J. Stephan, *Survey of Inmates of State Correctional Facilities, 1974* National Prisoner Statistics Special Report No. SD-NPS-SR-R, March, 1976 (Washington, D.C.: Government Printing Office, 1976), p. 24.

[70]*California Prisoners, 1972* (Sacramento: California Department of Corrections, 1973), p. 27.

California, but no comparable information for the general state populations is available.

A large proportion of delinquents do poor school work, and they are retarded in reading, writing, and arithmetic. In Ghana, 25 percent of a group of delinquents had never attended school, and 52 percent had four years or less of schooling; but only 1 percent of a control group made up of nondelinquents had as little as four years of schooling.[71] Among the males who were born in Norway in 1933 and who had become offenders by the time they were 25 years old, 32 percent had some education beyond elementary school, as compared to 52 percent of the nonoffenders who were born in 1933. Two percent of the offenders and 10 percent of the nonoffenders had four or more years of education beyond elementary school.[72] A similar study of all boys born in Stockholm in 1940 indicated that among those who had acquired a criminal record by age 21, the conviction rate among those who had completed only primary school was ten times as great as the rate among those who had graduated from *gymnasium* (roughly equivalent to junior college).[73] The incidence of juvenile delinquency among the 30 to 40 percent of American children who drop out of high school is about ten times higher than the rate in the total youth population or for high school graduates.[74] Interviews with a sample (N = 2510) of all American men who were 20 to 30 years old in 1974 showed high negative correlations between educational level and arrest, juvenile court appearances, conviction for a crime, and imprisonment.[75] The percentages are shown in Table 19.

If these differences are viewed uncritically, the institution of education may be considered a tremendous success in preventing delinquency and crime. After all, the higher the educational level, the lower the crime rate. But in fact these differences do not show that formal education, in itself, stops people from committing crimes, for the formal educational level may merely reflect economic status, home conditions, and several other conditions which affect the probabilities for contacts with delinquent and criminal behavior patterns, as well as the

---

[71]S. Kirson Weinberg, "Juvenile Delinquency in Ghana: A Comparative Analysis of Delinquents and Non-Delinquents," *Journal of Criminal Law, Criminology, and Police Science,* 55:471–81, 1964.

[72]Nils Christie, *Unge Norske Lovovertredere* [Young Norwegian lawbreakers] (Oslo: Universitetsforlaget, 1960), pp. 144–47.

[73]Jackson Toby, "Affluence and Adolescent Crime," appendix H in President's Commission, *Task Force Report: Juvenile Delinquency and Youth Crime,* pp. 132–44.

[74]Lucius F. Cervantes, *The Drop Out* (Ann Arbor: University of Michigan Press, 1965), p. 197. See also Daniel Schreiber, "Juvenile Delinquency and the School Dropout Problem," *Federal Probation,* 27:15–19, 1963; Delbert S. Elliott, "Delinquency, School Attendance, and Dropout," *Social Problems,* 13:307–14, 1966; Jon E. Simpson and Maurice D. Van Arsdol, Jr., "Residential History and Educational Status of Delinquents and Nondelinquents," *Social Problems,* 15:25–40, 1967; and C. Ray and Ina A. Jeffery, "Delinquency and Dropouts: An Experimental Program in Behavior Change," *Canadian Journal of Corrections,* 12:47–58, 1970.

[75]John A. O'Donnell, Harwin L. Voss, Richard R. Clayton, Gerald T. Slatin, and Robin G. W. Room, *Young Men and Drugs—A Nationwide Survey* (Washington, D. C.: National Institute on Drug Abuse, Research Monograph No. 5, 1976), pp. 89–93.

Table 19 *Official Actions Accounted for by Different Educational Levels*

Respondents' Education	Total	Nontraffic Arrest (Percent)	Juvenile court Appearance (Percent)	Conviction of Crime (Percent)	Sentenced Served (Percent)
Less than high school	394	53	22	27	18
High school graduate	933	32	8	11	5
Some college	713	28	5	10	2
College graduate	470	17	2	4	—
Total	2510	31	8	12	6

SOURCE: O'Donnell et al., *Young Men and Drugs*, pp. 89–93.

probabilities of being arrested. Like the home, the school (1) may be located in a delinquency area, (2) may affect the prestige values of various types of persons the child later will encounter, (3) may fail to present antidelinquency behavior patterns, or (4) may provide pleasant or unpleasant experiences which affect the child's associations with delinquency behavior patterns.[76]

Perhaps the school's influence on delinquency rates has been largely through the last process, and in this respect it is a failure. The fact that truancy and delinquency are closely correlated by area, and the fact that truancy so frequently precedes delinquencies involving acts which would be crimes if committed by adults is evidence of this. Among some groups of juveniles appearing before juvenile courts, as many as 60 percent have truanted habitually. Frum found that 23 percent of 148 cases of adult recidivism started with juvenile truancy or incorrigibility.[77]

Moreover, the way the school handles its academic work, and the way it structures relationships between students and students as well as between students and teachers, is highly relevant to explanation of why school "successes" (persons with much education) have lower delinquency and crime rates than school "failures" (persons who, in a system supposedly requiring much education for all, have only little education). A sequence along the following lines seems to be at work: (1) Some students, especially working-class students, lack the role-playing abilities necessary to meet the demands of the teachers and, especially, of the other students in school. (2) These students enter school at a competitive disadvantage because their life experiences have not provided the social skills; verbal skills; attitudes toward students, teachers, and scholarship; and familiarity with pencils and reading materials that are common among other students. To

[76]See Chapter 10 above.

[77]Harold S. Frum, "Adult Criminal Offense Trends Following Juvenile Delinquency," *Journal of Criminal Law, Criminology, and Police Science,* 49:29–49, 1958.

take a simple example, some first-graders have never seen an adult reading a newspaper, magazine, or book. (3) These disadvantages are enlarged rather than diminished when teachers and other students assume that the students experiencing them are bad, undesirable, stupid, or even sick, and then devote their time, attention, and affection to students assumed not to have these characteristics.[78] In high schools, this "locking out" process has been shown to occur even among students who have verbal abilities such that they are capable of excellent work.[79] (4) The eventual outcome is alienation from school, truancy, drop out, or the passive compliance necessary to graduate from high school, but without the social skills necessary for getting along with employers, fellow workers, and in unfamiliar settings generally.[80] (5) Some such youngsters do not become delinquent; they are so well integrated into families or peer groups placing a high value on conformity and educational success that they do not even become truant.[81] But others are not thus "held into" the legitimate system for achieving success, and they drift into association with delinquent subcultures.[82]

The school experience, thus, is neither interesting nor pleasant for some students. Indeed, as schools themselves have in recent years increasingly become centers of delinquency, including violent delinquency, the educational experience is becoming unpleasant for more and more students. A survey of 750 school districts suggested that in the three years between 1970 and 1973 assaults on students increased by 85 percent, assaults on teachers by 77 percent, robberies by 37 percent, and rapes and attempted rapes by 40 percent.[83] The nature of formal school activities is probably related to these and other delinquencies, as is the fact that no employment is available for students who might otherwise drop out.

A study of 21,720 boys and girls in grades seven through twelve in the schools of Nashville indicated that delinquents and truants are more likely to want to quit school and accept the conforming goal of getting a job than they are to want to quit school because they regard the norm of compulsory school attendance as

[78] Walter E. Schafer and Kenneth Polk, "Delinquency and the Schools," in President's Commission, *Task Force Report: Juvenile Delinquency and Youth Crime*, pp. 222–77. See also John B. Braithwaite, "Competitiveness in Schools and Delinquency," *Australian Journal of Social Issues*, 10:107–10, 1975.

[79] Delbert S. Elliott, Harwin L. Voss, and Aubrey Wendling, "Capable Dropouts and the Social Milieu of the High School," *Journal of Educational Research*, 60:180–86, 1966; and Harwin L. Voss, Aubrey Wendling, and Delbert S. Elliott, "Some Types of High School Dropouts," *Journal of Educational Research*, 59:363–68, 1966.

[80] See James F. Short, Jr., and Fred L. Strodtbeck, *Group Process and Gang Delinquency* (Chicago: University of Chicago Press, 1965), pp. 214–47; Robert A. Gordon, "Social Level, Disability, and Gang Interaction," *American Journal of Sociology*, 73:42–62, 1967; and Jack L. Roach and Orville R. Gursslin, "The Lower Class, Status Frustration, and Social Disorganization," *Social Forces*, 43:506–17, 1974.

[81] See David H. Hargreaves, *Social Relations in a Secondary School* (London: Routledge, 1967); and Travis Hirschi, *Causes of Delinquency* (Berkeley: University of California Press, 1969), pp. 157–58.

[82] Schafer and Polk, "Delinquency and the Schools," pp. 230–31. See also Kenneth Polk and William Pink, "Youth Culture and the School: A Replication," *British Journal of Sociology*, 22:160–71, 1971.

[83] United States Senate Subcommittee to Investigate Juvenile Delinquency, *Preliminary Report* (Washington, D. C.: Government Printing Office, April, 1975).

coercive.[84] This suggests that truancy and delinquency might be ameliorated by an opportunity to undertake a productive role in the labor force.

For four years Elliott and Voss followed about 2600 students who entered eight different junior high schools as ninth graders in 1963. They found that the delinquency rate was significantly higher among those who continued in high school than it was among those who dropped out. Further, there was considerable evidence that the dropouts' involvement in delinquency began while the subjects were still in school and was primarily a response to experiences in the school. Departure from school reduced the dropouts' delinquent behavior and the likelihood of police contact.[85] This finding is consistent with the observation that there is a temporary decline in delinquency during the summer months, and that it reaches its peak in the hours immediately after school and decreases during the weekend.[86]

In a study of the male high school students in a small city in the Pacific Northwest, Polk and Halferty found that blue-collar students who made A's and B's had the same low rate of delinquency (4 percent) as did the white-collar students earning the same grades. However, about one-fifth to one-fourth of the students doing poor or failing work in school became delinquent, whether they were blue collar or white collar, and the remaining four-fifths to three-fourths did not.[87] In explaining these and other findings, Polk noted that in small towns some but not all school failures are locked out of the system which supports accomplishments by legitimate means, and some but not all of the locked-out students drift into trouble-making subcultures.[88] Thus, about 80 percent of the students who did poor and failing work in school either were not locked out of the legitimate system or did not participate in the delinquent subculture and therefore did not become delinquent, regardless of social class. Karacki and Toby have made essentially the same observation about the relationship between commitment to school, participation in a delinquent subculture (which they unfortunately called "the youth culture"), and delinquency:

[84] Albert Lewis Rhodes and Albert J. Reiss, Jr., "Apathy, Truancy, and Delinquency as Adaptations to School Failure," *Social Forces*, 48:12–22, 1969.

[85] Elliott and Voss, *Delinquency and Dropout*, pp. 121, 206.

[86] Delbert S. Elliott, "Delinquency, School Attendance, and Dropout," *Social Problems*, 13:307–14, 1966; William C. Kvaraceus, *Juvenile Delinquency and the School* (New York: World Book Company, 1945).

[87] Kenneth Polk and David S. Halferty, "Adolescence, Commitment, and Delinquency," *Journal of Research in Crime and Delinquency*, 3:82–96, 1966. See also Walter E. Schafer and Kenneth Polk, eds., *Schools and Delinquency* (Englewood Cliffs, N. J.: Prentice-Hall, 1972); M. Gold and D. Mann, "Delinquency as Defense," *American Journal of Orthopsychiatry*, 42:463–79, 1972; D. H. Kelly and R. W. Balch, "Social Origins and School Failure: A Re-examination of Cohen's Theory of Work ng-Class Delinquency," *Pacific Sociological Review*, 14:413–30, 1971; and D. H. Kelly and W. T. Pink, "School Commitment, Youth, Rebellion, and Delinquency," *Criminology*, 10:473–85, 1973.

[88] Kenneth Polk, "Delinquency and Community Action in Nonmetropolitan Areas," appendix R in President's Commission, *Task Force Report: Juvenile Delinquency and Youth Crime*, pp. 343–52.

It is our impression that the Dukes failed to develop early in adolescence commitments to adult roles and values which would have mobilized their interests and energies and which would have served to relate them to school and work. In lieu of this, they drew instead upon the youth culture for meaning and purpose, and out of this emerged a delinquent gang. . . . This involvement in the youth culture was incompatible with diligent performance in school.[89]

The findings of the Elliott and Voss study, which used both official delinquencies and self-reported delinquent acts as measures of delinquency, are consistent with these observations. However, Polk and Halferty, like Karacki and Toby, give the impression that the delinquent subculture is "out there" somewhere, existing rather independently of the school, and Elliott and Voss show that this is not the case. Moreover, they show that the locking-out process and exposure to delinquent behavior patterns occur simultaneously, and within the context of the school. For the males in their study, the most powerful predictors of delinquency were found to be limited academic achievement, alienation in school, association with delinquent classmates, and commitment to peers. For females, the best predictors were found to be parental rejection, alienation in school, association with delinquent classmates, and commitment to peers.[90]

Association with delinquent classmates or having friends who have been picked up by the police is not necessarily association with delinquent behavior patterns. The relationship may be a peripheral one, as in the case of students who are "friends" but do not hang out together. On the other hand, once boys or girls are delinquent, they are likely to select as friends other delinquent boys and girls. For statistical purposes, however, it is not incorrect to assume that the more delinquent friends a student has, the greater is the exposure to behavior patterns favorable to delinquency. These behavior patterns are what constitute a delinquent subculture, and they thrive in the school as well as on the street, as part of what has been called the "youth culture." Elliott and Voss have shown that failure and social isolation in school are not sufficient to account for a capable student's decision to drop out of school, and their observation about dropouts can, with the changes in wording inserted in brackets, be read as a statement about delinquent behavior generally:

Exposure to dropout is a necessary variable in the causal chain leading to dropout. The argument is essentially the same as the one developed for patterns of differential association and exposure to delinquency. . . . The probability of dropout [delinquency] is maximized when an individual has contact with peers, parents or siblings who have dropped out [participated in delinquency] and who encourage dropping out [delinquency] by placing little value on education [antidelinquent behavior patterns].[91]

[89]Larry Karacki and Jackson Toby, "The Uncommitted Adolescent: Candidate for Gang Socialization," *Sociological Inquiry*, 32:203–15, 1962.

[90]Elliott and Voss, *Delinquency and Dropout*, pp. 186, 204.

[91]Ibid., p. 34. See also pp. 157–159.

WAR

Many persons have asserted that crimes increase during war and postwar periods. This assertion is not necessarily incorrect, but it is an oversimplification of a very complex relationship. The following five propositions are a more adequate statement of the facts.

First, the official statistics on juvenile delinquency show a general trend toward an increase in wartime.[92] The trend, however, is a statistical artifact: rates go down in some communities within a nation, while going up in a larger number of communities. Furthermore, the statistics of arrests and convictions of juveniles are not a certain measure of the delinquent behavior of juveniles. In Liverpool, England, the number of convictions of juveniles increased during the First World War, but the number of unofficial actions in the form of warnings decreased by approximately an equal amount.

Four explanations of the apparent increase in juvenile delinquency in wartime have been suggested.

1. One theory attributes the rise to an increase in a "contagion of violence." Children in wartime develop an admiration for the soldier. They are furnished with war toys; they play war games and in other ways carry the patterns of warfare into their lives. This theory makes sense of increases in assaults and similar crimes of violence among juveniles during wartime, but it does not explain the rises in rates of nonviolent offenses.

2. Another explanation, popular between World War I and World War II, was that the increase in delinquency is due to an increase in economic hardships due to blockades, rationing systems, and reduced earnings. This notion may have some relevance for devastated areas, but in the United States during World War II, the Korean War, and the Vietnam War, delinquency increased in the midst of unusual prosperity.

3. A third explanation is that the increase in juvenile delinquency is due to emotional strain in wartime. The inadequacy of this explanation is seen in the fact that some kinds of delinquency increase and some kinds decrease in wartime. It is difficult to understand why emotional strain should produce an increase in one kind of delinquency and a decrease in another kind.

4. The explanation which seems to best fit the facts is that juvenile delinquency increases in wartime as a result of changes in the family and other local community institutions.[93] Parents join the army, engage in war industries and other war activities, and neglect the supervision of their children. At the same

[92]See Edward R. Schwartz, "Statistics of Juvenile Delinquency in the United States," *Annals of the American Academy of Political and Social Science,* 261:9–13, 1949; Martin H. Neumeyer, "Delinquency Trends in Wartime," *Sociology and Social Research,* 29:262–75, 1945; Walter C. Reckless, "The Impact of War on Crime, Delinquency and Prostitution," *American Journal of Sociology,* 48 378–86, 1942.

[93]See Edith Abbott, "Juvenile Delinquency During the First World War: Notes on the British Experience, 1914–1918," *Social Service Review,* 17:192–212, 1943.

time, many other agencies which ordinarily present antidelinquency values break down as a result of the withdrawal of personnel, lack of interest of adults, and the diversion of money to other uses. With increased mobility, children more frequently come into contact with persons who have delinquent values, and they assimilate delinquent ways of behaving. In invaded and occupied territories, children learn that it is not immoral to steal from, or even to kill, the invader. It has been determined, moreover, that these changes also affect the postwar delinquency rates of children too young to get very involved in delinquency during the war years. In a study of England, Wales, and Scotland, Wilkins found that the highest postwar (1948–1957) delinquency rates occurred among those children who were 4 or 5 years old during some part of World War II (1939–1945). Further, youths aged 17 and 21 in 1955 had delinquency rates higher than would be expected on the basis of the delinquency rates of youths whose seventeenth and twenty-first birthdays fell in other years.[94] A study of children reared in Denmark during the nation's critical war years (1943–1944) showed similar results.[95]

Second, the absolute number of adult crimes decreases during wartime because of the mobilization of the young-adult population, but the ratio of crimes committed by adult civilians to the number of adult civilians in the population remains relatively constant.[96] The adult-female crime rate increased greatly in Germany and Austria during both world wars, presumably because females assumed the economic and social roles of the males. To a lesser extent, this also occurred in the United States during World War II.

Third, special wartime regulations are violated with great frequency. There is widespread evidence of extensive violation of price-ceiling and rationing regulations in the United States during World War II.[97] Similarly, the Vietnam War was accompanied by widespread violations of the Selective Service Act. The number of defendants who appeared before U.S. District Courts for draft evasion soared from 516 in 1966 to 2973 in 1971.

Fourth, postwar crime waves are confined largely to countries which suffer rather complete disintegration of their economic, political, and social systems as a result of the war. Earlier studies have shown that serious crimes increased significantly in France after the Revolution of 1884, in the United States after the Civil War, in Germany and Austria after the war of 1866, in Germany and France

[94]Leslie T. Wilkins, *Delinquent Generations* (London: Home Office Studies in the Causes of Delinquency and the Treatment of Offenders, Report No. 3, 1961), pp. 3, 7–9.

[95]Karl O. Christiansen, "Delinquent Generations in Denmark," *British Journal of Criminology*, 3:259–64, 1964.

[96]Edwin H. Sutherland, "Crime," in *American Society in Wartime*, ed. William F. Ogburn (Chicago: University of Chicago Press, 1943), pp. 185–206; and Yael Hassin and Menashem Amir, "Business (Crime) As Usual in Wartime Conditions Among Offenders in Israel," *Journal of Criminal Law and Criminology*, 66:491–95, 1976.

[97]Frank E. Hartung, "White-Collar Offenses in the Wholesale Meat Industry in Detroit," *American Journal of Sociology*, 56:25–35, 1950; Clinard, *Black Market*, pp. 28–50, 115–204.

after the Franco-Prussian War of 1870–1871, and in Germany and Austria after the First World War.[98] But in nations which did not experience a great disintegration of social institutions, such as England and the United States after both world wars, the crime rates seem to remain rather constant in prewar, war, and postwar periods.

This seems to be adequate rebuttal of the argument that young men who have engaged in physical violence during wars will continue similar activities when they return to civilian life. Furthermore, after World War I it was observed that when former servicemen were committed to prison, they were most likely, in comparison with those who had not seen war service, to be committed for fraud, embezzlement, and nonsupport, and least likely to be imprisoned for homicide, burglary, assault, and rape. After World War II this same tendency was found. James V. Bennett, then director of the United States Bureau of Prisons, reported that the offenses most commonly committed by veterans sentenced to federal prisons were embezzlement, fraud, and forgery, while "robbery and homicide, the violent crimes for which one might expect a high proportion of veterans, were well down the list."[99] Bennett indicated further that the imprisonment rate for veterans in all age groups from 25 to 54 was lower than the rate for nonveterans; the 20 to 24 age category, however, had a larger proportion of veterans among the prisoners than were in the general population. He explained these variations in terms of the selective processes of the armed forces.

Fifth, there is a tendency for *homicide* to increase in postwar periods as compared to prewar periods, especially in victorious nations suffering heavy wartime casualties. Further, a recent study of 110 nations and 14 different wars found that a postwar increase in the rate of homicides known to the police was much more likely to characterize combatant nations than neutral nations, such as Norway in World War I, Switzerland in World War II, Turkey in the Middle East Six-Day War of 1967, and Burma in the Vietnam War.[100]

The extensive statistics on homicide collected for this important and difficult study are inconsistent with six of the seven popular explanations of wartime increases and decreases in general crime rates, some of which are mentioned above. Either the theories are incorrect or changes in homicide rates are not generated by the same conditions generating changes in general crime rates. First,

---

[98]Edith Abbott, "The Civil War and the Crime Wave of 1860–1870," *Social Service Review*, 1:212–34, 1927; Franz Exner, *Krieg und Kriminalität in Oesterreich* (Vienna: Hölder-Pichler-Tempsky, 1972); Moritz Liepman, *Krieg und Kriminalität in Deutschland* (Stuttgart: Deutsche Verlagsanstalt, 1930).

[99]James V. Bennett, "The Ex-GI in Federal Prisons," *Proceedings of the American Correctional Association*, 1953, pp. 131–36; and idem, "The Criminality of Veterans," *Federal Probation*, 28:40–42, 1954. See also John C. Spencer, *Crime and the Services* (London: Routledge and Kegan Paul, 1954); and Harry Willbach, "Recent Crimes and the Veterans," *Journal of Criminal Law and Criminology*, 38:501–08, 1948.

[100]Dand Archer and Rosemary Gartner, "Violent Acts and Violent Times: A Comparative Approach to Postwar Homicide Rates," *American Sociological Review*, 41:937–63, 1976.

the *social solidarity model*, which suggests that wars increase social solidarity and, as a result, reduce crime rates, was not supported because postwar homicide rates were generally higher than prewar rates for combatant nations. Second, the *social disorganization model*, which suggests that wars increase crime because they lessen social integration, especially among defeated nations, was not supported because postwar increases in homicide rates were more frequent among victorious nations than defeated ones. Third, the *economic conditions model*, which suggests that crime rates decrease in periods of economic health (whether during a war or shortly thereafter), was not supported because nations with improved economies as well as nations with worsened economies experienced postwar increases in homicide rates. Fourth, the *catharsis model*, which suggests that wars substitute public violence for private violence, was not supported because the nations with the most fatal experiences in war were precisely those most likely to show homicide increases. Fifth, the *violent veterans model*, which suggests that men who kill during wartime will continue to kill after the armistice, was not supported because the postwar changes in the homicide rates of women were comparable to those of men. Sixth, the *statistical artifacts model*, which suggests that changes in wartime or postwar crime rates are due to demographic artifacts such as changes in age structure and sex structure, was not supported because homicide rates in the United States increased among all age groups during the Vietnam war.

The Archer and Gartner analysis of homicide statistics *did* support the *legitimation of violence model*, which suggests that some members of a warring society are influenced by lessons learned in wartime, when a society reverses its customary prohibitions against killing and instead honors acts of violence that would be regarded as murderous in peacetime. The authors found, as indicated above, that most of the combatant nations in their study experienced substantial postwar increases in their rates of homicide, and that these increases did not occur as frequently among a control group of noncombatant nations. Indeed, postwar increases were more frequent among warring nations with large numbers of combat deaths. The legitimation of violence model suggests that sanctioned wartime killing depicted in literature, news stories, billboards, songs, and propaganda has a residual effect on the level of homicide in peacetime because the wartime activities increase the probability that violence will be regarded as a justifiable means of settling disputes among relatives and acquaintances. It does *not* suggest a comparable mechanism whereby sanctioned wartime violence has a residual effect on the levels of theft, burglary, and white-collar crimes, which also increase among many combatant nations in postwar periods.

THE MASS MEDIA

In 1892 Enrico Ferri, the Italian criminological pioneer, directed attention to what he called the "unfavorable effect" of popular literature, daily newspapers, and illustrated journals on the crime problem.[101] Almost a century later, most Americans place at least some of the blame for delinquency and crime on the mass media of communication, and especially on television. Placing such blame is justified, but it says nothing about how media presentations might "work" to produce either individual criminality or high crime rates. Little direct support for the idea that the mass media overcome the influences of the family, school, and other social institutions and thereby produce individual cases of delinquency or criminality can be found in the statistics on delinquency and crime. People all over the United States read the same newspapers and see the same movies and television shows, and yet they differ greatly among themselves in regard to criminality. Even when the communicator deliberately intends to modify people's attitudes, which is certainly not the case among the personnel of the communication agencies which are said to contribute to crime, there is a great deal of variation in the response. Berelson, an American expert on such matters even before television became prominent, said that "effects upon the audience do not follow directly from and in correspondence with the intent of the communicator and the content of the communication. The predispositions of the reader or listener are deeply involved in the situation, and may operate to block or modify the intended effect or even to set up a boomerang effect." This is the same as saying that only "some kinds of communication on some kinds of issues, brought to the attention of some kinds of people under some kinds of conditions, have some kinds of effects."[102] Hundreds of laboratory experiments and other studies on the effects of film presentations have confirmed this observation.[103]

News Media and Crime

American newspapers and television news programs have been severely criticized for the part they play in relation to crime. The following charges are made against them. First, they promote crime by constantly advertising it and exaggerating its incidence. Second, they interfere with justice by "trial by news media," by distortion of news, and by providing advance information to the public, including criminals, regarding the plans of the police and prosecutors. Third, they ordinarily promote indifference to crime, but on occasion create public panic with reference to crime, both of which interfere with efforts to prevent crime and in other ways to reduce its incidence.

[101]Enrico Ferri, "Les Microbes de Monde Criminel et l'art Populaire," in idem. *Les Crimenels dans l'art et la Litérature,* trans. Euguen Laurent, 2d ed. (Paris, 1902). Cited by Stephen Schafer, *Introduction to Criminology* (Reston. Va.: Reston Publishing Company, 1976), p. 96.

[102]B. Berelson, "Communications and Public Opinion," in *Communications in Modern Society,* ed. W. Schramm (Urbana, Ill.: University of Illinois Press, 1948), pp. 168–85.

[103]Many of these studies have been summarized and analyzed in Gary Steiner, *People Look at Television* (New York: Knopf, 1963); Harry Skornia, *Television and Society* (New York: McGraw-Hill, 1965); Robert M. Liebert, Emily S. Davidson, and John M. Neale, *The Early Window: Effects of Television on Children and Youth* (New York: Pergamon, 1973); and Victor B. Cline, ed., *Where Do You Draw the Line? An Exploration into Media Violence, Pornography, and Censorship* (Provo, Utah: Brigham Young University Press, 1974).

The desirability of publishing crime news is not here in question. Rather it is the amount and style of the crime news. English newspapers and television programs present crime news in the form of brief factual statements. American crime news is presented vividly and sometimes not distastefully to the reader.[104] Because nothing is said about the millions of persons who lead consistently law-abiding lives, the impression is created that crime is the customary mode of life. Conceivably, this publicity given to crime creates and perpetuates an attitude of indifference to ordinary criminal offenses among persons who are not the direct victims of them. On the other hand, the publicity given to certain sensational crimes does rouse the public to action, and this action could culminate in the creation of strong anticriminal influences in the community. Usually, however, the public action merely consists of requesting the legislatures to increase the severity of punishments for the type of crime in question, after which the whole thing is forgotten.[105]

The direct effect of the constant presentation of crime news to the public cannot be demonstrated in specific criminal cases. Occasionally, a criminal states that he got the idea for a crime from a newspaper or television account of the activities of another criminal. But most "crime waves" are fabrications of the press: a sensational crime is committed and given wide publicity in one community; that type of crime becomes news; editors begin publicizing hitherto unnoticed crimes of the same type in other parts of the country; and newspaper readers get the impression that the influence of the criminal whose offense was first publicized is spreading throughout the country.

On occasion, news media glorify specific criminals and, consequently, increase their prestige among other criminals and among youths residing in high delinquency areas. Newspaper and television publicity, like commitment to a prison for adults, contributes immensely to one's status in some delinquent groups. Further, news accounts contribute considerably to the self-esteem of professional criminals, who generally are among the most enthusiastic followers of the crime news.

Also, newspapers sometimes interfere with the course of justice by what has been called "trial by newspaper," but which now must also be called "trial by television." Prior to the trial and during the trial, the reporters present such evidence as they have, which is likely to be partisan information, again and again, until the public accepts the implied verdict of the news media and thereafter cannot easily be shaken in its opinion. The news persons' sources of information are almost always the office of the prosecuting attorney or the police; the defendant's version of the case is ignored until the time of the trial itself. A fair

[104]See Alfred Friendly and Ronald Goldfarb, *Crime and Publicity: The Impact of News on the Administration of Justice* (New York: Twentieth Century Fund, 1967).
[105]See Edwin H. Sutherland, "The Diffusion of Sexual Psychopath Laws," *American Journal of Sociology*, 56:142–48, 1950.

trial under such circumstances becomes almost imposs ble, especially in communities where the judges are elected and where they are afraid of arousing public antagonism. It is quite certain that under such circumstances some innocent persons are convicted, and that many persons who are punished severely would otherwise be given light penalities. However, the number of cases which attract this detailed and continued attention is not large.

President Johnson's National Crime Commission pointed out that newspaper, television, and radio reporting are essential to the administration of justice, but the commission also pointed out that a fair trial can be held only if the evidence is presented in the courtroom, not in the press, and jurors do not come to their task prejudiced by publicity. The conflict is not between a hero and a bad guy; it is between two good guys—free press and free trial. The commission cited two recent United States Supreme Court decisions which held that the defendant did not get a fair trial because of prejudicial publicity. In one case, the trial was turned into a "Roman holiday" by the press, and in the other case the presence of television and still cameras in the courtroom during the trial destroyed the "judicial serenity and calm" necessary for a fair trial. Several agencies, including the New York City Police Department and the United States Department of Justice, have restricted the information which law-enforcement officers can disclose to the press prior to a trial.[106] The American Bar Association, similarly, has published rules regarding the release of information to the press by law-enforcement officers and judicial employees.

News media, because they are business concerns operated for the purpose of profits, are concerned with arousing emotions rather than giving the reader an understanding of the crime situation. Their primary interest is in increasing their own circulation or audiences so that advertising rates can be raised. Public welfare is secondary. Accordingly, presentation of crime news sometimes is designed to throw the public into a panic. In England, reporters deal with crime news as they do with sickness and financial dangers, that is, quietly and factually. American newspersonnel, on the other hand, either have not realized the dangers of panics of this nature, or they do not care about them, and continue to make the crime stories as colorful as possible.[107] Moreover, the public gets outmoded notions of "inborn criminality," distorted notions about the nature and success of probation and parole, and sensational, "tough" punitive policies rather than a constructive approach to problems of crime causation, law enforcement, and crime control. Taft and England have observed that reporters have a tendency to find trivial motives for crime because the more shockingly trivial the alleged motive, the

---

[106]President's Commission on Law Enforcement and Administration of Justice, *Task Force Report: The Courts* (Washington, D.C.: Government Printing Office, 1967), pp. 48–50.

[107]National Advisory Commission on Civil Disorders, *Report* (Washington, D.C.: Government Printing Office, 1968), pp. 201–2. See also American Newspaper Publishers Association, *Reporting the Detroit Riot* (New York: American Newspaper Publishers Association, 1968).

more newsworthy it becomes, especially when heinous offenses are involved—"I wanted to see what it was like to kill someone," "I stabbed Pa because he was always criticizing me," "We set fire to the school because the gym teacher bawled us out."[108]

Crime Dramatization

Judicial, psychological, sociological, and literary experts continue to disagree about the effect of television dramas on delinquency and crime, just as a generation ago they disagreed as to the effects of movies, radio, and comic books, and before that were in disagreement about the effects of dime novels and pulp magazines.

The extent of the disagreement seems to have been reduced by an extensive study launched in 1969 by the Surgeon General's Scientific Advisory Committee on Television and Social Behavior, but the controversy continues to thrive nevertheless, perhaps because the committee gave so little time and attention specifically to delinquency and crime. The study was of the characteristics of television programs and their audiences, and of the potential impact of violent programs on the behavior of viewers. Most of the work was done by independent researchers who seemed preoccupied with aggression, whether of the criminal variety or not. The committee published an official report and five volumes of research papers in 1972.[109] There is little or no disagreement about one set of the committee's findings, namely that television has since the time of its commercialization about thirty years ago, become an increasing part of the lives of an increasing number of people, and that its dramatic content is highly laced with violence. These findings may be summarized in three propositions.

First, more and more people have ready access to the medium. Youngsters 16 years of age have spent as much time watching television as they have spent in school and have spent more time watching it than they have in any other single activity except sleep. Second, for most persons, but particularly for the poor, television is perceived as the most credible and believable source of information concerning the world as it really is. Third, the menu offered by television is saturated with violent content, including incidents of persons intentionally doing injury to each other. Between the ages of 5 and 14 the average American child witnesses on television the destruction of about thirteen thousand human beings.

Implied in these propositions is a hint at what is perhaps the major effect of crime dramatization generally, not just of the dramatization of violence—creation

---

[108]Donald R. Taft and Ralph W. England, Jr., *Criminology*, 4th ed. (New York: Macmillan, 1964), p. 211. See also Britt-Mari Persson Blegvad, "Newspapers and Rock and Roll Riots in Copenhagen," *Acta Sociologica* (Copenhagen), 7:151–78, 1964.

[109]Surgeon General's Scientific Advisory Committee on Television and Social Behavior, *Television and Growing Up: The Impact of Televised Violence* (Washington, D.C.: Government Printing Office, 1972); and George A. Comstock and Eli Rubenstein, eds., *Television and Social Behavior*, vols. 1–5 (Washington, D.C.: Government Printing Office, 1972).

and perpetuation of an attitude of indifference to ordinary delinquency and crime among persons who are not the direct victims of delinquents or criminals. The committee did not study this subject directly. However, it is reasonable to infer that, because television dramas create the impression that crime is rather routine fare, the viewing public becomes indifferent about ordinary offenses such as burglary and larceny, and does not even show much concern for any but the most sensational crimes of violence. In this respect, television dramatizations of crime have effects similar to the effects of the way news about crime is presented in newspapers and on radio and television. The two sources of information about crime—news and dramatization—seem to complement each other in this respect.

In courthouses, prosecutors, public defenders, and judges are likely to see so many cases of criminality that they experience a blunting of the indignation regarding crime that persons in, say, a university are likely to have. Several studies have shown that a similar kind of psychological blunting, a kind of "tuning out," occurs as persons watch frequent dramatizations of violence on television. One such study even found that physiological changes accompanying emotional reactions to violence were diminished in a "high TV exposure" group of children, as compared with a "low TV exposure" group.[110] Thus, it is not unreasonable to believe that frequent dramatizations of crime, violent or not, reduce the degree of conscience and concern when real crimes are committed and, therefore, contribute indirectly to high crime rates.[111] A population for whom crime is routine has become desensitized to crime and cannot present a consistent front against it.

A second possible important effect of television dramatizations is more direct, but even here a specific relationship to criminality and crime has not been demonstrated. Albert Bandura and his associates, and many other researchers in the social-learning field called *behaviorism* or *operant conditioning*, have shown that children imitate models they have just observed in contrived sequences presented to them on a laboratory TV screen.[112] One does not need a laboratory experiment, however, to observe that television dramas teach people the words of popular songs, techniques of lovemaking, and even certain criminal techniques, and that they affect fashions in dress, etiquette, language, and child rearing. Thus, children impersonate actors in play, and both children and adults imitate them in

[110]Victor B. Cline, Roger G. Croft, and Steven Courier, "The Desensitization of Children to Violence," *Where Do You Draw the Line?*, ed. Cline, pp. 147–55.

[111]See D. M. Holland, "Television and Crime—A Causal Link?" *Auckland [New Zealand] University Law Review*, 2:53–61, 1975; and Steven Arons and Ethan Katsh, "How TV Cops Flout the Law," *Saturday Review*, March 19, 1977, pp. 10–19.

[112]Many of these studies are summarized in Albert Bandura and Richard H. Walters, *Adolescent Aggression* (New York: Ronald Press, 1959); Bandura and Walters, *Social Learning and Personality Development* (New York: Holt, Rinehart and Winston, 1963); Bandura, *Principles of Behavior Modification* (New York: Holt, Rinehart and Winston, 1969); and Bandura, ed., *Psychological Modeling: Conflicting Theories* (Chicago: Aldine, 1972). See also Stanley Milgram and R. Lance Shotland, *Television and Antisocial Behavior* (New York: Academic Press, 1973).

their everyday language and conduct. It should not be surprising to find that television dramas also provide people with temporary philosophies of life, with ideas about their rights and privileges and, generally, with ideas about possible ways of resolving interpersonal disputes, clashes, and conflicts. Consistently, if the legitimation of violence during time of war has a residual effect on the homicide rate, which Archer and Gartner have suggested is the case,[113] it should be expected that legitimation of violence in television dramas will increase the probability that violence will be regarded by viewers as a justifiable means of settling disputes in everyday life and, therefore will increase the probability that violence will be used as a method of conflict resolution. Several studies have shown that continued exposure to violence in ordinary (not laboratory) television dramatizations is correlated with increased willingness to use violence, to suggest it as a solution to conflict, and to perceive it as effective.[114]

No studies seem to have been made of an even more general way in which television dramatizations may be functioning to increase the incidence of violence. It seems possible that television dramas, through the modeling process, increase the probability that viewers will "go berserk" and thus increase the proportion of berserk incidents in the lives of viewers. Television dramas rarely show characters demonstrating alternatives to aggression in frustrating circumstances. Instead, television characters who are frustrated or provoked often go berserk—they strike out, smash, and even kill in what looks like blind, uncontrollable rage. The viewer thus learns that it is "natural" for persons to go berserk, thus increasing the probability that the viewer will, when frustrated or provoked, go berserk.

For example, one message of televised professional ice-hockey games (which to old ice-hockey players are as much stage productions as athletic contests) is this: People are "supposed to" have fits of uncontrollable anger under certain circumstances. Another message is that these fits are bound to have aggression as a

[113] Archer and Gartner, "Violent Acts and Violent Times."

[114] J. R. Dominick and B. S. Greenberg, "Attitudes Toward Violence: The Interaction of Television Exposure, Family Attitudes, and Social Class," in *Television and Social Behavior*, ed. Comstock and Rubenstein, vol. 3, pp. 314–25; F. B. Steur, J. M. Applefield, and R. Smith, "Televised Aggression and the Interpersonal Aggression of Preschool Children," *Journal of Consulting Psychology*, 11:442–47, 1971; R. M. Liebert and R. A. Baron, "Some Immediate Effects of Televised Violence on Children's Behavior," *Developmental Psychology*, 6:469–75, 1972; Jennie J. McIntyre and James J. Teevan, Jr., "Television Violence and Deviant Behavior," in *Television and Social Behavior*, ed. Comstock and Rubenstein, vol, 3, pp. 383–435; L. D. Eron, et al., "Does Television Violence Cause Aggression?" *American Psychologist* 27:253–63, 1972. Many of these studies are summarized in Liebert, Davidson, and Neale, *The Early Window*. It should be noted that Klapper, a sociologist who works for CBS, evaluated the results of five early studies which contrasted people habitually exposed to media with a violent content and people who were not; he found no significant differences between the two groups and therefore concluded that mass media are not a primary factor in deviant behavior and not, per se, a cause of crime and delinquency. Joseph T. Klapper, *The Effects of Mass Communication* (Glencoe, Ill.: Free Press, 1961), p. 37. See also Timothy F. Hartnagel, James J. Teevan, Jr., and Jennie J. McIntyre, "Television Violence and Violent Behavior," *Social Forces*, 54:341–51, 1975.

consequence. Young ice-hockey players watching these dramas are likely to have fits of uncontrollable anger when they later get on the ice because they have learned that players are supposed to have them, naturally. Even children (and adults as well) who do not play hockey are presented with these behavior patterns favorable to going berserk, and a nation of people who have been exposed to this behavior pattern is likely to have a high rate of what television news reporters are prone to call "senseless violence."

We earlier presented evidence that drug addicts who are "forced to steal" in order to maintain their supplies of drugs are persons who have *learned* in association with the addicts' street culture that they, as addicts, are forced to steal for this purpose. We also showed, more generally, that people who have *not* learned that they are "supposed to" steal when hungry have starved to death. By the same reasoning, which stems from differential association theory, it is probable that at least some of the people who go berserk have *learned* that they are supposed to go berserk under certain circumstances. It also is probable that television dramas have increased the number of people who are exposed to this message.

It should not be concluded from these observations and studies that exposure to dramatizations of crime, even repeated exposure, will change given individuals from noncriminals into criminals. It was long ago shown that what persons perceive when they watch dramatizations varies with socioeconomic, ethnic, religious, and cultural background.[115] It is also reasonable to assume that such perception varies with personal background. Behavior patterns favorable to a crime such as assault or theft are presented on television, but these behavior patterns are only isolated items in the huge repertoire of behavior patterns unfavorable to such crimes which most viewers have learned in the course of their life experiences. Whether the viewer is reinforced to the extent that he or she will follow the pattern presented, then, will depend upon the ratio of that person's prior associations with delinquent and antidelinquent behavior patterns, especially as they have been presented in primary groups. Perhaps it is for this reason that many adolescents and college students make love after seeing violent television shows as well as after seeing dramatizations of dramatic lovemaking, while children play cops and robbers after seeing love stories as well as after seeing violent cops and robbers stories. Older studies suggested, in fact, that children who resided in areas where delinquency rates are high were influenced more significantly by crime movies and radio crime dramas than were those who lived in areas with low delinquency rates.[116] This, in general, is what the differential

[115]Theodore M. Newcomb, *Social Psychology* (New York: Dryden Press, 1950), pp. 90–96. See also Eunice Cooper and Helen Dinerman, "Analysis of the Film 'Don't Be a Sucker': A Study in Communication," *Public Opinion Quarterly*, 15:243–64, 1951.

[116]Paul G. Cressey, "The Motion Picture Experience as Modified by Social Background and Personality," *American Sociological Review*, 3:516–25, 1938; Ethel Shanas and C. E. Dunning, *Recreation and Delinquency* (Chicago: Chicago Recreation Commission, 1942); Howard Rowland, "Radio Crime Dramas," *Educational Research Bulletin*, 23:210–17, 1944.

association theory would predict, and what it continues to predict about the specific effects on individuals of crime dramatizations on television.

CONCLUSION

The general argument of this chapter has been that the causes of crime lie primarily in the area of personal interaction, and that personal interaction is confined almost entirely to local communities and neighborhoods. Negatively, criminal behavior is not affected directly or significantly by variations in the form of the general social institutions—economics, government, religion, and education—or by the media of mass communication. This negative proposition does not deny that the general institutions and mass media have some significance for crime, and certain exceptions and qualifications should be noted. First, the crime rate does increase when the general institutions are suddenly disrupted. Second, the efficiency of the police system and of the entire system of criminal justice does have an effect on the crime rate. Third, the institutions and mass media have a very important indirect effect in that they determine the social organization and interaction patterns of local communities.

SUGGESTED READINGS

Archer, Dane, & Rosemary Gartner "Violent Acts and Violent Times: A Comparative Approach to Postwar Homicide Rates." *American Sociological Review*, 41:937–63, 1976.

Bonger, W. A. *Criminality and Economic Conditions.* Trans. H. P. Horton. Boston: Little, Brown, 1916. (Abridged ed., with an introduction by Austin T. Turk. Bloomington, Ind.: Indiana University Press, 1969.)

Callow, Alexander B., Jr., ed. *The City Boss in America.* New York: Oxford University Press, 1976.

Clark, John P., & Eugene P. Wenninger. "Socio-Economic Class and Area as Correlates of Illegal Behavior Among Juveniles." *American Sociological Review*, 27:826–34, 1962.

Cline, Victor B., ed. *Where Do You Draw the Line? An Exploration into Media Violence, Pornography, and Censorship.* Provo, Utah: Brigham Young University Press, 1974.

Conner, Walter D. *Deviance in Soviet Society: Crime, Delinquency, and Alcoholism.* New York: Columbia University Press, 1972.

Elliott, Delbert S., & Harwin L. Voss. *Delinquency and Dropout.* Lexington, Mass.: Lexington Books, 1974.

Flango, Victor Eugene, & Edgar L. Sherbenou. "Poverty, Urbanization, and Crime." *Criminology,* 14:331–46, 1976.

Fleisher, Belton M. *The Economics of Delinquency.* Chicago: Quadrangle Books, 1966.

Gardiner, John A. *The Politics of Corruption: Organized Crime in an American City.* New York: Russell Sage Foundation, 1970.

Gardiner, John A., & David J. Olson. *Theft of the City.* Bloomington, Ind.: Indiana University Press, 1974.

Gould, Leroy C. "The Changing Structure of Property Crime in an Affluent Soceity." *Social Forces,* 48:50–59, 1969.

Hanawalt, Barbara A. "Economic Influences on the Pattern of Crime in England, 1300–1348." *American Journal of Legal History,* 18:281–97, 1974.

Henry, Andrew F., & James F. Short, Jr. *Suicide and Homicide.* Glencoe, Ill.: Free Press, 1954.

Larsen, Otto N., ed. *Violence and the Mass Media.* New York: Harper and Row, 1968.

Liebert, Robert M., Emily S. Davidson, and John M. Neale. *The Early Window: Effects of Television on Children and Youth.* New York: Pergamon, 1973.

McDonald, Lynn. *Social Class and Delinquency.* London: Faber & Faber, 1969.

Monkkonen, Eric H. *The Dangerous Class: Crime and Poverty in Columbus, Ohio, 1860–1885.* Cambridge, Mass.: Harvard University Press, 1975.

Polk, Kenneth, & David S. Halferty. "Adolescence, Commitment, and Delinquency." *Journal of Research in Crime and Delinquency,* 3:82–96, 1966.

Reiss, Albert J., Jr., & Albert Lewis Rhodes. "The Distribution of Juvenile Delinquency in the Social Class Structure." *American Sociological Review,* 26:720–32, 1961.

Rhodes, Albert Lewis, & Albert J. Reiss, Jr. "Apathy, Truancy, and Delinquency as Adaptations to School Failure." *Social Forces,* 48:12–22, 1969.

Schafer, Walter E., & Kenneth Polk, eds. *Schools and Delinquency.* Englewood Cliffs, N. J.: Prentice-Hall, 1972.

Sellin, Thorsten. *Research Memorandum on Crime in the Depression.* New York: Social Science Research Council, 1937.

Silverman, Robert A. "Criminality Among Jews: An Overview." *Issues in Criminology,* 6:1–38, 1971.

Stefens, Lincoln. *Autobiography.* New York: Harcourt, Brace, 1931.

Vaz, Edmund W., ed. *Middle-Class Juvenile Delinquency.* New York: Harper and Row, 1967.

12

Behavior Processes and Systems

In the life histories of criminals, in the interaction between criminals and others, and in the interaction among criminals, all the processes observed in other areas of social participation may be discovered. The psychological, social, economic, and political lives of criminals, thus, are not abnormal. They are patterned by processes common to the lives of everyone. For example, criminals mature or do not mature in their criminal development, just as they, like noncriminals, mature or do not mature in their emotional and intellectual development. Similarly, segregation, conflict, and competition—processes common in every society—appear among criminals as well as in the interaction between criminals and noncriminals. Fashion, organization, and professionalization also appear among criminals just as they appear among noncriminals. Although noting that criminals do not differ from noncriminals in intelligence or personality traits, as was shown in Chapter 8, does not explain criminal behavior, it does help in the understanding of such behavior and, further, focuses attention on the importance to criminality of social learning. Similarly, noting that the social processes among criminals are not significantly different from the processes occurring among the noncriminal population, again calls attention to the fact that crime and criminality are neither abnormal nor deviant.

MATURATION

A process which may be called *maturation* appears in the life histories of persisting criminals. This means merely that the criminal conduct of such persons develops in a somewhat consistent course. It does not mean that an individual who starts on this course must or will follow it to the end, or that the person may not begin at some point other than that at which most other criminals begin. Like other terms borrowed from biology by the social and behavioral sciences, the term *maturation* is misleading, but it is used for want of a better term.

A person's criminal age is determined by the point the person has reached in this process of maturation. The process refers to the development of attitudes toward criminality and to the use of techniques which make crime both safe and profitable. A boy who is reared in an area of high delinquency might reach criminal maturity by age twelve or fourteen. He has reached criminal maturity because criminality has become an integrated part of his lifestyle. He plans his offenses, knows how to "fix" things if caught, and thinks of himself as delinquent or bad.[1] When convicted, he takes imprisonment philosophically as a part of his life, just as a newspaper boy who has made what provision he can against snow and rain takes inclement weather as a part of his life. An adult female shoplifter or an adult male embezzler, on the other hand, may be four times as old as this delinquent, but with no provision for immunity in case of detection and with no occupational orientation to be used for support during trial and punishment; the character of such a person is not integrated—it is immature.

The development of criminal methods in relation to chronological age varies in different crimes. Life histories of persons who in young adult life become robbers and burglars show that criminality proceeds from trivial to serious, from occasional to frequent, from sport to business, and from crimes committed by isolated individuals or by very loosely organized groups to crimes committed by rather tightly organized groups.[2] In such crimes of violence as robbery, this process reaches its height when the offender is about nineteen years of age and then remains constant for five or ten years, when it either changes into crimes which require less agility and daring, or into the kind of criminal behavior connected with politics, gambling, liquor, and usury, or is abandoned entirely.

The process in the life history of embezzlers is decidedly different. Persons who have previous histories of rectitude accept positions of financial trust with no intention of committing a crime, then later become embezzlers by criminally violating their positions of trust. The persons who occupy positions of financial responsibility seldom are psychopathic, feeble-minded, residents of deteriorated

[1] Walter C. Reckless, Simon Dinitz, and Ellen Murray, "Self-Concept as an Insulator Against Delinquency," *American Sociological Review*, 21:744–46, 1956. See also Reckless, Dinitz, and Barbara Kay, "The Self Component in Potential Delinquency and Potential Non-Delinquency," *American Sociological Review*, 22:566–70, 1957; and Dinitz, F. R. Scarpitti, and Reckless, "Delinquency Vulnerability: A Cross Group and Longitudinal Analysis," *American Sociological Review*, 27:515–17, 1962.

[2] See Hutchins Hapgood, *The Autobiography of a Thief* (New York: Fox, Duffield, 1930); Stephen Burroughs, *Memoirs of the Notorious Stephen Burroughs of New Hampshire* (New York: L. MacVeagh, Dial Press, 1924); John Bartlow Martin, *My Life in Crime* (New York: American Library, 1952); Claude Brown, *Manchild in the Promised Land* (New York: Macmillan, 1965); Bill Chambliss, ed., *Box Man: A Professional Thief's Journey* (New York: Harper and Row, 1972); and Pedro R. David, ed., *The World of the Burglar: Five Criminal Lives* (Albuquerque, N. M.: University of New Mexico Press, 1974).

slum areas, or in other ways personally or situationally pathological. Consequently, few embezzlers have such characteristics. Usually embezzlements are committed by employees who have held positions of financial responsibility for many years, rather than by recent recruits. Occasionally, embezzlers snatch a large sum of money, or whatever money is on hand, and abscond. The more usual procedure is to abstract relatively small sums over a long period of time. The embezzlement process has three phases.

First, potential trust violators define financial problems which confronts them as "unshareable," that is, as problems which cannot be shared with persons who, from a more objective point of view, could aid in their solution. In many cases these unshareable financial problems arise from obligations incurred in gambling or extravagant living, but they also arise in other ways.

Second, potential trust violators realize that they have the ability and opportunity to solve the unshareable problem by violating the position of trust. Each realizes that the unshareable financial problem can be solved by using the same technical skills which were formerly used legitimately.

Third, trust violators define embezzlement in terms which enable them to look upon it as essentially noncriminal, as justified, or as part of a general irresponsibility for which they are not completely accountable.[3] One popular notion among embezzlers, for example, is that they are merely "borrowing," not "stealing," the entrusted funds. Use of this rationalization enables them to look upon themselves as borrowers and to take relatively small amounts of money over a period of time, always with the intention of repaying it. It is the popularity of this notion, in fact, which accounts for the relatively small proportion of "snatch-and-run" embezzlers. In some cases the embezzler repays the "borrowed" money and the embezzlement goes undetected.

Among apprehended embezzlers, a few are found to have kept a careful record of their amount of "indebtedness," but most state that after a few abstractions they lost track of the total amount of their "debt." A considerable amount of money may be taken before the embezzler realizes that the amount taken cannot possibly be repaid. This realization, which is described by embezzlers as recognition of the fact that they are "in too deep," does not occur in all cases, since some violators are arrested before it takes place; and its absence enables these trust violators to continue rationalizing, even after apprehension, that they were merely borrowing. But when embezzlers discover that they are "in too deep" they are forced to abandon the notion that they are borrowing and to face the fact that an "honest and respectable person" has committed a crime. By using the rationaliza-

---

[3]Use of such definitions has been described as a "technique of neutralization." See Gresham M. Sykes and David Matza, "Techniques of Neutralization: A Theory of Delinquency," *American Sociological Review*, 22:664–70, 1957. See also David Matza, *Delinquency and Drift* (New York: Wiley, 1964), pp. 60–62, 175–77; and Travis Hirschi, *Causes of Delinquency* (Berkeley, Calif.: University of California Press, 1969), pp. 24–25, 199–212. For an excellent general analysis of criminalistic vocabularies of motive, see Frank E. Hartung, *Crime, Law, and Society* (Detroit: Wayne State University Press, 1965), pp. 62–83, 125–36.

tion that they are borrowing, then, embezzlers are able to remain in full contact with the values and ideals of former and present associates who condemn crime, and when they find that they are "in too deep" and have slipped into a category (criminal) which they know is regarded as undesirable according to that set of values and ideals, they rebel against it. They usually describe themselves as being extremely nervous, tense, emotionally upset, and unhappy. To get rid of these symptoms they may report their behavior to the police, quit taking funds, speculate or gamble wildly in an attempt to regain the stolen funds, or commit suicide. On the other hand, they may identify themselves with criminals and thus become reckless in their defalcations, taking larger amounts than formerly and with less attempt to avoid detection and with no notion of repayment.

Thus, in the absence of the rationalization that she is borrowing, a female embezzler of this kind cannot reconcile the fact that she is converting money while at the same time she is an "honest and trusted person"; consequently, she either (1) readopts the attitudes of the noncriminal groups with which she identified herself before she violated her trust, or (2) adopts the attitudes of the new category of persons (criminals) with whom she now finds herself identified. After apprehension, those embezzlers who finally come to look upon their behavior as criminal express disapproval of crime and embezzlement, just as do noncriminals. The crimes are generally committed individually, but occasionally two or more persons act in collusion. Embezzlers are scorned by professional criminals but are regarded by prison officers as model prisoners. A comparatively small proportion of them become recidivists, for the discovery of an embezzlement generally precludes further employment in positions of financial trust.[4]

The processes in the life histories of other types of criminals might also be described. The legal offense category is not the best unit to use in these descriptions. Rather, sociological categories which combine several legal categories should be used as the unit. After a sufficient number of such units have been defined and described, the types which appear can be differentiated from each other with little reference to the legal category.[5]

A few statistical studies have been made from the point of view of the sequential relations between crimes. Some years ago, the Austrian criminologist Grassberger made a study of the arrest records of habitual criminals in New York City which showed that the habitual criminal during his lifetime spreads his crimes over almost the entire field of illegality, and does not confine himself to a single specialty.[6] More recently, however, a Dutch study of all 21-year-old recidivists (three or more convictions) showed that 75 percent of all their offenses

[4]For an extended discussion of embezzlement, see Donald R. Cressey, *Other People's Money: A Study in the Social Psychology of Embezzlement* (Glencoe, Ill.: Free Press, 1953). Paperback edition, (Belmont, Calif.: Wadsworth Publishing Co., 1971). Reissued by the Patterson Smith Publishing Co., Montclair, N. J., 1973.
[5]See the discussion of behavior systems, below.
[6]Roland Grassberger, "Gewerbs- und Berufsverbrechertum in den Vereinigten Staaten von Amerika," *Kriminologische Abhandlungen*, Vienna, No. 8, 1933.

were in the same general category—property crimes, violence, sexual crimes, or traffic violations.[7] Frum found that 63 percent of 148 cases of adult recidivism began with some type of juvenile stealing, 23 percent with truancy or incorrigibility, 13 percent with drunk-vagrancy, and 1 percent with robbery.[8] It is often said that children with problems become "problem children," that these problem children become delinquents, and that these delinquents become criminal adults. But, as our discussion in earlier chapters has indicated, this common belief is misplaced. Studies of the careers of adult criminals show the importance of delinquency as a forerunner of adult crime, but they do not show the immense proportion of delinquents who never reach criminal maturity and, hence, do not move into adult criminality.

SEGREGATION

Segregation may be observed in the interaction between criminals and the public. The extent to which segregation occurs is determined largely by the frequency and intensity of hatred of criminals by persons with the power to segregate them.[9] The very term *outlaw* was apparently invented to picture persons completely segregated from routine social life.[10] White-collar criminals are not intensely hated by most businessmen, are not considered outlaws, and are not ostracized in the way that even juvenile shoplifters may be. Sex offenders were completely ostracized in many communities two generations ago, much less completely now. The person with a prison record is still almost completely ostracized in most small communities and in many occupational groups, but may become a political leader in larger communities. In 1974 Hawaii enacted the nation's first law prohibiting discrimination against ex-convicts in private employment, and New York passed similar legislation in 1975. Thus segregation as a process does not apply universally to all criminals in all groups.

In some earlier societies, outlaws lived entirely apart from law-abiding groups, in remote regions from which they might issue to make raids upon travelers or householders. Today most criminals live in the midst of society, where they have developed a symbiotic relation with many kinds of businessmen. While known working-class criminals tend to be segregated in slum areas, the portion of American society that used to be called the "underworld" has blended into the

---

[7] W. Buikhuisen and R. W. Jongman, "A Legalistic Classification of Juvenile Delinquents," *British Journal of Criminology*, 10:109–23, 1970. See also Julian B. Roebuck, *Criminal Typology* (Springfield, Ill.: Charles C. Thomas, 1967); Marshall B. Clinard and Richard Quinney, *Criminal Behavior Systems*, 2d ed. (New York: Holt, Rinehart and Winston, 1973); and Jack P. Gibbs and James F. Short, Jr., "Criminal Differentiation and Occupational Differentiation," *Journal of Research in Crime and Delinquency*, 11:89–100, 1974.

[8] Harold S. Frum, "Adult Criminal Offense Trends Following Juvenile Delinquency," *Journal of Criminal Law, Criminology, and Police Science*, 49:29–49, 1958.

[9] Pauline Morris, *Prisoners and Their Families* (London: Allen and Unwin, 1965).

[10] See Mary McIntosh, *The Organization of Crime* (London: Macmillan, 1975); and E. J. Hobsbawm, *Primitive Rebels: Studies in Archaic Forms of Social Movement in the 19th and 20th Centuries* (New York: Norton, 1959).

portion considered to be the respectable "upperworld." Nevertheless, admission to the company of thieves is still restricted. It may be secured only by those who have certain abilities, skills, and demeanors that make them acceptable.

By the same token, persons who do not have other abilities, skills, and demeanors are segregated from middle-class and upper-class society. For example, taken as a group, important American organized-crime figures have not been accepted into the social life of the suburban societies where they reside. By exhibiting humility and understatement in social relationships, especially in relationships of power, they seek acceptance. Before one Cosa Nostra boss went to prison, his wealth totalled between $20 million and $30 million. But he lived in a modest house, drove a two-year-old Ford, and owned not more than ten suits, none of which had been purchased for more than about a hundred dollars. He, like other organized crime leaders, followed a pattern set by American businessmen, whose methods and demeanor became smoother, more subtle, and more gentlemanly as they achieved some measure of success.[11] As Daniel Bell has put it,

As American society became more "organized," as the American businessman became more "civilized" and less "buccaneering," so did the American racketeer. And just as there were important changes in the structure of business enterprise, so the "institutionalized" criminal enterprise was transformed too.[12]

Such crime "bosses" were once geographically segregated, and they lived in tenement apartments, each in his own territory. But as their illicit businesses have expanded and become bureaucratized, as organized criminals have moved into legitimate businesses, and as the need for personal supervision and control has diminished, they have joined the move of respectable citizens to suburbs like Detroit's Grosse Point, New York's Westchester County, and Chicago's River Forest.

Yet organized crime leaders remain socially segregated. They are excluded from offices in civic improvement associations and parent-teacher associations, from sailing weekends and from debutante balls. Perhaps they are excluded not because they make their living in crime but because they do not have the social background and social graces which would make them eligible to participate. One New York Cosa Nostra boss even went to a psychiatrist to try to overcome his inferiority feelings about his inadequacy in social situations. As such feelings are overcome among the organized crime leaders—as they become "white-collar criminals" rather than "organized criminals" by gaining more power, and as they extend their influence to wider and wider circles of economic, political, and social

---

[11] See Donald R. Cressey, *Theft of the Nation: The Structure and Operations of Organized Crime in America* (New York: Harper and Row, 1969), pp. 214–20.

[12] Daniel Bell, "Crime as an American Way of Life," *Antioch Review*, 13:131–54, 1953. At p. 131. See also Mark H. Haller, "Organized Crime in Urban Society: Chicago in the Twentieth Century," *Journal of Social History*, 5:210–34, 1971.

activities—they probably will attain the self-confidence and poise necessary for complete assimilation by the "respectables."

PROGRESSIVE CONFLICT

Although some individual criminals and some individual law-enforcement officials live side-by-side in a corrupter-corruptee relationship, criminals and law-enforcement agents collectively are engaged in continuous conflict. In this conflict each side tends to drive the other side to greater violence unless the conflict becomes stabilized, on a recognized level, as was the case in Great Britain for years. In Britain, police and criminals both went without guns, and the danger of death was practically eliminated. But now the criminals are beginning to arm themselves, and it is quite likely that before long the police will start shooting back, or shooting first.

When police officers handle criminals violently, the criminals react violently when they have an opportunity. This spurs police officers to greater violence, which again produces more violence by criminals. It is not evident and perhaps makes no difference which side is responsible for the beginning of this process.

In American cities, for example, the declaration of a "war on crime" has led to progressive armament of both sides and progressive rapidity of shooting. Some participants on each side of the "war" adopted the slogan "Shoot and shoot first," as people are likely to do in time of war. As a consequence, participation on each side became increasingly dangerous to those on the opposing side, thus making it dangerous for each side not to be dangerous. This escalation has affected not only the police but also that part of the general public which was repeatedly victimized by criminals. The result has been an increasing death rate on both sides. Between about 1960 and 1970 the number of policemen killed by criminals and the number of criminals killed by policemen in the United States almost doubled. However, the *rate* of citizens killed by police probably was higher than the rate of policemen killed by citizens, for the number of policemen in the nation increased tremendously during the decade.

In the absence of settled traditions, this process of progressive conflict begins with arrest, which is interpreted as defining a person as an enemy of society, and which calls forth hostile reactions from representatives of the state prior to and regardless of proof of guilt. It is not surprising that the arrested person reacts with hostility. Thus, in areas where arrests are frequent, especially the ghetto residential areas of blacks, a tradition of hostility has developed and is assimilated by many persons who have had no personal experiences with the procedures of arrest. During the last generation, as the police have found it necessary to deal with more and more automobile drivers and, thus, with a wider and wider cross section of the society, rather widespread hostility toward the police has developed.[13]

[13]For a history and analysis of motoring offenses, see T. C. Willett, *Criminal on the Road* (London: Tavistock, 1964); and Donald R. Cressey, "Law, Order, and the Motorist," in *Crime, Criminology, and Public Policy: Essays in Honour of Sir Leon Radzinowicz*, ed. Roger Hood (London: Heinemann, 1974), pp. 213–34.

Competitive Development of Technology

Both criminals and law-enforcement officers gradually adopt the relevant inventions of modern technology. In early days both traveled on foot or horseback, then both used bicycles, and now automobiles, with the occasional use of an airplane or helicopter. In the early days both used clubs as weapons, and now both use guns and chemical mace, with an occasional survival of the knife. Both use bulletproof vests and armored cars. Both, on some occasions, use tear-gas bombs and both may be equipped with gas masks. Today kidnapers use adhesive tape to bind the eyes, mouth, and hands of victims; adhesive tape was practically unknown seventy-five years ago, even to physicians.

When police develop an invention for the detection or identification of criminals, criminals find a device to protect themselves. When police began to use the fingerprint technique, criminals began to wear gloves and to wipe surfaces that they had touched. When police utilized the radio to despatch squad cars to the location of a crime being committed and to direct those cars in the pursuit of criminals, criminals began equipping themselves with shortwave radio sets, tuned them to police frequencies, and are informed of an alarm as quickly as are the police. Police technicians are now trying to develop selective devices for radio calls which will restrict the calls to police cars. As soon as such a device is perfected, criminals will devise methods of overcoming it.

The history of the strong box furnishes one of the best illustrations of this alternation of progress in the techniques of protection and of crime. A hundred years ago, the safe was locked with a key. Full-time safe-burglars learned how to pick these locks, and the combination lock was invented. The criminals rigged a lever by means of which the whole spindle of the combination could be pulled out and the safe opened. When correction was made to prevent this, the burglars drilled holes in the safe and inserted gunpowder or dynamite. Then the manufacturers made the safe "drill-proof," and the burglars secured harder drills with more powerful leverage. When the manufacturers used harder materials, the burglars cleverly turned to nitroglycerine, which could be inserted in minute crevices around the door where powder and dynamite cannot be used. Then safemakers developed doors that fitted so perfectly that even nitroglycerine could not be inserted in the cracks. The burglars then adopted the oxyacetylene torch and turned it against the safe, and the manufacturers devised a compound which was proof against the torch.

Somewhere in this process, the burglars began to kidnap bankers and compel them to open the safe, and to prevent this, the timelock was invented. Also, when the manufacturers made the safes difficult to open, the burglars hauled the safes away and opened them at their leisure. The manufacturers countered by making the safes too heavy to move, and banks installed night depositories so that businessmen would not have to leave money in their own small safes. The safemakers experimented with safes which would release gas or great clouds of smoke when disturbed, and burglars then went equipped with gas masks. Some twenty years ago an electronic lock for safes was invented, but the inventor declared that within a short time someone certainly would design tools and devices to pick it. The thermic lance burner, an extraordinarily powerful cutting tool, has recently put the safe-makers on the defensive.

Bank robbery and defense against this crime also show competitive technological trends. For example, small task forces of criminals organized themselves to take advantage of the newly developed automobile before police departments did. In Chicago, especially, criminals jumped in a car, roared into nearby states, robbed a bank and then roared back into Chicago while the local police, still riding bicycles, were pedalling toward the scene of the crime. As soon as the police became technologically and organizationally equal to these bank robbers, the robbers were out of business. Secret pushbuttons to call the police or guards were developed, but bank robbers then took hostages. Also, secret pushbuttons to release tear gas were utilized, but the robbers wore small gas masks, leaving only bank employees, customers, and security personnel to suffer the ill effects of the gas. When efforts were made to secure automatic photographs of the scene in order to identify the robbers, the criminals started wearing grotesque masks. When the protective devices against both burglary and robbery became well developed in the larger banks, robbers turned to the smaller banks, whose owners could not afford such expensive equipment. And as the smaller banks improved their protective devices, the criminals directed their attacks against business firms which lacked adequate protection, and the competitive process started all over again. For example, American supermarkets became a prime target for organized robbers, partly because they began providing a payroll-check cashing service. When the robbers returned to the banks, the bankers—who had learned to insure themselves against robbery—more or less gave up. Now many banks keep only small amounts of money outside their strong boxes and the tellers simply and quietly hand a small sum to any robber who comes in and demands it. The bank robbery rate has risen enormously as a result, but the character of the offense has changed too. Working groups and task forces of robbers have moved to more lucrative fields, leaving the small sums in banks to less dedicated criminals.[14]

FASHIONS IN CRIME

Certain types of crimes have disappeared almost entirely. This has generally been due to changes in economic and social conditions, rather than to improved law-enforcement techniques or protective devices. Piracy has practically disappeared, and its disappearance was due to the development of steamships, which were too large and fast for attack by pirates. Train robberies in which a train was stopped and the mail car and the passengers were robbed have been discontinued, but this kind of attack is now sometimes made on bus passengers. Cattle stealing in the

---

[14]See Donald R. Cressey, *Criminal Organization: Its Elementary Forms* (London: Heinemann, 1972; and McIntosh, *The Organization of Crime.*

form of driving away a herd has ceased, but for it has been substituted the loading of two or three cattle into a truck and delivering them to the city. Robbery of bus drivers has disappeared in cities that require passengers to deposit exact change in a strongbox. Prostitution in the form of residential houses has all but disappeared in American cities as job opportunities for women have opened up, as immigration of large numbers of single men has diminished, and as sex standards have changed in such a way that the services of prostitutes are no longer in great demand.

In addition, however, the type and method of crime vary in ways which closely resemble fashion in other affairs. A criminal makes an attack on a gambling place, and within a short time dozens of other gambling places are attacked. Some criminal selects a hotel for robbery, and quickly dozens of other hotels are robbed. A pickpocket secures a thousand dollars in a certain airport terminal and other pickpockets flock to that terminal. A wanted criminal hijacks an airplane, and the airlines soon have a hijacking problem of serious dimensions. A criminal makes an unusually successful gain by a method which was not customary; other criminals try the method. In recent years, robbery of banks by lone-wolf criminals who demand the money in the cash drawer of a teller seems to have become fashionable.

BEHAVIOR SYSTEMS

Most of the work in theoretical criminology has been directed at explaining crime in general. But criminal statutes label a wide variety of acts as crimes. These acts have very little in common except that they are violations of law, and the statistics pertaining to each of them are not assembled uniformly or with equal vigor. The outlawed behaviors differ among themselves in the motives and characteristics of the offenders, the characteristics of the victims, the situations in which they occur, the techniques used, and the reactions of the victims and various segments of the public. Even the legal definitions of specific crimes, such as kidnapping, do not always delimit categories of conduct which have many behavioral characteristics in common.

Accordingly, burglary, robbery, embezzlement, kidnapping, and rape are all crimes, but it is almost obvious that they are homogeneous with respect to etiology only in a very general way. This commonality, we have repeatedly demonstrated in previous chapters, lies in the fact that the behavior necessary for each of these offenses, and others, is learned in a process of social interaction, just as other social behavior is learned. But although a general theory of criminal behavior and crime, such as the theory of differential association and differential social organization, organizes criminological knowledge and is therefore helpful in making sense of the gross facts about crime, it also is desirable to break crime into more homogeneous units and to develop explanations of these units.[15]

---

[15] See Don C. Gibbons, *Changing the Lawbreaker* (Englewood Cliffs, N. J.: Prentice-Hall, 1965).

In this respect, explaining crime is like explaining disease—development of the germ theory of disease radically altered the approach to illness by making sense of sicknesses which were regarded as the outcome of mere happenstance, or of a wide variety of "factors," including evil spirits. But once germ theory was developed, progress was made, and is being made, by studying specific diseases and specific germs, not by continuing to study the relationship between diseases and germs in general. Further, it was discovered that even the germ theory of disease does not apply to some diseases, and great modifications in medicine have been made through study of these exceptions. In criminology, similarly, it seems desirable to continue the development of general theory comparable in scope to germ theory, but it also seems desirable to concentrate research work on specific crimes and on specific sociological units within the broad area of crime and also within the statutory definitions of such specific offenses as burglary, robbery, kidnapping, and rape.

Several procedures for locating and studying such sociological units within the broad field of crime and within the definitions of specific crimes have been suggested. The typological approach is one such procedure. It has been used by Riemer and by Lottier to define homogeneous units within a specific offense category, embezzlement, and it has been used by Clinard and Wade to define a homogeneous unit, vandalism, as a specific type of delinquency.[16]

A second procedure involves *combining* legal categories of crime in such a way that some of the crimes in each of several legal categories are made into a sociological unit. In the course of an attempt to formulate a sociological theory of embezzlement, for example, it was discovered that the legal term *embezzlement* did not describe a homogeneous class of behavior. Persons whose illegal behavior was not covered by the legal definition were found to have been convicted of embezzlement, and the behavior of some persons who were convicted of offenses such as forgery and confidence game was found to come within the definition of embezzlement. Consequently, a new, sociological, definition of the behavior under study was made. This definition enabled the investigator to study certain cases from each of several legal categories, including embezzlement, forgery, and confidence game, and to develop a causal theory about this new sociological unit.[17]

[16]Svend Riemer, "Embezzlement: Pathological Basis," *Journal of Criminal Law and Criminology*, 32:411–23, 1941; S. Lottier, "Tension Theory of Criminal Behavior," *American Sociological Review*, 7:840–48, 1942; Marshall B. Clinard and Andrew L. Wade, "Toward the Delineation of Vandalism as a Sub-type in Juvenile Delinquency," *Journal of Criminal Law, Criminology, and Police Science*, 48:493–99, 1958. See also Theodore N. Ferdinand, *Typologies of Delinquency* (New York: Random House, 1966); Richard F. Sparks, "Types of Treatment for Types of Offenders," *Collected Studies in Criminological Research* (Council of Europe), 3:129–69, 1968; Clinard and Quinney, *Criminal Behavior Systems*; and Don C. Gibbons, "Offender Typologies—Two Decades Later," *British Journal of Criminology*, 15:97–108, 1975.

[17]Donald R. Cressey, "Criminological Research and the Definition of Crimes," *American Journal of Sociology*, 56:546–51, 1951; and Guy Houchon, "Contribution à la Methode Differentielle en Criminologie," *Revue Internationale de Criminologie et de Police Technique*, 18:19–32, 1964.

A third procedure suggested by sociologists for breaking crime into homogeneous units is the study of "behavior systems." Just as is the case when the typological approach is used, these systems of criminal behavior ordinarily have been defined in such a way that the behavior becomes homogeneous within the definition of a specific legal category. An example of this may be seen in the work of Jerome Hall, who found several behavior systems within the legal category of larceny.[18] Perhaps this procedure holds the greatest promise for criminological research, for by taking the behavior system as the unit of study it is possible to break away from the legal limitations that have often impeded scientific work in criminology. A behavior system can be studied wherever it exists, whether as crime or not crime.

Behavior systems have three characteristics. First, they are integrated units of individual acts, codes, traditions, esprit de corps, and social relationships. A behavior system thus is not merely an aggregation of individual acts. It is a group way of life. Behavior systems in crime may be illustrated by professional theft, organized sale of illicit goods and services, fraudulent advertising, systematic violation of antitrust laws, and organized manipulation of corporate securities.

Second, common and joint participation in the system is an essential characteristic of a behavior system. The crimes committed in a behavior system are not simply the behaviors of individuals. The criminal behavior is common behavior, shared by many persons.

Third, the boundaries of a behavior system are defined psychologically, rather than physically, by the feeling of identification of those who participate in the system. If the participants feel that they belong together they do belong together. Professional confidence men and professional forgers feel that they belong together, even though they use different techniques, because they have many interests and standards in common; they refer to themselves as "thieves." On the other hand, an embezzler does not identify himself with an automobile thief. When these two meet in prison they have no common reactions or sentiments growing out of their crimes except those which are common to practically all persons who violate the laws.

If a behavior system can be isolated, the problem is to explain that system as a unit. In crime, a behavior system would in this respect be similar to a disease, which is differentiated from other diseases by the causal process common to it regardless of the person in whom it occurs. To use another analogy, the attempt to explain a behavior system in crime is similar to an attempt to explain baseball in America. Such explanation does not involve a listing of the many reasons why particular persons become baseball players and in fact merely assumes the existence and persistence of baseball as a system. By taking the behavior system as

---

[18]Jerome Hall, *Theft, Law, and Society*, 2d ed. (Indianapolis: Bobbs-Merrill, 1952).

a problem, it is possible to avoid some of the methodological difficulties which arise when the act of specific persons is taken as the problem.[19]

Professional Theft as a Behavior System

Professional theft is presented as an illustration of a behavior system which can be defined and explained as a unit.[20] The sociological question regarding professional theft is similar to the sociological question about baseball: How did the behavior system originate, and how is it perpetuated in our culture?

The term *professional* when applied to a criminal refers to the following things: the pursuit of crime as a regular, day-by-day occupation; the development of skilled techniques and careful planning in that occupation; and status among criminals.[21] The professional criminal is differentiated from the occasional criminal, the amateur criminal, the unskilled and careless criminal, and the organized criminal. The term *profession* does not carry with it the ideal of public service which is supposed to be characteristic of the legitimate professions, but the professional criminal argues that the ideal of public service is no more developed in these professions than in the criminal profession.

Certain types of crimes can be committed without previous experience in crime. Murder by shooting, for instance, may be committed by a woman who has no previous experience in murder, and even if she has no experience in shooting. Most crimes, however, require training. Boys in high delinquency areas are taught how to commit thefts of various kinds. The boy who moves into an area at, say, the age of 10 without previous experience in stealing has to learn many criminal techniques and attitudes in order to keep his new-found friends. The other boys show him how to steal articles from department stores, how to steal from a truck, how to steal an automobile. The training extends to knowledge of methods of behavior in case he is caught, knowledge of when to cry and when not to cry, what types of lies to tell the police or the court. Although, from the standpoint of the mature professional criminal, such devices are on a relatively crude and low plane, as is the work of older amateur burglars and robbers, the criminal maturation of such criminals is much greater than that of episodic offenders such as murderers, embezzlers, and rapists.

Professional theft is a rational extension of this training. Each professional criminal has a highly skilled occupation. At one time the safecracker stood at the

---

[19]See Robert Dubin, "Deviant Behavior and Social Structure," *American Sociological Review*, 24:147–64, 1959; and J. Milton Yinger, "Contraculture and Subculture," *American Sociological Review*, 25:625–26, 1960.

[20]See Edwin H. Sutherland, *The Professional Thief* (Chicago: University of Chicago Press, 1937); and Chambliss, ed., *Box Man*.

[21]Reckless has used essentially the same criteria to differentiate "career criminals." Walter C. Reckless, *The Crime Problem*, 5th ed. (New York: Appleton-Century-Crofts, 1967), pp. 250–52. See also Don C. Gibbons, *Society, Crime, and Criminal Careers* (Englewood Cliffs, N. J.: Prentice-Hall, 1968) pp. 245–52.

head of the criminal professions, for his skill was unusually great, and his plans had to be made with unusual care. Thieves whose occupation requires both manual skill and skill in social manipulation also have high status. These include pickpockets, shoplifters, and confidence men. The crime of picking pockets requires manual skill, but it also requires occupational specialization within a working group and ability to manipulate victims. Most shoplifting is of the casual amateur kind, but some of it involves the use of sophisticated equipment and highly skilled techniques, including social skills which enable the thief to give store clerks the impression that he or she is a regular customer. The confidence games are based essentially on salesmanship, and they often involve convincing the victim that he or she should engage in what appears to be an illegitimate manipulation.

The rationality of a professional criminal extends beyond acquisition of the manual and social skills necessary for executing the crime itself. It includes planning, prior location of spots and victims, and prior preparation for avoiding punishment in case of detection. Arrangements are made in advance for bail, legal services, and fixing the case. It is the rational system for making these arrangements, as well as the use of technical skills, which distinguishes professional thieves from ordinary thieves.

Professional thieves, like members of Cosa Nostra "families" (to be discussed below) and other criminals, follow specialized codes of behavior. The codes are not the same for all types of crime or all types of criminals. There are, however, two very general rules. One is a prohibition against informing. "Be a stand-up guy," "Keep your eyes and ears open and your mouth shut," and "Don't sell out" are variations on this theme. The second is a prohibition against dishonesty. "Don't burn your partner," "Be loyal to the mob," and "Be a man of honor," are some of the variations.[22] Unquestionably, these commandments are violated frequently. On the other hand, it is sometimes surprising how much punishment criminals will endure rather than inform on other criminals.

The commandments are enforced by direct and violent punishment in Cosa Nostra "families" and other criminal organizations, whose table of organization provides for "enforcers" (who make the arrangements for inflicting punishments) and "executioners" (who actually carry out the punishments ordered by enforcers and those above them in the hierarchy). Professional thieves are likely to take punitive action against any member of a working group who betrays the group to the police or who holds out more than a fair share of the spoils. But professional criminals have not been organized in advance to enforce the rules prohibiting organizational disloyalty and organizational dishonesty. They do not, among other things, recruit persons to, or train persons for, well-established enforcer positions. Indeed, many professional thieves work alone.

---

[22]For elaboration of the criminal code and its functions, see Cressey, *Theft of the Nation*, pp. 162–220; and John K. Irwin and Donald R. Cressey, "Thieves, Convicts, and the Inmate Culture," *Social Problems*, 10:142–55, 1962. See also the discussion, in Chapter 24 below, of the inmate code in prisons.

Among professional criminals, a certain lack of concern and sympathy is displayed in dealing with the public, and especially in dealing with victims. This is in part a consequence of, and in part a form of, the segregation of criminals and criminal behavior. Just as a businessman acts on the principle that "business is business," the professional criminal acts on the principle that "crime is crime." There is no place for sentiment in either case.

Amateur criminals, not professionals, stir up the police and public by displays of toughness and bravado. A group of young criminals made a successful daylight robbery of a store across the street from a police station, and as they drove away they shot out the window of the station. A young criminal was angered at the way the police had treated his brother, so he set fire to a police car parked in front of the police station. Automobile thieves sometimes make a special effort to steal police cars. Robbers sometimes punish the victim who turns out to have very little or no money. Similarly, burglars may destroy property in a store if they find no money in the cash register or the safe. A man on trial in a courtroom filled with police, bailiffs, and spectators secured a gun and tried to shoot his way out of the room. Such acts give the criminal high status in a group, but not in the profession of theft. Professionals avoid "heat." Professional pickpockets, for example, could easily pick the pockets of police officers, but they refrain from doing so because this would antagonize the police and, in the long run, would lead to restraints on the pocket-picking profession.

The principal, but not the only, occupations of professional thieves are confidence games, shoplifting, and pocket-picking. Not all persons who commit these specific crimes are professional thieves. Professional thieves make a regular business of theft. They use techniques which have been developed over a period of centuries and transmitted to them through traditions and personal association. They have codes of behavior, esprit de corps, and consensus. They have high status among other thieves and in the political and criminal underworld in general. They associate with each other and do not associate with outsiders on the same basis, and they carefully select their colleagues. They tend to look down on amateur thieves, because the crude crimes committed by amateurs arouse the public and make the professional practice of theft more difficult and less profitable. Because of this differential association they develop a common language or argot which is relatively unknown to persons not in the profession. And they have organization.

A man is a professional thief when he has these five characteristics: regular work at theft, technical skill, consensus, status, and organization. The amateur thief is not a professional, even if he or she steals frequently; neither is the consistently dishonest bond salesperson, neither is the Cosa Nostra member who sells illicit goods and services. The case is not quite so clear for the persistent burglar or robber, for there the principal differential is the nature of the technique and the identification. The techniques of the professional thief are much the same as those of the salesperson and the actor; they consist of methods of manipulating the interests, attention, and behavior of the victim. The professional thief depends on cleverness and wits, while the robber resorts to force or threat of force, and the burglar relies on both stealth and force. Professional thieves have their group ways of behavior for the principal situations which confront them in their criminal activities. Consequently professional theft is a behavior system and a sociological entity.[23]

The motives of professional thieves are much the same as the motives of other occupational groups: they wish to make money in safety. These desires require no specific explanation. The specific problem is: How do professional thieves remain secure in their violations of the law? Many professional thieves have conducted their illegal activities for a normal lifetime and have never been locked up for more than a few days at a time; others have had one or two terms over a period of twenty or thirty years.

Security in professional theft is attained in three ways. First, the thieves select crimes that involve a minimum of danger. The confidence game is relatively safe because the victims generally agree to participate in a dishonest transaction, and when they find that they are victims, they cannot make a complaint without disgracing themselves.[24] For example, the three principal types of big confidence game—the "wire," the "pay-off," and the "rag"—all involve victims who believe they are defrauding someone. In the "wire" the swindler convinces the victim that they can delay the telegrams of race results long enough so that the victim can make bets with bookmakers after the race is run, thereby defrauding the bookmakers; in the "pay-off" the victim believes a large racing syndicate is being defrauded; in the "rag" the victims believe they have inside information regarding the great value of apparently worthless stock.[25]

Some confidence games do not depend upon the victim's willingness to do something dishonest, but all of them are quite safe. In one recent version of an ancient confidence game, for example, a confidence man telephones a woman at her home and represents himself as a radio announcer who is conducting a quiz program; after the victim answers a simple question, the announcer tells her that she has won an amount of money equal to the amount of money she has in the house and asks her to name that amount; if $100 is mentioned the announcer says he will deliver that amount by messenger; when the messenger arrives he has two checks, one for $100 and the other for $200, and the latter is represented as a "double dividend" which the victim has won instead of the $100; after the victim gives the confidence man the $100 in cash, to prove that she actually had that amount in the house, she receives the bogus $100 check and a receipt for her money, plus the bogus check for the $200 prize; the confidence man then safely

[23]See David W. Maurer, *Whiz Mob: A Correlation of the Technical Argot of Pickpockets with Their Behavior Pattern* (Gainesville, Fla.: American Dialect Society, 1955), pp. 19–28; and Robert L. Gasser, "The Confidence Game," *Federal Probation*, 27:47–54, 1963.

[24]See Arthur A. Leff, *Swindling and Selling* (New York: Free Press, 1976).

[25]David W. Maurer, *The Big Con* (Indianapolis: Bobbs-Merrill, 1940).

disappears. Similarly, shoplifting is relatively safe because store managers do not wish to run the risk of accusing legitimate customers of stealing, and the professional shoplifter makes it a point to look and act like a legitimate customer.[26] Picking pockets is relatively safe because the law requires direct evidence that the thief withdrew the money from the pocket, and that evidence is seldom secured.

As a second means of attaining security, professional thieves develop clever and skilled techniques for executing the crimes they select. They do this through tradition and tutelage. Cleverness and skill may merely mean brashness, as in the case of the man who, in the sporting-goods section of a large department store, balanced an aluminum kayak on his head and walked out with it. Cleverness and skill also include such things as the utilization of one person to maneuver a man so that another person can pick his pocket; the dexterity required to steal a victim's wristwatch; working with a partner who kicks a child to cause a commotion, thereby allowing the shoplifter to operate unobserved; and the ability to identify, observe, outtalk, and outmaneuver store clerks and detectives. Similarly, many ingenious devices for obtaining and carrying shoplifted goods have been invented. These include innocent-looking boxes with false bottoms so that they can be placed over counter merchandise, trousers with hidden pockets and linings, "belly pockets" worn around the waist, false arms, and rubber suction cups attached to strings and elastic bands.

As a third source of security, the professional thief makes arrangements to fix those cases in which there is a chance of being caught. The professional thief expects to fix every such case. Generally thieves do not fix these cases themselves but employ a professional fixer. The techniques of fixing crimes are as important as the techniques of executing crimes.[27] Whether the fixing is done by the thieves themselves or by their fixer, it is generally accomplished by the direct or indirect payment of money. Usually a promise is made to the victim that the stolen property will be returned, sometimes with a bonus, if the victim will refuse to press the prosecution or to testify in a way that would damage the thief.

The police are sometimes the agents of the criminals in persuading victims to accept restitution. They inform the victim that a criminal trial will cause great inconvenience and expense, and may be continued for months, after which the victim will have no prospect of recovering the stolen money or property. A large proportion of cases are fixed in this manner, for the victim is generally more interested in the return of the stolen property than in seeing that justice is done to the thieves. If this fails, a police officer may be induced not to make a complaint, or, if a complaint is made, not to testify truthfully, or to give evidence which conflicts with that of the victim or other witnesses. The prosecutor may be

---

[26] See Mary Owen Cameron, *The Booster and the Snitch: Department Store Shoplifting* (New York: Free Press, 1964).

[27] Erving Goffman, "On Cooling the Mark Out: Some Aspects of Adaptation to Failure," *Psychiatry*, 15:451–63, 1962.

induced not to prosecute or, if prosecution is inevitable, to make a very weak effort to bring out evidence which is damaging to the thief. As a last resort, the judge may be bribed to render a decision in favor of the thief, or to impose a minor penalty. It is not necessary that all persons associated with a prosecution act dishonestly. The only thing necessary is to find one of them who will twist or pervert evidence or decisions. As Maurer has said, "The dominant culture could control the predatory cultures without difficulty, and what is more, it could exterminate them, for no criminal subculture can operate continuously and professionally without the connivance of the law."[28] President Johnson's commission agreed, saying, "Professional crime would not exist except for two essential relationships with legitimate society: the 'fence' and the 'fix.' "[29]

As a behavior system, then, the profession of theft exists in modern society because victims are more interested in getting their property back than in abstract justice, because police and other officeholders are under the control of political organizations with predatory interests, and because some officials themselves have predatory personal interests. Also, professional theft exists because individuals and business concerns are willing to purchase stolen commodities.[30] In Los Angeles some years ago, "legitimate businessmen," mostly used car dealers, who purchased stolen automobile radios and other accessories had to be put out of the "fence" business before thefts from automobiles could be reduced. Professional theft exists not only because persons are willing to steal, but also because the rest of society does not present a solid front against theft.

ORGANIZATION OF CRIMINALS

There is a broad range of informal and formal organization among criminals, just as there is a broad range of organization among businessmen, government officials, and other citizens.[31] One kind of organization is simply a stabilized pattern of interaction based on similarities of interests and attitudes, and on mutual aid. Many street-corner groups of delinquents are organized in this way. These groups have their own standards, attitudes, and public opinions, an effective system of communication, the shared danger of arrest and incarceration, the common experience of having encounters with the police, and common attitudes about outsiders. Yet the participants in many of these groups are so loosely affiliated that

---

[28] Maurer, *Whiz Mob*, p. 129.

[29] President's Commission on Law Enforcement and Administration of Justice, *The Challenge of Crime in a Free Society* (Washington, D.C.: Government Printing Office, 1967), p. 46.

[30] See Carl B. Klockars, *The Professional Fence* (New York: Free Press, 1974); and Mary McIntosh, "Thieves and Fences: Markets and Power in Professional Crime," *British Journal of Criminology*, 16:257–66, 1976.

[31] Parts of this section are adapted from Cressey, *Theft of the Nation*; from idem, "The Functions and Structure of Criminal Syndicates," appendix A in President's Commission on Law Enforcement and Administration of Justice, *Task Force Report: Organized Crime* (Washington, D.C.: Government Printing Office, 1967), pp. 25–60; and from idem, *Criminal Organization*.

it is not proper to call these street-corner associations an organization.[32] Similarly, the juveniles who associate in street groups know that each of the several groups has its own turf, and the participants in the several territorial groups of a city or area have many attitudes in common, but all these juveniles are in no sense members of *an* organization that encompasses all the street-corner groups. Thus, although there is organization among street-corner juveniles, *an* organization in which all such juveniles have membership does not exist.

This observation is relevant, also, to "underworld" matters. It is correct to say that there is *organization* among a very wide range of individual criminals, some of them portrayed as respectable businessmen or governmental officials, but it is not proper to say that all these persons are linked together in *an* organization, as is erroneously implied whenever the phrase *"the* underworld" is used. More specifically, a pattern of organization is characteristic of Mafia behavior in contemporary Sicily; and in the United States, a similar pattern of organization is apparent in much of what is commonly called "organized crime."[33] Thus, there are understandings and even agreements about where a particular Sicilian Mafia unit or American organized-crime unit will operate, but all the persons who are party to these understandings and agreements are so loosely affiliated that the entire enterprise cannot properly be called *an* organization. As among juvenile gangs, the organizational principle in such alliances is more territorial than occupational, more attitudinal than operational.

In other cases, organization means a particular set of roles that has come to be seen as serving express purposes by the persons playing the roles. An enterprise of this kind qualifies as *an* organization because specific tasks are allocated to individuals, entrance into the organization is limited, and survival and maintenance rules are delineated. More specifically, such units have three important characteristics. First, a division of labor is present. This means that there is occupational specialization, with each specialty fitting into the whole. Second, the activities of each person in the organization are coordinated with the activities of other participants by means of rules, agreements, and understandings which support the division of labor. Third, the entire enterprise is rationally designed to achieve announced objectives.[34]

These features are matters of degree. Among criminal organizations, the degree to which they are present affects the character of the crimes perpetrated. The criminal tribes of India, the bandits of pre-Communist China, the brigands of southeastern Europe, the smugglers in America and in many European countries

---

[32] See Lewis Yablonsky, "The Delinquent Gang as a Near-Group," *Social Problems*, 7:106–17, 1959.

[33] See Norman Lewis, *The Honored Society* (New York: Putnam, 1964); Luigi Barzini, *The Italians* (New York: Atheneum, 1964); Robert T. Anderson, "From Mafia to Cosa Nostra," *American Journal of Sociology*, 71:302–10, 1965; and Henner Hess, *Mafia and Mafiosi: The Structure of Power* (Lexington, Mass.: Lexington Books, 1973).

[34] See S. J. Udy, Jr., "The Comparative Analysis of Organizations," chap. 6 in *Handbook of Organizations*, ed. James G. March (Chicago: Rand McNally, 1965), p. 687.

in the last century, the Ku Klux Klan, vigilante groups, and feuding families engaged in guerilla warfare were earlier forms of criminal organization. All these units had occupational specialization, rules of conduct, and the objective of committing crime safely (and profitably). The geographically based Cosa Nostra "families"[35] of criminals now operating in the United States have the same characteristics and, thus, qualify as criminal organizations. Each family has specialized positions, such as "boss," "soldier" and others (to be described later), who collectively commit several kinds of crime. Also, within each family the members' organizational activities are coordinated and controlled, not only by the structure itself, but also by a criminal code, the values of which govern many of the interpersonal relationships in which members engage both on and off the job.

Small criminal organizations, dedicated to perpetrating particular types of crimes, have existed for centuries. Some of those operating in England during the Elizabethan period have been described in detail.[36] Similar groups exist today for the purposes of burglary, robbery, shoplifting, confidence games, picking pockets, and stealing automobiles. The organization may be on a craft basis (picking pockets, confidence games), on a project basis (robbery, some burglary), or on a marketing basis (automobile theft, some burglary, and the sale of illicit goods and services). Some of these groups have become "professionalized." Participants in small groups organized on a craft basis, especially, are prone to consider themselves professional thieves, and to be considered professional thieves by persons skilled in similar crafts, as well as by police officers.

These small working groups of criminals have the three characteristics of formal organizations. They have divisions of labor based on the requirements of specific team operations, but controls over job responsibilities and daily activities are neither extensive nor precise. For example, the fundamental form of organization among pickpockets is the "troupe," "tribe," or "team" of two, three, or four crafts persons. The relationships between the persons occupying the positions making up the troupe are "loose, ephemeral, and highly insecure," but there is organization nevertheless.[37] The duties and responsibilities of each position are finely detailed. There is, for example, a position for a criminal whose duty it is to locate the prospective victim and distract his or her attention. A second position requires a specialist skilled in actually removing the wallet from the victim's pocket. A third position demands skills in receiving the wallet or other goods from the person who took it from the victim. The persons who fill these positions, even

---

[35] Because the "families" are fictive in the sense that members are not all blood relatives, it is proper to refer to them in quotation marks. To improve readability, however, we shall not continue to do so.

[36] A. V. Judges, *The Elizabethan Underworld* (London: Routledge, 1930). See also Mary McIntosh, "Changes in the Organization of Thieving," in *Images of Deviance*, ed. Stanley Cohen (Hammondsworth: Penguin, 1971), pp. 98–133; and Kellow Chesney, *The Anti-Society: An Account of the Victorian Underworld* (Boston: Gambit, 1970).

[37] Maurer, *Whiz Mob*, p. 84.

temporarily, are specialists. As in any legitimate craft organization, a variety of skills is required for effective operations.

Organization, whether it be that of a working group of criminals or of a legitimate corporation, means rationality. The rationality behind the operations of working groups of criminals can be observed in three different contexts.[38] First, the crimes committed by teams of criminals tend to be those whose nature makes it difficult to apprehend and prosecute the perpetrators. Second, the divisions of labor are such that all incumbents must be skilled in the use of techniques which in combination make the whole group's work safe and, therefore, profitable. In project robberies and kidnappings, for example, provision is made for a planner, whose job is to select rich targets; in project burglaries, provision is made for a "fence," whose job is to accept and resell stolen goods. Third, rational organization for safety and profit is indicated in some, but not all, working groups of criminals by the establishment of at least one position for a "corrupter" and one or more positions for "corruptees." Corruptee positions are occupied by public officials who, for a fee, will insure that the group can operate with relative immunity from the penal process. It is as much a part of the criminal organization as any other position.[39]

The "market" form of organized crime is a system based on a further extension of this rational design for safety and profit. Although it is true that the division of labor in Cosa Nostra families has been designed for the perpetration of crimes which cannot be perpetrated profitably by small working groups of criminals, let alone by criminals working outside an organization, the critical difference is not merely a difference in size. Small firms selling stolen goods or illicit goods and services must, if they are to capitalize on the great demand for their wares, expand by establishing a division of labor which includes positions for financiers, purchasing agents, supervisors, transportation specialists, lawyers, accountants, and employee-training specialists. The next rational move is to allocate specific territories to each of the separate divisions of labor, thus minimizing competition and maximizing the profits of all. Such a monopolistic move, of course, is also a rational decision for peaceful coexistence. As such, it necessarily involves governmental considerations as well as business considerations.

Investigations of American Organized Crime

Some criminals, law-enforcement officials, political figures, and others insist that a nationwide cartel and confederation of criminals was established in the United States in 1931 and that it is more powerful today than it has ever been. Some law-enforcement officials and political figures have denied the existence of such an apparatus because they, as criminals, participate in organized crime and profit

[38] See Sutherland, *The Professional Thief*, pp. 217–18.
[39] See William J. Chambliss, "Vice, Corruption, Bureaucracy, and Power," *Wisconsin Law Review*, 1150–73, 1971.

from it. Still others believe that such terms as *cartel* and *confederation* (and even *alliance*) imply more organizational rationality than actually exists. But for more than thirty years government officials and others have been trying to convince the American public that the activities of organized crime are threatening the foundations of American economic, political, and legal order. The authors of these warnings have been handicapped by their failure to distinguish between organization of criminals who sell illicit goods and services on the one hand, and *an* organization which sells such things on the other. To some observers, the words *cartel, confederation* and *alliance* imply only that territories have been marked out and understandings about peaceful coexistence have been reached. To others, these words imply that a nationwide criminal organization has taken the form of a legitimate labor union or corporation.[40]

The latter interpretation, though erroneous, has been by far the most popular one, perhaps because few persons are familiar with the sociological notion that there can be organization of criminals even if the activities of these criminals are not controlled by a governing board. Further, even experts have difficulty in maintaining this distinction because our language is biased in favor of the "corporate" image. Thus, organizational titles such as *the* syndicate, *the* Mafia, and *La* Cosa Nostra necessarily suggest formal and hierarchical organization, even if none exists. To complicate matters even further, a contemporary alliance of some organized criminals, commonly called Cosa Nostra, is more than just informal organization. For example, members of local units (families) believe that a "commission" tries to settle organizational disputes, and this structure gives Cosa Nostra some of the characteristics of formal organizations.

The Cosa Nostra alliance grew out of the gangs organized to meet the demand for illicit alcohol during the period of national prohibition. Almost from the first, the manufacture, distribution, and sale of prohibited alcohol was in the hands of organized groups, rather than of isolated individuals. There were many such groups, at first organized primarily on an occupational basis but also on a neighborhood and ethnic basis. With increasing competition, violent warfare broke out. Some of the smaller units were fused together into larger units, and some of these larger units then made arrangements for peaceful coexistence. These alliances for reducing competition came to be called *syndicates*.[41] The process was exactly the same as in legitimate business, though the methods inclined more to violence and less to fraud than in legitimate business.

While the groups engaged in the production and sale of illicit alcohol were using warnings, destruction of property, and murder as means of stifling competi-

[40]See Lowell L. Kuehn, "Syndicated Crime in America," chap. 4 in *Deviants: Voluntary Actors in a Hostile World*, ed. Edward Sagarin and Fred Montanino (Morristown, N. J.: General Learning Press, 1977), pp. 157–219; and Denny F. Pace and Jimmie C. Styles, *Organized Crime. Concepts* (Englewood Cliffs, N. J.: Prentice-Hall, 1975).

[41]See Cressey, *Theft of the Nation*, pp. 29–53.

tion, law-enforcement agents, acting under orders of political leaders, were harassing new manufacturers or dealers who tried to enter the illicit liquor business. For a considerable part of the period of national prohibition, the leading manufacturer of alcohol was in charge of enforcing the law against illicit manufacture and sale of alcohol. Nevertheless, the syndicates were never secure, even within a given territory. Subordinates were ambitious, and some of the gangs were rebellious. Because the entire business was illegal, control depended finally on violence. Near the end of the prohibition period, the basic framework of the current organizational arrangements was established as the final product of a series of "gangland wars" in which an alliance of Italians and Sicilians first conquered other groups, then fought each other. A decision for peaceful coexistence was made in 1931, and that decision, which amounted to a peace treaty, has determined the shape of American organized crime ever since. When the period of national prohibition ended, organized criminals moved into other illicit fields.

Participants in the Cosa Nostra alliance now control much of the illegal gambling in the United States. They engage in usury (loan sharking) and in the importation and wholesaling of illicit drugs. They are active in project crimes, especially those involving thefts of cargoes and bankruptcy fraud. They have infiltrated certain labor unions, where they extort money from the employers and, at the same time, cheat the members of the union. In some areas, the members of local families have a virtual monopoly on some legitimate enterprises, such as cigarette vending machines and jukeboxes, and they own a wide variety of legitimate retail firms, restaurants, bars, hotels, trucking companies, food companies, linen-supply houses, garbage-collection routes, and factories. They have corrupted officials in the legislative, executive, and judicial branches of government at the local, state, and federal levels.

One of the earliest warnings about organization for reducing competition in the sale of illicit goods and services was made by a defector. In a series of articles appearing in 1939, the former attorney for an illicit New York organization, a man who was a "corrupter" for the organization, disclosed that a nationwide alliance between criminal businesses in the United States was in operation. While in jail he wrote an exposé of political corruption and crime in New York and also drew the conclusion about a nationwide alliance. This was not the first time such a conclusion was drawn, but it dramatically foreshadowed statements which have been made in more recent years. His statement vacillates between the conception of organization as mere understandings and agreements ("framework," "system of alliances") and the notion that a governing body was established to direct criminal activities ("centralization of control," "the organization"):

When I speak of the underworld now, I mean something far bigger than the Schultz mob. The Dutchman was one of the last independent barons to hold out against a general centralization of control which had been going on ever since Charlie Lucky became leader of the Unione Siciliana in 1931. . . . The "greasers" in the Unione were killed off, and the organization was no longer a loose, fraternal order of Sicilian black handers and alcohol cookers, but rather the framework for a system of alliances which were to govern the underworld. In Chicago, for instance, the Unione no longer fought the Capone mob, but pooled strength and worked with it. . . . It still numbers among its members many old-time Sicilians who are not gangsters, but anybody who goes into it today is a mobster, and an important one. In New York City the organization is split up territorially into districts, each led by a minor boss, known as the *"compare,"* or godfather. . . . I know that throughout the underworld the Unione Siciliana is accepted as a mysterious, all-pervasive reality, and that Lucky used it as the vehicle by which the underworld was drawn into cooperation on a national scale.[42]

More than a decade after this statement appeared in a popular magazine of the time, many members of the public (and some law-enforcement officers) still had no notion that several territorial criminal organizations had implicitly or explicitly agreed to stop competing with each other and had thus become allies rather than enemies. If they heard of "the Mafia" or "the syndicate" or "the outfit" or "the mob" or "the brotherhood" or "the *fratellanza,"* they did not believe what they heard, perhaps because the word *the* in each of the titles too strongly suggested formal hierarchical organization, rather than mere organizational arrangements for peaceful coexistence. The famous Kefauver Committee in 1951 did not help matters much when it drew the following four conclusions from the testimony of some eight hundred witnesses who appeared before it:

(1) There is a Nation-wide crime syndicate known as the Mafia, whose tentacles are found in many large cities. It has international ramifications which appear most clearly in connection with the narcotics traffic.

(2) Its leaders are usually found in control of the most lucrative rackets in their cities.

(3) There are indications of a centralized direction and control of these rackets, but leadership appears to be in a group rather than in a single individual.

(4) The Mafia is the cement that helps to bind the Costello-Adonis-Lansky syndicate of New York and the Accardo-Guzik-Fischetti syndicate of Chicago as well as smaller criminal gangs and individual criminals throughout the country. These groups have kept in touch with Luciano since his deportation from this country.[43]

In the next decade, investigating bodies were able to overcome some of the handicaps of the Kefauver Committee, which "found it difficult to obtain reliable data concerning the extent of Mafia operation, the nature of Mafia organization, and the way it presently operates." While *all* such handicaps will not be overcome for some years, there no longer is any doubt that several regional organizations, rationally constructed for the control of the sale of illicit goods and services, are in operation. Neither is there any doubt that these regional organizations are linked together by understandings and agreements, but the "centralized direction and

---

[42]J. Richard Davis, "Things I Couldn't Tell Till Now," *Collier's,* July 22, July 29, August 12, August 19, and August 26, 1939. The quote is from pp. 35–36 of the August 19 issue.

[43]Special Committee to Investigate Crime in Interstate Commerce (Kefauver Committee), *Third Interim Report* (U.S. Senate Report No. 307, 82d Congress 1st Session, 1951), p. 150.

control" noted by the Kefauver Committee has been shown to be an exaggeration.[44]

Another series of investigations was set off in 1957, when at least seventy-five of the nation's organized crime leaders were discovered at a meeting in Apalachin, New York. At least twenty-three came from New York City or New Jersey, nineteen from upstate New York, eight from the Midwest, three from the West, and two from the South. At least two "delegates" were from Cuba, and one was from Italy. No one has been able to prove the nature of the conspiracy involved at Apalachin, but no one believes that the men all just happened to drop in on the host at the same time. Two of the men attending the meeting had met at a somewhat similar meeting of criminals in Cleveland in 1928. The Italian police revealed that some of them also attended a 1957 meeting in a Sicilian motel.

Discovery of the Apalachin meeting stimulated increased investigative action by the United States Attorney General, the Federal Bureau of Narcotics, the Federal Bureau of Investigation, the Internal Revenue Service, and several state and local agencies. Starting about 1961, these investigating agencies began to receive intelligence information about the existence of an alliance now commonly labeled "Cosa Nostra." In 1963 the McClellan Committee portrayed this syndicate to a nationwide television audience.[45] Once again, a considerable number of citizens had forgotten, or had never heard, the information on organized crime presented to them over a period of thirty years. They were shocked and surprised when they heard Joseph Valachi, an active member of an organized group of criminals, describe the skeletal structure of the organization, its operations, and its membership. The basic points in Mr. Valachi's testimony have now been validated by a wide variety of law-enforcement agencies.[46]

The Structural Skeleton

Valachi used the name "Cosa Nostra" when describing the alliance. While it continues to be called the Mafia or the syndicate in some parts of the country, some members and law-enforcement officers now use the "Cosa Nostra" title. Extensive investigations and studies of the structure of Cosa Nostra justify the conclusion that it has the characteristics of *an* organization. When there are specialized but integrated positions for bosses, foremen, and workers, there is economic organization. When there are specialized but integrated positions for statesmen and administrators of criminal justice, there is political organization.

[44]Joseph L. Albini, *The American Mafia: Genesis of a Legend* (New York: Appleton-Century-Crofts, 1971); Francis A. J. Ianni, *A Family Business: Kinship and Social Control in Organized Crime* (New York: Russell Sage Foundation, 1972); Dwight C. Smith, *The Mafia Mystique* (New York: Basic Books, 1975); and Frederic D. Homer, *Guns and Garlic: Myths and Realities of Organized Crime* (West Lafayette, Ind.: Purdue University Press, 1973).

[45]Permanent Subcommittee on Investigations of the Senate Committee on Government Operations, *Organized Crime and Illicit Traffic in Narcotics* (U.S. Senate, 88th Congress, 1st Session, 1963, 1964, 1965).

[46]See Peter Maas, *The Valachi Papers* (New York: Putnam, 1968).

Cosa Nostra has both kinds of positions, giving it the characteristics of both a business organization and of a government. Further, Cosa Nostra and its constituent families exist independently of current personnel; its activities go on despite complete turnover in the personnel occupying the various positions making up the organization. As in the nationwide alliances of police officers, no person is indispensable. Organization, or structure, not persons, gives Cosa Nostra its self-perpetuating character.

It should be noted, however, that La Cosa Nostra, like the "nationwide crime syndicate" discussed by the Kefauver Committee, has not been shown to be characterized by the "centralized direction and control" also discussed by the Kefauver Committee. It is deserving of the word "it," meaning that the characteristics of *an* organization are present, but La Cosa Nostra is organized more like the International Conference of Police Associations, or like Phi Beta Kappa, than like a nationally operated corporation. Phi Beta Kappa chapters, like police departments, may be said to be in an alliance, and collectively they comprise a nationwide cartel, confederation, or syndicate. But the activities of neither local Phi Beta Kappa chapters nor of their members are directed or otherwise controlled by a centralized "home office" or board of directors in the way the local activities of units in a nationwide corporation are directed and managed. Instead, the national board merely sets standards and, in so doing, determines where local chapters shall thrive.

In Cosa Nostra, a "commission" similarly functions more as a standard-setting and dispute-arbitrating body than anything else. It has national influence, like Phi Beta Kappa's national board, but it does not direct or control individual criminal activities within the various Cosa Nostra "chapters," which are called families. But because criminals who consider themselves members of Cosa Nostra look to the commission as the ultimate authority on territorial disputes between families, and even as the ultimate authority on organizational disputes within families, it serves as something of a combined legislature, supreme court, and arbitration board all rolled into one. It is made up of the rulers of the most powerful Cosa Nostra families, the name given to the geographical units of the alliance. From nine to twelve men usually sit on the commission. The commission is not a representative body, and its members do not necessarily regard each other as equals.

Beneath the commission are twenty-four families each of which is *an* organization, and each of which is headed by a *boss*. (Italian words often are used interchangeably with each of the English words designating a position in the division of labor. Rather than "boss," the words *il capo*, *don*, and *rappresentante* are used.) The boss's primary function is to maintain order while at the same time maximizing profits. He is the final arbiter in most matters relating to his branch of the confederation.

Beneath each boss of at least the larger families, is an *underboss*, or *sottocapo*. The man occupying the position often collects information for the boss; he relays messages to him; and he passes his orders down to the men occupying positions below him in the hierarchy. He acts as boss in the absence of the boss.

On the same level as the underboss there is a position for a *counselor* or *adviser*. The person occupying this position is likely to be an elder member who is partially retired after a career in which he did not quite succeed in becoming a boss. He gives advice to family members, including the boss and underboss, and he therefore enjoys considerable influence and power. In some families the positions of underboss and counselor are occupied by the same person; he "wears two hats," so to speak.

Also at about the same level as the underboss is a "buffer" position. The top members of the family hierarchy, particularly the boss, avoid direct communication with the lower-echelon personnel, the workers. They are insulated from the police. To obtain this insulation, information, money, and complaints generally flow back and forth through the buffer, who is a trusted and clever go-between. However, the buffer does not make decisions or assume any of the authority of his boss, as the underboss does.

To reach the working level, a boss usually goes through channels. For example, a boss's decision on the settlement of a dispute involving the activities of the "runners" (ticket sellers) in a particular numbers lottery game, passes first to his buffer, then to the next level of rank, which is *lieutenant* or *capodecina* or *caporegima*. The person occupying this position is the chief of at least one business operation, such as an illegal lottery or betting office. The lieutenant usually has one or two assistants who work closely with him, serving as messengers and buffers. They carry orders, information, and money back and forth between the lieutenant and the men belonging to his regime, but they do not share the lieutenant's administrative power.

Beneath the lieutenants there might be one or more *section chiefs*. A section chief may be deputy lieutenant. He is in charge of a section of the lieutenant's operations. In smaller families, the position of lieutenant and the position of section chief are combined. In general, the larger the regime, the stronger the power of the section chief.

About five *soldiers, buttons,* or just *members* report to each section chief or, if there is no section chief, to a lieutenant. The number of soldiers in a family varies; some families have as many as six hundred members, some as few as twenty. A soldier might operate an illicit business for a boss, on a commission basis, or he might "own" the business and pay homage to the boss for "protection," the right to operate. Partnerships between two or more soldiers, and between soldiers and men higher up in the hierarchy, including bosses, are common. A "business" could be a usury operation, a dice game, a lottery, a bookie operation, a smuggling operation, or a vending machine company. Some soldiers and most upper-echelon family members have interests in more than one business.

Family membership ends at the soldier level, and all members are of Italian or Sicilian descent. About five thousand men are members of families. But beneath the soldiers in the hierarchy of operations are large numbers of employees and commission agents who are not necessarily of Italian-Sicilian descent. These are the persons carrying on most of the work "on the street." They have no "buffers" or other forms of insulation from the police. They are the relatively unskilled workmen who actually take bets, answer telephones, drive trucks, sell narcotics, and so on. In Chicago, for example, the workers in a major lottery business operated in a black neighborhood were blacks; the bankers for the lottery were Japanese-Americans; but the game, including the banking operation, was licensed, for a fee, by a family member. The entire operation, including the bankers, was more or less a "customer" of the Chicago family, in the way any legitimate enterprise operating under a franchise is a customer of the parent corporation.

As just presented, this authority structure constitutes the "organizational chart" of Cosa Nostra as it is described by its members. Four things are missing. First, there is no description of the many organizational positions necessary to actual street-level operation of illicit enterprises such as bookmaking establishments and lotteries. As indicated, many of the positions in such enterprises are occupied by persons who are not Cosa Nostra members. Second, and more importantly, there is no description of the actual behavior of the men who occupy the formally established positions making up the organization. Third, the structure as described by members is the structure of membership roles, not of the relationships between members and indispensable outsiders such as street-level workers, attorneys, accountants, tax experts, and corrupt public officials.[47] These outsiders play roles in organized crime, even if they are not members of a criminal organization. Fourth, even a complete picture of the structure and operations of Cosa Nostra would not be a description of "organized crime." All of the activities and positions we have described are also found in organized crime units operating independently of the Cosa Nostra alliance, and even in competition with it.[48]

Corruption of Law-Enforcement and Political Systems

Cosa Nostra families and other organized crime units have some of the attributes of government. However, they are not in competition with the established agencies of legitimate government and are not interested in political and economic reform. Their political objective is a negative one: nullification of government.

Nullification is sought at two different levels. At the lower level are the agencies for law enforcement and the administration of criminal justice. When an organized criminal bribes a police officer, a police chief, a prosecutor, a judge, or a license administrator, he does so in an attempt to nullify the law-enforcement

[47] For these details, see Cressey, *Theft of the Nation*, pp. 126–85.
[48] See Francis A. J. Ianni, *Black Mafia: Ethnic Succession In Organized Crime* (New York: Simon and Schuster, 1974).

process. At the upper level are legislative agencies, including federal and state legislatures as well as city councils and county boards of supervisors. When a family boss supports a candidate for political office, he does so in an attempt to deprive honest citizens of their democratic voice, thus nullifying the democratic process.

The two levels are not discrete. Organized criminals engage in all seven forms of corruption outlined in the previous chapter. If an elected official can be persuaded not to represent the honest citizens of his district on matters pertaining to the interests of organized criminals, he is, at the same time, persuaded that he should help insure that some laws are not enforced, or are enforced selectively. When the political "representative" of a district works to prevent the passing of laws which would damage organized criminals but help honest citizens, the political process has been nullified. But when the same "representative" is paid by criminals to block appropriations for law-enforcement agencies which would fight organized crime, to block the promotion of policemen who create "embarrassing incidents" by enforcing antigambling statutes, and to use his political position to insure that dishonest or stupid administrators of criminal justice are appointed, he is being paid to nullify the law-enforcement process. The operations of organized crime should not be referred to as the operations of the "underworld." The activities of Cosa Nostra members are so interwoven with the activities of so-called respectable businessmen and government officials that doing so directs our attention to the wrong places.

Every Cosa Nostra family has in its division of labor at least one position for a corrupter. The person occupying this position bribes, buys, intimidates, threatens, negotiates, and sweet-talks himself into relationships with police, public officials, and anyone else who might help family members maintain immunity from arrest, prosecution, and punishment. The corrupter is not depicted on the organizational charts which informants and others have sketched out as they have described Cosa Nostra. It is an essential, but unofficial, functional position, like that of the buffer. It might be occupied by a person who is a soldier, a lieutenant, an underboss, or even a boss.

For every corrupter, there must be at least one corruptee. Most corrupt police officers and public officials have been sought out and wooed into the position of corruptee. Persons must be recruited and selected for this position just as they must be recruited and selected for such positions as bookmaker or lieutenant. While the officials occupying corruptee positions are not ordinarily members of Cosa Nostra families, their positions are part of the division of labor in each family, just as are low-level positions for street workers. Occasionally, a corrupter does not have to recruit a particular man to a corruptee position because the corrupter's family has, with the help of the corrupter, recruited him in advance and put him in office.

Demand, Supply, and Profit

As a behavior system, the "marketing" form of criminal organization thrives in the United States because a large number of citizens demand the illicit goods and services they have for sale. As Walter Lippmann observed at the end of the prohibition era, the basic distinction between ordinary criminals and organized criminals in the United States turns on the fact that the ordinary criminal is wholly predatory, while the person participating in crime on a rational, systematic basis offers a return to the respectable members of society.[49] If all burglars were miraculously abolished, they would be missed by only a few persons to whose income or employment they contribute directly—burglary insurance companies, manufacturers of locks and other security devices, police, prison personnel, and a few others. But if the establishment of men and women employed in illicit business were suddenly abolished, it would be sorely missed because it performs services for which there is a great public demand.

It is true, of course, that criminals who do not occupy positions in any organization also supply the kinds of illicit goods and services supplied by criminal organizations. A gray-haired old lady who accepts a few horse-racing bets from the patrons of her neighborhood grocery store performs an illegal service for those patrons, just as does the factory foreman who sells his own home-made whiskey to his friends at the plant. Law violators of this kind do not seem very dangerous and, if treated in isolation, such persons cannot be perceived as a serious threat to social order. Accordingly, they tend to be pampered in various ways by criminal justice personnel. The police officer is inclined to overlook the bookmaker's offenses or merely to insist that they be conducted in another precinct, the judge is likely to invoke the mildest punishment the legislature has established, and the jailer is likely to differentiate such offenders from "real criminals."

But such providers of illegal services cannot be individual entrepreneurs for long. The nature of the illegal lottery and bookmaking business is such that bookmakers must join hands with others in the same business. Bookmakers and lottery operators are organized to insure that *making* bets is gambling but *taking* bets is not. Other illicit businesses have the same character. Free enterprise does not exist in the field of illicit services and goods—any small illicit business must soon take in, voluntarily or involuntarily, an organized criminal as a partner.

By joining hands, the suppliers of illicit goods and services (1) cut costs, improve their markets, and pool capital; (2) gain monopolies on certain of the illicit services or on all of the illicit services provided in a specific geographic area, whether it be a neighborhood or a large city; (3) centralize locally the procedures for stimulating the agencies of law enforcement and administration of justice to

---

[49] Walter Lippmann, "Underworld: Our Secret Servant," and "The Underworld: A Stultified Conscience," *Forum*, 85:1–4 and 65–69, 1931. See also Homer, *Guns and Garlic*.

overlook the illegal operations; and (4) accumulate vast wealth which can be used to attain even wider monopolies on illicit activities, and on legal businesses as well. In the long run, then, the "small operation" corrupts the traditional economic and political procedures designed to insure that citizens need not pay tribute to a criminal in order to conduct a legitimate business. The demand, and the profits, are too great to be left in the hands of small operators.

Thus, it is the American demand for illicit goods and services which produces illicit businesses. These businesses, in turn, invest part of their profits in legitimate commercial enterprises and in politics. Robert F. Kennedy made the following statement while he was attorney general of the United States: "What is at least disturbing—and for me insidious—is the increasing encroachment of the big businessmen of the rackets into legitimate business."[50] Cosa Nostra members have been, and are, acquiring and operating legitimate enterprises, ranging from Las Vegas casinos to huge corporations. Moreover, some of them have deposited huge sums in Swiss banks, and they draw on these fruits of crime whenever they want to buy or corrupt another large piece of America. The distinction between white-collar crime and organized crime is rapidly disappearing.

CONCLUSION

Most theories of crime and criminal behavior have tried to account for criminal behavior in general, to account for variations in general crime rates, or to account for both of these. Because the phenomena to be explained are quite general, the explanations of them must also be quite general. The theoretician's problem will become easier when uniformities in crime and criminal behavior have been identified and described. Then, efforts to explain these uniformities can be made, by means of specific theory which is consistent with general theory such as differential association and differential social organization. The social processes and behavior systems which have been discussed above are illustrations of some of the uniformities which may be perceived in criminal behavior, and in noncriminal behavior as well.

Professional theft and organized crime have been briefly used as illustrations of the procedure for studying behavior systems in crime. Neither of these topics has been investigated exhaustively, and the interpretations are therefore tentative and hypothetical. More intensive studies of these two behavior systems and of other behavior systems in crime are needed before general propositions can be developed.

It is not likely that the entire area of crime can be covered in this manner. Certain crimes cluster in systems, are organized, or can logically be combined with other crimes to form systems. But other crimes stand somewhat isolated and outside of systems. Behavior systems in crime may be understood more readily than isolated crimes, and therefore the study of them may yield general

[50]Permanent Subcommittee on Investigations, *Organized Crime and Illicit Traffic in Narcotics*, 1963, p. 12.

propositions that apply to a considerable range of criminal offenses. Then legal categories designating less systemic crimes can be combined or redefined in such a way that the behavior designated by them can be studied scientifically and related to the general propositions.

SUGGESTED READINGS

Albini, Joseph L. *The American Mafia: Genesis of a Legend*. New York: Appleton-Century-Crofts, 1971.

Arnold, David O. *The Sociology of Subcultures*. Berkeley, Calif.: Glendessary Press, 1970.

Cameron, Mary Owen. *The Booster and the Snitch: Department Store Shoplifting*. New York: Free Press, 1964.

Chambliss, Bill, ed. *Box Man: A Professional Thief's Journey*. New York: Harper and Row, 1972.

Clinard, Marshall B., & Richard Quinney. *Criminal Behavior Systems: A Typology*. 2d ed. New York: Holt, Rinehart and Winston, 1973.

Cressey, Donald R. *Criminal Organization*. London: Heinemann, 1972.

Cressey, Donald R. *Other People's Money: A Study in the Social Psychology of Embezzlement*. Glencoe, Ill.: Free Press, 1953.

Cressey, Donald R. *Theft of the Nation: The Structure and Operations of Organized Crime in America*. New York: Harper and Row, 1969.

Einstadter, Werner J. "The Social Organization of Armed Robbery." *Social Problems*, 17:64–82, 1969.

Hess, Henner. *Mafia and Mafiosi: The Structure of Power*. Lexington, Mass.: Lexington Books, 1973.

Hobsbawm, E. J. *Primitive Rebels: Studies in Archaic Forms of Social Movement in the 19th and 20th Centuries*. New York: Norton, 1959.

Homer, Frederic D. *Guns and Garlic: Myths and Realities of Organized Crime*. West Lafayette, Ind.: Purdue University Press, 1973.

Ianni, Francis A. J. *A Family Business: Kinship and Social Control in Organized Crime*. New York: Russell Sage Foundation, 1972.

Ianni, Francis A. J. *Black Mafia: Ethnic Succession in Organized Crime*. New York: Simon and Schuster, 1974.

Inciardi, James A. *Careers in Crime*. Chicago: Rand McNally, 1975.

Klockars, Carl B. *The Professional Fence*. New York: Free Press, 1974.

Leff, Arthur A. *Swindling and Selling*. New York: Free Press, 1976.

Lemert, Edwin M. "The Behavior of the Systematic Check Forger." *Social Problems*, 6:141–49, 1958.

Mack, John A. "The Able Criminal." *British Journal of Criminology*, 13:44–54, 1972.

Mack, John A. *The Crime Industry*. London: Saxon House, 1975.

Mack, John A., & H. J. Kerner. "Professional and Organized Crime: A Comparative Approach," *International Journal of Criminology and Penology*, 4:113–28, 1976.

Maurer, David W. *The Big Con*. Indianapolis: Bobbs-Merrill, 1940.

Maurer, David W. *Whiz Mob: A Correlation of the Technical Argot of Pickpockets with Their Behavior Pattern*. Gainesville, Fla.: American Dialect Society, 1955.

McIntosh, Mary. *The Organization of Crime*. London: Macmillan, 1975.

McKenzie, Donald. *Occupation: Thief*. Indianapolis: Bobbs-Merrill, 1955.

Mollenhoff, Clark R. *Strike Force: Organized Crime and the Government*. Englewood Cliffs, N. J.: Prentice-Hall, 1972.

Moore, William H. *The Kefauver Committee and the Politics of Crime, 1950–52.* Columbia, Mo.: University of Missouri Press, 1974.

Robin, Gerald D. "Patterns of Department Store Shoplifting," *Crime and Delinquency,* 9:163–72, 1963.

Salerno, Ralph F., & John S. Tompkins. *The Crime Confederation.* New York: Doubleday, 1969.

Shover, Neal. "The Social Organization of Burglary." *Social Problems,* 20:499–514, 1973.

Smigel, Erwin O., & H. Laurence Ross. *Crimes Against Bureaucracy.* New York: Van Nostrand, 1970.

Smith, Dwight C. *The Mafia Mystique.* New York: Basic Books, 1975.

Snodgrass, Jon. "The Criminologist and His Criminal: The Case of Edwin H. Sutherland and Broadway Jones." *Issues in Criminology,* 8:1–17, 1973.

Steffens, Lincoln. *Autobiography.* New York: Harcourt, Brace, 1931.

Sutherland, Edwin H. *The Professional Thief.* Chicago: University of Chicago Press, 1937.

Talese, Gay. *Honor Thy Father.* New York: World, 1971.

Teresa, Vincent. *My Life in the Mafia.* New York: Doubleday, 1973.

Yeager, Matthew G. "The Gangster as White Collar Criminal: Organized Crime and Stolen Securities," *Issues in Criminology,* 8:49–73, 1973.

PART TWO

THE PROCESSING OF DELINQUENCY AND CRIME

13

Variations in Punitive Policies

With this chapter we begin the study of various methods of dealing with crime and with apprehended criminals. These methods may be described as societal reactions to crime and criminality, and, as such, they are subject to analysis and explanation, just as are criminal reactions. However, until quite recently, social scientists concentrated on understanding and explaining lawbreaking rather than on understanding and explaining the societal reactions to lawbreaking. Now, advocates of the labeling approach and the conflict approach, discussed in earlier chapters, call for correction of this deficiency. Indeed, most current criminological research focuses on the reactions of the many agencies engaged in processing criminals, rather than on criminals themselves.[1]

Nevertheless, the research data and other information about societal reactions to lawbreaking has not been organized or integrated, and theoretical problems in this area are therefore not as sharply delimited as are theoretical problems in criminal etiology. Systematic organization of knowledge about societal reactions to crime, or about interactions between criminal conduct and societal reactions to it, is a prerequisite for understanding and explaining present and future policies. As a preliminary step toward such integration, four general problems will be specified.

The first problem in the study of societal reactions is closely analogous to the problem of observing variations in the incidence of crime and delinquency. Just as we have described many variations in delinquency and crime rates, careful descriptions of variations in societal reactions to crime should be made. The varieties of methods and policies used in attempts to minimize crime are

---

[1] See Stanton Wheeler, "Trends and Problems in the Sociological Study of Crime," *Social Problems*, 23: 525–34, 1976.

enormous, if they are considered in detail, and it is necessary to classify and generalize these variations in a manner which will make them easier to study and understand. For instance, we can readily observe a great number of variations in reactions to lawbreaking, not only in the United States at present, but in the history of mankind. In some social systems the reaction to lawbreaking is annihilation, in some systems it is severe corporal punishments, while in yet others, it is imprisonment or probation, and so on. Similarly, the number of variations in the official policies for implementing the societal reactions to delinquency and crime—such as policies for police, courts, institutions—is enormous. For example, in some prisons the inmates are tortured, in others they are studiously ignored except when they try to escape, and in still others positive efforts are made to change them.

These many variations can be classified tentatively according to their position on a scale ranging from a purely *punitive* reaction or policy to a purely *interventionist* reaction or policy, although this classification does not summarize all the differences. Some societal reactions to crime and, hence, some policies and organizations for dealing with crime and criminals, have been and continue to be negative, directed primarily by concern for punishing criminals; others are positive, directed primarily by concern for intervening in the processes by which crime and criminality are produced; and a final category is produced by a mixture of punitive and interventionist considerations.

Second, the general problem of "efficiency" must be analyzed if the materials on the state's effort to control crime are to be integrated. Is the true crime rate really reduced when police and prosecutors enforce the law rather than using discretion and common sense in deciding who should be arrested? Do crime rates go down when punitive police policies are used, as compared to when interventionist policies are used? Until about 1970, official policies showed a distinct trend toward intervention and away from punishment, but this trend was not based on a demonstration of the superiority of interventionist methods. The criteria of efficiency have not been precisely established nor agreed upon, and for that reason what is said to be "efficient" is often more a matter of politics than of science.[2]

One preliminary and general criterion is that the system is most efficient which results in the smallest number of crimes, other things being equal. A small number of crimes may result from either of two things: few people who commit crimes, or few repetitions of crimes by those who commit at least one crime. Hence, according to this criterion an efficient system would reform those who commit crimes, so that they do not commit additional crimes; and the system would also keep others from committing their first crimes, either by *deterrence* (which has to do with refraining from crime due to fear of punishment), or by

[2] See Kurt Weis and Michael Milakovich, "Political Uses of Crime Rates," *Transaction*, 11:27–33, 1977; and David Seidman and Michael Coozens, "Getting the Crime Rate Down: Political Pressures and Crime Reporting," *Law and Society Review*, 8:457–93, 1974.

prevention (which has to do with changing the conditions which produce crime and delinquency in the first place).

In dealing with problems of efficiency, however, the question must be raised as to whether the most efficient method for reducing crime rates has a chance of being adopted in a given society at a given time. For example, even if it were shown with complete certainty that crime would be greatly reduced by implementation of a policy which is much less punitive than the policies now being used in the United States, this new policy might not be adopted. In view of what appears to be a punitive societal reaction to lawbreaking, our lawmakers would probably reject such a method. Similarly, a policy of extremely severe punishment might be rejected even if it were shown to be the most efficient method of dealing with criminals, for government officials also possess certain humanitarian attitudes. Further, a policy of strict enforcement or full enforcement of current laws probably would be rejected because it would interfere with those rights summarized by the phrase "due process of law." Or government officials might formally adopt the policy of severe punishment, only to wink at its enforcement. There is doubt as to whether such a policy would, in the circumstances in which it would be expected to operate, be superior to some other policy which would be carried out in a straightforward manner.[3]

A third general problem is that of establishing a relationship between varying reactions to lawbreaking on the one hand, and existing knowledge about crime causation on the other. However, changes in policies do not immediately follow new discoveries or theories about crime causation. Some present methods are clearly based on erroneous theories, but this apparent contradiction stems in part from the fact that some of the more fruitful theories, such as differential association, cannot readily be used as a basis for social policy.[4] Many modifications would be made if police departments, courts, probation departments, and prisons operated strictly in accordance with the criminological theory of emotional disturbances, or with the theory of economic determinism, or with the differential association theory.

The fourth general problem is not unlike the general problem of explaining crime and criminality. The problem may be summarized by the question, Why do the policies and methods for dealing with crime vary from time to time and from place to place? At present, the United States is witnessing a shift toward the punitive reaction to lawbreaking, and away from the interventionist reaction and the "due process of law" reaction. The problem is to locate the social origins of this trend. Generally speaking, the variations in policies and methods, and in the

---

[3]See Arthur Rosett and Donald R. Cressey, *Justice by Consent: Plea Bargains in the American Courthouse* (Philadelphia: Lippincott, 1976).

[4]James Q. Wilson, *Thinking About Crime* (New York: Vintage Books, 1977), pp. 52–58. See also Walter B. Miller, "Ideology and Criminal Justice Policy: Some Current Issues." *Journal of Criminal Law and Criminology*, 64:141–62, 1973.

frequency with which various methods are employed, will be accounted for by exploring the nature of the social organization of the societies in which they appear. Thus, for example, Kennedy has noted that penal sanctions as we know them arose in Western Europe in the fifteenth century, the time of the emergence of several other social forms, including concepts of citizenship, formal (rational) states, and the institutions of capitalism.[5]

More specific or detailed subsidiary problems that require explanation include the following: (1) Variations in the traditional modalities of punishment: severity, uniformity, celerity, and certainty. In some societies, punishments may be comparatively severe, uniform, swift, or certain, while in other societies the reaction to lawbreaking may be punitive but not so severe, so uniform, so swift, or so certain. Is it possible to make sense of such differences? (2) Variations in specific methods of implementing the punitive reaction, such as the death penalty, corporal punishment, imprisonment, and fines. (3) Variations in specific methods of implementing the positive interventionist reaction, such as individual case-work and community work with criminals, group therapy, community reorganization, and restructuring the economic and political-social order. (4) Variations between the official or formal reactions to crime and the unofficial or informal reactions.

The present chapter supplies some of the data on variations in the general punitive reaction to crime, as well as on variations in the use of specific methods of punishment, in different times and places. Chapters 14 and 15 are concerned with variations in other specific aspects of the punitive reaction, with variations in the interventionist reaction, with the comparative efficiency of punitive and interventionist policies, and with explanation of variations in punishment and intervention. After this "introduction," the interventionist and punitive aspects of the various agencies and institutions which deal with criminals, from the time of apprehension to the time of discharge from parole, will be discussed.

DEFINITION OF PUNISHMENT

Two essential ideas are contained in the concept of punishment as an instrument of public justice. First, it is deliberately inflicted by officials of the state upon one who is regarded as subject to the laws of the state. Killing enemies and destroying their property during times of war is not punishment, for the actions are directed against persons who are not state subjects. The loss of status which often follows commission of a crime is not punishment, except insofar as it is administered in measure by state officials. Second, punishment involves pain or suffering produced by design and justified by some value that the suffering is assumed to have. This is the conventional conception used in the criminal law. If the pain or suffering is merely accidental, to be avoided if possible, it is not punishment. A

[5] Mark C. Kennedy, "Beyond Incrimination: Some Neglected Facts of the Theory of Punishment," *Catalyst*, 5:1–37, 1970.

surgical operation performed on a prisoner to correct a physical defect is not punishment, for the pain is not regarded as valuable or desirable. Similarly, the confinement of a psychotic person usually involves suffering for that person, but the suffering is not punishment because judges and other officials do not assume that suffering is what the psychotic deserves, do not assume that locking up a psychotic will reduce the incidence of psychoses in the community, and do not assume that the suffering will "teach" the psychotic not to repeat the psychosis. All these assumptions are made about the value of the physical pain or psychological suffering imposed on criminals. Indeed, pain and suffering are deliberately imposed on criminals for these reasons.

VARIATIONS IN THE PUNITIVE REACTION TO LAWBREAKING

Many authorities have maintained that deliberately hurting criminals is an expression of an instinct of vengeance or of a desire for vengeance which is made up of a complex of instincts or urges. Some crimes upset the interests of dominant social groups, and various punitive responses—which partially restore the interests, at least symbolically—take place. However, there is no evidence that these reactions are directed by an instinct of vengeance or by a basic desire for punishment of the offender. Punishing people cannot be instinctual because it is only one of many reactions to lawbreaking, and it is not at all important in the reactions to offenses occurring among nonliterate peoples.

Three types of wrongs, followed by three types of reactions, no one of which is clearly punitive, were found in nonliterate societies. The first includes tribal and sacral offenses, such as treason, witchcraft, and sacrilege. Although such offenses seldom occurred in small, homogeneous groups, when they did occur the reaction was annihilation. The group might annihilate the offender by either death or exile; either reaction rendered the offender nonexistent so far as the group was concerned. The reaction of annihilation was closely related to war, social hygiene, and sacrifice. The offender was regarded as an enemy and was processed as an enemy. Offenders also were thought to be polluted, and the tribe attempted to get rid of them and of everything connected with them as a social hygiene measure. Thus, in many societies witchcraft was followed by death, and the body of the offender was thrown into the sea, which was supposed to have cleansing power, or it was buried on foreign soil. The offender's name could not even be mentioned for fear that it might carry pollution with it. An element of sacrifice also was present; annihilation by death or exile was designed to please the gods.[6]

The second group of wrongs were injuries to private individuals who were not in the same family. In contemporary terms, these offenses would be defined as assault, murder, and theft. Generally, they provoked feuds between families. The attitude in these feuds was largely vengeance, and severe suffering was involved.

[6]Gunter Wagner, "The Political Organization of the Banto of Kavirondo," Chapter 6 in *African Political Systems*, ed. E. E. Evans-Pritchard and Meyer Fortes (London: Oxford University Press, 1958).

But the reaction to the perceived harms was not punishment by state officials acting in the name of the whole society; it was private, involving two individuals and their relatives. By and large, the members of the community—including so-called "chiefs" and other leaders—were mere spectators, although one or the other of the opposing parties was likely to enjoy the approval or tacit support of these "disinterested" community members.[7] This seems to have been the origin of the system of payment of damages in civil courts, but not of punishment by criminal courts.[8]

The third group of wrongs consisted of injuries to other members of the same family. These wrongs were neither regarded as crimes nor followed by punishment in the sense that the word is used today. In the family, as in the tribe generally, ridicule was the most powerful method of control and was generally sufficient to secure observance of rules. This is illustrated by the Andaman Islanders:

> There is no such thing as the punishment of a crime by the society. If one person injured another, it was left to the injured one to seek vengeance if he wished and if he dared. There were probably always some who would side with the criminal, their attachment to him overcoming their disapproval of his actions. The only painful result of antisocial actions was the loss of the esteem of others. This in itself was a punishment that the Andamanese, with their great personal vanity, would feel keenly, and it was in most instances sufficient to prevent such actions. For the rest, good order depended largely on the influence of the more prominent men and women.[9]

Even if a young man killed his father, which was in many nonliterate groups regarded as a horrible offense, he was not punished by the other members of the family or by the tribe. The members of the family felt that since the family had already been weakened by the loss of one member, it would be foolish to weaken it still more by injuring the offender. They looked upon such acts, however, with great surprise and disgust.

Similarly, among modern nonliterate peoples who are fairly well segregated from civilization, as among primitive peoples, punishment of children seldom occurs:

> Travelers everywhere have remarked upon the extreme indulgence toward children. This is very marked among the Eskimos, though perhaps not more so than among the Fuegians of South America. Wherever we have data parents almost never punish or even severely reprove, but such pressure as may be needed is exercised by certain relatives. . . . Chastising the young seems to have been practised in the centres of higher culture, but outside of these limits was practically unknown. . . . In short, the same principles applied to control

[7] E. Adamson Hoebel, *The Law of Primitive Man: A Study in Comparative Legal Dynamics* (Cambridge, Mass.: Harvard University Press, 1954), pp. 329–30. See also Rafael Karsten, "Blood Revenge Among the Jibako Indians of Eastern Ecuador," in *Law and Warfare*, ed. Paul Bohannan (Garden City, N.Y.: Natural History Press, 1967), pp. 312–13.

[8] See Chapter 1 above.

[9] A. Radcliffe-Brown, *The Andaman Islanders* (Cambridge: University Press, 1922), p. 52.

of the young as to adults, *viz.*, admonition and ridicule. In fact, the whole control of the local group in aboriginal days seems to have been exercised by admonition and mild ridicule instead of by force and punishment.[10]

The Winnebago Indian had the following precepts:

If you have a child and it is naughty do not strike it. In old times if a child was naughty the parents did not strike it but made it fast. When it is quite hungry it will reflect upon its disobedience. If you hit him you will merely put more naughtiness into him. It is said that mothers should not lecture the children, that they merely make the children bad by admonishing them.[11]

In these nonliterate groups, therefore, we find certain motives and attitudes which apparently preceded the punitive reaction to lawbreaking but were not, in themselves, punishment: desire to annihilate an enemy of the group, sacrifice to appease or fend off the wrath of the gods, social hygiene measures to rid the community of pollution, self-redress in cases of private injury, and surprise and disgust at persons who injured their own families. Deliberate and "just" infliction of pain by the group in its corporate capacity was not invented until later.[12]

With the rise of kingship and the king's authority, disposition of wrongdoers became a public matter. The "court" arose and was backed by central authority, the state. The reaction to wrongs became collective or social rather than private, and wrongs were viewed as crimes—that is, as offenses against the state as well as against the victim.[13] The reaction approached the punitive reaction as we now know it, for severe corporal punishments were inflicted by state officials, but the notion that the pain imposed has some value in itself was not necessarily present. This kind of reaction is illustrated in the following statement about the Anglo-Saxon period in England:

A detected criminal was either fined, mutilated, or killed, but punishment, as we now understand the term, was seldom inflicted; that is to say, the dominant idea was neither to reform the culprit nor to deter others from following in his footsteps. If a man was killed it was either to satisfy the bloodfeud or to remove him out of the way as a wild beast would be destroyed; if a man was mutilated by having his fore-finger cut off or branded with a red-hot iron on the brow, it was done not so much to give him pain as to make him less expert in his trade of thieving and to put upon him an indelible mark by which all men should know that he was no longer a man to be trusted; if a fine were levied, it was more with a view to

---

[10]C. Wissler, *The American Indian* (New York: Oxford University Press, 1922), pp. 177–78.

[11]Paul Radin, *Crashing Thunder: The Autobiography of a Winnebago Indian* (New York: D. Appleton-Century, 1926), p. 463.

[12]For a discussion of feudal justice see Marc Bloch, *Feudal Society* (Chicago: University of Chicago Press, 1964).

[13]See E. Faris, "The Origin of Punishment," *International Journal of Ethics*, 25:54–67, 1914; Max Radin, "Enemies of Society," *Journal of Criminal Law and Criminology*, 27:328–56, 1936; Hans von Hentig, *Punishment: Its Origin, Purpose, and Psychology* (London: William Hodge, 1937); and Kennedy, "Beyond Incrimination."

the satisfaction of the recipients of the money or cattle or what not, than with the intention of causing discomfort or loss to the offender.[14]

It was not until the modern period that the clearly punitive reaction to crime—the purposive infliction of pain on the offender because of some assumed value of the pain—became popular. Debates regarding the wisdom and efficiency of this reaction and of specific policies and methods consistent with it gave rise to three schools of penology: the classical, the neoclassical, and the positive or Italian. The principal arguments of these schools will be used here as illustrations of variations in the punitive reaction to crime, on the assumption that each of the schools arose as a result of or in connection with a variation in reaction to crime, rather than on the assumption that the arguments of the schools caused the variations. The basic ideas about punishing criminals reflected in the writings of the members of the neoclassical and the positive schools are conflicting, but both are characteristic of the United States at present. They were discussed earlier in the section on schools of criminology.[15]

The classical school, to which Beccaria made one of the first significant contributions, and to which Rousseau, Montesquieu, and Voltaire belonged, maintained the doctrine of psychological hedonism, that the individual calculates pleasures and pains in advance of action and regulates his conduct by the results of his calculations. The implication was that it is necessary to make undesirable acts painful by attaching punishment to them, and to make the amount of pain thus attached knowable to all, so that prospective criminals can make rational calculations. Further, the amount of pain to be imposed on each of those committing a specific crime is to be such that the pain following the commission of the prohibited act will exceed the pleasures of committing the act. Consistently, the doctrine of the classical school was that the reaction to every crime should be administration of a measured amount of pain on the criminal by state officials. Because the punishment must be one that can be calculated in advance, it must be the same for all individuals, regardless of age, sex, mentality, social status, or other considerations. Bentham, the great reformer of the criminal law in this period, tried to extend hedonistic calculus by working out precise mathematical laws for the infliction of punishment. The question of individual responsibility was not considered, just as it had not been considered in the earlier period when offenders were annihilated.[16]

---

[14] W. L. M. Lee, *History of Police in England* (London: Methuen, 1901), p. 10. See also Linton C. Freeman and Robert F. Winch, "Societal Complexity: An Empirical Test of a Typology of Societies," *American Journal of Sociology*, 62:461–66, 1957; and Steven Spitzer, "Punishment and Social Organization: A Study of Durkheim's Theory of Penal Evolution," *Law and Society Review*, 9:613–37, 1975.

[15] See Chapter 3 above.

[16] In the earlier period, this lack of consideration for responsibility can best be shown by the penalties imposed upon inanimate objects, insects, and lower animals. Ives reported a number of instances in which inanimate objects were punished, and Evans collected a mass of materials regarding the medieval and modern practice of punishing animals. Much doubt was cast on the authenticity of Evans's account by Liquori, however, and it is highly probable that the few cases which may have occurred have little significance from a theoretical

The neoclassical school, which arose at the time of the French Revolution and the period immediately following, maintained that while the classical doctrine was correct in general, it should be modified in certain details: because children and "lunatics" cannot calculate pleasures and pains, they should not be regarded as criminals and thus should not be punished. This principle was occasionally extended to others by the practice of taking into account certain "mitigating circumstances." The reaction to crime, therefore, was no longer purely punitive; punishment was imposed on some lawbreakers but not on others. Recognition of the exceptions meant that individual responsibility was to be taken into account, and subsequently it was necessary for administrators of justice to consider the psychology and sociology of crime. The neoclassical argument became the basic principle of the judicial and legal system of Western civilization during the last century.

The positive school, in contrast to the neoclassical school, denied that even sane and mature persons are individually responsible for their criminal acts. Consistently, members of the positive school reflected an essentially nonpunitive reaction to crime and criminality. If criminals are not responsible for their acts, it follows logically that they should not be punished for those acts. The adherents of this doctrine maintained that a crime is a natural phenomenon, just like a tornado, a flood, a stroke of lightning, or the bite of a snake. In self-protection, the group might put criminals to death or incarcerate them, but those precautions were not considered to be punishment.[17] Criminals who could be reformed were to be reformed, and those who could not be reformed were to be segregated or killed. Denial of personal responsibility for individual criminals blurs the concept of guilt; it therefore seriously flaws the accused person's rights to jury trial, to counsel, to confront witnesses, and to other safeguards of "due process of law."[18]

Following the reactions to lawbreaking reflected in these three early schools of penology, two different reflections of a nonpunitive reaction to crime appeared. The first of these is treatment by individual casework, which substituted psychological determinism for the biological determinism of the early positivists. Thus this approach is based on the premises of the positive school, but differs from it as to procedures. The second is social psychological and sociological. Here,

---

point of view. George Ives, *A History of Penal Methods* (London: Stanley Paul, 1914), p. 254; E. P. Evans, *The Criminal Prosecution and Capital Punishment of Animals* (London: W. Heinemann, 1906), pp. 143, 175; Sister Mary Liquori, "The Trial and Punishment of Animals," *America*, February 1, 1936, pp. 395–96. Until the last two centuries, intent was generally not an issue in the determination of whether or not a person should be convicted of a crime. Intensive studies of particular communities indicate, however, that generalizations of this nature are subject to many exceptions.

[17] In Europe, recent attempts to introduce this idea into penal legislation are properly characterized as pleas for "social defense" against criminals. For a history of the "new social defense" movement, see Marc Ancel, *Social Defence* (London: Routledge and Kegan Paul, 1965).

[18] See Jerome Hall, "Science and Reform in Criminal Law," *University of Pennsylvania Law Review*, 100:787–804, 1952; and Sidney J. Kaplan, "Barriers to the Establishment of a Deterministic Criminal Law," *Kentucky Law Journal*, 26:103–11, 1957.

crime and criminality are seen as products of group relations, not of individual choice or defect. For this reason, criminality cannot be treated effectively by psychotherapy or by other forms of casework; it must be handled as a problem of culture-bearing groups. This might be called group work, but it is different from the group work of most social workers. Its interventions include modifications of society as well as modifications of the group relations of criminals. These two procedures and the societal reaction of which they are a part will be discussed later.[19]

VARIATIONS IN USE OF METHODS FOR IMPLEMENTING THE PUNITIVE REACTION

Like the general punitive reaction to lawbreaking, the specific techniques for implementing or expressing the punitive reaction has varied from time to time and place to place. During the history of mankind, four principal methods of implementing the punitive policy have been used, but there has been no distinct evolution of any one system from the others. Removal from the group by death, by exile, or by imprisonment; physical torture; social degradation; and financial loss all have been used differentially in various historical periods, and they are used differentially today. While it cannot be maintained that any one type of punitive reaction is exclusively characteristic of any one historical period or of any one society, certain emphases upon the different methods can be observed. In the United States at present, for example, all four of the systems are used to some degree, but certainly imprisonment is emphasized.

The Death Penalty

The prevalence of capital punishment has varied a great deal in different societies.[20] Such techniques of inflicting death as burning, boiling in oil, breaking at the wheel, the iron coffin, drowning, and impaling have had their greatest frequency not in the earliest or in the more recent societies, but in the society of the medieval period. Impaling and immuring were practiced in Switzerland until about 1400, and death by drowning until about 1600. The last case of burning at the stake in Berlin was in 1786. In Frankfurt, Germany, the number of executions was 317 in the fifteenth century, 248 in the sixteenth, and only 140 in the seventeenth.[21] In the cantons of Zurich and Schwyz, 572 executions occurred in the sixteenth century, 336 in the seventeenth, and only 149 in the eighteenth.[22]

---

[19] See Chapter 15 below.

[20] As suggested above, it is not always clear that execution of a criminal is punishment in the strict sense of the word. A rather intensive study of the circumstances of the executions must be made to determine whether the executions in certain historical periods were punishments. Such a study has not been made, and it will be necessary, therefore, to accept the uncritical statements now available.

[21] G. L. Kriegk, *Deutsches Bürgerthum im Mittelalter* (Frankfurt, Germany: Rütten und Löning, 1868–1871), vol. I, pp. 200–1.

[22] Karl L. von Bar, *A History of Continental Criminal Law* (Boston: Little, Brown, 1916), p. 299.

In England, however, the situation is somewhat different, for there were only seventeen capital offenses in the early part of the fifteenth century, about 350 in 1780, and then, by 1839, the number was reduced again to about the same as it had been four centuries before.[23] In the earlier part of this period in England, the death penalty was frequently inflicted for religious offenses, but most of the later inflictions were for offenses against property, and many of them for very trivial offenses. In 1814, three boys—aged eight, nine, and eleven—were sentenced to death for stealing a pair of shoes. This was not unusual.[24] During the early part of the modern period, the corpse was gibbeted, that is, remained hanging in chains, and was sometimes soaked in tar so that it would remain for a long time as a warning to evildoers. These objects were seen so frequently that landscape painters considered them an essential part of the scenery and not infrequently introduced them into their landscapes.[25]

Under the leadership of Romilly, Bentham, Peel, McIntosh, Montagu, Cruickshank, and others, and as the power of the common people increased, the use of capital punishment decreased. But as late as 1814, Romilly tried in vain to substitute simple hanging as the official reaction to treason, in place of the existing penalty of hanging, cutting down alive, disemboweling, cutting off the head, and quartering the body. Although the later penalty was not actually carried out, members of Parliament were afraid that treason would be greatly increased if the law were modified.

During the course of the last century, a distinct trend away from the death penalty has occurred. The Economic and Social Council of the United Nations, as well as the General Assembly, has several times passed resolutions encouraging abolition. Sweden in 1975 became the tenth nation in the world to eliminate the death sentence from its law books. Canada became the eleventh in 1976. About twenty-five other countries have removed capital punishment from civilian penal codes but retained it in military codes. Venezuela did so in 1863, Argentina in 1973. In many other nations the offenses for which the death penalty may be imposed have been limited, usually to murder or some specific form of murder, such as killing a police officer.[26]

Of the fifty-two jurisdictions in the United States in 1971, only one (the District of Columbia) had a mandatory death penalty; thirty-six had a permissive death penalty; nine jurisdictions did not permit the death penalty; and six severely restricted its use. The states which in 1971 did not permit the death penalty or which limited it to crimes such as killing a police officer were Alaska,

[23]See Leon Radzinowicz, *A History of English Criminal Law and Its Administration from 1750* (New York: Macmillan, 1948), vol. 1, pp. 42–79, 611–59.

[24]See Douglas Hay, "Property, Authority, and the Criminal Law," chap. 1 in Douglas Hay, Peter Linebaugh, John G. Rule, E. P. Thompson, and Cal Winslow, *Albion's Fatal Tree: Crime and Society in Eighteenth-Century England* (New York: Pantheon, 1975), pp. 17–63.

[25]W. Andrews, *Old-Time Punishments* (London: Hull, W. Andrews, 1890), pp. 211–12.

[26]James McCafferty, "Major Trends in the Use of Capital Punishment," *Federal Probation*, 25:15–21, 1961.

Arizona, Hawaii, Iowa, Maine, Michigan, Minnesota, North Dakota, Oregon, Rhode Island, Vermont, Wisconsin, New Mexico, New York, and West Virginia. Puerto Rico and the Virgin Islands also had abolished capital punishment legislatively. In 1972, certain death penalty laws were declared unconstitutional, and thus abolished, by the U.S. Supreme Court, but in 1976 the Court held that some of the new death penalty laws, enacted in response to the 1972 decision, were constitutional. The Court's decision was complex but, generally speaking, it invalidated *mandatory* death penalty statutes and upheld *guided-discretion* statutes giving juries or judges the power to choose between death and life imprisonment after considering, in individual cases and according to statute, certain aggravating and mitigating conditions.

Several variations may be observed in the use of the death penalty in the United States during the last century. First, there was a fluctuating tendency to abolish it. Between 1847, when the first state abolished the death penalty, and 1876, four states prohibited capital punishment. One addition to this list was made in 1907 and another in 1911. From 1913 to 1918, seven other states were added, but five of them restored the penalty after an average experience of two and a half years. Delaware joined the abolition states in 1958, being the first state to do so since 1918. However, in 1961 Delaware restored the death penalty. There are periodic attempts to abolish capital punishment in those states retaining it, and to restore it in those states which have abolished it.

Second, a more pronounced recent variation was substitution of a permissive death penalty law for the mandatory one. Courts and juries were given the power of deciding whether one who has committed a capital offense must be executed. In 1918, the death penalty was mandatory on conviction of capital crime in twelve states, in 1938 in five states, and in 1964 and thereafter in none of the states.

Of the states which permitted capital punishment, an average of about one-third each year had no executions. In 1945–1959, Illinois imposed the death penalty on only 1.2 percent of those eligible for it.[27] Maryland in 1936–1961 executed 56 percent of those sentenced to death; in 1936–1940 this percentage was 69; in 1946–1950 it was 56; and in 1956–1960 it was 23.[28] In 1967 there were only two executions by the federal government or by the states which permitted the death penalty, and between 1967 and 1976—when Utah officials shot a convicted murderer—there were no executions in the United States. Thus, to some extent the introduction of permissive clauses was a technique for abolishing capital punishment in practice while retaining it in law.

Third, public opinion concerning capital punishment shifts with the times and especially with changing perceptions of increasing crime rates.[29] For the last

---

[27] Daniel Glaser, "Survey of the Death Sentence in Illinois" (Chicago: John Howard Association, 1959. Mimeographed).

[28] Legislative Council of Maryland, *Report of the Committee on Capital Punishment* (Baltimore: Legislative Council of Maryland, 1962), p. 54.

[29] Charles W. Thomas and Samuel C. Foster, "A Sociological Perspective on Public Support for Capital Punishment," *American Journal of Orthopsychiatry*, 45:641–57, 1975.

twenty-five years, the Gallup poll has, at intervals, asked a representative sample of the United States population aged twenty-one and over a standardized question on capital punishment: "Are you in favor of the death penalty for persons convicted of murder?" In 1953, 68 percent of those polled answered yes. In 1960, this percentage was 52; in 1965, it had declined to 45, and in 1966, to 42. In 1969 the percentage answering yes had climbed again to 51; in 1972 the percentage of yes opinions was 57, and by 1976 the percentage climbed back to 65, almost as high as it was in 1953. A 1972 poll by the American Institute of Public Opinion found that among persons with incomes over $15,000, 52 percent favored the death penalty, while among persons with incomes under $3000 only 43 percent favored it.[30]

Fourth, the number of capital crimes has been reduced. In 1970, there were in the fifty states only twelve capital offenses, and no one state had declared all of these to be capital offenses. Only one crime was punishable by death in fourteen states, two in eight states, and only nine states had as many as six capital crimes.[31] In practice, however, between 1930 and 1967 less than two percent of the 3857 executions were for crimes other than murder and rape.

Fifth, over the last century the annual number and proportion of executions decreased, largely as a result of the changes mentioned above. The number of executions in the United States decreased rather consistently each year after 1935. Table 20 shows that in Ohio the number of death sentences decreased very greatly in proportion to the number of admissions to prison for first-degree murder, while the percent of the death sentences which were actually executed decreased from 1900 to 1915, increased decidedly until 1940, and then declined.

Sixth, executions were closed to the public. While executions were at one time public spectacles, the number of witnesses was increasingly restricted.[32]

Seventh, in place of prolonged torture, the method of execution was made as swift and painless as possible in a large proportion of the states. Electrocution was adopted in New York in 1888, and by 1970 this method was being used by twenty-three states. Ten states now provide for execution by deadly gas, while eight authorize hanging and one (Utah) offers a choice between hanging and firing squad. In other nations, hanging is the most widely used method of execution. Garrotting survives as the means of execution in only one country, Spain.

In 1930–1975, 3857 executions by civil authorities occurred in the United States, of which 86 percent were for murder and 12 percent for rape. Of the executed persons, 45 percent were white, 54 percent black, and 1 percent other

---

[30] Michael J. Hindelang, "Public Opinion Regarding Crime, Criminal Justice, and Related Topics," *Journal of Research in Crime and Delinquency,*" 11:101–16, 1974.

[31] The exact number of capital offenses is difficult to determine because of the tendency to specify subcategories. For example, Ohio specified first-degree murder as a capital offense, but it also specified that killing of a policeman (a form of first-degree murder) is a capital offense. See Leonard D. Savitz, "Capital Crimes as Defined in American Statutory Law," *Journal of Criminal Law, Criminology, and Police Science,* 46:355–63, 1955.

[32] See John Lofland, *The Dramaturgy of State Executions* (Montclair, N. J.: Patterson Smith, 1977).

races. Fewer than 1 percent were female. About 60 percent of the executions carried out each year since 1930 occurred in seventeen southern and south-western states, which contain about one-third of the nation's population.[33]

Physical Torture

Societies have implemented to varying degrees the punitive reaction by corporal punishment. Branding, stocks, pillory, mutilation, confinement in irons and cages, and whipping were used extensively in the medieval and early modern periods. Such penalties, in general, have increased and decreased in prevalence as the death penalty has increased or decreased in prevalence.

Whipping is the only one of the many varieties of corporal punishment which has been officially retained in Western civilization, and the trend of opinion is very much against it. In Great Britain it was a legal penalty for certain adult crimes and juvenile delinquencies until 1948.

In the United States, whipping is authorized in only one state. Until 1952 it could be used on wife-beaters in Maryland, but it seldom was inflicted. It is authorized in Delaware for several crimes. Of the 7302 offenders convicted in Delaware in 1900–1942 for crimes which called for whipping, 22 percent were whipped; this percentage was 70 in 1900, 55 in 1910, 30 in 1921, 15 in 1930, 7 in 1940. Few floggings, however, have taken place in Delaware since 1950.[34]

Social Degradation

Shame and humiliation have been used to impose suffering by reduction of the social status of the offender, sometimes temporarily, sometimes permanently. In general, this method of punishment flourished from the beginning of the sixteenth to the end of the seventeenth century, but it is not absent even today. Many techniques for reducing prestige have been used in various societies. Some were used extensively in the societies in which physical torture was the primary method for implementing the punitive reaction. For example, the ducking stool, the stocks, the pillory, the brank, and other devices were not only instruments of corporal punishment, but were used to reduce the status of the offender as well. They were used for minor offenses, such as scolding, giving short weights, forgery, and blasphemy. In the seventeenth century one offender who had stolen cabbages from his neighbor's garden in New York was ordered to stand in the pillory with the cabbages on his head, and in addition was banished from the colony for five years.[35] The brank was a cagelike device placed over the head; it was provided with a bar which was thrust into the mouth of the offender, thus holding down the

[33] Federal Bureau of Prisons, "Capital Punishment 1930–1970," *National Prisoner Statistics Bulletin*, No. 46, August, 1971.

[34] Robert G. Caldwell, *Red Hannah: Delaware's Whipping Post* (Philadelphia: University of Pennsylvania Press, 1947), pp. 69–70. For an analysis of the decline of corporal punishment, see Ernest van den Haag, *Punishing Criminals: Concerning a Very Old and Painful Question* (New York: Basic Books, 1975), pp. 196–206.

[35] Phillip Klein, *Prison Methods in New York State* (New York: Columbia University Press, 1920), p. 23.

Table 20 Admissions to Ohio Penitentiary for First-Degree Murder, Percent of These Admissions with Death Sentences, and Percent of Death Sentences Executed, by Five-Year Periods, 1896–1968

Years	Number of Admissions for First-Degree Murder	Percent of First-Degree Murder Admissions with Death Sentences	Percent of Death Sentences Which Were Executed
1896–1900	33	58	58
1901–1905	44	43	74
1906–1910	55	40	59
1911–1915	43	21	45
1916–1920	118	27	59
1921–1925	151	41	82
1926–1930	197	26	69
1931–1935	189	31	78
1936–1940	178	21	84
1941–1945	110	21	87
1946–1950	229	21	77
1951–1955	167	12	60
1956–1960	102	25	54
1961–1965	117	19	21
1966–1968	91	24	0

Source: Data for 1896–1930 compiled by the Ohio Institute; 1931–1968 data compiled by the Bureau of Research and Statistics, Ohio Department of Mental Hygiene and Correction. Some imprecision in column four is introduced by the fact that the persons executed in any five-year period were not necessarily the same persons admitted during that period.

tongue. Occasionally this bar had spikes on it to prevent any use of the tongue. This device was regarded as superior to the ducking stool in dealing with scolds, because the scold could talk between ducks.

The marks of degradation, temporary or permanent, inflicted in an effort to reduce the social status of offenders often made them into outlaws. An English statue of 1698, which provided for branding on the left cheek, was repealed after eight years with the explanation that this penalty

had not had its desired effect of deterring offenders from the further committing of crimes and offenses but, on the contrary, such offenders, being rendered thereby unfit to be entrusted in any service or employment to get their livelihood in any honest and lawful way, became the more desperate.[36]

[36]Luke O. Pike, *A History of Crime in England* (London: Smith, Elder, 1873–1876), Vol. 2, p. 280.

Another way of degrading criminals is to deprive them of rights of various kinds following commission of "infamous" and certain other crimes. In the Roman Republic, infamy as the result of the conviction of crime meant loss of the right to vote, to hold office, to represent another in the courts, to be a witness, to manage the affairs of another, and the abridging of the right to marry. During the early modern period certain crimes also resulted in infamy. This infamy was produced to some extent merely by the publicity of the trial, but also by the subsequent loss of rights of citizenship. In addition, offenders were branded or mutilated, so that everyone might know that they had been guilty of crimes, and so that they were exposed to continuing suffering. Loss of rank, mutilation of the body after death, and other methods were used to produce a greater infamy than the public would naturally or ordinarily attribute to the offender. During the feudal period, by bills of attainder, persons convicted of treason or felony might be deprived of their real and personal property, their right to inherit or transmit property, and all rights in the courts. This was known as "civil death."

In the United States, various traces of the "civil death" concept are still observable in thirteen states; other states have disavowed the concept but nevertheless provide for specific disabilities.[37] The following are the principal rights which, at present, may be lost in various states by the commission of serious crimes. (1) The right to vote is lost upon conviction of almost all felonies in all states except Indiana, Massachusetts, New Hampshire, and Vermont. (2) The right to hold public office is lost in most states. Public offices are generally restricted to electors, and therefore the loss of suffrage carries with it the loss of the right to hold office. In addition, certain other restrictions are specified in some states, such as incapacity to serve on a jury or to testify as a witness. (3) The right to practice certain professions or occupations. In addition, in a few states the convicted felon loses the right to make a contract, to marry, or to migrate to a foreign country.[38]

The disabilities produced as the result of conviction are terminated automatically in some states when the sentence is served; in other states they are terminated if the person is not indicted or convicted for another crime within a specified time after the completion of the sentence. In most states the disabilities are removed only by pardon, and in some of them not even by pardon. The validity of various disability statutes have recently been challenged in the courts.[39] However, as Garfinkel has shown, successful degradation ceremonies destroy old identities and create new, and disabling, ones; because such degradation is part of the punishment mandated by each criminal law, it cannot be erased by repeal of disability statutes.[40]

[37] Neil Cohen and Dean Hill Rivkin, "Civil Disabilities: The Forgotten Punishment," *Federal Probation*, 35:19–25, 1971.

[38] Ibid. See also Mirjam R. Damaska, "Adverse Legal Consequences of Conviction and Their Removal: A Comparative Study," *Journal of Criminal Law, Criminology, and Police Science*, 59:347–60, 542–68, 1968.

[39] Sol Rubin, "The Man with a Record: A Civil Rights Problem," *Federal Probation*, 35:3–7, 1971.

[40] Harold Garfinkel, "Conditions of Successful Degradation Ceremonies," *American Journal of Sociology*, 61:420–24, 1956.

Banishment and Transportation

Practically all societies have banished some criminals, especially political criminals, but wholesale deportation of offenders is a rather recent invention.[41] Banishment was used in early societies and in ancient Rome, where it was either a prohibition against coming into a specified territory, generally the city of Rome, or a prohibition against going outside a specified territory, such as an island to which the offender had been removed; in either case, banishment might be for life or for a short time. After a long period during which this method for expressing the punitive reaction to crime was seldom used, the method was revived. In England the first modern legalization of transportation was in 1598, and concerned "rogues, vagabonds, and sturdy beggars." However, the law was not often used until the period during which America was colonized. From that time until the American Revolution a considerable proportion of England's criminal population was sent to America. The Transportation Act of 1718 declared that its purpose was both to deter criminals and to supply the colonies with labor.[42]

In 1786, after the American colonies had become independent, the policy of transportation to Australia was adopted, and this practice continued until 1867. The total number transported during this period was 134,308, but the average number per year was 474 during the period 1787–1816, and about 3000 between 1816 and 1838. In England in 1834, the sentence of transportation was imposed on 4053 persons, death on 480, and imprisonment on 10,716. This shows that at the time, transportation, though at its height, was not being used as frequently as imprisonment. But all except 314 of those sentenced to prison had terms of one year or less, which means that imprisonment was used almost entirely for offenses considered to be relatively trivial.

Transportation was abandoned by England because it was found not to be a good method of reformation or deterrence, because it was expensive, and primarily because it was strenuously opposed by the Australian colonies. John Mitchel, a convict transported for aiding in the Irish rebellion, described the conditions in Australia in 1851 as follows:

> There is but one political question now existing—the transportation system. Most of the decent colonists, having families growing up, and feeling the effects of the moral and social atmosphere that surrounds them, and the ignominy of having no country but a penal colony, no servants, no laborers, few neighbors even, who are not men fairly due to the gallows—ardently desire to use this new Constitution, such as it is, to make vigorous protest against the continuance of the penal system.[43]

Many other countries have used transportation in the modern period. In the sixteenth century, Portugal sent criminals and women of ill repute to Brazil and later sent criminals to Angola. Spain tried transportation in a limited way in the eighteenth century. Russia has used Siberia as a penal colony since 1823. Italy has

[41]See Spitzer, "Punishment and Social Organization."
[42]A. G. L. Shaw, *Convicts and the Colonies* (London: Faber and Faber, 1966), p. 25.
[43]John Mitchel, *Jail Journal* (Dublin: J. Corrigan, 1864), p. 264.

transported some convicts to the islands along her coast since 1865; and France from 1763 to 1766, in 1824, and from 1851 to the present has used transportation to some extent.

Banishment, which is closely related to transportation, is still used as part of the penalty for certain types of crimes. It is never certain, however, that banishment is intended to cause criminals to suffer, rather than merely to get rid of them. In 1637, in one of the earliest criminal prosecutions on American soil, the sentence imposed was that the defendant was to be "banished from out of our jurisdiction as being a woman not fit for our society."[44] In 1969–1971, 826 alien criminals were deported from the United States; an additional 589 persons were deported as narcotic addicts.[45] A modified form of banishment also is used constantly in the United States at present. It consists of giving a person accused or convicted of a minor offense a specified number of hours in which to leave the country, town, or state.

Imprisonment

Early Uses   In ancient and medieval societies, and in nonliterate societies in general, imprisonment was rarely used as a penalty. Similarly, the penalty of imprisonment hardly ever occurred in early Greece; and it was not used at all in the Roman Republic but was used for minor offenses in the Empire. The last code of laws in France previous to the Revolution was made in 1670 and contained no mention of imprisonment as a penalty. Incarceration was sometimes used in France and other countries, however, either as a means of enforcing the payment of fines or as a commutation of death sentences when mitigating circumstances were found.

In England, imprisonment was used in a few cases in the Anglo-Saxon period, as in a law providing that persons convicted of murder or theft should be imprisoned for 120 or 40 days respectively, before they could be redeemed by their kinsmen. Henry II provided a penalty of imprisonment for one year for perjury, and Henry III provided the same penalty for breaches of the forest law. In 1241 some Jews convicted of circumcising a Christian child were ordered either to pay twenty thousand marks "or else be kept perpetual prisoners." But it was in the reign of Edward I in the latter half of the thirteenth century that incarceration came into extensive use in England, though even in this period it was used primarily as a "squeezer," or means of securing fines.

Thus, in general, until about the last part of the thirteenth century in England, and probably a little later in some of the Continental countries, imprisonment as a penalty was used only for very restricted groups of offenders. It is, therefore, a comparatively modern method of dealing with offenders, though its roots run back to ancient societies.

[44] William O. Douglas, *An Almanac of Liberty* (New York: Doubleday, 1954) p. 135.
[45] Immigration and Naturalization Service, Department of Justice, *Annual Report, 1971* (Washington: Department of Justice, 1972), p. 81.

Imprisonment by the Church   The early church authorities did use imprison-ment, partly because they were not permitted by law to kill offenders, and partly because they believed that isolation from others was rehabilitative. In 1283, a certain Brother John bit his prior's finger "like a dog," and the bishop gave orders to

> keep the said Brother John in prison under iron chains in which he shall be content with bread, indifferent ale, pottage, and a pittance of meat or fish (which on the sixth day he shall do without) until he is penitent.[46]

Though this method was used by the church as early as the fifth century, it was used most extensively during the Inquisition, when it was the most severe penalty that could be inflicted for any offense on those who professed conversion. In 1229, Gregory IX ordered that all who were converted after arrest because of fear of death should be imprisoned for life; this rule was stated by several councils, also. In the Inquisition of Toulouse from 1246 to 1248, of 192 known sentences, all were imprisonment except 43 death penalties imposed on persons who refused to appear; of the 149 prison sentences, 127 were for life, 6 for ten years, and 16 for an indefinite period. Of the 636 sentences imposed by the medieval inquisitor Bernard Gui from 1308 to 1322 (of which 88 were imposed on persons already dead), 300 were imprisonment. Many of these sentences were commuted, however. Such releases were necessary in part because of the lack of prisons, but in general the idea of reformation was taken into account. St. John Chrysostom, the early Christian philosopher, said: "I require not continuance of time, but the correction of your soul; demonstrate your contrition, demonstrate your reforma-tion, and all is done."[47]

Ecclesiastical imprisonment varied from strict confinement in absolute soli-tude, known as *in pace*, to congregate life in the corridors of the prisons, with occasional retirement to a cell, which was known as *murus largus.* As a matter of fact there was much association between prisoners in many institutions, some gambling and feasting, and some grafting by jailers who kept the money of prisoners or food that had been sent to the prison for them, and ordered supplies for prisoners who had long been dead.

Imprisonment in the Galleys   Huge boats propelled by oars as well as by sails were used considerably as places of confinement for criminals from about 1500 to the early part of the eighteenth century. This practice was a revival of the ancient method of forced labor, although in the earlier period galley slaves were not necessarily criminals. The practice continued until large sailing vessels were developed to such an extent that the galleys could not successfully compete with them. In 1602, Queen Elizabeth appointed a commission to make arrangements for commuting other penalties to galley labor, so that offenders may be "in such

---

[46]Quoted in Ives, *History of Penal Methods*, p. 43.
[47]Ibid., p. 38.

sort corrected and punished that even in their punishment they may yeld more profitable service to the Common welth."[48]

In seventeenth-century France, the courts were ordered to refrain from other methods of punishment as much as possible in order to provide crews for galleys. Those who could not work in the galleys, such as women, aged, and infirm convicts, were frequently imprisoned on land during this period, and when the galleys were abandoned, many former slaves were transported or were held in hulks on the shores or in arsenals.[49]

Imprisonment in Houses of Correction[50]   The house of correction appeared in England about the middle of the sixteenth century, when, on the petition of Bishop Ridley of London for help in dealing with the "sturdy vagabonds" of the city, the king gave his palace at Bridewell to be one of the "hospitals of the city," for the "lewd and idle" and a place for the employment of the unemployed and the training of children. By act of 1576, Parliament provided that a house of correction should be erected in each county, and in 1609 provided penalties for counties that failed to erect such institutions. The assumption was that hard work at rather unpleasant tasks would reform criminals, but the possibility of profits was not overlooked. Also, in addition to punitive labor, corporal punishments were used. Justices were ordered to search for "rogues, vagabonds, and idle persons" and to commit them to institutions, but the institutions also were used for confinement of "lewd women" with illegitimate children who might become a charge on the community and for men who deserted their families. By an act of 1711 the maximum period of confinement in these houses of correction was fixed at three years, and by subsequent legislation the number of offenses for which persons might be committed was greatly enlarged. By the early part of the eighteenth century, the house of correction and the common jail were practically the same in discipline and character of inmates.

This system for implementation of the punitive reaction to lawbreaking also was used on the Continent during the same period. It began a little later, but was used more extensively than in England. In 1669 one Peter Rentzel established a workhouse in Hamburg at his own expense because he had observed that thieves and prostitutes were made worse instead of better by the pillory, and he hoped that

---

[48] Ibid., pp. 103–104.

[49] See W. Branch-Thompson, *The English Prison Hulks* (London: Christopher Johnson, 1957).

[50] It is necessary to make a distinction between the house of correction and the workhouse. Technically the workhouse was an institution in which employment was furnished to those able and willing to work, and industrial training was furnished for the young; consequently, it was a part of the "welfare" system. The house of correction, on the other hand, was a part of the penal system, designed to protect the poor-relief funds against encroachments by those able but unwilling to work. Thus, the house of correction was designed to compel "sturdy beggars" to work. But as a matter of fact, the two institutions are hardly distinguishable during the larger part of their history in England and America, and no attempt is made in the present discussion to differentiate them precisely. However, no attention is paid to the workhouse in its pure form.

they might be improved by work and religious instruction in the workhouse.[51] A house of correction was established in Waldheim in 1716 with the lower floor for criminals and the upper floor for paupers and orphans, and with complete separation of the sexes on both floors. On entrance the criminals received a "welcome" of ten lashes; work was compulsory and silence was the rule. The staff of the institution included a chaplain, a teacher, and a physician, which was distinctly noteworthy at that time. During the first century of its history this institution received 13,954 persons, of whom 7921 were criminals, 4642 paupers, and 1391 orphans. Almost half of the criminals were convicted of theft, a fourth of begging and vagrancy, and an eighth of sexual offenses; 270 of them were convicted of homicide, which was usually infanticide. Perhaps the most famous house of correction on the Continent was the one established in Ghent in 1775.

Early Prison Reforms   The early "prison reform" movement, which reached its peak in the last part of the eighteenth century and the first part of the nineteenth century, actually was a movement for the popularization of a relatively new punitive method: imprisonment as a system of punishment. Although imprisonment as punishment was in part the basis of the system of committing offenders to houses of correction, jails, and hulks in the seventeenth and eighteenth centuries, the primary use of imprisonment at that time was for persons awaiting trial. The reforms advocated and accomplished were primarily in reference to the prison as a place of detention, and they may be seen best in England and America. Chapter 21 explores the changing character of imprisonment in America.

In England, from the middle of the seventeenth century there had been considerable publicity regarding prison practices and various suggestions for methods of improvement. Geoffrey Mynshal, committed to prison as an insolvent debtor, while in prison wrote "Certain Characters and Essays of Prison and Prisoners," which was published in 1618. This was the first regular treatise on prison abuses; it describes most of the practices and conditions of prison life which John Howard found a century and a half later. In 1699, the Society for the Promotion of Christian Knowledge, with a committee on prisons, was formed. This committee visited many prisons and presented a report in 1702, under the title "Essay towards the Reformation of Newgate and other Prisons in and about London." The following conditions are mentioned: the old criminals corrupt the new; swearing, blasphemy, and gambling; unlimited use of intoxicating liquors; personal lewdness of officers and keepers; and the cooperation of officers with the prisoners in their vices. The committee suggested methods of reducing these conditions as follows: separate confinement in cells, labor while in prison, regular religious services, abolition of fees, prohibition of liquor in prison, retention of hardened offenders until evidence is furnished that they will secure decent

[51] F. H. Wines, *Punishment and Reformation* (New York: Crowell, 1895), pp. 115–16.

employment when released and until they give security for good behavior, and advertisement to the public of the names of those prisoners who have lived decently in prison with the object of securing help for these prisoners after their release.

During the next century, the investigations, reports, and discussions continued; a few laws were passed; a few individuals in control of prisons undertook to make improvements as suggested by committees. In 1773, Parliament authorized magistrates to appoint chaplains in their jails. This was the first official recognition of the desirability of attempting to reform the prisoners. But in some institutions the felons were not permitted to attend religious services as late as 1808.

The great prison reformer of England was John Howard, who in 1777 wrote *The State of Prisons in England* after a personal investigation of practically all the prisons of England. This book contains, after a short summary, a description of each prison, so that it is a mass of concrete details. His general conclusion was:

If it were the wish and aim of magistrates to effect the destruction present and future of young delinquents, they could not devise a more effectual method, than to confine them so long in our prisons, those seats and seminaries . . . of idleness and every vice.[52]

Howard's work was supplemented by that of other leaders, and several societies for prison reform were formed. Substantial changes were made in prisons, as may be determined by a comparison of Dixon's account of the prisons in 1850[53] with Howard's account of 1777. In fact, Beaumont in 1821 lamented that prisons had changed so much that they were no longer a deterrent. He argued that workmen preferred prison life to the life of freedom, and he urged a return to the earlier methods.[54] Another author berated justices of the peace for indulging "in such costly fads as the separation of male prisoners from females, of adults from children, and of the convicted from the unconvicted, whilst altogether disapproving the extravagant cubic space required either for the cellular confinement or for the useful employment of any prisoners."[55]

This sketch shows that imprisonment as a method of implementing the punitive reaction to lawbreaking rarely occurred in earlier societies. It was adopted by the church and used quite extensively, and then common jails and special prisons for larger and larger proportions of criminals arose, until in the early nineteenth century, imprisonment came to be the principal method of punishing serious offenders. In England there has been an unbroken downward trend in the use of imprisonment by superior courts since 1900. Along the same lines, more than half of Dutch prison sentences since about 1965 have been for under a month; sentences of more than one year run about five percent of all prison sentences. In the United States, the number of youths confined in state institu-

---

52 John Howard, *The State of Prisons in England and Wales*, 2d ed. (London: Cadell and Conant, 1780), p. 13.
53 W. Hepworth Dixon, *The London Prisons* (London: Jackson and Walford, 1850).
54 B. Beaumont, "Essay on Criminal Jurisprudence," *Pamphleteer* (1821), pp. 1873 ff.
55 Edward Mullins, *A Treatise on the Magistracy of England* (London, 1836).

tions, camps, and ranches in 1969 was 43,500, but by 1974 this number had decreased to 28,000; some states send up to twenty times as many youths to institutions as other states (adjusting for population sizes), and these proportions have no relationship to the states' crime rates. The wealthier, more urbanized and industrial states have the lowest incarceration rates.[56]

Financial Penalties

Reaction to criminality by general confiscation of property or by imposition of a fine has existed in most literate societies, but there have been great variations in the emphasis placed on this system. The practice developed somewhat as the general punitive reaction developed. When a person was injured by another, damages might be claimed, the amount depending on the injury done and the social position of the injured party. Then the king claimed a part of this payment or an additional payment for the participation of the state in the trial and for the injury done to the state by the disturbance of the peace. About the twelfth century, the victim's share began to decrease and the king's share to increase, until finally the king took the entire payment. These payments became one of the principal sources of revenue, and imprisonment was used largely at this time as a means of compelling the defendant to pay the fine. Fines, therefore, developed out of private damages or civil actions and were in their origin a part of the civil law rather than of the criminal law.[57]

This method became frequent only at the end of the last century, and the current trend toward its greater use is apparent in the following statistics:[58] In Germany in 1882, fines were 22.2 percent of all penalties imposed, while in 1934, 54.7 percent; in France in 1900, 35.8 percent, and in 1934, 47.8 percent; in Belgium in 1905, 48.0 percent, while in 1933, 66.5 percent. In Sweden in 1953, and in Finland in 1959, fines were 95 percent of all sentences imposed.[59]

If we consider a particular crime, the same trend is apparent. In Germany, of all penalties for fraud, 11.0 percent were fines in 1882, and 47.5 percent were fines in 1932. In Finland in 1935, 23 percent of the persons convicted of drunkenness were fined; by 1959 the percentage had increased to 58.[60] Fines then are being substituted for other penalties. In the United States there seems to be a variation in this trend. Until quite recently the imposition of a fine was the most frequent method of reacting punitively to crime, probably because of the increase in trivial

---

[56] Robert D. Vinter, George Downs, and John Hall, *Juvenile Corrections in the United States: Residential Programs and Deinstitutionalization* (Ann Arbor, Mich.: National Assessment of Juvenile Corrections, 1975) pp. 13, 17, 18.

[57] L. T. Hobhouse, G. C. Wheeler, and M. Ginsberg, *The Material Culture and Social Institutions of the Simpler Peoples* (London: Chapman and Hall, 1915), pp. 86–119.

[58] George Rusche and Otto Kirchheimer, *Punishment and Social Structure* (New York: Columbia University Press, 1939), pp. 147–50.

[59] Thorsten Sellin, *The Protective Code: A Swedish Proposal* (Stockholm: Department of Justice, 1957), p. 17; and Inkeri Anttila, "Fines for Drunkenness—An Expensive and Ineffective System," *Alkoholpolitik* [Finland], 3:2–3, 1960.

[60] Anttila, "Fines for Drunkenness."

offenses growing out of an increased number of technical regulations. But the proportion of punishments which are fines seems to have declined in the last decade.

Courts at present are generally given authority to impose fines within maximum and minimum limits set by legislatures. Sometimes only the maximum level is fixed, sometimes only the minimum. The constitutions of several American states provide that fines "shall not be excessive." In Scandinavian countries the amount of a fine is adjusted to the defendant's income and wealth.

At common law, fines were collected by confiscation of property, but in more recent times offenders were usually imprisoned in a jail or house of correction if they defaulted in payment of their fine. About 60 percent of the persons committed to the Philadelphia County Jail in 1960 were committed for nonpayment of fines. In the Baltimore City Jail on one day in 1970, 410 inmates—about 30 percent of the jail population—were in jail for not paying fines, at the rate of $2.00 per day, and 170 of that number were traffic offenders. When a fine is imposed, the action is tantamount to a declaration that neither the safety of the community nor the reformation of the criminal requires the imprisonment of the offender and that the assumed values of punishment can be accomplished without imprisonment. Imprisonment for failure to pay fines is therefore only a means of collecting a debt to the state.[61] Moreover, this type of sentence is inherently discriminatory because severity of punishment is determined solely by the defendant's wealth, and it is being abandoned.

The justifications given for this method of implementing the punitive reaction have varied, but at present they consist of the following: First, the fine is the most easily and thoroughly remissible of any of the penalties; capital punishment, whipping, or imprisonment once administered cannot be remitted effectively, but a fine that has been paid can be repaid. Second, the fine is a most economical penalty; it costs the state practically nothing when used without imprisonment for default. Third, the fine is easily divisible and can be adjusted to the enormity of the offense, the character and wealth of the offender, the state of public opinion, and other conditions more easily than any other penalty. Fourth, it does not carry with it the public stigma and disgrace that imprisonment does, and therefore does not hamper reformation of the offender. Fifth, it affects one of the most general interests of mankind and causes a kind of suffering that is universal; therefore it is efficacious in dealing with the great majority of mankind. Finally, it provides an income for the state, county, or city.

Restitution

In the previous discussion it was observed that the imposition of financial penalties appeared in clear-cut form when the state appropriated all of the payment made by an offender; what had previously been a combination of civil

---

[61] Robert G. Fisher, "Comment," in *Mass Production of Justice and the Constitutional Ideal*, ed. Charles E. Whitebread II (Charlottesville, Va.: Michil, 1970), p. 175.

and criminal procedures became thereby distinctly a criminal procedure. The offense came to be regarded as an offense against the state alone; the victim had to initiate a separate civil action to recover damages for the injury done to her or him. It was found in practice, however, that the injured party had very little success in securing damages under this system, because of the insolvent condition of the typical criminal and the opportunity to hide or transfer personal property. Consequently, victims usually made no effort to recover by civil process, or settled out of court by threatening to report the crime to the criminal court if the civil damages were not paid.

For over a century, opinion has been developing in favor of restitution by order of the criminal court. At the beginning of the nineteenth century, several American states had laws which provided that a person convicted of larceny should return to the owner twice the value of the property stolen. This kind of reaction to crime is essentially nonpunitive, and it probably is a system for implementation of the general nonpunitive reaction which was characteristic of the positive school and which has been gaining popularity in recent times.[62] The advantages of the sanction, for victims as well as offenders, have been summed up as follows:

> First, the requirements of restitution can be logically and rationally related to the damages done. Second, the use of restitutive procedures would require the offender to engage in constructive acts that may lead to greater integration with, as opposed to alienation from, the larger social order. Furthermore, restitution can be concrete and specific, thus allowing offenders to know clearly at all times where they stand relative to completing the adjudicated penalty. Finally, restitution addresses itself to the strengths of offenders and rests upon the assumption that individuals either possess or are able to acquire the requisite skills and abilities to redress the wrongs done.[63]

It is probable that the system of restitution is used much more frequently than official records indicate. One of the prevalent methods used by professional thieves when they are arrested is to suggest to the victim that the property will be restored if the victim refuses to prosecute. This results in release in a large proportion of cases, for most victims are more interested in regaining their stolen property than in seeing justice done. Also, many persons are protected against crime by insurance. The insurance company is interested primarily in restitution, and in many cases the crime probably is not reported, or criminal prosecution is not urged, if restitution is made. Similarly, there are thousands of cases of shoplifting, embezzlement, and automobile theft annually which are not reported to the police by the victim because restitution is made. Restitution is most

---

[62] Stephen Schafer, *Restitution to Victims of Crime* (London: Stevens and Sons, 1960), pp. 3–7. See also idem, "Restitution to Victims of Crime—An Old Correctional Aim Modernized," *Minnesota Law Review*, 50:243–54, 1965; and Kathleen J. Smith, *A Cure for Crime: The Case for the Self-Determinate Prison Sentence* (London, 1965).

[63] David Fogel, Burt Galaway, and Joe Hudson, "Restitution in Criminal Justice: A Minnesota Experiment," *Criminal Law Bulletin*, 8:681–83, 1972.

frequently used, both officially and unofficially, in connection with minor cases. In the United States, probation is often granted on the condition that the offender make restitution. Probation departments then become collection agencies.

CONCLUSION

The general theme of this chapter has been that neither the punitive reaction to lawbreaking nor any specific method of implementing that reaction is rooted in the human organism or in universal traits of human nature. On the contrary, reactions to crime change with variations in economic, political, and social conditions. Some kind of reaction to criminal behavior is universal, but that reaction may be either punitive or nonpunitive. Even when the official reaction is punitive, there are great variations in the specific methods used to implement the reaction.

SUGGESTED READINGS

Ancel, Marc. *Social Defence.* London: Routledge and Kegan Paul, 1965.

Andenaes, Johannes. *Punishment and Deterrence.* Ann Arbor, Mich.: University of Michigan Press, 1974.

Aschaffenburg, G. *Crime and Its Repression.* Boston: Little, Brown, 1913.

Bedau, Hugo Adam, & Chester M. Pierce, eds. *Capital Punishment in the United States.* New York: AMS Press, 1976.

Berk, Richard A., Harold Brackman, & Selma L. Lesser. *A Measure of Justice: An Empirical Study of Changes in the California Penal Code—1955–1971.* New York: Academic Press, 1977.

Bittner, Egon, & Anthony Platt, "The Meaning of Punishment." *Issues in Criminology,* 2:79–99, 1966.

Bloch, Marc, *Feudal Society.* Chicago: University of Chicago Press, 1964.

Bohannan, Paul, ed., *Law and Warfare.* Garden City, N.Y.: Natural History Press, 1967.

Chambliss, William J. "A Sociological Analysis of the Law of Vagrancy," *Social Problems,* 12:67–77, 1964.

Garfinkel, Harold. "Conditions of Successful Degradation Ceremonies." *American Journal of Sociology,* 61:420–24, 1956.

Hentig, Hans von. *Punishment: Its Origin, Purpose, and Psychology.* London: William Hodge, 1937.

Hoebel, E. Adamson. *The Law of Primitive Man: A Study in Comparative Legal Dynamics.* Cambridge, Mass.: Harvard University Press, 1954.

Ives, George. *A History of Penal Methods.* London: Stanley Paul, 1914.

Juviler, Peter H. *Revolutionary Law and Order: Politics and Social Change in the USSR.* New York: Free Press, 1976.

McCafferty, James A., ed. *Capital Punishment.* Chicago: Aldine-Atherton, 1972.

Mead, G. H. "The Psychology of Punitive Justice." *American Journal of Sociology,* 23:577–602, 1918.

Moberly, Walter. *The Ethics of Punishment.* London: Faber and Faber, 1968.

Oppenheimer, H. *The Rationale of Punishment.* London: University of London Press, 1913.

Packer, Herbert L. *The Limits of the Criminal Sanction.* Stanford: Stanford University Press, 1968.

Quinney, Richard. *Class, State, and Crime: On the Theory and Practice of Criminal Justice.* New York: David McKay, 1977.

Rothman, David J. *The Discovery of the Asylum.* Boston: Little, Brown, 1971.

Rusche, George, & Otto Kirchheimer. *Punishment and Social Structure.* New York: Columbia University Press, 1939.

Saleilles, R. *The Individualization of Punishment.* Translated by R. S. Jastrow. Boston: Little, Brown, 1911.

Sellin, Thorsten, ed. *Capital Punishment.* New York: Harper and Row, 1967.

Spitzer, Steven. "Punishment and Social Organization: A Study of Durkheim's Theory of Penal Evolution," *Law and Society Review,* 9:613–37, 1975.

Van den Haag, Ernest. *Punishing Criminals: Concerning a Very Old and Painful Question.* New York: Basic Books, 1975.

14

Punitive Policies
and Social Structure

Severity (handwritten)

Social Deviance (handwritten)

378 (handwritten)

Severity (handwritten)

In the previous chapter we were primarily concerned with general variations in the punitive reaction to crime and with variations in specific methods of expressing that reaction. Here we will be concerned with the extent to which official reactions are the actual reactions to lawbreaking and with variations in the justifications given for the punitive reaction. In closing the chapter, we will summarize several theories which have tried to account for the wide range of variations.

VARIATIONS IN EXECUTION OF OFFICIAL PUNITIVE REACTIONS

The founders of the classical school, whose doctrines remain as the backbone of modern criminal law and its administration, argued strenuously that if every crime were followed immediately by extreme suffering on the part of the criminal, crime would practically disappear. The ideal was a punitive societal reaction which would approach as closely as possible an assumed law of nature. The desired attributes of punishment were *uniformity*, *certainty*, *celerity* (swiftness), and *severity*, and the basic objective of the classical school was to make these the characteristics of the official, legal system of dealing with lawbreakers.

With the rise of the positive school, on the other hand, any method of punishment was regarded with considerable skepticism. The early positivists pointed to intoxication, which often is rather promptly followed by suffering, but which is continued nevertheless. They maintained that a society has the amount of crime it deserves in view of its biological composition and its economic, political, and social conditions, leading to the conclusion that any policy for punishing individual criminals is relatively unimportant in determining behavior. Perhaps the same social conditions which gave life to the positive school in the

328

first place also effectively blocked the development of a uniform, certain, swift, and severe punitive reaction to lawbreaking.

The basic arguments of the classical school and the positive school have not changed much over the years. Currently, legislators and other policy makers frequently call for more efficient machinery for terrorizing the citizenry, claiming that swift and severe punishment of all wrongdoers will reform them and, at the same time, frighten onlookers into conformity. Others claim in opposition that such repression is and always will be ineffective, given the fact that crime has its roots in conditions of morality and inequality. Extreme terror might reduce crime, the argument goes, but at the cost of sacrificing basic rights and liberties.

Uniformity in the tradition of the classical school refers to two different ideas. The first is the notion that criminal laws apply to rich and poor alike. Even kings and presidents are criminals if they violate the criminal law. The second idea is that punishment of all persons who violate a particular law must be equal, regardless of their social status. The early emphasis on the first kind of uniformity was an expression of the spirit of democracy then strong in European countries. The second kind of uniformity was justified on the ground that specific punishments must be announced in advance for each type of crime, thus enabling prospective offenders to enter it into their calculations of the pleasures and pains which would result from a criminal act. Contemporary criminal laws, based as they are on these principles, do not prohibit anything. They merely mandate state officials to punish in a certain way whoever behaves in a certain way, leaving people free to choose which acts they will commit (or not commit). In reacting to those who choose crime, say the contemporary proponents of the classical position, state officials cannot give any consideration to social status, wealth, religion, previous behavior, age, sex, or any other characteristics or circumstances of the criminal.

Certainty of punishment refers to the probability that a violator will be detected, arrested, convicted, and punished. Certainty cannot be attained in modern societies, especially for such crimes as business fraud, larceny, and political corruption, although there probably are great variations in its approximation. Some of these variations were noted earlier, in the discussions of crime statistics, age, sex, race, and social class. Probably not more than 5 to 10 percent of all law violations by Americans result in an arrest. Further, of every one hundred Americans arrested for felonies, only two or three receive the lengthy prison term stipulated by statute as appropriate for felonies.

Severity and celerity of punishment have, of necessity, varied with uniformity and certainty. It is, in fact, impossible to separate any one of these attributes from the others. Many observations of severity have been attempted in support of arguments for and against the effectiveness of punishment as a deterrent. But such arguments have never been supported by conclusive evidence, probably because the relationship of severity to the other attributes cannot be controlled. Perhaps severe and swift punishment would be effective in deterrence if all offenders were punished in the same way. A recent Polish study noted, however, that such tactics of terror are effective only if the person exposed to them feels respect either toward the punitive agent or toward the norm underlying the penalty.[1] Given such respect, which means that the punishments are not considered unjust by the recipient, it is likely that even mild punishments would be effective deterrents for many crimes, especially white-collar crimes, if they were swift and certain.[2] When police and court practices and policies significantly reduce the uniformity, certainty, and celerity of punishment, there is a tendency for legislatures to try to make up for these reductions by increasing statutory severity.[3]

Officially prescribed punishments, whether severe or not, were not imposed with certainty or with any fixed degree of uniformity during earlier historical periods, and surely they are not imposed certainly or uniformly in the United States at the present.[4] This can be observed in the practice of mitigating official penalties and in the practice of imposing punitive policies differentially.

Mitigation of Penalties

Penalties officially prescribed as a part of the general punitive reaction to lawbreaking have been softened in various ways. One of the early methods used for this purpose was *securing sanctuary*. In the thirteenth century, an English criminal could avoid punishment by claiming refuge in a church for a period of forty days, at the end of which time the offender was compelled to leave the realm by an assigned road or port. In the early sixteenth century, instead of being permitted to leave the realm, criminals who had secured sanctuary might be compelled to spend the rest of their lives in an assigned locality in England, the name of which was branded on the offender's thumb for identification. The entire

[1] Adam Podgorecki, *Law and Society* (London: Routledge and Kegan Paul, 1974), p. 29. See also Michael R. Geerken and Walter R. Gove, "Deterrence: Some Theoretical Considerations," *Law and Society Review*, 9:497–513, 1975; Matthew Silberman, "Toward a Theory of Criminal Deterrence," *American Sociological Review*, 41:442–61, 1976; and S. Giora Shoham, Nehemia Geva, Rachel Markowski, and Nava Kaplinsky, "Internalization of Norms, Risk-perception and Anxiety as Related to Driving Offenses," *British Journal of Criminology*, 16:142–55, 1976.

[2] See William J. Chambliss, "The Deterrent Influence of Punishment," *Crime and Delinquency*, January, 1966, pp. 70–75; Gilbert Geis, "Deterring Corporate Crime," in *Corporate Power in America*, ed. Ralph Nader and Mark J. Green (New York: Viking Press, 1973); Charles H. Logan, "General Deterrent Effects of Imprisonment," *Social Forces*, 51:64–73, 1972; William C. Bailey, J. David Martin, and Louis N. Gray, "Crime and Deterrence: A Correlational Analysis," *Journal of Research in Crime and Delinquency*, 11:124–43, 1974; and Anthony R. Harris, "Imprisonment and the Expected Value of Criminal Choice: A Specification and Test of Aspects of the Labeling Perspective," *American Sociological Review*, 40:71–87, 1975.

[3] Arthur Rosett and Donald R. Cressey, *Justice By Consent: Plea Bargains in the American Courthouse* (Philadelphia: Lippincott, 1976), pp. 150–59.

[4] Jack P. Gibbs, "Crime, Punishment, and Deterrence," *Southwestern Social Science Quarterly*, 48:515–30, 1968; Charles R. Tittle, "Crime Rates and Legal Sanctions," *Social Problems*, 15:409–23, 1969; Theodore G. Chiricos and Gordon P. Waldo, "Punishment and Crime: An Examination of Some Empirical Evidence," *Social Problems*, 18:200–17, 1970; and Ruel and Shlomo Shinnar, "The Effects of the Criminal Justice System on the Control of Crime: A Quantitative Approach," *Law and Society Review*, 9:581–611, 1975.

system of securing sanctuary began to decline in the last part of the fifteenth century, and by the middle of the sixteenth century murder, rape, burglary, arson, and a few other offenses no longer carried the right of sanctuary. The whole system was abandoned when the monasteries were broken up.

A second system for mitigation of penalties was *right of clergy*. This grew out of the original demand of the church to try its own officers. To be tried by an ecclesiastical court was a distinct advantage, for, as we have already said, the church was not permitted to impose the death penalty during a part of the period of its supremacy, and its penalties in general were less severe, except for the offenses of heresy and witchcraft.[5] The clergy were defined at first in the strict sense, but later the term came to include all who had the clerical tonsure, then all who could read. The test used in determining whether a person could read was generally the first verse of the fifty-first psalm, and a little coaching would enable almost anyone to pass this test. Finally the peers who could not read received the same benefit of clergy by nature of their position.

Right of clergy or benefit of clergy was a device by which those who were similar to the lawmakers were made exempt from the more severe penalties. The elites who were responsible for expressing the official punitive reaction did not inflict severe penalties upon members of their own class; instead, they reserved these punishments for the lower classes. While the number of persons who could claim right of clergy increased, the number of times a person could claim the right and the number of offenses for which this right could be claimed were gradually reduced. Thus, as the power of the church elite declined, penalties came to be more nearly the same for those who had the benefit of clergy and those who did not. An act of 1705 provided that even those who claimed the right of clergy might be punished by secular authorities at least to the extent of confinement in a house of correction for not less than six months or more than two years. By the end of the eighteenth century the right of clergy meant nothing.[6]

A third method for softening penalties was the *pardon*. The prescribed penalties were severe, but the king was permitted to relax the severity in individual cases. The pardoning power had its origins in the king's desire to exempt from punishment those criminals who were of high social status, and the social status of the criminal continues to affect the decision to pardon.[7] But in eighteenth-century England pardons were extended to many of the lower-class criminals convicted of capital offenses, thus functioning to secure the power of the ruling class.[8] The general rule of pardons was, and is, that the more serious the

---

[5] See Joel Samaha, *Law and Order in Historical Perspective: The Case of Elizabethan Essex* (New York: Academic Press, 1974), pp. 59–63.

[6] See Jerome Hall, *Theft, Law, and Society*, 2d ed. (Indianapolis: Bobbs-Merrill, 1952), pp. 110–18, 356–63; and George Dalzell, *Benefit of Clergy in America* (Winston-Salem, N. C.: Blair, 1955).

[7] See Chapter 25 below.

[8] Douglas Hay, "Property, Authority, and Criminal Law," in Douglas Hay, Peter Linebaugh, John G. Rule, E. P. Thompson and Cal Winslow, *Albion's Fatal Tree: Crime and Society in Eighteenth-Century England* (New York: Pantheon Books, 1975), pp. 17–63.

crime and the more severe the sentence, the more probable is release by pardon.[9] Statistics recorded by the state prison of Massachusetts from 1828 to 1866 showed that pardons were granted to 20 percent of the prisoners on terms of from five to ten years, 32 percent of those on terms of ten years or more but not including life sentences, and 50 percent of those serving life sentences. The average time served before pardon by those on life sentences was six years and three months.

In the Anglo-American legal system, the power of an executive to grant pardons was derived from the time when the power of the crown was almost absolute.[10] In the American colonies the pardoning power was generally vested in the royal governor, acting either alone or with the governor's council. After the Revolution, because of the fear of executives, the pardoning power was at first retained by the legislative assemblies, but it soon passed to the governors, generally as an expression of the doctrine of separation of powers. In the middle of the nineteenth century the use of pardons dramatically decreased when American courts were authorized to fix penalties not uniformly but within limits set by legislatures, and in this manner to adjust the penalty to the characteristics of individual offenders and the circumstances of their offenses.

A fourth method of mitigating penalties was simple refusal to execute the punishments officially prescribed and imposed. The seventeenth and eighteenth centuries in England were a period of rapidly shifting standards. Property owners sought to protect their wealth by demanding that even minor property offenders be killed. Indeed, most offenders were sentenced to die. But because the common people were increasing in political and social power, and perhaps because the need for labor made executions seem wasteful, the sentences were not executed in a large proportion of the cases, as is shown by the statistics for England in Table 21.[11]

Corporal punishments disappeared from England, just as did the death penalty, because even when courts imposed the sentences, public sentiment prevented their execution. In the last part of the eighteenth century Bentham made the following statement regarding the penalty of branding:

Burning in the hand, according as the criminal and the executioner can agree, is performed either with a cold or a red-hot iron; and if it be with a red-hot iron, it is only a slice of ham which is burnt; to complete the farce, the criminal screams, whilst it is only the fat which smokes and burns, and the knowing spectators only laugh at this parody of justice.[12]

Similarly, as opposition to the policy of quartering the corpse after execution developed, the method became more and more symbolic until, in 1820, "quartering" consisted merely of scratching a cross on the neck of the corpse.

[9] This rule was stated by Henry Cabbt Lodge, "Naval Courts-Martial and the Pardoning Power," *Atlantic Monthly,* 50:43–50, 1882.

[10] Lewis Mayers, *The American Legal System,* rev. ed. (New York: Harper and Row, 1964), p. 138.

[11] See also Leon Radzinowicz, *A History of English Criminal Law and its Administration from 1750* (New York: Macmillan, 1948), Vol. I, pp. 143–64.

[12] Jeremy Bentham, "Principles of Penal Law," in *The Works of Jeremy Bentham* ed. John Bowring (Edinburgh: W. Tait, 1843), p. 550.

Table 21   Changes in the Proportion of Capital Penalties Executed

Years	Percent
1689–1718[a]	52.6
1755–1784[a]	28.3
1785–1814[a]	25.6
1815–1819	10.5
1820–1826	6.9
1827–1833	4.1

[a]Counties of Essex, Herts, Kent, Surrey, and Sussex only.

Even fines may be remitted by executive or judicial acts. At present, usually the governor alone has power to remit fines in state cases, but some variations are found. A practice has developed in some courts of imposing a fine and then, in chambers, allowing a motion in mitigation, by which the fine is reduced. This method was used extensively during the period of national prohibition; publicity was secured by imposing very large fines for alcohol violations, and justice was done by secretly reducing the fines.

Differential Imposition of Punishments

There is a great deal of evidence that current statutes calling for punishment of lawbreakers are not administered uniformly, or with celerity or certainty. This suggests that the actual reactions to crime are not really reflected in the laws governing the administration of justice. The statutes are so severe they must be mitigated in the interests of justice, and in order to maintain the consent of the governed.[13] Further, the idea of uniformity has all but disappeared in practice. The reactions to the crimes of persons of one status are different from the reactions of persons of another status. Discriminations have been made and are made because of the age, sex, wealth, education, political prestige, race, nationality, and other characteristics of the offender. For example, in the United States, female offenders are less likely than men to be arrested, and female prisoners are held in prison on the average about two-thirds as long for a specified type of offense as male prisoners. It is very difficult to convict females of capital offenses when the death penalty is mandatory, for juries refuse to find them guilty. In fact, for most major crimes, the ratio of convictions to arrests is lower for females than for males.

Powerful groups are usually punished less frequently and severely than less powerful groups, as may be observed in the differential punishments of white-collar criminals compared with other criminals, and of rich and poor persons who commit the same offense, be it drunken driving or embezzlement.[14] Also,

[13]Rosett and Cressey, *Justice By Consent*, pp. 182–84.

[14]See Alan M. Dershowitz, "Increasing Community Control Over Corporate Crime: A Problem in the Law of Sanctions," *Yale Law Journal*, 71:289–306, 1961; Theodore G. Chiricos, Phillip D. Jackson, and Gordon P.

numerous studies have shown that the official punitive reaction is more frequently applied to lawbreaking by blacks than it is to lawbreaking by whites. The following conclusions have been drawn by so many investigators that they may be accepted as factual: (1) Blacks are more likely to be arrested than whites. (2) Blacks are more likely to be indicted than are whites. (3) Blacks have a higher conviction rate than whites. (4) Blacks are usually punished more severely than whites, but this is not true for all crimes, especially those in which a black person victimizes a black person. (5) Blacks are less likely to receive probation and suspended sentences. (6) Blacks receive pardons less often than do whites. (7) Blacks have less chance of having a death sentence commuted than do whites.[15]

VARIATIONS IN THE JUSTIFICATIONS OF PUNITIVE REACTIONS
Not only have both official and actual reactions to crime varied, but the rationale given for those reactions has varied as well. At various times and places, expiation, deterrence, retribution, reformation, income for the state, restoring or promoting the solidarity of the group, and other things have all been offered as justifications for the punitive reaction.[16]

Such justifications are not merely ex post facto rationalizations but, instead, are the reasons or motives men have for punishing in the first place. The particular form the punitive reaction takes depends upon the reasons offered for it or, in other words, upon the kind of value which the punishment is assumed to have.

No consistent course of development can be discerned, and certainly at any given time, especially at present, all the members of a given society do not have the same reason for using the punitive reaction, even if they agree that such a reaction is desirable. Even individuals probably have more than one motive for punishing. Usually investigators infer merely that one or more of the motives is dominant, but not exclusive, in a society. Thomas and Znaniecki, two pioneering sociologists whose work on immigration has attained classic status, argued, for example, that among the Polish peasants they studied, the motive for punishment of crime was the restoration of the situation which existed before the crime and renewal of the solidarity of the group, and that revenge was a secondary consideration.[17]

Exner, the noted German penal law scholar, once remarked, "So far as we can look back, men have always punished and have never ceased to dispute their

---

Waldo, "Inequality in the Imposition of a Criminal Label," *Social Problems* 19:553–72, 1972; and Daniel Swett, "Cultural Bias in the American Legal System," *Law and Society Review*, 5:79–110, 1969.

[15] Many of these studies are either reproduced in, or commented upon, in Charles E. Reasons and Jack L. Kuykendal, eds., *Race, Crime, and Justice* (Pacific Palisades, Calif.: Goodyear, 1972); and in Elton Long, James Long, Wilmer Leon, and Paul B. Weston, *American Minorities: The Justice Issue* (Englewood Cliffs, N. J.: Prentice-Hall, 1975).

[16] Egon Bittner and Anthony M. Platt, "The Meaning of Punishment," *Issues in Criminology*, 2 (1966): 79–99.

[17] W. I. Thomas and F. Znaniecki, *The Polish Peasant in Europe and America* (Chicago: University of Chicago Press, 1927), 2:1254–255.

reasons for so doing."[18] After the early attempts to rationalize punishments by considerations of a transcendental nature, the leading writers in this field were political philosophers who insisted that certain social benefits resulted from punishment and constituted the justification of punishment. But little of this literature faced the issue of punishment *versus* other methods of dealing with criminals. It was assumed without argument that punishment is necessary, and the problem was to formulate an acceptable statement of this necessity. Thus, the controversy was largely between adherents of rival concepts of punishment, not between the adherents and opponents of punishment.

The political philosophers were also concerned with the abstract right of the state to punish for crime, and hundreds of essays on this subject were written. However, these works mostly miss the point, because they avoid the problem of determining whether punishment is either wise or economical in the larger sense. Moreover, these philosophical discussions, like those dealing with the reasons for punishing, have been concerned primarily with the amount and nature of punishment, not with its value in comparison with other methods of minimizing crime and coping with criminals. The following values of punishment have been indicated by those who insist on the desirability of hurting criminals.[19]

Punishment as Retribution

At least since the formulation (in about 1875 B.C.) of the Code of Hammurabi ("an eye for an eye and a tooth for a tooth"), it has been urged by leaders and accepted by the general public that the criminal deserves to suffer. The suffering imposed by the state in its corporate capacity is considered the political counterpart of an assumed instinct for individual revenge. One of England's greatest criminal law scholars, Sir James Stephen, stated: "Criminal procedure is to resentment what marriage is to affection: namely, the legal provision for an inevitable impulse of human beings." This, of course, is not a justification of punishment in terms of the social utilities allegedly produced by it. By way of contrast, John Dewey argued that we are not relieved of the responsibility for the consequences of our procedures by the fact that the offender is guilty.[20] A justification of punishment must state what future effects punishment is likely to have on criminals and on social order. The future is not often considered by those who insist that the criminal deserves to be punished. It sometimes is urged, negatively, that unless the criminal is punished, the victim will seek individual revenge, which may mean lynch-law; or the victim will refuse to make complaint or offer testimony, and the state will therefore be handicapped in dealing with criminals.

18 Franz Exner, *Gerechtigkeit und Richteramt* (Leipzig: F. Meiner, 1922), p. 6.
19 See Gertrude Ezorsky, ed., *Philosophical Perspectives on Punishment* (Albany, N. Y.: State University of New York Press, 1972); and John Kleinig, *Punishment and Desert* (The Hague: Martinus Nijhoff, 1973).
20 John Dewey, *Human Nature and Conduct* (New York: Henry Holt, 1930), pp. 18–19.

Punishment as a General Deterrent

Beginning with the Age of Reason in the eighteenth century, the aim of the criminal law has gradually changed from punishment for its own sake to punishment as a means for improving social behavior. Punishment is designed to deter future crime by making an example of each defendant, thus frightening citizens so much that they will not do what the defendant did (general deterrence). Beyond this, punishment is designed to educate and therefore to reform the criminals subjected to it (specific deterrence). The basic argument for general deterrence is that inflicting suffering upon those convicted of crime serves to terrorize others, and that punishment has great value for that reason, even if some individuals are not deterred. Ohio's Attorney General, William J. Brown, recently made this claim in the following dramatic terms:

I am firmly convinced that the mandatory-type penalty structure will actually deter crimes of intent. . . . We're talking about the first offender, first crack at crime, you go right to the can. Pure and simple . . . he knows that if he gets caught he's going to jail. . . . And nobody's going to help him. The parole board can't help him, the judge can't help him, his priest can't help him. That's the frame of mind we want the criminal to be in. So that when he commits a crime, he knows what he's going to get. . . .

What we're trying to do is this: Make sure that the criminal who stands before the judge knows that the judge doesn't have any discretion. . . .

The guy who uses a gun should be put in jail . . . forever. That's how I feel. I think that anyone who wants to use a gun in the commission of a crime, goes. That's all. . . . And he stays. Forever and ever and ever. . . .

That's the only way you're going to be able to solve the crime problem.[21]

There seems to be no question that if punitive terror is great enough, most people will dread the punishers, and will conform. But the hundreds of essays and studies devoted to the general deterrence idea have mostly addressed a different question, namely whether existing systems of punishment have any significant effect on existing crime rates.[22] This question is important because it challenges the assumption that state officials can control crime by creating the degree of terror that is needed to control it, and no more.[23] The deterrence principle is mechanistic, holding that varieties of crime and varieties of punishment are to be so finely balanced that each punishment imposed on a criminal will have a

---

[21] Quoted by John P. Conrad, "We Should Never Have Promised a Hospital," *Federal Probation*, 39:3–9, 1975.

[22] For summaries and bibliographies, see Charles R. Tittle, "Punishment and Deterrence of Deviance," in *The Economics of Crime and Punishment*, ed. Simon Rottenberg (Washington, D. C.: American Enterprise Institute for Public Policy Research, 1973), pp. 85–102; Richard L. Henshel and Robert A. Silverman eds., *Perception in Criminology* (New York: Columbia University Press, 1975) Frank Zimring and Gordon Hawkins, *Deterrence: The Legal Threat in Crime Control* (Chicago: University of Chicago Press, 1973); Bailey, Martin, and Gray, "Crime and Deterrence"; Jack P. Gibbs, *Crime, Punishment, and Deterrence* (New York: Elsevier, 1975); and Jan Palmer, "Economic Analyses of the Deterrent Effect of Punishment: A Review," *Journal of Research on Crime and Delinquency*, 14:4–21, 1977.

[23] See Walter D. Connor, *Deviance in Soviet Society: Crime, Delinquency, and Alcoholism* (New York: Columbia University Press, 1972), p. 250.

significant impact on citizens at large, as well as directly on the criminal. In this view, the calculus of deterrence is the basis of criminal law; lawmakers and others need only do their sums carefully in order to insure that appropriate amounts of pain are inflicted on wrongdoers, thus convincing bystanders that the costs of committing a crime outweigh the benefits.

The general deterrence principle is stated in economic terms, apparent in such phrases as "pay the price of crime" and "pay his debt to society." Perhaps it is for that reason that nowadays economists are leading a drive seemingly designed to show that high crime rates stem from policies which make crime too cheap.[24] Thus, the economic hypothesis seems to be based on the hedonistic assumption that people regulate their behavior by calculations of pleasure and pain. To these economists, all men are businessmen: "The potential criminal evaluates all possibilities within the limits of all information which he possesses and chooses that activity which maximizes his utility."[25]

This hedonistic assumption has been under attack for at least fifty years. Dewey emphasized the general fallacy in this assumption:

Deliberation no more resembles the casting-up of accounts of profit and loss, pleasure and pain, than an actor engaged in a drama resembles a clerk recording debit and credit items in his ledger.[26]

More recently, Horton and Leslie put the matter this way:

This misplaced faith in punishment may rest upon the unrealistic assumption that people *consciously decide* whether to be criminal—that they consider a criminal career, rationally balance its dangers against its rewards, and arrive at a decision based upon such pleasure-pain calculation. It supposedly follows that if the pain element is increased by severe punishments, people will turn from crime to righteousness. A little reflection reveals the absurdity of this notion.[27]

The use of the word "absurdity" here does not seem to have reference to the question of whether terror works. Terror does work. Instead, "absurdity" refers to the simplicity of the assumption that any given punishment is effective in crime control because people rationally weigh it as a cost of doing business. Anyone making this assumption must necessarily conclude that punishment deters. No research is necessary. As Charles R. Tittle has pointed out, "The crucial question is not simply whether negative sanctions deter, but rather under what conditions

[24] See, for example, Gary Becker, "Crime and Punishment: An Economic Approach," *Journal of Political Economy*, 76:169–217, 1968; Gordon Tullock, "Does Punishment Deter Crime?" *The Public Interest*, 36:103–11, 1974; and Llad Phillips, 'Crime Control: The Case for Deterrence," in *The Economics of Crime and Punishment*, ed. Rottenberg, pp. 65–84; and I. Ehrlich, "Participation in Illegitimate Activities: A Theoretical and Empirical Investigation," *Journal of Political Economy*, 81:521–65, 1973.

[25] William E. Cobb, "Theft and the Two Hypotheses," in *The Economics of Crime and Punishment*, ed. Rottenberg, p. 19. See also Palmer, "Economic Analyses of the Deterrent Effect of Punishment."

[26] Dewey, *Human Nature and Conduct*, p. 199.

[27] Paul B. Horton and Gerald R. Leslie, *The Sociology of Social Problems*, 4th ed. (New York: Appleton-Century-Crofts, 1970), p. 167.

are negative sanctions likely to be effective."[28] Henshel and Carey go further, noting that negative sanctions are negative only if people know about them, and that prospective criminals can judge the profits of crime only if they know what those profits are likely to be. Thus, the critical weakness of deterrence studies "is that they ignore the central theoretical conception that deterrence is in the eyes of the beholder. Deterrence, when and if it exists, is a state of mind."[29]

The basic problem in settling the general deterrence argument one way or the other seems to stem from the fact that deterrence theory is psychological rather than economic, or political, or sociological. Consistently, the parameters of this theory—celerity, certainty, severity—are psychological variables, drawn from hedonism. Thus, proponents of punishment argue that Johnny goes wrong because he is not afraid to go wrong, and opponents argue that Johnny's psychology is such that he will go wrong (or not) regardless of the potential penalty. Resolution of this argument would be helped by research in which deterrence theory is used in the study of individual cases.[30] But a variation in a crime rate is a social fact, not a psychological one. Accordingly, it should be accounted for by reference to variations in culture or social structure, not by reference to the psychological make up of individuals.[31]

However, a final refutation of hedonistic psychology and its conceptions probably would not justify rejection of the broader aspects of the deterrence argument. In a broader perspective, the criminal law and its application by police and courts seem to have great effects upon public morality. Although specific punishments may have little immediate demonstrable effect in deterring specific persons from committing crimes, the existence of the criminal code with its penal sanctions probably has a long-run negative effect upon the development of criminalistic ideologies. Andenaes has called this the "moral or socio-pedagogical influence of punishment."[32] By means of the criminal law and the procedures for implementing the criminal law, including the imposition of swift and certain punishments, the undesirability and impropriety of certain behavior is emphasized.

Not the crimes punished, but the crimes prevented should measure the worth of the law. . . . If out of a score of law-abiding persons, only one obeys the law from fear of its

[28] Charles R. Tittle, "Crime Rates and Legal Sanctions."

[29] Richard L. Henshel and Sandra H. Carey, "Deviance, Deterrence, and Knowledge of Sanctions," in *Perception in Criminology*, ed. Henshel and Silverman, pp. 54–73. Ibid., pp. 56–57. See also Maynard L. Erickson, Jack P. Gibbs, and Gary F. Jensen, "The Deterrence Doctrine and the Perceived Certainty of Legal Punishments," *American Sociological Review*, 42:305–17, 1977.

[30] See Robert F. Meier and Weldon T. Johnson, "Deterrence as Social Control: The Legal and Extralegal Production of Conformity," *American Sociological Review*, 42:292–304, 1977.

[31] See Michael R. Geerken and Walter R. Gove, "Deterrence: Some Theoretical Considerations"; and Silberman, "Toward a Theory of Criminal Deterrence."

[32] Johannes Andenaes, *Punishment and Deterrence* (Ann Arbor, Mich.: University of Michigan Press, 1974), p. 35. See also H. Laurence Ross, "The Scandinavian Myth: The Effectiveness of Drinking-and-Driving Legislation in Sweden and Norway," *Journal of Legal Studies*, 4:285–310, 1975.

penalties, it does not follow that the penal system occupies a correspondingly insignificant place among the supports of social order. For the rules of the social game are respected by the many good men chiefly because they are forced upon the few bad. If the one rascal among twenty men might aggress at will, the higher forms of control would break down, the fair-play instinct would cease to bind, and, between bad example and the impulse of retaliation, man after man would be detached from the honest majority. Thus, the deadly contagion of lawlessness would spread with increasing rapidity till the social order lay in ruins. The law, therefore, however minor its part at a given moment in the actual coercion of citizens, is still the cornerstone of the edifice of order.[33]

When general deterrence was regarded as the principal purpose of punishment, penalties were made as public and as brutal as possible—witness the ducking stool, the stocks, the pillory, the public hangings, and the gibbeting of the body so that it might remain as long as possible as an example to the public. Whenever a community experiences a significant increase in its crime rate—however that rate may be produced—a demand for an increase in certainty and severity of penalties arises, based on the assumption that if more criminals are punished more severely, other persons will be more effectively deterred from similar crimes.[34] These demands ordinarily are based on a confusion of penal sanctions as general expressions of hostility to crime on the one hand, and severe punishments as deterrence for persons who might be contemplating prohibited acts on the other.[35]

Punishment as a Specific Deterrent

It is also maintained that punishment reforms criminals and that it does this by creating fear of repetition of the punishment. Until recently, this presumed value of inflicting physical pain or psychological suffering on criminals was called *reformation*, suggesting that hurting criminals changes them into noncriminals. But this value is coming to be called *specific deterrence*, thus likening it to the general deterrence assumed to be operating as citizens watch criminals being punished, learn their lesson, and become afraid to do what the criminal did.

Whether called reformation or specific deterrence, illustrations such as the following are given in support of the stress on fear: When a boy touches a hot stove, he is painfully burned, and in that way learns to avoid hot stoves. A city attorney, speaking more generally, used the logic of this illustration in advocating punishment of criminals, and as a general practice in child rearing:

> You must inflict pain to get results. It was that way with me when I was a boy: I had been misbehaving and my father gave me an awful whaling and he had to do it only once. I had

---

[33] E. A. Ross, *Social Control* (New York: Macmillan, 1916), p. 125.

[34] See Barry Schwartz, "The Effect in Philadelphia of Pennsylvania's Increased Penalties for Rape and Attempted Rape," *Journal of Criminal Law, Criminology, and Police Science*, 59:509–15, 1968; and Glenn W. Samuelson, "Why Was Capital Punishment Restored in Delaware?" *Journal of Criminal Law, Criminology, and Police Science*, 60:148–51, 1969.

[35] See Ted Honderich, *Punishment: Its Supposed Justifications* (London: Hutchinson, 1969), pp. 76–93.

the same experience in dealing with my son. It is the same way with criminals. You must inflict pain to get results. It is the only language they understand.

Similarly, it is said that if honey bees swarm out of their hive and sting the girl who molests them, she will not trouble the bees in the future; if, on the other hand, the bees retreat from the hive on the approach of the girl, leaving their honey at her disposal, they will be troubled again and again. Beyond such folksy illustrations, it is said to have been established that experiments with animals have shown that animals more frequently learn an operation when they are punished for failure than when they are not punished.

Recently, thousands of experiments have been run in the effort to determine the relative values of rewards and punishments in human learning and performance, and these studies are considered pertinent to policies for the reformation of criminals.[36] But the effects of punishment, even in these experimental situations, cannot be stated as a simple proposition. A mild punishment may promote learning, but a more severe punishment may cause terror and panic which interfere with the whole learning process. Moreover, the social situations in which punishments for crime are inflicted involve variables which are lacking in punishments administered in experimental laboratories.[37]

Changes in schoolchildren's behavior in spite of, or because of, the disappearance of corporal punishment are more relevant to the issue than are laboratory experiments. An eighteenth-century schoolteacher left an itemized list of 1,423,100 corporal punishments which he had inflicted on schoolchildren during his career.[38] A century ago most of the teachers' time in almost all schools was devoted to the maintenance of order and infliction of punishments. The average number of whippings per day in 1845 in a school of about 250 pupils near Boston was 65.6. Nevertheless, nearly four hundred Massachusetts schools were broken up annually because the teacher was unable to maintain discipline. The behavior of schoolchildren in modern schools, in which corporal punishment is seldom inflicted, is much better than in the schools of a century ago, when corporal punishment was extremely frequent. It is evident that the effect of punishment on reformation depends very much on the situation in which the punishment is inflicted.

Punishment and Social Solidarity

It is also asserted that respect for law grows largely out of opposition to those who violate the law. The public's disapproval or even hatred of criminals is expressed by

[36] See Harvey Wheeler, ed., *Beyond the Punitive Society: Operant Conditioning—Social and Political Aspects* (San Francisco: W. H. Freeman, 1973).

[37] For an analysis of the complexities in the effects of punishment see Barry F. Singer, "Psychological Studies of Punishment," *California Law Review*, 58:405–43, 1970. See also Stanley Milgram, *Obedience to Authority: An Experimental View* (New York: Harper and Row, 1974); and J. M. Johnson, "Punishment of Human Behavior," *American Psychologist*, 27:1033–54, 1972.

[38] Henry Barnard, *English Pedagogy*, 2d ser. (Hartford, Conn.: Brown and Gross, 1876), p. 327.

punishing some of them, and this collective action against violators develops respect for the values which were violated.[39] Thus, as suggested earlier in this section, law-abiding behavior might develop because the penal law process reaffirms law-abiding ideals and attitudes, not because punishment terrorizes near-criminals into conformity. Lundstedt a half-century ago argued eloquently that the significant contribution of punishment is not fear of punishment, but rather the legal sentiments, legal conscience, or moral feeling which have been developed in the general public by the administration of the criminal law during previous generations, and which have become so organized that they regulate behavior spontaneously, almost like an instinct.[40]

TESTING THE EFFECTIVENESS OF PUNISHMENT

Most of the justifications of punitive reactions and policies have not been made in the abstract but, instead, have been given as rather specific arguments for such methods as corporal punishment, the death penalty, or imprisonment. At present each of these methods is advocated by some on the ground that it has a deterrent effect, an effect on social solidarity, or other desirable effects, just as they were advocated a century or more ago. In the earlier period, the arguments were challenged only by counter-arguments, while in the recent period the challenges have been based at least in part upon examination and analysis of such empirical data as can be found. Such analyses of evidence amount to attempts to test the arguments, to treat them as hypotheses. This is a scientific procedure, and some of the arguments for the death penalty, together with some of the kinds of data used to refute the arguments, are presented here to illustrate the procedure. Arguments and data regarding the effectiveness of imprisonment will be given later.[41]

The most popular arguments currently made in favor of the death penalty are:

(1) It is more effective than any other penalty in deterring from murder.
(2) It is necessary in order to prevent the public from lynching criminals.
(3) It is the only certain penalty, for murderers who are sentenced to life imprisonment frequently secure paroles or pardons.
(4) It is more economical than imprisonment.

On the other hand, those who oppose the death penalty argue that the death penalty is not more effective than imprisonment as a deterrent, that the abolition

---

[39] See Lewis A. Coser, "Some Functions of Deviant Behavior and Normative Flexibility," *American Journal of Sociology*, 68:172–82, 1962. For a case study of this proposition, see Kai T. Erikson, *Wayward Puritans: A Study in the Sociology of Deviance* (New York: Wiley, 1966). See also Pat Lauderdale, "Deviance and Moral Boundaries," *American Sociological Review*, 41:660–76, 1976; and James Inverarity, "Populism and Lynching in Louisiana 1889–96: A Test of Erickson's Theory of the Relationship Between Boundary Crises and Repressive Justice," *American Sociological Review*, 41:262–80, 1976.

[40] A. V. Lundstedt, *Superstition or Rationality in Action for Peace?* (London: Longmans, Green, 1925), pp. 47–49, 190–192.

[41] See Chapter 22, below.

of the death penalty does not promote lynchings, that it reduces the certainty and speed of punishment, that by breaking down respect for human life it tends to promote murder, that errors of justice are irreparable, and that it has undesirable effects on the prisoners and the staff in institutions in which it is inflicted.[42] Of these arguments, the one about the deterrent effect of the death penalty is by far the most important.

The Death Penalty as a Deterrent

The most common method of testing the deterrent effect of the death penalty is to compare the homicide rate in states which have abolished the death penalty with rates in states which retain it. In general, such comparisons (which refer to the period before 1972, when the Supreme Court outlawed many death penalty statutes) show that in abolition states the homicide rate is only about one-third to one-half as high as it is in other states. However, such comparisons are somewhat biased because the death penalty is authorized in all of the southern states, and the southern states have the highest homicide rate.[43] A more justifiable comparison is between states in a particular section of the United States. Figure 1 shows that there is no significant difference in the homicide rates of states which have abolished the death penalty and adjoining states which have retained the death penalty.[44] Bailey studied the number of first-degree murderers committed to American penal institutions in 1967 and 1968, and found that the murder rate is higher in the death-penalty states than in the abolitionist states, and also that the rate is consistently higher in retentionist states than in their contiguous abolitionist neighbors. "In sum," he concluded, "the evidence reported here falls within the pattern of previous death penalty investigations which span five decades."[45]

The significant difference is not between states which have the death penalty and those which do not, but between the different sections of the country, regardless of whether the states have or do not have the death penalty. The composition and customs of the population are much more important than the presence or absence of the death penalty in determining homicide rates. For example, Brown has linked the tradition of violence in Central Texas to an ethic of self-redress and self-defense which flourishes there.[46]

[42] For bibliographies on capital punishment see James A. McCafferty, ed., *Capital Punishment* (Chicago: Aldine-Atherton, 1973); Thorsten Sellin, ed., *Capital Punishment* (New York: Harper and Row, 1967); and Ernest van den Haag, *Punishing Criminals: Concerning a Very Old and Painful Question* (New York: Basic Books, 1975).

[43] See Shelton Hackney, "Southern Violence," *American Historical Review*, 74:906–25, 1969.

[44] Figure 1 is from Thorsten Sellin, "Homicide in Retentionist and Abolitionist States," in idem, ed., *Capital Punishment*, pp. 135–38. See also James Boudouris, *Trends in Homicide: Detroit, 1926–1968* (Ph.D. diss., Wayne State University, 1970).

[45] William C. Bailey, "Murder and the Death Penalty," *Journal of Criminal Law and Criminology*, 65:416–23, 1974.

[46] Richard Maxwell Brown, *Strain of Violence: Historical Studies of American Violence and Vigilantism* (New York: Oxford University Press, 1975), pp. 236–99.

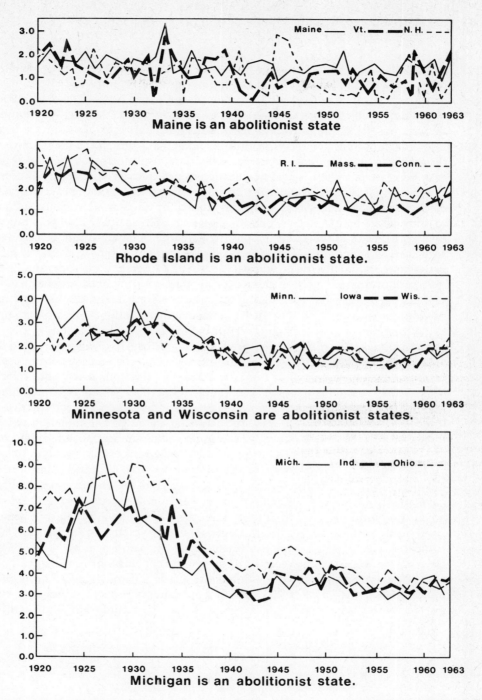

Figure 1 *Homicide Death Rates (per 100,000 Population) in Contiguous Abolitionist and Retentionist States, 1920–1963*

Similar differences are found within states. Vold compared two states which, at the time, had the death penalty. He found the average homicide rate to be 3.9 percent per 100,000 population in the southernmost counties of Iowa, and 3.5 in the adjoining counties of Missouri. But in the southern tier of Missouri counties the rate was 10.5. The northern tier of Missouri counties is very similar to the southern tier of Iowa counties in culture and composition of the population, but the southern tier of Missouri counties is significantly different.[47]

A second method for testing the deterrent effect of the death penalty is comparison of crime rates just before and just after one or more executions has taken place. If the death penalty has any deterrent value, it presumably lies more in knowledge about actual executions than in awareness of the legal possibility of execution. Areas in which murderers are actually executed should be compared with areas in which the law prohibits such executions. Moreover, the areas should be sufficiently small (say, counties), so that an execution will produce some influence on the potential murderers in that area. No significant difference was found in this respect in a study of homicide rates sixty days prior and sixty days subsequent to five executions in Philadelphia.[48] In another Philadelphia study, Savitz analyzed the rate of capital crimes for a period of eight weeks just before and eight weeks after the sentencing of four men to death. He hypothesized that the greatest deterrence would occur in the locality where the crimes were committed and where the criminal was known. The four cases were selected because the sentencing was given great publicity in the newspapers. No significant increase or decrease in the murder rate occurred; there was no pattern that would indicate deterrence.[49] A Chicago study also indicated that homicide fluctuates independently of news coverage, executions, and commutations of sentences in capital cases.[50]

The results of these comparisons in the United States are reinforced by comparisons in European countries. On the average, the European states which have abolished the death penalty have lower homicide rates (which generally means lower murder rates in Europe) than states which retain the death penalty.

A third method for testing the deterrent value of the death penalty is by comparing, in the states which have abolished the death penalty, the homicide rates before and after the abolition. The general conclusion from such comparisons is that the states which abolished the death penalty have had no unusual increase in homicide rates. Eleven states abolished the death sentence only to restore it after a few years, on the ground that the murder rate had increased

[47] George B. Vold, "Can the Death Penalty Prevent Crime," *Prison Journal*, October, 1932, pp. 3–8.

[48] Robert H. Dann, "The Deterrent Effect of Capital Punishment," *Friends' Social Service Series*, Bulletin No. 29, 1935.

[49] Leonard D. Savitz, "A Study of Capital Punishment," *Journal of Criminal Law, Criminology, and Police Science*, 49:338–41, 1958; Karl F. Schuessler, "The Deterrent Influence of the Death Penalty," *Annals of the American Academy of Political and Social Science*, 284:54–62, 1952.

[50] Hans W. Mattick, *The Unexamined Death*, 2d ed. (Chicago: John Howard Association, 1966), pp. 12–15.

greatly after the abolition. The statistics show, however, that the changes in homicide rates were almost exactly parallel in other states which made no changes in their laws regarding the death penalty. For instance, Missouri abolished the death penalty in 1917 and restored it in 1919 on the ground that murders had increased greatly. But the changes in the homicide rate in Missouri from 1910 to 1924 were almost exactly the same in direction and amount as in Ohio, which retained the death penalty throughout this whole period, and were very much like the changes in the United States in general. Comparison of the "before and after" homicide rates of European countries which have abolished the death penalty also shows that the presence or absence of the death penalty has no perceptible effect on the incidence of murder.

The available statistics do not justify an absolute conclusion regarding the value of the death penalty as a deterrent. The evidence, such as it is, shows a relatively unimportant relation between the murder rate and the death penalty. The argument that the death penalty is an effective deterrent over and above life imprisonment is not, at least, substantiated by the data available.[51] This argument is based on preconceptions rather than on data, and the preconceptions are taken from hedonistic psychology which assumes that the psychological processes are much less complex than they are in fact.

The Death Penalty and Certainty of Punishment

The advocates of the death penalty argue that it is more certain than imprisonment, because imprisonment is frequently terminated by escape, pardon, or parole. Actually, the death penalty is very uncertain, because it is so severe and repulsive that it is seldom imposed even when it is authorized. For this reason, the deterrent effect of this sanction is difficult to measure. As Andenaes has said,

There is much historical evidence to show that capital punishment in war, revolution and similar situations may have a much stronger effect than any other measure. The main reason is probably that execution is definitive, whereas a threat of life imprisonment under the uncertainty of future developments lacks its normal credibility.[52]

Calvert cites a petition by English bankers in 1830 for abolition of the death penalty for forgery, on the ground that convictions could not be secured because of the severity of the penalty, and for the authorization of a less severe penalty in order that their property might be protected more adequately.[53] Bye found, over a half-century ago, that a slightly larger proportion of murder convictions was secured in states which had abolished the death penalty than in states which

---

[51] Jack P. Gibbs, "Crime, Punishment, and Deterrence."

[52] Johannes Andenaes, "General Prevention Revisited: Research and Policy Implications," *Journal of Criminal Law and Criminology*, 66:338–65, 1975. See also Paul E. Meehl, "Law and the Fireside Inductions: Some Reflections of a Clinical Psychologist," *Journal of Social Issues*, 27:65–100, 1971.

[53] E. R. Calvert, *Capital Punishment in the Twentieth Century* (London: Putnam's Sons, 1927), p. 15.

retained it.[54] Many jurors are less willing to convict and witnesses less willing to testify when the penalty is death than when it is a less irreparable penalty. Until recently in death-penalty states prospective jurors opposed to the death penalty were excused from serving in capital cases, and in some instances this weeding-out process produced biased juries which were most likely to convict the accused.[55] Moreover, the percentage of defendants found guilty in murder cases varies widely from county to county even in states which have the death penalty. For example, during a fifteen-year period, Middlesex County, Massachusetts, found 16.8 percent of its cases guilty of murder in the first degree, while in adjacent Suffolk County, the corresponding percentage was only 3.9.[56]

The uncertainty of the death penalty also is indicated by the fact that many of the persons sentenced to death are not executed. Of the 124 persons convicted of first-degree murder between 1898 and 1971 in Massachusetts, which had a mandatory death penalty until 1951, 65 were executed, 37 had their sentences commuted, and two died awaiting execution.[57] In Maryland in 1936–61, 59 percent of those sentenced to death for murder and 51 percent of those sentenced to death for rape were executed.[58] Only one execution has been carried out in the United States since 1967.

Schuessler devised an index of the certainty of the death penalty and showed that the murder rate has a slight tendency to decrease as the probability of execution increases. He found that among the death-penalty states, those which executed the largest proportion of the persons convicted of homicide in the period 1937–49 generally had the lowest homicide rates. However, the correlation coefficient of −.29 was not statistically significant. Nor did the homicide rate drop consistently as the risk of execution increased. Also, he found that when a state executes a relatively large proportion of its murderers in one year, the homicide rate does not necessarily drop during the following year.[59]

The Death Penalty and Financial Economy
The death penalty often is defended on the ground that it is less expensive than life imprisonment. The per capita cost of imprisonment is about ten thousand

[54] R. T. Bye, *Capital Punishment in the United States* (Philadelphia: Committee on Philanthropic Labor, Philadelphia Yearly Meeting of Friends, 1919), pp. 47 ff.

[55] Hans Zeisel, *Some Data on Juror Attitudes Toward Capital Punishment* (Chicago: University of Chicago Law School—Center for Studies in Criminal Justice, 1968). See also Walter E. Oberer, "Does Disqualification of Jurors for Scruples Against Capital Punishment Constitute Denial of Fair Trial on Issue of Guilt?" *Texas Law Review*, 39:545–53, 1961.

[56] Herbert B. Ehrmann, "The Death Penalty and the Administration of Justice," *Annals of the American Academy of Political and Social Science*, 284:73–84, 1952.

[57] Massachusetts Department of Correction, "Some Notes on Death Row and the Death Penalty in Massachusetts," Document No. 5678, June, 1971, p. 1.

[58] Legislative Council of Maryland, *Report of the Committee on Capital Punishment* (Baltimore: Legislative Council of Maryland, 1962), p. 35.

[59] Schuessler, "The Deterrent Influence of the Death Penalty," See also Savitz, "A Study of Capital Punishment."

dollars per year, and the life term may amount to an average of twenty years, making a total of two hundred thousand dollars. But there is some doubt as to whether execution actually is cheaper than imprisonment. First, the trials of death-penalty cases are ordinarily much longer than trials of other cases. As many as a thousand jurors may be examined before twelve are chosen, and a year or more intervenes between arrest and sentencing. Second, although the maintenance cost per prisoner may be high, this does not mean that it would increase appreciably if those now executed were committed to prisons. Third, in considering the cost of executions, the expenditures for death houses and for the closer custody which must be maintained are usually not computed.

But it is fallacious to debate the capital-punishment issue as though the matter were one of getting the most for the taxpayer's money. If executions could be purchased for less money than life imprisonment, that fact would not make them fair, humane, or just. Indeed, if financial economy were the only issue, and if citizens could be killed cheaply, then it would follow that we should kill insane and mentally retarded persons, as well as all criminals whose institutional maintenance would cost more than their execution.

The Irreparability of Error with the Death Penalty

Those who advocate capital punishment consider wrongful conviction as only a remote possibility.[60] But although most mistakes are prevented by the judicial system or by executive clemency, some do occur, due to mistaken identification, inadequate circumstantial evidence, framed and simulated evidence, perjury, unreliable expert evidence, overlooking and suppressing of evidence, and excessive zeal on the part of investigators and prosecutors.[61] In a forty-year period, 12.3 percent of the 406 persons sent to New York's Sing Sing Prison for execution were found, upon reconsideration, to have been sentenced in error.[62] Hartung found that in Michigan, which does not have the death penalty, judges and juries erred in 10.9 percent of 759 life-imprisonment convictions for first-degree murder in a ten-year period.[63]

THEORIES OF PUNISHMENT

Our previous discussion has indicated that there has been no constant desire to make all criminals suffer and that the system used for inflicting suffering on those criminals who are thought to deserve suffering has changed from time to time.

[60] See Bernard Lande Cohen, *Law Without Order: Capital Punishment and the Liberals* (New Rochelle, N. Y.: Arlington House, 1970), pp. 24–28.

[61] Charles L. Black, Jr., *Capital Punishment: The Inevitability of Caprice and Mistake* (New York, Norton, 1974).

[62] Lewis E. Lawes, *Twenty Thousand Years in Sing Sing* (New York: R. Long and R. R. Smith, 1932), pp. 146–47, 156.

[63] Frank E. Hartung, "Trends in the Use of Capital Punishment," *Annals of The American Academy of Political and Social Science*, 284:8–19, 1952. See also Otto Pollak, "The Errors of Justice," *Annals of the American Academy of Political and Social Science*, 284:115–23, 1952; and Jerome and Barbara Frank, *Not Guilty* (New York: Doubleday, 1957).

The punitive reaction to lawbreaking has not been present in all societies; the methods for implementing the punitive reaction which are predominant in some societies are not predominant in others; the extent to which official punitive policies are carried out in practice varies from time to time even within a given society; and the rationale for punishment has taken many forms. A theory which precisely explains or accounts for all of these variations has not been developed. Preliminary attempts to account for at least some of the variations have been made, however, and the major cultural, psychoanalytic, and sociological explanations will be described briefly.

Cultural Consistency

One theory which partially accounts for the many variations in the presence and implementation of the punitive reaction to lawbreaking may be termed a theory of cultural consistency. The societal reactions to lawbreaking and the methods used to implement or express those reactions show a general tendency to be consistent with other ways of behaving in the society. This may be observed in a number of ways.

First, when criminals were disemboweled, hung in chains, branded, and in other ways tortured and mutilated, suffering was widely regarded as the natural lot of mankind. Torture merely increased the level of physical pain experienced in everyday life by slaves, serfs, and working-class persons everywhere. Physical suffering has been reduced in most parts of the world, and is now being reduced even more. Consider the conditions under which people earn their daily bread. Punishment "at hard labor" in galleys, houses of correction, and prisons might have been reasonable when most work was toil. Such punishment is no longer reasonable. Most workers outside prisons no longer sweat in a dawn-to-dusk tedium of toil. Thanks to labor unions, improved production technology, and increased governmental concern, they do comparatively easy forty-hour-a-week shifts in relatively comfortable surroundings. Physical suffering by criminals cannot be harmonized with the general interest in reducing fatigue, disease, and poverty throughout the world.

Second, the price system—with all its market implications—developed at about the time modern criminal law theory developed. Hence the monetary implications in the terms of imprisonment—"debt to society," "pay the price." Just as a price was assumed to bear a relationship to the demand for a commodity, so, it was assumed, punishment should bear a relationship to the demand for a crime. But now more and more prices are being fixed by governmental boards, agreements among businesses, and negotiations between groups (for example, labor and management), rather than by agreements between individuals. Accordingly, it is no longer reasonable to think of punishment in the framework of classical economics. For example, a person can no longer be sent to prison to pay a debt, and then released when the account is settled. There is no such account.

Third, the ideal of equal punishment for all criminals committing the same technical offense was stated at about the time of the French Revolution, when democracy meant the equality of all persons. Political leaders of democratic nations now rarely talk about "classless society" or, for that matter, about "liberty, equality, fraternity." Accordingly, if it ever was reasonable to believe that a criminal's background and the circumstances of the offense should not be taken into account in deciding on the punishment, this is no longer the case. Consider, similarly, the notion that there should be uniformity in punishments and the very notion that, as an ideal, all crimes should be followed by pain. Both ideas developed when only one cure, bloodletting, was uniformly used by physicians for all kinds of diseases and all kinds of patients. We now know that this cure was worse than disease. We also know that it is neither necessary nor desirable to punish all criminals, as if this single "cure" were appropriate for everyone. Neither is it now reasonable to assume that one person convicted of stealing should be punished as severely as another person convicted of the same crime.

Fourth, in the last few generations punishment as a means of social control has dramatically declined in the home, the school, and the church. When fathers were totalitarians, school teachers authoritarian taskmasters, and preachers spreaders of rumors about the horrors of hell, it was reasonable that state officials also should be champions of terror. Now the state's punitive policy is inconsistent with the practices of other social institutions, and it is being abandoned. If the changes in the other institutions may be taken as evidence, then there is no danger that a deluge of crime will follow. As we suggested earlier, school discipline is much better now than it was when punitive methods were the order of the day. Similarly, men are no less moral now than they were when immoral persons were threatened with hellfire and damnation.

Fifth, the more brutal punishments flourished at a time when the social distance between the punishers and the punished was great. Although the development of democracy obviously can be said to lie behind the continuing reduction of this social distance, development of the means of communication is contributing its part, too. The printed page, telephone, radio, motion picture, and television now enable a larger proportion of a population to appreciate the situation of those who have committed crimes, so that imposing the pain of punishment is no longer indifferently viewed as the injuring of an animal or a savage creature from another planet. This keener sympathy for criminals, if greater social integration may be called that, is still restricted by prejudice against blacks, against the "poor ways" of poor people, and against ethnic cultures, but even such blind bigotry seems to be diminishing. Further, improved communication devices are permitting a broader segment of the population to get inside police departments, courts, jails, and prisons, figuratively speaking, and to report their dislike for what they see.

Sixth, and somewhat more specifically, imprisonment as a method of implementing the punitive reaction has in the last two centuries been substituted for physical torture and death. The explanation for this increase in the use of imprisonment is not entirely clear, but three suggestions seem in order.

Negatively, imprisonment of most criminals was practically impossible before the age of industrialization. No buildings secure enough for confinement of masses of criminals had been constructed, and the technology of the times made their development impractically expensive. More importantly, with many wars, shifts in power, and lack of police or other guardians such buildings, even if constructed, would have been quite useless. It was necessary for social life to become more settled before imprisonment could become a popular reaction to lawbreaking.

More positively, a greater appreciation of freedom developed in the modern period, and deliberate restriction of freedom has increasingly come to be regarded as suffering. During the medieval period, which was characterized by an interest in theology, severe suffering could be imposed by excommunication. Similarly, with the rise of an interest in democracy and freedom at the time of the French and American Revolutions, intense suffering could be imposed by imprisonment. Loss of liberty came to be regarded as sufficiently punitive even for the worst criminals. Moreover, in the medieval period the suffering following excommunication was much greater than the suffering following the same action nowadays. By the same token, but in reverse, the amount of suffering stemming from a given term of imprisonment is much greater now than it was only fifty years ago, when there was less freedom, and less valuation of freedom, in the world.[64] The trend, therefore, is toward reducing prison terms.

Further, imprisonment developed at about the time the slave-labor system was beginning to wane.[65] Life and labor became valuable. Despite the revolutionary stress on painful deprivation of liberty when imprisonment was invented, the modern form developed when state officials learned how to use convict labor in the production of wealth. Because the labor of criminals became valuable, it was logical to conserve it instead of destroying it by death or mutilation.[66] But now that the industrial community has no need for convict labor—and in fact has effectively outlawed prison labor in many areas of the world—it is no longer economically reasonable to commit criminals to institutions designed to use their labor. For that matter, it is hardly reasonable even to try to train prisoners to be "productive members of society." Owing to improved technology and increasing automation, industrial society now needs far fewer productive members than it once did. The trend, therefore, seems to be toward committing criminals to prison for reasons of punishment and incapacitation, thus reducing unemployment rates when need be, rather than for reasons pertaining to the value of convict labor.

[64] See David J. Rothman, *The Discovery of the Asylum* (Boston: Little, Brown, 1971), chap. 4.

[65] See Thorsten Sellin, *Slavery and the Penal System* (New York: Elsevier, 1976).

[66] See Martin B. Miller, "At Hard Labor: Rediscovering the Nineteenth Century Prison," *Issues in Criminology*, 9:91–114, 1974.

Seventh, both the punishments stipulated by statute and the punishments actually imposed tend to be more certain and severe for acts which endanger the values held in high esteem by lawmakers and other persons of power, and these values change. Erikson has argued, for example, that the "moral boundaries" of communities shift over time, and as these boundaries change, the varieties of behavior sanctioned, and the severity of punishment, also change.[67]

The Scapegoat Theory

Psychoanalysts have advanced a theory which correlates the many variations in the punitive reaction with variations in the alternative systems for satisfying aggressive and libidinal instincts.[68] The general notion is that (1) these instincts are present in all persons; (2) these instincts must be expressed in some fashion; and (3) the criminal serves as a scapegoat for their legitimate expression. Thus, it is maintained that in punishing criminals, society expresses the same urges which are expressed, among criminals, in committing crime. One of America's leading psychiatrists has said, "We need criminals to identify ourselves with, to envy secretly, and to punish stoutly. They do for us the forbidden, illegal things we *wish* to do and, like scapegoats of old, they bear the burdens of our displaced guilt and punishment—'the iniquities of us all.' "[69]

One form of this theory holds that the urge to punish criminals is closely related to sexuality and that the variations in the punitive reaction to lawbreaking tend to follow the variations in social prohibitions against sexual behavior. In societies in which sex taboos are few and lax, punishment is absent or lenient; in periods when sex and sexuality are loudly declaimed, punishment is frequent, open, and severe; in periods when sex becomes more suppressed as a topic of public discussion, punishment is suppressed or hidden. One author accounts for variations in the methods of implementing the punitive reaction in terms of the suppression of a rather fixed amount of libidinal "urge" which is assumed to be present in the human organism. It is his contention that in the recent period the punitive reaction to lawbreaking is as prevalent as it was in the period when corporal and capital punishments were most popular, but that the method of punishment has merely gone underground. Thus, we no longer openly whip or torture criminals but, instead, torture them secretly, behind prison walls.[70]

A more popular version of this theory deals more directly with aggression. Again, the essential notion is that the human organism, because of unconscious conflicts, contains a fixed amount of aggression, which must be expressed. It may

---

[67] Erikson, *Wayward Puritans*. See also Lauderdale, "Deviance and Moral Boundaries"; Inverarity, "Populism and Lynching in Louisiana 1889–96"; and Austin T. Turk, "Law as a Weapon in Social Control," *Social Problems*, 23:276–91, 1976.

[68] For an excellent introduction to psychoanalytic theory, see Charles Brenner, *An Elementary Textbook of Psychoanalysis* (Garden City, N. Y. Doubleday, 1974).

[69] Karl Menninger, "The Crime of Punishment," *Saturday Review*, September 7, 1968, pp. 21–25 ff. See also idem, *The Crime of Punishment* (New York: Viking, 1968).

[70] Charles Berg, "The Psychology of Punishment," *British Journal of Medical Psychology*, 20:295–313, 1945.

be expressed in criminality; it may be expressed in punishment of criminals; or it may be expressed in other ways.[71] Variations in the punitive reaction to crime, then, depend upon the availability of alternative outlets for aggressions. The reverse is also thought to be true: limitations on the expression of aggression through punishment of lawbreakers results in the expression of aggression in other ways, perhaps in criminality itself. It has been intimated that the First World War (aggression) was a substitute for punitive aggression against criminals. That is, the punitive reaction of aggression could not be expressed during the period just prior to the war, but since the aggression had to be expressed, enemies, rather than criminals, became the scapegoats.[72] Hence, it is concluded that societies need criminals for emotional reasons, and they organize the fight against them in such a way that crime is actually maintained.[73]

Punishment of criminals, then, is considered a system for sublimation of aggressive tendencies; persons who are aggressive secure satisfaction in the punishment inflicted, and this satisfaction is socially proper. In this way, many persons can avoid illegal aggressions, just as they avoid them by other kinds of sublimation.[74] The analogy here is with the psychoanalytic theory of the development of the individual. Society is said to have advanced through the same three stages as are said to be present in the psychological development of the human organism. First, there was in social life a stage in which there was free expression of the instincts of sexuality and aggressiveness and this was the period of no punishment. Next, the expression of the instincts was repressed and, hence, the instincts obtained their outlet in superego activities, directed against their original form; this was the period of severe and open punishments. In the third stage there has been a further degree of repression, and an open expression of the libidinal and aggressive instincts is no longer tolerated, even in the indirect or symbolic form of punishment. Just as the libidinal and aggressive instincts are said to be repressed and hidden in the unconscious of the individual, the societal expression of such instincts is repressed and hidden behind prison walls. "Inside the prison—the objective equivalent of the unconscious—the same process [instinctual expression] goes on unseen by consciousness and inaccessible to ego-interference."[75]

Social Structure Theories

A few social scientists, largely European, have attempted to relate the many variations in the punitive reaction and its expression and implementation to

---

[71] David Abrahamsen, *Who Are the Guilty: A Study of Education and Crime* (New York: Rinehart, 1952), p. 287.

[72] Paul Reiwald, *Society and Its Criminals* (New York: International Universities Press, 1950).

[73] Ibid., p. 235.

[74] F. Alexander and H. Staub, *The Criminal, the Judge, and the Public*, rev. ed. (Glencoe, Ill.: Free Press, 1956), pp. 213–23; C. G. Schoenfeld, "Psychoanalysis, Criminal Justice Planning and Reform, and the Law," *Criminal Law Bulletin*, 7:313–27, 1971.

[75] Berg, "Psychology of Punishment."

variations in social structure. The variations have been accounted for by the availability of labor supply, the presence of the lower middle class, the division of labor, and social disorganization.

Punishment and Economic Conditions   One theory of punishment is analogous to, or a part of, the economic theory of crime causation. The general notion is that both the punitive reaction itself and the specific methods of implementing that reaction are very much affected, if not determined, by the general economic conditions of the society. Rusche, for example, has advanced the thesis that the primary determinant of the societal reaction to crime is the condition of the labor market.[76] He contends that when the labor market is glutted, and labor therefore is cheap, the reaction to lawbreaking tends to be punitive; but when the labor supply is scarce, and labor therefore is at a premium, the reaction becomes nonpunitive. Substantiation of this point was recently documented for the county of Essex, England, during the reign of Elizabeth (1559–1603). In this agricultural county, the number of criminals taken before the courts during the winter months—when farm labor was not essential—was more than twice the number during the months of the harvest.[77] It is probable, of course, that the figures also reflect fluctuations in the actual number of crimes committed, not merely a fluctuation in prosecutions.[78]

Also, the *methods* of implementing the punitive reaction vary with the condition of the labor market. For instance, the galleys were substituted for corporal and capital punishment when it was necessary to secure men for rowing. The workhouse developed when the state did not have sufficient labor. Transportation began as a means of providing labor for the colonies and stopped because of increased demand for labor at home. Solitary confinement was abandoned as a prison regime because under that system the labor of the prisoners could not be utilized, and fines developed as revenue measures.[79]

The basic assumption in this theory is that crime is a lower-class phenomenon, and that the societal reaction is a phenomenon of the upper classes, who have political power, and for that reason comprise a ruling class. When economic conditions are poor and the labor market is glutted, the upper classes impose severe punishments upon the lower classes; but when the economic need of the upper classes for labor cannot be satisfied, they impose few and mild punishments. Actually, the theory can be broken down into two arguments, the second of which is as follows: When economic conditions are good, there is no economic need to commit crime, and the crime rate is low; but when there is widespread unemployment, the temptation to commit crime is great. If, ruling-class persons believe, in times of unemployment criminals can illegally obtain economic

[76]George Rusche, "Arbeitsmarkt und Strafvollzug," *Zeitschrift für Sozialforschung*, 2:63–78, 1933.

[77]Joel Samaha, *Law and Order in Historical Perspective: The Case of Elizabethan Essex*, p. 171.

[78]Ibid., pp. 23–24.

[79]George Rusche and Otto Kirchheimer, *Punishment and Social Structure* (New York: Columbia University Press, 1939).

necessities in exchange for mild punishments, the crime rate will be high. Therefore, they impose severe penalties in order to counteract the temptations of the lower classes.

When the two arguments are put together, the formula takes the following form: When poverty increases, crime increases, and, also, the labor market is glutted; and when crime increases and the labor market is glutted, the official reaction to crime is punitive rather than nonpunitive. Whether it is the crime rate or the condition of the labor market that determines the societal reaction, then, is not clear. However, most economic determinists are not concerned with this lack of clarity, for it is their contention that it is general economic conditions and power differences which determine both crime and unemployment rates and, thereby, determine the official reaction to crime and the means used to implement that reaction. The studies of the crime rate in relation to business cycles, reviewed in Chapter 11, throw much doubt upon this assumed relationship between economic conditions and crime, but there is considerable evidence that unemployment and imprisonment are correlated, as Rusche and Kirchheimer predicted.[80]

Punishment and the Middle Class Another theory of punishment relates variations in the punitive reaction to the presence or absence of a lower middle class. The chief proponent of this theory, however, uses the term *middle class* in a sense uncommon in the United States; also, there is some doubt as to whether he is considering the middle class or something else. The theory is summarized in the following statement: "The disinterested tendency to inflict punishment is a distinctive characteristic of the lower middle class, that is, of a social class living under conditions which force its members to an extraordinary high degree of self-restraint and subject them to much frustration of natural desires."[81]

This statement actually has three component parts: (1) The punitive reaction to lawbreaking ("the disinterested tendency to inflict punishment") grows out of the moral indignation of the public; it does not grow out of the indignation of the person who has been injured by a crime. (2) Moral indignation is found almost exclusively in the lower middle class and is the product of self-imposed frustration among members of this class. (3) The punitive reaction increases in frequency and severity when the lower middle class is in control and decreases when the lower middle class loses power.

In connection with the second point, it is assumed that moral indignation— which is the emotion behind the disinterested tendency to inflict punishment and is a kind of disguised envy—is caused by the repression of natural desires. The

---

[80] Ivan Jankovic, *Punishment and the Post-Industrial Society: A Study of Unemployment, Crime and Imprisonment in the United States* (Ph.D. diss., University of California, Santa Barbara, 1977). See also Richard Quinney, *Class, State, and Crime: On the Theory and Practice of Criminal Justice* (New York: David McKay, 1977) pp. 131–35.

[81] Svend Ranulf, *Moral Indignation and Middle Class Psychology: A Sociological Study* (Copenhagen: Levin and Munksgaard, 1938), p. 198. See also idem, *The Jealousy of the Gods and the Criminal Law of Athens* (Copenhagen: Levin and Munksgaard, 1933).

natural desires of lower-middle-class persons are repressed; the members of the class are morally indignant when crime occurs; and lower-middle-class persons react punitively to lawbreaking. In this view, the theory is not a social structure theory but, instead, a variation of the scapegoat theory.

However, in connection with the third point, it is argued that even if the above psychological interpretation is omitted, a correlation between the presence of the lower middle class and the frequency and severity of the punitive reaction to lawbreaking still can be observed. At least the literature suggests that the punitive reaction has always been popular in that social class which may be loosely described as the "petit bourgeoisie," and that it does not prevail in communities where this social class is of little significance. The punitive reaction to crime is said to have been absent among the Teutons, the Chinese, the Hindus, and among primitive groups, which had no class of this kind. Among the Israelites, the punitive reaction did develop strongly, but not until a social class comparable to the lower middle class of modern Europe had grown influential.[82]

One difficulty with this suggestive theory is the lack of precision in the definition of *lower middle class*. Ranulf does not define this term precisely, and consequently it is not possible to appraise the theory. Probably what he means by "middle-class psychology" is similar to what is meant by "Puritanism" or "Victorianism." If this be true, then recent variations in the punitive reaction and the methods of implementing it could be related to the rise of the Protestant ethic, in much the same way that Max Weber linked the rise of the spirit of capitalism to the Protestant ethic.[83] The development of an appreciation of the value of labor was shown by Weber to be correlated with the rise of Protestantism, especially Calvinism, and it is not inconceivable that houses of correction and other systems for utilizing the labor of criminals developed along with Calvinism, which emphasized the spiritual value of labor.

Punishment and the Division of Labor   Emile Durkheim, one of sociology's pioneers, attributed fluctuations in the punitive reaction to changes in the division of labor of society. His theory may be stated briefly in three propositions: (1) Offenses which attack the collective values of a society elicit more severe punitive reactions than those which attack individual values. (2) Punishments for crime may be ordered by tribunals made up of all the people or of only a select number, but in either case they are imposed primarily for the purpose of reinforcing collective values, not for vengeance, intimidation or reformation. "We must not say that an action shocks the common conscience because it is criminal, but rather that it is criminal because it shocks the common conscience."[84] (3) As

[82] Ranulf, *Moral Indignation*, pp. 174–86.

[83] For a discussion of Weber's work, see Talcott Parsons, *Structure of Social Action* (New York: McGraw-Hill, 1937), chaps. 14–17.

[84] Emile Durkheim, *The Division of Labor in Society*, trans. George Simpson (Glencoe, Ill.: Free Press, 1947), p. 81. (This book was first published in 1893.) See also Emile Durkheim, "Deux lois de l'evolution penale," *L'Anne Sociologique*, 14:65–95, 1900.

the principle of social organization changes from mechanical solidarity to organic solidarity, the punitive reaction to lawbreaking tends to disappear, and in its place is substituted restitution and reparations.

The final proposition is the one used to account for many of the variations in the punitive reaction to crime. The type of societal reaction to crime is determined by the social structure, and the important aspect of the social structure is the complexity of the division of labor. When a society has mechanical solidarity, a solidarity based not upon division of labor but upon similarity of behavior and attitudes, the reaction to legal wrongs is punitive. This punitive reaction is formalized in the criminal law. But in societies in which the solidarity is organic, a solidarity based upon specialization or division of labor, the reaction is nonpunitive, for the desire is to return things to the condition they were in before the offense. However, state officials in this case are not merely third-party arbitrators, intervening to compromise disputes between individuals; instead, they apply general and traditional rules of law to particular cases. This nonpunitive restitutive reaction is formalized in the rules of civil law, procedural law, administrative law, and constitutional law. Since organic solidarity is becoming more and more the essential characteristic of the social structure of modern societies, the idea goes, the punitive reaction of repressive criminal law is decreasing, and the restitutive law and nonpunitive reaction are increasing.

Several researchers have tried to test this theory or some aspect of it, with varying results. Spitzer, for example, recently studied forty-eight societies and concluded, "The severity of punishment does not decrease as societies grow more concentrated and complex. On the contrary, greater punitiveness is associated with higher levels of structural differentiation."[85] Another empirical study noted that restitutive sanctions—damages and mediation—occur in many societies that lack even rudimentary specialization, and that police ("specialized armed forces used partially or wholly for norm enforcement") are found only in societies characterized by a "substantial division of labor."[86]

But empirical testing is very difficult because in fact Durkheim's theory is not as straightforward as our presentation of it. In the first place, Durkheim noted that political organization need not develop consistently with social organization and may, indeed, counteract nonpunitive restitutive trends stemming from changes in

[85] Steven Spitzer, "Punishment and Social Organization: A Study of Durkheim's Theory of Penal Evolution," *Law and Society Review*, 9:613–37, 1975.

[86] Richard D. Schwartz and James C. Miller, "Legal Evolution and Societal Complexity," *American Journal of Sociology*, 70:159–72, 1964. See also Linton C. Freeman and Robert F. Winch, "Societal Complexity: An Empirical Test of a Typology of Societies," *American Journal of Sociology*, 62:461–66, 1957; Stephen D. Webb, "Crime and Division of Labor: Testing a Durkheimian Model," *American Journal of Sociology*, 78:127–32, 1972; Howard Wimberly, "Legal Evolution: One Further Step," *American Journal of Sociology*, 79:78–83, 1973; Upendra Baxi, "Durkheim and Legal Evolution: Some Problems of Disproof," *Law and Society Review*, 8:112–25, 1974; and Richard D. Schwartz, "Legal Evolution and the Durkheim Hypothesis: Reply to Professor Baxi," *Law and Society Review*, 8:126–27, 1974.

the division of labor. In other words, organization of government sometimes neutralizes the effects of social organization. For this reason, he said, complex societies do not always exhibit a decrease in the severity of punishment. Durkheim also suggested that the effects of type of crime (point 1 above) and the effects of societal complexity (point 3) may also counteract each other, thus complicating matters even more. He distinguished between "religious criminality," which attacks public authority (treason, heresy), and "human criminality," which attacks individuals (murder, theft). Because, he theorized, the things affronted by religious crimes are held in greater esteem and reverence than those attacked by human crimes, the reaction to religious crimes is more severe. Further, religious crimes characterize the less-developed societies and human crimes characterize the more complex ones. Any shift toward less severity in complex societies, then, is a consequence of the change in the type of criminality as well as of changes in governmental organization and division of labor.

Punishment and Social Disorganization   Another theory which attempts to account for many of the variations in the punitive reaction is stated in terms of the heterogeneity of societies. In general, the notion is that in homogeneous societies the punitive reaction is infrequent and mild, while in heterogeneous societies it is frequent and severe. While heterogeneity does not necessarily imply social disorganization, heterogeneous societies are often considered as being in a condition of social disorganization, and homogeneous societies are considered as organized.

Sorokin has stated a social disorganization theory somewhat consistent with Rusche's theory and somewhat inconsistent with Durkheim's.[87] He refers to variations in the "ethico-juridical heterogeneity and antagonism" of social groups, and argues that whenever this heterogeneity increases, whatever the reason for the increase, the frequency as well as the severity of the punitive reaction to lawbreaking increases. The greater the increase in the heterogeneity and antagonism, the greater is the increase in the punitive reaction, as formalized in the imposition of punishments by one part of the group upon the other.[88] The ethico-juridical heterogeneity and antagonism is increased by social crises, including those affecting the economy.[89]

In simple statement, this theory of conflict holds that the quantity and severity of punishments tend to vary directly with the heterogeneity and antagonism within a society. When a society has homogeneous morality, violations of that morality are infrequent; they do not greatly endanger the group; and the political reaction to them is essentially nonpunitive. Thus, as Spitzer has put it, "Beliefs act as legitimations or rationalizations which bolster a specific set of social arrange-

---

[87] Pitirim A. Sorokin, *Social and Cultural Dynamics* (New York: American Book Company, 1937), vol. II, pp. 523–632.

[88] Ibid., p. 595.

[89] Cf. Gaston Richard, "Les Crises Sociales et les conditions de la criminalité," *L'Anne Sociologique*, 4:17–28, 1900.

ments."[90] But when this network of social relations is broken up, and there is an increase in moral and legal heterogeneity—a condition of conflict which may be called disorganization—the official reaction to violations becomes punitive.

The evidence Sorokin advanced in support of this explanation of variations in the punitive reaction is largely the fluctuations of the reaction in periods of revolution, when conflict and heterogeneity increase and the punitive reaction increases. Following the revolution, heterogeneity decreases and the punitive reaction decreases. In periods of revolution the use of capital punishment, imprisonment, banishment, transportation, confiscation of property, and all other methods of implementing the punitive reaction increases enormously. For example, in Russia the number of executions averaged about ten to twenty per year in the years 1880–1905; during the revolution of 1905–07 they were up to about five hundred per year, and even to about thirteen hundred in 1908, thereafter dropping to about one hundred.[91] The same trends have been found in other revolutions.[92]

These theories are all based on the principle that characteristics of the culture and social structure determine the way criminality is handled in a society. But none of the theories specifies the *process* by which cultural and social conditions produce the societal reactions. For example, the cultural consistency theory does not indicate how culture "works" to change the reactions to crime and criminality, just as the economic determinism theory of crime causation does not indicate how poverty "works" to produce criminality in individuals. By shifting to the social psychological level, all the theories could be supplemented by study of the processes by which persons learn to react differentially to crime. Perhaps we learn to react punitively or in some other way just as we learn to speak English, German, or Japanese. If this is true, it could be maintained that the "societal" reactions to crime represent the outcome of negotiations between persons possessing various learned reactions to crime and various degrees of power to implement their reactions. This application of the differential association principle would place the emphasis upon study of the process by which societal reactions to criminality change; it would supplement the theories outlined, and it would not necessarily contradict any of them.

SUGGESTED READINGS

Andenaes, Johannes. *Punishment and Deterrence.* Ann Arbor, Mich.: University of Michigan Press, 1974.

Bedau, Hugo A. *The Death Penalty.* New York: Anchor Books, 1967.

Black, Donald, & Maureen Mileski, eds. *The Social Organization of Law.* New York: Academic Press, 1973.

---

[90] Spitzer, "Punishment and Social Organization," p. 632.

[91] Sorokin, *Social and Cultural Dynamics,* p. 601.

[92] See John N. Hazard, "Trends in the Soviet Treatment of Crime," *American Sociological Review,* 5:565–76, 1940.

Boshier, Roger, & Camille Ray. "Punishing Criminals: A Study of the Relationship Between Conservativism and Punitiveness." *Australian and New Zealand Journal of Criminology,* 8:37–45, 1975.

Bowers, William J. *Executions in America.* Lexington, Mass.: D. C. Heath, 1974.

Brehm, Jack W. *Responses to Loss of Freedom: A Theory of Psychological Reactance.* Morristown, N. J.: General Learning Press, 1972.

Bromberg, Walter. "Is Punishment Dead?" *American Journal of Psychiatry,* 127:245–48, 1970.

Chapman, Denis. *Sociology and the Stereotype of the Criminal.* London: Tavistock, 1968.

Dalzell, George. *Benefit of Clergy in America.* Winston-Salem, N. C.: Blair, 1955.

Ezorsky, Gertrude, ed. *Philosophical Perspectives on Punishment.* Albany, N. Y.: State University of New York Press, 1972.

Gerber, Rudolph J., & Patrick D. McAnany, eds. *Contemporary Punishment: Views, Explanations, and Justifications.* Notre Dame, Ind.: University of Notre Dame Press, 1972.

Gibbs, Jack P. *Crime, Punishment and Deterrence.* New York: Elsevier, 1975.

Goldberg, Steven. "On Capital Punishment," *Ethics,* 85:67–74, 1974.

Hibbert, Christopher. *The Roots of Evil: A Social History of Crime and Punishment.* London: Weidenfeld and Nicolson, 1963.

Honderich, Ted. *Punishment: The Supposed Justifications.* London: Hutchinson, 1969.

Levitt, A. "Some Social Aspects of the Criminal Law," *Journal of Criminal Law and Criminology,* 13:90–104, 1922.

Meehl, Paul E. "Law and the Fireside Inductions: Some Reflections of a Clinical Psychologist," *Journal of Social Issues,* 27:65–100, 1971.

Palmer, Jan. "Economic Analysis of the Deterrent Effect of Punishment: A Review," *Journal of Research on Crime and Delinquency,* 14:4–21, 1977.

Pepinsky, Harold E. *Crime and Conflict: A Study of Law and Society.* New York: Academic Press, 1976.

Samaha, Joel. *Law and Order in Historical Perspective: The Case of Elizabethan Essex.* New York: Academic Press, 1974.

Shinnar, Ruel, & Shlomo Shinnar. "The Effects of the Criminal Justice System on the Control of Crime: A Quantitative Approach," *Law and Society Review,* 9:581–611, 1975.

Silberman, Matthew. "Toward a Theory of Criminal Deterrence," *American Sociological Review,* 41:442–61, 1976.

Singer, Barry F. "Psychological Studies of Punishment," *California Law Review,* 58:405–43, 1970.

Tittle, Charles R. "Deterrents or Labeling?" *Social Forces,* 53:399–410, 1975.

Waldo, Gordon P., & Theodore G. Chiricos. "Perceived Penal Sanction and Self-Reported Criminality: A Neglected Approach to Deterrence Research," *Social Problems,* 19:522–40, 1972.

Wines, F. H. *Punishment and Reformation.* New York: Crowell, 1875.

Zimring, Franklin E., & Gordon Hawkins. *Deterrence: The Legal Threat in Crime Control.* New York: Columbia University Press, 1973.

15

Intervention and Treatment

Until about two hundred years ago, there were few alternatives to the punitive reaction. It was usually assumed that criminals would change their ways if they were punished. Consistently, it was usually assumed in official policies that punishment of criminals would deter potential criminals, thus keeping crime rates low. Therefore, state officials had the apparent choice of imposing punishments or doing nothing to reform criminals or to prevent crime. Although in many areas of the world there still is no positive alternative to the punitive reaction, a distinct trend during the last century has been toward policies and programs designed to help rather than merely to punish the criminal, and toward congruent policies and programs for changing the economic, political, and social conditions associated with high crime rates.

This recent societal reaction is basically a two-step process—studying the conditions in which persons become delinquents and criminals, and then utilizing the knowledge thus secured in attempts to modify these conditions. Positive, constructive programs are implied, in contrast with the rather negative programs of punishment. Such positive programs range from individual psychotherapy to drastic alterations of class structure.

Over the years, however, this reaction to criminality and crime has come to be dominated by a medical model in which the stress is on the notion that individual criminals should be cured of what ails them. For this reason, it has been called a "treatment reaction," even when the help given to offenders consists merely of finding them jobs or teaching them arithmetic. Use of the medical model distracts from the idea that it is both possible and desirable for state officials and others to implement the positive, interventionist reaction by initiating programs designed to change crime rates by changing the social order.

If there is one key to understanding present-day practices in criminal-justice agencies, and in legislation concerning delinquency and crime, it is the conflict between the notion that crime and criminals should be modified by punitive actions, and the notion that they should be modified by positive actions. One popular contemporary reaction to crime is hostility, with insistence that the criminal be made to suffer. Every criminal law specifies that a penalty should be imposed for violation, so everyone convicted of violating the law is at least threatened with punishment. As we have seen, the pain or suffering is justified in various ways: vengeance, retribution, deterrence, reformation. The following statement advocates the punitive policy:

> I warn you to stay unswerving to your task—that of standing by the man on the firing line—the practical, hard-headed, experienced, honest policemen who have shown by their efforts that they, and they alone, know the answer to the crime problem. That answer can be summed up in one sentence—adequate detection, swift apprehension, and certain, unrelenting punishment. That is what the criminal fears. That is what he understands, and nothing else, and that fear is the only thing which will force him into the ranks of the law-abiding. There is no royal road to law enforcement. If we wait upon the medical quacks, the parole panderers, and the misguided sympathizers with habitual criminals to protect our lives and property from the criminal horde, then we must also resign ourselves to increasing violence, robbery, and sudden death.[1]

But another popular contemporary reaction to crime is one of inquiry designed to secure comprehension of the conditions under which criminal laws are enacted, enforced, and broken, and of working out methods of change based on this comprehension. Pain and suffering may be necessary to the process of change, but they are incidental, not a direct aim of the process. This second reaction is the foundation of a psychology of offenders—and of a sociology of criminal law, criminal behavior, and criminal justice as well. It was reflected most clearly in the invention of juvenile-court procedures and in the abolition of child-labor laws, and it was rapidly extended into adult courts, institutions, and systems of probation and parole. It also appears in programs for decriminalizing drunkenness and marijuana use, for enlarging the economic opportunities of youth, for developing a sense of community in urban districts, and for redistributing economic wealth and political power.

One form of this reaction locates the cause of criminality in the offender's psychological makeup and consistently calls for treatment and cure of the diagnosed ailment:

> . . . imprisonment and punishment do not present themselves as the proper methods of dealing with criminals. We have to treat them psychically as sick people, which in every respect they are. It is no more reasonable to punish these individuals for a behavior over which they have no control than it is to punish an individual for breathing through his

---

[1]J. Edgar Hoover, "Patriotism and the War Against Crime," an address given before the annual convention of the Daughters of the American Revolution, Washington, D.C., April 23, 1936. Quoted by permission of the late Mr. Hoover.

mouth because of enlarged adenoids. . . . It is the hope of the more progressive elements in psychopathology and criminology that the guard and the jailer will be replaced by the nurse, and the judge by the psychiatrist, whose sole attempt will be to treat and cure the individual instead of merely to punish him. Then and then only can we hope to lessen, even if not entirely to abolish, crime, the most costly burden that society has today.[2]

Although the *methods* advocated in this statement are quite different from those advocated by persons who would eradicate crime by reducing inequalities, the principle is the same: Change the crime rate by treating the conditions believed to create and maintain it. A half-century ago an eminent philosopher and social psychologist argued that this reaction to crime, which shall be called the "interventionist reaction" for want of a better term, cannot be combined with the punitive reaction:

. . . the two attitudes, that of control of crime by the hostile procedure of the law, and that of control through comprehension of social and psychological conditions, cannot be combined. To understand is to forgive, and the social procedure seems to deny the very responsibility which the law affirms, and on the other hand the pursuit by criminal justice inevitably awakens the hostile attitude in the offender and renders the attitude of mutual comprehension practically impossible.[3]

This is a fashionable view at present. It is apparent in the many presentations of the notion that, because our efforts to change criminals and the society that produces them have been ineffective, we must retain punishment and abandon the effort to understand and do something about changing crime and criminals. For example, it has become fashionable for radicals and liberals to announce that the rehabilitative idea—as it pertains to *criminals*—has failed, that criminals suffer under it, and that criminal justice should therefore return to the policies of the classical school.[4] The search for the cause or causes of crime is futile, it is said, and one implication is that the agents of the state should therefore merely punish evil persons who have drifted into delinquency and crime.[5] Similarly, it has become fashionable for reactionaries and conservatives to announce that the rehabilitative idea—as it pertains to *society*—has failed, and that powerful persons should therefore continue to punish blacks, poor people, and a few others.[6] Earlier, of course, the fashionable argument was that the punitive reaction should be abandoned and the effort to understand the conditions spawning crime and criminals enlarged. David Bazelon, chief judge of the United States Court of

---

[2]Benjamin Karpman, "Criminality, Insanity and the Law," *Journal of Criminal Law and Criminology*, 39:584–605, 1949.

[3]George H. Mead, "The Psychology of Punitive Justice," *American Journal of Sociology*, 23:577–602, 1918.

[4]See American Friends Service Committee, *Struggle for Justice* (New York: Hill and Wang, 1971); and James Q. Wilson, *Thinking About Crime* (New York: Basic Books, 1975).

[5]See Patrik Törnüdd, "The Futility of Searching for Causes of Crime," *Scandinavian Studies in Criminology*, vol. 3, pp. 23–33, 1971.

[6]See Ernest van Den Haag, *Punishing Criminals: Concerning a Very Old and Painful Question* (New York: Basic Books, 1975).

Appeals for the District of Columbia, recently warned that when the study of crime causation is ignored, repressive measures flourish:

> Today street crime has replaced anarchism and communism as our cause for alarm. . . . And in the legislatures there is a rush to adopt tougher sentencing provisions. The spirit of our response to previous demons can be discerned in our reaction to the crime threat.
>
> Our libertarian tradition would tell us to get tough with the "deprivations that caused the disease" rather than with those who manifest the symptoms.
>
> Mandatory incarceration, determinate sentencing, and the like are the first steps in a thousand-mile journey, but in precisely the wrong direction: towards repression. Mandatory incarceration means nothing more than locking up those manifesting symptoms of the underlying ill. If it reduces crime, and it probably can, it will only be because repression and fear can be effective.
>
> Our last best hope is to seek out the causes of the criminal act. . . . To do that effectively, however, will require (1) a major commitment of resources to produce probing presentencing reports that permit critical insights; and (2) an erosion of the obdurate resistance of almost all sentencing judges to systematically spelling out exactly what has been learned about the individual and exactly what facts and reasoning led to the exercise of their sentencing discretion.[7]

But one can agree that the two reactions—punishment and intervention—are logically incompatible while at the same time implementing both of them in practice. In fact, the differential-association theory implies that this seemingly contradictory position is the correct one.[8] The implication is that crime as well as individual criminal acts must be understood if they are to be modified, and that the most important conditions in *preventing* crime are expressions of disapproval and those most effective in *causing* crime are expressions of appreciation.

This principle applies to making and enforcing criminal laws as well as to violating them. Thus a legislature is expressing hostility to burglary when it makes burglary behavior punishable by law, and it is not expressing hostility to exploitative business practices when it does not outlaw them.[9] Similarly, a police officer, prosecutor, or judge expresses appreciation for misconduct when the official concludes that the behavior of a respectable middle-class person is not "really crime," and the same person expresses hostility when perceiving behavior of a working-class person as "real crime" that must be punished. And of course it

---

[7] Quoted by Stephen A. Bennett, "A Bicentennial Inquiry into American Law," *Trial*, 12:16–33, 1976. See also David L. Bazelon, "Street Crime and Correctional Potholes," *Federal Probation*, 41:1–9, 1977.

[8] See Chapter 4, above.

[9] Disapprobation can be expressed in nonpunitive ways, including the withholding of praise and other rewards. See Albert Bandura, *Principles of Behavior Modification* (New York: Holt, Rinehart and Winston, 1969), pp. 293–354; idem, *Social Learning Theory* (New York: General Learning Press, 1971); Vitali Rozynko, Kenneth Swift, Josephine Swift, and Larney J. Boggs, "Controlled Environments for Social Change," in *Beyond the Punitive Society*, ed. Harvey Wheeler (San Francisco: W. H. Freeman, 1973), pp. 71–100; and Robert F. Meier and Weldon T. Johnson, "Deterrence as Social Control: The Legal and Extralegal Production of Conformity," *American Sociological Review*, 42:292–304, 1977.

is obvious that once a behavior pattern such as stealing a neighbor's television set or mugging an old lady has been outlawed by a legislature and declared to be "real" crime by criminal-justice agents, persons will engage in it or not depending on whether they are encouraged to do so or discouraged from doing so.

Thus, the differential-association principle supports systems for expressing disapprobation, just as it supports programs for expressing appreciation of noncriminal and anticriminal attitudes. Accordingly, it is possible to combine the notion that crime and criminals should be understood in general with the notion that there should be a certain hostility toward crime and criminals in general. What really is at issue is the effectiveness and the justice of expressing disapprobation by imposing state punishments on individual lawbreakers rather than by more peaceful means. Also at issue is the effectiveness and justice of constructive programs based on various theories of what crime and criminality are all about.

INTERVENTION AND THE STUDY OF CRIME CAUSATION

The development of causal explanations of crime probably is more a part of than an explanation for the development of the interventionist reaction. Nevertheless, on a formal level it may be observed that attempts to explain criminal behavior have greatly abetted at least the official policy of intervention. In the eighteenth and early nineteenth centuries the will, assumed to be isolated from all other psychological conditions and from social processes and conditions, was practically the only element considered in discussions of behavior, both criminal and noncriminal. The Lombrosian brand of positivism denied the doctrine of free will and attempted to explain crime in terms of biological determinism. The explanation was not at all satisfactory, but it resulted in a demand that crime and criminality be regarded as explainable and, hence, changeable. Accordingly, the validity of the punitive reaction was denied, and what is now commonly called the "treatment reaction" was supported.

To the logic of the Lombrosian school was added the immense weight of authority in the last half-century. By many methods, conditions associated with crime were isolated, and a valid principle that would make sense of these relationships was sought. The emphasis on mental deficiency, emotional disturbances, differential association, and status frustration as explanations of delinquency and crime during the last fifty years has helped establish the view that if criminals are to become noncriminals they must first be understood and then assisted. Further, because criminal-law policies have been based on the doctrine of free will, the conclusion that crime and delinquency can be accounted for by looking at economic, political, and social arrangements helped establish the view that if crime and delinquency rates are to be reduced, they must first be understood. Recent developments in theories of crime, criminality, delinquency and delinquent behavior—especially theories stressing normative conflict, differential social organization, restricted opportunities for social mobility, labeling, and economic and political exploitation—have important implications for changing societies rather than personalities.

It is important to note, however, that implementing the interventionist reaction has not been a simple matter of developing theory and then basing policy on it. On the contrary, criminological theory has been greatly affected by changing methods of dealing with criminals and crime. A bit at a time, methods for implementing the interventionist reaction encroached on the methods used to implement the punitive reaction, and it appeared that some of them seemed more successful than the punitive policies of earlier days. Then, in an effort to account for the apparent success of the new methods, new criminological theory was developed. There are three good examples of this interaction between practice and theory.

First, the theory of differential association and differential social organization grew out of the efforts to get the residents of several Chicago areas to do something about delinquency in the neighborhood, rather than relying on police officers, prosecutors, judges, probation workers, and other state agents to repress it by punishing delinquents. The Chicago Area Projects, as these experiments were called, seemed to work. In trying to tell why they seemed to work, Clifford R. Shaw, Henry D. McKay, and Edwin H. Sutherland developed a powerful set of explanatory principles.[10]

Second, and more generally, ideas about why boys and girls become delinquents were profoundly influenced by the invention of the juvenile court at the turn of the century. What the new procedure did, basically, was to accompany the punitive methods of dealing with delinquents with nonpunitive methods such as vocational guidance, counseling, and a helping hand. The juvenile-court movement, of course, stemmed from theory stressing the despair rather than the evil of children in court, but once the court was in operation, new theories of delinquency developed and then maintained, essentially, that delinquent behavior is a product of emotional maladjustments.[11] Then juvenile courts and correctional agencies were enthusiastically "psychiatrized"—nonpunitive psychotherapy, not punishment, was to cure the ills of bad girls and boys. It then came to be said that if the delinquent behavior of persons under sixteen years of age could be cured psychiatrically, it logically followed that the criminality of older persons could also be cured. The medical model had been established.

Third, some persons have long argued that delinquency and crime rates will go down if a policy of social change replaces both the punitive reaction and the

---

[10] See James F. Short, Jr., "Introduction to the Revised Edition" of Clifford R. Shaw and Henry D. McKay, *Juvenile Delinquency and Urban Areas* (Chicago: University of Chicago Press, 1969), pp. xxv–liv. See also Harold Finestone, "The Delinquent and Society: The Shaw and McKay Tradition," chap. 1 in James F. Short, Jr., ed., *Delinquency, Crime and Society* (Chicago: University of Chicago Press, 1976), pp. 23–48.

[11] See Anthony M. Platt, *The Child Savers: The Invention of Delinquency* (Chicago: University of Chicago Press, 1969).

methods based on the idea that the offender is somehow sick. They observed, as we have, the low delinquency and crime rates of nonliterate and peasant societies where the influences surrounding a person are relatively steady, uniform, and consistent, and from these observations developed the theory that crime rates are high when participation in economic, political, and social affairs is low.[12] Similar communal policies and practices in contemporary China and Cuba are said to be working to produce low delinquency and crime rates. From such observations, sociologists have developed a theory that attributes crime to class conflict, the basic idea being that such conflict underlies the formulations and definitions of what is called crime, the application of these definitions, and the development of behavior patterns in violation of the definitions.[13]

THE CONFLICT BETWEEN PUNITIVE AND INTERVENTION METHODS

The punitive reaction is still very popular. Many leaders, both liberal and conservative, argue for the social utility of punishment by maintaining that high crime rates are a consequence of the interventionist reaction to crime and criminals. Actually, there is no available proof that the change toward nonpunitive methods has either increased or decreased crime rates. It is just as logical to assert that crime rates are high because the effectiveness of methods based on the interventionist reaction have been blocked by surviving structures and processes based on the punitive reaction.[14] Although many of the arguments against change and attempts at change are only repetitions of the justifications for punishment that were used when introducing interventionist programs was not an alternative, a more detailed consideration of some of the objections helps clarify the nature of the conflict.

(1) It is asserted by those whose reaction to crime is punitive that the general public cannot be prevented from engaging in a general debauch of crime except by fear of punishment; state officials must continue to terrorize the citizenry. The reply to this objection is that not all of the unpleasantness and suffering would be removed even if the present form of punishment for criminals were completely abandoned. On the basis of the situation experienced in Denmark when the country was without police during a part of the Nazi occupation, it may be concluded that the penal process, including arrest, does deter.[15] Other more recent studies also show that terror works—some people are deterred from some crimes

---

[12] W. I. Thomas and F. Znaniecki, *The Polish Peasant in Europe and America* (Chicago: University of Chicago Press, 1927).

[13] Richard Quinney, *Criminology: Analysis and Critique of Crime in America* (Boston: Little, Brown, 1975), pp. 33–41; idem, *Class, State and Crime: On the Theory and Practice of Criminal Justice* (New York: David McKay, 1977); and Harold E. Pepinsky, *Crime and Conflict: A Study of Law and Society* (New York: Academic Press, 1976).

[14] See Donald R. Cressey, "The Nature and Effectiveness of Correctional Techniques," *Law and Contemporary Problems*, 23:754–771, 1958.

[15] Jorgen Trolle, *Syv Maaneder under Politi [Seven Months Without Police]* (Copenhagen, 1945).

by some punishments. Yet none of these studies has weighed a deterrence system against some other system.

But the real reason for believing that the substitution of positive programs for punishment would not result in a debauch of crime is that social control, after all, lies in the recognition and reward secured by lawful conduct rather than in direct fear of punishment. Not the fear of legal penalties, as such, but the fear of loss of status in the group is the effective deterrent. But this is not really fear; what really occurs is that a girl or woman, for example, feels that doing a specified thing in violation of a group standard, which also happens to be in violation of the law, would not be in harmony with her self-image, would demean her. It does not occur to her to do such a thing. She would feel uncomfortable in violating such a norm and would secure no reward from it. This is the principal method of control, whether or not the conduct is regulated by law.

Some men and women never even think of breaking into a jewelry store or robbing a liquor store. Such actions simply are not in their behavioral repertoires. Nevertheless, a person to whom such street crime is unthinkable will violate the law by smuggling jewelry into the country upon returning from a trip to Europe, and also will frequently violate the laws regulating business and then brag about the crimes at cocktail parties. Such a person's reference groups regard the first violations, but not the second, as beneath the dignity of its members. Accordingly, the person has a stake in conformity to statutes outlawing burglary and robbery but little or no stake in conformity to statutes pertaining to other outlawed conduct. Regardless of official methods of state control, we have retained this informal but highly effective method of control by rewarding conformity rather than by punishing nonconformity.

It is quite possible that, as Wheeler maintains, crime rates are high because we have not yet invented the nonpunitive society:

Just as prisons teach criminals how to be criminals, not how to be good citizens, so punishment teaches persons how to punish; how to punish themselves by haranguing themselves with guilt feelings, as well as how to punish others retributively. When interrelations are complex, each punishment may have a multiplier effect. The result is a society characterized by punishing; repressive behavior produces a suppressive society. Such a society is dysfunctional; no species can survive in such an environment. The human being, marvelously subtle and resourceful creature that he is, has been able to accommodate much more suppression than can other living things, but even he can take only so much.[16]

If attitudes of appreciation for certain values could be developed, laws pertaining to those values would be unnecessary. For example, if everyone in a society had an

---

[16] Harvey Wheeler, "Introduction: A Nonpunitive World?" in Harvey Wheeler, ed., *Beyond the Punitive Society* (San Francisco: W. H. Freeman, 1973), pp. 5–6. See also Manuel Lopez-Rey, "Quelques Observations Critiques sur Violence et Justice," *Etudes Internationales de Psycho-Sociologie Criminelle*, 27:3–27, 1975; and Harold E. Pepinsky, *Crime and Conflict: A Study of Law and Society* (New York: Academic Press, 1976).

equal stake in the concept of private property, then trying to terrorize people into respecting property rights would become obsolete.

(2) A second objection is that, if criminals are not punished, victims will take the law into their own hands, thus engaging either in self-redress or in lynch law. This assertion is based on the belief that there is an unalterable demand for vengeance that will be satisfied by illegal means if it is not satisfied by legal means, and it is consistent with the "scapegoat" theory described in the previous chapter. Most persons demand vengeance under certain circumstances. In offenses involving social relations between blacks and whites in the South, in certain brutal sex offenses and offenses that victimize children or older people, and in criminal attempts to change the social order, a rather widespread demand for vengeance may arise. Individuals who take the law into their own hands in response to such crimes may receive the support of a group, especially when the crime has political overtones. But most crimes—probably more than 75 percent— arouse the resentment of no particular individual. And even when resentment is aroused, it is generally confined to a small number of persons, whose resentment is likely to be counteracted by a nonpunitive reaction on the part of other members of the society.

The vengeance reaction is not instinctive. It is the product of social contacts and interactions. The very fact that the interventionist reaction exists is evidence of this.[17] Even if an unconscious desire for vengeance be assumed, it cannot be said that this drive determines its own method of expression. One may secure revenge by a blow with the fist, by spitting, by calling names, by shooting with a gun, by spreading calumny, by voting, by bringing the offender to trial, and, perhaps, by assisting the state to use methods that will change the offender.

(3) It is believed that victims will be unwilling to testify or make complaint if they cannot see their opponents suffer; they will take the loss and remain silent rather than go to the trouble of initiating procedures that will give no satisfaction. However, no private vengeance is necessary to the official processing of the vast majority of all offenders. For such offenses as drunkenness, prostitution, gambling, abortion, traffic violations, and the use, possession, and sale of illicit drugs, the complaint usually is initiated by an officer of the state; testimony regarding the offense is furnished by the same officer and by others subpoenaed to appear in court. Moreover, friends and even the victim of the criminal are currently likely to rally in the criminal's support in opposition to the hostile procedure of the criminal law and the very severe consequences of conviction. If these persons had any reason to believe that the community is really concerned about the welfare of its members, including those who deviate from its norms, they would be much more inclined to get involved.

(4) Another objection to the interventionist method is that group solidarity

---

[17] See Adam Podgorecki, Wolfgang Kaupen, J. Van Houtte, P. Vinke, and Berl Ktchinsky, *Knowledge and Opinion About Law* (South Hackensack, N.J.: Rothman, 1973).

and respect for the law, now developed and maintained by the punitive reaction, would decrease in the absence of this reaction. As we said earlier, these conditions can be developed and maintained in a great variety of other ways. The only thing needed is issues or events on which persons can act collectively, thus developing or maintaining or reinforcing a sense of community among them. Social solidarity might be enhanced by pursuing and hurting criminals, but it also is enhanced by collective action to cure and prevent disease, prevent catastrophes and environmental pollution, save crops from insects, correct injustices, and other actions where comprehension, not punishment, is involved. It also can be enhanced by collective action toward comprehending the causes of crime and utilizing the knowledge thus obtained.

But the weakest part of this objection is its assumption that crime upsets group solidarity. In the first place, there is not much solidarity to be upset. In the second place, punishment seldom restores the equilibrium of a community, such as it is, because this equilibrium is not much disturbed by crime. Crime is an impersonal event, and no direct collective reaction occurs. Many persons carry burglary, robbery, and larceny insurance; for them, crime is not a shocking event—the burden of loss is distributed over a period of years in the premiums paid to the insurance company. Even victims not protected by insurance are generally willing to drop the case if restitution can be secured. They usually are interested only secondarily in the offense against the peace and dignity of the community. In general, whole communities are seldom disturbed by individual crimes or even by high crime rates except in spectacular cases, and infliction of punishment therefore has little effect on the community.

As these opposing arguments show, punitive reactions and interventionist reactions are both sanctioned ways of behaving in present-day society. For that reason, crime-control procedures and programs are not exclusively punitive nor exclusively interventionist, even when they are formally set up to operate in one of the alternative ways.

LIMITATIONS OF PUNISHMENT

As the constructive, interventionist, positive reaction to lawbreaking became more popular, many arguments (again based on very shaky empirical evidence) were advanced in support of the proposition that punishment is relatively ineffective either as an instrument of specific deterrence (reformation of the offender) or as an instrument of general deterrence (frightening citizens). It has been pointed out in this connection that punishment often has unanticipated effects, and that these effects are the opposite of those expected when the punishment was imposed. Thus the general argument is that the interventionist reaction should be substituted for the punitive reaction, since it would not, at least to the same extent, produce these undesirable effects. The following are some of the types of unanticipated consequences produced by punishment.

(1) Punishment often isolates individuals who are punished, making them

confirmed enemies of society. When the sole reaction is punitive, criminals are isolated from law-abiding groups and neither understand nor are understood by these groups. Hatred of the criminal by society results in hatred of society by the criminal.

In this respect, a war on crime is similar to a real war, which produces isolation and dissociation of the citizens of warring nations, as well as hatred, atrocities, and the killing of enemies. When individual criminals are declared enemies and are effectively ostracized, they have only two alternatives They may associate with other criminals, among whom they can find recognition, prestige, and criminal means to a livelihood, thus becoming the enemy they have been declared to be. Or they may become asocial, unstable, or even psychotic isolates. The current practice is to permit almost all criminals to return to the streets in a physical sense, but to hold them off, make them keep their distance, segregate them, deny them jobs, and otherwise isolate them psychologically from law-abiding groups. If they are to be turned into law-abiding citizens, they must be assimilated, which means that they must be given a stake in the society, like all other citizens.[18]

(2) Punishment develops caution. A painful experience, such as being punished by the state or being stung by honey bees, will make most persons "think twice" before repeating the behavior. But, in the case of the bees, "thinking twice" might be a means of securing immunity from the bees while grabbing their honey. The actor has been made cautious by the previous suffering, but has not been reformed. Similarly, an unanticipated consequence of current systems for punishing criminals might be caution rather than specific deterrence. Differences between unorganized crime and various forms of organized crime, for example, are principally differences in organizing to avoid punishment while maximizing profit from crime. After a few convictions, the amateur criminal develops both the professional criminal's caution and the professional criminal's techniques for avoiding punishment.

(3) Punishment often gives offenders high status. In some neighborhoods, going to a boys' school or a prison is a sign of manliness. In states whose prisons are scaled from tough maximum-security institutions down to relaxed minimum-security institutions, youthful offenders frequently request assignment to the maximum-security institutions, because such assignment will result in high status among their friends when they are released.

(4) Punishment generally stops constructive efforts. If the members of a group, in a spirit of hatred, inflict punishment on an offender in their midst, they can relax after the penalty is inflicted, confident that the matter is now settled. But the situation remains, in general, just about what it was before the punishment was

---

[18] See Donald R. Cressey, "Changing Criminals: The Application of the Theory of Differential Association," *American Journal of Sociology,* 61:116–20, 1955; and Rita Volkman and Donald R. Cressey, "Differential Association and the Rehabilitation of Drug Addicts," *American Journal of Sociology,* 69:129–42, 1963.

inflicted. Such a punitive reaction may produce fear in the offender, but more than fear is required for an alteration of character, personality, and behavior. Reformation involves more than a determination to change one's behavior because it is painful to do otherwise. It involves a constructive process of reorganizing the conditions that produced the criminal behavior in the first place.[19] Individuals must have stimulations, patterns, suggestions, sentiments, and ideals presented to them. They must be given an appreciation of the values that are conserved by the law, and this can occur only if they assimilate the culture of the group that passed the law, or, stated otherwise, only if they themselves become part of the powerful group that decides which conduct is to be regulated by law. The negative act of prohibiting certain conduct is not sufficient because it does not promote assimilation.

Simple incapacitation of criminals by locking them up temporarily or permanently—with no thought of punishing them for deterrence purposes—also stops constructive efforts. A recent study concluded that a prison stay of five years for muggers and robbers would reduce mugging and robbery by a factor of four or five.[20] But the study pays little attention to the negative effects of such incapacitation on prisoners, and it implicitly recommends that political policy makers cease or diminish constructive programs for reorganizing the society in ways that will reduce the perceived need to lock up so many people. Such a policy would be comparable to a system for isolating all persons with a venereal disease while paying little or no attention to public-health measures that would decrease the incidence of such disease.

(5) Punishment creates other unanticipated attitudes. Even if some acts are forestalled by terror, this does not necessarily promote the public interest. Whatever is accomplished by terror may be more than offset by attitudes and other behavior patterns produced by the terror. For instance, the state could at least temporarily cut down a neighborhood burglary rate if it dramatically executed ten citizens every time a burglary occurred. Soon the neighborhood would organize against burglary. On a less dramatic level, a boy's practice of lying might be stopped by whipping him, but he might then come to fear the parent who inflicted the punishment, with the result that both his welfare and the welfare of his family are jeopardized. And thus the punitive reaction frequently diminishes the consent of the governed even as particular crimes are successfully forestalled—lack of respect for law, lack of patriotism, lack of willingness to sacrifice for the state, and lack of initiative. Real efficiency in dealing with delinquents and criminals involves not only the stopping of specific violations of law, but the accomplishment of this result without the loss of other social values.

---

[19] See Chapter 26, below.

[20] Ruel Shinnar and Shlomo Shinnar, "The Effects of the Criminal Justice System on the Control of Crime: A Quantitative Approach," *Law and Society Review,* 9:581–611, 1975.

IMPLEMENTATION OF THE INTERVENTIONIST REACTION: INDIVIDUALIZATION

The official policy of providing individualized programs for offenders developed out of the positive school's arguments against the practice of attempting to impose uniform punishments on all persons violating a particular law. It was, and is, argued that policies calling for uniform punishments are as obviously ineffective as would be a policy calling for uniform treatment of all medical patients, no matter what their ailments. This led some persons to advocate that the type of punishment and the severity of punishment be adapted to the individual offender; even today "individualization" sometimes refers to a system for imposing punishments.

As the interventionist reaction increased in popularity, however, "individualization" came to designate a process in which the handling of each case of criminality would include expert diagnosis of individual problems and needs, expert prescription of therapy, and expert therapy—just as clinical medicine includes diagnosis, prescription, and therapy. This is by far the most common meaning of the term in modern correctional parlance.

"Individualization," then, usually means any positive procedure for trying to change criminals into noncriminals. There are hundreds of such procedures, ranging from vocational education and the lending of a helping hand to psychoanalysis and aversion therapy. These methods fall into two principal categories—clinical casework and alteration of group structures—and the basic difference between the two lies in the conception of the process by which crime and criminality originate and flourish.

The Clinical Method

In the early part of the present century, constructive attempts to change criminals were based almost exclusively on the assumption that criminality is strictly an individual disorder that can, therefore, be treated in a clinic just as syphilis can be treated in a clinic. The model was a medical one, even when the so-called "disorder" was poor work habits and the so-called "treatment" consisted of finding a proper job for the offender. It was correctly pointed out that two or three centuries ago diseases were not differentiated from each other or explained as natural phenomena; bloodletting was almost the only treatment, varying in amount with the seriousness of the ailment. Since then the germ theory of disease and experimental methods have produced a great variety of treatment methods adapted to particular diseases. By analogy, until recently in the modern world punishment was the sole "cure" for criminality, and—like bloodletting—it was varied in amount depending on the seriousness of the offense. The focus then officially shifted from offense to offender, and the amount of pain heaped on, say, one robber was greater or less than that imposed on another robber, depending on someone's assessment of the circumstances of the offense and the background of the offender. In the name of justice, punishments were no longer to be uniform, whether ordered by judges or by parole boards. One consequence was the current practice of punishing powerless people much more severely than the powerful.[21] Another consequence was logical extension of the notion of individualization into rehabilitation work, so that it came to be assumed that each criminal should be personally corrected.

Ideally, each offender was to have his or her own correctional program. There was to be an intensive study of why a burglar or thief "turned to crime," followed by a program for change. For example, if the diagnosis was that a boy burned down the schoolhouse in order to get attention, the prescription might be to give him tender loving care, and the "therapy" might consist of placing him with foster parents. Although the program prescribed and carried out for a criminal was a personal one, it might be identical to that into which other criminals were placed. As in medicine, where treatment of diseases does not imply an entirely different policy for each patient, a unique program for each offender was not implied.[22]

But in the clinical method this medical analogy was then carried to its logical extreme. Because the original arguments for individualization were based on an analogy with clinical medicine, the *methods and theory* used in diagnosing and treating cases of criminality and delinquency came to resemble those used in clinical medicine. That is, each delinquent and criminal was assumed to be suffering from a personal disorder, defect, maladjustment, disease, or sickness. Accordingly, the diagnosis became similar to diagnoses of various medical ailments of patients, and the recommendations for treatment became similar to medical prescriptions for clinical treatment. Indeed, when the process was orchestrated by psychiatrists, it was identical to that used in the treatment of noncriminal and nondelinquent sick people. Usually, however, social caseworkers dominated—because there were not enough psychiatrists to go around—but they tended to use the psychiatric framework and terminology. A diagnosis made in clinical terms will be followed, obviously, by clinical treatment of the individual.[23]

Even today this medical model has great popularity among judges, probation agents, directors of institutions for delinquents, prison social workers and psychologists, parole-board members, parole officers, and other personnel involved in correctional work. Some cases of criminality are assumed to be generated by disorders that are quite independent of the criminal's social contacts, somewhat as anemia is independent of group life. More commonly, delinquents and criminals are viewed as persons who have caught an infectious disease such as syphilis. Although group contacts of certain kinds are necessary to individual

[21] See Austin T. Turk, "Conflict and Criminality," *American Sociological Review*, 31:338–52, 1966.

[22] See Marguerite Q. Grant, "Interaction Between Kinds of Treatments and Kinds of Delinquents" (California Board of Corrections, Monograph No. 2, July, 1961), pp. 5–14; and Keiichi Mizushima and Richard L. Jenkins, "Treatment Needs Corresponding to Varieties of Delinquents," *International Journal of Social Psychiatry*, 8:91–103, 1962.

[23] See Michael Hakeem, "A Critique of the Psychiatric Approach to Crime and Correction," *Law and Contemporary Problems*, 23:550–82, 1958.

cases of syphilis and to most individual cases of criminality, the idea goes, both ailments can be "cured" in a clinic. Thus a delinquent's relations with his or her parents might be diagnosed as the cause of a specific psychological problem that, in turn, caused the delinquency. But the clinician is not immediately concerned with the relevant parent-child relations. As in medicine, such problems are to be attacked by public-health officials, not by the doctors who are treating and curing patients within the walls of clinics.

The following description of the method once used in the New Jersey Home for Boys illustrates the clinical procedure. The obvious assumption behind the program is that the offender's delinquency can be cleared up by taking steps, within institutional walls, to cure what ails him. Although the statement was made over a half-century ago, it indicates the method officials of correctional institutions said they were using as recently as the 1970s, when the idea that prisons correct, rehabilitate, or cure criminals went out of style.[24] Directors of both private and public "community treatment programs" continue to use the same method, and with the same vagueness as to the specifics.

First: We make a definite study of each boy when he enters the institution. This study extends over a period of several weeks and is conducted by trained people (psychiatrist, psychologist, director of education, etc.). . . . During the period of these examinations we secure from the Central Parole Bureau, probation officers, and other sources, all the information possible about the ward's earlier history, his home and community relations, and other vital facts.

Second: Once a week all of the people concerned with the examinations named in the last paragraph meet with the Superintendent for the purpose of comparing reports and consulting as to the best means of promoting the welfare of the ward while in the institution—this is called our Classification Meeting.

Third: We make a definite plan for the development and training of the boy. This plan, or parts of it, at least, are discussed with the boy. We try to secure his cooperation with us for his own development, with a definite purpose in his mind and ours of preparing him for a successful parole. Every boy's case is reconsidered by the Classification Committee within three months, and if the case presents unusual factors, it may be reconsidered several times.

Fourth: As time for his parole approaches, each boy's case is taken up for preparole investigation. . . . Home investigations are made, employment and friendly counselors are secured, and the family prepared for the return of the boy. Sometimes the Central Parole Bureau has to prepare the neighborhood or move the family to a new locality, in order to further the interests of the boy.[25]

The Group-Relations Method

The methods of implementing the punitive reaction were and are applied to offenders without regard for their relationships in social groups. A basic assumption underlying criminal laws is that every person possesses the ability to refrain

[24]See the discussion in Chapter 22, below.
[25]State of New Jersey, *Report of State Home for Boys*, 1921, pp. 19–20.

from delinquency and crime, regardless of the values and influences of the person's membership groups and reference groups. It is only a matter of making up your mind not to do evil, and the law specifies some of the bad things that will happen to you, ideally, if you do not make this free choice. Similarly, clinical treatment methods were and are applied to the offender in isolation. Gradually these methods for punishing individual offenders and, alternatively, for curing individual offenders were supplemented by methods based on a very different principle, namely that criminality is a group product and therefore can be modified in individual cases only if the criminal's relations with social groups are modified.

The proponents of the group-relations principle have not extended the medical analogy to include the methods and theory used in diagnosing, prescribing, and treating. Rather, they contend, as is made explicit in the differential-association theory, that persons become criminals principally because they have been relatively isolated from the culture of the groups that make, enforce, and obey laws because it is in their self-interest to do so, or else have been in frequent and intimate association with rival criminalistic behavior patterns. The isolation is on a class basis, and is manifest in segregated residential areas, schools, churches, jobs, and political participation.

If crime and criminality are products of isolation from law-abiding behavior patterns and association with behavior patterns favorable to crime, it cannot be expected that they will be overcome by more isolation. On the contrary, assimilation is essential, and a melding can come only if there is contact. As early as 1868 Desprez stated the argument against isolation from the standpoint of an elitist, and with special reference to isolation of prisoners from each other and from the public:

> All isolation, even if voluntary, is bad. There is no idea more fallacious than that isolation from the world by prolonged imprisonment will produce moral meditations in the culprit which will be the source of his reformation. It is not sufficient to place a person between four walls in order to improve him. . . . How is it possible to hope or believe for a single moment that gross natures, uncultured and degraded, can find in themselves the force to condemn and sincerely detest their faults, and maintain a firm resolution during the years of detention, in the midst of all the elements of corruption, if the imprisonment is in common, or in apathy and despair, if the imprisonment is in cells?[26]

The group-relations method focuses on reducing isolation. Diagnosis is directed at analysis of the criminal's attitudes, motives, and rationalizations regarding criminality, with recognition that the character of these behaviors depends on the kinds of groups in which individuals have memberships, with which they identify themselves, and to which they owe allegiance and loyalty. If the criminality of an individual depends on such group relations, then the

---

[26] E. Desprez, *De l'abolition de l'emprisonment* (Paris: E. Dentu, 1868), pp. 18–19.

prescription for "treatment" must be a prescription for modification of group relations.[27] As to the "treatment" itself, it is suggested that the group relations that support criminality cannot be directly modified in a clinic in the way that the condition of a person suffering from syphilis can be modified in a clinic; they can be modified only by providing the criminal with new social relations or in some way changing the nature of present group relations A procedure for such modification is outlined in Chapter 26.

Numerous policies and programs arising in correctional work during the last hundred years have been explicitly or implicitly based on recognition of the necessity for modifying criminality by changing the social relationships of delinquents and criminals. Among these are probation, which is supposed to help offenders come in contact with law-abiding groups instead of isolating them behind prison walls; education, self-government, and group therapy in prison, which are supposed to develop social interaction even while the prisoners are physically isolated; parole, which is supposed to act in the same way as probation; and various other efforts to assist the offender after release from prison to gain or regain contacts with law-abiding groups.[28]

This method of implementing the treatment reaction by providing contact with the law-abiding culture is important, but it has two shortcomings. First, the presence of a cultural pattern does not necessarily result in its adoption. Acculturation comes only as the result of contact, but contact does not necessarily result in acculturation. All persons are in contact with law-abiding culture, and all persons are in contact with criminal culture. Something more than contact is needed.[29] Second, offenders usually find it almost impossible to secure intimate associations with law-abiding groups even if they are receptive to the notion that conformity to criminal laws is desirable. Neighbors openly display prejudice against ex-convicts. Law-enforcement officers, fearful that offenders will repeat their crimes or contaminate others, hound them until they become convinced that the values embodied in the criminal law support injustice rather than justice. Third, the notion that criminals can and should be changed by modifying their group relations does not directly address the problem of altering the conditions that created the criminality in the first place.[30]

In view of these shortcomings, the group-relations principle has been used to approach crime itself, not just criminality. Calls for institutional reorganization such that the United States, or the world, would be either a "brotherhood of mankind" or a "classless society" (which seem to mean about the same thing) are,

[27] Cf. Dorwin Cartwright, "Achieving Change in People: Some Applications of Group Dynamics Theory," *Human Relations*, 4:381–92, 1951.

[28] Cressey, "Nature and Effectiveness of Correctional Techniques."

[29] See Elihu Katz, Martin L. Levin, and Herbert Hamilton, "Traditions in Research on the Diffusion of Innovation," *American Sociological Review*, 28:237–52, 1963.

[30] See Richard A. Cloward and Frances Fox Piven, "The Acquiescence of Social Work," *Transaction: Social Science and Modern Society*, 14:55–63, 1977.

among other things, calls for eliminating or at least reducing the cultural, economic, and political differences that make crime a social problem. This reaction to crime is one of intervention by modifying group relations, but the focus is on the social order rather than on individual criminals. The reaction will be explored in Chapter 26.

STATUTORY BASIS OF THE CONFLICT

Contemporary criminal law is ambivalent about what should be done to, with, and for criminals. Our forefathers were convinced, and most lawmakers and enforcers are still convinced, that conduct described by criminal statutes can be minimized by swift, certain, and uniform punishment of those who deviate. Everything is to be reasonable. Each criminal law stipulates that a certain type of conduct is punishable, thus serving to warn citizens that such conduct will be punished. If criminal-justice administrators calmly, rationally, swiftly, and certainly impose punishments on those who do not heed the warnings, the deterrence argument goes, the undesirability and impropriety of the outlawed behavior is emphasized.

This idea, which is one of the pillars of modern systems of justice, assumes that appropriate punishments can be stipulated in advance of any display of the outlawed conduct. It views the criminal-justice system as a well-programmed computer that scans its memory bank for the punishment set down as correct for the conduct displayed by an offender, and then imposes the described punishment. The idea also incorporates the assumption that the computer programmers—the legislators—will rapidly change both the kinds of behavior outlawed and the prescribed punishments whenever the law on the books is inconsistent with the law on the street. In other words, the assumption is that the persons being governed always want the law to be that which is contained in the statutes. This is rarely the case.

Criminal statutes necessarily speak in generalities.[31] A machinelike set of precise stipulations covering all varieties of crime and punishment cannot be set down, even by omnipotent legislatures. Punishments that seem appropriate in one time or place are too severe, or not severe enough, in another time or place. Whether the punishment stipulated for robbery is appropriate or not depends on the circumstances of the offense and the characteristics of the offender. No legislature, far removed from the conduct it defines as criminal, can incorporate enough justice-producing nuances and behavioral clues in its statutory statements. No two robberies are the same. A brutal armed holdup and a scuffle in which one boy in a schoolyard takes a basketball from another are both defined as robberies by statutes prescribing punishment for the offense. Yet these two

---

[31] The following material is adpated from Arthur Rosett and Donald R. Cressey, *Justice by Consent: Plea Bargains in the American Courthouse* (Philadelphia: Lippincott, 1976), pp. 37–9.

robberies bear little resemblance to each other when criminal intent, degree of guilt, and personal character are taken into account.

Accordingly, modern criminal codes represent a rather crude attempt to satisfy both the sense of justice which demands that similar people (robbers) be treated alike, and the sense of justice which demands that each person be treated according to his or her deserts. They call for uniformity but make room for diversity in three principal ways. First, they stress equality by outlawing all robbery and other crimes, but they also stress individual differences by subdividing and grading offenses in terms of a range of culpability. For example, the punishment for robbery with a gun is more severe than that for unarmed robbery, and the punishment for burglary of someone's home is more severe than burglary of a warehouse. Second, criminal codes universally ask for punishment of the guilty, but they also set a range of minimum and maximum punishments for particular offenses, rather than setting a fixed penalty for all. One kind of robbery may be punishable by a prison term ranging from five years to life, another by one to ten years, another by one to three years. Third, criminal codes make all criminal acts punishable by law, but they also authorize judges to suspend punishment and place the criminal on probation, as well as authorizing members of the executive branch to mitigate the severity of a prison sentence by softening the pangs of imprisonment and by releasing prisoners on parole.

It must be concluded that an "adjustment principle" lies at the base of contemporary legislation about criminal matters, just as does the "law-enforcement" or "deterrence" principle. Our forefathers were convinced of the efficiency of swift, certain, severe, and uniform punishment, but they also were convinced that law violations and law violators must be handled individually, so far as punishment is concerned. The stipulations of criminal statutes give advance notice that convicted wrongdoers will be punished in prescribed ways, but laws providing for suspended sentences, indeterminate sentences, probation, and parole—among others—stipulate that the penalties may be officially mitigated.[32]

Moreover, the content of criminal statutes is very uncertain. Everyone agrees that the state should outlaw the unlawful killing of human beings, but is a fetus a human being? Everyone agrees that the state should outlaw stealing, but what is stealing? The concept has changed over the years as ideas about property and its values have changed, and it continues to change. If a student takes a library book and puts it on his or her own shelf, it is stealing, but is it stealing if the person takes the book without properly checking it out, reads it, and returns it? Is it stealing if the student takes the book, photocopies it, and returns it? If a factory worker takes tools home from the plant, it is stealing, but is it stealing if the employee loafs on the job? If a legislator or a city-council member sells favors, it is stealing, but is it stealing if the official profits politically by flouting the will of the people?

Such questions must be decided by someone. Justice is the process by which such decisions are made. A system of criminal justice that did not take into

[32]See J. Thibault and L. Walker, *Procedural Justice: A Psychological Analysis* (New York: Halsted Press, 1975).

account people's individuality would be so unmerciful and wasteful of human lives that few thinking citizens would support it. Similarly, criminal-justice workers want the power to control, or at least to bend, the process of catching and disposing of offenders. They want this power because, put simply, it allows them to do justice. Morris Cohen, the distinguished legal philosopher, long ago pointed out that the idea of individualization and adjustment of penalties is but a reassertion of the old idea of equity as a corrective of undue rigor of law, "a corrective to the injustice which results from the fact that the abstract rule cannot take into account all the specific circumstances that are relevant to the case."[33]

In recent times, then, criminal laws have asked state officials to treat criminals, in addition to punishing them justly. To the degree that treatment is an alternative to punishment, not a supplement to it and not merely punishment in disguise, its introduction into the legal process was, like the introduction of the adjustment principle, an attempt to soften the harsh penalties prescribed by statute. Probation, prison, and parole workers, especially, are expected to modify the statutory punishments so that offenders will be corrected, rehabilitated, or cured, and the amount of conformity thereby increased.

OBSTACLES TO INNOVATION

Because of these conflicts in criminal law itself, it is not surprising to find that criminal-justice work has been, almost from the beginning, characterized by ambivalent values, conflicting goals and norms, and contradictory ideologies.[34] Such conflict is not necessarily an impediment to innovation. On the contrary, it provides unusual opportunities for innovation. For example, an analysis of the Soviet industrial system concluded that conflicting standards and selective enforcement of an organization's rules permits supervisors to transmit changes in their objectives to subordinates without disrupting the operation of the system; permits subordinates to take initiative, be critical, make innovations, and suggest improvements; and permits workers who are closest to the problem field (usually subordinates) to adapt their decisions to the ever-changing details of circumstances. The following comment about the last point is especially relevant to criminal-law administration:

The very conflict among standards, which prevents the subordinate from meeting all standards at once, gives him a high degree of discretion in applying received standards to the situation with which he is faced. Maintenance of conflicting standards, in short, is a way of decentralizing decision-making.[35]

---

[33] Morris R. Cohen, *Reason and Law* (Glencoe, Ill.: Free Press, 1950), p. 53.

[34] Parts of this section are adapted from Donald R. Cressey, "Sources of Resistance to the Use of Offenders and Ex-Offenders in the Correctional Process," in *Offenders as a Correctional Manpower Resource*, Keith A. Stubblefield and Larry L. Dye, eds., (Washington: Joint Commission on Correctional Manpower and Training, 1968), pp. 31–49.

[35] Andrew Gunder Frank, "Goal Ambiguity and Conflicting Standards: An Approach to the Study of Organization," *Human Organization*, 17:8–13, Winter, 1958–59.

As conceptions of "the good society" have changed, conceptions of "good penology" and, more recently, "good corrections" also have changed. This has meant, by and large, that interventionist conceptions and services have been added to the criminal-justice process. But these additions have been made without much regard for the services and roles already existing. The modification seems different from that accompanying similar growth of manufacturing and sales corporations, for the new state services have been organized around purposes that are only remotely related to the old punitive and custodial ones. This could mean, as in the case of Soviet industry, that anything goes.

But change toward intervention and away from punishment has been slow and sporadic despite conflicting principles that seem to make anything possible. Ambivalence and conflict in social values and penal theories have produced state interventionist organizations that are, at least inadvertently, designed to resist change.

In the first place, a shift toward interventionist objectives requires changes in organization, not merely in the attitudes or work habits of employees. In police departments and prisons, for example, there is a line organization of ranks, and salary differentials and descriptive titles (usually of a military nature) indicate that a chain of command exists within this hierarchy. Any police or prison innovation whose goals cannot be achieved by means of this organization must surmount the difficult task of modifying or somehow evading the hierarchy of punitive-custodial personnel.

Second, most innovations in criminal-justice work can be introduced and implemented only if the participation, or at least the cooperation, of all employees is secured. In factories, there are separate but integrated hierarchies of management personnel and of workers, and many kinds of orders for innovation can flow freely downward from management offices to factory floors. For example, if the manager of an aircraft factory decides to innovate by manufacturing boats instead of airplanes, a turret-lathe operator can readily accept the order to change the setup of the machine in such a way that part of a boat is manufactured. But in probation, parole, and prison work, at least, management is an end, not a means. Accordingly, management hierarchies extend down to the lowest level of employee. Thus criminal-justice personnel are both managers and workers. They are managed in a system of controls and regulations from above, but also they manage the suspects, inmates, probationers, or parolees in their charge. Criminal-justice personnel are low-status workers in interaction with chiefs, wardens, and directors, but they are managers in relationships with criminals. Because they are managers, they cannot be ordered to accept a proposed innovation, as a turret-lathe operator can be ordered. They can only be persuaded to do so, and gaining such consensus is extraordinarily difficult.

Third, even though all criminal-justice employees are managers as well as workers, they do not own the agencies and institutions they manage. Each agency has a number of absentee owners, and these owners have varying conceptions about policy, program, and management procedures. If they were questioned, it is probable that each would have a distinct opinion about what should be done to, with, and for criminals. Because of differences in theoretical conceptions in the broader society and in the criminal law, the contemporary environment of criminal-justice agencies contains overlapping groups with interests in seeing that physical punishments are imposed, groups with interests in reducing physical punishments, and groups with varying ideas for implementing the interventionist notion that criminals can be reformed only if they are provided with positive, nonpunitive services. The interests of such groups converge in any particular criminal-justice agency, and the means used by administrators for handling their contradictory directives gives these agencies their organizational character.[36]

One type of interest group emerges when an existing group sees present or possible activities of a criminal-justice program as a means for achieving its own objectives. In prisons, for example, inmate leaders sometimes operate as an interest group and press for control over routine decisions because such control gives them additional power to exact recognition and conformity from other inmates. Similarly, prison guards become an interest group when they perceive that prison discipline for inmates is becoming so relaxed that the guards might be in danger. Political leaders become an interest group when they see a parole agency as a resource for discharging political obligations, and they demand that the agency be so organized that the skills of political appointees, not experts, can be used. Church groups and other groups sometimes band together to support or oppose a police or prosecutorial program on moral grounds. Because there is a strong belief in our society that criminality, like laziness and lack of "self-discipline," is sinful, such groups tend to support punishment, custody, and routinization rather than positive programs for intervening in the process that produces crime and criminals.

Another type of interest group is directly concerned with preventing innovations that threaten the group's existing activities or plans. With reference to courts, probation, prisons, and parole, some police departments constitute an interest group of this kind. They, even more than correctional workers, are charged with keeping the crime rate low by apprehending offenders and presenting them for punishment, and they tend to oppose any change that might reduce the degree of punishment, custody, and surveillance. Similarly, social-welfare groups and educational groups oppose any correctional changes that threaten to upset clinical treatment and vocational training; industrial groups oppose any organization of employment or employment services that will compete with them; and labor groups oppose any innovation that might reduce the number of jobs for noncriminals.

[36] See Philip Selznick, *Leadership and Administration* (Evanston, Ill.: Row, Peterson, 1957); and Mayer N. Zald, "The Correctional Institution for Juvenile Offenders: An Analysis of Organizational 'Character,' " *Social Problems*, 8:57–67, 1960.

In this situation, effective positive action on the part of a criminal-justice administrator depends on realistic assessment of the power possessed by interest groups. When an administrator makes a commitment to any given group or coalition of groups, the person's freedom of action is henceforth limited. If, at the same time, the administrator decides not to be committed to other groups or coalitions, then freedom to introduce innovations is limited even more. Administrators are able to make innovative moves only because the mandates given by powerful punitive and custodial interest groups ordinarily are stated in broad terms and consequently have broad tolerance limits. For example, the directives asking a judge or prison warden to be punitive usually ask for increased punishment, but ordinarily do not specify the means to be used for achieving it. Accordingly, in minor ways, the administrator can accommodate interventionist interest groups that have little power.

If the administrator is skillful, and if the organization is big enough, the manager can segregate audiences by giving one part of the organization to one interest group while giving another part to a group with conflicting interests. For example, a director of institutions might maneuver an interest group of social workers so that it concentrates its concern on the boys' school or on correctional work with children generally, while an interest group of law-enforcement personnel might have its interests reflected in a particular prison. Even an entire criminal-justice agency, such as a probation department, may be given to interests supporting an interventionist policy, while another unit is given to interests supporting a punitive and surveillance policy. But the specialization of correctional units should not be overemphasized. Every unit reflects powerful punitive interests, making change difficult.

Fourth, the ambivalence and conflict in penal theory, together with a complex structure of criminal-justice organizations, seems to have produced an attitude of "standing by" among criminal-justice workers. As we have seen, the ambivalence in theory has permitted various interest groups collectively to establish organizational structures that are extraordinarily difficult to change. But criminal-justice personnel themselves do not seem to have tried very hard. There certainly is variation from state to state and from agency to agency, but among criminal-justice workers in general there has been very little concern for the design of innovations that would put real rehabilitative processes into prisons and probation-parole agencies, or real crime-prevention processes in crime-prevention agencies. As indicated, the mandates given correctional administrators by interest groups tend to be stated in broad terms. Consequently, the mere creation of so-called treatment programs within institutions and agencies, and so-called prevention programs in communities, has pacified some of the groups that supported the interventionist reaction. By and large, however, groups pressuring for positive programs for dealing with crime and criminals left invention of the processes for administering them to correctional workers themselves, and correctional workers have not been innovative.

Criminal-justice workers should not be attacked or blamed, however, for what appears to be a lack of serious interest in developing or even utilizing basic interventionist principles concerning the processes by which societies can lower their crime rates. Obstacles to progress in preventing crime and changing criminals seem to be rooted in the very nature of criminal-justice occupations and organizations.[37] At least an attitude of "standing by" seems to be rooted in criminal-justice work in a way that experimental and innovative attitudes about intervention are not.[38]

SUGGESTED READINGS

Allen, Francis A. "Criminal Justice, Legal Values and the Rehabilitative Ideal." *Journal of Criminal Law, Criminology, and Police Science,* 50:226–32, 1959.

American Friends Service Committee. *Struggle for Justice.* New York: Hill and Wang, 1971.

Bailey, Robert, Jr. *Radicals in Urban Politics: The Alinsky Approach.* Chicago: University of Chicago Press, 1974.

Boshier, Roger, & Camille Ray. "Punishing Criminals: A Study of the Relationship Between Conservatism and Punitiveness." *Australian and New Zealand Journal of Criminology,* 8:37–45, 1975.

Cantor, Nathaniel. "Conflicts in Penal Theory and Practice." *Journal of Criminal Law and Criminology,* 26:330–50, 1935.

Cartwright, Dorwin. "Achieving Change in People: Some Applications of Group Dynamics Theory." *Human Relations,* 4:381–92, 1951.

Cressey, Donald R. "Changing Criminals: The Application of the Theory of Differential Association." *American Journal of Sociology,* 61:116–20, 1955.

Cressey, Donald R. "The Nature and Effectiveness of Correctional Techniques." *Law and Contemporary Problems,* 23:754–71, 1958.

Empey, La Mar T. *Alternatives to Incarceration.* Washington: Government Printing Office, 1967.

Eriksson, Torsten. *The Reformers: An Historical Survey of Pioneer Experiments in the Treatment of Criminals.* New York: Elsevier, 1976.

Fogel, David. *We Are the Living Proof: The Justice Model for Corrections.* Cincinnati: Anderson, 1975.

Harlow, Eleanor, & J. Robert Weber. *Diversion from the Criminal Justice System.* Washington: Government Printing Office, 1971.

Lipton, Dorothy, Robert Martinson, & Judith Wilks. *The Effectiveness of Correctional Treatment: A Survey of Treatment Evaluation Studies.* New York: Praeger, 1975.

Meier, Robert F., & Weldon T. Johnson. "Deterrence as a Social Control: The Legal and Extralegal Production of Conformity." *American Sociological Review,* 42:292–304, 1977.

---

[37] See Donald R. Cressey, "Professional Correctional Work and Professional Work in Correction," *National Probation and Parole Association Journal,* 5:1–15, 1959; and idem, "Nature and Effectiveness of Correctional Techniques."

[38] See Stanley Cohen and Laurie Taylor, *Psychological Survival: The Experience of Long-Term Imprisonment* (New York: Pantheon Books, 1972), pp. 201–07; George I. Diffenbaucher, "Settling for 'Humanization': Evidence of Despair or of Facing 'Reality'?" *Federal Probation,* 40:25–8, 1976; Thomas Murton, *The Dilemma of Prison Reform* (New York: Holt, Rinehart and Winston, 1976); and John P. Conrad, "We Should Never Have Promised a Hospital," *Federal Probation,* 30:3–9, 1975.

Meyer, Joel. "Reflections on Some Theories of Punishment." *Journal of Criminal Law, Criminology, and Police Science,* 59:595–99, 1968.

Miller, David, "The Ideological Backgrounds to Conceptions of Social Justice," *Political Studies,* 22:387–99, 1974.

Orland, Leonard. *Justice, Punishment, Treatment.* New York: Free Press, 1976.

Quinney, Richard. *Class, State and Crime: On the Theory and Practice of Criminal Justice.* New York: David McKay, 1977.

Rose, Gordon. *The Struggle for Penal Reform.* London: Stevens and Sons, 1961.

Rosett, Arthur, & Donald R. Cressey. *Justice by Consent: Plea Bargains in the American Courthouse.* Philadelphia: Lippincott, 1976.

Saleilles, R. *The Individualization of Punishment.* Trans. by R. S. Jastrow. Boston: Little, Brown, 1911.

Schwitzgebel, Ralph K. *Development and Legal Regulation of Coercive Behavior Modification Techniques with Offenders.* Washington: Government Printing Office, 1971.

Sellin, Thorsten. "Correction in Historical Perspective." *Law and Contemporary Problems,* 23:585–93, 1958.

Stubblefield, Keith A., & Larry L. Dye, eds. *Offenders as a Correctional Manpower Resource.* Washington: Joint Commission on Correctional Manpower Training, 1968.

Von Hirsh, Andrew. "Prediction of Criminal Conduct and Preventive Confinement of Convicted Persons." *Buffalo Law Review,* 21:717–58, 1972.

Wheeler, Harvey, ed. *Beyond the Punitive Society.* San Francisco: W. H. Freeman, 1973.

Wilkins, Leslie T. "Current Aspects of Penology: Directions for Corrections." *Proceedings of the American Philosophical Society,* 118:235–52, 1974.

Wilson, James Q. *Thinking About Crime.* New York: Basic Books, 1975.

16

Policing

After criminals have been detected, they become, successively, the concern of many agencies that are organized for the direction and implementation of societal reactions to crime. Hypothetically, a criminal could come into contact with at least one police department, jail, courthouse, probation department, prison, and parole department. However, only serious offenders and repeaters are likely to encounter all the agencies in the series. Many guilty persons are discharged by the police or courts; others are sentenced to jail terms or placed on probation and, consequently, do not come into contact with the prison system; others are sent to prison directly and have no contact with probation or parole agencies.

But in almost all instances, contact with a police department precedes contact with any subsequent agency or agencies. For this reason, and because contact with police officers is often terminal, the officers are in a strategic position with reference to the subsequent behavior of apprehended offenders. In some instances, the fact that a person's delinquent or criminal behavior is forgiven by a police officer leads to further offenses, but in other instances this action leads to lawfulness. Sometimes the process of *labeling* a person delinquent or criminal in the course of arrest, detention, and interrogation by police officers causes the person to identify with delinquents or criminals and therefore to get into further trouble. But sometimes police methods, including labeling persons as delinquents or criminals, cause suspects to disavow their proclaimed deviance and to stay out of further trouble.[1]

Police officers are also in a strategic position regarding the presentation of criminal and anticriminal behavior patterns in society. Among both criminals

[1] See Ross Hampton, "Labeling Theory and the Police Decision to Prosecute Juveniles," *Australian and New Zealand Journal of Sociology*, 11:64–6, 1975.

and noncriminals, police officers frequently are personified as "the law," and respect for law depends on the behavior of police officers more than on any other agents of the state. Most noncriminals have at least casual contact with the police, and anticriminal behavior among such persons, as among apprehended offenders, is not effectively reinforced if police officers are held in low esteem because of their prior conduct.

During the course of the last century, police departments have also become increasingly important in the total official process of crime control. Punishments have become milder and milder. Imprisonment was substituted for the stock, the whip, and the gallows, and then the conditions of prison life were gradually improved. As Bittner and Platt have observed, "Reform followed reform, and every generation of penologists found the devices of their predecessors barbaric." This development has been matched, step by step, by the growth and increasing influence of organized police departments:

The very same forces that advocated the reduction of severity of punishment also advocated the establishment of a stable police force, while their opponents were as much opposed to mild treatment of offenders as they were opposed to the police.[2]

Currently, the wide distribution of police control, together with mild forms of punishment, probably has given us an internal pacification of society hitherto unknown in the civilized world. In other words, despite high crime rates—which are manufactured in part by police departments—and despite widespread fear of crime, it appears that police officers are managing to protect us from street crime more effectively and efficiently than severe punishments ever did.

There are in the advanced nations no longer any hobo jungles, or city slums, or districts of any sort that lie outside the purview of control of the administration of justice. Life and property of everybody, but especially the life and property of the middle and lower classes, are today safer than they were at any time in the past. Indeed, it is fair to say that modern law enforcement has achieved virtually complete control over crime and thus reduced it to a minor social problem.[3]

COMPOSITION OF THE POLICE

The term *police* refers primarily to agents of the state whose official function is maintenance of law and order and enforcement of the regular criminal code. Each governmental unit, under the American Constitution, may have its own police force. The city has a police department, the small town has a marshal, and the township has a constable. The county may have an organized, uniformed, police force in the form of a sheriff and deputies. Each separate state may have its highway patrol or other police force. The police work of the federal government is concentrated in the Federal Bureau of Investigation of the Department of Justice,

---

[2]Egon Bittner and Anthony M. Platt, "The Meaning of Punishment," *Issues in Criminology,* 2:79–99, 1966.
[3]Ibid., pp. 95–6.

but most federal departments have agents for enforcement of particular laws, including those regulating the currency, narcotic drugs, alcohol, firearms, tobacco, internal revenue, customs, and immigration. States and cities also employ such special-purpose police forces, illustrated by the campus police of some state universities and by the New York City Transit Police. State militias and the air force, army, and navy police their own ranks and may perform general police functions in emergencies.

In the United States there are about 40,000 local law-enforcement agencies, employing in 1975 at least 350,000 police officers, sheriffs, constables, and marshals, and at least another 110,000 support personnel. The vast majority of these agencies—about 30,000—have no more than five employees. In 1975 there were 2.5 local police personnel, excluding support personnel, for each 1,000 inhabitants of the 7,477 cities reporting crime statistics to the FBI. In addition, state governments employ at least 39,000 uniformed police, some of whom are limited to traffic regulation. The federal government employs at least 36,000 law-enforcement personnel, not counting military policemen, but only an unknown fraction of these have full police powers. Another 130,000 persons are employed as guards by local, state, or federal governments, or as support personnel for those guards.

In addition, two other types of agents engage in police work. The first of these is private police. These security personnel are privately selected, financed, and controlled, although they are sometimes licensed or commissioned as public agents. Industrial plants, business firms, schools and universities, and even individuals have organized their own private police forces because they feel they are not adequately protected by the public police. In the United States in 1969, about 290,000 persons (excluding part-time workers) were employed as private detectives, investigators, and guards, as compared to about 400,000 sworn public police officers and about 120,000 personnel employed as government guards. About 40,000 firms such as Pinkerton's, Burns, Brink's, and Wackenhut provide contract guard and investigative services.

Only a small percentage of private police officers have ever applied for a public police job; 40 percent of the 275 private officers studied in one survey said they were working at their job because they had been unemployed and it was the best job they could find.[4] The training a private guard receives before beginning work typically takes no more than eight to twelve hours, and many guards, some of whom are armed, receive less than two hours of training.[5] The survey of 275 private officers found that two-thirds had received *no* training and another 20 percent were simply put to work on their own on the first day; half of those in the survey were armed, but less than one-fifth reported any firearms training.

[4]James S. Kakalik and Sorrel Wildhorn, *Private Police in the United States: Findings and Recommendations* (Santa Monica, Calif.: Rand Corporation, 1971), p. 31.
[5]Ibid., p. 34.

Private police are expected to be concerned with private interests, and their major functions are said to be prevention and detection of crime on private property and the gathering of information for private purposes. Public police, on the other hand, are said to be primarily concerned with public interests such as keeping the peace and protecting consumers. But private police also serve what may be called public interests, and public police, when acting as watchmen and patrolmen, and even when making arrests for thefts and burglaries, serve private interests.[6] For this reason, perhaps, cooperative arrangements between private and public police are common. Public police may provide private police with arrest records and FBI records even when access to such records is prohibited by law, operate nightly call-in services for security agencies and dispatch patrol cars to check on those guards who fail to call in periodically, complete investigations begun by private police, provide private police with radios preset to the police frequency, and permit, require, or even pay for the installation of direct-dial alarms and central alarms that notify the police department of burglaries, robberies, or prowlers. Reciprocally, private police act as extended eyes and ears for public police, assist in serving warrants and citations on private property or in traffic control around private property, report suspicious persons and circumstances to public police, make preliminary investigations of crime, make arrests or assist in making arrests, and apprise public police of impending strikes and riots.[7] Further, private police keep the official crime rate down by devising their own criminal-justice procedures, most of which involve handling employee thefts, shoplifting, and other crimes as private matters.

The second type of special police consists of inspectors and examiners who are appointed by public authorities: game wardens, bank examiners, factory and dairy inspectors, and inspectors of weights and measures. The staffs of the Securities and Exchange Commission, the Federal Trade Commission, and analogous state and federal commissions perform police functions in relation to white-collar crimes. By and large, examiners and inspectors officially function to protect consumers from being cheated by businessmen. Because they perform such protective services, they are regarded with antagonism by many businessmen. At the same time, their work for the consumer is relatively unknown to consumers themselves. If members of the regular police departments enforced laws calling for special inspections and examinations, and publicized this activity as protection of the poor and uninformed, perhaps the ghetto image of the police officer as an adversary would change to an image of the officer as an ally. Should this occur, however, the officer's status might decline in the eyes of the businessmen whose taxes contribute heavily to police salaries.

In summary, police business is big business. It is estimated that in 1977 at least a million people in the United States were employed in security-related occupa-

---

[6] See Theodore M. Becker, "The Place of Private Police in Society: An Area of Research for the Social Sciences," *Social Problems*, 21:438–55, 1974.

[7] Kakalik and Wildhorn, *Private Police in the United States*, p. 20.

tions. This estimate is very rough and also very conservative in the sense that it does not include part-time workers, military police officers, many if not most federal, state, county, and city inspectors and examiners, nor all the factory workers, clerical workers, sales personnel, and administrative personnel engaged in the manufacture and distribution of security equipment such as electronic detection devices, burglar alarms, police cars, guns, and uniforms. Of the million persons estimated to be engaged in police work in 1977, about 465,000 were employed by local police agencies, 55,000 by state police agencies, and 40,000 by federal police agencies. About 130,000 were government-employed guards, and 310,000 were employed by private organizations or persons.[8]

Between 1960 and 1969, the last year for which estimates on private police forces are available, the number of identifiable public law-enforcement personnel employed at all levels of government increased 42 percent while the population grew 12 percent. During the same period, publicly employed guards increased 40 percent, and private guards, watchmen, and investigators increased about 7 percent. Public law-enforcement expenditures increased about 90 percent, rising to over $8 billion. In the same period, private-sector expenditures (including those for equipment) increased at least 150 percent.[9] There is no reason to believe that this trend has not continued since 1969, nor to doubt that now the people of the United States are spending about 1 percent of the gross national product on domestic security services.[10]

CONFLICTS BETWEEN POLICE RESPONSIBILITY AND POWER

American police officers are in a difficult position, for in order to do their work efficiently they must use more power than the law seems to give them. They are responsible for maintaining order and for catching and arresting people suspected of violating the criminal law, but they cannot meet these responsibilities under the power and authority granted them. At the same time, if they exceed their authority when dealing with certain suspects and offenders, they are subject to severe public criticism.[11] They can safely exceed their legal authority only when dealing with people who are not powerful politically and who are, therefore, relatively helpless.

Furthermore, although police officers are expected to help make crime dangerous for all, they are to use discretion and to exercise certain judicial functions as they do so. They must decide whether a certain act is in violation of the law, and also whether it probably can be proved that the law has been violated. They must rigorously enforce the law, yet they also must determine whether a

---

[8]Based on 1969 estimates presented in ibid., p. 11.

[9]Ibid., pp. 10–13.

[10]The remainder of this chapter will be concerned with the work of regular police officers, and no further attention will be given to private police or specialized public agents who perform police functions for the various divisions of federal, state, and local government.

[11]See Herbert T. Klein, *The Police: Damned If They Do, Damned If They Don't* (New York: Crown, 1963).

particular violation of law should be handled by dismissal, warning, or arrest, for police officers are not expected to arrest everyone who is known to have violated a law. The courts would find it impossible to do their work if police officers brought all suspects into court, and officers would be in court so much of the time that the police force would have to be enlarged enormously. Consequently, police officers must judge and informally settle more cases than they take into court, but the processes by which such settlements are made have not been spelled out formally.[12]

Social scientists and others have in recent years shown considerable indignation about this situation, and there have been many calls for elimination, reduction, or monitoring of police discretion.[13] One basis of these requests is the commonplace assumption that police agencies are supposed to be ministerial, acting in strict accord with legislative provisions.[14] As one police chief recently put it:

A police officer does not have the discretion to arrest or not to arrest any more than a judge has the discretion to judge or not to judge. . . . When some people advocate the philosophy that a police officer has discretion in the field to arrest an individual or to take him home, they are talking about *discriminatory law enforcement*, which is *police corruption*.[15]

Another basis of the requests for control of discretion is the commonplace conclusion, drawn from many studies, that as police officers exercise discretion they discriminate against blacks and other poor and powerless people. Discretionary decision making by police officers does not square with the notion that the punishments stipulated by legislatures are supposed to be imposed certainly and uniformly on all who violate the law. We have seen, however, that the "adjustment principle" is as much a part of the criminal law as is the "law-enforcement principle," so the controversy is necessarily about whether police officers exercise their discretion wisely and fairly, not about whether their discretion is unauthorized.[16] As one of America's leading experts on administrative law has said:

Every governmental and legal system in world history has involved both rules and discretion. No government has ever been a government of laws and not of men in the sense of eliminating all discretionary power. Every government has always been a *government of laws and men*.[17]

Police discretion invites scandal. "It invites arbitrariness, favoritism, corruption, and injustice. Even when it is exercised evenhandedly, it can create the ap-

---

[12]See Egon Bittner, "Police Discretion in Emergency Apprehension of Mentally Ill Persons," *Social Problems*, 14:278–92, 1967; idem, *The Functions of Police in Modern Society* (Washington: Government Printing Office, 1970), pp. 36–47, 95–106; and Kenneth Culp Davis, "An Approach to Legal Control of the Police," *Texas Law Review*, 52:703–25, 1974.

[13]For a bibliography, see Clarence Schrag, *Crime and Justice: American Style* (Washington: Government Printing Office, 1971).

[14]Herman Goldstein, *Policing a Free Society* (Cambridge, Mass.:Ballinger, 1977), p. 12.

[15]A. O. Archuleta, "Police Discretion v. Plea Bargaining," *Police Chief*, April, 1974, p. 78.

[16]See Chapter 15, above.

[17]Kenneth Culp Davis, *Discretionary Justice* (Baton Rouge, La.: Louisiana State University Press, 1969), p. 17.

pearance of injustice."[18] Nevertheless, police discretion will always be with us, for no legislature, far removed from the street, can precisely and unequivocally stipulate in advance just which behavior is supposed to have an arrest as its consequence. As Reiss has noted:

> It is incumbent upon a police officer to enter upon a variety of social stages, encounter the actors, determine their roles, and figure out the plot. Often, before they can act, the police must uncover the "plot" and identify the roles and behavior of the actors. This is true even in emergency situations where an officer is expected to assess the situation almost immediately and make judgments as to what he must do.[19]

Further, it is doubtful that even the current arrangement, in which police officers have almost unbridled discretion, produces more injustice and invites more arbitrariness, favoritism, and corruption than would a system in which arrests and punishments were centrally administered.[20]

The prevailing image of criminal-justice work generally and of police work particularly is an erroneous one. It pictures a "criminal-justice system" as well as a "police system" in which persons of superior rank control the practices of persons of lower ranks, somewhat as an army colonel is said to control the practices of captains, captains are said to control the practices of sergeants, and sergeants are said to control the practices of corporals. This image does not square with reality; it is not even a correct portrayal of army discipline. Rather than a "criminal-justice system" centrally controlled by legislators (colonels) in a fashion such that the low-level personnel of each agency (sergeants, corporals) are under the command of an officer (captain) who is responsible to the legislature, there is only a loose collection of agencies whose personnel often work at cross-purposes and in a spirit of competition rather than cooperation.[21] And rather than a police system operating through a hierarchy of ranks, there is a collection of patrol officers (corporals) who make discretionary decisions, ignoring or evading the sergeants, lieutenants, captains, and colonels (now with genuine military titles) who presumably control them.

In reality, then, the power in a police department is held by the personnel of lowest rank, the officers on the street. Their superiors give them orders about keeping their shoes shined and their hair trimmed, admonish them in general terms to enforce all laws, and give them general instructions on how to behave in a variety of general situations.[22] But the street-level officers must ignore or dismiss

---

[18] William F. McDonald, "Administratively Choosing the Drug Criminal: Police Discretion in the Enforcement of Drug Laws," *Journal of Drug Issues*, 3:123–134, 1973. See also James Q. Wilson, *Varieties of Police Behavior: The Management of Law and Order in Eight Communities* (New York: Atheneum, 1972), p. 181.

[19] Albert J. Reiss, Jr., *The Police and the Public* (New Haven, Conn.: Yale University Press, 1971), p. 45.

[20] See Gary T. Marx, "Thoughts on a Neglected Category of Social Movement Participant: The Agent Provocateur and the Informant," *American Journal of Sociology*, 80:402–42, 1974.

[21] See James P. Driscoll, *No One to Count Cadence: The Police Officer as Law Maker* (unpublished Ph.D. dissertation, University of California, Santa Barbara, 1977).

[22] See Nathan Joseph and Nicholas Alex, "The Uniform: A Sociological Perspective," *American Journal of Sociology*, 77:318–26, 1972.

without arrest a great deal of what others might call "crime" because to them the behavior in question—considering all the contingencies operating at the moment—is not crime "really" and "after all." In some jurisdictions, such as Washington, D. C., the "police system" image has been crystallized in laws making it a crime, punishable by imprisonment, for a police officer to ignore a crime committed in his or her presence. Considered from the standpoint of hierarchical organization, such laws make criminals of all police officers because the assumption is that persons of high rank know what crime is and that police officers—persons of lower rank—ignore it. But in practice such extensive criminalization of police officers does not occur. Unless officers on the street take bribes or otherwise display evidence of corruption, their behavior is almost always in compliance with laws and rules stipulating that they should not ignore crimes. This is true because such laws and rules are necessarily vague. Accordingly, when an officer ignores an act, then the ignored act is by definition not a crime and the officer has committed no offense.[23]

After Professor Davis had made a study of discretionary practices among Chicago police officers, he recommended (1) that police executives make rules regarding selective enforcement of statutes and (2) that these be made public. These recommendations were based in part on his assumption that "The quality of enforcement policy will be improved because it will be made by top officers instead of by patrolmen."[24] But there is no clear evidence that top-level police officers are any more knowledgeable about discretionary matters than are street-level officers. Neither is there any real evidence in support of the assumption that such administrative rules will "reduce injustice by cutting out unnecessary discretion, which is one of the prime sources of injustice."[25] It is quite possible that a "criminal-justice system" made up of a hierarchy of command running down from a legislature to judges, prosecutors, police executives, and so on, and from these officers to their subordinates, would punish many more persons than

---

[23]This point has been substantiated in a series of recent studies that elaborated on the work of Egon Bittner, "The Police on Skid Row: A Study of Peace Keeping," *American Sociological Review*, 32:699–715, 1967; Howard C. Daudistel and William B. Sanders, "Police Discretion in Application of the Law," *et al.*, 3:26–40, 1974 [reprinted in Sanders and Daudistel, *The Criminal Justice Process: A Reader* (New York; Praeger, 1976), pp. 96–107]: Sanders and Daudistel, "Detective Work: Patterns of Criminal Investigations," ch. 8 in Sanders, ed., *The Sociologist as Detective: An Introduction to Research Methods* (New York: Praeger, 1974), pp. 166–83; Sanders, *Detective Story: A Study of Criminal Investigations* (unpublished Ph.D. dissertation, University of California, Santa Barbara, 1974); Daudistel, *Deciding What the Law Means: An Examination of Police-Prosecutor Discretion* (unpublished Ph.D. dissertation, University of California, Santa Barbara, 1976); Michael J. Williams, "*Playing It by Ear: The Functions of Typified Knowledge in Police Patrol*" (unpublished Ph.D. dissertation, University of California, Santa Barbara, 1976); and W. Clinton Terry III and David F. Luckenbill, "Investigating Homicides: Police Work in Reporting and Solving Murders," in Sanders and Daudistel, *The Criminal Justice Process*, pp. 79–95.

[24]Kenneth Culp Davis, *Police Discretion* (St. Paul, Minn.: West, 1975), p. 113 For analysis of proposals and programs based on similar assumptions, see Goldstein, *Policing a Free Society*, pp. 116–117.

[25]Ibid., p. 119.

are now being punished. That would not necessarily mean, however, that injustices were being reduced. It is quite possible, too, that formulating department rules to be followed by all officers in selective enforcement practices might help patrol officers carry out what Davis calls "community desires,"[26] but this would not necessarily be a sign that injustice had diminished. For example, suppose that "community desires" were such that police officers were asked to dismiss middle-class suspects and to arrest lower-class suspects. Would departmental rules for implementing those desires reduce injustices?

There is at least a possibility, then, that current discretionary police practices are less discriminatory than would be the practices of a police system that operated the way the hierarchy-of-ranks image suggests a police department is supposed to operate. There is no doubt that contemporary practices result in a disproportionate number of arrests of the poor.[27] This injustice seems to be systemic rather than merely a consequence of bigotry on the part of individual officers.[28] The fact is that the ideal of civil order, which is supposed to be maintained or at least defended by police officers, is primarily a middle-class ideal. Its main features, Bittner and Krantz have pointed out, are "a stable income, interest in property, the structuring of all social relations with full regard to membership in nuclear families in which the breadwinner has a stable occupational career, and the allocation of an extraordinarily large share of the general wealth to freely chosen private consumption."[29] Behavior that seems consistent with this order—such as gainful employment and budgeted household spending—is right and proper. And behavior that seems incongruous with it is suspect, if not outright deviant. Thus, Bittner and Krantz continue, "Poor people who are incapable of, or uninterested in, maintaining middle-class aspirations live under the stigma of opprobrium, even though they are no longer spoken of quite as unabashedly as the 'dangerous classes' they used to be in the past."[30]

From this perspective, which is dominant in the United States, poor people do not cause trouble, they *are* trouble. Judged by middle-class ideals, their lives are full of chaos, they live in ghettos, they do not come from respectable families, and they do not seem interested in "getting ahead." Put generally, they are vulgar because they necessarily display the manners and customs of the *vulgus*—that is, "the common people," "the masses." As police officers exercise discretion, they sometimes enforce this institutionalized bias against the poor, but sometimes they

---

[26] Ibid., p. 115.

[27] See the summaries in Chapters 7 and 11, above.

[28] See, for example, Norman C. Weiner and Charles V. Willie, "Decisions by Juvenile Officers," *American Journal of Sociology*, 77:199–210, 1971.

[29] Egon Bittner and Sheldon Krantz, *Standards Relating to Police Handling of Juvenile Problems*, manuscript prepared for the Juvenile Justice Standards Project, Institute of Judicial Administration, New York, July, 1976, p. 11.

[30] Ibid. See also William J. Goode, "The Protection of the Inept," *American Sociological Review*, 32:5–19, 1967; and Donald J. Black, "The Social Organization of Arrest," *Stanford Law Review*, 23:1087–1111, 1971.

use their discretionary power to soften the harsh consequences to poor people of the middle-class conception of order. Should a police department become an organization that strictly enforced the law that attempts to control the *vulgus*, or strictly enforced administrative orders formulated by police commanders in response to "community desires," the probability is high that the difference between the proportion of poor people arrested and the proportion of others arrested would be much greater than it now is. What is needed is a set of laws and rules that would effectively restrain more police behavior, as the United States Constitution does, not laws and rules mandating specific police actions.[31]

The various impediments to performance of the law-enforcement duties that citizens ordinarily expect of police officers are all related, in one way or another, to this tension between the demand for uniform and certain punishments (arrests) and the demand for adjustment and the exercise of discretion. These impediments include the assignment of administrative duties to police departments, the law of arrest, antiquated legal systems, and political control of police activities.

Administrative Tasks

Many administrative tasks have been assigned to police departments, and this imposition has been made without regard to what the police function is or should be. Some of these tasks are concerned with public order, but not with crime, as in the direction of traffic (including installation and maintenance of traffic lights and signals, and designation of one-way streets and of zones); granting permits or licenses for taxicabs, taxidrivers, and taxistands, parades, and similar activities; restraining crowds at fires; and aiding in emergencies. Other administrative tasks are even less directly concerned with keeping the peace and enforcing the criminal law. They include licensing of amusement parks, dance halls, theaters, property for advertising purposes, auctioneers, places for handling explosives, and also inspecting theaters and a great variety of other places and activities. The laws that require licensing are increasing rapidly, but the budgets and staffs of police departments are not being increased proportionately, so that inefficiency is almost a necessity. Officers must select the laws they will enforce. Suggestions have been made that the regular police should confine their activities to the enforcement of laws against "serious" crimes, and that separate organizations should be developed for dealing with "morals," traffic, and licensing.[32]

The public also has failed to recognize that catching of criminals in modern times is extremely difficult and that it can be attained only by continuous, patient effort. Such effort requires a large staff and expensive equipment. The develop-

---

[31] See Isidore Silver, "Restraining the Police," *The Massachusetts Review*, 40:587–600, 1970.

[32] Raymond T. Nimmer, *Two Million Unnecessary Arrests: Removing a Social Service from the Criminal Justice System* (Chicago: American Bar Foundation, 1971); Edwin M. Schur and Hugo Adam Bedau, *Victimless Crimes: Two Sides of a Controversy* (Englewood Cliffs, N.J.: Prentice-Hall, 1974); and Alexander B. Smith and Harriet Pollack, *Some Sins Are Not Crimes: A Plea for Reform of the Criminal Law* (New York: Franklin Watts, 1975).

ment of modern means of transportation and the resulting mobility of people has immensely increased the difficulties of detecting and apprehending criminals. City residents are anonymous. Two generations ago criminals wore masks, but this practice occurs only infrequently today. The criminal is a stranger, and it is difficult to identify a stranger.

Moreover, the very number of crimes impedes the solution of any one of them, yet the police department is responsible for the solution of all. In large American cities, at least one murder occurs, on the average, almost every day. A small, specialized homicide squad therefore has little time for study of a particular murder but must rush from one case to another. In England, on the other hand, where murders are less frequent, a specialized force can concentrate on one murder until it is solved. This difference would not be as significant if it were not for the American demand that someone be arrested for each spectacular crime. Such demands are championed by, if not instigated by, the news media. During "crusades" inaugurated in response to media pressure for the solution of a spectacular crime, police rules asking for calm, deliberate, dignified, and legal police work are likely to be suspended:

> Even if the force has but one set of consistent ends specified for it by the commissioner or superintendent, and even if adherence to those ends is enforced as far as is possible, it is almost inevitable that there will come a time when the commissioner will decide that something must be done "at all costs"—that some civic goal justifies any police means. This might be the case when a commissioner is hard pressed by the newspapers to solve some particularly heinous crime (say, the rape and murder of a little girl). A "crusade" is launched. Policemen who have been trained to act in accord with one set of rules ("Use no violence." "Respect civil liberties." "Avoid becoming involved with criminal informants.") are suddenly told to act in accord with another rule—"catch the murderer"—no matter what it costs in terms of the normal rules.[33]

The Law of Arrest

Arrests can be made on warrants, or written orders of the court, by anyone authorized to serve them. Upon application, a warrant may be obtained from a judge when the judge is convinced that there is "probable cause" that a particular person is guilty of an offense. Under certain conditions, both private citizens and police officers can arrest without a warrant. Private citizens without a warrant, however, have no authority to arrest for misdemeanors, except in some states where they are allowed to arrest for a breach of peace committed in their presence. Officers can arrest for misdemeanors without a warrant if the misdemeanor is committed in their presence.

For felonies, in some states, arrest by a private person without a warrant is not lawful unless the arresting person (1) has reasonable grounds for believing the arrestee is guilty, and (2) the arrestee is guilty. In a greater number of states, a

[33]James Q. Wilson, "The Police and Their Problems: A Theory," *Public Policy*, 12:189–216, 1963.

private citizen may arrest for a felony if (1) the arresting person has reasonable grounds for believing the arrestee is guilty, and (2) a felony has been committed. In about five other states, private persons have the same powers as police officers generally have in regard to felonies: they can arrest for a felony when they have (1) reasonable grounds for believing that a felony has been committed, and (2) reasonable grounds for believing that the arrestee committed it. Under common law, neither police officers nor private citizens could arrest for a felony without a warrant unless there were *positive* knowledge that a felony had been committed and there were reasonable grounds for believing that the arrestee was the guilty person.

The law is frequently violated by police officers in making arrests. In most police departments, for instance, officers make arrests on suspicion quite in opposition to the law.[34] In those rural areas where officers are paid by fees—one fee for making an arrest, another for discharging a person from jail, and so on—the officers are induced to make unjustifiable and illegal arrests in order to get the fees. However, not all of the thousands of unlawful arrests made by urban police officers in "dragnet raids" and in the arrests of drunks, vagrants, and other minor offenders are equally sinister. These arrests are often based on the mere hope that arrests for minor offenses will lead to evidence about major offenses, or are mere public-relations measures designed to put the police department in a good light at budget-allocation time.[35] But dragnet arrests also reflect, in many cases, "a praiseworthy zeal in the pursuit of the criminal, leading the zealous officer to chafe against, to strain, and occasionally to break the shackles which the law has thrown about his operations."[36] The number of illegal arrests probably would be even greater if more suspects made it necessary for a police officer to make an actual arrest before taking them to the police station for questioning or investigation. Often the officer merely says, "You had better talk to the captain about this," or "We had better take a ride down to the station," rather than actually placing the suspected person under arrest, but in many cases the person in question believes that an arrest is being made.

Officers are severely criticized for making illegal arrests, and they are subject to damage suits by the illegally detained persons. Yet they also are severely criticized for not arresting persons who apparently have violated the law.[37] Under the law of

---

[34] See Paul Chevigny, *Police Power: Police Abuses in New York City* (New York: Vintage Books, 1969), pp. 136–60; and Ed Cray, *The Enemy in the Streets: Police Malpractice in America* (Garden City, N.Y.: Anchor Books, 1972), pp. 36–63.

[35] See Donald J. Black, "Production of Crime Rates," *American Sociological Review,* 35:733–48, 1970; H. Taylor Bruckner, *Deviance, Reality, and Change* (New York: Random House, 1971), pp. 245–9; David W. Britt and Charles R. Tittle, "Crime Rates and Police Behavior: A Test of Two Hypotheses," *Social Forces,* 54:441–51, 1975; and Lois B. DeFleur, "Biasing Influences on Drug Arrest Records: Implications for Deviance Research," *American Sociological Review,* 40:88–103, 1975.

[36] Lewis Mayers, *The American Legal System,* rev. ed. (New York: Harper and Row, 1964), p. 55.

[37] See Wilson, *Varieties of Police Behavior,* pp. 95–110.

arrest, if a man were detained by a private citizen who saw him commit a misdemeanor, and a police officer subsequently arrived on the scene and arrested the offender for the misdemeanor, the arrest probably would be illegal. But a police officer who did not make an arrest under such circumstances would be subject to severe criticism, and it is not inconceivable that the officer would be accused of being in collusion with the offender. Persons charged with concealed weapons are frequently discharged from court on the ground that the officer had no reasonable ground for making an arrest; the fact that concealed weapons were found in the search subsequent to the arrest is of no legal importance, for such evidence is held to have been illegally secured and therefore may not be introduced in the court. In some police departments, however, an officer who did not take such a suspect to court would be reprimanded. Police leaders have resisted recent U. S. Supreme Court decisions holding that evidence secured through unreasonable search and seizure, in violation of the Fourth Amendment, shall not be admitted in court against the accused.[38]

Legal Restrictions

Although police officers are expected to reduce crime rates by making crime dangerous and painful, they are expected to do so within the framework of criminal law and criminal procedure. Among persons who have studied policing, there is almost unanimous agreement that frustrated police see many criminals escape conviction because of this system. Skolnick has suggested that this frustration stems from a conflict between a set of forces stressing initiative and efficiency and another set of forces stressing the "rule of law":

> The police in democratic society are required to maintain order and to do so under the rule of law. As functionaries charged with maintaining order, they are part of the bureaucracy. The ideology of democratic bureaucracy emphasizes initiative rather than disciplined adherence to rules and regulations. By contrast, the rule of law emphasizes the rights of individual citizens and constraints upon the initiative of legal officials. The tension between the operational consequences of ideas of order, efficiency, and initiative, on the one hand, and legality, on the other, constitutes the principal problem of police as a democratic legal organization.[39]

The "tension" noted by Skolnick was discussed by Herbert Packer, a professor of criminal law, in terms of a conflict between what he called a "crime-control

[38] See O. W. Wilson, "Police Arrest Privileges in a Free Society: A Plea for Modernization," in *Police Power and Individual Freedom: The Quest for Balance*, ed. Claude R. Sowle (Chicago: Aldine, 1962), pp. 21–8; Caleb Foote, "The Fourth Amendment: Obstacle or Necessity in the Law of Arrest?" ibid., pp. 29–36; Reiss, *The Police and the Public*, pp. 125–34; and Jan Gorecki, "Miranda and Beyond—The Fifth Amendment Reconsidered," *University of Illinois Law Forum*, 1975:295–312, 1975.

[39] Jerome H. Skolnick, *Justice Without Trial*, 2nd ed. (New York: John Wiley, 1975), p. 6. See also Maureen E. Cain, *Society and the Policeman's Role* (London: Routledge and Kegan Paul, 1973), pp. 21–25; and Chevigny, *Police Power*, pp. 276–83.

model" and a "due-process model."[40] On the one hand, there are demands that police departments control crime by managing the criminal-justice process in such a way that a maximum number of criminals are punished, thus discouraging them and deterring others. But a series of U. S. Supreme Court decisions handed down in the last two decades stresses "constitutionalizing" each stage of the criminal process, thus enhancing the capacity of accused persons, rich and poor alike, to challenge the operation of the process on the ground that it invades their rights to privacy, liberty, dignity, and equality (due-process model).

For example, in the *Mallory* case, a defendant was tried for rape and sentenced to death. Under procedures consistent with the crime-control model, he had been detained from early afternoon until the next morning at police headquarters without being taken before a magistrate, although magistrates were available nearby. He was not told of his right to remain silent, to have counsel, or to be arraigned before a magistrate. By the time he was arraigned, he had made a confession, which was used as evidence to convict him. The Supreme Court reversed the conviction, holding in essence that only the courts can decide to deprive a person of liberty, and that an illegal detention for "investigation" invalidates an otherwise legal confession.[41]

In a second important case, that of *Mapp*, the defendant was convicted of possessing lewd and lascivious pictures and books. She had refused to admit police officers to her home, so they entered forcibly, without a search warrant, and seized the illegal material. In reversing the conviction, the Supreme Court held that "all evidence obtained by searches and seizures in violation of the Constitution is, by the same authority, inadmissible in a state court."[42]

The *Gideon* and *Miranda* decisions also stressed the importance of due process of law. Gideon was charged with breaking and entering a Florida poolroom. At his trial, he asked the court to appoint a lawyer for him, but the judge refused. The Supreme Court reversed his conviction, stating, "The right of one charged with crime to counsel may not be fundamental and essential to fair trial in some countries, but it is in ours."[43] In the *Miranda* case, a confession was admitted as evidence against a man charged with rape, but he had not been informed of his constitutional rights to remain silent and to have legal counsel. The Supreme Court reversed the conviction on the ground that he should have been so informed.[44]

[40] Herbert L. Packer, "Two Models of the Criminal Process," *University of Pennsylvania Law Review*, 118: 1–68, 1964. See also idem, *The Limits of the Criminal Sanction* (Stanford, Calif.: Stanford University Press, 1968).

[41] *Mallory v. United States* 354 U.S. 449 (1957). Interpretation of this and the following cases follows closely the analysis by George Edwards (Judge, U.S. Court of Appeals), *The Police on the Urban Frontier* (New York: Institute of Human Relations Press, 1968), pp. 13–17.

[42] *Mapp* v. *Ohio*, 367 U.S. 643 (1961).

[43] *Gideon* v. *Wainwright*, 372 U.S. 335 (1963).

[44] *Miranda* v. *Arizona*, 384 U.S. 436 (1966).

Packer summarized as follows the important differences between the due-process model used by the Supreme Court and the crime-control model used by police officers and court officials in the cases overruled:

> The choice, basically, is between what I have termed the Crime Control and the Due Process models. The Crime Control model sees the efficient, expeditious and reliable screening and disposition of persons suspected of crime as the central value to be served by the criminal process. The Due Process model sees that function as limited by and subordinate to the maintenance of the dignity and autonomy of the individual. The Crime Control model is administrative and managerial; the Due Process model is adversary and judicial. The Crime Control model may be analogized to an assembly line, the Due Process model to an obstacle course.[45]

Besides being necessarily restricted by laws requiring that they show concern for the rights of accused and suspected persons, police officers are unnecessarily hampered by an antiquated system of local boundaries. In the area within fifty miles of the center of Chicago, more than 400 independent police forces are operating with no central control or organization. In Cook County alone more than 12,000 police officers are employed as members of about 200 separate and uncoordinated agencies. The result is a system of duplicating and conflicting efforts that is necessarily inefficient. Police try to offset the inefficient system by violating the law. When local boundaries seriously hamper their efforts to control crime, they ignore them.

Police officers also violate the law in other ways. Because they operate part of a process designed to deter citizens by terrorizing them but are also thwarted in their attempts to do so by the law, they sometimes take it upon themselves to terrorize by extralegal methods. For instance, violence that is not legally justified is sometimes used at the time of arrest or between the arrest and the court hearing. When such violence, including protracted questioning and various psychological tortures, is used to get confessions from suspected persons, the Fifth, Sixth, and Fourteenth Amendments to the Constitution usually are violated. Those amendments safeguard the rights of suspected persons in courts and make it illegal for a state to deprive any citizen of life, liberty, or property without due process of law. The methods by which these constitutional safeguards are violated in order to obtain confessions from suspects were once referred to as the "third degree." Third-degree practices have declined dramatically in the last thirty years, and especially since 1966, when the U. S. Supreme Court handed down the *Miranda* decision—which makes it necessary for the police to warn suspects that they have a right to remain silent, that anything they say may be used against them, that they have a right to have an attorney present during any questioning, and that, if a suspect cannot afford to hire a lawyer, one will be appointed and compensated by

[45]Herbert L. Packer, "The Courts, the Police, and the Rest of Us," *Journal of Criminal Law, Criminology, and Police Science*, 57:238–43, 1966.

the state. Ordinarily, third-degree methods were and are used against rather powerless and inconspicuous persons.

Although violence designed to coerce confessions has declined, some police departments have been severely criticized in recent years for using excessive force at the times of apprehension, arrest, booking, and detention. President Johnson's Crime Commission reported on national surveys that found "brutality" and "intimidation" at these points to be common in many police departments across the country.[46] In a study made some years ago, 37 percent of the police officers questioned believed that "roughing a man up" is justified if he has shown disrespect for the police, and 19 percent believed that such violence is justified when the objective is to obtain information from the subject.[47] A more recent study of police-citizen encounters in Boston, Chicago, and Washington, D.C., suggested that what citizens object to and call "police brutality" is sometimes something less than "roughing a man up." Those complaining of brutality were really making the judgment that they had not been treated with the full rights and dignity owing citizens in a democratic society.[48]

The study found that the most common citizen complaints refer to traditional and common police practices such as the use of profane and abusive language, commands to move on or get home, stopping and questioning people on the street or searching them and their cars, threats to use force if not obeyed, prodding with a nightstick or approaching with a pistol, and the actual use of physical force or violence itself. Members of minority groups and those seen as nonconformists are the most likely targets of status degradation involving treatment as nonpersons, harassment, and unnecessary searches.

The observers who rode in police cars and monitored booking and lockup procedures in high-crime precincts of Boston, Chicago, and Washington judged the force used by police to be "improper" or "unnecessary" only if it were used in one or more of the following ways:

(1) If a police officer physically assaulted a citizen and then failed to make an arrest; proper use involves an arrest.

(2) If the citizen being arrested did not, by word or deed, resist the police officer; force should be used only if it is necessary to make the arrest.

(3) If the police officer, even though there was resistance to the arrest, could easily have restrained the citizen in other ways.

(4) If a large number of police officers were present and could have assisted in subduing the citizen in the station, in lockup, and in the interrogation rooms.

[46] President's Commission on Law Enforcement and Administration of Justice, *Task Force Report: The Police* (Washington: Government Printing Office, 1967), pp. 144–9, 178–90.

[47] William A. Westley, "Violence and the Police," *American Journal of Sociology*, 56:34–41, 1953.

[48] Albert J. Reiss, Jr., "Police Brutality—Answers to Key Questions," *Trans-Action*, July–August, 1968, pp. 10–19. See also Peter H. Rossi and Richard A. Berk, "Local Political Leadership and Popular Discontent in the Ghetto," *Annals of the American Academy of Political and Social Science*, 391:111–27, 1970; and James R. Hudson, "Police-Citizen Encounters That Lead to Citizen Complaints," *Social Problems*, 18:179–93, 1970.

(5) If an offender was handcuffed and made no attempt to flee or offer violent resistance.

(6) If the citizen resisted arrest, but the use of force continued even after the citizen was subdued.

In a seven-week period, the observers noted thirty-seven cases, involving forty-four citizens, in which force was used improperly, by these definitions. In three cases, the amount of force was so great that the citizen had to be hospitalized. Encounters with 643 white suspects and 751 black suspects were observed. Twenty-seven of the white suspects experienced undue use of force, for a rate of 41.9 per 1,000. The comparable rate for the black suspects, of whom seventeen experienced undue use of force, was 22.6 per 1,000. Thus the rate of excessive force on the white citizens alleged by police officers to be offenders was almost twice that of black suspects. Sixty-seven percent of the citizens victimized by white police officers were white, and 71 percent of the citizens victimized by black police officers were black. The study concluded, "The most likely victim of excessive force is a lower-class man of either race."

The most injurious aspect of police violence is that it tends to alienate the public; yet that same public applauds violence when it is used officially and legally, and on the more unpopular criminals. Some years ago, a bill to ban third-degree tactics was passed by the lower house of an eastern state, but it was killed when a state senator asked, "Are we to give the criminal an even break? Does the criminal give the law-abiding citizen an even break?" In the 1970s, a period characterized by great fear of crime, this sentiment was echoed by thousands of police officers, politicians, and ordinary citizens.

Politics

The most serious impediments to efficient crime control by police officers stem from improper political control of police organizations. In some cities, the police force is under the control of politicians who do not wish and will not permit the enforcement of some laws. Appointments of commissioners and superintendents and advancement of police officers from one rank to another are controlled largely by politicians. The politicians therefore control the fundamental policies and practices of the police department.[49] Formally, the police department is organized and operates for the welfare of society; informally, it is organized for the welfare of police, politicians, and other special interests. This means both that some crimes are unjustifiably overlooked and that some criminals are corruptly protected.

Under the control of corrupt politicians, police departments become systematically lawless. This does not mean that every police officer is lawless, but that, as a system, the police department operates in a lawless manner. Such lawlessness falls into two major categories: external corruption, involving relations between police and public; and internal corruption, involving the relationships among police

[49] See Virgil W. Peterson, "The Chicago Police Scandals," *Atlantic Monthly*, 206:58–64, 1960.

officers. External corruption has been found to consist of one or more of the following activities:[50]

(1) Payoffs to police by essentially noncriminal elements who fail to comply with stringent statutes or city ordinances or payoffs to those in particular need of police protection, who are willing to pass money to individual officers or groups of officers (for example, businessmen dispensing liquor, businessmen located in high-crime areas, individuals operating any type of business requiring a license, automobile-towing operations, attorneys who represent those guilty of minor violations of law where police testimony constitutes most of the state's case, and individuals who repeatedly violate traffic laws).

(2) Payoffs to police by individuals who continually violate the law as a method of making money (for example, prostitutes, narcotic addicts and pushers, and professional burglars).

(3) "Clean graft" in which money is paid to police for services or courtesy discounts are given routinely to the police.

Internal corruption is closely related to external corruption. For example, an officer who charges a tavern owner a fee for overlooking law violations may in turn be charged a fee by the commander for the lucrative assignment. Internal corruption has been found to include the following:[51]

(1) Payment of money to pay the police force.
(2) Payment of money to higher-ranking officers for better shifts or assignments.
(3) Payment for choice vacation time.
(4) Strict adherence to a code of silence concerning external police corruption.
(5) Payment for promotions.
(6) Payment for an assignment that will yield lucrative kick-backs.

Illegal activity in police departments is not a recent phenomenon. Federal and state investigating committees have revealed graft and corruption almost every time they have looked for them. In New York City in 1894–1895, for example, the Lexow Committee found that graft was characteristic of the police system rather than of isolated patrol officers.[52] The Seabury Committee a generation later found

[50] Herbert Beigel, "The Investigation and Prosecution of Police Corruption," *Journal of Criminal Law and Criminology*, 65:135–56, 1974. See also the discussion in Chapter 11, above.

[51] Ibid., p. 136. See also Barbara R. Price, "Police Corruption: An Analysis," *Criminology*, 10:161–76, 1972; Julian B. Roebuck and Thomas Barker, "A Typology of Police Corruption," *Social Problems*, 21:423–37, 1974; Lawrence W. Sherman, *Police Corruption: A Sociological Perspective* (New York: Anchor Press, 1974); and Peter K. Manning and Lawrence John Redlinger, "Invitational Edges of Corruption: Some Consequences of Narcotic Law Enforcement," in *Politics and Drugs*, ed. Paul Rock (New York: Dutton, 1976), pp. 284–305.

[52] New York Legislature, *Report and Proceedings of the Senate Committee Appointed to Investigate the Police Department of the City of New York* [Lexow Committee] (Albany: State Printing Office, 1895), vol 5, pp. 5311–388. For a brief description of this investigation, see Lincoln Steffens, *Autobiography* (New York: Harcourt, 1931), pp. 247–84.

the same situation persisting.[53] In 1915 the Chicago City Council Commission on Crime found much evidence of collusion between police officers and professional criminals.[54] The 1950 investigations of the U. S. Senate Committee to Investigate Crime in Interstate Commerce revealed extensive collusion between criminals and law-enforcement officers and extensive graft by law-enforcement officers.[55] The committee found evidence of corruption and connivance at all levels of government—federal, state, and local. In the federal government the corruption was found to be primarily in connection with the enforcement of income-tax laws, but evidence of illegal activities on the state and local levels took four different forms: (1) direct bribe or protection payments made to the police by criminals; (2) politicians using their influence to protect criminals and further the interests of criminals; (3) police possessing unusual and unexplained wealth; and (4) police participating directly in the business of organized crime.[56]

Twenty years later, the Knapp Commission found corruption to be widespread in the New York City Police Department.[57] Appointed in 1970 by the mayor of New York City, the commission found that "almost all policemen" accepted a variety of favors as a kind of "natural perquisite of the job." The officers divided themselves into "grass eaters," who accept payoffs when the right circumstances arise, and "meat eaters," who aggressively misuse their police powers for personal gain. Individual detectives engaged in shakedowns of "individual targets of opportunity," but in the Narcotics Division extortion of money from drug dealers was systematic, with several officers sharing the proceeds whenever a "score" was made. Corruption appeared in its most sophisticated form among plainclothes officers assigned to enforce gambling laws. The monthly payments made by illegal gambling establishments were coordinated and shared equally by the officers, except that supervisors got a share and a half, and a newly assigned officer was not entitled to a share for about two months. The commission concluded that corruption could not be explained away by reference to a few "rotten apples" in an

[53] New York Legislature, *Report of the Joint Committee on the Government of the City of New York*, 5 vols. (Albany: State Printing Office, 1932). This report has been summarized, interpreted, and amplified in several unofficial books, of which the following are the most important: W. B. Northrop and J. B. Northrop, *The Insolence of Office* (New York: Putnam's Sons, 1932); Raymond Moley, *Tribunes of the People* (New Haven: Yale University Press, 1932); Norman Thomas and Paul Blanshard, *What's the Matter with New York?* (New York: Macmillan, 1932).

[54] Chicago City Council, *Report of the Commission on Crime* (Chicago: Author, 1915).

[55] Special Committee to Investigate Organized Crime in Interstate Commerce, *Third Interim Report*, U.S. Senate Report No. 307, 82d Congress (Washington: Government Printing Office, 1951); *Final Report*, U.S. Senate Report No. 257, 82d Congress (Washington: Government Printing Office, 1951). See also Norton Mockridge and Robert H. Prall, *The Big Fix* (New York: McGraw-Hill, 1957); Estes Kefauver, *Crime in America* (New York: Doubleday, 1951); and William H. Moore, *The Kefauver Committee and the Politics of Crime* (Columbia: University of Missouri Press, 1974).

[56] *Third Interim Report*, pp. 183–84.

[57] New York City Commission to Investigate Allegation of Police Corruption and the City's Anti-Corruption Procedures, *The Knapp Commission Report* (New York: George Brazilier, 1972).

otherwise clean barrel. Instead, each corrupt officer was "only one part of an apparatus of corruption."

In 1973 the Police Foundation arranged to receive clippings of newspaper articles about police corruption across the United States. In a period of two months, clippings were received from thirty states. They reported on alleged corruption in small cities, sheriffs' offices, state police forces, and suburban departments, and they reflected corrupt practices ranging from accepting bribes from traffic offenders to accepting payment to alter testimony at trials.[58] At about the same time, an astute observer of police practices in Philadelphia noted that officers saw themselves "operating in a world where 'notes' are constantly floating about, and only the stupid, the naive, and the fainthearted are unwilling to allow some of them to stick to their fingers."[59]

The Lexow Committee found that the same system of bribery used by criminals was also used by contractors and others. The Seabury Committee reported more specifically that the bribery of public officers was the method used in securing special privileges regarding building-zone ordinances, bus franchises, waterfront leases, condemnation cases, weights and measures, taxi regulations, and many other things. The Knapp Commission also found a close connection between police corruption and more general corruption, and white New York police officers interviewed shortly after the time of the commission's hearings complained bitterly that police officers were unfairly singled out from the huge mass of corrupt public officials.[60] Similarly, a study of Reading, Pennsylvania, a middle-sized industrial city, revealed that most of the crimes perpetrated by city officials during a period of almost total corruption were committed in order to facilitate the gambling offenses of organized criminals. But the same officials charged under-the-table fees for building permits, for liquor licenses, for employment in city hall, and for contracts to supply the city with goods and services. A follow-up survey revealed that the residents of Reading approved of gambling or were tolerant of it, but were hostile toward corruption. The citizens, in other words, "display both a desire for or toleration of illicit services and a demand for honesty on the part of local officials." The residents of the city failed to see that widespread illegal gambling is accompanied by widespread taking of bribes.[61]

[58]Herman Goldstein, *Police Corruption: A Perspective on Its Nature and Control* (Washington: Police Foundation, 1975), p. 55.

[59]Jonathan Rubenstein, *City Police* (New York: Farrar, Straus and Giroux, 1973), p. 400.

[60]William P. Brown, *A Study of the New York City Police Department Anti-Corruption Campaign October 1970–August 1972* (New York: New York State University at Albany, 1972); idem, "Police Corruption: The System Is the Problem," *Nation*, April, 1973, pp. 456–59; and Nicholas Alex, *New York Cops Talk Back: A Study of a Beleaguered Minority* (New York: Wiley, 1976), pp. 87–113.

[61]John A. Gardiner, with the assistance of David J. Olson, "Wincanton: The Politics of Corruption," Appendix B in President's Commission on Law Enforcement and Administration of Justice, *Task Force Report: Organized Crime* (Washington: Government Printing Office, 1967), pp. 61–79. See also John A. Gardiner, *The Politics of Corruption: Organized Crime in an American City* (New York: Russell Sage Foundation,

Another consequence of the fact that police departments sometimes are organized for the welfare of corrupt police officers and politicians, rather than of the people, is inefficient and unqualified personnel. This is unquestionably linked with police dishonesty, for only police officers who are "right" will be employed by those in political power. Civil-service systems that have been set up for the selection and promotion of qualified officers are sometimes ignored or circumvented. The public loudly demands that police officers catch criminals, keep the peace, and provide welfare services, but the same people fail to ensure that police officers are selected carefully, to provide appropriate training, to furnish adequate salaries and conditions of employment, and to make possible continuous policies. The average term of office of the chief official of police departments in American cities of a half-million population or more is only about two years, while in London it has been about fifteen years. Even police departments that do not select officers on the basis of political patronage usually are inadequately staffed. This inadequacy arises, we shall see, because there has been widespread failure of police administrators and other public officials to acknowledge the fact that most police work consists of providing social services and that very little of it is concerned with detecting and arresting criminals.

In general, police officers are inefficient in performing their law-enforcement duties, as these duties are formally defined, but the inefficiency is due to the fact that the public does not want to sacrifice individual rights and liberties to the cause of crime control. Some officials believe, for example, that a universal registration system would facilitate efficient police work. The ordinary American interprets this as an imposition on personal liberty. In the same spirit, citizens are often unwilling to assist the police in other respects. It is extremely difficult for police officers to secure the cooperation of witnesses and victims, let alone the active assistance of bystanders in the pursuit of a criminal or the detection of crime. Indeed, as Turk has pointed out, one of the most troublesome aspects of contemporary life is the tendency for citizens to let police officers, as agents of the state, try to settle their disputes, rather than trying to iron them out themselves.[62]

THE PUNITIVE REACTION AND THE POLICE

From the time of the formation of the United States there has been a tradition of narrow and restricted authority and power on the part of administrators and executives. At the same time, the persons occupying such positions are expected to play their roles as administrators skillfully. For this reason they tend to take attitudes of superordination and to assume unofficial powers, often in opposition to the desires of many of their constituents. In this respect police officers are no different than other administrators—in city halls, governmental bureaus,

1970); and John A. Gardiner and David J. Olson, eds., *Theft of the City: Readings on Corruption in Urban America* (Bloomington: Indiana University Press, 1974).

[62] Austin T. Turk, "Law as a Weapon in Social Conflict," *Social Problems*, 23:276–91, 1976.

churches, schools, and elsewhere. However, as police officers assume postures of superiority, rather than remaining as servants of the public, they often adopt punitive measures.

According to legal and political theory, the rights and duties of police officers to inflict punishments must be sharply limited.[63] The police are to maintain order, serve the public, and capture suspected criminals and take them to courts for trial. Formally, authority to implement anything approaching a punitive reaction to law violation is restricted to four main areas. (1) In some jurisdictions a limited judicial authority has been conferred on the police department, primarily in connection with minor offenses such as traffic violations, and the exercise of this authority in "police courts" usually involves a punitive reaction to the offenses. (2) Police are expected to punish by destroying property that is prohibited by law, such as gambling devices, unregistered equipment for making alcohol, and marijuana gardens. (3) Police are authorized to confiscate or impound property that is being used in violation of law, with the result that the owner loses the property or is required to pay a fee for its recovery. This may be illustrated by the impounding of arms and by the towing away of illegally parked cars. (4) County jails are administered by sheriffs, and the personnel employed to implement the punitive reaction in these institutions are police officers, acting as jailers.

Because police officers are expected to make crime dangerous, however, they in fact implement a punitive reaction to crime in many additional ways. The third degree, which entails pain and suffering for the purpose of extorting a confession, is punitive in nature, as is collecting a bribe from a guilty person in lieu of arrest. Brutality in the process of arrest or detention is deliberate infliction of pain by state agents who assume that the pain has some utility. So far as brutality is defended by police officers, it is said to be justified by the fact that many guilty persons escape conviction through technicalities or corruption and thus escape official punishment. Police officers say, in effect, "We will see that he gets this much punishment anyway."

Even when arrests and detention do not incorporate brutality, they often include intentional imposition of suffering. Police are likely to be discourteous, sarcastic, or rude when encountering or arresting persons of lower socioeconomic classes, but courteous and lenient when dealing with persons of high social status. The fact that courtesy was first emphasized in police departments when officers came into frequent contact with automobile drivers, who were not ordinarily of the lower classes, is evidence of this discrimination.[64] In fact, until the police

---

[63] See Jerome Hall, "Police and Law in a Democratic Society," *Indiana Law Journal*, 28:133–77, 1953; and Frank J. Remington, "The Role of the Police in Democratic Society," *Journal of Criminal Law, Criminology and Police Science*, 56:361–65, 1965.

[64] See Donald R. Cressey, "Law, Order and the Motorist," in *Crime, Criminology and Public Policy: Essays in Honour of Sir Leon Radzinowicz*, ed. Roger Hood (London: Heinemann, 1974), pp. 213–34. See also T. C. Willett, *Criminal on the Road* (London: Tavistock, 1964); idem, *Drivers After Sentence* (London:

started dealing with automobile drivers, they were mostly workingmen employed by the upper classes and middle classes to control other workingmen. The first police department, established in England in 1829, had something of this form, as did the first regular police forces in New York (1844) and Chicago (1855). The fact that southern California, with the highest number of automobiles per capita in the world, also has the police with the highest average educational level in the world shows one effect of the encounter between the police and upper- and middle-class automobile drivers. Undoubtedly, police officers make distinctions in favor of upper socioeconomic classes because making such distinctions is part of our culture. Similarly, police officers use punitive methods because the punitive reaction to crime is popular in our culture.

It should not be concluded, however, that all the force and violence used by police officers is necessarily "brutality," motivated by a desire to inflict pain or suffering. Because some of the persons with whom police officers deal are dangerous, the officers must as a matter of survival learn how to make themselves violent and dangerous. Confronting and subduing certain suspects, criminals, and crazy people is a hazardous business, and police officers cannot be expected to be gentle at all times. When a police officer's life is at stake, he or she should not be expected to follow either the rules of boxing or the rules governing the behavior of television characters, both of which stress the propriety of fighting "fairly," like ladies or gentlemen. Officers who fought by these rules would soon use up all their sick leave. The first chapter of a "practical handbook" for American police officers is exclusively devoted to the use of force, and its instructions range from details about how to use an opponent's clothing for restraint, to how to use a nightstick and how to kill with a gun.[65] On the latter point, the authors give police officers the following lesson:

> You don't have to wait until a suspect is actually assaulting you before you draw your gun. In fiction and on film, the actor portraying a western marshal can afford to wait until his assailant has started to draw before he goes for his gun. You cannot. You are in a real-life drama; there are no rehearsals or retakes and mistakes can be fatal.[66]

THE INTERVENTIONIST REACTION AND THE POLICE

Every police department arrests criminals and takes them to judges who in turn order the imposition of appropriate punishments. Accordingly, the law-enforcement work of a department is by definition designed to help implement the punitive reaction to crime. But during the last fifty years there has been a slight

Heinemann, 1973); and Allan Silver, "The Demand for Order in Civil Society: A Review of Some Theories in the History of Urban Crime, Police and Riot," in *The Police: Six Sociological Essays*, ed. David J. Bordua (New York: Wiley, 1967), pp. 1–24.

[65] David H. Gilston and Lawrence Podell, *The Practical Patrolman* (Springfield, Ill.: Charles C Thomas, 1959), pp. 5–28.

[66] Ibid., p. 23. It should be noted, however, that police work in general is not a hazardous occupation. See Ronald K. Tauber, "Danger and the Police: A Theoretical Analysis," *Issues in Criminology*, 3:69–81, 1967.

trend toward implementing the interventionist reaction to lawbreaking as well. Changes in police departments in this connection, of course, correspond to changes in other areas. As the treatment reaction became more popular in the courts and correctional agencies, it also became popular in police organizations. However, like direct implementation of the punitive reaction by police officers, direct implementation of the interventionist reaction is largely unofficial. The activities of police officers in this area are usually called "crime prevention"— discouraging or hindering crime by methods not designed to produce fear in the recipients.

Most of the activities of crime-prevention divisions of police departments are directed toward what are considered the social conditions leading to delinquency and crime, but the interventionist reaction also is implemented in other ways. In exercising their judicial authority, police officials certainly screen offenders on the basis of whether or not it is thought that punishment is warranted, but they also sometimes evaluate offenders according to whether or not it is thought that a "rehabilitation program" is needed. Especially in dealing with juveniles, police officers screen offenders by using discretion as to whether a youngster should be released or diverted to a guidance clinic for personality help, to a youth agency for club contacts, to some other agency, or to a court.[67] Many police departments now use a quite unofficial process of placing boys on "police probation," sometimes requiring them to do punitive labor such as washing police cars or raking leaves. Guilt usually is assumed, but even if guilt is not assumed, and the police officer makes a decision on the basis of mere probabilities or symptoms of delinquency, expostulation and referral are part of the interventionist reaction to crime, just as the deliberate infliction of illegal punishments on innocent persons is part of the punitive reaction to crime.[68]

In general, police departments have applied selected principles of social science to their work, and, in so doing, they have put some emphasis on reducing delinquency and crime by attacking their alleged causes. But for the most part police officers deal with persons who have not yet been convicted of crime, and they are expected to treat these persons as though they were innocent. Although in a strict sense it is impossible to implement such a policy, the possibility for development of interventionist programs within police departments is severely limited by it. Some persons have, in fact, criticized police departments for

---

[67] See Irving Piliavin and Scott Briar, "Police Encounters with Juveniles," *American Journal of Sociology*, 70:206–14, 1964; Aaron Cicourel, *The Social Organization of Juvenile Justice* (New York: Wiley, 1968); Donald J. Black and Albert J. Reiss, Jr., "Police Control of Juveniles," *American Sociological Review*, 35:63–77, 1970; Donald R. Cressey and Robert A. McDermott, *Diversion from the Juvenile Justice System* (Washington: Government Printing Office, 1973); and John Stratton, "Crisis Intervention Counseling and Police Diversion from the Juvenile Justice System: A Review of the Literature," *Juvenile Justice*, 25:44–53, 1974.

[68] Norman L. Weiner and Charles V. Willie, "Decisions by Juvenile Officers," *American Journal of Sociology*, 77:199–210, 1971.

developing social-work and social-reform programs, on the ground that other agencies exist for this purpose and that such programs are extraneous to the official duties of the police. This criticism is similar to the arguments of persons who criticize police officers for unofficially inflicting punishments. In the words of a policy statement issued by the International Association of Chiefs of Police, "The police are not in the punishing business any more than they are in the rehabilitating business. The police job is to prevent crime and to detect and apprehend offenders. Treatment of the offender is someone else's job."[69]

TRENDS IN POLICE WORK

Plans for improving police departments have been developed by various persons and agencies, and there has been a slight and inconsistent trend toward following them. This program includes freedom from corrupt politics; larger territorial organization; improvements of personnel, systems of assignments, equipment, and scientific techniques; development of preventive police work; cordial relations between police and public; and development of police morale and of police work as a profession.

Politics

The fundamental requirement for good police work is freedom from corrupt politics. Any other parts of a program for the improvement of a police department are likely to be futile unless the impediments caused by corrupt politics are reduced.

Corruption in municipal politics seems to be decreasing. The strength of party affiliations and, therefore, the strength of local political control has diminished rather steadily since the Civil War, which left a heritage of party loyalty. Civil-service measures have made great inroads on patronage in the last fifty years. Municipal, state, and federal welfare agencies now distribute goods and services to the needy, where fifty years ago these things were distributed by political machines, in exchange for votes. Also, businessmen are beginning to revolt against the old system of corruption of government, especially local government, for special privilege.

Further, police officers may now secure a measure of freedom even in cities where politics remain corrupt. The executive officer of the police department was traditionally a political appointee, but such officers are increasingly being selected by civil service and given permanent tenure, subject to removal for cause. Consistently, as compared with the situation fifty years ago, police officers are inactive and uninfluential in political campaigns. For example, the Hatch Act forecloses political activity by federal police, and in many states police are

---

[69] International Association of Chiefs of Police, *The Police and the Civil Rights Act* (New York: Author, 1964), p. 15.

forbidden by law or police regulations to participate in such activity. The Illinois State Police are by law 50 percent Democrats and 50 percent Republicans. Also, graft has been increasingly centralized and syndicated, with the result that police officers secure little of the proceeds. Accordingly, more police officers are more inclined to view graft as crime.

Freedom from corrupt politics does not, of course, mean freedom from outside control. It is to be expected that powerful people, especially, will always demand and receive special privileges from police officers. Accordingly, police departments always will in this sense be corrupt, even if there is no bribe taking. Moreover, as police executives have secured freedom from traditional corrupt politics, they have become politicians themselves and have gained a much stronger voice in legislative and executive policies. In doing so, they have gained a degree of immunity from interference with their activities by ordinary citizens, and it is not certain that ordinary citizens now have more influence on police practices than they did when police executives reported to corrupt mayors and the men of their machines.

Police executives have gained this power primarily by catering to repressive law-and-order interests, creating and exploiting fears of a crime wave, and picturing criminals as violent, mad-dog, predatory enemies.[70] Consistently, they have portrayed police officers as soldiers at war with criminals when in fact most police work consists of rendering social services rather than with detecting, catching, and arresting criminals. By such political tactics (including, as we noted earlier, the shaping of crime statistics so that a distorted and misleading picture of "the crime problem" emerges),[71] police executives have gained enormous increases in budgetary support, manpower, and equipment for police departments across the United States and in foreign countries as well. It may be concluded, then, that as police executives have been freed from traditional corrupt politics they have to a large degree become their own bosses, rather than becoming servants of all the politicians elected by the people in honest elections.

Coordination

There are about 40,000 public law-enforcement organizations in the United States, ranging from one-person village units to New York City's 30,000-person department. No national law or coordinating agency sets standards for all these units, but over the years there have been three tendencies toward their amalgamation and coordination. One is to develop a regular uniformed county police or else to place all the constables and marshals of the county under the direction of the sheriff. This trend is seen principally in the development of narcotics squads made

---

[70] See Arthur Rosett and Donald R. Cressey, *Justice by Consent: Plea Bargains in the American Courthouse* (Philadelphia: Lippincott, 1976), pp. 175–80; Leonard Ruchelman, *Police Politics: A Comparative Study of Three Cities* (Cambridge, Mass.: Ballinger, 1974); and idem, ed., *Who Rules the Police?* (New York: New York University Press, 1973).

[71] See Chapter 2, above.

up of police officers from each of the agencies in a county.[72] A second trend is to develop single police systems for metropolitan areas. Cooperative efforts among the police forces in the metropolitan area of Chicago have been developed, while in Cincinnati a cooperative organization which includes officers in Ohio, Kentucky, and Indiana is now operating. Similarly, metropolitan "strike forces" dealing with organized crime in some metropolitan areas are made up of federal officers from several agencies, and of state, county, and local police officers as well. Under a different arrangement, some small police jurisdictions contract with large jurisdictions for specific police services.

A third trend is to develop state police departments and enlarge their powers. In 1934, forty-seven state police systems were found in thirty-eight states, of which eleven were regular state police systems, nine highway patrol systems with general powers over crimes, twenty highway patrol systems with powers restricted to regulation of traffic, four state sheriffs, and three governors' reserves. By 1971, there were fifty state police, highway patrols, or criminal-investigation agencies. In about one-third of the states, these agencies had full law-enforcement authority.[73] The principal opposition to the extension of state police has come from labor unions, whose members fear their use as strikebreakers, as occurred in the 1930s.

Related to this development of regional and state police forces is the tendency toward increased participation of federal police in the total law-enforcement effort. Federal police go into operation only when the crimes are of an interstate nature or when federal activities are involved. But in recent years there has been a tremendous increase in the scope of federal criminal jurisdiction, brought about by new federal legislation. Federal action against crime is made possible by the commerce clause of the Constitution and also by the postal, taxing and regulating powers of Congress.

An enormous amount of crime is now of an interstate nature. Because of the mobility of criminals, local agencies are seriously handicapped. There is no logical reason why all serious crimes should not be defined by federal laws, as is done in Canada, and it is at least an open question whether centralization of police administrative work would be a greater threat to civil liberties and human rights than is the current decentralized arrangement.[74]

Personnel

It goes without saying that a good police department has good personnel. Careful selection, adequate training, and appropriate remuneration of police officers are essential. In about three-fourths of the cities at present, police officers are at least

---

[72]Driscoll, *No One to Count Cadence;* for a description of a similar development in Great Britain, the establishment of regional police, see Leon Radzinowicz, "The Dangerous Offender," *The Police Journal* (England), 41:411–47, 1968.

[73]See Schrag, *Crime and Justice*, p. 130.

[74]See Ben Whitaker, *The Police* (London: Eyre and Spottiswoode, 1964), pp. 87–109.

selected by civil-service examinations, though some cities still have a large turnover on change of political administration. The civil-service examinations and other screening devices are highly selective. Of the 3,714 men who applied for positions with the Detroit Police Department in one year, only 4 percent were placed on the eligible list for appointment. In 1965, the Washington, D.C., Police Department found 10 percent of its applicants to be eligible for police work; Los Angeles accepted only 2.8 percent of its applicants. A President's Commission survey indicated that, as a result of such selective practices, two-thirds of American police forces were under their authorized strength.[75] There is no assurance, however, that the screening devices are selecting the best persons for police work, and it could well be that they select an undue proportion of persons who are not qualified to perform the many social-service tasks that police officers must perform.

Police training, like selection for police work, has developed extensively during the last fifty years. Most metropolitan police departments offer standardized training programs for recruits and regularly give additional in-service training to established officers. Researchers who have examined recruit-training programs in recent years have found them defective, if not irrelevant. Herman Goldstein, a noted police expert, has described the training as follows:

Extraordinarily heavy emphasis is placed on maintaining neat notebooks and on committing to memory large numbers of irrelevant facts. Technical subjects are emphasized over basic principles of law, democracy, and human relations. The military atmosphere and the prevailing teaching techniques make the training process a very passive one for the recruit. And the programs are structured to convey only one point of view on controversial matters in a manner intended to avoid open discussion. Beyond these observations there is an unreal quality in the training programs—in the emphasis placed on military protocol, in their narrow concept of the police function, and in their according-to-the-book teaching of police operations. In addition to the emphasis on the police function relative to crime, they often dwell on specific topics of little practical value and ignore large areas to which officers devote most of their time. They create the impression that the highly structured organization of the police agency results in a highly structured work environment as well. And they tend to portray the police officer's job as a rigid one, largely dictated by law, ignoring the tremendous amount of discretion officers are required to exercise.[76]

Most colleges and universities now offer courses designed primarily for police officers, but most of the courses are mere in-service training classes that have moved in the last decade from the police academy to the campus. Many are taught by retired police officers or by senior officers who earn a few extra dollars by teaching on a college campus in the evenings, and the curriculum covers subjects such as elementary criminal law, criminalistics and identification techniques,

[75]President's Commission, *Task Force Report: Police*, p. 9.
[76]Goldstein; *Policing a Free Society*, pp. 274–5.

patrol administration, police management, and control of drug abuse.[77] The officers taking these courses are paid by the Law Enforcement Assistance Administration and receive credit toward graduation. This proof that they are raising their level of education helps get them promoted. Many departments now require at least some college training for entrance into police work or for promotion, but there is no evidence that persons with college or university experience make better police officers. Moreover, when such regulations pertain to genuine college or university work (courses in science, literature, and the arts) rather than in-service courses for working officers, the regulations favor middle-class persons as compared to working-class persons, for the former are more likely to be able to afford a leisurely liberal education. Further, there is a possibility that any minimal educational requirement will be greatly exceeded by women and other minorities who become "overqualified" in order to get the attention of recruiting authorities. Twenty years ago, when the New York City Police Department required a high-school education for entrance, nearly 40 percent of the blacks who were appointed had attended college for at least one year, compared to about 20 percent of the whites.[78]

Perhaps the most basic assumption of police administrators, police reformers, and ordinary police officers alike is that police practices will improve if the quality of personnel is improved. It is difficult to quarrel with this assumption, for concentration on personnel matters certainly is a route to "change" and "improvement." But determining just what is changed or improved by a new personnel policy is another matter for these things can be measured only if the goal sought by the policy is spelled out.[79] Indeed, unless goals are specified, it cannot be determined whether any change has occurred at all.

For example, suppose that a particular police department uses procedures that reject as unfit for police work 90 percent of the persons who apply. Suppose further that the police chief, pressured by reformers, decides to "upgrade" or "improve" the quality of the staff and then a year later cites as evidence of this improvement the fact that now the selection procedures reject 95 percent of the applicants. Is the chief of police correct? Have police services improved? Have the personnel been upgraded? The answer to these questions must be, "Not necessarily." It could well be that the changed entrance tests weeded out even more of the best-qualified personnel than did the old tests, if police work is identified for what it is—namely,

[77] See Robert W. Ferguson and Allan H. Stoke, *Concepts of Criminal Law* (Boston: Holbrook Press, 1976); Kevin P. O'Brien and Robert C. Sullivan, *Criminalistics: Theory and Practice*, 2nd ed. (Boston: Holbrook Press, 1976); Harrison C. Allison, *Personal Identification* (Boston: Holbrook Press, 1973); Donald T. Shanahan, *Patrol Administration* (Boston: Holbrook Press, 1975); Ronald G. Lynch, *The Police Manager* (Boston: Holbrook Press, 1975); and Robert W. Ferguson, *Drug Abuse Control* (Boston: Holbrook Press, 1975).

[78] Bernard Cohen and Jan M. Chaiken, *Police Background Characteristics and Performance* (New York: New York City Rand Institute, 1972), p. xi.

[79] See Alex, *New York Cops Talk Back*, pp. 28–53.

a combination of rendering social services and catching criminals, with a much greater emphasis on the former than the latter.

Similarly, because police work requires extensive exercise of individual judgment and discretion, it is not reasonable to say that an officer who has become a good marksman, a judo expert, or a criminal-law specialist is more deserving of promotion than an officer who has not done any of these things but who has a great deal of "street sense." And because no relationship between educational level and good police work has been identified, it is not reasonable, either, to say that police work has improved because the average educational level of the officers has been raised, or to promote a person who has attended college over a person who has not. Put another way, "improving the quality of personnel" or "upgrading the caliber of officers" wins prestige for a police department but this policy does so only because few people ask what the improvement, if any, is all about. Goldstein has summarized his observations regarding personnel reforms as follows:

Inherent in the various programs designed to improve the caliber of police personnel is the assumption that the personnel who are recruited, selected, and trained according to the recommended procedures will be different from those who have entered police service in the past. But the nature of this difference is rarely articulated. And if it is, it is usually set forth in such general terms (e.g., individuals with a higher level of intelligence) that people can agree in supporting the new program although they may disagree if pressed to define the objectives they have in mind. Many people in police service, for example, have the limited objective of using personnel reforms to realize greater prestige, better public relations, and improved salaries. They have no desire to alter the form of police service. Others—police personnel and citizens alike—see personnel reforms as a way of perfecting police performance, but they mean by this the prevailing standards of good performance. Still others—including especially those outside police agencies who advocate police reform—see improvements in personnel administration as a way of bringing about radical change in policing. They propose to achieve such change by attracting and promoting officers who have different values and different attitudes toward their jobs and toward the communities they serve.

One of the consequences of this lack of agreement on specific objectives is that advocated programs are frequently subverted when implemented, because those who would carry them out tend, intentionally or unintentionally, to substitute their own objectives for the goals of those who initially supported them. Emphasis is often shifted from content to form.[80]

What is at stake here is the image of the police officer as a soldier in a war on crime. This image is incorrect. In their daily work, most police officers must behave more like social workers than like soldiers or even the principals in a game of cops and robbers.[81] But police executives, eager to maintain the "crime fighter" image because it is popular and profitable, construct selection and training programs that stress the notion that every officer is merely a tough, authoritarian,

---

[80] Goldstein, *Policing in a Free Society*, p. 258.

[81] Elaine Cumming, Ian Cumming, and Laura Edell, "Policeman as Philosopher, Guide and Friend," *Social Problems*, 12:276–86, 1965.

cog in a military machine that is trying to conquer crime.[82] Moreover, officers are not likely to be rewarded for outstanding performance in the social-service role, either by the police department or by the persons helped.[83] Accordingly, recruit-training programs, even those requiring many hours in classrooms, fail to introduce new officers to the work they actually will do, and new officers find it necessary to learn about police work primarily by using more experienced officers as models. A recent Los Angeles survey of juvenile-justice personnel suggested that the respondents were dissatisfied with this kind of training, at least for police juvenile specialists. The area of knowledge they considered most important to the training of police officers dealing with juveniles was information about the juvenile-justice system itself, including the political, institutional, and economic realities of juvenile delinquency. The second most important area was said to be causal theory, the third was knowledge of "analytical tools" (research methods and statistics), and the fourth was skill in interpersonal relations and organizational skills.[84]

Assignments

The assignment of police officers to specific tasks and the organization of police work have changed significantly in the years since the automobile, the telephone, and the police radio became popular. August Vollmer developed a program for statistical and ecological studies of crimes as a basis of assignments. His system is still widely used. If the records of the police department indicate that robberies are concentrated in certain areas, at certain hours, and on certain days of the week, the police force is also concentrated at those places and times. Thus the neighborhood patrol officer is tending to disappear, and specialized squads are increasing in number. The word *patrolman* is becoming little more than a designation of rank and no longer describes a type of work. The small number of officers now assigned to regular patrol duty is explained in part by the fact that a citizen in trouble can telephone police headquarters, which can dispatch a radio car to give help. Formerly, the patrolman had to be available on the beat if the citizen were to get help.

Improved communication and transportation have made the use of specialized squads possible, while changes in the technology of police work have made them necessary.[85] The most important of these squads is the traffic squad. In some

---

[82] See Arthur Niederhoffer, *Behind the Shield: The Police in Urban Society* (New York: Doubleday, 1967), pp. 118–29.

[83] Jesse Rubin, "Police Identity and the Police Role," ch. 2 in *The Police and the Community*, ed. Robert F. Steadman, (Baltimore: Johns Hopkins University Press, 1972), pp. 25–8. See also Jack J. Preiss and Howard J. Ehrlich, *An Examination of Role Theory: The Case of the State Police* (Lincoln: University of Nebraska Press, 1966).

[84] Steven M. Ward, "The Delinquency Control Institute: A Participant in the Debate," *Crime Prevention Review* (California), 3:30–6, 1975.

[85] See Michael Banton, *The Policeman in the Community* (London: Tavistock, 1964), pp. 7, 127; and Rubenstein, *City Police*, pp. 26–68.

communities, regulation of traffic now occupies the time of as much as 25 percent of the police force. In addition, large cities have pickpocket squads, vice squads, forgery squads, narcotics squads, an aviation police squad, and other squads and divisions. Because the members of these squads are mobile experts, the neighborhood patrol officer is less important.

Moreover, the formation of specialized squads and divisions has meant that a much larger percentage of police law-enforcement work is now "proactive" (initiated by police officers out looking for trouble) and a smaller percentage is "reactive" (responding to citizens' calls for help, in the manner of a fire department).[86] One of the first controversies about Boston's newly established nineteenth-century police department occurred because a law regulating liquor licensing and consumption in effect called upon police officers to be proactive, to act as detectives on their own initiative, to enter private places without a warrant, and to seize evidence of crime no one had complained about.[87] Similar poor relationships between police and public, stemming from assignment of similar proactive responsibilities to police officers, seem to have become the heritage of modern American cities.[88]

It has long been assumed that what American police executives call "preventive patrolling" and what British police administrators call "showing the flag"—deploying uniformed police officers in marked cars over geographic areas in systematic ways—cuts crime rates by creating impressions of a police omnipresence which, in turn, convinces potential offenders that the risks of committing crime are great. However, a year-long experiment conducted in Kansas City, Missouri, suggested that this assumption is not warranted. Fifteen police beats were computer matched on the basis of crime data, number of calls for service, ethnic composition, median income, and transience of population. The matching produced five groups of beats, each consisting of three beats. In each of the groups, one beat was designated reactive, one control, and one proactive. In each reactive beat, the patrol cars were removed and entered the area only to answer citizens' requests for services. In each proactive beat, patrol cars were added, increasing the level of visibility two or three times. In each control beat, police cars continued to patrol in the usual manner. The essential finding, following careful measurement of possible effects, was that decreasing or increasing routine preventive patrol had no effect on crime, arrests, citizen fear of crime, citizen attitudes toward the

[86]The "proactive" and "reactive" terminology was introduced by David Bordua and Albert J. Reiss, Jr., "Environment and Organization: A Perspective on Police," in *The Police: Six Sociological Essays*, ed. Bordua, p. 40. Wilson used different terminology—"police-invoked action" and "citizen-invoked action"—to indicate these two styles of law enforcement and order maintenance: *Varieties of Police Behavior*, pp. 83–9.

[87]Roger Lane, *Policing the City: Boston, 1822–1885* (Cambridge, Mass.: Harvard University Press, 1967), pp. 39–44.

[88]See Arthur Stinchcombe, "Institutions of Privacy in the Determination of Police Administrative Practices," *American Sociological Review*, 69:150–60, 1963; and Walter Ryland, "Police Surveillance of Public Toilets," *Washington and Lee Review*, 23:265–8, 1966.

that their members must be polite and courteous, and attention is being paid to special problems of dealing with minority groups, demonstrators, pickets, and automobile drivers. More fundamentally, however, demonstration of coordinated efforts to keep the peace while efficiently protecting civil liberties of citizens has more influence than anything else in reducing public antagonism. An earlier observation on the inadequacies of police training in the United States still holds true:

> It can be said of police training schools that the recruit is taught everything except the essential requirement of his calling, which is how to secure and maintain the approval and respect of the public whom he encounters daily in the course of his duties.[110]

One of the advantages stemming from good relations with the public is high police morale. More and more, high police morale is being seen to stem from efficient public service and not from tight military discipline and stress on firepower, physical strength, and bravery.[111]

SUGGESTED READINGS

Alex, Nicholas. *New York Cops Talk Back: A Study of a Beleaguered Minority.* New York: Wiley, 1976.

Bent, Alan Edward. *The Politics of Law Enforcement.* Lexington, Mass.: Lexington Books, 1974.

Bittner, Egon. *The Functions of the Police in Modern Society.* Washington: Government Printing Office, 1970.

Cain, Maureen E. *Society and the Policeman's Role.* London: Routledge & Kegan Paul, 1973.

Cobb, R. C. *The Police and the People: French Popular Protest, 1789–1820.* Oxford: Clarendon Press, 1970.

Cohen, Bernard. "The Police Internal System of Justice in New York City." *Journal of Criminal Law, Criminology, and Police Science,* 63:53–67, 1972.

Davis, Kenneth Culp. *Police Discretion.* St. Paul, Minn.: West, 1975.

Driver, Edwin D. "Confessions and the Social Psychology of Coercion." *Harvard Law Review,* 82:42–61, 1968.

Goldstein, Joseph. "Police Discretion Not to Invoke the Criminal Process: Low-Visibility Decisions in the Administration of Criminal Justice." *Yale Law Journal,* 69:543–94, 1960.

Grosman, Brian A. *Police Command: Decisions and Discretion.* Niagara Falls, N.Y.: MacLean-Hunter Press, 1975.

Jagiello, Robert J. "College Education for the Patrolman: Necessity or Irrelevance?" *Journal of Criminal Law, Criminology and Police Science,* 62:114–21, 1971.

LaFave, Wayne R. *Arrest: The Decision to Take a Suspect Into Custody.* Boston: Little, Brown, 1965.

Lane, Roger. *Policing the City: Boston, 1822–1885.* New York: Atheneum, 1971.

---

110 Charles Reith, *The Blind Eye of History: A Study of the Origins of the Present Police Era* (London: Faber and Faber, 1952), pp. 115–16.

111 Robert L. Peabody, "Authority Relations in Three Organizations," *Public Administration Review,* 23:87–92, 1963; idem, "Perceptions of Organizational Authority: A Comparative Analysis," *Administrative Science Quarterly,* 6:477–82, 1962; and Nicholas Alex, *Black in Blue: A Study of the Negro Policeman* (New York: Appleton-Century-Crofts, 1969), pp. 57–84.

Neubauer, David W. *Criminal Justice in Middle America*. Morristown, N.J.: General Learning Press, 1974.

Niederhoffer, Arthur. *Behind the Shield: The Police in Urban Society*. New York: Doubleday, 1967.

Niederhoffer, Arthur, & Abraham S. Blumberg, eds. *The Ambivalent Force: Perspective on the Police*. Waltham, Mass.: Xerox Publishing, 1970.

Pepinsky, Harold E. "Policing Patrolmen's Offense-Reporting Behavior." *Journal of Research in Crime and Delinquency*, 13:33–47, 1976.

Platt, Anthony, & Lynn Cooper, eds. *Policing America*. Englewood Cliffs, N.J.: Prentice-Hall, 1974.

Reiss, Albert J. *The Police and the Public*. New Haven: Yale University Press, 1971.

Schwartz, Louis B., & Stephen R. Goldstein. *Law Enforcement Handbook for Police*. St. Paul, Minn.: West, 1970.

Sherman, Lawrence W. *Police Corruption: A Sociological Perspective* New York: Anchor Books, 1974.

Skolnick, Jerome H. *Justice Without Trial: Law Enforcement in Democratic Society*. 2nd ed. New York: Wiley, 1975.

Skolnick, Jerome H., & Thomas C. Gray, eds. *Police in America*. Boston: Educational Associates, 1975.

Smith, Bruce. *Police Systems in the United States*. 2nd rev. ed. New York: Harper, 1960.

Sowle, Claude R., ed. *Police Power and Individual Freedom: The Quest for Balance*. Chicago: Aldine, 1962.

Stark, Rodney. *Police Riots: Collective Violence and Law Enforcement*. Belmont, Calif.: Wadsworth, 1972.

Steadman, Robert F., ed. *The Police and the Community*. Baltimore: Johns Hopkins University Press, 1972.

Steffens, Lincoln. *Autobiography*. New York: Harcourt Brace, 1931.

Unger, Sanford J. *FBI*. Boston: Atlantic—Little, Brown, 1975.

Vollmer, August. "Police Progress in the Past Twenty-five years." *Journal of Criminal Law and Criminology*, 24:161–75, May–June, 1933.

Wilson, James Q. *Varieties of Police Behavior: The Management of Law and Order in Eight Communities*. New York: Atheneum, 1972.

17

Pretrial Release and Detention

After suspected persons have been arrested, it is the duty of police officers to take them promptly to a magistrate. This duty often is ignored, and arrested persons are sometimes discharged by the police without a court appearance. If the alleged crime of the person taken before a magistrate is a minor one, the magistrate either discharges or convicts the accused. But if the alleged crime is serious, the magistrate merely considers the conditions under which temporary release on bail or on the suspected person's own recognizance can be granted.

Whether the person accused of serious crime is released on bail or not, he or she is entitled to a preliminary hearing, also before a magistrate. At this hearing the magistrate determines whether the known evidence against the accused is sufficient to justify further legal proceedings. Defendants who have been denied bail or who cannot meet the requirements for bail must remain in custody while arrangements are made for this preliminary hearing, and the practice of holding accused persons in this way is detention.

The preliminary hearing is wholly for the benefit of the suspect and never results in an official decision that the suspect is guilty. Its purpose is to save obviously innocent persons the expense and trouble of a lengthy trial. The magistrate makes no effort to obtain new evidence and deals only with probability of guilt or innocence. Some states bar newsmen from preliminary hearings, primarily because readers are likely to interpret a "probable cause" action as a finding of guilt. If the known evidence against the accused is not sufficient to justify further court proceedings, the suspect is discharged from custody or from the conditions of bail. However, if there is probable cause to believe the suspect is guilty, the accused person is held for further proceedings by a higher court or is temporarily released on bail. The practice of holding suspected persons for further legal proceedings after the preliminary hearing also is called detention.

425

RELEASE BEFORE TRIAL

A person who has been arrested may be held at the police station for a few hours or days and then released without a court appearance. Alternatively, the person may secure a release on a writ of habeas corpus, may secure a temporary release on bail by giving financial security for return, or may secure temporary release on his or her own recognizance or promise to return.

Unofficial Release

Suspects are frequently released by the police without court appearance. In some instances such release follows illegal arrest and, hence, illegal detention, but in other cases it is considered the most practical system for dealing with persons rightfully arrested for minor offenses. Illegal arrests include those made for failing to bribe an officer, those made for the purpose of forcing gambling places to pay graft, and those made when there is no evidence of crime. They are followed by illegal detention and, usually, release without trial. This system of release is also used in most cases of juvenile delinquency, and in many cases of intoxication, disorderliness, vagrancy, and other misdemeanors. When so used, it is known as the golden-rule disposition.

Intoxicated persons are often held in the police lockup only until they are sober, vagrants are held until they agree to leave the community, and disorderly persons are held until it is believed that their behavior will be orderly. Only about 10 percent of all juvenile-delinquency cases (not counting traffic, dependency, and neglect cases) that come to the attention of large urban police departments are referred to a juvenile court or a criminal court. Formally, these releases are, with a few exceptions, unjustified. Informally, however, the unofficial release procedure often represents the selection of the best method available at the time. For example, the arrest and temporary detention of inebriates protects them as well as the public. If these persons were taken into court, they would either be dismissed or fined, and since most of them would be unable to pay fines, they would be committed to a house of correction for a short period. None of these methods is of great value in solving the problem of drunkenness and alcoholism, and in many cities police officers are now required to take inebriates to detoxification centers rather than to a detention institution.

Some of the other unofficial releases are probably much like those that occur in cases of intoxication. Thus most are straight discharges from detention, sometimes accompanied by a referral to an appropriate community agency. But in a few cities the discharges are conditional, despite the fact that the accused person has not been found guilty of any crime. The threat of prosecution is used to guarantee that the offender follows through with a proposed program of treatment, submits to supervision, makes restitution, or performs some other condition of release. In Baltimore, this kind of informal adjustment, now likely to be called "diversion," is performed by a magistrate, who holds court in a police precinct station. Ten years ago, a special unit of the Detroit probation department disposed of nearly 5,000 criminal complaints monthly, mainly complaints of nonsupport or other domestic problems. Warrants of arrest were issued for only about 3 percent of the complaints filed.[1] These systems for making the decision about whether an offender should be charged with crime are, like the golden-rule disposition by the police, without the benefit of guidelines from legislatures or top-level policymakers. "Decisions are to a great extent fortuitous because they are made on inadequate information about the offense, the offender, and the alternatives available."[2] Nevertheless, the decisions manage to soften the harsh effects of a severe statutory system.

Release by Writ of Habeas Corpus

In recent years, most habeas corpus writs have been filed by convicted prisoners claiming error in trial proceedings. But the traditional use of the writ has been in connection with pretrial detention. So that citizens are protected from false arrest and illegal detention, habeas corpus writs may be obtained from courts to force the detaining officials to bring the arrested person before a magistrate immediately for a preliminary hearing. If no just reason for holding a citizen can be shown, the person must be discharged from custody.

The "root principle" of habeas corpus, the U.S. Supreme Court has noted, "is that in civilized society, government must always be accountable to the judiciary for a man's imprisonment; if the imprisonment cannot be shown to conform with the fundamental requirements of law, the individual is entitled to his immediate release."[3]

Although the arrested person usually must apply to the court for a writ, some judges are known to have issued them informally from their homes, and writs also have been issued immediately after arrest. Some professional and organized criminals have attorneys constantly prepared to secure a writ, and sometimes the attorney arrives at the police station with the writ even before police officers arrive with the suspect. Some years ago a series of fifteen outlying station houses in Detroit constituted a "loop," and suspects were shifted from one to another of these stations for a period of a week or ten days and then released. The abuse of the use of the habeas corpus writ by attorneys, then, prompted police to use illegal methods to avoid its use. Both kinds of abuse have been greatly reduced by recent Supreme Court decisions regarding the rights of suspects and detained persons.[4]

Release on Bail

The principal official method of securing release before trial is the use of bail. A promise is made to pay the state a specified sum of money if the accused person

---

[1] President's Commission on Law Enforcement and Administration of Justice, *Task Force Report: The Courts* (Washington: Government Printing Office, 1967), p. 6.
[2] Ibid., p. 7.
[3] *Fay* v. *Noia*, 372 U.S. 391, 402 (1963).
[4] See Chapter 16, above.

does not appear for trial. *Bail* is the term for the financial security that is pledged, but it also is used to describe the entire system whereby one is released after having given such security.

As a general rule, magistrates are required by law to grant release on bail, but the law also gives them wide discretion as to the amount and character of the bail. They can effectively prevent release by setting the bail at a high figure, or by requiring security of a kind that is extremely difficult to obtain. The United States Constitution stipulates that "excessive bail shall not be required, nor excessive fines imposed, nor cruel and unusual punishments inflicted."

In early English law, a man charged with a crime could be released if a friend would act as his keeper and thus act as surety for his appearance in court. The person who acted as surety was liable for the punishment if the accused was not delivered. Later the surety pledged property, which generally consisted of a house or land, but still remained essentially the keeper of the accused person. The real estate of friends is still used as security in small towns and to some extent in cities, but in the city many defendants have no friends who own property available for bail. Professional bondsmen and corporate surety companies have filled this gap, and such agencies now provide surety. There are about 3,000 bondsmen in the United States. Most of them act as semi-independent agents of about a dozen surety companies.

In most places, an accused person can pay a relatively small fee to a company or to a professional bondsman for providing the financial security necessary for release. The security thus obtained is called a *bond* or a *bail bond,* and it has become customary to refer to the status of one who has been released on bail as "out on bond." The usual bail for a person charged with burglary is about $5,000. Surety companies generally will provide a $5,000 bond for about $100 or $150, but in some communities the rates are much higher than this. In Illinois, a defendant can obtain release by depositing with the court a down payment of 10 percent of the total amount. A refund of 90 percent of the down payment is given if the defendant appears in court at the appointed time.

In some jurisdictions it has become common practice to require persons charged with traffic offenses to provide what is called "cash bail." This is a sum fixed at an amount approximately equal to the fine customarily imposed for the offense of which the person is accused. If a person who has paid such a sum desires a trial, the person appears in traffic court at a specified time, but if there is no desire for a trial, the person simply does not appear, forfeiting the cash. The great majority of persons who post such sums forfeit them, and a large proportion of offenders consider them as fines. In practice, one who forfeits such a cash sum is absolved from further liability for the offense, forfeiture of the cash being tacitly accepted by the courts as satisfactory. Although the "cash bail" procedure relieves police and courts of a great deal of work, there is no legal basis for this custom. Ordinarily, bail is not a punitive measure, and the forfeiture of bail does not absolve the offender from prosecution. A person who forfeits bail can be rearrested and tried, and, even if acquitted, the forfeited bail is not returned.

The ordinary system of providing financial security for persons charged with crimes has been criticized on several points. The chief criticism is that police departments and courts have inadequate facilities for determining whether financial security is needed, how much security is needed, and how adequate the security that is offered may be. The amount required is therefore generally determined by the charge against the suspect rather than by assessment of the person's character and responsibility. This bears heavily on the poor and makes bail practically prohibitive for them.

Although the proportion of persons failing to make bail varies widely from place to place, a recent study of large and small counties shows that it often is substantial:[5]

	Percentage of felony defendants unable to make bail
Large counties:	
Cook (Chicago)	75
Hennepin (Minneapolis)	71
Jefferson (Louisville)	30
Philadelphia (Philadelphia)	14
Small counties:	
Brown, Kansas	93
Rutland, Vermont	83
Putnam, Missouri	36
Anchorage, Alaska	28
Catoosa, Georgia	6

A study of New York City bail practices found that almost half of all defendants could not obtain the funds for bail: 25 percent failed to make bail at $500; 45 percent failed at $1,500; and 63 percent at $2,500. Thirty-eight percent of the persons unable to post bail in New York City were detained for from fifty to ninety-nine days prior to the trial. The investigators believed that bail was often intentionally set so high that the accused would not be able to obtain the necessary funds, so as to give the offender a "taste of jail" or to "protect society." This practice was condemned in the following terms: "It is fundamental that the state has no right to punish a person until his guilt has been established beyond a reasonable doubt. And there is no support in the law for the proposition that a

---

[5] President's Commission, *Task Force Report: The Courts*, p. 37.

person may be imprisoned because of the speculative possibility that he may commit a crime."[6]

In effect, therefore, an indigent man of excellent character and responsibility charged with a crime of which he is completely innocent has no alternative to detention in an institution. This hardship cannot be defended by the argument that poor persons should not commit crimes, for many of them are actually innocent. Indeed, statistical studies have shown that defendants are more likely to plead guilty as the time spent in jail awaiting trial increases. Thus the period of detention following denial of bail coerces persons into pleading guilty.[7]

A second criticism of the bail system is that it involves collusion between police officers, judges and other court officials, and professional bondsmen. The offender asks a police officer, jailer, or lawyer how to secure bail, and that person suggests a bondsman or informs a runner for a bondsman that the defendant has no bondsman. Fees are than divided, a practice that is illegal. Dill has shown that there are nonfinancial exchanges too. For example, bondsmen help officials control arrestees, help move defendants through the courts, and on occasion refuse to write a bond for a defendant an official wants detained; in exchange, judges overlook the collection of forfeited bail bonds.[8] Suffet has noted, more generally, that bail setting diffuses the responsibility for release of a defendant; he argues that this accounts for the persistence of the bail system and shows why judges usually side with prosecutors in bail hearings.[9]

Several suggestions for improving the bail system have been made, and there has been a slight tendency to follow them in practice. First, it has been proposed that one bureau should have complete control of all the work of granting bail, recommending forfeitures, and collecting forfeited bonds in a city. This organization has been arranged in several cities with varying degrees of success. It results in better inspection of securities, so that bonds can always be kept within the value of the securities listed, and it prevents bondsmen from peddling bonds from one court to another. It appears to have no effect on other aspects of the bail problem.

Second, it is argued that this bureau, or a section of it, should be responsible for investigating the character of the defendant for the purpose of determining whether release should be granted without financial security, or under no conditions at all. Under present constitutional provisions, an outright refusal of bail is not permissible in the United States in most cases, but such refusal is

[6]Caleb Foote, James P. Markle, and Edward A. Wooley, "Compelling Appearance in Court: Administration of Bail in Philadelphia," *University of Pennsylvania Law Review*, 102:1031–79, 1954. See also Charles Ares and Herbert Sturz, "Bail and the Indigent Accused," *Crime and Delinquency*, 8:12–20, 1962.

[7]Anne Rankin, "The Effect of Pretrial Detention," *New York University Law Review*, 39:641–64, 1964; New York Legal Aid Society, "The Unconstitutional Administration of Bail," *Criminal Law Bulletin*, 8:459–72, 1972.

[8]Forrest Dill, "Discretion, Exchange and Social Control: Bail Bondsmen in Criminal Courts," *Law and Society Review*, 9:639–74, 1975.

[9]Frederic Suffet, "Bail Setting: A Study of Courtroom Interaction," *Crime and Delinquency*, 12:318–31, 1966.

permissible in England. Probably a great proportion of offenders could be released on their own recognizance, a system that eliminates the necessity for bail and for detention. Under the sponsorship of the Manhattan Bail Project, law students interviewed and appraised the responsibility of adult prisoners appearing in magistrates' felony courts and then either recommended or did not recommend that the person be released on promise to return to court at a given time for trial. Of the first 275 defendants released under this system, only three did not fulfill their promises.[10] Congress introduced a similar program into the federal court system in 1966, and many cities have introduced similar programs. More than 100 such bail-reform projects were operating in the late 1960s, but one study of them concluded that they are not effective because the main criteria imposed for release are linked to the middle-class life style: length of residence at current address, family ties, prior criminal record.[11] A 1970 survey showed that cities with these programs detained only 23 percent of their defendants while cities with traditional bail practices detained 36 percent.[12] Nevertheless, detention institutions remain clogged with suspects who are detained because they are unable to post bail.

Third, it has been suggested that bail would not be necessary if hearings and trials were more prompt.

As an alternative to the existing conditions of detention, bail has decided advantages. Perhaps the most important of these is that it permits persons who are merely accused of crime to avoid the financial hardships, the physical unpleasantness, and the punitive aspects of being detained in a police lockup, jail, or other detention institution.

PUNITIVE ASPECTS OF DETENTION

It is obviously important that all persons accused of crimes be available for hearings and trials. It is equally important, however, that the method of securing the presence of accused persons at the court proceedings should involve a minimum of hardship on them, since they might be innocent. Strictly speaking, the British and American policy of presuming innocence until guilt is proved refers only to the preponderance of evidence in a trial in court. The rule is that the defendant is assumed to be innocent rather than guilty, and the evidence must then be sufficient to convict. The policy of presuming innocence is, with limitations required by practical considerations, considered sound social policy in other situations. But if the rule were made absolute, there would be no justification even for arrest. Similarly, practical considerations make it necessary

10Herbert Sturz, "An Alternative to the Bail System," *Federal Probation*, 23:12–17, 1962.

11Paul B. Wice, *Freedom for Sale* (Lexington, Mass.: Lexington Books, 1974).

12Paul Wice and Rita James Simon, "Pretrial Release: A Survey of Alternative Practices," *Federal Probation*, 34:60–3, 1970.

that the state detain some of the persons suspected of crime, thus imposing hardships on persons who might be innocent.

The imposition of these hardships could be nonpunitive, but it is, in fact, punitive. The constitutional view is that even when persons are actually guilty, they are to be dealt with, so far as practicable, on the presumption of innocence. In this view, detention is something like confiscation of property for public purposes, or drafting men for the army in time of war, or requiring attendance at public schools, or summoning citizens for service on a jury. These legal actions impose hardships on citizens, but the hardships are reduced to a minimum consistent with public purpose, and they are not deliberately imposed on the assumption that the hurt will be good for society or the individual being hurt. Furthermore, the person arrested for the first time is likely to be in a very impressionable condition, and sympathetic handling and understanding will have great effect at this point, just as unnecessary and unwarranted hardships will be very damaging. In general, therefore, the official view is that those suspects who are detained awaiting trial should be treated at least as well as citizens who are drafted into the army, and that the conditions of life in a detention institution should be at least equal to those in an army camp.

Just as police officers sometimes argue that punitive arrest methods are justified because many guilty persons avoid conviction, it is sometimes suggested that the hardships of detention should be severe and punitive. Generally, the argument is that a large proportion of guilty persons avoid official punishment and that they should at least be made to suffer severe hardships in detention, as a deterrent to others or as a retributive or reformative measure. Any hardship imposed with this argument in mind is punishment. Even when this unofficial policy is not voiced, it is the informal principle on which most detention institutions are operated. The innocent are punished along with the guilty. This may be observed in the types of institutions that are used as places of detention and in the manner in which these institutions are maintained and operated.

Types of Detention Institutions

The institutions used for detention are of the following four types: station lockups, small-town municipal jails or lockups, county jails, and special detention institutions for women and children.

Station lockups are maintained in connection with police precinct stations in large cities. Few criminals serve sentences in these institutions, and few suspected persons are held for court proceedings for more than a few days. Persons arrested in the precinct are kept in custody until arrangements for a preliminary hearing or a trial can be made, or they are released without trial after a few hours.

Small-town municipal jails usually are under control of police departments or marshals, and they resemble city police-station lockups. However, in addition to persons awaiting hearings or trials, the populations of these institutions include offenders serving short sentences usually in lieu of payment of fines ordered by the court. Ordinarily the personnel of these institutions make few, if any, distinctions between those persons awaiting court proceedings and those being punished. There are about 11,000 police and village lockups in the United States.

County jails usually are under the control of the sheriff, and they generally are used for three different purposes. First, they serve as lockups for persons arrested by the sheriff's staff and awaiting trials or hearings. Ordinarily, if the court to which a person is taken after having been detained in a police, village, or county lockup has final jurisdiction, as in misdemeanor cases, it tries the case and either releases the individual or fixes a penalty. But if the court does not have final jurisdiction in a case and serves to provide a preliminary hearing only, it may discharge the suspect from custody or release the suspect on bail, or commit the suspect to the county jail to await further proceedings by a higher court. A second purpose of county jails, then, is to serve as detention institutions for persons who are accused of felonies, who have been unable to post bail, and who, in preliminary hearings, have been ordered to await disposition by higher courts. Third, county jails are used as penal institutions, ordinarily for misdemeanants whose sentences are under one year. No serious attempt is made to change or help these offenders, and they are not ordinarily carefully segregated from those persons merely awaiting court proceedings.

Special institutions for children have been developed in about 10 percent of the juvenile-court jurisdictions (usually counties) in the United States. These jurisdictions have established about 300 special juvenile detention institutions.[13] Youngsters of juvenile-court age are generally permitted to remain at home after a complaint is made against them; a summons is issued for the parents to bring the children to court at the appointed time. But it is frequently necessary to detain juveniles because of the serious nature of the offense, the condition of the home, or the possibility that the youth will run away from the jurisdiction of the court. In about 90 percent of all juvenile-court jurisdictions, ordinary jails and lockups are used as places of detention for juveniles, but in most states recent laws have placed restrictions on this use of such institutions. In general practice, however, these laws are frequently violated, especially in districts that do not have specially organized juvenile courts.[14] In at least forty-five states, juveniles are confined in local and county jails along with adults.[15] The personnel of juvenile detention institutions usually consider mere detention to be insufficient, just as do the personnel of detention institutions for adults. The important difference between

13National Criminal Justice Information and Statistics Service, Law Enforcement Assistance Administration, U.S. Department of Justice, *Children in Custody: A Report on Juvenile Detention and Correctional Facilities* (Washington: Government Printing Office, 1971).

14Daniel Skoler, "Future Trends in Juvenile and Adult Community-Based Corrections," *Juvenile Court Judges Journal*, 21:99–103, 1971.

15Rosemary C. Sarri, *Under Lock and Key: Juveniles in Jails and Detention* (Ann Arbor, Mich.: National Assessment of Juvenile Corrections, University of Michigan, 1974), pp. 5, 29. See also Thomas R. Phelps, *Juvenile Delinquency: A Contemporary View* (Pacific Palisades, Calif.: Goodyear, 1976), pp. 157–85.

them is that in most adult institutions the desire is to supplement detention with punishment, while in most juvenile institutions the desire is to supplement detention with a positive interventionist program.

The Maintenance and Operation of Detention Institutions

On any given day, about 150,000 persons are confined in the nation's jails; about 60 percent of these persons are awaiting trial or are in other stages of adjudications, and about 40 percent are serving sentences. About ten years ago, more than 19,000 persons were employed to staff American lockups, jails, and workhouses. Of these, only 500—about 3 percent—performed rehabilitative duties, and some of the 500 were employed on a part-time basis. The national average is one psychologist for each 4,300 inmates and one teacher for each 1,300 inmates. However, most of the professional personnel work in the larger institutions, leaving the vast majority of local institutions with custodial personnel only.[16] The overwhelming majority of the persons employed in jails are persons whose primary duties are elsewhere but happen to include the handling and servicing of prisoners. Most of these persons are law-enforcement officers.

In general, the physical conditions in the county and city detention institutions are decidedly worse than the conditions in the state prisons where criminals are confined after conviction of serious offenses. Those who are officially presumed to be innocent, some of whom are actually innocent and almost all of whom are detained because they do not have the money or influence to obtain release on bail, are subjected to conditions much worse than those for persons already convicted of serious crimes. Criticisms of these conditions have been made for nearly a century, by both American and foreign observers. The president of the International Prison Congress in 1907 said that nothing as bad as the American jails had been known in the history of the world except in the prisons of Turkey in the thirteenth century. The conditions most frequently criticized at present are filth, vermin, fire hazard, inadequate food, inadequate plumbing, inadequate lighting and ventilation, lack of segregation of persons with infectious diseases, universal idleness, lack of provision for medical care, special privileges for favored prisoners (sometimes including a key to the prison door), and inadequate security against escape. The 1970 national jail census found that 86 percent of the nation's jails had no recreational facilities, 89 percent no educational facilities, and 49 percent no medical facilities.[17]

Fishman, who was inspector of jails for the federal government for some time, defined the jail thus:

Jail: An unbelievably filthy institution in which are confined men and women serving sentences for misdemeanors and crimes, and men and women not under sentence who are

---

[16]President's Commission on Law Enforcement and Administration of Justice, *Task Force Report: Corrections* (Washington: Government Printing Office, 1967), p. 75.

[17]Sarri, *Under Lock and Key,* pp. 11–12.

simply awaiting trial. With few exceptions, having no segregation of the unconvicted from the convicted, the well from the diseased, the youngest and most impressionable from the most degraded and hardened. Usually swarming with bedbugs, roaches, lice, and other vermin; has an odor of disinfectant and filth which is appalling; supports in complete idleness countless thousands of able-bodied men and women, and generally affords ample time and opportunity to assure inmates a complete course in every kind of viciousness and crime. A melting pot in which the worst elements of the raw material in the criminal world are brought forth blended and turned out in absolute perfection.[18]

Almost fifty years later, a federal judge characterized an Ohio jail as follows, and his description fits most other American jails at present:

When the total picture of confinement in the Lucas County Jail is examined, what appears is confinement in cramped and over crowded quarters, lightless, airless, damp and filthy with leaking water and human wastes, slow starvation, deprivation of most human contacts, except with others in the same subhuman state, no exercise or recreation, little if any medical attention, no attempt at rehabilitation, and for those who in despair or frustration lash out at their surroundings, confinement, stripped of clothing and every last vestige of humanity in a sort of oubliette. . . . If the constitutional provision against cruel and unusual punishment has any meaning, the evidence in this case shows that it has been violated. The cruelty is a refined sort, much more comparable to the Chinese water torture than to such crudities as breaking on the wheel. The evidence also shows that, in this case at least, the punishment is unusual.[19]

From the viewpoint of differential association, the fundamental criticism of the jail is that it permits association of convicted and unconvicted prisoners. About one-fourth of the inmates in county jails are awaiting trial, and most of the others are serving sentences imposed after conviction. This official system of blending suspects and criminals together physically and psychologically, and of thereby labeling suspects as criminals, probably influences many suspects to identify with criminals. The sheriff directing one of the nation's largest county jails, in Cook County (Chicago), Illinois, criticized his own and other county jails as follows:

County jails, as presently constituted, are for all practical purposes agencies for the creation of a community of interest on the part of those who violate the law. They establish contacts and a continuing association among law violators. They afford a machinery for perpetuating and transmitting the culture and tradition of crime. And they insure the maturation of delinquent and criminal attitudes as well as professional criminal skills among the young by the indiscriminate lodging of all types of persons under one framework of concrete and steel.[20]

It is possible to exaggerate the importance of contacts with convicted criminals, however. It is not clear that detention in a city police lockup in which no

---

[18]Joseph F. Fishman, *Crucibles of Crime* (New York: Cosmopolis Press, 1923), pp. 13–14.
[19]*Jones* v. *Wittenberg*, 323 F. Supp. 93 (N.D. Ohio 1971). At p. 99.
[20]Joseph D. Lohman, *Mid-Term Report* (Chicago: Cook County Sheriff's Office, 1956), p. 23.

convicted prisoners are held is any less injurious than detention in a county jail in company with convicted prisoners. Detention under existing conditions involves association with behavior patterns favorable to crime even when it does not involve association with criminals. Inmates confined in detention institutions where there are no convicted criminals can learn to identify with criminal types, can learn criminal techniques, and can learn verbalizations favorable to violation of the law.[21] It is reasonable to assume that jails are even more important than prisons in providing opportunities for these types of learning.

Explanations of Punitive Conditions in Jails

Punitive and repulsive physical conditions in detention institutions have existed for centuries and have become traditional. In England, John Howard's investigations during the latter part of the eighteenth century and Elizabeth Fry's work during the early part of the nineteenth century were investigations of institutions similar to our police lockups, for the prisons in those periods were used primarily for detention prior to trial. Criticisms of the jails in America—made three-quarters of a century ago, a half-century ago, a quarter of a century ago, and only a few years ago—all sound very familiar. The persistence of physically unpleasant punitive conditions may be explained partially by the expense of improvements and by inertia among officials. As one authority stated: "Jails mean *jobs*. Jails mean *income*. Jails mean *power*. Jails mean *influence*. Jails mean *patronage*. Jails mean *votes*. Against such a formidable defense the offense must devise an attack of atomic power."[22] Thus sheriffs and other officials responsible for detention institutions resist change because the existing conditions are highly profitable, both in the form of influence and power and in income. Some jailers are paid "turnkey" fees and are granted a certain sum for the daily maintenance of each prisoner in their custody. If the sum is five dollars and the daily costs can be reduced to three dollars, the jailer is able to pocket two dollars per prisoner per day. In some communities numerous arrests are made solely to maximize these fees. Although the incumbents have merely inherited, not created, such a system, it is understandable that they should resist attempts to improve the physical conditions in prisons by eliminating it.

Resistance of officials, however, is not a sufficient explanation; there is some popular sympathy with existing conditions. This sympathy takes two different forms. First, accusation is, in fact, taken as equivalent to proof of criminality. The person who is arrested and detained for court proceedings is identified with the persons already convicted of crime. Then, because the societal reaction to the crimes of persons confined in jails usually is punitive, those who are accused but

[21]See Gerald G. O'Connor, "The Impact of Initial Detention upon Male Delinquents," *Social Problems*, 18:194–9, 1970.

[22]Roberts J. Wright, "The Jail and Misdemeanant Institutions," in *Contemporary Correction*, ed. Paul W. Tappan (New York: McGraw-Hill, 1951), pp. 310–22.

not convicted are punished. Most ordinary citizens have so few contacts with suspects and criminals that they cannot make a clear distinction between them. They know only that jails, like prisons, are for bad people. The mass communication media ordinarily report in some detail the cases of persons who have been convicted, but only in the most sensational cases are acquittals reported. Also, many citizens take the strange position that a person who is accused of crime is somehow at fault and, hence, deserving of punishment. This assumption is usually stated as a rhetorical question: "If he isn't guilty, why would the police arrest him and lock him up?"

Second, only the poor are held in jail without bail, and it is traditional to discriminate against the poor. A person of wealth or moderate comfort can secure release on bail in most instances. Persons in detention institutions, then, are not likely to be middle class; they are likely to be unemployed and unattached, and therefore to be viewed as undesirable if not deviant simply because they do not conform to middle-class ideals regarding "respectability." They cannot reasonably expect middle-class citizens to be anything other than indifferent. The poor do not have the power or influence to change the situation. Those few persons who do have power and influence and who have been in jail, whether they were found guilty or not, try to conceal this fact rather than advertise it. Perhaps the situation will be improved in this country as in England, where Bernard Shaw said that the day of improvement was at hand because in a short time every honest man would have spent some time in jail and would know what jails were like.

ALTERNATIVES TO PRESENT-DAY DETENTION INSTITUTIONS

Many persons and agencies have suggested programs for modifying the methods of detention. In general, these suggestions have been made with consideration for the view that the methods of detention should conform to the constitutional notion that accused persons should be handled as though they were innocent. Also, it is commonplace to say that certain modifications will reduce the crime rates by eliminating many contacts with criminal-behavior patterns and by increasing the prestige of law-enforcement officers. Finally, it is believed that detention facilities for adults should, like those for juveniles, adopt methods that will at least assist accused persons with the problems arising from the fact that they have been detained. The following are some of the suggestions that have been made:[23]

(1) Bail and release on personal recognizance should be used more extensively.

(2) The number of arrests should be reduced. In some cities, well over half of the arrests result in release without prosecution. In addition, between a third and a

---

[23]This list is adapted from a more inclusive list of recommendations for reform by Hans W. Mattick, "The Contemporary Jails of the United States: An Unknown and Neglected Area of Justice," in *Handbook of Criminology*, ed. Daniel Glaser (Chicago: Rand McNally, 1974), pp. 777–848.

half of the persons who are prosecuted are dismissed without conviction. It is not possible to determine what proportion of the dismissals results from inefficiency of the courts, but it is probable that both the courts and the police share responsibility. The summons and on-the-spot citation by a police officer may be substituted for arrest in many cases. Citations are now used almost exclusively for violations of traffic regulations, but use of the summons in lieu of an arrest warrant is authorized in the federal system. A Department of Justice study found no substantial default problem in any of the sixty federal districts that use the summons, or even a mere letter, to bring to court those accused of misdemeanors or of violations of regulatory statutes.[24] Contra Costa County, California, uses citations extensively for all misdemeanor offenses. Unless an arrest is considered necessary to the protection of the community, court processes, or the defendant, misdemeanor suspects are released at the scene of their alleged offenses if they can identify themselves. The police officer checks with headquarters through a computer-based record system, and if the defendant is not wanted for another crime, a summons is issued.

(3) The courts should dispose of cases more rapidly. The shorter the period of detention of the average prisoner, the smaller is the number detained at a particular time. A survey of the Cook County, Illinois, jail reported that the jail would contain only 29 people at one time if the average period of detention were one day, 200 if it were one week, 887 if it were one month, and 10,642 if it were one year. A recent study of pretrial delay in felony cases shows that the procedures now in use were designed for an eighteenth-century agrarian society that no longer exists.[25] Detained defendants should be given priority in setting trial dates, and the states should impose a statutory limit on the length of time an unconvicted person may be detained, as the federal government has done. Moreover, persons detained prior to trial and thereafter sentenced should be given full credit for all time spent in custody prior to commencement of sentence.

(4) The physical conditions and the programs of jails and lockups should be improved. Perhaps this is the suggestion that is made most frequently. Even if the number of persons committed and the length of the period of detention were greatly reduced, it would still be sound policy to improve the health and sanitary conditions of the places of detention. However, this is not at all an easy suggestion to follow, because the detained persons include many who are intoxicated at the time of arrest, or are diseased, or are ignorant of the conditions of hygiene. But institutions can be made fireproof; sanitary plumbing can be installed; facilities for bathing can be made available; heat and light can be provided; sick and diseased persons can be segregated; organized activities can be provided. Some jails provide opportunities for employment, recreational activities, reading,

---

[24]President's Commission, *Task Force Report: The Courts*, p. 41.

[25]Lewis R. Katz, Lawrence B. Litwin, and Richard H. Bamberger, *Justice Is the Crime: Pretrial Delay in Felony Cases* (Cleveland, Ohio: Case Western Reserve Press, 1976).

organized educational classes, moving pictures, and counseling. The complete and practically universal idleness of the jail and lockup could be eliminated.

It is suggested, further, that such standards should be maintained by a system of inspection by state officials, who would have authority to close the jails and lockups that do not meet requirements. Indiana, Minnesota, New Jersey, Oklahoma, and Wisconsin now have regular state supervision of jails and lockups, and certain other states inspect jails and lockups "on complaint." Virginia has adopted a plan whereby a state board is given almost complete control over jails and lockups; the board is authorized to prescribe minimum standards for the institutions and to prohibit the confinement of prisoners in institutions not meeting the standards. In Connecticut, Delaware, and Rhode Island, the state has assumed responsibility for jail operations.[26]

Also, it is pointed out that if the standards mentioned are to be maintained, it probably will be necessary to enlarge the geographical area served by particular detention institutions. The county apparently is too small a unit to maintain an institution of this nature, especially if the convicted prisoners and the responsible unconvicted prisoners are removed. Counties could combine, or the state could establish jail districts, or the state could own and operate the places of detention in which persons are held awaiting trial for longer than two or three days.[27] Moreover, if larger units were organized, specialized institutions for special classes could be established. This has already started in the detention institutions for women and children but can be developed outside of the large cities only by state management of the places of detention.

(5) Persons awaiting trial should be separated from convicted criminals. Ordinarily, authorities believe that this could best be accomplished by maintaining convicted prisoners in one institution and detained persons in another. Indiana, California, Wisconsin, Virginia, and numerous other states operate camps, farms, and colonies that take many of the convicted misdemeanants out of the county jails. Some cities and counties have provided farm work for convicted prisoners, who are housed separately from those awaiting trial. Numerous jurisdictions have established halfway houses and detoxification centers for chronic alcoholics, thus removing them from detention centers.

In Wisconsin, misdemeanants sentenced under the Huber law are permitted to work at regular jobs outside the jail. About one-third of the persons sentenced to Wisconsin's county jails are sentenced under this law; of these persons, about 40 percent actually are employed outside the jails. Work furlough, work release, or

---

[26] National Criminal Justice Information and Statistics Service, Law Enforcement Assistance Administration, U.S. Department of Justice, *National Jail Census, 1970* (Washington: Government Printing Office, 1970). See also idem, *The Nation's Jails* (Washington: Government Printing Office, 1975); and *Survey of Inmates of Local Jails* (Washington: Government Printing Office, 1972).

[27] This suggestion is not necessarily at variance with the current argument that more convicted felons should be kept in their home counties rather than transported to state and federal prisons. See John Conrad, "Counties and the Correctional Crisis," *American County*, 37:15–19, 1972.

community work programs—the terms are synonymous—are now operating in about 40 percent of the nation's jails. A study of a California program found the recidivism rates to be about the same for a work-furlough group and a non-furlough group.[28]

(6) Dependents of those detained in jail awaiting trial should be cared for by the state or other governmental unit in charge of the jail. If the state finds it necessary to detain in an institution a person against whom a charge of crime is made, the duty of providing for those dependent upon the detained person follows logically as a corollary. Whether the person is subsequently found guilty should make no difference in the care during the period of detention before trial.

(7) Those who are acquitted should be indemnified for financial losses suffered as the result of the detention. Such a system has prevailed for many years in some European countries. Massachusetts, in 1911, authorized indemnification, in case of acquittal or discharge, for financial losses if the detention in awaiting trial exceeded six months. But there is no reason for such a long minimum period. The general arguments in favor of indemnification are as follows: First, when private property is taken for public use, the owner is compensated; likewise, when the state requires individuals to give time or services to the state, they are compensated. The state does not in these cases compensate the person who is deprived of property because the state was enriched, but because the individual suffered a loss at the hands of the state. The person detained for trial is deprived of his or her liberty for the sake of public welfare; if the trial shows that this detention was not justified, the accused should be compensated for the loss suffered in the public interest. Second, in workmen's-compensation laws the state has ruled that an employer, though not at fault, must compensate a worker for injuries. The principal involved in indemnification is the same as that of workmen's compensation laws—spread the loss on the public rather than impose it on one individual. Third, indemnification would be desirable because it would tend to prevent needless arrests, speed up the courts, and create a public opinion favorable to greater efficiency in police departments, detention institutions, and courts.

DETENTION OF WITNESSES

The material witness who is detained in a city or county jail awaiting trial has received little consideration. Some years ago the newspapers reported a case of a man who was knocked down and robbed; he could not furnish financial security for his appearance at the trial, and he was therefore detained in jail for three months as a material witness, while the person accused of the crime was released on bail. Although witnesses make up an insignificant percentage of the persons handled by law-enforcement and detention personnel, it is important that their rights be respected. Performance of the task of testifying for purposes of public

---

[28] Alvin Rudolph, T. C. Esselstyn, and George L. Kirkham, "Evaluating Work Furlough," *Federal Probation*, 35:34–8, 1971.

justice should not impose a hardship on these persons. They, like the persons accused of the crimes, are held at the demand of the state and likewise should not be detained unless the necessity is definite; if detained they should be treated in a decent manner. The American Law Institute has proposed that if a witness is unable to secure financial sureties within three days, he or she should be examined in the presence of the defendant and the deposition thus obtained should be used in further court proceedings if the witness is unable to attend.

SUGGESTED READINGS

Ares, Charles, & Herbert Sturz. "Bail and the Indigent Accused." *Crime and Delinquency*, 8:12–20, 1962.

Cromwell, P. F., Jr., ed. *Jails and Justice*. Springfield, Ill.: Charles C Thomas, 1975.

Flynn, Edith Elizabeth. "Jails and Criminal Justice." Chap. 2 in *Prisoners in America*, ed. Lloyd E. Ohlin, pp. 49–85. Englewood Cliffs, N.J.: Prentice-Hall, 1973.

Freed, Daniel J., & Patricia Wald. *Bail in the United States*. Washington: National Conference on Bail and Criminal Justice, 1964.

Friedland, Martin L. *Detention Before Trial: A Study of Criminal Cases Tried in the Toronto Magistrates' Courts*. Toronto: University of Toronto Press, 1965.

Goldfarb, Ronald L. *Ransom: A Critique of the American Bail System*. New York: Harper and Row, 1965.

Goldfarb, Ronald L. *Jails: The Ultimate Ghetto of the Criminal Justice System*. Garden City, N.Y.: Doubleday, 1975.

Mattick, Hans W., & Alexander B. Aikman. "The Cloacal Region of American Corrections," *Annals of the American Academy of Political and Social Science*, 381:109–18, 1969.

Mattick, Hans W., & Ronald P. Sweet. *Illinois Jails: Challenge and Opportunity for the 1970's*. Chicago: Center for Studies in Criminal Justice, University of Chicago Law School, 1970.

McGee, Richard A. "Our Sick Jails." *Federal Probation*, 35:3–8, 1971.

Neubauer, David W. *Criminal Justice in Middle America*. Morristown, N.J.: General Learning Press, 1974.

Newman, Charles L., & Barbara R. Price. *Jails and Drug Treatment*. Beverly Hills, Calif.: Sage, 1977.

O'Connor, Gerald G. "The Impact of Initial Detention upon Male Delinquents." *Social Problems*, 18:194–9, 1970.

Pappas, Nick, ed. *The Jail: Its Operation and Management*. Washington: U.S. Bureau of Prisons, 1970.

Queen, S. A. *The Passing of the County Jail*. Menasha, Wis.: Banta, 1920.

Rudoff, Alvin, T. C. Esselstyn, & George L. Kirkham. "Evaluating Work Furlough." *Federal Probation*, 35:34–8, 1971.

Suffet, Frederic. "Bail Setting: A Study of Courtroom Interaction." *Crime and Delinquency*, 12:318–31, 1966.

Wice, Paul B. *Freedom for Sale*. Lexington, Mass.: Lexington Books, 1974.

Wice, Paul, & Rita James Simon. "Pretrial Release: A Survey of Alternative Practices." *Federal Probation*, 34:60–3, 1970.

18

The Criminal Court

The substantive laws with which criminal courts are concerned all contain threats of punishment for infraction of specified rules. The courts thus are organized primarily for implementing the punitive reaction to crime. But the organization of courts also allows court personnel to use discretion both as to what the punishment shall be and which guilty persons actually are to be punished. Also, in recent years a number of provisions for the use of nonpunitive and interventionist methods by the criminal courts have been made, but the threat of punishment remains, even for the recipients of the interventionist measures. For example, it has become possible for courts to grant probation to some offenders, but the probationer is constantly under the threat of punishment; probationers who do not maintain the conditions of their probation are imprisoned. Further, as the clinical or treatment method of intervention became more popular, many persons believed the criminal courts should be solely concerned with determining the guilt or innocence of accused persons, leaving the problem of sentencing criminals entirely to persons in the executive branch of government. Under these conditions, the organization of the court system, the duties and activities of court personnel, and even the nature of the trial took on bureaucratic characteristics more in keeping with the "adjustment principle" than with the "law-enforcement principle" of criminal-law administration.[1]

ORGANIZATION OF THE AMERICAN COURT SYSTEM

Although there are variations among the states, the organization of the criminal courts includes the following types: (1) *Lower courts*, such as justice-of-the-peace courts, police courts, magistrates' courts, municipal courts, and recorders' courts.

[1] See Chapter 15, above.

These inferior courts serve the dual purpose of rendering final decisions, subject to appeal, in minor cases and holding preliminary hearings in felony cases. They also consider release on bail or on the suspected person's own recognizance. (2) *Trial courts*, such as county courts, district courts, circuit courts, superior courts, and quarter-sessions courts. The county is usually taken as the unit, even when the circuit includes several counties. These courts render final decision, subject to appeal, in cases that have come up for trial from the preliminary hearings. They also dispose of cases appealed from the inferior courts. (3) *Specialized branches* of the above-mentioned courts, such as traffic courts, morals courts, and domestic-relations courts. These courts deal only with specified types of offenses. (4) *Appellate courts and supreme courts.* Such courts take cases on appeal from the trial courts and have original jurisdiction in a restricted field.

Each of these courts is customarily a separate unit. The justices of the peace and the magistrates in a particular city ordinarily act without reference to each other or to other courts, except to consider the possibility of reversal of decisions by higher courts. Proposals for unification and simplification of court structures have long been part of suggestions for court reform. A slight trend toward coordination of the different courts is evident. In many jurisdictions, for example, municipal courts or magistrates' courts are now organized on a city or county basis, replacing scattered and uncoordinated justices of the peace and police courts. The chief magistrates of these lower-court systems have wide powers in regard to the assignment of magistrates and cases and in regard to organization of work, but they have very little power concerning the actual work of judging. The federal courts were unified in 1922. In 1962 Colorado transferred the work of its justice-of-the-peace courts to county courts; Vermont created district courts to replace municipal courts in 1965; and in the late 1970s Alabama, Indiana, Iowa, Kansas, and Kentucky streamlined their judicial systems, primarily by elimination of some or all of the limited- and special-jurisdiction courts.[2]

The development of state judicial councils is another example of the trend toward centralization of court administration. Such councils collect statistics and make suggestions for new legislation dealing with changes in court procedures and administration. Also, in some states, associations of judges and prosecuting attorneys have taken positive action toward coordination of the various units in the court system.

It is frequently suggested that all the work of criminal-justice agencies should be integrated. In recent years, especially, it has been commonly assumed that there is a unitary "criminal-justice system" and that this system ought to be made to operate more efficiently, thus punishing a larger percentage of all persons arrested, and inflicting more pain on them as well. According to this plan, each legislature

[2] National Criminal Justice Information and Statistics Service, Law Enforcement Assistance Administration, U.S. Department of Justice, *National Survey of Court Organization, 1977 Supplement to State Judicial Systems* (Washington: Government Printing Office, 1977).

would be in command of the police departments, courts, jails and prisons, probation and parole bureaus, and related agencies in its territory, somewhat as a colonel commands the army troops in a specific area.

But this assumption is unrealistic, as is the "war on crime" plan implicitly or explicitly based on it. The principle holding that legislative, executive, and judicial powers should be separated and balanced means that criminal-justice agencies frequently must be working at cross-purposes. Moreover, as we noted earlier, to demand that a rank-oriented bureaucracy conduct a war on crime is to ignore the fact that criminal-justice personnel are experts who, for that reason, cannot simply be commanded or otherwise ordered to perform their duties in a specified way.[3] In courthouses, specifically, grave injustices would be done if judges, prosecutors, defense attorneys, and others were all under the command of one officer; if, consistently, all judges were told that they must either decide cases in a way specified by a chief judge or risk punishment; if all prosecutors were told that they must prosecute in a specified way, and so on. The courthouse is above all a place where each juror, judge, probation officer, prosecutor, and defense lawyer is to be wise, judicious, and compassionate, thus in practice softening some of the harsh punishments that legislators have stipulated as appropriate for various crimes.

INITIATION OF PROSECUTION AND THE GRAND JURY

Prosecution in misdemeanor cases is customarily initiated by complaint of a victim or a witness; frequently the police officer who makes the arrest is the complaining witness. The complaint and evidence are presented in the lower court, and the whole matter is settled there, subject to an occasional appeal.

In felony cases the procedure is more complicated. The complaint is made by a victim or witness and a prosecuting attorney hears the evidence. If this official, who like police officers is a member of the executive branch of government, decides that the case should be prosecuted, the evidence is presented to a lower court. If the lower court decides that the evidence is sufficient, the prosecutor must, in some states, present the evidence again to a grand jury.[4] If the grand jury regards the evidence as sufficient, the offender is indicted[5] and then arraigned. The arraignment is a ritualistic procedure seemingly based on the assumption that

---

[3]See Chapter 15, above.

[4]The term *grand* came into use because in England the number of jurors, originally, was twenty-three, almost double the number composing the trial, or *petit*, jury—twelve. In some states, twenty-three is still the rule, but in other states, sixteen or less are required. In Michigan a single judge can perform the functions of a grand jury. See Seymor Gelber, "A Reappraisal of the Grand Jury Concept," *Journal of Criminal Law, Criminology, and Police Science*, 60:24–7, 1969; and LeRoy D. Clark, *The Grand Jury: The Use and Abuse of Political Power* (Chicago: Quadrangle Books, 1975).

[5]A charge issued by a grand jury on its own motion is called a *presentment* to distinguish it from an *indictment*, which is a charge requested by a prosecutor.

the defendants or their attorneys cannot read. The charges are read aloud in the courtroom and the defendant is asked to plead guilty or not guilty. If the defendant pleads not guilty, the case is scheduled for trial; and if it actually goes to trial, the prosecutor must present the evidence in a trial court, usually in several pretrial hearings as well as at the trial itself. The entire felony procedure thus involves (1) an informal hearing of the evidence by the prosecutor, (2) a formal preliminary hearing before a lower court, (3) a formal hearing before a grand jury, (4) pretrial hearings about the legality of the arrest, admissibility of the evidence, or other matters, and (5) the trial itself. Usually there are also several informal conferences of judge, prosecutor, and defense lawyer. The whole procedure is sometimes necessary even if the accused person pleads guilty.

The tendency, however, is toward permissive use of formal accusation by "information," and away from requirement of an indictment by a grand jury. At present only five states require indictments in all felony cases; twenty-two states demand that only serious offenses be initiated by grand-jury indictment; and twenty-three states permit prosecution of substantially all crimes by either information or indictment.[6] Those who favor the use of the information claim that the indictment does not protect the accused person, that it encumbers the whole process, that it delays decisions and thus facilitates the acquittal of the accused, that it is generally a perfunctory rubber-stamping of the prosecutor's evidence, and that it is a useless expense.[7] Those favoring the grand-jury system argue that the validity of these criticisms has by no means been demonstrated. The possibility of the indictment as a check on the prosecutor's information is desirable, even if it is seldom used.

The grand jury also has authority to initiate general investigations, but, since the evidence in most cases must be collected and presented by the prosecutor, this work has not been very effective. A severe criticism of the grand jury from this point of view was made some years ago by a grand-jury foreman, who showed the helplessness of a grand jury that was eager to make an investigation of banking practices, racketeering, police corruption, and other serious and organized forms of lawlessness. Because of the inactivity of the prosecutor in regard to these forms of lawlessness, the grand jury was confined to minor routine cases.[8]

Since about 1940 the Supreme Court has been holding that grand juries and trial juries alike should be bodies truly representative of the community, in the sense of being cross sections or representative samples from the community.

---

[6] W. Spain, "The Grand Jury Past and Present: A Survey," *American Criminal Law Quarterly*, 119:126–42, 1964.

[7] See William J. Campbell, "Eliminate the Grand Jury," *Journal of Criminal Law and Criminology*, 64:174–82, 1973; and Robert Gilbert Johnson, "The Grand Jury—Prosecutorial Abuse of the Indictment Process," *Journal of Criminal Law and Criminology*, 65:157–69, 1974.

[8] William Feathers, *Grand Jury Report* (Cuyahoga County, Ohio, December 21, 1933).

However, analyses of jury service in the United States have shown that the principle of a representative jury had not been operative.[9] Instead, the membership of grand juries and other juries still shows considerable economic and social bias. For example, until recently a Louisiana law automatically exempted women from jury service unless they volunteered to serve, and as a consequence in one parish less than 10 percent of the persons on jury lists were women, and no women were on the panels from which some juries were selected. The U. S. Supreme Court determined in 1975 that the Louisiana law was unconstitutional.[10]

THE PROSECUTOR

The prosecutor is the most important person working in the courthouse. This executive or his or her representative—an assistant or deputy district attorney—determines whether a particular case brought in by the police shall be prosecuted.[11] If it is determined that the case shall be prosecuted, the prosecutor then decides what crime or crimes the suspect shall be accused of. The rules governing the wording of felony accusations are very technical and legalistic, particularly those for indictments, in which even a misplaced comma can be a prosecutor's undoing. The technicalities have developed over the years as lawyers have found loopholes in formal accusations and other lawyers have closed them. They reflect a constitutional concern that the accused have precise and definite notice of the charges. The power of prosecutors is thus restricted by a requirement that they tell each defendant exactly what it is that the defendant must defend against.

On the other hand, the prosecutor is given tremendous power by the fact that a single act can involve more than one serious crime. For example, an ordinary burglary might involve burglary in the first degree (occupied dwelling at night), which carries a penalty, say, of imprisonment for from five years to life. This burglary might at the same time be simple burglary (any building, any time), which carries a penalty, say, of from one to five years. And the burglary might also involve grand larceny (stealing property worth a certain amount, such as $200), which carries a penalty, say, of from one to three years. The prosecutor handling the case thus has the power to charge the defendant with a crime potentially punishable by imprisonment for life or with a crime punishable by only a

---

[9] W. S. Robinson, "Bias, Probability, and Trial by Jury," *American Sociological Review*, 15:73–8, 1950; John S. De Cani, "Statistical Evidence in Jury Discrimination Cases," *Journal of Criminal Law and Criminology*, 65 234–8, 1974; and Hayward R. Alker, Jr., Carl Hosticka, and Michael Mitchell, "Jury Selection as a Biased Social Process," *Law and Society Review*, 11:9–41, 1976.

[10] Note, *Women's Rights Law Reporter*, 2:33–6, 1975. See also Adeline Gordon Levine and Claudine Schweber-Koren, "Jury Selection in Erie County: Changing a Sexist System," *Law and Society Review*, 11:43–55, 1976.

[11] Such prosecutorial discretion to prosecute or not to prosecute does not exist in all nations. In Sweden, for example, prosecutors are required to prosecute offenses that come to their knowledge; and in Denmark and Norway, prosecutors have a "relative duty" to prosecute. Paul C. Friday, "Sanctioning in Sweden: An Overview," *Federal Probation*, 40:48–55, 1976. See also Howard K. Becker and Einar O. Hjellemo, *Justice in Modern Sweden: A Description of the Components of the Swedish Criminal Justice System* (Springfield, Ill. Charles C. Thomas, 1976).

maximum of three years in prison. Indeed, in the example given, a prosecutor is authorized to charge all three crimes and to recommend that the sentences for them be served consecutively, so that the defendant could receive a sentence of one to three years, to be followed by a sentence of one to five years, to be followed by imprisonment for from five years to life.

Every information filed by a prosecutor automatically includes charges of all "lesser included offenses" that are linked with the more serious offenses that are charged, and this fact loads the prosecutor with additional discretionary power. Burglary charges, for example, imply misdemeanor charges of unlawful entry and trespassing because it is impossible to burglarize without entering unlawfully and trespassing. For that matter, it is impossible to enter unlawfully without trespassing. Similarly, a grand-theft charge automatically accuses the defendant of misdemeanor petty theft as well—it is impossible to steal a lot (grand) without stealing a little (petty).

A prosecutor's charge of burglary may easily be reduced to a charge of trespassing, but it is more difficult, technically, to raise a charge of trespassing to burglary. Accordingly, permitting prosecutors to include misdemeanor charges in their felony accusations enables a prosecutor to say, "If I can't get the defendant on the formal charge, I'll get him on something else." Or "If I formally charge the defendant with a felony or two, maybe he'll plead guilty to a misdemeanor." Further, the rules encourage prosecutors to play it safe, saying, "I really don't know whether to charge him with a serious crime or a minor one, so I'll hit him with the serious one and wait for developments."

It is nearly impossible to determine which of these concerns, if any, a prosecutor has in mind when an information is filed. Is the prosecutor merely trying technically to make the accusation fit the evidence? Is the prosecutor using the accusation of serious crime as a bludgeon for persuading the defendant to plead guilty to a lesser charge? Is the prosecutor looking for justice, hoping that later developments in the case will better enable the prosecutor, judge, and defense attorney to match the punishment to the criminal and the criminal's behavior?[12]

If a case goes to trial before a judge or a jury, the prosecutor is responsible for the organization and presentation of evidence before the court. This fact gives prosecutors additional power, for the technical efficiency of this enterprise greatly affects the decision of the judge or jury. The prosecutor is generally very influential in regard to sentencing also, suggesting to judge and jury the appropriate penalty. In addition, the prosecutor is tending to become a criminal investigator. Several prosecutors have made great reputations by vigorous law-and-order campaigns in which they have made investigations, secured evidence, and initiated prosecutions. In many counties the prosecutor has a staff of investigators. Also, the police departments in some jurisdictions assign a number of officers

[12]See Norman Abrams, "Prosecutorial Charge Decision Systems," *UCLA Law Review*, 23:1–56, 1975.

to the prosecutor's office for this work, and the number thus assigned seems to be increasing.

The prosecutor who does all these things is generally elected, and, as is true of other elected officials, this means that attention must be given to the wishes of politicians. It also means distraction of attention from official business for the sake of political activities. Small-county prosecutors work on a part-time basis for low salaries that are supplemented by income from private practice, often involving conflict of interest. The urban prosecutor must be careful not to antagonize any large organized group, and the record must show a large proportion of convictions in cases that go to trial. It is customary at election time for the prosecutor to present statistics on this point. Accordingly, prosecutors are in the business of producing favorable statistics. They avoid trials unless they are confident of conviction, or unless the case is well publicized. Also, it has been shown that the prosecutor's decision to prosecute is best understood in terms of an exchange system existing between the prosecutor's office and various groups that supply resources to it.[13]

Thus the prosecutor's reaction to crime must be, and is, selectively punitive. If a prosecutor is to continue in office or advance to a higher political office, it is necessary to seek the severest possible punishments in some cases, while intentionally failing to prosecute other cases. While he was on the Supreme Court, Justice William O. Douglas claimed that the quality of prosecutors had "markedly declined," and he observed that prosecutors "sometimes treat the courtroom not as a place of dignity, detached from the community, but as a place to unleash the fury of public passion."[14] The American Bar Association has noted, in this connection, that the prosecutor is expected to serve more than one end:

> The prosecutor has a dual role which reflects in a sense the ambivalence of public attitudes on law enforcement and is the source of some difficulties. On the one hand, the prosecutor is the leader of law enforcement in the community. He is expected to participate actively in marshaling society's resources against the threat of crime. . . . On the other hand, the office demands, and on sober thought the public expects, that the prosecutor will respect the rights of persons accused of crime. . . . The conflicting demands on a prosecutor may exert pressures on him which his sense of fairness as a lawyer rejects. Both his public responsibilities as well as his obligations as a member of the bar require that he be something more than a partisan advocate intent on winning cases.[15]

In larger communities the prosecutor has a staff of assistants—as many as 400 in Los Angeles. The assistant prosecutors secure their positions in many cases because they have been active in political organizations, and their reactions to crime must be similar to those of the prosecutor. They are generally inexperienced

---

[13]George P. Cole, "The Decision to Prosecute," *Law and Society Review,* 4:331–43, 1970. See also idem, ed., *Criminal Justice and Politics* (New York: Duxbury Press, 1972).

[14]William O. Douglas, "A Challenge to the Bar," *Notre Dame Lawyer,* 28:497–508, 1953.

[15]American Bar Association Project on Minimum Standards for Criminal Justice, *The Prosecution Function and the Defense Function* (New York: Institute of Judicial Administration, 1970).

in the work at the time they are appointed; those in small towns engage in private practice while in office, and they are dismissed when the political administration changes.

Although each state has a single code of criminal laws, the prosecutorial function, like the police and the courts, is fragmented. Texas has 317 county or local prosecutors. There is need for, at least, statewide coordination of and assistance to the many local prosecutors' offices. In Alaska, Delaware, and Rhode Island, state attorneys general have full responsibility for all prosecutions. This centralized procedure takes prosecutors out of local politics but it does not, of course, remove the office of prosecutor from the political arena in a larger sense. As Klonoski and Mendelsohn have noted, "Political considerations, broadly conceived, explain to a large extent who gets—and in what amounts and how—the 'good' [justice] that is produced by the legal system in the setting of local communities."[16] Further, the internal organization of the prosecutorial work in any courthouse must adjust to the work of police agencies, whether it is under the official direction of a local district attorney or the official direction of a state attorney general.

Like a corporation lawyer paid to do legal work for a company, the prosecutor is retained to do legal work for police agencies. Corporation lawyers come to identify with their clients, the corporations, and prosecuting attorneys come to identify with their clients, police officers. For this reason, perhaps, many prosecuting attorneys like to refer to themselves as "the chief law-enforcement officers" of their counties. This means, by and large, that they, like police executives, believe (or at least maintain publicly) that they are engaged in a war on crime in which they are commanding officers of a sort.[17] In fact, however, the prosecuting attorney or attorney general has little direct control over the everyday work of the assistant prosecutors, just as the police chief has little control over the routine on-the-street conduct of police officers. As Rosett and Cressey have pointed out, the administrator can use statistics to measure bureaucratic and technical efficiency in a prosecutorial agency—how many cases were prosecuted, how many trials were won—but such statistics cannot be the sole measures of an individual assistant's worth because every assistant district attorney, like every police officer and every other expert, must "play it by ear."[18]

THE LAWYER FOR THE DEFENSE
Legal defense for a person on trial was generally prohibited in early English law but has now become a general right. As early as 1701 the Pennsylvania legal code

---

[16] James Klonoski and Robert Mendelsohn, eds., *The Politics of Local Justice* (Boston: Little, Brown, 1970), p. xx.

[17] See David W. Neubauer, *Criminal Justice in Middle America* (Morristown, N.J.: General Learning Press, 1974), pp. 46–50.

[18] Arthur Rosett and Donald R. Cressey, *Justice by Consent: Plea Bargains in the American Courthouse* (Philadelphia: Lippincott, 1976), p. 128.

provided for the right of defendants to be represented by counsel. The Sixth Amendment to the United States Constitution provides, "In all criminal prosecutions, the accused shall enjoy the right . . . to have the assistance of counsel for his defence." It was some years, however, before this provision was held to be an aspect of due process of law binding on the states as well as the federal government, and to require that counsel be provided defendants who are indigent. The defendant's right to a lawyer in all felony cases was recognized as a principle of constitutional law in 1962. In 1972, the same right was extended to misdemeanor cases in which a jail term is possible, but most communities had been furnishing legal services to at least some indigent defendants for years. Most commonly, a judge simply assigned to a private attorney the duty of defending a person accused of crime.[19]

Unlike such assigned lawyers, public defenders work full time as government employees, just as prosecutors do. The public-defender system was found in ancient Rome, in fifteenth-century Spain, and in many European countries before it was adopted in Los Angeles (in 1913) and then spread to about half the states. In 1963, every state was required by court decision to provide public money for defense services for poor people accused of felonies, and the effect has been to create agencies that, whatever their name, tend to look like public defender's offices. These offices attract lawyers who are much more interested in doing justice than in processing legal cases, but indigent defendants tend to view them as incompetent bureaucrats.[20] In a few recent cases, state prisoners have won new trials after appeals based on the claim that, though they were furnished counsel at the trial, the service rendered by such counsel was so incompetent that the petitioner was in effect without the assistance of counsel.

Before the arrival of public defenders, a large proportion of all criminal cases was in the hands of a small number of criminal lawyers. Sixty percent of the offenders defended by private counsel in the Cook County (Chicago) Criminal Court during a two-year period were represented by the same thirty-five attorneys. Eighty percent were represented by forty-two attorneys.[21] Such specialists often were recommended to the accused persons by police officers and court attendants, and in more general ways were dependent on cooperation of government officials. For example, they had to deal with officials in arranging for interviews with their clients, in negotiating bail, in negotiating for a charge or a sentence, and in many other ways. Accordingly, they tended to be more active in politics than other lawyers, tended to find their friends among persons whose social status was lower than that of businessmen, and tended to substitute social skills of dealing with

---

[19]Studies of the comparative merits of different methods of providing legal services to the indigent are generally inconclusive. See Lee Silverstein, *The Defense of the Poor in Criminal Cases in American State Courts* (Chicago: American Bar Foundation, 1965).

[20]Jonathan Caspar, "Did You Have a Lawyer When You Went to Court? No, I Had a Public Defender," *Yale Review of Law and Social Action*, 4:127–36, 1971.

[21]Don T. Blackiston, *The Judge, the Defendant, and Criminal Law Administration* (unpublished Ph.D. dissertation, University of Chicago, 1952).

officials for the professional technical skills of dealing with the law.[22] Criminal lawyers were at one time as influential in preventing the enactment of bills for the reform of criminal procedure and of court organization as police executives and bail bondsmen now are.

Bar associations in some states have advocated voluntary defenders paid by the bar association or some other group as preferable to public defenders paid by the state. Under this method, popularly known as "judicare," a defendant who is unable to retain a lawyer would be permitted to select one from a list maintained by the court or some other public or private agency. This method is currently used only with reference to indigent persons involved in civil cases. It would be superior to the public-defender system, because under that system the defense attorney and the prosecutor are likely to be members of the same political party and therefore under political control.

Moreover, even when prosecutors and public defenders are somewhat free of politics, public defenders are likely to be at a great disadvantage simply because their budgets are so low. In 1971–1972, the various states, counties, and municipalities of the United States spent about $473 million on prosecution and $87 million on defense of the indigent; in terms of manpower, prosecution at all levels of government employed nearly 44,000 persons while indigent defense employed slightly more than 4,000.[23] Further, persons who work together on a day-to-day basis, even in a so-called adversary system, are likely to reach understandings and agreements that are not necessarily in the best interests of defendants. Because most cases are settled in conferences between the prosecution and the defense, these are important considerations.[24]

The role of the public defender and of other defense attorneys is quite ambiguous. As attorneys, defense lawyers are supposed to represent their clients to the best of their ability. But this duty is at variance with the need to dispose of cases quickly and cheaply. Consequently, unless an attorney's client is rich, the lawyer always balances a desire to ensure a just result for an individual client against a desire to move the case along. This conflict is most apparent among public defenders, whose clients are poor. They must meet the demands of clients as well as the demands of the government bureaus for which they work.

[22] Two good examinations of criminal lawyers are Jerome Carlin, *Lawyers on Their Own* (New Brunswick, N.J.: Rutgers University Press, 1962); and Arthur Lewis Wood, *Criminal Lawyer* (New Haven, Conn.: College and University Press, 1967). However, these studies were completed before the recent explosion in criminal-defender programs that followed constitutional rulings greatly expanding the right of poor defendants to a lawyer at public expense.

[23] National Criminal Justice Information and Statistics Service, Law Enforcement Assistance Administration, U.S. Department of Justice, *Expenditure and Employee Data for the Criminal Justice System 1971–72* (Washington: Goverment Printing Office, 1974).

[24] See David Sudnow, "Normal Crimes: Sociological Features of the Penal Code in a Public Defender Office," *Social Problems*, 12:255–76, 1965; and Jerome Skolnick, "Social Control in the Adversary System," *Journal of Conflict Resolution*, 11:52–61, 1967. The literature is reviewed in Olavi Maru, *Research on the Legal Profession* (Chicago: American Bar Foundation, 1972).

Generally speaking, the defense attorney tries to poke holes in the prosecutor's case but is seldom able to present witnesses or other affirmative proof of the client's innocence. Rather than trying to improve the client's situation, then, the attorney merely tries to prevent police officers and district attorneys from taking legal action against the client. Thus the attorney's work is *defense* in the strict sense of the term. Stated simply, the defense lawyer's duty is to hold the cruel aspects of the criminal law at bay, to get the client off, to get leniency, to get a lighter punishment. Often, then, the lawyer is in opposition to the criminal law itself, or at least to the aims of specific statutes.

A problem arises when the defense lawyer thinks the client is guilty, and most defense lawyers think most of their clients are guilty though not necessarily guilty as charged by the prosecutor. This opinion is not irrational. In the selective processes occurring soon after arrest, the cases of obviously innocent persons are dismissed by police officers and prosecutors. Further, the cases of persons whose arrests were obviously illegal are dismissed at pretrial hearings. Few defendants insist that they are blameless, or even that they should be presumed blameless. Given these facts, the defense lawyer is tempted to cooperate with the prosecutor, to "go along," to try to ensure that the client will get the punishment the client deserves and no more. The attorney must walk a tightrope, maintaining a balance between adversary defense on the one hand and cooperation on the other.[25]

Equally important to the defense lawyer's role is the fact that the attorney is bound to lose most cases. This is true because criminal cases are handled as though they are sporting events, with a winner and a loser, rather than as matters of justice. This structuring may or may not be based on the assumption that the state and the defendant are equals. Whatever the assumption in this respect, the fact of inequality is quite obvious in most cases: the indigent defendant with a somewhat indigent lawyer is no match for the majesty and power of the state. Further, the defense lawyer is not likely to identify with clients in the way that a prosecuting attorney identifies with police officers. Judged by middle-class standards, the clients are, generally speaking, too unattractive. They are unkempt, undisciplined, unattached, and—summarizing all these things—poor and "common." Moreover, they are criminals. "It is because defendants are poor that they are made the clients of an organization [public defender's office] rather than of men. Indigent defendants are perceived as welfare recipients, and guilty, undeserving ones at that, not as lawyer's clients."[26]

In some cases, such perceptions of defendants dampen defense attorneys' enthusiasm about "winning." In drug cases, for example, a defense attorney occasionally "wins" by showing a judge, in a pretrial hearing, that the evidence must be suppressed because it was obtained illegally, thereby making it necessary

[25] See Douglas E. Rosenthal, *Lawyer and Client: Who's in Charge?* (New York: Russell Sage Foundation, 1974).
[26] Rosett and Cressey, *Justice by Consent*, p. 139. See also Anthony Platt and Randi Pollock, "Channeling Lawyers: The Careers of Public Defenders," *Issues in Criminology*, 9:1–31, 1974.

for the judge to order the defendant released. But the defense attorney knows that such winning is also a form of losing—tomorrow the client will be back on the street dealing or stealing or pimping or prostituting to get money for drugs. There are few opportunities to advise such "winners" of their needs for assistance, as a corporation lawyer might do for a client, nor are there many opportunities for defense attorneys to obtain any assistance for defendants if they accept the advice. Given this fact, plus the realistic assumption that only a few clients are not guilty of *something*, the defense lawyer's job becomes more a matter of arranging pleas for the guilty than of defending the innocent.[27] Speaking of public defenders, Rosett and Cressey characterized the defense attorney's plight as follows:

Experience teaches the public defender that vigorously protecting each client from conviction and punishment will advance the criminal careers of some of them. He has trouble identifying with unattractive criminals of low social class. It is easy for him to identify more strongly with fellow lawyers—including judges and prosecutors—who symbolize law-abiding society. Moreover, he needs accolades from his fellow professionals more than he needs them from defendants. As time passes, he learns that he must be a good fellow, a moderate rather than an extremist, if he is to win these accolades. He might aspire to be either an adversary tiger or a man of justice—or some combination of both—but experience teaches him that his career will not be furthered by taking the most vigorous position in a case, especially if doing so means antagonizing the judge, the politically potent prosecutor, powerful law-and-order interest groups, or his boss.[28]

THE JUDGE

At present each American judge has two rather distinct and separate duties. First, the judge must preside over the proceedings for determining whether defendants are guilty, and in some such proceedings the judge must make the decision as to innocence or guilt. If the case is tried before a jury, the judge must supervise selection of jurors, enforce the rules of evidence, and declare law to the jury. In the courts of some states the judge may even express opinions to the jury about the innocence or guilt of the accused person, provided that it is made clear that the jury need not follow the opinion. The judge may order a jury to acquit a defendant, and when a jury returns a verdict of guilty, the judge who believes there is no evidence of guilt may set it aside and order a new trial. However, a judge may not order a jury to convict, and cannot set aside a verdict that is favorable to the defendant unless the verdict has been induced by fraud.

If the case is tried before a judge in what is called a "bench trial," as distinguished from a jury trial, the judge must similarly interpret the law and enforce the rules of evidence designed to ensure that innocent defendants are not found guilty and guilty defendants are not found innocent. In bench trials, judges also determine whether or not the defendant is guilty.

[27] See Neubauer, *Criminal Justice in Middle America*, pp. 210–16.
[28] Rosett and Cressey, *Justice by Consent*, p. 126.

Most judges, especially superior-court judges, are well qualified to perform this first duty. In some lower courts the magistrates are uneducated and even corrupt, but in most contemporary courts judges who are honest and capable are in control of a careful investigation of defendants who are tried, and they also attempt to ensure that defendants who plead guilty are in fact guilty and know the consequences of the plea. An approach to the Continental system, in which the judge actually directs the trial, would appear to be desirable. A former federal prosecutor and keen observer of the criminal-justice processes of France has gone even further, proposing that the primary responsibility for investigating crime, preparing accusations, and proving guilt be removed from the executive branch of government and assigned to the judicial branch. One judge would be in charge of this investigative agency and another would preside at the trial.[29]

The second duty of the judge is to impose just sentences according to the law on those persons who plead guilty or are found guilty.[30] When the influence of the classical school was at its height, such imposition of sentences was considered rather routine. Because the law ordained specific punishments for specific offenses, when it had been legally determined that the defendant had perpetrated an offense, the judge simply ordered administration of the appropriate punishment. In theory, the judge of two centuries ago had no choice in the matter, just as the present-day judge in some states theoretically has no choice about the imposition of a mandatory minimum for some offenders. Although there were many exceptions in practice, the offense, not the offender, was technically the object of attention.

But with the development of the neoclassical and positivist schools, and especially with the development of the interventionist reaction to crime, the offender became more important, and the judge was given a wide range of alternative methods for dealing with criminals. Generally speaking, the severity of the sentence is supposed to be matched with the background of the offender as well as the circumstances of the offense, in addition to being matched with the seriousness of the crime. Thus a judge may be permitted to place one murderer on probation, commit another murderer to prison for a year, and order the execution of still a third.

The consensus seems to be that contemporary judges do not impose sentences fairly, and there is a current trend toward narrowing their range of alternatives.[31] However, it is not at all certain that a return to a system of automatic sentences,

[29] Lloyd R. Weinreb, *Denial of Justice: Criminal Process in the United States* (New York: Free Press, 1976).

[30] For bibliographies, see Dorothy L. Tompkins, *Sentencing the Offender* (Berkeley: University of California Institute of Governmental Studies, 1971); and John Hogarth, *Sentencing as a Human Process* (Toronto: University of Toronto Press, 1971).

[31] See Marvin E. Frankel, *Criminal Sentences: Law Without Order* (New York: Hill and Wang, 1973); Julian C. D'Esposito, Jr., "Sentencing Disparity: Causes and Cures," *Journal of Criminal Law, Criminology and Police Science* 60:182–95, 1969; and W. Zumwalt, "The Anarchy of Sentencing in the Federal Courts," *Judicature,* 57:96–104, 1973.

stipulated in advance by legislatures, would be any more effective or fair.[32] The reasons for this are clear: if sentences are to be fair according to modern standards, it is necessary to know the background and character of the offender, and the possible effects on the offender and the community of punishing the offender in various ways. But such information is not available in most courthouses now, and it clearly would not be available if judges had no sentencing discretion at all.[33] Despite the modern emphasis on adjusting the penalty to the offender rather than to the general character of the crime the offender has committed (e.g., burglary), the fact is that courtroom procedures are designed merely to show the fact of guilt or innocence. Such evidence is not relevant to the task of determining what policy should be used in ordering the specific punishments of the persons who plead guilty or are proven guilty.

Attempts have been made to assist the judges by field investigations conducted by probation officers, by recommendations of psychiatrists, and in other ways. In California, judges must order an investigation by a probation officer before judgment is passed in felony cases, and presentence investigations are similarly required in about one-quarter of the states for certain classes of offenses, generally those punishable by imprisonment in excess of one year. Presentence reports are made in about 90 percent of federal felony cases. But in misdemeanor courts systematic gathering of sentencing information is virtually nonexistent, and even in superior courts the availability of the background information contained in presentence reports does not prevent wide variations from occurring in the individual sentencing behavior of judges.[34] Some judges sentence as many as 60 percent of the persons coming before them to imprisonment, while others in adjacent courts send only 30 percent to prison; some use probation in almost half the cases, while others use it in only 5 or 10 percent.[35]

For years it has been repeatedly recommended that the sentencing function be transferred to a dispositions board composed of representatives of disciplines concerned with human behavior, such as a psychiatrist, a social worker, a psychologist, a sociologist, and an educator.[36] To a degree, these recommendations have been followed, principally by permitting parole boards to determine the time

[32] See the arguments made by Edith Flynn, "Turning Judges into Robots?" *Trial*, 12:17–18, March 1976.

[33] Some philosophers are convinced that such information *never* will be available because it really is not possible to award an individual convicted of crime an equitable and just sentence. See Walter Kaufmann, *Without Guilt or Justice* (New York: Wyden, 1973), pp. 35–64.

[34] See Robert M. Carter and Leslie T. Wilkins, "Some Factors in Sentencing Policy," *Journal of Criminal Law, Criminology and Police Science*, 58:503–14, 1967.

[35] See, as an example of the many studies in sentencing disparities, K. D. Harris and R. P. Lura, "The Geography of Justice—Sentencing Variations in U.S. Judicial Districts," *Judicature*, 57:392–401, 1974.

[36] Nathaniel Cantor, "A Dispositions Tribunal," *Journal of Criminal Law and Criminology*, 29:51–61, 1931; Theodore Levin, "Sentencing the Criminal Offender," *Federal Probation*, 13:3–6, 1949; Richard A. Doyle, "A Sentencing Council in Operation," *Federal Probation*, 25:27–30, 1961; and John S. Palmore, "Sentencing and Correction: The Black Sheep of Criminal Law," *Federal Probation*, 26:6–14, 1962.

of release of the defendants who are sentenced to prison.[37] Similarly, many sentencing institutes and sentencing councils have been established, and some of them receive advice from behavioral scientists and social workers.[38] But no dispositions tribunal composed of behavioral scientists has appeared in a court-house, probably because there is doubt as to whether such tribunals could be any more effective and fair than the current system.

The fact is that the role of the sentencing authority is an ambiguous one, whether that authority be a judge acting alone, a judge acting with the assistance of probation officers and other experts, or a sentencing tribunal made up of experts. This ambiguity arises because of conflict between the "law-enforcement principle" and the "adjustment principle" we discussed earlier. Both principles are at work in all courthouses. There is widespread belief in the wisdom of the law-enforcement principle, namely that all persons should be punished equally, no matter what their social status. But there also is widespread belief in the wisdom of the adjustment principle, namely that punishments should vary because some burglars and burglaries are very different from other burglars and burglaries, some murderers and murders are very different from other murderers and murders, and so on. Judges, then, are supposed to order uniform punishments for burglaries or murders, no matter what the circumstances of the offense or the background of the offender, but they also are supposed to order different punishments for the various persons convicted of violating the same statute.

In satisfying these conflicting demands and directives, judges or other sentencing authorities are bound to be denounced as unfair. If a judge routinely and mechanically ordered each burglar coming before the court to serve the severe sentence prescribed by statute, the results clearly would be viewed as unjust. A professional burglar and a youth who broke into a neighbor's garage to steal some tools would be treated equally. But if the same judge noted differences among offenders and sentenced to prison a black indigent youth who broke into his neighbor's apartment while placing on probation a white middle-class youth who broke into his neighbor's garage, the results would clearly be viewed as unjust too.

In ordering punishments, the judge's task is to walk a thin line between these two conceptions of justice and injustice. (We have seen that this is the primary task of police officers, prosecutors, and defense lawyers as well.) A judge who leans too far toward uniformity and law enforcement is not displaying the judicious-ness, wisdom, and compassion that Americans expect of their judges. A judge who leans too far toward disparities in sentences is not exhibiting these characteristics either.

Judges' judicial and sentencing behavior is influenced by participation in social relationships, just as the behavior of other persons is influenced by their social

---

[37] See the discussion of the indeterminate sentence in Chap. 25, below.

[38] Walter Evans and Frank S. Gilbert, Jr., "The Sentencing Process: Better Methods Are Available," *Federal Probation*, **39**:36–42, 1975.

participation. Among judges as well as laymen, social-class membership affects interpretations of law and colors attitudes toward various types of offenses and offenders.[39] A judge's prior associations with punitive and nonpunitive behavior patterns, for example, affect the particular way the judge reacts to a particular offender as well as affecting the judge's sentencing record. Whether a person is a "hanging judge," a "bleeding heart," or something in between, then, is affected by the person's background characteristics as well as by the position the person takes regarding the relative importance of the law-enforcement and adjustment principles. Indeed, the position one takes with reference to a balance between uniformity and individualization of punishments is greatly affected by personal background too.

The judge's training as a lawyer does not ordinarily include studies in anthropology, psychology, and sociology, which would tend to promote an appreciation for the wide variations found in the behavior of persons belonging to different social classes, ethnic groups, occupational groups, and so on. These variations are present in a wide range of behavior, including, significantly, attitudes toward evidence, guilt, and punishment. Thus a study of the decisions of 313 state and federal judges indicated that decisions for or against the defense in criminal cases are significantly related to membership in various groups.[40] For example, there was a greater tendency to decide for the defense among Democrats as opposed to Republicans, among nonmembers of the American Bar Association as opposed to members, among judges who had served as prosecutors as opposed to those who had not, and among Catholics as opposed to Protestants. On their responses to a mailed questionnaire, 119 of the judges were scored on "general liberalism" and on "criminal liberalism." The first score was determined by responses to questions measuring the degree of sympathy for less-privileged groups and the degree of acceptance of social change, while the second score was determined by the degree of agreement with this statement: "Our treatment of criminals is too harsh; we should try to cure, not punish, them." Judges with a high "general liberalism" score had a significantly greater tendency to decide for the defense than did judges with low scores on this measure, and this was true also for judges with a high "criminal liberalism" score.

However, one of the best studies of the sentencing of juveniles showed almost the opposite, so far as "criminal liberalism" is concerned. The study was concerned with severity of sentences rather than with findings for the defense. It compared juvenile-court judges who wore robes and ran their court in a formal

---

[39] See Martin Levin, "Urban Politics and Judicial Behavior," *Journal of Legal Studies*, 1:193–225, 1972; Alexander Smith and Abraham Blumberg, "The Problem of Objectivity," *Social Forces*, 46:96–105, 1967; and Neubauer, *Criminal Justice in Middle America*, pp. 89–93.

[40] Stuart S. Nagel, "Judicial Backgrounds and Criminal Cases," *Journal of Criminal Law, Criminology and Police Science*, 53:333–9, 1962. See also idem, "Testing Relations Between Judicial Characteristics and Judicial Decision-Making," *Western Political Science Quarterly*, 15:425–37, 1962.

manner with judges who followed a more informal procedure. The judges using formal procedures were found to be more punitive in their attitudes, and those using informal procedures were more "professional," in the sense that they read more literature with an aim to understanding delinquents and delinquency. But the "punitive" judges committed fewer juveniles to institutions than did the "professional" judges:

The judges who have taken the more severe sanctions are those who read more about delinquents, who read from professional journals, who do not wear their robes in court and who are more permissive in outlook. . . . Severity of the sanctions, therefore, appears to be positively related to the degree to which a judge uses a professional, humanistic, social welfare ideology in making his decisions.[41]

The authors suggest that the differences appeared because the "professional" judges considered institutionalization as therapeutic or, at least, as a shelter from bad homes, and therefore saw themselves as acting in behalf of the child. The punitive judges perceived institutions as hurtful, suitable only for "bad" children, and so used them more sparingly.[42]

Many studies have shown that the general sentencing practices of judges tend to be biased against the poor and the black. Green found that Philadelphia judges favored females, youths, and whites, as compared with males, older offenders and blacks, but he concluded that these differences were due to the crime rate among the various groups rather than to bias among the judges.[43] The significant issue, however, is not that of determining whether individual judges are biased. It is that of determining whether, in view of the way courthouse procedures are arranged, it "just happens" that people with little power are more frequently found guilty and more frequently given severe punishments than are people with much power.[44] The lawyers in one courthouse characterized the chief judge as "prejudiced against psychiatrists, psychologists, sociologists, clergy, trailer courts, small loans, small claims cases, and, of course, people on welfare."[45]

In more than half the states, judges are selected by popular election, and their terms are relatively short. In nineteen states, candidates for the bench run in

[41]Stanton Wheeler, Edna Bonacich, M. Richard Cramer, and Irving K. Zola, "Agents of Delinquency Control: A Comparative Analysis," ch. 3 in *Controlling Delinquents*, ed. Stanton Wheeler (New York: Wiley, 1968), p. 55.

[42]For a summary of this and other studies of sentencing disparities, see Roger Hood and Richard Sparks, *Key Issues in Criminology* (London: Weidenfeld and Nicholson, 1970), pp. 141–70.

[43]Edward Green, *Judicial Attitudes in Sentencing* (New York: St. Martin's Press, 1961), p. 63. See also John Hagan, "Extra-legal Attributes and Criminal Sentencing: An Assessment of a Sociological Viewpoint," *Law and Society Review*, 8:357–83, 1974; William R. Arnold, "Race and Ethnicity Relative to Other Factors in Juvenile Court Dispositions, *American Journal of Sociology*, 77:211–27, 1971; and Theodore G. Chiricos and Gordon P. Waldo, "Socioeconomic Status and Criminal Sentencing: An Empirical Assessment of a Conflict Proposition," *American Sociological Review*, 40:753–72, 1975.

[44]See the discussion of police discretion in Chapter 16, above.

[45]Neubauer, *Criminal Justice in Middle America*, p. 92.

partisan elections after winning a primary election or receiving their party's nomination at a political convention. In other states, candidates run without party designation. More than 80 percent of the judicial positions in the United States are elective. Voters cannot always know the qualities essential in a good judge, such as personal integrity, adequate legal training, and judicial temperament. Accordingly, some judges try to win votes by self-advertisement, by attending banquets, weddings, funerals, sports events, and lodge entertainments, by sensational behavior on the bench, and in other ways. Judges have asked to be transferred from the civil to the criminal branch of the court shortly before elections because of the better opportunity for publicity in the criminal court. With the exception of parts of Switzerland, the United States is the only democracy in the world where the practice of selecting judges by popular vote still survives.

In 1940, Missouri adopted a plan whereby judges are nominated by a commission of outstanding citizens, including lawyers. The names of three nominees are submitted to the governor, who selects one. After a judge selected in this manner has served for one year, the judge's name is placed on the ballot, and the voters decide whether the person should be retained in office. This plan does away with the defects and disadvantages of both the appointment system and the election system of selecting judges. Ten other states have adopted it. The nominating-commission procedure is also used on a voluntary basis in other states.

CLERKS AND ATTENDANTS

The importance of clerks and attendants in the judicial process ordinarily is rarely acknowledged. Some clerks and bailiffs steer cases to professional bondsmen and to lawyers who will split fees with them. Clerks can manipulate complaint forms so that discharges result. Dates for which trials are set may be changed by clerks without the knowledge of the complaining witnesses so that the defendants will be discharged for lack of prosecution. In some cases, judges look to their clerks for sentencing advice, and in lower courts the clerks sometimes know more about the technicalities of criminal procedure than do the magistrates. Moreover, clerks and other nonjudicial agents are in charge of court administration, and, even when no dishonesty is involved, the management of most courts is archaic and inefficient. As the President's Commission stated, "Operation of today's courts requires the professional and continuous gathering and assessment of up-to-date information and statistics for scheduling, calendaring, and budgeting. Business affairs of the courts not directly related to the disposition of cases must also be taken care of."[46] Many hospitals and clinics now employ administrators to handle the business and organizational aspects of medical treatment, but few courts have employed skilled administrators to oversee the organizational aspects of justice. Although the trend is toward the employment of administrators, the judges, lawyers, and other

---

[46]President's Commission, *Task Force Report: The Courts*, p. 81.

courthouse personnel tend to resist organizational charges that would inconvenience them rather than the defendants and witnesses.[47]

THE TRIAL

Except in very serious cases, such as capital offenses, a plea of guilty makes a trial unnecessary. A defendant who pleads not guilty is entitled to a jury trial, but in many instances this right can be waived. The defendant then stands trial before a judge. Recent statistics show that the trial plays a very small part in the system of criminal justice, and that the jury plays a small part in the trial. In 1974, 85 percent of the persons convicted in the United States district courts were convicted on pleas of guilty, 10 percent on findings of a jury, and 5 percent on finding of the court.[48] The President's Commission presented similar statistics on the number and percentage of guilty-plea convictions in trial courts of general jurisdiction in those states in which reliable statistical information was available.[49]

The Jury

The jury originated as a protection against the despotism of the king and frequently has been acclaimed as the "palladium of our liberties." According to legal theory, the business of the jury is to determine, on the basis of evidence, a question of fact: Did the accused person commit the crime? It is supposed to be a problem in logic similar to the problem confronting a scientist in a laboratory. In practice, however, the prosecutor tries to select jurors who will be antagonistic to the accused, and the attorney for the defense tries to select jurors who will be sympathetic. One tries to exclude all persons not of the same race, religion, politics, or occupation as the accused, and the other tries to exclude all persons who are of the same race, religion, politics, or occupation. A famous criminal lawyer, Clarence Darrow, described the process of selecting a jury in the following terms:

Jurymen seldom convict a person they like, or acquit one that they dislike. The main work of a trial lawyer is to make a jury like his client, or, at least, to feel sympathy for him; facts regarding the crime are relatively unimportant.

I try to get a jury with little education but with much human emotion. The Irish are always the best jurymen for the defense. I don't want a Scotchman, for he has too little human feeling; I don't want a Scandinavian, for he has too strong a respect for law as law. In general I don't want a religious person, for he believes in sin and punishment. The defendant should avoid rich men who have a high regard for the law, as they make and use it. The smug and ultrarespectable think they are the guardians of soceity, and they believe the law is for them.

---

[47] Rosett and Cressey, *Justice by Consent*, pp. 172–5.
[48] *Federal Offenders in the United States District Courts, 1974* (Washington: Administrative Office of the U.S. Courts, 1975), p. 14.
[49] President's Commission, *Task Force Report: The Courts*, p. 9.

The man who is down on his luck, who has trouble, who is more or less a failure, is much kinder to the poor and unfortunate than are the rich and selfish.[50]

In some cases, several thousand prospective jurors have been examined before twelve were secured. In one Chicago trial, 9,425 persons were summoned for jury duty, and 4,821 were examined before twelve were finally selected. Ninety-one days were required to select a jury in one San Francisco case. However, this procedure is not due to the jury system as such, for there is evidence that in some courts, especially the federal courts, juries are generally selected expeditiously. In several celebrated trials in recent years, a team of psychologists and sociologists has studied prospective jurors and, on the basis of this study, helped defense attorneys select jurors who will be most favorable to the defense.[51]

Trial by jury is necessarily slower and more cumbersome than trial before a judge, and about two-thirds of the states have made legislative provision for waiver of the jury trial and substitution of trial by the judge. Few cases are tried by jury in states where this legislation has been in existence for some time. More than 48 percent of the persons who pleaded not guilty in Massachusetts superior courts in 1970 waived the jury trial.[52] As Newman has pointed out, "Waiver of the jury is often felt to be an advantage to the defendant in cases which have received a great deal of negative publicity, when a highly technical defense is going to be raised, or when it is believed laymen are otherwise unlikely to be sympathetic to the defense."[53] Nevertheless, recent studies have shown that while judges and juries agree on the outcome of cases about 75 percent of the time, juries are significantly more lenient than judges in the remaining cases.[54] The weight of opinion is distinctly in favor of retaining the right to a jury trial but of facilitating the waiver of the jury.

A series of studies done twenty years ago suggested both that juries tend to follow the technical instructions given them by the judges and that the leaders in jury deliberations are those who are most articulate and assertive, which means that the leaders tend to come from the upper socioeconomic levels.[55] It also was found that male jurors tend to try to complete the jury's task, while female jurors tend more to react to the other jurors and to display social solidarity.[56] More

---

[50] From a statement made at an anniversary dinner of the Quadrangle Club, Chicago, in 1933. See also James A. Dooley, "The Trial Court," *The Law School Record* (University of Chicago), vol. 3 (1954), no. 2. pp. 1 ff.

[51] Tom Goldstein, "The Science of Jury Selection," *New York Times*, February 16, 1975, sect. 4, p. 6.

[52] Commissioner of Correction, *Statistical Reports 1970* (Boston: Massachusetts Public Document No. 115), p. 70.

[53] Donald J. Newman, *Introduction to Criminal Justice* (Philadelphia: Lippincott, 1975), p. 220.

[54] Harry Kalven and Hans Zeisel, *The American Jury* (Boston: Little, Brown, 1966), p. 59.

[55] Rita M. James, "Jurors' Assessment of Criminal Responsibility," *Social Problems*, 7:58–69, 1959; and Fred L. Strodtbeck, Rita M. James, and Charles Hawkins, "Social Status in Jury Deliberations," *American Sociological Review*, 22:713–19, 1957; Rita M. James,"Status and Competence of Juries," *American Journal of Sociology*, 64:563–70, 1959.

[56] Fred L. Strodtbeck and Richard D. Mann, "Sex Role Differentiation in Jury Deliberations," *Sociometry*, 19:3–11, 1956.

recently, it has been argued that the jury role is one of conflict—jurors are expected to follow the instructions given them by a judge, but they are also expected to use their own judgment as to whether to follow them or not.[57]

Evidence and Testimony

The great proportion of evidence in a trial is furnished by the witnesses for the two sides. Several problems arise in regard to such evidence. The first is that it is very difficult to induce witnesses to appear in court and give testimony. In cases involving organized crime, terrorism may be involved. In other types of cases, witnesses are reluctant to go to court because of the great inconvenience involved. They may be required to go to court again and again, at great financial loss to themselves. Defense attorneys often attempt to obtain as many continuances as possible, on the theory that witnesses for the prosecution, including victims, eventually will grow tired of the inconvenience of coming to court. In addition to being subjected to losses of time and income, witnesses often are insulted, manipulated, and otherwise treated as pawns in a game. Consequently, many witnesses do not disclose to anyone the fact that they have important evidence, and many crimes are not reported to the police. Much of the evidence provided by witnesses could be supplied by means of deposition, telephone, two-way radio, or two-way television.

A second problem is the honest mistakes that witnesses frequently make. Often what a person remembers is a combination of what was witnessed and of other things that were heard or imagined subsequent to the occurrence. The only check on mistakes in testimony in court is the testimony of other witnesses, but this adversary system places undue stress on the witnesses and makes it difficult for them to contribute in a meaningful way to the proceedings. Under the heading "How to Humiliate and Subdue a Recalcitrant Witness," a book written for prosecutors and defense attorneys contains the following advice:

> When you have forced the witness into giving you a direct answer to your question you really have him under control; he is off-balance, and usually rather scared. This advantage should be followed up with a few simple questions such as, "You did not want to answer that question, did you?" If the witness says that he wanted to answer it, ask him in a resounding voice, "Well, why did you not answer it when I first asked you?" Whatever his answer is you then ask him, "Did you think that you were smart enough to evade answering the question?" Again, whatever the answer is you ask him, "Well, I would like for the jurors to know what you have behind all this dodging and ducking you have done!" . . . This battering and legal-style "kicking the witness around" not only humiliates but subdues him.[58]

[57] Mortimer R. Kadish and Sanford H. Kadish, "The Institutionalization of Conflict: Jury Acquittals," *Journal of Social Issues*, 27:199–217, 1971. See also Sanford H. Kadish, *Discretion to Disobey* (Stanford, Calif.: Stanford University Press, 1973).

[58] Lewis W. Lake, *How to Win Lawsuits Before Juries* (Englewood Cliffs, N.J.: Prentice-Hall, 1954), pp. 164–65.

A third problem is dishonesty in testimony. The only official check on dishonesty is the oath and the possibility of prosecution for perjury. In a few famous cases, witnesses have not been permitted to testify because they were atheists, to whom the oath would have no meaning. But the oath probably has little significance to a large proportion of the witnesses in courts. Judges and others believe that there is an immense amount of perjury in testimony, but few persons are convicted of perjury.

For some time, efforts have been made to invent devices that will detect guilty knowledge. The "lie detector" currently has the best standing of any of these devices. This instrument registers physiological measurements of emotional changes that occur as the result of questions presented, but, unfortunately, the emotional changes are not necessarily due to lies. Probably the "lie detector" is of less value in the direct detection of lies than in the detection of emotional conditions that may be utilized by the examiner to induce a confession. Various drugs are being used to some extent for the same purpose.

The Audience and Publicity

One of the rights for which the common people fought two centuries ago was the right to a public trial. This right is no longer highly prized by accused persons. On the contrary, a few defendants currently secure the highly prized privilege of being tried in the judge's chambers or of having the judge come to the courtroom at an unusual hour so that they are protected against a public trial. The right to a private trial has been granted in the juvenile court, and it has been argued that restrictions similar to those in the juvenile court should be authorized for all trials, so that the audience could be confined to those who have a particular and justified interest in the case. Many trials are unquestionably an invasion of the accused person's right to privacy. Probably the most notorious offenders in this respect are reporters and photographers.

THE "SPORTING THEORY" OF JUSTICE

Formally, the essential business of a trial is to determine a question of fact: Did the accused commit the crime? In the performance of that duty, tricks and surprises are no more justifiable than in determining a fact in a laboratory. In practice, however, the criminal trial is regarded as a game between two lawyers, who pose as adversaries. Large audiences were attracted in the past, and in some sections of the country criminal trials still are an important source of amusement. Each side tries to win the case and takes advantage of every possible trick, surprise, and technical device. It is not at all unusual for as many as fifteen formal motions to be introduced in a case, each of which involves debate, possible continuances, and decisions by the court. When a case is continued, witnesses disappear and public sentiments weaken, and the chance for conviction decreases. One legal writer used an analogy with warfare, stating that the trial involves scouting the enemy's position and strength, stratagems, tactics, skirmishes, and battles. "Opposing

counsel are charged with the responsibility of so conducting their campaign that ultimate victory will result."[59]

THE "BARGAIN THEORY" OF JUSTICE

Most of the conflicts that took place in the courtroom in earlier days in accordance with the sporting theory of justice are now avoided. Most cases are settled in the office of the prosecutor in a process commonly called "plea bargaining." Among prisoners, the process is known as "copping a plea." In one form of settlement, the defendant pleads guilty to a lesser included offense or to a separate misdemeanor that has been charged along with one or more felonies. A charge of burglary may be reduced to unlawful entry; a charge of grand larceny may be reduced to petty larceny; theft of an automobile may be reduced to joyriding, tampering with an automobile, or theft of a tire; murder may be reduced to manslaughter, and so on. In another form of settlement, the prosecutor promises a specific sentence to persons who plead guilty as charged, and the promised sentence, of course, is less severe than the most severe sentence a judge could impose following a finding of guilt.

The first form of settlement is ordinarily portrayed as a system for informally haggling about the price of a crime. Prosecutors want to reduce their workloads and want to save the state the expenses of trials. Defense lawyers, knowing this, ask the prosecutors to reduce the charge in exchange for a plea of guilty to the reduced charge. The two attorneys then bargain about just which crime the defendant will plead guilty to, for the statute defining one crime calls for a less severe penalty than does the statute defining another crime. The statistics showing differences between original charges and the crimes to which defendants eventually plead guilty are taken as evidence that such haggling is extensive. For example, in New York City a few years ago, 18 percent of all defendants indicted for first-degree robbery, which carried a ten-to-thirty-year sentence, pleaded guilty to a misdemeanor carrying a one-year maximum. More than half of all defendants indicted for grand theft, which carried a ten-year maximum, pleaded guilty to various misdemeanors subject to no more than one year in jail. Three-quarters of all defendants indicted for felonies such as assault pleaded guilty to misdemeanor offenses, thereby ensuring no more than one year rather than a five-year sentence.[60]

The practices resulting in such statistics are currently under severe attack. Legislators say they have mandated that all felons should be imprisoned. Their watchword is efficiency. Any digression from rapid and impersonal processing of felons from arrest to imprisonment is undesirable. So-called "plea bargaining" by

[59]Leonard Moore, "Modern Practice and Strategy," *Practicing Law Institute*, 1946, p. 1; quoted in Jerome Frank, *Courts on Trial* (Princeton: Princeton University Press, 1949), p. 8.

[60]James E. Bond, *Plea Bargaining and Guilty Pleas* (New York: Clark Boardman, 1975), p. 15. See also idem, "Plea Bargaining in North Carolina," *North Carolina Law Review*, 54:823–43, 1976.

prosecutors is being viewed as a rip in the net which legislators have woven to ensure that few felons escape the severe punishment said to be due them.

Rosett and Cressey have shown, however, that this image of the settlement process is incorrect. Their study noted that out-of-court settlements between prosecutors and defense attorneys sometimes reflect a desire of expediency on the part of court personnel, and it was further noted that charges are sometimes dropped or reduced in the cases of criminals who are informers. But the study showed that in the overwhelming majority of cases the reductions represent informal attempts to soften the severe penalities set down in statute books.[61] Similarly, a study of courthouse practices in an Illinois city noted that prosecutors look at the background of the offender and the character of the offense, and adjust the penalty accordingly:

> Prosecutors mention two primary factors that are involved in the exercise of discretion: the nature of the defendant and the nature of the event. One assistant commented that he tends to charge a misdemeanor if the defendant is a little down-and-out, a little stupid, a first-time offender, or the case is unclear. The nature of the event also plays a part. An attempt is made to interpret the cold law in light of what happened. A prosecutor pointed to a recent aggravated battery case stemming from a barroom brawl. While the evidence could have established a felony, the office chose to file a misdemeanor because the victim had provoked the defendant. A special example of the prosecutor looking at the nature of the event rather than the sterile law involves aggravated battery charges involving police officers. While it is a felony to cause bodily harm to a police officer, the state's attorney does not treat this protection as sacrosanct. Instead, he inquires into the nature of the event. Did the defendant take a good swing at the cop with evil intent? Or, did he just struggle a little? Was he too drunk to know what he was doing? As one assistant stated it, the police want an aggravated battery charge every time a drunk lurches at them. But the more dispassionate prosecutor tends to examine the events from a broader perspective.[62]

Consistently, a recent historical study of Connecticut courts suggests that it is not correct to attribute so-called "plea bargaining" to a high volume of cases and a burden of overwork on court officials—low-volume courthouses settle their cases without trials just as do high-volume courts, and in about the same proportions.[63] In American courthouses, then, prosecutors modify the law as they engage in practices that are called "plea bargaining," but not necessarily for reasons of

[61] Rosett and Cressey, *Justice by Consent*, pp. 145–59. See also H. Laurence Ross, "The Neutralization of Severe Penalties: Some Traffic Law Studies," *Law and Society Review*, 10:403–13, 1976; Neal Shover, William B. Bankston, and J. William Gurley, "Responses of the Criminal Justice System to Legislation Providing More Severe Threatened Sanctions," *Criminology*, 14:483–500, 1977; and The Association of the Bar of the City of New York, Drug Abuse Council, *The Effects of the 1973 Drug Laws on the New York State Courts* (New York: Author, 1976).

[62] Neubauer, *Criminal Justice in Middle America*, p. 121.

[63] Milton Heumann, "A Note on Plea Bargaining and Case Pressure," *Law and Society Review*, 9:516–28, 1975. See also Thomas W. Church, Jr., "Plea Bargains, Concessions and the Courts: Analysis of a Quasi-experiment," *Law and Society Review*, 10:377–401, 1976.

expediency. Instead, they seem to reduce charges and thus modify the law as a way of doing justice and maintaining the consent of the governed.

Every modern criminal-justice system employs persons to reduce the severity of the punishments that are mandated by lawmakers. Judges, for example, soften harsh penalties whenever they suspend a sentence, place a criminal on probation, or otherwise divert the criminal from the hurt that is stipulated by statute as appropriate for the crime committed. Personnel in the executive branch of government—police officers, parole boards, prosecuting attorneys—also are authorized to make discretionary judgments about punishments, and they make them with great frequency. Currently, American legislators and others seem to be rushing to close this breach, to eliminate, or at least drastically narrow, discretionary decision-making regarding actual punishments. In keeping with the law-enforcement principle, legislators think that crime rates would not be so high if prosecutors, judges, and parole-board members would stop softening the penalties they have prescribed. Accordingly, judges are being mandated to send certain kinds of offenders—especially habitual ones—to prison for fixed terms, with no possibility of probation or parole. Parts of the parole system are being abolished and parole boards eliminated. Consistently, prosecutors are being told to stop bargaining with criminals who offer to plead guilty if the charge against them is reduced from a serious to a less serious crime. President Nixon's National Advisory Commission on Criminal Justice Standards and Goals called for abolition of all guilty-plea negotiations.[64] Several jurisdictions are now trying to implement that recommendation.

In the legislators' quest for efficiency, they tend to forget that mechanical law enforcement is both undesirable and impossible. The question is whether the law—considered simply as statutes defining crimes, specifying punishments for them, and listing the formal procedures that must be used for dealing with suspects and defendants—can be fair and just. Many authorities, including some Biblical ones, have concluded that it cannot, and the adjustment principle has been inserted in criminal-law administration for this reason. No social system or organization has ever operated on the basis of formal rules alone, partly because such rigidity is impossible and partly because, if successful, it would result in gross injustices.

The very term "plea bargaining" stacks the cards in this argument. It makes it hard for many people to see that the winnowing effect in the criminal-justice process is essential to justice. Plea bargaining conjures the image of prosecutors and murderers haggling over the price to be paid for having taken a human life. In fact, the Rosett and Cressey study showed that this image is a distortion of what happens when criminal defendants plead guilty and are sentenced to something less than the most severe crime for which they could have been charged. There are

[64]National Advisory Commission on Criminal Justice Standards and Goals, *Courts* (Washington: Government Printing Office, 1973), p. 48.

at least three senses in which these arrangements have little to do with pleas and are in no sense bargaining.

In the first place, screening is necessary because the events reported by a police officer do not always constitute the crime the officer says they constitute. Prosecutors dismiss many felony charges and reduce many others to misdemeanors on the basis of evidence rather than bargaining.[65]

In the second place, a single set of events can be either one crime or another, depending on how it is interpreted. Prosecutors must decide whether a crime is in fact a felony even when the evidence indicates that it is. For example, a prosecutor filed a misdemeanor charge of disorderly conduct against an old man who had stumbled drunkenly around a liquor store, waving a toy pistol over his head, demanding a bottle of whiskey. Clearly, the evidence could support the charge of either armed robbery or disorderly conduct. The latter offense was selected, but not because of a bargaining session between prosecution and defense (neither the defendant nor his attorney had even talked to the prosecutor before this decision was made). Nor was it selected as a concession to the defendant in exchange for his plea of guilty to the lesser charge. The disorderly conduct charge was selected because it seemed fair; the prosecutor considered that the penalty for that offense—a few days in the county jail—was about right.

In the third place, decisions as to which crime, if any, has taken place necessarily vary from day to day. In the above example, another prosecutor might have charged the old man with armed robbery and then later, when the circumstances of the offense and the character of the offender were known, might have reduced it to disorderly conduct. Such a change might show up in court statistics, and be interpreted to mean that yet another robber has been allowed to escape the dragnet of the law, that an inefficient prosecutor has let a proper charge of robbery be bargained down to a misdemeanor charge. In reality no bargaining takes place in such cases. The prosecutor simply files the most severe charge the evidence seemingly will support, and later reduces it in the name of justice.

It should not be concluded that because plea bargaining, in the literal sense, is rare in American courthouses, negotiations between prosecution and defense are also rare. On the contrary, a dominant concern of both defendants and courthouse personnel is discussion, debate, and negotiation about what the facts are in a case. In many, if not most, cases the prosecutor and the defense lawyer quickly negotiate out a set of facts acceptable to both. For example, the attorneys might agree, without much discussion, that the defendant is a "bad guy" or a "punk" who ought to be imprisoned. If they do, the defendant will be encouraged to plead to a felony. On the other hand, both lawyers might acknowledge that the defendant is not really a "bad guy" and thus agree that a plea of guilty to disorderly conduct is appropriate even if the defendant technically committed robbery.

[65]See William F. McDonald, "Prosecutorial Decisions and Case Mortality at the Initial Screening," paper read at the annual meetings of the American Criminological Society, New York, November 5, 1973.

In still other cases, there is heated argument about whether a defendant's character and the circumstances of the crime are such that the person should be sent to prison for ten years rather than to a county jail for ten days, and about what really happened on the night of the alleged crime.[66]

The issue in such debates is always the amount of punishment that is appropriate for *this* defendant. A case is likely to go to trial only if prosecution and defense cannot negotiate a mutually acceptable set of facts legitimating one degree of punitive severity or another. If the facts agreed upon suggest that the defendant is a robber who should be sent to prison, the defense lawyer is not likely to ask for a trial or to bargain for a charge of disorderly conduct. On the other hand, if the facts suggest that justice would be done if the defendant were punished by a few days in jail, the prosecutor is not likely to demand that the suspect either plead guilty to robbery or go to trial on a robbery charge. Such out-of-court settlement techniques are commonly used with reference to civil suits and seem to have been adapted to criminal procedures.[67]

It is only a slight oversimplification to conclude that courthouse personnel first decide what a defendant's punishment shall be and then hunt around to find a charge that is consistent with their decision. One of the best studies of prosecutorial discretion suggested that this practice is part of the "living law," in contrast to the law as set down in statutes:[68]

Adversarial conflict and its ritualization at trial is incompatible with the more satisfactory conciliatory adjustments which assure more consistent and reliable outcomes. As long as reciprocal relationships and compromise provide more benefits to defense and prosecution than those provided by the trial process, criminal cases will continue to be adjusted outside the courtroom.[69]

In the second form of settlement, a plea of guilty to the offense charged is entered, but the prosecutor promises probation or a light sentence. Such "sentence bargaining" occurs much less frequently than the first kind of settlement. Even a defendant who is guilty has a legal and moral right to plead not guilty and to require the state to prove its case. The prosecutor not only must know that the defendant committed the offense, but must prove that fact. District attorneys are

---

[66] See Lynn Mather, "Some Determinants of the Method of Case Disposition: Decision Making by Public Defenders in Los Angeles," *Law and Society Review*, 8:187–216, 1973. See also Neubauer, *Criminal Justice in Middle America*, pp. 216–23.

[67] Marian Neef and Stuart Nagel, "The Adversary Legal System in a Changing Society," *et al.*, 3:50–5, 1974; John W. Palmer, "Pre-Arrest Diversion: Victim Confrontation," *Federal Probation*, 38:12–18, 1974; Neubauer, *Criminal Justice in Middle America*, pp. 222–3; and Suzann R. Thomas Buckle and Leonard G. Buckle, *Bargaining for Justice: Case Disposition and Reform in the Criminal Courts* (New York: Praeger, 1976). For an excellent account of the transformation of a welfare agency into a court of law, with dire consequences for the flexibility so essential to justice, see Philippe Nonet, *Administrative Justice: Advocacy and Change in a Government Agency* (New York: Russell Sage Foundation, 1969).

[68] See the discussion in Chapter 1, above.

[69] Brian A. Grosman, *The Prosecutor: An Inquiry into the Exercise of Discretion* (Toronto: University of Toronto Press, 1969), p. 96.

willing to recommend probation or a light sentence in cases of offenders who, in the district attorneys' judgment, do not deserve to be labeled as felons, do not deserve the severe penalty the law allows for such felons, and who admit their guilt.

It is the prosecutor's privilege to recommend a light or a heavy sentence to the judge, but the judge, of course, need not follow the recommendation. In practice, however, judges usually go along with the arrangements made between the defendant and the prosecutor, because considerable saving to the state is effected by a guilty plea, which makes a lengthy trial unnecessary, and because there usually is no evidence that a judge's guess as to an appropriate sentence is any better than a prosecutor's guess. Many prisoners insist that prosecuting attorneys do not always keep their promises to recommend a light sentence, but, instead, merely use the promise as a device to trick the defendant into pleading guilty.[70] Also, defendants who have pleaded guilty on the assumption that the sentence will be light are shocked when the judge imposes a heavier sentence than the one recommended by the prosecutor. Although it would be difficult to prove, it is probable that a grave injustice is done to many defendants who insist on their right to a jury trial and refuse to plead guilty. An extreme penalty is sometimes ordered not solely because a crime has been committed but in part as punishment for refusing to plead guilty, thus causing the court personnel the inconvenience of holding a trial. For example, two men who had refused to accept an offer of two-year sentences in exchange for pleas of guilty to robbery were sentenced to twenty years by a trial judge.

It is not possible to determine what proportion of the reductions of charges and the promises of light sentences involve corruption. Not all charge reductions, however, are equally honest. In one study of ninety-seven felony convictions, plea arranging was acknowledged in 56.7 percent of the cases, but there was no evidence of bribery.[71] Neither is it possible to determine how much corruption is involved in the cases that are dismissed by motion of the prosecutor. Certainly corruption is involved in some of them, but it is equally certain that the prosecutor performs an important public service in sifting out the cases that should not go to trial, either because of the innocence of the accused, the triviality of the offense, the inadequacy of the evidence, or the undue severity of the potential punishment.[72]

The principal danger of so-called "plea bargaining," the President's Commis-

---

[70] Alan F. Arcuri, "Lawyers, Judges, and Plea Bargaining: Some New Data on Inmates' Views," *International Journal of Criminology and Penology*, 4:177–91, 1976. See also Geoffrey P. Alpert and Donald A. Hicks, "Prisoners' Attitudes Toward Components of the Legal and Judicial Systems," *Criminology*, 14:461–82, 1977.

[71] Donald J. Newman, "Pleading Guilty for Considerations: A Study of Bargain Justice," *Journal of Criminal Law, Criminology and Police Science*, 46:780–90, 1956. See also idem, *Conviction: The Determination of Guilt or Innocence Without Trial* (Boston: Little, Brown, 1966).

[72] See Donald J. Newman and Edgar C. NeMoyer, "Issues of Propriety in Negotiated Justice," *Denver Law Journal*, 47:367–407, 1970.

sion concluded, "lies in the fact that it is so informal and invisible that it gives rise to fears that it does not operate fairly or that it does not accurately identify those who should be prosecuted and what disposition should be made in their cases.[73] Viewed in its best light, plea bargaining is a system for adjusting the general criminal-law rules to the circumstances of specific offenses and the characteristics of individual offenders.

"CASH REGISTER" JUSTICE

Some cases are rushed through the courts with scant attention of any court official. This type of justice is well known in the traffic courts, where the whole procedure is mechanical. Perhaps the assembly-line procedure is inevitable, in view of the large number of traffic cases, but many citizens are irritated by it.[74] The poor and uninfluential persons accused of other minor offenses, are rushed through the regular criminal courts in exactly the same manner.[75]

The volume of misdemeanor cases is overwhelming. In one year three Atlanta judges of the municipal court disposed of more than 70,000 cases; in Detroit more than 20,000 misdemeanor and nontraffic petty offenses were handled by a single judge each year; the District of Columbia Court of General Sessions at one time had four judges to process the preliminary stages of more than 1,500 felony cases, and to hear and determine 7,500 serious misdemeanor cases, 38,000 petty offenses, and an equal number of traffic offenses per year.[76] A Philadelphia judge disposed of fifty-five cases of vagrancy, drunkenness, and disorderly conduct in fifteen minutes; four men were tried, found guilty, and sentenced in seventeen seconds. From the standpoint of the number of cases settled and the number of persons affected, these magistrates' courts are "supreme courts." They are inferior courts only with reference to the character and training of the judges, the efficiency of the machinery, and the type of justice dispensed. At no point, in a very large proportion of cases, is there an opportunity for an adequate consideration of the facts in the case either by the prosecutor or by the court. In many superior courts, too, "clearing the docket" is a primary objective. Cases are dismissed, guilty pleas are entered, and sentences are imposed with a view to "moving the cases," rather than with a view to dispersing justice. Clearly, new methods are needed to decrease discrimination against the weak, upgrade

---

[73]President's Commission, *Task Force Report: The Courts*, p. 4. See also Charles W. Thomas and Anthony Fitch, "Prosecutorial Decision Making," *American Criminal Law Review* 13:507–52, 1976; and Kenneth Kipnis, "Criminal Justice and the Negotiated Plea," *Ethics*, 86:93–106, 1976.

[74]Stephen L. Brickey and Dan E. Miller, "Bureaucratic Due Process: An Ethnography of a Traffic Court," *Social Problems*, 22:688–97, 1975.

[75]Maureen Mileski, "An Observation of a Lower Criminal Court," *Law and Society Review*, 5:473–538, 1971. See also Stephen R. Bing and S. Stephen Rosenfeld, *The Quality of Justice* (New York: Lawyer's Committee for Civil Rights Under Law, 1970); John A. Robertson, ed., *Rough Justice: Perspectives on Lower Criminal Courts* (Boston: Little, Brown, 1974); and Jacqueline P. Wiseman, *Stations of the Lost: The Treatment of Skid Row Alcoholics* (Englewood Cliffs, N.J.: Prentice-Hall, 1970), pp. 86–103.

[76]President's Commission, *Task Force Report: The Courts*, p. 31.

courthouse personnel, improve procedural efficiency, and increase compliance with the law.[77] Rosett and Cressey have recommended, with such ends in mind, that the oversized, remote, and impersonal downtown courthouse be replaced with small-volume courthouses located closer to the homes of the people brought into them, thus making them accessible to witnesses, victims, and observers. "Courthouses have reached a size that effectively precludes either efficiency or humanity."[78]

THE COURT AS A WELFARE AGENCY

The criminal-court system is an expression of a conflict principle of social organization. The theory is that the state has been injured by a crime and therefore should injure the offender by punishment, and also that the truth regarding guilt can best be determined by a combat between opposed lawyers. The juvenile court, on the other hand, has been built on a different principle. Its work is supposed to proceed on the assumption that the delinquent and the state have much in common, and that the interests of both will be promoted by efforts to help rather than to injure the delinquent. Some branches of the criminal court, also, have adopted the interventionist theory that future crime can best be prevented by assisting the accused. Provision for probation is the best illustration of this, and probation practices are to be discussed in Chapter 20. "Family courts" and divorce courts are organized on somewhat the same principle as the juvenile court. In ordinary criminal courts, too, the prosecutor frequently brings together persons who have been quarreling and, through conciliation, induces them to settle the quarrel without prosecution. In many so-called "plea-bargaining" cases, the prosecutor actually dismisses charges or reduces them, with no hint of adversary bargaining, so that nonpunitive, rehabilitative methods can be used. It is certainly possible that this procedure will become more prominent in the future.[79] However, criminal courts will not become generally nonpunitive and interventionist in their methods of dealing with criminals as long as punitive sanctions are an intrinsic part of the criminal law.

SUGGESTED READINGS

Bing, Stephen R., & S. Stephen Rosenfeld. *The Quality of Justice.* New York: Lawyer's Committee for Civil Rights Under Law, 1970.

Bond, James E. *Plea Bargaining and Guilty Pleas.* New York: Clark Boardman, 1975.

Buckle, Suzann R. Thomas, & Leonard G. Buckle. *Bargaining for Justice: Case Disposition and Reform in Criminal Courts.* New York: Praeger, 1976.

Cole, George P., ed. *Criminal Justice and Politics.* New York: Duxbury Press, 1972.

---

[77] Stuart S. Nagel, *Improving the Legal Process: Effects of Alternatives* (Lexington, Mass.: Lexington Books, 1975).

[78] Rosett and Cressey, *Justice by Consent,* p. 175.

[79] See John Griffiths, "Ideology in Criminal Procedure or a Third 'Model' of the Criminal Process," *Yale Law Journal,* 79:359–95, 1970.

Dawson, Robert O. *Sentencing: The Decision as to Type, Length and Conditions of Sentence.* Boston: Little, Brown, 1969.

Dershowitz, Alan. "Criminal Sentencing in the United States: An Historical and Conceptual Overview," *Annals of the American Academy of Political and Social Science,* 23:117–32, 1976.

D'Esposito, Julian C., Jr. "Sentencing Disparity: Causes and Cures." *Journal of Criminal Law, Criminology and Police Science,* 60:182–94, 1969.

Frankel, Marvin E. *Criminal Sentences: Law Without Order.* New York: Hill and Wang, 1973.

Gaylin, Willard. *Partial Justice: A Study of Sentencing.* New York: Vintage Books, 1975.

Grosman, Brian A. *The Prosecutor: An Inquiry into the Exercise of Discretion.* Toronto: University of Toronto Press, 1969.

Hogarth, John. *Sentencing as a Human Process.* Toronto: University of Toronto Press, 1971.

Hood, Roger. *Sentencing the Motoring Offender.* London: Heinemann, 1972.

Kadish, Sanford, H. *Discretion to Disobey.* Stanford, Calif.: Stanford University Press, 1973.

Kaufmann, Walter. *Without Guilt or Justice.* New York: Wyden, 1973.

Mather, Lynn. "Some Determinants of the Method Case Disposition by Public Defenders in Los Angeles." *Law and Society Review,* 8:187–216, 1973.

Mayers, Lewis. *The American Legal System.* Rev. ed. New York: Harper and Row, 1964.

Miller, Frank W. *Prosecution: The Decision to Charge a Suspect with Crime.* Boston: Little, Brown, 1969.

Nagel, Stuart S., ed. *The Rights of the Accused: In Law and Action.* Beverly Hills, Calif.: Sage, 1972.

Neubauer, David W. *Criminal Justice in Middle America.* Morristown, N.J.: General Learning Press, 1974.

Newman, Donald J. *Conviction: The Determination of Guilt or Innocence Without Trial.* Boston: Little, Brown, 1966.

Poulos, John W. *The Anatomy of Criminal Justice.* Mineola, N.Y.: Foundation Press, 1976.

Robertson, John A., ed. *Rough Justice: Perspectives on Lower Criminal Courts.* Boston: Little, Brown, 1974.

Rosenthal, Douglas E. *Lawyer and Client: Who's in Charge?* New York: Russell Sage Foundation, 1974.

Rosett, Arthur, & Donald R. Cressey. *Justice by Consent: Plea Bargains in the American Courthouse.* Philadelphia: Lippincott, 1976.

Rubin, Jeffrey Z., & Bert R. Brown. *The Social Psychology of Bargaining and Negotiation.* New York: Academic Press, 1975.

Simon, Rita James, ed. *The Jury System in America.* Beverly Hills, Calif.: Sage, 1975.

Sudnow, David. "Normal Crimes: Sociological Features of the Penal Code in a Public Defender Office." *Social Problems,* 12:255–76, 1965.

Walker, Nigel. *Sentencing in a Rational Society.* London: Penguin, 1972.

Weinreb, Lloyd L. *Denial of Justice: Criminal Process in the United States.* New York: Free Press, 1976.

Wilkins, Leslie T. "Equity and Republican Justice." *Annals of the American Academy of Political and Social Science,* 423:152–61, 1976.

Wilson, Amy Auerbacher, Sidney Leonard Greenblatt, & Richard Whittingham Wilson, eds. *Deviance and Social Control in Chinese Society.* New York: Praeger, 1977.

19

The Juvenile Court

Changing views of children and of childhood have been accompanied by changing relations between juveniles and the state. Our present conception of childhood developed in the seventeenth century, when children began to be regarded as persons deficient in rationality or the powers of discernment and, therefore, as not completely responsible for their acts. This notion eventually became the foundation of the juvenile court, which made the conception an official one, enforced by the coercive power of the state. But shifting ideas about just which young persons are to be considered children have given the court an ambivalent character.[1]

From the beginning, the backers of the juvenile-court movement have been unsure about which categories of youngsters are innocents who are not capable of formulating criminal intent. Juveniles of certain ages are considered not responsible for their acts, but they also are considered "responsible enough" to be answerable to the state for their deviations. They are exempt from the harsh effects of the criminal law because they are "mere children" or even "infants," but they are incarcerated and otherwise controlled if they deviate significantly from the way state officials expect them to behave. They are not officially considered responsible enough to behave like adults, but they are officially considered responsible enough to behave like children. Boys, for example, were once expected to leave home and seek their fortunes, and to behave like "little men" in other ways, but after the juvenile court was invented they became subject to arrest for

[1] June Fielding, *The Social Control of Female Delinquency: Occupational Ideologies of Policewomen, Welfare Workers and Magistrates* (unpublished M. A. thesis, Australian National University, Canberra, 1975). See also P. Boss, *Social Policy and the Young Delinquent* (London: Routledge and Kegan Paul, 1967), p. 32; and Meda Chesney-Lind, "Judicial Enforcement of the Female Sex Role: The Family Court and the Female Delinquent," *Issues in Criminology*, 8:51–69, 1973.

thus taking the adult role. Girls, similarly, are likely to be locked up if they start behaving like women too early in life.

Currently, there is widespread disenchantment with the juvenile court, and this suggests that the conception of childhood is again undergoing significant change. There is a move toward again holding youngsters responsible for violations of criminal laws and toward punishing them for these crimes like adults, despite the fact that the same youngsters are by law excluded from the labor market, required to attend school, considered incapable of making contracts, and in other ways prohibited from full participation in economic, political, and social life.

ORIGINS AND DEVELOPMENT OF THE JUVENILE COURT

At common law a century and a half ago, most children were tried and punished for violations of law in the same way as adults. However, all children under seven years of age were regarded as not responsible and therefore as incapable of committing a crime; children between the ages of seven and fourteen were regarded as having the possibility of being responsible, and this was decided in each case by examination. A child under seven years of age, therefore, could not be punished by order of the court, while a child between the ages of seven and fourteen could be subjected to all forms of punishment that were used for adults. In the course of time the maximum age was raised in some American states from seven to ten or some other age, but it still happens that children under fourteen years of age are arrested, held in jail, tried in court, and punished in the same ways as adult criminals.

Differential reactions to the offenses perpetrated by children and those committed by adults have been developing for centuries. Although the official reaction to the offenses of both groups has been slowly changing from a punitive to a nonpunitive reaction, this change has been much more pronounced in the case of juveniles. At least the official policies for dealing with delinquents and delinquency have incorporated more interventionist methods than have the official policies for dealing with adult offenders. As early as 1824 a house of refuge was established in New York state so that children, after conviction, would not be confined with adult criminals.[2] The laws of Illinois in 1831 provided that for certain offenses the penalties for minors might differ from those for adults. In 1861 the legislature of Illinois authorized the mayor of Chicago to appoint a commissioner before whom boys between the ages of six and seventeen could be taken on charges of petty offenses; this commissioner had authority to place the boys on probation, to send them to reform schools, and generally to use

[2]See Robert S. Pickett, *House of Refuge: Origins of Juvenile Reform in New York State, 1815–1857* (Syracuse, N. Y.: Syracuse University Press, 1969); and Joseph M. Hawes, *Children in Urban Society: Juvenile Delinquency in Nineteenth-Century America* (New York: Oxford University Press, 1974).

nonpunitive methods. In 1867 this work was transferred to the regular judges of the courts. Separate hearings for juvenile offenders were required in Boston in 1870 and in all parts of the state of Massachusetts in 1872. In 1877 both Massachusetts and New York authorized separate sessions with separate dockets and records for juvenile cases. During the last quarter of the nineteenth century, cases of truancy and incorrigibility of children were heard in some places by probate courts, without juries or the ordinary legal technicalities and formalities.[3]

These policies were combined and were supported by a consistent theory, which had been lacking in the earlier developments, and thus the juvenile court came into existence in 1899 in Chicago. The two significant points about this new court were: (1) The age below which a child could not be a criminal was advanced from seven to sixteen years, which was in line with changes that had been made elsewhere. But whereas the previous law had made no definite provision for dealing with culprits below the age of responsibility, the new law did make provision for dealing with them under the softer name *delinquents*. (2) The work of the court was placed under chancery, or equity, jurisdiction. For several centuries dependent children had been under chancery jurisdiction; in principle all children were wards of the state if their parents were not willing or able to care for them; in practice the protection of dependent children was confined almost entirely to those who had property. The juvenile-court law of Chicago was a logical extension of this principle of guardianship by the court of chancery to all children who were in need of the protection and guardianship of the state, and thus was made to include delinquent children.

The juvenile-court movement developed rapidly after the Chicago court was authorized. Twenty-two states had somewhat similar laws within ten years. By 1925 all except two states—Maine and Wyoming—had such laws, and by 1945, when Wyoming passed its law, all states had juvenile-court laws. The juvenile-court movement spread to other continents, and most developed countries now have specialized juvenile courts.

The juvenile court has developed administratively as well as geographically. The age of the children coming under the court's jurisdiction has been raised from sixteen to seventeen or eighteen and in some places even to twenty-one. Adults who commit crimes against children or contribute to the delinquency or dependency of children are included in the jurisdiction of some juvenile courts. Many administrative tasks have been assumed by the juvenile court, including adoption proceedings, recreational work, and educational work. These tasks are ordinarily administered as part of the preventive program of the court.

[3]For discussions of the history, trends, and problems of the juvenile court, see Anthony M. Platt, *The Child Savers: The Invention of Delinquency* (Chicago: University of Chicago Press, 1969); Sanford J. Fox, "Juvenile Justice Reform: An Historical Perspective," *Stanford Law Review*, 22:1187–1239, 1970; and Robert M. Mennel, *Thorns and Thistles: Juvenile Delinquents in the United States, 1825–1940* (Hanover, N.H.: University Press of New England, 1973).

CHARACTERISTICS OF THE JUVENILE COURT

A comparison of the juvenile court with the criminal court is difficult because of the large number of variations in the procedure and organization of each court. At present, the actual practices of some juvenile courts do not differ a great deal from the practices of some criminal courts. Perhaps there is as much variation among juvenile courts as there is between juvenile and criminal courts. The following comparison refers to the conventional criminal court, without its unofficial modifications, and to the juvenile court in its ideal form.

Criminal Court	*Juvenile Court*
1. Trial characterized by contentiousness; two partisan groups in conflict.	1. Hearing characterized by scientific methods of investigation.
2. Purpose of trial to determine whether the defendant committed the crime charged.	2. Purpose of hearing to determine whether the youth is delinquent and the general condition and character of the youth.
3. Limited procedures for securing information regarding the character of the defendant.	3. Elaborate procedures for securing information regarding the character of the juvenile.
4. Such information, if secured, may not be introduced as a part of the evidence.	4. Such information is the basis on which a decision is made.
5. Punishment if convicted.	5. Protection, guardianship, and treatment by the state if the existing conditions show the need.
6. Correctional methods in a specific case determined not by the needs of the particular individual but by the possibilities of using such methods within the framework of specific deterrence and general deterrence.	6. Correctional methods in a specific case determined by the needs of the particular individual without reference to specific deterrence or general deterrence.

Broad Definition of Delinquency

The expected reaction of criminal-court personnel to crime is punitive—they seek, with some exceptions, to implement a punitive reaction to an offense. In contrast, the expected reaction of juvenile-court personnel is that of treatment—they seek, with some exceptions, to implement an interventionist reaction to the offender. The *ideal* of the juvenile courts is that the personnel "are not looking outwardly at the act, but scrutinizing it as a symptom, are looking forward to what the child is to become."[4] The characteristics of the juvenile court in practice, however, are

[4] White House Conference on Child Health and Protection, *The Delinquent Child* (New York: Appleton-Century-Crofts, 1932), p. 257.

quite similar in some respects to those of the criminal court in practice. For example, a very broad definition of "delinquent child" ordinarily is provided, but in practice juvenile-court officials look for violations of specific statutes, just as do criminal-court officials. The state of Illinois, for example, once used the following definition of a delinquent child:

A delinquent child is any male who while under the age of 17 years, or any female child who while under the age of 18 years, violates any law of this state; or is incorrigible, or knowingly associates with thieves, vicious or immoral persons; or without just cause and without the consent of its parents, guardian or custodian absents itself from its home or place of abode, or is growing up in idleness or crime; or knowingly frequents a house of ill repute; or knowingly frequents any policy shop or place where any gambling device is operated; or frequents any saloon or dram-shop where intoxicating liquors are sold; or patronizes or visits any public pool room or bucket shop; or wanders about the streets in the night time without being on any lawful business or lawful occupation; or habitually wanders about any railroad yards or tracks or jumps or attempts to jump onto any moving train; or enters any car or engine without lawful authority; or uses vile, obscene, vulgar, or indecent language in any public place or about any school house; or is guilty of indecent or lascivious conduct.[5]

In the standard juvenile-court law formulated by the National Probation Association and in many states, the concept of delinquency is similarly avoided. These laws are even more general than the Illinois law. They simply establish the fact that juvenile courts have jurisdiction over children who behave in certain general ways. For example, in the standard act, jurisdiction is established over "predelinquents . . . whose occupation, behavior, environment, or associations are injurious to his welfare," as well as over delinquents "who violate any state law or municipal ordinance."[6] Definitions of the dependent child also are stated in general terms. Supporters of the standard act argued, and still argue, that the broad definition of who is a delinquent enables the court to help and protect juveniles without stigmatizing them.[7]

The behavior of "predelinquent" and dependent children is quite different from behavior that, except for the age of the offender, would be crime. However, it was not through oversight that the juvenile court was given jurisdiction over all three categories of children and youth. The purpose is supposed to be the same in all three cases: to determine whether the child needs special guardianship by the state. The elements of guilt, responsibility, criminal intent, and punishment are,

---

[5] *Illinois Revised Statutes* (Chicago: Burdette Smith, 1949), pp. 1315–16. Several states continue to use "delinquent child" statutes that are very similar to this one. See Mark M. Levin and Rosemary C. Sarri, *Juvenile Delinquency: A Comparative Analysis of Legal Codes in the United States* (Ann Arbor, Mich.: University of Michigan National Assessment of Juvenile Corrections, 1974), pp. 10–12.

[6] National Probation Association, *A Standard Juvenile Court Act* (New York: Author, 1959), p. 10. For an enumeration of items mentioned in juvenile-court laws as constituting delinquency, see Sol Rubin, "Legal Definitions of Offenses by Children and Youth," *Illinois Law Forum*, 16:512–23, 1960.

[7] The problems associated with broad definitions of juvenile delinquents are discussed by Thorsten Sellin and Marvin E. Wolfgang, *The Measurement of Delinquency* (New York: Wiley, 1964), pp. 71–86.

theoretically, not considered. The omnibus definitions of delinquency are a logical extension of this theory. The assumption is that the results of contact with the juvenile court are beneficial, not harmful or punitive, and, consequently, precise descriptions of proscribed acts are not necessary.

In practice, some criteria for distinguishing between lawbreakers and nondelinquents must be used by the courts, and, although the result is called "adjudication" or "finding" rather than "conviction" or "acquittal," the criteria used are quite similar to those used in the criminal courts. For example, a juvenile court using the Illinois statute quoted above would have to consider the question of guilt or intent in order to determine whether a child has *knowingly* associated with thieves or *knowingly* frequented a gambling house.[8] Thus *delinquency* becomes a mere softening of the word *crime*, for in distinguishing between delinquency and predelinquency, the juvenile court in fact considers delinquents as "young criminals." Of the 407,223 juveniles arrested in California in 1974, 74 percent were detained for specific offenses, such as assault, burglary, and automobile theft, and 26 percent were detained for "delinquent tendencies" indicated by behavior such as truancy, incorrigibility, and hitchhiking.[9] In the United States, about 75 percent of the children referred to juvenile courts are predelinquency or lawbreaking cases; about 20 percent are dependency and neglect cases; and about 5 percent are involved in special proceedings, such as adoption. In many states, dependent children (e.g., orphans) have been removed from juvenile-court jurisdiction, and there is a current trend toward removing "predelinquent" youngsters as well (e.g., runaways, truants, incorrigibles, and others said to be "in-need of supervision").[10]

Equity, or Chancery, Jurisdiction

Equity courts stand for flexibility, guardianship, and protection, rather than rigidity and punishment. Consequently, friends of the juvenile court insist that children's cases should fall within the equity jurisdiction rather than the criminal jurisdiction. Supreme courts approved of this in several early decisions about the constitutionality of juvenile-court procedures. But the methods used in juvenile courts actually are not chancery procedures, and it appears that the analogy was used merely to rationalize the abandonment of the basic elements of due process of law. In many jurisdictions almost all the procedural safeguards of the criminal law were removed in children's cases, so that the court became a child-saving agency whose decisions were supported by the coercive power of the state.

Informal Procedures

Whether the jurisdiction is that of equity or not, the procedures in the juvenile court ordinarily are "summary" or informal. The proceedings begin with a

---

[8] See Sanford J. Fox, "Responsibility in the Juvenile Court," *William and Mary Law Review*, 11:659–84, 1970.
[9] *Crime and Delinquency in California, 1974* (Sacramento: Department of Justice), pp. 29–30.
[10] See R. Hale Andrews, Jr., and Andrew H. Cohn, "Ungovernability: The Unjustifiable Jurisdiction," *Yale Law Journal*, 83:1383–1409, 1974.

complaint against a child or youth. The juvenile may be arrested and detained in a jail or a juvenile hall, but usually is merely summoned to appear in court with his or her parents. Next, the juvenile is *arraigned.* Juveniles who have been locked up in detention usually are entitled to an arraignment within forty-eight hours, just as are adult suspects. The charging and arraignment procedure, called "initial hearing" or "intake interview," is quite informal. A court official—often a probation officer—tells the juvenile of the charge. Then the intake officer—usually a social worker rather than a lawyer—either dismisses the juvenile entirely, disposes of the case with an action called "counseled, warned, and released," or files an official petition for a court hearing. In thirty-four states the intake officer also can officially place the juvenile on probation—called "informal probation" because there has been no adjudication of delinquency—and the juvenile becomes part of the caseload of a regular probation officer. The juvenile and the parents or guardian must consent to this action. Most delinquency cases are settled by intake officers, just as most criminal cases are settled by prosecuting attorneys. Thus the hearing and adjudication process is avoided by dealing with the juvenile unofficially.[11] In recent years, about half the delinquency cases reported to the U.S. Children's Bureau by juvenile courts around the nation have been unofficial.

For those cases not disposed of at the time of intake, a *hearing* may be held immediately. More commonly, the intake officer files an official *petition in behalf* of the juvenile at this stage. This actually is a petition for a future hearing before a judge. Next, there is a *social investigation* by a probation officer. In some states this investigation is not held until after the court has indicated that a youth is delinquent, but the trend is toward prehearing investigations. The investigations involve not merely the questions of fact regarding a specified offense, but the whole social situation of the youth—especially the home and neighborhood conditions. Physical and psychiatric examinations sometimes are made also. The information secured in this way is supposed to be the basis of decisions and policies. A Minnesota study suggested that probation officers believe that analysis of the juvenile's attitude toward the offense, family data, and previous delinquent problems are the most important parts of the investigation reports; but the same officers believed that juvenile-court judges were most interested in present offense data, previous delinquency problems, and the juvenile's attitude toward the offense.[12] A San Diego, California, study produced similar findings, but also noted that judges granted 83 percent of the requests for probation and 75 percent of the recommendations for institutional commitment. In the 20 percent of the cases in which the probation officer's recommendation was not followed, a more lenient disposition was made three times as often as a more severe disposition.[13] Whether

---

[11] See Donald R. Cressey and Robert A. McDermott, *Diversion from the Juvenile Justice System* (Washington: Government Printing Office, 1974), pp. 7–17.

[12] Seymour Z. Gross, "The Prehearing Juvenile Report: Probation Officers' Conceptions," *Journal of Research in Crime and Delinquency,* 4:212–17, 1967.

[13] Richard M. Ariessohn, "Offense vs. Offender in Juvenile Court," *Juvenile Justice,* 23:17–22, 1972.

the investigation comes after a hearing or before a hearing, juveniles are either placed in detention or released on their own recognizance, called "parole" in some juvenile courts, until the time of trial (called "adjudication") and sentencing (called "disposition"). Most are entitled to bail, but this procedure is seldom used.[14]

Following the social investigation, a *hearing*, corresponding to the trial in adult courts, is held. The juvenile-court judge may hear the case either in chambers or in the courtroom, but the courtroom is generally arranged so that spectators are so far removed from the bench or table at which the judge is sitting that they cannot hear the conversation. The records are customarily regarded as confidential, and most states prohibit the publication of information on juvenile-court cases or printing a photograph of a child in the juvenile court. The general practice in the hearings is to exercise care in weighing evidence, but without the same observance of forms as in the criminal courts. Juveniles do not have a federal constitutional right to trial by jury under the due-process clause of the Fourteenth Amendment, but a statutory right to trial by jury exists in ten states. A nationwide survey of 266 juvenile courts found that, on the average, the courts dismissed 12 percent of the cases brought to the adjudication stage, but the rate was higher (19 percent) in the largest courts.[15]

The procedure called *sentencing* in the criminal courts generally is named *disposition* in the juvenile courts. The disposition of a case and the treatment of the juvenile theoretically are determined by the whole investigation, of which the court procedure is only a part. The major methods used in disposing of the cases that are given a hearing are continuance, probation, and commitment to an institution. The continuance is designed as a test of the offender and the parents without special assistance or supervision by the court. It differs from dismissal of the petition (often called "adjustment" or "discharge") largely in that the judge feels that further action of the court *might* be necessary. It also differs from probation, which includes, theoretically at least, supervision and guidance by a probation officer. Probation is used in a large proportion of the cases in places where juvenile-court methods are well developed. But in places where the judge has no special training in the problems of juvenile delinquency, where there are no social workers, psychologists, or psychiatrists, the juvenile is more likely either to be dismissed or to be committed to an institution. In ten states the juvenile-court judge is authorized to commit juveniles directly to institutions for adult offenders. In another third of the states a child committed by the juvenile court to an institution for delinquent children may be administratively transferred to an

[14] Allene K. Richardson Hill, "The Constitutional Controversy of a Juvenile's Right to Bail in Juvenile Preadjudication Proceedings," *Hastings Constitutional Law Quarterly*, 1:215–33, 1974.

[15] Yeheskel Hasenfeld, "Youth in the Juvenile Court: Input and Output Patterns," ch. 4. in *Brought to Justice? Juveniles, the Courts, and the Law*, eds. Rosemary Sarri and Yeheskel Hasenfeld (Ann Arbor, Mich.: University of Michigan National Assessment of Juvenile Corrections, 1976), pp. 69–70.

institution for adults convicted of crime.[16] Referral to a social-work agency, to a foster home, or to a qualified individual often is a condition of probation.

Criminal Procedures

Even in the juvenile courts said to operate under equity jurisdiction, many elements of criminal procedure may be found. First, the rights to counsel and trial by jury are retained, largely because of the fear that the Supreme Court might otherwise find the law unconstitutional.[17] The necessity of exercising such rights is minimized, however, and few children or parents demand an attorney or a jury trial. It has long been the rule that jury trials are inconsistent with both the law and the theory upon which juvenile courts were founded, and the Supreme Court recently affirmed that rule.[18]

Second, juvenile-court decisions may be appealed to the criminal courts. Among the states, only Delaware has no statutory provision relating to appeals. The number of appeals has always been very small, however. Of 277 juvenile-court judges who responded to a recent national survey, 58 percent said they had no appeals the previous year or had no information about appeals. Of the 120 courts with appeals, the median number of appeals was three. Seventy-two percent of the part-time judges reported no appeals, as compared with 40 percent of the full-time judges.[19] The proportion of juvenile-court cases appealed steadily declined during the first sixty years of juvenile-court history, but it is now increasing.[20]

Third, delinquency, though given a blanket definition by some phrases, is defined also by some specific phrases, in imitation of the criminal law.

Fourth, in their reports the juvenile courts frequently classify offenses in terms of the criminal law, such as grand larceny, burglary, etc. Similarly, in an early New York case it was stated by a criminal court that an adult defendant charged with receiving stolen property could not offer the defense that since the property had been purchased from a "juvenile delinquent," not from a "thief" or a "criminal," it was not "stolen."[21]

Fifth, most judges impose sentences that are distinctly those of the criminal court, including imprisonment. From the point of view of juvenile-court theory, commitment to an institution is a substitute for family life and home training, not an infliction of punishment. But almost everyone—especially juvenile delinquents—views institutionalization as punishment. For example, juveniles placed on probation are threatened with incarceration if they get into trouble again.

[16]President's Commission on Law Enforcement and Administration of Justice, *Task Force Report: Juvenile Delinquency and Youth Crime* (Washington: Government Printing Office, 1967), p. 6.

[17]National Council of Juvenile Court Judges, *Counsel for the Child* (Chicago: American Bar Center, 1966).

[18]*McKeiver* v. *Pennsylvania*, 403 U. S. 528 (1971).

[19]Michael Sosin and Rosemary Sarri, "Due Process—Reality or Myth?" ch. 9 in *Brought to Justice? Juveniles, the Courts, and the Law*, eds. Sarri and Hasenfeld, pp. 176–206.

[20]Addison M. Bowman, "Appeals from Juvenile Courts," *Crime and Delinquency*, 11:63–77, 1977.

[21]*Pollack* v. *People*, Supreme Court of New York, Appellate Division, 1913. 154 App. Div. 716.

Sixth, despite welfare ideology, the juvenile-justice processes are generally regarded as procedures for punishing bad children. In the minds of the juvenile, the parents, the neighbors, the police, and others, juvenile-court action is a criminal process.[22] That this belief is not unrealistic is seen in the fact that most complaints against or petitions in behalf of juveniles are filed by police officers. In California, about 90 percent of the male delinquency cases and 80 percent of the female delinquency cases are referred by police.

Seventh, and more generally, because juvenile courts in fact deprive persons of their liberty, as do criminal courts, they now must show concern for due process of law. Ten years ago the Supreme Court rendered a highly significant decision in the area of juvenile-court procedure. It ruled in the *Gault* case that juvenile courts must grant to children many of the procedural protections required in criminal trials by the Bill of Rights.[23] The Court was impressed with the kind of observations made above, and with the kind of observation made by the President's Commission:

> In theory the juvenile court was to be helpful and rehabilitative rather than punitive. In fact the distinction often disappears, not only because of the absence of facilities and personnel but also because of the limits of knowledge and technique. In theory the court's action was to affix no stigmatizing label. In fact a delinquent is generally viewed by employers, schools, the armed services—by society generally—as a criminal. In theory the court was to treat children guilty of criminal acts in noncriminal ways. In fact it labels truants and runaways as junior criminals. In theory the court's operations could justifiably be informal, its findings and decisions made without observing ordinary procedural safeguards, because it would act only in the best interests of the child. In fact it frequently does nothing more nor less than deprive a child of liberty without due process of law—knowing not what else to do and needing, whether admittedly or not, to act in the community's interest even more imperatively than the child's.[24]

The *Gault* decision specified that the juvenile and the parent must be given specific notice in writing of the specific charges that must be met at the hearing; that the juvenile and the parent must be notified of the juvenile's right to be represented by counsel; that a lawyer must be appointed if the parents are unable to afford one; that juveniles and parents must be advised of the juvenile's privilege against self-incrimination, such as the right to remain silent rather than be a witness against one's self; that admission or confessions obtained from a juvenile

[22]See Martha Baum and Stanton Wheeler, ''Becoming an Inmate,'' ch. 7 in *Controlling Delinquents*, ed. Stanton Wheeler (New York: Wiley, 1968), pp. 153–85; Eloise Snyder, ''The Impact of the Juvenile Court Hearing on the Child,'' *Crime and Delinquency*, 17:180–7; and Jack D. Foster, Simon Dinitz, and Walter C. Reckless, ''Perceptions of Stigma Following Public Intervention for Delinquent Behavior,'' *Social Problems*, 20:202–9, 1972.

[23]*In Re Gault*, 387 U.S. 1 (1967).

[24]President's Commission, *Task Force Report: Juvenile Delinquency and Youth Crime*, p. 9. See also Edwin M. Schur, *Radical Non-Intervention: Rethinking the Delinquency Problem* (Englewood Cliffs, N.J.: Prentice-Hall, 1973), pp. 29–78.

without the presence of counsel must be given the greatest scrutiny in order to ensure reliability; and that, in the absence of a valid confession, confrontation and sworn testimony by witnesses available for cross-examination are essential for a finding of "delinquency."

The extension of these rights, long available to adults, would seem to require an overnight transformation of juvenile-court procedures. As indicated, juvenile courts were founded on the notion that strict application of the ordinary rules of criminal procedure would interfere with the desired relationship between the juvenile and the court officials. The *Gault* decision demands that these rules be applied. But a study of hearings in three urban juvenile courts indicated that the Supreme Court directives were being avoided.[25] In keeping with the Court's decision, the study covered only those hearings in which individuals were charged with delinquency, who were subject to commitment to an institution, and who were not represented by an attorney. The general finding was that the courts were not systematically applying the principles of the *Gault* decision. For example, in two of the courts, parents were fully informed of the juvenile's right to retained or appointed counsel in only two of 131 cases. Informing the juvenile of the right to silence occurred in only twenty of 121 relevant cases, and in seventeen of these cases—all in one court—the advice given by the judge was prejudicial. Of the 122 cases deemed relevant for purposes of the right to confrontation, full opportunity for cross-examination of witnesses was found in thirty-seven, or 30 percent. The investigators concluded, "Despite the Supreme Court's concern for protecting youths in jeopardy of losing their liberty, juveniles were at the time of this study and presumably still are remanded to peno-custodial institutions without being afforded their constitutional rights."[26] Consistently, a recent survey of juvenile-court practices suggested that no revolution has occurred in the implementation of due process. Most judges agreed that juvenile rights should be acknowledged and protected, but they agreed far less about how and to what extent procedural safeguards must be implemented.[27] It should be noted, further, that most juvenile-court cases are disposed of informally, with no hearing before a judge and, hence, with few procedural safeguards.

THE COURT HAVING JURISDICTION

Jurisdiction over children's cases varies widely from state to state and even from county to county within a state. Independent juvenile courts have been created in

[25]Norman Lefstein, Vaughan Stapleton, and Lee Teitelbaum, "In Search of Juvenile Justice: Gault and Its Implementation," *Law and Society Review*, 3:491–562, 1969.

[26]Ibid., p. 535. See also Paul Lerman, "Beyond Gault: Injustice and the Child," in *Delinquency and Social Policy*, ed. Paul Lerman (New York: Praeger, 1970), pp. 236–50; Charles E. Reasons, "Gault: Procedural Change and Substantive Effect," *Crime and Delinquency* 16:163–71, 1970; D. Dufee and L. Siegal, "The Organization Man: Legal Counsel in the Juvenile Court," *Criminal Law Bulletin*, 7:544–53, 1971; and Elyce Zenoff Ferster, and Thomas F. Courtless, "Pre-dispositional Data, Role of Counsel and Delinquency in Juvenile Court," *Law and Society Review*, 7:195–222, 1972.

[27]Sosin and Sarri, "Due Process—Reality or Myth?" p. 205.

about half the states, but in many of these states the juvenile court is independent only in certain counties. The juvenile court usually is a specialized branch of some other court, generally a county court or a probate court. Because county-court judges preside over many of the independent courts, the independent courts are scarcely distinguishable from the others. Connecticut, Delaware, Rhode Island, and Utah have statewide juvenile courts, one for each of a number of geographical districts; these courts are funded and operated at the state level, as opposed to the county or municipal level.

In thirty-seven states, the District of Columbia, and in parts of another state, the juvenile court has exclusive jurisdiction in children's cases, with certain exceptions. In the other states, the juvenile may be taken either to the juvenile court or to a branch of the criminal court. Also, provision is frequently made in states in which the juvenile court has exclusive original jurisdiction that the judge may transfer cases involving serious offenses to the criminal court. The Supreme Court held in 1968 that such a transfer must be preceded by a judicial hearing, with counsel, testing the necessity for the transfer.[28] In some states the juvenile court has no jurisdiction over juveniles charged with offenses that, if committed by adults, would be punishable by death or by life imprisonment.

Good reasons exist for the opinion that the juvenile court should have original, exclusive, and complete jurisdiction over all cases of delinquency of juveniles. The fact that in some states the jurisdiction of the juvenile courts and the criminal courts is concurrent, as well as the fact that serious offenses are excepted from the jurisdiction of the juvenile court, reveals that the authors of juvenile statutes obviously were confused. It is asserted that the juvenile is not responsible for crime and should not, therefore, be punished; yet violations that call for the most severe punishments in the criminal law are excepted.

AGE JURISDICTION

Age jurisdiction also varies widely from state to state. The maximum age for original jurisdiction is seventeen in thirty-three states, sixteen in twelve states, and fifteen in the remaining states. Three states (Illinois, Oklahoma, and Texas) still set a lower maximum age for males than for females despite the fact that such a distinction has been held unconstitutional by several state supreme courts.[29] In some states a youth taken into the juvenile court before reaching the maximum age of juvenile-court jurisdiction remains within the jurisdiction of the juvenile court until a later age, generally twenty-one.

Many juvenile courts also have jurisdiction over certain adults. Forty-three states have laws that make it possible to deal through the courts with parents or others who contribute to the delinquency or dependency of children, and in thirty-one states and parts of six others it is the juvenile courts that have this jurisdiction, with limitations in some states. The juvenile court in a few states is

---

[28] *Kent* v. *United States*, 401 F. 2d 408 (1968).
[29] Levin and Sarri, *Juvenile Delinquency*, p. 13.

given jurisdiction over the following specified groups: adults deserting or failing to support juveniles, adults accused of crimes against children, adults violating child-labor laws, parents failing to comply with the compulsory school law or concealing the birth of a child, adults aiding a child to escape from an institution, and adults furnishing children in institutions with contraband items.

The justifications offered for extending the jurisdiction of the juvenile court to these adults are that it keeps the juvenile, even as a witness, out of the criminal court; that it is easier to deal with all the significant personnel together, and that judges in other courts hesitate to use the ordinary criminal sanctions in dealing with such offenders, and consequently discharge them with a futile warning. However, the informal procedures of the juvenile court do not necessarily safeguard civil rights, and many persons have therefore argued that the juvenile-court hearing should not be used in dealing with adults.

THE JUDGE

The judge of the juvenile court is elected to that post in certain cities or counties in six states, is appointed by the governor in certain cities or counties in nine states, by the president of the United States in the District of Columbia, by the public-welfare commissioner in Utah, and by the presiding superior-court judge in each judicial district in Alaska. In by far the largest proportion of counties, the judge is elected as judge of the ordinary local court, then later assumes the duties of a juvenile-court judge. In most rural counties there is only one judge for all types of cases; the judge of the county circuit, or district court, of which the juvenile court is a part, acts ex officio as judge of the juvenile court. In the larger cities where the juvenile court is more completely separated from the court of which it is a branch, and one judge gives full time to juvenile-court work, the judge of the juvenile court is appointed by his or her associates in most cases. When the appointment is not made in this way, the judges frequently rotate, each one taking one month, two months, or perhaps a year in the juvenile court.

This method of rotation does not necessarily select judges who are best able to deal with juveniles, but one study indicated that Iowa juvenile-court judges conceive of their role as one approximating the role defined in juvenile-court philosophy, rather than as one approximating that of the criminal-court judge.[30] A recent survey of juvenile-court judges revealed that one-third had not received undergraduate degrees, 5 percent had no college education at all, and 15 percent were not members of the bar. Two-thirds of the judges devoted one-fourth time or less to juvenile matters.[31] In attitudes and behavior patterns, juvenile-court judges

[30] F. James Davis, "The Iowa Juvenile Court Judge," *Journal of Criminal Law, Criminology, and Police Science,* 42:338–50, 1951.

[31] Kenneth Cruce Smith, "A Profile of Juvenile Court Judges in the United States," *Juvenile Justice,* 25:27–38, 1974. See also Howard James, *Children in Trouble* (New York: David McKay, 1969), ch. 4; Robert M. Emerson, *Judging Delinquents: Context and Process in Juvenile Court* (Chicago: Aldine, 1969), ch. 7; and Josefina McDonough, "Structural and Staff Characteristics of Juvenile Courts," ch. 6 in *Brought to Justice? Juveniles, the Courts, and the Law,* eds. Sarri and Hasenfeld, pp. 96–118.

are less restrictive than police officers, but they are more likely than social workers to favor external controls.[32] A Washington, D.C., study found that experienced juvenile-court judges, having learned a criminal-court role, showed a more punitive attitude than did inexperienced judges, who showed a more prominent treatment orientation.[33] However, Wheeler and his associates found that judges with punitive attitudes did not impose sentences as severe as those imposed by judges who were more permissive in outlook, probably because the more punitive judges saw incarceration as hurtful while the more "professional" judges saw it as therapeutic or protective.[34]

But the behavior of juvenile-court judges also is affected by the environment in which they work. Emerson noted that although the juvenile-court judges he studied were oriented toward a rehabilitation ideology, they were obliged to make accommodations to other users of the court, such as police officers, parents, welfare workers, and school officials. When such interest groups made specific demands for imposition of sanctions, judges frequently satisfied them: "Thus, the problem for the court is not to decide between punishing or treating a particular delinquent. Rather it is to identify the alternative courses of action open to it and to choose the one that both satisfies the various interests represented in the case and affords the best chance of 'helping' the youth involved."[35] A survey of juvenile-court judges, court administrators, and probation officers found that about half of these personnel believed that the community wants the court "to protect the community at any cost" and "to make an example of those committing the most serious offenses," and about 90 percent believed that the community wants the court "to remove offenders with serious behavior problems from the community."[36] In general, "Juvenile court staff tend to perceive the mandate from the community to be that of social control and deterrence, despite the fact that most juvenile court cases referred to the courts are for minor and status offenses."[37]

Because the definitions of delinquency and the rules of law regarding juvenile-court procedures are not precisely stated in most instances, the judge plays an

---

[32]R. H. Walther and S. C. McCune, "Juvenile Court Judges in the United States: Working Styles and Characteristics," *Crime and Delinquency*, 11:384–93, 1965; Ariessohn, "Offense vs. Offender in Juvenile Court," p. 19; and Michael Sosin, "Staff Perceptions of Goal Priorities," ch. 3 in *Brought to Justice? Juveniles, the Courts, and the Law*, eds. Sarri and Hasenfeld, pp. 38–59.

[33]Jackwell Sussman, "Juvenile Justice: Even-handed or Many Handed? An Empirical Investigation of Decision Processes in Disposition Hearings," *Crime and Delinquency*, 19:493–507, 1973.

[34]Stanton Wheeler, Edna Bonacich, M. Richard Cramer, and Irving K. Zola, "Agents of Delinquency Control: A Comparative Analysis," ch. 3 in *Controlling Delinquents*, ed. Stanton Wheeler (New York: Wiley, 1968), pp. 31–60.

[35]Emerson, *Judging Delinquents*, p. 29. See also Michael Lanley, "The Juvenile Court: Making a Delinquent," *Law and Society Review*, 7:268–82, 1972.

[36]Yeheskel Hasenfeld, "The Juvenile Court and Its Environment," ch. 5. in *Brought to Justice? Juveniles, the Courts, and the Law*, eds. Sarri and Hasenfeld, pp. 72–95.

[37]Ibid., p. 93.

exceedingly important role in the official proceedings. It is the judge's duty to order that the best available social-work and social-welfare programs be utilized in dealing with juveniles. At the same time, it is the judge's duty to protect the rights of all juveniles coming before the court, and to declare juveniles "delinquent" and, hence, subject to supervision, only when there are legal grounds for doing so. Familiarity with behavioral science is considered necessary to the efficient performance of the first duty, and some persons have recommended that judges should be persons trained in principles of child welfare rather than in law. The second duty, however, requires decisions on issues of law. In view of the *Gault* decision, it is not possible to dispense with the legal character of the juvenile court.[38]

It is possible, however, for much of the work to be done under the supervision of the judge by persons who have not had legal training. Most cases are now settled by intake officers who are not lawyers. In twenty-eight states, the law gives juvenile-court judges authority to appoint referees, who make tentative disposals of the cases petitioned for a hearing, subject to the judge's subsequent approval. This power to appoint referees makes it possible to extend the court to rural districts that are far from the place where the sessions of the court are held. If no such arrangement is made, offenses are passed over, or a justice of the peace is appealed to for the exercise of coercive power, or some other unsatisfactory method is adopted because of the inconvenience of attending the sessions of the juvenile court.

THE SUCCESS OF THE JUVENILE COURT

If it could be demonstrated that the juvenile-offense rate in areas possessing juvenile courts is lower than the rate in areas without such courts, then, all other things being equal, there would be little question about the success of the juvenile court. This fact has not been demonstrated, however, for two reasons. First, in order to make such a study it would be necessary to locate two areas comparable in every significant respect, so that only the presence of a juvenile court was the differentiating factor. Second, it would be necessary to measure the amount of juvenile delinquency in each case. Although the first difficulty could be partially surmounted by comparing an area before and after it established a juvenile court, experience has indicated that judicial statistics do not measure the amount of crime or delinquency. In most towns and cities, most of the children who commit delinquencies serious enough to result in arrests are kept at the police station and then unofficially released by the police. Also, broad definitions contribute to the difficulty of comparing the juvenile-offense rates at various places and times. Consequently, the effects of juvenile-court work must be measured in some other way.

[38] The conflict here is essentially the same as the conflict between the role of the criminal-court judge as an umpire in the attempt to determine guilt or innocence, and the same judge's role in sentencing. See the discussion in Chapter 18, above.

Two alternative methods, both severely limited by the fact that many youths under the care of the juvenile court commit delinquencies that do not come to the attention of the juvenile court, have been used. First, studies have been made of the subsequent "success" or "failure" of cases handled by juvenile courts. Numerous surveys indicate that about one-third of all juvenile-court cases involve repeaters. In the District of Columbia the figure has reached 60 percent, and in one year more than a quarter of the cases involved juveniles who had been referred to the court three or more times before.[39] A recent Philadelphia study found that 84 percent of the delinquencies were committed by repeaters, who composed 54 percent of the sample; offenders with five or more offenses composed 18 percent of the sample but were responsible for 51 percent of the delinquent acts.[40]

A second method of appraising the success of the juvenile court is by enumerating the offenders in criminal courts who have previously been in juvenile court. About 3 percent of the 39,600 defendants convicted in the United States district courts in 1972 had a prior juvenile record. A study of Ohio prisoners disclosed that 25 percent of the males and 28 percent of the females had been arrested at least once as juveniles.[41] Similarly, the Massachusetts prison reports show that approximately 25 percent of the offenders sentenced to the state prison and the state reformatories have previously been committed to institutions for delinquent children. Such statistical enumerations, of course, do not precisely test the effects of the juvenile court, since it is not clear what proportion of the subjects involved would have become repeaters if they had been dealt with in some other way. Also, insofar as the wards of the juvenile court refrain from subsequent delinquency, it is not clear why they do so. The assumption has been that the methods used in connection with the juvenile court are the explanation. But serious questions have been raised regarding the validity of the belief that individualized treatment methods are valuable in a large proportion of cases, even if they are used. For example, some years ago it was proposed that an intensive study be made of the Cincinnati court, which had a reputation for unusual success in preventing repeated delinquencies among its wards. But a preliminary investigation showed that the court was far inferior to the Boston juvenile court in its standards of casework and facilities for casework, despite the fact that the Cincinnati court secured at least equally successful results. Consequently, it was concluded that the success of the Cincinnati court could not be explained by its casework methods.

[39] President's Commission, *Task Force Report: Juvenile Delinquency and Youth Crime*, p. 23.

[40] Marvin E. Wolfgang, Robert M. Figlio, and Thorsten Sellin, *Delinquency in a Birth Cohort* (Chicago: University of Chicago Press, 1972), p. 88. See also Elyce Zenoff Ferster and Thomas F. Courtless, "Post-dispositional Treatment and Recidivism in the Juvenile Court," *Journal of Family Law*, 11:683–709, 1972; and Anne Rankin Mahoney, "The Effect of Labeling upon Youths in the Juvenile Justice System: A Review of the Evidence," *Law and Society Review*, 8:583–614, 1974.

[41] Barbara Ann Kay, "Attitudes Toward Law and Moral Values: Men versus Women Prisoners of Ohio," paper presented at the meetings of the American Society of Criminology, Montreal, 1964.

On the basis of such information as has been presented, some authorities have stated that the juvenile court is a dismal failure, while others have become convinced that it is highly successful. Those considering it a success point out that it is unfair to the court to test it in terms of absolute cessation of delinquency. Taft used an analogy with illness, stating that "a hospital is not a complete failure if its patients leave in better health, even though they again contract the same disease for which they were treated."[42] Those who speak most frequently of the failure of the juvenile court ordinarily believe that it is a failure because it has not been punitive enough, permitting too many youngsters to avoid the hurt stipulated in the criminal law for all who transgress in certain ways. Their "war on crime" includes a "war on juvenile delinquency." But others consider the juvenile court a failure because it has in practice coerced and punished youngsters and has done most of this in the name of treatment and rehabilitation. These persons, like the Supreme Court justices who rendered the *Gault* decision, ask that juveniles be handled as though they were criminal-court suspects and defendants when they are accused of acts that would be called crimes if they were adults, and ask that juveniles not be interfered with at all by coercive state agents if they have not been accused of committing such acts.[43]

PROPOSED MODIFICATIONS

Among the plans suggested for changes, the three most important proposals are (1) a merger of the juvenile court with a general family court; (2) a transfer of most of the work of the juvenile court to social-welfare agencies or to the schools; and (3) a merger of the juvenile court with the criminal court.

The proposal that the juvenile court be merged with the general family court is made because of the conviction that the various problems of the family are related and should all be handled by one agency. Juvenile courts would handle all cases of domestic difficulty, including nonsupport, desertion, paternity, divorce, alimony, custody of children, guardianship of children, adoption of children, neglect of children, dependency, contributing to the delinquency of children, and delinquency itself. A court organized along these lines has been operating in Cincinnati since 1914, and such courts are found in parts of at least eighteen states, chiefly in the larger urban areas, and throughout New Jersey and Virginia. In its extreme form, however, such a court would be one in which juveniles would be given many of the rights now reserved for adults (e.g., the right to sue for separate maintenance), rather than a traditional family court, domestic-relations court, or juvenile court where things are done to, with, and for juveniles whether the juveniles want these things done or not.

The second suggestion is that the work of the juvenile court be confined to the

---

[42]Donald R. Taft, *Criminology* (New York: Macmillan, 1950), p. 577.

[43]See, for example, Patrick T. Murphy, *Our Kindly Parent—The State: The Juvenile Justice System and How It Works* (New York: Viking Press, 1973).

performance of judicial functions, and that all casework functions be transferred to social-work agencies. The suggestion is contrary to the "social agency" view that as a public agency the court cannot refuse to accept any case that might come to it for aid, and it is an endorsement of the legal view that the courts should limit their intake to cases in which there is a specific issue of delinquency.[44] As early as 1903, Aschaffenburg urged that the discipline of school-age children should be transferred to the schools, and that they should not be tried at all in the courts. In recent years, the tendency has been to suggest that the cases of children in trouble be diverted to social-welfare agencies, rather than to the school.

The argument for these changes is based on the observation that court labeling of a juvenile as a delinquent often does more harm than good. The idea is to find alternative means of directing the behavior of minors. As has been indicated, of the selected cases that go to the juvenile court, the large proportion are settled unofficially, without an appearance before the judge. It is proposed, therefore, that this unofficial work be expanded.[45] The proposal does not assume, of course, that no cases need go to the juvenile court for adjudication. It is an expression of a belief that it is undesirable for a child to appear in a court of any kind, juvenile or criminal, and that such appearances should be obviated as far as possible by the development of extracourt methods of dealing with juvenile behavior. Lemert has noted that this proposal, which he helped to formulate, calls for fundamentally different ways of *perceiving what juvenile delinquency is*, not just for different methods of dealing with youngsters who are referred to official agencies:

Categorically different ways of perceiving delinquency need to be found, ways which give prominence to the definitional processes, and to the ramified consequences of the policy and actions of those agencies which feed cases into the juvenile justice system. An operational perspective is needed to replace that of treatment and reform. . . . The things which have been called delinquency are with a small exceptionable portion normal problems of socialization, and should be so conceived. From such a view, all children are delinquency prone and at the same time none are, hence such invidious terms are bereft of their meaning and should be discarded. This is not to insist that children's serious problems should be ignored, but rather that they meet objective criteria in order to make youths candidates for the official justice system. . . . If forms of delinquency have been defined into existence they can be defined and administered out of existence by those with power to do so. Statutes need changing in such a way that specified procedures rather than substantive statements make it difficult, costly, or impossible to process truants, runaways, incorrigibles, and "moral danger" cases from police departments or other sources to

---

[44]For discussion of these two views, see H. Warren Dunham, "The Juvenile Court: Contradictory Orientations in Processing Offenders," *Law and Contemporary Problems*, 23:508–27, 1958. See also Edwin M. Lemert, *Social Action and Legal Change: Revolution Within the Juvenile Court* (Chicago: Aldine, 1970).

[45]See Edwin M. Lemert, *Instead of Court: Diversion in Juvenile Justice* (Washington: Government Printing Office, 1971); Robert M. Carter, "The Diversion of Offenders," *Federal Probation*, 36:31–6, 1972; and Ross E. Hampton, *Sentencing in a Children's Court and Labeling Theory* (Wellington, New Zealand: Department of Justice, 1975).

juvenile courts. . . . Ideally, the diversion of minors from juvenile courts will become a state of mind, an unquestioned moral position held by all child and youth welfare organizations, considered as a good in itself rather than a means to an end. Problems will be absorbed informally into the community, or if they are deemed sufficiently serious they will be funnelled into some type of diversion institution, staffed and organized to cope with problems on their own terms rather than as antecedents to delinquency.[46]

Of the hundreds of "diversion" programs and projects inaugurated and sponsored by juvenile courts in recent years, only a few have been consistent with this proposal. Rather than redefining delinquency in a way that is consistent with what a "child" or a "youth" actually is in the twentieth century, legislators and others have, by and large, merely extended the reach of the juvenile court by handling perceived delinquents more informally than before. Police departments have long been diverting from the juvenile court the vast majority of the juveniles they encounter. Nejelski and LaPook have noted that for every 500 possible arrests of juveniles, there are only about 200 police contacts, resulting in about 100 arrests; of these, only forty youths reach the intake stage, only twenty have adjudicatory hearings, and only one or two are sent to an institution.[47] Perhaps eight out of ten youths encountering police officers are released without any formal processing or recording. They are lectured, sent home, referred to social-work agencies, threatened, or even punished administratively, but they are not arrested or booked.

But this action, or lack of it, does not necessarily involve a redefinition of delinquency. Juveniles who "fail to take advantage" of a police diversion policy or program are likely to find themselves before a probation officer serving as intake officer for a juvenile court. Such intake officers are authorized to make a wide range of decisions pertaining to what is now called diversion, ranging from dismissal, "counsel, warn, and release," informal probation, and referral to a special diversion unit or diversion program. There is a distinct possibility that juveniles who would have been informally dismissed by police officers or formally dismissed by court intake officers are now being required to participate in "diversional programs," with the result that there is more state interference in

[46]Lemert, *Instead of Court*, pp. 91–2.

[47]Paul Nejelski and Judith LaPook, "Monitoring the Juvenile Justice System: How Can You Tell Where You're Going, If You Don't Know Where You Are?" *American Criminal Law Review*, 12:9–31, 1974. See also Donald J. Black and Albert J. Reiss, Jr., "Police Control of Juveniles," *American Sociological Review*, 35:211–27, 1970; Theodore N. Ferdinand and Elmer G. Luchterhand, "Inner-City Youth, the Police, the Juvenile Court, and Justice," *Social Problems*, 17:510–27, 1970; Norman L. Weiner and Charles V. Willie, "Decisions by Juvenile Officers," *American Journal of Sociology*, 77:199–210, 1971; William R. Arnold, "Race and Ethnicity Relative to Other Factors in Juvenile Court Dispositions," *American Journal of Sociology*, 77:211–27, 1971; Jay R. Williams and Martin Gold, "From Delinquent Behavior to Official Delinquency," *Social Problems*, 20:209–29, 1972; Terrence P. Thornberry, "Race, Socioeconomic Status and Sentencing in the Juvenile Justice System," *Journal of Criminal Law and Criminology*, 64:90–8, 1973; and Charles W. Thomas and Christopher M. Sieverdes, "Juvenile Court Intake: An Analysis of Discretionary Decision-Making," *Criminology*, 12:413–32, 1975.

their lives, and in the lives of their parents, than there was before the diversion concept became popular.[48] If, at the level of the intake officer, the juvenile fails or in some other way forgoes a chance to avoid the juvenile court itself, the case is likely to become truly official—a petition charging delinquency will be filed with the court. When, after completion of the official social investigation, the juvenile appears in a courtroom, there is still a slight chance that the youth will be "diverted" by a referee or judge. But by then the juvenile will have had so many contacts with juvenile-justice agents that it is doubtful whether the "diversion" action can be called diversion without putting the word in quotation marks.

When true diversion occurs, the juvenile is safely out of the official realm of the juvenile-justice apparatus and is immune from incurring the delinquent label or any of its variations—predelinquent, delinquent tendencies, diverted delinquent, person in need of supervision, troublemaker, hard-core, unreachable. In one community, for example, some females who have run away from home, or exhibited other behavior traditionally identified as diagnostic of delinquency or predelinquency, are taken by police officers to a detention center, but from there they are accompanied in a walk down the street to a house maintained by a private Good Neighbor Agency, and their cases are dismissed. Thus no official action is taken. The young women are free to leave the house immediately if they wish, but few of them do so. There is no limit to the number of times an individual may be referred to the program.[49] Consistently, California recently removed "predelinquency" cases such as runaways, truants, and girls who are "out of control" from the jurisdiction of juvenile courts, and many communities have established Youth Service Bureaus whose functions are similar to those of the Good Neighbor Agency program.[50] Perhaps the most outstanding success of such Youth Service Bureaus has been in the area of image change. The personnel of public and private agencies and, what is more, a significant number of minors have learned that youth problems are family and community problems and that they are usually easier to resolve outside the traditional authoritarian framework than within it.

But Cressey and McDermott found very little such diversion in the communities they studied. They found, instead, that juveniles are labeled as delinquents and then required to participate in one of the many new diversion programs maintained by the court system at some level short of official court action—

---

[48]See Paul Nejelski, "Diversion: The Promise and the Danger," *Crime and Delinquency*, 22:393–410, 1976.

[49]Cressey and McDermott, *Diversion from the Juvenile Justice System*, pp. 20–1.

[50]See Elaine B. Duxbury, *Youth Service Bureaus in California: A Progress Report* (Sacramento, Calif.: Department of the Youth Authority, 1971); J. R. Seymour, "Youth Service Bureaus," *Law and Society Review*, 7:247–72, 1972; Arnold Binder, John Monahan, and Martha Newkirk, "Diversion from the Juvenile Justice System and the Prevention of Delinquency," in *Community Mental Health and the Criminal Justice System*, ed. John Monahan (New York: Pergamon Press, 1974); Richard Ku and Carol Holliday Blew, *The Adolescent Diversion Project: A University's Approach to Delinquency Prevention* (Washington: Government Printing Office, 1977); and Thomas R. Phelps, *Juvenile Delinquency: A Contemporary View* (Pacific Palisades, Calif.: Goodyear, 1976), pp. 89–127.

informal probation, a diversion unit for predelinquents, a family-counseling center, a drug-abuse prevention program, etc. Consistently, a California project dedicated to evaluating diversion programs stresses the coercive nature of such programs: "Any diversion involves a decision not to further process youth accused or convicted of an offense into the justice system *on the condition that the individual participates in a diversion program.*"[51] Canada is currently considering legislation which in one respect would regularize this practice of merely pretending that juveniles will be diverted away from the juvenile-court bureaucracy in the way they were, at the time of the invention of the juvenile court, diverted away from the criminal-court bureaucracy. The Canadian legislation would limit delinquency to offenses against the regular criminal code, thus diverting so-called "predelinquents" or "status offenders" from the court system. But the legislation also would require attorneys general to "lay charges" against young people accused of violating this code and would establish formal screening agencies "to facilitate the diversion of young persons from the court process."[52] Such practices probably would increase rather than decrease the number of code violators labeled as delinquents because youths now handled informally by police officers and others would be accused of an offense of some kind. The discretionary procedures now used by intake officers would be formalized, with the result that the screening agencies would become courts in themselves, functioning as juvenile courts now function when they hold hearings to determine whether certain juveniles should be turned over to the criminal-court system.

In the United States, the process proposed for Canada is called "minimization of penetration," and it is used for assuming control over juveniles and then keeping them under control by allowing them to avoid court by participating in an official or semiofficial program, to avoid formal probation by going on informal probation, to avoid institutionalization by going on formal probation, and so on. All this is being done in the name of diversion, and such diversion policies have, among other things, diverted away from the juvenile court the accusations that the court has inadvertently been harming young children and teenagers as well as helping them. Cressey and McDermott concluded, "The faddist nature of diversion has produced a proliferation of diversion units and programs without generating a close look at whether the juvenile subject to all this attention is receiving a better deal. It is quite possible that participating personnel have revamped terminology and procedures without seriously altering what happens to the juvenile."[53] It is quite possible, also, that establishing diversion units has

---

[51] Marvin Bohrnstedt, Roy Lewis, Gary Miyao, Lin Moon, Carolyn Moore, Ted Palmer, and Cliff Zerikotes, *The Evaluation of Juvenile Diversion Programs, Second Annual Report* (Sacramento, Calif.: Department of the Youth Authority, 1976), p. 2 (italics added).

[52] Solicitor General's Committee on Proposals for New Legislation to Replace the Juvenile Delinquents Act, *Young Persons in Conflict with the Law* (Ottawa: Solicitor General of Canada, 1976), pp. 7, 25–7.

[53] *Diversion from the Juvenile Justice System*, p. 34.

become a means of expanding intervention in the lives of juveniles rather than a means of officially ignoring much of what for a century has been called delinquency: "As long as mainstream America continues to view all deviations from a narrowly defined acceptable norm as evidence of pathology requiring some kind of control response (whether punitive or rehabilitative), diversion is likely to remain largely a technique of enforcing conformity by alternate means."[54]

The third proposal for juvenile-court modification—that juvenile courts and criminal courts be merged—has taken two quite different forms, as suggested by the differing opinions regarding the success of the juvenile court. In the first form, it is observed that the rights of children to due process of law have been neglected by juvenile courts, and it is proposed that they no longer be neglected, thus making the juvenile court more like the criminal court. In the second form, it is observed that the distinction between the juvenile court and the criminal court is not a logical one, and it is proposed that both kinds of courts be modified, resulting in a merger.

The statements made above regarding the characteristics of the juvenile court give an incorrect impression of the present methods of dealing with juvenile delinquents because attention is fixed on the well-organized courts in a few large cities. But most of the courts that hear children's cases are in counties that have no city of more than 25,000 population, and in such areas few courts can afford even the bare essentials of a juvenile court: separate hearings for children, probation service, and records of social information. Thousands of children are deprived every year of rights that are guaranteed to them by law—the right not to be detained in jails with adult offenders, the right to a separate hearing, the right to be regarded as the ward of the court in need of protection and help rather than of punishment. The loss of these rights causes little protest, because few people speak for such children. If the rights of a professional or other influential class were so denied or abridged, a howl of protest would compel the authorities to obey the law. It is this situation that has prompted proposals for organization of the juvenile court on a statewide rather than on a countywide basis, and also for merger with the criminal-court system where, presumably, civil liberties are more carefully safeguarded than in the juvenile-court system.

The problem of extending the juvenile court may be approached from another standpoint. Why should not the methods now used in juvenile courts be extended to adults? If we do this, does the separate existence of the juvenile court have an adequate justification? Two principles have been used to justify the handling of juvenile offenders separately from adults, and both of them are under attack.

First, children have been regarded as not capable of committing crime because they do not have sufficient intelligence and experience to formulate an essential element in every crime—criminal intent. But the juvenile court has retained the element of intent in the distinction between delinquency and "predelinquency,"

---

[54]Eleanor Harlow, *Diversion from the Criminal Justice System* (Washington: 1971), p. 26.

and whether a particular juvenile is treated as one or the other is determined largely by a judgment as to intent. Moreover, if the youngster under sixteen or even under eighteen or twenty-one is, by law, incapable of having criminal intent, it would appear that many persons over the juvenile-court age are similarly incapable. No logical method exists for setting an age level that will separate those who are responsible from those who are not. Juvenile-court methods based on the principle of lack of responsibility are, therefore, either not justified or else their very existence logically indicates that they should be extended to adults.

Second, juvenile courts developed because it was believed that criminal courts were based on the assumption that criminals were vicious and depraved, and on the assumption that severe penalties efficiently deter others from crime. It was insisted that the best policy for dealing with children would be to guard and protect them rather than punish them.[55] But recent changes have made it impossible to state the function of the criminal law solely in terms of punishment. For example, presentence investigations are required by law in the adult courts of some states, and in many states certain offenders, especially sex offenders, are accorded psychiatric treatment rather than punishment. Also, in many of the specialized courts, such as morals courts and domestic-relations courts, the methods are very similar to those of the juvenile court. It may be observed these are largely formal changes only, and that in practice the object of the law is punishment. But it may also be observed that in practice the object of most institutions and programs for juvenile delinquents also is punishment. The differences between the criminal courts and the juvenile courts are not nearly as great as they were when the juvenile court was invented.[56] Social investigations in keeping with the adjustment principle, use of the summons instead of arrest, bail and detention, informal procedures, and private sessions—all of these could be used advantageously by the criminal court.[57]

SUGGESTED READINGS

Beemsterboer, Matthew J. "The Juvenile Court—Benevolence in the Star Chamber." *Journal of Criminal Law, Criminology, and Police Science*, 50:464–75, 1960.

Cicourel, Aaron. *The Social Organization of Juvenile Justice*. New York: Wiley, 1968.

Coffey, Alan R. *Juvenile Justice as a System: Law Enforcement to Rehabilitation*. Englewood Cliffs, N.J.: Prentice-Hall, 1974.

Cressey, Donald R., & Robert A. McDermott. *Diversion from the Juvenile Justice System*. Washington: Government Printing Office, 1974.

Emerson, Robert M. *Judging Delinquents: Context and Process in the Juvenile Court*. Chicago: Aldine, 1969.

---

[55]For an elaboration and critique of this assumption, see Anna Louise Simpson, "Rehabilitation and the Justification of a Separate Juvenile Court System," *California Law Review*, 64:984–1017, 1976.

[56]See George Edwards, "In Defense of the Juvenile Court," *Juvenile Justice*, 23:2–6, 1972.

[57]See John Griffiths, "Ideology in Criminal Procedure, or a 'Third' Model of the Criminal Process," *Yale Law Journal*, 79:359–95, 1970.

Empey, Lamar T. "Juvenile Justice Reform: Diversion, Due Process, and Deinstitutionalization." Chapter 4 in *Prisoners in America*, ed. Lloyd E. Ohlin. Englewood Cliffs, N.J.: Prentice-Hall, 1973.

Faust, Frederic L., & Paul J. Brantingham, eds. *Juvenile Justice Philosophy: Readings, Cases and Comments*. St. Paul, Minn.: West, 1974.

Fox, Sanford J. "Juvenile Justice Reform: An Historical Perspective." *Stanford Law Review*, 22:1187–1239, 1970.

Klein, Malcolm W. *The Juvenile Justice System*. Beverly Hills, Calif.: Sage, 1976.

Lemert, Edwin M. *Social Action and Legal Change: Revolution Within the Juvenile Court*. Chicago: Aldine, 1970.

Lemert, Edwin M. *Instead of Court: Diversion in Juvenile Justice*. Washington: Government Printing Office, 1971.

Lerman, Paul, ed. *Delinquency and Social Policy*. New York: Praeger, 1970.

Lerman, Paul. *Community Treatment and Social Control*. Chicago: University of Chicago Press, 1975.

Mennel, Robert M. *Thorns and Thistles: Juvenile Delinquents in the United States, 1825–1940*. Hanover, N.H.: University Press of New England, 1973.

Platt, Anthony M. *The Child Savers: The Invention of Delinquency*. Chicago: University of Chicago Press, 1969.

Reinemann, John. "Fifty Years of the Juvenile Court Movement in the United States." *Mental Hygiene*, 34:391–9, 1950.

Rosenheim, Margaret K., ed. *Pursuing Justice for the Child*. Chicago: University of Chicago Press, 1976.

Sarri, Rosemary, & Yeheskel Hasenfeld. *Brought to Justice? Juveniles, the Courts, and the Law*. Ann Arbor, Mich.: University of Michigan National Assessment of Juvenile Corrections, 1976.

Waite, E. F. "How Far Can Court Procedure Be Socialized Without Impairing Individual Rights?" *Journal of Criminal Law and Criminology*, 12:339–48, 1921.

20

Probation

Although probation is primarily a nonpunitive method of handling offenders, it has developed within the framework of a legal system that is basically punitive. Probation methods represent a distinct break with the classical theory on which the criminal law is based, for an attempt is made to deal with offenders as individuals rather than as classes or concepts, to select certain offenders who can be expected, with assistance, to change their attitudes and other behavior patterns while residing in the free community, and to use a great variety of nonpunitive methods in rendering assistance to those offenders selected. Probation thus is a system for implementing the interventionist reaction to lawbreaking. It does not attempt to make criminals suffer; it attemps to shield them from suffering. Some suffering results from having been placed in the probationer status, but, in theory at least, this suffering is not intentional and is avoided as far as possible. Consequently there is no reason for insisting that probation is punishment, as some authors have done in an effort to win approval for the system.

THE NATURE OF PROBATION

From the constitutional point of view, probation is the suspension of a sentence during a period of liberty in the community conditional upon good behavior of the convicted offender. The courts have, without exception, found the constitutional justification of probation in the right of the court to suspend sentence. Ancel has shown that the suspended sentence was invented as an "alternative sentence"; nowadays it would be called a diversion program or an alternative to prison.[1] But mere suspension of sentence is an act of mercy or judicial leniency that allows "hopeful cases" or first offenders "another chance." Probation is

[1] Marc Ancel, *Suspended Sentence* (London: Heinemann, 1971), p. 7.

clearly different from the suspended sentence alone, because in principle it includes a positive method of dealing with offenders. Although a conditional suspension of sentence by the court is necessary, probation includes supervision, guidance, and assistance to the offender. This assistance has come to be the important part of the probation system. Probation thus is a diversion program and an alternative to prison, but it also is a program of what recently has been named "community-based corrections."[2]

The suspension of sentence, and hence the threat of punishment, is always present in probation, and this is a reflection of a punitive reaction to crime. In some states, however, a suspended sentence now can be granted only if the offender is placed on probation; this notion that the offender should be guided and assisted is a reflection of the interventionist reaction to crime. Probation, then, represents a kind of compromise between the punitive reaction and the interventionist reaction.

A definition of probation that reveals this compromise may be stated as follows: Probation is the status of a convicted offender during a period of suspension of sentence, in which the criminal is given liberty conditioned on good behavior, and in which the state, by personal supervision, attempts to help the offender maintain good behavior. Court decisions based on information obtained in presentence investigations of the offender's personality and background are implied. The U.S. Supreme Court has stated that probation is to be used "to provide an individualized program offering a young or unhardened offender an opportunity to rehabilitate himself without institutional confinement under the tutelage of a probation officer and under the continuing power of the court to impose institutional punishment for his original offense in the event he abuses the opportunity."[3]

The suspension of sentence that permits positive action to be taken may be either a suspension of the *imposition* of the sentence or the suspension of the *execution* of the sentence. Most states suspend the execution, but others suspend the imposition, and still others use both methods. In California, about 80 percent of the probation grants to adults by superior courts are suspensions of the imposition of sentence, 10 percent are suspensions of the execution of a jail sentence, and 5 percent are suspensions of a sentence to prison. If the judge imposes a sentence and then suspends the execution of the sentence, and if the offender violates the probation, the judge merely orders the execution of the original sentence. If the judge suspends the imposition of the sentence, the court will, in case of violation of probation, have additional information on which to base a decision regarding the sentence that should be imposed.

Whichever method of suspending the sentence is used, it is a method of

---

[2] See Gary R. Perlstein and Thomas R. Phelps, eds., *Alternatives to Prison: Community-Based Corrections* (Pacific Palisades, Calif.: Goodyear, 1975).

[3] *Roberts* v. *United States*, 320 U.S. 264, 272 (1943).

suspending punishment, and thus it is to be regarded as an alternative to imprisonment and to release without supervision. It is important to judge probation in relation to these two alternatives; it is frequently judged as though it were an alternative to imprisonment alone.

Some questions of law have arisen regarding probation. A federal court sentenced an offender to serve two years in a penitentiary and then provided that he be released on probation at the end of six months and kept on probation during the remainder of the two years. The higher court held that this was illegal, because the court was really ordering the offender paroled, and the court had no jurisdiction in regard to parole. However, Ohio recently enacted a "shock probation" law under which judges are authorized to release convicted felons from prison after 130 days or less, and place them on probation. The rationale behind the law is that limited exposure to prison is enough for deterrence and retributive purposes. Between 1966 and 1974, 5,509 criminals were sent to prison and then released under the "shock probation" law; 10 percent of them violated the terms of probation, some by committing new crimes.[4] Again, the court may convict a woman on two counts, then commit her to an institution on the first count and place her on probation on the second count. This apparently is not illegal, but like "shock probation" it is contradictory to the principle that probation is to be used as a system for keeping offenders out of prison while at the same time giving them assistance. In some jurisdictions, offenders frequently are granted probation with the stipulation that they spend part of the probationary period in the county jail. Forty percent of the persons granted probation by California superior courts in 1972 were given jail sentences as part of the conditions of probation. Six counties gave jail sentences to over 80 percent of their probationers, but one county used this sentence with 29 percent.[5]

THE ORIGIN, DEVELOPMENT, AND SCOPE OF PROBATION

As was observed in Chapter 14, the punitive reaction was at one time mitigated by methods such as securing sanctuary, right of clergy, judicial reprieve, and technical circumvention of statutes. Probation can be traced to such practices.[6] The common-law practice of suspending sentences for short periods was extended, and courts began to suspend sentences indefinitely, permitting convicted offenders to remain at large on good behavior. Some offenders were compelled to furnish a financial guarantee that they would maintain good behavior, and in

[4]Nick Gatz, "First Shock Probation; Now Shock Parole," *American Journal of Corrections*, 37:20–1, 1975. See also David M. Peterson and Paul C. Friday, "Early Release from Incarceration: Race as a Factor in the Use of 'Shock Probation,'" *Journal of Criminal Law and Criminology*, 66:79–87, 1975; and Paul C. Friday and David M. Peterson, "Shock Imprisonment: Short-Term Incarceration as a Treatment Technique," *International Journal of Criminology and Penology*, 1:319–426, 1973.

[5]*Adult and Juvenile Probation* (Sacramento: California Department of Justice, 1972), p. 27.

[6]Frank W. Grinnell, "The Common Law History of Probation," *Journal of Criminal Law and Criminology*, 32:15–34, 1941.

some instances restrictions were placed on their freedom. Then volunteers began to assist such offenders during the period of the suspension of the sentence. Among the early volunteers was John Augustus, a shoemaker of Boston, who in 1841 secured the release of a confirmed drunkard from the police court of Boston by acting as surety for him. This offender turned out to be a "sober, industrious citizen" under his care. During the next seventeen years Augustus acted as surety for 1,152 males and 794 females and gave less formal aid to many others.[7] Such volunteers became more numerous and were, in effect, probation officers before probation had been authorized by statute.

In 1869, a Massachusetts state social agency was authorized by the legislature to accept the custody of juvenile offenders, with the right of placing them in private families. This amounted to probation, and 23 percent of the juvenile offenders convicted in the courts of Boston in 1869–1870 were dealt with in this manner. But the first statutory provision for probation with publicly paid officers was the Massachusetts law of 1878, which authorized the mayor of Boston to appoint and pay a probation officer and authorized the municipal court to place offenders on probation. No restrictions were made, as in many subsequent probation laws, regarding the term of probation, the age, previous record, or other characteristics of the offender. The legislature extended this power to all other mayors of the state in 1880, and in 1891 it made mandatory the appointment of probation officers by lower-court judges.

By 1917, twenty-one states had provided for adult probation, and all states had authorized, at least, the suspension of sentences. The states with the highest percentage of urban population developed probation first, and it gradually spread to the more rural states. Probation was authorized in the federal courts in 1925, but those courts had used it without statutory authority for some years before that. Most European nations have provision for suspension of sentence, and many have volunteer or philanthropic assistance for persons during the period of suspension of sentence, but few have provided for publicly paid probation officers.

In 1925 probation for juveniles was available in every state, and by 1956 all states had made probation available to adult felons as well. However, use of probation in many of these states is limited by statute, and in only fifteen states may probation be granted regardless of type of crime. Crimes of violence, crimes involving the use of a deadly weapon, and crimes carrying a certain penalty often are excepted. Furthermore, in some states probation may be used only by courts in cities or counties of a specified size or by courts with specified types of jurisdiction. These statutory restrictions ordinarily are indicative of a conflict between the punitive and interventionist reactions to crime, for they are based on the assumption that

[7] *John Augustus, First Probation Officer* [reprint of a report by Augustus, with an introduction by Sheldon Glueck] (New York: National Probation Association, 1939), p. vi. See also N. S. Timasheff, *One Hundred Years of Probation* (New York: Fordham University Press, 1941); and Donald W. Moreland, "John Augustus and His Successors," *National Probation Association Yearbook, 1941*.

probation is mere judicial leniency, which should not be available to certain offenders.

Evidence of the conflict also may be found in the failure of courts to appoint and pay authorized probation officers and in the failure to use probation when it is authorized by law and when probation officers are provided. The rural districts are far behind the urban communities in this respect. In 165 counties in four states, no juvenile probation services were available in 1966.[8] No general statistics covering the entire United States are available. In the federal-court system in recent years, about 40 percent of those convicted in district courts have been placed on probation. The district courts of Massachusetts grant probation to about two-thirds of the cases coming before them, and the superior courts use probation in about 45 percent of their cases. Probation probably is used more generally in this state than in many others. In England's superior courts there has been an increase in the proportion of offenders given probation in the years since World War II, but in magistrates' courts (which include juvenile courts), there has been a steady decrease. Table 22 shows that in Michigan the number of prisoners per 100,000 population decreased regularly in a thirty-year period, while the number of probationers per 100,000 population steadily increased.

ORGANIZATION OF PROBATION DEPARTMENTS

Two agencies have been suggested as the proper bodies to control probation work— the court and an independent administrative body. Because probation originated in the suspended sentence and hence is regarded as an extension of the judicial function, the control of probation work usually is in the hands of the court. This has carried with it the decision in some states that probation officers can be appointed by no agency except the court. The stated objections to the method are: (1) The work of supervision is essentially administrative, not judicial. There is no more reason for having probation administered by the courts than for having prisons or reformatories so administered. (2) Judges are not able to handle this administrative work efficiently. They have other duties that interfere with supervision of probation, and the probation department really becomes an independent administrative body. Consequently there has been a trend toward the other method of appointment and supervision of probation officers. The Los Angeles County probation department, for example, is completely separate from the courts and is under the control of a county board of supervisors. It serves the juvenile courts as well as the adult courts. In the juvenile field, sixteen states have centralized state administration for probation services, while in the adult field, thirty-seven states are so organized.[9]

[8]National Council on Crime and Delinquency, "Correction in the United States," appendix A in President's Commission on Law Enforcement and Administration of Justice, *Task Force Report: Corrections* (Washington: Government Printing Office, 1967), p. 134.

[9]President's Commission, *Task Force Report: Corrections*, p. 36.

Table 22 Rates for Convicted Offenders Granted Probation, Parole, or Sentenced to Prison in Census Years, Michigan, 1930–1960

Census Years as of January 1	Rates per 100,000 General Population for Offenders			
	Total	On Probation	On Parole	In Prison
1930	270	72	38	159
1940	286	84	56	147
1950	299	105	59	135
1960	363	173	67	123

SOURCE: Robert J. Glass, *Review of Trends in Adult Corrections over Thirty Years* (Lansing: Michigan Department of Corrections, 1961), table A-3.

Probation, like the maintenance of detention institutions and the administration of juvenile courts, is primarily a municipal or county responsibility. Most probation workers argue that administration of probation should be a function of the state, and in states that have a strongly centralized system the probation system has operated most effectively. Many counties cannot support the services of full-time probation officers, and in other counties there are so few criminal cases that employment of a full-time, paid worker is not justified. Because parole is almost always administered on a statewide basis, thirty of the fifty states combine felony probation and parole services for adults, and thirteen do so wholly or in part for juveniles.

SELECTION OF PROBATIONERS

In almost all jurisdictions adult probation is granted only after the offender has been found guilty. There must be a conviction of a specific offense. A few jurisdictions, however, use a procedure comparable to that of the juvenile courts. Thus, persons merely *charged* with crime are placed on probation. For example, in magistrates' courts of Maryland, the defendant may receive the disposition of "probation before conviction." A similar disposition in lower courts in Massachusetts is termed "case continued without finding." In both instances, if an individual stays out of difficulty for a given period of time and follows a recommended course of action, such as outpatient psychotherapy, attendance at Alcoholics Anonymous, or participation in some other diversion program, the case is closed.[10] Newman gives examples of similar procedures in the lower courts of Kansas, Michigan, and Wisconsin.[11] This "deferred prosecution" procedure

[10] President's Commission on Law Enforcement and Administration of Justice, *Task Force Report: The Courts* (Washington: Government Printing Office, 1967), p. 6.

[11] Donald J. Newman, *Conviction: The Determination of Guilt or Innocence Without Trial* (Boston: Little, Brown, 1966), pp. 160–5.

enables the accused person to maintain certain rights that might be forfeited by a conviction, and it eliminates expensive trials, but these advantages might be completely offset by the denial of the traditional rights to due process of law.

Statutes or procedural rules make a presentence report mandatory for certain classes of offenses in about one-quarter of the states. In most states and in the federal system a request for a presentence report is discretionary with the judge, although in some of these states probation may not be granted unless a presentence report has been prepared. This investigation is for the purpose of determining the characteristics of the prospective probationer and of the circumstances of the offense, so that the judge will have factual information on which to make a decision. Even in states where the report is mandatory, many judges do not wait for an investigation; instead, they base their decisions on the offender's statement, criminal record, personal appearance, social status, the nature of the offense, and the recommendations of persons outside the probation department. These criteria are likely to be decidedly inadequate as a basis for sentencing, and it is largely because of this inadequacy that probation has been brought into ill repute.

Preprobation investigations are mandatory in Illinois, yet in a two-year period 13 percent of the probations granted to felons in Cook County were granted without proper continuance of court proceedings so that the investigation could be made.[12] In Great Britain, "social enquiry" reports (essentially presentence reports but sometimes used to assess culpability as well) were prepared for about 40 percent of all the cases tried and sentenced in higher courts in 1956, but by 1971 this proportion had increased to about 80 percent.[13] A recent study of probation reports filed in seventeen Canadian cities revealed that presentence investigations were requested by judges in two-thirds of the cases, and that probation investigators' recommendations had a strong direct effect on judges' sentencing dispositions.[14] In the federal courts of the United States, as in California, judges almost always follow the probation officer's recommendation for probation, but when the officer recommends against probation the recommendation is followed in about 80 percent of the cases.[15]

When investigations are made, they usually are made by regular probation officers. Using an analogy with medicine, these investigations are sometimes referred to as "diagnosis" because they provide the factual basis for later individual or group treatment. Reckless has formulated the scientific, interven-

[12]Don T. Blackiston, "The Judge, the Defendant, and Criminal Law Administration" (unpublished Ph.D. dissertation, University of Chicago, 1952).

[13]Martin Davies and Andrea Knopf, *Social Enquiry Reports and the Probation Service*, Home Office Research Unit Report No. 18 (London: Her Majesty's Stationery Office, 1973), p. 4. See also Mary Daunton Fear, "Social Enquiry Reports: Comprehensive and Reliable?" *British Journal of Criminology*, 15:128–39, 1975.

[14]John Hagan, "The Social and Legal Construction of Criminal Justice: A Study of the Pre-Sentencing Process," *Social Problems*, 22:620–37, 1975.

[15]Robert M. Carter and Leslie T. Wilkins, "Some Factors in Sentencing Policy," *Journal of Criminal Law, Criminology, and Police Science*, 58:503–14, 1967.

tionist principle as follows: "An adequate presentence investigation not only indicates whether the defendant is probationable; it also gives clues as to the causes of the criminal behavior, the possible extent to which he may be reformed or rehabilitated, and his need for a constructive probation program."[16] Gross has similarly stressed the idea that a presentence investigation seeks the cause of the criminality and then recommends a program of intervention based on this knowledge: "The main function of the prehearing report in juvenile court proceedings is to present the sociocultural and psychodynamic factors which influence the juvenile's alleged delinquent behavior. The prehearing report is supposed to give an objective, integrated, and perceptive evaluation so that the court can arrive at an individualized and rehabilitative disposition."[17] The ideal investigation covers such things as the person's attitude toward the offense, previous criminal record, family situation, neighborhood and other group associations, educational and work history, personal habits (particularly in reference to the use of alcohol and drugs), physical and mental health, and perspective on life. Such ideal investigations are occasionally conducted in large probation departments where specialized officers can be assigned to the work, but in smaller departments the investigations are likely to be mere routine interviews with the prospective probationer. Cohn's study of probation officers' recommendations suggested that the officers are likely to collect objective information about the offender (e.g., age, sex, religion), but to base their recommendations on subjective assessments of data not collected in a systematic fashion.[18]

Probation departments characteristically have insufficient funds for the employment of adequate personnel. In this situation adequate investigation of each case is, of course, impossible. Probation investigation often is handicapped also by the fact that the investigator frequently is regarded as a detective by the offender and the other persons interviewed. This attitude is not without some justification, for in some cases, especially when the prospective probationers have insisted that they are innocent of the crimes for which they have been found guilty, the investigation takes on some of the characteristics of a retrial. After such an investigation, supervisory work will be extremely difficult, particularly in small departments where investigation and supervision are performed by the same officer.

The absence of organized and central records is a further detriment to probation investigation. In some communities official records are not available to probation investigators. Juvenile-court files frequently cannot be cited in preparation of reports of adult probation investigations. Educational and social-service

16 Walter C. Reckless, *The Crime Problem*, 5th ed. (New York: Appleton-Century-Crofts, 1973), p. 469.

17 Seymour Z. Gross, "The Prehearing Juvenile Report: Probation Officers' Conceptions," *Journal of Research in Crime and Delinquency*, 4:212–17, 1967.

18 Yona Cohn, "Criteria for the Probation Officer's Recommendations to the Juvenile Court Judge," *Crime and Delinquency*, 9:262–75, 1963. See also idem, *The Court and the Probation Officer: Two Interacting Systems* (Jerusalem: Ministry of Social Welfare, 1970).

records usually are scattered throughout the community, although in large cities social-service records are now centralized. The Los Angeles County probation department maintains a confidential central registry of all juveniles handled by the law-enforcement agencies in the county, but the registry information is destroyed when the juvenile reaches eighteen. Where probation is administered on a statewide basis, records ordinarily are maintained in a central state file. The maintenance of centralized records aids in the investigation of individual cases and makes statistical comparison of certain types of classes of offenders possible, but in the opinion of many, such records also give the state too much power over individual citizens.

Probation is used, as explained previously, primarily as a substitute for discharge without supervision and for imprisonment. The principle that should be used in determining whether probation should be substituted for discharge without supervision is: Does this offender need supervision and assistance in adjusting to community conditions, and will the offender benefit from this assistance and supervision? The principle that should be used in determining whether probation should be substituted for imprisonment is essentially the same, but includes also the seriousness of the offense. For both groups these questions can be answered best by intensive study of individual cases supplemented by analysis of the rates of probation violation by offenders in the past.

THE TERMS OF PROBATION

The terms of probation are generally fixed jointly by the legislature, the court, and the probation department or staff. The following are generally included: observance of all laws, good habits, keeping good company, regular reports as required, regular work or school attendance, payment of fines or reparation, abstinence from the use of alcohol and drugs, avoidance of unnecessary debts.[19] Often the probationer may not marry, may not become divorced, or may not change residence without permission of the probation department. Sometimes the probationer is required to live in a specified place. It may be necessary to require the person to live at home, not to live at home, or to live in some philanthropic institution. The probationer may be required to undergo specific medical or psychiatric treatment. In some states these terms must be communicated to the probationer in writing.

Payment of restitution, fines, or costs is frequently imposed not as a sentence, but as a condition for being placed on probation. Of the persons granted probation by California superior courts in one year, about 58 percent received a fine, an order to pay restitution, or both. In England it is not legally possible to impose a fine on an offender for the same offense resulting in a probation order; nevertheless, a study of a sample of probationers from eight probation areas showed that 56

[19]See Judah Best and Paul Birzon, "Conditions of Probation," *Georgetown Law Journal*, 51:809–36, 1963.

percent of them had been fined at the time they were placed on probation, usually for a second offense associated with the first one.[20] Though restitution or reparation is a valuable requirement in many cases, two objections have been made regarding the method by which this is enforced. (1) Probationers may be required to pay so much that their dependents suffer seriously. In Los Angeles County, the probation department investigates all pertinent claims against the offender and regulates payments according to ability to pay. (2) This frequently interferes with other work of the probation department and makes it primarily a collecting agency. Probation officers object to acting as collecting agents, principally on the ground that the assumption of such duties destroys the confidential relationship necessary to constructive casework. Persons who have been imprisoned after failing to make restitution payments, thus violating the conditions of their probation, often believe they are being punished not for crime but for failure to pay their debts.

The maximum probationary period is generally fixed by law and is the same as the maximum prison sentence for the offense. Within that limit the court may fix the period of probation and, after fixing it once, may subsequently alter it. In many states the average period of probation for all offenders is less than one year.

About 30,000 probation revocation hearings are held in the United States each year. The probation officer has the duty of informing the court if the probationer does not maintain the conditions imposed. Thus probation workers are expected to be police officers in addition to being welfare workers.[21] At a hearing, the court either warns the probationer or orders execution of the sentence for the original offense, in which case the time served on probation ordinarily is not counted as part of the prison term. The U.S. Supreme Court has ruled that persons on probation have a right to counsel in proceedings to revoke their probation or to reimpose a suspended sentence.[22] Some probationers arrested for a new crime merely have their probation revoked, but others are tried for the new offense. A probationer who is convicted may again apply for probation. If a prison term is ordered, the sentence that was suspended for purposes of probation may be ignored, or it may be made to run either concurrently or consecutively with the new sentence. If the probationer does not violate the conditions of probation, discharge may, depending on the jurisdiction, come automatically at the end of the probationary period, be ordered by the court before or at the end of the period, or be ordered by the probation officer without court action.

SUPERVISION AND GUIDANCE OF PROBATIONERS

After a person has been granted probationary status by the court, the probationer is assigned to a specified probation officer who administers the probation program.

[20] Martin Davies, *Financial Penalties and Probation*, Home Office Research Unit Report No. 5 (London: Her Majesty's Stationery Office, 1970).
[21] Carl B. Klockars, "A Theory of Probation Supervision," *Journal of Criminal Law, Criminology, and Police Science*, 63:550-7, 1972.
[22] *Mempa v. Rhay*, 389 U.S. 128 (1967).

In many instances this is the same officer who made the original probation investigation for the court.

Assignment

Three systems of probation assignments are used: by districts; by sex, ethnic status, or religion; and by problems. The first method, which is used most frequently, gives to one officer all probationers living in a particular district. The second method makes assignments of male probationers to male officers, female probationers to female officers, and similarly for ethnic status and religion. A 1974 survey found that probation agencies in four states do not allow probation officers to supervise persons of the opposite sex.[23] A national survey found 61 percent of the line probation officers to be male, 89 percent white; probation supervisors were 72 percent male, 93 percent white.[24] The specialization of probation work by problems is possible only in the larger urban probation departments.

Fifty probationers are now generally given as the recommended number to be assigned to one officer, provided the officer has a densely populated territory and is paid to give full time to supervision and guidance. In practice, most full-time probation officers have several times that number of probationers under supervision; in some departments the average case load is as high as four hundred. When the case load is more than about fifty, work with each probationer is impossible. This is not consistent with the principle of probation, for release without supervision and guidance is mere suspension of sentence. According to probation principles, if offenders do not need supervision and guidance, they should not be placed on probation; if they do need supervision and guidance, then the number assigned to one worker should be restricted so that the work will be effective.

Ordinarily, each probationer is assigned to the case load of a paid probation officer. Early experience with unpaid and untrained volunteers in the United States resulted in the almost unanimous conclusion that paid workers are essential and, beginning in the 1930s when social work started becoming a profession, volunteers were gradually replaced with paid probation officers. This conclusion and the policy stemming from it were both based on the assumption that probation workers, like physicians, administer individual treatment and therefore should, like physicians, be highly skilled and highly paid.

But in the 1960s volunteerism reemerged as a mode of public participation in the criminal-justice processes. Since that time there has been a steady increase in the extent and in the diversity of the work done by volunteers. Probationers continue to be assigned to the case loads of paid government employees, but these employees are being assisted by volunteers. In 1970 there were about 50,000

[23] Niyressa H. Schoonmayer and Jennifer S. Brooks, "Women in Probation and Parole, 1974," *Crime and Delinquency*, 21:98–106, 1975.

[24] Josefina McDonough, "Structural and Staff Characteristics of Juvenile Courts," ch. 5 in *Brought to Justice? Juveniles, the Courts, and the Law*, eds. Rosemary Sarri and Yeheskel Hasenfeld (Ann Arbor, Mich.: University of Michigan National Assessment of Juvenile Corrections, 1976), pp. 96–118.

citizens contributing millions of hours as probation volunteers throughout the country in all types of communities; at least fifty types of skills were donated.[25] Some paid and professional workers resisted the new volunteerism, which was implicitly implementing the theory that criminality and delinquency stem from the actor's social relationships and not from personal maladjustment or other illness. Scheier, an expert on volunteerism, has assured paid probation officers that volunteer work is similar to the work of paramedics and nurses' aides, and therefore should not be threatening to those in charge: "Your staff is the community, a reservoir of skills which can be orchestrated to probation planning."[26] By 1972 it was estimated that more than 200,000 volunteers were donating their time and efforts in some 2,000 court systems throughout the United States.[27] In Royal Oak, a Detroit suburb, sponsorship of probationers by unpaid volunteers is said to be highly successful, apparently because the program stresses involvement of the community in caring relationships with offenders.[28] However, courts continue to assign cases to probation departments, and these in turn assign them to paid probation officers, who enlist the assistance of volunteers. In Australia and in some European countries, probationers are directly assigned to volunteers, each of whom has a very small case load. There is no evidence that paid, specialized probation workers are more effective than are these persons, but evaluation of volunteer programs has proven to be peculiarly difficult.[29]

Routine Reports

Contacts between the paid probation officer and the probationer are generally made either in the office of the probation officer or the home of the probationer. Home visits are more effective because they enable the probation officer to come into contact with this most important part of the offender's environment, thus making possible a better understanding of the offender. Also, since the attitudes of the probationer's family and other close associates are important in determining the person's criminality or noncriminality, contacts with these associates are important in any effort to modify the offender's criminal attitudes. Yet the number of home visits per month and the amount of time per visit usually are so small as to be insignificant.

[25] Thomas J. Cook and Frank P. Scioloi, Jr., "Public Participation in the Criminal Justice System: Volunteers in Police, Courts, and Correctional Agencies," ch. 9 in *Crime and Criminal Justice: Issues in Public Policy Analysis*, eds. John A. Gardiner and Michael A. Mulkey (Lexington, Mass.: Lexington Books, 1975), pp. 107–12.

[26] Ivan H. Scheier, "The Professional and the Volunteer in Probation: An Emerging Relationship," *Federal Probation*, 12:27–34, 1970.

[27] *Volunteers in Law Enforcement Programs* (Washington: Law Enforcement Administration, Division of Program and Management Evaluation, 1972), p. 17.

[28] Joe Alex Morris, *First Offender* (New York: Funk and Wagnalls, 1970), p. 122.

[29] Hans W. Mattick and Broderick E. Reischl, *Some Problems in the Evaluation of Criminal Justice Programs: The Case of Volunteer Court Counselors and Volunteers in Probation* (Chicago: University of Illinois at Chicago Circle, Center for Research in Criminal Justice, 1975).

Most probationers are required by court order to report at regular intervals to the probation officer. Sometimes these reports are made once a week, sometimes once a month; at one time in Detroit the probationers who were not working were required to report daily. The procedure in making these reports varies widely. In some places the officer merely checks a card that the probationer hands through a window. In slightly less perfunctory systems the officer questions the probationer about work, companions, recreations, habits, and other things, and gives advice on many topics—economic, family, legal, habits, reading, self-improvement, and so on. Probationers are frequently required to bring written reports, such as school reports, reports from employers, receipts for payment toward support of the family or for restitution or reparation. Since "supervision" in such systems is practically nonexistent, it has been suggested that the system not be called "probation" and that, instead, it be called what it is, the suspended sentence.

Material Assistance

Probation officers also serve as welfare workers. They make efforts to give material assistance to probationers, principally in the form of jobs and welfare payments. Some probation departments maintain regular employment agencies, and others have small-loan programs. Some probation officers lend probationers money out of their own pockets and in other ways give a helping hand. In earlier years, probation officers administered the county welfare program as it pertained to probationers and their dependents, and in a few places this still occurs. Such duplication of the work of other community agencies is wasteful, and probation departments now generally refer their probationers to these other agencies.

Intervention

For about a quarter of a century, the fieldwork of probation officers has been called *treatment*, just as the work of probation investigators has been called *diagnosis*. This terminology, based on a medical analogy, is incorrect in at least four respects. (1) As already indicated, few if any presentence reports are, or can be, specific enough to be called "diagnoses." (2) Even if the ailment said to produce a person's delinquency or criminality were specifically diagnosed as, say, a defective ego, the probability is low that the diagnosis would be correct. (3) The efforts of probation workers are mostly given over to surveillance or to the direct opposite, shielding the probationer from arrest, not to making the probationer into a nondelinquent or a noncriminal.[30] (4) The efforts of probation officers that are not dedicated to surveillance matters or to routine report writing are principally educational, and we do not ordinarily think of education as "treatment."

The notion that criminals and delinquents should be placed on probation and

---

[30]See Dale G. Hardman, "The Function of the Probation Officer," *Federal Probation*, 24:3–10, 1960; Louis Tomaino, "The Five Faces of Probation," *Federal Probation*, 39:42–5, 1975; and Klockars, "A Theory of Probation Supervision."

thus guided and assisted is, however, a part of the interventionist reaction to crime. Even the naive notions about changing criminals used in some probation departments are scientific, for they involve the assumption that criminality is caused by something and can be modified if that cause is modified. For example, it is not difficult to find probation officers who say they use rehabilitation methods such as "gaining their confidence and friendship," "stimulating their self-respect, ambition, and thrift," "relieving their emotional tensions," and "counseling them on personal matters." These simplistic methods have two things in common: (1) they are nonpunitive and (2) they are based on the positivistic notion that crime and criminality can be reduced by dealing with the conditions that produce them.

Less simplistic methods are also interventionist, even if they are outdated theoretically. For example, the psychiatric school of criminology has popularized the conception of "treatment" by insisting that proper probation work consists of giving the probationer insight into his or her emotional problems and thus into the personal motivations for committing crimes. A probationer who gains such insight, the idea goes, will be unlikely to violate the law in the future. The probation officer can understand the client or patient only through intensive sessions that probe the basic motivations of the criminal, and these sessions at the same time give the criminal insight into personal dynamics and motivations. A further value of these sessions, according to this line of reasoning, is that the probationer will develop an identification with the probation worker, and through this identification will tend to behave as the probation worker behaves. The probation worker later breaks up this relationship so the probationer can make independent decisions. Although something akin to this conception of intervention continues to dominate professional probation work in the United States, the value of the techniques has not been demonstrated, and the validity of the theories is open to question. The principal reason for skepticism is that the procedure is, like most other conceptions of treatment or therapy for criminals, based on the mistaken idea that delinquency and criminality can be treated in an office or a clinic just as infectious diseases can be.

Differential-association theory and more general modern learning theory ask probation workers to see the attitudes and other behaviors of individuals as products of reinforcements occurring in the course of everyday social interactions. The learning processes that are of greatest importance in determining criminal behavior patterns are those that are frequent and intimate, as in the family, the play group, the old-fashioned neighborhood. The procedure for modifying these behavior patterns necessarily involves changing the person's group relations. For this purpose it is necessary either to remove the probationer from the web of former relations or to insert new elements into that web of relations. Although it is easier to remove the probationer from the interactions that are reinforcing the delinquency or criminality, modification of interactions is more effective in the long run.

If it be true that behavior is determined largely in local, personal groups, and that a probation officer can accomplish little by individual therapy, the policy of probation must be implemented principally by organization of the local community for helping the delinquent or criminal. Efforts of this type have been made in the Chicago Area Projects, where for almost fifty years local communities have been organized for probation work as well as for other programs for the reduction of delinquency.[31] Probation officers are selected, so far as practicable, from the local community. This selection is based on the belief that such officers will be culturally homogeneous with the community and therefore more effective than officers imported from other groups both in influencing the delinquents who are on probation and in inducing other residents of the community to participate in programs for presenting alternative behavior patterns to probationers.[32] Although little objective evidence of the success of the Area Projects in this respect is available, the principle seems to be correct, and it seems to be the principle underlying the development of halfway houses and other self-help programs for criminals.[33]

Community Corrections

England has long maintained hostels for youthful probationers, who may be sentenced to reside in them for a period of up to a year while working or attending school.[34] These hostels are "halfway houses" in the sense that they are intermediate between closed institutions and the community. Similarly, England has long maintained day-care centers and group homes for some juvenile probationers. In the United States in the last decade, similar programs have been introduced as "community corrections" and "diversion," and probation workers have increasingly become involved in them.[35]

"Community corrections" and "diversion" have never been precisely defined, but each refers to systems for keeping delinquents and criminals out of traditional institutions, and usually something more than straight probation is implied.[36]

[31] See James F. Short, Jr., "Introduction" in *Juvenile Delinquency and Urban Areas*, rev. ed., by Clifford R. Shaw and Henry D. McKay (Chicago: University of Chicago Press, 1969), pp. xxv–liv; and Harold Finestone, "The Delinquent and Society: The Shaw and McKay Tradition," ch. 1 in *Delinquency, Crime, and Society*, ed. James F. Short, Jr. (Chicago: University of Chicago Press, 1976), pp. 23–49.

[32] See Donald W. Beless, William S. Pilcher, and Ellen T. Ryan, "Use of Indigenous Nonprofessionals in Probation and Parole," *Federal Probation*, 36:10–15, 1972.

[33] See Donald R. Cressey, "Social Psychological Foundations for Using Criminals in the Rehabilitation of Criminals," *Journal of Research in Crime and Delinquency*, 2:49–59, 1965.

[34] Ian Sinclair, *Hostels for Probationers*, Home Office Research Unit Report No. 6 (London: Her Majesty's Stationery Office, 1971).

[35] Robert D. Vinter, George Downs, and John Hall, *Juvenile Corrections in the States: Residential Programs and Deinstitutionalization* (Ann Arbor, Mich: University of Michigan National Assessment of Juvenile Corrections, 1975). See also Robert D. Vinter, ed., *Time Out: A National Study of Juvenile Correctional Programs*, (Ann Arbor, Mich.: University of Michigan National Assessment of Juvenile Corrections, 1976).

[36] See Margaret K. Rosenheim, "Youth Service Bureaus: A Concept in Search of Definition," *Juvenile Court Judges Journal*, 20:69–74, 1969; and Elizabeth W. Vorenberg and James Vorenberg, "Early Diversion from the Criminal Justice System: Practice in Search of a Theory," ch. 5 in *Prisoners in America*, ed. Lloyd E. Ohlin (Englewood Cliffs, N.J.: Prentice-Hall, 1973), pp. 151–83.

Thus community corrections and diversion are not just new names for probation. They are, ideally, what probation should have been all along, namely "intensive intervention in lieu of institutionalization."[37] Included are specialized units of probation and parole agencies, nonresidential schools and counseling centers, and residential centers and out-of-home placements.[38]

In England, as in New Zealand, convicted offenders are sentenced to work alongside volunteers (or to do work that would be appropriate for volunteers if any were available), sometimes as a condition of probation, sometimes as a sentence in its own right.[39] Similar programs are being introduced in the United States as "community treatment" or "diversion." Connor has shown, in a study of the Soviet Union, that such forced public-participation programs have ideological as well as economic implications: "Part of the significance of public participation may lie in its relation to the attempt to form and solidify attitudes the regime wishes to create: to build, Soviet style, a 'collective conscience.' "[40] Whether this actually takes place is another question—in one Soviet city, factory directors sent a hundred persons to act as "guardians" under the local police, but only one showed up.

In the United States, adults as well as juveniles are diverted from institutions to these "probation plus" programs, but the programs are used primarily for juveniles. Adults are more often handled in "prison plus" or "parole plus" programs—selected inmates are partially released on furlough to halfway houses and other programs, and parolees participate in intensive intervention programs resembling those for juveniles on probation. A national survey showed that, for juveniles at least, these community treatment and diversion programs have significantly increased the overall number of persons who are adjudicated as delinquents and then put under the custody and direction of state agencies.[41]

Surveillance

Probation workers are expected to be police officers as well as diagnosers and interveners. As in parole, "supervision" is sometimes taken to mean zealous police work designed to determine whether the conditions of probation have been violated, sometimes as watchful waiting for violations coupled with helping the probationer in material ways, sometimes as methods for improving the welfare of the probationer through interventionist methods.[42]

[37] Eleanor Harlow, J. Robert Weber, and Leslie T. Wilkins, *Community-Based Correctional Programs: Models and Practices* (Washington: Government Printing Office, 1971), p. 3.

[38] Irving A. Spergel, "Community-Based Delinquency-Prevention Programs: An Overview," *Social Service Review*, 47:16–31, 1973.

[39] Kenneth Pease, P. Durkin, Douglas Payne, and J. Thorpe, *Community Service Orders*, Home Office Research Unit Report No. 29 (London: Her Majesty's Stationery Office, 1975). See also Kenneth Pease and Jenny S. M. West, "Community Service Orders: The Way Ahead," *Home Office Research Unit Bulletin*, 4:16–21, 1977.

[40] Walter D. Connor, *Deviance in Soviet Society: Deviance, Delinquency, and Alcoholism* (New York: Columbia University Press, 1972), p. 123.

[41] Vinter, Downs, and Hall, *Juvenile Corrections in the States*, p. 15.

[42] See Chapter 25, below.

As we indicated previously, the "police officer" role is played whenever the probation worker reports to the court that the probationer has committed a new crime or has otherwise violated the terms of the probation contract. Some judges, some probation officers, and others bound by the principles of the classical school see such surveillance and threat of punishment, rather than intervention, as the essence of probation. These persons contend that any achievements of probation departments stem from fear of punishment. Fear of imprisonment and fear of the probation officer because the officer has the power to recommend imprisonment is considered the essential factor in reformation. The logic of this argument leads to universal imprisonment of offenders; the logic of probation is that contacts and assimilation in noncriminal groups are most important in modifying behavior; fear places social distance between probationer and probation officer and retards contact and assimilation. Terror unquestionably has value in deterring persons from violations of law, and the question is whether it cannot be replaced generally by methods that are more effective than terror, and, specifically, whether it is not inconsistent with the principles of probation work and does not interfere with the efficiency of probation work.

SUCCESS AND FAILURE ON PROBATION

Probation departments generally report that about 75 percent of their probationers succeed on probation. The lowest success rates are for persons convicted of forgery, bad checks, burglary, and automobile theft; the highest success rates are for persons convicted of manslaughter. The 75 percent general figure is a rough average of the reports of many departments in many different years. Even in this sense it is inadequate in at least three respects. First, the number reported to be failures is incomplete because the probation officer is not in sufficiently close contact with probationers to know how many of them commit crimes and also because the identification records of police departments have been so restricted that they do not adequately supplement the knowledge of the probation officer. These inadequacies in the official records are rapidly being corrected by computerized record-keeping systems, and probation violation rates probably will go up as a result. Departments that have had the reputation of doing the best probation work show the smallest proportion of successes, probably because they have had more complete information regarding the behavior of their probationers than have other departments.

Second, the statistics of probation departments are confined to behavior during the period of probation and do not include the behavior subsequent to release from probation. Many studies of convictions have been made for the purpose of supplying this information, and they suggest that the number of failures is not greatly increased after the end of the probation period. However, probationers and former probationers do not avoid arrest as readily as they avoid conviction. An FBI follow-up study of 78,143 offenders who were released in 1972 showed that 21 percent of those released on parole, 57 percent of those placed on probation, and

67 percent of those acquitted or who had their cases dismissed were rearrested by the end of 1975. When repeaters were ranked by crime, burglars ranked first with 81 percent, embezzlers lowest with 28 percent.[43]

Third, the "success" of probation logically should be determined by comparing the effects of probation with the effects of alternative methods of dealing with offenders. Since probation is generally a substitute either for release without supervision or for imprisonment, efforts should be made to compare the subsequent behavior of probationers with the subsequent behavior of those released without supervision and those committed to institutions. Such comparison is extremely difficult, however, since probationers generally are selected from the criminal population as those least likely to become recidivists. It is probably for this reason that few comparisons have been made.[44] The FBI study indicated that 75 percent of the automobile thieves, 81 percent of the burglars, and 65 percent of the narcotics offenders released at the expiration of their sentences in penal institutions in 1970 had been arrested by the end of 1975, but it is not possible to tell whether these percentages would be higher or lower if the criminals had been placed on probation rather than imprisoned. Conclusions regarding the value of probation are sometimes erroneously based on the number of prison or reformatory inmates who are ex-probationers. Such statistics are inadequate, for they show nothing regarding the number of probationers who do not appear subsequently in institutions.

Almost everyone agrees that probation should be used to some extent. The important question, therefore, is not whether probation in general is a success or failure, but what type of offenders succeed on probation and under what conditions. Many studies contain organized information on this point, and they agree in the conclusion that the highest rates of violation of probation are found among the probationers who had previous criminal records, previous records of irregular work, low economic status, low occupational level, previous institutional placement, residence in deteriorated or commercial areas, families with records of crime, criminal associates, great mobility in residences, and few or irregular contacts with schools or churches. Reiss, for example, found that among the probationers from the Chicago juvenile courts, 44.8 percent of those who resided in areas with the highest delinquency rates violated probation, as compared with 30.7 percent of those who resided in the areas of lowest delinquency rates.[45] Similarly, Glaser and Hangren found that probation was violated by 80 percent of thirty cases whose leisure time was spent predominantly in association with

---

[43]Federal Bureau of Investigation, U.S. Department of Justice, *Uniform Crime Reports for the United States, 1975* (Washington: Government Printing Office, 1976), pp. 44–5.

[44]For an excellent example of this kind of comparison, see Dean V. Babst and John W. Mannering, "Probation Versus Imprisonment," *Journal of Research in Crime and Delinquency*, 2:61–9, 1965.

[45]Albert J. Reiss, Jr., "Delinquency as the Failure of Personal and Social Controls," *American Sociological Review*, 16:196–207, 1951; and idem, "The Accuracy, Efficiency, and Validity of a Prediction Instrument," *American Journal of Sociology*, 56:552–61, 1951.

persons describable as "criminogenic," or in opposition to "respectable" moral standards, while it was violated by only 7 percent of sixty-nine offenders whose recreational activities were describable as taking place in groups predominantly oriented toward socially approved patterns of behavior.[46] These studies make specific the general proposition that excessive intimate association with criminal behavior patterns characterizes second offenders as well as first offenders.

When data on probation violators and nonviolators are organized in statistical form, courts have a basis for intelligent selection of offenders to be placed on probation, and probation officers have a fund of information on which interventionist policies might be based.[47] By analyzing the backgrounds of probationers who were reconvicted and comparing them with persons who were not reconvicted, Davies has developed an index that purportedly measures environmental conditions that are important to a probationer's subsequent criminality. The index includes conditions such as criminal record, friends who are known criminals, family cohesiveness, and school or work attendance.[48] Prediction studies utilizing such statistical data have been carried somewhat further in regard to parole than in regard to probation, and these studies will be discussed in Chapter 25. The statistical information on probation is not adequate at present from the point of view of reliability, classifications, or significance, but these defects can be corrected.[49]

APPRAISAL OF PROBATION

The advocates of probation do not insist that all offenders should be placed on probation, but rather that certain types of offenders will get along better and do less injury to society if they are placed on probation than if they are imprisoned or dismissed without supervision. The probation policy enables these offenders to remain somewhere in the general society, which ordinarily is better than prison as a character-developing institution, and at the same time to receive assistance in modifying the conditions that produced their delinquency or criminality.

Probation, furthermore, has the advantage that the probationer, being at liberty, has a better opportunity to make payments toward family support or toward restitution. As it is now administered, probation also is much cheaper than imprisonment. In general terms, imprisonment is about ten times more costly

[46] Daniel Glaser and Richard F. Hangren, "Predicting the Adjustment of Federal Probationers," *National Probation and Parole Association Journal*, 4:258–67, 1958. See also Judson R. Landis, James D. Mercer, and Carole E. Wolff, "Success and Failure of Adult Probationers in California," *Journal of Research in Crime and Delinquency*, 6:34–40, 1969.

[47] Robert H. Fosen and Jay Campbell, Jr., "Common Sense and Correctional Science," *Journal of Research in Crime and Delinquency*, 3:73–81, 1966.

[48] Martin Davies, *An Index of Social Environment*, Home Office Research Unit Report No. 17 (London: Her Majesty's Stationery Office, 1973). See also idem, *Probationers in Their Social Environment*, Home Office Research Unit Report No. 2 (London: Her Majesty's Stationery Office, 1969).

[49] William E. Hemple, William H. Webb, Jr., and Stephen W. Reynolds, "Researching Prediction Scales for Probation," *Federal Probation*, 40:32–7, 1976.

than probation, but exactly how much more expensive it is depends on the prison, the probation program, and the method of computing the costs. In Tennessee it costs about $8,700 more to keep a person in prison for eighteen months than to keep the same person on probation for that time, which is the average length of a prison term.[50] North Carolina spends about 45 cents a day on each probationer, in contrast to $13.12 a day for a prisoner.[51] Ten years ago, the President's Commission estimated that the national average cost for institutionalization of adult felons was about $1,900; for probation services to adults it was about $140.[52] More recently it was estimated that community-based corrections for juveniles, which include probation, cost an average of $5,500 per offender in the United States, while the average cost per juvenile in an institution was $11,650.[53] Probation would cost more if it were properly administered. However, a study in Saginaw County, Michigan, indicated that reducing case loads and improving the quality of probation services actually reduces the total cost of correctional programs.[54]

Certain objections have been raised against probation, of which the most important are the following: (1) probation decreases the average penalty for crime and therefore tends to increase crime; (2) probation replaces offenders in the environment that produced them and is not likely to modify their behavior; (3) probation does not satisfy the desire for revenge and therefore tends to eliminate the incentive for prosecution.

The first objection, as has been shown previously, has little basis in fact. Extensive use of probation does not in itself result in an increase of serious crimes. A study of California counties indicated that there is no correlation between the percentage of convicted superior-court defendants placed on probation and the rate of failure among these probationers.[55] The recent California "probation subsidy" program also suggests that probation can safely be used for more cases in most counties. Under that program, the state pays counties a fixed sum for retaining in the community on probation felons who otherwise would be committed to state prison.[56]

The argument that probation does not alter the environment of the offender is sound, and it is presented primarily by those who insist that casework must be expanded to include the family, other intimate groups, and the larger neighbor-

[50] Tennessee Law Enforcement Planning Commission, *Evaluation Report: Probation and Parole* (Nashville: Author, 1975).

[51] North Carolina Adult Probation and Parole Division, *Probation and Parole: Invisible Bars* (Raleigh: Author, 1975).

[52] President's Commission, *Task Force Report: Corrections*, p. 28.

[53] Vinter, Downs, and Hall, *Juvenile Corrections in the States*, pp. 25, 40.

[54] Alfred C. Ball, *The Saginaw Probation Demonstration Project* (East Lansing: Michigan Crime and Delinquency Council, 1963), pp. 2–3.

[55] Special Study Commission, *Probation in California*, pp. 93–4.

[56] Robert L. Smith, *A Quiet Revolution: Probation Subsidy* (Washington: U.S. Department of Health, Education and Welfare, 1971).

hood if it is to be effective. It is not an argument against probation, but against the specific methods of probationary work.

The last of the objections requires additional comment. The basic idea is that as probation increases, the number of injured persons who will be willing to go to the trouble of prosecuting offenders will decrease, because they will secure so little satisfaction from it. But the amount of injury that must be inflicted in order to satisfy any desire for revenge is variable; a few centuries ago nothing short of the death of the offender would satisfy; at present the desired injury is much less, and it seems to be decreasing. Further, it is quite fallacious to assume that at present the desire for revenge is the only or most important reason for prosecution. Despite the fact that a large proportion of criminal cases involves no particular injured party, if court procedures were humanized, the number of persons, whether motivated by revenge or something else, who would be willing to participate in courthouse affairs probably would be greatly increased.[57] The desire for restitution also is a general motive, alternative to revenge, for prosecution. Resort to civil courts will not generally serve the purpose of the victim because, though the judgment of the court may be more certain if the process is civil, most of the offenders are impecunious, and the judgment is worthless to the victim. The criminal court, with its combination of probation and restitution, could be a more effective means of securing financial compensation for injury than the civil court in a large proportion of cases.

SUGGESTED READINGS

Alper, Benedict S. *Prisons Inside-Out: Alternatives in Correctional Reform.* Cambridge, Mass.: Ballinger, 1974.

Ancel, Marc. *Suspended Sentence.* London: Heinemann, 1971.

Bates, Sanford. "The Establishment and Early Years of the Federal Probation System." *Federal Probation,* 14:16–21, 1950.

Carter, Robert M., & Leslie T. Wilkins, eds. *Probation and Parole: Selected Readings.* New York: Wiley, 1970.

Cohn, Yona. "Criteria for the Probation Officer's Recommendations to the Juvenile Court Judge." *Crime and Delinquency,* 9:262–75, 1963.

Cressey, Donald R. "Professional Correctional Work and Professional Work in Correction." *National Probation and Parole Association Journal,* 5:1–15, 1959.

Duffee, David, & Robert Fitch. *An Introduction to Corrections: A Policy and Systems Approach.* Pacific Palisades, Calif.: Goodyear, 1976.

Empey, Lamar T. *Alternatives to Incarceration.* Washington: Government Printing Office, 1967.

Empey, Lamar T., & Maynard L. Erickson. *The Provo Experiment: Evaluating Community Control of Delinquency.* Lexington, Mass.: Lexington Books, 1972.

Grinnell, Frank W. "The Common Law History of Probation." *Journal of Criminal Law and Criminology,* 32:15–34, 1941.

---

[57] See Arthur Rosett and Donald R. Cressey, *Justice by Consent: Plea Bargains in the American Courthouse* (Philadelphia: Lippincott, 1976), pp. 172–80.

Landis, Judson R., James D. Mercer, & Carole E. Wolff. "Success and Failure of Adult Probationers in California." *Journal of Research in Crime and Delinquency*, 6:34–40, 1969.

Lerman, Paul. *Community Treatment and Social Control: A Critical Analysis of Juvenile Correctional Policy*. Chicago: University of Chicago Press, 1975.

Meyer, Charles H. Z. "A Half Century of Probation and Parole." *Journal of Criminal Law, Criminology, and Police Science*, 42:707–28, 1952.

Ohlin, Lloyd E., Herman Piven, & Donnell M. Pappenfort. "Major Dilemmas of the Social Worker in Probation and Parole." *National Probation and Parole Association Journal*, 2:211–25, 1956.

Peoples, Edward E., ed. *Readings in Correctional Casework and Counseling*. Pacific Palisades, Calif.: Goodyear, 1975.

Scarpitti, Frank R., & Richard M. Stephenson. "A Study of Probation Effectiveness." *Journal of Criminal Law, Criminology, and Police Science*, 59:361–9, 1968.

Schafer, Stephen. *Restitution to Victims of Crime*. London: Stevens and Sons, 1960.

Timasheff, N. S. *One Hundred Years of Probation*. New York: Fordham University Press, 1941.

21

Development of American Prisons

We have considered previously the development of imprisonment until it became an established and generally used policy in England about the beginning of the nineteenth century. This chapter continues the discussion with reference to the development of prisons in the United States, especially after the beginning of the nineteenth century.

EARLY AMERICAN PRISONS

Jails and houses of correction were established in the American colonies soon after settlement. The jail was designed originally for the detention of persons awaiting trial. It soon came to be used as a place of punishment after conviction. As in England, this change accompanied increasing opposition to the use of corporal and capital punishments, and it was thus a modification of the prevailing system for implementing the punitive reaction to lawbreaking. Convicted drunkards and vagrants, especially, were confined in these institutions. The house of correction began as an institution for vagrants, but before long was not different except in name from many of the jails. The modification of the punitive reaction was made only gradually. For example, the number of persons confined either in jails or workhouses after conviction was small throughout the eighteenth century, and in New York State it was not until 1788 that a general law was passed for the use of jails or workhouses as places of punishment. Previously, commitments to those institutions were made only by a special law in each case.[1]

By present-day standards, the conditions in these jails and houses of correction

[1] P. Klein, *Prison Methods in New York State* (New York: Columbia University Press, 1920), pp. 25–6. See also E. W. Capen, *The Historical Development of the Poor Law of Connecticut* (New York: Columbia University Press, 1905).

were horrible. The prisoners spent their time in association, without labor, depending on charity for their maintenance. There was no attempt to treat sick inmates; even religious services were absent. Drunkenness and vice generally prevailed, as had been customary in England. The following description of the Walnut Street (county) Jail in Philadelphia at the end of the Revolutionary War could be duplicated with regard to many other institutions of the time:

It is represented as a scene of promiscuous and unrestricted intercourse, and universal riot and debauchery. There was no labor, no separation of those accused, but yet untried, nor even of those confined for debt only, from convicts sentenced for the foulest crimes; no separation of color, age or sex, by day or by night; the prisoners lying promiscuously on the floor, most of them without anything like bed or bedding. As soon as the sexes were placed in different wings, which was the first reform made in the prison, of thirty or forty women then confined there, all but four or five immediately left it; it having been a common practice, it is said, for women to cause themselves to be arrested for fictitious debts, that they might share in the orgies of the place. Intoxicating liquors abounded, and indeed were freely sold at a bar kept by one of the officers of the prison. Intercourse between the convicts and persons without was hardly restricted. Prisoners tried and acquitted were still detained till they should pay jail fees to the keeper; and the custom of garnish was established and unquestioned; that is, the custom of stripping every newcomer of his outer clothing, to be sold for liquor, unless redeemed by the payment of a sum of money to be applied to the same object. It need hardly be added, that there was no attempt to give any kind of instruction, and no religious service whatsoever.[2]

The Quakers of Philadelphia made decided efforts to change these conditions. In 1776 Richard Wistar at his own expense provided soup for some of the prisoners in the county jail, when it became known that some of them had died of starvation. Others became interested in his efforts, and in that year the Philadelphia Society for Alleviating Distressed Prisoners was formed. Its activities were stopped by the war. It was revived in 1787 with the name Philadelphia Society for Alleviating the Miseries of Public Prisons. About half of its members were Quakers. It had the primary purpose of relieving the physical suffering of prisoners, but soon attempted, in addition, to modify the punitive reaction, largely by advocating reduction of the number of capital penalties and substitution of imprisonment in solitary confinement for the death penalty.

During the colonial period no institutions similar to the present state prison were established until, in 1773, Connecticut purchased an old mine near

---

[2]F. C. Gray, *Prison Discipline in America* (London: J. Murray, 1848); reissued, with an Introduction by Donald R. Cressey (Montclair, N.J.: Patterson Smith, 1973); pp. 15–6. It has been reported that when the first attempt was made to preach to the prisoners in this Walnut Street Jail, the prison authorities opposed it for fear of an outbreak by the prisoners, but finally agreed on condition that the preacher leave all his valuables outside and that a loaded cannon be placed facing the prisoners, with a man standing ready with a lighted fuse to touch it off. It seems probable that this was more a device of the warden to frighten the preacher rather than the prisoners. J. Thomas Scharf and Thompson Westcott, *History of Philadelphia, 1609–1884* (Philadelphia: L. H. Everts, 1884), vol. 1, pp. 144–45.

Simsbury and turned it into a prison. This was used by the state as a prison until 1827. The prisoners were fastened during the night by heavy chains attached to their necks at one end and the heavy beams above them at the other; in addition, heavy iron bars were fixed to their feet. In 1785 Massachusetts provided that persons sentenced to solitary confinement and hard labor should serve the sentence on Castle Island, a military post in Boston harbor, instead of in the county jails and houses of correction, most of which were insecure. Massachusetts authorized a new state prison in 1803. The movement spread rapidly during the last part of the eighteenth and the first part of the nineteenth century. New York erected a state prison in 1796, New Jersey in 1798, Virginia in 1800, Vermont in 1808, Maryland in 1812, New Hampshire in 1812, and Ohio in 1816. The following inscription, placed over the door of the New Jersey state prison, indicates the punitive philosophy that prevailed in such institutions: "Labor, silence, penitence. 1797. That those who are feared for their crimes may learn to fear the laws and be useful. *Hic labor, hoc opus.*"

The immediate motive for the erection of state prisons was not humanitarian concern for prisoners' welfare. Instead, the motive was to centralize the power of the state and to obtain greater security for persons sentenced to long terms of imprisonment.[3] The number of prisoners with long sentences was increasing because of the development of opposition to the death penalty. Zephaniah Swift said that Connecticut authorized a state prison because of opposition to the death penalty and because long-term imprisonment was the only available substitute for the death penalty.[4] This motive stands out more clearly in Pennsylvania than in any other state. The constitution of that state in 1776 directed that imprisonment at hard, punitive labor be substituted for capital punishment. Immediately after the war, under the direction of Benjamin Rush, Benjamin Franklin, William Bradford, Caleb Lownes, and others, a plan was prepared, made law in 1786, and amended several times during the next decade. By these laws, capital punishment was abolished for all crimes except murder; corporal punishment was abolished, and fines and imprisonments were the only penalties left. It was directed that imprisonment should be "with hard labor, public and disgracefully imposed." At first this resulted in gang labor on the streets, with the prisoners restrained by ball and chain, dressed in a distinctive garb, and with heads shaved. Philadelphia citizens were outraged, and the policy and practice were soon abandoned. Because there was no state prison to be used as a replacement for the labor gangs, arrangements were made to keep state prisoners in county jails.

In addition to this desire to obtain more secure places of confinement for long-term prisoners, the hope that these prisoners, because they were confined for long

[3]See Paul Takagi, "The Walnut Street Jail: A Penal Reform to Centralize the Powers of the State," *Federal Probation*, 39:18–26, 1975.

[4]Zephania Swift, *A System of the Laws of the State of Connecticut* (Windham: Byrne, for the author, 1796), vol. 2, p. 295; L. N. Robinson, *Penology in the United States* (Philadelphia: Winston, 1921), p. 69.

periods, might be able to pay the expenses of the institution by their labor was instrumental in the development of the state prison.[5] Undoubtedly, also, labor was introduced because imprisonment was not believed to be sufficient punishment in itself.

THE PENITENTIARY

About the time the state became interested in the maintenance of prisons of its own, there appeared a new conception of prison discipline, which resulted in the designation of these institutions as penitentiaries. The word *penitentiary* had a significance then that it has generally lost now—that is, it meant an institution not for retribution but for producing penitence or penitentiary reformation. As indicated earlier, the medieval prisons under the control of the church had this ideal, and the same purpose was reflected in the law of England passed in 1778 authorizing a penitentiary. The purpose of this institution was stated by the law to be: "By sobriety, cleanliness, and medical assistance, by a regular series of labour, by solitary confinement during the intervals of work, and by due religious instruction to preserve and amend the health of the unhappy offenders, to inure them to habits of industry, to guard them from pernicious company, to accustom them to serious reflection and to teach them both the principles and practice of every Christian and moral duty."

This law was framed by Blackstone, Eden, and Howard. Howard stated: "The term penitentiary clearly shows that Parliament had chiefly in view the reformation and amendment of those to be committed to such places of confinement."

This institution was not erected, but the law incorporated the idea that prisoners should be "amended" and "inured" by constructive action, and it probably influenced the Quakers of Pennsylvania. They developed not only a state prison, but also a new conception of prison discipline that made their institution, and others modeled on it, penitentiaries. These innovators looked upon imprisonment as a sufficiently severe penalty in itself, and they insisted that prisoners should be assisted in their efforts to become rehabilitated. This notion, which is indicative of the rise in popularity of the interventionist reaction to crime, was in opposition to the opinion of many persons of the time. Judge Walworth, in declaring whipping in prison a proper punishment, stated in 1826:

That confinement with labor merely had no terrors for the guilty; that the labor which the human body was capable of performing without endangering its health was but little more than many of the virtuous laboring class of the community daily and voluntarily perform, for the support and maintenance of their families; that to produce reformation in the guilty or to restrain the vicious from the perpetration of crime by the terrors of punishment, it was absolutely necessary that the convict should feel his degraded situation . . .; that the system of discipline adopted by the inspectors under the sanction of the laws was well calculated to have the desired effect of reforming the less vicious offenders and of

[5]See Thorsten Sellin, *Slavery and the Penal System* (New York, Elsevier, 1976).

deterring others from the commission of crime . . .; that it was, however, through terror of bodily suffering alone that the proper effect upon the mind of the convict was produced.[6]

THE PENNSYLVANIA SYSTEM

The prison leaders in Pennsylvania contended that association of all types of criminals in prisons is disastrous. They suggested, as had been suggested frequently for several centuries, that prisoners should be kept in solitary confinement. Arrangements for this were made in the Walnut Street Jail, in which the state prisoners were confined. Solitary confinement, it was contended, not only prevented undesirable association of criminals, but also had the positive virtue of forcing the prisoners to reflect on their crimes, and therefore of producing reformation. During a part of the history of the system of solitary confinement, the prisoners were not permitted to work, and when they later were permitted to do so, the work was made subordinate to reflection. It was realized that solitude would be injurious if too long continued, and provision was therefore made for association with the following official visitors: the governor of the state, the members of the state legislature, the judges of all courts, the mayors of Philadelphia, Pittsburgh, and Lancaster, the county commissioners and sheriffs, and a committee of the Philadelphia Society for Alleviating the Miseries of Public Prisons. The relations between the prisoners and these official visitors could not have been very intimate. The committee of the society did very well to average four and a half hours a year per prisoner, and their conversation was confined largely to theological exhortations. The solitude was not frequently broken, therefore. But it was argued that the effect of this solitude was to cause an appreciation of these good men when they did come.

The Western State Penitentiary at Pittsburgh, Pennsylvania, which opened in 1826, adopted this "separate and silent" system. As in the Walnut Street Jail, the prisoners were at first kept in idleness. After a few years, however, they were permitted to work in their cells. But it was in the Eastern State Penitentiary, which was opened in Philadelphia in 1829, that the "Pennsylvania system" really developed. As in the other institutions, the prisoners were to work alone at such occupations as spinning, weaving, and shoemaking, and were to do maintenance work outside their cells only when blindfolded. The system was not practical, and it was formally abolished in 1913. However, strict solitude probably never was enforced.[7]

THE AUBURN SYSTEM

On the demand of Governor John Jay for the improvement of the criminal law of New York State, a commission was sent to Pennsylvania in 1794 to study the new

---

[6] Reported by Klein, *Prison Methods in New York State*, p. 206.

[7] For a detailed description of the Pennsylvania system and its development, see Harry Elmer Barnes, *The Evolution of Penology in Pennsylvania: A Study in American Social History* (Indianapolis: Bobbs-Merrill, 1927); reissued by Patterson Smith, Montclair, N.J., 1968.

system. After the report of this commission in 1796, a law was passed in New York, reducing the capital offenses to two and substituting imprisonment for the death penalty and for corporal punishment. The construction of two prisons was also authorized. However, Newgate Prison, which opened in 1797, was the only one erected. The institution was small, and there were no provisions for solitary confinement. Newgate proved to be inadequate, and in 1816 another prison was authorized at Auburn. A part of this institution was to be used for solitary confinement. By a law of 1821, the prisoners in Auburn were divided into three classes. The first class, composed of the "oldest and most heinous offenders," was to be kept in solitary confinement continuously; those in second class were to be kept in their cells three days a week; and the others one day a week. The cells were small and dark, and no provision was made for work in the cells.

This experiment with strict solitary confinement proved to be a dismal failure. Of eighty prisoners who were kept in solitary confinement continuously, all except two were out of the prison within two years, as the result of death, insanity, or pardon. A legislative commission investigated the policy in 1824 and recommended that it be abandoned at once; this recommendation was adopted. Being now thoroughly opposed to the method of solitary confinement, which had not, however, been tried under as favorable conditions as in Pennsylvania, the Auburn authorities provided for work by the prisoners in association but in silence during the day and solitary confinement during the night. This has been known as the Auburn system, in contrast to the Pennsylvania system, which was solitary confinement by day and night.

THE CONTROVERSY BETWEEN THE AUBURN
AND PENNSYLVANIA SYSTEMS

The literature of criminology during the forty years subsequent to the establishment of the Auburn system is devoted almost entirely to a hot controversy between these two systems. It was carried on largely by two prison-reform associations: the Philadelphia Society, mentioned above, which supported the Pennsylvania system, and the Boston Society for the Improvement of Prison Discipline and for the Reformation of Juvenile Offenders, which supported the Auburn system.[8] Both societies were intensely interested in the reformation of offenders; each was convinced of the merits of its method and the demerits of the other method; and both were entirely unscrupulous in their use of statistics to prove their arguments. When Dickens, after a visit to America, wrote his *American Notes*, he included a severe arraignment of the Pennsylvania system, which still further increased the antagonism between the two groups.

The Pennsylvania system was tried in a number of the states, but was generally abandoned in favor of the Auburn system after a short trial. The principal advantages claimed for the Auburn system were economic; that is, it cost less to

[8] See Stewart H. Holbrook, *Dreamers of the American Dream* (New York: Doubleday, 1957), pp. 240–4.

construct the congregate-type prison, and the congregate system made possible more efficient utilization of the labor of prisoners for production of wealth. At the same time, the system of silence was thought to be sufficient for reformation through reflection. European visitors, however, generally secured and carried away an impression that the Pennsylvania system was superior. In 1835, commissioners were sent from England, France, Prussia, and Belgium to examine the American prison systems; they made their visits together and presented practically identical reports to their home governments in favor of the Pennsylvania system. These reports produced a great effect in Europe, and most of the European countries adopted the Pennsylvania system in a modified form.

The controversy between these two systems, after raging for more than half a century, was diverted by the importation of a new system from Europe and Australia. This system was started in an organized manner in the Australian convict camps.[9] It was imported into Ireland and England and, under the name of the "Irish system," became known to and was discussed by American leaders shortly before the Civil War.

The Irish system consisted of the indeterminate sentence, the "mark system," whereby prisoners could gain their freedom by earning a certain number of credits, and a form of parole. The first institution using these methods was the Elmira Reformatory in New York, created by law in 1869 but not opened until 1876. Emphasis was placed on education, productive labor, the mark system, the indeterminate sentence, and parole, all of which were designed to produce reformation. It is not correct to think of this as the first reformatory, for the penitentiaries three-quarters of a century earlier were designed to produce reformation. But with the establishment of the Elmira system, the rehabilitative ideal was more explicitly incorporated into institutional policy. Also, the conflict between the interventionist and punitive reactions became institutionalized. It is significant in this connection that the Elmira Reformatory was constructed as a maximum-security penal institution, and that efforts at rehabilitation were made in this setting. Similarly, corporal punishment was a part of the Elmira routine.

Almost all reformatories constructed in the United States since 1875 have been based on the Elmira system, including the conflict between rehabilitation as an ideal and punishment as an ideal. This system of organized conflict between the methods for implementing each of these ideals also spread rather quickly to state prisons, so that it is now difficult to draw a line between state prisons and state reformatories so far as methods are concerned. Fifty years after Elmira was opened, New York prisoners were begging the sentencing judges to send them to Auburn Prison, rather than to Elmira Reformatory, because the disciplinary system at

[9]See John V. Barry, "Pioneers in Criminology: XII, Alexander Maconochie (1787–1860)," *Journal of Criminal Law, Criminology, and Police Science*, 47:145–61, 1956; idem, *Alexander Maconochie of Norfolk Island* (Melbourne: Oxford University Press, 1958); and Stephen White, "Alexander Maconochie and the Development of Parole," *Journal of Criminal Law and Criminology*, 67:72–88, 1976.

Elmira was so severe. A high official at Elmira boasted of this fact, believing that such a state of affairs was a credit to his institution.

JUVENILE REFORMATORIES AND INDUSTRIAL SCHOOLS

The first American institution specifically for juvenile delinquents was opened in New York City in 1825 after more than a generation of discussion. It was under the control of a private society called the New York Association for the Prevention of Pauperism, but the state made annual grants for its maintenance. A similar institution under private control was started in Philadelphia in 1826. The first institution of this type under state control was started in Massachusetts in 1847, but even this institution received assistance from private funds. Seven institutions had been opened by 1850, thirty-two more by 1875, and sixty-six more by 1900. At present there are about three hundred state and local training schools.

From the first, it was contended that these institutions were not penal institutions or prisons, but schools. The children were to be educated, not punished. In certain respects the institutions incorporated nonpunitive policies, and many efforts were made to reform the delinquents by methods other than solitary confinement: they had self-government, religious teaching, academic teaching, indeterminate sentences, and release on good behavior, which was similar to parole. In the second year of the New York House of Refuge, the president of the board made the following statement, which was quite opposed to the prevailing punitive reaction to lawbreaking: "A child may be made quiet and industrious by beating, but it seldom happens, I believe, that kindheartedness, morality, and intelligence are induced by whipping."[10] Some of these nonpunitive policies were only temporary, and in some respects the rationale of these institutions was punitive from the time of their origin.

The earliest institutions for juvenile delinquents were organized under the dominance of the prison idea. . . . In all regards this was true; the establishments were distinctly prison enclosures, the dormitories were blocks of cells, the dining-rooms were chambers of silence, with only the meagerest provision of the crudest table furniture; the earning capacity of those confined was exploited to the highest possible figure, and education in letters was only provided for during such hours as could not be profitably employed in work; and the greatest ambition and strongest claim for popular approval was a low per capita cost of maintenance.[11]

Thus it seems probable that, with temporary exceptions in regard to certain punitive policies, these institutions were primarily prisons during the first half-century of their history, and their principal contribution was the removal of

[10]B. K. Peirce, *A Half Century with Juvenile Delinquents, or the New York House of Refuge and Its Times* (New York: Appleton-Century-Crofts, 1869), p. 120. See also Robert S. Pickett, *House of Refuge: Origins of Juvenile Reform in New York State, 1815–1857* (Syracuse, N.Y.: Syracuse University Press, 1969).

[11]F. H. Nibecker, "Education of Juvenile Delinquents," *Annals of the American Academy of Political and Social Science,* 23:483, 1904.

juvenile prisoners from association with adult prisoners. The punitive reaction to crime was modified first in connection with juvenile offenses; the modifications spread to offenses of youths, and then to adult offenses. But in no case was the punitive reaction completely replaced.[12] Even today some institutions for juveniles can best be described as congregate prisons.

One of the important developments in juvenile reformatories was the cottage system of architecture, in place of the old cell-block structure. In America the first examples of the cottage system, which was copied from European systems, were a Massachusetts institution for girls and the Ohio School for Boys at Lancaster, established in 1858. This system won general approval, probably because it was cheap, and most of the state institutions have adopted a similar plan because of the more homelike surroundings and the greater ease of classification. Such surroundings, however, do not necessarily mean that the conflict between interventionist and punitive policies is absent.

SPECIALIZATION OF PRISONS

As the previous discussion implies, one of the evident trends accompanying the development of American prisons has been toward specialization of institutions. The jail once was the only penal institution. In the past two hundred years various groups of prisoners have been withdrawn from the jail for incarceration in specialized institutions. Vagrants were first withdrawn and placed in houses of correction. This proved to be abortive, and the houses of correction have now either been abandoned or become identical with the jail except in name. Then state prisons, with differing names, were established for juvenile delinquents, for insane prisoners, for young adults, for women, for blacks, for defective delinquents, for misdemeanants, for the sick, and for other groups of criminals. Thus, in the development of these specialized institutions, the principles used in the selection of offenders have included the governing unit, the seriousness of the crime, and the age, race, sex, and mental or physical condition of the offenders. The motives for specialization have included the prevention of contamination of one type of offenders by another and the adaptation of methods of work and of facilities to the characteristics of the special groups of offenders.

Until recent years the principles used in specialization had little, if anything, to do with special programs. Even now the most prevalent principle of specialization is the seriousness of the particular offense of which the prisoner was convicted; the state institutions generally care for felons, the county and municipal institutions for misdemeanants. This kind of differentiation is unsound, for the particular offense is not a suitable index of character, dangerousness, or needs of the offender. The misdemeanant generally violates a law of the state as well as of the municipality, and the state would therefore be justified in taking charge of the

[12]See Robert M. Mennel, *Thorns and Thistles: Juvenile Delinquents in the United States, 1825–1940* (Hanover, N.H.: University Press of New England, 1973), chs. 1 and 2.

prisoner rather than transferring this work to the local community. The local prisons of England were taken over by the national government and have been thus operated for more than half a century with improvement in efficiency and great decrease in expense.[13]

Several states in America have established state farms for misdemeanants, which to some extent take the place of county jails. Indiana, for example, established a state farm for misdemeanants in 1915. The law provides that male misdemeanants are to be sent to this state farm unless their sentences are thirty days or less, in which case they may be retained in the county jail or sent to the state farm at the discretion of the judge. The expenses of transportation are paid by the county, the expenses of maintenance by the state. But state farms, like county jails, are seldom specialized except in respect to the age and sex of inmates.

Specialization of institutions by sex of inmates is now characteristic of all types of prisons—jails, houses of correction, reformatories, and state prisons. When both sexes are confined in one institution, the two departments are separated almost as completely as though they were different institutions.

Another principle of specialization is by age. The desirability of special institutions for juveniles, if they are to be kept in institutions at all, is beyond question. However, the state reformatory for young adults is not clearly justified. It was established on the theory that it would serve younger, less criminal, and more easily reformable men. But 62 percent of the men committed to the Massachusetts State Reformatory at Concord in 1970 were recidivists, as compared to 72 percent of the men sentenced to the Massachusetts State Prison at Walpole. Also, there is considerable overlapping in age. In 1970, 80 percent of the persons sentenced to the Concord reformatory were under twenty-five, and 40 percent of those sentenced to the state prison were under twenty-five.[14] Thus the distinction between the state prison and the state reformatory is not at all clear. It has never been drawn as clearly for women as for men offenders, and at present practically every institution for women offenders might be called a reformatory.

Still another principle of specialization is by the personal characteristics of offenders. The federal government and states with large populations, like California, have been able to establish a series of prisons, graded from "maximum security" to "minimum security" and with quite different programs. Some special institutions have been established for vagrants, some for insane prisoners, some for defective delinquents, some for alcoholics, and some for drug addicts. Such arrangements could be considered as specialization on the basis of the kind of punishment considered necessary in each case, but they also are considered specialization according to the kind of treatment method deemed advisable for

[13]See Richard F. Sparks, *Local Prisons: The Crisis in the English Penal System* (London: Heinemann, 1971).
[14]Commissioner of Correction, *Statistical Report, 1970* (Commonwealth of Massachusetts, Public Document No. 115), pp. 33–4, 43.

the various categories of offenders.[15] In relatively recent years, "classification" of prisoners has come to include recommendation as to the kind of specialized institution in which an offender should be incarcerated, as well as recommendation for a particular kind of program within the institution. Classification will be discussed in the next chapter.

SOCIAL CONTACTS FOR PRISONERS

The solitary confinement of the early Pennsylvania system has been generally abandoned in the United States except as punishment for infraction of prison regulations. Even the rule of silence, which was substituted for this, has been abandoned. Unquestionably, the horrors of prison life have been reduced. Improvements have been made in diet, cleanliness, ventilation, lighting, and methods of discipline. The clearest marks of degradation, such as shaving of the head, the lockstep, striped clothing, and the ball and chain, have been eliminated. Also, the monotony of prison life has been reduced. Entertainments have been provided, athletics and other recreations developed, libraries and educational classes provided. Visiting and correspondence privileges have been introduced, and college students, potential employers, peer counselors, and others are permitted to enter many prisons for discussions with inmates. These are efforts to promote contacts between the inmates and the outside world, and they are in part based on the conviction that reformation is a process of assimilating certain cultural patterns of the outside world. Assimilation of culture is promoted by contact with that culture and not by isolation from it.

IMPRISONMENT AS PUNISHMENT

The major changes occurring in prisons in the course of their history have been directed, explicitly or implicitly, by the doctrine that restriction of a criminal's liberty is, by itself, punishment, and that this punishment is adequate for meeting the demand for retribution, deterrence, and reformation.[16] In the early days of their existence, democratic societies were not sure of themselves—they deprived criminals of their freedom and inflicted physical suffering on them. American prisons have abandoned corporal punishments as a regime for supplementing the suffering that "mere imprisonment" is expected to produce. Most prison officials now maintain that men are committed to prisons *as* punishment rather than *for* punishment.

Yet "mere imprisonment" continues to be ordered because it is painful to offenders. It is no coincidence that imprisonment as a system for dealing with criminals arose with the democratic revolutions of the eighteenth century.

---

[15]See Richard O. Nahrendorf, "A Correctional Dilemma: The Narcotics Addict," *Sociology and Social Research*, 53:21–33, 1968.

[16]See the discussion in Chap. 22, below.

Neither is it a coincidence that imprisonment has remained as the principal method for dealing with serious offenders in democratic societies. As democracy developed, so did an appreciation of liberty, and restriction of freedom by imprisonment came to be regarded as a proper system for imposing pain on criminals. It was in this period that our current system of criminal laws, each law calling for a measured amount of loss of freedom and thus a measured amount of pain, was initiated.

Of course, "mere imprisonment" has never been consistently defined and has meant many things to many people, as has been true of the concept "liberty." In the Walnut Street Jail it meant only perimeter control, with freedom to commit crime and engage in debauchery within prison walls. At the other extreme, it meant confinement of all prisoners in solitary, as in the Pennsylvania system. Now we adopt, or try to adopt, a middle-of-the-road position, allowing inmates physical mobility within the walls but directing their actions and choices. Nevertheless, incarceration is intended as punishment in contemporary American society.

In the quarter of a century following World War II, prison workers were admonished to treat criminals as well as to punish them. In the 1940s and 1950s the traditional notion that prisoners should be "amended" by constructive action such as religious exhortation, penitence, and education was gradually replaced by the idea that they should be changed by nonpunitive treatment methods.[17] Although these methods were never defined precisely, the emphasis was on psychotherapy. The mental hospital was often used as a model of what the prison should be.[18] Nevertheless, the prison remained as a place of punishment because the act of taking away a criminal's liberty remained an act performed by the state in a deliberate attempt to make the criminal suffer.

The principal difference between committing a criminal to a prison and a psychotic to a mental hospital lies in the fact that we want the prisoner, but not the psychotic, to suffer from the incarceration. Patients in mental hospitals may suffer from confinement behind bars, but the suffering is not deliberately imposed by the state. Psychotics who are so disturbed that they are dangerous may be incapacitated by placement behind bars. But no mental patients are committed to institutions on the assumption that the suffering resulting from the incarceration will have some positive value in their rehabilitation or in deterring others from becoming patients. This is precisely the assumption behind committing criminals to prison, and it is this assumption that makes the prison a place of punishment.

SUGGESTED READINGS

Barnes, Harry Elmer. *The Evolution of Penology in Pennsylvania.* Indianapolis: Bobbs-Merrill, 1927.

---

[17] See Torsten Eriksson, *The Reformers: An Historical Survey of Pioneer Experiments in the Treatment of Criminals* (New York: Elsevier, 1976).

[18] See the discussion in Chapter 15, above.

Berk, Richard A., & Peter H. Rossi. *Prison Reform and State Elites*. Cambridge, Mass.: Ballinger, 1977.

Brockway, Zebulon R. *Fifty Years of Prison Service*. New York: Charities Publication Committee, 1912.

Carleton, Mark T. *Politics and Punishment: The History of the Louisiana Penal System*. Baton Rouge: Louisiana State University Press, 1971.

De Beaumont, Gustave, & Alexis de Tocqueville. *On the Penitentiary System in the United States and Its Application to France*. Translated by Francis Lieber. Philadelphia: Carey, Lea and Blanchard, 1833. (Reissued by Southern Illinois University Press, Carbondale, 1964.)

Eriksson, Torsten. *The Reformers: An Historical Survey of Pioneer Experiments in the Treatment of Criminals*. New York: Elsevier, 1976.

Gray, Francis C. *Prison Discipline in America*. London: J. Murray, 1848. (Reissued by Patterson Smith, Montclair, N.J., 1973.)

Heath, James, ed. *Eighteenth Century Penal Theory*. London: Oxford University Press, 1963.

Ives, George. *A History of Penal Methods*. London: Stanley Paul, 1914.

Jobes, Patrick C. "Historical Development of Causal Theories of Rational Man." *California Youth Authority Quarterly*, 26:18–27, 1973.

Johnston, Norman. *The Human Cage: A Brief History of Prison Architecture*. Philadelphia: The American Foundation, 1973.

Klein, P. *Prison Methods in New York State*. New York: Columbia University Press, 1920.

Lewis, O. F. *The Development of American Prisons and Prison Customs, 1776–1845*. Albany: Prison Association of New York, 1922.

McKelway, Blake. *American Prisons: A History of Good Intentions*. Montclair, N.J.: Patterson Smith, 1977.

Robinson, L. N. *Penology in the United States*. Philadelphia: Winston, 1921.

Rose, Gordon. *The Struggle for Penal Reform*. London: Stevens and Sons, 1961.

Rothman, David J. *The Discovery of the Asylum: Social Order and Disorder in the New Republic*. Boston: Little, Brown, 1971.

Sellin, Thorsten. *Slavery and the Penal System*. New York: Elsevier, 1976.

Smith, Joan, & William Fried. *The Uses of American Prisons: Political Theory and Penal Practice*. Cambridge, Mass.: Lexington Books, 1974.

Teeters, Negley K. *The Cradle of the Penitentiary: The Walnut Street Jail at Philadelphia, 1773–1835*. Philadelphia: Pennsylvania Prison Society, 1955.

Wines, E. C. *Punishment and Reformation*. New York: Crowell, 1895.

22

Objectives and Conditions
of Imprisonment

The history of imprisonment in the United States reveals a trend toward emphasis on interventionist methods. For years the view formally expressed by most prison leaders was that the prison should make every possible effort to treat prisoners, within the framework of a system of security. It was correctly observed that practically all prisoners return to free society sooner or later, and that the use of punitive methods alone does not produce the desired reformation. Consequently it was emphasized that positive, nonpunitive, interventionist methods should be used. As in probation work, the personal conditions that led to each inmate's crime were to be determined (diagnosis), and the knowledge thus obtained was to be used to help the inmate overcome these conditions (treatment). Rather than punishment, or in addition to it, there was to be scientific inquiry and an intimate, free, confidential, and amoral relationship in which therapists and clients exchanged information. Punishment was to be minimal because it detracts from such inquiry and also because it alienates inmates from prison personnel, making it difficult for the latter to take positive action for inmate rehabilitation.[1]

But treatment was never defined. Psychotherapy and counseling were viewed as treatment, but so were vocational education, library privileges, work assignments, a balanced diet, and softball games. These programs have one thing in common: they are all nonpunitive. They were called treatment because they were nonpunitive, not because they had been shown to be effective ways of implementing scientific diagnoses of the cause of an inmate's criminal conduct. True interventionist methods were (and are) rare, but in some prisons the inmates who wished

---

[1] For a recent statement of these arguments, see Ludwig Fink and J. Peter Martin, "Psychiatry and the Crisis of the Prison System," *American Journal of Psychiatry*, 27:171–84, 1972.

to be released on parole nevertheless had to show evidence of having tried to better themselves by participating in a correctional program.

In the 1970s it became popular for prison reformers and prison administrators to acknowledge what most inmates, guards, and administrators—and many outside observers—had known all along, namely that prison programs rarely rehabilitate anyone. The misguided idea that a criminal can be treated for criminality in the way that a mental patient can be treated for schizophrenia is no longer popular in prison circles. Appearing in its place is the idea that the prison is a place for hurting bad people, and nothing else. Punitive conditions that had been tempered on the ground that they interfered with the use of positive (nonpunitive) measures are being restored.

The interventionist idea has left its mark in prison, however. In the first place, prisons are still organized as though significant rehabilitation work is being done. For example, one senior official is still designated as the deputy warden in charge of "care and treatment" even though this role is not as important as that of the official designated as the deputy warden in charge of "custody." Similarly, inmates are still "classified" and "reclassified," and these processes continue to show some concern for inmate needs (diagnosis) as well as for institutional needs. In the second place, prisons continue to provide programs called "treatment"—psychotherapy, counseling, vocational education, reading, and recreation. In principle, participation in such nonpunitive programs is no longer compulsory for inmates who wish to be released on parole.

OBJECTIVES OF IMPRISONMENT

Contemporary lawmakers and other political leaders seem to have a variety of objectives in regard to control of crime, and they consider imprisonment the means for achieving each of them.[2] (1) They want retribution. The prison is expected to make life unpleasant for people who, by their crimes, have made others' lives unpleasant. (2) They want to frighten noncriminals so much that they will be afraid to commit crimes. The prison is expected to reduce crime rates by deterring the public from behavior that is punishable by imprisonment (general deterrence). (3) They want protection from criminals. The prison is expected to isolate criminals so they cannot commit crimes during the period of incarceration. (4) They want criminals changed, so they will commit no more crimes. The prison is expected to reform criminals by hurting them so much they will desist from crime (specific deterrence). It also is supposed to ensure that the bad people confined in the institution do not become even worse—at a minimum, bad criminals are to be isolated from criminals who are *really* bad. And the prison is still supposed to change criminals by interventionist methods—a recent

---

[2]See the discussion by Gordon Hawkins, *The Prison: Policy and Practice* (Chicago: University of Chicago Press, 1976), pp. 30–45.

Pennsylvania public-opinion survey suggested that prisons are still expected to do things to, with, and for prisoners in order to rehabilitate them.[3]

The first two goals, retribution and deterrence by purposeful infliction of suffering always, obviously, necessitate punitive prison conditions, even if the suffering results merely from the severe limitations on personal freedom imposed by incarceration. Moreover, restrictions on freedom-within-walls are deliberately imposed. Some prisons whose administrators stress only perimeter control are often referred to by outsiders and by old-time prison administrators as country clubs, and others—those in which inmates engage in petty rackets and debauchery—are viewed as too lax or even corrupt. As a result, systems of punitive control and discipline supplement the punitive conditions brought about by the mere fact of incarceration.

The third goal, incapacitation of criminals, has two distinct subgoals. The first is incapacitating criminals so they will not be able to commit crimes against free citizens. Such incapacitation need not include purposefully inflicted suffering, any more than the incapacitation of psychotics by confinement in a hospital need include such suffering. But achieving the second subgoal—incapacitating inmates so they will not commit crimes against each other—usually does involve the intentional infliction of suffering. So far as the inmate community is concerned, prison workers play the roles of police officers, prosecutors, judges, and jailers, for the law-enforcement and criminal-justice processes inside a prison are not very different from those on the outside. A prisoner who steals, for example, is arrested, tried, sentenced, and punished by confinement in a solitary cell. Thus the law-enforcement principle, with its emphasis on certain, rapid, severe, and uniform punishments, is at work inside the prison as well as outside. Moreover, the prison's punitive criminal-justice processes are designed in part to prevent escapes and to prevent frauds against outsiders, so incapacitation to meet the first subgoal actually does involve the intentional infliction of suffering. It is almost impossible to determine, however, whether punitive discipline and control are considered part of the routine necessary for achieving the incapacitation goal or whether, instead, they are considered necessary only to achieving the retribution and deterrence objectives. Probably most prison personnel consider them essential to the attainment of all these goals.

The fourth goal, changing criminals into noncriminals, has come to require prison conditions quite different from those necessary for exacting retribution, for general deterrence, and for incapacitation. The essence of the interventionist idea is that, so far as changing criminals is concerned, the pain of punishment can at most be neutral. Negative punishment does not by itself produce change, and it might even be counterproductive. Positive, nonpunitive interventionist programs must be administered, whether they be old-fashioned attempts to give inmates a

[3]David Duffee and Richard Ritti, "Correctional Policy and Public Values," *Criminology*, 14:449–60, 1977. See also Richard Kwartler, *Behind Bars: Prisons in America* (New York: Vintage Books, 1977), pp. 124–45.

moral education, more modern attempts to give them a vocational education, or recent professional attempts to give them psychotherapy.

It should be noted, however, that the idea that criminals can be changed by sending them to prison has not always been in conflict with the idea that criminals should be punished by sending them to prison. In early American prisons, few organizational problems arose as the wardens tried to accomplish the four tasks. Within the walls protecting society from criminals, a rigorous, monotonous, and unpleasant regime—spiced with floggings—was said to change criminals as well as to hurt them and to make examples of them. Even subsidiary programs, such as work and school, were punitive rather than interventionist. At Auburn and Elmira, for example, retribution was exacted and both general deterrence and specific deterrence were promoted by the labor program. It was clear to everyone except the prisoners that inmate employment to produce wealth should be toil, their labor weariness. Closely supervised and regimented congregate labor, performed in silence, kept inmates out of mischief, and for that reason was considered part of the prison's program of incapacitation. At the same time, punitive toil, like systems of rigid military discipline, was justified on the ground that it develops habits of industry, obedience, perseverance, and conformity, thus having a reformative effect. Punitive school work also was considered reformative. In Elmira's school, as in the public schools of the time, boys were made to study because it was more painful to study than to loaf, because classroom confinement in silence kept them off the streets and out of trouble, and because their school habits of obeying the teacher (on pain of punishment if they did not) could be taken as evidence of reform.

Gradually, organizational strain crept into this harmonious if miserable setting, first as a consequence of doubts about the use of physical punishments within prisons, then as a consequence of doubts about how severe prison punishments had to be if the prison was to accomplish its four goals, and finally by interventionist doubts that reformation can be achieved by punishment of any kind—physical or psychological, severe or mild.

First, as we have seen, came questioning of the idea that there is a need for retributive, deterrent, and reformative punishment more severe than "mere" deprivation of liberty. This questioning, transformed into action, asked wardens to reduce physical tortures such as whipping, hanging in chains, baking, freezing, electric shock, squirting with a fire hose, forced walks in a squatting position (duck walk), and forced standing at rigid attention for hours. These and other modern prison tortures still occur on occasion, but they are not routine, as they were as recently as the 1940s. They were used to inspire conformity to prison rules as well as to criminal laws. That is, they were to exact retribution, inflict deterrent pain, incapacitate, and reform prison-rule violators as well as doing these things as more general crime-control measures.

As the tortures diminished, many wardens were confident that "disciplinary problems" would arise, and they did. But things did not turn out as badly as some old-time wardens predicted. Some feared that without the threat that nonconformists would be tortured, prisoners could not be made to obey staff rules. Consequently, criminals would avoid some of the pains the general prison regime was supposed to impose for retribution and for both general and specific deterrence. Further, they would hardly be incapacitated if they went over the wall, killed each other, stabbed each other, stole from each other, and hit guards over the head with clubs. In short, nothing painful would result if discipline became lax and prisons accordingly became "country clubs," even if perimeter control were maintained.

Something did result, however. For one thing, use of psychological punishments increased. For another, in response to removal of physical tortures has come development of a system of internal control that boils down to a matter of divide and conquer. These trends will be discussed in the next chapter. Here it need only be noted that both psychological punishments and psychological controls have been used since the day inmates were let out of the solitary-confinement cells of the early Pennsylvania prisons, but that the general trend toward the contemporary view that criminals are sent to prison *as* punishment rather than *for* punishment greatly increased their frequency.

But the conflict between the fourth goal of prisons (changing criminals) and the other three goals became, in the 1940s and 1950s more than a controversy about alternative kinds and degrees of punishment in prison. The idea of intervention hit at the very roots of the idea that prisons would change criminals by hurting them. Rather than being *reformed* (i.e., changed through punishment producing specific deterrence), prisoners were to be *rehabilitated* or *corrected* (i.e., changed by nonpunitive means). Still, prisons remained punitive. Every criminal law specifies that any person behaving in a stipulated way shall be punished, and for felonies imprisonment is specified as the proper means of inflicting this pain. We offer accused persons the right to be tried by jury, to confront witnesses, and to have counsel because we do not want the pain of imprisonment to be experienced by those who are not guilty. With the coming of the interventionist notion of rehabilitation and treatment, then, prisons did not become places of treatment, like hospitals. They came to be seen as places of punishment *and* of nonpunitive treatment. Wardens were not asked to replace programs designed to produce reformation through punishment with programs implementing the theory of reformation through treatment. They were asked to set the new programs alongside the old ones and thus to be punitive and nonpunitive at the same time.

The administrative problems brought about by this contradiction have been attacked in many ways. A most common system of resolving the conflict was compromise—punitive conditions were softened in favor of interventionist conditions, and interventionist conditions were modified in favor of the punitive aspects of imprisonment. This really did not resolve the conflict; it merely made it less intense. The contradiction also was resolved by formally maintaining that the prison both rehabilitates and punishes, while informally abandoning almost all conditions conducive to effective intervention. Another solution could have resolved the dilemma by open abandonment of all punitive aspects of incarceration, but this was unrealistic and it never was tried in adult prisons.[4] However, some attempts were made to transform juvenile institutions into hospitals, in keeping with the early philosophy of juvenile courts. A final solution was to abandon any serious attempt to change inmates by any means of intervention, including treatment. This solution became increasingly popular in the 1970s, and it was stimulated by reviews purporting to show that the programs attempting to change prisoners by nonpunitive means had failed.[5]

But, as indicated earlier, prison administrators have not yet completely abandoned the idea of intervention and returned to the notion that prisons should be run on only the punitive principle that crime and criminality should be controlled by terror alone.[6] The contradiction continues to pose administrative problems, and all of the alternative kinds of solutions to these problems may be observed in the varied uses of "classification" in prisons.

CLASSIFICATION

The primary condition against which early American prison reformers argued was the association of all types of criminals in a conglomerate group. At first, "classification" consisted of mere segregation, for purposes of discipline and administrative control, of prisoners according to such criteria as age, sex, race, and dangerousness.[7] Formally, this kind of definition and practice was soon abandoned, but, as we shall see, it has remained in practice. Next, programs considered helpful to inmates—primarily schools and vocational training—were introduced. Such programs were administered on a shotgun basis to all criminals or to all criminals of a certain class, such as an age group, and "classification" consisted of putting persons into such categories. Finally, in the 1920s and 1930s the medical model of intervention was introduced. It was decided that treatment is not possible without knowledge of the persons being treated, so facilities and procedures aimed at "diagnosis" were set up. Once the classification procedures

---

[4]See Don C. Gibbons, *Changing the Lawbreaker: The Treatment of Delinquents and Criminals* (Englewood Cliffs, N.J.: Prentice-Hall, 1965), pp. 130–5.

[5]Walter C. Bailey, "Correctional Outcome: An Evaluation of 100 Reports," *Journal of Criminal Law, Criminology, and Police Science,* 57:153–60, 1966; Robert Martinson, "What Works? Questions and Answers About Prison Reform," *The Public Interest,* 35:22–54, 1974; Douglas Lipton, Robert Martinson, and Judith Wilks, *The Effectiveness of Correctional Treatment: A Survey of Evaluation Studies* (New York: Praeger, 1975); and Norval Morris, *The Future of Imprisonment* (Chicago: University of Chicago Press, 1974).

[6]See the arguments by Ted Palmer, "Martinson Revisited," *Journal of Research in Crime and Delinquency,* 12:133–52, 1975; and by Judith Wilks and Robert Martinson, "Is the Treatment of Criminal Offenders Really Necessary?" *Federal Probation,* 40:3–9, 1976.

[7]See Frank Loveland, "Classification in the Prison System," in *Contemporary Correction,* ed. Paul W. Tappan (New York: McGraw-Hill, 1951), pp. 91–106. For a short history of classification concepts and procedures, see Stephen Schafer, *Introduction to Criminology* (Reston, Va.: Reston Publishing Co., 1976), pp. 229–35.

were said to be diagnostic, it was just a short step to the idea that the personnel making the diagnoses should ensure that "cures" or "corrections" based on the diagnoses should be introduced also. "Classification" then came to refer to the system of making differentiations according to inmates individual needs, and for execution, on an individualized basis, of programs consistent with these needs, as in medicine. The term is now used to designate the entire process by which prisons attempt to attain the objective of reformation through intervention. This process is said to consist of four separate but coordinated procedures.[8]

First, the prisoner's case history is taken, repeating in many cases the "diagnoses" made earlier by probation officers who wrote presentence reports. In addition, intelligence tests and personality tests are administered and the results assessed. This work is usually performed by a staff of psychologists and social workers; in a few prisons there also is a part-time psychiatrist on the team. The diagnostic procedure ideally involves "the use of every available technique, such as social investigations; medical, psychiatric, and psychological examinations; and educational, vocational, religious, and recreational studies."[9]

Second, the information regarding the prisoner is presented to a classification committee. This committee is said to decide on a program of individualized treatment and training based on the diagnosis. Sometimes the classification committee is made up of only the professionally trained staff, but ordinarily it also includes the warden or superintendent, the deputy warden or wardens, the superintendent of industry, the educational director, and the chaplain. Generally, the warden is chairman of a committee consisting of representatives of all administrative departments. The committee assigns the inmate to a designated type of custody—usually minimum, medium, or maximum—to a certain kind of cell or living quarters, to a job, to health services, to educational classes, to recreations, and to other activities and services. The inmate usually appears before the committee within sixty days after arrival from court.

The third step is application of the corrective measures. The classification committee has the responsibility of seeing that its recommendations are carried out. The diagnostic analysis of the inmate is said to be utilized not only as a basis for a decision as to how the individual *should* be treated, but also as a basis for actual treatment.

Finally, the correctional program is supposed to be kept current with the inmate's changing needs and with new analyses, based on any information concerning the inmate's case that was not available at the time of the initial meeting of the classification committee. This procedure is known as "reclassifica-

---

[8] See the statement, in Chap. 15 above, of the clinical procedure used in the New Jersey Home for Boys during the early 1920s. For a review of several classification schemes, see Marguerite Q. Warren, "Classification of Offenders as an Aid to Efficient Management and Effective Treatment," *Journal of Criminal Law, Criminology, and Police Science*, 62:239–58, 1971.

[9] Robert G. Caldwell, "Classification: Key to Effective Institutional Correction," *American Journal of Correction*, 20:10 ff., 1958.

tion," and it is carried out by the classification committee. Presumably it guarantees that there will be no dead-end placements or forgotten men in the prison. The reclassification procedure continues from the time of the first classification until the inmate is released. Consequently the diagnostic report (generally called, more accurately, an "admission summary"), the initial classification report, and the reclassification reports presumably constitute a complete preinstitutional and institutional history of the individual.

The classification system and consequently the treatment program can and does break down at any point in the process. Obviously the entire program depends to a large extent on the original diagnosis. Yet it is axiomatic that most prisons have insufficient diagnostic personnel. Of the 46,680 persons employed in state institutions for adults about a decade ago, only 1,124 (2.4 percent) were psychologists, psychiatrists, social workers, or counselors. Thus, for the United States, 1,124 professional personnel carried diagnostic and treatment responsibilities for over 201,000 misdemeanants and felons, a ratio of 1 to 179. In southern states the ratio was 1 to 930; in eleven states it was higher than 1 to 500, and in two states it was 1 to 2,000.[10]

Even when diagnostic personnel are present, diagnoses accurate enough for treatment planning are rarely made. The very notion that the cause of an individual's criminality can be diagnosed, in the manner of a biological disease, is open to question. Inmates often are available for diagnostic interviews only for about two hours in the morning and two hours in the afternoon, the remainder of the time being given over to routine prison activities such as "count," "yard," "bath," "barber," and meals. Accordingly, much of the case history is hurriedly collected in the allotted periods, often with the aid of inmate clerks. The diagnostic interviews themselves sometimes are only five to fifteen minutes in duration, and on the basis of them an appraisal is made of the inmate's home and community life, and the etiology of the offense. Also on the basis of these brief contacts the interviewer makes a prognosis as to the probabilities for reformation of each offender, classifies them as to personality type, decides whether the inmate is improvable, unimprovable, or somewhere in between, makes a recommendation for a program of treatment and training, and does many other things.

Even if the diagnoses are assumed to be accurate, the planning for institutional treatment is rarely based on them. In some institutions the classification committee never meets, or meets only rarely, and the decisions regarding program planning are made by one person. In other institutions the classification committee meets regularly but bases its decisions on custodial and punitive considerations rather than on treatment or correctional considerations. That is, rather than reading diagnostic reports for evidence of inmates' individual needs for specific

---

[10]National Council on Crime and Delinquency, "Correction in the United States," in President's Commission on Law Enforcement and Administration of Justice, *Task Force Report: Corrections* (Washington: Government Printing Office, 1967), Appendix A, p. 180.

kinds of treatment, these committees read them for evidence of the kinds of precautions that must be taken to ensure incapacitation and just punishment.

Probably most classification committees have based their decisions on considerations of custody, convenience, discipline, and treatment, in that order. Thus it may be decided that a particular inmate must be handled as a maximum security risk, and if, for example, psychiatric services are not available to maximum-risk prisoners, then that decision will mean that psychiatric help will not be available to the inmate in question, no matter what the person's treatment needs.[11] Stated more realistically, all the programs the institution has developed to keep the inmates busy are likely to be called treatment programs, but even assignment to these programs is restricted by custody considerations. For example, a classification committee may for some unstated reason decide that for maximum effect on an inmate's rehabilitation the prisoner should work on the prison farm; but if the "patient" who is the subject of this diagnosis and prescription is not considered a minimum security risk, an assignment to the farm will not be made. When a warden, who knows that wardens lose their jobs when escapes occur, is the chairperson of the classification committee, security against escapes takes precedence over everything else. The warden or the deputy warden in charge of custody can, in effect, veto the recommendations of the professional staff or the deputy warden in charge of care and treatment. In this way many institutions that appeared to both treat and punish prisoners long ago abandoned any real attempts at rehabilitation.

Also, classification committees may operate merely as assignment boards, in which case the requirements of the institution, rather than the needs of the prisoners, determine the program that is recommended. An inmate who needs vocational training may be assigned to kitchen duties because "someone has to do the maintenance work." In some prisons, the official responsible for custody brings to the classification committee meetings a list of the institutional jobs that are "open," and inmates are only rarely given an assignment not on the list. Many institutions have established industries that require a certain quota of men for operation, and it sometimes appears that the task of the classification committee is that of keeping the industries going, regardless of whether assignment of an inmate to the industry will aid in rehabilitation. In the autumn, incoming inmates will be assigned to the cannery, because "if we don't get someone in the cannery, the tomatoes will spoil." Ordinarily, when convenience is the criterion used for assignment, a compromise is made in regard to the rehabilitative ideal. The inmate may be required to devote mornings to labor that everyone recognizes as having no rehabilitative value, but be given the option of participating in something called a rehabilitative program during the afternoons. Or the person may be assigned to the cannery in the autumn, to the nursery in the summer, and

---

[11] See Eric H. Steele and James B. Jacobs, "Untangling Minimum Security: Concepts, Realities and Implications for Correctional Systems," *Journal of Research in Crime and Delinquency*, 14:68–83, 1977.

to the vocational school in the winter. Again, the inmate may be given a full-time assignment as a janitor, with a recommendation for school attendance in the evenings.

It is at the third step in the process that classification has most frequently broken down. When the classification committee does not include custodial personnel, such as the warden or deputy warden, the recommendations of that committee are likely to be ignored. In such instances the classification committee is merely advisory; it is an addition to the institutional program but not an integral part of it. Sometimes the so-called diagnoses of inmates' needs for particular kinds of treatment are never read by the personnel who are expected to administer the appropriate programs. Sometimes the recommendations are impractical because the institution does not have the facilities for carrying them out; sometimes the recommendations are considered to be impractical by custodial personnel because they conflict with custodial and punitive programs.[12] Often the assignments to workshops, to cellblocks, to educational grades, and to counseling are made by a custodial officer whose chief criteria for assignment are, again, custody, convenience, and discipline.

Even when both professional and custodial personnel are involved in program planning, there is no guarantee that the committee's recommendations will be carried out. Interventionist recommendations that are not vetoed in the committee might be in conflict with recommendations based on custody and convenience, in which case the latter recommendations are most likely to be acted upon. Also, prisoners may be removed from any program as a form of punishment, and they are permitted to enroll in educational or vocational programs as a reward for "good behavior" with reference to the punitive aspects of imprisonment. Similarly, participation in a counseling, educational, or group-therapy program may be interpreted by individual guards as a form of malingering.

Professional staff members themselves have been extremely negligent in carrying out their own recommendations for treatment. It is apparent, for example, that staff members who are so occupied with report writing and meetings that they are unable to perform their diagnostic duties also will be too busy to perform their duties as administrators of the recommended programs. The treatment programs then become meaningless and superficial. Even prison educational and medical programs are usually inefficiently administered. The existence of such conditions again illustrates a procedure for informally abandoning interventionist programs while maintaining in the formal organization of the institution the ideology that the prison should both punish and intervene in the processes producing criminality.

The final step in the classification process, reclassification, also is a point at which the interventionist principle of crime control was, and is, rejected. When

---

[12]See Stephan G. Seliger, "Toward a Realistic Reorganization of the Penitentiaries," *Journal of Criminal Law, Criminology, and Police Science*, 60:47–58, 1969.

periodic reclassification is required, the classification committee sometimes merely examines the inmate's record for evidence of infraction of custodial rules, or simply rubber-stamps whatever it is that the inmate is doing. When reclassification is not required at periodic intervals, the inmate is likely to see the classification committee only at the time of initial classification and at the time of preparole consideration. An inmate who wants a reclassification usually can apply to the committee, but the request can be denied on the ground that the inmate's work record is poor, that the inmate has violated custodial rules, or that it would not be convenient for the institution if the assignment were changed, as well as on the ground that the desired program, in the opinion of the committee, would be useless to the inmate. Frequently it is difficult to determine just which grounds are used for reclassification, just as it is difficult to determine the grounds for the original classification. Probably the order of precedence is, again, custody, convenience, discipline, and intervention.

The reception center, sometimes called a "diagnostic center," is the most recent development in the field of classification. The principal difference between classification systems that use reception centers and those that do not is that in the former the inmates are sent to specialized *institutions* on the recommendation of classification committees. All inmates in the state are committed to the reception center and, after a period of about sixty days, during which the diagnostic studies are made, the reception-center staff assigns them to appropriate institutions where local classification committees take over.

In some jurisdictions, offenders are referred to reception and classification centers before final sentencing disposition. Under federal sentencing procedures, for example, judges can make a final decision as to disposition after committing an offender to the Bureau of Prisons for study and diagnosis. Kansas also provides this service. Persons committed to prison and then studied in the reception center may be referred back to the court with a recommendation for "recall from commitment." The final decision remains with the judge. California's youth authority and department of corrections have developed reception centers that assign offenders to any of a range of institutions. They also refer cases back to the courts with recommendations for probation rather than institutionalization. In addition to diagnosis, the California reception-center staffs conduct an admission-orientation program, a counseling program, and a group-therapy program. In general, an institutional treatment program is supposed to be initiated at these centers.

It is clear that, for most prisoners, the rehabilitative or treatment objective of imprisonment cannot be attained. The conflict with efforts to achieve retribution, deterrence, and incapacitation is so great that no prison reasonably should be expected to provide effective rehabilitative programs, let alone effective treatment programs based on the medical model.[13] The prison may be said to have failed as an agency of rehabilitation because the attitudes toward crime of the interest

---

[13]See the analysis in Rick Carlson, *The Dilemmas of Corrections* (Lexington, Mass: Lexington Books, 1976).

groups that employ the personnel, ascribe their duties, and provide them with funds never have supported the ideas of the positive, interventionist school of criminology, but have, instead, supported the theories of the negative, punitive, classical school. Put another way, when a society sends to an institution only persons whose behavior is punishable by law, it is to be expected that those persons will be punished while in the institution, even if such punishment interferes with programs introduced on the assumption that the cause of a person's criminality can be clinically diagnosed and tested. More specifically, however, treatment programs—symbolized by classification programs—probably have failed because they have been based on the false assumption that criminality is caused by something in the criminal rather than by something in the society where the criminal resides. In the United States, the principal and most important function of classification committees, professional personnel, and so-called treatment programs has been that of softening the harsh severity of an official system that sends to prison more persons per capita than any other nation in the Western world.[14] It is probably for the same reason that California, with the highest imprisonment rate of all the fifty states, has been the state where classification, treatment, and rehabilitation have been most stressed.

DISCIPLINE AND CONTROL

Prison disciplinary systems reflect the criminal-justice processes used in the society that maintains the prison—arrest, adjudication, sentencing, and punishment. But in prison one sees these processes in their extremes. Prison discipline means, conventionally, the regulation or attempt at regulation of the details of prisoners' lives by means of punishment for infraction of rules. Such regulation on the outside would mean that all the berserk demands for law and order had been granted.

In any prison, as in any society, some minimum organization is necessary. The prison must have a division of labor for the staff and for inmates, a schedule of work and meals, a satisfactory relationship with the outside community, and similar arrangements. In addition, it is assumed as a matter of course that employee and inmate work schedules must be closely coordinated; meals for inmates must be served and eaten at scheduled times; baths and haircuts must be taken at an assigned period rather than at will; and almost all activities involving choice must be rationed. Although different physical plants, budgets, and personnel alter the degree of precision believed to be needed, the perceived necessity for dominating inmates makes essential a degree of scheduling and coordinating that is higher than the degree ordinarily experienced in democratic societies.

Probably no topic of conversation is as popular, general, or unsettled among

[14]See Irving Waller and Janet Chan, "Prison Use: An International Comparison," *Criminal Law Quarterly* (Canada), 17:47–71, 1975.

prison workers as discussion of the degree and kind of organization that is best for institutional operation and for rehabilitation of inmates. Almost all relations between staff members, between staff and inmates, and even between inmates are colored by the positions taken, in conversation and in action, on this subject. As our discussion of classification has shown, these positions seem to be based on a variety of conceptions of the proper relationships between security and punitive measures and rehabilitation measures.

There are many ramifications, however. Such conceptions, when generalized, are notions about the proper balance between responsibility to the group (organization) on the one hand and individual freedom on the other. Put another way, they are arguments about totalitarianism and democracy. Among prison workers, variation in the value placed on individual liberty appears in reference to many aspects of the total program, just as such variations appear on the outside with reference to economic, political, religious, and social affairs. For example, there are wide differences in evaluations of various "creative activities," such as art, music, hobby-craft, and even school work. One opinion is that such behavior is psychologically therapeutic—it enables inmates to express themselves (minimal restriction), or it enables them to escape momentarily from the repressive organization of prison life. From another viewpoint, however, such activities are viewed as frivolous "wasting of time," as a means of escaping work tasks that need to be accomplished, or as opportunities for inmates to 'blow off steam'' so that they will more readily accept the organization of the society in which they live.

More significantly, contradictory notions about the proper degree of organization are illustrated by alternative positions taken in reference to inmate discipline itself. Everyone connected with prisons, including inmates, agrees that there must be "discipline" among the inmates and among staff members, just as everyone on the outside agrees that the proclivities of individuals must be restrained. However, there are wide variations in the meanings of the term and thus in the opinions about the degree to which organization is vital to institutional functioning.

The American Correctional Association's early official statement on discipline is couched in language that identifies, but by no means solves, the problem. "Prison discipline," the association said, is concerned with "the reasonable regulation of everyday institutional life so that the institution will be an orderly, self-respecting community." The aim of discipline, so far as the individual inmate is concerned, is "self-reliance, self-control, self-respect, self-discipline; not merely the ability to conform to institutional rules and regulations, but the ability and *desire* to conform to accepted standards for individual and community life in free society."[15]

[15] American Correctional Association, *Model of Suggested Standards for a State Correctional System* (New York: Author, 1946), p. 61. The statement was later modified as follows: Prison discipline is "treatment oriented toward enabling the inmate to clarify his self-concept and toward enabling him to practice new methods of adjustment in a protected setting. Even more important than imposed disciplinary rules, however, is the necessary development of self-discipline and self-controls within the inmate: Not merely the

The principal difficulty here is with the word *reasonable*. Three basic questions arise: (1) Shall the regulation be reasonable only in the way that the requirement that guards be to work on time and work an eight-hour day is reasonable? (2) Or shall it reasonably attempt to control almost all the details of the prisoner's life by means of punishment for rule infractions? (3) Can "self-reliance," "self-control," and "the desire to conform to accepted standards," effectively be induced by either reasonable regulation of the kinds implied in the first two questions, or can it more efficiently be induced by nonpunitive measures? These are questions on which prison personnel disagree, and which most prison workers have not satisfactorily resolved even for themselves.

But prison personnel are not alone in their dilemma about prison organization or the desirable degree of restrictive discipline. In their attempts to arrive at a solution regarding the degree to which inmate actions should be regulated (and, therefore, the degree to which regulation is valuable), prison personnel are participating in an unsettled controversy about democratic social order. They also are participating in a behavioral-science debate about the relationship between personality and the organization of social relationships.

As Stanton and Schwartz long ago pointed out, there are social scientists at one extreme who think of the organization of social interaction and personality as two facets of the same thing.[15] The person is viewed as a product of the kinds of social relationships and values in which he or she participates; people obtain their satisfactions and, in fact, their essence from participation in the rituals, schedules, customs, rules, and regulations of various sorts that surround them. Moreover, the person (personality) is not separable from the social relationships in which he or she lives. Persons behave according to the rules (which sometimes are contradictory) of the large organization (society) in which they participate; they cannot behave any other way.

On the other hand, social scientists at the opposite pole think of the individual as essentially autonomous, and they view relationships with the rules and regulations of society and other organizations as *submission* rather than participation. Personality is an outgrowth of the effect that the restrictions necessary to organization have on individuals' expressions of their own pristine needs. These social scientists emphasize individual self-determination and attempt to make a distinction between the "real" or "natural" part of the person and the "spurious," "artificial," or "consensual" part. The former is viewed as primary, free, and spontaneous; the latter (obtained from the social relationships making up society) is formal, secondary, and restrictive. In discussing prison organization,

ability to conform to institutional rules and regulations, but the ability and *desire* to conform to accepted standards for individual and community life in a free society." Idem, *Manual of Correctional Standards* (Washington, D.C., 1966), p. 402.

16 Alfred H. Stanton and Morris S. Schwartz, *The Mental Hospital* (New York: Basic Books, 1954), pp. 37–8. See also Neil J. Smelser and William S. Smelser, eds., *Personality and Social Systems*, 2nd ed. (New York: Wiley, 1970).

these persons are likely to emphasize rigidity, cruelty, unresponsiveness, and sadism, without recognizing the usefulness of the organization to the broader society or to the inmates.

Certainly the two theories of the relationship between personality and culture are more complex than this simple statement implies, and probably no social scientist maintains one or the other of them explicitly and with no qualifications. But these ideas, in form even more garbled and unqualified than they have been stated here, have made their way into the policies of prisons. They have come into the prison precisely because members of our society subscribe to both of them. The prison is assigned punitive functions because of concern for the criminal's disruption of the ongoing organization—that is, society. But at the same time the prison is asked to reform criminals by means that are consistent with the theory that the prison's rules and regulations are harsh, restrictive, and punitive. While groups external to the prison demand that it perform interventionist functions, other groups, or perhaps the same groups at a different time, demand that the institution be restrictive and, hence, punitive.

When a prisoner breaks the rules of some prisons, punishment follows as a matter of course. Reports of infractions ordinarily are given to a senior custodial officer or to a subcommittee of the classification committee. A hearing is held and the inmate is allowed to present a defense and, if the offense is a serious one, to call witnesses. The guard reporting the infraction also makes a statement to the disciplinary officer or committee. Inmates who are found guilty are punished. In the earlier days, punishment almost always meant some form of physical suffering. At present, punishment more frequently consists of loss of privileges that are most appreciated by children, such as movies, television, athletic contests, radio earphones, visiting and correspondence, and educational classes. Also, the "good time" that has been credited to the inmate for early release frequently is revoked, and solitary confinement is used in serious cases. But such practices as confinement in cramped sweat boxes, exposure to extreme heat or cold, standing on a line or in a circle for hours, spraying with a firehose, and stringing up by the wrists are occasionally used even today.

This system for administration of discipline corresponds roughly to the general system of policing, arresting, trying, convicting, and punishing criminals. But there are three great differences between the contemporary legal system and current prison disciplinary systems. First, in prison the inmate is expected to obey not only all laws, but a host of additional rules. Many of these rules and regulations stem from the mere fact that a large number of people must live together within rather narrow quarters, but others are designed to aid the prison in attaining its punitive objectives. Some rules are very general in nature, such as: "Inmates are expected at all times and in all parts of the institution to conduct themselves in an orderly manner and to respect the rights of others." Much behavior that is routine and customary in free society—such as cutting across a lawn, running if one is late for work, leaving unwanted food on a plate, horseplay, personal untidiness, evading work, and oversleeping—is a violation of prison rules. Second, inmates accused of rule violations are not ordinarily represented by counsel, and in fact the procedures summarized in the expression "due process of law" are generally ignored.[17] Third, the reaction to a violation of a prison rule is almost never one of nonpunitive intervention, but in the contemporary legal system there are at least formal provisions for such intervention, as in probation. An inmate who is found guilty by the disciplinary board or officer is almost always punished, even if the punishment is a mere reprimand.

Four principal attitudes or conditions enter into maintenance of the punitive system of discipline: (1) the ideal of reformation by denial of choice, (2) the attitude of dominance, (3) the attitude of retaliation, and (4) the danger of escapes.

(1) The earlier psychology of reformation was based on the assumption that a habit formed by compulsion would be retained after the compulsion was removed. It was believed that prisoners had failed to make the proper choices before entrance into the prison, and therefore should be given no opportunity to make such bad choices while in the institution. Instead, all decisions should be imposed upon them. Brockway, the first superintendent of the Elmira Reformatory, stated this ideal as follows:

In order to train criminals for social life they must have a strict regime and learn quick and accurate self-adjustment to a uniform requirement, habituation to the yoke of established custom. Exactness of observance is of the greatest importance . . . so that the newly formed habit of precision calls up the instinctive impulse to social orderliness quite independent of conscious volition.[18]

It is now generally agreed that this theory is incorrect, and policies based on it have been abandoned in most institutions. Indeed, in some contemporary jails and prisons the disciplinary system can only be characterized as "permissive." Such disciplinary systems, in which the guards essentially retreat to the walls, give inmates an easy opportunity to exploit other inmates. If criminals, while in prison, learn that they can use murder, brute strength, stealing, cheating, and lying to get what they want from other inmates, they certainly cannot be said to be undergoing rehabilitative experiences. Similarly, poor disciplinary control that permits inmates to use fraud and other crimes to obtain goods, services, and privileges denied them by the prison and society cannot be conducive to the rehabilitation of people who have been sentenced to prison precisely because they obtained such things in an illegal manner while on the outside. It is necessary to abandon the idea that habits are formed by compulsion, but it is not necessary to abandon the notion that criminality should not be made attractive to prisoners.

---

17 See Sheldon Krantz, Robert A. Bell, Jonathan Brant, and Michael Macgruder, *Model Rules and Regulations on Prisoners' Rights and Responsibilities* (St. Paul: West, 1973).

18 Zebulon R. Brockway, *Fifty Years of Prison Service* (New York: Charities Publication Committee, 1912), p. 355.

(2) The crime rate in prison is likely to be high unless inmate activities are carefully policed. Just as saturation of a high-crime area in a city with police officers is considered by many persons to be a desirable way to prevent crime, so careful scrutiny and regulation of inmate actions is viewed as a necessary and desirable system for preventing prisoners from attacking each other and stealing from each other. In a general sense, prison officials are hired to dominate convicted criminals, just as police officers are hired to dominate citizens at large. It is not surprising, therefore, that some guards attempt to dominate inmates in a specific sense.

A guard who is responsible for keeping inmates inside the walls cannot be expected to have the same attitudes toward inmates as a psychologist who has the duty of providing the nonjudgmental, relaxed atmosphere considered necessary for psychotherapy and counseling. Personnel who are hired to guard believe that they, to be effective, must view inmates as dangerous, scheming, conniving criminals who need close surveillance and domination. They are convinced that they cannot just watch and wait, in the way traffic police sometimes hide behind parked cars waiting for violations, for this would grant inmates an opportunity to gamble the advantages of nonconformity against the disadvantages of possible detection and punishment. They become proactive, thus trying to minimize *potential* violations by maximizing the domination of individual inmates. This means that they must show their authority, and the making and enforcing of rules and the infliction of punishment are methods of showing this authority. The officer also may express this attitude in subtle ways, such as by saying, "Keep your hands at your sides," to prisoners who are not doing so as they walk by, and then saying, "That's right, keep your hands at your sides," to inmates who have not even thought of having their hands anywhere else. Inmates are believed to have come into the prison because they could not or would not respect the rights of others, and domination of their activities is considered corrective of these deficiencies in social relationships.

(3) Prison officers often have an attitude of retaliation toward prisoners. Restriction of freedom within walls, like the general restriction of freedom stemming from incarceration itself, is imposed because it is painful to the recipient. The pain may or may not be viewed as having a reformative effect; it is desired as retribution and as a general deterrent. Individual officers reporting an infraction of the rules often are disappointed or angry if the offender is not punished. This attitude tends to perpetuate the system of punitive discipline, even when there is a "court" that hears cases of alleged infractions. Something like the following takes place. First, the persons on the disciplinary board ordinarily are the superior prison officials, and, consequently, some guards are eager to report infractions because they believe that such reports indicate that they are alert and capable. Next, because offenders "should get what's coming to them," nonpunishment of an offender is likely to be interpreted by the reporting guard as a reprimand for overzealousness in reporting offenses, even if that is not the motive of the board. Finally, the board is likely, then, to use punitive rather than

nonpunitive methods in handling infractions because its members believe that employee morale will suffer if there is no punishment.

(4) The great threat to American prison administrators, which is perhaps the principal source of rigid discipline in American prisons, is escapes. Security against escape takes precedence over everything else, and all programs are limited by considerations of the danger of escape. Emphasis on prevention of escapes results from the attempt to attain the objective of incapacitation, but it also results from the attempt to obtain the retaliation and deterrence objectives. Although some prisoners have become so adapted to institutional life that they do not wish to escape, in the appropriate circumstances a large number would even attempt to escape from a prison that is as delightful as some of the newspapers picture the actual prisons. Escape by a prisoner is not a crime in England, Germany, Mexico, Spain, and other nations. "It is regarded as something to be expected of confined men and is punishable by some such method as isolation on reduced rations for two weeks."[19] Yet extreme measures are taken by some European prison directors to prevent escapes, just as is the case in the United States. The fundamental reason for opposition to confinement is the fact of confinement, and the most delightful entertainments, recreations, and food will not make such a place desirable to most inmates. Permitting prisoners to determine their own schedules, rules, and routines is thus likely to be dangerous, for it allows inmates to join forces.

Although it would be absurd to contend that the antagonism between prison officials and inmates cannot possibly be eliminated, it appears to be inherent in prison systems in a way that unsanitary conditions or poor food are not. This does not make it impossible to eliminate brutal disciplinary practices. But as long as prisons are considered the means for attaining punitive objectives, some aspects of Zebulon Brockway's system of rigid discipline must remain.

ADMINISTRATIVE AND CUSTODIAL PERSONNEL

Efficient administration of prisons has been generally lacking. When personnel are selected on the basis of political patronage, it is all but impossible to secure efficiency, even in routine matters. A warden who is a political appointee appoints guards and administrative personnel who have shown some evidence of loyalty to the political party that selected the warden. Sometimes the county or state committee of the political party in office submits a list of loyal party workers from which the warden must make appointments. When the party in power changes, the warden changes or, at least, there is a general shakeup of the prison personnel. Over a period of fifty years, the average tenure of 612 wardens was 5.2 years. Only 13 percent held their jobs for ten years or more, and 22 percent were in office one year or less.[20]

---

[19]Norman S. Hayner, "Correctional Systems and National Values," *British Journal of Criminology*, 3:163–75, 1962.
[20]Walter A. Lunden, "The Tenure and Turnover of State Prison Wardens," *American Journal of Correction*, 19:14–15 ff., 1957.

In only twenty-three states are the superintendents of institutions for adults covered by a civil-service or merit system, and such a system for institutional employees does not exist in thirteen states. Professional workers such as psychologists and teachers have civil-service appointments in thirty-six states, custodial workers in thirty-seven states.[21] But even civil-service examinations do not necessarily assure appointments on the basis of merit. In the first place, such examinations and requirements are routinely circumvented by making "temporary" appointments. Second, examinations for a high position, such as warden or deputy warden, may be rigged, so that a particular person will almost certainly make the best score and thus become qualified for the position. Even when examinations are administered fairly, they may do little more than eliminate the obviously unfit rather than assure the appointments of the most capable personnel. One study in a maximum-security prison indicated that the best guards, as judged by rating scales, tended to score only average or below average on the civil-service examination. Conversely, many of the guards who were rated as "poor" had received high scores on the examination.[22]

Unqualified personnel obviously cannot, by reason of sheer indifference or ignorance, perform the duties necessary for prevention of waste and for efficient, businesslike operation of an institution. Moreover, filling institutional positions on the basis of political patronage often means that the personnel will be corrupt as well as inefficient.

Appointment of unqualified personnel also necessarily means that the prison cannot attain its rehabilitative objective. Guards probably have more opportunities for changing inmates' attitudes than any other class of prison workers, yet they are seldom equipped for this exceedingly difficult task.[23] Many released prisoners report that, even under the present system, guards and industrial workers have more impact on the inmates than do professional treatment specialists. However, 77 percent of the inmates engaged in a special counseling program chose their counselors as the persons who helped them most; 4 percent chose correctional officers. Twenty-one percent of a control group chose correctional officers, and 45 percent chose vocational instructors or job supervisors.[24]

Generally speaking, the status of custodial officers underwent a significant change in the 1950s and 1960s. In many states they became "correctional officers" rather than "guards," in keeping with their new responsibilities, just as institutions became "correctional facilities" rather than "prisons." The basic motivation

[21] National Council on Crime and Delinquency, "Correction in the United States," p. 181.

[22] Richard R. Korn and Lloyd W. McCorkle, *Criminology and Penology* (New York: Holt, 1959), p. 503.

[23] Donald R. Cressey, "Social Psychological Foundations for Using Criminals in the Rehabilitation of Criminals," *Journal of Research in Crime and Delinquency*, 2:49–59, 1965. See also Charles W. Slack, "Experimenter-Subject Psychotherapy: A New Method of Introducing Intensive Office Treatment for Unreachable Cases," *Mental Hygiene*, 44:238–56, 1960.

[24] Alvin Rudoff, *The PICO Project: A Measure of Casework in Corrections*, Second Technical Report (Sacramento: Department of Corrections, 1959), pp. 16–17.

for these title changes was to publicize the idea that every worker in an institution was to be part of a therapeutic community that would try to make noncriminals out of criminals. Many administrators believed that, for effectiveness as a rehabilitative agency, the prison must have guards who relax in custodial and disciplinary matters, take the personality needs of each inmate into account, and individualize the handling of inmates accordingly. These practices were viewed either as constituting treatment itself or as a means of assisting (or at least not hindering) the therapeutic practices of social workers and psychologists. Preservice and in-service training classes were designed to make guards correctional rather than custodial, the general idea being that if custody and punishment could be made subordinate to treatment, prisoners would become rehabilitated. Further, a conscious effort to improve the quality of guards was made, and in states such as Massachusetts, New Jersey, New York, California, and Wisconsin, as well as the federal prison system, capable leaders were able to secure personnel who gave promise of being relaxed and therapeutic. But the institutions in these states did not become outstanding successes as rehabilitation agencies, at least in part because the custodial and punitive functions of the institutions remained, resulting in an institutional environment in which guards and work supervisors never really understood what the psychologists, social workers, and administrators expected them to do.[25]

But even when guards are not expected to play a therapeutic role, their job is an extraordinarily difficult one. Most guards do not "use" inmates productively any more than they, in their roles as guards, are used productively by prison wardens. They manage and are managed in an organization where management is an end, not a means. It is this fact that makes the guard's job so difficult. Unlike popular stereotypes that picture the guard as either a brutal sadist with a club or as a robot standing on a wall with a rifle, guards are personnel managers. They are responsible for keeping convicted criminals quiet and secure and for supervising groups of inmates who have no loyalty to the prison. Yet they do not have the help of ordinary "incentives" such as wages, promotions, threat of discharge, or even force.

Moreover, in their attempt to maximize conformity to prison rules, prison officers must balance strict law enforcement with individualization of punishments, just as police officers and others must use the "adjustment principle" as well as the "law-enforcement principle" in the general attempt to maximize conformity to criminal laws.[26] Further, custodial practices are limited by conceptions of human rights, civil liberties, and humanitarianism. For these reasons,

---

[25] See George H. Weber, "Conflicts Between Professional and Non-Professional Personnel in Institutional Delinquency Treatment," *Journal of Criminal Law, Criminology, and Police Science*, 48:26–43, 1957. See also idem, "Emotional and Defensive Reactions of Cottage Parents," in *The Prison: Studies in Institutional Organization and Change*, ed. Donald R. Cressey (New York: Holt, Rinehart and Winston, 1961), pp. 189–228.

[26] See the discussion in Chapter 16, above.

inmates cannot be kept docile by cruel punishments or severe deprivations; neither can a large number be kept in solitary confinement. Considerations of a humanitarian nature therefore have had as one of their effects the introduction of conflicting directives for prison guards. They are to minimize friction between inmates and staff but they also are expected to exact compliance to rules and restrictive conditions that have been deliberately designed to make inmates' lives unpleasant. They are to contribute to humanitarianism and rehabilitation by relaxing, and by showing concern for inmates' individual personality problems. But they also are expected to act as police officers, protecting inmates from each other.[27] On top of all this, they are to keep inmates busy at maintenance, housekeeping, and production tasks, to administer justice, and to ensure that escapes do not occur.

These and similar conflicting directives make it almost impossible for the guard to do anything that will be judged to be correct by the lieutenants, captains, and wardens. If guards attempt to get strict conformity to institutional rules, they risk being accused of antagonizing inmates. Rules must be enforced, but the enforcement must not be so rigid and arbitrary that the inmates are stimulated to riot, rebel, or ask the courts for relief. If they attempt to use common sense and discretion in attempting to get conformity to rules, then they risk being accused of not being alert to potential danger or even of corruption. If they enforce discipline and insist on inmate orderliness, they risk undesirable diagnosis as "rigid," "punitive," or "neurotic," for such enforcement theoretically interferes with individualized treatment. But if they relax to a degree that institutional security and organization seem to be threatened, then they risk undesirable diagnosis as "lazy" or "unmotivated."

OBSTACLES TO INTERVENTION

In Chapter 15 we noted four principal obstacles that block the path of anyone trying to introduce and utilize interventionist methods in the criminal-justice processes.[28] One such obstacle is the fact that an interventionist organization must have characteristics quite different from those of punitive or custodial organizations. Another is the fact that personnel cannot simply be ordered to make changes; their cooperation and even permission must be secured. The third obstacle is the fact that criminal-justice agencies necessarily reflect the desires and demands of groups with conflicting interests in what should be done to, with, and for criminals. Finally, attitudes of "standing by" seem to have characterized

---

[27] See David Duffee, "The Correctional Officer Subculture and Organizational Change," *Journal of Research in Crime and Delinquency,* 11:155–72, 1974; Donald R. Cressey, "Contradictory Directives in Complex Organizations: The Case of the Prison," *Administrative Science Quarterly,* 4:1–19, 1959; and idem, "Prison Organizations," in *Handbook of Organizations,* ed. James G. March (Chicago: Rand McNally, 1965), pp. 1023–70.

[28] See also the more general discussion in Chapter 26, below.

criminal-justice personnel, just as they have characterized personnel working in other kinds of governmental bureaus and agencies.

These observations are especially relevant to prisons, where interventionist programs have been introduced and called "treatment" despite the fact that the specifics regarding how such programs are supposed to change criminals have never been spelled out. Because treatment programs have been introduced in defiance of interest groups demanding that prisons be organized for punishment and custody, there has been a tendency on the part of prison workers to define treatment negatively. Rather than specifying what treatment *is*, they have been content to assert what it *is not*: Any method of dealing with offenders that involves purposive infliction of pain and suffering, including psychological restrictions, is not treatment. Thus psychotherapy, counseling, vocational education, and working in a prison factory are viewed as treatment principally because they are nonpunitive, not because they have been demonstrated to be effective methods of changing criminals into noncriminals, and not even because there are good theoretical grounds for believing that they ought to be effective in this regard.[29] In the processes and programs designed to implement the idea that treatment is an absence of punishment rather than something positive, there seems to be a mixture of humanitarianism and ethics of the middle class, with some psychiatric theory thrown in for good measure. By and large, prison personnel have not introduced many programs based on the premise, used in probation work, that intervention requires that something positive be done, and that mere absence of punishment—as in the suspended sentence—is not enough. Put more generally, in matters of changing criminals, prisons have been characterized by rather extreme conservativism.[30] Five principal conditions seem to be associated with this conservativism: humanitarianism, poor advertising, bureaucracy, professionalization, and inmate resistance.

Humanitarianism as "Treatment"

One of the principal handicaps to developing and utilizing interventionist methods in prisons, reformatories, and institutions for juvenile delinquents arises from the fact that humane handling of criminals and delinquents was introduced and justified by calling that humanitarianism "treatment." The "barbaric" and "cruel" conditions of nineteenth-century prisons were contrasted with the enlightened "treatment methods" of more recent times. Yet at no time has more

---

[29] See Donald R. Cressey, "The Nature and Effectiveness of Correctional Techniques," *Law and Contemporary Problems*, 23:754–71, 1958; and idem, "Limitations on Organization of Treatment in the Modern Prison," in *Theoretical Studies in Social Organization of the Prison*, by Richard A. Cloward, Donald R. Cressey, George H. Grosser, Richard McCleery, Lloyd E. Ohlin, Gresham M. Sykes, and Sheldon L. Messinger (New York: Social Science Research Council, 1960), pp. 78–110.

[30] See Thomas Murton, *The Dilemma of Prison Reform* (New York: Holt, Rinehart and Winston, 1976); and Lonnie H. Athens, "Differences in the Liberal-Conservative Political Attitudes of Prison Guards and Felons: Status versus Race," *International Journal of Group Tensions*, 5:143–55, 1975.

than an insignificant proportion of all persons employed in American prisons been directly concerned with the administration of treatment or any other form of positive intervention. Perhaps when it was said that prisoners were being treated, the statement meant something like, "They are being treated well"—that is, handled humanely.[31]

Prison workers are increasingly being asked to show the effects of treatment, but they can produce little evidence of success because much of what has been called treatment is either mere humanitarianism or punishment. Budgets for treatment greatly expanded in the 1950s and 1960s, but the recidivism rate remained about the same. Over the years, punitive measures, custodial routines, and surveillance measures were relaxed on the ground that such humanitarian relaxation is treatment, but it is reasonable to assume that no prison guard and no prison social worker has ever been fired because so many of the inmates became repeaters. Now that policy makers are beginning to learn what researchers have known all along, namely that such "treatment" does not rehabilitate, repression is again coming into style. Occasionally someone still argues, usually in connection with a budget request, that no treatment principles have been formulated and that, therefore, treatment or other forms of intervention never have been tried in prisons. More often, it is indirectly argued that humanitarianism disguised as treatment has not worked because "inhumane" persons and policies in prison work have opposed it. Perhaps the best argument is this: Treatment methods (considered as something more than mere relaxation of punishment and discipline) have not worked because they have in practice been only thinly disguised punishments.[32]

Poor Advertising

The second condition associated with conservatism in correctional theory and practice, poor advertising, is closely related to the first. Humanitarians have left to prison administrators the problems of both justifying humanitarianism on the ground that it is treatment and implementing that humanitarianism. But prison workers by their very nature are poor propagandists for the humanitarian view, even if it is called "treatment." Correctional agencies are political units whose budgets and activities are, in the last analysis, controlled by politicians. And most politicians who want to continue being politicians must be opposed to crime as well as to sin and man-eating sharks. It simply is not expedient for governmental workers to advocate being "soft" on criminals, even if they think they can show that being "soft" is more efficient than not being "soft." Police and prosecuting

[31] See George I. Diefenbaucher, "Settling for 'Humanization': Evidence of Despair or of Facing 'Reality'?" *Federal Probation*, 40:25–8, 1976; and Paul C. Friday, "Sanctioning in Sweden: An Overview," *Federal Probation*, 40:48–55, 1976.

[32] American Friends Service Committee, *Struggle for Justice: A Report on Crime and Punishment in America* (New York: Hill and Wang, 1971), pp. 83–98. See also L. Coleman, "Prisons: The Crime of Treatment," *Psychiatric Opinion*, 2:3–16, 1974; and F. Rundle, "Prisons: The Crime of No Treatment," *Psychiatric Opinion*, 2:17–29, 1974.

attorneys are excellently organized for promotion of the view that criminals should be dealt with harshly, but prison workers are not, and probably cannot be, as efficiently organized for promotion of *either* the humanitarian point of view or the interventionist point of view. Now that it is generally agreed that treatment methods do not rehabilitate prisoners, some prison officials are arguing that their institutions never should have been considered anything but places of punishment.[33]

Bureaucracy and Housekeeping

The third condition associated with the conservatism about theory and practice in prison work is the bureaucratic organization necessary to the continuation of correctional agencies themselves. There is no reason to believe that the bureaucratization of prisons should involve processes different from the processes of bureaucratization elsewhere. One effect of bureaucratization is conservatism and routinization. On a simple level, any interventionist work done by correctional employees must be performed within the framework of an eight-hour day and a forty-hour week, and it must usually be performed at a special work station. On a more complex level, it may be observed that a bureaucracy involves bureaucrats, and bureaucrats are primarily concerned with housekeeping. Thus individual innovation, experimentation, and attempted implementation of new interventionist ideas must necessarily be controlled. If this is not done, organizational routines might be embarrassingly upset. One control procedure is creation of a "research team," a "research division," or a "planning and development section," which is to contain the experimenters.[34] This custom can block innovation, for the larger the team, the more difficult it is to get concurrence that radically new concepts are worth risking the team's reputation on. After all, if the new plan goes sour, is attacked, ridiculed, and deprecated, the time and energy of all the team members, not just one crackpot, are brought into question.

Profession Versus Occupation

The fourth condition associated with conservatism among prison workers is professionalization. Because personnel such as social workers, psychologists, and psychiatrists have constituted an interest group pressuring for treatment in prisons, it is somewhat paradoxical to observe that strong resistance to further change is characteristic of this group. There is no doubt that such professional personnel have agitated for diminishing the punishment-custody-surveillance aspects of imprisonment, largely in the name of clinical treatment. However, the same personnel tend to be conservative with reference to changes in professional practices themselves. "Professionalization" implies standardization of practice,

[33] See John P. Conrad, "We Should Never Have Promised a Hospital," *Federal Probation*, 39:3–9, 1975.
[34] See Stanley Cohen and Laurie Taylor, *Psychological Survival: The Experience of Long-Term Imprisonment* (New York: Pantheon Books, 1972), pp. 201–7.

with the result that the kind of bureaucratization just discussed is perhaps more characteristic of professional personnel than anyone else working in prisons.

Among the characteristics of a profession is monopolization of specialized knowledge, including theory and skills. When an occupation is professionalized, access to its specialized knowledge is restricted; definition of the content of the knowledge is uniform; and determination of whether a specific person possesses the knowledge is made by examination. Further, professional personnel ordinarily establish formal associations, with definite membership criteria based on possession of the specialized knowledge and specifically aimed at excluding "technically unqualified" personnel. Neither practitioners nor trainees can be allowed to "go it alone" in such a way that new or different standards are developed. They must learn the established code and behave according to the standards it implies. They must, in other words, accept the professional culture.

Moreover, "professionalization" implies that personnel will *not* engage in certain practices, just as it implies that certain practices are reserved to an elite group of personnel. Status as a professional person implies a position of high rank involving little or no dirty work. An admiral does not expect to chip paint, and a doctor does not expect to carry bedpans. As nursing has become professionalized in recent years, nurses do not expect to carry bedpans either. And as social work has become professionalized, social workers do not expect to carry baskets of food to the poor. Such activities are "unprofessional." In prison work, innovations that require the professionals to perform the equivalent of chipping paint, carrying bedpans, and carrying baskets of food to the poor are resisted by the professionals.

In the 1950s and 1960s, prison administrative positions were increasingly being assigned to professional personnel. When this was the case, an administrator's income and status often depended on the ability to maintain professional practices that over the years have been defined as "standard" and "good." A person who is the director of a nonpunitive rehabilitation program or crime-prevention program does more than try to change criminals or prevent crime. He or she administers an organization that provides employment for its members, and confers status on these members as well as on the administrator. In other words, personal and organizational needs supplement the societal needs being met by administration of a program.

By utilizing or advocating use of "professional methods" in prisons, a person could secure employment and income, a good professional reputation, scholarly authority, prestige as an intellectual, the power stemming from being the champion of a popular cause, and many other personal rewards. A prison organized around administration of "professional methods" could fill such needs for hundreds of employees. Nevertheless, because of personal and organizational investments, personnel dedicated to changing criminals were likely to maintain that change was accomplished by whatever they were doing. Vague statistical measures of efficiency were valuable and useful because they decreased the range of points on which disagreements and direct challenges could occur.[35] Most importantly, any suggestion for meaningful change could be countered by announcing that the proposed change would introduce "substandard" or "unprofessional" procedures.

Prisoner Resistance

Prisoners, like parolees and probationers, are notoriously resistant to correctional programs that would change them significantly. First, they usually have good reasons for not trusting the personnel paid to implement any treatment program. Most procedures used in the administration of criminal justice necessarily are based on the theory that the state must hurt criminals in order to emphasize the undesirability of nonconformity. Criminals are committed to prisons against their will, and no amount of sugar-coating hides from them the fact that the first duty of prison personnel is to deliberately restrict the freedom of criminals so they will suffer. Prisoners often find it difficult to distinguish between correctional procedures designed to punish them and those designed to help them.

Similarly, they are not at all confident that prison personnel ostensibly engaged to help them are not actually engaged to assist in punishing them and keeping them under control. They note, for example, that in most prisons the so-called rehabilitation specialists are subordinate to officials who emphasize the necessity for restricting freedom, even if such restriction interferes with interventionist practices. They know that the prison psychiatrist or social worker might have the task of stopping "rumbles" or of "cooling out" threatening inmates, rather than of rehabilitating criminals. They know that being released on parole depends as much on the attitudes of parole-board members as on the behavior of the prisoner. Further, they know that the pressures put on them to reform or become rehabilitated have as much to do with the good of "society" or the good of middle-class property owners as they have to do with the good of the individual criminal.

Most prisoners have very little confidence that the immense amount of data collected on them will be used for their benefit. As a sophisticated ex-convict has written, "The prisoner's need to live and the system's attempt to live for him (and off him) can never be reconciled."[36] In contemporary prisons, the inmates have a minimal sense of obligation to the personnel controlling their fate. If, as McCorkle and Korn argued some years ago, prisoners are intent on rejecting their rejectors,[37] interventionist programs will succeed only if the degree of rejection is diminished.

[35] See Donald R. Cressey, "The State of Criminal Statistics," *National Probation and Parole Association Journal*, 3:230–41, 1957; and idem, "Nature and Effectiveness of Correctional Techniques."

[36] W. H. Kuenning, "Letter to a Penologist," in *Prison Etiquette*, eds. Holley Cantine and Dachine Rainer (Bearsville, N.Y.: Retort Press, 1959), p. 132. See also Bengt Börjeson, "Type of Treatment in Relation to Type of Offender," *Collected Studies in Criminological Research* (Council of Europe), 3:174–236, 1968.

[37] Lloyd E. McCorkle and Richard Korn, "Resocialization Within Walls," *Annals of the American Academy of Political and Social Science*, 293:88–9, 1954.

Second, prisoners are by no means convinced that they need either existing treatment programs or any positive program that might be invented in the future. They cooperate with prison workers not to facilitate their own reformation, but to secure release from surveillance and punishment as quickly and as unscathed as possible. Prisoners, for example, participate in group therapy, group counseling, and individual treatment programs more from a belief that doing so will impress the parole board than from a conviction that they, as individuals, need to change.

Once a man has gone through the impersonal procedures necessary to processing and labeling him as a criminal and a prisoner, about all he has left in the world is his "self." No matter what that self may be, he takes elaborate steps to protect it, to guard it, to maintain it. If it should be taken away from him, even in the name of rehabilitation or treatment, he will have lost everything. Old-fashioned punishment-custody-surveillance procedures were designed to extermi-nate each criminal's self. Modern clinical programs are designed to do the same thing. Although many criminals, especially inmates, have favored "rehabilita-tion" and "treatment," strong resistance has occurred whenever the rehabilitation technique hints at "brainwashing" or any other procedure that would change the essence of "what I am." A pill or an injection that would miraculously change a criminal into a noncriminal without changing the rest of the self might be accepted with enthusiasm by most prisoners. But attempts to change prisoners into noncriminals by significantly changing their personalities or life styles threaten to take away all they have left in the world.

Third, prisoners are not likely to become very excited about any program that expects them to look upon the task of becoming a noncriminal as a full-time job. Criminals, like others, have been taught that efforts at rehabilitation involve "technical," "professional," or even medical work on the part of a high-status employee, not hard work on the part of the person to be changed. Moreover, for most prisoners, crime has been at most a moonlighting occupation or a brief, temporary engagement, and it follows that any personal involvement in their own rehabilitation also should be a part-time affair.

Fourth, a special kind of resistance is encountered in those prisons where inmates are in close interaction and have developed their own norms, rules, and belief systems. Wheeler has shown that inmate attitudes are not as opposed to staff norms as even inmates believe.[38] Nevertheless, for most prisoners, "adjust-ment" means attachment to, or at least acceptance by, an inmate group. Moreover, an inmate participating in a program designed to change criminals, no matter what its character, is likely to be viewed as a nut, a traitor, or both. Strong resistance will be encountered when efforts to change individual prisoners would,

---

[38]Stanton Wheeler, "Role Conflicts in Correctional Communities," chap. 6 in *The Prison: Studies in Institutional Organization and Change*, ed. Donald R. Cressey (New York Holt, Rinehart and Winston, 1961), pp. 229–59.

if successful, have the result of making them deviate from the norms of their membership groups and reference groups.[39]

Fifth, the use of individualized procedures with some prisoners is resisted by other prisoners because the special handling is viewed as unfair. Criminals, perhaps more than other citizens, are concerned with justice, and one conception of justice views "special treatment" as unjust "special privilege" or "special favor." In prisons, the punitive-custodial-administrative view is that all prisoners are equal and equally deserving of any "special privileges." They are not, of course. But when treatment criteria cannot be understood, handling inmates as special cases is likely to be interpreted to mean that the inmates in question are being given special privileges with reference to restrictive punishment. Prisoners who are released from prison because they have become "adjusted" or "rehabilitated" are not, from a clinical point of view, being granted a special privilege. But as they are being discharged for treatment reasons, they also are being released from the punitive restrictions deliberately imposed on them. Accordingly, the discharge is likely to be viewed as a reward for good behavior. More significantly, the prisoners who remain behind are likely to view their continued incarceration as unjust punishment, imposed not because of their crimes but because of their prison conduct or the prejudice of the releasing authorities. It is this view that has led, in recent years, to increased criticism of the indeterminate-sentence system.[40]

THE SUCCESS AND FAILURE OF IMPRISONMENT

The success or failure of imprisonment should be judged according to the four principal goals assigned to prisons—retribution, general deterrence, incapacitation, and reformation (specific deterrence and intervention).

As a retributive machine, the prison seems highly successful. Prisoners lead miserable lives even in the minimum-security institutions likely to be called "country clubs" by those who want imprisonment to be even more painful than it is. We send men and women to prison because we want them hurt, and we succeed.

The success of the prison in deterring the general public from crime is probably much less than its success in exacting retribution. Imprisonment certainly has some deterrent effect, but it is difficult to compare the terrorizing effects of different prison policies or to isolate the effect of any prison policy from the whole process of arrest, conviction, and incarceration.[41] The general deterrent effect of imprisonment probably increases slightly with the horrors of prison life, though

---

[39] See Harold H. Kelley and Edmund H. Volkart, "The Resistance to Change of Group-Anchored Attitudes," *American Sociological Review*, 17:453–65, 1952.

[40] See the discussion in Chapter 25. See also American Friends Service Committee, *Struggle for Justice;* and David Fogel, *We Are the Living Proof: The Justice Model for Corrections* (Cincinnati: W. H. Anderson, 1975).

[41] See the discussion of deterrence in Chapter 14.

this is likely to be offset by the difficulty of securing convictions if the horrors of imprisonment are too much greater than the horrors of the crimes. Perhaps the fact of incarceration, regardless of the conditions within prisons and regardless of the length of prison terms, is the most important element in general deterrence.

As a means of incapacitation, imprisonment has not been very successful. A recent statistical study suggests that the collective incapacitative effect of imprisonment, quite apart from any deterrent effects, is quite small. It was concluded that the amount of serious crime forestalled by taking the present prison population off the streets amounted to no more than 8 percent of the total.[42] Further, the crime rate in prisons is high, and it is quite possible that, for many prisoners, the prison is just another location in which to commit crime, not an incapacitator. Prison property is seldom safe from theft. Prisoners frequently commit crimes against each other in the form of theft, assault, and murder. In the years 1970–1974, 88 inmates and 11 staff members were killed in California prisons; there were 809 assaults with weapons, for a total average of one killing or serious assault every other day.[43] Forced homosexual practices and the use of narcotic drugs flourish in many prisons and exist to some extent in most prisons. Intramural crimes, as well as extramural crimes, vary in frequency in different prisons and are affected by the prison policies. Probably the strict isolation of the original Pennsylvania system was more effective than any other prison policy in incapacitating prisoners. This does not justify a conclusion that the Pennsylvania system is in general most efficient, for other values must be considered.

The success of imprisonment as a means of reformation is very slight. The statistics on this point are inadequate, but they indicate that the methods thus far developed have not been attended by very significant changes in recidivism. In 1972, 72 percent of the persons convicted in federal courts had records of commitments to penal or reformatory institutions, and this record is certainly incomplete.[44] In California during 1971, 65,236 felony defendants were disposed of in the superior courts. Of these, 22 percent had no institutional record. Thirty percent had been convicted of minor charges for which the penalty assessed was less than ninety days; 32 percent had previously been convicted and sentenced for periods of ninety days or more, and 16 percent had served a prior prison term.[45] A

[42] David F. Greenberg, "The Incapacitative Effect of Imprisonment: Some Estimates," *Law and Society Review*, 9:541–80, 1975. See also Isaac Ehrlich, "Participation in Illegitimate Activities: A Theoretical and Empirical Investigation," *Journal of Political Economy*, 81:521–65, 1973; Ruel Shinnar and Shlomo Shinnar, "The Effects of the Criminal Justice System on the Control of Crime: A Quantitative Approach," *Law and Society Review*, 9:581–611, 1975; and Stephan Van Dine, Simon Dinitz, and John Conrad, "The Incapacitation of the Dangerous Offender: A Statistical Experiment," *Journal of Research in Crime and Delinquency*, 14:22–34, 1977.

[43] California Legislature, Senate Subcommittee on Civil Disorder, *Report to the Senate* (Sacramento: State Printing Office, 1975), p. 2.

[44] *Federal Offenders in the United States District Courts, 1972* (Washington: Administrative Office of the U.S. Courts, 1975), p. 24.

[45] *Crime and Delinquency in California, 1971* (Sacramento: Department of Justice, 1972), p. 127.

three-year follow-up study of offenders released from penal institutions in 1972 indicated that 74 percent had been arrested by December 31, 1975.[46]

In the most comprehensive study that has been made on recidivism, Glaser studied a sample of 1,015 men drawn by taking every tenth case from a list of adult males released from federal prisons four years earlier. He found that 35 percent of these men could be classed as "failures," a category including persons returned to prison for new offenses or as parole violators, and persons given nonprison sentences for felonylike offenses. The "successes" included 52 percent who had no further criminal record whatsoever and 13 percent who had been convicted for misdemeanors or arrested (but not convicted) on felony charges.[47] The failure rate was greater for younger offenders than for older offenders, greater for those who served more than eighteen months than for those who served shorter terms, greater for those whose first arrest occurred at age sixteen or under, and greater for those who had received prior sentences than for those who had not.[48]

The high failure rates should not be regarded as the responsibility of the last institution that dealt with these offenders. No institution, receiving the failures of the rest of society, should be expected to change a very large proportion of them. Also, the institution cannot properly be given the credit for those who stop committing crimes after imprisonment. Persistence in crime and desistance from crime are affected by conditions other than the institutional programs. Further, fundamental and relatively inherent characteristics of imprisonment mean that the prison must necessarily have a low degree of efficiency as a rehabilitative agency. There is a tendency to believe that a prison is a success if it does not make offenders worse. An institutional psychiatrist recently reviewed the programs of American prisons and drew the following conclusion:

> I am convinced that no effective psychiatric intervention exists or can exist in our present correctional system. The absence of psychiatry from the system is not due to lack of effort, either in the past or present, on the part of health workers; rather, it is the result of the basic antitherapeutic nature of the correctional system. So, rather than trying to attract psychiatric, mental health, and rehabilitative professionals into our present system, I suggest we spend our efforts on attempting to change the system itself.[49]

DECARCERATION

In the 1960s and early 1970s, there was a distinct trend in the direction of closing prisons. The population of American prisons rose steadily from about 130,000 in 1945 to about 225,000 in 1960. Then the population declined steadily each year; it

---

[46] Federal Bureau of Investigation, *Uniform Crime Reports, 1975* (Washington: Government Printing Office, 1976), p. 46.

[47] Daniel Glaser, *The Effectiveness of a Prison and Parole System* (Indianapolis: Bobbs-Merrill, 1964), pp. 19–20. See also Andrew Hopkins, "Imprisonment and Recidivism: A Quasi-experimental Study," *Journal of Research in Crime and Delinquency*, 13:13–32, 1976.

[48] Glaser, ibid., p. 474.

[49] Francis A. J. Tyce, "Psychiatry in Correctional Systems," *Psychiatric Annals*, 7:281–91, 1977.

went down to 200,000 in 1967 and remained at about that level until 1973. Similar trends took place in the individual states in essentially the same years. California, for example, had 25,600 felons locked in prisons in 1968 and 17,750 in 1972; the prison population of Illinois dropped from 10,000 in 1962 to 6,000 in 1973; in New York there were 19,400 prisoners in 1964 and only 12,400 in 1972.[50]

These trends took place during a period when crime rates were increasing. Prison officials, political leaders, and criminologists seemed to agree that imprisonment as a method of changing criminals had been demonstrated to be almost irrelevant, and that interventionist goals could better be achieved by community programs. Further, it was acknowledged that incarceration is very hurtful, and that the idea that institutions are rehabilitative had for too long made it easy for judges and others to overlook the fact that prisons are in fact maintained in order to make criminals suffer. Thus, when politicians and other state officials finally recognized what sociologists had been saying for half a century, namely that prisons do not rehabilitate, the prevailing policy seemed to be that imprisonment should be reserved for only the small number of convicted criminals who should be hurt for reasons of revenge and deterrence, and for only the small number of convicted criminals who have demonstrated that they are too dangerous to be left on the streets. In keeping with this policy, probation and other community programs were substituted for imprisonment.[51] Juveniles and adults alike were diverted from institutions by police, courts, and probation offices.[52]

Another line of reasoning took the following form: A criminal who is no danger to the community while working in a camp or minimum-security place on the edge of town will not become a danger if released to live in the town itself. Alternatively, a criminal who can safely be released from a prison at intervals in order to work in the community or attend college can safely be released completely. In keeping with this logic, many camps and minimum-security institutions for adults were closed, and many institutions for juveniles also were abandoned. In Massachusetts, all the institutions for juveniles were closed, primarily on the ground that institutions do not help the individuals they incarcerate and are not needed for vengeance and deterrence purposes. As Martinson put it, "If we can't do more for (and to) offenders, at least we can safely do less."[53] The children and youths were placed in alternative programs, and the

[50]John Flanagan, "Imminent Crisis in Prison Populations," *American Journal of Corrections*, 37:20–1 ff., 1975. See also idem, "Projection of Prison Populations," *American Journal of Corrections*, 39:11–12 ff., 1977.

[51]Many of the policy issues are discussed in Gary R. Perlstein and Thomas R. Phelps, eds., *Alternatives to Prison: Community Based Corrections, a Reader* (Pacific Palisades, Calif.: Goodyear, 1975); in Calvert R. Dodge, ed., *A Nation Without Prisons: Alternatives to Incarceration* (Lexington, Mass.: Lexington Books, 1975); and in Robert M. Carter and Leslie T. Wilkins, eds., *Probation, Parole and Community Corrections* 2d ed. (New York: Wiley, 1976).

[52]See Kevin E. O'Brien, *Juvenile Diversion: A Selected Bibliography*, 2d ed. (Washington: National Criminal Justice Reference Service, 1977).

[53]Martinson, "What Works?" p. 48.

recidivism rate did not seem to increase.[54] Correctional interest groups such as the National Council on Crime and Delinquency and the National Advisory Commission on Criminal Justice Standards and Goals called for a moratorium on the construction of new prisons, believing that a shortage of cells might stimulate legislators and other officials to invent and utilize more alternatives to prisons, with great financial savings to taxpayers and with more justice to criminals.

But in 1973 the prison population increased dramatically, shooting up from about 200,000 in 1973 to about 230,000 in 1974. By 1976, about 250,000 persons were confined in state and federal prisons, and on January 1, 1977, this number had risen to 283,000. (Included in the 1977 figure were 7,700 persons sentenced to the prisons of eight states but held in county jails because the prisons were too full.) Again, similar trends occurred in individual states. California's prison population rose from 17,750 to 22,700 between 1972 and 1975; Illinois saw an increase of 1,400 prisoners—from 6,000 to 7,400—between 1973 and 1975; in New York there were 12,400 prisoners in 1972, 15,800 in 1975, and 17,800 in 1977.

Six interrelated and overlapping conditions seem to produce this new trend. First, it was part of a more general trend toward punishment and away from intervention and even humanitarianism. Liberals and conservatives alike called for mandatory and longer sentences. Second, the general population contained an undue proportion of persons in the crime-committing and prison-going ages, thus overcrowding community treatment programs and prisons alike. There were 21.7 million persons aged 20–29 in the United States in 1960 and 29.9 million in 1970. Third, the proportion of all criminals who were processed by a correctional agency of some kind probably *increased* with the invention of so-called "diversion" programs and "community treatment" programs; the effect of this would be to produce more persons who could reasonably be committed to institutions on the ground that they are recidivists.[55] Fourth, there seemed to be an increase in the number of repetitively violent criminals whom judges and others considered unsuitable for placement in probation, parole, and other community programs. Fifth, the economy took a downward turn and unemployment rates increased. Jankovic recently showed that unemployment is highly correlated with the imprisonment rate, but hardly correlated at all with the crime rate.[56] Sixth, the

---

[54] See Lloyd E. Ohlin, Robert B. Coates, and Alden D. Miller, "Evaluating the Reform of Youth Corrections in Massachusetts," *Journal of Research in Crime and Delinquency*, 12:3–16, 1975. See also Yitzhak Bakal, ed., *Closing Correctional Institutions: New Strategies in Youth Services* (Lexington, Mass.: Lexington Books, 1973); and Bakal and Howard W. Polsky, *Correctional Youth Reform: The Massachusetts Experience* (Lexington, Mass.: Lexington Books, 1975).

[55] See Robert D. Vinter, George Downs, and John Hall, *Juvenile Corrections in the States: Residential Programs and Deinstitutionalization* (Ann Arbor, Mich.: University of Michigan National Assessment of Juvenile Corrections, 1975), pp. 15–16.

[56] Ivan Jankovic, *Punishment and the Post-Industrial Society* (unpublished Ph.D. dissertation, Department of Sociology, University of California, Santa Barbara, 1977). See also Richard Quinney, *Class, State and Crime: On the Theory and Practice of Criminal Justice* (New York: David McKay, 1977), pp. 131–40.

widely publicized but not surprising conclusion that prisons do not rehabilitate was taken to mean that nothing else will rehabilitate either.[57] All at once, it seemed, everyone—from the International Association of Chiefs of Police to the American Friends Service Committee—was declaring rehabilitation a failure. What was left was punishment, the pain of incarceration. Norman Carlson, director of the United States Bureau of Prisons, can be used as an example of the many persons and groups believing that interventionist goals can best be achieved outside prisons. "I always tell judges you should never send a man to prison so he can be rehabilitated," he said. "If rehabilitation is your goal, it ought to be done in the community." William Saxbe, who was United States Attorney General for a short time, can be used as an example of the many persons and groups that saw *all* interventionist goals as foolhardy. In 1974 Mr. Saxbe began barnstorming the nation with speeches attacking lenient judges, lazy prosecutors, and community-centered rehabilitation programs, saying that these divert or release from prisons tens of thousands of dangerous criminals. The solution to the crime problem was not more rehabilitation programs, he maintained, but more punishment.

SUGGESTED READINGS

Buffum, Peter C. *Homosexuality in Prisons*. Washington: Government Printing Office, 1972.

Carter, Robert M., Daniel Glaser, & Leslie T. Wilkins, eds. *Correctional Institutions*. Philadelphia: Lippincott, 1975.

Cohen, Stanley, & Laurie Taylor. *Psychological Survival: The Experience of Long-Term Imprisonment*. New York: Pantheon Books, 1972.

Cressey, Donald R., ed. *The Prison: Studies in Institutional Organization and Change*. New York: Holt, Rinehart and Winston, 1961.

Fox, Vernon. *Introduction to Corrections*. Englewood Cliffs, N.J.: Prentice-Hall, 1972.

Gallington, Daniel J. "Prison Disciplinary Decisions." *Journal of Criminal Law, Criminology, and Police Science*, 60:152–64, 1969.

Gibbons, Don C. *Changing the Lawbreaker: The Treatment of Delinquents and Criminals*. Englewood Cliffs, N.J.: Prentice-Hall, 1965.

Glaser, Daniel. *The Effectiveness of a Prison and Parole System*. Indianapolis: Bobbs-Merrill, 1964.

Hawkins, Gordon. *The Prison: Policy and Practice*. Chicago: University of Chicago Press, 1976.

Hazelrigg, Lawrence E., ed. *Prison Within Society: A Reader in Penology*. New York: Doubleday, 1968.

Hippchen, Leonard J., ed. *Correctional Classification and Treatment*. Cincinnati: Anderson, 1975.

Jacobs, James B. *Stateville: The Penitentiary in Mass Society*. Chicago: University of Chicago Press, 1977.

Lipton, Douglas, Robert Martinson, & Judith Wilks. *The Effectiveness of Correctional Treatment: A Survey of Evaluation Studies*. New York: Praeger, 1975.

Mann, Dale, ed. *Intervening with Convicted Serious Juvenile Offenders*. Washington: Government Printing Office, 1976.

---

[57] The remainder of this paragraph is an adaptation of Richard Kwartler, ed., *Behind Bars: Prisons in America* (New York: Vintage Books, 1977), pp. 126–7, 132.

Mathiesen, Thomas. *The Politics of Abolition*. New York: Wiley, 1974.

Morris, Norval. *The Future of Imprisonment*. Chicago: University of Chicago Press, 1974.

Nagel, William G. *The New Red Barn: A Critical Look at the Modern American Prison*. Philadelphia: The American Foundation, 1973.

Ohlin, Lloyd E., ed. *Prisoners in America*. Englewood Cliffs, N.J.: Prentice-Hall, 1973.

Orland, Leonard. *Justice, Punishment, Treatment*. New York: Free Press, 1973.

Orland, Leonard. *Prisons: Houses of Darkness*. New York: Free Press, 1976.

Schneller, Donald P. "Some Social and Psychological Effects of Incarceration on the Families of Negro Prisoners." *American Journal of Correction*, 37:29–33, 1975.

Sparks, Richard F. *Local Prisons: The Crisis in the English Penal System*. London: Heinemann, 1971.

Sykes, Gresham M. *The Society of Captives: A Study of a Maximum Security Prison*. Princeton: Princeton University Press, 1958.

Thomas, Charles W., & David M. Petersen. *Prison Organization and Inmate Subcultures*. Indianapolis: Bobbs-Merrill, 1977.

Ward, David A. "Inmate Rights and Prison Reform in Sweden and Denmark." *Journal of Criminal Law, Criminology, and Police Science*, 63:240–55, 1972.

Wilkins, Leslie T. *Evaluation of Penal Measures*. New York: Random House, 1969.

Wilkins, Leslie T. "Directions for Corrections." *Proceedings of the American Philosophical Society*, 118:235–47, 1974.

Wright, Erik Olin. *The Politics of Punishment*. New York: Harper and Row, 1973.

Zimring, Franklin E., & Gordon Hawkins. *Deterrence: The Legal Threat in Crime Control*. Chicago: University of Chicago Press, 1973.

23

Prison Labor, Education, and Group Programs

Prison administrators over the years have used three principal means of keeping inmates busy—work, school, and group discussions. All three have been said to be rehabilitative, but they also have been used as control measures. They are by far the most common and most pervasive activities found in prisons today. Perhaps they were, and are, called rehabilitative because the inmates participating in them show outward signs that they are not rejecting the middle-class ideal—a life of hard work, self-support, rationality, discipline, and a desire to "get ahead" through self-improvement, all of which are ways of "making a contribution to society."

Although the three programs dominate contemporary prisons, their appearance was in chronological order. Until the 1930s, inmates were expected to work, and labor in prison factories was called rehabilitation. Then restrictive legislation closed the factories, the idle inmates were shunted into prison schools, and education was called rehabilitation. Then the conception of poor people and criminals as ignorant, unsocialized children shifted to an image of them as sick adults, and inmates were denied paroles if they did not show signs of having the "insight" or "maturity" or "mental health" that enable most people to see that criminal behavior is irrational and stupid. Although the sequence of progression overlapped much more than this portrayal suggests, it nevertheless seems clear that programs inside prisons have been consistent with prevailing attitudes about the duties of all citizens and the propriety of personal conduct of various kinds among rich and poor alike.

It is a worthy hypothesis, at least, that when work activities dominated the prison, the industrial system needed productive labor, and laziness was denounced as immoral; when the prison school dominated the prison, the industrial system needed educated technologists who could use rulers and wrenches; and when group discussions (social education, group therapy) dominated the prison, the industrial system needed "adjusted" persons skilled in personal relations and knowledgeable about how to render services. The chronological sequence of these concerns should not be exaggerated, however. The primary programs of contemporary prisons continue to be labor, education, and group discussions, all of which, it is hoped, will help criminals see that sober industry and service to humankind are reasonable alternatives to criminality.

PRISON LABOR

The notion that work should be provided for prisoners is almost as old as the prison system itself. When institutions became places of punishment, rather than places of detention for persons awaiting trial, systems for occupying the time of prisoners also arose. This tendency was offset to some extent by the theory on which the early Pennsylvania prisons were based—namely, that labor interfered with the meditation considered essential for penitence. Idleness as a prison regime is no longer defended on any ground, and, on the contrary, the value of prison labor to inmates and to society is stressed. Despite this emphasis, idleness in prisons has become increasingly prevalent during the last fifty years.

When labor was introduced into prison, it was regarded primarily as a means of punishment, although the possibilities for profits were not overlooked.[1] Prisoners were sentenced to the pain of incarceration, but on top of this was piled the pain of bodily suffering. Some prisoners were forced to perform such tasks as carrying a cannonball back and forth along a corridor, walking treadmills, turning cranks, and smashing boulders with mauls and sledge hammers. Sometimes a quota of such labor had to be accomplished as payments for each day's meals and lodging, but often it was purely punitive, in the sense that it was useless. The laws required that the labor should be "hard and servile" or "publicly and disgracefully imposed."

Although the idea that labor should be provided primarily for punishment was soon superseded by concern for utilization of labor in the production of wealth, the punitive element in labor is still retained in many institutions. Currently, the weight of opinion is that prison labor must be "useful" and must train inmates for postrelease vocations, but the idea that monotonous, hard, unpleasant work is necessary, if the prison is to perform its retributive and deterrent functions, also is popular. Further, systems of monotonous or punitive work, like systems of monotonous discipline and punishment generally, are still justified on the ground that they develop habits of industry, obedience, perseverence, and conformity and, hence, have a reformative or rehabilitative effect. Despite the fact that most inmates are now idle, one of the most common punishments in modern prisons is for "refusal to work." Similarly, the fact that routine prison labor often is defended on the ground that it "keeps inmates out of mischief" is evidence that it

---

[1] George Rusche and Otto Kirchheimer, *Punishment and Social Structure* (New York: Columbia University Press, 1939), pp. 41–52; and Thorsten Sellin, *Slavery and the Penal System* (New York: Elsevier, 1976).

is, to some extent, considered part of the prison's program of incapacitation. Prison labor systems, then, are expected to accomplish the same goals—retribution, general deterrence, incapacitation, and reformation (specific deterrence and intervention)—as is imprisonment itself.

Trends in Labor Systems

Concern for profits was important in the development of imprisonment as a replacement for corporal punishment and the death penalty, and this concern has remained. Although in recent years restrictive legislation has seriously curtailed the amount of wealth that can be produced with convict labor, prisoners are expected to at least "pay their way" by producing goods or performing services that will reduce the number of tax dollars necessary for support of the prison. Even in institutions whose programs were said to be those of treatment, inmates were considered as "owing" the state a proportion of their time.

As a method for production of wealth, prison labor may be either public or private with reference to three items: the maintenance and discipline of the prisoners, the control of the employment, and the control and sale of the products. As may be seen in Table 23, the lease system gives a private individual or firm control over all three of these. The contract system gives a private individual control over the employment and the sale of the products, while the state retains control over the maintenance and discipline. The piece-price system gives the private sector control over the sale of the products, but not over the employment or the maintenance and discipline. The state retains control over all three of these in the public-account, state-use, and public-works systems.

The three public systems differ from each other in the extent of the market. In the public-account system the market is entirely unrestricted. In the state-use system the market is restricted to the public institutions in the state in which the goods are produced. In the public-works system the market is restricted to the state, and in addition to the "sale" of public buildings or roads. The last system, therefore, is merely a specialized form of the state-use system.

The first system of convict labor in America was the public-works system. After several temporary experiments with this system during the seventeenth and eighteenth centuries, before the great development of prisons, it was practically abandoned until late in the nineteenth century. It was not until about 1880, when the advent of the bicycle helped create a demand for good roads, that the system flourished. The demand was further increased after the invention of the automobile. The "road gangs" employed by southern states and counties are examples of this system. Some states now make extensive use of the public-works system by maintaining forestry camps where prisoners are employed in fire fighting, insect control, and clearance work. In many counties and cities, juvenile delinquents are required to work in parks and zoos, county hospitals, or nonprofit private agencies in lieu of fines or incarceration. Similarly, the principle behind the early public-works, convict-labor system was recognized by President Ford in

Table 23 **Prison labor systems**

System	Maintenance and Discipline of Prisoners	Control of Employment	Control of Sale of Products	Market Area
Lease	Private	Private	Private	Open
Contract	Public	Private	Private	Open
Piece-price	Public	Public	Private	Open
Public account	Public	Public	Public	Open
State use	Public	Public	Public	State
Public works	Public	Public	Public	State

1974 when he announced that draft evaders and deserters might be required to perform community work for specified periods of time, without pay.

The public-account system was used generally in the early state prisons from about 1800 to 1825. Prison officials were responsible for the labor of the prisoners and the sale of the products; sometimes they were given commissions on the sales. The system failed because inadequate equipment, capital, transportation facilities, and demand for prison-made goods made it impossible to keep the prisoners steadily employed. Also, the introduction of machinery in outside industries resulted in production of goods at prices so low that the prisons, which depended on hand labor, could not compete. After the failure of the system in this early period, it was resumed in the decade of the 1880s as a substitute for contract labor and has been utilized to some extent since that time. Perhaps the best current example of this system is the state prison at Stillwater, Minnesota, where farm machinery and binder twine are produced for sale to Minnesota farmers.

The next system in order of appearance was the contract system, which was authorized as early as 1798 in Massachusetts and was actually used there in 1807. However, the system did not begin to flourish until about 1820. Up to this time it was difficult to use prison labor to advantage, and there was no market for prison products. The merchant-capitalist appeared, and he found that he could use cheap prison labor profitably and could enable the institution to make a profit on it. Thus he supplied the production and marketing organizations that had been lacking in the public-account system.[2] The contract system flourished until about 1880, when it was attacked by the rising labor organizations. Auburn prison utilized this system, and the fact that the prison paid for itself was an important stimulus to the diffusion of the "Auburn system" to other states and nations. At the Auburn institution, prisoners were released from the solitary confinement characterizing the Pennsylvania prisons, but they were not given unfettered freedom within the institution's boundaries. Instead, they were forced to work

[2]J. R. Commons, *History of Labour in the United States* (New York: Macmillan, 1918), vol. 1, pp. 153–5.

like slaves. The rules called for downcast eyes, lockstep marching, no prisoners ever face to face, no talking, and constant work when outside the cells, which were used only at night. The punishment for rule infractions was the lash, and most of the whippings were for failure to do satisfactory work. The number of prisoners employed in contract systems steadily declined after 1880, and since about 1940 no inmates in United States prisons have been employed in them.

A fourth system was the piece-price system, which was similar to the contract system except that the state directed the labor of the convicts, turning over the finished product to a contractor at a specified price per piece. This system was used in the prisons of Pennsylvania in the beginning of the nineteenth century and in New Jersey from 1798 to 1838 in connection with the public-account system. Except for a few such temporary trials, it had its greatest development in the 1880s, when the agitation against the contract system broke out. Although contractors paid for labor on the basis of output, rather than according to the number of hours worked, the piece-price system was merely a subterfuge—really the contract system under a different name and in a somewhat preferable form. This system also steadily declined during the twentieth century; less than 1 percent of the prisons in the United States are now employed in it, and their work consists primarily of clerical jobs such as addressing envelopes.

The lease system, which also is similar to the contract system, was authorized in Massachusetts in 1798, and in Kentucky and a few other states in about 1825. The lease system had its greatest development in the South after the Civil War, where convicts were leased to private parties who used their labor in lumber camps, turpentine camps, or other camps, but it is related to the indenture system used in the colonies, generally as a substitute for fines. This system is still authorized by law and used somewhat in the county jails of several southern states. In South Africa, modified forms of the lease system are used extensively. In one form, farmers' associations construct buildings for the accommodation of prisoners and personnel, and turn them over to the Department of Prisons, which puts its own officers in control. Black male recidivists are assigned to these "labor outposts," and the farmers' associations pay fixed daily rates for their labor. In another form, prisoners with short sentences give their permission to be assigned to individual farmers, who pay them a small wage and provide food, clothing, housing, and medical care. Some contemporary work-release programs in the United States and elsewhere are related to the lease system in that prisoners nearing the end of their term are permitted to work for private parties under conditions closely approximating those of complete freedom.

The state-use system came into prominence in the decade of the 1880s, when the contract system began to decline. By 1899, the system had been authorized by twenty-four states, and at present in about half the states it is mandatory that state agencies and institutions purchase prison-made products, such as furniture, inmate clothing, and printed materials, if they are available. In practice, evasions are frequent, and prisons sometimes find it difficult to sell goods that compete with commercially produced products, usually because the prison products are inferior. The antagonism of trade unions and manufacturers has been aroused by this sytem, just as it was aroused by the contract and lease systems. If a prison makes furniture for state agencies, privately manufactured furniture cannot be sold to these same agencies. Of the prisoners who are now employed, about 90 percent are in the state-use system or the public-works system.

Most prison inmates do not work, however, and those who are employed work haphazardly. The Hawes-Cooper Law of 1934 authorized the states to regulate the sale within their boundaries of commodities made in the prisons of other states, and shortly thereafter every state enacted laws that prohibited or restricted the sale in the open market of goods made in prisons. These state laws were then supplemented by federal laws barring from interstate commerce most goods made in state prisons. This restriction of the market for prison-made goods has contributed to increased idleness. Glaser's survey showed that less than a fourth of the inmates in state and federal prisons were employed in prison industries, which ordinarily do not include prison housekeeping and food-service tasks, and the work of maintaining prison plants.[3] Moreover, the number engaged in productive labor is padded by overassignment, and probably at least two-thirds of the prisoners are, in fact, idle on an average day. Although the assignments of prisoners to educational activities, to counseling programs, and to institutional maintenance have increased, they have not increased sufficiently to compensate for the reduction in productive employment. A recent study of California prison industries found that the employment provided for inmates is little different from idleness, and a national survey concluded that prison factories are more like hobby shops than like industries.[4]

Wage Payments to Prisoners

Payment of wages to prisoners is not a new device. As early as 1700, Massachusetts provided that inmates of the houses of correction should received eight pence out of every shilling they made, under a system in which the masters or relatives furnished tools and materials. For a time, prisoners were held until they paid for their maintenance, but the prisons soon became congested, and the system was modified. After a general failure of the wage system in the colonial period, it disappeared almost entirely for half a century. But in 1853 the Eastern Penitentiary of Pennsylvania began to pay small wages to prisoners. Other states gradually adopted the same policy. A recent survey showed that six states do not pay wages

---

[3]Daniel Glaser, *The Effectiveness of a Prison and Parole System* (Indianapolis: Bobbs-Merrill, 1964), p. 226.
[4]California Assembly, Office of Research, *Report on the Economic Status and Rehabilitative Value of California Correctional Industries* (Sacramento: California Legislature, 1969), p. 5; John R. Stratton and Jude P. West, *The Role of Correctional Industries: A Summary Report* (Washington: Government Printing Office, 1972), p. 25.

to inmates and that the remaining states pay from two cents to three dollars per day; sixteen states pay less than sixty cents per day.[5]

Among the states, wages depend on a variety of things other than the efficiency of the inmate—for example, good conduct, the number of children in the prisoner's family, and especially the profits of the institution. The institution may fail to make a profit because of conditions over which the prisoner has no control, such as inadequate working capital, poor location of the prison, poor choice of industries, poor salesmanship, or poor organization of the work. If prisoners are to be paid at all, they should be paid even when idle, if their idleness is no fault of their own. This principle is currently used in twenty states and the District of Columbia, where 90 to 100 percent of the inmates earn money in prison.[6] These include states with above-average per capita revenue, such as Massachusetts and New York, as well as some of the lower-income states, such as Kentucky and South Carolina. In five states, however, no more than 10 percent of the inmates earn money.

The former chief of the Section on Social Defense in the United Nations argued that labor is a right of prisoners under the Universal Declaration of Human Rights adopted by the United Nations. He stated, further, that prison labor is not treatment, that prisoners should receive the same pay as free men if they do the same work, and that prison labor should be a part of labor in general.[7]

Administrative Problems

Three general problems confront the administrative officers and professional workers of a prison with reference to the employment of prisoners, even after the system of labor is settled. One of the problems is the assignment of prisoners to their tasks in the prison industry and to institutional maintenance tasks such as cleaning, cooking, and clerical work. With the development of classification committees, a few prisons have developed personnel programs that compare favorably with personnel programs in private industry. The various kinds of jobs are analyzed, and prisoners are studied on entrance to determine the kind of work each is equipped to do. The prisoner's preferences and needs are noted, and, in the ideal system, each prisoner is given the preferred job if it is possible to do so in view of the person's ability and the institutional opportunities. In practice, however, the needs of the institution almost always are given priority over the needs or desires of the inmate. As was pointed out in Chapter 22, the criteria used for assignment of inmates to specific tasks probably are custody, convenience, discipline, and treatment, in that order.

A second problem is keeping the prison industries efficient enough to be

---

[5] Norman C. Colter, "Subsidizing the Released Inmate," *Crime and Delinquency*, 21:282–91, 1975.

[6] Glaser, *Effectiveness of a Prison and Parole System*, p. 235.

[7] Manuel Lopez-Rey, "Some Considerations on the Character and Organization of Prison Labor," *Journal of Criminal Law, Criminology, and Police Science*, 49:10–28, 1958.

competitive with outside industries, in face of the low educational levels and poor skills of the inmates who must be employed. So that work can be provided for inmates, prisons use obsolete hand operations. Further, most inmates have little skill, little work experience, poor work habits, and little academic training. They are not able to operate the modern automated equipment that characterizes efficient industrial organizations. Twenty-five years ago, 150 to 180 Michigan prisoners picked sweet corn and green beans by hand; today these crops are harvested by complex mechanical pickers operated by only two inmates. Most inmates cannot qualify as operators of the machines. If prison industries are to compete with private industries, inmates must first be trained in the most basic manual work skills, taught to read operators' manuals, trained to write reports, and instructed in such basic mechanical skills as the use of a ruler and a wrench. Thus, in the modern age, the vocational training given in prison schools is almost as essential to employment in the prison as it is to employment outside prison.

Organization of working time poses a third general administrative problem. If prison industry is to be efficient and profitable, interference with work must be reduced to a minimum. At the same time, the reduction in work interference must be consistent with the performance of other necessary activities. It is extremely difficult to organize an efficient prison industry because men are frequently called from work for interviews, visits, band practice, group therapy, school, sick call, discipline, or other routine prison activities. Certain custodial practices also are conducive to inefficiency in inmate work. For example, time must be taken for counts; the inmates must be in their cells at 4:00 P.M. or 4:30 P.M., when the guard is changed; and, for security reasons, inmates usually must bathe, play baseball and basketball, visit the barber, and patronize the commissary during working hours. The rate of absenteeism in the San Quentin prison's correctional industries in one year was about 12 percent, and on any given day only about two-thirds of the inmates worked a full shift.[8] The rate of sick-leave absenteeism in government and private industry is about 3 percent.

Canada recently tried to overcome many of these obstacles by introducing a penitentiary industry system modeled on outside industry rather than on traditional prison industries. Initially, only about eighty inmates have been employed, but the plans are to build prison factories at several prisons and to reduce the number of different products from 700 to 100, thus enabling the factories to concentrate on profit making. Candidates for all jobs must apply in the same manner as they do in private industry, and they must meet the basic requirements for each position. Hours of work are similar to those in commercial industry. Interruptions are kept to a minimum by scheduling as many prison services as possible in evenings and on weekends for factory workers. Inmates are paid the federal minimum hourly wage, and they must meet all usual require-

[8]California Assembly, Office of Research, *Report on Economic Status*, p. 9.

ments for income tax, unemployment insurance, the Canada Pension Plan (social security), etc., and must pay the prison for their room, board, and clothing. Further, the workers are subject to dismissal. The hiring and firing of inmate employees is done by a three-man committee.[9]

A more fundamental administrative problem involves a question of the priority of prison work over other programs. Although the increasing idleness in prisons in recent years has been rightfully viewed with alarm, revival of the industrial prison might not, by itself, produce the rehabilitative effects that are expected of our prisons. Instead, the interventionist reaction to crime seems to imply a reduction in the amount of prison labor, so that time can be devoted to more efficient programs. Gill was arguing on this ground for a reduction of prison labor over forty years ago:

> The industrial prison has not proven a success penologically. In the early days hard work was the panacea for all ills—especially crime. In these days of social work, scientific medicine and psychiatry, we have come to realize that the cause and cure of crime are by no means merely economic. Practically everyone admits that most men leave prison worse than they enter. This is not the fault of the industries, but it is a strong indication that the present emphasis on industries does not produce the desired results penologically.[10]

Despite this argument, most classification committees and prison administrators still operate as though work were the most important activity in the institution, regardless of whether or not the work is of any value to the inmates. In some institutions, the assumption is that industries that are profitable to the institution must be manned, even if the value of the work to the inmates cannot be rationalized at all. The interventionist principle is not yet so pervasive that a prison administrator can choose to assign inmates to specific rehabilitation programs at the cost of closing down an industry such as a cannery. Similarly, the notion that free laborers should be hired to perform the prison maintenance tasks, thereby releasing inmates for treatment, would find few supporters today, even though most persons readily accept such a policy as it pertains to inmates of mental hospitals.

Training and Rehabilitation
In recent times, labor usually has been characterized as part of the prison treatment program. Ordinarily, the assumption is that nonpunitive labor of almost any kind will instill in inmates habits of industry, so that in the postrelease period they will work at socially acceptable occupations and will not commit crimes.[11]

---

[9] Note, "Canada Launches New Approach to Inmate Employment," *American Journal of Correction*, 38:10–11, 1976.

[10] Howard B. Gill, "The Future of Prison Employment," *Proceedings of the American Prison Association, 1935*, pp. 179–85.

[11] See Ralph D. Edwards, "Correctional Industries and Inmate Training," *Proceedings of the American Correctional Association, 1963*, pp. 197–200.

This conception of reformation is very similar to conceptions regarding the reformative effect of punitive labor, or of punishment of any kind. Another popular assumption is that through prison labor inmates learn skills that enable them, in the postrelease period, to support themselves and their families by legitimate means, so that they "do not have to turn to crime." Both assumptions, in turn, are based on the notion that economic need and attitudes toward work, not attitudes toward legal norms, produce crime. The assumption regarding the "habit-forming" values of prison labor was stated as follows by James V. Bennett, former director of the United States Bureau of Prisons:

> The great necessity in prison is work. If I had to manage a prison upon condition that I make my choice of one thing, and only one, as an aid to discipline, as an agency for reform, for its therapeutic value, I would unhesitatingly choose work—just plain, honest-to-goodness work. Of course, I wouldn't like to have to concentrate so on a choice and it would be unwise to be so restricted. Physical examinations, medical treatments, bodily repairs, educational opportunities, spiritual guidance, psychiatry, psychology, are necessary and helpful. But the habit of work is what men most need.

An alternative statement regarding the indirect rehabilitative value of prison labor may be made as follows: Work in prison affects reformation largely to the extent that it is conducive to changes in associations upon discharge from prison, but it also contributes to the morale of the inmates, so that they are psychologically better equipped for making such changes in associations. Many prisoners learn skills that could be used after discharge. But the possession of these skills does not, by itself, produce reformation. Instead, it is at least probable that possession of the skills affects the social mobility of discharged inmates and that moving from the status of an unskilled worker or unemployed person to the status of a skilled worker changes their associations and consequently their attitudes toward legal norms. Rather than return to the social situation that produced criminality in the first place, the discharged inmate who has been trained in a standard occupation conceivably will move into a new social situation, perhaps one not conducive to criminality.

Also, the work provided in prisons is indirectly important to reformation because, under current prison practices, absence of work means idleness, not participation in programs aimed more directly at rehabilitation. Because idleness in prisons undoubtedly contributes to the incidence of "prison stupor," and because it contributes to low prisoner morale and affects the incidence of prison riots, it may be concluded that idleness seldom equips inmates for shifts in loyalties from criminal groups to law-abiding groups. Until the interventionist reaction and programs based on it become much more dominant than at present, prisons will necessarily have to provide work programs that contribute to the psychological well-being of inmates who are merely "doing time."[12] Perhaps it is

[12] See Stanley Cohen and Laurie Taylor, *Psychological Survival: The Experience of Long-Term Imprisonment* (New York: Pantheon, 1972), pp. 100–4.

for this reason that prisoners in Scandinavian countries and in Mexico possess the right to work.

Prison labor, then, can contribute to rehabilitation by providing inmates with skills that, in turn, might affect their associations and consequently their attitudes toward criminality. It also can contribute to rehabilitation, in a rather negative sense, by keeping inmates occupied so that they leave the prison in good psychological and physical condition.[13]

There is no good evidence, however, that either of these changes flow from work programs in contemporary prisons. In the first place, as suggested previously, most inmates do not work. Second, few ex-prisoners are employed at jobs related to the work they did in prison. They do not wish to tell where they have been, wish to throw off everything that reminds them of prison, and, further, rarely have learned a trade sufficiently to pursue it after release. Glaser interviewed 140 men four months after they had been released from federal prisons to the supervision of the United States Probation Offices in Chicago, Detroit, Cleveland, and St. Louis.[14] Of these men, twenty-four had not yet found any postrelease employment, and two had had no work assignment in prison, due to hospitalization. Of the 114 men who had worked in prison and who had postrelease jobs, thirty-three reported that some job they had held for a week or longer after having been released from prison was related in some way to a job they had had in prison. The 114 men had held a total of 184 postrelease jobs; forty-seven, or about a quarter of these jobs, were related to prison work experience. Among the forty-seven, twenty-four (51 percent) were considered by the men to be related to relatively unskilled prison work, such as construction labor or unskilled kitchen or dining-room work; 31 percent of the forty-seven references (fifteen cases) were to relatively skilled work in the prison, such as machinist, electrician, printer, cook, and baker assignments. The remaining 18 percent (eight cases) of the forty-seven references were to white-collar assignments in the prison, predominantly clerical jobs. However, of the forty-seven men who said their postrelease jobs were related to their prison jobs, twenty-five (52 percent) reported that they had had preprison experience with the job they held in prison. From these data and from responses to a question about the usefulness of the prison work to the forty-seven jobs, Glaser concluded that in about one-tenth of inmate postrelease jobs there are benefits from new learning acquired in prison work; in about 3 or 4 percent of these jobs there are benefits from the preservation of old skills through practice in prison; and in about 5 or 6 percent of the postrelease jobs the prison had provided useful physical or psychological conditioning.

PRISON EDUCATION

Education, as popularly understood, means the process or product of formal training in schools or classrooms. In a broader sense, education includes all the life

[13]Stratton and West, *The Role of Correctional Industries*, p. 26.
[14]Glaser, *Effectiveness of a Prison and Parole System*, pp. 250–1.

experiences that shape a person's attitudes and behavior. Education in prison has been viewed in both ways. On one hand, prison education was once taken to mean little more than the academic school programs that were offered to inmates. This conception of education still persists in most prisons. On the other hand, all intentional efforts to direct inmates away from crime by means of nonacademic, as well as academic, measures are now sometimes considered as prison education. From this point of view, "education" of prisoners is almost synonymous with "treatment" of prisoners. This broad conception of prison education may be observed in the New York State Correctional Law:

> The objective of prison education in its broadest sense should be the socialization of the inmates through varied impressional and expressional activities, with emphasis on individual inmate needs. The objective of this program shall be the return of these inmates to society with a more wholesome attitude toward living, with a desire to conduct themselves as good citizens and with the skill and knowledge which will give them a reasonable chance to maintain themselves and their dependents through honest labor. To this end, each prisoner shall be given a program of education which, on the basis of available data, seems most likely to further the process of socialization and rehabilitation. The time daily devoted to such education shall be such as required for meeting the above objective.[15]

In this broad sense, the problem of prison education is essentially a problem in rehabilitation. This involves a conversion, a transference of allegiance from one group to another so that the person is not receptive to criminal-behavior patterns, and a redirection of those specific interests and attitudes conducive to contacts with criminal-behavior patterns. Little specific knowledge has been acquired regarding the techniques for producing the required identification of self with law-abiding groups. Probably the best way to accomplish this would be by providing inmates with frequent and intimate contacts with people who have the traditions; this is limited by considerations of custody and punishment. An alternative is to provide the contacts, meager and ineffective as they must be in the prison community, by means of educational facilities. Reading and writing can assist in producing the contacts, but contacts also can be provided by means of movies, library facilities, lectures, classroom instruction, discussions with volunteer groups, religious exercises, certain recreations and entertainments, and even individual psychotherapy. Participation in such activities, like participation in prison industries, gives the offender an opportunity, after release, to change social position and, conceivably, to associate with persons having strong anticriminal biases.

Trends

The church has been interested in the religious instruction of prisoners since the origin of imprisonment. During the medieval and early modern periods, preachers

[15] New York Correctional Law, chap. 864, sect. 136.

and priests visited the lockups more or less regularly and conversed with prisoners in congregate or separate meetings. Some of the early houses of correction had resident chaplains who, in addition to holding regular religious services, attempted to teach the elementary subjects, especially to the children confined in these institutions. The first recorded instance of regular visitation of prisoners in America was by the Quakers of Philadelphia just before the Revolutionary War. These laymen, like the preachers after them, distributed Bibles and theological tracts and talked with the prisoners in the cells. Before 1845, few prisons had resident chaplains.

The development of secular educational work in prisons resulted directly from the effort to teach prisoners to read the Bible and the tracts. This effort to introduce secular education met with some resistance. The warden of Auburn prison in 1824 successfully opposed an attempt to teach the younger convicts to read and write. His opposition was based on the "increased danger to society of the educated convict." The same fear was expressed in England about this time.[16]

The first organized educational work in America started in the New York House of Refuge. Provision was made for two hours of school a day for each child; one hour of this consisted of learning to read the New Testament, the other of lectures and talks by the superintendent. The following year, the school period was increased to four hours a day, and the work consisted of the three R's, geography, and bookkeeping.[17]

In practically all institutions for adults up to the middle of the nineteenth century, prisoners were not permitted to meet in groups, and the school work was done at night. As late as 1845, few institutions taught even the three R's, and these few gave a very small amount of time to formal educational work. The first legal recognition of academic education as desirable in penal or reformatory institutions was in 1847, when the legislature of New York provided for the appointment of two teachers for each of the state prisons to give instruction in English for not less than an hour and a half a day. Within a short time, prisons in other states made similar provisions. In most places, the educational work continued to be confined to the evening, and no congregate groups were permitted.

The greatest stimulation to the development of prison schools and other educational activities in prisons came with the increasing popularity of the interventionist philosophy after the War Between the States. The nonpunitive, constructive measures advocated for use in the attempt to change inmates were largely educational. A growing faith in the importance of academic education to

[16] Orlando F. Lewis, *The Development of American Prisons and Prison Customs, 1776–1845* (Albany: Prison Association of New York, 1922), p. 95; Sidney and Beatrice Webb, *English Prisons Under Local Government* (London: Longmans, 1922), p. 157.

[17] Philip Klein, *Prison Methods in New York State* (New York: Columbia University Press, 1920), pp. 308, 311. See also Robert S. Pickett, *The House of Refuge: Origins of Juvenile Reform in New York State, 1815–1857* (Syracuse, N.Y.: Syracuse University Press, 1969).

all citizens in a democracy and to the "good life" also permeated prison and reformatory systems. The logic was something like this: If the good citizens are the educated citizens, then the education of bad citizens (prisoners) should make them good. The Elmira Reformatory, which opened in 1876, had a "school of letters" as well as a trade school. Elmira's first warden, Zebulon Brockway, described the changes in his own attitude toward reformation during the last half of the nineteenth century, and this description may be taken as an illustration of the changes in public opinion taking place at the time. He said he had at first placed his dependence on regular labor, with the expectation that it would form habits that would persist after release; then he was converted in a religious meeting and, for a time, had great faith in the power of religion to modify the behavior of the prisoners; by 1885, he had developed a greatly enhanced estimation of the reformative value of rational education. By rational education, he meant education in its broadest sense, including vocational education, lectures, certain entertainments, group discussions, and the teaching of ethics, as well as the ordinary academic courses.

The Prison School
In many state prisons any academic training is confined to the first three, five, or eight grades, and the time spent in the classroom is generally no more than five or ten hours per week. The primary objective in such schools is to teach the use of the tool subjects—reading, writing, and arithmetic. In view of the fact that about half of the inmates in America's correctional institutions throughout the country are functionally illiterate, these are important subjects.[18] The level of educational achievement in California is higher than in most states. Yet in California prisons in 1972, 4 percent of the male felons received from court were illiterate; the median level of educational achievement was the eighth grade, and about 25 percent of the men fell below the sixth grade.[19]

Other popular subjects include bookkeeping, stenography, and civics. Comparatively few institutions give courses in any of the social sciences other than civics, although several advisory commissions that have made surveys of education in correctional institutions have recommended that much more emphasis should be placed on the social studies, and especially on those social studies that deal with contemporary life, namely, sociology, economics, and political science. These recommendations have been made on the principle that inmates should understand the social world in which they live and especially should understand and appreciate the traditions of law-abiding society. It is doubtful, however, that even university students gain an understanding of such things from courses in economics, political science, and sociology.

[18]Janet K. Carsetti, *Literacy Problems and Solutions: A Resource Book for Correctional Educators* (Washington: American Bar Association, 1975).
[19]*California Prisoners, 1972* (Sacramento: California Department of Corrections, 1973), p. 27.

A few institutions for adults have developed school programs that compare favorably with the school programs of many cities. In California, the prison schools are a part of the school system of the city in which the prison is located, and both the administration of the school and the instruction are under the direction of the State Board of Education. The students and equipment are provided by the prison, the teachers and program by the school district. Regular courses from the first grade through high school are given by teachers certified by the board. The content, methods, and procedures employed in the ordinary public schools are followed, and certificates and diplomas are granted by the regular school district, rather than by the prison. In addition to the courses leading to a diploma, a wide variety of the general cultural and technical subjects usually included in adult-education programs, such as French literature, social living, and accounting, are offered. New York State and the Federal Bureau of Prisons also have excellent, well-organized school systems. Institutions for juvenile delinquents have the most adequate schools, while formal education in jails and workhouses is almost entirely lacking.

An innovative educational program was recently conducted for inmates of the Robert F. Kennedy Youth Center, a federal institution for boys in Morgantown, West Virginia. The project, which was conducted over a period of two years, used "programmed learning" coupled with personal counseling and instruction. Boys could choose how to occupy themselves, but they were paid in "points" equivalent to money for their accomplishments. They earned no points if they were lazy, and they were fined points for misbehavior. In school, points were awarded to boys who passed a test with a score of 90 percent or higher. Boys also could earn points by working in the cafeteria as janitors before or after school. Bonus points were given for exemplary behavior. By spending the points like money, the inmates could "rent" individual cells, buy special meals, and purchase special items from the commissary and a mail-order catalog. Jukeboxes and pool tables also were available for rental. With these incentives, inmates averaged a grade advancement of one year's academic level in about five months.[20]

Some prisons now give college-level instruction. The most common form of instruction is correspondence courses, then live instruction by visiting college staff members, television, and then a furlough system that allows inmates time out of prison to attend classes. Adams estimated that, in 1967, 850 inmates were enrolled in college-level correspondence courses, and about two thousand were taking regular classes taught by college and university instructors.[21] The numbers have at least doubled since that time.

---

[20] Presidents Commission on Law Enforcement and Administration of Justice, *Task Force Report: Corrections* (Washington: Government Printing Office, 1967), p. 53.

[21] Stuart Adams, *College-Level Instruction in U.S. Prisons* (Berkeley: University of California School of Criminology, 1968), pp. 1–14. See also Marjorie J. Seashore, Steven Haberfeld, John Irwin, and Keith Baker, *Prisoner Education: Project Newgate and Other College Programs* (New York: Praeger, 1976).

A common practice in the state prisons is to employ one teacher or superinten- dent and inmate assistants. Most of the inmate teachers are poorly equipped for the work, although it was once reported that the Oklahoma prison had such success with inmate teachers that they were preferred to civilian teachers. The inmate teachers interviewed by Glaser, however, reported pressure from inmates to give good grades, to allow cheating, and to let class discussions wander for indefinite periods to sports, crime, or other topics irrelevant to the assigned study topic. The inmate teachers who balked at such practices were subject to reprisals, but those who complied received favors. In general, it is distinctly preferable to have teachers who represent ordinary society and who have had sufficient experience with delinquents and criminals to be able to understand them and to present the school work in ways that appeal to them. Some reformatories for males now use female teachers.

Vocational Education

The best prison vocational-training programs are those in which trade training is correlated with related academic subjects, and in which a serious attempt is made to teach vocational skills. Only a small number of prisons have such vocational programs. In the vast majority of institutions, "vocational training" is merely the maintenance, industrial, or agricultural work to which inmates are assigned. It is possible to assign inmates to routine prison work—such as painting, baking, barbering, electrical and mechanical repairing, and tailoring—that will furnish the basis for training. For example, the New Jersey Division of Correction and Parole recently set up, at each of nine prisons, a basic six-month on-the-job training program in the field of cooking, baking, meat cutting, table waiting, and sanitation. Over 350 trained workers were placed with members of the New Jersey Restaurant Association in the first thirty months of operation. In one fifteen- month period, 69 percent of the graduate releasees were placed in apprenticeship- level jobs.[22]

But in most institutions participation in such prison work hardly deserves the name "vocational education." Even in institutions where inmates are assigned to certain work activities on the basis of their needs, the training has not been developed in proportion to the development of techniques for classification and assignment. Inmates are likely to be assigned to painting because they are painters, not because they need training in painting. A California study found, more generally, that the tendency is for vocational-training programs to select inmates who show some evidence of already possessing job-oriented motivations, atti- tudes, and habits, but who are lacking in certain trade skills, thus ignoring the inmates who have never been exposed to middle-class work values:

[22]Robert R. Walton, "Culinary Arts Training," *American Journal of Correction*, 38:25–6, 1976.

What seems to be happening in institutional vocational training is the same thing that happens in all programs for the disadvantaged; there is a kind of "skimming" going on where those who are most similar to the middle class in attitudes, motives, and values are motivated to respond to and to utilize the vocational training. . . . The effect of the vocational training is to move the socialization along a little more to give the trainee skills he needs to realize the already acquired motives, attitudes, and values which are centered around performance on the job in terms of standards which are to some extent characteristic of the middle class. What needs to be emphasized among other things in vocational training is a system of behavior modification which will lead to the development of performance-related motives among those trainees who are generally lacking in them. Unfortunately, it is just at this point that the system of vocational education in the Department of Corrections has its greatest weakness—a weakness it shares with virtually all educational systems working with the disadvantaged.[23]

The vocational training in reformatories for young adults and in institutions for juveniles is not much better, on the whole, than in state prisons. The greatest difficulty is that the inmates either stay in the institution for too short a time to acquire a trade, or else shift from one trade to another. Jails and workhouses characteristically give no vocational training.

Perhaps the most serious current problem regarding vocational education in prisons is that of determining the amount of emphasis that should be placed on this subject in the total correctional program. Forty years ago, vocational training was considered the most essential kind of education, and almost all rehabilitative efforts in the prison were vocational. In the 1950s, emphasis on treatment—sometimes called social education—superseded the earlier emphasis on vocational training, but did not make the prison rehabilitative either. Nevertheless, such interventionist ideas made it necessary to reexamine the aims of vocational education, and as a result we no longer are satisfied if the prison produces competent bricklayers; we want it to produce honest bricklayers. After a careful survey of fifteen state reformatories a half-century ago, Nadler concluded that the industrial training in those institutions was not successful, and that it would be preferable to devote the time to changing inmates' attitudes.[24] Although vocational education has been greatly improved in recent years, the notion that prisoners' major difficulties can be resolved by vocational training has declined in popularity. It now appears that vocational education is not important to rehabilitation because of the skills it might provide. Instead, it is important to the extent that it, like both work and academic education, affects the inmate's conception of self and influences postrelease associations [25]

[23]Robert M. Dickover, Verner E. Maynard, and James A. Painter, *A Study of Vocational Training in the California Department of Corrections*, Research Report No. 40 (Sacramento: California Department of Corrections, 1971), p. 55.

[24]F. F. Nadler, "The American State Reformatory," *University of California Publications in Education*, vol. 5, no. 3 (1920), p. 420.

Obstacles to Educational Work

Among the obstacles to educational work in prisons are the attitudes of the prisoners and the unofficial organization of the prison, to be discussed in Chapter 24. Some of the attitudes are developed outside the institution, but many of them are produced by the prison regime and by the conception that the prisons are primarily places of punishment. The walls and bars needed to prevent escapes keep the punitive and protective functions of the prison continually before the attention of the inmates. Prisoners conventionally react by assuming hostile attitudes toward the institution and all its activities. The school, recreational programs, religious instruction, and other activities struggle against this attitude, but generally with little success. Educational administrators, like wardens and guards, are considered outsiders by inmates. Prisoners who participate in educational activities are looked down upon and, in some prisons, suspected of being stool pigeons.

A second obstacle is inadequate equipment and organization. Some libraries are housed in the visiting room, chaplain's office, or a storage room. Money is not available for vocational educational materials or instructors. In some institutions, no room is provided for school except the cafeteria or chapel. In other institutions, children's school desks are used for adult prisoners. The textbooks are sometimes those used in the public schools for children. Some years ago, a class of prisoners was engaged in copying from the blackboard a sentence that read, "How swiftly and pleasantly the hours fly by."

A third obstacle to educational work is the productive industry and maintenance activities of the institution. The custodial practices that interfere with prison industrial systems—baths, haircuts, counts, recreation hours, etc.—also interfere with prison educational systems. And, of course, work and educational activities interfere with each other. This involves a difficult problem in the comparative importance of labor and of educational activities. School authorities generally insist that the work should not interfere with the school; the warden, interested in the financial status and the smooth operation of the institution, insists that the school should not interfere with prison labor.

Results of Prison Education

Although most existing academic, social, and vocational-education programs, like most existing work programs, probably are of slight and indirect value in modification of attitudes and other behavior patterns, many prison administrators and many prisoners cling to the belief that well-organized prison schools are excellent agencies of change. Few attempts have been made to measure this influence, and most of these attempts have not been reliable.

[25] See Michael J. Miller, "Vocational Training in Prisons: Some Policy Implications," *Federal Probation*, 36:19–21, 1972.

An interview study of 120 parolees who had graduated from the trade-training programs of various Michigan institutions indicated that only 14 percent were using their training; 38 percent had not even applied for a job in their area of training.[26] Similarly, Glaser found that of 114 men who had been released from prison four months earlier, and who had found postrelease employment, ninety-five (83 percent) had been involved in some sort of educational activity in prison. These ninety-five men had held 156 postrelease jobs. Of the ninety-five men, twenty-six (27 percent) reported that their prison education had helped them in thirty-one of their 156 jobs. The men said that elementary-school education was helpful in nine of the thirty-two jobs, high-school education in three, white-collar training such as bookkeeping in another nine, personality-improvement courses in five, and mechanical trade courses in the remaining five.[27] Glaser's more general data on the relationship between prison education and recidivism indicate that 39 percent of 361 men enrolled in prison education were "failures" (returned to prison or received a nonprison sentence for a felonylike offense within four years), while 33 percent of 654 men who never enrolled in prison school programs were failures.[28]

GROUP-RELATIONS WORK

The policy of individualized treatment developed as a reaction to eighteenth-century attempts to impose uniform penalties on criminals. Members of the positive school argued that uniform punishments for all criminals could be no more effective than a policy calling for uniform handling of all medical patients, and the alternative eventually proposed was the system of individualized treatment based on the medical model. In the early period under this system, little or no attention was paid to the offender's relations with groups, primarily on the assumption that personality and behavior disorders have little to do with groups and can, consequently, be treated in a clinic, just as tuberculosis can be treated in a clinic. Gradually, the interventionist methods based on this "clinical principle" were supplemented by methods based on the "group-relations principle" that criminality is social in nature and, therefore, can be modified in individual cases only if the criminal's relations with social groups are modified.[29] This trend may be observed in prison programs as well as in correctional work generally.

When considered as a general system for handling criminals, comparable to probation, imprisonment cannot operate on the group-relations principle. Because

---

[26]James Gillham and William L. Kime, *The Use of Correctional Trade Training* (Lansing: Michigan Department of Corrections, 1970), p. 19.
[27]Glaser, *Effectiveness of a Prison and Parole System*, pp. 271–2.
[28]Ibid., p. 276.
[29]See the discussion in Chapter 15, above.

prisoners, by definition, must in many respects be isolated from law-abiding persons, the reformative influences of any prison are distinctly limited by the very nature of imprisonment. But for at least a century some persons have recognized that the offender can most effectively be trained for participation in law-abiding society by being provided with membership in that society, and this acknowledgment of the importance of group relations to behavior has led to many modifications of the conditions of imprisonment. Implicitly, at least, the group-relations principle has become the basis of many contemporary prison practices and policies. In recent years there has been a growing awareness among prison workers of the necessity for promoting informal contacts between prisoners and law-abiding groups and for studying and developing interaction among the prisoners themselves.

Reduction of Prisoner Isolation

Although prisoners for the most part continue to be separated from law-abiding groups and from most kinds of social relations in which they will be expected to participate after release, isolation of inmates has gradually been reduced by "prison reforms" undertaken for humanitarian reasons during the last century. For example, visiting and correspondence privileges are restricted in all prisons, yet the very fact that they exist and are being extended reveals implicit recognition of the importance of reducing the degree of prisoner isolation.[30] Mexico and some American states permit prisoners with records of good behavior to have private visits with their wives and families. Home visits are permitted prisoners in England, Sweden, Poland, and Argentina. Many American jails, and a few prisons, have introduced work-release programs that permit inmates to work in private industry outside the institution during the weekday. In New Zealand, first offenders who have been convicted of offenses punishable by imprisonment may be sentenced to "periodic detention" for up to a year; this means, by and large, that they must spend their weekends restoring old government buildings, in which they are confined, or must engage in other community service. Of the persons so sentenced in a five-year period, about 70 percent committed no serious crimes in the two-year period following completion of sentence.[31] On the other hand, a study of work-release in Santa Clara County, California, concluded that work-furlough programs are associated with a deterioration of law-abiding attitudes.[32]

Furthermore, prison administrators usually take precautions to see that visitors

30 See David Rudovsky, *The Rights of Prisoners: The Basic ACLU Guide to a Prisoner's Rights* (New York: Avon, 1973), pp. 41–68.
31 Eric A. Missen, "Periodic Detention in New Zealand," *United Nations Asia and Far East Institute for the Prevention of Crime and the Treatment of Offenders, Resource Materials*, No. 10, October, 1975, pp. 99–106.
32 Alvin Rudoff, *Work Furlough and the County Jail* (Springfield, Ill.: Charles C. Thomas, 1975).

and correspondents *are* law-abiding, again implicitly recognizing the effects of group relations upon criminality and reformation. Also, obviously, the general provision in prisons of newspapers, books, magazines, television, movies, and extramural athletic events reduces the inmates' isolation. Even classification, which frequently is used as the best example of a treatment method based on the clinical principle, involves recognition of group effects on the criminality or noncriminality of the prisoners. The separation, by means of classification, of first offenders and habitual criminals must be based on the notion that the behavior of individual first offenders will be positively affected by placing them in association with persons having relatively few criminal attitudes or, at least, that the behavior of first offenders should not be adversely affected by forcing them into membership in groups composed of experienced criminals. Similarly, educational, vocational, religious, and even individual psychotherapy programs may be interpreted as efforts to reform inmates by providing them with associations representative of the noncriminal world and by modifying their skills in such a way that upon release they will abandon membership in the groups that promoted their criminality. All such privileges and treatment programs are administered, of course, within the framework of prison security, discipline, and punishment.

Self-government by Prisoners

The group-relations principle of intervention also has been recognized in programs designed to develop a prison social life somewhat comparable to the social life outside prisons. One basis for such programs is the notion that if prisoners are to be changed, they must be permitted to participate in social situations that are to some extent representative of the kinds of noncriminal social interaction in which they will be expected to participate upon release. Another basis, of course, is the hope that inmate-participation programs will simplify administrative problems of discipline and control.[33] One of the earliest specific attempts to promote social interaction among prisoners was the development of self-government systems.

As early as 1793, a modified system of self-government was used in the Walnut Street Jail in Philadelphia. In the institutions for juvenile delinquents in New York and Boston in the first few years of their history, the delinquents had a self-governing court and voting participation in the election of some of the officers. In the Massachusetts state prison, about 1845, the prisoners were organized into a society for improvement and mutual aid, primarily by discussion of topics of interest to the prisoners; the warden was president of the organization, and it was clearly not spontaneous, but was imposed upon the prisoners.[34] In the 1860s, Brockway organized a system in the Detroit House of Correction which he

[33]See Alan K. Klaus, *Assessment of Participatory Management System at O. H. Close School* (Sacramento: California Department of the Youth Authority, 1976), pp. 34–5.
[34]Lewis, *The Development of American Prisons and Prison Customs*, pp. 169–70.

described as "almost complete self-government."[35] In 1895, William George founded the George Junior Republic at Freeville, New York, with the principle of self-government very prominent. Apparently it was this institution, rather than the earlier precedents, that was important in the development of self-government in the next two generations, for one of the directors of this Republic was Thomas M. Osborne, who became the chief advocate of self-government.[36]

Despite favorable accounts of the custodial accomplishments of a system of self-government in some institutions, and despite the theoretical value of a system that stimulates participation in groups holding noncrimiality as an ideal, many students of prison systems have grave doubts about it. A poll of fifty-two state penitentiary wardens brought replies from forty-four, only seven of whom had inmate councils in their institutions.[37] At about this same time, only eight of the thirty-two federal prisons had inmate councils.[38]

There are two principal objections to inmate councils and other forms of self-government. First, if the council in fact has any power to govern, it tends to be controlled by inmates who manipulate it to their own advantage. Powerful prisoners use the weapons of imprisonment, including solitary confinement and deprivation of privileges, against inmates who do not do their bidding. The system of inmate government used by Brockway in a Boston house of correction some years ago resulted in frequent escapes; the officers of the league were arrogant toward the prison officials and lorded it over the inmates, locking up more in solitary confinement than had ever been locked up under the control of the prison officials. The prisoners finally pleaded to have it abolished. After a trial of self-government for about a year, the inmates of the New Jersey State Reformatory at Rahway abandoned it by a vote that was practically unanimous. Ward politics had developed; cliques were formed; the shrewd prisoners were elected to offices; and prisoners against whom grudges were held were punished. When, shortly after World War II, Oahu Prison in Hawaii moved away from an authoritarian system of administration to a more democratic system, an inmate council was established with unusually broad responsibilities and direct access to the warden on policy matters. At first, this did not disturb the order of the prison, for the old, custodially oriented inmates gained election to a majority of the seats. Gradually, however, the council was taken over by younger inmates, who referred to themselves as a "syndicate," and who used the privileges granted as devices for demanding even more privileges; a wave of violence, disorder, and anarchy then

[35] Zebulon R. Brockway, *Fifty Years of Prison Service* (New York: Charities Publication Committee, 1912), p. 97.

[36] See Thomas M. Osborne, *Society and Prisons* (New Haven: Yale University Press, 1916); W. D. Lane, "Democracy for Law Breakers," *New Republic*, 18:173, 1919; and Frank Tannenbaum, *Osborne of Sing Sing* (Chapel Hill: University of North Carolina Press, 1933).

[37] J. E. Baker, "Inmate Self-Government," *Journal of Criminal Law, Criminology, and Police Science*, 55:39–47, 1964.

[38] Glaser, *The Effectiveness of a Prison and Parole System*, p. 219.

occurred.[39] A similar sequence took place in other prisons. It is quite possible that these experiments with self-government "failed" because they came to resemble the politics of local governments on the outside, where political processes also are manipulated to the advantage of the powerful.

Second, in response to incidents such as those indicated above, inmate councils have tended to become mere window dressing. They are made up principally of inmates called "square Johns" or "do-rights," and these types of inmates do not have the respect of the real inmate leaders. They take actions that are of little significance to the government of the prison, and all their actions are subject to veto by the warden. A principal activity of contemporary inmate councils, for example, is one of communicating inmate preferences in respect to recreational matters—the movies and television programs to be shown, and the radio programs to be received on the headsets provided in the cells. The councils also organize various safe activities, such as athletic tournaments and campaigns for blood-bank donations.

These experiences with self-government do not necessarily show that it will be impossible to establish successful self-government systems in the future. It should be recalled, however, that the current system of imprisonment is so designed that inmates can have no loyalty to the prison that keeps them confined, and no loyalty to any majority of their fellow prisoners.

The Honor System

The honor system is similar to self-government only in that it places responsibility upon prisoners and gives them a chance to make choices. Under the honor system, the prison officials grant, as rewards for good behavior and loyalty, privileges that are conditional upon continued good behavior and loyalty. The loyalty is partly to the officials and partly to other inmates. The prisoners who are given privileges or other rewards in return for a promise not to escape or violate prison rules do not want other trusted prisoners to suffer in case they break the trust. Further, because the other prisoners want the privileges, they help the officials control the potential violator. It is obvious that most criminals cannot be converted into persons of honor and transformed into noncriminals simply by saying, "From now on I am going to trust you." Although inmates released from honor camps and minimum-security honor institutions have lower parole-violation rates and recidivism rates than do other prisoners, this record might be due merely to the fact that only those who are considered most likely to reform are permitted to participate in such programs.

Group Therapy

In the two decades following World War II, group therapy became relatively popular in prisons, and it often was considered a system, similar in principle to

---

[39]Richard H. McCleery, "The Governmental Process and Informal Social Control," chap. 4 in *The Prison: Studies in Institutional Organizations and Change*, ed. Donald R. Cressey (New York: Holt, Rinehart and Winston, 1961), pp. 171–81.

self-government, for changing prisoners by giving them experience in social groups. Although there were many forms of group therapy, it usually consisted of a program in which small groups of inmates met regularly and discussed their problems; a therapist—either trained or untrained—guided the discussion but did not restrict it. Such programs are still found in many prisons but, as compared to the 1950s and 1960s, inmates are not as frequently coerced into participating in them.

The emphasis on group therapy—also called "group psychotherapy," "group counseling," and "group psychoanalysis,"—grew out of the difficulty of treating cases of mental disorder individually during World War II. There is an almost unanimous opinion that group therapy is a markedly effective technique for dealing with mental patients. In this area, the chief contribution of group therapy has been elimination or reduction of social isolation and egocentricity, or, stated positively, the assimilation of isolated or egocentric patients into clinical groups.

The group-relations principle applied to intramural treatment of prisoners ideally went beyond this program of group integration in the narrow sense and tried, by means of prison groups, to present inmates with anticriminal behavior patterns. The aim was not mere reduction of isolation and belligerence among prisoners as they operate in the prison situation, but the provision of positive contacts with groups that will directly or indirectly implant in the prisoner the anticriminal values of the larger society.[40] In California, for example, Department of Corrections administrators were convinced, or said they were convinced, that participation in their group-counseling program lessened endorsement of the inmate code (positive attitude change), reduced prison disciplinary reports, and lowered the likelihood of being returned to prison.[41] It is probable that group-therapy programs in prisons do not ordinarily have this positive objective but, instead, merely attempt to provide permissive situations that enable inmates both to discuss their problems with each other freely and to "ventilate" their "suppressed hostilities" toward the courts, the police, and the prison. According to the proponents of the clinical principle, but not those of the group-relations principle, this "reforms" inmates by enabling them to rid themselves of certain individual emotional disorders that are considered the causes of their criminality. There is little difference between the aims of such programs and the aims of individual, clinical psychotherapy.

Group therapy was used extensively in the California institutions, where it was called "group counseling." The therapists in these programs were primarily prison guards and tradesmen. They tried to go beyond mere ventilation and reduction of isolation, attempting in a more positive way to utilize the group for reformation of

---

[40] See Lloyd W. McCorkle, Albert Elias, and F. Lovell Bixby, *The Highfields Story* (New York: Holt, 1958), pp. 68–80; and Don C. Gibbons, *Changing the Lawbreaker: The Treatment of Delinquents and Criminals* (Englewood Cliffs, N.J.: Prentice-Hall, 1965), pp. 146–7.

[41] Gene Kassebaum, David A. Ward, and Daniel M. Wilner, *Prison Treatment and Parole Survival: An Empirical Assessment* (New York: John Wiley, 1971), p. 14.

offenders.[42] It was not clear how such reformation was specifically to be accomplished, but group-counseling programs seem to have been based, and still are based, implicitly or explicitly, on four principal assumptions about the processes by which the group sessions contribute to individual reformation. Three of these assumptions are consistent with the clinical principle, only one with the group-relations principle.

First, there was an assumption that free discussion of an inmate's problem and personality characteristics by and with an inmate group and a therapist will both enable and force the inmate to "face the facts" by "getting beneath the surface." Inmates who have had similar experiences will not let the individual lie, bluff, or provide ex post facto justifications for criminal behavior. Presumably, the inmate eventually will accept fellow inmates' friendly denunciations of criminal behavior and rationalizations more readily than would be the case if the rejections and denunciations were made by an outsider.

Second, it was assumed that stimulation to "face the facts" will give inmates "insight" by enabling each to see that problems of criminality are due to such attitudes as "resentment of authority," or "feelings of guilt," or "frustration." Such insight, combined with the opportunity to ventilate, presumably will reform the individual.[43] This is obviously in keeping with the notion, based on clinical principle, that criminals who are able to dissipate the "tensions" and "anxieties" arising from emotional disturbances will be reformed.

Third, it was assumed that group counseling will give each inmate experience in accepting the analyses, opinions, and arguments of others in the inmate group, and that this, in turn, will give each person needed practice in accepting the general "restrictions of society." This assumption is consistent with the individualistic, clinical notion that there is a war between "the individual" and "society." One variety of this idea in criminology is that the individual, because of something *in the makeup of the individual*, "breaks through" the restrictions of society and follows criminal patterns. For reformation, the something *in that person* must be modified, and this can be done in a clinic.[44] Another variety, possibly the one used in group counseling, is that the criminal's character makeup is egocentric rather than altruistic—the person thinks in terms of "I" rather than "we" and, consequently, follows delinquent patterns. In group counseling, this individualistic makeup, viewed as being in opposition to the spirit of "society" and "group living," purportedly is removed by the therapist and the fellow inmates, who will not let the individual "get away with" the expression of an egocentric character. But according to the group-relations principle, the problem is not one of "individual versus society," but, instead, of one kind of values

[42] See James Robinson and Marimette Kevorkian, *Intensive Treatment Project, Phase II, Parole Outcome: Interim Report* (Sacramento: California Department of Corrections, 1967).
[43] See the discussion in Chapters 15 and 26.
[44] See Hans J. Eysenck, "The Effects of Psychotherapy," *International Journal of Psychiatry*, 1:102–16, 1965.

(criminal) versus another kind of values (anticriminal). What we attempt to correct in our prisons is not nonconformity or lack of satisfaction in conformity to "social rules" or "restrictions of society," but, instead, conformity and satisfaction in conformity to the norms and values that we, the lawmakers, do not approve.

A fourth implicit assumption was consistent with the group-relations principle. It was expected that each participant in the group sessions gains experience in the role of a law-abiding person, and that this experience will carry over to the life outside the session and outside the prison. Here, the reformative effect of the sessions was considered as operating not on the inmate whose criminal behavior and attitudes are analyzed and denounced, but on the inmate doing the analyzing and denouncing.[45] Any person who attempts to change the behavior of others necessarily recognizes that behavior as undesirable. When the undesirable behavior is criminal, the change agent necessarily identifies with and takes the side of anticriminal groups. Perhaps it is for this reason that so few probation and parole officers are criminals. In effective group-relations work with criminals, the reformers become reformees; they denounce their own criminality whenever they denounce the criminality of others. Possibly, the entire group will become "anticriminal," thus supporting the new anticriminal views of individual participants. Status in the group may be assigned according to the degree of "pro-reform" behavior exhibited. If this occurs, there has been a real modification of the social relations of each participant in the group, and the group itself has become an effective medium of change. The personal satisfaction that a participant now obtains from denouncing criminal behavior and values actually is satisfaction in conforming to anticriminal social norms.

It is by no means certain that group counseling and similar group-therapy programs in prisons transfer allegiance from criminal to anticriminal values, despite the fact that group-relations programs are quite effective outside of prisons. An extensive and careful study of a California prison in which inmates were randomly selected to participate or not participate in group counseling and "group living" showed that the experimental group did not subsequently have lower parole violation rates.[46] Group therapy rarely deals with "natural groups" in the prison. Perhaps it is for this reason that any anticriminal attitudes acquired in the group sessions receive little support in the general prison community, and rarely carry over to situations outside the prison. Wheeler has shown that the

[45]See Donald R. Cressey, "Changing Criminals: The Application of the Theory of Differential Association," *American Journal of Sociology*, 61:116–20, 1955; Rita Volkman and Donald R. Cressey, "Differential Association and the Rehabilitation of Drug Addicts," *American Journal of Sociology*, 69:129–42, 1963; Donald R. Cressey, "Social Psychological Foundations for Using Criminals in the Rehabilitation of Criminals," *Journal of Research in Crime and Delinquency*, 2:49–59, 1965; and Ronald Huff, "Programs Based on Sociology and Social Work," chap. 3 in *Intervening with Convicted Serious Juvenile Offenders*, ed. Dale Mann (Washington: Government Printing Office, 1976), pp. 32–49.

[46]See Kassebaum, Ward, and Wilner, *Prison Treatment and Parole Survival*, pp. 207–51.

private attitudes of prisoners are quite different from the attitudes they express publicly, and that in their private attitudes many inmates are not antagonistic to being changed.[47] Consistently, Garabedian found that recalcitrant, "antisocial" inmates join counseling programs when they are sponsored by inmates, but are reluctant to participate in those initiated by officials.[48] Inmate critics of group counseling in California noted that the class line between inmates and staff effectively blocked group-oriented efforts, and that too often staff attitudes toward inmates were sterile, clinical, and devoid of human warmth.

SUGGESTED READINGS

Akman, Dogan D., André Normandeau, & Marvin E. Wolfgang. "The Group Treatment Literature in Correctional Institutions: An International Bibliography, 1945–1967." *Journal of Criminal Law, Criminology, and Police Science*, 59:41–56, 1968.

Baird, Russell N. *The Penal Press*. Evanston, Ill.: Northwestern University Press, 1967.

Barnes, Harry E. "Economics of American Penology: State of Pennsylvania." *Journal of Political Economy*, 29:614–42, 1921.

Engelbarts, Rudolf. *Books in Stir: A Bibliographic Essay About Prison Libraries and About Books Written by Prisoners and Prison Employees*. Metuchen, N.J.: The Scarecrow Press, 1972.

England, Ralph W., Jr. "New Departures in Prison Labor." *Prison Journal*, 41:21–6, 1961.

Gillham, James, & William L. Kime. *The Use of Correctional Trade Training*. Lansing: Michigan Department of Corrections, 1970.

Hiller, E. T. "Development of the Systems of Control of Convict Labor in the United States." *Journal of Criminal Law and Criminology*, 5:241–69, 1914.

Lopez-Rey, Manuel. "Some Considerations on the Character and Organization of Prison Labor." *Journal of Criminal Law, Criminology, and Police Science*, 49:10–28, 1958.

Mann, Dale, ed. *Intervening with Convicted Serious Juvenile Offenders*. Washington: Government Printing Office, 1976.

Rudoff, Alvin, T. C. Esselstyn, & George L. Kirkham. "Evaluating Work Furlough." *Federal Probation*, 35:34–8, 1971.

Rusche, George, & Otto Kirchheimer. *Punishment and Social Structure*. New York: Columbia University Press, 1939.

Seashore, Marjorie J., Steven Haberfeld, John Irwin, & Keith Baker. *Prisoner Education: Project Newgate and Other College Programs*. New York: Praeger, 1976.

Sellin, Thorsten. *Slavery and the Penal System*. New York: Elsevier, 1976.

Steiner, Jesse F., & Roy M. Brown. *The North Carolina Chain Gang*. Chapel Hill: University of North Carolina Press, 1927.

Vinter, Robert D., ed. *Time Out: A National Study of Juvenile Correctional Programs*. Ann Arbor: University of Michigan National Assessment of Juvenile Corrections, 1976.

West, Jude P., & John R. Stratton, eds. *The Role of Correctional Industries*. Iowa City: University of Iowa Press, 1971.

---

[47] Stanton Wheeler, "Role Conflict in Correctional Communities," chap. 6 in *The Prison*, ed. Cressey, pp. 234–40.

[48] Peter G. Garabedian, "Legitimate and Illegitimate Alternatives in the Prison Community," *Sociological Inquiry*, 32:172–84, 1962.

24

Prison Life

Very little is known, even by prisoners and prison workers, about the kinds of social interaction that take place among inmates. Prisoners, by definition, are persons who have been forcibly removed from the social relations in which they have been participating and locked in institutions where they "serve their time," "pay their debt to society," and, perhaps, "learn their lesson." But they do more than pay, and serve, and learn in the institutions. They *live* in them. For varying periods of time, each prisoner participates in an extraordinarily complex set of social relations, including a wide variety of social contacts, associations, bonds, alliances, compromises, and conflicts between hundreds of prisoners, guards, administrators, teachers, tradesmen, and professional personnel like social workers, psychologists, and physicians.

During the period of participation in this set of social relations, some prisoners apparently become "reformed" or "rehabilitated," while others become "confirmed" or "hardened" criminals. For still others, prison life has no discernible effect on subsequent criminality or noncriminality. In the last twenty years, social scientists have studied inmate participation in prison life in some detail, and they are beginning to establish as fact the idea that whether any particular prisoner becomes "reformed," or becomes "hardened," or remains neutral during a prison experience depends on the specific nature of the prisoner's participation in the prison culture.[1]

[1] For bibliographies of the extensive literature in this area, see Gresham M. Sykes and Sheldon L. Messinger, "The Inmate Social System," in *Theoretical Studies in Social Organization of the Prison*, by Richard A. Cloward, Donald R. Cressey, George H. Grosser, Richard McCleery, Lloyd E. Ohlin, Gresham M. Sykes, and Sheldon L. Messinger (New York: Social Science Research Council, 1960), pp. 5–7; T. P. Morris, "Research on the Prison Community," *Collected Studies in Criminological Research* (Council of Europe), vol. I, 1967, pp.

These studies have made two principal points. First, the prison, like other organizations, has distinctive sets of values, norms, positions, and roles—the elements that make up a social system. Second, in the course of incarceration, not all inmates come into association with the same sets of norms and values in the same way; they hold different positions and play different roles in sets of relationships that are so confused, entangled, complicated, and subtle that even the participants are unable to see and describe clearly their own involvements.[2]

THE SOCIAL SYSTEM

A chart of a prison's administrative hierarchy, showing the lines of authority, does not begin to describe how the prison is organized, who is responsible to whom, or who influences whom. It is even difficult to draw a picture of the official parts of the organization in this way, although these are the least complex aspects of the system. In addition, there are unofficial components of institutional structure, and it is these that are most complicated and, usually, unstated. In one sense, in fact, whether specific aspects of organization are "official" or "unofficial" depends on whether or not they are clear and observable. If a prison warden can do something about some aspects of the institution—such as issuing an order that a certain practice is to be changed—the warden is dealing with official organization. If there is something going on, the nature of which cannot be clearly stated and which, consequently, cannot be changed by order, the warden is dealing with unofficial organization.

Both the official and unofficial aspects of social organization are important determinants of behavior, including attitudes, opinions, and beliefs. It is likely, however, that unofficial arrangements are of most significance to inmates, for most of their time is spent in them. The good or bad feeling between an inmate and a guard, between two inmates, or between the warden and the chef, the vocabulary of the psychologists and the social workers, and the sense of justice among inmates and guards are all part of each inmate's world, and they have a powerful effect on the form of the inmate's adjustment in the institution and on subsequent criminality as well. Similarly, while prison officers have some control over much of the inmate's behavior, mostly in the form of authority to punish for deviation, their control is negligible compared to control by prisoners themselves. In a system of friendships, mutual obligations, statuses, reciprocal relations, loyalties, intimidation, deception, and violence, inmates learn that conformity to prisoner expectations is just as important to their welfare as is conformity to the

123–56; Esther Heffernan, *Making It in Prison: The Square, the Cool, and the Life* (New York: John Wiley, 1972); and Charles W. Thomas and David M. Petersen, *Prison Organization and Inmate Subcultures* (Indianapolis, Bobbs-Merrill, 1977).

[2]See Donald R. Cressey, "Adult Felons in Prison," in *Prisoners in America*, ed. Lloyd E. Ohlin (Englewood Cliffs, N.J.: Prentice-Hall, 1973), pp. 117–50.

formal controls exerted by outsiders.[3] Powerful prisoners insist that inmates be orthodox in their statements and actions. And orthodoxy is more important in prison than in outside life, because in outside life a person has freedom of mobility not possible in prisons. Orthodoxy in the ways of behaving of prisoners is promoted by a system of rewards and punishments, the latter emphasizing gossip, laughter, and ridicule, but including corporal punishments and, occasionally, execution.

Informal control may be seen in the persistence of the fundamental principles of prisoner organization, called "the code." An examination of many descriptions of prison life has suggested that the chief tenets of the inmate code can be classified roughly into five major groups.[4] First are those maxims that caution: *Don't interfere with inmate interests.* These center on the idea that inmates should serve the least possible time, while enjoying the greatest possible number of pleasures and privileges. Included are directives such as, *never rat on a con; don't be nosy; don't have a loose lip; keep off a man's back; don't put a guy on the spot.* Put positively, *be loyal to your class, the cons.* A second set of behavioral rules asks inmates to refrain from quarrels or arguments with fellow prisoners: *Don't lose your head; play it cool; do your own time; don't bring heat.* Third, prisoners assert that inmates should not take advantage of one another by means of force, fraud, or chicanery: *Don't exploit inmates.* This injunction sums up several directives: *Don't break your word; don't steal from cons; don't sell favors; don't be a racketeer; don't welsh on debts; be right.* Fourth, some rules have as their central theme the maintenance of self: *Don't weaken; don't whine; don't cop out* (plead guilty). Stated positively: *Be tough; be a man.* Fifth, prisoners express a variety of maxims that forbid according prestige or respect to the guards or the world for which they stand: *Don't be a sucker; skim it off the top; never talk to a screw* (guard); *have a connection; be sharp.*

All inmates learn the code by word of mouth, and, to varying degrees, prisoners are guided by the code in their relationships both within the prison and in the free community after release. There is no question that the code is frequently violated, just as the formal legal code is violated. Moreover, during the last decade the inmates of many prisons have become increasingly factionalized, so that the tenets of the code seem relevant only to inmates of a certain faction rather than all inmates. Whites, for example, are likely to believe only that they should not interfere with the interests of other whites, blacks are likely to believe that "playing it cool" pertains only to relationships among blacks, and Latino inmates are likely to believe that the code means only that they should not exploit other Latinos. Further, there are factions within each of these factions, and the code

---

[3]See Barry Schwartz, "Peer versus Authority Effects in a Correctional Community," *Criminology*, 11:233–57, 1973.

[4]Sykes and Messinger, "The Inmate Social System," pp. 6–10.

often is interpreted as being pertinent only to the inmates having membership in a specific gang or clique. But the fact that a code is violated does not mean that it is not prescribed, nor does it mean that it has no important effects on the behavior of persons sharing it. For example, no matter what the ethnic or other status of persons who violate the code by becoming "finks," "rats," or "stool pigeons," all known informers are ostracized, ridiculed, hissed, scoffed, and generally made to feel miserable. An informer may be given the "silent treatment," a system in which the ostracism is so complete that other inmates do not even acknowledge the informer's presence. In extreme cases, informers are murdered, and many prison systems have a special cellblock or a special institution for the protection of informers.

The code is not necessarily a "code of honor," and persons accused of violating it have no rights to due process of law. A man is guilty if he is not above suspicion or if his associates are not above suspicion. An inmate who has been a witness for the state against another criminal usually is treated as an informer or, at least, as an outsider. To be seen speaking to a guard is a social error, and frequent conversation with guards is in most prisons unthinkable, on the part of both the prisoners and the guards.[5] Professional persons are considered hardly different from guards, and inmates are suspicious of fellow inmates who participate in research projects or rehabilitation programs. The code thus makes inmates suspicious of all outsiders, and it also makes them suspicious of each other. The members of any given faction must be constantly on guard to prevent individuals from seeking an advantage with the officials by betraying the group.

The code, like other behavior patterns among inmates, arises in part out of conditions in the prison. It symbolizes a situation in which an official and dominant government (the prison administration) has failed to obtain the consent of the governed. Prisoners have learned how to evade the government in power and have learned to devise their own ways of providing the services official governments ordinarily provide their citizens. Not the least of these are law-enforcement and criminal-justice services.[6] By withholding their consent to be governed and developing their own unofficial government, elite prisoners accomplish precisely what prison officials say they do not want them to accomplish—illegally obtained status symbols, power, and an unequal share of goods and services in short supply. Yet it should not be concluded that the code is necessarily as "anti-administration" in emphasis as it appears to be. On the contrary, the code reflects an important alliance between inmate leaders and prison officials.

We observed earlier that humanitarian and treatment considerations have

[5]See Robert Sommer and Humphrey Osmond, "Symptoms of Institutional Care," *Social Problems*, 8:254–63, 1960–61; Elmer H. Johnson, "Sociology of Confinement: Assimilation and the Prison 'Rat,' " *Journal of Criminal Law, Criminology, and Police Science*, 51:528–33, 1961; and Harry A. Wilmer, "The Role of the 'Rat' in the Prison," *Federal Probation*, 29:44–9, 1965.

[6]See Donald R. Cressey, *Theft of the Nation: The Structure and Operations of Organized Crime in America* (New York: Harper and Row, 1969), pp. 171–5.

effectively limited the punitive means available to prison administrators for keeping inmates quietly confined, yet these officials continue to be held responsible for the prisoners' orderly confinement.[7] One solution to this problem is to keep inmates unorganized. This practice permits inmates to work together and to participate in other group activities, but it minimizes the danger of escape or riot. Thus "incentives" such as parole, good-time allowances, and privileges of various sorts are administered as rewards to inmates who heed the administrators' admonition to "do your own time."[8]

The very first intensive study of an American prison (done in the 1930s) estimated that in an Illinois prison about 40 percent of the prisoners were not in any way intimately integrated in groups in which strong social relationships existed, and that another 40 percent engaged in some of the superficial practices of group life but were not genuinely affiliated with primary groups.[9] This high percentage of "ungrouped" inmates has continued. It seems attributable to the official system of maintaining control by psychological isolation of inmates. It is much easier to control individual prisoners than to control groups of prisoners.

A second, and more complex, kind of solution to the problem is to enlist, unofficially at least, the aid of some of the inmates. When prisoners far outnumber staff members, it is extremely difficult, if not impossible, to keep each of them psychologically isolated. But control is facilitated if factions of inmates fight each other and betray each other. And control is further facilitated if inmate elites develop and enforce norms and values that promote psychological isolation among the other inmates.

Actually, the inmate code that puts emphasis on being an astute criminal, on maintaining social distance from the guards, and on inmate solidarity promotes both factionalism and individual isolation. Thus inmate leaders operate in such a manner that the important administrative task of maintaining a quiet, secure institution is indirectly supported, rather than subverted. As Sykes showed long ago, the values and type of organization that inmate elites attempt to maintain are to a large degree systems for exploiting fellow captives, a condition attended by control and repression of inmates by inmates rather than by administrators.[10] For example, the advice inmate elites give to other inmates almost duplicates the admonitions that prison officers give to all inmates. Such advice includes directives to be rational, not to bring "heat" by antagonizing employees, not to cause trouble by stealing from fellow inmates, and, generally, to "do your own time."[11] In enforcing the code, of course, the inmate elites necessarily violate it.

---

[7] See Chapter 22, above.

[8] See Richard A. Cloward, "Social Control in the Prison," chap. 2 in *Theoretical Studies in Social Organization of the Prison*, by Cloward et al., pp. 41–8.

[9] Donald Clemmer, *The Prison Community* (Boston: Christopher Publishing House, 1940), p. 129.

[10] Gresham M. Sykes, "Men, Merchants, and Toughs: A Study of Reactions to Imprisonment," *Social Problems*, 4:130–8, 1956; and idem, *The Society of Captives: A Study of a Maximum Security Prison* (Princeton: Princeton University Press, 1958), pp. 76–8.

[11] Daniel Glaser, *The Effectiveness of a Prison and Parole System* (Indianapolis: Bobbs-Merrill, 1964), p. 99.

When they insist that inmates "do their own time," inmate leaders are not doing their own time.

Because inmate control of other inmates is valuable to prison administrators, it should be expected that power of various kinds will unofficially, and perhaps unintentionally, be *assigned* to inmate elites, rather than seized by them. This seems to be the case. Judicious distribution of goods in short supply, including measures of freedom and symbols of power and status, enables administrators to enlist the aid of certain inmates in the task of controlling other inmates. In return for some of the scarce goods, usually called "favors," inmate leaders control the bulk of other inmates. As Cloward has said, "Stability depends upon reciprocal adjustments between formal and inmate systems." McCorkle and Korn studied the prison as a rehabilitative organization and concluded, "Prison officials have generally tended to use the inmate power structure as an aid in prison administration and the maintenance of good order."[12] McCleery has summarized the relationship between administrative organization and inmate organization in the following terms: "The processes by which the formal hierarchy is sustained create the conditions for a parallel hierarchy in the inmate community. Exploitive and authoritarian inmate leaders may be removed to segregation, but others rise to fill their place because their role is necessary in the situation."[13]

Many inmate elites have vested interests in maintaining the status quo, just as administrators do. A basic tenet in their code is that prisoners must stick together and must not use official channels to gain advantages over other inmates, but this is exactly what the leaders do. Officials insist that guards must not fraternize with inmates, and inmate elites insist that prisoners must not fraternize with guards; in this way, both officials and elites control the channels of communication, an important source of power.[14] Like administrators, some convicts insist that all inmates are equal, but by this they mean that "outside" criteria such as occupation, wealth, or criminal notoriety shall not be used to determine the power, prestige, and special privileges within the institution. Such rules for the behavior of prisoners protect the elite convict's privileged positions and are necessary to the maintenance of organizational status quo; when they exist, few inmates can seriously threaten the power positions of the leaders. If special

---

[12] Lloyd E. McCorkle and Richard Korn, "Resocialization Within Walls," *Annals of the American Academy of Political and Social Science*, 293:88–98, 1954.

[13] Richard H. McCleery, "Communication Patterns as Bases of Systems of Authority and Power," chap. 3 in *Theoretical Studies in Social Organization*, by Cloward et al., p. 76; see also Gresham M. Sykes, "The Corruption of Authority and Rehabilitation," *Social Forces*, 34:257–62, 1956.

[14] McCleery, "Communication Patterns as Bases of Systems of Authority and Power," pp. 52–6. See also McCleery, "The Governmental Process and Informal Social Control," chap. 4 in *The Prison: Studies in Institutional Organization and Change* ed. Donald R. Cressey (New York: Holt, Rinehart and Winston, 1961), pp. 149–88; and Merle R. Schneckloth, "Why Do Honest Employees React Dishonestly?" *American Journal of Correction*, 21:6 ff., 1959.

privileges and power were awarded solely on the basis of extra-institutional criteria, the result would be chaotic dethroning of inmate elites at frequent intervals and, consequently, destruction of cooperative alliances between elites and administrators. At the same time, the inmates' rules operate to keep the bulk of the inmates unorganized.

To take an oversimplified example of administrative-inmate alliances, an inmate might be allowed by a guard to steal a little coffee from the kitchen in return for being cooperative, working hard, discouraging other inmates from violence, and generally making the guard's job an easy one. This inmate then has a vested interest in the coffee-stealing privileges and is likely to take a dim view of other inmates who would steal coffee in such manner and measure that the guard and the superiors would put all coffee under strict control. The inmate then makes the guard's job even easier, for the coffee thief guards the coffee. But the inmate really doesn't guard it—other inmates are prohibited from making inroads on the thief's coffee-stealing privileges by a code that emphasizes the importance of doing one's own time, not bringing heat, sticking together against the administration, and not ratting. Both the prison's coffee supply and the inmate's special coffee ration are thus protected by a prisoner who steals from the supply while enforcing a code that, in these circumstances, prohibits others from doing the same. The thief exploits other inmates by stealing coffee allotted for their use, and is permitted to do so by a guard who implicitly recognizes that such exploitation keeps the bulk of the inmates unorganized and thus under control.

PRISONIZATION

One of the amazing things about prisons is that they "work" at all. Any prison is made up of the synchronized actions of hundreds of people, some of whom hate and distrust each other, love each other, fight each other physically and psychologically, think of each other as stupid or mentally disturbed, manage and control each other, and vie with each other for favors, prestige, power, and money. Often the personnel involved do not know with whom they are competing or cooperating and are not sure whether they are the managers or the managed. But despite these conditions, the social system that is a prison does not degenerate into a chaotic mess of social relations that have no order and make no sense. Somehow the personnel, including the prisoners, are bound together enough so that most conflicts and misunderstandings are not crucial—the personnel remain "organized," and the prison continues to "work." Viewed in this way, the prison is a microcosm of the larger society that has created it and that maintains it, for this larger society also is a unit that continues to "work" despite numerous individual disagreements, misunderstandings, antagonisms, and conflicts.

Offenders entering a prison for the first time are introduced to the culture in much the way children are introduced to the ways of behaving of their elders. The general process by which children are taught the behavior patterns of the group is called *socialization*, and the somewhat comparable process among inmates has been named *prisonization*.[15] However, like a person moving into a new culture, the new inmate usually must unlearn some former behavior patterns in addition to learning new ways of behaving. Also unlike the situation in socialization is the fact that inmates are by no means neutral toward accepting or rejecting the behavior patterns presented to them. Among incoming inmates there is variation in the social class of attainment, social class of origin, age at first conviction, number of contacts with persons outside the prison, postprison expectations, and in other personal characteristics acquired prior to imprisonment. All of these affect the degree of prisonization.[16] Regardless of these personal characteristics, however, all persons entering a penitentiary undergo prisonization to some extent, if only because they must undergo the process of being assigned a number, a standard set of clothing, and a standard haircut.

All inmates who are new to a particular prison, even if they have been previously incarcerated, must learn "the rules" and the many technical details of prison living. In this phase of prisonization, which continues for only a few days or weeks, the inmates are essentially outsiders: They maintain the bulk of the attitudes and behavior patterns they possessed upon admission to the prison but change their personal habits to comply with the folkways of the prison.

Gradually, new inmates are subject to other, more pervasive, influences. They accept their inferior status and grow accustomed to having their names replaced by numbers. They wear clothing that is not significantly different from that worn by the other inmates, and realize that, from the guard's point of view, each prisoner is an anonymous figure. They come to know the meanings of prison slang or argot, and, no matter how aloof they may try to be, they find themselves using some of that slang. They begin to recognize the fact that in many respects the prisoners, not the administrators, control the life in the prison. They become aware of their security, realizing that they owe nothing to anyone for such food, entertainment, recreation, education, and living accommodations as are furnished. They begin to look for comfortable jobs where, as one inmate said, "I can do my time without any trouble and get out of here." All inmates are subject to these pervasive aspects of prisonization. They are swallowed up by the prison.

For many inmates, prisonization does not cease when there is mere engulfment by the rather routine prison life. The prison culture contains other patterns that are learned and accepted by some prisoners. These prisoners learn to gamble, to participate in homosexual activities, to rape, and to hate and distrust prison officials and generally outsiders. They not only accept the prescribed prison code, they attempt to enforce it. They not only hear the prison dogma, they begin to spread it. They not only believe that the environment should administer to them,

[15]Clemmer, *The Prison Community*, p. 298.
[16]Charles W. Thomas, "Prisonization or Resocialization? External Factors Associated with the Impact of Imprisonment," *Journal of Research in Crime and Delinquency*, 10:13–21 1973.

they attempt to control the environment through prison politics and conniving. These and similar changes do not occur in every prisoner, and all of them usually do not occur in any one prisoner. They are, nevertheless, characteristic of the prison culture. The inmates who participate in these aspects of prison life differ from those subjected only to what Clemmer called the "universal factors of prisonization," largely in attitudes of allegiance to prisoners. Thomas and Poole found a correlation of .48 between degree of prisonization and opposition to prison organization, a correlation of .53 between prisonization and opposition to the legal system, and a correlation of .51 between prisonization and criminal identification.[17]

The general effect of prisonization is the introduction, with varying degrees of efficiency, of all inmates to attitudes, codes, norms, and values that are in many ways contradictory to anticriminal norms.[18] Because it causes prisoners to identify themselves as persons quite different from noncriminals, even contact with the "universal factors" will render difficult any effort at rehabilitation. As Clemmer said:

> Even if no other factor of the prison culture touches the personality of an inmate of many years of residence, the influences of these universal factors are sufficient to make a man characteristic of the penal community and probably so disrupt his personality that a happy adjustment in any [outside] community becomes next to impossible. On the other hand, if inmates who are incarcerated for only short periods, such as a year or so, do not become integrated into the culture except insofar as these universal factors of prisonization are concerned, they do not seem to be so characteristic of the penal community and are able when released to take up a new mode of life without much difficulty.[19]

The prisoners who are most efficiently or completely prisonized adopt the ideology characteristic of their prison. Most of those who are integrated to a lesser extent at least outwardly espouse the same ideology. A series of studies has demonstrated, however, that inmates show a U-shaped pattern of maximum aloofness to the ideology at the beginning and the end of the prison term.[20] Wheeler concluded from his study that at the beginning and end of their terms, most inmates are primarily influenced by reference groups outside the prison— relatives, friends, and employers whom they have just left or whom they are anxious to rejoin.

[17] Charles W. Thomas and E. D. Poole, "The Consequences of Incompatible Goal Structures in Correctional Settings," *International Journal of Criminology and Penology*, 3:27–42, 1975.

[18] See Thomas and Peterson, *Prison Organization and Inmate Subcultures*.

[19] Clemmer, *The Prison Community*, p. 300.

[20] Stanton H. Wheeler, "Socialization in Correctional Communities," *American Sociological Review*, 26:697– 712, 1961; Peter G. Garabedian, "Social Roles and Processes of Socialization in the Prison Community," *Social Problems*, 11:139–52, 1963; Charles Wellford, "Factors Associated with Adoption of the Inmate Code," *Journal of Criminal Law, Criminology, and Police Science*, 58:197–203, 1967; and Sheldon L. Messinger, "Issues in the Study of the Social System of Prison Inmates," *Issues in Criminology*, 4:133–41, 1969.

PRISON CULTURE

Despite the fact that all inmates undergo prisonization, much of the inmate behavior ordinarily considered part of the prison culture is not peculiar to the prison at all. Some aspects of the prison code are part of a *criminal code*, existing outside prisons. Similarly, many inmates come to any given prison with a record of several terms in correctional institutions, and they bring with them a ready-made set of patterns which they apply to the new situation, just as is the case with participants in various outside criminal subcultures Several recent research studies have shown that a clear understanding of inmate conduct cannot be obtained simply by viewing "prison culture" or "inmate culture" as an isolated system springing solely from the conditions of imprisonment.[21] An early analysis that stimulated much of this research suggested that a distinction must be made between the *convict subculture*, which arises within institutions, and the *thief subculture* and *straight subculture*, both of which are carried into prisons by criminals.[22]

In the late 1960s and in the 1970s prisons seemed to change dramatically as more and more outside behavior patterns became operative within institutions. It became obvious that the values of "thieves" and "straights" are not the only

[21]Charles R. Tittle and Drollene Tittle, "Social Organization of Prisoners: an Empirical Test," *Social Forces*, 43:216–21, 1964; Thomas Mathiesen, *The Defences of the Weak: A Sociological Study of a Norwegian Correctional Institution* (London: Tavistock, 1965); Wellford, "Factors Associated with Adoption of the Inmate Code," 1967; Robert Atchley and Patrick M. McCabe, "Socialization in Correctional Communities: A Replication," *American Sociological Review*, 33:774–86, 1968; Hugh Cline, "The Determinants of Normative Patterns in Correctional Institutions," *Scandinavian Studies in Criminology*, 2:173–84, 1968; Charles Tittle, "Inmate Organization: Sex Differentiation and the Influence of Criminal Subcultures," *American Sociological Review*, 29:492–505, 1969; Stanton Wheeler, "Socialization in Correctional Institutions," chap. 25 in *Handbook of Socialization Theory and Research*, ed David Goslin (Chicago: Rand McNally, 1969), pp. 1005–23; Anne R. Edwards, "Inmate Adaptation and Socialization in the Prison," *Sociology*, 4:213–25, 1970; Charles W. Thomas, "Toward a More Inclusive Model of the Inmate Culture," *Criminology*, 8:251–62, 1970; Barry Schwartz, "Pre-Institutional vs. Situational Influence in a Correctional Community," *Journal of Criminal Law, Criminology, and Police Science*, 62:532–42, 1971; Heffernan, *Making It in Prison*, 1972; Charles R. Tittle, *Society of Subordinates* (Bloomington: Indiana University Press, 1972; Charles W. Thomas and Samuel C. Foster, "Prisonization in the Inmate Contraculture," *Social Problems*, 20:229–39, 1972; Thomas, "Prisonization or Socialization?" 1973; Charles W. Thomas and Samuel C. Foster, "The Importation Model Perspective on Inmate Social Roles: An Empirical Test," *Sociological Quarterly*, 16:226–34, 1973; Ronald L. Akers, Norman S. Hayner, and Werner Gruninger, "Homosexual and Drug Behavior in Prison: A Test of the Functional and Importation Models of the Inmate System," *Social Problems*, 21:410–22, 1974; Thomas and Poole, "The Consequences of Incompatible Goal Structures in Correctional Settings," 1975; Charles W. Thomas, "Theoretical Perspectives on Alienation in the Prison Community," *Pacific Sociological Review*, 18:483–99, 1975; Nicholas R. Curcione, "Social Relations Among Inmate Addicts," *Journal of Research in Crime and Delinquency*, 12:61–74, 1975; Charles W. Thomas and Matthew T. Zingraff, "Organizational Structure as a Determinant of Prisonization," *Pacific Sociological Review*, 19:98–116, 1976; and Gary F. Jensen, "Age and Rule-Breaking in Prison: A Test of Sociocultural Interpretations," *Criminology*, 14:555–68, 1977.

[22]John Irwin and Donald R. Cressey, "Thieves, Convicts and Inmate Culture," *Social Problems*, 10:142–55, 1962.

behavior patterns imported from the outside to affect relations among inmates. Racial and ethnic consciousness in American society has always been reflected in racial-ethnic identities within prisons; these supplement other identities, including those of "thieves," "convicts" and "straights." Now, Latinos, blacks, and others constitute three rather separate and conflicting societies, inside as well as outside prisons.[23] Further, in some prisons even these societies are factionalized by membership in "supergangs," resulting in inmate organization resembling that of multinational prisoner-of-war camps. These gangs thrive outside prisons, and their organizational structure, leadership hierarchies, and activities have been imported.[24] Further, religious sects such as Jehovah's Witnesses, Black Muslims, and Church of the New Song also have been imported. On top of all this, radical groups have seen prisoners as a revolutionary force to be mobilized, and as a result radical and revolutionary politics have become a part of prison society. "The prison experience becomes defined as a period for the development of political consciousness and revolutionary organization. Under such circumstances, the 'program' of the prison administrator interested in rehabilitation is interpreted as irrelevant and counter-revolutionary. Political radicals do not want to be adjusted to the system."[25]

In general, the old picture of prisoner society as an integrated, normative, and moral community is not accurate. It never was accurate. Fifty years ago American prisons were characterized by competing inmate groups with no functional relevance to the prison, just as contemporary prisons are so characterized. At that time, as in the years when Clemmer did his pioneering study, the dominant ethnic groups in conflict were Irish and Italian, and they fought each other with the same vigor now exhibited in the competition between blacks, whites, and Latinos.[26] Blacks inside prisons were as powerless as blacks outside prisons. Only twenty-five years ago no black inmates participated in what was described as a "general riot" in the Missouri State Prison. In the same years, religious conflict between Catholics and Protestants was as rife on the inside as it was on the outside. Further, the political radicals imprisoned in the 1930s were no less radical than contemporary radical prisoners. And members of bootlegging groups, other organized crime groups, political groups, and even street gangs were no less

[23]James B. Jacobs, "Stratification and Conflict Among Prison Inmates," *Journal of Criminal Law and Criminology*, 66:476–82, 1976; Lec Carroll, *Hacks, Blacks, and Cons: Race Relations in a Maximum Security Prison* (Lexington, Mass.: Lexington Books, 1974); R. Theodore Davidson, *Chicano Prisoners: The Key to San Quentin* (New York: Holt, Rinehart and Winston, 1974); and Hans Toch, *Police, Prisons, and the Problem of Violence* (Washington: Government Printing Office, 1977). See also David A. Ward and Gene G. Kassebaum, *Women's Prison: Sex and Social Structure* (Chicago: Aldine, 1965).

[24]James B. Jacobs, "Street Gangs Behind Bars," *Social Problems*, 21:395–410, 1974.

[25]Jacobs, "Stratification and Conflict Among Prison Inmates," p. 481. See also Gresham Sykes, "Prison Is a Perfect Culture for Growing Conspiracies," *New York Times*, April 21, 1974.

[26]See James B. Jacobs, *Stateville: The Penitentiary in Mass Society* (Chicago: University of Chicago Press, 1977), pp. 22–7.

oriented to their membership in "supergangs" than are contemporary youthful prisoners. Despite such factionalism in the prison cultures of a half-century ago, a quarter-century ago, and a decade ago, the thief subculture, the convict subculture and the straight subculture were all present, and these subcultures continue to be present in the more factionalized cultures of contemporary prisons.

The Thief Subculture

The core values of thieves operating on the street correspond closely to the values that prison observers have ascribed to the type of inmate called the "right guy" or "real man." Things have not changed much since the 1930s, when the sociologist Hans Riemer secured a prison commitment for the purpose of studying the prison community and spent about four months in a state prison without the knowledge of any prisoner or administrative officer that he was not a bona fide offender. He described the two principal types of inmate leaders as follows:

> The prison population is largely in the control of a small group of men which has two divisions. There are the "politicians," "shots," or whatever they may be called in varying institutions, who hold key positions in the administrative offices of the prison. They wield a power to distribute special privileges, to make possible the circulation of special foods or other supplies. They in frequent instances become "racketeers" and use their positions to force money and services from less powerful inmates. These men are seldom trusted by the top level of the prison hierarchy, are frequently hated by the general population because of the exclusiveness and self-seeking behavior characteristic of them. . . . The other section of this controlling power is held by the so-called "right guys." These men are so known because of the consistency of their behavior in accordance with the criminal or prison code. They are men who can always be trusted, who do not abuse lesser inmates, who are invariably loyal to their class—the convicts. They are not wanton trouble makers but they are expected to stand up for their rights as convicts, to get what they can from the prison officials, to never permit an opportunity to pass from which they might secure anything from a better job to freedom. . . . These men, because of their outright and loyal behavior, are the real leaders of the prison and impose stringent control upon the definitions of proper behaviors from the convicts.[27]

Similarly, Clemmer found that the most important characteristic of prison leaders was "being right," although the leaders also were above average in intelligence, experienced in crime, and city-bred.[28]

High status as a "politician," "shot," "merchant," "peddler," or even as a "tough," "hood," or "gorilla" is based principally on conduct within the prison, but status as a "right guy" depends as well upon participation in the "criminal" or

---

[27] Hans Riemer, "Socialization in the Prison Community," *Proceedings of the American Prison Association*, 1937, pp. 151–5.

[28] Donald Clemmer, "Leadership Phenomena in a Prison Community," *Journal of Criminal Law and Criminology*, 28:861–72, 1938. See also Clarence Schrag, "Leadership Among Prison Inmates," *American Sociological Review*, 19:37–42, 1954.

"thief" subculture that exists outside prisons.[29] In the thief subculture, as it exists on the street, a person who is known as "right" or "solid" is one who can be trusted and relied upon. High status is also awarded to those who possess skill as thieves, but to be just a successful thief is not enough; there must be solidness as well. A solid person is respected even if unskilled, and no matter how skilled in crime a stool pigeon may be, the informer's status is low.

Despite the fact that adherence to the norms of the thief subculture is an ideal, and the fact that the behavior of the great majority of persons arrested or convicted varies sharply from any "criminal code" that might be identified, a proportion of the persons arrested for "real crime," such as burglary, robbery, and larceny, have been in close contact with the values of the subculture. Many criminals, while not following the precepts of the subculture religiously, give lip service to its values and evaluate their own behavior and the behavior of their associates in terms relating to adherence to "rightness" and being "solid." It is probable, further, that use of this kind of values is not even peculiarly "criminal," for policemen, prison guards, college professors, students, and almost all other persons evaluate behavior in terms of in-group loyalties. In his classic study, Whyte noted the mutual obligations binding corner boys together and concluded that status depends on the extent to which a boy lives up to his obligations, a form of "solidness."[30] More recently, Miller identified "toughness," "smartness," and "autonomy" among the focal concerns of lower-class adolescent delinquent boys; these also characterize prisoners who are oriented to the thief subculture.[31] Wheeler found that half the custody staff and 60 percent of the treatment staff in one prison approved the conduct of a hypothetical inmate who refused to name an inmate with whom he had been engaged in a knife fight.[32]

Imprisonment is one of the recurring problems with which *thieves* must cope. It is almost certain that a *thief* will be arrested from time to time, and the subculture provides members with patterns to be used in order to help solve this problem. Norms that apply to the prison situation, and information on how to undergo the prison experience—how to do time "standing on your head"—with the least suffering and in a minimum amount of time are provided. Of course, the subculture itself is both nurtured and diffused in the different jails and prisons of the country.

[29]The argot terms for types of prisoners vary from institution to institution. The terms used above do not include all the inmate types identified by prisoners. For example, terms such as *wolf, punk,* and *fag* refer to roles in homosexuality, and *ding* and *rapo* refer to mentally disturbed inmates and sex offenders, respectively.

[30]William Foote Whyte, "Corner Boys: A Study of Clique Behavior," *American Journal of Sociology,* 46:647–63, 1941.

[31]Walter B. Miller, "Lower Class Culture as a Generating Milieu of Gang Delinquency," *Journal of Social Issues,* 14:5–19, 1958.

[32]Stanton Wheeler, "Role Conflict in Correctional Communities," chap. 6 in *The Prison,* ed. Cressey, p. 235.

The Convict Subculture

As Riemer's discussion of "politicians" and "shots" indicates, there also exists in prisons a subculture that is by definition a set of patterns that flourishes in the environment of incarceration. This is the "convict subculture," which can be found wherever people are confined, whether it be in city jails, state and federal prisons, army stockades, prisoner-of-war camps, concentration camps, or even mental hospitals. Such organizations are characterized by deprivations and limitations on freedom, and in them available wealth must be competed for by inmates supposedly on an equal footing. It is in connection with the *maintenance* (but not necessarily with the *origin*) of this subculture that it is appropriate to stress the notion that a minimum of outside status criteria are carried into the situation.

The convict subculture is oriented to manipulating the conditions of prison life, not to an honorable and proud life as a thief. As indicated, prison argot identifies some of the prisoners participating in this subculture as "merchants," "peddlers," "shots," and "politicians." Nowadays, inmates tend to use a single term to refer to all of them—"convicts." Prisoners playing this role do favors for their fellow prisoners in direct exchange for favors from them, or for payment in cigarettes, the medium of exchange in most prisons. Many if not most of the favors involve distribution of goods and services that are supposed to go to inmates without cost—the "merchant" charges a price for dental care, laundry, food, library books, a good job assignment, and so on. The central value of the convict subculture is utilitarianism, and the most utilitarian individuals win the available wealth, privileges, and positions of influence.

Also oriented to the convict subculture and to manipulating prison life are inmates who exhibit highly aggressive behavior against other inmates and against officials. They are likely to be called "gorillas," "ballbusters," "outlaws," or some similar name, depending on the prison. The terms are all synonyms referring to inmates, likely to be diagnosed as psychopaths by psychiatrists, who hijack their fellow inmates when the latter are returning from the commissary, who attack guards and fellow inmates verbally and physically, who force other inmates to pay for cell and job assignments, who run any kangaroo court, who smash up the prison at the beginning of a riot. These *convicts* offer protection to weak inmates for a fee, but, like "merchants," they actually exploit other inmates while seeming to help make prison life easier for them.

Although the *convicts* in a prison achieve status within that prison through the displayed ability to manipulate the environment, win special privileges through a system of illegal exchange, and assert influence over others through political control and violence, it is not correct to conclude that these behavior patterns arise simply from the conditions within any particular prison. In the first place, such utilitarian and manipulative behavior probably is characteristic of the urban lower class in the United States, and most prisoners come from this class. After discussing the importance of toughness, smartness, excitement, and fate in this group, Miller makes the following significant observation:

. . . in lower class culture a close conceptual connection is made between "authority" and "nurturance." To be restrictively or firmly controlled is to be cared for. Thus the overtly negative evaluation of superordinate authority frequently extends as well to nurturance, care, or protection. The desire for personal independence is often expressed in terms such as "I don't need *nobody* to take care of me. I can take care of myself!" Actual patterns of behavior, however, reveal a marked discrepancy between expressed sentiment and what is covertly valued. Many lower class people appear to seek out highly restrictive social environments wherein stringent external controls are maintained over their behavior. Such institutions as the armed forces, the mental hospital, the disciplinary school, the prison or correctional institution, provide environments which incorporate a strict and detailed set of rules defining and limiting behavior, and enforced by an authority system which controls and applies coercive sanctions for deviance from these rules. While under the jurisdiction of such systems, the lower class person generally expresses to his peers continual resentment of the coercive, unjust, and arbitrary exercise of authority. Having been released, or having escaped from these milieux, however, he will often act in such a way as to insure recommitment, or choose recommitment voluntarily after a temporary period of "freedom."[33]

In the second place, the dedicated participants in the convict subculture, as it exists in American prisons for adults, are likely to be inmates who have a long record of confinement in county jails and institutions for juveniles. McCleery observed that, in a period of transition, reform-school graduates all but took over inmate society in one prison. These youths called themselves a "syndicate" and engaged in a concentrated campaign of argument and intimidation directed toward capturing the inmate council and the inmate craft shop that had been placed under council management. "The move of the syndicate to take over the craft shop involved elements of simple exploitation, the grasp for a status symbol, and an aspect of economic reform."[34]

Persons with long histories of institutionalization, it is important to note, might have had little contact with the thief subculture. The thief subculture does not flourish in institutions for juveniles, and graduates of such institutions have not necessarily had extensive criminal experience on the outside. However, some form of the convict subculture *does* exist in institutions for juveniles, though not to the extent characterizing prisons for felons. Further, in places of short-term confinement the convict subculture is dominant, for the thief subculture involves status distinctions that are not readily noticeable or influential in the short run. Some of the newcomers to a prison for adults are, in short, persons who have been oriented to the convict subculture, who have found the utilitarian nature of this subculture acceptable, and who have had little contact with the thief subculture. In California prisons, the "right guys" and others refer to them as "state-raised youths" because they have spent too much time in institutions. A background of this kind makes a difference in their behavior.

---

[33] Miller, "Lower Class Culture as a Generating Milieu of Gang Delinquency," pp. 12–13.
[34] McCleery, "The Governmental Process and Informal Social Control," p. 179.

The "Straight" Subculture

A final category of inmates is oriented to legitimate activities. Prisoners with this orientation are called "straights," "square Johns," "do-rights," and so on. This category includes inmates who are not members of the thief subculture upon entering prison, and who isolate themselves—or are isolated—from the thief and convict subcultures. They make up a large percentage of the population of any prison, but they present few problems to prison administrators. Whatever their ethnic status, the inmates who share the straight subculture of a prison are oriented to the problem of achieving goals through means that are legitimate outside prisons.

DIFFERENTIAL PARTICIPATION

There are great differences in the prison behavior of prisoners oriented to one or another of the three subcultures. The hard-core member of the convict subculture finds reference groups inside the institution, and, as indicated, seeks status through means available in the prison environment. But it is important for the understanding of inmate conduct to note that the hard-core member of the thief subculture seeks status in the broader criminal world of which prison is only a part. The *thief's* reference groups include people both inside and outside prison, but the *thief* is committed to criminal life, not prison life. Similarly, a prisoner oriented to legitimate subculture is, by definition, committed to the values of persons outside the prison.

On the other hand, within any given prison, it is the inmates oriented to the convict subculture who seek positions of power and influence and sources of information. A job as secretary to the captain or warden, for example, gives an aspiring prisoner information and consequent power, and enables the *convict* to influence the assignment or regulation of other inmates. In the same way, a job that allows the incumbent to participate in a racket, such as clerk in the kitchen storeroom, where one can steal and sell food, is highly desirable to an inmate oriented to the convict subculture. With a steady income of cigarettes, ordinarily the prisoners' medium of exchange, he can assert a great deal of influence and purchase those things that are symbols of status among persons oriented to the convict subculture. These include information and such items as specially starched, pressed, and tailored prison clothing, fancy belts, belt buckles, billfolds, special shoes, or any other type of dress that will set the inmate apart and indicate that the *convict* has both the influence to get the goods and the influence necessary to keeping and displaying them despite prison rules that outlaw doing so.

Because prisoners oriented either to a legitimate subculture or to a thief subculture are not seeking high status within any given prison, they do not look for the kinds of positions considered so desirable by *convicts*. Those oriented to legitimate subcultures take prison as it comes and seek status through channels provided for that purpose by prison administrators—running for election to the inmate council, to the editorship of the institutional newspaper, and so on—and, generally, by conforming to what they think administrators expect of good prisoners.

Long before *thieves* have come to prison, their subculture has defined proper prison conduct as behavior rationally calculated to "do time" in the easiest possible way. This means that the *thief* wants a prison life containing the best possible combination of a maximum amount of leisure time and a maximum number of privileges. Accordingly, the privileges sought by the *thief* are different from the privileges sought by the *convict* oriented to prison itself. The *thief* wants things that will make prison life a little easier—extra food, a maximum amount of recreation time, a good radio, a little peace. One *thief* serving his third sentence for armed robbery was a dishwasher in the officers' dining room. He liked the eating privileges, but he never sold food. Despite his "low-status" job, he was highly respected by other *thieves*, who described him as "right," and "solid."

Members of the convict subculture, like the *thieves*, seek privileges. There is a difference, however, for the *convict* seeks privileges that will enhance a person's position in the inmate hierarchy. *Convicts*, like *thieves*, want to do easy time, but, as compared with the *thief*, desirable privileges are more likely to involve freedom to amplify one's store, such as stealing rights in the kitchen and freedom of movement around the prison. Obtaining an easy job is managed because it is easy and therefore desirable, but it also is managed for the purpose of displaying the fact that it can be obtained.

In the routine prison setting, the two deviant subcultures exist in a balanced relationship. It is this total setting that has been observed as "inmate culture." There is some conflict because of the great disparity in some of the values of *thieves* and *convicts*, but the two subcultures share other values. *Thieves* are committed to keeping their hands off other people's activities, and *convicts*, being utilitarian, are likely to know that it is better in the long run to avoid conflict with *thieves* and confine one's exploitation to the "do-rights" and to the members of the convict subculture. Of course, the *thief* must deal with the *convict* from time to time, and in doing so the *thief* adjusts to the reality of imprisonment. Choosing to follow prison definitions usually means paying for some service in cigarettes or in a returned service; this is the cost of doing easy time. Some *thieves* adapt in a more general way to the ways of convicts and assimilate the prisonized person's concern for making out in the institution.[35] On an ideal-type level, however, *thieves* do not sanction exploitation of other inmates, and they simply ignore the "square Johns," who are oriented to legitimate subcultures. Nevertheless, their subculture, as it operates in prison, has exploitative effects.

Numerous studies have documented the fact that "right guys," many of whom can be identified as leaders of the *thieves*, not of the *convicts*, exercise the greatest influence over the total prison population. The influence is the long-run kind

[35] See John Irwin, *The Felon* (Englewood Cliffs, N.J.: Prentice-Hall, 1970), pp. 61–85.

stemming from the ability to influence notions of what is right and proper, what McCleery calls the formulation and communication of definitions.[36] The *thief*, after all, has the respect of many inmates who are not themselves *thieves*. The "right guy" carries a set of attitudes, values, and norms that have a great deal of consistency and clarity. He acts, forms opinions, and evaluates events in the prison according to them, and over a long period of time he in this way influences behavior patterns in the institution. In what the *thief* thinks of as "small matters," however—getting job transfers, enforcing payment of gambling debts, selling narcotics, making cell assignments and leading racial feuds and fights—members of the convict subculture run things.

It is difficult to assess the direct lines of influence the two deviant subcultures have over those inmates who are not members of either subculture when they enter a prison. It is true that if a new inmate does not have definitions to apply to the new prison situation, one or the other of the deviant subcultures is likely to supply them in the prisonization process. On the one hand the convict subculture is much more apparent than the thief subculture; its roles are readily visible to any new arrival, and its definitions are readily available to one who wants to "get along" and "make it" in a prison. Moreover, the inmate leaders oriented to the convict subculture are eager to get new followers who will recognize the existing status hierarchy in the prison. *Thieves*, on the other hand, tend to be snobs. Their status in prison is determined in part by outside criteria, as well as by prison conduct, and it is therefore difficult for a prisoner, acting as a prisoner, to achieve these criteria. At a minimum, newcomers can fall under the influence of the thief subculture only if they have intimate association over a period of time with some of its members who are able and willing to impart some of its subtle behavior patterns to them.

It seems clear that *thieves, convicts,* and *straights* all bring certain values and behavior patterns to prison with them, and that total "inmate culture" represents an adjustment or accommodation of these three subcultures within the official administrative framework of deprivation and control. The "inmate culture" of any given prison, then, will depend on the nature of the balance between the three subcultures. Doing time in minimum-security institutions, in prisons for women, and in federal prisons for gentleman criminals is much easier than doing time in maximum-security prisons because the proportion of inmates oriented to the straight subculture is much greater in the former than in the latter. Similarly, doing time in institutions for youthful offenders is more difficult than in institutions for mature criminals because there are fewer *thieves* to help the administrators maintain peace and keep order. Indeed, it seems likely that in the last decade doing time in prisons generally has become more difficult because a larger proportion of all inmates are now *convicts*, and particularly *convicts* of the "gorilla" type. Probation and parole policies, supplemented with diversion

---

[36] McCleery, "The Governmental Process and Informal Social Control," p. 154.

programs and community-treatment programs, have drained off many criminals who formerly strengthened the straight subculture. Further, the number of recidivists who have committed drug-related crimes, muggings or similar violent crimes, and cheap burglaries and robberies—and who, thus, are likely to be supporters of the convict subculture—has increased in proportion to the number of persons committed to prisons because they have committed the classy larcenies, burglaries, and robberies typical of *thieves*. The "politicalization" of prisoners also has strengthened the convict subculture as compared with the other two subcultures. There is something to be said in favor of the notion that life in prison is more unpleasant and dangerous than it was only twenty years ago because the moral and ethical standards of the inmate body have deteriorated, making it much more difficult for prison administrators to protect inmates from each other.

REFORMATION IN THE PRISON CULTURE

Inmates learn many criminal techniques from each other and often form alliances for the perpetration of crimes after release. However, retention and development of criminal attitudes and other criminal-behavior patterns in prison does not result primarily from mere contamination and individual tutelage of one prisoner by another. Instead, these processes take place in response to participation in a culture in which persons have *collectively* developed traditions favorable to crime and to the repression of any tendency toward reformation. An inmate of the United States Penitentiary at Atlanta long ago noted this fact in the following terms:

I know that prisons are wrong because it is self-manifest that were society to attempt to devise a process for the development of the criminal personality; were society to attempt to perfect curricula for the dissemination of anti-social attitudes; were society to attempt to create institutions for the mass production of criminals; then no finer nor no more effective agency for the attainment of these aims could have been evolved than the prison.

This is no attempt to rejuvenate the corny old chestnut about older prisoners teaching the younger ones techniques toward the more effectual penetration of strong-boxes and recipes for outwitting the gendarmerie. Such phenomena serve only for the theses of the more junior penologists and viewers-with-alarm in the ranks of the earnestly public-spirited but sadly misinformed committees for the study and improvement of this and that. . . .

It is not the possibility of a non-legitimate vocational training that makes the prison a man-perverting agency of great power and efficiency. It is the doleful fact that some nebulous something happens to a man between the time that he checks into and checks out of a prison; some inculcation of the essence of bitterness and social antagonism, an inculcation that is not merely a veneering process but a deep inoculation. And this "something" spawns a man who is invariably less desirable as a citizen than he was at the time he stood before the bar of justice.[37]

[37] Richard Jordan, "Traumatic Trivia," *The Atlantian*, 3:26–7 ff., July-August, 1941.

The "nebulous something" that happens to the inmate is participation in a prison group—ethnic or otherwise—that has developed an *esprit de corps*, with crime and violation of official prison rules as the common interest. The net effect of extensive participation in a group with such an *esprit de corps* is likely to be a definition of one's self as an "elite," as one who has few, if any, obligations to "outsiders" who conform to legal norms. This conception of self is both stimulated and reinforced not only by inmates, but also by the attitudes of prison officials. The social distance between inmates as a class and officials as a class lengthens the social distance between inmates and law-abiding persons generally.[38]

We have already noted, however, that there are variations in the extent to which inmates participate in the antireform and essentially procriminal *esprit de corps* of the thief subculture and the convict subculture. Wheeler has shown that inmate attitudes and loyalties most closely resemble those of elite *thieves* and *convicts* when the inmates in question occupy positions that make the elite deviant subcultures most visible to them.[39] Similarly, noting that inmate culture is a balance between the thief subculture, the convict subculture, and the legitimate subculture has implications for predicting the behavior of prisoners when they are released. Most inmates are under the influence of *both* the thief subculture and the convict subculture. Without realizing it, inmates who have served long prison terms are likely to move toward the middle, toward a compromise between the directives coming from the two sources. A member of the convict subculture may come to see that *thieves* are the persons with the prestige; a member of the thief subculture or even a *do-right* may lose the ability to sustain status needs by outside criteria.

Despite these differences, in any prison the inmates oriented to legitimate subcultures should have a low recidivism rate, while the highest recidivism rate should be found among participants in the convict subculture. The hard-core members of this subculture are being trained in manipulation, duplicity, and exploitation; they are not sure they can make it on the outside; and even when they are on the outside, they continue to use *convicts* as a reference group. This sometimes means that there will be a wild spree of crime and dissipation that takes the members of the convict subculture directly back to the prison. Members of the thief subculture, to whom prison life represents a pitfall in outside life, also should have a high recidivism rate. However, the *thief* sometimes "reforms" and tries to succeed in some life within the law. Such behavior, contrary to popular notions, is quite acceptable to other members of the thief subculture, so long as the new job and position are not "anticriminal" and do not involve regular, routine, "slave labor." Suckers work, but a person who, like a *thief*, "skims it off

---

[38]Joseph C. Mouledous, "Organizational Goals and Structural Change: A Study of the Organization of a Prison Social System," *Social Forces*, 41:283–90, 1963; and Mathiesen, *Defences of the Weak*, pp. 11–16.

[39]Wheeler, "Role Conflict in Correctional Communities," pp. 250–6. See also Jon E. Simpson, Thomas G. Eynon, and Walter C. Reckless, "Institutionalization as Perceived by the Juvenile Offender," *Sociology and Social Research*, 48:13–23, 1963.

the top" is not a sucker. At any rate, the fact that *convicts*, to a greater extent than *thieves*, tend to evaluate things from the perspective of the prison and to look upon discharge as a short vacation from prison life suggests that their recidivism rate should be higher than that of *thieves*.

No study of the recidivism rates of *thieves*, *convicts*, and *do-rights* has been made. However, a significant analysis has been made of the recidivism rates, and of the tendencies for these rates to increase or decrease with increasing length of prison terms, for each of four inmate types identified by Schrag.[40] This typology classifies inmates of close-custody prisons as *prosocial*, *antisocial*, *pseudosocial*, and *asocial*.[41] These types correspond closely to the argot labels used for various types of inmates by prisoners themselves. Thus *prosocial* inmates are those who fall within the "square John," "do-right," or "hoosier" configurations; *antisocial* inmates are the "right guys" and "real men"; *pseudosocial* prisoners are the "con politicians," "merchants," and "peddlers"; and *asocial* prisoners are the "outlaws," "hoods," "gorillas," and "ballbusters"; also in the *asocial* category are disturbed inmates, usually called "dings" or "rapos." Unfortunately, this typology does not clearly make the distinction between the thief subculture and the convict subculture. Schrag's "right guys" (*antisocial* offenders) thus might include both men who perceive role requirements in terms of the norms of the convict subculture, and men who perceive those requirements in terms of the norms of the thief subculture. Similarly, neither his "con politician" (*pseudosocial* offender) nor his "outlaw" (*asocial* offender) seem to be ideal-type members of the convict subculture. Schrag's "square Johns" (*prosocial* offenders) closely resemble the "legitimate subcultures" category.

Garrity found that a group of "square Johns" had a low parole-violation rate, and that this rate remained low no matter how much time was served. "Right guys" had a high violation rate that decreased markedly as time in prison increased. In Garrity's words, this was because "continued incarceration [served] to sever his connections with the criminal subculture and thus increase the probability of successful parole."[42] The rates for the "outlaw" were very high and remained high as time in prison increased. The parole-violation rates of the "con politician" were low if the sentences were rather short, but increased systematically with time served. Many studies have shown, more generally, that there is

[40] Donald L. Garrity, "The Effects of Length of Incarceration upon Parole Adjustment and Estimation of Optimum Sentence: Washington State Correctional Institutions" (unpublished Ph.D. dissertation, Department of Sociology, University of Washington, 1956); and idem, "The Prison as a Rehabilitation Agency," chap. 9 in *The Prison*, ed. Cressey, pp. 358–80.

[41] Clarence C. Schrag, "Social Types in a Prison Community" (unpublished M.A. thesis, Department of Sociology, University of Washington, 1944); idem, "Leadership Among Prison Inmates"; idem, "Some Foundations for a Theory of Correction," chap. 8 in *The Prison*, ed. Cressey, pp. 346–56; and idem, "A Preliminary Criminal Typology," *Pacific Sociological Review*, 4:11–16, 1961. See also Glaser, *Effectiveness of a Prison and Parole System*, pp. 575–83.

[42] Garrity, "The Prison as a Rehabilitation Agency," p. 377.

only a slight, if any, relationship between the amount of time served and recidivism when selected background factors are held constant.[43]

Noting that the origins of the thief subculture and the convict subculture are both external to a prison should change expectations regarding the possible reformative effect of that prison. The recidivism rates of neither *thieves, convicts,* nor *straights* are likely to be significantly affected by incarceration in any particular traditional prison. This is not to say, of course, that the *entire system* of imprisonment, in which both the thief subculture and the convict subculture are nurtured, does not contribute significantly to recidivism. In reference to the ordinary custodially oriented prison, the "right guy" says he can do his time "standing on his head," and it appears that he *is* able to do the time "standing on his head"—except for long-termers, imprisonment has little effect on the *thief* one way or the other. Similarly, the routine of any particular prison is not likely to have significant reformative effects on members of the convict subculture; they return to prison because, in effect, they have found a home there. And the individuals oriented to legitimate subcultures maintain low recidivism rates even if they never experience imprisonment.

PRISON RIOTS

Occasionally the relationships between the inmate body, inmate elites, and officials are dramatized in a prison riot. During a riot, the loyalty of inmates to inmates and to criminals, the exploitation of prisoners by their leaders, the antagonistic attitudes of guards and officials toward inmates, and the alliances between elites and officials all become manifest.[44] Thus a prison riot, confrontation, or demonstration is likely to be much more than a mere conflict between the keepers and the kept. For about twenty years it has been an established fact—with reference to mental hospitals as well as to prisons—that disturbances among institutionalized inmates follow disturbances among staff members.[45] Perhaps the greatest significance of prison riots is the awakening of the public to the fact that

[43]See Don M. Gottfredson, M. G. Neithercutt, J. Nuffield, and Vincent O'Leary, *Four Thousand Lifetimes: A Study of Time Served and Parole Outcome* (Davis, Calif.: National Council on Crime and Delinquency, 1973); James L. Beck and Peter B. Hoffman, "Time Served and Release Performance," *Journal of Research in Crime and Delinquency,* 13:127–32, 1976; and Anthony R. Harris, "Imprisonment and the Expected Value of Criminal Choice: A Specification and Test of Aspects of the Labeling Perspective," *American Sociological Review,* 40:71–87, 1975.

[44]See Donald R. Cressey, "A Confrontation of Violent Dynamics," *International Journal of Psychiatry,* 10:109–24, 1972.

[45]Alfred H. Stanton and Morris S. Schwartz, *The Mental Hospital* (New York: Basic Books, 1954), pp. 378–400; Lloyd E. Ohlin, *Sociology and the Field of Corrections* (New York: Russell Sage Foundation, 1956), pp. 22–6; Maurice Floch and Frank E. Hartung, "A Sociological Analysis of Prison Riots: A Hypothesis," *Journal of Criminal Law, Criminology, and Police Science,* 47:51–7, 1956; Richard H. McCleery, *Policy Change in Prison Management* (East Lansing: Michigan State University Governmental Research Bureau, 1957), pp. 28–34; Clarence Schrag, "The Sociology of Prison Riots," *Proceedings of the American Correctional Association, 1960,* pp. 138–45; and Vernon Fox, "Why Prisoners Riot," *Federal Probation,* 35:9–14, 1971.

prison life, for both inmates and officers, is full of more misery than most middle-class citizens can imagine.

The contemporary pattern of riots in American prisons was established about twenty-five years ago. It became common shortly after Chinese prisoners of war held by Americans during the Korean War seized hostages and made demands of their captors. In the spring of 1952, sixty-nine prisoners at the Trenton, New Jersey, State Prison seized four guards as hostages, barricaded themselves in the prison print shop, and stated that they would not surrender until a committee of citizens investigated the conditions of the prison. Within a week, 232 prisoners at the New Jersey Prison Farm in Rahway barricaded themselves in a dormitory with nine hostages and demanded changes in prison conditions; they smashed all the dormitory windows, tore up the plumbing and heating systems, and destroyed their own lockers. A few days later 176 inmates at the Southern Michigan Prison in Jackson seized eleven hostages, barricaded themselves in a cellblock, and wrecked whatever was wreckable; prisoners in other sections of the prison armed themselves with makeshift weapons, wrecked the dining hall, set fire to the laundry, tore up the chapel, library, and gymnasium, and broke thousands of windows. Within a few months similar riots occurred in Idaho, Illinois, Kentucky, Louisiana, Massachusetts, New Mexico, North Carolina, Ohio, and Utah. In addition, potentially serious disturbances were quelled in one prison in California, one in Oregon, and two federal institutions.

The pattern was thus established. None of the riots involved attempts at mass escape. Each seemed to be a semiplanned strike or demonstration designed to call public attention to the conditions of prison life. Hostages were seized; the prisoners barricaded themselves; all destructible property in reach was destroyed; demands were issued, followed by bargaining with prison officials or political officials of the state. The formal demands were for better food, better medical care, better recreational facilities, segregation of sex offenders, less rigid disciplinary practices, and more liberal parole practices. This pattern also characterizes contemporary riots, including the 1971 riot taking place in the prison at Attica, New York, where forty-three citizens died. Thirty-nine of that number were killed by gunfire, eighty others suffered gunshot wounds during an assault on prisoners holding several dozen hostages, and almost half of the participating inmates suffered bruises, lacerations, abrasions, and broken bones.[46] An authority on prison riots has noted that recent riots tend to pattern in five stages:

First, there is a period of undirected violence like the exploding bomb. Secondly, inmate leaders tend to emerge and organize around them a group of ringleaders who determine inmate policy during the riot. Thirdly, a period of interaction with prison authority, whether by negotiation or by force, assists in identifying the alternatives available for the resolution of the riot. Fourthly, the surrender of the inmates, whether by negotiation or by

[46] New York State Special Commission on Attica, *Attica* (New York: Bantam, 1972), pp. 114–206.

force, phases out the violent event. Fifthly, and most important from the political viewpoint, the investigations and administrative changes restore order and confidence in the remaining power structure by making "constructive changes" to regain administrative control and to rectify the undesirable situation that produced the riot.[47]

Riots make visible the contradictory and even conflicting orientations of the three principal prison staff organizations—the one for keeping inmates, the one for using them, and the one for serving them. They also shed light on the orientations of "right guys," "merchants" and "gorillas," and on the exploitative relationship between elite inmate leaders and their followers. And riots most dramatically reveal the principal control measure used to keep the peace during less tumultuous times—witting or unwitting cooperative alliances between staff members and inmates.

The explosion of a prison powder keg into a riot has potential benefits for guards as well as for inmates. Moreover, a riot's possible benefits are greater for the "old guard" among guards than for others. This is true because riots are, among other things, reactions to prison reform movements that would take power away from the staff hierarchy dedicated to keeping inmates and give it to the hierarchy dedicated to serving them. A working-class prison guard who has learned what is "right" and "proper" in the world is likely to implement in his or her work a strong moral code that stresses righteous indignation about crime, hatred of rapists and robbers, intolerance of slovenliness and laziness, disdain for acquisition except by the slow process of honest labor, and "self-discipline" rather than "self-expression."[48] Any prison reformer who tries to implement a program at variance with such attitudes must expect resistance. Should the reformer be a warden, the reform efforts will be resisted by old-guard staff members who know their legal and moral duty is to cage bad men and women. Should the reformer be a director of an entire system of prisons, the wardens themselves might be members of the old guard.

The old guard does not "start" or "stimulate" or "incite" or "instigate" an inmate riot in order to counter the revolution a reformer promotes and leads. There is no doubt, however, that inmate riots help guards stop changes they consider undesirable. Neither is there any doubt that past riots have functioned to produce the demotion or discharge of prison wardens and commissioners who have introduced too many changes too fast. The Massachusetts Commissioner of Corrections, John O. Boone, in 1972 began an eighteen-month term in which he tried to loosen up the rigid rules that had governed life at Walpole prison. During that period there were two major riots, in which inmates took complete control of

---

[47] Fox, "Why Prisoners Riot," p. 10.

[48] See R. Rice, "Intentions and the Structure of Attitudes Among Inmates and Noninmates," *Journal of Research in Crime and Delinquency*, 10:203–7, 1973; and Lonnie H. Athens, "Differences in the Liberal-Conservative Political Attitudes of Prison Guards and Felons: Status versus Race," *International Journal of Group Tensions*, 5:143–55, 1975.

the prison, and a half-dozen lesser disturbances.[49] The commissioner was fired, and the new commissioner appointed a warden who reintroduced rigid controls. Boone contended that the violence was a direct result of sabotage by some guards and elements of the guards' union who, he said, were "willing to go to any lengths to resist his attempts to loosen up the rigid rules that had governed life at Walpole." All of the troubles at Walpole, he added, could be traced to the fact that the "guards stopped guarding." By early 1976, the Walpole prison was more custody-oriented and security-oriented than it had been before Boone became commissioner. The deputy warden said that "morale among the officers is one hundred and fifty percent better," and he credited the new warden with "taking positive action to get things stabilized the way they should be."

The principle behind the firing of Commissioner Boone has for at least twenty years been the one used to fire other prison reformers whose changes were followed by riots. "We didn't have all this trouble when Old Joe was here," riot-investigating committees have in essence concluded. "So let's replace this official with someone who, like Old Joe, knows how to control inmates." Just prior to the Attica riot, the New York Commissioner of Corrections, Russell G. Oswald, tried to institute humanitarian changes designed to make the prison less unpleasant, to start a group-counseling program, and, generally, to stress "rehabilitation" rather than mere custody. He encountered resistance from guards, who stressed the need for custody and security:

What [an ex-convict] admires and what others—including guards and townspeople—deplore have been the attempts made in Mr. Oswald's tenure to use new approaches and recruit new personnel. In conversations around this village, people talk of the toughness that the system had under the former commissioner, Paul D. McGinnis, who, unlike Mr. Oswald, came up through the ranks. They view the new commissioner as too permissive, too lenient. . . . In less troubled times than these, Commissioner Oswald has frequently indicated the need to change the thinking of correctional officers, shifting away from "custodial aspects" to more training and rehabilitation.[50]

Months after the Attica riot, the President of the American Association of Wardens and Superintendents was *still* telling correctional commissioners and guards to leave prison matters in the hands of the wardens "at the helm," implying that resistance by subordinates (either guards or wardens) in the employee hierarchy might have an inmate riot as its consequence:

I am convinced that on the whole most institutions in the United States have shown great improvement in the past 10 years and will continue to show good progress if the people at the helm of the correctional institutions will be given support by their subordinates *as well*

---

[49] See the description of these and other disturbances in Richard Kwartler, ed., *Behind Bars: Prisons in America* (New York: Vintage Books, 1977), pp. 11–21.
[50] Michael Kaufmann, *New York Times*, September 15, 1971.

as by those above them, in attempting to continue on the progressive course which they have started.[51]

Some inmates, like some guards, stand to benefit if a prison reformer can be frustrated in the attempt to change the social structure of a prison. Just after inmates in one prison had seized hostages, barricaded themselves in a cellblock, torn up the plumbing and heating system in their own cells, and wrecked whatever else was wreckable, an experienced warden professed himself baffled by the uprising: "This prison is their home," he said. "I don't know why they want to tear it up." Why, indeed, would inmates destroy their own living quarters and, more generally, shake up the conditions of peaceful coexistence usually prevailing among inmates and guards in prisons? Perhaps because old-guard inmates like old-guard guards unwittingly anticipate that losing a battle might win a war—a war against "oppressive conditions" but also a war against reformers who would more permanently destroy the alliances that serve to maintain the peace and privileges of the old-guard inmates' "home."

In many prisons, "right guys" and "merchants" are allied with guards, as noted earlier. Any prison reformer whose program would break up these alliances—which give inmate leaders an undue share of a prison's scarce goods—must promise the involved inmates a substitute for their special privileges. Usually what is explicitly or implicitly promised in exchange for the good life "right guys" and "convicts" are living is a program of "rehabilitation" or, generally, "better living conditions." If the reformer cannot produce the promised change, "right guys" and "convicts" alike are in a position to withdraw their stabilizing influence and to flit around the edges of the kind of violent demonstration commonly called a "spontaneous riot."[52]

Recall the prison "gorilla" who quite regularly violates both prison rules and the inmate code. An inmate of this type is even likely to hit a guard over the head with a club, knowing full well (if rationality is assumed) that the guard and the prison system the guard represents have more than enough power to crush the attacker. Because "gorillas" bring heat (close surveillance) rather than playing it cool, *thieves*, "right guys," and other inmates see them as losers. They know that one belief enforced by prison staff members and endorsed by the general public always has been that the prisoner who aggresses against the prison ought to remain in prison. "Gorilla" behavior and staff reaction to it, then, is viewed as undesirable because it makes prison life uncomfortable and also because it is likely to keep a criminal off the streets, where one can acquire a bit of money through criminal means. But at riot time "gorillas" and their tactics can be useful.

Although a reformer's proposed changes are not very threatening to "gorillas," they do, as indicated, threaten the peace and the status of *thieves*. They also

---

[51] Don R. Erickson, "Don't Run Scared or Sell Corrections Short," *American Journal of Correction*, 33:11, 1971 (italics added).

[52] Sykes, *The Society of Captives*, pp. 109–29.

threaten "merchants" and *convicts* generally, inmates who have learned to adjust to prison life and enjoy it, such as it is. Prison reform might break up their homosexual partnerships, deprive them of the starched and well-pressed uniforms they consider symbols of status, decrease their profits from gambling, cut off their sources of illegal alcohol and drugs, and so on. Thus, like the old guard among staff members, the inmate old guard—"right guys" and "merchants"—stand to reap certain benefits if "gorillas" initiate a riot that will stop or slow down a reformer's program. If reform has been progressing for some time, a riot might even restore the conditions of the good old days. For this reason, riots are—to some inmates as well as to some staff members—more like antirevisionist confrontations or even counterrevolutions than they are like revolutions.

The pattern of inmate conduct during riots has been uncannily uniform for about two decades. Three rather distinct stages have been noted.[53] First, during the initial stage, "gorillas" are in charge. It is during these days that sex, alcohol, and drug orgies occur, cells are wrecked and buildings burned, hostages are threatened and (on rare occasions) murdered, and inmates armed with knives and clubs settle old grudges among themselves. In days of calm, guards spend some of their time trying, with various degrees of efficiency and enthusiasm, to function as police officers who protect inmates from each other.[54] But when, during a riot, this police force withdraws to the walls, the crime rate goes up.

Second, *thieves* then seize the leadership from "gorillas." They are assisted by "merchants" and "politicians," many of whom aspire to "right guy" status. At this juncture there is likely to be additional maiming and even an inmate murder or two—by-products of the fight for leadership—and the persons maimed or murdered are likely to be either "merchants" or "gorillas." At this juncture, also, *thieves* note for the ears of one and all that any half-baked revolutionary scheme or escape plot that might have existed early in the riot has been thoroughly squashed. No violent confrontation will succeed when *we* are sitting here as open targets in a burning prison and *they* have speckled the wall with machine gunners and flecked the sky with armed helicopters. But peaceful negotiations over inmate "demands" might now direct attention to needed prison programs.

Third, the "right guy" leaders draw up lists of demands and negotiate with public officials. The negotiations with prison administrators, politicians, and news personnel are not concerned with changes that would shake up the inmate social structure or the alliances between staff and inmate elites. Instead, the elites demand better food, better parole practices, better law libraries, better trade training, and so forth, all of which amount to requests that liberal prison administrators be given the enlarged budgets they have been seeking for years. Official responses to these demands have, as indicated earlier, helped old-guard

---

[53] Cressey, "A Confrontation of Violent Dynamics."

[54] Donald R. Cressey, "Achievement of an Unstated Organizational Goal: An Observation on Prisons," *Pacific Sociological Review*, 1:43–9, 1958.

employees and old-guard inmates resist more significant structural changes. Rarely, if ever, do riot-investigation committees seeking the causes of riots look back to complex staff organization, complex inmate organization, and complex bonds between staff and inmates. Instead, they look for ways of restoring peace, and these range from firing the reformer who caused all the trouble to trying to buy inmates off with superficial improvements.

But this three-stage pattern is of less relevance today than formerly. In the Attica riot, for example, it appears that *thieves* and "merchants" never did seize control from the "gorillas," and that the slaughter of inmates was a result. Owing to what is commonly called "politicalization" of prisoners, especially blacks, the proportion of "gorillas" in most prisons has increased in recent years, while the proportion of "right guys" has decreased, as we noted earlier. Thus, because the prison now, as always, is a microcosm of the society in which it sits, militancy on the outside is inevitably reflected on the inside. Numerous observers of recent change in prisons have considered the new militancy a sign of new prisoner power. But prisoner power is nothing new. Inmates have dominated the internal affairs, and have had a strong voice in the external affairs, of prisons during most of their two-hundred-year history. What is new is the shift of inmate power from "right guys" to "gorillas," and this shift has done what prison reformers have rarely done—disrupted the privileged prison lives of *thieves* and their allies A black man who is convinced that he has been victimized by white society and then imprisoned only because he tried to undo some of the effects of that victimization is not likely to play it cool in prison, as *thieves* and old-guard staff members would have him do. In short, more prisoners are now opposed to imprisonment as a general principle, not just because proposed programs of rehabilitation and better living conditions threaten to break up old coalitions of power.[55]

"No longer do black prisoners play the sycophant's game of 'pleasing the powers,'" said a former prisoner who served ten years in a California prison for armed robbery and murder.[56] In an interview with a *New York Times* reporter, the warden of a California prison put the matter in a different way: "Our prisoners are consumed with bitterness and resentment and are ideal recruits for the more sophisticated radicals on the outside who cloak their real intentions with talk of humanitarian reform."[57] The former inmate seemed to be saying that black prisoners are no longer going to be Uncle Toms, and the warden seemed to be saying that this admirable resolution is somehow nefarious.

But, in prison or elsewhere, one need not be a "gorilla," a "hero," or a loser in order to avoid being a sycophant or an Uncle Tom. Inmates of Swedish prisons are by no means happy prisoners, but at least a decade ago they won humane

[55] John P. Spiegel, "The Dynamics of Violent Confrontation," *International Journal of Psychiatry*, 10:93–108, 125–128, 1972.
[56] *New York Times*, September 16, 1971.
[57] *New York Times*, December 19, 1971.

conditions and many rights denied to almost all American prisoners, and they did so by means of peaceful confrontations of a kind that is characteristic of the recent "prisoner union" movement in the United States.[58] Perhaps prisoner unions are merely the most recent manifestation of the *thieves'* desire to maintain conditions of peaceful coexistence between inmates and staff, with obvious benefits to the old guard of both camps.

ATTEMPTS TO MODIFY THE PRISON CULTURE

If the prison is to be efficient as an institution for changing criminals, the *esprit de corps* or public opinion among prisoners must be changed. No amount of individual therapy, vocational education, or coercion will do this. In addition, there is little reason to think that the prisoners themselves will develop self-government or other community organization favorable to changing the prison subcultures. The leaders of the prison population look upon themselves as enemies of society, and on society as an enemy of prisoners. They are not to be induced in ordinary prison circumstances to shift their attitudes. Similarly, so long as the prison is expected to perform its retribution and deterrence functions, it is doubtful that the prison community can be greatly modified to bridge the chasm separating the social worlds of the insiders and the outsiders. The organization of prisoners is in part a reaction to the repressive aspects of the prison's administrative organization, and it therefore seems to be modifiable only slightly or not at all as long as the administrative organization efficiently performs the duties society assigns to it.[59]

In the United States, the most impressive attempts to change prisoner organization by modifying the administrative organization have been made in minimum-security institutions. One of the earliest attempts was made by Howard B. Gill, some years before study of the prison community became popular, at the Norfolk Prison Colony in Massachusetts.[60] The Norfolk program differed from honor systems and self-government systems in that the staff was made a part of the community. Twenty-five inmates were assigned to each "house officer" or caseworker. These officers did not wear uniforms, and their primary duty was to

[58] David A. Ward, "Inmate Rights and Prison Reform in Sweden and Denmark," *Journal of Criminal Law, Criminology, and Police Science,* 63:240–55, 1972. See also Thomas Mathiesen, *The Politics of Abolition* (New York: Wiley, 1974); Robert Minton and Stephen Rice, "Using Racism at San Quentin," chap. 7 in *Prison Life: A Study of Explosive Conditions in America's Prisons,* ed. Frank Browning (New York: Harper and Row, 1972), pp. 104–14; and Erik Olin Wright, *The Politics of Punishment: Prisons in America* (New York: Harper and Row, 1973), pp. 100–24.

[59] See Eliot Studt, Sheldon L. Messinger, and Thomas P. Wilson, *C-Unit: Search for Community in Prison* (New York: Russell Sage Foundation, 1968).

[60] See Howard B. Gill, "The Norfolk State Prison Colony at Massachusetts," *Journal of Criminal Law and Criminology,* 22:107–12, 1931; and W. H. Commons, T. Yahkub, E. Powers, and C. R. Doering, *A Report on the Development of Penological Treatment at Norfolk Prison Colony in Massachusetts* (New York: Bureau of Social Hygiene, 1940).

maintain a friendly, cooperative, and sympathetic relationship with the inmates. "Watch officers," whose duties were custodial, were used, but almost all of them remained on, or outside, the wall. They were not considered part of the community. From the standpoint of conventional prison organization, the caseworkers became a part of the informal prison social life, while the watch officers represented a modified type of repressive formal organization. The overall plan thus was to give inmates experience in noncriminal social activities and especially to modify inmates' attitudes in the direction of noncriminality by placing them in intimate, informal contact with sympathetic persons possessing a strong bias against criminality. Today it would be considered a large-scale group-therapy program that handled "natural groups," included all inmates, and operated on principles similar to those used by Alcoholics Anonymous. The Norfolk program was subjected to severe and caustic criticism almost from its beginning, largely because it did not perform the retributive and deterrent functions that the taxpayers demanded. Superintendent Gill was discharged, and a more conventional type of prison organization was established.

Sykes and Messinger, among others, have suggested that the inmate code and status system arise as responses to the deprivations imposed on prisoners.[61] The implication is that the inmate system of organization would decline in importance if the pains of imprisonment were reduced, and that, therefore, the degree of deprivation ought to be reduced if reformation is a goal. Currently, this system for attempting to modify the traditional inmate structure is one of the principal features of prison camps, prison honor farms, institutions for juveniles, and so-called "therapeutic communities" in prison.[62]

The relatively relaxed discipline of such institutions, as well as the effort to understand rather than blame the inmates, weakens the "antireform" organization among the inmates.[63] However, it is possible that such institutions merely select a disproportionate number of inmates oriented to legitimate values and do not select many prisoners who bring with them to the prison an orientation either to the thief subculture or to the convict subculture. Because many of the attitudes, values, and other behavior patterns of inmates are carried into the prison from the outside, reducing the pains of imprisonment will not by itself result in modification of these behavior patterns. As Wheeler has noted:

[61] Sykes and Messinger, "The Inmate Social System."

[62] See Oscar Grusky, "Some Factors Promoting Cooperative Behavior Among Inmate Leaders," *American Journal of Correction,* 21:8–9 ff., 1959; idem, "Organizational Goals and the Behavior of Informal Leaders," *American Journal of Sociology,* 65:59–67, 1959; Howard W. Polsky, *Cottage Six* (New York: Russell Sage Foundation, 1962); Mayer N. Zald, "The Correctional Institution for Juvenile Offenders: An Analysis of Organizational 'Character,' " *Social Problems,* 8:57–67, 1960; and John M. Wilson and Jon D. Snodgrass, "The Prison Code in a Therapeutic Community," *Journal of Criminal Law, Criminology, and Police Science,* 60:532–42, 1971.

[63] David Street, Robert D. Vinter, and Charles Perrow, *Organization for Treatment* (New York: Free Press, 1966), pp. 225–7; Thomas P. Wilson, "Patterns of Management and Adaptations to Organizational Roles," *American Journal of Sociology,* 74:146–57, 1968; and Studt, Messinger, and Wilson, *C-Unit,* pp. 192–228.

While little is known about the relationship between roles played inside and outside the prison, there is a strong suggestion that the visible inmates are those who have had most experience in exploitative and manipulative roles prior to imprisonment—those most schooled in techniques of aggression and deceit. The combination of greater motivation and more well-developed skills among the more criminalistic inmates suggests the difficulties facing administrative attempts to decrease their visibility and power.[64]

McCleery's reports on changes in Oahu prison indicated that the orientation of inmates can to some degree be shifted by opening new channels of communication between staff and inmates.[65] By means of these channels, Oahu staff members presented their behavior patterns to inmates, and at the same time the "anti-reform" and "antiadministration" behavior patterns ordinarily circulating among prisoners were choked off. Because in any prison it is almost literally true among inmates that "knowledge is power," a shift in the distribution of knowledge about appropriate ways of behaving in the prison changed the distribution of power. Although merely reducing the pains of imprisonment does not change the patterns of behavior brought in from the outside, changing the system of communication produces some of the desired effects. This kind of program was pioneered at Highfields, a New Jersey institution housing twenty boys, where the entire program was oriented toward piercing the boys' strong defenses against rehabilitation.[66] It has been used, with varying degrees of specificity and success, in many institutions. However, most such attempts to change inmate cultures by fostering participatory democracy have been handicapped by the notion that such changes in communication are somehow "therapeutic," as noted earlier in our discussion of group programs in prisons.[67]

Such programs also have been handicapped by the fact that prisons are fundamentally and basically institutions for implementing the doubtful assumption that mere negative, punitive action is all that is needed to change criminals.[68] For centuries the whole system of imprisonment has been based on this assumption that criminals will stop committing crimes if they are presented with painful evidence that criminal behavior is undesirable. Accordingly, almost all prisons have permitted and even encouraged inmates to maintain the same deviant attitudes and other behavior patterns they possessed when they arrived. The antireform emphasis in inmate cultures—much of it brought in from the outside—has persisted, and attempts to change it have been sabotaged, whether

[64] Wheeler, "Role Conflict in Correctional Communities," p. 257.

[65] McCleery, "The Governmental Process and Informal Social Control"; idem, "Communication Patterns as Bases of Systems of Authority and Power"; and idem, *Policy Change in Prison Management*.

[66] Lloyd W. McCorkle, Albert Elias, and F. Lovell Bixby, *The Highfields Story* (New York: Holt, 1958). See also H. Ashley Weeks, *Youthful Offenders at Highfields* (Ann Arbor: University of Michigan Press, 1958).

[67] See Chapter 23, above.

[68] See Thomas and Poole, "The Consequences of Incompatible Goal Structures in Correctional Settings"; and Ronald Akers, Norman Hayner, and Werner Gruninger, "Prisonization in Five Countries," *Criminology*, 14:527–54, 1977. See also Thomas Mathiesen, *The Politics of Abolition* (New York: Wiley, 1974).

the attempts were based on a medical model, a political model, a humanitarian model, or a sociological model. The prison thus has remained irrelevant to the reformation of criminals. "In a less than perfect society where confinement is used as a means of deterrence and reform, it is possible that the prison is a 'success' if only it does not make the offender worse. However, it does not seem overly optimistic to suppose that the prison can do more than simply stand still."[69]

SUGGESTED READINGS

Akers, Ronald L., Norman S. Hayner, & Werner Gruninger. "Prisonization in Five Countries: Type of Prison and Inmate Characteristics." *Criminology*, 44:527–54, 1977.

Bondeson, Ulla. "Argot Knowledge as an Indicator of Criminal Socialization." *Scandinavian Studies in Criminology*, 2:73–107, 1968.

Bowker, Lee H. *Prison Subcultures*. Lexington, Mass.: Lexington Books, 1977.

Brodsky, Stanley L. *Families and Friends of Men in Prison: The Uncertain Relationship*. Lexington, Mass.: Lexington Books, 1975.

Carroll, Leo. *Hacks, Blacks and Cons: Race Relations in a Maximum Security Prison*. Lexington, Mass.: Lexington Books, 1974.

Chang, Dae H., & Warren B. Armstrong, eds. *The Prison: Voices from the Inside*. Cambridge, Mass.: Schenkman, 1972.

Clemmer, Donald. *The Prison Community*. Boston: Christopher, 1940. Reissued by Rinehart, 1958.

Cohen, Albert K., George F. Cole, & Robert G. Bailey, eds. *Prison Violence*. Lexington, Mass.: Lexington Books, 1976.

Cohen, Stanley, & Laurie Taylor. *Psychological Survival: The Experience of Long-Term Imprisonment*. New York: Pantheon, 1972.

Cressey, Donald R. "Prison Organizations." Chap. 24 in *Handbook of Organizations*, ed. James G. March, pp. 1023–70. New York: Rand McNally, 1965.

Davidson, R. Theodore. *Chicano Prisoners: The Key to San Quentin*. New York: Holt, Rinehart and Winston, 1974.

Elli, Frank. *The Riot*. New York: Coward-McCann, 1966.

Fox, Vernon. "Why Prisoners Riot." *Federal Probation*, 35:9–14, 1971.

Garabedian, Peter G. "Social Roles and Processes of Socialization in the Prison Community." *Social Problems*, 11:139–52, 1963.

Gibbons, Don C. *Changing the Lawbreaker: The Treatment of Delinquents and Criminals*. Englewood Cliffs, N.J.: Prentice-Hall, 1965.

Glaser, Daniel. *The Effectiveness of a Prison and Parole System*. Indianapolis: Bobbs-Merrill, 1964.

Hall, Jay, Martha Williams, & Louis Tomaino. "The Challenge of Correctional Change: The Interface of Conformity and Commitment," *Journal of Criminal Law, Criminology, and Police Science*, 57:493–503, 1966.

Hazelrigg, Lawrence, ed. *Prison Within Society: A Reader in Penology*. New York: Doubleday, 1968.

Heffernan, Esther. *Making It in Prison: The Square, the Cool, and the Life*. New York: John Wiley, 1972.

Irwin, John. *The Felon*. Englewood Cliffs, N.J.: Prentice-Hall, 1970.

---

[69] Sykes, "Men, Merchants, and Toughs."

Jacobs, James B. *Stateville: The Penitentiary in Mass Society.* Chicago: University of Chicago Press, 1977.

Kassebaum, Gene G., David A. Ward, & Daniel M. Wilner. *Prison Treatment and Parole Survival: An Empirical Assessment.* New York: John Wiley, 1971.

Kwartler, Richard, ed. *Behind Bars: Prisons in America.* New York: Vantage Books, 1977.

Manacchio, Anthony J., & Jimmy Dunn. *The Time Game: Two Views of a Prison.* Beverly Hills, Calif.: Sage Publications, 1970.

Mathiesen, Thomas. *The Defences of the Weak: A Sociological Study of a Norwegian Correctional Institution.* London: Tavistock, 1965.

Minton, Robert J., ed. *Inside: Prison American Style.* New York: Random House, 1971.

Moos, Rudolf H. *Evaluating Correctional and Community Settings.* New York: John Wiley, 1975.

Peretti, Peter O. "A Critique of the Prison and Prisoner Communities as Generating Milieu of Anti-Social and Anti-Legal Attitudes Among Inmates." *Acta Criminologiae et Medicinae Legalis Japonica,* 37:1–14, February, 1971.

Petersen, David M., & Marcello Truzzi, eds. *Criminal Life: Views from the Inside.* Englewood Cliffs, N.J.: Prentice-Hall, 1972.

Polsky, Howard W., Daniel S. Claster, & Carl Goldberg, eds. *Social System Perspectives in Residential Institutions.* East Lansing: Michigan State University Press, 1970.

Scacco, Anthony M. *Rape in Prison.* Springfield, Ill.: Charles C. Thomas, 1975.

Street, David, Robert D. Vinter, & Charles Perrow. *Organization for Treatment.* New York: Free Press, 1966.

Thomas, Charles W., & David M. Petersen. *Prison Organization and Inmate Subcultures.* Indianapolis: Bobbs-Merrill, 1977.

Ward, David A., & Gene G. Kassebaum. *Women's Prison: Sex and Social Structure.* Chicago: Aldine, 1965.

Wilkins, Leslie T. *Evaluation of Penal Measures.* New York: Random House, 1969.

Williams, Vergil L., & Mary Fish. *Convicts, Codes and Contraband: The Prison Life of Men and Women.* Cambridge, Mass.: Ballinger, 1974.

Wright, Erik Olin. *The Politics of Punishment: A Critical Analysis of Prison in America.* New York: Harper and Row, 1973.

25

Release from Prison

The exits from prison are more numerous than the entrances. Inmates always enter prisons by way of the courts, in accordance with conditions fixed by a legislature. But an inmate may be released from prison by completion of the full term imposed by the court, or before the end of the full term by an executive who grants a pardon or commutation or by an administrative board that grants a parole or a release on good time. That is, acting by authority of a constitution or statutes, the legislature, the court, an executive, or an administrative board may determine the time of release of a prisoner. Table 24 shows the methods of release for felons in 1970, as reported by the Federal Bureau of Prisons.[1]

PARDON AND RELATED CONCEPTS

Modification of penalties by an executive official may take the form of pardon, commutation, or amnesty. A pardon is an act of mercy or clemency, ordinarily by an executive, by which a criminal is excused from a penalty that has been imposed by a court. It has been held in court decisions that the pardon wipes away guilt and makes the person who committed the crime as innocent as though a crime had not been committed. Pardons may be either conditional or absolute. The conditional pardon is one in which the guilt is wiped away on condition that the offender perform certain acts or refrain from certain acts specified by the pardoning power, such as leaving the country or abstaining from intoxicating liquors. For example, in 1974 President Ford pardoned certain draft evaders on the condition that they return to the United States and perform some service for the country. If a man who has received a conditional pardon fails to perform the

[1] Federal Bureau of Prisons, "Prisoners in State and Federal Institutions, 1968–1970," *National Prisoner Statistics*, No. 47, April, 1972, p. 6.

Table 24 **Types of Departures from State and Federal Institutions, 1970**

Type of Departure	All Institutions		Federal Institutions		State Institutions	
	Number	Per-cent	Number	Per-cent	Number	Per-cent
Conditional releases (includes parole)[a]	61,877	24.4	5,696	21.0	56,181	24.8
Unconditional releases[b]	29,855	11.7	5,993	22.1	23,862	10.5
Deaths, except executions	663	.3	36	.1	627	.3
Executions	—	—	—	—	—	—
Other departures[c]	61,530	24.2	4,988	18.4	56,542	24.9
Transferred	99,912	39.4	10,414	38.4	89,498	39.5
Total departures	**253,837**	**100.0**	**27,127**	**100.0**	**226,710**	**100.0**

[a]Also includes 49 conditional pardons.
[b]Includes 16 full pardons.
[c]Includes escapes, court orders, and authorized temporary absences.

required acts, the pardon becomes void, and he may be returned to prison for the remainder of his original term.

Commutation of sentence is a reduction of the penalty by executive order. A sentence is frequently commuted so that it expires at once. Commutation differs from conditional pardon in that it does not wipe away guilt in the eyes of the law, and consequently does not restore civil rights as does a pardon. Massachusetts governors commuted to life imprisonment 50 percent of the death sentences imposed by juries and courts from 1947 to 1971.[2]

Amnesty is a pardon applied to a group of criminals. After World War II, the president of the United States restored civil rights to all federal ex-prisoners who had served honorably in the armed forces for one year or more, and Britain granted amnesty to 14,260 wartime deserters from the armed forces. Israel declared a general amnesty in July, 1967, to celebrate its victory in a six-day war. More than five hundred prisoners were released, and the police closed their files on about seventy thousand cases, of which about fifteen thousand were cases of felonies and misdemeanors. Suspended sentences were annulled, fines forgiven, and jail sentences reduced by 25 percent.[3]

In twenty-one states, the governor shares the power to pardon with a board or

[2]Massachusetts Department of Correction, "Some Notes on Death Row and the Death Penalty in Massachusetts," Document No. 5678, 1971, p. 1.
[3]*Amnesty in Israel* (Jerusalem: Institute of Criminology, The Hebrew University, 1968).

council, and has no more power than any other member of the board in eight of these states. In twenty-seven states, the governor has the sole and complete power to pardon except in impeachment cases. In seventeen of these states in which the governor has final authority, a pardon board or other assistants are appointed for advisory purposes. Some advisory pardon boards, in practice, have complete control of pardons because the governor always adopts the recommendations of the board. On the other hand, some governors rarely accept the recommendations of their advisory boards.

The use of pardons began to decrease steadily about a century ago, and currently pardons are seldom used. In the years 1905–1909, 3 percent of those released from federal prisons were released through pardon by the president of the United States. This percentage decreased to 0.009 percent by 1940, when 313 pardons (including 235 restorations of civil rights) were granted, and since then the number of releases by pardon has been insignificant. The same decrease is found in many states. In 1970, only forty-nine conditional pardons and sixteen full pardons were granted to all the adult felons in the United States.

Blacks are pardoned less frequently than whites, especially in southern states, and gentlemen criminals more frequently than criminals of the lower socio-economic class. Also, in areas where parole is used frequently, pardons are used infrequently. Wolfgang examined recommendations for commutation of sentence, by judges and district attorneys, in the cases of 368 prisoners who had been convicted of murder. The opinion of the judge differed significantly from that of the district attorney in two-thirds of the cases, a situation arising principally because the attorneys supported the pardon board's decision in significantly more cases than did the judges. In only 7 percent of the cases did the board grant commutation when the judge and the attorney both recommended that it not be granted.[4]

GOOD-TIME LAWS

Under good-time laws a prison board may release prisoners before they have served their full sentences if they have maintained good conduct in prison. Generally, for every month of satisfactory conduct, a certain number of days is deducted from the inmate's sentence. A usual procedure is to deduct one month from the first year of satisfactory conduct, two months for the second year, and so on, up to six months for the sixth and each succeeding year. A three-year sentence can thus be reduced to two years and six months by good behavior; a ten-year sentence can be reduced to six years and three months. A prison board determines whether or not the prisoner has earned the reduction in time, but the legislature makes the schedule of reductions in time. Granting "time off for good behavior" differs, in this respect, from commutation of sentence by executive order, in which the

---

[4] Marvin E. Wolfgang, "Murder, the Pardon Board, and Recommendations by Judges and District Attorneys," *Journal of Criminal Law, Criminology, and Police Science,* 50:338–46, 1959.

sentence is shortened because the inmate's behavior has been good, or for other reasons.

As early as 1817, a good-time law was passed in New York State, which provided that first-term prisoners on sentences of five years or less could abridge their sentences by one-fourth for good behavior. Apparently the law was not used. The good-time principle was soon adopted in several other places. In 1821 Connecticut passed a good-time law pertaining to inmates of workhouses. Tennessee passed its good-time law in 1833, Ohio in 1856. The good-time system was used in 1842 in the convict colonies in Australia, and Marsangy advocated this method in France in 1846. Despite the earlier precedents in the United States, "time off for good behavior" did not become generally known in American prisons until just after the Civil War, when the news regarding the famous Irish system spread. By 1868, twenty-four states had made provision for reduction of prison terms by good behavior, and at present all states except California have good-time laws.

In addition to "statutory good time," as the general system is called by inmates, prisoners in some states may earn "merit good time" for extraordinary behavior and "industrial good time" for participation in the prison industries. Merit good-time and industrial good-time laws usually operate to reduce the period of time to be served before inmates are entitled to have their cases reviewed by the parole board, rather than to reduce the actual sentence. Inmates are eager to work at jobs carrying this special good-time allowance, thus forgoing training programs designed to provide them with trades, skills, and attitudes that will be valuable upon release.[5]

Good-time laws represent an attempt to mitigate the severity of sentences, to get good work from the prisoners, to assist in reformation, and, above all, to solve the problem of prison discipline. The two principal objections to good-time laws are that they tend to become mechanical and that they place emphasis on routine conformity to prison rules, rather than on reformation. Prisoners then come to view good time as a right. The usual practice is to credit the new inmate with the maximum amount of good time permitted by law and then to deduct a certain number of days from that time whenever the disciplinary court finds the inmate guilty of serious infraction of the prison rules. Good time may be deducted from the amount of time imposed in a definite sentence, or it may be applied to either the minimum or the maximum period of an indefinite sentence, according to the laws of the state.

THE INDETERMINATE SENTENCE

The release time of a prisoner may be determined by the legislature, which fixes a definite sentence for the offense, by the court, which receives authority from the legislature to fix definite penalties within the limits set by the legislature, or by an administrative board, which receives from the legislature authority to fix definite

[5]Daniel Glaser, *The Effectiveness of a Prison and Parole System* (Indianapolis: Bobbs-Merrill, 1964), pp. 234–6.

penalties within the limits set by the legislature or by the court. When the time of release is determined by an administrative board, and the court merely imposes minimum and maximum limits of the penalty, the sentence is known as an indeterminate sentence. Strictly speaking, the sentence is not indeterminate if the limits are fixed by the court or by the legislature, and it should be called indefinite rather than indeterminate. With the exception of Maryland, which sets neither a minimum nor maximum in sentencing "psychopaths," no state has sentences that are completely indeterminate, and the general practice is to call indefinite sentences indeterminate.

The administrative board that fixes the penalties is called a parole board, but there is no necessary connection between parole and the indeterminate sentence. *Indeterminate sentence* refers to the fact that the exact period of custody is not fixed before the custody begins, while the term *parole* refers to the fact that a portion of the period of custody may be spent outside the institution. Either may be used independently of the other.

The federal government and some states have parole systems but no indeterminate sentences; it would be possible to have indeterminate sentences with complete and final release without supervision. Parole is the status of the prisoner after release from the walls of the institution, while still under the special guardianship of the state. It may be granted either to the prisoner on a definite sentence, though this is usually restricted to the period of freedom granted by the good-time allowance,[6] or to the prisoner on an indeterminate sentence. A person on an indeterminate sentence may be released either conditionally on parole or unconditionally and completely without parole. The two methods, though distinct in principle, are generally combined in practice

Originally, legislators fixed a definite penalty for each offense. In this system all armed robbers, for example, received the same sentence no matter what the circumstances of the crime or the background of the individual offender. In attempts to reduce the injustices accompanying such procedures, legislatures transferred first to the court and then to the parole board the authority to impose sentences within limits set by the legislature for each offense or class of offenses. Currently, there are six major variations in the combinations of the authority of the legislative, judicial, and executive branches of governments to fix sentences.

First, for some crimes, legislatures have set mandatory and flat sentences, with no judicial or executive discretion permitted except reduction of sentence on the basis of "good time." In a second system, judges are authorized to fix flat sentences, with no possibility of early release, within the minimum and maximum limits set by the legislature. Third, in other states, or for other crimes, judges set maxima and minima within limits set by the legislature, and an administrative board has discretion to release within the range set by the judge.

---

[6]In the federal system and in Wisconsin, an inmate who has served one-third of a sentence is eligible for release on parole, but if parole is denied or if the inmate waives parole, he or she may be "conditionally released" for a period of time equal to the good-time allowance.

When this form was introduced, some judges who viewed it as an intrusion into their rights and responsibilities made the minimum almost identical with the maximum, giving such sentences as two years and nine months to two years and ten months, thirty to thirty-one years, 150 to 160 years. To correct these abuses, some legislatures at first provided that the minimum set by the court may not be more than one-half, or some other fraction, of the maximum. Then they introduced the fourth system, in which the legislature sets the maxima and minima, the court sentences to the "term prescribed by law," and the board determines the time of release. In a fifth variation, recommended in the Model Penal Code, the legislature sets the maximum, the court sets the minimum, and the board sets the date of release. The sixth system, tried in a few states for a few crimes and then generally abandoned, is the truly indeterminate-sentence system, whereby neither legislature nor court sets maxima or minima, in effect authorizing the executive branch to release a convicted criminal with no punishment at all or to hold the prisoner for life.[7]

For about fifty years, the important policy issue regarding such variations has been: Why should either the legislature or the court fix the limits? Until recently, this issue was addressed principally by asking the question: Why should not the sentences be completely indeterminate and the parole board given complete and unlimited authority to determine the time of release? Now, the issue of indeterminacy is being addressed by asking the same question in reverse order: Why should not the sentences be made absolutely determinate, so that neither courts nor administrative board have authority to determine the time of release?[8] The problem of the minimum limit is somewhat different from the problem of the maximum limit.

The principal argument for the minimum limit is that it is needed as a check in case a court or parole board should become sentimental, inefficient, or corrupt. Generally, this argument is part of the punitive reaction to crime. The assumption is that all criminals should be punished and, further, that they will not be punished severely enough if no minimum is set. There is no evidence, however, that legislators—who tend to set more severe penalties than do judges or parole boards—are more effective at making the punishment fit the crime and criminal than are members of the judicial and executive branches. Moreover, the few states in which the minimum limit has been removed have witnessed no wholesale release of criminals.[9] It is probable that, bureaucratically speaking, the very existence of the minimum sentence serves as a convenient time of release of all offenders against whom no bad behavior in prison has been recorded. On the

[7] Other permutations are noted by Daniel Glaser, Fred Cohen, and Vincent O'Leary, *The Sentencing and Parole Process* (Washington: Government Printing Office, 1966), pp. 10–15.

[8] See David Fogel, "The Case for Determinacy in Sentencing and the Justice Model in Corrections," *American Journal of Correction*, 38:25–8, 1976.

[9] See Norman S. Hayner, "Sentencing by an Administrative Board," *Law and Contemporary Problems*, 23:477–94, 1958.

other hand, when no minimum is provided, then courts and boards are free to discriminate against poor and black criminals by releasing affluent and white criminals after short prison terms.[10]

The absolute maximum limit probably results in more unnecessary pain and suffering than does the minimum. On the one hand, it often seems clear to prison and parole authorities that certain offenders will repeat their offenses as soon as they are released. Nevertheless, the existence of a maximum limit requires that state officials release these criminals when a certain period of imprisonment has been served. In this respect, the fixed-maximum sentence is identical to the flat sentence, and it is said to interfere with long-range treatment practices.[11] The indefinite-sentence system was introduced in response to arguments to the effect that, among other things, it can in individual cases be more severe than the flat-sentence system, enabling the state to keep in prison for life those dangerous criminals who will commit new crimes, especially violent ones, upon release. Gradually it came to be held that the function of the indeterminate sentence is to hold inmates in prison until the programs there have rehabilitated them; now that it is acknowledged that these programs have not been effective, there is a cry for return to the system of flat sentences.[12]

On the other hand, the legal maximum was expected to reduce pain and suffering by guaranteeing that the administrative board will not keep confined for life some prisoners who would not commit new crimes if released. Thus the maximum limit—given the existence of a system of indefinite sentences—prohibits state agents from keeping specific inmates in prison because they do not like the inmates' politics, religion, skin color, ethnic status, life style, or other nonlegal characteristics. Further, when the legislature does not by law specify that no prisoners shall be released before a flat term or a maximum term has been served, the board can use the indeterminate-sentence system as a means of maintaining prison discipline, threatening to hold in prison for life those inmates

[10]Good summaries of the issues in the determinate versus the indeterminate sentence controversy are I. J. "Cy" Shain, "The Indeterminate Sentence Concept: A Reexamination of the Theory and Practice," *United Nations Asia and Far East Institute for the Prevention of Crime and the Treatment of Offenders Resource Material Series*, No. 12, 1976, pp. 77–91; David B. Wexler, *Criminal Commitments and Dangerous Mental Patients: Legal Issues of Confinement, Treatment and Release* (Washington: Government Printing Office, 1976); and Alan M. Dershowitz, "Background Paper," in *Fair and Certain Punishment*, The Twentieth Century Fund Task Force on Criminal Sentencing (New York: McGraw-Hill, 1976), pp. 68–142.

[11]See F. L. Carney, "The Indeterminate Sentence at Patuxent," *Crime and Delinquency*, 20:135–43, 1974; and E. F. Hodges, "Crime Prevention by the Indeterminate Sentence Law," *American Journal of Psychiatry*, 128:291–5, 1971.

[12]See Richard A. McGee, "A New Look at Sentencing, Part I and Part II," *Federal Probation*, 38:3–8, 1974; Anne M. Heinz, John P. Heinz, Stephen J. Senderowitz, and Mary Anne Vance, "Sentencing by Parole Board: An Evaluation," *Journal of Criminal Law and Criminology*, 67:1–22, 1976; Andrew Von Hirsch (The Committee for the Study of Incarceration), *Doing Justice: The Choice of Punishments* (New York: Hill and Wang, 1976); and Edward M. Kennedy, "Making Time Fit the Crime," *Trial*, 12:14–15 ff., 1976.

who rebel against the prison routine.[13] Prisoners are then held in prison as punishment for violating prison rules, not for violating the criminal law. Put in the most favorable light, this is an error in "diagnosis" rather than a blatant effort to use imprisonment to maintain conformity in prisons—inability to adjust to prison life is erroneously taken as evidence of inability to live a law-abiding life outside prison.

The broad issues in this controversy cannot be settled by empirical research. Currently, there is a move toward abandoning the indefinite sentence and returning to flat sentences. California and Maine, for example, have recently reduced drastically the discretionary range in the sentences judges and parole boards are authorized to impose. But these legislative changes have been based on shifts in conceptions of justice, not on research regarding the efficacy of the two systems. One unanswerable question is whether more injustice is done under the indeterminate system than under the determinate system in which a legislature prescribes the sentence for an entire class of criminals. Another question not answerable on the basis of empirical evidence is whether parole boards with broad discretionary powers produce more injustice than do courts that, having only superficial knowledge of individual offenders, fix minimum and maximum sentences within broad limits set by a legislature.[14]

To the many persons who think that justice should consist of machinelike imposition of specific punishments listed in legislative statutes, any significant adjustments made by the judicial or executive branch necessarily means that criminals are not being brought to justice.[15] When sentences are determinate, however, the flat sentences imposed are in many cases unjustifiably severe and repressive because unlike cases are handled as though they were alike.[16]

The indeterminate-sentence system, which is in accordance with the "adjustment principle" discussed earlier, is designed to reduce the number of such injustices.[17] But sentencing based on the adjustment principle produces injustices

[13] See M. B. Miller, "The Indeterminate Sentence Paradigm: Resocialization or Social Control?" *Issues in Criminology*, 7:101–24, 1972; and B. Crowley, "Maryland's Defective Delinquent Law: Nightmarish Prelude to 1984," *Correctional Psychiatry*, 18:15–20, 1972.

[14] See L. Cargan and M. A. Coates, "The Indeterminate Sentence and Judicial Bias," *Crime and Delinquency*, 20:144–55, 1974.

[15] See American Friends Service Committee, *Struggle for Justice: A Report on Crime and Punishment in America* (New York: Hill and Wang, 1971); James Q. Wilson, *Thinking About Crime* (New York: Basic Books, 1975); Ernest van den Haag, *Punishing Criminals: Concerning a Very Old and Painful Question* (New York: Basic Books, 1975); David Fogel, *We Are the Living Proof: The Justice Model for Corrections* (Cincinnati: W. H. Anderson, 1975); and The Twentieth Century Fund Task Force on Criminal Sentencing, *Fair and Certain Punishment* (New York: McGraw-Hill, 1976).

[16] See E. B. Spaeth, Jr., "A Response to *Struggle for Justice*," *Prison Journal*, 52:4–32, 1972; and Arthur Rosett and Donald R. Cressey, *Justice by Consent: Plea Bargains in the American Court House* (Philadelphia: Lippincott, 1976).

[17] See Chapter 15, above. See also David L. Bazelon, "Street Crime and Correctional Potholes," *Federal Probation*, 41:3–9, 1977.

too. In practice, when sentencing is left to the discretion of a judge or board, with or without minimum and maximum limits, the sentences imposed on the poor and least powerful tend to be unjustifiably severe in comparison with the punishments accorded the affluent and powerful.[18] The important, and unresolvable, issue is whether the amount of unnecessary pain and suffering produced by one of these unjust systems is greater than the amount produced by the other.

One thing is clear: Courts and parole boards must be able to do much better work than they have done if they expect to continue to be trusted with the authority to decide that it is fair to hold some offenders in prison for long periods of time while releasing other offenders immediately or after a short term in prison. Political radicals, liberals, and conservatives are currently joining hands to abolish the indeterminate sentence and to return to flat, retributory sentences, and their principal argument is that the indeterminate-sentence system, even with its minima and maxima, has been unjustly and inefficiently administered.[19] By this logic, we also should be abolishing schools, universities, hospitals, police departments, welfare programs, and most other public institutions and services, all of which are unjustly and inefficiently administered. Moreover, it is highly probable that if judges and parole-board members are prohibited from tempering the severity of the punishments prescribed in statutes by legislators, someone else will do so.[20] The fact is that few, if any, criminal laws really can specify in detail what it is that judges and executives are supposed to punish. The fact is that the legislators setting the penalties for criminal behavior do not want all criminal laws enforced with equal vigor, no matter how flat and how severe the sentence stipulated for each crime. The fact is that legislators do not automatically and systematically change and adapt criminal laws whenever a penalty gets out of date.

The mechanical, flat-sentence image of the criminal-justice process either assumes that a given set of punishments is good for all times, or it portrays legislators as computer programmers who quickly change both the kinds of behavior outlawed and the prescribed punishments whenever the law on the books is not consistent with the living law. Neither assumption is accurate. By and large, legislators let the penalties they have prescribed become too severe, and when that happens, judges and parole boards bring them up to date by softening them. Members of the judicial and executive branches of government also

---

[18]See D. Bailey, "Inequities of the Parole System in California," *Howard Law Journal*, 17:797–804, 1973; and Leo Carroll and Margaret E. Mondrick, "Racial Bias in the Decision to Grant Parole," *Law and Society Review*, 11:93–107, 1976.

[19]See David T. Stanley, *Prisoners Among Us: The Problems of Parole* (Washington: Brookings Institution, 1976).

[20]See Neal Shover, William B. Bankston, and J. William Gurley, "Responses of the Criminal Justice System to Legislation Providing More Severe Threatened Sanctions," *Criminology*, 14:483–500, 1977; and The Association of the Bar of the City of New York, Drug Abuse Council, *The Effects of the 1973 Drug Laws on the New York State Courts* (New York: Author, 1976).

implement, by means of the indeterminate sentence, their interpretations of just which criminal laws the legislators and the people want punished, and with what severity. If judges and parole boards are prohibited from making such adjustments, perhaps pardon boards will once again make them.[21] In the years before the indeterminate sentence, harsh sentences were mitigated in about the only way they could be mitigated—through pardon by the governor of a state or the president of the United States. A distinguished judge believes, alternatively, that returning to a flat-sentence system would merely shift sentencing discretion from judges and parole boards to prosecuting attorneys:

> At present, sentencing discretion is shared by prosecutors, judges, parole boards, and others. Uniform and mandatory sentencing would merely transfer most of this discretion to prosecutors, who would in effect set sentences by their decisions about whom to charge with what crime and whether to plea bargain. Remember that prosecutorial discretion is not reviewable and subject to very few checks.[22]

PAROLE

Parole is the act of releasing or the status of being released from a penal institution in which a criminal has served a part of a maximum sentence, on condition of maintaining good behavior and remaining in the custody and under the guidance of the institution or some other agency approved by the state until a final discharge is granted. The term *parole* is used in analogous manner with reference to institutions for mentally disturbed and retarded persons. The conditional pardon, now rarely used, is similar to parole in that both are liberation from an institution on conditions, with restoration of the original penalty if the conditions of liberation are violated. They differ in that a conditional pardon carries with it the remission of guilt, and a parole does not; parole refers to release from imprisonment only, while conditional pardon may refer to other penalties also.

Parole is related to, but should be distinguished from, probation. Like probation, it represents a break with the classical theory of the criminal law, since an attempt is made to adjust the societal response to the circumstances of the offense and the characteristics of the offender. Also, parole ideally includes guidance and assistance to the offender, just as probation ideally includes such guidance and assistance. Thus both systems attempt to implement the interventionist reaction to crime and criminality.

On the other hand, the influence of the punitive reaction to crime is more clearly present in parole than in probation. Parole is granted by an administrative board or an executive, and it is always preceded by serving part of a sentence in a prison or in a similar institution, while no formal penalty is imposed in probation, or, if imposed, is not executed. Probationers are considered as receiving assistance

---

[21] See Chapter 13, above.
[22] Bazelon, "Street Crime and Correctional Potholes," p. 5.

while under the threat of punishment, should they violate the conditions of their probation, but probation is granted by the courts as a substitute for punishment as well as for mere suspension of sentence. Parolees are considered as "in custody" and undergoing both punishment and assistance while under the threat of more severe punishment—return to the institutions from which they have been released. Without the threat of return to prison, release from prison before the maximum term was served would merely represent the workings of the indeterminate sentence, not parole. Since parole is expected both to punish and to rehabilitate, the conflicts between punishment and intervention found in prisons are also found in parole.

Parole is a combination and extension of earlier practices, although the idea of giving guidance and assistance is relatively new. The first trace of parole was the system of indenturing prisoners. By this means prisoners were removed from institutions and placed under the supervision of masters or employers and could be returned to the institution if they did not behave properly. Later, the supervision was centralized by appointment of state visiting agents with the special function of protecting the juvenile wards of institutions against cruelty. Several other systems for handling prisoners were combined with the indenture system before a parole system for adults was formed. One of these was after-care of discharged convicts. As early as 1776 American philanthropic societies attempted to help ex-prisoners. Such societies worked most energetically in the 1840s and 1850s.[23] Later the state made efforts in the same direction. In 1845 Massachusetts appointed a state agent for discharged convicts, and this agent used public funds to assist ex-prisoners to secure employment, tools, clothing, and transportation to places of employment. Other states appointed similar agents, and they began to ask for continuing custody over the ex-prisoners. For example, a New York agent for discharged convicts pointed out in his reports that his work could be greatly improved if the state retained custody over prisoners for some time after their release; he suggested that good-time allowances should be used merely to determine the time of release from the institutions, but not from custody.

In the early nineteenth century the English convict colonies in Australia developed a primitive parole system, with little supervision or guidance after release, under the name of ticket-of-leave. This was later made a part of the Irish system and in that form became known to American penologists. When members of the Massachusetts prison board made a plea for a parole system in 1865, they called it "the English ticket-of-leave system." The English Prevention of Crimes Act of 1871 also helped create a demand for a parole system in the United States. That act provided for surveillance by the police for a period of seven years after release from prison of all except those on their first terms. The Massachusetts

---

[23] For a history of such societies, see H. H. Hart, "Prisoners' Aid Societies," *Proceedings of the National Prison Association, 1889,* pp. 270–87.

prison board called attention to this act repeatedly and urged the adoption of a similar law.

Parole in its developed form was first adopted by New York State in the 1869 law that authorized the Elmira Reformatory. It was hailed at the time as a great invention. But it is evident that the system had existed for more than fifty years in European countries and, as indicated, in its essential features had a long history in the United States. The parole method was first extended to state prisons by Ohio in 1884, and by 1898 it had been adopted in twenty-five states.

Although parole and the indeterminate sentence are now generally combined in practice, in 1898 only five states had indeterminate-sentence laws. By 1922, parole laws had been passed by forty-five states, and since 1922 by all the other states, the last being Mississippi, which enacted a parole law in 1944. Many states make extensive use and others little use of it. In eighteen states, more than 75 percent of the releases from state prisons and reformatories in 1970 were by parole, while in two states less than 10 percent of the releases were by parole; in one state, New Hampshire, 100 percent of the discharges were by parole.[24] Parole is used most extensively in the New England and Middle Atlantic states, and in a few states scattered among the North Central, Pacific, and Mountain regions.

The Parole Board

The parole board has the duty of determining when a prisoner shall be released on parole. Parole boards are of three principal types, with various combinations of these types: (1) a special parole board limited to one institution, which is sometimes composed of institutional staff members, and at other times includes only the warden of the institution as one member of the board; (2) a general state parole board that is located in the state department of correction and has authority to release from any state institution; (3) a general state parole board that is located outside the department of correction and has authority to release from any state institution. In four states the power of the parole board is limited to recommending a disposition to the governor.[25]

The trend during the last fifty years has been toward centralization of parole authority and toward removal of the parole board from the department of correction. Although this movement was supported by some prison workers on the ground that it relieved them of a troublesome responsibility that interfered with their efficiency in the institutional work, it was criticized by others on the ground that the prison staff knows better than any other agency when a prisoner should be released. In forty-one states today the parole board is an independent agency; in seven states it is a unit within a larger department; and in two states it is

---

[24] U. S. Department of Justice, Bureau of Prisons, "Prisoners in State and Federal Institutions for Adult Felons, 1968–1970," *National Prisoner Statistics*, No. 47, April, 1972, pp. 22–3.

[25] President's Commission on Law Enforcement and Administration of Justice, *Task Force Report: Corrections* (Washington: Government Printing Office, 1967), p. 65.

the same body that regulates the correctional institutions. In no jurisdiction in the adult field is the final power to grant or deny parole given to the staff directly involved in the operation of a correctional institution, but in the juvenile field the great majority of the releasing decisions directly involve the staff of training schools.

Parole boards that were restricted to considering release of only the inmates confined in a single institution usually were dominated by the institution staff. In some states this meant that the classification committee that directed and supervised the prisoners also determined when they were released. In this way, it was said, the prison rehabilitation programs were closely coordinated with parole selection and supervision. But domination of the parole board by the institution staff also meant that the board granted parole as a reward for good conduct in the prison, rather than as a correctional device, that the board tried to maintain discipline by means of threats in regard to chances for parole, or that the board granted paroles indiscriminately when the institution was overcrowded.

At the other extreme is the parole board that is entirely independent of the department of correction. In some states, this type of parole board, like governors' advisory boards, is concerned less with the progress of the prisoner than with the possible reactions of the public toward parole. Further, even independent boards use parole to maintain prison discipline, and to keep the total prison population at some desired level.

Parole boards currently include members from all walks of life. There has been an increasing trend among the states to require that a particular profession be represented on the board—for example, attorney, penologist, peace officer, psychiatrist, sociologist.[26] When various court, probation, parole, police, and institutional staff members and prison inmates were asked to select the best occupational training for an ideal parole board, there was little consensus.[27] Although all the respondents favored training in law, sociology, and psychiatry, there was a tendency for each respondent to select a representative of his or her own occupation.

DETERMINING THE TIME OF RELEASE

Most contemporary criminologists agree that all released prisoners could benefit from assistance and guidance by parole officers. It is obvious, also, that recidivism rates would go down if all offenders were kept under close surveillance during the period immediately following incarceration. But parole, as currently administered, gives very little assistance to parolees. Accordingly, many prisoners are opposed to parole, and some of them, when the time between eligibility for parole

[26]Charles L. Newman, *Personnel Practices in Adult Parole Systems* (Springfield, Ill.: Charles C. Thomas, 1971), p. 26.

[27]Joseph W. Rogers and Norman S. Hayner, "The Ideal Parole Board: Views from the Correctional World and the Society of Captives," *Proceedings of the American Correctional Association, 1963*, pp. 287–300.

and final discharge is not too great, waive the parole hearing. This opposition is based on the observation that parole really does not provide assistance or treatment, and it therefore merely helps police officers keep ex-convicts under surveillance.[28] Some criminologists are beginning to adopt a similar view. One proposed alternative is return to the system of after-care—all discharged prisoners would be entitled but not required to participate in programs established for guidance and assistance of discharged prisoners.

Many laymen and legislators also are opposed to the policy of paroling prisoners, but this opposition is based on the belief that parole is a form of leniency. Such opposition is reflected in statutes that exclude certain types of criminals from parole. These are generally the prisoners convicted of the more serious crimes, such as murder, rape, or any offense for which life imprisonment is imposed. Often these offenders are in great need of the guidance and assistance that could be afforded in efficient parole work.

The American Parole Association stated in 1933 that fitness for limited freedom should be the principle used in determining the release time of particular offenders:

> Has the institution accomplished all that it can for him; is the offender's state of mind and attitude toward his own difficulties and problems such that further residence will be harmful or beneficial; does a suitable environment await him on the outside; can the beneficial effect already accomplished be retained if he is held longer to allow a more suitable environment to be developed?[29]

Although parole boards have generally given lip service to this principle, they usually depart from it in practice. A recent study of three prisons showed that seriousness of offense was the best indicator that the parole board would deny a parole: "Parole board members appear to believe that an inmate is not ready for parole until he has suffered commensurately for the crime he has committed."[30] The same study found only a weak relationship between prior criminal record and severity of punishment, but it found a moderate relationship ($r = .24$) between the number of disciplinary reports and severity. Generally speaking, parole applicants are not as well protected, procedurally, as are defendants.[31] A 1972

28 See C. P. Nuttall et al., *Parole in England and Wales*, Home Office Research Study No. 38 (London: Her Majesty's Stationery Office, 1977), pp. 40–64.

29 Note, *Journal of Criminal Law and Criminology*, 24:791, 1933.

30 Joseph E. Scott, "The Use of Discretion in Determining the Severity of Punishment," *Journal of Criminal Law and Criminology*, 65:214–24, 1974. See also Vincent O'Leary and Daniel Glaser, "The Assessment of Risk in Parole Decision Making," in *The Future of Parole*, ed. Donald J. West (London: Duckworth, 1972), pp. 136–98; Peter B. Hoffman, "Paroling Policy Feedback," in *Parole Decision-Making Project, Report No. 8* (Davis, Calif.: National Council on Crime and Delinquency Research Center, 1973); and P. A. Banister, K. J. Heskin, N. Bolton, and F. V. Smith, 'A Study of Variables Related to the Selection of Long-Term Prisoners for Parole," *British Journal of Criminology*, 14:359–68, 1974.

31 David Gilman, "Developments in Correctional Law," *Crime and Delinquency*, 21:163–73, 1975; and W. Ernsthaft, "The Prisoner's Right to a Statement of Reasons for Parole Denial: Silence Is Not Always Golden," *Buffalo Law Review*, 24:567–94, 1975.

survey of fifty-one state and federal parole boards revealed that twenty-one of them permitted the inmate to have counsel at the hearing, seventeen permitted the inmate to present witnesses, and eleven recorded the reasons for the decision; twenty of the fifty-one boards made a verbatim record of the proceedings.[32]

A second form of departure from principle arises from interpretation of the phrase, "does a suitable environment await him on the outside?" Two specific prerequisites of parole are frequently made. One is that there be no "detainer" against the prisoner. This requirement is made partly out of courtesy to the jurisdiction in which the prisoner is wanted for a former crime, and partly because success on parole is unlikely if the prisoner goes immediately into another trial or another prison. The second specific requirement is a guarantee of employment. Three objections have been made to this requirement. First, many of the positions that are guaranteed are fictitious. Second, many prisoners who have reached the point where they are best prepared to go out are detained in prison because no jobs are available. Third, the parolee is exploited because the employer must be notified of the prison record.

Everyone agrees that prisoners should have employment into which they can go immediately after release. However, a California study has shown that releasing those who have no employment does not necessarily increase recidivism.[33] Several states have modified the employment requirement. New York uses a plan called "release on reasonable assurance," under which selected parolees are released without a job guarantee if they have a stable home situation, a skill or a trade that reasonably assures employment, or the help of an outside community agency in obtaining employment. It has been found that inmates released under this plan do not have a higher violation rate than those who are assured of a job before they are paroled.[34] A United States Department of Labor experiment found, more generally, that providing ex-prisoners with money and assistance in finding jobs significantly reduces recidivism rates.[35]

Parole boards also depart from principle when it would be politically or administratively disadvantageous to release a prisoner, even if the board is convinced that the offender will not commit another serious crime. This is especially the case when the board is dealing with inmates who have committed notorious crimes—release of one inmate, even if the person is rehabilitated, might result in such severe attacks on the board and on the indeterminate-sentence system that the opportunity to use the principle in other cases would be lost. A

---

[32] Vincent O'Leary and Joan Nuffield, "Parole Decision-Making Characteristics: Report of a National Survey," *Criminal Law Bulletin*, 8:651–78, 1972.

[33] Ernest Riemer and Martin Warren, *Special Intensive Parole Unit, Phase II, Thirty-Man Caseload Study* (Sacramento: Department of Corrections, 1958), p. i. See also William L. Jacks, "Release on Parole to Plans with and without Employment," *American Journal of Correction*, 24:12 ff., 1962.

[34] John M. Stanton, "Is It Safe to Parole Inmates Without Jobs?" *Crime and Delinquency*, 12:147–50, 1966.

[35] Kenneth J. Lenihan, *Unlocking the Second Gate: The Role of Financial Assistance in Reducing Recidivism Among Ex-prisoners* (Washington: U. S. Department of Labor Research and Development Monograph No. 45, 1977).

person must be sacrificed for the system. Similarly, if persons of power react to crime punitively and insist on long terms for certain types of offenders, the parole board may not openly and repeatedly insist on short terms. The policies and actions of parole boards are usually carefully watched by police, district attorneys, newspapers, prison boards, crime commissions, and other agencies that believe certain offenders should not be released. These interests must be balanced against the interests of groups that clamor for the idea that the board should release prisoners whenever the board believes they are ready to be released.

No matter what the system for measuring "institutional accomplishment" and "the offender's state of mind," fitness for release cannot be determined by looking at the prisoner's conduct in an institution. Four types of prisoners behave well in prisons: (1) those who attempt to secure an early release by good behavior in order to return more quickly to crime; (2) those who are quite comfortable and conforming while under close control; (3) those who, as "square Johns," are quite docile inside prison as well as outside; and (4) those who really profit from institutionalization. The good behavior of only the last two groups indicates fitness for release. On the other hand, some prisoners who behave badly under the surveillance of prison guards get along satisfactorily in the general community.

In a number of institutions, a "progressive merit system" or "graduated release program" has been tried. The prisoner might pass through special "prerelease" classes inside the walls, an honor camp outside the walls, a work furlough program, and a halfway house.[36] Although there is widespread enthusiasm for graduated-release programs, a review of the research and experiments undertaken with regard to them found that the more rigorous the evaluation methods the more ambivalent or negative are the findings regarding the efficacy of such programs.[37] An intensive study of sixty parolees in San Diego, California, has documented what most inmates and parolees have known for years, namely that neither institutional programs nor graduated-release programs nor parole programs prepare persons for "making it" on the outside.[38]

Suffering on the part of prisoners is increased by indeterminate sentences and parole. Most prisoners would prefer sentence of a fixed term in prison plus a fixed term on parole to the agony of indeterminacy.[39] Some would even prefer a long term fixed in advance to a short term accompanied by a period of worry and anxiety while they await a decision or "setting" by the parole board. Using a

---

[36] See Oliver J. Keller and Benedict S. Alper, *Halfway Houses: Community Centered Correction and Treatment* (Lexington, Mass.: Lexington Books, 1970). See also James A. Beha, II, "Testing the Functions and Effect of the Parole Halfway House: One Case Study," *Journal of Criminal Law and Criminology,* 67:335–50, 1976.

[37] Eugene Doleschal and Gilbert Geis, *Graduated Release* (Washington: Government Printing Office, 1971), p. 23.

[38] Rosemary J. Erickson, Wayman J. Crow, Louis A. Zurcher, and Archie V. Connett, *Paroled But Not Free: Ex-offenders Look at What They Need to Make It Outside* (New York: Behavioral Publications, 1973).

[39] See E. Barrett Prettyman, "The Indeterminate Sentence and the Right to Treatment," *American Criminal Law Review,* 11:7–37, 1972; and American Friends Service Committee, *Struggle for Justice,* pp. 83–98.

semifree interviewing technique based on some one hundred standard questions, Farber years ago found that the following five things are significantly related to the degree of suffering of prisoners: indefiniteness of knowledge as to time of release, feeling of injustice of sentence, feeling of injustice of length of time served, lack of hope of getting a break, and apparent unfriendliness on the outside.[40] The following statement by an ex-prisoner illustrates the effect of the first three of these:

I was sentenced to San Quentin on an indefinite term. The prisoner there has no notion during the entire year regarding the term the parole board will set for him to do. At the end of that year the parole board fixes his maximum, and may later reduce it. That first year is a perfect hell for the prisoner. He keeps asking others who were convicted of a similar offense about the details of their crimes and of their maximum sentences. One man committed the same crime I did and he received a sentence of nine years but he had a long previous record and he was armed. Another man who was a first offender and was not armed got four years. I was a first offender and was armed. Consequently I figured that I will get between four and nine years. But I keep thinking and worrying about it, for every year in prison makes a big difference. My worry interferes with my work, and I get sent to the "hole" for inefficiency in work. That looks bad on my record and I wonder whether it will increase my maximum sentence. This worry drives a person mad. As soon as the sentence is fixed the prisoner can settle down to serve his time, and it is a great relief to have it settled.

Prisoners must be released by some agency unless they are to be held for life. No one can now determine in advance how long any individual prisoner should be held, and there is little possibility of developing a prediction instrument for doing so. When the sentence is definite, the criminal is given a right to feel that when the fixed term of imprisonment has been served, the prisoner has paid the penalty and balanced the account. This is a dangerous doctrine for criminals or others to hold. There is no such account. Nevertheless, when the sentence is indefinite many criminals are made to suffer unnecessarily and to believe that they are not being treated fairly, with the result that they see the criminal-justice system, if not the whole society, as unjust, bigoted, and even corrupt.

PAROLE SUPERVISION

Parole is "conditional liberation"—that is, liberation on condition that the prisoner live in accordance with specified rules. The conditions are sometimes fixed by law, sometimes by the parole board, and sometimes by other agencies. These conditions may include leading a law-abiding life, abstaining from intoxicating liquors and drugs, keeping away from bad associates, spending evenings at home, refraining from gambling, supporting legal dependents, remaining in a specified territory, not changing residence or employment without permission

---

[40] M. F. Farber, "Suffering and Time Perspectives of the Prisoner," *University of Iowa Studies in Child Welfare,* 20:153–227, 1944. See also Stanley Cohen and Laurie Taylor, *Psychological Survival: The Experience of Long-Term Imprisonment* (New York: Pantheon, 1972), pp. 86–111.

(sometimes merely without reporting the change), attending church at least once each Sunday, not marrying without permission, not becoming dependent on welfare, making reparation or restitution for the crime, and making written or personal reports as required. A recent survey showed that more than one-half the states forbid cohabitation of unmarried persons on parole, and that only seven states allow cohabitation without qualification.[41] The attempt to impose on parolees standards of conduct not imposed on law-abiding persons is absurd. Unrealistic rules and conditions usually are mitigated informally by parole officers, who count as "parole violation" only the more serious violations of rules.[42]

Parole supervision is little more than nominal in most states, for very few have a sufficient number of officers to make adequate supervision possible. As in probation, caseloads sometimes run as high as two or three hundred per officer. In California, the usual load in recent years has been ninety parolees. An experimental program showed that when the caseloads were reduced to fifteen, and parolees were accorded intensive supervision during the first ninety days after release and then transferred to the regular ninety-person caseloads for regular supervision, only slight reductions in parole-violation rates occurred. It also was found that parolees whose parole-release dates were advanced three months violated parole slightly less frequently than did those whose release dates were not advanced.[43] A follow-up study indicated that intensive supervision—defined as a caseload of thirty with frequent controls during the first six months—did not produce rates significantly lower than the rates of those in ninety-person caseloads; about 55 percent of each group violated parole in the first year.[44] In Pennsylvania, the caseload is about sixty, but a study indicated that even with this number, adequate supervision is difficult—only 34 percent of work time was spent in contact with parolees.[45]

Principles and Methods of Supervision

At least three different views of supervision, differentially emphasizing punishment and treatment, are found among lay and professional parole workers.[46] One

[41] Mary C. Schwartz and Laura Zeisel, "Unmarried Cohabitation: A Nationwide Study of Parole," *Crime and Delinquency*, 22:18–24, 1976.

[42] See Deborah Star and John E. Berecochea, *Rationalizing the Conditions of Parole: Some Recommended Changes* (Sacramento: California Department of Corrections, Research Report No. 58, 1977).

[43] Ernest Riemer and Martin Warren, "Special Intensive Parole Unit: Relationship Between Violation Rate and Initially Small Caseload," *National Probation and Parole Association Journal*, 3:1–8, 1957.

[44] Riemer and Warren, *Special Intensive Parole Unit, Phase II, Thirty-Man Caseload Study*, pp. 13–16.

[45] William L. Jacks, *A Time Study of Parole Agents* (Harrisburg, Pa.: Pennsylvania Board of Parole, 1961), pp. 4–5.

[46] See Lloyd E. Ohlin, Herman Piven, and Donnell M. Pappenfort, "Major Dilemmas of the Social Worker in Probation and Parole," *National Probation and Parole Association Journal*, 2:211–25, 1956; Carl B. Klockars, Jr., "A Theory of Probation Supervision," *Journal of Criminal Law, Criminology, and Police Science*, 63:550–7, 1972; and Richard Dembo, "Orientation and Activities of the Parole Officer," *Criminology*, 10:193–215, 1972.

conception, currently popular among "war on crime" enthusiasts, is based on the assumption that parole is a system of leniency that permits the early release of many dangerous criminals who should continue to suffer punishment. Consequently, in parole work based on this view, emphasis is placed on supervision rather than assistance, and "supervision" is taken to mean zealous "police work," "parole officer" to mean "police officer." It is assumed that most parolees have not reformed, and that they will commit new crimes if given the opportunity. The parole officers are charged, then, with the duty of keeping parolees under close surveillance and coercing the offender into conformity by threats of punishment.

A second conception is based on the assumption that reformation is a matter of individual self-determination to "make good" in free society. The essential notion is that reformation is practically complete at the time of release, and that the function of the parole officer is to watch parolees to determine whether they are maintaining the conditions fixed for parole. A supervisory system based on this view may be characterized as "watchful waiting." Coupled with the idea that society must be protected by a careful watch over the parolee is a belief that the parolee must be protected from society. Parole officers using this system are likely to give direct help and assistance in locating jobs or solving other problems, to lecture, and to use both praise and blame. They believe that frequent contacts will destroy the parolee's initiative and confidence.

The third conception is based on the belief that essential work of promoting adjustment has to be done after release from an institution, and that this requires assistance, not to prevent parolees from exercising their own initiative, but to assist them in exercising it correctly, so that crimes will not be repeated. Although it is not assumed that all parolees are dangerous criminals, it is recognized that "reformation" in the form of self-resolution to "make good" is not always sufficient to prevent recidivism. Parole is viewed as a system for using the interventionist policy of trying to change criminal behavior by locating its cause and then eliminating or modifying that cause. In the recent version of this process, based on the medical model, a client's needs are diagnosed and a program of "treatment" is prescribed and administered, at least on paper. In either case, assistance rather than surveillance is emphasized, on the ground that we already have police to act as surveillants and detectives. In parole work based on this conception, parole officers are social workers.[47]

As in probation work, however, it never has been clear just what a parole worker is to do in order to produce the desired rehabilitation of the parolee. As noted above, a California experiment long ago indicated that if parole caseloads are reduced to fifteen and parolees are accorded "intensive supervision" during the first ninety days after release and then transferred to the normal ninety-person caseloads for regular supervision, only slight reductions in parole-violation rates occur.[48] But no one knows *why* this experiment, like others, turned out the way it

[47] See Eliot Studt, *Surveillance and Service in Parole* (Washington: Government Printing Office, 1973).
[48] Riemer and Warren, "Special Intensive Parole Unit."

did, principally because no one knows what, specifically, was involved in "intensive supervision" that is not included when the procedure is not "intensive." Perhaps parole officials do not want to know. As things now stand, the parole budget and bureaucracy can be enlarged by ignoring the results of the experiment and continuing to demand that "intensive supervision" be expanded. A recent New York study concluded that parole workers cannot even provide needed social services, let alone "treatment" or "intensive supervision," and it was recommended that these workers be replaced by community-services advisors.[49] A Canadian study and a British study concluded, similarly, that the parole officer is of little importance in affecting the behavior of parolees.[50]

In practice, of course, it is difficult to separate surveillance and assistance or treatment, and even in parole systems emphasizing assistance, the parole officer must do some policing. Also, from the parolee's viewpoint almost any contacts, whether called "assistance" or something else, are regarded as snooping. Parole officers, like prison officials, are charged with maintaining a delicate balance between punishment and treatment. That balance seems to be most effectively maintained in supervisory systems where the dominant view is that parolees must be given assistance within the framework of the punitive restrictions imposed as conditions of their parole, thus protecting society.

If the parole officer is to be of real assistance to the person on parole, the officer should have an intimate acquaintance with the personality and background of the offender. This information must be secured before a proper method for dealing with the offender can be determined. In addition, an efficient parole officer must have an intimate knowledge of the family and other personal groups into which the individual will go, so that the officer can attempt to prepare these groups for the parolee's return before parole begins. It is ridiculous to return the parolee to the very circumstances that produced the individual's criminality in the first place.

A study of fifty male prisoners in the District of Columbia revealed that they had four main areas of concern about their release on parole—community acceptance, employment, family relationships, and relationships with police and parole officers.[51] The important thing is to make parolees feel that they are part of society. This is easier said than done, for the criminal-justice system up to this point has done much to convince them that they are outcasts and outlaws. Further, they are likely to be ostracized while on parole. The following statement from a prisoner's letter reveals the feelings of being set apart from law-abiding groups:

[49] Citizens' Inquiry on Parole and Criminal Justice, *Prison Without Walls: Report on New York Parole* (New York: Praeger, 1975).

[50] Irwin Waller, *Men Released from Prison* (Toronto: University of Toronto Press, 1974); Pauline Morris and Farida Beverly, *On License: A Study of Parole* (New York: Wiley, 1975).

[51] Reuben S. Horlick, "Inmate Perception of Obstacles to Readjustment in the Community," *Proceedings of the American Correctional Association, 1961*, pp. 200–5. See also Erickson et al., *Paroled But Not Free*, pp. 64–73.

We are the anonymous ones who move amongst you with wary eyes. We are among you but not of you; constantly on guard, lest by an incautious word or gesture we may betray ourselves to you, and thereby lose our anonymity—and your respect. You may find us in your factories, in your garages, on your farms, and, sometimes in your offices and places of business. We live next door, work at the next lathe, sit next to you in the movies. In short— we are your neighbors. Yet we are a group of men set apart, divided by our experiences from those around us. We are the parolees from your prisons; still doing time, still paying our debt to society. Although we walk the streets to all outward appearances free men, we wear invisible numbers. . . .[52]

Supervision in the form of close surveillance is likely to contribute to this attitude, and mere inspection of the parolee's activities will do little to reduce it. In order to reduce the feeling of isolation, and in order that the parolee will not, in fact, be isolated, positive, constructive action must be taken. Contacts with groups that possess a bias against criminality must be developed. The larger the number of intimate associations that can be formed between the parolee and law-abiding groups, the more likely the parolee is to become and remain a law-abiding person. To this end, as indicated above, the federal system and most states have opened halfway houses where parolees can live while they attempt to reenter the community.

Violation of Parole

The law usually states that any violation of the conditions imposed upon the person on parole constitutes a violation of parole, and that for a violation of parole the person is to be returned to prison. In practice, the supervising parole agent generally uses discretion and permits some violations. Also, many violations are not observed by the parole officer. Nevertheless, Takagi has shown, differences in revocation decisions are as dependent on the status of parole officers as on the behavior of parolees.[53] When a formal declaration of violation of parole is made, a warrant for the arrest of the parolee is issued and served if the parolee can be located.

When an alleged parole violator is arrested, a court trial is not necessary in order to return the parolee to prison, and the decision of the supervising authority usually is final. However, a parolee who has allegedly violated parole by committing a new crime may be tried and sentenced for that crime. Until recently, most violators were returned to the prison with no hearing at all. Even when hearings were held, the usual rights to counsel and to other court procedures designed for protection of accused persons were denied, ordinarily on the ground that persons on parole are still being punished. In 1972 the Supreme Court held that there must

---

[52] Quoted in James V. Bennett, "Wise Men Have Enough to Do . . . ," *Federal Probation*, 14:25–9, 1950.

[53] Paul T. Takagi, "The Effect of Parole Agents' Judgment on Recidivism Rates," *Psychiatry*, 32:192–9, 1969; and Takagi and James Robison, "The Parole Violator: An Organizational Reject," *Journal of Research in Crime and Delinquency*, 6:78–86, 1969.

be a hearing with most of the due-process safeguards, but the Court remained silent on the question of whether the parolee is entitled to the assistance of counsel.[54]

A parole violator who is returned to prison may be required to serve the remainder of a definite sentence or the remainder of the maximum term of an indeterminate sentence. The violator may lose the good time earned prior to parole, or may be denied the privilege of earning good time after return to prison, thus lengthening the prison term. In a few states, violators lose the right to be considered for another parole, or may not be allowed to apply for a new parole until a certain period of time has elapsed. In some states the length of time to be served in prison after parole violation is determined by statute, in other states by the supervising authority, and in others by the parole board that controls releases.

In a few states, the prisoner may be returned to the prison without a violation of parole. This may occur in several ways. The parolee may ask to return because of unemployment, for medical care, or to complete a course in trade training. Other parolees may be returned by action of the supervisor because the supervisor believes the parolee needs additional training or needs medical care or for other reasons that do not involve a formal violation of the conditions of parole.

Parolees may not be kept on parole beyond the end of the maximum sentence to prison. In some states, they cannot be discharged from parole before the end of that maximum period; in others they can be discharged when they have served a shorter period specified by law or by the regulations of the parole board; in still others the parole board has complete authority to determine, within the limits of the maximum sentence, how long parole should continue.

Civil rights, which are lost in most states on conviction of certain types of crimes, are restored in some states automatically when parole is granted; in others they are restored only when one is discharged from parole; and in others they are restored, if at all, only by a pardon by the governor. In California, the parole board is authorized to restore civil rights to persons on parole at such time and to such a degree as they see fit, except that they cannot restore the right to be an elector, hold public office, or act as trustee.

The deprivation of civil rights was originally devised as a punitive system for placing social distance between the offender and law-abiding citizens. As the interventionist reaction to crime has become more popular, however, it became apparent that prisoners who are to be released to the community should be members of that community and should be made to feel that they are members of it. To this end, prisoners should be permitted to vote and exercise some of the other rights, even if they cannot hold office. For the maximum degree of reformation and, hence, protection of society, all the prisoners' rights should be automatically restored as soon as they are placed in the outside community. Criminals are returned to the community so that law-abiding groups may

54 *Morrissey* v. *Brewer,* 408 U. S. 471 (1972).

assimilate them. Assimilation is not promoted by treating them as second-class citizens.

SUCCESS OR FAILURE ON PAROLE

The annual reports of parole departments customarily state the parole-violation rate as the ratio between paroles granted during a year and paroles violated during the same year. Calculated by this method, the parole-violation rates in the several states tend to cluster around 25 percent, with a range of 10 to 40 percent. Even these percentages include only the violations known to parole officers and, in general, are restricted to the relatively serious violations for which paroles are revoked. In many areas the parole staff is not sufficient in numbers or activities to have reliable or complete information regarding the conduct of the parolees. Consequently, considerable skepticism regarding the stated violation rates has developed.[55] In the states in which parolees are kept under close surveillance, the percentages of success are generally lower than in the states where surveillance is superficial.

Also, questions have been raised as to the adequacy of the usual method of measuring parole violations, since most prisoners remain on parole for many years. The proportion of parolees released in a specified year who subsequently violate parole sometime during the parole period generally is higher than the ratio of paroles violated to paroles granted in a certain year. In a pioneering study, the Gluecks made an analysis of the careers of five hundred young adult male offenders paroled from the Massachusetts reformatory and reported that 55.3 percent violated paroles, as recorded by the parole department of the state, and 5.3 percent more violated paroles by new crimes committed during the parole period which were not known to the parole department but which were discovered by the Gluecks in independent investigations. Thus they concluded that the parole-violation rate was 60.6 percent, while the state department was reporting a parole-violation rate of about 25 percent.[56] Later studies have revealed lower rates. For example, of 1,803 persons released from federal prisons in 1970, 33 percent were judged to be "failures" by 1972. The "failure" rate (parole revocation and a sentence of sixty days or more) was higher for youths than for mature adults, higher for males than for females, higher for Indians than for blacks, higher for blacks than for whites, and higher for automobile thieves than for persons who had been imprisoned for other offenses.[57] Of 6,700 male offenders paroled in California in 1972, 39 percent had been declared violators by the end of 1973, and

[55] See Richard McCleary, "How Structural Variables Constrain the Parole Officer's Use of Discretionary Powers," *Social Problems*, 23:209–25, 1975; and idem, "How Parole Officers Use Records," *Social Problems*, 24:576–89, 1977.

[56] Sheldon and Eleanor T. Glueck, *Five Hundred Criminal Careers* (Cambridge: Harvard University Press, 1930), p. 169.

[57] U. S. Department of Justice, Bureau of Prisons, *Success and Failure of Federal Offenders in 1970* (Washington: Government Printing Office, 1974), Tables 1–8.

of 5,553 male offenders released in 1969, 54 percent had been declared violators by 1973.[58] Precise comparisons of reports are not possible because the definitions of "violation" and "failure" are not the same in all studies.

The parole-violation rate, however it may be computed, refers only to the period of parole and does not include the career of the offender after release from parole. Numerous studies have been made of the subsequent careers of ex-prisoners, beyond the period of parole. One of the first was made in 1888 by Brockway regarding former inmates of Elmira Reformatory. He concluded that 78.6 percent of those released during the preceding decade were leading law-abiding lives and were self-supporting at the time of the investigation.[59] The most intensive studies of this type were made by Sheldon and Eleanor Glueck and refer to five hundred young adult male offenders over a fifteen-year period, and one thousand juvenile delinquents over a ten-year period.[60] They reported that 79 percent of the five hundred young male offenders committed new crimes during the first five-year period after parole, 68 percent during the second five-year period, and 68 percent during the third five-year period. Three and one-half years after release from a Borstal institution in England, 45 percent of a group of 720 boys had no further record of crime.[61]

A Minnesota study compared the subsequent careers of a group of prisoners released on parole with the subsequent careers of a group released unconditionally without parole. Five years after discharge from a reformatory, 30 percent of the men released on expiration of sentence and 21.4 percent of those released on parole had been convicted, sentenced, returned to custody, or had paroles revoked for felonies. In addition, 7.3 percent of those released on expiration of sentence and 4.9 percent of those released on parole had been fingerprinted for felonies, but there was no record of conviction.[62] A Canadian study examined the recidivism rates of 210 men released from federal penitentiaries on parole and 213 men discharged from prison after having completed their sentences. Forty-four percent of the parolees and 68 percent of the dischargees had been rearrested and reconvicted of an indictable (serious) offense within two years.[63] These differences, however, may not be due to any assistance given while on parole; the

58 *California Prisoners, 1973* (Sacramento: Department of Corrections, 1973), p. 87.

59 Zebulon R. Brockway, *Fifty Years of Prison Service* (New York: Charities Publication Committee, 1912), p. 297.

60 *Five Hundred Criminal Careers; Later Criminal Careers* (New York: Commonwealth Fund, 1937); *Criminal Careers in Retrospect* (New York: Commonwealth Fund, 1943); *One Thousand Juvenile Delinquents* (Cambridge: Harvard University Press, 1934); *Juvenile Delinquents Grow Up* (New York: Commonwealth Fund, 1940).

61 Hermann Mannheim and Leslie T. Wilkins, *Prediction Methods in Relation to Borstal Training* (London: Her Majesty's Stationery Office, 1955), pp. 53, 65.

62 Stanley B. Zuckerman, Alfred J. Barron, and Horace B. Whittier, "A Follow-up Study of Minnesota State Reformatory Inmates," *Journal of Criminal Law, Criminology, and Police Science*, 43:622–36, 1953.

63 Waller, *Men Released from Prison.*

inmates least likely to commit new crimes probably are selected for parole, while the inmates most likely to commit new crimes remain in prison until the end of the maximum sentence.

During the last generation, over six hundred statistical studies have been made of the factors associated with success or failure on parole.[64] The criterion of failure used in most of these studies is a violation of parole by behavior that is noticed by the parole authorities and that leads to the issuance of a parole-violation warrant. Such warrants ordinarily are requested and issued only when the parole agent is reasonably certain that the parolee cannot make an adequate social adjustment, or when a new crime is committed. Consequently, parole-violation warrants as a measure of outcome tend to overestimate the actual adjustment achieved by parolees. Information regarding many of the "factors" or conditions that are said to affect success or failure—such as "home status" and "previous work record"— are customarily taken from unverified statements made by the inmates. Others, such as "social type," "type of offense," and "personality rating," are taken from the official prison documents or from classification committee reports.

These statistical studies are consistent in their conclusions in certain respects and inconsistent in other respects. They show considerable consistency in the conclusion that failures decrease as the age of first delinquency increases, and increase as the number of previous arrests, the irregularity of previous work habits, the frequency of contacts with associates from the institution, and the size of the community in which the offender resided increase. Generally, older offenders succeed on parole more often than do the young offenders, white offenders more often than blacks, and sex offenders and murderers more often than those engaged in crimes against property.

The studies either show no consistent relation or a very slight relation between failure on parole and such characteristics as height and weight, intelligence, religious preference, occupational classification, and work habits in the institution, On the other hand, the studies that are pertinent to this point show a close association between success on parole and postrelease behavior such as regular work habits, abstinence from alcohol and drugs, and constructive use of leisure time, as well as between parole success and such conditions as close family ties and residence in low-delinquency areas.[65]

[64] Bibliographies of such studies are given in Robert M. Allen, "A Review of Parole Prediction Literature," *Journal of Criminal Law and Criminology*, 32:548–54, 1942; Michael Hakeem, "Prediction of Criminality," *Federal Probation*, 9:31–8, 1945; Lloyd E. Ohlin and Otis Dudley Duncan, "The Efficiency of Prediction in Criminology," *American Journal of Sociology*, 54:441–52, 1949; Karl F. Schuessler, "Parole Prediction: Its History and Status," *Journal of Criminal Law, Criminology, and Police Science*, 45:425–31, 1954; Mannheim and Wilkins, *Prediction Methods in Relation to Borstal Training*; Charles Dean and Thomas J. Duggan, "Problems in Parole Prediction: A Historical Analysis," *Social Problems*, 15:450–8, 1968; and Don M. Gottfredson, Leslie T. Wilkins, Peter B. Hoffman, and Susan M. Singer, *The Utilization of Experience in Parole Decisions* (Washington: Government Printing Office, 1974).

[65] Gottfredson et al., *The Utilization of Experience in Parole Decisions*; and Herbert Solomon, "Parole Outcome: A Multidimensional Contingency Table Analysis," *Journal of Research in Crime and Delinquency*, 13:107–26, 1976.

Prediction of Success on Parole

The information regarding the conditions of success or failure on parole of those who have been paroled in earlier years has been organized into experience tables and used to predict probable success or failure on parole and the probable violation rates for specific groups of parole applicants.[66] For example, in one of the earlier prediction studies, Burgess found that parolees who had more than fifteen "unfavorable" factors (e.g., poor work record, previous criminal career, institutional punishments, and residence in a deteriorated neighborhood) violated parole in 98.5 percent of the cases, while those who had less than five unfavorable factors violated parole in only 24.0 percent of the cases.[67] On the basis of this experience, he predicted that a person who had more than fifteen unfavorable factors was almost certain to violate parole, and that a person who had less than five unfavorable factors had three chances out of four of success on parole.

The reliability of the original data, the methods of classification, and the statistical methods of organizing the information were improved by further studies. Six states have for fifty years been producing most of the parole-prediction studies. These are California, Illinois, Massachusetts, Minnesota, Washington, and Wisconsin. The improvement of prediction techniques has been strongly stimulated by the state of Illinois. Since 1933, this state has employed actuarial sociologists to conduct research on parole prediction and to assist the parole board by preparing a prediction of the success or failure of each person who comes before the board. This gives the board organized information, which may or may not be used as the basis of decision by the board.

Although the prediction technique has customarily been considered as a device for selecting for parole those prisoners who are most likely to succeed, it is potentially more useful as a device for directing the supervision and guidance of prisoners who are placed on parole. That is, parolees who are "poor risks" could be given close parole supervision and careful guidance, and those who are "good risks" could be given a minimum of supervision and guidance. In an experimental study, California placed good parole risks under minimal supervision and found that they did as well as they were predicted to do under regular supervision.[68]

Four principal criticisms have been made of this prediction technique as a method of selecting persons for parole. The first is that it does not provide a standard for selecting parolees. Should the parole board grant parole to those who have fifty chances out of a hundred or only to those who have seventy-five or ninety chances out of a hundred? The prediction technique, if adequately

---

[66] For an exceptionally clear description of how experience tables are constructed and used in parole, see Lloyd E. Ohlin, *Selection for Parole* (New York: Russell Sage Foundation, 1951).

[67] A. A. Bruce, E. W. Burgess, and A. J. Harno, *The Workings of the Indeterminate-Sentence Law and the Parole System in Illinois* (Springfield, Ill.: State of Illinois, 1928).

[68] Joan Havel, *Special Intensive Parole Unit, Phase IV, The High Base Expectancy Study*, Research Report No. 10 (Sacramento, Calif.: Department of Corrections, 1963), and *The Parole Outcome Study*, Research Report No. 13 (Sacramento, Calif.: Department of Corrections, 1965).

developed, may be able to give information regarding the chances of success, but it cannot provide a standard. Moreover, the question recurs: Should prisoners who have little chance of success on parole be held to the end of the maximum sentence and then released without supervision, or should they be released on parole anyhow? It is clear that the prediction technique cannot provide the standards, but prediction studies may assist the parole board in defining the standards.

The second criticism is that this technique largely neglects the fact that every prisoner reaches a point where he or she is a better risk on parole than at any other time.[69] The prediction technique is concerned principally with events and characteristics that preceded the period of imprisonment, only to a slight extent with behavior while in prison, and not at all with the changing attitudes of the prisoner while in prison.[70] In a pioneering study, Laune attempted to take these attitudes into account and to base predictions on them.[71] But a later check on the parolees whose success or failure was predicted by Laune indicated that, in general, prediction by use of objective factors would have been more efficient than the prediction based on inmate attitudes.[72] This does not mean, however, that prediction systems using objective factors are necessarily more valuable than the systems using attitudinal factors when the aim is the efficient *selection* of parolees.

A third criticism, especially strong among inmates, notes the injustice of telling inmates that they will be paroled when they have changed their attitudes and other behavior patterns, and then actually releasing them on the basis of criteria over which they have no control. For example, the United States Parole Board now takes nine "salient factors" into account in determining the time of release, but eight of these are not in any way modifiable by prisoners or anyone else—prior convictions, prior incarcerations, age at first commitment, full-time employment (or school) before incarceration, offense involving automobile theft, prior parole, and a release plan to live with spouse and/or children. The modifiable "salient factor" is education—inmates who have a twelfth-grade education have been found to have a lower parole-violation rate than those who do not.[73] It is

[69] Norman S. Hayner, "Why Do Parole Boards Lag in the Use of Prediction Scores?" *Pacific Sociological Review*, 1:73–6, 1958; and Jerome K. Skolnick, "Toward a Developmental Theory of Parole," *American Sociological Review*, 25:542–9, 1960.

[70] See Ralph W. England, "Some Dangers in Parole Prediction," *Crime and Delinquency*, 8:265–9, 1962.

[71] F. F. Laune, *Predicting Criminality: Forecasting Behavior on Parole*, Northwestern University Studies in the Social Sciences, No. 1 (Evanston, Ill: Northwestern University Press, 1936); idem, "The Application of Attitude Tests in the Field of Parole Prediction," *American Sociological Review*, 1:781–96, 1936.

[72] Lloyd E. Ohlin and Richard A. Lawrence, "A Comparison of Alternative Methods of Parole Prediction," *American Sociological Review*, 17:268–74, 1952.

[73] See Peter B. Hoffman and L. K. DeGostin, "Parole Decision-Making: Structuring Discretion," *Federal Probation*, 38:7–15, 1974; Hoffman and J. L. Beck, "Parole Decision-Making: A Salient Factor Score," *Journal*

theoretically possible for inmates to graduate from prison high schools, thus improving their chances for parole. But even this "salient factor" is not modifiable by the great proportion of prisoners who are intellectually incapable of doing even the watered-down academic work that passes for education in most prison high schools. Clearly, if there is no way to improve inmates' chances for parole while they are in prison, it is unfair to tell them that they will be released when they have become "adjusted," "rehabilitated," or "reformed."

A fourth criticism is that prediction methods do not predict. The predictive efficiency of an experience table can be measured by comparing (1) the number of errors in prediction occurring when the table is used with (2) the number of errors that would have occurred had the prediction been based on the crudest method available—prediction from total violation rates alone. For example, it might be found, after the parole results are in, that an actuary using an experience table had predicted incorrectly in, say, 30 percent of the cases. On the other hand, it might be observed that 40 percent of the parolees under consideration actually violated parole, so that the best possible prediction for each individual case, on the basis of this total violation rate alone, would have been "nonviolation." If the actuary had predicted "nonviolation" for all the parolees, on the basis of the total violation rate, the person would have been incorrect in 40 percent of the cases. By using the experience table, then, the actuary reduces the percentage of error from 40 to 30, an improvement of 25 percent. Ohlin and Duncan reported that all of the twenty-six major experience tables that had been used in research studies produced some reduction in the error of prediction for the original samples; the percentage reduction of error in the various studies ranged from 43 percent down to only 3 percent, with an average of about 12 percent. Hence, it may be concluded that the experience tables do have some predictive efficiency.[74]

However, the predictive ability of the tables generally fails to stand up in follow-up samples to which the tables are applied for the purpose of validation. For example, in the Gluecks' study of five hundred young adult male offenders over a fifteen-year period, the factors that were selected as most highly associated with failure in the first five-year period did not apply to the second five-year period, and an almost completely new set of factors was adopted; neither the first nor the second set of factors applied satisfactorily to the third five-year period, and a third set of factors was therefore adopted. When existing experience tables are applied to new samples of parolees, some of them do not significantly decrease the amount of error that would have been present had prediction been based simply on

of Criminal Justice, 2:195–206, 1974; William J. Genego, Peter D. Goldberger, and Vicki C. Jackson, "Parole Release Decisionmaking and the Sentencing Process," *Yale Law Journal,* 84:809–902, 1975; and Don M. Gottfredson, Peter B. Hoffman, Maurice H. Sigler, and Leslie T. Wilkins, "Making Paroling Policy Explicit," *Crime and Delinquency,* 21:34–44, 1975.

[74]Ohlin and Duncan, "Efficiency of Prediction in Criminology."

knowledge of the total violation rates alone, and others even *increase* the amount of error.[75]

The general failure of the prediction instruments to predict for new samples may be attributed to four principal kinds of error that occur in practice.[76] First, there are many errors that result from lack of association between the "factors" and the actual outcome on parole. At best, the predictive techniques rest on the assumption that some categories of individuals will get involved and other categories of individuals will not get involved in the unknown causal systems that lead to parole violation.[77] Intensive analysis of the cause of parole violation probably would reduce the incidence of this type of error.

Second, errors arise because of sampling fluctuations; that is, the characteristics of the new sample may differ from those of the first sample in such a way that the predictive efficiency of the instrument is reduced.

Third, errors occur because of the unreliability of the information used to establish the "factors" and of the "factors" themselves. Although the extent of the unreliability of prison records cannot be precisely determined, research workers agree that these sources of information are notably unreliable. This source of error can be corrected by basing prediction on data collected for the specific purpose of making predictions. Scientific prediction can hardly be based on data collected by prisons for nonscientific purposes. The unreliability of the "factors" is due to lack of rigorous definition and to lack of knowledge of the cause of parole violation.

Fourth, errors correlated with time frequently occur. The prediction tables are based on the assumption that parole conditions remain constant over the years. Actually, many conditions that affect violation rates, but which do not affect the factors used in prediction, occur from time to time. Among these are the effectiveness of the treatment measures used in the prison, the policy of the parole board, the employment possibilities for parolees, the policy of the parole agent, the policy of law-enforcement officers, the policy of the supervising agent in regard to what constitutes "violation," and the attitude of the community toward parole. This type of error constitutes perhaps the most serious obstacle to efficient parole prediction. Ohlin developed a technique for routine adjustment of the prediction instrument so that it will take account of such changes in parole conditions.[78]

However, the condition that probably has the most effect on violation and nonviolation is the behavior of the persons with whom the parolee interacts, and

[75] Andrew von Hirsch, "Prediction of Criminal Conduct and Preventive Confinement of Convicted Persons," *Buffalo Law Review*, 21:717–58, 1972; David F. Greenberg, "The Incapacitative Effect of Imprisonment: Some Estimates," *Law and Society Review*, 9:541–80, 1975; and Arthur S. Elstein, "Clinical Judgment: Psychological Research and Medical Practice," *Science*, 194:696–700, 1976.

[76] Lloyd E. Ohlin, "The Routinization of Correctional Change," *Journal of Criminal Law, Criminology, and Police Science*, 45:400–11, 1954.

[77] See Robert M. Martinson, Gene G. Kassebaum, and David A. Ward, "A Critique of Research in Parole," *Federal Probation*, 28:34–8, 1964.

[78] Ohlin, *Selection for Parole*, pp. 62–4, 119–21.

this social interaction is not precisely taken into account in most prediction systems. Some of the prediction systems in criminology attempt to predict behavior on parole and even thoughout life from traits and circumstances in infancy and early childhood. Although certain behaviors may be fixed in infancy and remain relatively inflexible throughout life, behaviors like crime and serious infraction of parole regulations are not among them. These actions develop in a complex process of continuing social interaction. Accordingly, the criminal behavior of a person can be accurately predicted only if the behavior of those with whom the person will come in contact is known. Glaser examined the effects of social interaction on parole violation by deriving his prediction factors from the differential-association theory, and he found that such factors are more efficient predictors than are case-study personality ratings.[79] A study of parolees from a state training school also concluded that "parolees' social relations rather than their personal characteristics are decisive in determining their success or failure on parole."[80] A recent analysis of parole-prediction studies in California similarly concluded:

If a particular individual's recidivism depends not only on his or her own personal traits, but also on largely unforseeable contingencies such as how others (spouses, prospective employers, etc.) behave toward that individual, the information that would be essential for an accurate prediction would be omitted from the actuarial analysis that forms the basis for a prediction. The meager results obtained from the characteristics of individual parolees strongly suggest that these contingencies may be at least as important as biographical data in determining parole success or failure.[81]

SUGGESTED READINGS

Amos, William E., & Charles L. Newman, eds. *Parole: Legal Issues, Decision-making, Research.* New York: Aberdeen Press, 1976.

Arluke, Nat R. "A Summary of Parole Rules." *Crime and Delinquency*, 15:267–74, 1969.

Arnold, William R. *Juveniles on Parole.* New York: Random House, 1970.

Bailey, Walter C. "Correctional Outcome: An Evaluation of 100 Reports." *Journal of Criminal Law, Criminology, and Police Science*, 57:153–60, 1966.

Barnett, J. D. "The Grounds of Pardon." *Journal of Criminal Law and Criminology*, 17:490–530, 1927.

Cohen, Bernard, with the assistance of Stephen H. Leinen. *Research on Criminal Justice Organizations: The Sentencing Process.* Santa Monica, Calif.: Rand, 1976.

---

[79] Daniel Glaser, "A Reconsideration of Some Parole Prediction Factors," *American Sociological Review*, 19:335–41, 1954; and idem, "The Efficacy of Alternative Approaches to Parole Prediction," *American Sociological Review*, 20:283–7, 1955.

[80] William R. Arnold, "A Functional Explanation of Recidivism," *Journal of Criminal Law, Criminology, and Police Science*, 56:212–20, 1965; and idem, *Juveniles on Parole: A Sociological Perspective* (New York: Random House, 1970), pp. 96–105, 111–32. See also Joseph W. Rogers, "Parole Prediction in Three Dimensions: Theory, Prediction, and Perception," *Sociology and Social Research*, 52:377–91, 1968; and Thomas J. Duggan and Charles V. Dean, "Statistical Interaction and Parole Prediction," *Social Forces*, 48:45–9, 1969.

[81] Greenberg, "The Incapacitative Effect of Imprisonment," p. 549.

Doleschal, Eugene, & Gilbert Geis. *Graduated Release*. Washington: Government Printing Office, 1971.

Fogel, David. *We Are the Living Proof: The Justice Model for Corrections*. Cincinnati: W. H. Anderson, 1975.

Gaylin, Willard. "No Exit—The Turf of the Federal Parole Board Is a Landscape of Illogic." *Harper's Magazine*, 243:86–94, 1971.

Gottfredson, Don M., & Kelley B. Ballard, Jr. "Differences in Parole Decisions Associated with Decision-Makers." *Journal of Research in Crime and Delinquency*, 3:112–19, 1966.

Kassebaum, Gene, David A. Ward, & Daniel M. Wilner. *Prison Treatment and Parole Survival: An Empirical Assessment*. New York: John Wiley, 1971.

Lipton, Douglas, Robert M. Martinson, & Judith Wilks. *The Effectiveness of Correctional Treatment*. New York: Praeger, 1975.

Martin, John P., & D. Webster. *Social Consequences of Conviction*. London: Heinemann, 1971.

Martinson, Robert M. "What Works: Questions and Answers About Prison Reform." *The Public Interest*, 35:22–54, 1974.

Martinson, Robert M., Gene G. Kassebaum, & David A. Ward. "A Critique of Research in Parole." *Federal Probation*, 28:34–8, 1964.

McCleary, Richard. "How Structural Variables Constrain the Parole Officer's Use of Discretionary Powers." *Social Problems*, 23:209–25, 1975.

Meyer, Charles H. Z. "A Half-Century of Federal Probation and Parole." *Journal of Criminal Law, Criminology, and Police Science*, 42:707–28, 1952.

Moran, F. A. "The Origins of Parole." *National Probation Yearbook*, 1945, pp. 71–98.

Neithercutt, M. G. "Parole Violation Patterns and Commitment Offense." *Journal of Research in Crime and Delinquency*, 9:87–98, 1972.

Schoonmaker, Meyressa H. "Women in Probation and Parole." *Crime and Delinquency*, 21:109–15, 1975.

Scott, Joseph E. *Ex-offenders as Parole Officers: The Parole Officer Aide Program in Ohio*. Lexington, Mass.: Lexington Books, 1975.

Shover, Neal, William B. Bankston, & J. William Gurley. "Responses of the Criminal Justice System to Legislation Providing More Severe Threatened Sanctions." *Criminology*, 14:483–500, 1977.

Sklar, Ronald B. "Law and Practice in Probation and Parole Revocation Hearings." *Journal of Criminal Law, Criminology, and Police Science*, 55:175–98, 1964.

Soothill, Keith. *The Prisoner's Release: A Study of the Employment of Ex-prisoners*. London: Allen and Unwin, 1974.

Stanley, David T. *Prisoners Among Us: The Problems of Parole*. Washington: Brookings Institution, 1976.

Takagi, Paul, & James Robison. "The Parole Violator: An Organizational Reject." *Journal of Research in Crime and Delinquency*, 6:78–86, 1969.

Von Hirsch, Andrew. *Doing Justice: The Choice of Punishments*. New York: Hill and Wang, 1976.

West, Donald, ed. *The Future of Parole*. London: Duckworth, 1972.

Wilkins, Leslie T. "Equity and Republican Justice." *Annals of the American Academy of Political and Social Science*, 423:152–61, 1976.

26

Prevention of Crime and Delinquency

We have already noted, several times, that two general systems for reducing the frequency of delinquency and crime have been tried. One system is concerned with reducing the amount of repeated crime, the other with reducing the frequency of first crimes. There are hundreds of variations in the procedures and policies used within each of these two systems, but they can be divided into three categories—*punitive methods, defense methods, and interventionist methods.*

Punitive methods of reacting to delinquency and crime are all based on the assumption that inflicting severe pain on lawbreakers both reforms those who are punished (specific deterrence) and frightens others so much that they do not commit first crimes (general deterrence). Most legislation aimed at doing something dramatic about a crime problem that has been publicized—for example, a "wave" of rapes or robberies or kidnappings—simply attempts to increase the certainty or severity of punishment.

The segregation of criminals by locking them behind bars so they cannot commit many crimes against outsiders is a good example of the many methods of defending against criminals. In principle, the defense methods do not punish criminals and do not try to intervene in the processes generating crime and criminal behavior. In practice, as we have seen, it is often difficult to determine whether criminals are intentionally hurt because the pain is assumed to have some deterrent value, or are unintentionally hurt as a mere adjunct to incapacitating them. The uncertainty is most striking in policies regarding imprisonment, but it may also be seen in other policies. Thus, if a thief's right hand is cut off, the criminal will no longer be in good shape to steal (defense), but the amputation ceremony also is assumed to hurt so much that the thief will be afraid to steal again, and to frighten others so much that they will not steal for the first time. Similarly, killing criminals is a defense against repeated crime but the method is called capital *punishment*, probably because it is assumed to have a general deterrent effect. Other measures—such as lighting the streets, searching airline passengers, and keeping citizens under surveillance—are concerned with reducing opportunities for crime but also with increasing the certainty of punishment for anyone who commits crime. Still other defense measures are more purely nonpunitive. These include locking doors and windows, outlawing guns, putting valuables in strong boxes, building fences and walls, and packaging small retail items in boxes so large they are difficult to shoplift.[1]

Interventionist methods are based on the observation that mere negative action (punishment) and mere neutrality (defense) are not enough. Rather, as we have already noted, the assumption is that criminality and crime rates can be reduced significantly only by determining the conditions that produce them and then changing those conditions. Treatment methods based on the medical model assume that criminals are sick or maladjusted and thus in need of a "cure." Alternatively, probation, parole, diversion programs, halfway houses, and work-release schemes are all designed, in part, to implement the assumption that if criminals are to change there must be interaction between them and persons who appreciate and support the values the lawmakers have tried to establish and preserve by means of the criminal law. As to reducing the frequency of first crimes, numerous policies have been implemented following the observation that, though punishment of criminals has educative effects on noncriminals, this policy must be supplemented by interventionist methods of developing "moral character" in the family, school, and religious institution. More generally, interventionist methods assume that high crime rates are a product of economic, political, and social organization, and that it is therefore rather silly to leave this organization intact and hope to reduce crime rates either by punishing the criminals produced by it, or by defending against them.

Because punishment, defense, and intervention are all concerned with reducing the amount of repeated crime as well as the amount of first crime, all are said to be concerned with crime prevention. Crime is prevented when criminals are so terrorized that they reform, and crime is prevented when other citizens are so terrorized that they are afraid to commit crimes. Crime also is prevented when criminals are executed or kept behind locked doors and steel bars, and when citizens lock up their valuables and themselves, thus frustrating other citizens who would behave criminally. Finally, crime is prevented when the personal and social relationships of criminals are changed in ways such that criminal behavior

[1] See Clarence R. Jeffery, *Crime Prevention Through Environmental Design* (Beverly Hills, Calif.: Sage Publications, 1971); Oscar Newman, *Defensible Space: Design for Improvement of Security in Urban Residential Areas* (New York: Macmillan, 1972); J. L. Grenough, "Crime Prevention: A New Approach," *Journal of Police Science and Administration*, 2:339–43, 1974; and P. Mayhew, R. V. G. Clarke, A. Sturman, and J. M. Hough, *Crime as Opportunity*, Home Office Research Study No. 34 (London: Her Majesty's Stationery Office, 1976).

is extinguished, and crime is prevented when the economic, political, and social order that generates high crime rates is modified so that it no longer does so.

The previous chapters have presented many arguments and much evidence in support of the proposition that, of the three methods, intervention is, or could be, the most effective system for reducing crime rates. For this reason, we will be primarily concerned here with *crime prevention* only in the interventionist sense. Thus some criminals might be *reformed* by punishment, but we will be concerned with how repeated criminal behavior can be prevented by using nonpunitive methods to change criminals. Also, crime rates might be reduced if the citizenry were effectively *deterred* by agents of the state, but we will be concerned with the more realistic alternative, in democratic societies, of how first crimes can be prevented by nonpunitive methods based on comprehension of crime causation. Further, criminal behavior and crime might be *frustrated* by various measures of defense, but we will be concerned with interventionist methods that are hoped to reduce the need for so many bars, locks, and surveillance procedures. In short, *crime prevention* here will be taken to mean nonpunitive means for reducing the amount of repeated crime and for forestalling first crimes.

PREVENTION POLICIES

As we find out more about criminal behavior and crime, we shall have a better basis for interventionist policies. These policies, if carried out consistently, would protect society from crime in three ways.

First, they would secure the segregation of persons who have demonstrated their dangerousness by persistent involvement in serious crime. Segregation will not reform these offenders, but it will protect society by incapacitating them and by indicating disapproval of serious deviance from legal norms. Apparently, in the present state of politics and behavioral science, we neither can change some persistent offenders nor significantly modify the social situations spawning them. We can only defend ourselves from this small category of dangerous persons, and segregation is the most extreme measure of defense. It must be stressed that the persons to be detained must have *demonstrated* their dangerousness. *Predicted* dangerousness must unequivocally be excluded as a criterion for social defense because no prediction instrument—scientific or clinical—for predicting dangerousness has been devised.[2] Moreover, such an instrument never will be devised; the assumption that dangerousness can accurately be predicted in individual cases is, like "treatment" and "cure" theory, based on a misconception of the nature of criminality and of personality. We must use each person's track record. All other methods of determining dangerousness have tended to be political—they

---

[2]See Andrew von Hirsch, "Prediction of Criminal Conduct and Preventive Confinement of Convicted Persons," *Buffalo Law Review*, 21:717–58, 1972; and Arthur S. Elstein, "Clinical Judgment: Psychological Research and Medical Practice," *Science*, 194:696–700, 1976.

select out for severity the poorest and least powerful persons in a criminal population.

Second, these policies would integrate into law-abiding society a larger proportion of citizens, including the vast majority of those who have committed crimes but have not demonstrated that they are serious threats to the anticriminal culture. As we noted earlier, social control stems from the recognition and rewards secured by lawful conduct—or apparently lawful conduct—rather than from direct fear of punishment.[3] The effective deterrent is not the fear of legal penalties as such, but the fear of loss of status. But this is not really fear. Rather, the conforming person is one who feels that doing certain things is unthinkable. The policies for crime prevention must, if they are to be effective, give more citizens a stake in conformity to the statutes that outlaw criminal conduct.

Third, these policies would define and identify the social situations from which crimes are most likely to issue, and would make it possible to attack and eliminate those social situations. A low crime rate is a desirable social objective. But rather than trying to smash the economic, political, and social attitudes, conditions, and injustices that generate crime, political leaders have, by and large, preferred to rely on fear. Terror seems to be cheaper but it is not. Moreover, the stress on punishment distracts from the need for developing the conditions necessary to domestic tranquility. If attitudes of appreciation for certain values could be developed, punitive criminal laws pertaining to those values would be unnecessary. For example, if everyone in a society had an equal stake in the concept of private property, then trying to terrorize people into respecting property rights would be obsolete.

Thus crime would be reduced by absorbing those criminals who can and should be absorbed, segregating for social defense but not punishment those who cannot be absorbed, and eliminating the conditions that are most conducive to crime and thus produce the need to absorb some criminals and segregate others.

Vigorous implementation of such policies would be as much evidence of social disapproval of crime as would punishment. It is approbation and disapprobation, rather than punishment of individual criminals, that forestall crime among the large majority of citizens, including the vast majority of the poor and the powerless, from whose ranks most criminals come.

The police officer's uniform and armament, the drama of the courtroom, the prison, and most other criminal-justice institutions and processes are now symbols of authoritarianism, coercion, condemnation, and rejection. These symbolic messages influence how we see criminal-justice agencies and also determine what they become. For example, concrete walls, armed men on catwalks, and cages of reinforced steel suggest that criminals are uncommitted, alien, wild. They therefore are to be isolated and punished by concrete walls, armed men on catwalks, and cages of reinforced steel.

[3]See the discussion in Chapter 15, above.

A very different perception would be both promoted and supported by an explicit and displayed process of social control that emphasized other aspects of the complex reality of crime. If the control system put more emphasis on social absorption of criminal behavior, crime would still be called crime, meaning that certain conduct would be condemned. But the stress would be on forgiveness, on the *similarities* between criminals and others, not on their differences. This is not unrealistic because, after all, most people who commit bad acts are not intrinsically bad. And even now most crimes—including so-called serious ones—do not in fact lead to condemnation and punishment. Unreported, undetected, or unrecorded, they are absorbed by the community, and their perpetrators are absorbed with them. Additionally, most people who have at one time engaged in predatory, damaging behavior no longer do so, whether they were punished or not.

RECIDIVISM

As our discussion of probation, prisons, and parole has shown, a large proportion of the offenders under the care of any agency are recidivists. In a special study of about 256,000 persons arrested in 1970–1975, the FBI found that at least 64 percent had been arrested on a prior charge. Fifty-seven percent of those arrested for murder, 74 percent of those arrested for robbery, 53 percent of those arrested for burglary, 82 percent of those arrested for forgery, and 45 percent of those arrested for rape had been convicted of some prior charge.[4] Similarly, of the persons arrested for robbery in New York City in 1970, 86 percent had been arrested previously on a felony charge; for burglary, the percentage with at least one prior felony arrest was 70; for homicide 65, and for felonious assault 50.[5] About 85 percent of the offenders admitted to the prisons and reformatories of Massachusetts in 1971, and about 84 percent of the male felons admitted to California prisons in 1973 had previously been confined in a jail, prison, or institution for juveniles.[6] Similar rates have been compiled for several European countries.

This high rate of recidivism is extremely important, for it means that a large proportion of the crimes committed can be attributed to repeaters. A large part of the work of police, courts, and penal and reformatory institutions must be devoted to recidivists. Moreover, recidivists take more than their share of the time and efforts of agency personnel. Recidivists are overrepresented among the failures

---

[4] *Uniform Crime Reports, 1975* (Washington: Government Printing Office, 1976), pp. 42–3.

[5] Ruel Shinnar and Shlomo Shinnar, ' The Effects of the Criminal Justice System on the Control of Crime: A Quantitative Approach," *Law and Society Review*, 9:581–611, 1975. Much lower proportions of recidivists were found among the adults arrested and charged for murder and manslaughter, aggravated assault, robbery, and sex offenses in Franklin County (Columbus) Ohio in 1973; see Stephan Van Dine, Simon Dinitz, and John Conrad, "The Incapacitation of the Dangerous Offender: A Statistical Experiment," *Journal of Research in Crime and Delinquency*, 14:22–34, 1977.

[6] Massachusetts Department of Correction, *Criminal Statistics, 1971* (Boston: Author, 1972), table B5; *California Prisoners, 1973* (Sacramento: Department of Corrections, 1974), p. 22.

on probation and parole, and among prisoner populations. Massive walls, steel cages, and electronic locks are needed only for dangerous recidivists.

The persistence of criminals in their crimes may be explained either in terms of the characteristics and conditions of offenses and offenders or in terms of the inadequacy of agencies of reformation. The first involves a social psychology of the recidivist, the second an analysis of the techniques of reformation.

Social Psychology of Recidivism

One of the findings of the prediction studies is that, with some exceptions, the social situations associated with criminality in the first place are also associated with persistence in crime. Persons who live in areas having low crime rates, who are reared in nondelinquent homes, and who have a comfortable scale of living are least likely to return to crime after any method of punishment, intervention, or treatment. They, like persons with minor physical ailments, probably "cure" themselves. Repeaters frequently were reared in deteriorated areas, in homes where destitution, vice, and criminality were usual, in isolation from law-abiding groups of the community. Several studies of delinquents indicate that nonrecidivists, as compared to recidivists, are older, have older mothers, are better educated, have fewer known delinquencies, are more intelligent, and are less likely to have a father with a criminal record.[7] Blacks have a higher rate of recidivism than whites, males have a higher rate of recidivism than females, and urban-dwellers have a higher rate than rural-dwellers.

One common explanation of recidivism is stated in terms of simple habit formation; persistence in crime is merely persistence of habits. Some of the habits were formed prior to the official reaction, others during the course of the processing. Drug addiction and drunkenness are illustrations of offenses that persist after official treatment as the result of habit formation. It is doubtful, however, whether the term *habit formation* is an adequate explanation of the persistence even of drug addiction or drunkenness. This concept implies physiological mechanisms and leaves the social conditions in obscurity. Both the recidivism of any individual and the high rate of recidivism in some groups are much more complex than is ordinarily conceived when explained in terms of habit formation.

Similarly, persistence in criminal behavior has been attributed to personality traits, most frequently to pathological traits of personality such as mental defectiveness, emotional instability, egocentrism, and psychosis. Personality characteristics, whether pathological or not, tend to persist in spite of the punishment or treatment currently given in any of the correctional processes.

[7] Dugald S. Arbuckle and Lawrence Litwack, "A Study of Recidivism Among Juvenile Delinquents," *Federal Probation*, 24:45–8, 1960; and Jerome Laulicht, "Problems of Statistical Research and Its Correlates," *Journal of Criminal Law, Criminology, and Police Science*, 54:163–74, 1963.

Neither first crimes nor repeated crimes, however, have been found to be associated with any specific traits of personality.

Isolation from law-abiding society has been suggested as another explanation of recidivism. Ordinarily the offender acquires no facility in the manners of law-abiding groups and has little opportunity to come in contact with them after or during the period of official handling. Upon discharge by an agency, offenders are restricted in their group memberships by their occupational skills, table manners, methods of conversation, manners in recreation and in wearing clothes, and other characteristics. Offenders who lived previously in law-abiding groups are likely to be ostracized, while those who lived previously in criminal groups may acquire status by further crime. By their manners, skills, life styles, stigma, and other traits, they are confined to social groups that reinforce their criminal behavior. If they get out of these groups, they will do so slowly. This isolation from law-abiding groups occurs more frequently after imprisonment than after other methods of punishment or correction, but it exists to some extent in connection with every method.

At the same time, criminality and the methods of dealing with crime stimulate criminals to form associations, loyalties, and friendships with each other, and as a result their attitudes and other behavior patterns tend to persist. The offender who manifests a desire to change is called "yellow," "rat," "square," or "stool pigeon" by associates. Even violence or threats of violence may be used to keep a person a criminal. Parolees often say that while on parole they have dozens of opportunities for crime suggested to them but receive few offers of legitimate work. Of great significance in this connection is the criminal's feeling of obligation and loyalty to criminals who have given assistance in the past.[8] Duffee and Fitch have made the following proposal about intervention in the processes that isolate offenders and thus contribute to their recidivism:

It is possible that the final solution to the problem of criminality will be found in the community. It appears that no significant change in the criminal justice system will take place without citizen influence and citizen participation. It is becoming apparent that "experts" and professionals in the field of corrections lack the means by which we can either reduce recidivism or rehabilitate offenders. The present system cannot function in a meaningful way as long as it remains isolated from the community. Attempts are now being made to end this isolation and permit a greater interaction between the system and the community. It has been discovered that the community can be used as a change agent. As a result of this discovery, less faith is being placed in the traditional model for corrections based on the segregation of the offender. . . . Not only does the end to isolation have a significant impact on the way in which offenders are treated; it also opens to the

[8]See John Irwin and Donald R. Cressey, "Thieves, Convicts and the Inmate Culture," *Social Problems*, 10:142–55, 1962; and Bill Chambliss. ed., *Box Man: A Professional Thief's Journey* (New York: Harper and Row, 1972).

scrutiny of the public and the courts a system which has been favored by a "hands-off" policy and left to function in an atmosphere of almost complete autonomy.[9]

Another explanation of the persistence of the criminal is found in the criminality and near-criminality in the general society. Just as a person would secure no satisfaction from smoking in church because a church is not a suitable situation for smoking, an offender can feel comfortable in committing crimes only in situations where that behavior has become customary. The urban areas with high rates of crime and delinquency are also areas with high rates of recidivism in crime and delinquency. Mack found that among the delinquents residing on the street with the highest crime rate in a Scottish city, 29 percent became adult criminals; the comparable figure for all Scottish delinquents is less than 5 percent.[10] Patterns of dishonesty, however, are prevalent outside deteriorated areas as well as within them. Advertisements of toothpaste, medicines, and hundreds of other commodities are notoriously fraudulent in their claims and suggestions. The bribery of purchasing agents by business concerns is almost universal in many trades. In some lines of business, ruthlessness in making money has become an important part of the business code. Trade unions have become involved in racketeering. Political graft and corruption are widespread. Evasion of taxes is commonplace. Thus lying, cheating, fraud, exploitation, violation of trust, and graft are prevalent in the general society. Offenders who become noncriminals must be superior to the society in which they live.[11]

INTERVENTION

The second general type of explanation of recidivism is stated in terms of the inadequacy of the methods of intervention. If offenders were changed by the first agency with which they came in contact, the crime rate would be greatly reduced. As our previous discussion has indicated, every major policy (e.g., corporal punishment, fines, imprisonment, probation, and parole) has resulted in a large proportion of failures. Further, the specific methods used in probation, prisons, and parole have had a high failure rate, too. Such failures may be due to the inefficiency of the theories of change that are used, or they may be due to the inability to apply the theories when adequate facilities and personnel are not available.[12] In the following review, we shall be concerned with the theories of

[9]David Duffee and Robert Fitch, *An Introduction to Corrections: A Policy and Systems Approach* (Pacific Palisades, Calif.: Goodyear, 1976), p. 278.

[10]John Mack, "Full-time Miscreants, Delinquent Neighbourhoods, and Criminal Networks," *British Journal of Sociology*, 15:38–53, 1964.

[11]See David Matza and Gresham M. Sykes, "Juvenile Delinquency and Subterranean Values," *American Sociological Review*, 26:712–19, 1961. See also David Matza, *Delinquency and Drift* (New York: John Wiley, 1964); and idem, *Becoming Deviant* (Englewood Cliffs, N.J.: Prentice-Hall, 1969).

[12]See Joel Meyer, "Reflections on Some Theories of Punishment," *Journal of Criminal Law, Criminology, and Police Science*, 59:595–99, 1968; and Douglas Lipton, Robert M. Martinson, and Judith Wilks, *The Effectiveness of Correctional Treatment* (New York: Praeger, 1975).

change and the technical policies based on such theories, rather than with personnel and facilities.

Mechanical Methods

Until the present century, almost all attempts to change criminals were mass methods designed to modify the criminal in some mechanical manner. In the light of contemporary psychological and sociological knowledge, these methods of reformation are obsolete. However, they maintain a certain popularity among laymen, and they continue to be used, on an individual basis, by many correctional workers.

The classical theory was that reformation would occur if enough pain were inflicted on the offender. This was a strictly hedonistic theory, and it is still held by considerable numbers in the general public. It has generally been discarded by psychologists and sociologists. Pain clearly is effective in modifying behavior, but the value is more or less completely balanced by the antagonism, isolation, and group loyalties it produces. Further, punishing offenders does not change the situations that produce criminality. In some cases there is not much more justification for punishing a criminal than for punishing a person with tuberculosis or smallpox.

A second method designed to change criminals was meditation, generally enforced by isolation from all or almost all other persons. The theory was that crime was due to a failure to think, and that meditation would develop remorse and repentance. Early in the nineteenth century Mease made a clear-cut statement of this method of producing reformation. He maintained that repentance was produced by:

(1) A tiresome state of mind from idle seclusion; (2) self-condemnation arising from deep, long-continued and poignant reflections upon a guilty life. All our endeavors, therefore, ought to be directed to the production of that state of mind, which will cause a convict to concentrate his thoughts upon his forlorn condition, to abstract himself from the world, and to think of nothing except the suffering and the privations he endures, the result of his crimes. Such a state of mind is totally incompatible with the least mechanical operation, but is only to be brought about, if ever, by complete mental and bodily insulation.[13]

Some prisoners have testified that during the period of solitude they thought over their careers, and that this resulted in decisions to desist from crime. In general, however, this procedure has not been effective. Many years ago Hobhouse and Brockway accumulated considerable documentary evidence that isolation results in deterioration and degradation, not reformation.[14] Saleilles maintained that

---

[13] James Mease, *Observations on the Penitentiary System and Penal Code of Pennsylvania* (Philadelphia, 1828), p. 73. Quoted in Francis C. Gray, *Prison Discipline in America* (Boston: Little, Brown, 1847), p. 30.
[14] Stephen Hobhouse and A. Fenner Brockway, *English Prisons Today, Being the Report of the Prison System Enquiry Committee* (London: Longmans, Green, 1922), pp. 476–589.

"The constant thought of remorse and, still more, of shame, becomes the greatest hindrance to individual regeneration."[15]

A third method, used in earlier and in later times, was moralizing. By tracts, sermons, and personal exhortations, in the name of God, mother, and country, appeals were made to the offenders. These exhortations generally produce antagonism in prisoners. Exhortation is an important method of social control when it is used by members of a group upon other members of the same group. It is seldom effective when used by one group upon another group.

A fourth method asked the offender to sign a pledge or in some other way make resolutions to live a law-abiding life. This method was based on the assumption that change can be accomplished merely by inducing offenders to "make up their minds" to change. The fallacy of this assumption is abundantly illustrated every New Year's Day. Personal change involves a complex array of social relationships and reinforcements that is not altered by resolutions.

A fifth method of reformation was mechanical habituation, produced by various punitive regimes, including hard and dreary work in the prison and rigid prison discipline. Bentham justified constant surveillance of the offender on the ground that it results in the formation of good habits:

To render a man totally unable to do mischief, you have only to keep him constantly in sight, after depriving him of such offensive instruments as would render him dangerous to you. Place a man by himself, in an iron cage, for example, and keep him every hour and every minute of his life in sight, and it is evident you can prevent him from doing mischief, whether by making his escape to prey again upon society, or by exerting his powers to any pernicious effect where you have him confined.

To place criminals then under perpetual inspection is the object, the all-powerful object, which it is required to accomplish. If this can be done, without loading society with exorbitant expense, the problem respecting a better disposal of criminals than killing them is already resolved.[16]

Bentham's plan included a prison constructed in circular form with a central guard tower, from which one guard could look into all the cells and thus keep all the prisoners under constant surveillance. When this prison architecture was used in the prison at Joliet, Illinois, it was found that the construction that enabled the guard to watch all of the prisoners also enabled any prisoner to watch the guard, and therefore prisoners could do whatever mischief they pleased while the guard's back was turned. In addition, the condition of constant mutual surveillance produced antagonism in both the guard and the prisoners. The panopticon plan has been abandoned.

These five methods are examples of the efforts to change criminals in the past.

[15]Raymond Saleilles, *The Individualization of Punishment*, trans. from the second French edition (1908) by Rachel Szold Jastrow (Boston: Little, Brown, 1911), p. 195. This book was originally published in Paris in 1898.
[16]Jeremy Bentham, "On Houses of Safe-Custody and Industry," *Philanthropist*, 1:229, 1811.

Although they have carried over to the present, they reveal the importance of knowing more about human behavior than was known in the last century.

The Clinical Method

Strictly speaking, adherence to the policy of intervention does not imply the use of any specific technique or theory. Rather, commitment to this policy means only that those conditions considered as causing criminals to behave criminally will be considered in the attempt to change them. Attention is focused on the criminal rather than on the crime. Generally, an attempt is made to diagnose the cause of criminality and to base the technique of reformation on the diagnosis. An analogy with the *method* of diagnosis, prescription, and therapy for medical patients is apparent.[17]

The clinical method of changing criminals has extended this medical analogy, and it has become similar to clinical medicine in theory and content as well as in procedures. Criminality is considered as a defect or disorder, or as a symptom of a defect or disorder, which can be treated on an individual basis without reference to the offender's groups, just as biological disorders can be treated on an individual basis. An extreme position in this regard is that criminality actually *is* a biological disorder, treatable by modification of the physiology or anatomy of the individual through lobotomy, castration, interference with glandular functioning, or something else. However, the much more popular view is that criminality is an individual psychological disorder that may or may not have a strictly biological basis. According to this view, the essential difference between clinical medicine and the proper system for treatment of criminals lies in the nature of the disorder being treated—clinical medicine deals with organic disorders, clinical treatment for criminals with psychological disorders, with "mental disease." The clinical method is thus based on an individualistic, psychiatric theory of criminality.

The essence of the popular individualistic theory is that criminality is an expression of emotional disorders or conflicts in the makeup of the individual. Criminals may be considered as persons who are unable to canalize or sublimate "primitive," antisocial impulses or tendencies; or they may be considered as expressing symbolically in criminal behavior some unconscious wish or urge created by an early traumatic emotional experience; or they may be considered as possessing some other kind of defective personality component.[18] In any event, the implication for treatment is that the internal emotional maladjustment must be eradicated before the external, behavioral maladjustment (criminality) will be corrected.[19]

---

[17] See the discussion in Chap. 15, above. See also Theodore S. Donaldson and Gail L. Zellman, "Programs Based on Psychology and Sociology," in *Intervening with Convicted Serious Juvenile Offenders*, ed. Dale Mann (Washington: Government Printing Office, 1976), pp. 19–31.

[18] See R. C. Marohn, O. Dalle-Molle, D. Ofler, and E. Ostrov, "A Hospital Riot: Its Determinants and Implications for Treatment," *American Journal of Psychiatry*, 130:631–6, 1973.

[19] See Don C. Gibbons, *Changing the Lawbreaker* (Englewood Cliffs, N.J.: Prentice-Hall, 1965), pp. 143–57.

The specific techniques for changing criminals, then, make no attempt to modify the offender's group relations in any direct way. Rather, the techniques used for treating criminals are the same as the techniques used for treating emotionally maladjusted noncriminals. The many clinical techniques for administering therapy to emotionally disturbed persons cannot be reviewed here. Psychoanalysis stresses internal states originating in the distant past, but other forms of psychotherapy, transactional analysis, gestalt therapy, counseling programs, and other clinical methods focus on present experiences. Generally, the emotional disorders that are thought to produce criminality are now usually recognized to be the result of social conditions, but the treatment is aimed at modification and correction of the criminal's purported emotional maladjustments rather than the social conditions. For example, rejection by parents might be considered the source of the emotional disorder that produced a child's delinquency, yet the therapy might be directed exclusively at the emotional disorder rather than at the social relationships in the family. The parental rejection is considered as having produced a defect in the individual's personality, a defect that will continue to direct and determine overt behavior until such time as it is modified by treatment. Behavioristic approaches, however, are not based on the assumption that emotional disorders precede delinquent and criminal conduct, and they rely primarily on response-reinforcement techniques to alter the occurrence of delinquency or criminality itself.[20]

One clinical system or technique for modification of criminality through modification of emotional maladjustments or disorders can be broken down into five steps or stages. Although this analysis greatly oversimplifies the procedures used in clinical therapy, it illustrates the basic operations performed. First, in discussions with a therapist, criminals are urged to talk freely about their personal criminality and the conditions they think are responsible for it. Second, the therapist identifies a character defect. This defect may be labeled "feelings of guilt," "resentment of authority," or any of a host of other terms. Third, this interpretation of the interview materials is communicated to the criminal, providing "insight" into the "basic motivation" for the person's criminal behavior. Fourth, the criminal is urged to recall life experiences in an attempt to discover the original source of the emotional defect. Fifth, the subject's awareness of the source of the emotional disorder may alone "cure" that disorder, and "cure" of the disorder, in turn, "cures" the criminality. In some cases however, merely raising unconscious emotional circuits to the surface of consciousness so that they are observed by the individuals in whom they occur will not be sufficient for

---

[20] See W. Davidson and E. Seidman, "Studies of Behavior Modification and Juvenile Delinquency: A Review, Methodological Critique, and Social Perspective," *Psychological Bulletin*, 81:998–1011, 1974; W. Gaylin and H. Blatte, "Behavior Modification in Prisons," *American Criminal Law Review*, 13:11–36; and S. B. Stoltz, L. Wienckowski, and B. S. Brown, "Behavior Modification: A Perspective on Critical Issues," *American Psychologist*, 30:1027–48, 1975.

eradication of the emotional defects produced by these traumatic experiences, and further guidance and counseling may be necessary.

This system may be seen in the following description, by a psychiatrist, of psychotherapy and "intensive treatment" for prisoners:

> The purpose of this discipline is the uncovering of unconscious material which has been expressed in the form of disordered behavior, of disabling subjective symptoms, or demonstrable derangements of function. This material is uncovered in order to bring it to the awareness of the person suffering from the disability, and for the purpose of helping him to alter favorably his behavior patterns; of effecting as deeply ranging a change as is possible and is necessary, of the disposition and expression of his impulses. . . . To put it differently, the aim of this therapy would be to assist a person toward the goal of socially acceptable behavior, through his understanding of the unconscious purposes served by his former unacceptable behavior.[21]

The Group-Relations Method

Modern sociological and psychological discoveries about the nature of personality have provided an alternative theory on which to base diagnosis and treatment of criminals. The personality is viewed as "situation determined" rather than "trait determined"; the behavior of an individual is said to be the product of group relationships rather than of the presence of specific individual traits or characteristics. The traits an individual exhibits are the properties of groups, not of the individual alone. About a half-century ago and about a quarter-century ago, John Dewey and Dorwin Cartwright, respectively, expressed this viewpoint as follows:

> To change the "working character" or will of another, we have to alter objective conditions which enter into his habits. Our own schemes of judgment, of assigning blame and praise, or awarding punishment and honor are part of these conditions. . . . We cannot change habit directly: that notion is magic. But we can change it indirectly by modifying conditions, by an intelligent selecting and weighing of the objects which engage attention and which influence the fulfillment of desires.[22]

> The behavior, attitudes, beliefs and values of the individual are all firmly grounded in the groups to which he belongs. How aggressive or cooperative a person is, how much self-respect or self-confidence he has, how energetic and productive his work is, what he aspires to, what he believes to be true and good, whom he loves or hates, and what beliefs and prejudices he holds—all these characteristics are highly determined by the individual's group membership. In a real sense, they are properties of groups and of the relationships between people. Whether they change or resist change will, therefore, be greatly influenced by the nature of these groups. Attempts to change them must be concerned with the dynamics of groups.[23]

[21] David Sherbon, "Definition of 'Intensive Treatment,' " in *Intensive Treatment Program: Second Annual Report*, by Harold B. Bradley and Jack D. Williams (Sacramento, Calif.: Department of Corrections, 1958), pp. 23–4.

[22] John Dewey, *Human Nature and Conduct* (New York: Henry Holt, 1922), pp. 19–20.

[23] Dorwin Cartwright, "Achieving Change in People: Some Applications of Group Dynamics Theory," *Human Relations*, 4:381–92, 1951.

In criminology, the differential-association theory is consistent with this conception of the nature of individual behavior. Also, as was pointed out in Chapter 15, the general implication of the differential-association theory for reformation of criminals is that relations in the culture of law-abiding groups must be promoted, and relations in procriminal culture must be discouraged. Negatively, this means that criminality cannot be modified to any significant extent in a clinic, for clinical methods do not deal with group relations.

Although correctional programs are including more and more provisions for contacts with anticriminal culture, a specific set of techniques for changing criminals by this method has not been worked out. Instead, the contacts provided have been promoted in a rather haphazard fashion, often with no explicit acknowledgment of the group-relations theory of criminality and change. Perhaps a general statement of some principles consistent with the group-relations theory of behavior in general and with differential-association theory in particular will provide a basis for explicit attempts to utilize the group-relations principle in correctional programs. Research and experimentation may eventually produce precise, detailed rules of action for correctional workers interested in achieving change in criminals, but current knowledge of the techniques of change is very scanty. The following statement, adapted from a more general statement by Dorwin Cartwright,[24] should be regarded as tentative, as directing attention to areas where research and experimentation should prove fruitful:

(1) Criminals who are to be changed and the persons who are to exert influence in this direction must have a strong sense of belonging to the same group. The two general processes are *alienation* of the criminal from groups that support values conducive to criminality and, concurrently, *assimilation* of the criminal into groups supporting values conducive to law-abiding behavior. The latter process can be accomplished only when the social distance between the criminals and the change agents is small enough to permit a genuine "we" feeling. Consequently, the reformers and the reformees should be similar in social status and ethnic backgrounds; ideally, they would be similar in all respects except attitudes toward law violation. Neither the view that all criminals are "outsiders" nor the view that correctional workers are "hoosiers," "screws," or "cops" is conducive to change. However, these two views currently prevail, and it is probably for that reason that nonprofessional persons, such as the family of a person with whom the criminal is in love, often exert more influence than do correctional workers.

(2) The more attractive the group to the criminal, the greater is the influence that the group can exert on the criminal. The group must be so constituted that the criminal desires and can achieve status in it. The reformee must be given recognition for anticriminal and noncriminal behavior. In psychiatric terminology, the group must fill the offender's "unmet needs," "provide an opportunity for ego expansion," and so on. Not all persons are attracted to the same groups, and it

[24] Ibid.

can be safely asserted that few criminals are attracted to groups in which they are made the object of ridicule, hate, sermons, or tear-jerking sympathy. A New York judge sent a man who had shown remarkable organizing ability in the field of crime to oversee the reclamation of large tracts of abandoned farm land. The criminal acquired status in the community by this method, and his opinion of the behavior that was appropriate to the status no longer included crime. He came to think of himself as a useful member of society. Similarly, the provision of material services by the group may serve to attract criminals to a network of anticriminal personal relations. The correctional worker must appeal to criminals with as much skill as salespersons use in appealing to customers, and must produce an effect that will be much more permanent than that produced by salespersons. This appeal must be based on study of the offender's background and past experiences. For example, a delinquent boy who thinks that Boy Scouts are sissies is not likely to join the Scouts. But if he should join, the group probably will change him only very slowly, for he will resist entering into intimate personal relationships with the other boys.

(3) The more relevant the basis of attraction of the group to the reformation of criminals, the greater will be the influence that the group can exert on the criminal's attitudes and values. This means that groups organized largely for the purpose of occupying the criminal's time—such as hobby and recreational groups—will not have the influence of a group organized for the explicit purpose of changing criminals. If the basis of attraction of the group is some tangential interest that the criminal might have (e.g., an interest in music), the criminal's criminality is likely to remain unchanged, while the person's behavior patterns regarding the tangential interest are changed. The reformee might become a criminal educated in music, rather than a noncriminal. A group in which "Criminal A" and some noncriminals join together to change "Criminal B" probably is most effective in changing "Criminal A." This system is sometimes rather inadvertently used in institutions for delinquents, where one of the older children is appointed as "monitor" or "big brother" for each newcomer. The newcomer takes personal troubles to the monitor, and, more significantly, the monitor, even when not consulted, tries to direct and protect the newcomer. The monitor probably benefits more than does his charge. The system also is effective in Alcoholics Anonymous and in Synanon, a self-help organization for drug addicts.[25] It has been tried, in modified form, in several institutions and programs.[26] It probably is at the base of whatever success halfway houses and other

---

[25] Rita Volkman and Donald R. Cressey, "Differential Association and the Rehabilitation of Drug Addicts," *American Journal of Sociology*, 69:129–42, 1963; and Michael M. Jasinsky, "Die Anwendungsmöglichkeit der Theorie der differentiellen Assoziation in der Kriminalpädagogik," *Monatsschrift für Kriminologie und Strafrechtsreform*, 53:238–50, 1970.

[26] See Keith A. Stubblefield and Larry L. Dye, eds., *Offenders as a Correctional Manpower Resource* (Washington: Joint Commission on Correctional Manpower and Training, 1968). See also Andrew Rutherford, "New Careers for Ex-offenders," *Prison Service Journal* (England), 1971, pp. 2–5; and Barry Sugarman, *Daytop Village: A Therapeutic Community* (New York: Holt, Rinehart and Winston, 1974).

programs run by ex-convicts have had. A parolee who becomes a parole officer is likely to assume the attitudes and other behavior patterns of a "square John," not of a "thief."[27]

(4) The greater the prestige of a group member in the eyes of those who are to be reformed, the greater the influence the person can exert. The prestige assigned to a group member may spring from the member's social position outside the group, or it may spring from some attribute or trait the member seems to possess. In assigning prestige, reformees may use criteria different from those used by other reformers.

(5) Strong resistance will be encountered when the efforts to change individual criminals or the criminal members of a group would, if successful, have the result of making them deviate from the norms of the group.[28] The group must be, first of all, a strongly anticriminal group, so that deviation from group norms will be deviation in the direction of criminality. If the reformers are in such a minority—in numbers, influence, or prestige—that exhibition of essentially "antichange" attitudes is the real basis of group cohesion, any reformation of individuals will be extremely unlikely. The offender who understands the social-psychological mechanisms involved in criminal conduct and who has a stake in the prohibitions against that conduct probably will accept anticriminal values more readily than an offender who does not. Sometimes an understanding of the situation can be secured only if offenders' rationalizations, by which they justify criminality and defend themselves, are broken down. Such an understanding can be promoted only by persons who themselves have some understanding of the psychology and sociology of crime.

(6) The source of pressure on the criminal whose change is sought must lie within the group. The group must not rely on criminals to change themselves. So far as the processes are concerned, there is no essential difference between abandoning crime and backsliding in church. Persons who change transfer their loyalties from one group to another. The change is sometimes rapid, sometimes gradual. Often reformees do not repent and resolve to do right. Instead, their behavior is modified by shifts in group relations. Perhaps the most effective group for changing criminals would be one in which status is achieved by exhibition of "prochange" attitudes. That is, those persons who show the most marked tendency toward anticriminal values, attitudes, and behavior would become leaders. Criminality is learned in intimate, personal groups, and noncriminality and anticriminality are learned in similar groups.

This last principle was demonstrated in an early but highly significant

[27]Joseph E. Scott, *Ex-offenders as Parole Officers: The Parole Officer Aide Program in Ohio* (Lexington, Mass.: Lexington Books, 1974). See also Donald R. Cressey, "Social Psychological Foundations for Using Criminals in the Rehabilitation of Criminals," *Journal of Research in Crime and Delinquency*, 2:49–59, 1962.

[28]See Harold H. Kelley and Edmund H. Volkart, "The Resistance to Change of Group-Anchored Attitudes," *American Sociological Review*, 17:453–65, 1952.

experiment with hospitalized drug addicts. When the experiment began, the hospital wards contained an essentially "antichange" culture, and the ward leaders were the older, more experienced addicts. The social organization in the wards was described as follows:

> Pro-social attitudes, such as a desire for psychotherapy or real cooperation with hospital authorities, were frowned upon. Patients who held these beliefs were "squares" or "chickens" and were ostracized by the dominant antisocial group on the ward. On the regular wards, it was found that the bulk of the patients' free time was spent in "breaking up jack pots" (group discussion of past addiction or plans for future use of the drug), group expressions of hatred and contempt for authority (hospital and community), and how to do "easy time" (devices for seducing authority so as to get easy or pleasant jobs in the hospital).[29]

In connection with a group-therapy program, this antichange culture was modified so that prestige was assigned by ward members to persons exhibiting signs of abandoning the use of drugs, rather than to persons exhibiting antichange attitudes:

> Continuous observation of the Treatment Ward revealed a significant change in the subculture developed on this ward. On the Treatment Ward, a premium was placed by the patients "on getting better," as evidenced by realistic relations with other patients on the ward and with authority figures. Group discussions of drugs for their own sake were discouraged. The leaders that evolved were people who could demonstrate by their relations to others that they had utilized and benefited from "treatment." All the patients on this ward were in a [therapy] group. The group was used to explore the personal problems and interpersonal experiences on the ward. . . . [The treatment] ward developed a pro-social therapeutic climate that fostered psychotherapy. This was not true of the other wards of the hospital.[30]

This experiment has great significance for a theory of reformation, for almost all of the participants were reformees. The culture observed among the addicts was not unlike that existing in many prisons, making the task of reformation exceedingly difficult. When the reformees are probationers or released prisoners, the change agent has the advantage of being able to direct reformees to an anticriminal group or to draw them into group relations that are already anticriminal. Under such circumstances, achievement of personal change should be much easier than it is under conditions in which the subculture itself must be changed.[31]

[29] James J. Thorpe and Barnard Smith, "Phases in Group Development in the Treatment of Drug Addicts," *International Journal of Group Psychotherapy*, 3:66–78, 1953. See also Lamar T. Empey and Jerome Rabow, "The Provo Experiment in Delinquency Rehabilitation," *American Sociological Review*, 26:679–95, 1961; and Lamar T. Empey and George E. Newland, "Staff-Inmate Collaboration—A Study of Critical Incidents and Consequences in the Silverlake Experiment," *Journal of Research in Crime and Delinquency*, 5:1–17, 1968.
[30] Ibid.
[31] See Gibbons, *Changing the Lawbreaker*, pp. 163–74.

CRIME PREVENTION

The methods of changing criminals, like the methods of punishment, have not been notably successful in reducing crime rates. They have failed most frequently in changing offenders who have been reared in the situations where crime flourishes most. Thus they have been least effective in dealing with the offenders who come from the most potent crime-breeding situations, from which a considerable proportion of all the criminals who are dealt with by official methods do come.

Moreover, a very small proportion of those who commit crimes have interventionist methods applied to them. Perhaps as few as 10 percent of all crimes result in arrests, and a small percentage of arrests result in official action. This is especially true of fraud, bribery, and similar white-collar crimes that flourish in the business world and the political world, and which almost never result in arrest. The implication of these facts is that the policy of prevention must be emphasized if the crime rate is to be reduced significantly. Punishment and procedures for changing criminals are, at best, methods of coping with the products of a crime-generating social system. It is futile to take individual after individual out of the situations that produce criminals and permit the situations to remain as they were. A case of delinquency or crime is more than a physiological act of an individual. It involves a whole network of social relations. If we deal with this set of social relations, we shall be working to prevent crime.

The superiority of prevention to reformation and to correction by nonpunitive methods may be illustrated in the problem of school discipline. Two generations ago corporal punishment was used with great frequency in the schools, and disorder was generally prevalent in spite of the punishment. Orderly behavior then developed, but it did not develop by increasing the severity and frequency of punishment or by "treating" unruly students. Rather the improvement in the behavior of schoolchildren came as the result of improvement in the teachers and the curricula, and in the gradual development of a tradition of orderly behavior, together with liberality in the criteria of good behavior. The school system was adjusted to the needs of the students much better than it had been previously. It is probable that analogous changes must be made in the social organization before great reductions can be made in crime rates. Even the school must again make readjustments if recent increases in disorderliness are to be checked.

Most criminals, in their earlier stages, are probably much like the person who is dishonest in reporting personal property to the tax assessor. This person would be willing to make an honest report if others made honest reports. Individuals are driven to dishonesty because dishonesty is prevalent. In that sense most criminals probably do not need to be changed or reformed, at least in their earlier stages of criminality. Instead, the prevalence of dishonesty needs to be modified so that individual crime is prevented.[32]

---

[32] See Joseph W. Rogers, *Why Are You Not a Criminal?* (Englewood Cliffs, N.J.: Prentice-Hall, 1977), pp. 115–17.

Almost everything in the universe has been found to be associated in some direct or indirect manner with criminality. These multiple factors have not been reduced to a clear-cut system, with immediate and remote relationships established. Although the differential-association theory is a step in this direction, no universals have been discovered. Until they are discovered, programs of prevention as well as programs of punishment and programs changing criminals must operate on the trial-and-error principle. No one can show in advance that crime will be significantly reduced if a particular program of prevention is adopted.

General Programs

Many general programs of crime prevention have been outlined. For example, Bentham, in the last part of the eighteenth century, made a comprehensive outline of the "indirect methods" (that is, methods other than punishment) that might be used to prevent crime. He included both social-defense items and interventionist items, such as taking away the capacity to injure, diverting the course of dangerous desires, decreasing susceptibility to temptations, general education, and a code of morals similar to a code of laws.[33] Ferri, a leader of the Italian school, in the last part of the nineteenth century paid considerable attention to the prevention of crime. He had a doctrine of criminal saturation—namely, that a group has the crimes it deserves in view of the type of people and the conditions of the group, and that as long as the type of people and the conditions remain constant, crime will remain constant regardless of methods of punishment. Consequently, he insisted that methods of modifying the conditions and traits of people should be used. He outlined a long list of these, including free trade, reduction in consumption of alcohol, metal (instead of paper) money, street lights, reduction in hours of labor, lower interest on public securities, local political autonomy, and many other things.[34]

Many other elaborate programs for the prevention of crime have been proposed, and these programs have included practically every reform that has been suggested by anyone. The programs tend to be somewhat utopian, principally because their relationship to knowledge of crime causation has not been spelled out. Yet every policy for the prevention of crime necessarily is based, implicitly or explicitly, on a theory or theories of the causes of crime. Those who believe that crime is due to innate defects advocate a policy of sterilization. Those who believe that it is due to acquired personal defects advocate agencies for education or psychiatric clinics. Those who believe that it is due to the immediate personal groups advocate modification of the family, neighborhood, or school. Those who believe that it is due to poverty and conditions of inequality advocate modification of the

[33]Jeremy Bentham, "Principles of Penal Law," in *The Works of Jeremy Bentham*, ed. John Bowring (Edinburgh: W. Tait, 1843).

[34]Enrico Ferri, *Criminal Sociology*, trans. by Joseph I. Kelly and John Lisle (Boston: Little, Brown, 1917), pp. 209–87. This book was first published in Rome in 1881.

economic and political systems or a more general economic, political, and social reorganization.

The greatest need in crime prevention now is, and always has been, irrefutable facts about crime causation and sound means for transforming that knowledge into a program of action.[35] Until such information is secured, and perhaps even after it is secured, most taxpayers will be opposed to modifications of the status quo. Citizens are opposed to crime, to be sure, but they are also opposed to high taxes and individual financial sacrifice. It is easier to make punitive and emotional gestures in regard to crime than to risk capital on studies and changes that might prevent crime. If reliable information on which to base programs of prevention were available, the political decision-makers probably could be educated and induced to carry out programs based on such information. However, in view of the fact that persons administering crime-prevention programs have vested interests in maintaining only vague procedures for measuring the effectiveness of the programs, such reliable information is not likely to be forthcoming.[36]

Local Community Organization

Previous chapters have documented the idea that the sources of delinquency and crime lie principally in the personal groups within local communities. It was shown that delinquent and criminal behavior are explained principally by an excess of associations with criminal-behavior patterns over associations with anticriminal-behavior patterns. In such associations, intimacy and the prestige of the source of a pattern are the principal characteristics that result in behavior concordant with that pattern. Moreover, it was shown that the condition in these local and personal groups that has the greatest significance is the definition of behavior as desirable or undesirable. For example, even in the most deplorable family, school, and neighborhood situations, girls are less delinquent than boys, and this is due to the fact that delinquency is defined as more undesirable for girls than for boys.

The closest approximation to a general formula for the prevention of crime and delinquency that presently can be made on the basis of these findings is that criminal and delinquent behavior must be defined as undesirable by the personal groups in which a person participates. The correlate of this is that lawful behavior must be defined as desirable by such groups. The personal groups in question may be the family, school and neighborhood groups, work or recreational groups, religious groups, or others. Policies for prevention of delinquency and crime, therefore, should be directed primarily at these personal groups. In this sense,

[35] See Lamar Empey and Steven G. Lubeck, *Delinquency Prevention Strategies* (Washington: Government Printing Office, 1970).
[36] See Donald R. Cressey, "The Nature and Effectiveness of Correctional Techniques," *Law and Contemporary Problems*, 23:754–71, 1958; and James C. Hackler, "Evaluation of Delinquency Prevention Programs: Ideals and Compromises," *Federal Probation*, 31:22–6, 1967.

control of delinquency and crime lies within the local community. This means, first, that the local community must be the active agency in reducing its own delinquency. Second, modifications of the general institutional structure are important in reducing crime and delinquency rates to the degree that they affect local community organization.

Experiments in preventing delinquency along the lines suggested in the preceding paragraph were developed in Chicago under the guidance of the sociologists in the Institute for Juvenile Research.[37] The principle involved in these "Chicago Area Projects" is that the persons who reside in an area of high delinquency are induced to form an organization for the purpose of reducing their own delinquency rates. The "natural leaders" in these areas direct the organizations, with some suggestions from outsiders and with financial aid from agencies outside the area. The groups that are most important in the lives of the residents of an area become the agencies through which operations are conducted.

These Area Projects have been in operation for over forty years. The approach has remained the same over the years, although the community committees now assist in the rehabilitation of parolees as well as trying to prevent delinquency and crime. The community units seem to be as important in modifying the attitudes and behavior of the adult participants as in directly changing the activities of children and youth.[38] Adults who band together to prevent delinquency in their community rather automatically modify their own attitudes. An antidelinquency group is formed, and status in the group is achieved by expressions of antidelinquent behavior.

This subtle modification of adults' attitudes of indifference to delinquency is itself delinquency prevention, for a new set of social influences for juveniles is created. Young people begin to live in an antidelinquency setting where they, also, gain status by nondelinquent or antidelinquent activities, in contrast to delinquent activities. Even probationers, parolees, and ex-criminals may work to improve the community and to keep others out of delinquency, thus reforming themselves. In addition, the attempts to deal directly with the behavior of children and youth probably are most effective when the cultural differences between the adults and the children are at a minimum, as is the case in the Area Project communities. The Area Projects, and many similar programs developed in the last decade, have been criticized for using "untrained" workers and "bad"

[37] See E. W. Burgess, J. D. Lohman, and Clifford R. Shaw, "The Chicago Area Project," *National Probation Association Yearbook*, 1937, pp. 8–28; Fred A. Romano, "Organizing a Community for Delinquency Prevention," *National Probation Association Yearbook*, 1940, pp. 1–12; Clifford R. Shaw and Jesse A. Jacobs, "The Chicago Area Project," *Proceedings of the American Prison Association*, 1939, pp. 40–53; Clifford R. Shaw and Henry D. McKay, *Juvenile Delinquency and Urban Areas* (Chicago: University of Chicago Press, 1942), pp. 442–6. (Rev. ed., with a new introduction by James F. Short, Jr., 1969); and James F. Short, Jr., ed., *Delinquency, Crime, and Society* (Chicago: University of Chicago Press, 1976).

[38] See Solomon Kobrin, "The Chicago Area Project—A 25-Year Assessment," *Annals of the American Academy of Political and Social Science*, 322:19–29, 1959.

people as leaders, yet the use of such natural leaders is one of the program's greatest assets.

Unfortunately, there is little objective evidence that the projects have reduced the delinquency rates of the subject areas. Some persons connected with the program believe that significant reductions in delinquency rates have resulted, while others connected with the program are skeptical as to the results. Delinquency rates have shown a greater decrease in project areas than in nearby areas, but this difference may be due merely to a difference in delinquency reporting in the two kinds of areas. Spergel recently concluded, "It is possible that the Chicago Area Projects, now largely under state government auspices, has become too simplistic, routinized, and perhaps apolitical in dealing with urban problems more complex than those of an earlier period."[39] Perhaps the best that can be said in appraisal of the Area Projects and similar programs is that they are consistent with an important theory of criminal behavior and with the ideals of democracy. Communities that have been indifferent to high delinquency rates must gradually be converted to a set of values that places a premium on nondelinquency.[40]

Establishing such an antidelinquency public opinion obviously is very difficult in areas with highly mobile populations, made up of persons with little stake in conformity to the dominant society. These areas, then, must be brought into the dominant society. The Anti-Crime Crusade of Indianapolis made progress in this direction. The organization was founded by thirty women the day after a ninety-year-old woman was beaten and robbed on the street. Four years later, about fifty thousand women were participating. Among the activities of the organization are securing jobs for young people, helping school dropouts return to school, involving adolescents in volunteer work for social agencies and clinics, campaigning for slum cleanups, sponsoring police recruits, publicizing the shortcomings of the courts, assisting probation and parole workers, forming block clubs to improve slum neighborhoods, and campaigning for police pay raises. After a few months or years, most such organizations collapse for lack of membership, change goals, regain members, then collapse again.[41]

Organized Recreation
One feature of most programs for preventing delinquency is emphasis on athletics and other leisure-time activities. The stress on recreation is essentially negative, in the sense that it implies that juveniles who are engaged in conventional recreation activities will not, at the same time, engage in delinquency. It is a method of occupying the time of children; as such, it does not change attitudes or tendencies

[39] Irving A. Spergel, "Community-Based Delinquency-Prevention Programs: An Overview," *Social Service Review*, 47:16–31, 1973.

[40] See Walter B. Miller, "The Impact of a 'Total-Community' Delinquency Control Project," *Social Problems*, 10:168–91, 1962.

[41] See Ivan Jankovic, "The Natural History of a Social Control Agency" (Cambridge, England: Institute of Criminology, mimeographed, 1971).

regarding delinquent behavior. Youth centers, recreational groups, and youth clubs have been established by social agencies, churches, police departments, and other organizations as a means of "keeping them off the streets." Claims have been made that delinquency rates have been greatly reduced in neighborhoods where recreation centers have been established. On the other hand, many recreational centers have become sources of infection for delinquency. The successful recreation centers are those that somehow manage to provide participants with an excess of definitions unfavorable to delinquency.[42]

Casework with Near-Delinquents

Certain children have been called *potential delinquents* or *predelinquents*. These terms are misleading, for every child is a potential delinquent; every child in earlier years is a predelinquent, and every able-bodied person who has passed the earlier years of childhood commits delinquencies more or less frequently. The terms are used, however, to refer to the children who are believed to be extraordinarily likely to become confirmed delinquents. These predelinquents have not been definitely identified, but are believed by certain psychiatrists and social workers to be the children who manifest emotional problems such as enuresis, temper tantrums, sullenness, timidity, and, in later years, difficulties in school and with companions. It is believed that if these problems can be corrected in early childhood by appropriate procedures, the child will develop into a less delinquent adult.

The principal agency that has developed in the attempt to turn these near-delinquents away from their trend toward delinquency is the guidance clinic. Some guidance clinics, often called by other names such as "youth service bureaus," have been operated by the public schools, some by juvenile courts, some by public welfare departments, some by private welfare agencies, some by state hospitals and mental-health organizations, and some by independent agencies organized for this purpose. The clinic staff usually is made up of psychiatrists, psychologists, and social workers. Problem children are referred to the clinic by parents who are anxious about their children, by police, judges, and probation officers, by kindergartens and schools, by welfare agencies, and by other agencies and persons. Some of them are referred because they have been delinquent, some because of behavior that is not in violation of the law, such as temper tantrums, bed-wetting, or bashfulness. These children are sometimes divided into behavior problems and personality problems.

Studies of child-guidance clinics generally indicate that from a fourth to a third of the children who attend them continue to have problems, and that approximately a third manifest no further difficulties. One study showed no significant

---

[42]See the discussion in Chap. 9, above. See also Roscoe C. Brown, Jr., and Dan W. Dodson, "The Effectiveness of a Boys' Club in Reducing Delinquency," *Annals of the American Academy of Political and Social Science,* 322:47–52, 1959.

difference in the outcome of a group of children receiving psychiatric treatment in a clinic and a group not receiving such treatment.[43] Another study found that 47 percent of a group treated in a psychiatric clinic thirty years earlier had been arrested, as compared with 16 percent of a control group; 60 percent of the persons referred to the clinic for delinquency had arrests, as compared to 20 percent of those referred for neuroses or learning problems.[44] Modification of an "undesirable personality trait" undoubtedly is valuable to the individual and to society, but such modification does not necessarily mean that the individual in question will refrain from law violation.

In general, the child-guidance clinic seems to be only slightly more successful in dealing with youth problems than are institutions for delinquents and criminals. Probably this failure is due to the fact that the source of delinquency is not to be found in the organism of the juvenile, but involves wider social relationships in the family, the neighborhood, the institutions, and the general culture. However, the child-guidance clinic is at a great disadvantage, both in preventing delinquency and in aiding emotionally disturbed children, for it cannot initiate action. It must wait for cases to be referred to it. Accordingly, the delinquents seen in clinics are not likely to be drawn from all segments of the population, and, in fact, the clinics might not be serving the delinquents who are most in need of their services.

An old but definitive ten-year experiment in delinquency and crime prevention by methods that can best be described as casework outside a clinic setting revealed that the professional workers' efforts were not highly successful.[45] A group of 650 boys under twelve years of age were selected for the project from a list of about 1,900 names submitted by teachers, social workers, police officers, and probation officers. Some of these boys were believed destined to become delinquent, and others were not. The 650 boys were paired on the basis of about one hundred factors, such as age, religion, intelligence, educational performance, personality, neighborhood, and social adjustment. The information regarding these factors was obtained from social-work agencies, schools, interviews with parents, and physical and psychological examinations of the boys. On the basis of these factors, prognostications as to probable delinquency were made. One set of the matched pairs was randomly selected as the "treatment group," while their "diagnostic twins" became the "control group."

[43] LaMay Adamson and H. Warren Dunham, "Clinical Treatment of Male Delinquents: A Case Study in Effort and Result," *American Sociological Review*, 21:312–20, 1956.

[44] Lee N. Robins and Patricia O'Neal, "Mortality, Mobility, and Crime: Problem Children Thirty Years Later," *American Sociological Review*, 23:162–71, 1958.

[45] Edwin Powers, "An Experiment in Prevention of Delinquency," *Annals of the American Academy of Political and Social Science*, 261:77–88, 1949; Edwin Powers and Helen L. Witmer, *An Experiment in the Prevention of Delinquency—The Cambridge-Somerville Youth Study* (New York: Columbia University Press, 1951). See also William McCord and Joan McCord, *Origins of Crime: A New Evaluation of the Cambridge-Somerville Youth Study* (New York: Columbia University Press, 1959); and Jackson Toby, "Early Identification and Intensive Treatment of Predelinquents: A Negative View," *Social Work*, 6:3–13, 1961.

The members of the treatment group were given help in educational problems, were given special counseling, guidance, and health services, were taken on camping trips, and so on. The control group was given none of these services. After two or three years, 65 of the boys in the treatment group were dropped because they presented no special problems and were definitely nondelinquent; this left 260 boys in the treatment group. At the end of the experimental period, 76, or 23.4 percent, of the 325 treatment-group members had appeared in court for serious offenses, and 90, or 27.7 percent, had committed either serious or minor offenses. Among the 325 control-group members, the proportions were slightly *less* in each instance: 67, or 20.6 percent, had court appearances for serious offenses, and 85, or 26.1 percent, had committed either serious or minor offenses.

At the time of the original diagnosis, delinquent careers were predicted for 70 boys in the treatment group and for 68 in the control group; 23 (32.9 percent) of the members of this treatment subgroup became delinquent, and 27 (39.7 percent) of the control subgroup became delinquent. Similarly, "probable delinquency" was predicted for 163 members of the treatment group and for 165 members of the control group; 14.1 percent of the treatment subgroup became delinquent, as compared to 13.3 percent of the control subgroup. These differences are hardly significant, indicating that the "treatment" had little effect; they also cast doubt on the feasibility of identifying "predelinquents" accurately. There was evidence, however, that the control-group members who became delinquent were more persistent offenders than the treatment-group members who became delinquent.

Group Work with Near-Delinquents
One of the significant developments in social work during the last two decades is group work. The development is to some extent based on the desirability of extending casework beyond the person and family to groups of approximately the same age as the delinquent or near-delinquent who is being helped. Group work with delinquents and near-delinquents may be regarded as falling into two types, both of which are now being used in most large urban communities. First, an individual is induced to become a member of a group, as a means of satisfying his or her needs as a person. The group may be a ball team, a hiking club, an art-crafts class, or it may be concerned with some other activity. While in this group, the person is given aid in adjusting to the group and in overcoming tendencies considered to be conducive to delinquency. At its best, this type of group work does more than merely provide recreational opportunities. It uses an individualistic psychology, and is based on the same general theory as is clinical treatment. A principal problem is that of inducing children to participate in the groups. Generally, group-work agencies using this approach are not identified closely with the underprivileged and deprived, nor with the age groups among which delinquency is most prevalent.

A second type of group work consists of redirecting the activities of a group of persons, all or nearly all of whom are delinquents or near-delinquents. One of the early applications of this procedure was made by Keltner in St. Louis under the sponsorship of the YMCA. In a deteriorated section of St. Louis, which had been the headquarters of a notorious adult gang, Keltner attempted to redirect the boys' gangs so that they would be assets to the community. After a period of fifteen years, forty of these gangs, now turned into boys' clubs, were carrying on their activities in this section, with an average membership of about twenty-five. Keltner stated that the members were seldom in difficulties with the police, that the older members assisted in developing similar groups for their younger brothers, and that the businessmen of the district wholeheartedly cooperated with the project.[46]

Most cities now have agencies using this kind of group work, primarily with relationship to delinquent gangs or street-corner groups, rather than with reference to a community or neighborhood. The essential characteristic of this policy, as differentiated from other policies, is that some person attempts to enter into friendly participation with the gang in order to try to change the members into law-abiding citizens.[47] In a pioneering program conducted in central Harlem years ago, trained workers were assigned to five street gangs, and these workers attempted by informal methods to influence the activities of the gang. At the end of its third year, the program was judged successful.[48] This program set the pattern for many subsequent programs in other areas.[49] However, the strategy whereby street-corner workers make contact with juvenile gangs, gain their confidence, and then direct their energies into nondelinquent channels has not proven to be effective.[50] Malcolm Klein, one of the leading experts in this area, has noted that street-gang workers have neither the time nor the ability to be effective:

> Gang workers in this project spent one-fifth of their time with gang members (and a few siblings, cousins, friends, or schoolmates from time to time). With 50 to 100 gang members in the neighborhood, and eight hours a week spent in contact with them, how much impact can reasonably be expected? It seems presumptuous to think that an average of five

[46] Harold S. Keltner, "Crime Prevention Program of the YMCA, St. Louis," in *Preventing Crime*, eds. Sheldon and Eleanor Glueck (New York: McGraw-Hill, 1936), chap. 24.

[47] See David M. Austin, "Goals for Gang Workers," *Social Work*, 2:43–50, 1957; and David J. Bordua, *Sociological Theories and Their Implications for Juvenile Delinquency* (Washington: U.S. Children's Bureau, 1960).

[48] Paul L. Crawford, Daniel I. Malamud, and James R. Dumpson, *Working with Teen-age Gangs* (New York: Welfare Council of New York City, 1950); and James R. Dumpson, "An Approach to Anti-Social Street Gangs," *Federal Probation*, 13:22–9, 1949.

[49] See Irving Spergel, *Street Gang Work: Theory and Practice* (Reading, Mass.: Addison-Wesley, 1966); Malcolm W. Klein and Barbara G. Meyerhoff, eds., *Juvenile Gangs in Context: Theory, Research, and Action* (Los Angeles: University of Southern California Youth Studies Center, 1964); Malcolm W. Klein, "Juvenile Gangs, Police, and Detached Workers: Controversies in Gang Intervention," *Social Service Review*, 39:183–90, 1965; and Solomon Kobrin, "Sociological Aspects of the Development of a Street Corner Group: An Exploratory Study," *American Journal of Orthopsychiatry*, 31:685–702, 1961.

[50] See William E. Wright and Michael C. Dixon, "Community Prevention and Treatment of Juvenile Delinquency," *Journal of Research in Crime and Delinquency*. 14:35–67, 1977.

minutes per week per boy would somehow result in a reduction in delinquent behavior, even if it is matched by half again as much time with some of the significant adults around him. It may be the peculiar conceit of the social scientist and the social worker to think that his five minutes can overcome the forces that have been at work for 10 or 20 years to bring a client to the point at which he can be labeled delinquent or gang member or criminal offender. As one of our colleagues succinctly put it, "Just who the hell do we think we are, what do we think we've got, to change all this?"[51]

The emphasis on gangs, rather than on neighborhoods, probably has arisen in part because lower-class areas of large cities have become more unstable or less strongly organized—family, ethnic, political, and religious organizations are all weak. Another reason is the pervasive tendency of social agencies to push middle-class patterns of control and conformity:

The social agency is *society's* instrument for support, rehabilitation and control of deviant population segments. Agencies which serve primarily low-income persons derive their major source of funds from middle-class people and groups. Policies are determined and programs controlled by a board representing extra-local or nonlower-class interests. Staff are recruited for ability to assist a *lower-class* population, but within a professional outlook fundamentally determined by *middle-class* norms and values. Therefore, the basic structure and dynamic of social agencies has not allowed for determination of policy and program by the local residents of low-income areas.[52]

Institutional Modification

The structural-frustration theory developed by Merton and by Cloward and Ohlin is widely considered to be a theory of delinquency and crime as well as a theory about the origin of deviant subcultures.[53] The basic notion, when viewed from this perspective, is that when a cultural system extols common success goals for all but restricts or blocks access to the means of achieving these goals, delinquency and crime appear among those persons whose access to legitimate means for achieving success has been frustrated. It follows that much of a nation's delinquency and crime would be prevented if the economic institution were modified in such a way that opportunities for achieving success by legitimate means became more nearly equal.

Mobilization for Youth, a program run in the Lower East Side area of New York City during the 1960s, tried to implement this idea on a local level. As Quinney has pointed out, the basic theory underlying this prevention program was "that obstacles to economic and social betterment are chiefly responsible for crime and delinquency among low-income groups."[54] The expectation was that delinquency

---

[51] Malcolm W. Klein, "Gang Cohesiveness, Delinquency, and a Street Work Program," *Journal of Research in Crime and Delinquency*, 6:135–66, 1969. See also idem, *Street Gangs and Streetworkers* (Englewood Cliffs, N.J.: Prentice-Hall, 1971).

[52] Spergel, *Street Gang Work*, p. xvi.

[53] See the discussions in Chapters 5 and 9, above.

[54] Richard Quinney, *Criminology: Analysis and Critique of Crime in America* (Boston: Little, Brown, 1975), p. 246.

rates would go down if the employability of youths from low-income families was increased, training and work-preparation facilities were improved and made more accessible to the poor, young people were assisted in achieving employment goals consistent with their capabilities, employment opportunities for youth were increased, minority-group youngsters were helped to overcome discrimination in hiring, and so on.[55] The Mobilization for Youth organization itself provided paid community-service employment for several hundred out-of-school youths who otherwise would have been unemployed, hired working-class high-school students to tutor elementary-school students, set up a laboratory school to demonstrate effective methods of teaching lower-income students, and engaged in many similar activities.[56] Despite an extensive literature on Mobilization for Youth, it is not clear whether the multifaceted program prevented delinquency or not.[57] Clearly it incorporated so many components that it cannot be considered a good test of structural-frustration theory.

The problem of measuring the effects of the Mobilization for Youth program on delinquency and crime rates was complicated by the fact that it soon became a community-action project, aimed at helping poor people achieve their legal rights. The prevention of delinquency apparently became a long-range goal rather than a direct one. Thus opportunities for poor people were improved by hiring a staff of lawyers to serve welfare recipients, another staff that collected data on landlord violations and took action against them, a third staff of organizers who advised and helped the poor organize to improve their lot, and so on. Apparently it was assumed that these aspects of the "war on poverty" would in the long run reduce delinquency rates by reducing the degree of inequality in the area. However, the Mobilization for Youth project was so threatening to entrenched political and economic interests that it soon became embroiled in local, state, and federal political feuds, with the result that its effectiveness as an antipoverty program, let alone its effectiveness as a delinquency-prevention program, could not be measured.

Projects similar to Mobilization for Youth have been conducted in many other areas. Each stresses community action to improve the economic opportunities for lower-class youth, and in one way or another the programs have tried to do this by providing improved work and educational experiences. For example, a Kansas City

[55] *Action on the Lower East Side: Program Report, July, 1962–January, 1964* (New York: Mobilization for Youth, 1964, mimeographed).

[56] *Counter-Attack on Delinquency* (Washington: President's Committee on Delinquency and Youth Crime, 1965, mimeographed); and Don C. Gibbons, *Delinquent Behavior*, 2d ed. (Englewood Cliffs, N.J.: Prentice-Hall, 1976), pp. 278–9.

[57] See, for example, George A. Brager and Francis P. Purcell, eds., *Community Action Against Poverty* (New Haven, Conn.: College and Universities Press, 1967); Harold H. Weissman, ed., *Individual and Group Services in the Mobilization for Youth Experience* (New York: Association Press, 1969); idem, ed., *Justice and the Law* (New York: Association Press, 1969); and idem, ed., *Community Development in the Mobilization for Youth Experience* (New York: Association Press, 1969).

project gave special work experience and a modified school program to male youths regarded as potential delinquents. The experimenters concluded that "all these efforts and expenditures of money had remarkably little effect."[58]

Many attempts to prevent delinquency and crime by modifying some aspect of the educational institution also have been made. Indeed, the proposal that schools be used more effectively in delinquency prevention is probably the most frequently voiced suggestion for reducing delinquency and crime rates. As Gibbons has pointed out, there are two quite different schools of thought about the school and delinquency:

One batch of proposals assumes that American schools are viable and healthy institutions but are called upon to deal with a group of unruly, predelinquent youths. Accordingly, in this view, schools are asked to use their positive resources in the effort to curb the delinquent tendencies of the aberrant, nonconformist youths. In the second grouping of preventive proposals involving schools, the schools themselves are seen as fundamentally implicated in delinquency because of the various shortcomings and inadequacies within the American educational institution. It follows from these premises that the target of change ought to be schools and their programs, more than unruly, recalcitrant youths.[59]

Generally speaking, experiments focusing on the idea that some students are in need of correction because they are "just plain bad," or will become bad unless the school does something to them, have failed. In Columbus, Ohio, for example, an attempt was made to change the negative self-images of delinquents and "predelinquents," thereby reducing the delinquency rate, by placing them in special seventh-grade classes staffed by special teachers. A control group attended regular classes.[60] The follow-up data suggested that the predicted changes did not occur.[61]

It is failures such as these, viewed in conjunction with the findings of studies such as those we reviewed in Chapter 11, which have stimulated requests that the educational system be modified with a view to reducing its delinquency-generating aspects.[62] Duffee and Fitch have stated this need in terms going beyond the educational institution:

There is much that corrections can do to help individuals more effectively within our present social structure. But helping individuals reenter the marketplace does nothing to

[58] Winston M. Ahlstrom and Robert J. Havighurst, *400 Losers: Delinquent Boys in High School* (San Francisco: Jossey-Bass, 1971), p. 2. See also C. R. Jeffery and I. R. Jeffery, "Dropouts and Delinquents: An Experimental Program in Behavior Change," *Education and Urban Society,* 1:325–36, 1969; and James C. Hackler, "Boys, Blisters, and Behavior—The Impact of a Work Program in an Urban Central Area," *Journal of Research in Crime and Delinquency,* 3:155–64, 1966.

[59] Gibbons, *Delinquent Behavior,* p. 280.

[60] Simon Dinitz, Frank R. Scarpitti, and Walter C. Reckless, "Delinquency Vulnerability: A Cross Group and Longitudinal Analysis," *American Sociological Review,* 27:515–17, 1962.

[61] Walter C. Reckless and Simon Dinitz, *The Prevention of Juvenile Delinquency: An Experiment* (Columbus: Ohio State University Press, 1972).

[62] Kenneth Polk and Walter E. Schafer, eds, *Schools and Delinquency* (Englewood Cliffs, N.J.: Prentice-Hall, 1972), pp. 240–77.

change the basic mode of exchange in the market. Thus, if it is a goal of corrections to reduce crime rather than merely to help individual criminals, corrections must be reorganized so that it can deal with deviance-generating patterns of behavior, rather than focusing on the deviant behavior of individuals who have already been caught and isolated. In short, corrections, to be a crime-reducing institution of society, must be in a position to change society.[63]

Institutional Reorganization

Many persons have advocated widespread reorganization of the general institutional structure. Some have done so in connection with preventing crime and delinquency. Many criminologists have suggested that only partial and temporary reduction in crime rates can be expected from the programs currently employed in the attempt to prevent crime and delinquency: repression, clinical treatment, special school classes for "predelinquents," character education, education of parents, casework and group work with parents and children, domestic-relations courts, foster homes, club and camp programs, neighborhood and school modification, and others. All of these, it is said, are based on a theory that attributes delinquency and crime to some kind of defect in an accepted social system; the prevention programs consistently try to correct these defects without disturbing the status quo. Currently, "remedying minor institutional defects" is by far the most common sociological approach to crime prevention in the United States, where criminologists and politicians alike seem intent on eliminating crime without destroying "the American way of life." In the Soviet Union, too, delinquency and crime are attributed to defects in socialization processes and other social-control mechanisms, and prevention consists of trying to improve those mechanisms rather than changing the economic, political, and social order.[64]

Donald R. Taft, an American sociologist who did extensive research on crime among immigrants and culture conflict during the first half of this century, argued persuasively that none of the remedial crime-prevention programs cuts the deeper roots of crime. After acknowledging the tremendous difficulties and opposition that institutional reorganization would entail, he made the following statement regarding the characteristics of a "crimeless society":

Since social change implies maladjustment, a crimeless society had best be static. To avoid culture conflict it should be internally homogeneous. On the economic side, a crimeless society must avoid excessive competition and greed for material gain and must be planned rather than chaotic. This would be essential to avoid such sources of maladjust-

---

[63] Duffee and Fitch, *An Introduction to Corrections*, p. 375.

[64] Francis T. Cullen, Jr., and John B. Cullen, "The Soviet Model of Deviance," *Pacific Sociological Review*, 20:389–410, 1977. See also Austin T. Turk, "The Problem of Legal Order in the United States and South Africa: Substantive and Analytical Considerations," *Sociological Focus*, 10:31–41, 1977; and Ralf Dahrendorf, *Class and Class Conflict in Industrial Society* (Stanford, Calif.: Stanford University Press, 1959), pp. 234–8.

ment as relative failure, city slums, struggle for speculative gains, monopolistic advantages, and various types of exploitation.

A crimeless society might have to reverse the trend toward impersonal relationships and restore the personalized culture of the past. It might need to restrict human freedom. It might resort to a return to religious superstitions as agencies of social control. Though different in some respects, such a crimeless society would seem more nearly to approximate primitive or peasant society, than does modern society. . . .

A crimeless society should also be largely free from preferential group loyalties which we have found to be at once so cherished and so productive of strife and crime. A society so homogeneous as we have indicated might perhaps accept and enforce a puritanical morality, otherwise it would seem to need a "new morality" permitting considerable freedom of sex and other personal behavior.

Perhaps the most basic change needed in the interest of crime prevention would be the incorporation in our culture of a genuinely scientific point of view which sees criminals as products. Such a society would not hold the individual criminal responsible, though it would continue to hold him in every way accountable for his behavior.

The reader may decide for himself, first which of the changes needed to prevent crime he desires, and second whether the criminogenic conditions he would hate to sacrifice are or are not more desirable than crime prevention. A program of cultural change solely in the interest of crime prevention would be based upon the, perhaps false, assumption that a crimeless society is the one great good. It is not the task of the criminologist to determine what is the major social good.[65]

Saul Alinsky, a Chicago sociologist who became disillusioned with the remedial philosophy inherent in the Chicago Area Projects, similarly suggested that crime and delinquency must, in the last analysis, be prevented through institutional reorganization, and he initiated a program to achieve that reorganization. His program, variously known as the "Back of the Yards Project," the "Industrial Areas Foundation," and the "People's Organization," was not aimed directly at control of delinquency and crime. Instead, it attempted to eradicate "unemployment, undernourishment, disease, deterioration, demoralization, and other aspects of social disorganization." The implication is that as these conditions are altered, crime and delinquency rates will decrease. The essence of the following statement, made about thirty years ago, has become the rallying cry for those who subscribe to the now-popular idea that delinquency and crime will be prevented only when basic social injustices are eradicated:

It is very clear that if any intelligent attack is to be made upon the problem of youth or the causes of crime the community council will have to concern itself with the basic issues of unemployment, diseases, and housing, as well as all other causes of crime. This the conventional community council cannot do. It is not equipped to attack basic social issues, and its very character is such that it never was meant to do that kind of job. The

---

[65] Donald R. Taft, *Criminology: A Cultural Interpretation* (New York, Macmillan, 1950), pp. 666–7. See also the third edition of this book (1956), pp. 756–7; and Edwin Schur, *Our Criminal Society: The Social and Legal Sources of Crime in America* (Englewood Cliffs, N.J.: Prentice-Hall, 1969), pp. 15–22.

community council organized to prevent crime will tell you that its function is in the field of crime purely and it has no place in such controversial fields as conflict between labor and capital, private *vs.* government housing, public health, and other fundamental issues. Intellectually and logically members of such council will admit that one cannot hope to attack the causes of crime unless one gets into all the related fields, yet in actual practice they will vigorously abstain from entering any controversial field. . . . You don't, you dare not, come to a people who are unemployed, who don't know where their next meal is coming from, whose children and themselves are in the gutter of despair—and offer them not food, not jobs, not security, but supervised recreation, handicraft classes and character building! Yet *that is what is done!* Instead of a little bread and butter we come to them with plenty of bats and balls![66]

Modern radical criminologists have gone beyond Alinsky and Taft, who did not recommend revolution, apparently believing that crime rates can and should be reduced by reorganizing American society in such a way that its essence remains but some of its crime-generating aspects are eliminated. Contemporary radicals tend to go further than this, saying that the capitalistic order that is synonymous with American society must be brought to its knees if the American crime problem is to be solved. Quinney, for example, maintains that crime exists because the criminal-law apparatus is a tool used by the state and the "ruling class" to secure the survival of the capitalist system. And, he says, "as capitalist society is further threatened, criminal law is increasingly used to attempt to maintain domestic order." To remove the oppression and to eliminate what he calls "the need for further revolt" would necessarily mean the end of the dominant class and the capitalist economy. Quinney has presented a summary of these ideas in six assertions:

(1) American society is based on an advanced capitalist economy.

(2) The state is organized to serve the interests of the dominant economic class, the capitalist ruling class.

(3) Criminal law is an instrument that the state and dominant ruling class use to maintain and perpetuate the social and economic order.

(4) Crime control in capitalist society is accomplished by institutions and agencies established and administered by a governmental elite, representing dominant ruling-class interests, to establish domestic order.

(5) The contradictions of advanced capitalism—the disjunction between existence and essence—requires that the subordinate classes remain oppressed by whatever means necessary, especially by the legal system's coercion and violence.

(6) Only with the collapse of capitalist society, based on socialist principles, will there be a solution to the crime problem.[67]

[66] Saul D. Alinsky, *Reveille for Radicals* (Chicago: University of Chicago Press, 1946), pp. 81–2. See also Robert Bailey, Jr., *Radicals in Urban Politics: The Alinsky Approach* (Chicago: University of Chicago Press, 1974).

[67] Quinney, *Criminology: Analysis and Critique of Crime in America*, p. 291. See also idem, *Class, State and Crime: On the Theory and Practice of Criminal Justice* (New York: David McKay, 1977), pp. 108–9.

The author of an early criminology textbook—published almost half a century before Quinney's textbook was published—was much less pessimistic and sour than Quinney seems to be. He thought he had already witnessed the end of autocratic government disguised as democracy—the end of oppression by what Quinney calls "the capitalist ruling class," "a governmental elite," and "dominant ruling-class interests." Further, he predicted an inevitable rise of what contemporary persons call "participatory democracy," and he saw this change in the direction of equality as a preventer of crime, one of the faults of an incomplete democracy:

> The day of autocratic government is gone. What the *Chicago Tribune* in 1914 described as the "twilight of the kings" has settled into complete darkness. Self-government in industry, among students, and in penal and reformatory institutions is inevitable, although the process will be an evolutionary one. The cures for the faults of democracy must be more democracy unless we are ready to believe that all the progress of recent centuries is an illusion or delusion.[68]

SUGGESTED READINGS

Alinsky, Saul D. "Community Analysis and Organization." *American Journal of Sociology*, 46:797–808, 1941.

Amos, William E., & Charles F. Wellford, eds. *Delinquency Prevention: Theory and Practice*. Englewood Cliffs, N.J.: Prentice-Hall, 1967.

Beless, Donald W., William S. Pilcher, & Ellen Jo Ryan. "Use of Indigenous Nonprofessionals in Probation and Parole." *Federal Probation*, 36:10–15, 1972.

Black, Donald. *The Behavior of Law*. New York: Academic Press, 1976.

Bordua, David J. *Sociological Theories and Their Implications for Juvenile Delinquency*. Washington: U.S. Children's Bureau, 1960.

Conklin, John E. "Dimensions of Community Response to the Crime Problems." *Social Problems*, 18:373–85, 1971.

Cressey, Donald R. "The Nature and Effectiveness of Correctional Techniques." *Law and Contemporary Problems*, 23:754–71, 1958.

Empey, Lamar T., & Steven G. Lubeck. *Delinquency Prevention Strategies*. Washington: Government Printing Office, 1970.

Gibbons, Don C. *Changing the Lawbreaker*. Englewood Cliffs, N.J.: Prentice-Hall, 1965.

Glaser, Daniel. "National Goals and Indicators for the Reduction of Crime and Delinquency." *Annals of the American Academy of Political and Social Science*, 371:104–26, 1967.

Hackler, James C. "Evaluation of Delinquency Prevention Programs: Ideals and Compromises." *Federal Probation*, 31:22–6, 1967.

Hills, Stuart L. *Crime, Power, and Morality: The Criminal-Law Process in the United States*. San Francisco: Chandler, 1971.

Irwin, John. *The Felon*. Englewood Cliffs, N.J.: Prentice-Hall, 1970.

Jacobs, Alfred, & Wilford Spradlin, eds. *The Group as an Agent of Change*. New York: Behavioral Publications, 1973.

---

[68] Fred E. Hayes, *Criminology* (New York: McGraw-Hill, 1930), p. 298.

Kassebaum, Gene, David A. Ward, & Daniel M. Wilner. *Prison Treatment and Parole Survival: An Empirical Assessment.* New York: John Wiley, 1971.

Kittrie, Nicholas N. *The Right to Be Different: Deviance and Enforced Therapy.* Baltimore: Johns Hopkins Press, 1971.

Klein, Malcolm W., ed. *Juvenile Gangs in Context.* Englewood Cliffs, N.J.: Prentice-Hall, 1967.

McKay, Henry D. "Differential Association and Crime Prevention: Problems of Utilization." *Social Problems,* 8:25–37, 1960.

Palmer, Stuart. *The Prevention of Crime.* New York: Behavioral Publications, 1973.

Quinney, Richard. *Class, State and Crime: On the Theory and Practice of Criminal Justice.* New York: David McKay, 1977.

Schur, Edwin M. *Radical Non-Intervention: Rethinking the Delinquency Problem.* Englewood Cliffs, N.J.: Prentice-Hall, 1973.

Spergel, Irving. *Street Gang Work: Theory and Practice.* Reading, Mass.: Addison-Wesley, 1966.

Stratton, John R., & Robert M. Terry, eds. *Prevention of Delinquency: Problems and Programs.* New York: Macmillan, 1968.

Toby, Jackson. "Early Identification and Intensive Treatment of Predelinquents: A Negative View." *Social Work,* 6:3–13, 1961.

Volkman, Rita, & Donald R. Cressey. "Differential Association and the Rehabilitation of Drug Addicts." *American Journal of Sociology,* 69:129–42, 1963.

Warren, Marguerite Q. *Correctional Treatment in Community Settings: A Report of Current Research.* Washington: Government Printing Office, 1972.

Wright, William E., & Michael C. Dixon. "Community Prevention and Treatment of Juvenile Delinquency: A Review of Evaluation Studies." *Journal of Research in Crime and Delinquency,* 14:35–67, 1977.

Index of Names

Index of Subjects